More praise for Robert Alter's
The Five Books of Moses

"[An] astonishing translation. Out of Mr. Alter's close reading and translation, something grander really does take shape, along with a conviction that the Bible is not just incidentally mysterious, posing challenges because of its antique references and sources. It is essentially mysterious."   —Edward Rothstein, *New York Times*

"[A] remarkable new translation of the Pentateuch, a monument of scholarship. . . . The result greatly refreshes, sometimes productively estranges, words that may now be too familiar to those who grew up with the King James Bible. . . . Alter's translation brings delight because it follows the precepts of the committee of King James, but is founded on a greatly deeper conversance with Hebrew than the great 17th-century scholars could summon. And Alter . . . brings to his own English a scholarly comprehension of the capacities of literary usage. . . . Especially fine is the way Alter seems to dig into the earth of the Hebrew to recover, in English, its fearless tactility."
                              —James Wood, *London Review of Books*

"In the ancient Hebrew, Alter discovers a profound music. He can raise an already beloved text to new heights of resonance and reality. . . . Alter's combination of a freshly minted text and splendidly concise commentaries makes the biblical words resonate."
                              —Thomas D'Evelyn, *Christian Science Monitor*

"This is a masterpiece of clarity, erudition, and synthesis. Alter uses his talent as a literary critic to inspire in the reader a passion for studying the text. . . . This work abounds in stimulating thinking and eloquent writing. He honors those he invites not just to follow him but to accompany him."   —Elie Wiesel, *Bible Review*

"The arrival of this new translation of *The Five Books of Moses*— a heroic and literary achievement that captures in almost standard English the rhythms, repetition, and beauty of the Hebrew original—is cause for celebration. . . . [This translation] well might become the definitive text for readers and scholars alike."

—Pearl Abraham, *The Forward*

"Alter has admirably—one could say miraculously—succeeded."

—Earl L. Dachslager, *Houston Chronicle*

"The renowned scholar Robert Alter has produced a fresh translation [and] backed it up with an enlightening commentary. The result offers Old Testament newcomers, long-term absentees, and veterans a compelling reading experience." —Matt Love, *Sunday Oregonian*

"*The Five Books of Moses* is a fine work that deserves admiration for its sheer scale and literary power. The commentary is at least as important as the translation, and the two together make up a unique contribution both to biblical studies and to the understanding and appreciation of a text that is central to Western culture."

—John Barton, *Times Literary Supplement*

"Magisterial . . . an extraordinary achievement by any measure. Alter is indeed a magician with words." —Diana Lipton, *Booklog*

"Alter has succeeded admirably in conveying to English readers something of the flair, mystery, majesty, and power of the original Hebrew."

—John W. Rogerson, *Church Times*

"Has a story ever been at once so comprehensive, so intricate, and so integral as the one Alter gives us here? One is tempted to call it inspired." —Alan Jacobs, *First Things*

"Alter demonstrates a general reverence for literature that is complete, and his reverence for the power of the original text is compelling as well. The thrill of discovery occurs often."

—David M. Levine, *Congress Monthly*

"Alter's accomplishment is immense. He has produced a translation of the Pentateuch that respects and captures the beauty and majesty of the original." —Eric Ormsby, *New Criterion*

THE
FIVE BOOKS
OF MOSES

ALSO BY ROBERT ALTER

CANON AND CREATIVITY:
MODERN WRITING AND THE AUTHORITY OF SCRIPTURE

THE DAVID STORY

GENESIS

HEBREW AND MODERNITY

THE WORLD OF BIBLICAL LITERATURE

NECESSARY ANGELS: TRADITION AND MODERNITY IN KAFKA,
BENJAMIN, AND SCHOLEM

THE PLEASURES OF READING IN AN IDEOLOGICAL AGE

THE LITERARY GUIDE TO THE BIBLE
(coeditor with Frank Kermode)

THE INVENTION OF HEBREW PROSE

THE ART OF BIBLICAL POETRY

MOTIVES FOR FICTION

THE ART OF BIBLICAL NARRATIVE

A LION FOR LOVE: A CRITICAL BIOGRAPHY OF STENDHAL

DEFENSES OF THE IMAGINATION

PARTIAL MAGIC: THE NOVEL AS SELF-CONSCIOUS GENRE

MODERN HEBREW LITERATURE

AFTER THE TRADITION

FIELDING AND THE NATURE OF THE NOVEL

ROGUE'S PROGRESS: STUDIES IN THE PICARESQUE NOVEL

THE
FIVE BOOKS
OF MOSES

A Translation with Commentury

ROBERT ALTER

W·W·Norton & Company NEW YORK LONDON

Copyright © 2004 by Robert Alter

Portions previously published in *Genesis: Translation and Commentary*
by Robert Alter copyright © 1996 by Robert Alter.

For information about permission to reproduce selections from this book, write to Permissions,
W. W. Norton & Company, Inc., 500 Fifth Avenue, New York, NY 10110

Manufacturing by RR Donnelley, Crawfordsville
Book design by Margaret Wagner
Production manager: Julia Druskin

Library of Congress Cataloging-in-Publication Data

Bible. O.T. Pentateuch. English. Alter. 2004.
The five books of Moses : a translation with commentary / Robert Alter.
p. cm.
Includes bibliographical references.
ISBN 978-0-393-01955-1 (hardcover)
1. Bible. O.T. Pentateuch—Commentaries. I. Alter, Robert. II. Title.
BS1223.A48 2004
222'.1077—dc22

2004014067

ISBN 978-0-393-33393-0 pbk.

W. W. Norton & Company, Inc., 500 Fifth Avenue, New York, N.Y. 10110
www.wwnorton.com

W. W. Norton & Company Ltd., Castle House, 75/76 Wells Street, London W1T 3QT

1 2 3 4 5 6 7 8 9 0

CONTENTS

INTRODUCTION

GENESIS

EXODUS

LEVITICUS

NUMBERS

DEUTERONOMY

INTRODUCTION

I. APPROACHING THE FIVE BOOKS

The rabbinic sage Resh Lakish once wondered why the Hebrew text in Genesis used a seemingly superfluous definite article in the phrase "And it was evening and it was morning, the sixth day." (The definite article is not used for the preceding five days.) He took this to be a hidden reference to the sixth day of the month of Sivan, when according to tradition the Torah was given to Israel: "to teach us that the Holy One made a condition with all created things, saying to them, 'If Israel accepts the Torah, you will continue to exist. If not, I shall return you to welter and waste' " (Babylonian Talmud: Shabbat 88A). This is surely an extraordinary notion to entertain about the cosmic status of a book, imagining that the very existence of the world depends on it and on Israel's embrace of it.

Jewish tradition abounds in such extravagant celebrations of the supreme importance of this book. What is it about this text that led to such a vision of its unique standing? Are the five literary units it comprises in fact one book or five? How were they brought together? What are we to call them?

Let us begin with the question of the name for the whole. The fluctuations of the title reflect something of the oscillation of the text itself between multiplicity and unity. The Five Books of Moses does not translate any of the circulating Hebrew titles, though it does register the traditional attribution of authorship to Moses. The more compact English title, the Pentateuch, derives from a Greek equivalent for one popular Hebrew designation, the Humash.* Both names simply mean

---

*The symbol *h* represents the Hebrew consonant *het*, a light fricative that sounds something like *j* in Spanish.

the Five Books (though the "book" element is merely implied in the Hebrew term). "Pentateuch" was once the prevalent English title but has come to enjoy less currency, perhaps because faintly forbidding polysyllabic Greek terms are now less in favor. It does sound a little ponderous to the contemporary ear, and on those grounds it has not been adopted for this volume.

The fuller Hebrew designation is *Ḥamishah ḥumshey torah*, literally, the five fifths of the Torah. More simply, these five books are very often referred to in Hebrew and by Jews using other languages as the Torah. Torah means "teaching," or in biblical contexts involving specific laws, something like "regulation" or "protocol," i.e., that which is to be taught as proper procedure for a given topic. Of the Five Books, it is Deuteronomy that most often uses the term *torah*, sometimes joining it with *sefer*, "book" (as in "this book of teaching"), so that the reference widens at points from a specific teaching to all of Deuteronomy as a book. After Deuteronomy was brought together editorially with the four previous books, the designation Torah came to be extended to all five. In the traditional Hebrew division, the Torah then constituted the first, foundational unit of the three large units that make up the Hebrew Bible, which is called acronymically the Tanakh—that is, **Torah**, **Nevi'im*** (the Prophets, Former and Latter), and **Ketuvim** (the Writings, which is to say, everything else).

Scholarship for more than two centuries has agreed that the Five Books are drawn together from different literary sources, though there have been shifting debates about the particular identification of sources in the text and fierce differences of opinion about the dating of the sundry sources. Some extremists in recent decades have contended that the entire Torah was composed in the Persian period, beginning the late sixth century B.C.E., or even later, in Hellenistic times, but there is abundant evidence that argues against that view. Perhaps the most decisive consideration is that the Hebrew language visibly evolves over the nine centuries of biblical literary activity, with many demonstrable differences between the language current in the First Commonwealth—approximately 1000 B.C.E. to 586 B.C.E.—and the language

---

*The symbol ' designates the Hebrew letter *'aleph,* perhaps once a lightly aspirated sound but now a "silent" letter.

as it was written in the Persian and Hellenistic periods. There is very little in the Hebrew of the Torah that could have been written in this later era. (Ronald Hendel provides a concise and trenchant marshaling of the linguistic evidence against late dating in the appendix to his *Remembering Abraham*.) A recent revisionist approach, purportedly based on archeological evidence, places the composition of our texts as well as most of the Former Prophets in the seventh century B.C.E., during the reign of King Josiah, the period when, according to scholarly consensus, most of Deuteronomy was written. This contention, however, flatly ignores the philological evidence that Deuteronomy was responding to, and revising, a long-standing written legal tradition, and that the editors of the so-called Deuteronomistic History (the national chronicle that runs from Deuteronomy to the end of 2 Kings) were manifestly incorporating much older texts often strikingly different from their own writing both in style and in outlook.

The standard account offered by modern scholars of the Torah identifies four principal literary strands (together with a number of lesser ones): J, the Yahwistic strand (the divine name Yahweh is spelled with a J in German); E, the Elohistic strand; P, the Priestly strand; and D, for Deuteronomy. The first three are unevenly intertwined through Genesis, Exodus, and Numbers; P predominates in Leviticus; and all of Deuteronomy is D. J and E are so designated because of the name for the deity each characteristically uses, respectively, Yahweh and Elohim. J is sometimes thought to be the oldest of these strands, though J and E might have been approximately contemporary, the former a product of the southern kingdom of Judea, the latter deriving from literary activity in the northern kingdom of Israel. The composition of J and E, or at least of J, was once often dated to the tenth century B.C.E., perhaps even to the time of Solomon, and this is a view that still cannot be entirely dismissed. It is more common now, however, to put both a little later, perhaps in the ninth or eighth century. P, like everything else a bone of contention, seems to be both relatively early and late: some of it may have been written as early as the eighth century B.C.E., though the principal stratum is in all likelihood a product of the sixth century B.C.E., when these same Priestly writers were also drawing together editorially all the previous sources with their own work into a single text. Deuteronomy, or at any rate the bulk of Deuteronomy, is usually identified with the book purportedly discovered during the Temple renovations in the reign of Josiah in 621 B.C.E. The book presumably would have been written quite close to that date, though it might conceivably have utilized some literary materials going back as far as a century, to the reign of Hezekiah.

These sundry literary sources were probably edited and fashioned into a single book—the first properly canonical book with binding authority on the national community—sometime in the sixth century B.C.E., in the Babylonian exile. It has been proposed—not without challenge—that Ezra the Scribe, who instituted public readings of the Torah for the Judeans returned from the Babylonian exile, perhaps soon after 458 B.C.E., may have overseen the final redaction of the Torah. The finished product, as one might expect, exhibits a good many duplications, contradictions, and inconsistencies, which have been abundantly analyzed by modern scholarship. But it also possesses a degree of cohesiveness as a book, and I would like to sketch out here the general literary design, which will then receive more specific attention in the commentary and in the introductions to the individual books.

Genesis is the only one of the Five Books that is more or less continuous narrative from beginning to end, the only recurrent but limited exception being the genealogies (the "begats"), which, as I shall try to indicate in the commentary, have a function as structural and thematic markers. If this were the work of a single writer, one would say he begins at the top of his form, not slowly and circuitously, like the late Henry James, but with a tour de force, like Proust in the initial pages of *In Search of Lost Time*. Genesis opens with a narrative of origins— Creation and the Garden Story—that is compelling in its archetypal character, its adaptation of myth to monotheistic ends, and that has set the terms, not scientifically but symbolically, for much of the way we have thought about human nature and culture ever since.

This legendary sequence, which moves from Eden at the beginning to the Tower of Babel in chapter 11, is followed by a different kind of narrative in the Patriarchal Tales that begin with Abraham in chapter 12. Nowhere else in ancient literature have the quirkiness and unpredictability of individual character and the frictions and tensions of family life—sibling rivalry, the jealousy of co-wives, the extravagance of parental favoritism—been registered with such subtlety and insight. These stories were of course written more than half a millennium after

the time of the purported events, and many details reflect political considerations of a later era involving power relations among the tribes and
Israel's posture toward neighboring peoples. Yet the literary miracle of
the stories is that the chief personages are nevertheless imagined with
remarkable integrity and complexity as individual characters—Tamar
fiercely resolved to take into her own hands her personal cause of justice; Jacob, relentlessly calculating yet also imprudently loving, who as
an old man becomes a histrionic, tragically weakened father of the clan;
Joseph, evolving from spoiled brat to mature and shrewd administrator;
Judah, at first impetuous, in the end, penitent and lovingly devoted to
his father in all his weaknesses. Only the David story would equal the
Patriarchal Tales in psychological insight and in the representation of
character growing and changing through long stretches of life-
experience.

Genesis ends with the death of Joseph, and Exodus begins with an
Egyptian king who "knew not Joseph" and with a flurry of allusions to
early Genesis, so the two are clearly meant to be read in succession as
a continuous narrative. The focus of the narrative, however, shifts from
the emotionally fraught lives of the founding fathers and mothers to the
story of the origins of the nation. The account of the enslavement in
Egypt, the liberation from slavery through God's great signs and wonders wrought against Egypt, and the march of the people led by Moses
to the foot of Mount Sinai, is a kind of national epic, narrated in a
cadenced prose, punctuated with refrainlike rhetorical flourishes,
deploying a grand sweeping style only occasionally evidenced in Genesis. This imposing narrative has been shaped to show forth God's overwhelming power in history, exerted against one of the great ancient
kingdoms, and the forging of the nation through a spectacular chain of
divine interventions that culminates in the spectacle of the revelation
on the mountain of God's imperatives to Israel.

After the Sinai epiphany, Exodus takes a turn that may seem per-
plexing to modern readers. Narrative is dropped—to return briefly with
the arresting episode of the Golden Calf in chapters 32–34—and is
replaced first by the articulation of a code of civil and criminal law and
then by elaborate instructions for the erection of that Tabernacle that
will be implemented in the closing chapters of the book with word-for-
word repetition. Narrative continues to be set aside for almost all of the

next book, Leviticus, which is devoted to a complex body of legal injunctions, mainly but not exclusively cultic. Structurally, Leviticus is the capstone of the Five Books, balancing Genesis and Exodus on one side and Numbers and Deuteronomy on the other. It will strike many as an odd sort of capstone, given its concentration on sacrificial procedure, and one is inclined to suspect that the Priestly editors of the Torah are furthering the interests of their own guild in the central placement of this book.

It should be said, however, that if these Five Books are chiefly an account of the origins and definition of the nation from its first forebears who accepted a covenant with God to the moment when the people stands on the brink of entering the Promised Land, the ancient writers conceived three major constituents of national identity and cohesion. The first, and the one that we can most readily understand, is the trajectory of the collective and of its principal figures through the medium of history. In the tracing of this trajectory, the narrative shows us how historical events shape the people, how the people achieves a sense of its identity and purpose through the pressure of events. This, in essence, is the grand narrative arc from Genesis 12 to Exodus 20. But the biblical writers assumed that Israel's covenant with God had to be realized through institutional arrangements as well as through historical acts; and so the account of national origins and destiny required a body of cultic regulations, in which the people's relationship with God would be enacted regularly, repeatedly, through ritual, and a body of general law governing persons, property, acts of violence of man against man, social obligations, and ethical behavior. Although it is not clear whether all of these laws were actually implemented in ancient Israel, the effect of the lengthy legal passages, both cultic and civil or criminal, is to bridge the distance of the epic *illud tempus*, the time-back-when, of the narrative and bring the text into the institutional present of its audience.

The Book of Numbers begins with a long roll call of the tribes, what might be regarded as a statistically buttressed realization of the imposing extent of the Israelite hosts in the wilderness before the conquest of the land. After some intervening chapters of cultic and other laws, we at last return, with a few further interruptions, to narrative—a sequence of episodes in which the recalcitrant Israelites "murmur" against Moses and Aaron, the story of the twelve spies with its disastrous outcome, and, late in the book, a series of encounters between Israel and various hostile peoples of the trans-Jordan region that block their approach to Canaan. The excitements, the grave dangers, and the grand hopes of swimming in the tide of history are all powerfully at play here, and these are vividly brought forth in the evocative poetry of Balaam's oracles that take up chapters 23 and 24.

Although Deuteronomy, as we have already noted, was originally composed quite independently of the preceding four books and actually before a good many of the Priestly passages they contain were even written, in the place it has been given in the process of redaction, it comes to serve as a grand summary of the themes and story we have read up to this point. To be sure, this last book was intended as a fundamental revision of much earlier law, with the emphasis on one exclusive national sanctuary the principal item of revision. Nevertheless, read in sequence with the other four books, it comes across as a strong recapitulation and conclusion. Moses, standing across the Jordan from the land he will never enter and on the verge of his own death, speaks the message of the book as a long valedictory address or, perhaps more precisely, a series of addresses. He picks up, in first-person singular or plural report, some of the principal narrative elements of the preceding three books (the Genesis stories are not much involved), usually abridging them, sometimes subjecting them to revision according to the overall ideological aims of Deuteronomy. Because these speeches are represented as spoken words addressed to the people as audience, rhetoric is spectacularly prominent here in ways that have no counterparts in the first four books with their narrative and legal interests. The rhetoric itself makes this appropriate as a concluding book: after the narrative and the legislation of Genesis through Numbers, Moses on the rostrum in trans-Jordan delivers a tremendous peroration in which all the themes of liberation, revelation, and theological and ethical imperative of the previous books are deeply impressed on the imagination of the people.

All that I have said here of course does not constitute a claim that the Five Books from "When God began to create . . ." to "before the eyes of all Israel" form one continuous text. The Torah is manifestly a composite construction, but there is abundant evidence throughout the

Hebrew Bible that composite work was fundamental to the very conception of what literature was, that a process akin to collage was assumed to be one of the chief ways in which literary texts were put together. What we have, then, in the Five Books is a work assembled by many hands, reflecting several different viewpoints, and representing literary activity that spanned several centuries. The redacted whole nevertheless creates some sense of continuity and development, and it allows itself to be read as a forward-moving process through time and theme from book to book, yielding an overarching literary structure we can call, in the singular version of the title, the Torah. The Torah exhibits seams, fissures, and inner tensions that cannot be ignored, but it has also been artfully assembled through the ancient editorial process to cohere strongly as the foundational text of Israelite life and the cornerstone of the biblical canon.

II. THE BIBLE IN ENGLISH
AND THE HERESY OF EXPLANATION

Why, after so many English versions, a new translation of the Five Books of Moses? There is, as I shall explain in detail, something seriously wrong with all the familiar English translations, traditional and recent, of the Hebrew Bible. Broadly speaking, one may say that in the case of the modern versions, the problem is a shaky sense of English and in the case of the King James Version, a shaky sense of Hebrew. The present translation is an experiment in re-presenting the Bible—and, above all, biblical narrative prose—in a language that conveys with some precision the semantic nuances and the lively orchestration of literary effects of the Hebrew and at the same time has stylistic and rhythmic integrity as literary English. I shall presently give a more specific account of the kind of English I have aimed for and of the features of the Hebrew that have prompted my choices, but I think it will be helpful for me to say something first about why English translations of the Bible have been problematic—more problematic, perhaps, than most readers may realize.

It is an old and in some ways unfair cliché to say that translation is always a betrayal, but modern English versions of the Bible provide unfortunately persuasive evidence for that uncompromising generalization. At first thought, it is rather puzzling that this should be the case. In purely quantitative terms, we live in a great age of Bible translation. Several integral translations of the Bible have been done since the middle of the twentieth century, and a spate of English versions of individual biblical books has appeared. This period, moreover, is one in which our understanding of ancient Hebrew has become considerably more nuanced and precise than it once was, thanks to comparative Semitic philology aided by archeology, and also thanks to the careful reanalysis of the formal structures—syntax, grammar, morphology, verb tenses— of biblical Hebrew. One might have expected that this recent flurry of translation activity, informed by the newly focused awareness of the meanings of biblical Hebrew, would have produced at least some English versions that would be both vividly precise and closer to the feel of the original than any of the older translations. Instead, the modern English versions—especially in their treatment of Hebrew narrative prose—have placed readers at a grotesque distance from the distinctive literary experience of the Bible in its original language. As a consequence, the King James Version, as Gerald Hammond, an eminent British authority on Bible translations, has convincingly argued, remains the closest approach for English readers to the original— despite its frequent and at times embarrassing inaccuracies, despite its archaisms, and despite its insistent substitution of Renaissance English tonalities and rhythms for biblical ones.

Some observers have sought to explain the inadequacy of modern Bible translations in terms of the general decline of the English language. It is certainly true that there are far fewer people these days with a cultivated sensitivity to the expressive resources of the language, the nuances of lexical values, the force of metaphor and rhythm; and one is certainly much less likely to find such people on a committee of ecclesiastical or scholarly experts than one would have in the first decade of the seventeenth century. There are, nevertheless, still some brilliant stylists among English prose writers; and if our age has been graced with remarkable translations of Homer, Sophocles, and Dante, why not of the Bible?

Part of the explanation, I suspect, is in the conjunction of philological scholarship and translation. I intend no churlish disrespect to philology. On the contrary, without it, our reading of the Bible, or indeed of any older text, is no better than walking through a great museum on a very gloomy day with all the lights turned out. To read the Bible over the shoulder of a great philological critic, like Abraham ibn Ezra (1092–1167), one of the earliest and still eminently worth studying, is to see many important things in fine focus for the first time. There is, however, a crucial difference between philology as a tool for understanding literary texts and philology as an end in itself, for literature and philology work with extremely different conceptions of what constitutes knowledge. To be fair to the broad enterprise of philology, which has included some great literary critics, I use the term here as shorthand for "biblical philology," a discipline that, especially in its Anglo-American applications, has often come down to lexicography and the analysis of grammar.

For the philologist, the great goal is the achievement of clarity. It is scarcely necessary to say that in all sorts of important, but also delimited, ways clarity is indispensable in a translator's wrestling with the original text. The simplest case, but a pervasive one, consists of getting a handle on the meaning of particular terms. It is truly helpful, for example, to know that biblical *naḥal* most commonly indicates not any sort of brook, creek, or stream but the kind of freshet, called a *wadi* in both Arabic and modern Hebrew, that floods a dry desert gulch during the rainy months and vanishes in the heat of the summer. Suddenly, Job's "my brothers have betrayed like a *naḥal*" (Job 6:14) becomes a striking poetic image, where before it might have been a minor puzzlement. But philological clarity in literary texts can quickly turn into too much of a good thing. Literature in general, and the narrative prose of the Hebrew Bible in particular, cultivates certain profound and haunting enigmas, delights in leaving its audiences guessing about motives and connections, and, above all, loves to set ambiguities of word choice and image against one another in an endless interplay that resists neat resolution. In polar contrast, the impulse of the philologist is—here a barbarous term nicely catches the tenor of the activity—"to disambiguate" the terms of the text. The general result when applied to translation is to reduce, simplify, and denature the Bible. These unfortunate consequences are all the more pronounced when the philologist, however acutely trained in that discipline, has an underdeveloped sense of literary diction, rhythm, and the uses of figurative language; and that, alas, is often the case in an era in which literary culture is not widely disseminated even among the technically educated.

The unacknowledged heresy underlying most modern English versions of the Bible is the use of translation as a vehicle for *explaining* the Bible instead of representing it in another language, and in the most egregious instances this amounts to explaining away the Bible. This impulse may be attributed not only to a rather reduced sense of the philological enterprise but also to a feeling that the Bible, because of its canonical status, has to be made accessible—indeed, transparent—to all. (The one signal exception to all these generalizations is Everett Fox's 1995 American version of the Torah. Emulating the model of the German translation by Martin Buber and Franz Rosenzweig [begun in 1925, completed in 1961], which flaunts Hebrew etymologies, preserves nearly all repetitions of Hebrew terms, and invents German words, Fox goes to the opposite extreme: his English has the great virtue of reminding us verse after verse of the strangeness of the Hebrew original, but it does so at the cost of often being not quite English and consequently of becoming a text for study rather than a fluently readable version that conveys the stylistic poise and power of the Hebrew.) Modern translators, in their zeal to uncover the meanings of the biblical text for the instruction of a modern readership, frequently lose sight of how the text intimates its meanings—the distinctive, artfully deployed features of ancient Hebrew prose and poetry that are the instruments for the articulation of all meaning, message, insight, and vision.

One of the most salient characteristics of biblical Hebrew is its extraordinary concreteness, manifested especially in a fondness for images rooted in the human body. The general predisposition of modern translators is to convert most of this concrete language into more abstract terms that have the purported advantage of clarity but turn the pungency of the original into stale paraphrase. A good deal of this concrete biblical language based on the body is what a linguist would call lexicalized metaphor—imagery, here taken from body parts and bodily functions, that is made to stand for some general concept as a fixed item in the vocabulary of the language (as "eye" in English can be used to mean "perceptiveness" or "connoisseur's understanding"). Dead metaphors, however, are the one persuasive instance of the resurrection of the dead—for at least the ghosts of the old concrete meanings float over the supposedly abstract acceptations of the terms, and this is something the philologically driven translators do not appear to understand. "Many modern versions," Gerald Hammond tartly observes, "eschew anything which smacks of imagery or metaphor—based on the curious assumption, I guess, that modern English is an image-free language." The price paid for this avoidance of the metaphorical will become evident by considering two characteristic and recurrent Hebrew terms and the role they play in representing the world in the biblical story.

The Hebrew noun *zera*ʿ* has the general meaning of "seed," which can be applied either in the agricultural sense or to human beings, as the term for semen. By metaphorical extension, semen becomes the established designation for what it produces, progeny. Modern translators, evidently unwilling to trust the ability of adult readers to understand that "seed"—as regularly in the King James Version—may mean progeny, repeatedly render it as offspring, descendants, heirs, progeny, posterity. But I think there is convincing evidence in the texts themselves that the biblical writers never entirely forgot that their term for offspring also meant semen and had a precise equivalent in the vegetable world. To cite a distinctly physical example, when Onan "knew that the seed would not be his," that is, the progeny of his brother's widow should he impregnate her, "he would waste his seed on the ground, so to give no seed to his brother" (Genesis 38:9). Modern translators, despite their discomfort with body terms, can scarcely avoid the wasted "seed" here because without it the representation of spilling semen on the ground in coitus interruptus becomes unintelligible. E. A. Speiser substitutes "offspring" for "seed" at the end of the verse, however, and the Revised English Bible goes him one better by putting "offspring" at the beginning as well ("Onan knew that the offspring would not count as his") and introducing "seed" in the middle as object of the verb "to spill" and scuttling back to the decorousness of "offspring" at the end—a prime instance of explanation under the guise of

---

*The symbol ʿ represents the Hebrew consonant ʿ*ayin,* a glottal stop that might sound something like the Cockney pronunciation of the middle consonant of "bottle," in which the dentalized *t* is replaced by a gulping sound produced from the larynx.

translation. But the biblical writer is referring to "seed" as much at the
end of the verse as at the beginning. Onan adopts the stratagem of
coitus interruptus in order not to "give seed"—that is, semen—to
Tamar, and, as a necessary consequence of this contraceptive act, he
avoids providing her with offspring. The thematic point of this moment,
anchored in sexual practice, law, and human interaction, is blunted by
not preserving "seed" throughout.

Even in contexts not directly related to sexuality, the concreteness of
this term often amplifies the meaning of the utterance. When, for
example, at the end of the story of the binding of Isaac, God reiterates
His promise to Abraham, the multiplication of seed is strongly linked
with cosmic imagery—harking back to the Creation story—of heaven
and earth: "I will greatly bless you and will greatly multiply your seed,
as the stars in the heavens and as the sand on the shore of the sea"
(Genesis 22:17). If "seed" here is rendered as "offspring" or "descendants," what we get are two essentially mathematical similes of numerical increase. That is, in fact, the primary burden of the language God
addresses to Abraham, but as figurative language it also imposes itself
visually on the retina of the imagination, and so underlying the idea of
a single late-born son whose progeny will be countless millions is an
image of human seed (perhaps reinforced by the shared white color of
semen and stars) scattered across the vast expanses of the starry skies
and through the innumerable particles of sand on the shore of the sea.
To substitute "offspring" for "seed" here may not fundamentally alter
the meaning but it diminishes the vividness of the statement, making
it just a little harder for readers to sense why these ancient texts have
been so compelling down through the ages.

The most metaphorically extended body part in biblical Hebrew is
the hand, though head and foot are also abundantly represented in figurative senses. Now it is obvious enough, given the equivalent usages in
modern Western languages, that "hand" can be employed figuratively to
express such notions as power, control, responsibility, and trust—to
which biblical Hebrew adds one meaning peculiar to itself, commemorative monument. But most modern translators substitute one or
another of these abstract terms, introducing supposed clarity where
things were perfectly clear to begin with and subverting the literary
integrity of the story. In the two sequential episodes that end with

Joseph's being cast into a pit—the first is a dry cistern, the second an Egyptian prison, but the two are explicitly linked by the use of the term *bor* for both—the recurrently invoked "hand" is a focusing device that both defines and complicates the moral themes of the story. Reuben, hearing his brothers' murderous intentions, seeks to rescue Joseph "from their hands." He implores his brothers, "Lay not a hand upon him," just as, in the other strand of the story, Judah says, "Let not our hand be against him." E. A. Speiser, faithful to the clarifying impulse of the modern Bible scholar's philological imagination, renders both these phrases as "do away with," explaining that it would be illogical to have Reuben, or Judah, say "Don't lay a hand on him," since in fact the counsel proffered involves seizing him, stripping him, and throwing him into the pit. But in fact this alleged illogic is the luminous logic of the writer's moral critique. Reuben pleads with his brothers not to lay a hand on Joseph, that is, not to shed his blood (this is the phrase he uses at the beginning of his speech), but neither his plea nor Judah's proposal is an entirely innocent one: although each urges that the brothers lay no hand on Joseph, there is a violent laying on of hands necessitated by the course of action each proposes. Even more pointedly, once Joseph is headed south with the caravan, those same fraternal hands will take his ornamented tunic (the King James Version's "coat of many colors"), slaughter a kid, dip the garment in the blood, and send it off to Jacob.

The image of hands holding a garment belonging to Joseph that is turned into false evidence brilliantly returns at the climactic moment of the next episode involving him, in Genesis 39. When Joseph flees from the lust of his master's wife, "he left his garment in her hand" because she has virtually torn it off his back in trying to effect her reiterated "Lie with me" by seizing him. In her accusation of Joseph, she alters the narrator's twice-stated "in her hand" to "by me," implying that he disrobed deliberately before attempting to rape her. But the narrator's cunning deployment of repeated terms has conditioned us to zero in on these two pivotal words, *waya'azov beyad,* "he left in the hand of," for in the six initial framing verses of the story, "hand" appears four times, with the last, most significant occurrence being this summary of the comprehensiveness of Joseph's stewardship: "And he left all that he had in Joseph's hands" (39:6). (Hebrew idiom allows the writer to use "hand" in the singular, thus creating an exact phrasal identity between the figurative reference to the hand in which the trust of stewardship is left and the literal reference to the hand in which the garment belonging to the object of sexual desire is left.) The invocation of "hand" in chapters 37 and 39—the story of Judah and Tamar lies between them—forms an elegant A B A B pattern: in chapter 37 hands are laid on Joseph, an action carried forward in the resumptive repetition at the very beginning of chapter 39 when he is bought "from the hands of the Ishmaelites"; then we have the supremely competent hand, or hands, of Joseph, into which everything is placed, or left, and by which everything succeeds; then again a violent hand is laid on Joseph, involving the stripping of his garment, as in the episode with the brothers; and at the end of the chapter, Joseph in prison again has everything entrusted to his dependable hands, with this key term twice stated in the three and a half verses of the closing frame. A kind of dialectic is created in the thematic unfolding of the story between hand as the agency of violent impulse and hand as the instrument of scrupulous management. Although the concrete term is probably used with more formal precision in this particular sequence than is usually the case elsewhere, the hands of Joseph and the hands upon Joseph provide a fine object lesson about how biblical narrative is misrepresented when translators tamper with the purposeful and insistent physicality of its language, as here when "hand" is transmuted into "trust" or "care." Such substitutions offer explanations or interpretations instead of translations and thus betray the original.

There are, alas, more pervasive ways than the choice of terms in which nearly all the modern English versions commit the heresy of explanation. The most global of these is the prevalent modern strategy of repackaging biblical syntax for an audience whose reading experience is assumed to be limited to *Time, Newsweek,* and the *New York Times* or the *Times* of London. Now, it is often asserted, with seemingly self-evident justice, that the fundamental difference between biblical syntax and modern English syntax is between a system in which parallel clauses linked by "and" predominate (what linguists call "parataxis") and one in which the use of subordinate clauses and complex sentences predominates (what linguists call "hypotaxis"). Modern English has a broad array of modal and temporal discriminations in its system of verbs and a whole armament of subordinate conjunctions to stipulate different relations among clauses. Biblical Hebrew, on the other hand, has only two aspects* (they are probably not tenses in our sense) of verbs, together with one indication of a jussive mode—when a verb is used to express a desire or exhortation to perform the action in question—and a modest number of subordinate conjunctions. Although there are certainly instances of significant syntactic subordination, the characteristic biblical syntax is additive, working with parallel clauses linked by "and"—which in the Hebrew is not even a separate word but rather a particle, *waw*† (it means "hook"), that is prefixed to the first word of the clause.

The assumption of most modern translators has been that this sort of syntax will be either unintelligible or at least alienating to modern readers, and so should be entirely rearranged as modern English. There are two basic problems with this procedure. First, it ignores the fact that parataxis is the essential literary vehicle of biblical narrative: it is the way the ancient Hebrew writers saw the world, linked events in it, artfully ordered it, and narrated it, and one gets a very different world if their syntax is jettisoned. Second, rejection of biblical parataxis presupposes a very simplistic notion of what constitutes modern literary English. The implicit model seems to be, as I have suggested, the popular press, as well as perhaps high-school textbooks, bureaucratic directives, and ordinary conversation. But serious writers almost never accept such leveling limitation to a bland norm of popular usage. If one thinks of the great English stylists among twentieth-century novelists—writers like Joyce, Nabokov, Faulkner, and Virginia Woolf—there is not one among them whose use of language, including the deployment of syntax, even vaguely resembles the workaday simplicity and patly consistent orderliness that recent translators of the Bible have posited as the norm of modern English. It is also well to keep in mind that literary style, like many other aspects of literature, is constantly self-recapitulative, invoking recollections of its near and distant literary antecedents, so that modernists like Joyce and Faulkner sometimes

---

*Instead of a clear-cut expression of the temporal frame in which actions occur—past, present, future, past perfect, and so forth—aspects indicate chiefly whether the action has been completed or is to be completed.

†The modern Hebrew pronunciation is *vav*, with the vowel sounding like the short *a* in a French word like *bave*, with which it would rhyme.

echo biblical language and cadences, and a mannered stylist like Hemingway, in making "and" his most prominent connective, surely has the King James Version of the Bible in mind. And in any event, the broad history of both Semitic and European languages and literatures evinces a strong differentiation in most periods between everyday language and the language of literature.

The assumption of biblical philologists that parallel syntax is alien to modern literary English is belied by the persistent presence of highly wrought paratactic prose even at the end of the twentieth century and beyond. A variety of self-conscious English stylists in the modern era, from Gertrude Stein to Cormac McCarthy, have exhibited a fondness for chains of parallel utterances linked by "and" in which the basic sentence-type is the same structurally as that used again and again in biblical prose. What such a style makes manifest in a narrative is a series of more or less discrete events, or micro-events, in a chain, not unlike the biblical names of begetters and begotten that are strung one after another in the chains of the genealogical lists. The biblical writers generally chose not to order these events in ramified networks of causal, conceptual, or temporal subordination, not because hypotaxis was an unavailable option, as the opening verses of the second Creation story (Genesis 2:4–5) clearly demonstrate. The continuing appeal, moreover, for writers in our own age of this syntax dominated by "and," which highlights the discrete event, suggests that parallel syntax may still be a perfectly viable way to represent in English the studied parallelism of verbs and clauses of ancient Hebrew narrative.

Since a literary style is composed of very small elements as well as larger structural features, an English translator must confront the pesky question of whether the ubiquitous Hebrew particle that means "and" should be represented at all in translation. This is obviously not a problem when the *waw* simply connects two nouns—as in "the heavens and the earth"—but what of its constant use at the beginning of sentences and clauses prefixed to verbs? The argument against translating it in these cases is that the primary function of the *waw* appended to a verb is not to signify "and" but to indicate that the Hebrew prefix conjugation, which otherwise is used for actions yet to be completed, is reporting past events (hence its designation in the terminology of classical Hebrew grammar as "the *waw* of conversion").

It is far from clear, as modern Bible scholars tend to assume, that the fulfillment of one linguistic function by a particle of speech automatically excludes any others; on the contrary, it is entirely likely that for the ancient audience the *waw* appended to the verb both converted its temporal aspect and continued to signify "and." But, semantics aside, the general practice of modern English translators of suppressing the "and" when it is attached to a verb has the effect of changing the tempo, rhythm, and construction of events in biblical narrative. Let me illustrate by quoting a narrative sequence from Genesis 24 first in my own version, which reproduces every "and" and every element of parataxis, and then in the version of the Revised English Bible. The Revised English Bible is in general one of the most compulsive repackagers of biblical language, though in this instance the reordering of the Hebrew is relatively minor. Its rendering of these sentences is roughly interchangeable with any of the other modern versions—the Jerusalem Bible, the New Jewish Publication Society, Speiser—one might choose. I begin in the middle of verse 16, where Rebekah becomes the subject of a series of actions.

> And she came down to the spring and filled her jug and came back up. And the servant ran toward her and said, "Pray, let me sip a bit of water from your jug." And she said, "Drink, my lord," and she hurried and tipped down her jug on one hand and let him drink. And she let him drink his fill and said, "For your camels, too, I shall draw water until they drink their fill." And she hurried and emptied her jug into the trough, and she ran again to the well to draw water and drew water for all his camels.

And this is how the Revised English Bible, in keeping with the prevailing assumptions of most recent translations, renders these verses in what is presumed to be sensible modern English:

> She went down to the spring, filled her jar, and came up again. Abraham's servant hurried to meet her and said, "Will you give me a little water from your jar?" "Please drink, sir," she answered, and at once lowered her jar on her hand to let him drink. When she had finished giving him a drink, she said, "I shall draw water also for your camels until they have had enough." She quickly emptied her jar into the water trough, and then hurrying again to the well she drew water and watered all the camels.

There is, as one would expect, some modification of biblical parataxis, though it is not so extreme here as elsewhere in the Revised English Bible: "And she let him drink his fill" is converted into an introductory adverbial clause, "When she had finished giving him a drink" (actually in consonance with the otherwise paratactic King James Version): "and she hurried" is compressed into "quickly"; "and she ran again" becomes the participial "hurrying again." (Moves of this sort, it should be said, push translation to the verge of paraphrase—recasting and interpreting the original instead of representing it.) The most striking divergence between these two versions is that mine has fifteen "and's," corresponding precisely to fifteen occurrences of the particle *waw* in the Hebrew, whereas the Revised English Bible manages with just five. What difference does this make? To begin with, it should be observed that the *waw*, whatever is claimed about its linguistic function, is by no means an inaudible element in the phonetics of the Hebrew text: we must keep constantly in mind that these narratives were composed to be *heard*, not merely to be decoded by a reader's eye. The reiterated "and," then, plays an important role in creating the rhythm of the story, in phonetically punctuating the forward-driving movement of the prose. The elimination of the "and" in the Revised English Bible and in all its modern cousins produces   certainly to my ear—an abrupt, awkward effect in the sound pattern of the language, or to put it more strictly, a kind of narrative arrhythmia.

More is at stake here than pleasing sounds, for the heroine of the repeated actions is in fact subtly but significantly reduced in all the rhythmically deficient versions. She of course performs roughly the same acts in the different versions—politely offering water to the stranger, lowering her jug so that he can drink, rapidly going back and forth to the spring to bring water for the camels. But in the compressions, syntactical reorderings, and stop-and-start movements of the modernizing version, the encounter at the well and Rebekah's actions are made to seem rather matter-of-fact, however exemplary her impulse of hospitality. This tends to obscure what the Hebrew highlights, which is that she is doing something quite extraordinary. Rebekah at the well presents one of the rare biblical instances of the performance of an act of "Homeric" heroism. The servant begins by asking modestly to "sip a bit of water," as though all he wanted were to wet his lips. But we need to remember, as the ancient audience surely did, that a camel after a long desert journey can drink as much as twenty-five gallons of water, and there are ten camels here whom Rebekah offers to water "until they drink their fill." The chain of verbs tightly linked by all the "and's" does an admirable job in conveying this sense of the young woman's hurling herself with prodigious speed into the sequence of required actions. Even her dialogue is scarcely a pause in the narrative momentum, but is integrated syntactically and rhythmically into the chain: "And she said, 'Drink, my lord,' and she hurried and tipped down her jug. . . . And she hurried and emptied her jug into the trough, and she ran again to the well to draw water and drew water for all his camels." The parallel syntax and the barrage of "and's," far from being the reflex of a "primitive" language, are as artfully effective in furthering the ends of the narrative as any device one could find in a sophisticated modern novelist.

Beyond these issues of syntax and local word choice lies a fundamental question that no modern translator I know of has really confronted: what level, or perhaps levels, of style is represented in biblical Hebrew? There is no reason, I believe, to be awestruck by the sheer antiquity of the text. If biblical Hebrew could be shown to reflect a pungent colloquial usage in the ancient setting, or a free commingling of colloquial and formal language, it would be only logical to render it with equivalent levels of diction in modern English. As a matter of fact, all the modern translators—from Speiser to Fox to the sundry ecclesiastical committees in both America and England—have shown a deaf ear to diction, acting as though the only important considerations in rendering a literary text were lexical values and grammatical structures, while the English terms chosen could be promiscuously borrowed from boardroom or bedroom or scholar's word hoard, with little regard to the tonality and connotation the words carried with them from their native linguistic habitat.

Whatever conclusions we may draw about the stylistic level of biblical Hebrew are a little precarious because we of course have no record of the ancient spoken language, and if, as seems likely, there were extracanonical varieties or genres of Hebrew writing in the ancient world, the vestiges have long since crumbled into dust. Did, for example, the citizens of Judea in the time of Jeremiah speak in a parallel syntax, using the *waw* consecutive, and employing roughly the same vocabulary that we find in his prophecies, or in Deuteronomy and Genesis? Although there is no proof, my guess is that vernacular syntax and grammar probably differed in some ways from their literary counterparts. In regard to vocabulary, there is evidence that what we see in the canonical books would not have been identical with everyday usage. First, there is the problem of the relative paucity of vocabulary in biblical literature. As the Spanish Hebrew scholar Angel Sáenz-Badillos has observed in his *History of the Hebrew Language* (1993), the biblical lexicon is so restricted that it is hard to believe it could have served all the purposes of quotidian existence in a highly developed society. The instance of the poetry of Job, with its unusual number of words not found elsewhere in Scripture, is instructive in this regard: the Job-poet, in his powerful impulse to forge a poetic imagery that would represent humankind, God, and nature in a new and even startling light, draws on highly specific language from manufacturing processes, food preparation, commercial and legal institutions, which would never be used in biblical narrative. The plausible conclusion is that the Hebrew of the Bible is a conventionally delimited language, roughly analagous in this respect to the French of the neoclassical theater: it was understood by writers and their audiences, at least in the case of narrative, that only certain words were appropriate for the literary rendering of events.

There is evidence, moreover, that people in everyday life may have had different words for many of the basic concepts and entities that are mentioned in the Bible. This argument was persuasively made by the Israeli linguist Abba ben David in his still indispensable 1967 study, available only in Hebrew, *The Language of the Bible and the Language of the Sages*. Ben David offers a fascinating explanation for one of the great mysteries of the Hebrew language—the emergence, toward the end of the pre-Christian era, of a new kind of Hebrew, which became the language of the early rabbis. Now, it is widely recognized that this new Hebrew reflected the influence of the Aramaic vernacular in morphology, in grammar, and in some of its vocabulary, and that, understandably, it also incorporated a vast number of Greek and Latin loanwords. But what is puzzling is that rabbinic Hebrew also uses a good many indigenous Hebrew terms that are absent from the biblical corpus, or reflected only in rare and marginal biblical cognates. The standard terms in rabbinical Hebrew for sun and moon, and some of its frequently used verbs like to look, to take, to enter, to clean, are entirely different from their biblical counterparts, without visible influence from any of the languages impinging on Hebrew. Where did these words come from? Ben David, observing, as have others before him, that there are incipient signs of an emergent rabbinic Hebrew in late biblical books like Jonah and the Song of Songs, makes the bold and, to my mind, convincing proposal that rabbinic Hebrew was built upon an ancient vernacular that for the most part had been excluded from the literary language used for the canonical texts. This makes particular sense if one keeps in mind that the early rabbis were anxious to draw a line between their own "Oral Torah" and the written Torah they were expounding. For the purposes of legal and homiletic exegesis, they naturally would have used a vernacular Hebrew rather than the literary language, and when their discourse was first given written formulation in the Mishnah in the early third century C.E., that text would have recorded this vernacular, which probably had a long prehistory in the biblical period. It is distinctly possible that when a ninth-century B.C.E. Israelite farmer mopped his brow under the blazing sun, he did not point to it and say *shemesh,* as it is invariably called in biblical prose texts, but rather *ḥamah,* as it is regularly designated in the Mishnah.

There is, of course, no way of plotting a clear chronology of the evolution of rabbinic Hebrew from an older vernacular, no way of determining how far back into the biblical period various elements of rabbinic language may go. It is sufficient for our effort to gauge the level of style of the Bible's literary prose merely to grant the very high likelihood that the language of the canonical texts was not identical with the vernacular, that it reflected a specialized or elevated vocabulary, and perhaps even a distinct grammar and syntax. Let me cite a momentary exception to the rule of biblical usage that may give us a glimpse into this excluded vernacular background of a more formal literary language. It is well known that in biblical dialogue all the characters speak proper literary Hebrew, with no intimations of slang, dialect, or idiolect. The single striking exception is impatient Esau's first speech to Jacob in Genesis 25: "Let me gulp down some of this red red stuff." Inarticulate with hunger, he cannot come up with the ordinary Hebrew term for "stew," and so he makes do with *ha'adom ha'adom hazeh*—literally "this red red." But what is more interesting for our purpose is the verb Esau uses for "feeding," *hal'iteini*. This is the sole occurrence of this verb in the biblical corpus, but in the Talmud it is a commonly used term with the specific meaning of stuffing food into the mouth of an animal. One cannot be certain this was its precise meaning in the biblical period because words do, after all, undergo semantic shifts in a period of considerably more than a thousand years. But it seems safe to assume, minimally, that even a millennium before the rabbis *hal'it* would have been a cruder term for feeding than the standard biblical *ha'akhil*. What I think happened at this point in Genesis is that the author, in the writerly zest with which he sought to characterize Esau's crudeness, allowed himself, quite exceptionally, to introduce a vernacular term for coarse eating or animal feeding into the dialogue that would jibe nicely with his phrase "this red red stuff." After the close of the biblical era, this otherwise excluded term would surface in the legal pronouncements of the rabbis on animal husbandry, together with a host of vernacular words used in the ancient period but never permitted to enter the canonical texts.

All this strongly suggests that the language of biblical narrative in its own time was stylized, decorous, dignified, and readily identified by its audiences as a language of literature, in certain ways distinct from the language of quotidian reality. The tricky complication, however, is that in most respects it also was not a lofty style, and was certainly neither ornate nor euphemistic. If some of its vocabulary may have reflected a specialized literary lexicon, the language of biblical narrative also makes abundant use of ordinary Hebrew words that must have been in everyone's mouth from day to day. Just to mention the few recurrent terms on which I have commented, "hand," "house," "all," and "seed" are primary words in every phase of the history of Hebrew, and they continue to appear as such in the rabbinic language, where so much else is altered. Biblical prose, then, is a formal literary language but also, paradoxically, a plainspoken one, and, moreover, a language that evinces a strong commitment to using a limited set of terms again and again, making an aesthetic virtue out of the repetition. It should be added that the language of the Bible reflects not one level of diction but a certain range of dictions, as I shall explain presently.

What is the implication of this analysis for an appropriate modern English equivalent to ancient Hebrew style? The right direction, I think, was hit on by the King James Version, following the great model of Tyndale a century before it. There is no good reason to render biblical Hebrew as contemporary English, either lexically or syntactically. This is not to suggest that the Bible should be represented as fussily old-fashioned English, but a limited degree of archaizing coloration is entirely appropriate, employed with other strategies for creating a language that is stylized yet simple and direct, free of the overtones of contemporary colloquial usage but with a certain timeless homespun quality. An adequate English version should be able to indicate the small but significant modulations in diction in the biblical language— something the stylistically uniform King James Version, however, entirely fails to do. A suitable English version should avoid at all costs the modern abomination of elegant synonymous variation, for the literary prose of the Bible turns everywhere on significant repetition, not variation. Similarly, the translation of terms on the basis of immediate context—except when it becomes grotesque to do otherwise—is to be resisted as another instance of the heresy of explanation. Finally, the mesmerizing effect of these ancient stories will scarcely be conveyed if they are not rendered in cadenced English prose that at least in some ways corresponds to the powerful cadences of the Hebrew. Let me now comment more particularly on the distinctive biblical treatment of diction, word choice, syntax, and rhythm and what it implies for translation.

THE biblical prose writers favor what we may think of as a primary vocabulary. They revel in repetition, sometimes of a stately, refrainlike sort, sometimes deployed in ingenious patterns through which different meanings of the same term are played against one another. Elegant synonymity is alien to biblical prose, and it is only rarely that a highly specialized term is used instead of the more general word. Here is a characteristic biblical way of putting things: "And God made the two great lights, the great light for dominion of day and the small light for dominion of night, and the stars" (Genesis 1:16). In addition to the poised emphasis of the internal repetitions in the sentence, one should note that the primary term for a source of light—*ma'or,* transparently cognate with *'or,* the light that is divided from the darkness in 1:4—is placed in the foreground. In fact, there are half a dozen biblical synonyms for "light," suggesting a range roughly equivalent to English terms like "illumination," "effulgence," "brilliance," and "splendor," but these are all reserved for the more elaborate vocabulary of poetry, whereas in prose the writer sticks to the simplicity of *'or* and *ma'or,* and everywhere it behooves a translator to do the same with English equivalents.

Some biblical scholars might object that my example is skewed because it is taken from the so-called Priestly source (P), which has a stylistic predilection for high decorousness and cadenced repetitions. But the stylistic difference in this regard between P and the two other conjectured source documents of the Pentateuch, designated J and E, is one of degree, not kind. Thus, when the second version of the Creation story, commonly identified as J's, begins in Genesis 2:4, we do get some greater degree of specification in the language, in keeping with the way creation is here imagined. Instead of the verbs "to create" (*bara'*) and "to make" (*'asah*) that accompany God's speaking the world into being in chapter 1 we are given the potter's term "to fashion" (*yatsar*) and the architectural term "to build" (*banah*). These remain, however, within the limits of a primary vocabulary. The nuanced and specialized lexicon of manufacturing processes one encounters in the poetry of Job and of Deutero-Isaiah is firmly excluded from the stylistic horizon of this narrative prose, though the subject might have invited it.

The translator's task, then, is to mirror the repetitions as much as is feasible. Let me cite one small example, where I learned from my own mistake. When Joseph's brothers recount to Jacob what happened on their first trip to Egypt, they say, in the English of my first draft, "The man who is lord of the land spoke harshly to us and accused us of being spies in the land" (Genesis 42:30). (The verb "accused" is also used in the New Jewish Publication Society translation.) On rereading, I realized that I had violated the cardinal principle, not to translate according to context. The Hebrew says, very literally, "gave us as spies," "give" in biblical usage being one of those all-purpose verbs that variously means "to set," "to place," "to grant," "to deem." I hastened to change the last clause to "made us out to be spies" because "to make," with or without an accompanying preposition, is precisely such a primary term that serves many purposes and so is very much in keeping with biblical stylistic practice.

What is surprising about the biblical writers' use of this deliberately limited vocabulary is that it can be so precise and even nuanced. Our own cultural preconceptions of writers scrupulously devoted to finding exactly the right word are associated with figures like Flaubert and Joyce, who meticulously choose the terms of their narratives from a large repertory of finely discriminated lexical items. Biblical prose often exhibits an analogous precision within the severe limits of its primary vocabulary. There are, for example, two paired terms, masculine and feminine, in biblical Hebrew to designate young people: *na'ar/na'arah* (in this translation, "lad" and "young woman") and *yeled/yaldah* (in this translation, "child" and "girl"). The first pair is somewhat asymmetrical because *na'ar* often also means "servant" or anyone in a subaltern position, and sometimes means "elite soldier," whereas *na'arah* usually refers to a nubile young woman, and only occasionally to a servant girl. Though there are rare biblical occurrences of *yeled* in the sense of "young man," it generally designates someone younger than a *na'ar*— etymologically, it means "the one who is born," reflecting a development parallel to the French *enfant*.

With this little to work with, it is remarkable how much the biblical writers accomplish in their deployment of the terms. In the first part of the story of the banishment of Hagar and Ishmael (Genesis 21), Ishmael is referred to consistently as "the child," as was his infant half brother Isaac at the beginning of this chapter. The grief-stricken mother in the wilderness says to herself, "Let me not see when the child dies." From the moment God speaks in the story (verse 17), Ishmael is invariably referred to as "the lad"—evidently with an intimation of tenderness but also with the suggestion that he is a young man, *na'ar*, who will go on to have a future. In the elaborately parallel episode in the next chapter that features Abraham and Isaac in the wilderness, Isaac is referred to by man and God as "the lad," and the term is played off against "the lads" who are Abraham's servants accompanying him on his journey, and not his flesh and blood ("And Abraham said to his lads, 'Sit you here with the donkey and let me and the lad walk ahead'").

In the story of the rape of Dinah (Genesis 34), she is first referred to as "Leah's daughter"—and not Jacob's daughter, for it is Leah's sons, Simeon and Levi, who will exact vengeance for her. The initial designation of "daughter" aligns her with both "the daughters of the land" among whom she goes out to see, and Shechem, Hamor's son ("son" and "daughter" are cognates in Hebrew), who sees her, takes her, and rapes her. After the act of violation, Shechem is overcome with love for Dinah, and he implores his father, "Take me this girl [*yaldah*] as wife." Speaking to his father, then, he identifies—tenderly?—the victim of his own lust as a girl-child. When he parleys with Dinah's brothers, asking permission to marry her, he says, "Give me the young woman [*na'arah*] as wife," now using the term for a nubile woman that is strictly appropriate to betrothal negotiations. After the brothers stipulate their surgical precondition for the betrothal, the narrator reports, "And the lad [*na'ar*] lost no time in doing the thing, for he wanted Jacob's daughter." Suddenly, as the catastrophe of this gruesome tale becomes imminent, we learn that the sexually impulsive man is only a lad, probably an adolescent like Dinah—a discovery that is bound to complicate our task of moral judgment. And now Dinah is called Jacob's daughter, not Leah's, probably because that is how Shechem sees her, not realizing that the significant relationship is through her mother to her two full brothers who are plotting a terrible retribution for her violation.

It should be clear from all this that a translation that respects the literary precision of the biblical story must strive to reproduce its nice discrimination of terms, and cannot be free to translate a word here one way and there another, for the sake of variety or for the sake of context. It must be admitted, however, that some compromises are inevitable because modern English clearly does not coincide semantically with ancient Hebrew in many respects. The stuff from which the first human is fashioned, for example, 'adamah, manifestly means "soil," and it continues to have that meaning as it recurs at crucial junctures in the story of the Garden and the primordial banishment. But, alas, 'adamah also means "land," "farmland," "country," and even "earth," and to translate it invariably as "soil" for the sake of terminological consistency (as Everett Fox does) leads to local confusions and conspicuous peculiarities. To take a more extreme example, a term that has no semantic analogue in English, the Hebrew *nefesh,* which the King James Version, following the Vulgate, often translates as "soul," refers to the breath of life in the nostrils of a living creature and, by extension, "lifeblood" or simply "life," and by another slide of association, "person"; and it is also used as an intensifying form of the personal pronoun, having roughly the sense of "very self." In the face of this bewildering diversity of meaning, one is compelled to abandon the admirable principle of lexical consistency and to translate, regretfully, according to immediate context.

Finally, though many recurring biblical terms have serviceable English equivalents (like "lad" for *na'ar*), there are instances in which a translation must make another kind of compromise because, given the differences between modern and biblical culture, the social, moral, and ideological connotations of terms in the two languages do not adequately correspond. Consider the tricky case of verbs for sexual intercourse. In English, these tend to be either clinical and technical, or rude, or bawdy, or euphemistic, and absolutely none of this is true of the verbs used for sex in the Bible. In Genesis, three different terms occur: "to know," "to lie with," and "to come into." "To know," with one striking antithetical exception, indicates sexual possession by a man of his legitimate spouse. Modern solutions such as "to be intimate with," "to cohabit with," "to sleep with," are all egregiously wrong in tone and implication. Fortunately the King James Version has established a strong precedent in English by translating the verb literally, and "carnal knowledge" is part of our language, so it is feasible to preserve the literal Hebrew usage in translation. (There is, I think, a good deal to be said for the general procedure of Tyndale and the King James Version in imitating many Hebrew idioms and thus giving the English a certain Hebraic coloration.) "Lie with" is a literal equivalent of the Hebrew, though in English it is vaguely euphemistic, whereas in Hebrew it is a more brutally direct or carnally explicit idiom for sexual intercourse, without, however, any suggestion of obscenity. The most intractable of the three expressions is "to come into" or "to enter." In nonsexual contexts, this is the ordinary biblical verb for entering, or arriving. "To enter," or "to come into," however, is a misleading translation because the term clearly refers not merely to sexual penetration but to the whole act of sexual consummation. It is used with great precision—not registered by biblical scholarship—to indicate a man's having intercourse with a woman he has not yet had as a sexual partner, whether she is his wife, his concubine, or a whore. The underlying spatial imagery of the term, I think, is of the man's entering the woman's sphere for the first time through a series of concentric circles: her tent or chamber, her bed, her body. A translator, then, ought not surrender the image of coming into, but "come into" by itself doesn't quite do it. My own solution, in keeping with the slight strangeness of Hebraizing idioms of the translation as a whole, was to stretch an English idiom to cover the biblical usage: this translation consistently renders the Hebrew expression in question as "come to bed with," an idiom that in accepted usage a woman could plausibly use to a man referring to herself ("come to bed with me") but that in my translation is extended to a woman's reference to another woman ("come to bed with my slave-girl") and to a reference in the third person by the narrator or a male character to sexual consummation ("Give me my wife," Jacob says to Laban, "and let me come to bed with her").

Biblical syntax, beyond the basic pattern of parallel clauses, provides another occasion for what I have called a slight strangeness. The word order in biblical narrative is very often as finely expressive as the lexical choices. In many instances, the significant sequence of terms can be reproduced effortlessly and idiomatically in English, and it is a testament to the literary insensitivity of modern translators that they so often neglect to do so. Here, for example, is how the narrator reports Abimelech's discovery of the conjugal connection between Isaac and the woman Isaac had claimed was his sister: "Abimelech . . . looked out the window and saw—and there was Isaac playing with Rebekah his wife" (Genesis 26:8). The move into the character's point of view after the verbs of seeing is signaled by the so-called presentative, *wehineh* (rather like *voici* in French), which in this case I have represented by "there" but usually render as "look" (following the King James Version's "behold" and so deliberately coining an English idiom because the biblical term is so crucial for indicating shifts in narrative perspective). What follows "and there" is the precise sequence of Abimelech's perception as he looks out through the window: first Isaac, then the act of sexual play or fondling, then the identity of the female partner in the dalliance, and at the very end, the conclusion that Rebekah must be Isaac's wife. All this is perfectly fluent as English, and modern translations like the Revised English Bible, the New Jewish Publication Society, and Speiser that place "wife" before Rebekah spoil a nice narrative effect in the original.

But biblical syntax is also more flexible than modern English syntax, and there are hundreds of instances in the Five Books of Moses of significant syntactical inversions and, especially, emphatic first positioning of weighted terms. Syntactical inversion, however, is familiar enough in the more traditional strata of literary English, and if one adopts a general norm of decorous stylization for the prose of the translation, as I have done on the grounds I explained earlier, it becomes feasible to reproduce most of the Hebrew reconfigurations of syntax, preserving the thematic or psychological emphases they are meant to convey. The present translation does this, I think, to a greater degree than all previous English versions.

God repeatedly promises the patriarchs, "To your seed I will give this land" (e.g., Genesis 12:7), pointedly putting "your seed" at the beginning of the statement. Less rhetorically, more dramatically, when Hagar is asked by the divine messenger in the wilderness where she is going, she responds, "From Sarai my mistress I am fleeing" (Genesis 16:8), placing Sarai, the implacable source of her misery, at the beginning of the sentence. Still more strikingly, when Jacob is told by his sons that Simeon has been detained as a hostage in Egypt and that the Egyptian regent insists Benjamin be brought down to him, the old man begins his lament by saying, "Me you have bereaved" (Genesis 42:36). It is profoundly revelatory of Jacob's psychological posture that he should place himself as the object of suffering at the very beginning of his utterance (and again at the end, in a little formal symmetry). Normally, biblical Hebrew indicates a pronominal object of a verb by attaching a suffix to the verb itself. Here, however, instead of the usual accusative suffix we get an accusative first-person pronoun—'oti—placed before the verb, a procedure that beautifully expresses Jacob's self-dramatization as anguished and resentful father continually at the mercy of his sons. The "me" urgently needs to be thrust into the ear of the listener. Many translations simply suppress the inversion, but to put it decorously as "It is I" (Everett Fox) or paraphrastically as "It is always me" (New Jewish Publication Society) is to dilute the dramatic force of the original.

The sharpness and vividness of biblical style are also diluted when it is represented in English, as virtually all the versions do, by a single, indifferent level of diction. As I noted earlier, there seems to be nothing genuinely colloquial in the prose used by the narrator; but there is a palpable variation between passages that are more cadenced, more inclined to balanced structures of terms and elevated language, like the narrative of the Flood, and looser, more stylistically flexible passages. There are many instances, moreover, of single word choices that pointedly break with the stylistic decorum of the surrounding narrative, and for the most part these are fudged by the sundry English translations. When Hagar and Ishmael use up their supply of water in the wilderness, the despairing mother "flung the child under one of the bushes" (Genesis 21:15). The verb here, *hishlikh,* always means "to throw," usually abruptly or violently. This is somewhat softened by the King James Version and Fox, who use "cast." The Revised English Bible is uncomfortable with the idea of throwing a child and so translates "thrust." Speiser and the New Jewish Publication Society Bible altogether disapprove of spasmodic maternal gestures and hence dissolve "flung" into a gentler "left." In all such manipulation, the violence of Hagar's action and feelings disappears. When Laban berates Jacob for running off with his daughters, he says, "What have you done, . . . driving my daughters like captives of the sword?" (Genesis 31:26). All the English versions represent the verb here as "carrying away" or some approximation thereof, but *nahag* is a term for driving animals, and is used precisely in that sense earlier in this very chapter (verse 18). To translate it otherwise is to lose the edge of brutal exaggeration in Laban's angry words. In the throes of the great famine, the destitute Egyptians say to Joseph, "Nothing is left for our lord but our carcasses and our farmland" (Genesis 47:18). Most English versions use "bodies" instead of "carcasses," with a couple of modern translations flattening the language even more by rendering the term as "persons." But the Hebrew *gewiyah,* with the sole exception of one famous mythopoeic text in Ezekiel, invariably means "corpse" or "carcass." What the miserable Egyptians are saying to their great overlord is that they have been reduced to little more than walking corpses, and he might as well have those. This sort of pungency can be conveyed if the translator recognizes that the Hebrew does not operate at a single bland level and that literary expression is not inevitably bound to decorous "logic."

These last two examples were taken from dialogue, and it is chiefly in dialogue that we get small but vivid intimations of the colloquial. Again, these are eliminated in the flat regularity of conventional Bible translation. When God rebukes Abimelech for taking Sarah into his harem, the king vehemently protests that he has acted in good conscience: "Did not he say to me, 'She is my sister'? and she, she, too, said, 'He is my brother'" (Genesis 20:5). The repetition of "she, she, too" is a stammer or splutter of indignation clearly indicated in the Hebrew. In some English versions, it disappears altogether. The King James Version turns it into a rhetorical flourish: "she, even she herself." Everett Fox, because of his commitment to literalism, comes closer but without quite the requisite feeling of colloquial mimesis: "and also she, she said." The seventeen-year-old Joseph reports the first of his dreams to his brothers in the following manner: "And, look, we were binding sheaves in the field, and, look, my sheaf arose and actually [*wegam*] stood up, and, look, your sheaves drew round and bowed to my sheaf" (Genesis 37:7). The language here is surely crafted mimetically to capture the gee-gosh wonderment of this naive adolescent who blithely assumes his brothers will share his sense of amazement at his dream. The presentative *hineh* ("look") is the conventional term dreamers use to report the visual images of their dreams, perhaps partly because it readily introduces a surprising new perception, but here Joseph repeats the term three times in one breathless sentence, and the effect of naïve astonishment is equally expressed in his redundant "arose and actually stood up" (the Hebrew adverb *gam* most often means "also" but fairly frequently serves as well as a term of emphasis or intensification). The point is that the adolescent Joseph speaking to his brothers does not at all sound like the adult Joseph addressing Pharaoh, and a translation should not reduce either dialogue or narrator's language to a single dead level.

In the range of diction of the biblical text, the complementary opposite to these moments of colloquial mimesis occurs in the poetic insets. Most of these in the Torah are only a line or two of verse, though Genesis and Deuteronomy conclude with relatively long poems, and Exodus incorporates the Song of the Sea as Numbers does Balaam's oracles. Now, it has long been recognized by scholarship that biblical poetry reflects a stratum of Hebrew older than biblical prose: some of the grammatical forms are different, and there is a distinctive poetic vocabulary, a good deal of it archaic. No previous English translation has made a serious effort to represent the elevated and archaic nature of the poetic language in contradistinction to the prose, though that is clearly part of the intended literary effect of biblical narrative. The present translation tries to suggest this contrast in levels of style—through a more liberal use of syntactic inversion in the poetry, through a selective invocation of slightly archaic terms, and through the occasional deployment of rhetorical gestures broadly associated with older English poetry (like the ejaculation "O"). I wish I could have gone further in this direction, but there is a manifest danger in sounding merely quaint instead of eloquently archaic, and so the stylistic baggage of "anent" and "forsooth" had to be firmly excluded.

Two minute examples will illustrate how these discriminations of stylistic level are made in the Hebrew and how they might be conveyed in English. The enigmatic notice about the Nephilim, the human-divine hybrids of the primeval age, concludes with these words: "They are the heroes of yore, the men of renown" (Genesis 6:4). This line could conceivably be a fragment from an old mythological poem; more probably, it reads in the original as a kind of stylistic citation of the epic genre. The clearest clue to this in the Hebrew is the word "they," which here is *hemah* rather than the standard *hem*. This variant with the extra syllable is in all likelihood an older form: it occurs four times more often in poetry than in prose, and even in prose is often reserved for rather ceremonial gestures. There is no English variant of "they" that is similarly marked as poetic diction, and my translation compensates by using "of yore" instead of the phrase "of old" adopted by the King James Version and by most later English versions. In the next chapter, the unleashing of the Deluge is reported in this line of verse, with emphatic semantic parallelism and four Hebrew accents against three in the two halves of the line: "All the wellsprings of the great deep burst, / and the casements of the heavens opened" (7:11). In order to convey a sense that this is poetry, beyond the mechanics of typography, a translator of course has to create a good deal of rhythmic regularity, but there remains a problem of diction. The Hebrew word represented by "casements" is *'arubot*. It is a rare term, occurring only twice elsewhere in the Bible, and it clearly means "window" or "windowlike niche." The decision of several different modern translators to render it as "sluices" or "floodgates" has no philological warrant and is a conspicuous instance of translation by context. "Windows" in the King James Version is on target semantically but not stylistically. The occurrence of a cognate of 'arubot in Ugaritic poetry, several centuries before the composition of Genesis, is further indication that the term is poetic and probably somewhat archaic for the later Hebrew audience. "Casements," with its echoes of Keats and of Shakespeare behind Keats, seemed like a happy solution to the problem of diction. Though not all shifts in stylistic level in the Hebrew can be so readily represented by English equivalents, a translation that tries to do justice to the richness of the Hebrew must aim for some approximation of the nuances of diction in the original.

The most pervasive aspect of the magic of biblical style that has been neglected by English translators is its beautiful rhythms. An important reason for the magnetic appeal of these stories when you read them in the Hebrew is the rhythmic power of the words that convey the story. The British critic A. Alvarez has aptly described the crucial role of rhythm in all literary art: "the rhythm—the way the sounds move, combine, separate, recombine—is the vehicle for the feeling. . . . And without that inner movement or disturbance, the words, no matter how fetching, remain inert. In this way at least, the dynamics of poetry —and probably of all the arts—are the same as the dynamics of dreaming." I know of no modern English translation of the Bible that is not blotted by constant patches of arrhythmia, and the result is precisely the sense of inertness of which Alvarez speaks. The King James Version, of course, has its grand rhythmic movements—cultivated people around 1611 clearly had a much firmer sense of expressive sound in language than has been true of recent generations. But these rhythms are more orotund, less powerfully compact, than those of the Hebrew, and in fact there are far more local lapses in rhythm than nostalgic readers of the King James Version may recall.

The final arbiter of rhythmic effectiveness must be the inner ear of the sensitive reader, but I would like to show that there is a vital dimension of biblical prose that translation has to engage by quoting a couple of verses in transliteration and then in three English versions, together with my own. In regard to the transliteration, it should be kept in mind that we have an approximate notion, not an exact one, of how biblical Hebrew was originally pronounced. There is some question about vowels in particular because vowel points were added to the consonantal texts by the Masoretes—the Hebrew scholars of sixth- to tenth-century Tiberias who fixed the text of the Bible, with full punctuation, standard since then—more than a millennium after the texts were composed. There was, however, a continuous tradition for recitation of the texts on which the Masoretes drew, and anyone who has listened to the Masoretic Text read out loud can attest to its strong rhythmic integrity, which argues that its system of pronunciation was by no means an arbitrary imposition. Here is the narrative report of Noah's entering the ark as the Deluge is unleashed (Genesis 7:13–14). (Acute accents are used to indicate accented syllables. W is used for the letter waw [pronounced as v in modern Hebrew but as w in biblical times], especially to distinguish it from bet without dagesh, pronounced as v. Ḥ indicates a light fricative [something like Spanish j]; kh represents a heavier fricative, like the German ch in Bach.)

13. Be'élsem hayóm hazéh ba' nóaḥ weshém-weḥám wayéfet benci-nóaḥ we'éshet nóaḥ ushlóshet neshéi-vanáw 'itám 'el hateváh. 14. Hémah wekhol-haḥayáh lemináh wekhol-habehemáh lemináh wekhol-harémes haromés 'al-ha'árets leminéhu wekhol-ha'óf leminéhu kól tsipór kol-kanáf.

The Hebrew rhythm unfolds in groupings of three or four words marked by three or four stresses, usually with no more than one or two unstressed syllables between the stressed ones, and the sense of the words invites a slight pause between one grouping and the next. The overall effect is that of a grand solemn sweep, a sort of epic march, and that effect is reinforced in the diction by the use of *hemah* instead of *hem* for "they" at the beginning of the second verse.

Here is the King James Version:

13. In the selfsame day entered Noah, and Shem, and Ham, and Japheth, the sons of Noah, and Noah's wife, and the three wives of his sons with them, into the ark; 14. They, and every beast after its kind, and all the cattle after their kind, and every creeping thing that creepeth upon the earth after his kind, and every fowl after his kind, every bird of every sort.

The first of the two verses (up to "into the ark") is nearly perfect. I envy the freedom of the King James Version to follow the Hebrew syntax and write "entered Noah," an inversion feasible at the beginning of the seventeenth century but a little too odd, I am afraid, at the beginning of the twenty-first. But in the second verse rhythmic difficulties emerge. The repeated "after its kind," with its sequencing of a trochee and an iamb and its two stresses, is an ungainly equivalent of the Hebrew *lemináh*; "every creeping thing that creepeth upon the earth" is a whole mouthful of syllables in exchange for the compactness of the Hebrew; and "every bird of every sort" falls flat as a final cadence (apart from being inaccurate as a translation).

Here is E. A. Speiser's version of these two verses—a version, to be sure, intended to be accompanied by a philological commentary, but one that helped set a norm for recent Bible translations:

> 13. On the aforesaid day, Noah and his sons, Shem, Ham, and Japheth, Noah's wife, and the three wives of his sons had entered the ark—14. they as well as every kind of beast, every kind of creature that creeps on earth, and every kind of bird, every winged thing.

The initial phrase, "on the aforesaid day," is an ill-starred beginning in regard to diction as well as to rhythm. Something as mechanical as the list of the passengers of the ark is divided up in a way that undercuts its rhythmic momentum: at best, one can say that this version has intermittent moments of escape into rhythm.

Everett Fox, the most boldly literal of modern Bible translators, does a little better, but his attention to rhythm is by no means unflagging.

> 13. On that very day came Noah, and Shem, Ham, and Yefet, Noah's sons, Noah's wife and his three sons' wives with them, into the Ark, 14. they and all wildlife after their kind, all herd-animals after their kind, all crawling things that crawl upon the earth after their kind, all fowl after their kind, all chirping-things, all winged-things.

The first short clause, with the courageous inversion of verb and subject, rings nicely in the ear. But the simple deletion of the "and" between Shem and Ham collapses the rhythm, and Fox's grouping of the list is not much better rhythmically than Speiser's. As in the King James Version, the decision to use "after" four times introduces a series of unwelcome extra syllables, and rhythm is virtually lost in "all herd-animals after their kind, all crawling things that crawl upon the earth after their kind."

Here is my own version, far from perfect, but meant to preserve more of the phonetic compactness of the Hebrew and to avoid such glaring lapses into arrhythmia:

> 13. That very day, Noah and Shem and Ham and Japheth, the sons of Noah, and Noah's wife, and the three wives of his sons together with them, came into the ark, 14. they as well as beasts of each kind and cattle of each kind and each kind of crawling thing that crawls on the earth and each kind of bird, each winged thing.

Biblical Hebrew, in sum, has a distinctive music, a lovely precision of lexical choice, a meaningful concreteness, and a suppleness of expressive syntax that by and large have been given short shrift by translators with their eyes on other goals. The present translation, whatever its imperfections, seeks to do fuller justice to all these aspects of biblical style in the hope of making the rich literary experience of the Hebrew more accessible to readers of English.

III. ON TRANSLATING THE NAMES OF GOD

The God of Israel is referred to through a variety of names in these texts, and it is by no means self-evident how to render the names in English. The most difficult of them is the Tetragrammaton, YHWH. Modern biblical scholarship has agreed to represent this as "Yahweh," but there are problems with using that form in translation. The original Hebrew texts of the Bible were entirely consonantal, vowel-points having been added well over a millennium after the original composition of the texts. Because by then the Tetragrammaton was deemed ineffable by Jewish tradition, it was revocalized to be pronounced as though it read *'adonai*, LORD. The confidence of biblical scholarship that the original pronunciation was in fact Yahweh may not be entirely warranted. (See the comment on Exodus 3:14.) In any case, "Yahweh" would have given the English version a certain academic-archeological coloration that I preferred to avoid, and it would also have introduced a certain discomfort at least for some Jewish readers of the translation. I rejected the option of using "YHWH" because it cannot be pronounced whereas the dimension of sound seemed to me vital to the translation. I have therefore followed the precedent of the King James Version in representing YHWH as the LORD, in small uppercase letters to indicate that, like 'adonai, it is an anomaly, a substitution for another name.

The other most common designation of the deity is 'elohim, a word that is plural in form (perhaps, though this is far from certain, a plural of "majesty") but that is generally treated grammatically as a singular. "God" is the natural English equivalent, but in some contexts, where the generic character of the name seems prominent, I have rendered it with a lowercase g as "god," and when the name is treated as a plural, especially when the narrative context involves polytheism, I have translated it as "gods." Three other names for the deity, all borrowed from the Canaanite pantheon, occur in these books—El, Elyon, and Shaddai. Especially in poetry and at narrative moments of high solemnity, the writers appear to play on the archaic resonances of these names, and so for the most part I have given them in their Hebrew form, for in the particular contexts in which they typically appear a touch of linguistic archeology seemed to me entirely appropriate.

Admittedly, any of the choices I have described may be debatable, but in all of them my aim has been to name the deity in English in ways that would be in keeping with the overall concert of literary effects that the translation strives to create.

IV. ABOUT THE COMMENTARY

My original intention when I set out to translate Genesis in the mid-1990s had been simply to provide brief translator's notes. Puns, word-play in the sundry naming-speeches, and other untranslatable maneuvers of the Hebrew needed to be glossed. The reader also had to be informed, I felt, of the occasional junctures where I adopted a reading that varied from the Masoretic Text, the received Hebrew text of the Bible. Similarly, it seemed proper to offer some explanation for translation choices that were likely to surprise either the general reader or the scholarly reader, or both. In some instances, such a choice reflects a proposed new solution to a crux in the Hebrew text. More often, it is an effort to represent a more precise understanding of the Hebrew than previous translations have shown (e.g., the tree of knowledge is "lovely to look at," not "lovely to impart wisdom"; Pharaoh puts a "golden collar" around Joseph's neck, not a "gold chain"). And most pervasively, the little surprises in the translation are attempts to find English equivalents for the nuances of implication and the significant changes of diction in the Hebrew that have not been much regarded by previous translators. Finally, since this translation is, within the limits of readable English style, quite literal—not out of fundamentalist principle but in an effort to reproduce some of the distinctive literary effects of the original—when the interests of English intelligibility compelled me to diverge from a literal translation, I have alerted readers to the divergence and given the literal sense of the Hebrew words in a note. And beyond all such considerations of word choice and level of style, I thought it necessary to offer succinct explanations of some of the ancient Near Eastern cultural practices and social institutions that are presupposed by the narratives, for without an understanding of them it is sometimes hard to see exactly what is going on in the story.

This last category of explanation is, of course, standard fare in modern Bible commentaries, where it is sometimes dished out in very large portions, and it is admittedly intended here as an aid for the relatively uninitiated. But as I got caught up once again in this endlessly fascinating text, it struck me that there were important features that by and large had been given short shrift in the modern commentaries. In fact, a good many of my observations on stylistic choices already shaded into a discussion of the literary vehicle of the biblical narratives, and this was the point at which the tightly cinched annotation I had originally intended began to loosen its bonds and reach out to commentary. There were whole orders of questions, it seemed to me, that had been neglected or addressed only intermittently and impressionistically by the modern commentators. Where are there detectible shifts of stylistic level in the Hebrew, and why do they occur? What are the reasons for the small poetic insets in the prose narratives? What are the principles on which dialogue is organized, and how are the speakers differentiated? Where and why are there shifts from the narrator's point of view to that of one of the characters? What are the devices of analogy, recurrent motifs, and key words that invite us to link and contrast one episode with another? How is the poetry formally constructed? And do these books, granted their composite origins, exhibit overarching thematic and structural unities or lines of development?

On all these challenging questions I have surely not said the last word. Rather I have aspired to say some helpful first words in a commentary that I have sought to hold to modest proportions. Clearly, there is no way of separating a literary illumination of the biblical text from a confrontation with philological issues, on the one side, and, perhaps more indirectly, with historical issues, on the other. In any case, the exploration of the Torah as literary expression is the central focus of this commentary, and I would hope it would be of interest to everyone, from reader at large to scholar, who is drawn to the imaginative liveliness, the complexities, the stylistic vigor, and the sheer inventiveness of these splendid ancient stories and poems and legal and moral discourses.

ACKNOWLEDGMENTS

A project as daunting and complicated as this could scarcely have been completed without the help of a variety of people who saved me from my lapses in judgment, my gaps in knowledge, and my moments of inattention. The translation of Genesis, together with the commentary on Genesis, was the subject of lengthy, lively, and at times heated discussion with my late friend Amos Funkenstein. I continue to miss him sorely, and as I went on to tackle the four subsequent books of the Torah, I did my best to carry on the impulse he imparted to me to look at familiar problems in fresh ways. Another dear friend, Michael André Bernstein, scrupulously read through everything in draft and made valuable suggestions about certain stylistic decisions and about the logic or appropriateness of some of the notes. Stanley Burnshaw, Thomas G. Rosenmeyer, and Leonard Nathan went over parts of the manuscript and provided the assistance that highly attentive, literate readers can give. My colleague and friend Ronald Hendel painstakingly reviewed everything from Exodus to Deuteronomy and, with his vast fund of knowledge on biblical topics, helped me strengthen a series of vulnerable points in the commentary. Michael Ochs carefully checked the translation against the original and was especially helpful in detecting the all too numerous places in which my eye somehow skidded past words and phrases in the Hebrew. My copy editor, Trent Duffy, did a formidable job with a large mass of material, ferreting out inconsistencies in translations of the same phrases and inaccuracies in cross-references, and in many other ways saving me from embarrassment. The entire manuscript was typed with care and devotion by Janet Livingstone. Secretarial and related costs were covered by income from the Class of 1937 Chair of Hebrew and Comparative Literature at the

University of California at Berkeley. For all of the above I am deeply grateful. For the faults that remain, despite such lavish assistance, I of course must bear the blame.

Berkeley
December 2003

THE
FIVE BOOKS
OF MOSES

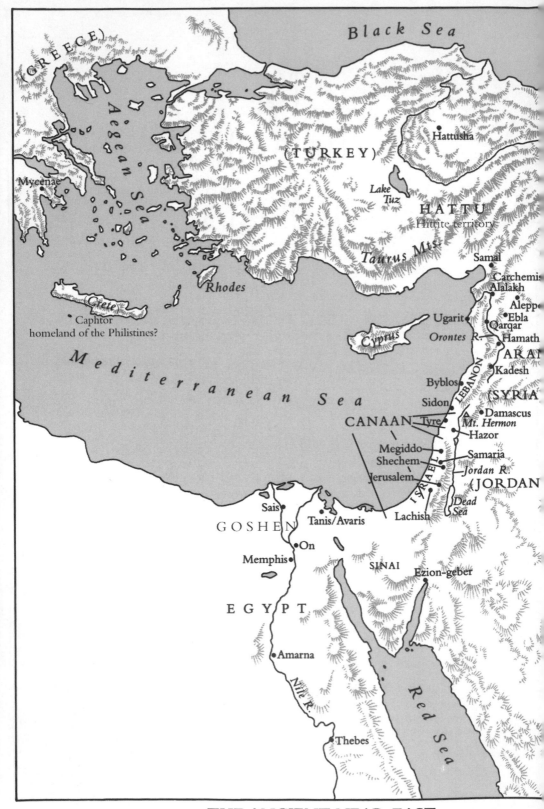

THE ANCIENT NEAR EAST

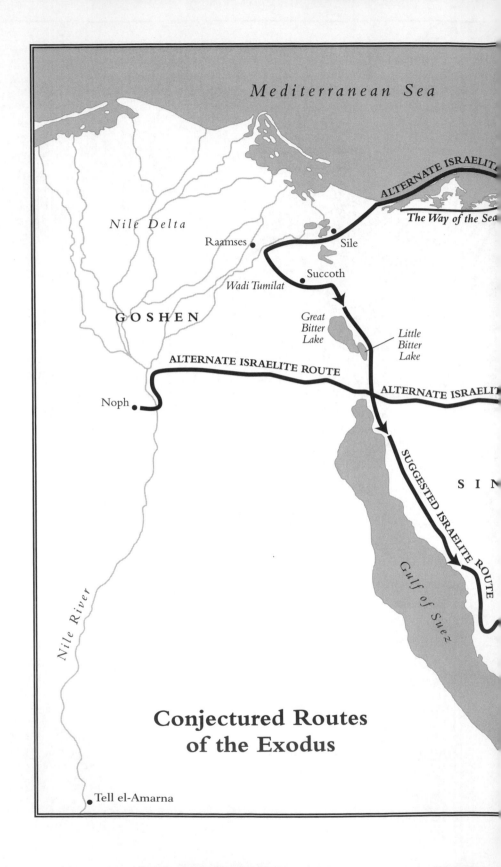

Mediterranean Sea

ALTERNATE ISRAELIT

The Way of the Sea

Nile Delta

Raamses

Sile

Succoth

Wadi Tumilat

GOSHEN

Great
Bitter
Lake

Little
Bitter
Lake

ALTERNATE ISRAELITE ROUTE

Noph

ALTERNATE ISRAELIT

SUGGESTED ISRAELITE ROUTE

S I N

Gulf of Suez

Nile River

Conjectured Routes
of the Exodus

Tell el-Amarna

GENESIS

INTRODUCTION

Much of what I have to say in my commentary about the details of the narrative presupposes that Genesis is a coherent book, what we moderns would think of as a work of literature. But, as many readers may be aware, two centuries of biblical scholarship have generally assumed that Genesis—and indeed each of the Five Books of Moses as well as most other biblical texts—is not strictly speaking a book but rather an accretion of sundry traditions, shot through with disjunctions and contradictions, and accumulated in an uneven editorial process over several centuries. There are knotty issues of the dating and the evolution of the text that have been debated by generations of scholars and that I shall not pretend to resolve, but I do think that the historical and textual criticism of the Bible is not so damaging to a literary reading of the text as is often assumed.

The biblical conception of a book was clearly far more open-ended than any notion current in our own culture, with its assumptions of known authorship and legal copyright. The very difference in the technology of bookmaking is emblematic. For us, a book is a printed object boxed in between two covers, with title and author emblazoned on the front cover and the year of publication indicated on the copyright page. The biblical term that comes closest to "book" is *sefer*. Etymologically, it means "something recounted," but its primary sense is "scroll," and it can refer to anything written on a scroll—a letter, a relatively brief unit within a longer composition, or a book more or less in our sense. A scroll is not a text shut in between covers, and additional swathes of scroll can be stitched onto it, which seems to have been a very common biblical practice. A book in the biblical sphere was assumed to be a product of anonymous tradition. The only ones in the biblical corpus that stipulate the names of their authors, in superscriptions at the

9

beginning, are the prophetic books, but even in this case, later prophecies by different prophet-poets could be tacked onto the earlier scrolls, and the earlier scrolls perhaps might even be edited to fit better into a continuous book with the later accretions.

Let me say just a few words about the different strands that are detectable in Genesis, Exodus, and Numbers, and then I shall explain why I make very little of them in my commentary. Since well back into the nineteenth century, it has been the consensus of biblical scholarship that Genesis, together with two of the next three books of the Pentateuch, is woven together from three distinct literary sources or "documents"—the Yahwistic document (spelled with an initial capital *J* in German and hence designated J), the Elohistic document (E), and the Priestly document (P). Most scholars have concluded that J and E are considerably earlier than P, which could be as late as the sixth century B.C.E. (the period after the return from the Babylonian exile). According to one older view, J would be a product of the tenth century B.C.E. (early in the Davidic dynasty) and E perhaps a century later, though many would make both at least several generations later; another common position is that J and E are roughly contemporary, the latter having been composed in the northern kingdom, Israel, the former in the southern kingdom, Judea. Scholars identify the different sources on the basis of different names used for the deity (emblematically, YHWH in J and Elohim in E), on the basis of certain stylistic features, and by virtue of what are claimed to be different ideological and historical assumptions. It is generally thought that the three sources were redacted into a single text quite early in the period of the Return to Zion, probably in Priestly circles.

This rapid summary may make matters sound pat, but in fact all the details of the Documentary Hypothesis are continually, and often quite vehemently, debated. There are strong differences of opinion about the dating of the various sources, especially J and E. Serious questions have been raised as to whether either J or E is the work of a single writer or school, and various scholars have contended that in fact there is a J[1], J[2], J[3], and so forth. Enormous energy has been invested in discriminating the precise boundaries between one document and the next, but disagreement on minute identifications continues to abound: one scholar will break down a particular text into an alternation between J and E, with an occasional conflation of the two and perhaps a brief intrusion from P, seeking to refine the documentary categories phrase by phrase, while another will call the whole passage "an authentic production of J." (I should add that efforts to distinguish between J and E on stylistic grounds have been quite unconvincing.) It is small wonder that the Documentary Hypothesis, whatever its general validity, has begun to look as though it has reached a point of diminishing returns, and many younger scholars, showing signs of restlessness with source criticism, have been exploring other approaches—literary, anthropolog ical, sociological, and so forth—to the Bible.

The informing assumption of my translation and commentary is that the edited version of Genesis—the so-called redacted text—which has come down to us, though not without certain limited contradictions and disparate elements, has powerful coherence as a literary work, and that this coherence is above all what we need to address as readers. One need not claim that Genesis is a unitary artwork, like, say, a novel by Henry James, in order to grant it integrity as a book. There are other instances of works of art that evolve over the centuries, like the cathedrals of medieval Europe, and are the product of many hands, involving an elaborate process of editing, like some of the greatest Hollywood films. From where we stand, it is difficult to know to what extent the biblical redactors felt free to modify or reshape their inherited sources and to what extent they felt obliged to reproduce them integrally, permitting themselves only an occasional editorial bridge or brief gloss. What seems quite clear, however, is that the redactors had a strong and often subtle sense of thematic and narrative purposefulness in the way they wove together the inherited literary strands, and the notion of some scholars that they were actuated by a mechanical compulsion to incorporate old traditions at all costs is not sustained by a scrutiny of the text, with only a few marginal exceptions.

It is quite apparent that a concept of composite artistry, of literary composition through a collage of textual materials, was generally assumed to be normal procedure in ancient Israelite culture. The technique of collage could come into play at two stages. A writer in the first instance might feel free to introduce into his own narrative, as an integral textual unit, a genealogy, an etiological tale, an ethnographic table, or a vestige of a mythological story, or perhaps to re-create one of the aforementioned without an explicit textual source. Then the redactor, in shaping the final version of the text, could place disparate textual materials at junctures that would give the completed text the thematic definition or the large formal punctuation he sought. I am deeply convinced that conventional biblical scholarship has been trigger-happy in using the arsenal of text-critical categories, proclaiming contradiction wherever there is the slightest internal tension in the text, seeing every repetition as evidence of a duplication of sources, everywhere tuning in to the static of transmission, not to the complex music of the redacted story.

The reader will consequently discover that this commentary refers only occasionally and obliquely to the source analysis of Genesis. For even where such analysis may be convincing, it seems to me a good deal less interesting than the subtle workings of the literary whole represented by the redacted text. As an attentive reader of other works of narrative literature, I have kept in mind that there are many kinds of ambiguity and contradiction, and abundant varieties of repetition, that are entirely purposeful, and that are essential features of the distinctive vehicle of literary experience. I have constantly sought, in both the translation and the commentary, to make this biblical text accessible as a book to be read, which is surely what was intended by its authors and redactors. To that end, I discovered that some of the medieval Hebrew commentators were often more helpful than nearly all the modern ones, with their predominantly text-critical and historical concerns. Rashi (acronym for Rabbi Shlomo Itshaqi, 1040–1105, France) and Abraham ibn Ezra (1092–1167, traveled from Spain to Italy, France, and England) are the most often cited here; they are two of the great readers of the Middle Ages, and there is still much we can learn from them.

A FEW brief remarks about the structure of Genesis as a book are in order. Genesis comprises two large literary units—the Primeval History (chapters 1–11) and the Patriarchal Tales (chapters 12–50). The two differ not only in subject but to some extent in style and perspective. The approach to the history of Israel and Israel's relationship with God that will be the material of the rest of the Hebrew Bible is undertaken through gradually narrowing concentric circles: first an account of the origins of the world, of the vegetable and animal kingdom and of humankind, then a narrative explanation of the origins of all the known peoples, from Greece to Africa to Mesopotamia and Asia Minor, and of the primary institutions of civilization, including the memorable fable about the source of linguistic division. The Mesopotamian family of Terah is introduced at the end of this universal history in chapter 11, and then when God calls Abraham out of Ur of the Chaldees at the beginning of chapter 12 we move on to the story of the beginnings of the Israelite nation, though the national focus of the narrative is given moral depth because the universal perspective of the first part of Genesis is never really forgotten. Some critics have plausibly imagined this whole large process of biblical literature as a divine experiment with the quirky and unpredictable stuff of human freedom, an experiment plagued by repeated failure and dedicated to renewed attempts: first Adam and Eve, then the generation of Noah, then the builders of the Tower of Babel, and finally Abraham and his seed.

Although the Creation story with which the Primeval History begins does look forward to the proliferation of humanity and the human conquest of the natural world, by and large the first eleven chapters of Genesis are concerned with origins, not eventualities—with the past, not the future: "he was the first of all who play on the lyre and pipe" (4:21), the narrator says of Jubal, one of the antediluvians. The literal phrasing of the Hebrew here, as in a series of analogous verses, is "he was the father of. . . ." That idiom is emblematic of the Primeval History, which is really a record of the archetypal fathers, a genealogy of human institutions and of ethnic and linguistic identity. Although the Patriarchal Tales are in one obvious way also the story of a chain of fathers—Abraham, Isaac, and Jacob—the horizon these tales constantly invoke is the future, not the past. God repeatedly tells Abraham what He intends to do with and for the offspring of Abraham in time to come, both in the impending near future of Egyptian enslavement and in the long-term future of national greatness. It is perfectly apt that the Patriarchal Tales should conclude with Jacob's deathbed poem envisaging the destiny of the future tribes of Israel, which he prefaces with the words, "Gather round, that I may tell you what shall befall you in the days to come" (49:1).

The Primeval History, in contrast to what follows in Genesis, cultivates a kind of narrative that is fablelike or legendary, and sometimes residually mythic. The human actors in these stories are kept at a certain distance, and seem more generalized types than individual characters with distinctive personal histories. The style tends much more than that of the Patriarchal Tales to formal symmetries, refrainlike repetitions, parallelisms, and other rhetorical devices of a prose that often aspires to the dignity of poetry, or that invites us to hear the echo of epic poetry in its cadences. As everywhere in biblical narrative, dialogue is an important vehicle, but in the Primeval History it does not have the central role it will play later, and one finds few of the touches of vivid mimesis that make dialogue in the Patriarchal Tales so brilliant an instrument for the representation of human—and human and divine—interactions. In sum, this rapid report of the distant early stages of the human story adopts something of a distancing procedure in the style and the narrative modes with which it tells the story.

God's very first words to Abraham at the beginning of chapter 12 enjoin him to abandon land, birthplace, and father's house. These very terms, or at least this very sphere, will become the arena of the narrative to the end of Genesis. The human creature is now to be represented not against the background of the heavens and the earth and civilization as such but rather within the tense and constricted theater of the paternal domain, in tent and wheatfield and sheepfold, in the minute rhythms of quotidian existence, working out all hopes of grand destiny in the coil of familial relationships, the internecine, sometimes deadly, warring of brothers and fathers and sons and wives. In keeping with this major shift in focus from the Primeval History to the Patriarchal Tales, style and narrative mode shift as well. The studied formality of the first eleven chapters—epitomized in the symmetries and the intricate repetition of word and sound in the story of the Tower of Babel—gives way to a more flexible and varied prose. Dialogue is accorded more prominence and embodies a more lively realism. When, for example, Sarai gives Abram her slavegirl Hagar as a concubine, and the proudly pregnant Hagar then treats her with disdain, the matriarch berates her husband in the following fashion: "This outrage against me is because of you! I myself put my slavegirl in your embrace and when she saw she had conceived, I became slight in her eyes" (16:5). Sarai's first sentence here has an explosive compactness in the Hebrew, being only two words, *ḥamasi 'alekha,* that resists translation. In any case, these lines smoldering with the fires of female resentment convey a sense of living speech and complexity of feeling and relationship one does not encounter before the Patriarchal Tales: the frustrated long-barren wife at cross-purposes with herself and with her husband, first aspiring to maternity through the surrogate of her slavegirl, then after the fact of her new co-wife's pregnancy, tasting a new humiliation, indignant at the slave's presumption, ready to blame her husband, who has been only the instrument of her will. Such vivid immediacy in the representation of the densely problematic nature of individual lives in everyday settings is an innovation not only in comparison with the Primeval History but also in comparison with virtually all of ancient literature.

What nevertheless strongly binds the two large units of the Book of Genesis is both outlook and theme. The unfolding history of the family that is to become the people of Israel is seen, as I have suggested, as the crucial focus of a larger, universal history. The very peregrinations of the family back and forth between Mesopotamia and Canaan and down to Egypt intimate that its scope involves not just the land Israel has been promised but the wider reach of known cultures. National existence, moreover, is emphatically imagined as a strenuous effort to renew the act of creation. The Creation story repeatedly highlights the injunction to be fruitful and multiply, while the Patriarchal Tales, in the very process of frequently echoing this language of fertility from the opening chapters, make clear that procreation, far from being an automatic biological process, is fraught with dangers, is constantly under the threat of being deflected or cut off. Abraham must live long years with the seeming mockery of a divine promise of numberless offspring as he and his wife advance childless into hoary old age. Near the end of the book, Jacob's whole family fears it may perish in the great famine, and Joseph must assure his brothers that God has sent him ahead of them to Egypt in order to sustain life. Genesis begins with the making of heaven and earth and all life, and ends with the image of a mummy—Joseph's—in a coffin. But implicit in the end is a promise of more life to come, of irrepressible procreation, and that renewal of creation will be manifested, even under the weight of oppression, at the beginning of Exodus. Genesis, then, works with dis-

parate materials, puts together its story with two large and very different building blocks, but nevertheless achieves the cohesiveness, the
continuity of theme and motif, and the sense of completion of an archi-
tectonically conceived book. Although it looks forward to its sequel, it
stands as a book, inviting our attention as an audience that follows the
tale from beginning to end.

CHAPTER 1

When God began to create heaven and earth, and the earth then [1,2] was welter and waste and darkness over the deep and God's breath hovering over the waters, God said, "Let there be light." [3] And there was light. And God saw the light, that it was good, and God [4] divided the light from the darkness. And God called the light Day, and [5] the darkness He called Night. And it was evening and it was morning, first day. And God said, "Let there be a vault in the midst of the waters, [6] and let it divide water from water." And God made the vault and it [7] divided the water beneath the vault from the water above the vault, and so it was. And God called the vault Heavens, and it was evening and it [8] was morning, second day. And God said, "Let the waters under the heav- [9] ens be gathered in one place so that the dry land will appear," and so it

---

2. *welter and waste.* The Hebrew *tohu wabohu* occurs only here and in two later biblical texts that are clearly alluding to this one. The second word of the pair looks like a nonce term coined to rhyme with the first and to reinforce it, an effect I have tried to approximate in English by alliteration. *Tohu* by itself means "emptiness" or "futility," and in some contexts is associated with the trackless vacancy of the desert.

hovering. The verb attached to God's breath-wind-spirit (*ruah*) elsewhere describes an eagle fluttering over its young and so might have a connotation of parturition or nurture as well as rapid back-and-forth movement.

5. *first day.* Unusually, the Hebrew uses a cardinal, not ordinal, number. As with all the six days except the sixth, the expected definite article is omitted.

6. *vault.* The Hebrew *raki'a* suggests a hammered-out slab, not necessarily arched, but the English architectural term with its celestial associations created by poetic tradition is otherwise appropriate.

10 was. And God called the dry land Earth and the gathering of waters He
11 called Seas, and God saw that it was good. And God said, "Let the earth
grow grass, plants yielding seed of each kind and trees bearing fruit
of each kind, that has its seed within it upon the earth." And so it was.
12 And the earth put forth grass, plants yielding seed, and trees bearing
13 fruit of each kind, and God saw that it was good. And it was evening and
14 it was morning, third day. And God said, "Let there be lights in the vault
of the heavens to divide the day from the night, and they shall be signs
15 for the fixed times and for days and years, and they shall be lights in the
16 vault of the heavens to light up the earth." And so it was. And God made
the two great lights, the great light for dominion of day and the small
17 light for dominion of night, and the stars. And God placed them in the
18 vault of the heavens to light up the earth and to have dominion over day
and night and to divide the light from the darkness. And God saw that
19,20 it was good. And it was evening and it was morning, fourth day. And God
said, "Let the waters swarm with the swarm of living creatures and let
21 fowl fly over the earth across the vault of the heavens." And God created
the great sea monsters and every living creature that crawls, which the
water had swarmed forth of each kind, and the winged fowl of each
22 kind, and God saw that it was good. And God blessed them, saying, "Be
fruitful and multiply and fill the water in the seas and let the fowl mul-
23,24 tiply in the earth." And it was evening and it was morning, fifth day. And
God said, "Let the earth bring forth living creatures of each kind, cattle
25 and crawling things and wild beasts of each kind. And so it was. And
God made wild beasts of each kind and cattle of every kind and all
crawling things on the ground of each kind, and God saw that it was
26 good. And God said, "Let us make a human in our image, by our likeness, to hold sway over the fish of the sea and the fowl of the heavens

---

24. *wild beasts*. Literally, the phrase would mean "beast of the earth," but the
archaic construct form for "beasts of," *ḥayto*, elsewhere regularly occurs in col-
locations that denote wild beasts. In verse 25, the archaic form is not used, but
given the close proximity of *ḥayat ha'arets* there to *ḥayto 'erets* here, it seems
likely that the meaning is the same.

26. *a human*. The term *'adam*, afterward consistently with a definite article,
which is used both here and in the second account of the origins of

and the cattle and the wild beasts and all the crawling things that crawl
upon the earth.

> And God created the human in his image,   27
>   in the image of God He created him,
>   male and female He created them.

And God blessed them, and God said to them, "Be fruitful and multi-   28
ply and fill the earth and conquer it, and hold sway over the fish of the
sea and the fowl of the heavens and every beast that crawls upon the
earth." And God said, "Look, I have given you every seed-bearing plant   29
on the face of all the earth and every tree that has fruit bearing seed,
yours they will be for food. And to all the beasts of the earth and to all   30
the fowl of the heavens and to all that crawls on the earth, which has
the breath of life within it, the green plants for food." And so it was.
And God saw all that He had done, and, look, it was very good. And it   31
was evening and it was morning, the sixth day.

---

humankind, is a generic term for human beings, not a proper noun. It also
does not automatically suggest maleness, especially not without the prefix hen,
"son of," and so the traditional rendering "man" is misleading, and an exclusively male 'adam would make nonsense of the last clause of verse 27.

   hold sway. The verb radah is not the normal Hebrew verb for "rule" (the latter is reflected in "dominion" of verse 16), and in most of the contexts in which
it occurs it seems to suggest an absolute or even fierce exercise of mastery.

   the wild beasts. The Masoretic Text reads "all the earth," bekhol ha'arets, but
since the term occurs in the middle of a catalogue of living creatures over
which humanity will hold sway, the reading of the Syriac Version, hayat
ha'arets, "wild beasts," seems preferable.

27. In the middle clause of this verse, "him," as in the Hebrew, is grammatically but not anatomically masculine. Feminist critics have raised the question
as to whether here and in the second account of human origins, in chapter 2,
'adam is to be imagined as sexually undifferentiated until the fashioning of
woman, though that proposal leads to certain dizzying paradoxes in following
the story.

CHAPTER 2

Then the heavens and the earth were completed, and all their array.
2 And God completed on the seventh day the task He had done, and
3 He ceased on the seventh day from all the task He had done. And
God blessed the seventh day and hallowed it, for on it He had ceased
4 from all His task that He had created to do. This is the tale of the heavens and the earth when they were created.

5 On the day the LORD God made earth and heavens, no shrub of the
field being yet on the earth and no plant of the field yet sprouted, for

---

4. As many modern commentators have noted, the first Creation account concludes with the summarizing phrase in the first half of this verse: "This is the
tale [literally, these are the begettings] of the heavens and the earth when they
were created," these two paired terms, "heavens" and "earth," taking us back
in an envelope structure to the paired terms of the very first verse of the Creation story. Now, after the grand choreography of resonant parallel utterances
of the cosmogony, the style changes sharply. Instead of the symmetry of
parataxis, hypotaxis is initially prominent: the second account begins with
elaborate syntactical subordination in a long complex sentence that uncoils all
the way from the second part of verse 4 to the end of verse 7. In this more
vividly anthropomorphic account, God, now called YHWH *'Elohim* instead of
'Elohim as in the first version, does not summon things into being from a lofty
distance through the mere agency of divine speech, but works as a craftsman,
fashioning (*yatsar* instead of *bara'*, "create"), blowing life-breath into nostrils,
building a woman from a rib. Whatever the disparate historical origins of the
two accounts, the redaction gives us first a harmonious cosmic overview of
creation and then a plunge into the technological nitty-gritty and moral ambiguities of human origins.

the LORD God had not caused rain to fall on the earth and there was
no human to till the soil, and wetness would well from the earth to   6
water all the surface of the soil, then the LORD God fashioned the   7
human, humus from the soil, and blew into his nostrils the breath of
life, and the human became a living creature. And the LORD God   8
planted a garden in Eden, to the east, and He placed there the human
He had fashioned. And the LORD God caused to sprout from the soil   9
every tree lovely to look at and good for food, and the tree of life was in
the midst of the garden, and the tree of knowledge, good and evil. Now   10
a river runs out of Eden to water the garden and from there splits off
into four streams. The name of the first is Pishon, the one that winds   11
through the whole land of Havilah, where there is gold. And the gold of   12
that land is goodly, bdellium is there, and lapis lazuli. And the name of   13
the second river is Gihon, the one that winds through all the land of
Cush. And the name of the third river is Tigris, the one that goes to the   14
east of Ashur. And the fourth river is Euphrates. And the LORD God   15
took the human and set him down in the garden of Eden to till it and
watch it. And the LORD God commanded the human, saying, "From   16
every fruit of the garden you may surely eat. But from the tree of knowl-   17
edge, good and evil, you shall not eat, for on the day you eat from it,
you are doomed to die." And the LORD God said, "It is not good for the   18

---

7. *the human, humus.* The Hebrew etymological pun is *'adam,* "human," from
the soil, *'adamah.*

16–17. *surely eat . . . doomed to die.* The form of the Hebrew in both instances
is what grammarians call the infinitive absolute: the infinitive immediately followed by a conjugated form of the same verb. The general effect of this repetition is to add emphasis to the verb, but because in the case of the verb "to
die" it is the pattern regularly used in the Bible for the issuing of death sentences, "doomed to die" is an appropriate equivalent.

19 human to be alone, I shall make him a sustainer beside him." And the
LORD God fashioned from the soil each beast of the field and each fowl
of the heavens and brought each to the human to see what he would
call it, and whatever the human called a living creature, that was its
20 name. And the human called names to all the cattle and to the fowl of
the heavens and to all the beasts of the field, but for the human no sus-
21 tainer beside him was found. And the LORD God cast a deep slumber
on the human, and he slept, and He took one of his ribs and closed over
22 the flesh where it had been, and the LORD God built the rib He had
taken from the human into a woman and He brought her to the human.
23 And the human said:

> "This one at last, bone of my bones
>   and flesh of my flesh,
> This one shall be called Woman,
>   for from man was this one taken."

18. *sustainer beside him*. The Hebrew *'ezer kenegdo* (King James Version "help
meet") is notoriously difficult to translate. The second term means "alongside
him," "opposite him," "a counterpart to him." "Help" is too weak because it
suggests a merely auxiliary function, whereas *'ezer* elsewhere connotes active
intervention on behalf of someone, especially in military contexts, as often in
Psalms.

22. *built*. Though this may seem an odd term for the creation of woman, it
complements the potter's term, "fashion," used for the creation of first human,
and is more appropriate because the LORD is now working with hard material,
not soft clay. As Nahum Sarna has observed, the Hebrew for "rib," *tsela'*, is also
used elsewhere to designate an architectural element.

23. The first human is given reported speech for the first time only when there
is another human to whom to respond. The speech takes the form of verse, a
naming-poem, in which each of the two lines begins with the feminine indicative pronoun, *zo't*, "this one," which is also the last Hebrew word of the poem,
cinching it in a tight envelope structure.

Therefore does a man leave his father and his mother and cling to his 24
wife and they become one flesh. And the two of them were naked, the 25
human and his woman, and they were not ashamed.

---

24. *Therefore.* This term, *'al-ken,* is the formula for introducing an etiological explanation: here, why it is that man separates from his parents and is drawn to join bodily, and otherwise, to a woman.

25. *And the two of them.* But characteristically, the narrative immediately unsettles the neatness of the etiological certainty, for the first couple are two, not one flesh, and their obliviousness to their nakedness is darkened by the foreshadow of the moment about to be narrated in which their innocence will be lost.

CHAPTER 3

ow the serpent was most cunning of all the beasts of the field that the LORD God had made. And he said to the woman, "Though God said, you shall not eat from any tree of the garden—" And the woman said to the serpent, "From the fruit of the garden's trees we may eat, but from the fruit of the tree in the midst of the garden God has said, 'You shall not eat from it and you shall not touch it, lest you die.'" And the serpent said to the woman, "You shall not be doomed to die. For God knows that on the day you eat of it your eyes will be opened and you will become as gods knowing good and evil." And the woman saw that the tree was good for eating and that it was lust to the eyes and the tree was lovely to look at, and she took of its fruit and ate,

---

1. *cunning*. In the kind of pun in which the ancient Hebrew writers delighted, *'arum*, "cunning," plays against *'arumim*, "naked," of the previous verse.

2. As E. A. Speiser has noted, the subordinate conjunction that introduces the serpent's first utterance does not have the sense of "truly" that most translators assign it, and is better construed as the beginning of a (false) statement that is cut off in midsentence by Eve's objection that the ban is not on *all* the trees of the Garden.

3. But, as many commentators have observed, Eve enlarges the divine prohibition in another direction, adding a ban on touching to the one on eating, and so perhaps setting herself up for transgression: having touched the fruit, and seeing no ill effect, she may proceed to eat.

6. *lust to the eyes*. There is a long tradition of rendering the first term here, *ta'awah*, according to English idiom and local biblical context, as "delight" or something similar. But *ta'awah* means "that which is intensely desired,"

and she also gave to her man, and he ate. And the eyes of the two were 7
opened, and they knew they were naked, and they sewed fig leaves and
made themselves loincloths.

And they heard the sound of the LORD God walking about in the gar- 8
den in the evening breeze, and the human and his woman hid from the
LORD God in the midst of the trees of the garden. And the LORD God 9
called to the human and said to him, "Where are you?" And he said, "I 10
heard Your sound in the garden and I was afraid, for I was naked, and
I hid." And He said, "Who told you that you were naked? From the tree 11
I commanded you not to eat have you eaten?" And the human said, 12
"The woman whom you gave by me, she gave me from the tree, and I
ate." And the LORD God said to the woman, "What is this you have 13
done?" And the woman said, "The serpent beguiled me and I ate." And 14
the LORD God said to the serpent, "Because you have done this,

---

"appetite," and sometimes specifically "lust." Eyes have just been mentioned
in the serpent's promise that they will be wondrously opened; now they are
linked to intense desire. In the event, they will be opened chiefly to see nakedness. *Ta'awah* is semantically bracketed with the next term attached to the
tree, "lovely," *nehmad,* which literally means "that which is desired."

to look at. A venerable tradition renders this verb, *lehaskil,* as "to make one
wise." But Amos Funkenstein has astutely observed to me that there is an
internal parallelism in the verse, "lust to the eyes . . . lovely to look at." Though
the usual sense of *lehaskil* in the *hiph'il* conjugation does involve the exercise
of wisdom, Funkenstein's suggestion leans on the meaning of the same root in
the *hitpa'el* conjugation in postbiblical Hebrew and Aramaic, "to look." And in
fact, the Aramaic Targums of both Onkelos and Yonatan ben Uziel render this
as *le'istakala beih,* "to look at." At least one other biblical occurrence is almost
certainly in the sense of look, the beginning of Psalm 41: "Happy is he who
maskil to the poor man"—surely, who looks at, has regard for, the poor man. A
correlation between verbs of seeing and verbs of knowledge or understanding
is common to many languages.

12. *gave by me, she gave me.* The repeated verb nicely catches the way the first
man passes the buck, not only blaming the woman for giving him the fruit but
virtually blaming God for giving him the woman. She in turn of course blames
the serpent. God's curse, framed in verse, follows the reverse order, from serpent to woman to man.

Cursed be you
  of all cattle and all beasts of the field.
On your belly shall you go
  and dust shall you eat all the days of your life.
15 Enmity will I set between you and the woman,
  between your seed and hers.
He will boot your head
  and you will bite his heel."

16 To the woman He said,

"I will terribly sharpen your birth pangs,
  in pain shall you bear children.
And for your man shall be your longing,
  and he shall rule over you."

17 And to the human He said, "Because you listened to the voice of your
wife and ate from the tree that I commanded you, 'You shall not eat
from it,'

---

15. *Enmity.* Although the serpent is by no means "satanic," as in the lens of
later Judeo-Christian traditions, the curse records a primal horror of
humankind before this slithering, viscous-looking, and poisonous representative of the animal realm. It is the first moment in which a split between man
and the rest of the animal kingdom is recorded. Behind it may stand, at a long
distance of cultural mediation, Canaanite myths of a primordial sea serpent.

boot . . . bite. The Hebrew uses what appear to be homonyms, the first verb
meaning "to trample," the second, identical in form, probably referring to the
hissing sound of the snake just before it bites.

17. *to the human.* The Masoretic Text vocalizes *le'adam* without the definite
article, which would make it mean "to Adam." But since Eve in the parallel
curse is still called "the woman," it seems better to assume the definite article
here.

Cursed be the soil for your sake,
   with pangs shall you eat from it all the days of your life.
Thorn and thistle shall it sprout for you   18
   and you shall eat the plants of the field.
By the sweat of your brow shall you eat bread   19
   till you return to the soil,
      for from there were you taken,
   for dust you are
      and to dust shall you return."

And the human called his woman's name Eve, for she was the mother   20
of all that lives. And the LORD God made skin coats for the human and   21
his woman, and He clothed them. And the LORD God said, "Now that   22
the human has become like one of us, knowing good and evil, he may

---

with pangs shall you eat. The noun *'itsavon* is the same used for the woman's birth pangs, confirming the lot of painful labor that is to be shared by man and woman.

18. The vista of thorn and thistle is diametrically opposed to the luscious vegetation of the garden and already intimates the verdict of banishment that will be carried out in verses 23–24.

20. *Eve . . . all that lives.* Like most of the explanations of names in Genesis, this is probably based on folk etymology or an imaginative playing with sound. The most searching explanation of these poetic etymologies in the Bible has been offered by Herbert Marks, who observes, "In a verisimilar narrative, naming establishes and fixes identity as something tautologically itself; etymology, by returning it to the trials of language, compromises it, complicates it, renders it potentially mobile." In the Hebrew here, the phonetic similarity is between *hawah,* "Eve," and the verbal root *hayah,* "to live." It has been proposed that Eve's name conceals very different origins, for it sounds suspiciously like the Aramaic word for "serpent." Could she have been given the name by the contagious contiguity with her wily interlocutor, or, on the contrary, might there lurk behind the name a very different evaluation of the serpent as a creature associated with the origins of life?

23 reach out and take as well from the tree of life and live forever." And
the LORD God sent him from the garden of Eden to till the soil from
24 which he had been taken. And He drove out the human and set up east
of the garden of Eden the cherubim and the flame of the whirling
sword to guard the way to the tree of life.

---

23. *the soil from which he had been taken.* This reminder of the first man's
clayey creatureliness occurs as a kind of refrain in this chapter, first in the act
of God's fashioning man, then in God's curse, and now in the banishment. It
is a mere thing shaped from clay that has aspired to be like a god.

24. The cherubim, a common feature of ancient Near Eastern mythology, are
not to be confused with the round-cheeked darlings of Renaissance iconography. The root of the term either means "hybrid" or, by an inversion of consonants, "mount," "steed," and they are the winged beasts, probably of awesome
aspect, on which the sky god of the old Canaanite myths and of the poetry of
Psalms goes riding through the air. The fiery sword, not mentioned elsewhere
but referred to with the definite article as though it were a familiar image, is a
suitable weapon to set alongside the formidable cherubim.

CHAPTER 4

And the human knew Eve his woman and she conceived and bore 1
Cain, and she said, "I have got me a man with the LORD." And she 2
bore as well his brother, Abel, and Abel became a herder of sheep
while Cain was a tiller of the soil. And it happened in the course of time 3
that Cain brought from the fruit of the soil an offering to the LORD.
And Abel too had brought from the choice firstlings of his flock, and 4
the LORD regarded Abel and his offering but He did not regard Cain 5

---

1. *knew*. The Hebrew verb suggests intimate knowledge and hence sexual possession. Amos Funkenstein notes that it is the one term for sexual intercourse associated with legitimate possession—and in a few antithetical instances, with perverse violation of legitimate possession. Given the clumsiness of modern English equivalents like "had experience of," "cohabited with," "was intimate with," and, given the familiarity of the King James Version's literal rendering, "to know" remains the least objectionable English solution.

I have got me a man with the LORD. Eve's naming-speech puns on the verb *qanah*, "to get," "to acquire," or perhaps, "to make," and *qayin*, "Cain." His name actually means "smith," an etymology that will be reflected in his linear descendant Tubal-cain, the legendary first metalworker. ("Tubal" also means "smith" in Sumerian and Akkadian.) Eve, upon bringing forth the third human being, imagines herself as a kind of partner of God in man-making.

2. *Abel*. No etymology is given, but it has been proposed that the Hebrew *hevel*, "vapor" or "puff of air," may be associated with his fleeting life span.

4–5. The widespread culture-founding story of rivalry between herdsman and farmer is recast in a pattern that will dominate Genesis—the displacement of the firstborn by the younger son. If there is any other reason intimated as to why God would favor Abel's offering and not Cain's, it would be in the narrator's stipulation that Abel brings the very best of his flock to God.

6 and his offering, and Cain was very incensed, and his face fell. And the
LORD said to Cain.

> "Why are you incensed,
>> and why is your face fallen?
7 > For whether you offer well,
>> or whether you do not,
> at the tent flap sin crouches
> and for you is its longing
>> but you will rule over it."

8 And Cain said to Abel his brother, "Let us go out to the field." And
when they were in the field, Cain rose against Abel his brother and
9 killed him. And the LORD said to Cain, "Where is Abel your brother?"
10 And he said, "I do not know. Am I my brother's keeper?" And He said,

---

6–7. This is the first of two enigmatic and probably quite archaic poems in the
chapter. God's initial words pick up the two locutions for dejection of the
immediately preceding narrative report and turn them into the parallel utterances of formal verse. The first clause of verse 7 is particularly elliptic in the
Hebrew, and thus any construction is no more than an educated guess. The
narrative context of sacrifices may suggest that the cryptic *s'eit* (elsewhere,
"preeminence") might be related to *mas'eit*, a gift or cultic offering.

8. *Let us go out to the field*. This sentence is missing in the Masoretic Text but
supplied in the Greek, Syriac, and Aramaic versions.
   his brother. In keeping with the biblical practice of using thematically
fraught relational epithets, the victim of the first murder is twice called "his
brother" here, and God will repeatedly refer to Abel in accusing Cain as "your
brother."

9–12. There are several verbal echoes of Adam's interrogation by God and
Adam's curse, setting up a general biblical pattern in which history is seen as
a cycle of approximate and significant recurrences. Adam's being driven from
the garden to till a landscape of thorn and thistle is replayed here in God's
insistence that Cain is cursed by—the preposition also could mean "of" or
"from"—the soil (*'adamah*) that had hitherto yielded its bounty to him. The
biblical imagination is equally preoccupied with the theme of exile (this is

"What have you done? Listen! your brother's blood cries out to me from
the soil. And so, cursed shall you be by the soil that gaped with its   11
mouth to take your brother's blood from your hand. If you till the soil,   12
it will no longer give you its strength. A restless wanderer shall you be
on the earth." And Cain said to the LORD, "My punishment is too great   13
to bear. Now that You have driven me this day from the soil and I must   14
hide from Your presence, I shall be a restless wanderer on the earth and
whoever finds me will kill me." And the LORD said to him, "Therefore   15
whoever kills Cain shall suffer sevenfold vengeance." And the LORD set
a mark upon Cain so that whoever found him would not slay him.

And Cain went out from the LORD's presence and dwelled in the land   16
of Nod east of Eden. And Cain knew his wife and she conceived and   17
bore Enoch. Then he became the builder of a city and called the name
of the city, like his son's name, Enoch. And Irad was born to Enoch, and   18

---

already the second expulsion) and with the arduousness or precariousness of
agriculture, a blessing that easily turns into blight.

11. *that gaped with its mouth to take your brother's blood from your hand.* The
image is strongly physical: a gaping *mouth* taking in *blood* from the murderer's
hand.

14. *whoever finds me.* This, and the subsequent report of Cain with a wife in
the land of Nod, are a famous inconsistency. Either the writer was assuming
knowledge of some other account of human origins involving more than a single founding family, or, because the schematic simplicity of the single nuclear-
family plot impeded narrative development after Cain's banishment, he
decided not to bother with consistency.

15. *a mark.* It is of course a mark of protection, not a stigma as the English
idiom "mark of Cain" suggests.

16. *the land of Nod.* Nod in Hebrew is cognate with "wanderer" in verse 12.

17. *the builder of a city.* The first recorded founder of a city is also the first murderer, a possible reflection of the antiurban bias in Genesis.

Irad begot Mehujael and Mehujael begot Methusael and Methusael
19 begot Lamech. And Lamech took him two wives, the name of the one
20 was Adah and the name of the other was Zillah. And Adah bore Jabal:
21 he was the first of tent dwellers with livestock. And his brother's name
    was Jubal: he was the first of all who play on the lyre and pipe. As for
22 Zillah, she bore Tubal-Cain, who forged every tool of copper and iron.
23 And the sister of Tubal-Cain was Naamah. And Lamech said to his
    wives,

> "Adah and Zillah, O hearken my voice,
>   You wives of Lamech, give ear to my speech.
> For a man have I slain for my wound,
>   a boy for my bruising.
24   For sevenfold Cain is avenged,
>   and Lamech seventy and seven."

---

20. *he was the first.* The Hebrew says literally "father of," in keeping with the
predisposition of the language and culture to imagine historical concatenation
genealogically.

22. *Naamah.* One might expect an identification that would align Naamah
with her siblings as a founder of some basic activity of human culture, but if
such an identification was part of the original epic roll call, it has been either
lost or deleted. The Midrash recognized that the root of her name can refer to
song: perhaps Naamah is meant to be associated with her half brother Jubal,
the founder of instrumental music—he as accompanist, she as singer.

23–24. The narrative context of this poem is long lost, but it looks like a warrior's triumphal song, cast as a boast to his wives. Unlike the looser form of the
earlier poetic insets, this poem follows the parallelistic pattern of biblical verse
with exemplary rigor. Every term in each initial verset has its semantic counterpart in the second verset. In the Hebrew, the first pair of versets has four
accented syllables in each; every subsequent verset has three accented syllables. The last pair of versets, with its numbers, provides a paradigm case for
poetic parallelism in the Bible: when a number occurs in the first half of the
line, it must be increased—by one, by a decimal, or by a decimal added to the
original number, as here, in the second half of the line. In the same way, there
is a pronounced tendency in the poetry to intensify semantic material as it is
repeated in approximate synonymity. Perhaps, then, what Lamech is saying

And Adam again knew his wife and she bore a son and called his name   25
Seth, as to say, "God has granted me other seed in place of Abel, for
Cain has killed him." As for Seth, to him, too, a son was born, and he   26
called his name Enosh. It was then that the name of the LORD was first
invoked.

(quite barbarically) is that not only has he killed a man for wounding him, he
has not hesitated to kill a mere boy for hurting him.

25. *Seth . . . granted me.* The naming pun plays on the similarity of sound
between "Seth," *shet,* and "granted," *shat.*

26. *Enosh.* The name is also a common noun in Hebrew meaning "man," and
that conceivably might explain why, from the universalist perspective of the
writer, the name YHWH began to be invoked in this generation. In any case,
the narrative unit that begins with one general term for human being, *'adam,*
in verse 1, here concludes with another, *'enosh,* and those two words elsewhere
are bracketed together in poetic parallelism.
   the name of the LORD was first invoked. That is, the distinctive Israelite designation for the deity, YHWH, represented in this translation, according to
precedent in the King James Version, as the LORD. The existence of primordial
monotheism is an odd biblical notion that seeks to reinforce the universalism
of the monotheistic idea. The enigmatic claim, made here with an atypical and
vague passive form of the verb, is contradicted by the report in Exodus that
only with Moses was the name YHWH revealed to man.

CHAPTER 5

1 This is the book of the lineage of Adam: On the day God created the
2 human, in the image of God He created him. Male and female He
created them, and He blessed them and called their name
3 humankind on the day they were created. And Adam lived a hundred
and thirty years and he begot in his likeness by his image and called his
4 name Seth. And the days of Adam after he begot Seth were eight hun-
5 dred years, and he begot sons and daughters. And all the days Adam
6 lived were nine hundred and thirty years. Then he died. And Seth lived
7 a hundred and five years and he begot Enosh. And Seth lived after he
begot Enosh eight hundred and seven years, and he begot sons and

---

NOTHING reveals the difference of the biblical conception of literature from
later Western ones more strikingly than the biblical use of genealogies as an
intrinsic element of literary structure. As J. P. Fokkelman (1987) has noted, the
genealogical lists or "begats" (*toledot*) in Genesis are carefully placed compositional units that mark off one large narrative segment from another: here, the
story of Creation and the antediluvian founding figures from the Deluge story.
As Fokkelman also observes, the begettings of the genealogical lists are linked
thematically with the initial injunction to be fruitful and multiply and with all
the subsequent stories of a threatened or thwarted procreative drive.

Repetition of formula dominates the genealogical list stylistically. Here the
procreative act and life span of each figure are conveyed in identical language,
and when there is a divergence from the formula, in the case of Enoch, it is
very significant. Formulaic numbers as well are characteristically used by the
biblical writer to give order and coherence to the narrated world. The seven
generations from Adam to Noah of chapter 4 are here displaced by a different
formulaic number, ten. (Some critics have argued that the two lists reflect
competing versions that deploy the same group of fathers and sons in different patterns: some of the names are identical in both lists, others—like Cain-

daughters. And all the days of Seth were nine hundred and twelve 8
years. Then he died. And Enosh lived ninety years and he begot Kenan. 9
And Enosh lived after he begot Kenan eight hundred and fifteen years, 10
and he begot sons and daughters. And all the days of Enosh were nine 11
hundred and five years. Then he died. And Kenan lived seventy years 12
and he begot Mahalalel. And Kenan lived after he begot Mahalalel 13
eight hundred and forty years, and he begot sons and daughters. And 14

Kenan, Irad-Jared—may well be variants of each other.) This list incorporates
both of the formulaic numbers: Lamech, the last of the antediluvians before
Noah, lives 777 years; Noah, unlike his predecessors, becomes a begetter at
the age of 500, halfway through a round millennium, which is the ten of the
ten generations with two decimal places added. A millennium is the age most
of the antediluvians come close to but never attain, as befits their mortality.

Surely part of the intention in using the genealogy is to give the history the
look of authentically archaic documentation. If, as many assume, Priestly circles in the Second Temple period were ultimately responsible for the list here,
they did not hesitate to include the fabulous ages of the antediluvians, which
must have had their origins in hoary Semitic antiquity (as the old
Mesopotamian parallels suggest), as well as the strange, evidently mythic fragment about Enoch, which could scarcely have been a late invention.

1. *This is the book.* The Hebrew *sefer,* which some render as "record," is anything written down, presumably in the form of a scroll. In any case, the introductory formula clearly announces this as a separate document.

Adam. The lack of a definite article would seem to indicate that the term is
being used as a proper name. But the two subsequent occurrences of *'adam,*
here and in the next verse, equally lack the definite article and yet clearly refer
to "the human creature" or "humankind." God's calling "them" by the name
'adam (verse 2) is also an explicit indication that the term is not exclusively
masculine, and so it is misleading to render it as "man."

1–2. *in the image of God . . . Male and female He created them.* The pointed
citation of the account in chapter 1 ties in the genealogical list with the initial
story of human origins: creation is recapitulated, and continues.

3. *in his likeness by his image.* Adam, then, replicates God's making of the
human being (with the order of "likeness" and "image" reversed) in his own act
of procreation.

all the days of Kenan were nine hundred and ten years. Then he died.
15,16 And Mahalalel lived sixty-five years and he begot Jared. And Mahalalel
lived after he begot Jared eight hundred and thirty years, and he begot
17 sons and daughters. And all the days of Mahalalel were eight hundred
18 and ninety-five years. Then he died. And Jared lived a hundred and
19 sixty-two years and he begot Enoch. And Jared lived after he begot
20 Enoch eight hundred years, and he begot sons and daughters. And all
the days of Jared were nine hundred and sixty-two years. Then he died.
21,22 And Enoch lived sixty-five years and he begot Methuselah. And Enoch
walked with God after he begot Methuselah three hundred years, and
23 he begot sons and daughters. And all the days of Enoch were three
24 hundred and sixty-five years. And Enoch walked with God and he was
25 no more, for God took him. And Methuselah lived a hundred and
26 eighty-seven years and he begot Lamech. And Methuselah lived after
he begot Lamech seven hundred and eighty-two years, and he begot
27 sons and daughters. And all the days of Methuselah were nine hundred
28 and sixty-nine years. Then he died. And Lamech lived a hundred and
29 eighty-two years and he begot a son. And he called his name Noah, as
to say, "This one will console us for the pain of our hands' work from

---

22. *And Enoch walked with God*. This cryptic verse has generated mountains
of speculative commentary, not to speak of two whole books of the Apocrypha.
The reflexive form of the verb "to walk" that occurs here is the same form used
for God's walking about in the Garden. Instead of the flat report of death, as
in the case of the other antediluvians, the euphemism "was no more" (literally
"was not"), which is also applied to Joseph, merely supposed by his brothers to
be dead, is used. "Walked with" surely implies some sort of special intimate
relationship with God, but what that might be is anyone's guess. This is one of
several instances in the early chapters of Genesis of a teasing vestige of a tradition for which the context is lost. Enoch is the seventh generation from
Adam, and some scholars have seen an instructive analogy in a Mesopotamian
list of kings before the Deluge, in which the seventh antediluvian king, a certain Enmeduranki, is taken up to sit before the gods Shamash and Adad, and
is granted preternatural wisdom. Shamash is the sun god, and the biblical
Enoch lives as many years as the days of the solar year.

29. *This one will console us*. As usual, the sound-play on the name Noah, which
lacks the final *mem* of the word for "console," *naḥem*, is loose phonetic asso-

the soil which the Lord cursed." And Lamech lived after he begot 30
Noah five hundred and ninety-five years, and he begot sons and daughters. And all the days of Lamech were seven hundred and seventy- 31
seven years. Then he died. And Noah was five hundred years old and 32
he begot Shem, Ham, and Japheth.

---

ciation. What the nature of the consolation might be is a cloudier issue.
Rashi's proposal that Noah was the inventor of the plow has scant support in
the subsequent text. Others, more plausibly, have linked the consolation with
Noah's role as the first cultivator of the vine. The idea that wine provides the
poor man respite from his drudgery (see Proverbs 31:6–7) is common enough
in the biblical world. Wine, then, might have been thought of as a palliative to
the curse of hard labor, which is also the curse of the soil: the language of Genesis 3:17–18 is explicitly echoed here.

   the pain of our hands' work. Most translations render this as "our toil, our
work," or something equivalent. But the second term *'itsavon,* does not mean
"labor" but rather "pain," and is the crucial word at the heart of Adam's curse,
and Eve's. Given that allusion, the two terms in the Hebrew—which reads literally, "our work and the pain of our hands"—are surely to be construed as a
hendiadys, a pair of terms for a single concept indicating "painful labor." It
should be noted that the "work of our hands" is a common biblical collocation
while "pain of our hands" occurs only here, evidently under the gravitational
pull of "work" with which it is paired as a compound idiom. Equally noteworthy is that the word *'itsavon* appears only three times in the Bible (other nom-
inal forms of the root being relatively common)—first for Eve, then for Adam,
and now for Noah.

CHAPTER 6

1   And it happened as humankind began to multiply over the earth
2   and daughters were born to them, that the sons of God saw that
    the daughters of man were comely, and they took themselves
3   wives howsoever they chose. And the LORD said, "My breath shall not
    abide in the human forever, for he is but flesh. Let his days be a hun-
    dred and twenty years."

1–4. This whole passage is obviously archaic and mythological. The idea of
male gods coupling with mortal women whose beauty ignites their desire is a
commonplace of Greek myth, and E. A. Speiser has proposed that both the
Greek and the Semitic stories may have a common source in the Hittite traditions of Asia Minor. The entourage of celestial beings obscurely implied in
God's use of the first-person plural in the Garden story (compare 3:22) here
produces, however fleetingly, active agents in the narrative. As with the
prospect that man and woman might eat from the tree of life, God sees this
intermingling of human and divine as the crossing of a necessary line of
human limitation, and He responds by setting a new retracted limit (three
times the formulaic forty) to human life span. Once more human mortality is
confirmed, this time in quantitative terms.

2. *man.* Here it seems better to render the generic *ha'adam* as "man" both
because in the patrilineal imagination (compare the immediately preceding
genealogy) males are seen as the begetters of daughters and sons, and because
the term "daughters of man" is played against "sons of God."

   comely. The Hebrew also means "good" but it very often occurs in the sense
of goodly appearance, and is sometimes explicitly paired with the word for
"beautiful." The same term is used for Eve's perception of the tree of knowledge (3:6).

3. *abide . . . is but.* Both pertinent Hebrew terms are cryptic, and the translation is somewhat speculative.

The Nephilim were then on the earth, and afterward as well, the sons   4
of God having come to bed with the daughters of man who bore them
children: they are the heroes of yore, the men of renown.

---

4. *Nephilim*. The only obvious meaning of this Hebrew term is "fallen ones"—
perhaps, those who have come down from the realm of the gods; but then the
word might conceivably reflect an entirely different, un-Hebraic background.
In any case, the notion of semidivine, heroic figures—in Numbers the
Nephilim are thought of as giants who are offspring of miscegenation between
gods and women—again touches on common ground with Greek and other
mythologies.

   come to bed with. The Hebrew idiom is literally "come into," that is,
"entered." It involves a more direct reference to the mechanics of the sexual
act than "to know" and thus has a more carnal coloration, but at the same time
it seems to be perfectly decorous. The English "entered" would be too clinical,
and, in any case, the Hebrew idiom refers to the whole act of intercourse, not
merely to penetration. Of the three expressions used for sexual intercourse in
Genesis—the other two are "to know" and "to lie with"—this one is reserved
for sexual intimacy with a woman with whom the man has not previously had
carnal relations, whether or not she is his legitimate wife. The spatial imagery
of the idiom of "coming into" appears to envisage entering concentric circles—
the woman's private sphere, her bed, her body.

   heroes of yore. The Hebrew style of this entire clause reflects a certain epic
heightening, hence the archaizing turn in the translation. One suspects that
these words are either a citation of an old heroic poem or a stylistic allusion to
the epic genre.

5 And the LORD saw that the evil of the human creature was great on the
earth and that every scheme of his heart's devising was only perpetually
6 evil. And the LORD regretted having made the human on earth and was
7 grieved to the heart. And the LORD said, "I will wipe out the human
race I created from the face of the earth, from human to cattle to crawling thing to the fowl of the heavens, for I regret that I have made them."
8,9 But Noah found favor in the eyes of the LORD. This is the lineage of
Noah—Noah was a righteous man, he was blameless in his time, Noah
10 walked with God—and Noah begot three sons, Shem and Ham and
11 Japheth. And the earth was corrupt before God and the earth was filled
12 with outrage. And God saw the earth and, look, it was corrupt, for all

---

5. *was great.* With a minor change in vocalization, this adjective could be read
as a verb, "multiplied": in any case, the whole phrase echoes the "multiply over
the earth" of verse 1. The nature of the evil, distinct from the preceding tale of
human-divine miscegenation, is not specified, and God's subsequent indict-
ment uses only general terms ("corruption" and "outrage"/"lawlessness"). It is
noteworthy that the sundry Mesopotamian Flood stories, on which this
account draws heavily, present the Deluge as the gods' response to overpopu-
lation or as an arbitrary act whereas here it is evil, not humankind, that multi-
plies and fills the earth.

heart's devising. In the Bible the heart is usually thought of as the seat of
intelligence, only occasionally as the seat of emotion; thus many modern translators use "mind" here. But man's evil heart is pointedly meant to stand in contrast to God's grieving heart (the same Hebrew word) in the next verse.

6. *grieved.* The same verbal root, '-*ts-b,* is reflected in Eve's pangs, Adam's pain,
and "the pain of our hands' work."

9. *lineage.* The listing of Noah's three sons in the next verse supports this sense
of *toledot,* but it might also mean "story."

11. *filled with outrage.* Humankind had been enjoined to multiply and fill the
earth, but the proliferation of human population leads to a proliferation of law-
less behavior. This is one of several verbal echoes of the Creation story, suggesting, first, a perversion of creation by man and, then, a reversal of creation
by God.

flesh had corrupted its ways on the earth. And God said to Noah, "The 13
end of all flesh is come before me, for the earth is filled with outrage
by them, and I am now about to destroy them, with the earth. Make 14
yourself an ark of cypress wood, with cells you shall make the ark, and
caulk it inside and out with pitch. This is how you shall make it: three 15
hundred cubits, the ark's length; fifty cubits, its width; thirty cubits, its
height. Make a skylight in the ark, within a cubit of the top you shall 16
finish it, and put an entrance in the ark on one side. With lower and
middle and upper decks you shall make it. As for me, I am about to 17
bring the Flood, water upon the earth, to destroy all flesh that has
within it the breath of life from under the heavens, everything on the
earth shall perish. And I will set up my covenant with you, and you shall 18
enter the ark, you and your sons and your wife and the wives of your
sons, with you. And from all that lives, from all flesh, two of each thing 19
you shall bring to the ark to keep alive with you, male and female they
shall be. From the fowl of each kind and from the cattle of each kind 20
and from all that crawls on the earth of each kind, two of each thing
shall come to you to be kept alive. As for you, take you from every food 21
that is eaten and store it by you, to serve for you and for them as food."
And this Noah did; as all that God commanded him, so he did. 22

13–21. God's pronouncement of imminent doom and His instructions about
the ark are the longest continuous speech up to this point in Genesis, considerably exceeding the triple curse in chapter 3. Most of the length is dictated
by the necessity to provide specifications for the construction of the ark and
the arrangements for the animals. But the writer also uses the speech as a
vehicle for realizing God's awesome presence in the story: the language is not
arranged in actual verse but it sounds a drumroll of grand formal cadences,
stressing repeated terms and phrases that are rhythmically or semantically
parallel.

13. *destroy*. The Hebrew verb is identical with the one used three times above
in the sense of "corrupt" and so inscribes a pattern of measure for measure.

CHAPTER 7

1   And the LORD said to Noah, "Come into the ark, you and all your
household, for it is you I have seen righteous before Me in this
2   generation. Of every clean animal take you seven pairs, each with
its mate, and of every animal that is not clean, one pair, each with its

---

1. *for it is you I have seen righteous before me in this generation*. God's words
here reflect a frequently used technique of biblical narrative, in which the narrator's report or evaluation is confirmed by a near verbatim repetition in dialogue, or vice versa. The judgment that Noah is "righteous in this generation"
explicitly echoes the narrator's declaration in 6:9 that Noah is "a righteous man
. . . blameless in his time" (the Hebrew for "time" is literally "generations").

2. *Of every clean animal take you seven pairs*. Clean and unclean evidently refer
to fitness for sacrificial use, not for eating, as in the later dietary prohibitions.
As scholarship has often noted, two versions of the Flood story, the Priestly
and the Yahwistic, are intertwined in a somewhat confusing fashion. According to the former, two of each species are to be brought into the ark and no
distinction is made between clean and unclean. According to the latter, seven
pairs of clean animals and one pair of the unclean are to be saved. Abraham
ibn Ezra and other medieval exegetes rescue consistency by proposing that
when God directed attention to the clean-unclean distinction, He had to add
the difference in numbers because more animals were needed to be sacrificed.
(Noah, like his counterpart in the Mesopotamian Flood stories, does in fact
offer a thanksgiving sacrifice after the waters recede.) But the tensions
between the two versions, including how they record the time span of the
Flood, persist, and there are some indications that the editor himself struggled
to harmonize them.

mate. Of the fowl of the heavens as well seven pairs, male and female, 3
to keep seed alive over all the earth. For in seven days' time I will make 4
it rain on the earth forty days and forty nights and I will wipe out from
the face of the earth all existing things that I have made." And Noah 5
did all that the LORD commanded him.

Noah was six hundred years old when the Flood came, water over the 6
earth. And Noah and his sons and his wife and his sons' wives came 7
into the ark because of the waters of the Flood. Of the clean animals 8
and of the animals that were not clean and of the fowl and of all that
crawls upon the ground two each came to Noah into the ark, male and 9
female, as God had commanded Noah. And it happened after seven 10
days, that the waters of the Flood were over the earth. In the six hun- 11
dredth year of Noah's life, in the second month, on the seventeenth day
of the month, on that day,

---

3. *seed*. The Hebrew term means both semen and the offspring that is its product. It is a very concrete way of conceiving propagation and the survival of a
line, and seems worth preserving in a literal English rendering.

4. *I will make it rain* The Hebrew uses a participial form indicating action virtually on the point of beginning, but in English the introductory temporal
clause requires a simple future.

7. *because of*. The Hebrew also means "in the face of" and may have the
implied sense here of fleeing from the rising waters, as ibn Ezra observes.

11. *In the six hundredth year*. The precise indications of age and date give the
report of the inception of the Flood a certain epic solemnity.

All the wellsprings of the great deep burst
and the casements of the heavens were opened.

12,13 And the rain was over the earth forty days and forty nights. That very
day, Noah and Shem and Ham and Japheth, the sons of Noah, and
Noah's wife, and the three wives of his sons together with them, came
14 into the ark, they as well as beasts of each kind and cattle of each kind
and each kind of crawling thing that crawls on the earth and each kind
15 of bird, each winged thing. They came to Noah into the ark, two by two
16 of all flesh that has the breath of life within it. And those that came in,
male and female of all flesh they came, as God had commanded him,
17 and the LORD shut him in. And the Flood was forty days over the earth,
and the waters multiplied and bore the ark upward and it rose above

---

All the wellsprings of the great deep burst. This line of poetry has been cited
by Umberto Cassuto and others as a fragment from an old epic poem on the
Flood. This is by no means a necessary assumption, however, because it is a
regular practice of biblical narrative to introduce insets of verse at moments of
high importance, and in many instances the composition of verse and prose
may be by the same hand. The grand flourish of this line of poetry is perfectly
consonant with the resonant repetitions and measured cadences of the surrounding prose. The surge of waters from the great deep below and from the
heavens above is, of course, a striking reversal of the second day of creation,
when a vault was erected to divide the waters above from the waters below.
The biblical imagination, having conceived creation as an orderly series of divisions imposed on primordial chaos, frequently conjures with the possibility of
a reversal of this process (see, for example, Jeremiah 4:23–26): biblical cosmogony and apocalypse are reverse sides of the same coin. The Flood story as
a whole abounds in verbal echoes of the Creation story (the crawling things,
the cattle and beasts of each kind, and so forth) as what was made on the six
days is wiped out in these forty.

17. *and the waters multiplied.* The very verb of proliferation employed in the
Creation story for living creatures is here attached to the instrument of their
destruction.

the earth. And the waters surged and multiplied mightily over the earth, 18 and the ark went on the surface of the water. And the waters surged 19 most mightily over the earth, and all the high mountains under the heavens were covered. Fifteen cubits above them the waters surged as 20 the mountains were covered. And all flesh that stirs on the earth per- 21 ished, the fowl and the cattle and the beasts and all swarming things that swarm upon the earth, and all humankind. All that had the quick- 22 ening breath of life in its nostrils, of all that was on dry land, died. And 23 He wiped out all existing things from the face of the earth, from humans to cattle to crawling things to the fowl of the heavens, they were wiped out from the earth. And Noah alone remained, and those with him in the ark. And the waters surged over the earth one hundred 24 and fifty days.

---

22. *the quickening breath of life.* The Hebrew, *nishmat ruah hayim,* is unusual, the first two terms in a way doubling each other ("the breath of the breath of life"). Some recent scholars construe this as a minimizing idiom that implies something like "the faintest breath of life." But the one other occurrence of the phrase *nishmat ruah,* in David's victory psalm (2 Samuel 22:16), is part of an anthropomorphic vision of God breathing fire on the battlefield ("From the LORD's roaring, / the blast of his nostril's breath"); and so it is more plausible that the doubled terms are intensifiers, underlining the physical exhalation of breath from the nostrils that is the sign of life. In fact, we shall encounter other instances, in the Plagues narrative and in the Sinai epiphany in Exodus, where two synonyms joined together in the construct state signify intensification.

CHAPTER 8

1 And God remembered Noah and all the beasts and all the cattle that were with him in the ark. And God sent a wind over the earth 2 and the waters subsided. And the wellsprings of the deep were dammed up, and the casements of the heavens, the rain from the heav- 3 ens held back. And the waters receded from the earth little by little, 4 and the waters ebbed. At the end of a hundred and fifty days the ark came to rest, on the seventeenth day of the seventh month, on the 5 mountains of Ararat. The waters continued to ebb, until the tenth month, on the first day of the tenth month, the mountaintops 6 appeared. And it happened, at the end of forty days, that Noah opened 7 the window of the ark he had made. And he sent out the raven and it went forth to and fro until the waters should dry up from the earth. 8 And he sent out the dove to see whether the waters had abated from 9 the surface of the ground. But the dove found no resting place for its foot and it returned to him to the ark, for the waters were over all the

---

2. *the wellsprings of the deep . . . and the casements of the heavens, the rain.* In keeping with the stately symmetry that governs the style of the whole Flood narrative, the ending of the Flood precisely echoes the terms in which its beginning was represented, in the same order: the poetic inset of 7:11 immediately followed by "rain" at the beginning of 7:12.

5. *the mountaintops appeared.* There is an echo here of "that the dry land will appear" of 1:9.

6. *at the end of forty days.* After the ark comes to rest, not the forty days of deluge.

earth. And he reached out and took it and brought it back to him into the ark. Then he waited another seven days and again sent the dove out 10 from the ark. And the dove came back to him at eventide and, look, a 11 plucked olive leaf was in its bill, and Noah knew that the waters had abated from the earth. Then he waited still another seven days and sent 12 out the dove, and it did not return to him again. And it happened in the 13 six hundred and first year, in the first month, on the first day of the month, the waters dried up from the earth, and Noah took off the covering of the ark and he saw and, look, the surface of the ground was dry. And in the second month, on the twenty-seventh day of the month, the 14 earth was completely dry. And God spoke to Noah, saying, "Go out of 15,16 the ark, you and your wife and your sons and your sons' wives, with you. All the animals that are with you of all flesh, fowl and cattle and every 17 crawling thing that crawls on the earth, take out with you, and let them swarm through the earth and be fruitful and multiply on the earth." And Noah went out, his sons and his wife and his sons' wives with him. 18

---

13. *in the six hundred and first year.* Of Noah's life. The Septuagint adds these words, though whether that reflects a gloss or a more reliable text at this point is unclear.

ground. The Hebrew is *'adamah,* the word that also means "soil" and that figures importantly in the Garden story and its immediate aftermath. It recurs again in verse 21 in God's vow not to destroy the earth again.

14. *completely dry.* There is no "completely" in the Hebrew but that may be implied by the verb used. The verb for "was dry" in the preceding verse is *harev;* the verb here is *yavesh.* The two are occasionally paired in poetic parallelism (e.g., Hosea 13:15), but they also occur twice in what looks like a temporal sequence (Isaiah 19:5 and Job 14:11): first a water source dries up (*harev*), then it is in a state of complete dryness (*yavesh*).

19 Every beast, every crawling thing, and every fowl, everything that stirs
20 on the earth, by their families, came out of the ark. And Noah built an
    altar to the LORD and he took from every clean cattle and every clean
21 fowl and offered burnt offerings on the altar. And the LORD smelled the
    fragrant odor and the LORD said in His heart, "I will not again damn the
    soil on humankind's score. For the devisings of the human heart are evil

---

19. The verb *ramas* and the noun *remes* usually refer to crawling life-forms, but
there are a few contexts in which they appear to designate any kind of moving
creature. (The meaning of the root is probably linked with minute movement,
shuffling, or trampling.) In Genesis 9:3, *remes* must indicate all kinds of animals because Noah's diet is surely not restricted to reptiles and insects. Here,
the initial *romes* seems to mean "crawling things," because it stands in contradistinction to "every beast," whereas *romes* in the next clause summarizes
the catalogue that precedes it, which includes birds.

21. *And the LORD smelled the fragrant odor.* Noah has followed in the literary
footsteps of the hero of the Mesopotamian Flood stories in offering thanksgiving sacrifice after the waters recede. The frankly anthropomorphic imagination that informs Genesis has no difficulty in conceiving God's enjoying the
aroma of the burnt offerings. What is rigorously excluded from the monotheistic version of the story is any suggestion that God eats the sacrifice—in the
Mesopotamian traditions, the gods are thought to be dependent on the food
men provide them through the sacrifices, and they swoop down on the postdiluvian offering "like flies." The word for "fragrance" (or perhaps, something
pleasing or soothing), *niḥoaḥ,* is always attached to "odor" as a technical term
linked with sacrifices, and it probably puns here on the name Noah.
    The thanksgiving sacrifice is evidently a requisite narrative motif taken
from the Mesopotamian antecedents, but the Hebrew writer's attitude toward
it may be more complicated than meets the eye. The first reported animal sacrifice, though equally pleasing to God, led to the murder of the sacrificer.
Noah is about to be warned about the mortal danger of bloodguilt, and he himself will become the victim of an act of violation, though not as a consequence
of his sacrifice. In any case, divine acceptance of ritual offerings does nothing
to mitigate man's dangerous impulses.
    and the LORD said in His heart. The idiom means "said to himself" but it is
important to preserve the literal wording because it pointedly echoes 6:6, "and
was grieved to the heart," just as "the devisings of the human heart are evil"
explicitly echoes 6:5. The Flood story is thus enclosed by mutually mirroring
reports of God's musing on human nature. Whether the addition here of "from

from youth. And I will not again strike down all living things as I did.
As long as all the days of the earth—   22

> seedtime and harvest
> and cold and heat
> and summer and winter
> and day and night
> shall not cease."

---

youth" means, as some commentators claim, that God now has a more qualified view of the human potential for evil, is questionable. But after the Flood,
God, once more recognizing the evil of which man is capable, concludes that,
given what man is all too likely disposed to do, it is scarcely worth destroying
the whole world again on his account.

damn. The Hebrew verb, from a root associated with the idea of lack of
importance, or contemptibility, may occasionally mean "to curse," as in the
Balaam story, but its usual meaning is to denigrate or vilify. Perhaps both
senses are intimated here.

I will not again. The repetition of this phrase may reflect, as Rashi suggests,
a formal oath, the solemnity of which would then be capped by the poetic
inset at the end (which uses an unconventional short-line form, with only two
accents in each verset). What is peculiar is that this is a pledge that God
makes to Himself, not out loud to Noah. The complementary promise to
Noah, in the next chapter, will be accompanied by the external sign of the
rainbow. The silent promise in God's interior monologue invokes no external
signs, only the seamless cycle of the seasons that will continue as long as the
earth.

CHAPTER 9

1   A nd God blessed Noah and his sons and He said to them, "Be fruit-
2   ful and multiply and fill the earth. And the dread and fear of you
shall be upon all the beasts of the field and all the fowl of the
heavens, in all that crawls on the ground and in all the fish of the sea.
3 In your hand they are given. All stirring things that are alive, yours shall
4 be for food, like the green plants, I have given all to you. But flesh with
5 its lifeblood still in it you shall not eat. And just so, your lifeblood I will
requite, from every beast I will requite it, and from humankind, from
every man's brother, I will requite human life.

6
> He who sheds human blood
>   by humans his blood shall be shed,
> for in the image of God
>   He made humankind.

1–7. God's first postdiluvian speech to Noah affirms man's solidarity with the
rest of the animal kingdom—the covenant He goes on to spell out is, emphatically, with all flesh, not just with humankind—but also modifies the arrangement stipulated in the Creation story. Vegetarian man of the Garden is now
allowed a carnivore's diet (this might conceivably be intended as an outlet for
his violent impulses), and in consonance with that change, man does not
merely rule over the animal kingdom but inspires it with fear.

6. *He who sheds human blood / by humans his blood shall be shed.* "by humans"
might alternately mean "on account of the human." In either case, a system of
retributive justice is suggested. As many analysts of the Hebrew have noted,
there is an emphatic play on *dam,* "blood," and *'adam,* "human," and the chiastic word order of the Hebrew formally mirrors the idea of measure for measure: *shofekh* [spills] *dam* [blood] *ha'adam* [of the human], *ba'adam* [by the

As for you, be fruitful and multiply,   7
   swarm through the earth, and hold sway over it."

And God said to Noah and to his sons with him, "And I, I am about to   8,9
establish My covenant with you and with your seed after you, and with   10
every living creature that is with you, the fowl and the cattle and every
beast of the earth with you, all that have come out of the ark, every
beast of the earth. And I will establish My covenant with you, that   11
never again shall all flesh be cut off by the waters of the Flood, and
never again shall there be a Flood to destroy the earth." And God said, 12
"This is the sign of the covenant that I set between Me and you and
every living creature that is with you, for everlasting generations: My 13

---

human] *damo* [his blood] *yishafekh* [will be spilled] (= A B C C' B' A'). Perhaps
the ban on bloodshed at this point suggests that murder was the endemic vice
of the antediluvians.

7. *hold sway.* The translation here follows some versions of the Septuagint,
which read *uredu,* "and hold sway," instead of *urevu,* "and multiply," as in the
Masoretic Text. The latter reading looks suspiciously like a scribal transposition of *urevu* from the end of the first clause. The entire line, of course, picks
up the language of 1:28 as the process of human history is resumed after the
Flood.

12. *And God said.* This is the first instance of a common convention of biblical
narrative: when a speaker addresses someone and the formula for introducing
speech is repeated with no intervening response from the interlocutor, it generally indicates some sort of significant silence—a failure to comprehend, a
resistance to the speaker's words, and so forth. (Compare Judges 8:23–24. First
Gideon declares to his men that he will not rule over them. Seeing their evident resistance, he proposes a concrete alternative they can understand, the
collection of gold ornaments to make an ephod.) Here, God first flatly states
His promise never to destroy the world again. The flood-battered Noah evidently needs further assurance, so God goes on, with a second formula for
introducing speech, to offer the rainbow as outward token of His covenant.
The third occurrence of the *wayomer* formula, at the beginning of verse 17,
introduces a confirming summary of the rainbow as sign of the covenant.

bow I have set in the clouds to be a sign of the covenant between Me
14 and the earth, and so, when I send clouds over the earth, the bow will
15 appear in the cloud. Then I will remember My covenant, between Me
and you and every living creature of all flesh, and the waters will no
16 more become a Flood to destroy all flesh. And the bow shall be in the
cloud and I will see it, to remember the everlasting covenant between
17 God and all living creatures, all flesh that is on the earth." And God said
to Noah, "This is the sign of the covenant I have established between
Me and all flesh that is on the earth."

18 And the sons of Noah who came out from the ark were Shem and Ham
19 and Japheth, and Ham was the father of Canaan. These three were the
20 sons of Noah, and from these the whole earth spread out. And Noah, a
21 man of the soil, was the first to plant a vineyard. And he drank of the
22 wine and became drunk, and exposed himself within his tent. And
Ham the father of Canaan saw his father's nakedness and told his two
23 brothers outside. And Shem and Japheth took a cloak and put it over
both their shoulders and walked backward and covered their father's
nakedness, their faces turned backward so they did not see their
24 father's nakedness. And Noah woke from his wine and he knew what
25 his youngest son had done to him. And he said,

"Cursed be Canaan,
the lowliest slave shall he be
to his brothers."

20–27. Like the story of the Nephilim, this episode alludes cryptically to narrative material that may have been familiar to the ancient audience but must
have seemed to the monotheistic writer dangerous to spell out. The big difference is that, for the first time in Genesis, the horizon of the story is the
national history of Israel: Ham, the perpetrator of the act of violation, is mysteriously displaced in the curse by his son Canaan, and thus the whole story
is made to justify the—merely hoped-for—subject status of the Canaanites in
relation to the descendents of Shem, the Israelites. (Ham also now figures as
the youngest son, not the middle one.) No one has ever figured out exactly
what it is that Ham does to Noah. Some, as early as the classical Midrash,
have glimpsed here a Zeus-Chronos story in which the son castrates the father

And he said,   26

> "Blessed be the LORD
>   the God of Shem,
>   unto them shall Canaan be slave.
> May God enlarge Japheth,   27
>   may he dwell in the tents of Shem,
>   unto them shall Canaan be slave."

And Noah lived after the Flood three hundred and fifty years. And all   28,29
the days of Noah were nine hundred and fifty years. Then he died.

---

or, alternately, penetrates him sexually. The latter possibility is reinforced by
the fact that "to see the nakedness of" frequently means "to copulate with,"
and it is noteworthy that the Hebrews associated the Canaanites with lascivi-
ousness (see, for example, the rape of Dinah, Genesis 34). Lot's daughters, of
course, take advantage of his drunkenness to have sex with him. But it is
entirely possible that the mere seeing of a father's nakedness was thought of
as a terrible taboo, so that Ham's failure to avert his eyes would itself have
earned him the curse.

27. *enlarge Japheth.* The Hebrew involves a pun: *yaft leyafet.*

28–29. These verses resume the precise verbal formulas of the antediluvian
genealogy in chapter 5. The story of Noah is given formal closure with this
recording of his age, and the stage is set for the Table of Nations of the next
chapter, which will constitute a historical divider between the tale of the Flood
and the next narrative episode, the Tower of Babel.

CHAPTER 10

₁ **A**nd this is the lineage of the sons of Noah, Shem, Ham, and
₂ Japheth. Sons were born to them after the Flood. The sons of
Japheth: Gomer and Magog and Madai and Javan and Tubal and
₃ Meshech and Tiras. And the sons of Gomer: Ashkenaz and Riphath and

---

As elsewhere, genealogy is adopted as a means of schematizing complex historical evolution, and thus the terms "father of" and "begot" are essentially metaphors for historical concatenation. The total number of figures in the Table of Nations (excluding Nimrod) comes to seventy, the biblical formulaic number for a sizeable and complete contingent of any sort. It should be observed that representing the origins of nations as a genealogical scheme preserves a thematic continuity with the divine injunction after creation to be fruitful and multiply and sets the stage for the history of the one people whose propagation is repeatedly promised but continually threatened.

In keeping with the universalist perspective of Genesis, the Table of Nations is a serious attempt, unprecedented in the ancient Near East, to sketch a panorama of all known human cultures—from Greece and Crete in the west through Asia Minor and Iran and down through Mesopotamia and the Arabian Peninsula to northwestern Africa. This chapter has been a happy hunting ground for scholars armed with the tools of archeology, and in fact an impressive proportion of these names have analogues in inscriptions and tablets in other ancient Near Eastern cultures. The Table mingles geographic, ethnic, and linguistic criteria for defining nations, and the list intersperses place-names and gentilic designations (the latter appearing first in plural forms and beginning with verse 16 in singular forms). Some analysts have argued for a splicing together of two different lists of nations. One may infer that the Table assumes a natural evolutionary explanation for the multiplicity of languages that does not involve an act of divine intervention of the sort that will be narrated in the next episode, the Tower of Babel.

Togarmah. And the sons of Javan: Elishah and Tarshish, the Kittites   4
and the Dodanites. From these the Sea Peoples branched out. [These   5
are the sons of Japheth,] in their lands, each with his own tongue,
according to their clans in their nations. And the sons of Ham: Cush   6
and Mizraim and Put and Canaan. And the sons of Cush: Seba and   7
Havilah and Raamah and Sabteca. And the sons of Raamah: Sheba and
Dedan. And Cush begot Nimrod. He was the first mighty man on   8
earth. He was a mighty hunter before the LORD. Therefore is it said: 9
Like Nimrod, a mighty hunter before the LORD. The start of his king-   10
dom was Babylon and Erech and Accad, all of them in the land of Shinar. From that land Asshur emerged, and he built Nineveh and   11
Rehoboth-Ir and Calah, and Resen, between Nineveh and Calah,   12
which is the great city. And Mizraim begot the Ludites and the Ana-   13
mites and the Lehabites and the Naphtuhites, and the Pathrusites and   14
the Casluhites, and the Caphtorites, from whom the Philistines

---

5. *the Sea Peoples.* The probable reference is to the migrants from the Greek islands ("Javan" is Ion, or Greece) who established a foothold in the coastal region of Palestine during the twelfth century B.C.E.

These are the sons of Japheth. These words do not occur in the Masoretic Text, but the scholarly consensus is that there is a scribal omission here, as this is part of the formula used in verse 20 and verse 31 to summarize the list of the descendants of each of Noah's other two sons.

8. *He was the first mighty man on earth.* The Hebrew, which says literally, "he began to be a mighty man," uses the same idiom that is invoked for Noah's planting a vineyard. The implication, then, is that Nimrod, too, was the founder of an archetypal human occupation. The next verse suggests that this occupation is that of hunter, with his founding of a great Mesopotamian empire then introduced in verses 10–12 as an ancillary fact. Perhaps his prowess as hunter is put forth as evidence of the martial prowess that enabled him to conquer kingdoms, since the two skills are often associated in the ruling classes of older civilizations. Numerous Neo-Assyrian bas-reliefs depict royal lion hunts or royal bull hunts. Nimrod has been conjecturally identified with the thirteenth-century B.C.E. Tukulti-Ninurta I, the first Assyrian conqueror of Babylonia.

10. *all of them.* This translation adopts a commonly accepted emendation *wekhulanah,* instead of the Masoretic Text's *wekhalneh,* "and Calneh."

15,16 emerged. And Canaan begot Sidon, his firstborn, and Heth and the
17 Jebusite and the Amorite and the Girgashite and the Hivite and the
18 Archite and the Sinite and the Arvadite and the Zemarite and the
19 Hamatite. Afterward the clans of the Canaanite spread out. And the
border of the Canaanite was from Sidon till you come to Gerar, as far
as Gaza, till you come to Sodom and Gomorrah and Admah and
20 Zeboiim, as far as Lasha. These are the sons of Ham according to their
21 clans and their tongues, in their lands and their nations. Sons were
born, too, to Shem, the father of all the sons of Eber, the older brother
22 of Japheth. The sons of Shem: Elam and Asshur and Arpachshad and
23 Lud and Aram. And the sons of Aram: Uz and Hul and Gether and
24,25 Mash. And Arpachshad begot Shelah and Shelah begot Eber. And to
Eber two sons were born. The name of one was Peleg for in his days
26 the earth was split apart; and his brother's name was Joktan. And Jok-
27 tan begot Almodad and Sheleph and Hazarmaveth and Jerah and
28,29 Hadoram and Uzal and Diklah and Obal and Abimael and Sheba and
30 Ophir and Havilah and Jobab. All these were the sons of Joktan. And
their settlements were from Mesha till you come to Sephar, in the east-
31 ern highlands. These are the sons of Shem according to their clans and

---

24. *Eber.* He is the eponymous father of the Hebrews, *'ibrim*. Whatever the
actual original meanings of the names, there is a clear tendency in the Table
to intimate exemplary meanings in the names of these mythic founders: elsewhere, "Eber" is explicitly linked with the term that means "from the other
side" (of the river).

25. *Peleg . . . in his days the earth split apart.* The three consonants of the name
Peleg, which as a common noun means "brook," form the verbal root that
means "to split." It is a stronger verb than "divide," the term used by most English translators. Rabbinic tradition construes the splitting here as a reference
to the Tower of Babel, but it is at least as plausible to see it as an allusion to
an entirely different epochal event of "division," such as a cataclysmic
earthquake.

tongues, in their lands and their nations. These are the clans of the 32
sons of Noah according to their lineage in their nations. And from these
the nations branched out on the earth after the Flood.

---

32. *branched out.* Literally, the Hebrew verb means "separated." The whole
Table of Nations is devised to explain how the many separate nations came
into being. The immediately following verse, which begins the tale of the
Tower of Babel, announces a primeval unity of all people on earth. This seeming flat contradiction might reflect a characteristically biblical way of playing
dialectically with alternative possibilities: humankind is many and divided, as
a consequence of natural history; and, alternately, humankind was once one,
as a consequence of having been made by the same Creator, but this God-
given oneness was lost through man's presumption in trying to overreach his
place in the divine scheme.

CHAPTER 11

1,2 **A**nd all the earth was one language, one set of words. And it happened as they journeyed from the east that they found a valley in
3 the land of Shinar and settled there. And they said to each other,
"Come, let us bake bricks and burn them hard." And the brick served
4 them as stone, and bitumen served them as mortar. And they said,
"Come, let us build us a city and a tower with its top in the heavens,

---

1–9. The story of the Tower of Babel transforms the Mesopotamian ziggurat,
built with bricks (in contrast to Canaanite stone structures) and one of the
wonders of ancient technology, into a monotheistic fable. Although there is a
long exegetical tradition that imagines the building of the Tower as an attempt
to scale the heights of heaven, the text does not really suggest that. "Its top in
the heavens" is a hyperbole found in Mesopotamian inscriptions for celebrating high towers, and to make or leave a "name" for oneself by erecting a lasting monument is a recurrent notion in ancient Hebrew culture. The polemic
thrust of the story is against urbanism and the overweening confidence of
humanity in the feats of technology. This polemic, in turn, is lined up with the
stories of the tree of life and the Nephilim in which humankind is seen aspiring to transcend the limits of its creaturely condition. As in those earlier
moments, one glimpses here the vestiges of a mythological background in
which God addresses an unspecified celestial entourage in the first-person
plural as He considers how to respond to man's presumption.

2. *a valley in the land of Shinar*. The Hebrew for "valley" might also mean
"plain," as was recognized as long ago as Abraham ibn Ezra in the twelfth century. That would fit the Mesopotamian setting better.

3. *Come, let us*. As many commentators have noted, the story exhibits an intricate antithetical symmetry that embodies the idea of "man proposes, God dis-
poses." The builders say, "Come, let us bake bricks," God says, "Come, let us

that we may make us a name, lest we be scattered over all the earth."
And the LORD came down to see the city and the tower that the human   5
creatures had built. And the LORD said, "As one people with one lan-   6
guage for all, if this is what they have begun to do, now nothing they
plot to do will elude them. Come, let us go down and baffle their lan-   7
guage there so that they will not understand each other's language."
And the LORD scattered them from there over all the earth and they left   8
off building the city. Therefore it is called Babel, for there the LORD   9
made the language of all the earth babble. And from there the LORD
scattered them over all the earth.

---

go down"; they are concerned "lest we be scattered," and God responds by
scattering them. The story is an extreme example of the stylistic predisposition
of biblical narrative to exploit interechoing words and to work with a deliberately restricted vocabulary. The word "language" occurs five times in this brief
text as does the phrase "all the earth" (and the "land" of Shinar is the same
Hebrew word as that for earth). The prose turns language itself into a game of
mirrors.

bake bricks and burn them hard. A literal rendering of the Hebrew would be
something like "brick bricks and burn for a burning." This fusion of words
reflects the striking tendency of the story as a whole to make words flow into
each other. "Bitumen," ḥeimar, becomes ḥomer, "mortar." The reiterated
"there," sham, is the first syllable of shamayim, "heavens," as well as an odd
echo of shem, "name." Meaning in language, as the biblical writer realized long
before the influential Swiss linguist Ferdinand de Saussure, is made possible
through differences between terms in the linguistic system. Here difference is
subverted in the very style of the story, with the blurring of lexical boundaries
culminating in God's confounding of tongues. The Hebrew balal, to "mix" or
"confuse," represented in this translation by "baffle" and "babble," is a polemic
pun on the Akkadian "Babel," which might actually mean "gate of the god." As
for the phonetic kinship of babble and balal, Webster's New World Dictionary
of the American Language (1966) notes that a word like "babble" occurs in a
wide spectrum of languages from Greek, Latin, and Sanskrit to Norwegian,
and prudently concludes, "of echoic origin; probably not of continuous derivation but recoined from common experience."

10   This is the lineage of Shem: Shem was a hundred years old when he
11   begot Arpachshad two years after the Flood. And Shem lived after
      begetting Arpachshad five hundred years and he begot sons and daugh-
12,13 ters. And Arpachshad lived thirty-five years and he begot Shelah. And
      Arpachshad lived after begetting Shelah four hundred and three years
14   and he begot sons and daughters. And Shelah lived thirty years and he
15   begot Eber. And Shelah lived after begetting Eber four hundred and
16   three years and he begot sons and daughters. And Eber lived thirty-
17   four years and he begot Peleg. And Eber lived after begetting Peleg four
18   hundred and thirty years and he begot sons and daughters. And Peleg
19   lived thirty years and he begot Reu. And Peleg lived after begetting Reu
20   two hundred and nine years and he begot sons and daughters. And Reu
21   lived thirty-two years and he begot Serug. And Reu lived after begetting
      Serug two hundred and seven years and he begot sons and daughters.
22,23 And Serug lived thirty years and he begot Nahor. And Serug lived after
      begetting Nahor two hundred years and he begot sons and daughters.
24,25 And Nahor lived twenty-nine years and he begot Terah. And Nahor
      lived after begetting Terah one hundred and nineteen years and he
26   begot sons and daughters. And Terah lived seventy years and he begot
      Abram, Nahor, and Haran.

10–26. There are ten generations from Shem to Abraham (as the universal history begins to focus down to a national history) as there are ten from Adam to
Noah. In another formal symmetry, the ten antediluvian generations end with
a father who begets three sons, just as this series of ten will end with Terah
begetting Abram, Nahor, and Haran. This genealogy, which constitutes the
bridge from the Flood to the beginning of the Patriarchal Tales, uses formulas
identical with those of the antediluvian genealogy in chapter 5, omitting the
summarizing indication of life span and the report of death of each begetter.
Longevity now is cut in half, and then halved again in the latter part of the list,
as we approach Abram. From this point, men will have merely the extraordinary life spans of modern Caucasian mountain dwellers and not legendary life
spans. The narrative in this way is preparing to enter recognizable human time
and family life. There is one hidden number-game here, as the Israeli Bible
scholar Moshe Weinfeld has observed: the number of years from the birth of
Shem's son to Abram's migration to Canaan is exactly a solar 365.

And this is the lineage of Terah: Terah begot Abram, Nahor, and Haran, 27
and Haran begot Lot. And Haran died in the lifetime of Terah his father 28
in the land of his birth, Ur of the Chaldees. And Abram and Nahor took 29
themselves wives. The name of Abram's wife was Sarai and the name
of Nahor's wife was Milcah daughter of Haran, the father of Milcah
and the father of Iscah. And Sarai was barren, she had no child. And 30,31
Terah took Abram his son and Lot son of Haran, his grandson, and
Sarai his daughter-in-law, the wife of his son Abram, and he set out
with them from Ur of the Chaldees toward the land of Canaan, and
they came to Haran and settled there. And the days of Terah were two 32
hundred and five years, and Terah died in Haran.

27–32. This is a second genealogical document, using different language, and
zeroing in on Abram's immediate family and its migrations.

31. *he set out with them*. Two small changes in the vocalization of the two
Hebrew words here yield "he took them out with him." This is the reading of
the Septuagint and the Samaritan Version.

Haran. In the Hebrew there is no confusion with the name of Abram's
deceased brother, because the latter begins with an aspirated *heh*, the former
with a fricative *ḥet*.

CHAPTER 12

1 And the LORD said to Abram, "Go forth from your land and your
2 birthplace and your father's house to the land I will show you. And
I will make you a great nation and I will bless you and make your
3 name great, and you shall be a blessing. And I will bless those who

---

1. *Go forth from your land . . . to the land I will show you*. Abram, a mere figure
in a notation of genealogy and migration in the preceding passage, becomes an
individual character, and begins the Patriarchal narratives, when he is here
addressed by God, though he himself as yet says nothing, responding only by
obedience. The name Canaan is never mentioned, and the divine imperative
to head out for an unspecified place resembles, as Rashi observes, God's terrible call to Abraham in chapter 22 to sacrifice his son on a mountain God will
show him. Rashi also draws a shrewd connection between the triplet here—
"your land and your birthplace and your father's house"—with the triplet in
chapter 22—"your son, your only one, whom you love." The series in each case
focuses the utterance more specifically from one term to the next. Thus the
Hebrew *moledet* almost certainly has its usual sense of "birthplace" and not its
occasional sense of "kinfolk," which would turn it into a loose synonym of
"father's house" (*beyt 'av*, a fixed term for the family social unit). In 11:28
moledet appears as part of a genetive construction, *'erets moladeto*, "land of his
birth." Here those two terms are broken out from each other to yield the focusing sequence: land–birthplace–father's house.

2. *you shall be a blessing*. The verb here as vocalized in the Masoretic Text literally means, "Be you a blessing," which makes the Hebrew syntax somewhat
problematic. A change in vocalization would yield, "and it [your name] will be
a blessing." The Israeli biblical scholar Moshe Weinfeld has aptly noted that
after the string of curses that begins with Adam and Eve, human history
reaches a turning point with Abraham, as blessings instead of curses are
emphatically promised.

bless you, and those who damn you I will curse, and all the clans of the earth through you shall be blessed." And Abram went forth as the LORD 4 had spoken to him and Lot went forth with him, Abram being seventy-five years old when he left Haran. And Abram took Sarai his wife and 5 Lot his nephew and all the goods they had gotten and the folk they had bought in Haran, and they set out on the way to the land of Canaan, and they came to the land of Canaan. And Abram crossed through the 6 land to the site of Shechem, to the Terebinth of Moreh. The Canaanite was then in the land. And the LORD appeared to Abram and said, 7 "To your seed I will give this land." And he built an altar there to the LORD who had appeared to him. And he pulled up his stakes from there 8 for the high country east of Bethel and pitched his tent with Bethel to the west and Ai to the east, and he built there an altar to the LORD, and he invoked the name of the LORD. And Abram journeyed onward by 9 stages to the Negeb.

---

3. *those who damn you.* The Masoretic Text uses a singular form, but the plural, attested in several manuscripts and ancient versions, makes better sense as parallelism. The balanced formulation of this and the preceding verse are almost scannable as poetry.

5. *the folk they had bought in Haran.* Slavery was a common institution throughout the ancient Near East. As subsequent stories in Genesis make clear, this was not the sort of chattel slavery later practiced in North America. These slaves had certain limited rights, could be given great responsibility, and were not thought to lose their personhood.

6. *The Canaanite was then in the land.* Abraham ibn Ezra famously detected a hint here that at the time of writing this was no longer the case. In any event, the point of the notation, as Gerhard von Rad has seen, is to introduce a certain tension with the immediately following promise that the land will be given to Abram's offspring.

8. *And he pulled up his stakes.* The Hebrew vocabulary (here, the verb *waya'teq*) in this sequence is meticulous in reflecting the procedures of nomadic life. The verb for "journey" in verse 9 also derives from another term for the pulling up of tent stakes, and the progressive form in which it is cast is a precise indication of movement through successive encampments.

10 And there was a famine in the land and Abram went down to Egypt to
11 sojourn there, for the famine was grave in the land. And it happened as
he drew near to the border of Egypt that he said to Sarai his wife,
12 "Look, I know you are a beautiful woman, and so when the Egyptians
see you and say, 'She is his wife,' they will kill me while you they will let
13 live. Say, please, that you are my sister, so that it will go well with me
14 on your count and I shall stay alive because of you." And it happened
when Abram came into Egypt that the Egyptians saw the woman was
15 very beautiful. And Pharaoh's courtiers saw her and praised her to
16 Pharaoh, and the woman was taken into Pharaoh's house. And it went
well with Abram on her count, and he had sheep and cattle and don-

---

10. *And there was a famine in the land.* The puzzling story of the sister-wife
occurs three times in Genesis (here, chapter 20, and chapter 26:1–12). It is the
first instance of type-scene in biblical narrative, in which the writer invokes a
fixed sequence of narrative motifs, familiar as a convention to his audience,
while pointedly modifying them in keeping with the needs of the immediate
narrative context. The Midrash recognized that the tale of going down to Egypt
at a time of famine was a foreshadowing of the sojourn in Egypt ("the actions
of the fathers are a sign for the sons"). But in contrast to the versions in chapters 20 and 26, here, at the beginning of the whole Patriarchal cycle, the writer
goes out of his way to heighten the connections with the Exodus story. Only
here is the land of sojourn Egypt and only here is the foreign potentate
Pharaoh. Only here does the narrator speak explicitly of "plagues" (though a
different term is used in Exodus). Only here is the danger of the husband's
death set off by the phrase "you they will let live" attached to the wife, a
pointed echo of Exodus 1:22, "Every boy that is born you shall fling into the
Nile, and every girl you shall let live." This is also the most compact, and the
most archetypal, of the three versions; the other two will elaborate and complicate the basic scheme, each in its own way.

11. *I know.* This is the construal of *yadaʿti* according to normative Hebrew
grammar. But the *ti* ending could be an archaic second-person singular feminine, and "you know" would make better conversational sense here.

13. *my sister.* Chapter 20 reveals that Sarah is actually Abraham's half sister. It
is not clear whether the writer means to endorse the peculiar stratagem of the
patriarch in any of these three stories.

keys and male and female slaves and she-asses and camels. And the 17
LORD afflicted Pharaoh and his household with terrible plagues
because of Sarai the wife of Abram. And Pharaoh summoned Abram 18
and said, "What is this you have done to me? Why did you not tell me 19
she was your wife? Why did you say, 'She is my sister,' so that I took her
to me as wife? Now, here is your wife. Take her and get out!" And 20
Pharaoh appointed men over him and they sent him out, with his wife
and all he had.

---

17. *plagues.* The nature of the afflictions is not spelled out. Rashi's inference
of a genital disorder preventing intercourse is not unreasonable. In that case,
one might imagine a tense exchange between Pharoah and Sarai ending in a
confession by Sarai of her status as Abram's wife. In the laconic narrative art
of the Hebrew writer, this is left as a gap for us to fill in by an indeterminate
compound of careful deduction and imaginative reconstruction.

19. *Take her and get out!* "Her" is merely implied in the Hebrew, which gives
us three abrupt syllables, two of them accented: *qákh walékh*. There may be
an intended counterpoint between the impatient brusqueness of this imperative, *lekh,* and the same imperative, softened by an ethical dative, *lekh lekha,*
"go forth" (literally, "go you"), in God's words to Abram that inaugurate the
Patriarchal cycle.

CHAPTER 13

¹ A nd Abram came up from Egypt, he and his wife and all he had,
² and Lot together with him, to the Negeb. And Abram was heavily
³ laden with cattle, with silver and gold. And he went on by stages
from the Negeb up to Bethel, to the place where his tent had been
⁴ before, between Bethel and Ai, to the place of the altar he had made
the first time, and Abram invoked there the name of the LORD.

⁵ And Lot, too, who came along with Abram, had flocks and herds and
⁶ tents. And the land could not support their dwelling together, for their
⁷ substance was great and they could not dwell together. And there was
strife between the herdsmen of Abram's flocks and the herdsmen of
Lot's flocks. The Canaanite and the Perizzite were then dwelling in the
⁸ land. And Abram said to Lot, "Pray, let there be no contention between
⁹ you and me, between your herdsmen and mine, for we are kinsmen. Is

---

7. *The Canaanite and the Perizzite.* This second notation of the indigenous
population of Canaan, at the moment of friction between the two immigrants
from Mesopotamia, suggests that they can scarcely afford such divisiveness
when they are surrounded by potential enemies. (In the next episode, Abram
will be compelled to bring military aid to his nephew.) There may also be a hint
of irony in their dividing up a land here that already has inhabitants.

8–9. This is only the second report of direct speech of Abram. The first, his
address to Sarai as they are about to enter Egypt, reveals a man fearful about
his own survival. Here we get a very different image of Abram as the reasonable peacemaker and as a man conscious of family bonds in alien surround-
ings. The language in which he addresses Lot is clear, firm, and polite.

not all the land before you? Pray, let us part company. If you take the
left hand, then I shall go right, and if you take the right hand, I shall go
left." And Lot raised his eyes and saw the whole plain of the Jordan,   10
saw that all of it was well-watered, before the LORD's destruction of
Sodom and Gomorrah, like the garden of the LORD, like the land of
Egypt, till you come to Zoar. And Lot chose for himself the whole plain   11
of the Jordan, and Lot journeyed eastward, and they parted from one
another. Abram dwelled in the land of Canaan and Lot dwelled in the   12
cities of the plain, and he set up his tent near Sodom

---

9. *Pray, let us part company*. The Hebrew is cast in the form of a polite imperative, literally: "Kindly part from me."

10. *saw that all of it was well-watered*. There is no repetition of "saw" in the
Hebrew; Hebrew grammar allows the single verb to govern simultaneously the
direct object ("the whole plain of the Jordan") and the relative clause that
modifies the direct object. What is significant thematically is that the point of
view of the entire clause is Lot's. The writer may well have drawn on a tradition that the whole plain of the Jordan down to the Dead Sea, before some
remembered cataclysm, was abundantly fertile, but it is Lot who sees the plain
in hyperbolic terms, likening it to "the garden of the LORD"—presumably,
Eden, far to the east—and to the fabulously irrigated Egypt to the south.
(Archeologists have in fact discovered traces of an ancient irrigation system in
the plain of the Jordan.)

12. *dwelled in the cities . . . set up his tent*. At least in this first phase of his habitation of the plain, Lot is represented ambiguously either living in a town or
camping near one. From the writer's perspective, abandoning the seminomadic life for urban existence can only spell trouble. The verb *'ahal* derived
from the noun "tent" is relatively rare, and seems to mean both to set up a tent
and (verse 18) to fold up a tent in preparation for moving on.

13 Now the people of Sodom were very evil offenders against the LORD.
14 And the LORD had said to Abram after Lot parted from him, "Raise your
   eyes and look out from the place where you are to the north and the
15 south and the east and the west, for all the land you see, to you I will
16 give it and to your seed forever. And I will make your seed like the dust
   of the earth—could a man count the dust of the earth, so too, your seed
17 might be counted. Rise, walk about the land through its length and its
18 breadth, for to you I will give it." And Abram took up his tent and came
   to dwell by the Terebinths of Mamre, which are in Hebron, and he
   built there an altar to the LORD.

---

13. *Now the people of Sodom.* This brief observation, as many commentators
have noted, suggests that Lot has made a very bad choice. The consequences
will become manifest in chapter 19.

14. *And the LORD had said to Abram.* Although all previous translations treat
this as a simple past, the word order—subject before verb—and the use of the
suffix conjugation instead of the prefix conjugation that is ordinarily employed
for past actions indicate a pluperfect. The definition of temporal frame is
pointed and precise: once Lot actually parts from Abram, heading down to his
fatal involvement in the cities of the plain, God proceeds to address His
promise of the land to Abram. The utterance of the promise is already an
accomplished fact as Lot takes up settlement in the plain to the east.
   Raise your eyes and look. The location between Bethel and Ai is in fact a
spectacular lookout point, and the already implicit contrast between Abram
and Lot is extended—Abram on the heights, Lot down in the sunken plain.

16. *could a man count the dust of the earth.* Unusually for the use of simile in
the Bible, the meaning of the simile is spelled out after the image is introduced. Perhaps this reflects the high didactic solemnity of the moment of
promise, though the comparison with dust might also raise negative associations that would have to be excluded. (The great Yiddish poet Yakov Glatstein
wrote a bitter poem after the Nazi genocide which proposes that indeed the
seed of Abraham has become like the dust of the earth.)

17. *walk about the land through its length and its breadth.* Walking around the
perimeter of a piece of property was a common legal ritual in the ancient Near
East for taking final possession, and the formula "I have given it to So-and-so
and to his sons forever" is a well-attested legal formula in the region for conveyance of property going back as far as the Ugaritic texts, composed in the
fourteenth and thirteenth centuries B.C.E.

CHAPTER 14

And it happened in the days of Amraphel king of Shinar, Arioch   1
king of Ellasar, Chedorlaomer king of Elam, and Tidal king of
Goiim. They made war on Bera king of Sodom and Birsha king of   2
Gomorrah, on Shinab king of Admah and Shemeber king of Zeboiim

---

1. *And it happened in the days of.* This introductory formula (just two words in
the Hebrew, *wayehi biymey*) signals a drastic stylistic shift to an annalistic narrative. Because verse 2 has no explicit subject, E. A. Speiser, followed by later
scholars, has conjectured that the first two Hebrew words of the text are a
somewhat awkward Hebrew translation of an Akkadian idiom used at the
beginning of literary narratives that simply means "when." This solution is a little strained, and would compromise the effect of introducing the audience to
a historical account that is conveyed by the formula "And it happened in the
days of such-and-such a king, or kings." Scholarship is virtually unanimous in
identifying this chapter as the product of a different literary source from the
three principal strands out of which Genesis is woven. The whole episode is
in fact a prime instance of the technique of literary collage that is characteristic of biblical narrative. Abram, having been promised national tenure in the
land in the immediately preceding episode, is now placed at the center of a
different kind of narrative that makes him a figure on the international historical scene, doing battle with monarchs from the far-flung corners of
Mesopotamia and treating with the king of Jerusalem (Salem), one of the principal cities of Canaan. The dating of the narrative is in dispute, but there are
good arguments for its relative antiquity: at least four of the five invading kings
have authentic Akkadian, Elamite, or Hittite names; and the repeated glossing
of place-names ("Bela, that is, Zoar") suggests an old document that invoked
certain names which usage had replaced by the time this text was woven into
the larger Abraham narrative.

3   and the king of Bela, that is, Zoar. All of them joined forces in the Val-
4   ley of Siddim, that is, the Dead Sea. Twelve years they had been sub-
5   ject to Chedorlaomer and in the thirteenth year they rebelled. And in
     the fourteenth year Chedorlaomer and the kings who were with him
     came and struck down the Rephaim at Ashteroth-Karnaim and the
6   Zuzim at Ham and the Emim at Shaveh-Kiriathaim, and the Horite in
     the high country of Seir as far as El-Paran which is by the wilderness.
7   And they swung back and came to En-Mishpat, that is, Kadesh, and
     they struck all the territory of the Amalekite and also the Amorite who
8   dwelt in Hazazon-Tamar. And the king of Sodom and the king of
     Gomorrah and the king of Admah and the king of Zeboiim and the king
     of Bela, that is, Zoar, went forth and joined battle with them in the Val-
9   ley of Siddim, with Chedorlaomer king of Elam and Tidal king of Goiim
     and Amraphel king of Shinar and Arioch king of Ellasar—four kings
10 against the five. And the Valley of Siddim was riddled with bitumen
     pits, and the kings of Sodom and Gomorrah fled there and leaped into
11 them, while the rest fled to the high country. And the four kings took
     all the substance of Sodom and Gomorrah and all their food, and went
12 off. And they took Lot, Abram's nephew, and all his substance, and
     went off, for he was then dwelling in Sodom.

---

3. *joined forces.* The verb is a technical military term and initiates a whole
chain of military or political terms not evident in the surrounding Patriarchal
narratives: "had been subject," "rebelled" (verse 4), "joined battle" (verse 8),
"marshaled his retainers" (verse 14), "fanned out against them" (verse 15). The
narrative perspective is geostrategic, and there is no dramatic engagement of
characters in dialogue until the rather ceremonial and didactic exchange
between Melchizedek and Abram at the end.

11. *the four kings.* The subject is supplied for clarity by the translation: the
Hebrew simply says "they." A similar employment of a verb without a stipulated subject, not uncommon in biblical usage, occurs at the end of verse 20,
where the Hebrew does not state what the context implies, that it is Abram
who gives the tithe.

And a fugitive came and told Abram the Hebrew, for he was then 13
encamped at the Terebinths of Mamre the Amorite, kinsman of Eshkol
and Aner, who were Abram's confederates. And Abram heard that his 14
kinsman was taken captive and he marshaled his retainers, natives of
his household, three hundred and eighteen of them, and gave chase up
to Dan. And he and his servants with him fanned out against them by 15
night and he struck them and pursued them up to Hobah, which is
north of Damascus. And he brought back all the substance, and also 16
Lot his kinsman and his substance he brought back, and the women
and the other people as well. And the king of Sodom went forth to meet 17
him after he came back from striking down Chedorlaomer and the
kings that were with him, to the Valley of Shaveh, that is, the Valley of
the King. And Melchizedek king of Salem brought out bread and wine, 18
for he was priest to El Elyon. And he blessed him, and he said, 19

13. *Abram the Hebrew.* Only here is he given this designation. Although scholars have argued whether "Hebrew" is an ethnic or social term or even the name
for a warrior class, it is clear that it is invoked only in contexts when Abraham
and his descendants stand in relation to members of other national groups.

14. *he marshaled his retainers.* The noun and the verb in this particular sense
occur only here. The former may derive from a root that means "to train," and
thus might imply "trained fighters." The latter is applied elsewhere to
unsheathing a sword, and thus may be metaphorically extended to the
"unsheathing" of warriors.

   three hundred and eighteen. This number sounds quite realistic, whereas
the geographical origins and the huge sweeping itinerary of the four kings,
coming hundreds of miles to subdue five petty princelets in eastern Canaan,
sound legendary.

18. *Melchizedek.* The name means "righteous king," which has suggested to
many commentators a Davidide agenda in this tale of the founder of the people of Israel in ceremonial encounter with a priest-king of Jerusalem.

"Blessed be Abram to El Elyon,
    possessor of heaven and earth,
20   and blessed be El Elyon
       who delivered your foes into your hand."

21 And Abram gave him a tithe of everything. And the king of Sodom said
22 to Abram, "Give me the folk, and the substance take for yourself." And
Abram said to the king of Sodom, "I raise my hand in oath to the LORD,
23 the Most High God, possessor of heaven and earth, that I will take not
a single thread or sandal strap of all that is yours, lest you say, 'I have
24 made Abram rich.' Nothing for me but what the lads have consumed.
And as for the share of the men who came with me, Aner, Eshkol, and
Mamre, let them take their share."

19–20. *El Elyon.* El is the proper name of the sky god in the Canaanite pantheon, and Elyon is evidently a distinct, associated deity, though here the two
appear as a compound name. But the two terms are also plain Hebrew words
that mean "God the Most High," and elsewhere are used separately or (once)
together as designations of the God of Israel. Whatever Melchizedek's theology, Abram elegantly co-opts him for monotheism by using *El Elyon* in its
orthodox Israelite sense (verse 22) when he addresses the king of Sodom.

19. *possessor.* Although conventional Semitic lexicography claims that the original meaning of this verb, *qanah,* is "to make," the overwhelming majority of
biblical occurrences reflect the meaning "to buy," "to acquire," "to gain possession," which is the standard acceptation of the word in postbiblical Hebrew.

24. *lads.* The primary meaning of the word is "lads" but it also has a technical
military sense of picked fighters. Its use here makes a neat contrast with "the
men," who do not belong to Abram's household and are entitled to a share of
the booty.
    In all this, it is a little surprising that Abram should figure as a military hero,
and some scholars (most forcefully, Yochanan Muffs) have seen this story as an
Israelite adaptation of an old Akkadian literary form, the *naru,* a historical
romance meant to glorify kings. One should note, however, that the military
exploit—apparently, a surprise attack by night—is dispatched very quickly
while the main emphasis is placed on the victorious Abram's magnaminity and
disinterestedness. Thus the idea of the patriarch's maintaining fair and proper
relations with the peoples of the land, already intimated in his dealings with Lot
in the previous chapter, comes to displace the image of mere martial prowess.

CHAPTER 15

After these things the word of the LORD came to Abram in a vision, 1
saying, "Fear not, Abram, I am your shield. Your reward shall be
very great." And Abram said, "O my Master, LORD, what can You 2
give me when I am going to my end childless, and the steward of my
household is Dammesek Eliezer?" And Abram said, "Look, to me you 3

---

1. *the word of the LORD came to Abram.* This is a formula for revelation characteristic of the Prophetic books, not of the Patriarchal Tales. It is noteworthy
that in Genesis 20 God refers to Abraham as a "prophet." The night-vision
(*maḥazeh*) invoked here is also a prophetic mode of experience.

2. *And Abram said.* Until this point, all of Abram's responses to God have been
silent obedience. His first actual dialogue with God—in this, too, Prophetic
precedents may be relevant—expresses doubt that God's promise can be realized: this first speech to God reveals a hitherto unglimpsed human dimension
of Abram.

I am going to my end. The Hebrew says simply "I am going," but elsewhere
"to go" is sometimes used as a euphemism for dying, and, as several analysts
have argued, the context here makes that a likely meaning.

steward. The translation follows a traditional conjecture about the anomalous Hebrew *mesheq,* but the meaning is uncertain. The word might be a
scribal repetition of the last three consonants in "Dammesek," or, alternately,
it could be a deliberate play on words (Dammesek and *mesheq,* "household
maintenance"). The enigma is compounded by the fact that only here is Abraham's majordomo named as Eliezer—a West Semitic name, moreover, that
would be surprising in someone from Damascus.

3. *And Abram said.* God remains impassively silent in the face of Abram's brief
initial complaint, forcing him to continue and spell out the reason for his skepticism about the divine promise.

have given no seed, and here a member of my household is to be my
4 heir." And now the word of the LORD came to him, saying, "This one
will not be your heir, but he who issues from your loins will be your
5 heir." And He took him outside and He said, "Look up to the heavens
and count the stars, if you can count them." And He said, "So shall be
6 your seed." And he trusted in the LORD, and He reckoned it to his
merit.

7 And He said to him, "I am the LORD who brought you out of Ur of the
8 Chaldees to give you this land to inherit." And he said, "O my Master,

---

5. *count the stars.* This is a complementary image to that of the numberless
dust in chapter 13 but, literally and figuratively, loftier, and presented to Abraham in the grand solemnity of a didactic display, not merely as a verbal trope
to be explained.

6. *And he trusted.* After his initial skepticism, Abram is reassured by the imposing character of God's reiterated promise under the night sky, which for the
first time stresses the concrete idea of Abram's biological propagation, "he who
issues from your loins."

7–21. Since this covenant is sealed at sunset, it can scarcely be a direct continuation of the nocturnal scene just narrated. The two scenes are an orchestration of complementary covenantal themes. In the first, God grandly
promises and Abram trusts; in the second, the two enter into a mutually binding pact, cast in terms of a legal ritual. In the first scene, progeny is promised;
in the second, the possession of the land, together with the dark prospect of
enslavement in Egypt before the full realization of the promise. The first scene
highlights dialogue and the rhetorical power of the divine assurance; the second scene evokes mystery, magic, the troubling enigma of the future.

7. *I am the LORD who brought you out.* This formula—the initial words of self-
identification are a commonplace of ancient Near Eastern royal decrees—
used here for the first time, looks forward to "who brought you out of the land
of Egypt" of the Decalogue and other texts. Compositionally, it also picks up
"He took him outside" (the same verb in the Hebrew) at the end of the preceding scene.

Lord, how shall I know that I shall inherit it?" And He said to him, 9
"Take Me a three-year-old heifer and a three-year-old she-goat and a
three-year-old ram and a turtledove and a young pigeon." And he took 10
all of these and clove them through the middle, and each set his part
opposite the other, but the birds he did not cleave. And carrion birds 11
came down on the carcasses and Abram drove them off. And as the sun 12
was about to set, a deep slumber fell upon Abram and now a great dark
dread came falling upon him. And He said to Abram, "Know well that 13
your seed shall be strangers in a land not theirs and they shall be
enslaved and afflicted four hundred years. But upon the nation for 14
whom they slave I will bring judgment, and afterward they shall come
forth with great substance. As for you, you shall go to your fathers in 15
peace, you shall be buried in ripe old age. And in the fourth generation 16
they shall return here, for the iniquity of the Amorites is not yet full."

---

8. *how shall I know that I shall inherit it?* In this instance, Abram's doubt is to
be assuaged by a formal pact. Covenants in which the two parties step
between cloven animal parts are attested in various places in the ancient Near
East as well as in Greece. The idea is that if either party violates the covenant,
his fate will be like that of the cloven animals. The Hebrew idiom *karat berit*,
literally "to cut a covenant" (as in verse 18), may derive from this legal ritual.

10. *each set his part.* Existing translations fudge the vivid anthropomorphism of
the Hebrew here: *'ish,* literally, "man," means "each" but is a word applied to
animate beings, not to things, so it must refer to the two parties to the
covenant facing each other, not to the animal parts.

11. *carrion birds.* Unaccountably, most English translators render this collective
noun as "birds of prey," though their action clearly indicates they belong to the
category of vultures, not hawks and eagles.

12. *deep slumber.* This is the same Hebrew word, *tardemah,* used for Adam's
sleep when God fashions Eve.

16. *the fourth generation.* This would seem to be an obvious contradiction of
the previously stated four hundred years. Some scholars have argued that the
Hebrew *dor* does not invariably mean "generation" and may here refer to "life
span" or "time span."

17 And just as the sun had set, there was a thick gloom and, look, a smok-
18 ing brazier with a flaming torch that passed between those parts. On
that day the LORD made a covenant with Abram, saying, "To your seed
I have given this land from the river of Egypt to the great river, the river
19,20 Euphrates: the Kenite and the Kenizite and the Kadmonite and the
21 Hittite and the Perizzite and the Rephaim and the Amorite and the
Canaanite and the Girgashite and the Jebusite."

---

17. *a smoking brazier with a flaming torch*. All this is mystifying and is surely
meant to be so, in keeping with the haunting mystery of the covenantal
moment. It seems unwise to "translate" the images into any neat symbolism
(and the same is true of the ominous carrion birds Abram drives off). There
may be some general association of smoke and fire with the biblical deity
(Nahmanides notes a link with the Sinai epiphany), and the pillars of fire and
cloud in Exodus also come to mind, but the disembodied brazier (or furnace)
and torch are wonderfully peculiar to this scene. The firelight in this preternatural after-sunset darkness is a piquant antithesis to the star-studded heavens of the previous scene.

18. *To your seed I have given*. Moshe Weinfeld shrewdly observes that for the
first time the divine promise—compare 12:1–3, 12:7, 13:14–17, 15:4–5—is stated
with a perfective, not an imperfective, verb—that is, as an action that can be
considered already completed. This small grammatical maneuver catches up a
large narrative pattern in the Abraham stories: the promise becomes more and
more definite as it seems progressively more implausible to the aged patriarch,
until Isaac is born.

CHAPTER 16

Now Sarai Abram's wife had borne him no children, and she had an   1
Egyptian slavegirl named Hagar. And Sarai said to Abram, "Look,   2
pray, the LORD has kept me from bearing children. Pray, come to
bed with my slavegirl. Perhaps I shall be built up through her." And

---

1. *slavegirl*. Hebrew *shifḥah*. The tradition of English versions that render this
as "maid" or "handmaiden" imposes a misleading sense of European gentility
on the sociology of the story. The point is that Hagar belongs to Sarai as property, and the ensuing complications of their relationship build on that fundamental fact. Later on, Hagar will also be referred to as *'amah*. The two terms
designate precisely the same social status. The only evident difference is that
'amah, the more international of the two terms, is often used in administrative
lists whereas *shifḥah* occurs in contexts that are more narrative and popular in
character.

2. *And Sarai said*. Sarai-Sarah's first reported speech, like that of Rachel later
on in the cycle, is a complaint about her childlessness. The institution of surrogate maternity to which she resorts is by no means her invention, being well
attested in ancient Near Eastern legal documents. Living with the human consequences of the institution could be quite another matter, as the writer
shrewdly understands: Sarai's first two-sided dialogue with her husband
(verses 5–6) vividly represents the first domestic squabble—her bitterness and
her resentment against the husband who, after all, has only complied with her
request; his willingness to buy conjugal peace at almost any price.
    be built up through her. The Hebrew *'ibaneh* puns on *ben*, "son," and so also
means, "I will be sonned through her."

3 Abram heeded the voice of Sarai. And Sarai Abram's wife took Hagar
the Egyptian her slavegirl after Abram had dwelt ten years in the land
4 of Canaan, and she gave her to Abram her husband as a wife. And he
came to bed with Hagar and she conceived and she saw that she had
5 conceived and her mistress seemed slight in her eyes. And Sarai said to
Abram, "This outrage against me is because of you! I myself put my
slavegirl in your embrace and when she saw she had conceived, I
became slight in her eyes. Let the Lord judge between you and me!"
6 And Abram said to Sarai, "Look, your slavegirl is in your hands. Do to
her whatever you think right." And Sarai harassed her and she fled from
7 her. And the Lord's messenger found her by a spring of water in the

---

3. *as a wife.* Most English versions, following the logic of the context, render
this as "concubine." The word used, however, is not *pilegesh* but *'ishah*, the
same term that identifies Sarai at the beginning of the verse. The terminological equation of the two women is surely intended, and sets up an ironic back-
drop for Sarai's abuse of Hagar.

4. *in her eyes.* It is best to leave the Hebrew idiom literally in place in English
because Hagar's sight will again be at issue in her naming of the divinity after
the epiphany in the wilderness.

5. *your embrace.* Literally, "your lap," often a euphemism for the genital area.
The emphasis is pointedly sexual.

7. *the Lord's messenger.* This is the first occurrence of an "angel" (Hebrew,
mal'akh, Greek, *angelos*) in Genesis, though "the sons of God," the members
of the divine entourage, are mentioned in chapter 6. "Messenger," or one who
carries out a designated task, is the primary meaning of the Hebrew term, and
there are abundant biblical instances of *mal'akhim* who are strictly human
emissaries. One assumes that the divine messenger in these stories is supposed to look just like a human being, and all postbiblical associations with
wings, halos, and glorious raiment must be firmly excluded. One should note
that the divine speaker here begins as an angel but ends up (verse 13) being
referred to as though he were God Himself. Gerhard von Rad and others have
proposed that the angel as intermediary was superimposed on the earliest biblical tradition in order to mitigate what may have seemed an excessively
anthropomorphic representation of the deity. But it is anyone's guess how the
Hebrew imagination conceived agents of the Lord three thousand years ago,
and it is certainly possible that the original traditions had a blurry notion of dif-

wilderness, by the spring on the way to Shur. And he said, "Hagar, 8
slavegirl of Sarai! Where have you come from and where are you
going?" And she said, "From Sarai my mistress I am fleeing." And the 9
Lord's messenger said to her, "Return to your mistress and suffer abuse
at her hand." And the Lord's messenger said to her, "I will surely mul- 10
tiply your seed and it will be beyond all counting." And the Lord's mes- 11
senger said to her:

> "Look, you have conceived and will bear a son
> and you will call his name Ishmael,
> for the Lord has heeded your suffering.

ferentiation between God's own interventions in human life and those of His
emissaries. Richard Elliott Friedman has actually proposed that the angels are
entities split off, or emanated, from God, and that no clear-cut distinction
between God and angel is intended.

in the wilderness, . . . on the way to Shur. Hagar is in the Negeb, headed
south, evidently back toward her native Egypt. Shur means "wall" in Hebrew,
and scholars have linked the name with the line of fortifications the Egyptians
built on their northern border. But the same word could also be construed as
a verb that occurs in poetic texts, "to see" (or perhaps, more loftily, "to espy"),
and may relate to the thematics of seeing in Hagar's story.

10. *And the Lord's messenger said to her.* The formula for introducing speech
is repeated as Hagar stands in baffled silence in response to the command that
she return to suffer abuse at Sarai's hand. Even the promise of progeny does
not suffice to allay her doubts, so, with still another repetition of the introductory formula, the messenger proceeds (verse 11) to spell out the promise in
a poetic oracle.

surely multiply. The repetition of the verb in an infinitive absolute could
refer either to the certainty of multiplication or to the scale of multiplication
("I will mightily multiply").

11. *Ishmael.* The name means "God has heard," as the messenger proceeds to
explain. The previous occurrence of hearing in the story is Abram's "heeding"
(*shama'*, the same verb) Sarai's voice. God's hearing is then complemented by
His and Hagar's seeing (verse 13).

your suffering. The noun derives from the same root as the verb of abuse (or,
harassment, harsh handling, humiliation) used for Sarai's mistreatment of
Hagar.

12   And he will be a wild ass of a man—
            his hand against all, the hand of all against him,
            he will encamp in despite of all his kin."

13 And she called the name of the LORD who had addressed her, "El-Roi,"
14 for she said, "Did not I go on seeing here after He saw me?" Therefore
    is the well called Beer-Lahai-Roi, which is between Kadesh and Bered.
15 And Hagar bore a son to Abram, and Abram called his son whom Hagar
16 had born Ishmael. And Abram was eighty-six years old when Hagar
    bore Ishmael to Abram.

---

12. *his hand against all.* Although this may be a somewhat ambiguous blessing,
it does celebrate the untamed power—also intimated in the image of the wild
ass or onager—of the future Ishmaelites to thrive under the bellicose conditions of their nomadic existence.

    in despite of. The Hebrew idiom suggests defiance, as E. A. Speiser has per-
suasively shown.

13. *El-Roi.* The most evident meaning of the Hebrew name would be "God
Who sees me." Hagar's words in explanation of the name are rather cryptic in
the Hebrew. The translation reflects a scholarly consensus that what is at issue
is a general Israelite terror that no one can survive having seen God. Hagar,
then, would be expressing grateful relief that she has survived her epiphany.
Though this might well be a somewhat garbled etiological tale to account for
the place-name Beer-Lahai-Roi (understood by the writer to mean "Well of the
Living One Who Sees Me"), it is made to serve the larger thematic ends of
Hagar's story: the outcast slavegirl is vouchsafed a revelation which she sur-
vives, and is assured that, as Abram's wife, she will be progenitrix of a great
people.

CHAPTER 17

And Abram was ninety-nine years old, and the LORD appeared to   1
Abram and said to him, "I am El Shaddai. Walk in My presence
and be blameless, and I will grant My covenant between Me and   2
you and I will multiply you very greatly." And Abram flung himself on   3
his face, and God spoke to him, saying, "As for Me, this is My covenant   4

---

1. *El Shaddai.* The first term, as in El Elyon (chapter 14), means God. Scholarship has been unable to determine the origins or precise meaning of the second term—tenuous associations have been proposed with a Semitic word meaning "mountain" and with fertility. What is clear (compare Exodus 6:3) is that the biblical writers considered it an archaic name of God.

Walk in My presence. Or "before me." In verse 18, the same preposition manifestly has the idiomatic sense of "in Your favor." The verb is the same used for Enoch's walking with God, but there the Hebrew preposition is actually "with." The meaning of this idiom is "to be devoted to the service of."

2. *My covenant.* The articulation of the covenant in this chapter is organized in three distinct units—first the promise of progeny and land, then the commandment of circumcision as sign of the covenant, then the promise of Sarah's maternity. The politics of the promise is now brought to the foreground as for the first time it is stipulated that both Abraham and Sarah will be progenitors of kings. Source critics have observed that this second covenantal episode, attributed to Priestly circles, abandons the sense of an almost equal pact between two parties of chapter 15 and gives us an Abraham who is merely a silent listener, flinging himself to the ground in fear and trembling as God makes His rather lengthy pronouncements. But Abraham's emphatic skepticism in verses 17–18 suggests that there is more complexity in his characterization here than such readings allow.

5 with you: you shall be father to a multitude of nations. And no longer
  shall your name be called Abram but your name shall be Abraham, for
6 I have made you father to a multitude of nations. And I will make you
  most abundantly fruitful and turn you into nations, and kings shall
7 come forth from you. And I will establish My covenant between Me
  and you and your seed after you through their generations as an ever-
8 lasting covenant to be God to you and to your seed after you. And I will
  give unto you and your seed after you the land in which you sojourn,
  the whole land of Canaan, as an everlasting holding, and I will be their
  God."

9 And God said to Abraham, "As for you, you shall keep My command-
10 ment, you and your seed after you through their generations. This is My
   covenant which you shall keep, between Me and you and your seed
11 after you: every male among you must be circumcised. You shall circumcise the flesh of your foreskin and it shall be the sign of the
12 covenant between Me and you. Eight days old every male among you

---

5. *Abram . . . Abraham.* The meaning of both versions of the name is something
like "exalted father." The longer form is evidently no more than a dialectical
variant of the shorter one. The real point is that Abraham should undergo a
name change—like a king assuming the throne, it has been proposed—as he
undertakes the full burden of the covenant. Similarly in verse 15, the only difference between Sarai and Sarah is that the former reflects an archaic feminine suffix, the latter, the normative feminine suffix: both versions of the name
mean "princess."

10. *every male among you must be circumcised.* Circumcision was practiced
among several of the West Semitic peoples and at least in the priestly class in
Egypt, as a bas-relief at Karnach makes clear in surgical detail. To Abraham
the immigrant from Mesopotamia, E. A. Speiser notes, it would have been a
new procedure to adopt, as this episode indicates. The stipulation of circumcision on the eighth day after birth dissociates it from its common function
elsewhere as a puberty rite, and the notion of its use as an apotropaic measure
(compare Exodus 4) is not intimated here. A covenant sealed on the organ of
generation may connect circumcision with fertility—and the threat against
fertility—which is repeatedly stressed in the immediately preceding and following passages. The contractual cutting up of animals in chapter 15 is now
followed by a cutting of human flesh.

shall be circumcised through your generations, even slaves born in the household and those purchased with silver from any foreigner who is not of your seed. Those born in your household and those purchased 13 with silver must be circumcised, and My covenant in your flesh shall be an everlasting covenant. And a male with a foreskin, who has not cir- 14 cumcised the flesh of his foreskin, that person shall be cut off from his folk. My covenant he has broken." And God said to Abraham, "Sarai 15 your wife shall no longer call her name Sarai, for Sarah is her name." And I will bless her and I will also give you from her a son and I will 16 bless him, and she shall become nations, kings of peoples shall issue from her." And Abraham flung himself on his face and he laughed, say- 17 ing to himself,

> "To a hundred-year-old will a child be born,
> will ninety-year-old Sarah give birth?"

---

13. *silver.* If the language of the text reflects the realia of the Patriarchal period, the term would refer to silver weights. If it reflects the writer's period, it would refer to money, since by then coins had been introduced. The weighing-out of silver by Abraham in chapter 23 argues for the likelihood of the former possibility.

16. *and I will bless him.* The Masoretic Text has "bless her," evidently to make the verb agree with the following clause, but this looks like a redundance in light of the beginning of the verse, and several ancient versions plausibly read here "bless him."

17. *and he laughed.* The verb *yitshaq* is identical with the Hebrew form of the name Isaac that will be introduced in verse 19. The laughter here—hardly the expected response of a man flinging himself on his face—is in disbelief, perhaps edged with bitterness. In the subsequent chapters, the narrative will ring the changes on this Hebrew verb, the meanings of which include joyous laughter, bitter laughter, mockery, and sexual dalliance.

To a hundred-year-old. Abraham's interior monologue is represented as a line of verse that neatly illustrates the pattern of heightening or intensification from first to second verset characteristic of biblical poetry: here, unusually (but in accord with the narrative data), the numbers go down from first to second verset, but the point is that, as incredible as it would be for a hundred-year-old to father a child, it would be even more incredible for a ninety-year-

18 And Abraham said to God, "Would that Ishmael might live in Your
19 favor!" And God said, "Yet Sarah your wife is to bear you a son and you
shall call his name Isaac and I will establish My covenant with him as
20 an everlasting covenant, for his seed after him. As for Ishmael, I have
heard you. Look, I will bless him and make him fruitful and will multiply him most abundantly, twelve chieftains he shall beget, and I will
21 make him a great nation. But My covenant I will establish with Isaac
22 whom Sarah will bear you by this season next year." And He finished
speaking with him, and God ascended from Abraham.

23 And Abraham took Ishmael his son and all the slaves born in his household and those purchased with silver, every male among the people of
Abraham's household, and he circumcised the flesh of their foreskin on
24 that very day as God had spoken to him. And Abraham was ninety-nine
25 years old when the flesh of his foreskin was circumcised. And Ishmael
was thirteen years old when the flesh of his foreskin was circumcised.
26,27 On that very day Abraham was circumcised, and Ishmael his son, and
all the men of his household, those born in the household and those
purchased with silver from the foreigners, were circumcised with him.

---

old woman, decades past menopause, to become a mother. The Abraham who
has been overpowered by two successive epiphanies in this chapter is now
seen as someone living within a human horizon of expectations. In the very
moment of prostration, he laughs, wondering whether God is not playing a
cruel joke on him in these repeated promises of fertility as time passes and he
and his wife approach fabulous old age. He would be content, he goes on to
say, to have Ishmael carry on his line with God's blessing.

20. *As for Ishmael, I have heard you.* Once again, the etymology of the name is
highlighted. These seven English words reflect just two Hebrew words in
immediate sequence, *uleyishma'el shema'tikha,* with the root *sh-m-'* evident in
both.

CHAPTER 18

And the Lord appeared to him in the Terebinths of Mamre when 1
he was sitting by the tent flap in the heat of the day. And he raised 2
his eyes and saw, and, look, three men were standing before him.
He saw, and he ran toward them from the tent flap and bowed to the
ground. And he said, "My lord, if I have found favor in your eyes, please 3

---

1. *And the* Lord *appeared.* The narrator at once apprises us of the divine character of Abraham's guests, but when Abraham peers out through the shim-
mering heat waves of the desert noon (verse 2), what he sees from his human
perspective is three "men." The whole scene seems to be a monotheistic adaptation to the seminomadic early Hebrew setting of an episode from the
Ugaritic *Tale of Aqhat* (tablet V: 6–7) in which the childless Dan'el is visited by
the craftsman-god Kothar. As Moshe Weinfeld has observed, there are several
verbal links between the two texts: Dan'el also is sitting by an entrance, over-
shadowed by a tree; he also "lifts up his eyes" to behold the divine visitor; and
similarly enjoins his wife to prepare a meal from the choice of the flock.

3. *My lord.* The Masoretic Text vocalizes this term of courtly address (*not*
YHWH) to read "my lords," in consonance with the appearance of three visitors. But the vocative terms that follow in this verse are in the singular, and it
is only in verse 4 that Abraham switches to plural verbs. Rashi, plausibly, suggests that Abraham initially addresses himself to "the greatest" of the three.
As verses 10 and 13–15 make clear, that greatest one is God Himself, who will tarry
to speak with Abraham while the two human-seeming angels of destruction
who accompany Him head down to the cities of the plain.

4 do not go on past your servant. Let a little water be fetched and bathe
5 your feet and stretch out under the tree, and let me fetch a morsel of
bread, and refresh yourselves. Then you may go on, for have you not
6 come by your servant?" And they said, "Do as you have spoken." And
Abraham hurried to the tent to Sarah and he said, "Hurry! Knead three
7 *seahs* of choice semolina flour and make loaves." And to the herd Abraham ran and fetched a tender and goodly calf and gave it to the lad,
8 who hurried to prepare it. And he fetched curds and milk and the calf
that had been prepared and he set these before them, he standing over
9 them under the tree, and they ate. And they said to him, "Where is
10 Sarah your wife?" And he said, "There, in the tent." And he said, "I will
surely return to you at this very season and, look, a son shall Sarah your

---

4. *Let a little water be fetched.* With good reason, the Jewish exegetical tradition makes Abraham figure as the exemplary dispenser of hospitality. Extending hospitality, as the subsequent contrasting episode in Sodom indicates, is
the primary act of civilized intercourse. The early Midrash (*Abot di Rabbi
Nathan*) aptly noted that Abraham promises modestly, a little water and a
morsel of bread, while hastening to prepare a sumptuous feast. "Fetch"
appears four times in rapid succession, "hurry" three times, as indices of the
flurry of hospitable activity.

9. *Where is Sarah.* The fact that the visitors know her name without prompt-
ing is the first indication to Abraham (unless one assumes a narrative ellipsis)
that they are not ordinary humans.

10. *he said, "I will surely return."* Evidently, one of the three visitors, unless the
text reflects a fusion of two traditions, one in which there were three visitors,
another in which there was one (which would then explain the switch from
singular to plural early in the story).
   at this very season. This phrase, or its equivalent, recurs in the various
annunciation type-scenes, of which this is the first instance. The narrative
motifs of the annunciation type-scene, in sequence, are: the fact of barren-
ness, the promise of a son by God or angel or holy man, and the fulfillment of
the promise in conception and birth. But only here is the emphatically matri-
archal annunciation displaced from wife to husband, with the woman merely
eavesdropping on the promise; only here is the barren woman actually postmenopausal; and only here is there a long postponement, filled in with seemingly unrelated episodes, until the fulfillment of the promise (chapter 21).

wife have," and Sarah was listening at the tent flap, which was behind
him. And Abraham and Sarah were old, advanced in years, Sarah no   11
longer had her woman's flow. And Sarah laughed inwardly, saying,   12
"After being shriveled, shall I have pleasure, and my husband is old?"
And the Lord said to Abraham, "Why is it that Sarah laughed, saying,   13
'Shall I really give birth, old as I am?' Is anything beyond the Lord? In   14
due time I will return to you, at this very season, and Sarah shall have
a son." And Sarah dissembled, saying, "I did not laugh," for she was   15
afraid. And He said, "Yes, you did laugh."

Thus the patriarch takes over the center-stage location of the matriarch, and
the difficult—indeed, miraculous—nature of the fulfillment is underscored.

11–13. This sequence of three utterances is a brilliant example of how much
fine definition of position and character can be achieved in biblical narrative
through variation in repetition. First the narrator informs us, objectively and
neutrally, of Abraham's and Sarah's advanced age, stating the fact, repeating it
with the emphasis of a synonym, and reserving for last Sarah's postmenopausal
condition, which would appear to make conception a biological impossibility.
When Sarah repeats this information in her interior monologue, it is given new
meaning from her bodily perspective as an old and barren woman: her flesh is
shriveled, she cannot imagine having pleasure again (the term 'ednah is cognate with Eden and probably suggests sexual pleasure, or perhaps even sexual
moistness), and besides—her husband is old. The dangling third clause hangs
on the verge of a conjugal complaint: how could she expect pleasure, or a
child, when her husband is so old? Then the Lord, having exercised the divine
faculty of listening to Sarah's unspoken words, her silent laughter of disbelief,
reports them to Abraham, tactfully editing out (as Rashi saw) the reference to
the patriarch's old age and also suppressing both the narrator's mention of the
vanished menses and Sarah's allusion to her withered flesh—after all, nothing
anaphrodisiac is to be communicated to old Abraham at a moment when he is
expected to cohabit with his wife in order at last to beget a son.

15. I did not laugh . . . Yes, you did laugh. Sarah's fearful denial and God's rejection of it afford an opportunity to foreground the verb of laughter, tsahaq,
already stressed through Abraham's laughter in chapter 17, which will become
the name of her son. After the birth, Sarah will laugh again, not in bitter disbelief but in joy, though perhaps not simply in joy, as we shall have occasion
to see in chapter 21.

16 And the men arose from there and looked out over Sodom, Abraham
17 walking along with them to see them off. And the LORD had thought,
18 "Shall I conceal from Abraham what I am about to do? For Abraham
will surely be a great and mighty nation, and all the nations of the earth
19 will be blessed through him. For I have embraced him so that he will
charge his sons and his household after him to keep the way of the
LORD to do righteousness and justice, that the LORD may bring upon
20 Abraham all that He spoke concerning him." And the LORD said,

"The outcry of Sodom and Gomorrah, how great!
Their offense is very grave.

21 Let Me go down and see whether as the outcry that has come to Me
22 they have dealt destruction, and if not, I shall know." And the men

---

17. *And the LORD had thought.* The verb *'amar,* "say," is sometimes used elliptically for *'amar belibo,* "said to himself," and that seems clearly the case here.
With the two divine messengers about to be sent off on their mission of
destruction, God will be left alone with Abraham, and before addressing him,
He reflects for a moment on the nature of His covenantal relationship with the
patriarch and what that dictates as to revealing divine intention to a human
partner. Abraham is in this fashion thrust into the role of prophet, and God will
so designate him in chapter 20.

19. *to do righteousness and justice.* This is the first time that the fulfillment of
the covenantal promise is explicitly made contingent on moral performance.
The two crucial Hebrew nouns, *tsedeq* and *mishpat,* will continue to reverberate literally and in cognate forms through Abraham's pleas to God on behalf of
the doomed cities, through the Sodom story itself, and through the story of
Abraham and Abimelech that follows it.

20. *outcry.* The Hebrew noun, or the verb from which it is derived, *tsa'aq* or
za'aq, is often associated in the Prophets and Psalms with the shrieks of torment of the oppressed.

21. *Let Me go down.* The locution indicating God's descent from on high
echoes the one in the story of the Tower of Babel.
    dealt destruction. Some construe the Hebrew noun as an adverb and render
this as "done altogether." But the verb "to do" (*'asah*) with the noun *kalah* as
direct object occurs a number of times in the Prophets in the clear sense of
"deal destruction."

turned from there and went on toward Sodom while the LORD was still
standing before Abraham. And Abraham stepped forward and said, 23
"Will You really wipe out the innocent with the guilty? Perhaps there 24
may be fifty innocent within the city. Will You really really wipe out the
place and not spare it for the sake of the fifty innocent within it? Far 25
be it from You to do such a thing, to put to death the innocent with the
guilty, making innocent and guilty the same. Far be it from You! Will not
the Judge of all the earth do justice?" And the LORD said, "Should I 26
find in Sodom fifty innocent within the city, I will forgive the whole
place for their sake." And Abraham spoke up and said, "Here, pray, I 27
have presumed to speak to my Lord when I am but dust and ashes.

---

22. *while the LORD was still standing before Abraham.* The Masoretic Text has
Abraham standing before the LORD, but this reading is avowedly a scribal
euphemism, what the Talmud calls a *tiqun sofrim,* introduced because the
original formulation smacked of *lèse-majesté.*

23. *And Abraham stepped forward.* The verb, often used for someone about to
deliver a legal plea, introduces an Abraham who is surprisingly audacious in
the cause of justice, a stance that could scarcely have been predicted from the
obedient and pious Abraham of the preceding episodes.
    the innocent. The term *tsadiq* has a legal usage—the party judged not guilty
in a court of law, though it also has the moral meaning of "righteous." Similarly, the term here for guilty, *rasha',* also means "wicked." *Tsadiq* is derived
from the same root as *tsedaqah,* "righteousness," the very term God has just
used in His interior monologue reflecting on what it is the people of Abraham
must do.

25. *the Judge of all the earth.* The term for "judge," *shofet,* is derived from the
same root as *mishpat,* "justice," which equally occurs in God's interior monologue about the ethical legacy of the seed of Abraham.

27. *Here, pray, I have presumed to speak to my Lord when I am but dust and
ashes.* Like the previous verbal exchange with the three divine visitors, this
whole scene is a remarkable instance of the use of contrastive dialogue in biblical narrative. In the preceding scene, Abraham is voluble in his protestations
of hospitable intention, whereas the three visitors only answer impassively and
tersely, "Do as you have spoken." Here, Abraham, aware that he is walking a
dangerous tight rope in reminding the Judge of all the earth of the necessity to

28 Perhaps the fifty innocent will lack five. Would you destroy the whole
city for the five?" And He said, "I will not destroy if I find there forty-
29 five." And he spoke to Him still again and he said, "Perhaps there will
be found forty." And He said, "I will not do it on account of the forty."
30 And he said, "Please, let not my Lord be incensed and let me speak,
perhaps there will be found thirty." And He said, "I will not do it if I
31 find there thirty." And he said, "Here, pray, I have presumed to speak to
my Lord. Perhaps there will be found twenty." And He said, "I will not
32 destroy for the sake of the twenty." And he said, "Please, let not my
Lord be incensed and let me speak just this time. Perhaps there will be
33 found ten." And He said, "I will not destroy for the sake of the ten." And
the LORD went off when He finished speaking with Abraham, and
Abraham returned to his place.

---

exercise justice, deploys a whole panoply of the abundant rhetorical devices of
ancient Hebrew for expressing self-abasement before a powerful figure. At
each turn of the dialogue, God responds only by stating flatly that He will not
destroy for the sake of the number of innocent just stipulated. The dialogue is
cast very much as a bargaining exchange—it is not the last time we shall see
Abraham bargaining. After Abraham's second bid of forty-five, each time he
ratchets down the number he holds back the new, smaller number, in good
bargaining fashion, to the very end of this statement.

32. *just this time . . . ten.* Abraham realizes he dare not go any lower than ten,
the minimal administrative unit for communal organization in later Israelite
life. In the event, Lot's family, less than the requisite ten, will be the only innocent souls in Sodom.

33. *and Abraham returned to his place.* The report of a character's returning to
his place or home is a formal convention for marking the end of an episode in
biblical narrative. But this minimal indication has a thematic implication
here—the contrast between Abraham's "place" in the nomadic, uncorrupted
existence in the land of promise and Lot's location in one of the doomed cities
of the plain.

CHAPTER 19

And the two messengers came into Sodom at evening, when Lot   1
was sitting in the gate of Sodom. And Lot saw, and he rose to greet
them and bowed, with his face to the ground. And he said, "O   2
please, my lords, turn aside to your servant's house to spend the night,
and bathe your feet, and you can set off early on your way." And they

---

1. *came into Sodom at evening, when Lot was sitting in the gate.* The whole
episode is framed in an elegant series of parallels and antitheses to Abraham's
hospitality scene at the beginning of chapter 18. Both men are sitting at an
entrance—the identical participial clause with the same verb—when the visitors appear. Lot's entrance is the city gate: he can sit "in" it because Canaanite cities had what amounted to a large chamber at the gateway; here people
gathered to gossip, to do business, and above all, to conduct justice; the gate
would have given on the town square, the area referred to by the messengers
in verse 2. There is an antipodal thematic distance from tent flap to city gate,
as the narrative quickly makes clear. Abraham's visitors, moreover, arrive at
midday, whereas Lot's visitors come as darkness falls—a time when it is as
dangerous to be out in the streets of Sodom as in those of any modern inner
city.

2. *turn aside.* Lot resembles his uncle in the gesture of hospitality. He uses the
verb "turn aside" (*sur*) instead of Abraham's "go on past" (*'avar*) because, unlike
the solitary tent in the desert, there are many habitations here, in addition to
the public space of the square.
  set off early. This may merely be to emphasize that he will not delay them
unduly, but it could hint that they can depart at daybreak before running into
trouble with any of the townsfolk.

3 said, "No. We will spend the night in the square." And he pressed them
   hard, and they turned aside to him and came into his house, and he
4 prepared them a feast and baked flatbread, and they ate. They had not
   yet lain down when the men of the city, the men of Sodom, surrounded
5 the house, from lads to elders, every last man of them. And they called
   out to Lot and said, "Where are the men who came to you tonight?
6 Bring them out to us so that we may know them!" And Lot went out to
7 them at the entrance, closing the door behind him, and he said,
8 "Please, my brothers, do no harm. Look, I have two daughters who have
   known no man. Let me bring them out to you and do to them whatever
   you want. Only to these men do nothing, for have they not come under

---

3. *a feast . . . flatbread.* Perhaps an ellipsis is to be inferred, but this is a scanty-
looking "feast." In contrast to Abraham's sumptuous menu, the only item mentioned is the lowly unleavened bread (*matsot*) of everyday fare, not even the
loaves from fine flour that Sarah prepares.

4–5. *the men of the city, the men of Sodom. . . . Where are the men.* Throughout
this sequence there is an ironic interplay between the "men" of Sodom, whose
manliness is expressed in the universal impulse to homosexual gang rape, and
the divine visitors who only seem to be "men."

7. *brothers.* Or "kinsmen," an appellation the Sodomites will vehemently reject
in verse 9.

8. *I have two daughters who have known no man.* Lot's shocking offer, about
which the narrator, characteristically, makes no explicit judgment, is too patly
explained as the reflex of an ancient Near Eastern code in which the sacredness of the host–guest bond took precedence over all other obligations. Lot
surely is inciting the lust of the would-be rapists in using the same verb of sexual "knowledge" they had applied to the visitors in order to proffer the virginity of his daughters for their pleasure. The concluding episode of this chapter,
in which the drunken Lot unwittingly takes the virginity of both his daughters,
suggests measure-for-measure justice meted out for his rash offer.
   for have they not come under the shadow of my roof-beam? This looks like a
proverbial expression for entering into someone's home and so into the bonds
of the host–guest relationship. But "roof-beam" implies a fixed structure and
so accords with the urban setting of Lot's effort at hospitality; Abraham, living
in a tent, in the parallel expression in his hospitality scene, merely says, "for
have you not come by your servant?"

the shadow of my roof-beam?" And they said, "Step aside." And they ₉
said, "This person came as a sojourner and he sets himself up to judge!
Now we'll do more harm to you than to them," and they pressed hard
against the man Lot and moved forward to break down the door. And ₁₀
the men reached out their hands and drew Lot to them into the house
and closed the door. And the men at the entrance of the house they ₁₁
struck with blinding light, from the smallest to the biggest, and they
could not find the entrance. And the men said to Lot, "Whom do you ₁₂
still have here? Your sons and your daughters and whomever you have
in the city take out of the place. For we are about to destroy this place ₁₃
because the outcry against them has grown great before the LORD and
the LORD has sent us to destroy it." And Lot went out and spoke to his ₁₄
sons-in-law who had married his daughters and he said, "Rise, get out
of this place, for the LORD is about to destroy the city." And he seemed
to his sons-in-law to be joking. And as dawn was breaking the messen- ₁₅

---

9. *came as a sojourner . . . sets himself up to judge!* The verb "to sojourn" is the
one technically used for resident aliens. "Judge," emphatically repeated in an
infinitive absolute (*wayishpot shafot*), picks up the thematic words of judge and
just from God's monologue and His dialogue with Abraham in chapter 18.

12. *Your sons and your daughters.* The Masoretic Text prefaces these words with
"son-in-law" (in the singular); but as numerous critics have observed, this
makes no grammatical sense, and this particular term would not belong at the
head of the list, before sons and daughters. It seems quite likely that the word
was erroneously transcribed from verse 14 and was not part of the original text.

13. *the outcry.* This term is a pointed repetition of the word God uses twice in
His initial speech about Sodom.

14. *his sons-in-law who had married his daughters.* Especially because of the reference to the two virgin daughters in the next verse as ones "who remain with
you" (literally, "are found with you"), it appears that Lot had other daughters
already married, and not that the two in the house were betrothed but still
unmarried.
   he seemed to his sons-in-law to be joking. The verb, though in a different
conjugation, is the same as the one used for Sarah's and Abraham's "laughter."
It is, of course, a wry echo—the laughter of disbelief of those about to be
divinely blessed, the false perception of mocking laughter by those about to be

gers urged Lot, saying, "Rise, take your wife and your two daughters who remain with you, lest you be wiped out in the punishment of the
16 city." And he lingered, and the men seized his hand and his wife's hand and the hands of his two daughters in the LORD's compassion for him
17 and led him outside the city. And as they were bringing them out, he said, "Flee for your life. Don't look behind you and don't stop anywhere
18 on the plain. Flee to the high country lest you be wiped out." And Lot
19 said to them, "Oh, no, my lord. Look, pray, your servant has found favor in your eyes, and you have shown such great kindness in what you have done for me in saving my life, but I cannot flee to the high country, lest
20 evil overtake me and I die. Here, pray, this town is nearby to escape there, and it is a small place. Let me flee there, for it is but a small
21 place, and my life will be saved." And he said, "I grant you a favor in this matter as well, and I will not overthrow the town of which you
22 spoke. Hurry, flee there, for I can do nothing before you arrive there."
23 Therefore is the name of the town called Zoar. The sun had just come

---

destroyed. The common denominator in the antithetical usages is skepticism about divine intentions, for good and for evil.

17. *he said.* The reader is meant to infer: one of the two of them.

19. *I cannot flee to the high country.* Lot seems a weak character—he has to be led out by the hand from the city—and his zigzagging determinations of flight make psychological sense. Accustomed to an urban setting, he is terrified at the idea of trying to survive in the forbidding landscape of cliffs and caves to the south and east of the Dead Sea. But once having settled in the little town of Zoar (verse 30), he has understandable premonitions of another cataclysm and so decides that, after all, the rocky wilderness is the lesser of two evils.

20. *a small place.* The Hebrew *miz'ar* plays on the name Zoar and for once this could be a correct etymology. Lot's point is that it is, after all, only a piddling town and so it would not be asking a great deal to spare it from destruction.

21. *overthrow.* This is the physical image presented by the Hebrew verb, though the obvious sense of the word throughout the story (and in later biblical references to Sodom) is something like "destroy by sudden cataclysm."

out over the earth when Lot arrived at Zoar. And the LORD rained upon 24
Sodom and Gomorrah brimstone and fire from the LORD from the
heavens. And He overthrew all those cities and all the plain and all the 25
inhabitants of the cities and what grew in the soil. And his wife looked 26
back and she became a pillar of salt. And Abraham hastened early in 27
the morning to the place where he had stood in the presence of the
LORD. And he looked out over Sodom and Gomorrah and over all the 28

---

24. *rained . . . brimstone and fire from the* LORD *from the heavens.* The slightly
awkward repetition of "from the LORD" with the added phrase "from the heavens," taken together with the verb "to rain" (*himtir*), underscores the connection with the Deluge story: the first time the Flood, the fire next time. Moshe
Weinfeld has aptly observed a whole series of parallels between the two stories. In each case, God wipes out a whole population because of epidemic
moral perversion, marking one family for survival. In each case, the idiom "to
keep alive seed" is used for survival. In each case, the male survivor becomes
drunk and is somehow sexually violated by his offspring, though only Lot is
unambiguously represented as the object of an incestuous advance. One
might add that the phrase used by the elder sister, "there is no man on earth
[or, "in the land," *ba'arets*] to come to bed with us" (verse 31), equally reinforces
the connection with the global cataclysm of the Flood story: she looks out
upon the desolate landscape after the destruction of the cities of the plain and
imagines that she, her sister, and their father are the sole survivors of
humankind.

26. *And his wife looked back and she became a pillar of salt.* As has often been
observed, this tale looks doubly archaic, incorporating both an etiological story
about a gynemorphic rock formation in the Dead Sea region and an old mythic
motif (as in the story of Orpheus and Euridyce) of a taboo against looking back
in fleeing from a place of doom. But the blighted looking of Lot's wife is antithetically integrated with the "looking out" (a different verb) of Abraham in the
next two verses over the scene of destruction from his safe vantage on the
heights of Hebron.

27. *early in the morning.* There is a nice temporal dovetailing of the two scenes.
Down in the plain, just as the sun rises, the LORD rains brimstone and fire. A
few minutes later, still early in the morning, Abraham hurries to take in the
awful panorama.

land of the plain, and he saw and, look, smoke was rising like the smoke from a kiln.

29 And it happened when God destroyed the cities of the plain that God remembered Abraham and sent Lot out of the upheaval as the cities in
30 which Lot dwelled were overthrown. And Lot came up from Zoar and settled in the high country, his two daughters together with him, for he was afraid to dwell in Zoar, and he dwelt in a certain cave, he and his
31 two daughters. And the elder said to the younger, "Our father is old, and there is no man on earth to come to bed with us like the way of all
32 the earth. Come, let us give our father wine to drink and let us lie with

---

28. *he saw and, look, smoke was rising*. The visual setup also represents the tight closing of an envelope structure. The Sodom episode began with Abraham's dialogue with God on the heights of Hebron. Now at the end, in a definition of visual perspective unusual for biblical narrative, Abraham, standing in the same place, makes out from a distance of forty or more miles the cloud of smoke rising from the incinerated cities.

30–38. The narrator withholds all comment on the incestuous enterprise of the two virgin sisters. Perhaps the story may draw on old—pre-Israelite?—traditions in which the supposed origins of these two peoples in incest were understood as evidence of their purity, or their vitality. (One recalls that Tamar, the progenitrix of the future kings of Judea, became pregnant by her father-in-law through pretending to be a whore.) But from the Israelite perspective, this story might well have cast a shadow of ambiguity over these two enemy peoples. Both names are etymologized to refer to incest: Moab (which probably means "desired place") is construed as *me-'ab*, "from the father," and Ben-Ammi (yielding the gentilic *benei-'ammon*) is construed as "my own kinsman's son."

32. *let us lie with him*. Although "lie with" is a somewhat euphemistic reference to coitus in English, its uses in Scripture suggest it is a rather coarse (though not obscene) verb for sexual intercourse in biblical Hebrew. Two linked sexual assailants, the Egyptian woman in Genesis 39 and Amnon in 2 Samuel 13, use it in urging the objects of their lust to submit to them. When the verb is followed by a direct object in sexual contexts, the meaning seems close to "rape." Ironically, the more decorous verb "to know" is used twice here asexually (verses 33 and 35) to indicate the drunken Lot's unconscious state as he deflowers each of his daughters.

him, so that we may keep alive seed from our father." And they gave 33
their father wine to drink that night, and the elder came and lay with
her father, and he knew not when she lay down or when she arose. And 34
on the next day the elder said to the younger, "Look, last night I lay with
my father. Let us give him wine to drink tonight as well, and come, lie
with him, so that we may keep alive seed from our father." And on that 35
night as well they gave their father wine to drink, and the younger arose
and lay with him, and he knew not when she lay down or when she
arose. And the two daughters of Lot conceived by their father. And the 36,37
elder bore a son and called his name Moab; he is the father of the
Moab of our days. And the younger as well bore a son and called his 38
name Ben-Ammi; he is the father of the Ammonites of our days.

---

37. *of our days.* The literal sense of the Hebrew is "to this day."

CHAPTER 20

I   And Abraham journeyed onward from there to the Negeb region and dwelt between Kadesh and Shur, and he sojourned in Gerar. 2 And Abraham said of Sarah his wife, "She is my sister." And Abim- 3 elech the king of Gerar sent and took Sarah. And God came to Abim- elech in a night-dream and said to him, "You are a dead man because 4 of the woman you took, as she is another's wife." But Abimelech had not come near her, and he said, "My Lord, will you slay a nation even

---

1. *And Abraham journeyed onward from there to the Negeb region.* This second instance of the sister-wife type-scene is in several ways fashioned to fit the particular narrative context in which it is inserted. The emphatic foreshadowing of the sojourn in Egypt of the episode in chapter 12 is deleted. Here there is no mention of a famine as the cause of the patriarch's migration, and the place he comes to is not Egypt but Gerar, a Canaanite city-state in the western Negeb.

3. *And God came to Abimelech.* This potentate is immediately given a higher moral status than Pharaoh in chapter 12: to Pharaoh God speaks only through plagues, whereas Abimelech is vouchsafed direct address from God in a night-vision.
    You are a dead man. Or, "you are about to die." Abimelech's distressed response to this peremptory death sentence is understandable, and leads back to the preceding episodes in the narrative chain.

4. *will you slay a nation even if innocent?* This phrase, which might also be construed "slay a nation even with the innocent," sounds as peculiar in the Hebrew as in translation, and has led some critics to see the word "nation" (*goy*) as a scribal error. But the apparent deformation of idiom has a sharp thematic point. "Innocent" (*tsadiq*) is the very term Abraham insisted on in questioning God as to whether He would really slay the innocent together with the

if innocent? Did not he say to me, 'She is my sister'? and she, she, too, 5
said, 'He is my brother.' With a pure heart and with clean hands I have
done this." And God said to him in the dream, "Indeed, I know that 6
with a pure heart you have done this, and I on My part have kept you
from offending against Me, and so I have not allowed you to touch her.
Now, send back the man's wife, for he is a prophet, and he will inter- 7
cede for you, and you may live. And if you do not send her back, know
that you are doomed to die, you and all that belongs to you."

And Abimelech rose early in the morning and called to all his servants, 8
and he spoke these things in their hearing, and the men were terribly
afraid. And Abimelech called to Abraham and said to him, "What have 9
you done to us, and how have I offended you, that you should bring
upon me and my kingdom so great an offense? Things that should not
be done you have done to me." And Abimelech said to Abraham, "What 10
did you imagine when you did this thing?" And Abraham said, "For I 11
thought, there is surely no fear of God in this place and they will kill
me because of my wife. And, in point of fact, she is my sister, my 12

---

guilty in destroying the entire nation of Sodom. If the king of Gerar chooses,
oddly, to refer to himself as "nation," leaning on the traditional identification
of monarch with people, it is because he is, in effect, repeating Abraham's
question to God: will not the Judge of all the earth do justice?

5. *and, she, she, too.* This repetitive splutter of indignation is vividly registered
in the Hebrew, though the existing translations smooth it over.

6. *I have not allowed you to touch her.* The means by which consummation is
prevented is intimated, cannily, only at the very end of the story.

9–10. *And Abimelech . . . said . . . and Abimelech said.* The repetition of the formula for introducing direct speech, with no intervening response from Abraham, is pointedly expressive. Abimelech vehemently castigates Abraham (with
good reason), and Abraham stands silent, not knowing what to say. And so
Abimelech repeats his upbraiding, in shorter form (verse 10).

11–12. When Abraham finally speaks up, his words have the ring of a speaker
floundering for self-justification. Introducing the explanation of Sarah's half-
sister status—there might be a Mesopotamian legal background to such a

father's daughter, though not my mother's daughter, and she became
13 my wife. And it happened, when the gods made me a wanderer from
my father's house, that I told her, 'This is the kindness you can do for
14 me: in every place to which we come, say of me, he is my brother.'" And
Abimelech took sheep and cattle and male and female slaves and gave
15 them to Abraham, and he sent back to him Sarah his wife. And Abimelech said, "Look, my land is before you. Settle wherever you want."

---

semi-incestuous marriage—he uses a windy argumentative locution, *wegam
'omnah,* "and, in point of fact," that may hint at a note of special pleading.

and they will kill me because of my wife. What Abraham fears is that Gerar,
without "fear of God," will prove to be another Sodom. In Sodom, two strangers
came into town and immediately became objects of sexual assault for the whole
male population. Here again, two strangers come into town, one male and one
female, and Abraham assumes the latter will be an object of sexual appropriation, the former the target of murder. In the event, he is entirely wrong: Abimelech is a decent, even noble, man; and the category of "Sodom" is not to be
projected onto everything that is not the seed of Abraham. On the contrary,
later biblical writers will suggest how easily Israel turns itself into Sodom.

13. *the gods made me a wanderer.* The word *'elohim,* which normally takes a singular verb (though it has a plural suffix) when it refers to God, as everywhere
else in this episode, is here linked with a plural verb. Conventional translation
procedure renders this as "God," or "Heaven," but Abraham, after all, is
addressing a pagan who knows nothing of this strange new idea of monotheism, and it is perfectly appropriate that he should choose his words accordingly, settling on a designation of the deity that ambiguously straddles
polytheism and monotheism. It is also noteworthy that Abraham, far from suggesting that God has directed him to a promised land, stresses to the native
king that the gods have imposed upon him a destiny of wandering.

in every place to which we come. The writer, quite aware that this episode
approximately repeats the one in chapter 12, introduces into Abraham's dialogue a motivation for the repetition: this is what we must do (whatever the
problematic consequences) in order to survive wherever we go.

14. *And Abimelech took sheep and cattle.* Unlike Pharoah in chapter 12, who
bestows gifts on Abraham as a kind of bride-price, the noble Abimelech offers
all this bounty *after* Sarah leaves his harem, as an act of restitution.

And to Sarah he said, "Look, I have given a thousand pieces of silver to 16
your brother. Let it hereby serve you as a shield against censorious eyes
for everyone who is with you, and you are now publicly vindicated."
And Abraham interceded with God, and God healed Abimelech and his 17
wife and his slave-women, and they gave birth. For the LORD had shut 18
fast every womb in the house of Abimelech because of Sarah, Abraham's wife.

---

16. *to your brother.* Surely there is an edge of irony in Abimelech's use of this
term.

    a shield against censorious eyes. The Hebrew, which has long puzzled schol-
ars, is literally "a covering of the eyes." That phrase may mean "mask," but its
idiomatic thrust seems to be: something that will ward off public disapproval.

18. *For the LORD had shut fast every womb.* Contrary to some textual critics who
conjecture that this verse was inadvertently displaced from an earlier point in
the story, it is a lovely piece of delayed narrative exposition. Shutting up the
womb is a standard idiom for infertility, which ancient Hebrew culture, at least
on the proverbial level, attributes to the woman, not to the man. But given the
earlier reference to Abimelech's having been prevented from touching Sarah,
this looks suspiciously like an epidemic of impotence that has struck Abimelech and his people—an idea not devoid of comic implications—from which
the Gerarite women would then suffer as the languishing partners of the
deflected sexual unions. (Nahmanides sees an allusion to impotence here.) It
is noteworthy that only in this version of the sister-wife story is the motif of
infertility introduced. Its presence nicely aligns the Abimelech episode with
what precedes and what follows. That is, first we have the implausible promise
of a son to the aged Sarah; then a whole people is wiped out; then the desperate act of procreation by Lot's daughters in a world seemingly emptied of
men; and now an entire kingdom blighted with an interruption of procreation.
The very next words of the story—one must remember that there were no
chapter breaks in the original Hebrew text, for both chapter and verse divisions were introduced only in the late Middle Ages—are the fulfillment of the
promise of progeny to Sarah: "And the LORD singled out Sarah as He had said."
As several medieval Hebrew commentators note, the plague of infertility also
guarantees that Abimelech cannot be imagined as the begetter of Isaac.

CHAPTER 21

1 And the LORD singled out Sarah as He had said, and the LORD did
2 for Sarah as He had spoken. And Sarah conceived and bore a son
to Abraham in his old age at the set time that God had spoken to
3 him. And Abraham called the name of his son who was born to him,
4 whom Sarah bore him, Isaac. And Abraham circumcised Isaac his son
5 when he was eight days old, as God had charged him. And Abraham
6 was a hundred years old when Isaac his son was born to him. And Sarah
said,

> "Laughter has God made me,
>   Whoever hears will laugh at me."

---

6. *Laughter has God made me*. The ambiguity of both the noun *tseḥoq* ("laughter") and the accompanying preposition *li* ("to" or "for" or "with" or "at" me) is wonderfully suited to the complexity of the moment. It may be laughter, triumphant joy, that Sarah experiences and that is the name of the child Isaac ("he-who-laughs"). But in her very exultation, she could well feel the absurdity (as Kafka noted in one of his parables) of a nonagenarian becoming a mother. *Tseḥoq* also means "mockery," and perhaps God is doing something *to* her as well as for her. (In poetry, the verb *tsaḥaq* is often linked in parallelism with *la'ag,* to scorn or mock, and it should be noted that *la'ag* is invariably followed by the preposition *l*ᵉ, as *tsaḥaq* is here.) All who hear of it may laugh, rejoice, with Sarah, but the hint that they might also laugh at her is evident in her language.

And she said, 7

> "Who would have uttered to Abraham—
> 'Sarah is suckling sons!'
> For I have borne a son in his old age."

And the child grew and was weaned, and Abraham made a great feast 8
on the day Isaac was weaned. And Sarah saw the son of Hagar the 9
Egyptian, whom she had borne to Abraham, laughing. And she said to 10
Abraham, "Drive out this slavegirl and her son, for the slavegirl's son
shall not inherit with my son, with Isaac." And the thing seemed evil in 11

---

7. *uttered.* The Hebrew *milel* is a term that occurs only in poetic texts and is
presumably high diction, perhaps archaic.

for I have borne a son in his old age. In a symmetrical reversal of God's report
in chapter 18 of Sarah's interior monologue, where Abraham's advanced age
was suppressed, Sarah's postpartum poem, like the narrator's report that precedes it, mentions only *his* old age. Hers is implied by her marveling reference
to herself as an old woman suckling infants, a pointed reversal of her own allusion in chapter 18 to her shriveled body.

9. *laughing.* Hebrew *metsaheq.* The same verb that meant "mocking" or "joking" in Lot's encounter with his sons-in-law and that elsewhere in the Patriarchal narratives refers to sexual dalliance. It also means "to play." (Although the
conjugation here is *pi'el* and Sarah's use of the same root in verse 6 is in the
qal conjugation, attempts to establish a firm semantic differentiation between
the deployment of the root in the two different conjugations do not stand up
under analysis.) Some medieval Hebrew exegetes, trying to find a justification
for Sarah's harsh response, construe the verb as a reference to homosexual
advances, though that seems far-fetched. Mocking laughter would surely suffice to trigger her outrage. Given the fact, moreover, that she is concerned lest
Ishmael encroach on her son's inheritance, and given the inscription of her
son's name in this crucial verb, we may also be invited to construe it as "Isaac-
ing-it"—that is, Sarah sees Ishmael presuming to play the role of Isaac, child
of laughter, presuming to be the legitimate heir.

10. *Drive out this slavegirl.* In language that nicely catches the indignation of
the legitimate wife, Sarah refers to neither Hagar nor Ishmael by name, but
instead insists on the designation of low social status.

12 Abraham's eyes because of his son. And God said to Abraham, "Let it not seem evil in your eyes on account of the lad and on account of your slavegirl. Whatever Sarah says to you, listen to her voice, for through
13 Isaac shall your seed be acclaimed. But the slavegirl's son, too, I will make a nation, for he is your seed."

14 And Abraham rose early in the morning and took bread and a skin of water and gave them to Hagar, placing them on her shoulder, and he gave her the child, and sent her away, and she went wandering through
15 the wilderness of Beersheba. And when the water in the skin was gone,
16 she flung the child under one of the bushes and went off and sat down at a distance, a bowshot away, for she thought, "Let me not see when the child dies." And she sat at a distance and raised her voice and wept.

---

12. *listen to her voice*. The Hebrew idiom has the obvious meaning "to obey," but the literal presence of hearing a voice is important because it resonates with the occurrence of the same verb and object at the heart of the wilderness scene that immediately follows.
    acclaimed. The literal meaning of the Hebrew is "called."

14. *rose early in the morning*. This is precisely echoed in the story of the binding of Isaac (22:3), as part of an intricate network of correspondences between the two stories.
    and he gave her the child. The Hebrew has only "the child," with an accusative prefix. This has led many commentators to imagine that Abraham is putting Ishmael on Hagar's shoulders together with the bread and water—a most unlikely act, since the boy would be about sixteen. But biblical syntax permits the use of a transitive verb ("gave [them] to Hagar") interrupted by a participial clause ("placing [them] on her shoulder"), which then controls a second object ("the child"). The only way to convey this in English is by repeating the verb.

16. *a bowshot away*. This particular indication of distance is carefully chosen, for it adumbrates the boy's vocation as bowman spelled out at the end of the story.
    when the child dies. Like the narrator in verses 14 and 15, Hagar refers to her son as *yeled*, "child" (the etymology—"the one who is born"—is the same as *enfant* in French). This is the same term that is used for Isaac at the beginning of verse 8. From the moment the angel speaks in verse 17, Ishmael is consis-

And God heard the voice of the lad and God's messenger called out 17
from the heavens and said to her, "What troubles you, Hagar? Fear not,
for God has heard the lad's voice where he is.

> Rise, lift up the lad 18
>> and hold him by the hand,
>>> for a great nation will I make him."

And God opened her eyes and she saw a well of water, and she went 19
and filled the skin with water and gave to the lad to drink. And God was 20
with the lad, and he grew up and dwelled in the wilderness, and he
became a seasoned bowman. And he dwelled in the wilderness of Paran 21
and his mother took him a wife from the land of Egypt.

---

tently referred to as *na'ar*, "lad"—a more realistic indication of his adolescent
status and also a term of tenderness, as in the story of the binding of Isaac in
the next chapter.

17. *And God heard the voice of the lad.* The narrator had reported only Hagar's
weeping. Now we learn that the boy has been weeping or crying out, and it is
his anguish that elicits God's saving response. In the earlier version of the banishment of Hagar (chapter 16), the naming of her future son Ishmael stands at
the center of the story. Here, as though the writer were ironically conspiring
with Sarah's refusal to name the boy, Ishmael's name is suppressed to the very
end. But the ghost of its etymology—"God will hear"—hovers at the center of
the story.

20. *a seasoned bowman.* There is an odd doubling of the professional designation in the Hebrew (literally "archer-bowman"), which I construe as an indication of his confirmed dedication to this hunter's calling, or his skill in
performing it.

22 And it happened at that time that Abimelech, and Phicol captain of his
troops with him, said to Abraham, saying, "God is with you in whatever
23 you do. Therefore swear to me by God that you will not deal falsely
with me, with my kith and kin. Like the kindness I have done you, so
you shall do for me, and for the land in which you have sojourned."
24,25 And Abraham said, "I indeed will swear it." But Abraham upbraided
Abimelech concerning the well of water that Abimelech's servants had
26 seized. And Abimelech said, "I do not know who has done this thing,
and you, too, have not told me, and I myself never heard of it till this
27 day." And Abraham took sheep and cattle and gave them to Abimelech,
28 and the two of them sealed a pact. And Abraham set apart seven ewes
29 of the flock, and Abimelech said to Abraham, "What are these seven
30 ewes that you set apart?" And he said, "Now, the seven ewes you shall
take from my hand, so that they may serve me as witness that I have
31 dug this well." Therefore did he call the name of that place Beersheba,

---

22. This episode is clearly a continuation of the Abimelech story in chapter 20,
interrupted by the linked episodes of the birth of Isaac and the expulsion of Ishmael. Abimelech had offered Abraham the right of settlement in his territories
("Look, my land is before you"). Now, as Abraham manifestly prospers ("God is
with you in whatever you do"), Abimelech proposes a treaty which will ensure
that the Hebrew sojourner does not unduly encroach on him or his land.

25. *concerning the well*. The particular instance of the clash between Abimelech's retainers and Abraham links this story with the immediately preceding
one, in which Ishmael is rescued by the discovery of a well in the wilderness.

31. *the name of that place Beersheba*. The Hebrew makes a transparent etymological pun. *Be'er* means "well." *Sheba'* can be construed as "oath" but it is also
the number seven, ritually embodied here in the seven ewes Abraham sets
apart. A second etymology may be intimated, not for the place-name Beersheba but for the term *shev'uah*, "oath," which seems to be derived by the
writer from the sacred number seven, made part of the oath-taking.

for there did the two of them swear. And they sealed a pact in Beer- 32
sheba, and Abimelech arose, and Phicol captain of his troops with him,
and they returned to the land of the Philistines. And Abraham planted 33
a tamarisk at Beersheba, and he invoked there the name of the LORD,
everlasting God. And Abraham sojourned in the land of the Philistines 34
many days.

---

32. *the land of the Philistines*. This is an often-noted anachronism, the incur-
sion of the Philistines from Crete to the coastal area of Canaan postdating the
Patriarchal period by more than four centuries. The writer may mean merely
to refer casually to this region in geographical terms familiar to his audience;
it is not clear that Abimelech with his Semitic name is meant to be thought of
as a "Philistine" king.

33. *at Beersheba*. The cultic tree is planted "at" rather than "in" Beersheba
because it is evident that the site of the oath is a well in the wilderness, not a
built-up town.

CHAPTER 22

1 ┃ nd it happened after these things that God tested Abraham. And
2 ┃ He said to him, "Abraham!" and he said, "Here I am." And He
┃ said, "Take, pray, your son, your only one, whom you love, Isaac,
and go forth to the land of Moriah and offer him up as a burnt offering
3 on one of the mountains which I shall say to you." And Abraham rose
early in the morning and saddled his donkey and took his two lads with

---

1. The abrupt beginning and stark, emotion-fraught development of this troubling story have led many critics to celebrate it as one of the peaks of ancient
narrative. Among modern commentators, Gerhard von Rad, Claus Westermann, and E. A. Speiser have all offered sensitive observations on the details
of the story, and the luminous first chapter of Erich Auerbach's *Mimesis,* which
compares this passage with one from the *Odyssey,* remains a landmark of
twentieth-century criticism.

2. *your son, your only one, whom you love, Isaac.* The Hebrew syntactic chain
is exquisitely forged to carry a dramatic burden, and the sundry attempts of
English translators from the King James Version to the present to rearrange it
are misguided. The classical Midrash, followed by Rashi, beautifully catches
the resonance of the order of terms. Rashi's concise version is as follows: "*Your
son.* He said to Him, 'I have two sons.' He said to him, '*Your only one.*' He said,
'This one is an only one to his mother and this one is an only one to his
mother.' He said to him, '*Whom you love.*' He said to him, 'I love both of them.'
He said to him, '*Isaac.*'" Although the human object of God's terrible imperative does not actually speak in the biblical text, this midrashic dialogue demonstrates a fine responsiveness to how the tense stance of the addressee is
intimated through the words of the addresser in a one-sided dialogue.
　　your only one. Some scholars, bothered by the technical inaccuracy of the
term, have followed an ancient reading of *yadid,* "favored one," instead of the
Masoretic *yaḥid.* This seriously misses the point that in regard to Abraham's

him, and Isaac his son, and he split wood for the offering, and rose and
went to the place that God had said to him. On the third day Abraham 4
raised his eyes and saw the place from afar. And Abraham said to his 5
lads, "Sit you here with the donkey and let me and the lad walk ahead
and let us worship and return to you." And Abraham took the wood for 6
the offering and put it on Isaac his son and he took in his hand the fire
and the cleaver, and the two of them went together. And Isaac said to 7
Abraham his father, "Father!" and he said, "Here I am, my son." And he

---

feelings, Isaac, this sole son by his legitimate wife, is his only one. The phrase
"your son, your only one," will return as a thematic refrain at the end of the
story (verses 12, 16).

    Moriah. Though traditional exegesis, supported by the reference to the
Mount of the LORD at the end of the tale, identifies this with Jerusalem, the
actual location remains in doubt. In any case, there is an assonance between
"Moriah" and *yir'eh,* "he sees," the thematic key word of the resolution of the
story.

3. *and Isaac his son.* The crucial item is left to the very end. The narrator does
not miss a chance in the story to refer to Isaac as "his son" and Abraham as
"his father," thus sharpening the edge of anguish that runs through the tale.

    and he split wood. In a narrative famous for its rigorous economy in report-
ing physical details, this act of Abraham, wielding an axe and cutting things
apart, is ominously singled out for attention.

5. *said to his lads . . . let me and the lad.* An identity of terms, an ironic divergence of meanings—the young men who are his servants (in fact, his slaves)
and the boy to whom he fondly refers, whom he thinks he is going to kill.

    let me. The Hebrew uses a jussive form for the three verbs, a gentler mode
of speech than a flat declarative about future actions.

6. *the cleaver.* E. A. Speiser notes, quite rightly, that the Hebrew term here is
not the usual biblical term for knife, and makes a good argument that it is a
cleaver. Other terms from butchering, rather than sacrifice, are used: to
slaughter (verse 10) and to bind (verse 9—a verb occurring only here but used
in rabbinic Hebrew for trussing up the legs of animals).

7. *Father!* The Hebrew is literally "My father," but that noun with the possessive ending is the form of intimate address in biblical Hebrew, like *Abba* in
postbiblical Hebrew.

said, "Here is the fire and the wood but where is the sheep for the offer-

8 ing?" And Abraham said, "God will see to the sheep for the offering, my

9 son." And the two of them went together. And they came to the place that God had said to him, and Abraham built there an altar and laid out the wood and bound Isaac his son and placed him on the altar on top

10 of the wood. And Abraham reached out his hand and took the cleaver

11 to slaughter his son. And the Lord's messenger called out to him from the heavens and said, "Abraham, Abraham!" and he said, "Here I am."

---

the fire and the wood. A moment earlier, we saw the boy loaded with the fire-wood, the father carrying the fire and the butcher knife. As Gerhard von Rad aptly remarks, "He himself carries the dangerous objects with which the boy could hurt himself, the torch and the knife." But now, as Isaac questions his father, he passes in silence over the one object that would have seemed scari-est to him, however unwitting he may have been of his father's intention—the sharp-edged butcher knife.

8. *God will see to.* Literally, "see for himself." The idiomatic force is "provide," but God's seeing lines up with Abraham's seeing the place from afar, his see-ing the ram, and the seeing on the Mount of the Lord. Beyond the tunnel vision of a trajectory toward child slaughter is a promise of true vision.

And the two of them went together. The impassive economy of this refrain-like repeated clause is haunting: two people, father and son, together for what threatens to be the last time, together "in one purpose" (Rashi), the father to sacrifice the son.

9–10. In contrast to the breathless pace of the narrative as a whole, this sequence inscribes a kind of slow motion: building the altar, laying out the wood, binding the child on top of the wood, reaching out the hand with the butcher knife—until the voice calls out from the heavens.

11. *and the Lord's messenger called out to him from the heavens.* This is nearly identical with the calling-out to Hagar in 21:17. In fact, a whole configuration of parallels between the two stories is invoked. Each of Abraham's sons is threatened with death in the wilderness, one in the presence of his mother, the other in the presence (and by the hand) of his father. In each case the angel intervenes at the critical moment, referring to the son fondly as *na'ar,* "lad." At the center of the story, Abraham's hand holds the knife, Hagar is enjoined to "hold her hand" (the literal meaning of the Hebrew) on the lad. In

And he said, "Do not reach out your hand against the lad, and do noth-   12
ing to him, for now I know that you fear God and you have not held
back your son, your only one, from Me." And Abraham raised his eyes   13
and saw and, look, a ram was caught in the thicket by its horns, and
Abraham went and took the ram and offered him up as a burnt offering instead of his son. And Abraham called the name of that place   14
YHWH-Yireh, as is said to this day, "On the mount of the LORD there
is sight." And the LORD's messenger called out to Abraham once again   15
from the heavens, and He said, "By My own Self I swear, declares the   16
LORD, that because you have done this thing and have not held back
your son, your only one, I will greatly bless you and will greatly multi-   17
ply your seed, as the stars in the heavens and as the sand on the shore
of the sea, and your seed shall take hold of its enemies' gate. And all the   18
nations of the earth will be blessed through your seed because you have
listened to my voice." And Abraham returned to his lads, and they rose   19
and went together to Beersheba, and Abraham dwelled in Beersheba.

---

the end, each of the sons is promised to become progenitor of a great people,
the threat to Abraham's continuity having been averted.

  Here I am. The third time Abraham pronounces this word—*hineni*—of
readiness: first to God, then to Isaac, now to the divine messenger.

13. *a ram.* The Masoretic Text reads "a ram behind [*aḥar*]," but scholarship is
virtually unanimous in following numerous ancient versions in reading *eḥad*,
"one," a very similar grapheme in the Hebrew.

14. *sight.* The place-name means "the LORD sees." The phrase at the end
means literally either "he sees" or "he will be seen," depending on how the verb
is vocalized, and this translation uses a noun instead to preserve the ambiguity. It is also not clear whether it is God or the person who comes to the Mount
who sees / is seen.

16. *because you have done this thing.* The LORD's invocation of causation thick-
ens the ambiguities of the story. Abraham has already been promised an innumerable posterity (chapters 15, 17). Perhaps now he has proved himself fully
worthy of the promise. One might note that here for the first time a future of
military triumph is added to the promise.

20 And it happened after these things that it was told to Abraham, saying,
21 "Look, Milcah, too, has born sons to Nahor your brother. Uz, his first-
22 born, and Buz his brother, and Kemuel the father of Aram. And Chesed
23 and Hazo and Pildash and Jidlaph, and Bethuel. And Bethuel begot
24 Rebekah. These eight Milcah bore to Nahor, Abraham's brother. And
his concubine, whose name was Reumah, she, too, gave birth—to
Tebah, and to Gaham, and to Tahash, and to Maacah."

20–24. The genealogical list inserted here, which reflects a Mesopotamian confederation of twelve tribes akin to the twelve tribes of Abraham's descendants, is directed toward the introduction of Rebekah (verse 23), soon to join the Patriarchal narrative as a principal figure. The genealogy marks a kind of boundary in the larger narrative. Abraham has accomplished his chief actions; all that is really left to him is to acquire a suitable burial plot for Sarah, which will be his final gesture in laying claim to the land. At that point, even before Abraham's death, the concerns of the next generation will take center stage (chapter 24).

CHAPTER 23

And Sarah's life was a hundred and twenty-seven years, the years of   1
Sarah's life. And Sarah died in Kiriath-Arba, which is Hebron, in   2
the land of Canaan, and Abraham came to mourn Sarah and to
keen for her. And Abraham rose from before his dead and he spoke to   3
the Hittites, saying: "I am a sojourning settler with you. Grant me a   4
burial-holding with you, and let me bury my dead now before me." And   5

---

1. *years, the years.* The Hebrew is still more extravagant in its use of repetition, unusually repeating "year" after a hundred, after twenty, and after seven. The same device of stylistic emphasis is used in the obituary notices of Abraham and Ishmael.

2. *Kiriath-Arba, which is Hebron.* The older name of the town means "city of four," perhaps a reference to its being a federation (a possible meaning of "Hebron") of four townlets. (Alternately, the name might refer to "four hills.") But some scholars think the earlier name is a Hebraization of a non-Semitic place-name, which would have been given to the town by its "Hittite" inhabitants.

3. *Hittites.* Whether these are actually Hittites who have migrated from Anatolia into Canaan or a loose Hebrew designation for non-Semitic Canaanites is unclear.

4. *sojourning settler . . . Grant me a burial-holding.* The Hebrew, which reads literally, "sojourner and settler," is a legal term that means "resident alien," but the bureaucratic coloration of that English equivalent misrepresents the stylistic decorum of the Hebrew. At the very beginning of Abraham's speech, he announces his vulnerable legal status, a hard fact of institutional reality which stands in ironic tension with his inward consciousness that the whole land has been promised to him and his seed. "Grant"—literally "give"—is pointedly

6   the Hittites answered Abraham, saying: "Pray, hear us, my lord. You are
     a prince of God among us! In the pick of our graves bury your dead. No
7   man among us will deny you his grave for burying your dead." And
8   Abraham rose and bowed to the folk of the land, to the Hittites. And
     he spoke with them, saying, "If you have it in your hearts that I should
     bury my dead now before me, hear me, entreat for me Ephron son of
9   Zohar, and let him grant me the cave of Machpelah that belongs to him,
     which is at the far end of his field. At the full price let him grant it to

---

ambiguous both here and in the subsequent exchange with Ephron. Abraham
avoids the frank term "sell," yet speaks of acquiring a "holding" (*'ahuzah*), a
word that clearly indicates permanent legal possession.

6. *Pray.* This translation follows E. A. Speiser, as well as the ancient Aramaic
version of Yonatan ben Uziel, in reading *lu* for *lo* ("to him") and moving the
monosyllabic term from the end of verse 5 to the beginning of verse 6. The
identical emendation is made at the end of verse 14 moving into the beginning of verse 15. Though one critic, Meir Sternberg (1991), has made an ingenious attempt to rescue the Masoretic Text at these two points, there is a
simple compelling argument against it: the formula for introducing direct
speech, *le'mor,* "saying," is always immediately followed by the direct speech,
not by a preposition "to him" (*lo*). And the repetition of the optative particle
lu, "pray," is just right for beginning each round of this elaborately polite
bargaining.
     You are a prince of God among us! In the pick of our graves bury your dead.
On the surface, this is a courtly gesture of extravagant generosity. But as Meir
Sternberg (1991), who provides an acute reading of the sinuous turns of the
subsurface bargaining, nicely shows, there is ambiguity of intention here: a
certain exaggeration in calling Abraham a prince of God—which could simply
mean "preeminent dignitary"—"among us" (*he* had claimed to be only "with"
them); and a pointed deletion of any reference to a "holding" or to transfer of
property.

9. *at the far end of his field.* In settling on this particular location for a burial
cave, Abraham wants to make it clear that he will not need to pass through or
encroach on the rest of the Hittite property. "Field," *sadeh,* a flexible term for
territory that stretches from field to steppe, could mean something like "land"
or "property" in context, but rendering it as "field" preserves the distinction
from *'erets,* "land," as in the repeated phrase, "folk of the land."
     At the full price. At this point Abraham makes it altogether unambiguous

me in your midst as a burial-holding." And Ephron was sitting in the 10
midst of the Hittites, and Ephron the Hittite answered Abraham in the
hearing of the Hittites, all the assembled in the gate of his town, saying: "Pray, my lord, hear me. The field I grant you and the cave that is 11
in it. I grant it to you in full view of my kinfolk. I grant it to you. Bury
your dead." And Abraham bowed before the folk of the land, and he 12,13
spoke to Ephron in the hearing of the folk of the land, saying: "If you
would but hear me—I give the price of the field, take it from me, and
let me bury my dead there." And Ephron answered Abraham, saying: 14

---

that the "grant" he has been mentioning means a sale. The Hebrew is literally
"with full silver," and the phrase in verse 16, "the silver that he spoke of," refers
back to this speech.

10. *in the hearing of the Hittites, all the assembled in the gate of his town.* Legal
business was conducted in the gateway: the men assembled there constitute,
as E. A. Speiser proposes, a kind of town council; and these two phrases in
apposition are a legal formula. Scholarship has abundantly observed that the
actual language used by Ephron and Abraham and the narrator bristles with
set terms familiar from other ancient Near Eastern documents for the conveyance of property.

11. *Pray, my lord, hear me.* Reading here *lu* for the Masoretic *lo'* ("no"). This
polite formula for initiating speech is not the sort of repetition that allows significant variation.

The field. As Meir Sternberg shrewdly notes, Abraham had wanted to buy
only the cave at the far end of the field, and so Ephron's seeming generosity in
throwing the unrequested field into the bargain is a ploy for demanding an
exorbitant price.

I grant you . . . I grant it . . . I grant it. This is a performative speech-act, the
repetition indicating that Ephron is formally conveying the plot to Abraham.
Ephron, of course, knows that what Abraham really wants is to be able to buy
the land and thus acquire inalienable right to it, and so this "bestowal" is really
a maneuver to elicit an offer from Abraham.

15 "Pray, my lord, hear me. Land for four hundred silver shekels between
16 me and you, what does it come to? Go bury your dead." And Abraham
heeded Ephron and Abraham weighed out to Ephron the silver that he
spoke of in the hearing of the Hittites, four hundred silver shekels at
17 the merchants' tried weight. And Ephron's field at Machpelah by
Mamre, the field and the cave that was in it and every tree in the field,
18 within its boundaries all around, passed over to Abraham as a possession, in the full view of the Hittites, all the assembled in the gate of his
19 town. And then Abraham buried Sarah his wife in the cave of the
Machpelah field by Mamre, which is Hebron, in the land of Canaan.
20 And the field and the cave that was in it passed over to Abraham as a
burial-holding from the Hittites.

---

15. *Land for four hundred silver shekels.* A comparison with the prices stipulated
for the purchase of property elsewhere in the Bible suggests that this pittance
is actually a king's ransom. Abraham, having twice declared his readiness to
pay "the full price," is in no position to object to the extortionate rate. In fact,
his only real bargaining aim has been to make a legitimate purchase, and he is
unwilling to haggle over the price, just as he refused to accept booty from the
king of Salem. Perhaps Ephron refers to the property as "land" (*'erets*) instead
of *sadeh* in order to provide rhetorical mitigation for the huge sum, intimating,
by way of a term that also means "country," that Abraham is free to imagine he
is getting more than a field with a burial cave for his money.

16. *heeded.* That is, agreed. But it is the same verb, "to hear" (*shama'*), repeatedly used at the beginning of the bargaining speeches.
   weighed out . . . four hundred silver shekels. The transaction antedates the
use of coins, and the silver is divided into weights (the literal meaning of
shekel).

17–20. The language of these concluding verses is emphatically legalistic, recapitulating the phraseology that would appear in a contract for the conveyance
of property. The verbal stem, *qanah,* "to buy," which was studiously avoided in
the bargaining, finally surfaces in the term for "possession" (*miqnah*). Many
interpreters view this whole episode as a final gesture of the aged Abraham
toward laying future claim to possession of the land. Meir Sternberg, on the
other hand, reads it as thematically coordinated with the previous episode of the
binding of Isaac: first the promise of seed seems threatened in the command to
sacrifice Isaac; then the promise of the land seems to be mocked in Abraham's
need to bargain with these sharp-dealing Hittites for a mere gravesite.

CHAPTER 24

And Abraham was old, advanced in years, and the LORD had 1
blessed Abraham in all things. And Abraham said to his servant, 2
elder of his household, who ruled over all things that were his,
"Put your hand, pray, under my thigh, that I may make you swear by the 3
LORD, God of the heavens and God of the earth, that you shall not take
a wife for my son from the daughters of the Canaanite in whose midst
I dwell. But to my land and to my birthplace you shall go, and you shall 4
take a wife for my son, for Isaac." And the servant said to him, "Perhaps 5
the woman will not want to come after me to this land. Shall I indeed
bring your son back to the land you left?" And Abraham said to him, 6
"Watch yourself, lest you bring my son back there. The LORD God of 7
the heavens, Who took me from my father's house and from the land
of my birthplace, and Who spoke to me and Who swore to me saying,

---

2. *Put your hand . . . under my thigh.* Holding the genitals, or placing a hand
next to the genitals, during the act of solemn oath-taking is attested in several
ancient societies (a fact already noted by Abraham ibn Ezra in the twelfth century), though here it may have the special purpose of invoking the place of procreation as the servant is to seek a bride for the only son Isaac.

4. *to my land and to my birthplace you shall go.* These words are still another
echo of the first words God speaks to Abraham at the beginning of chapter 12
sending him forth from his native land.

7. Abraham's language explicitly echoes the reiterated covenantal promises he
has received. Later in the story, when the servant gives the family a seemingly
verbatim report of this initial dialogue with his master, he discreetly edits out
this covenantal language.

'To your seed will I give this land,' He shall send His messenger before
8 you and you shall take a wife for my son from there. And if the woman
should not want to go after you, you shall be clear of this vow of mine;
9 only my son you must not bring back there." And the servant put his
hand under Abraham's thigh and he swore to him concerning this thing.
10 And the servant took ten camels from his master's camels, with all the
bounty of his master in his hand, and he rose and went to Aram-
Naharaim, to the city of Nahor.

11 And he made the camels kneel outside the city by the well of water at
12 eventide, the hour when the water-drawing women come out. And he

---

10. *camels*. The camels here and elsewhere in Genesis are a problem. Archeological and extrabiblical literary evidence indicates that camels were not
adopted as beasts of burden until several centuries after the Patriarchal period,
and so their introduction in the story would have to be anachronistic. What is
puzzling is that the narrative reflects careful attention to other details of historical authenticity: horses, which also were domesticated centuries later, are
scrupulously excluded from the Patriarchal Tales, and when Abraham buys a
gravesite, he deals in weights of silver, not in coins, as in the later Israelite
period. The details of betrothal negotiation, with the brother acting as principal agent for the family, the bestowal of a dowry on the bride and bethrothal
gifts on the family, are equally accurate for the middle of the second millennium B.C.E. Perhaps the camels are an inadvertent anachronism because they
had become so deeply associated in the minds of later writers and audiences
with desert travel. There remains a possibility that camels may have already
had some restricted use in the earlier period for long desert journeys, even
though they were not yet generally employed. In any case the camels here are
more than a prop, for their needs and treatment are turned into a pivot of the
plot.

11. *by the well of water at eventide, the hour when the water-drawing women
came out*. This is the first occurrence of the betrothal type-scene. The conventionally fixed sequence of motifs of this type-scene is: travel to a foreign
land, encounter there with the future bride (almost always referred to as
naʿarah, "young woman") at a well, drawing of water, "hurrying" or "running" to
bring the news of the stranger's arrival, a feast at which a betrothal agreement
is concluded. As a social institution, the well was probably a plausible place to
encounter nubile maidens, though the well in a foreign land also has an arche-

said, "LORD, God of my master Abraham, pray, grant me good speed
this day and do kindness with my master, Abraham. Here, I am poised 13
by the spring of water, and the daughters of the men of the town are
coming out to draw water. Let it be that the young woman to whom I 14
say, 'Pray, tip down your jug that I may drink,' if she says, 'Drink, and
your camels, too, I shall water,' she it is whom You have marked for Your
servant, for Isaac, and by this I shall know that You have done kindness
with my master." He had barely finished speaking when, look, Rebekah 15
was coming out, who was born to Bethuel son of Milcah, the wife of
Nahor, Abraham's brother, with her jug on her shoulder. And the young 16
woman was very comely to look at, a virgin, no man had known her.
And she came down to the spring and filled her jug and came back up.
And the servant ran toward her and said, "Pray, let me sip a bit of water 17
from your jug." And she said, "Drink, my lord," and she hurried and 18
lowered her jug onto her hand and let him drink. And she let him drink 19
his fill and said, "For your camels, too, I shall draw water until they

---

typal look, suggesting fertility and the nuptial encounter with the otherness of
the female. This version is the most elaborate and leisurely of the betrothal
type-scenes, rich in detail, full of stately repetition. It is also the only version
in which the bridegroom himself is not present but rather a surrogate, and in
which the young woman, not the man, draws the water, with the verb of hurrying that is linked with the bringing of the news amply describing her actions
at the well. There is surely some intimation in all this of the subsequent course
of the marriage of Isaac and Rebekah—he in most respects the most passive
of all the patriarchs, she forceful and enterprising.

17. *Pray, let me sip a bit of water.* With perfect politeness, the parched desert
traveler speaks as though he wanted no more than to wet his lips. In the event,
prodigious quantities of water will have to be drawn.

18–19. *Drink, my lord . . . and let him drink. And she let him drink his fill.* As
Meir Sternberg (1985) acutely observes, this long delay before she finally produces the requisite offer to water the camels is a heart-stopper, enough to
leave the servant in grave momentary doubt as to whether God has answered
his prayer.

    onto her hand. The motion, as Rashi notes, is lowering the jug from her
shoulder to her hand, so that she can pour water out.

20 drink their fill." And she hurried and emptied her jug into the trough
   and she ran again to the well to draw water and drew water for all his
21 camels. And the man was staring at her, keeping silent, to know
22 whether the LORD had granted success to his journey. And it happened,
   when the camels had drunk their fill, that the man took a gold nose
   ring, a *beqa* in weight, and two bracelets for her arms, ten gold shekels
23 in weight. And he said, "Whose daughter are you? Tell me, pray. Is there
24 room in your father's house for us to spend the night?" And she said to
   him, "I am the daughter of Bethuel the son of Milcah whom she bore
25 to Nahor." And she said to him, "We have abundance of bran and feed
26 as well and room to spend the night." And the man did obeisance and
27 bowed to the LORD, and he said, "Blessed be the LORD, God of my master Abraham, Who has not left off His steadfast kindness toward my
   master—me on this journey the LORD led to the house of my master's
   kinsmen."

28 And the young woman ran and told her mother's household about
29 these things. And Rebekah had a brother named Laban, and Laban ran

---

20. *and drew water for all his camels.* This is the closest anyone comes in Genesis to a feat of "Homeric" heroism (though the success of Rebekah's son Jacob
in *his* betrothal scene in rolling off the huge stone from the well invites comparison). A camel after a long desert journey drinks many gallons of water, and
there are ten camels here to water, so Rebekah hurrying down the steps of the
well would have had to be a nonstop blur of motion in order to carry up all this
water in her single jug.

22. *beqa.* The term *beqa'* is derived from a verb that means "to split" and so may
refer to half a shekel, the standard weight, though that is not certain. Following the convention of earlier English translations, I have not used the mark for
'*ayin* in the text.

25. *bran.* The Hebrew *teven* appears to have two different meanings in the Bible.
In the brickmaking process mentioned in Exodus, and in several other occurrences, it means "straw," and this becomes its only meaning in later Hebrew. But
there are several texts in which *teven* is clearly edible (Isaiah 11:7, 65:25; 1 Kings
5:8), and despite the preponderance of English versions, both Renaissance and
modern, that opt for "straw" here, edible grain makes more sense.

out to the man by the spring. And it happened, when he saw the nose 30
ring, and the bracelets on his sister's arms, and when he heard the
words of Rebekah his sister, saying, "Thus the man spoke to me," he
came up to the man and, look, he was standing over the camels by the
spring. And he said, "Come in, blessed of the LORD, why should you 31
stand outside, when I have readied the house and a place for the
camels?" And the man came into the house and unharnassed the 32
camels; and he gave bran and feed to the camels and water to bathe his
feet and the feet of the men who were with him. And food was set 33
before him. But he said, "I will not eat until I have spoken my word,"
and he said, "Speak." And he said, "I am Abraham's servant. The LORD 34,35
has blessed my master abundantly, and he has grown great. He has
given him sheep and cattle and silver and gold and male and female

---

30. *when he saw the nose ring, and the bracelets*. A brilliant moment of exposition of character. The narrator makes no comment about what kind of person
Laban may be. His sharp eye on the precious gifts surely invites us to wonder
about him—though for the moment, we might conclude that he simply sees
here evidence that Isaac comes of good family. Hovering suspicions about
Laban's rapacity will be confirmed many decades later in narrated time in the
course of his slippery dealings with Jacob. In contrast to the marriage so easily arranged for Isaac, Jacob will face immense difficulties, created by Laban,
in working out the terms of his betrothal.

31. *Come in, blessed of the LORD*. Laban's gesture of hospitality stands in a
direct sequence with Abraham's and Lot's. The language is courtly, the hospitality "Oriental," but we are not meant to forget his just noted observation of
the nose ring and bracelets.

32. *the men who were with him*. The servant would of course have had men
with him and his ten camels, but in keeping with the rigorous economy of biblical narrative, these are not mentioned until now, when they become requisite participants in the hospitality scene. Before this, they are only fleetingly
intimated in the "us" of verse 23.

35. The servant's speech, in keeping with the biblical technique of near verbatim repetition, echoes in detail the language first of the narrator and then of
his own dialogue with Abraham at the beginning of the chapter. But as several
modern commentators have noted, he makes numerous adjustments of the

36 slaves and camels and donkeys. And Sarah, my master's wife, bore a
son to my master after she had grown old, and he has given him all that
37 he has. And my master made me swear, saying, 'You shall not take a
wife for my son from the daughters of the Canaanite in whose land I
38 dwell, but to my father's house you shall go and to my clan, and you
39 shall take a wife for my son.' And I said to my master, 'Perhaps the
40 woman will not come after me.' And he said to me, 'The LORD, in whose
presence I have walked, shall send His messenger with you, and he
shall grant success to your journey, and you shall take a wife for my son
41 from my clan and my father's house. Then you shall be clear of my oath;
if you come to my clan and they refuse you, you shall be clear of my
42 oath.' And today I came to the spring and I said, 'O LORD, God of my
master Abraham, if You are going to grant success to the journey on
43 which I come, here, I am poised by the spring of water, and let it be
that the young woman who comes out to draw water to whom I say, 'Let
44 me drink a bit of water from your jug,' and she says to me, 'Drink, and
for your camels, too, I shall draw water,' she is the wife that the LORD

---

language he is quoting because of the practical and diplomatic requirements
of addressing this particular audience. Thus, the narrator simply said that "the
LORD had blessed Abraham in all things." The servant, cognizant that this is a
preamble to a proposal of marriage, fleshes out that flat statement by speaking
of how his master has "grown great" in sheep and cattle and other livestock, in
slaves and silver and gold.

40. *The LORD, in whose presence I have walked.* To "walk before," or live in
devoted service to, a particular deity is an idea that would have been perfectly
familiar to Abraham's polytheistic kinfolk back in Mesopotamia. What the servant is careful to delete in his repetition of the dialogue with his master are all
the monotheistic references to the God of heaven and earth and the covenantal promises to give the land to the seed of Abraham. Similarly excluded is
Abraham's allusion to having been taken by God from his father's house and
the land of his birth—a notion the family, to whom this God has not deigned
to speak, might construe as downright offensive.

from my clan and my father's house. Abraham had actually said, quite simply, "from there," but at this point the servant chooses to elaborate his master's
meaning in terms that emphasize to the kinfolk Abraham's admirable sense of
family loyalty.

has marked for my master's son.' I had barely finished speaking in my 45
heart and, look, Rebekah was coming out, her jug on her shoulder, and
she went down to the spring and drew water and I said to her, 'Pray, let
me drink.' And she hurried and tipped down the jug that she carried 46
and said, 'Drink, and your camels, too, I shall water,' and the camels,
too, she watered. And I asked her, saying, 'Whose daughter are you?' 47
and she said, 'The daughter of Bethuel son of Nahor whom Milcah
bore him.' And I put the ring in her nose and the bracelets on her arms,
and I did obeisance and bowed to the LORD and blessed the LORD, God 48
of my master Abraham Who guided me on the right way to take the
daughter of my master's brother for his son. And so, if you are going to 49
act with steadfast kindness toward my master, tell me, and if not, tell
me, that I may turn elsewhere." And Laban [and Bethuel] answered and 50
said, "From the LORD this thing has come; we can speak to you neither
good nor evil. Here is Rebekah before you. Take her and go and let her 51

---

47. *And I asked her. . . . And I put the ring in her nose.* The one significant divergence in the servant's report of the encounter at the well is that he claims to
have asked Rebekah about her lineage before placing the golden ornaments on
her, whereas he actually did this as soon as she had drawn water for all the
camels, and only afterward did he inquire about her family. This alteration of
the order of actions is again dictated by considerations of audience. The servant, having seen the stipulation of his prayer completely fulfilled by the beautiful girl at the well, is entirely certain that she is the wife God has intended
for Isaac. But to the family, he does not want to seem to have done anything
so presumptuous as bestowing gifts—implicitly betrothal gifts—on a young
woman without first ascertaining her pedigree. This is a small but strategic
indication of the precision with which social institutions and values are adumbrated in the dialogue.

49. *turn elsewhere.* The Hebrew says literally, "turn to the right or the left," a
biblical idiom for seeking alternatives to the course on which one is set.

50. *and Bethuel.* The convincing conclusion of many textual critics is that the
appearance of Bethuel is a later scribal or redactorial insertion. The surrounding narrative clearly suggests that Bethuel is deceased when these events
occur. Otherwise, it is hard to explain why the home to which Rebekah goes
running is referred to as "her mother's household." It is her brother who is the
male who speaks exclusively on behalf of the family; only her mother and

52 be wife to your master's son as the LORD has spoken." And it happened
when Abraham's servant heard their words, that he bowed to the
53 ground to the LORD. And the servant took out ornaments of silver and
ornaments of gold and garments and he gave them to Rebekah and he
54 gave presents to her brother and her mother. And they ate and drank,
he and the men who were with him, and they spent the night and rose
in the morning, and he said, "Send me off, that I may go to my master."
55 And her brother and her mother said, "Let the young woman stay with
56 us ten days or so, then she may go." And he said to them, "Do not hold
me back when the LORD has granted success to my journey. Send me
57 off that I may go to my master." And they said, "Let us call the young
58 woman and ask for her answer." And they called Rebekah and said to
59 her, "Will you go with this man?" And she said, "I will." And they sent
off Rebekah their sister, and her nurse, and Abraham's servant and his
60 men. And they blessed Rebekah and said to her,

"Our sister, become hence   myriads teeming.
May your seed take hold   of the gate of its foes."

---

brother are mentioned, never her father, elsewhere in the report of the
betrothal transaction, and even in this verse, "answered" is in the singular, with
an odd switch to the plural occurring only for "said."
   neither good nor evil. The sense of this idiom is "nothing whatsoever."

55. ten days or so. The time indication in the Hebrew is not entirely clear, as
the phrase—literally "days or ten"—has no parallels. The present translation
reflects a modern consensus, but some medieval commentators note, correctly, that "days" (precisely in this plural form) sometimes means "a year," in
which case the ten would refer to ten months. The request for such an
extended prenuptial period at home might be more plausible than a mere week
and a half.

59. her nurse. As in other societies, for a young woman to retain her old wet
nurse as permanent companion is a sign of social status (one recalls Shakespeare's Juliet). The nurse's name will be given when she is accorded an obituary notice in chapter 35.

And Rebekah rose, with her young women, and they mounted the 61
camels and went after the man, and the servant took Rebekah and went
off. And Isaac had come from the approach to Beer-Lahai-Roi, as he 62
was dwelling in the Negeb region. And Isaac went out to stroll in the 63
field toward evening, and he raised his eyes and saw and, look, camels
were coming. And Rebekah raised her eyes and saw Isaac, and she 64
alighted from the camel. And she said to the servant, "Who is that man 65
walking through the field toward us?" And the servant said, "He is my
master," and she took her veil and covered her face. And the servant 66

---

60. *Our sister*. Rebekah's family sends her off to her destiny in the west with a
poem that incorporates the twofold blessing of being progenitrix to a nation
multifarious in number and mighty in arms. The poem itself may in fact be
authentically archaic: the prosodic form is irregular—the two "lines," approximately parallel in meaning, are too long to scan conventionally and each
invites division into two very short versets—and the diction is elevated and
ceremonial. "Myriads teeming" is literally "thousands of myriads," and the
term for enemy at the end of the poem—literally, "haters"—is one that is generally reserved for poetry, hence the faintly archaic "foes" of this translation.
The virtually identical phrase in the prose blessing bestowed on Abraham in
22:17, uses the ordinary word for "enemy."

63. *to stroll*. The translation reproduces one current guess, but the verb occurs
only here, and no one is sure what it really means.
   and he raised his eyes and saw and, look, camels were coming. The formulaic
chain, he raised his eyes and saw, followed by the "presentative" *look* (rather
like *voici* in French), occurs frequently in these stories as a means of indicating a shift from the narrator's overview to the character's visual perspective.
The visual discrimination here is a nice one: in the distance, Isaac is able to
make out only a line of camels approaching; then we switch to Rebekah's point
of view, with presumably a few minutes of story time elapsed, and she is able
to detect the figure of a man moving across the open country.

65. *covered her face*. This is an indication of social practice, not of individual
psychology: unmarried women did not wear a veil, but there is evidence that
it was customary to keep the bride veiled in the presence of her bridegroom
until the wedding.

67 recounted to Isaac all the things he had done. And Isaac brought her
into the tent of Sarah his mother and took Rebekah as wife. And he
loved her, and Isaac was consoled after his mother's death.

---

67. *into the tent of Sarah his mother*. The proposal of some textual critics to
delete "Sarah his mother" as a scribal error should be resisted. Rebekah fills
the emotional gap left by Sarah's death, as the end of the verse indicates, and
with the first matriarch deceased, Rebekah also takes up the role of matriarch
in the family. It is thus exactly right that Isaac should bring her into his
mother's tent. Interestingly, no mention whatever is made of Abraham at the
end of the story. Many have construed his charging of the servant at the beginning of the story as a deathbed action: it would not be unreasonable to surmise
that he is already deceased when the servant returns (the genealogical notation concerning Abraham in the next chapter would be out of chronological
order—a kind of pluperfect that ends by placing Isaac around Beer-Lahai-Roi,
where in fact we find him upon Rebekah's arrival). The conclusion of the
betrothal tale in this way creates a curious symmetry between the household
of the bride and the household of the groom. She, evidently, is fatherless, living in "her mother's household." It is quite likely that he, too, is fatherless; and
though he was bereaved of his mother still earlier, it is to "his mother's tent"
that he brings his bride.

CHAPTER 25

And Abraham took another wife, and her name was Keturah. And 1,2
she bore him Zimran and Jokshan and Medan and Midian and
Ishbak and Shuah. And Jokshan begot Sheba and Dedan. And the 3
sons of Dedan were the Ashurim and the Letushim and the Leummim.
And the sons of Midian were Ephah and Epher and Enoch and Abida 4
and Eldaah. All these were the sons of Keturah. And Abraham gave 5
everything he had to Isaac. And to the sons of Abraham's concubines 6
Abraham gave gifts while he was still alive and sent them away from
Isaac his son eastward, to the land of the East. And these are the days 7

---

1. *And Abraham took another wife.* The actual place of this whole genealogical
notice in the chronology of Abraham's life might be somewhere after the burial of Sarah at the end of chapter 23, or perhaps even considerably earlier. The
genealogy is inserted here as a formal marker of the end of the Abraham story.
Perhaps a certain tension was felt between the repeated promise that Abraham
would father a vast nation and the fact that he had begotten only two sons.
This tension would have been mitigated by inserting this document at the end
of his story with the catalogue of his sons by Keturah. In this list, Abraham figures as the progenitor of the seminomadic peoples of the trans-Jordan region
and the Arabian Peninsula. The second genealogical notice (verses 12–18), that
of the descendants of Ishmael, covers a related group of tribes—twelve in
number, like the Israelite tribes—in the same geographical region, but also
extending up to northern Mesopotamia. Thus, as Ishmael definitively leaves
the scene of narration, the list provides a "documentary" confirmation of the
promise that he, too, will be the father of a great nation.

6. *concubines.* The plural form may imply that Keturah's status, like Hagar's,
was that of a concubine.

of the years of the life of Abraham which he lived: a hundred and
8 seventy-five years. And Abraham breathed his last and died at a ripe old
9 age, old and sated with years, and he was gathered to his kinfolk. And
Isaac and Ishmael his sons buried him in the Machpelah cave in the
10 field of Ephron son of Zohar the Hittite which faces Mamre, the field
that Abraham had bought from the Hittites, there was Abraham buried,
11 and Sarah his wife. And it happened after Abraham's death that God
blessed Isaac his son, and Isaac settled near Beer-Lahai-Roi.

12 And this is the lineage of Ishmael son of Abraham whom Hagar the
13 Egyptian, Sarah's slavegirl, bore to Abraham. And these are the names
of the sons of Ishmael, according to their lineage: Nebaioth, the first-
14 born of Ishmael, and Kedar and Adbeel and Mibsam, and Mishma and
15 Duma and Massa, Hadad and Tema, Jetur, Naphish, and Kedmah.
16 These are the sons of Ishmael and these are their names in their habitations and their encampments, twelve chieftains according to their
17 tribes. And these are the years of the life of Ishmael: a hundred and
thirty-seven years. And he breathed his last and died and he was gathered
18 to his kinfolk. And they ranged from Havilah to Shur, which faces Egypt,
and till you come to Asshur. In despite of all his kin he went down.

---

8. *sated with years*. The Masoretic Text has only "sated," but the Syriac, Samaritan, and Septuagint versions as well as some manuscripts read "sated with
years," which the context clearly requires.

16. *habitations*. The Hebrew term in urban architectural contexts means
"court," but the older meaning is "dwelling place," or perhaps something like
"unfortified village." The cognate in the Ugaritic texts means "house."

18. *And they ranged*. The verb *shakhan* suggests an activity less fixed than "to
settle" or "to dwell," and this translation follows the lead of E. A. Speiser in
using a verb that implies nomadism.
      In despite of all his kin he went down. The translation reproduces the enig-
matic character of the whole clause in the Hebrew. "In despite of all his kin"
repeats exactly the words of Ishmael's blessing in 16:12, and so the ambiguous
"he" here may also be Ishmael, who is mentioned in the previous verse. But
some construe the initial preposition of the clause as "alongside" or "in the
face of." The verb is equally opaque: its most common meaning is "to fall";

And this is the lineage of Isaac son of Abraham. Abraham begot Isaac. ₁₉
And Isaac was forty years old when he took as wife Rebekah daughter ₂₀
of Bethuel the Aramean from Paddan-Aram, sister of Laban the
Aramean. And Isaac pleaded with the LORD on behalf of his wife, for ₂₁
she was barren, and the LORD granted his plea, and Rebekah his wife
conceived. And the children clashed together within her, and she said, ₂₂
"Then why me?" and she went to inquire of the LORD. And the LORD ₂₃
said to her:

> "Two nations—in your womb,
> two peoples from your loins shall issue.
> People over people shall prevail,
> the elder, the younger's slave."

some have imagined it has a military meaning here ("to attack" or "to raid");
others have construed it as a reference to the "falling" of the inheritance.

19. *this is the lineage of Isaac.* Modern translations that render "lineage" (or,
"begettings") as "story" are misconceived. The formula is pointedly used to
suggest a false symmetry with "this is the lineage of Ishmael." In this case, the
natural chain of procreation is interrupted, and can proceed only through
divine intervention, as was true for Abraham.

21–23. In this second instance of the annunciation type-scene, the husband
intercedes on behalf of the wife, and the annunciation to the future mother—
here given the form of an oracle—is uniquely displaced from the period of bar-
renness to late pregnancy. The crucial point in this story of the birth of twins
is not the fact of birth itself but the future fate of struggle between the siblings, which is the burden of the oracular poem.

22. *Then why me?* Rebekah's cry of perplexity and anguish over this difficult
pregnancy is terse to the point of being elliptical. Her words might even be
construed as a broken-off sentence: Then why am I . . . ?

23. *the elder, the younger's slave.* Richard Elliott Friedman has made the interesting suggestion that the Hebrew oracle here has the ambiguity of its Delphic
counterpart: the Hebrew syntax leaves unclear which noun is subject and
which is object—"the elder shall serve the younger," or, "the elder, the younger
shall serve."

24 And when her time was come to give birth, look, there were twins in
25 her womb. And the first one came out ruddy, like a hairy mantle all
26 over, and they called his name Esau. Then his brother came out, his
hand grasping Esau's heel, and they called his name Jacob. And Isaac
was sixty years old when they were born.

27 And the lads grew up, and Esau was a man skilled in hunting, a man of
28 the field, and Jacob was a simple man, a dweller in tents. And
Isaac loved Esau for the game that he brought him, but Rebekah

---

25. *ruddy, like a hairy mantle . . . Esau.* There is an odd displacement of etymology in the naming sentence, perhaps because the writer was not sure what
"Esau" actually meant. "Ruddy," *'adom,* refers to another name for Esau, Edom
(as in verse 30), and the "hairy" component of the mantle simile, *se'ar,* refers
to Edom's territory, Seir.

26. *they called his name Jacob.* The Masoretic Text has a singular verb, but
some manuscript versions have the plural, as when the same phrase is used for
Esau. In this instance, the etymology is transparent: *Ya'aqob,* "Jacob," and
'aqeb, "heel." The grabbing of the heel by the younger twin becomes a kind of
emblem of their future relationship, and the birth, like the oracle, again
invokes the struggle against primogeniture. The original meaning of the name
Jacob was probably something like "God protects" or "God follows after."
   And Isaac was sixty years old. With the most deft economy of delayed exposition, the narrator reveals that Rebekah had been childless for twenty years—
an extraordinarily long period for a woman to suffer what in the ancient setting
was an acutely painful predicament.

27. *a simple man.* The Hebrew adjective *tam* suggests integrity or even innocence. In biblical idiom, the heart can be crooked (*'aqob,* the same root as
Jacob's name—cf. Jeremiah 17:9), and the idiomatic antonym is pureness or
innocence—*tom*—"of heart" (as in Genesis 20:5). There may well be a com-
plicating irony in the use of this epithet for Jacob, since his behavior is very far
from simple or innocent in the scene that is about to unfold.

28. *for the game that he brought him.* The Hebrew says literally, "for the game
in his mouth." It is unclear whether the idiom suggests Esau as a kind of lion
bringing home game in its mouth or rather bringing game to put in his father's
mouth. The almost grotesque concreteness of the idiom may be associated

loved Jacob. And Jacob prepared a stew and Esau came from the   29
field, and he was famished. And Esau said to Jacob, "Let me gulp   30
down some of this red red stuff, for I am famished." Therefore is his
name called Edom. And Jacob said, "Sell now your birthright to me."   31

---

with the absurdity of the material reason for Isaac's paternal favoritism. Pointedly, no reason is assigned for Rebekah's love of Jacob in the next clause.

29. *And Jacob prepared a stew,* Oraḥ Ḥaim, an eighteenth-century Hebrew commentary, brilliantly suggests that Jacob, seeing that Esau had won their father's heart with food, tries to compete by preparing his own (hearty vegetarian) culinary offering.

30. *Let me gulp down some of this red red stuff.* Although the Hebrew of the dialogues in the Bible reflects the same level of normative literary language as the surrounding narration, here the writer comes close to assigning substandard Hebrew to the rude Esau. The famished brother cannot even come up with the ordinary Hebrew word for "stew" (*nazid*) and instead points to the bubbling pot impatiently as (literally) "this red red." The verb he uses for gulping down occurs nowhere else in the Bible, but in rabbinic Hebrew it is reserved for the feeding of animals. This may be evidence for Abba ben David's contention that rabbinic Hebrew developed from a biblical vernacular which was excluded from literary usage: in this instance, the writer would have exceptionally allowed himself to introduce the vernacular term for animal feeding in order to suggest Esau's coarsely appetitive character. And even if one allows for semantic evolution of this particular verb over the millennium between the first articulation of our text and the Mishnah, it is safe to assume it was always a cruder term for eating than the standard biblical one.

    Edom. The pun, which forever associates crude impatient appetite with Israel's perennial enemy, is on *'adom-'adom,* "this red red stuff."

31. *Sell now your birthright to me.* Each of Jacob's words, in striking contrast to Esau's impetuous speech, is carefully weighed and positioned, with "me" held back until the end of the sentence. If Esau seems too much a creature of the imperious body to deserve the birthright, the dialogue suggests at the same time that Jacob is a man of legalistic calculation. Perhaps this is a quality needed to get and hold onto the birthright, but it hardly makes Jacob sympathetic, and moral ambiguities will pursue him in the story.

32 And Esau said, "Look, I am at the point of death, so why do I need a
33 birthright?" And Jacob said, "Swear to me now," and he swore to him,
34 and he sold his birthright to Jacob. Then Jacob gave Esau bread and
lentil stew, and he ate and he drank and he rose and he went off, and
Esau spurned the birthright.

---

32. *so why do I need.* The words he uses, *lamah zeh li,* are strongly reminiscent
of the words his mother used when she was troubled by the churning in her
womb, *lamah zeh 'anokhi.*

34. *and he ate and he drank and he rose and he went off.* This rapid-fire chain
of verbs nicely expresses the precipitous manner in which Esau gulps down
his food and, as the verse concludes, casts away his birthright.

CHAPTER 26

Ａnd there was a famine in the land besides the former famine that   1
was in the days of Abraham, and Isaac went to Abimelech king of
the Philistines in Gerar. And the LORD appeared unto him and   2

THIS chapter is the only one in which Isaac figures as an active protagonist.
Before, he was a bound victim; after, he will be seen as a bamboozled blind old
man. His only other initiated act is his brief moment as intercessor on behalf
of his wife in 25:21. Textual critics disagree about whether this chapter is a
"mosaic" of Isaac traditions or an integral literary unit, and about whether it is
early or late. What is clear is that the architectonics of the larger story require
a buffer of material on Isaac between Jacob's purchase of the birthright and
his stealing of the blessing—a buffer that focuses attention on Isaac's right to
the land and on his success in flourishing in the land. All of the actions
reported here, however, merely delineate him as a typological heir to Abraham.
Like Abraham he goes through the sister-wife experience, is vouchsafed a
covenantal promise by God, prospers in flock and field, and is involved in a
quarrel over wells. He remains the pale and schematic patriarch among the
three forefathers, preceded by the exemplary founder, followed by the vivid
struggler.

1. *besides the former famine.* The writer (some would say, the editor) signals at
the outset that this story comes after, and explicitly reenacts, what happened
before to Abraham.

king of the Philistines. In this version, the anachronistic identification of
Gerar as a Philistine city, not strictly intrinsic to the Abimelech story in chapter 20, is insisted on. There is no obvious literary purpose for this difference;
one suspects it simply reflects the historical context in which this version was
formulated, in which the western Negeb would have been naturally thought of
as Philistine country.

said, "Do not go down to Egypt. Stay in the land that I shall say to you.

3 Sojourn in this land so that I may be with you and bless you, for to you and your seed I will give all these lands and I will fulfill the oath that I

4 swore to Abraham your father, and I will multiply your seed like the stars in the heavens and I will give to your seed all these lands, and all

5 the nations of the earth shall be blessed through your seed because Abraham has listened to my voice and has kept My charge, My commandments, My statutes, and My teachings."

6,7 And Isaac dwelled in Gerar. And the men of the place asked of his wife and he said, "She is my sister," fearing to say, "My wife"—"lest the men

8 of the place kill me over Rebekah, for she is comely to look at." And it happened, as his time there drew on, that Abimelech king of the Philistines looked out the window and saw—and there was Isaac play-

---

2. *Do not go down to Egypt*. That is, emulate the pattern of Abraham's second sister-wife episode, not the first. Following a coastal route, Isaac could well have used Gerar as a way station to Egypt, and Abraham's pact with Abimelech (chapter 21) would have provided some assurance that the Gerarites would grant him safe transit.

4. *all these lands*. "lands" occurs in the plural in this version of the promise because Isaac is in the land of the Philistines.

7. *the men of the place*. The sexual threat against the matriarch is displaced in this final version from the monarch to the local male populace. The likely reference of "one of the people" in verse 10 is what it seems to say, any male Gerarite, despite an exegetical tradition (influenced by the earlier Abimelech story) that construes it as an epithet for the king.

she is comely to look at. Isaac's interior monologue uses the identical epithet invoked by the narrator in introducing Rebekah in chapter 24.

8. *as his time there drew on*. Rashi, with his characteristic acuteness of response to nuances of phrasing, construes this as a suggestion that Isaac became complacent with the passage of time ("From now on I don't have to worry since they haven't raped her so far") and so allowed himself to be publicly demonstrative with Rebekah.

ing with Rebekah his wife. And Abimelech summoned Isaac and he ⁹
said, "Why, look, she is your wife, and how could you say, 'She is my sister'?" And Isaac said to him, "For I thought, lest I die over her." And ₁₀
Abimelech said, "What is this you have done to us? One of the people
might well have lain with your wife and you would have brought guilt
upon us." And Abimelech commanded all the people saying, "Whoso- ₁₁
ever touches this man or his wife is doomed to die." And Isaac sowed ₁₂
in that land and he reaped that year a hundredfold, and the LORD
blessed him. And the man became ever greater until he was very great. ₁₃

---

looked out the window. This is the most naturalistic of the three versions of
the story. The matriarch's marital status is conveyed not by divine plagues, nor
by a dream-vision from God, but by ocular evidence.

playing. The meaning of the verb here is clearly sexual, implying either
fondling or actual sexual "play." It immediately follows the name "Isaac," in
which the same verbal root is transparently inscribed. Thus Isaac-the-laugher's
birth is preceded by the incredulous laughter of each of his parents; Sarah
laughs after his birth; Ishmael laughs-mocks at the child Isaac; and now Isaac
laughs-plays with the wife he loves. Perhaps there is some suggestion that the
generally passive Isaac is a man of strong physical appetites: he loves Esau
because of his own fondness for venison; here he rather recklessly disports
himself in public with the woman he has proclaimed to be his sister.

10. *One of the people might well have lain with your wife.* Though Abimelech's
words approximately mirror those of the indignant king in chapter 20, this version is pointedly devised to put the woman first announced as Isaac's beautiful, strictly virgin bride in less danger than Sarah was in chapters 12 and 20:
Rebekah is never taken into the harem; it is merely a supposition that one of
the local men might seize her for sexual exploitation.

12. *And Isaac sowed.* In keeping with the emphasis of this version on human
action, the bounty that comes to the patriarch after the deflection of the sexual danger to his wife is not a gift from the monarch but the fruit of his own
industry as agriculturalist and pastoralist. There is a continuity between his
sojourning in the western Negeb near Gerar and his movement somewhat to
the east, to Beersheba, where his father had long encamped. All this creates a
direct connection between the sister-wife episode and the theme of Isaac
inheriting and growing prosperous in the land.

14   And he had possessions of flocks and of herds and many slaves, and
15   the Philistines envied him. And all the wells that his father's servants
      had dug in the days of Abraham his father, the Philistines blocked up,
16   filling them with earth. And Abimelech said to Isaac, "Go away from
17   us, for you have grown far too powerful for us." And Isaac went off
      from there and encamped in the wadi of Gerar, and he dwelled there.
18   And Isaac dug anew the wells of water that had been dug in the days
      of Abraham his father, which the Philistines had blocked up after
      Abraham's death, and he gave them names, like the names his father
19   had called them. And Isaac's servants dug in the wadi and they found
20   there a well of fresh water. And the shepherds of Gerar quarreled with
      Isaac's shepherds, saying, "The water is ours." And he called the name
21   of the well Esek, for they had contended with him. And they dug
      another well and they quarreled over it, too, and he called its name
22   Sitnah. And he pulled up stakes from there and dug another well, and
      they did not quarrel over it, and he called its name Rehoboth, and he

---

14. *and the Philistines envied him.* The jealousy over Isaac's spectacular prosperity and the contention over precious water resources that follows lay the
ground for the story of the two brothers struggling over the blessing of land and
inheritance in the next episode. Isaac's being "sent away" by the Philistines
adumbrates Jacob's banishment to the east after having procured the blessing
by stealth.

17. *wadi.* The Arabic term, current in modern English and Hebrew usage, designates, as does the biblical *naḥal,* a dry riverbed that would be filled with
water only during the flash floods of the rainy season. But the floor of a wadi
might conceal, as here, an underground source of water.

20. *Esek.* Roughly, "contention," as in the verb that follows in the etiological
explanation of the name.

21. *Sitnah.* The transparent meaning is "accusation" or "hostility," though the
sentence lacks an etiological clause.

22. *another well.* The struggle over wells, which replays an episode in the Abraham stories but is given more elaborate emphasis, works nicely as part of the
preparation for the next round of the Jacob–Esau conflict: a water source is
not easily divisible; the spiteful act of the Philistines in blocking up the wells

said, "For now the LORD has given us space that we may be fruitful in the land."

And he went up from there to Beersheba. And the LORD appeared unto   23,24
him on that night and said, "I am the God of Abraham your father. Fear
not, for I am with you, and I will bless you and I will multiply your seed
for the sake of Abraham My servant." And he built an altar there and   25
he invoked the name of the LORD, and he pitched his tent there, and
Isaac's servants began digging a well there. And Abimelech came to him   26
from Gerar, with Ahuzzath his councillor and Phicol captain of his
troops. And Isaac said to them, "Why have you come to me when you   27
have been hostile toward me and have sent me away from you?" And   28
they said, "We have clearly seen that the LORD is with you, and we
thought—Let there be an oath between our two sides, between you
and us, and let us seal a pact with you, that you will do no harm to us,   29
just as we have not touched you, and just as we have done toward you
only good, sending you away in peace. Be you hence blessed of the
LORD!" And he made them a feast and they ate and drank. And they   30,31
rose early in the morning and swore to each other, and Isaac sent them
away, and they went from him in peace. And it happened on that day   32

---

expresses a feeling that if we can't have the water, nobody should; at the end,
Isaac's workers discover a new, undisputed well and call it Rehoboth, which
means "open spaces." We are being prepared for the story in which only one
of the two brothers can get the real blessing, in which there will be bitter jealousy and resentment; and which in the long run will end with room enough
for the two brothers to live peaceably in the same land.

27. *sent me away from you*. It is a mistake to render the verb, as several modern translations do, as "drive away." The verb Isaac chooses is a neutral one,
even though the context of the sentence strongly indicates hostile intention.
Abimelech in his response (verse 29) uses exactly the same word, adding the
qualifier "in peace" in order to put a different face on the action: this was no
banishment, we sent you off as a reasonable act of good will. The narrator then
uses the same verb and qualifier—which might conceivably be a formula for
parting after the completion of a treaty—in verse 31, "and Isaac sent them
away, and they went from him in peace." (Compare David and Abner in 2
Samuel 3.)

that Isaac's servants came and told him of the well they had dug and
33 they said to him, "We have found water." And he called it Shibah, therefore the name of the town is Beersheba to this day.

34 And Esau was forty years old and he took as wife Judith the daughter
35 of Beeri the Hittite and Basemath the daughter of Elon the Hittite. And
they were a provocation to Isaac and to Rebekah.

---

33. *Shibah*. Though the word in this form means "seven," the etiology of the
name intimated by the narrative context obviously relates it to *shevu'ah*, "oath,"
whereas the earlier story about Beersheba (chapter 21) appears to link the
name with both "seven" and "oath."

34. *And Esau . . . took as wife*. This brief notice about Esau's exogamous unions
obviously is distinct from the preceding stories about Isaac. It is probably
placed here to remind us of his unworthiness to be the true heir (thus forming a kind of envelope structure with the spurning of the birthright in the last
verse of chapter 25), and in this way serves to offer some sort of justification
in advance for Jacob's stealing the blessing in the next episode. It also lays the
ground for the end of the next episode in which Rebekah will invoke the need
for Jacob to find a wife from his own kin as an excuse for his hasty departure
for Mesopotamia.

35. *provocation*. Some commentators construe the first component of the compound noun *morat-ruah* as a derivative of the root *m-r-r*, "bitter"—hence the
term "bitterness" favored by many translations. But the morphology of the
word points to a more likely derivation from *m-r-h*, "to rebel" or "to defy," and
thus an equivalent such as "provocation" is more precise.

CHAPTER 27

And it happened when Isaac was old, that his eyes grew too bleary 1
to see, and he called to Esau his elder son and said to him, "My
son!" and he said, "Here I am." And he said, "Look, I have grown 2
old; I know not how soon I shall die. So now, take up, pray, your gear, 3
your quiver and your bow, and go out to the field, and hunt me some
game, and make me a dish of the kind that I love and bring it to me that 4
I may eat, so that I may solemnly bless you before I die." And Rebekah 5
was listening as Isaac spoke to Esau his son, and Esau went off to the
field to hunt game to bring.

---

1. *his eyes grew too bleary to see.* Isaac, the man of taste (25:28) and of touch
(26:8), is deprived of sight in his infirm old age. In the central episode of this
story, he will rely in sequence on taste, touch, and smell, ignoring the evidence
of sound, to identify his supposed firstborn.

4. *I may solemnly bless you.* The Hebrew says literally, "my life-breath [*nafshi*]
may bless you." *Nafshi* here is an intensive synonym for "I," and hence something like "solemnly bless" or "absolutely bless" is suggested.

5. *And Rebekah was listening as Isaac spoke to Esau.* According to the convention of biblical narrative, there can be only two interlocutors in a dialogue (as
in Aeschylean tragedy), though one of them may be a collective presence—
e.g., a person addressing a crowd and receiving its collective response. Within
the limits of this convention, the writer has woven an artful chain. The story,
preponderantly in dialogue, is made up of seven interlocking scenes: Isaac-
Esau, Rebekah-Jacob, Jacob-Isaac, Isaac-Esau, Rebekah-Jacob, Rebekah-
Isaac, Isaac-Jacob. (The last of these occupies the first four verses of chapter
28). The first two pairs set out the father and his favorite son, then the mother
and her favorite son, in opposing tracks. Husband and wife are kept apart until
the penultimate scene; there is no dialogue at all between the two brothers—

6 And Rebekah said to Jacob her son, "Look, I have heard your father
7 speaking to Esau your brother, saying, 'Bring me some game and make
me a dish that I may eat, and I shall bless you in the LORD's presence
8 before I die.' So now, my son, listen to my voice, to what I command
9 you. Go, pray, to the flock, and fetch me from there two choice kids
that I may make them into a dish for your father of the kind he loves.
10 And you shall bring it to your father and he shall eat, so that he may
11 bless you before he dies." And Jacob said to Rebekah his mother, "Look,
Esau my brother is a hairy man and I am a smooth-skinned man.
12 What if my father feels me and I seem a cheat to him and bring on

---

sundered by the formal mechanics of the narrative—or between Rebekah and
Esau. Although one must always guard against the excesses of numerological
exegesis, it is surely not accidental that there are just seven scenes, and that
the key word "blessing" (*berakhah*) is repeated seven times.

to bring. The Septuagint reads instead "for his father," which is phonetically
akin to the word in the Masoretic Text (either variant is a single word in the
Hebrew). The Septuagint reading has a slight advantage of syntactic com-
pleteness, but subsequent exchanges in the story insist repeatedly on the verb
"to bring" as an essential element in the paternal instructions.

7. *and I shall bless you in the LORD's presence*. Rebekah substitutes this for "that
I may solemnly bless you" in the actual speech on which she eavesdropped,
thus heightening the sense of the sacred and irrevocable character of the
blessing she wants Jacob to steal.

8. *So now*. There is a pointed verbal symmetry in Rebekah's use of the same
introductory term, *we'atah,* that Isaac used to preface his instructions to Esau.

9. *two choice kids*. Kids will again be an instrument of deception, turned on
Jacob, when his sons bring him Joseph's tunic soaked in kid's blood. And in the
immediately following episode (Genesis chapter 38), Judah, the engineer of
the deception, will promise to send kids as payment to the woman he imagines is a roadside whore, and who is actually his daughter-in-law Tamar, using
deception to obtain what is rightfully hers.

11. *Look, Esau my brother is a hairy man*. It is surely noteworthy that Jacob
expresses no compunction, only fear of getting caught.

myself a curse and not a blessing?" And his mother said, "Upon me 13
your curse, my son. Just listen to my voice and go, fetch them for me."
And he went and he fetched and he brought to his mother, and his 14
mother made a dish of the kind his father loved. And Rebekah took the 15
garments of Esau her elder son, the finery that was with her in the
house, and put them on Jacob her younger son, and the skins of the 16
kids she put on his hands and on the smooth part of his neck. And she 17
placed the dish, and the bread she had made, in the hand of Jacob her
son. And he came to his father and said, "Father!" And he said, "Here I 18
am. Who are you, my son?" And Jacob said to his father, "I am Esau 19
your firstborn. I have done as you have spoken to me. Rise, pray, sit up,
and eat of my game so that you may solemnly bless me." And Isaac said 20
to his son, "How is it you found it this soon, my son?" And he said,
"Because the LORD your God gave me good luck." And Isaac said to 21
Jacob, "Come close, pray, that I may feel you, my son, whether you are
my son Esau or not." And Jacob came close to Isaac his father and he 22
felt him and he said, "The voice is the voice of Jacob and the hands are

---

15–16. *the garments of Esau . . . the skins of the kids.* Both elements point forward to the use of a garment to deceive first Jacob, then Judah, with the tunic
soaked in kid's blood combining the garment motif and the kid motif.

18. *Who are you, my son?* The inclination of several modern translations to sort
out the logic of these words by rendering them as "Which of my sons are you?"
can only be deplored. Isaac's stark question, as Tyndale and the King James
Version rightly sensed, touches the exposed nerve of identity and moral fitness
that gives this ambiguous tale its profundity.

19. *I am Esau your firstborn.* He reserves the crucial term "firstborn" for the end
of his brief response. As Nahum Sarna notes, the narrator carefully avoids
identifying Esau as firstborn, using instead "elder son." The loaded term is
introduced by Jacob to cinch his false claim, and it will again be used by Esau
(verse 32) when he returns from the hunt.
    Rise, pray, sit up. It is only now that we learn the full extent of Isaac's infir-
mity: he is not only blind but also bedridden.

23 Esau's hands." But he did not recognize him for his hands were, like
24 Esau's hands, hairy, and he blessed him. And he said, "Are you my son
25 Esau?" And he said, "I am." And he said, "Serve me, that I may eat of
the game of my son, so that I may solemnly bless you." And he served
26 him and he ate, and he brought him wine and he drank. And Isaac his
father said to him, "Come close, pray, and kiss me, my son." And he
27 came close and kissed him, and he smelled his garments and he
blessed him and he said, "See, the smell of my son is like the smell of
the field that the LORD has blessed.

28   May God grant you
                from the dew of the heavens and the fat of the earth,
                    and abundance of grain and drink.
29   May peoples serve you,
                and nations bow before you.
            Be overlord to your brothers,
                may your mother's sons bow before you.
            Those who curse you be cursed,
                and those who bless you, blessed."

---

23. *he did not recognize him.* This crucial verb of recognition will return to haunt Jacob when he is deceived by his sons and then will play through the story of Judah and Tamar and of Joseph and his brothers.

24. *Are you my son Esau?* Doubt still lingers in Isaac's mind because of the voice he hears, and so he is driven to ask this question again. His doubt may seem assuaged when he asks his son to kiss him just before the blessing, but that, as Gerhard von Rad observes, is evidently one last effort to test the son's identity, through the sense of smell. The extent of Rebekah's cunning is thus fully revealed: one might have wondered why Jacob needed his brother's garments to appear before a father incapable of seeing them—now we realize she has anticipated the possibility that Isaac would try to smell Jacob: it is Esau's smell that he detects in Esau's clothing.

And it happened as soon as Isaac finished blessing Jacob, and Jacob   30
barely had left the presence of Isaac his father, that Esau his brother
came back from the hunt. And he, too, made a dish and brought it to   31
his father and he said to his father, "Let my father rise and eat of the
game of his son so that you may solemnly bless me." And his father   32
Isaac said, "Who are you?" And he said, "I am your son, your firstborn,
Esau." And Isaac was seized with a very great trembling and he said,   33
"Who is it, then, who caught game and brought it to me and I ate every-

---

30. *as soon as Isaac finished.* This entire sentence makes us aware of the break-
neck speed at which events are unfolding. Rebekah and Jacob have managed
to carry out her scheme just in the nick of time, and the physical "bind"
between this scene and the preceding one is deliberately exposed, just as the
bind between the first and second scene was highlighted by Rebekah's presence as eavesdropper.

31. *Let my father rise and eat of the game of his son . . . bless me.* Jacob's more
nervous and urgent words for his father to arise from his bed were cast in the
imperative (with the particle of entreaty, *na'*, "pray"). Esau, confident that he
has brought the requisites for the ritual of blessing, addresses his father more
ceremonially, beginning with the deferential third person. (The movement
from third person to second person at the end of the sentence is perfectly
idiomatic in biblical Hebrew when addressing a figure of authority.)

32. *Who are you?* This is the very question Isaac put to Jacob, but, significantly,
"my son" is deleted: Isaac is unwilling to imagine that a second "Esau" stands
before him, and so at first he questions the interlocutor as though he were a
stranger.
   I am your son, your firstborn, Esau. The small but crucial divergences from
Jacob's response (verse 18) could scarcely be more eloquent. Esau begins by
identifying himself as Isaac's son—the very term his father had omitted from
his question, and which Jacob did not need to invoke because it was part of
the question. Then he announces himself as firstborn—a condition to which
he has in fact sold off the legal rights—and, finally, he pronounces his own
name. Jacob, on his part, first got out the lie, "Esau," and then declared himself "firstborn."

33. *Who is it, then, who caught game.* As a final move in the game of false and
mistaken identities, Isaac pretends not to know who it is that has deceived
him, finding it easier to let Esau name the culprit himself. Isaac must of

34 thing before you came and blessed him? Now blessed he stays." When
Esau heard his father's words, he cried out with a great and very bitter
35 outcry and he said to his father, "Bless me, too, Father!" And he said,
36 "Your brother has come in deceit and has taken your blessing." And he
said,

> "Was his name called Jacob
>   that he should trip me now twice by the heels?
> My birthright he took,
>   and look, now, he's taken my blessing."

And he said, "Have you not kept back a blessing for me?"
37   And Isaac answered and said to Esau, "Look, I made him overlord to
you, and all his brothers I gave him as slaves, and with grain and wine
38 I endowed him. For you, then, what can I do, my son?" And Esau said
to his father, "Do you have but one blessing, my father? Bless me, too,

---

course realize at once who it is that has taken the blessing because he already
had his doubts when he heard the son speaking with the voice of Jacob.

34. *he cried out . . . "Bless me, too, Father!"* Esau, whose first speech in the narrative was a half-articulate grunt of impatient hunger, had achieved a certain
stylistic poise when he addressed his father after returning from the hunt,
imagining he was about to receive the blessing. Now, however, faced with irre-
versible defeat, his composure breaks: first he cries out (the Hebrew meaning
is close to "scream" or "shout"), then he asks in the pathetic voice of a small
child, "Bless me, too, Father." Esau strikes a similar note at the end of verse
36 and in verse 38.

36. *Was his name called Jacob / that he should trip me now twice by the heels?* At
birth, Jacob's name, *Ya'aqob,* was etymologized as "heel-grabber" (playing on
'aqeb, "heel"). Now Esau adds another layer of etymology by making the name
into a verb from *'aqob,* "crooked," with the obvious sense of devious or deceit-
ful dealing.

Father." And Esau raised his voice and he wept. And Isaac his father 39
answered and said to him,

> "Look, from the fat of the earth be your dwelling
>   and from the dew of the heavens above.
> By your sword shall you live 40
>   and your brother shall you serve.
> And when you rebel
>   you shall break off his yoke from your neck."

And Esau seethed with resentment against Jacob over the blessing his 41
father had blessed him, and Esau said in his heart, "As soon as the time
for mourning my father comes round, I will kill Jacob my brother."

---

39. *from the fat of the earth . . . from the dew of the heavens.* The notion put
forth by some commentators that these words mean something quite different
from what they mean in the blessing to Jacob is forced. Isaac, having recapitulated the terms of the blessing in his immediately preceding words to Esau
(verse 37), now reiterates them at the beginning of his blessing to Esau: the
bounty of heaven and earth, after all, can be enjoyed by more than one son,
though overlordship, as he has just made clear to Esau, cannot be shared. (The
reversal of order of heaven and earth is a formal variation, a kind of chiasm,
and it would be imprudent to read into it any symbolic significance.)

40. *By your sword shall you live.* Yet Esau's blessing, like Ishmael's, is an
ambiguous one. Deprived by paternal pronouncement of political mastery, he
must make his way through violent struggle.
    And when you rebel. The Hebrew verb is obscure and may reflect a defec-
tive text. The present rendering steps up the conventional proposal, "grow
restive," lightly glancing in the direction of an emendation others have suggested, *timrod,* "you shall rebel," instead of *tarid* (meaning uncertain). This
whole verse, however obscurely, alludes to the later political fortunes of Edom,
the trans-Jordanian nation of which Esau is said to be the progenitor. One of
the miracles of the story, and of the story of Joseph and his brothers that follows, is that the elements that adumbrate future political configurations in no
way diminish the complexity of these figures as individual characters. To the
extent that there is a kind of political allegory in all these tales, it remains a
secondary feature, however important it might have been for audiences in the
First Commonwealth period.

42   And Rebekah was told the words of Esau her elder son, and she sent
      and summoned Jacob her younger son and said to him, "Look, Esau
43   your brother is consoling himself with the idea he will kill you. So now,
      my son, listen to my voice, and rise, flee to my brother Laban in Haran,
44   and you may stay with him a while until your brother's wrath subsides,
45   until your brother's rage against you subsides and he forgets what you
      did to him, and I shall send and fetch you from there. Why should I be
46   bereft of you both on one day?" And Rebekah said to Isaac, "I loathe my
      life because of the Hittite women! If Jacob takes a wife from Hittite
      women like these, from the native girls, what good to me is life?"

---

42. *And Rebekah was told the words of Esau.* This is a shrewd ploy of oblique
characterization of Esau. He had "spoken" these words only to himself, in
what is presented as interior monologue. But one must infer that Esau was
unable to restrain himself and keep counsel with his own heart but instead
blurted out his murderous intention to people in the household.

43. *So now, my son, listen to my voice.* Introducing her counsel of flight,
Rebekah uses exactly the same words she spoke at the beginning of her
instructions to Jacob about the stratagem of deception to get the blessing.

45. *Why should I be bereft of you both on one day?* The verb *shakhal* is used for
a parent's bereavement of a child and so "you both" must refer to Jacob and
Esau: although a physical struggle between the two would scarcely be a battle
between equals, in her maternal fear she imagines the worst-case scenario, the
twins killing each other, and in the subsequent narrative, the sedentary Jacob
does demonstrate a capacity of unusual physical strength.

46. *I loathe my life because of the Hittite women!* Rebekah shows the same
alacrity in this verbal manipulation that she evinced in preparing the kidskin
disguise and the mock-venison dish, and, earlier, in her epic watering of the
camels. Instead of simply registering that Jacob ought not to take a wife from
the daughters of the Canaanite (compare 24:3 and 28:1), she brandishes a
sense of utter revulsion, claiming that her life is scarcely worth living because
of the native daughters-in-law Esau has inflicted on her. This tactic not only
provides a persuasive pretext for Jacob's departure but also allows her—
obliquely, for she does not pronounce his name—to discredit Esau.
    what good to me is life? The phrase she uses, *lamah li ḥayim*, contains an
echo of her question during her troubled pregnancy, *lamah zeh 'anokhi*, "why
then me?"

CHAPTER 28

A nd Isaac summoned Jacob and blessed him and commanded him   1
and said to him, "You shall not take a wife from the daughters of
Canaan. Rise, go to Paddan-Aram to the house of Bethuel your   2
mother's father, and take you from there a wife from the daughters of
Laban, your mother's brother. And may El Shaddai bless you and make   3
you fruitful and multiply, so you become an assembly of peoples. And   4
may He grant you the blessing of Abraham, to you and your seed as
well, that you may take hold of the land of your sojournings, which God

---

1. *and blessed him.* The Hebrew verb *berekh* also has the more everyday sense
of "to greet," but it is quite unnecessary to construe it in that sense here, as
some scholars have proposed. Isaac's clear intention is to give his son a parting blessing: the instructions about taking a wife from Mesopotamia intervene
in the last half of this verse and in verse 2 before we reach the actual words of
the blessing in verses 3 and 4, but this sort of proleptic introduction of a key
verb is entirely in accordance with Hebrew literary usage.

4. *And may He grant you the blessing of Abraham, to you and your seed as well.*
Documentary critics assign 27:46–28:9 to the Priestly source and argue that it
contradicts the logic of the story told in chapter 27. Such readings, however,
reflect an unfortunate tendency to construe any sign of tension in a narrative
as an irreconcilable contradiction, and underestimate the resourcefulness of
the Priestly writers in making their own version artfully answer the versions of
antecedent traditions. Sending Jacob off to Paddan-Aram to find a wife and
Jacob's flight from his vengeful brother are not alternate explanations for his
departure: the bride search is clearly presented as an *excuse* for what is actually his flight, an excuse ably engineered by Rebekah with her melodramatic
complaint (27:46). Now Isaac, whatever misgivings he may have about Jacob's
act of deception, knows that his younger son has irrevocably received the

5 granted to Abraham." And Isaac sent Jacob off and he went to Paddan-Aram to Laban son of Bethuel the Aramean, brother of Rebekah, mother of Jacob and Esau.

6 And Esau saw that Isaac had blessed Jacob and had sent him off to Paddan-Aram to take him a wife from there when he blessed him and charged him, saying, "You shall not take a wife from the daughters of 7 Canaan." And Jacob listened to his father and to his mother and he 8 went to Paddan-Aram. And Esau saw that the daughters of Canaan 9 were evil in the eyes of Isaac his father. And Esau went to Ishmael and he took Mahalath daughter of Ishmael son of Abraham, in addition to his wives, as a wife.

---

blessing, and he has no choice but to reiterate it at the moment of parting. He does so at this point in the lofty language of procreation and proliferation and inheritance, harking back to the first Creation story, that is characteristic of the Priestly style, which is in a different register from the earthy and political language of the blessing articulated in the previous chapter. But far from contradicting or needlessly duplicating the earlier blessing, this scene is a pointed, low-key replay of the scene in the tent. When Isaac tells Jacob he will become an assembly of peoples and his seed will take possession of the land promised to Abraham, he is manifestly conferring on him the blessing that is the prerogative of the elder son—something he would have no warrant to do were he not simply confirming the blessing he has already been led to pronounce, through Jacob's subterfuge, upon his younger son. Esau once again fails to get things right. Overhearing Isaac's warning to Jacob about exogamous unions, he behaves as though endogamy were a sufficient condition for obtaining the blessing, and so after the fact of his two marriages with Hittite women—perhaps even many years after the fact—he, too, takes a cousin as bride. There is no indication of his father's response to this initiative, but the marriage is an echo in action of his plaintive cry, "Do you have but one blessing, my Father? Bless me, too, Father."

And Jacob left Beersheba and set out for Haran. And he came upon a   10,11
certain place and stopped there for the night, for the sun had set, and
he took one of the stones of the place and put it at his head and he lay
down in that place, and he dreamed, and, look, a ramp was set against   12
the ground with its top reaching the heavens, and, look, messengers of
God were going up and coming down it. And, look, the LORD was   13
poised over him and He said, "I, the LORD, am the God of Abraham
your father and the God of Isaac. The land on which you lie, to you I

---

11. *a certain place.* Though archeological evidence indicates that Bethel had
been a cultic site for the Canaanites centuries before the patriarchs, this
pagan background, as Nahum Sarna argues, is entirely occluded: the site is no
more than an anonymous "place" where Jacob decides to spend the night.
Repetition of a term is usually a thematic marker in biblical narrative, and it is
noteworthy that "place" (*maqom*) occurs six times in this brief story. In part,
this is the tale of the transformation of an anonymous place through vision into
Bethel, a "house of God."

   one of the stones of the place. There is scant evidence elsewhere of a general
(and uncomfortable) ancient Near Eastern practice of using stones as pillows.
Rashi, followed by some modern scholars, proposes that the stone is not
placed under Jacob's head but alongside it, as a kind of protective barrier. The
stone by which Jacob's head rests as he dreams his vision will become the pillar, the commemorative or cultic marker (*matsevah*) at the end of the story.
J. P. Fokkelman (1975) astutely notes that stones are Jacob's personal motif:
from the stone at his head to the stone marker, then the stone upon the well he
will roll away, and the pile of stones he will set up to mark his treaty with Laban.

12. *a ramp.* The Hebrew term occurs only here. Although its etymology is
doubtful, the traditional rendering of "ladder" is unlikely. As has often been
observed, the references to both "its top reaching the heavens" and "the gate
of the heavens" use phrases associated with the Mesopotamian ziggurat, and
so the structure envisioned is probably a vast ramp with terraced landings.
There is a certain appropriateness in the Mesopotamian motif, given the destination of Jacob's journey. Jacob in general is represented as a border crosser,
a man of liminal experiences: here, then in his return trip when he is confronted by Laban, and in the nocturnal encounter at the ford of the Jabbok.

13. *the LORD was poised over him.* The syntactic reference of "over him" is
ambiguous, and the phrase could equally be construed to mean "on it" (i.e., on
the ramp).

14 will give it and to your seed. And your seed shall be like the dust of the
earth and you shall burst forth to the west and the east and the north
and the south, and all the clans of the earth shall be blessed through
15 you, and through your seed. And, look, I am with you and I will guard
you wherever you go, and I will bring you back to this land, for I will
16 not leave you until I have done that which I have spoken to you." And
Jacob awoke from his sleep and he said, "Indeed, the LORD is in this
17 place, and I did not know." And he was afraid and he said,

> "How fearsome is this place!
> This can be but the house of God,
>   and this is the gate of the heavens."

18 And Jacob rose early in the morning and took the stone he had put at
19 his head, and he set it as a pillar and poured oil over its top. And he
called the name of that place Bethel, though the name of the town
20 before had been Luz. And Jacob made a vow, saying, "If the LORD God

---

14. *And your seed shall be like the dust of the earth.* God in effect offers divine
confirmation of Isaac's blessing (verses 3 and 4) in language that is more
vivid—indeed, hyperbolic.

18. *took the stone . . . and he set it as a pillar.* Cultic pillars—Jacob ritually ded-
icates this one as such by pouring oil over its top—were generally several feet
high. If that is the case here, it would have required, as Gerhard von Rad
notes, Herculean strength to lift the stone. We are then prepared for Jacob's
feat with a massive weight of stone in the next episode.

19. *though the name of the town before had been Luz.* In fact, there is no indication of any "town" in the story, although Luz-Bethel would have been familiar to Israelite audiences as a town and cultic center. Perhaps Jacob's vision is
assumed to occur in the open, in the vicinity of Bethel.

20. *If the LORD God be with me.* The conditional form of the vow—if the other
party does such and such, then I on my part will do such and such in return—
is well attested elsewhere in the Bible and in other ancient Near Eastern texts.
But its use by Jacob has a characterizing particularity. God has already
promised him in the dream that He will do all these things for him. Jacob,
however, remains the suspicious bargainer—a "wrestler" with words and con-

be with me and guard me on this way that I am going and give me bread
to eat and clothing to wear, and I return safely to my father's house,   21
then the LORD will be my God. And this stone that I set as a pillar will   22
be a house of God, and everything that You give me I will surely tithe it
to You."

---

ditions just as he is a physical wrestler, a heel-grabber. He carefully stipulated
conditions of sale to the famished Esau; he was leery that he would be found
out when Rebekah proposed her stratagem of deception to him; now he wants
to be sure God will fulfill His side of the bargain before he commits himself
to God's service; and later he will prove to be a sharp dealer in his transactions
with his uncle Laban.

   on this way that I am going. The "way" replicates the mission of Abraham's
servant in chapter 24—to find a bride among his kinfolk in Mesopotamia. But
unlike the servant, who crosses the desert in grand style with a retinue of
camels and underlings, Jacob is fleeing alone on foot—in fact, it is a very dangerous journey. He will invoke an emblematic image of himself as refugee and
pedestrian border crosser in his reunion with Esau years later: "For with my
staff I crossed this Jordan" (32:11).

CHAPTER 29

¹ And Jacob lifted his feet and went on to the land of the Easterners.
² And he saw and, look, there was a well in the field, and, look, three flocks of sheep were lying beside it, for from that well they would water the flocks, and the stone was big on the mouth of the well. ³ And when all the flocks were gathered there, they would roll the stone from the mouth of the well and would water the sheep and put back ⁴ the stone in its place on the mouth of the well. And Jacob said to them, "My brothers, where are you from?" And they said, "We are from Haran." ⁵ And he said to them, "Do you know Laban son of Nahor?" And they ⁶ said, "We know him." And he said to them, "Is he well?" And they said, "He is well, and, look, Rachel his daughter is coming with the sheep."

---

1. *lifted his feet*. Although eyes are frequently lifted or raised in these narratives, the idiom of lifting the feet occurs only here. Rashi suggests that Jacob's elation after the Bethel epiphany imparted a buoyancy to the movement of his feet as he began his long trek to the east. Perhaps this is a general idiom for beginning a particularly arduous journey on foot. In any case, a symmetry of phrasing is created when, at the end of the journey, having discovered Rachel, Jacob "lifted his voice and wept."

2. *And he saw, and, look, . . .* These sentences are an interesting interweave of Jacob's perspective and the narrator's. It is Jacob who sees first the well, then the flocks. It is the narrator who intervenes to explain that from this well the flocks are watered, but it is in all likelihood Jacob who sees the stone, notes its bigness, observes how it covers the mouth of the well (the order of perception is precisely indicated by the word order). Then, in verse 3, the narrator again speaks out to explain the habitual procedures of the Haranites with the stone and the well.

And he said, "Look, the day is still long. It is not time to gather in the   7
herd. Water the sheep and take them to graze." And they said, "We can-   8
not until all the flocks have gathered and the stone is rolled from the
mouth of the well and we water the sheep." He was still speaking with   9
them when Rachel came with her father's sheep, for she was a shep-
herdess. And it happened when Jacob saw Rachel daughter of Laban his   10
mother's brother and the sheep of Laban his mother's brother that he
stepped forward and rolled the stone from the mouth of the well and
watered the sheep of Laban his mother's brother. And Jacob kissed   11
Rachel and lifted his voice and wept. And Jacob told Rachel that he was   12
her father's kin, and that he was Rebekah's son, and she ran and told her

---

7. *Look, the day is still long.* Jacob's scrupulousness about the shepherds' obligation to take full advantage of the daylight for grazing the flocks prefigures his
own dedication to the shepherd's calling and his later self-justification that he
has observed all his responsibilities punctiliously.

10. *he stepped forward and rolled the stone from the mouth of the well and
watered the sheep.* The "Homeric" feat of strength in rolling away the huge
stone single-handedly is the counterpart to his mother's feat of carrying up
water for ten thirsty camels. Though Jacob is not a man of the open field, like
Esau, we now see that he is formidably powerful—and so perhaps Rebekah
was not unrealistic in fearing the twins would kill each other should they come
to blows. The drawing of water after encountering a maiden at a well in a foreign land signals to the audience that a betrothal type-scene is unfolding. But
Jacob is the antithesis of his father: instead of a surrogate, the bridegroom
himself is present at the well, and it is he, not the maiden, who draws the
water; in order to do so, he must contend with a stone, the motif that is his
narrative signature. If, as seems entirely likely, the well in the foreign land is
associated with fertility and the otherness of the female body to the bridegroom, it is especially fitting that this well should be blocked by a stone, as
Rachel's womb will be "shut up" over long years of marriage.

11. *And Jacob kissed Rachel.* As Nahum Sarna notes, there is a pun between "he
watered" (*wayashq*) and "he kissed" (*wayishaq*). The same pun is played on by
the poet of the Song of Songs.

12. *and she ran and told.* The hurrying to bring home the news of the guest's
arrival, generally with the verb *ruts*, ("to run") as here, is another conventional
requirement of the betrothal type-scene.

13 father. And it happened, when Laban heard the report of Jacob his sister's son, he ran toward him and embraced him and kissed him and brought him to his house. And he recounted to Laban all these things. 14 And Laban said to him, "Indeed, you are my bone and my flesh."

15 And he stayed with him a month's time, and Laban said to Jacob, "Because you are my kin, should you serve me for nothing? Tell me 16 what your wages should be." And Laban had two daughters. The name 17 of the elder was Leah and the name of the younger Rachel. And Leah's eyes were tender, but Rachel was comely in features and comely to look 18 at, and Jacob loved Rachel. And he said, "I will serve seven years for 19 Rachel your younger daughter." And Laban said, "Better I should give

---

13. *he ran toward him.* This may be standard hospitality, but Rashi, exercising his own hermeneutics of suspicion, shrewdly notes that Laban could be recalling that the last time someone came from the emigrant branch of the family in Canaan, he brought ten heavily laden camels with him. Rashi pursues this idea by proposing that Laban's embrace was to see if Jacob had gold secreted on his person.

15. *Because you are my kin, should you serve me for nothing?* In a neat deployment of delayed revelation, a device of which the biblical writers were fond, we now learn that this "bone and flesh" of Laban's has already been put to work by his gracious host for a month's time.

17. *Leah's eyes were tender.* The precise meaning in this context of the adjective is uncertain. Generally, the word *rakh* is an antonym of "hard" and means "soft," "gentle," "tender," or in a few instances "weak." The claim that here it refers to dullness, or a lusterless quality, is pure translation by immediate context because *rakh* nowhere else has that meaning. Still, there is no way of confidently deciding whether the word indicates some sort of impairment ("weak" eyes or perhaps odd-looking eyes) or rather suggests that Leah has sweet eyes that are her one asset of appearance, in contrast to her beautiful sister.

18. *seven years for Rachel your younger daughter.* True to legalistic form, Jacob carefully stipulates the duration of the labor (in lieu of a bride-price that he does not possess), the name of the daughter, and the fact that she is the younger daughter. In the event, none of this avails.

her to you than give her to another man. Stay with me." And Jacob 20
served seven years for Rachel, and they seemed in his eyes but a few
days in his love for her. And Jacob said to Laban, "Give me my wife, for 21
my time is done, and let me come to bed with her." And Laban gath- 22
ered all the men of the place and made a feast. And when evening 23
came, he took Leah his daughter and brought her to Jacob, and he
came to bed with her. And Laban gave Zilpah his slavegirl to Leah his 24
daughter as her slavegirl. And when morning came, look, she was Leah. 25
And he said to Laban, "What is this you have done to me? Was it not
for Rachel that I served you, and why have you deceived me?" And 26
Laban said, "It is not done thus in our place, to give the younger girl
before the firstborn. Finish out the bridal week of this one and we shall 27

---

20. *they seemed in his eyes but a few days in his love for her.* The writer's eloquent economy scarcely needs comment, but it should be observed that "a few
days" (or, "a while," *yamim aḥadim*) is exactly the phrase his mother had used
in advising him to go off to stay with her brother (27:44).

21. *and let me come to bed with her.* The explicitness of Jacob's statement is sufficiently abrupt to have triggered maneuvers of exegetical justification in the
Midrash, but it is clearly meant to express his—understandable—sexual impatience, which is about to be given a quite unexpected outlet.

25. *why have you deceived me?* The verb Jacob uses to upbraid Laban reflects
the same root as the key noun Isaac used when he said to Esau, "Your brother
has come in deceit and has taken your blessing" (27:35).

26. *It is not done thus in our place, to give the younger girl before the firstborn.*
Laban is an instrument of dramatic irony: his perfectly natural reference to
"our place" has the effect of touching a nerve of guilty consciousness in Jacob,
who in *his* place acted to put the younger before the firstborn. This effect is
reinforced by Laban's referring to Leah not as the elder but as the firstborn
(*bekhirah*). It has been clearly recognized since late antiquity that the whole
story of the switched brides is a meting out of poetic justice to Jacob—the
deceiver deceived, deprived by darkness of the sense of sight as his father is
by blindness, relying, like his father, on the misleading sense of touch. The
Midrash Bereishit Rabba vividly represents the correspondence between the
two episodes: "And all that night he cried out to her, 'Rachel!' and she
answered him. In the morning, 'and, . . . look, she was Leah.' He said to her,

give you the other as well for the service you render me for still another
28 seven years." And so Jacob did. And when he finished out the bridal
29 week of the one, he gave him Rachel his daughter as wife. And Laban
gave to Rachel his daughter Bilhah his slavegirl as her slavegirl. And he
30 came to bed with Rachel, too, and, indeed, loved Rachel more than
31 Leah, and he served him still another seven years. And the LORD saw
that Leah was despised and He opened her womb, but Rachel was bar-
32 ren. And Leah conceived and bore a son and called his name Reuben,
for she said, "Yes, the LORD has seen my suffering, for now my husband
33 will love me." And she conceived again and bore a son, and she said,
"Yes, the LORD has heard I was despised and He has given me this one,

---

'Why did you deceive me, daughter of a deceiver? Didn't I call out Rachel in
the night, and you answered me!' She said: 'There is never a bad barber who
doesn't have disciples. Isn't this how your father cried out Esau, and you
answered him?'"

31. *Leah was despised and He opened her womb, but Rachel was barren.* The
Hebrew term for "despised" (or "hated") seems to have emotional implications,
as Leah's words in verse 33 suggest, but it is also a technical, legal term for the
unfavored co-wife. The pairing of an unloved wife who is fertile with a barren,
beloved co-wife sets the stage for a familiar variant of the annunciation type-
scene (as in the story of Peninah and Hannah in 1 Samuel 1). But, as we shall
see, in Rachel's case the annunciation is deflected.

32. *Reuben . . . seen my suffering.* All of the etymologies put forth for the names
of the sons are ad hoc improvisations by the mother who does the naming—
essentially, midrashic play on the sounds of the names. Thus "Reuben" is construed as *re'u ben,* "see, a son," but Leah immediately converts the verb into
God's seeing her suffering. The narrative definition of character and relationship continues through the naming-speeches, as, here, the emotionally
neglected Leah sees a kind of vindication in having borne a son and desperately imagines her husband will now finally love her.

33. *the LORD has heard . . . Simeon.* The naming plays on *shama',* "has heard,"
and *Shim'on.* It is noteworthy that Jacob's first two sons are named after sight
and sound, the two senses that might have detected him in his deception of
his father, were not Isaac deprived of sight and had not the evidence of touch
and smell led him to disregard the evidence of sound. Leah's illusion that bearing a son would bring her Jacob's love has been painfully disabused, for here

too," and she called his name Simeon. And she conceived again and 34
bore a son, and she said, "This time at last my husband will join me, for
I have borne him three sons." Therefore is his name called Levi. And she 35
conceived again and bore a son, and she said, "This time I sing praise
to the LORD," therefore she called his name Judah. And she ceased
bearing children.

---

she herself proclaims that she is "despised" and that God has given her another
son as compensation.

34. *my husband will join me . . . Levi.* The naming plays on *yilaveh,* "will join,"
and Levi. Once more, Leah voices the desperate hope that her bearing sons to
Jacob will bring him to love her.

35. *Sing praise . . . Judah.* The naming plays on *'odeh,* "sing praise," and *Yehudah,* "Judah." The verb Leah invokes is one that frequently figures in thanksgiving psalms. With the birth of her fourth son, she no longer expresses hope
of winning her husband's affection but instead simply gives thanks to God for
granting her male offspring.

she ceased bearing children. This may be merely the consequence of natural
process, though one possible reading of the mandrakes episode in the next
chapter is not that the two sisters had their conjugal turns but rather that
Jacob has ceased for a long period to cohabit with Leah.

CHAPTER 30

ᴀ nd Rachel saw that she had borne no children to Jacob, and
Rachel was jealous of her sister, and she said to Jacob, "Give me
sons, for if you don't, I'm a dead woman!" And Jacob was incensed
with Rachel, and he said, "Am I instead of God, Who has denied you

---

1. *Give me sons, for if you don't I'm a dead woman!* It is a general principle of
biblical narrative that a character's first recorded speech has particular defining force as characterization. Surprisingly, although Rachel has been part of
the story for more than a decade of narrated time, this is the first piece of dialogue assigned to her. It is a sudden revelation of her simmering frustration
and her impulsivity: in fact, she speaks with an impetuousness reminiscent of
her brother-in-law Esau, who also announced to Jacob that he was on the
point of death if Jacob did not immediately give him what he wanted.

2. *Am I instead of God.* Through Jacob's words, the writer shrewdly invokes a
fateful deflection of the annunciation type-scene. According to the convention
of the annunciation story, the barren wife should go to an oracle or be visited
by a divine messenger or a man of God to be told that she will give birth to a
son. Rachel instead importunes her husband, who properly responds that he
cannot play the role of God in the bestowal of fertility, or in the annunciation
narrative. Rachel is then forced to fall back on the strategy of surrogate maternity, like Sarai with Hagar. One should note that she demands "sons," not a
son. Eventually, she will have two sons, but will die in giving birth to the second one. Perhaps her rash words here, "Give me sons, for if you don't, I'm a
dead woman," are meant to foreshadow her premature death.

fruit of the womb?" And she said, "Here is my slavegirl, Bilhah. Come 3
to bed with her, that she may give birth on my knees, so that I, too, shall
be built up through her." And she gave him Bilhah her slavegirl as a 4
wife, and Jacob came to bed with her. And Bilhah conceived and bore 5
Jacob a son. And Rachel said, "God granted my cause. Yes, He heard 6
my voice and He gave me a son." Therefore she called his name Dan.
And Bilhah, Rachel's slavegirl, conceived again and bore a second son 7
to Jacob. And Rachel said, "In awesome grapplings I have grappled with 8
my sister and, yes, I won out." And she called his name Naphtali.
And Leah saw that she had ceased bearing children, and she took Zil- 9
pah, her slavegirl, and gave her to Jacob as a wife. And Zilpah, Leah's 10
slavegirl, bore Jacob a son. And Leah said, "Good luck has come." And 11
she called his name Gad. And Zilpah, Leah's slavegirl, bore a second 12
son to Jacob. And Leah said, "What good fortune! For the girls have 13
acclaimed me fortunate." And she called his name Asher.

---

3. *give birth on my knees.* Placing the newborn on someone's knees was a gesture of adoption.

   built up through her. As with Sarai in chapter 16, the verb, *'ibaneh,* puns on
ben, "son."

6. *God granted my cause.* The verb *dan* suggests vindication of a legal plea, and
is offered as the etymology of the name Dan.

8. *grapplings.* The Hebrew *naftulim* plays on Naphtali. It is noteworthy that
Rachel chooses an image of wrestling for her relationship with her sister that
marks a correspondence to the relationship of Jacob, the "heel-grabber," with
his older sibling.

11. *Good luck has come.* The translation follows a long-established practice in
separating the enigmatic single word of the Masoretic Text, *bagad,* into *ba' gad.*

13. *What good fortune! For the girls have acclaimed me fortunate.* Asher's name
is derived from *'osher,* "good fortune," and the entire naming is thus closely
parallel to the naming of Gad. This noun *'osher* produces a common biblical
verb *'isher,* the basic meaning of which is to call out to a lucky person, *'ashrei,*
"happy is he" (or, here, "happy is she").

₁₄ And Reuben went out during the wheat harvest and found mandrakes
in the field and brought them to Leah his mother. And Rachel said to
₁₅ Leah, "Give me, pray, some of the mandrakes of your son." And she
said, "Is it not enough that you have taken my husband, and now you
would take the mandrakes of my son?" And Rachel said, "Then let
₁₆ him lie with you tonight in return for the mandrakes of your son." And
Jacob came from the field in the evening and Leah went out to meet
him and said, "With me you will come to bed, for I have clearly hired
you with the mandrakes of my son." And he lay with her that night.
₁₇ And God heard Leah and she conceived and bore Jacob a fifth son.

---

14. *mandrakes.* As in other, later cultures, these plants with tomato-shaped
fruit were used for medicinal purposes and were thought to be aphrodisiac,
and also to have the virtue of promoting fertility, which seems to be what
Rachel has in mind. The aphrodisiac association is reinforced in the Hebrew
by a similarity of sound (exploited in the Song of Songs) between *duda'im,*
"mandrakes," and *dodim,* "lovemaking."

15. *Is it not enough that you have taken my husband.* The narrator has mentioned Rachel's jealousy of Leah, and Rachel has referred to "grappling" with
her sister, but this is the first actual dialogue between the sisters. It vividly
etches the bitterness between the two, on the part of the unloved Leah as well
as of the barren Rachel. In still another correspondence with the story of Jacob
and Esau, one sibling barters a privilege for a plant product, though here the
one who sells off the privilege is the younger, not the elder.

16. *With me you will come to bed . . . And he lay with her that night.* In his transactions with these two imperious, embittered women, Jacob seems chiefly
acquiescent, perhaps resigned. When Rachel instructs him to consort with her
slavegirl, he immediately complies, as he does here when Leah tells him it is
she who is to share his bed this night. In neither instance is there any report
of response on his part in dialogue. The fact that Leah uses this particular
idiom for sexual intercourse (literally, "to me you will come"), ordinarily used
for intercourse with a woman the man has not previously enjoyed, is a strong
indication that Jacob has been sexually boycotting Leah. That could be precisely what she is referring to when she says to Rachel, "You have taken my
husband."

And Leah said, "God has given my wages because I gave my slavegirl to 18
my husband," and she called his name Issachar. And Leah conceived 19
again and bore a sixth son to Jacob. And Leah said, "God has granted 20
me a goodly gift. This time my husband will exalt me, for I have borne
him six sons." And she called his name Zebulun. And afterward she 21
bore a daughter and she called her name Dinah.

---

18. *God has given my wages.* In this case, as again with the birth of Joseph,
there is a double pun in the naming-speech. The word for "wages" (or,
"reward") is *sakhar,* which also means a fee paid for hiring something. Leah
uses this same root when she tells Jacob (verse 16) that she has "clearly hired"
him (*sakhor sekhartikha*). Thus Issachar's name is derived from both the circumstances of his conception and his mother's sense of receiving a reward in
his birth. All this suggests that the naming etymologies may not have figured
so literally in the ancient Hebrew imagination as moderns tend to imagine: the
name is taken as a trigger of sound associations, releasing not absolute meaning but possible meaning, and in some instances, a cluster of complementary
or even contradictory meanings.

20. *a goodly gift . . . my husband will exalt me.* The naming of Zebulun illustrates how free the phonetic associations can be in the naming-speeches.
Zebulun and *zebed* ("gift") share only the first two consonants. The verb for
"exalt" (this meaning is no more than an educated guess), *zabal,* then exhibits
a fuller phonetic correspondence to Zebulun and evidently represents an alternative etymology of the name.
   This time my husband will exalt me. Having borne Jacob half a dozen sons,
half of the sanctified tribal grouping of twelve, Leah indulges one last time in
the poignant illusion that her husband will now love her.

21. *and she called her name Dinah.* The absence of a naming etymology for
Dinah is by no means an indication, as has often been claimed, that this verse
derives from a different source. There is no naming-speech for Dinah because
she is a daughter and will not be the eponymous founder of a tribe.

22 And God remembered Rachel and God heard her and He opened her
23 womb, and she conceived and bore a son, and she said, "God has taken
24 away my shame." And she called his name Joseph, which is to say, "May
the LORD add me another son."

25 And it happened, when Rachel bore Joseph, that Jacob said to Laban,
26 "Send me off, that I may go to my place and to my land. Give me my
wives and my children, for whom I have served you, that I may go, for
27 you know the service that I have done you." And Laban said to him, "If,
pray, I have found favor in your eyes, I have prospered and the LORD
28 has blessed me because of you." And he said, "Name me your wages

---

22–23. After the long years of frustrated hopes and prayers (the latter intimated by God's "hearing" Rachel), the gift of fertility is represented in a rapid-fire chain of uninterrupted verbs: remembered, heard, opened, conceived, bore.

23. *taken away my shame*. "Taken away," 'asaf, is proposed as an etymology of *Yosef*, Joseph.

24. *May the LORD add me another son*. "Add," *yosef*, Rachel's second etymology, is a perfect homonym in Hebrew for Joseph (and hence the odd name used among American Puritans, Increase). Leah's double etymology for Issachar had referred in sequence to conception and birth. Rachel's double etymology refers to birth and, prospectively, to a future son. She remains true to the character of her initial speech to Jacob, where she demanded of him not a son but sons. She will be granted the second son she seeks, but at the cost of her life.

26. *for whom I have served you . . . for you know the service that I have done you*. Jacob's speech repeatedly insists on the service (*'avodah*) he has performed for Laban, the same word used in the agreement about the double bride-price. He has worked seven years before marrying the two sisters and, given Leah's seven childbirths with a few years' hiatus between the fourth and fifth sons, several years beyond the second seven he owed Laban as Rachel's bride-price.

27. *If, pray, I have found favor in your eyes*. This formula of deference is normally followed by a request. If the text is reliable here, Laban begins with the deferential flourish and then, having mentioned how he has been blessed through Jacob, lets his voice trail off. A second formula for the introduction of speech ("and he said") is inserted, and only then does he proceed to his request: "Name me your wages." Could the thought of the prosperity he has

that I may give them." And he said to him, "You know how I have served 29
you and how your livestock has fared with me. For the little you had 30
before my time has swollen to a multitude and the LORD has blessed
you on my count. And now, when shall I, too, provide for my household?" And he said, "What shall I give you?" And Jacob said, "You 31
give me nothing if you will do this thing for me: Let me go back and
herd your flocks and watch them. I shall pass through all your flocks 32
today to remove from them every spotted and speckled animal and
every dark-colored sheep and the speckled and spotted among the
goats, and that will be my wages. Then my honesty will bear witness for 33
me in the days to come when you go over my wages—whatever is not
spotted and speckled among the goats and dark-colored among the
sheep shall be accounted stolen by me." And Laban said, "Let it be just 34
as you say."

---

enjoyed through Jacob's supervision of his flocks lead to this self-interruption,
a kind of hesitation before he asks Jacob to name the separation pay that he
knows he owes his nephew?

I have prospered. Everywhere else in the Bible, the verb *niḥesh* means "to
divine," but that makes little sense here, and so there is plausibility in the proposal of comparative semiticists that this particular usage reflects an Akkadian
cognate meaning "to prosper."

30. Once more in a bargaining situation, Jacob does not respond immediately
to the request to name his wages but lays out the general justice of his material claims on Laban, something Laban himself has already conceded.

31. *You need give me nothing.* In a classic bargainer's ploy, Jacob begins by making it sound as though Laban will owe him nothing. As he goes on to name his
terms, it seems as though he is asking for next to nothing: most sheep are
white, not dark-colored; most goats are black, not speckled; and, Laban, by
first removing all the animals with the recessive traits from the flocks, will
appear to have reduced to nil Jacob's chances of acquiring any substantial
number of livestock. One should note that, as in the stealing of the blessing,
Jacob is embarked on a plan of deception that involves goats.

35   And he removed on that day the spotted and speckled he-goats and all
     the brindled and speckled she-goats, every one that had white on it,
     and every dark-colored one among the sheep, and he gave them over to
36   his sons. And he put three days' journey between himself and Jacob
37   while Jacob herded the remaining flocks of Laban. And Jacob took him-
     self moist rods of poplar and almond and plane-tree, and peeled white
38   strips in them, laying bare the white on the rods. And he stood the rods
     he had peeled in the troughs, in the water channels from which the
     flocks came to drink—opposite the flocks, which went into heat when
39   they came to drink. And the flocks went into heat at the rods and the
40   flocks bore brindled, spotted, and speckled young. And the sheep Jacob

---

35–36. *And he removed . . . the spotted and speckled . . . And he put three days'
journey between himself and Jacob.* Laban, taking Jacob at his word, seeks to
eliminate any possibility of crossbreeding between the unicolored animals and
the others by putting a long distance between the spotted ones and the main
herds.

   that had white on it. The Hebrew "white," *lavan,* is identical with the name
Laban. As Nahum Sarna puts it, Jacob is beating Laban at his own game—or,
with his own name-color.

38. *he stood the rods he had peeled in the troughs . . . opposite the flocks, which
went into heat.* The mechanism of Jacob's ingenious scheme has long perplexed commentators. At least on the surface, it appears to involve the age-old
belief that sensory impressions at the moment of conception affect the
embryo—here, the peeled rods, with their strips of white against the dark
bark, would impart the trait of spots or brindle markings to the offspring conceived. (The same effect would then be achieved for the sheep by making
them face the flocks of speckled goats during their own mating time.) Yehuda
Feliks, an authority on biblical flora and fauna, has proposed that the peeled
rods are only a dodge, a gesture to popular belief, while Jacob is actually prac-
ticing sound principles of animal breeding. Using a Mendelian table, Feliks
argues that the recessive traits would have shown up in 25 percent of the animals born in the first breeding season, 12.5 percent in the second season, and
6.25 percent in the third season. Jacob is, moreover, careful to encourage the
breeding only of the more vigorous animals, which, according to Feliks, would
be more likely to be heterozygotes, bearing the recessive genes. It is noteworthy that Jacob makes no mention of the peeled rods when in the next chapter
he tells his wives how he acquired the flocks.

kept apart: he placed them facing the spotted and all the dark-colored in Laban's flocks, and he set himself herds of his own and he did not set them with Laban's flocks. And so, whenever the vigorous of the 41 flocks went into heat, Jacob put the rods in full sight of the flocks in the troughs for them to go in heat by the rods. And for the weaklings of 42 the flocks he did not put them, and so the feeble ones went to Laban and the vigorous ones to Jacob. And the man swelled up mightily and 43 he had many flocks and female and male slaves and camels and donkeys.

CHAPTER 31

1   And he heard the words of Laban's sons, saying, "Jacob has taken everything of our father's, and from what belonged to our father 2 he has made all this wealth." And Jacob saw Laban's face and, 3 look, it was not disposed toward him as in time past. And the LORD said to Jacob, "Return to the land of your fathers and to your birthplace and I will be with you."

---

1. *the words of Laban's sons.* It is a reflection of the drastic efficiency of biblical narrative that Laban's sons, who play only a peripheral role in the story, are not introduced at all until the point where they serve the unfolding of plot and theme. They are never given names or individual characters, and the first mention of them is in the previous chapter when Laban places the segregated particolored flocks in their charge. Here they are used to dramatize in a single quick stroke the atmosphere of suspicion and jealousy in Laban's household: they make the extravagant claim that the visibly prospering Jacob "has taken everything of our father's," thus leaving them nothing. The anonymous sons would presumably be members of the pursuit party Laban forms to go after the fleeing Jacob.

2. *Jacob saw Laban's face.* The physical concreteness of the image should not be obscured, as many modern translators are wont to do, by rendering this as "manner" or "attitude." Although the Hebrew *panim* does have a variety of extended or figurative meanings, the point is that Jacob looks at his father-in-law's face and sees in it a new and disquieting expression of hostility and suspicion.

3. *and I will be with you.* God's words recall the language of the divine promise to Jacob in the dream-vision at Bethel.

And Jacob sent and called Rachel and Leah out to the field, to his 4
flocks, and he said to them, "I see your father's face, that it is not dis- 5
posed toward me as in time past, but the God of my father has been
with me. And you know that with all my strength I have served your 6
father. But your father has tricked me and has switched my wages ten 7
times over, yet God has not let him do me harm. If thus he said, 'The 8
spotted ones will be your wages,' all the flocks bore spotted ones. And
if he said, 'The brindled ones will be your wages,' all the flocks bore
brindled ones. And God has reclaimed your father's livestock and given 9
it to me. And so, at the time when the flocks were in heat, I raised my 10
eyes and saw in a dream and, look, the rams mounting the flocks were
brindled, spotted, and speckled. And God's messenger said to me in the 11
dream, 'Jacob!' and I said, 'Here I am.' And he said, 'Raise your eyes, 12
pray, and see: all the rams mounting the flocks are spotted, brindled,
and speckled, for I have seen all that Laban has been doing to you.

---

4. *Jacob sent and called Rachel and Leah out to the field*. Jacob proceeds in this
fashion not only because he is busy tending the flocks, as he himself repeatedly reminds us in the dialogue, but also because he needs to confer with his
wives in a safe location beyond earshot of Laban and his sons.

11. *God's messenger said to me in the dream*. According to the source critics,
divine communication to men through dream-vision is a hallmark of the Elo-
hist, whereas the direct narrative report of the Speckled Flock story in the previous chapter makes no mention of either a dream or divine instructions and
is to be attributed to the Yahwist. Whatever the validity of such identifications,
they tend to scant the narrative integrity of the completed text, the ability of
the biblical Arranger—to borrow a term from the criticism of Joyce's *Ulysses*—
to orchestrate his sources. Jacob wants to make it vividly clear to his wives at
this tense juncture of imminent flight that God has been with him and will
continue to be with him. It serves this purpose to explain his spectacular prosperity not as the consequence of his own ingenuity as animal breeder but as
the revelation of an angel of God. It thus makes perfect narrative sense that
he should omit all mention of the elaborate stratagem of the peeled rods in the
troughs.

13 I am the God who appeared to you at Bethel, where you anointed a pillar and made me a vow. Now, rise, leave this land, and return to the

14 land of your birthplace.'" And Rachel and Leah answered and they said
to him, "Do we still have any share in the inheritance of our father's

15 house? Why, we have been counted by him as strangers, for he has sold

16 us, and he has wholly consumed our money. For whatever wealth God
has reclaimed from our father is ours and our children's, and so, what-

17 ever God has said to you, do." And Jacob rose and bore off his children

18 and his wives on the camels. And he drove all his livestock and all his
substance that he had acquired, his property in livestock that he had
acquired in Paddan-Aram, to go to Isaac his father in the land of
Canaan.

---

13. *the God who appeared to you at Bethel.* The Masoretic Text lacks "who
appeared to you at" (which in the Hebrew would be just two words plus a particle), but both major Aramaic Targums, that of Onkelos and Yonatan ben
Uziel, reflect this phrase, as does the Septuagint. Although the Targums are
often predisposed to explanatory paraphrase, in this instance the Masoretic
Hebrew sounds grammatically off, and it seems likely that they were faithfully
representing a phrase that was later lost in transmission. (The Targums, which
translated the Bible into the Aramaic that had become the vernacular of Pales-
tinian Jewry, were completed in the early centuries of the Christian Era—
Onkelos perhaps in the third century and Targum Yonatan at least a century
later.)

14. *any share in the inheritance.* The Hebrew, literally, "share and inheritance,"
is a hendiadys (two words for one concept, like "part and parcel"), with a deno-
tative meaning as translated here and a connotation something like "any part
at all."

15. *for he has sold us, and he has wholly consumed our money.* In a socially decorous marriage, a large part of the bride-price would go to the bride. Laban, who
first appeared in the narrative (chapter 24) eyeing the possible profit to himself in a betrothal transaction, has evidently pocketed all of the fruits of Jacob's
fourteen years of labor. His daughters thus see themselves reduced to chattel
by their father, not married off but rather sold for profit, as though they were
not his flesh and blood.

And Laban had gone to shear his flocks, and Rachel stole the house- 19
hold gods that were her father's. And Jacob deceived Laban the 20
Aramean, in not telling him he was fleeing. And he fled, he and all that 21
was his, and he rose and he crossed the Euphrates, and set his face

---

19. *Laban had gone to shear his flocks.* Rashi reminds us that Laban had earlier
set a precedent of grazing his herds at a distance of three days' journey from
Jacob's herds. In any case, other references to shearing of the flocks in the
Bible indicate it was a very elaborate procedure involving large numbers of
men, and accompanied by feasting, and so would have provided an excellent
cover for Jacob's flight.

   Rachel stole the household gods. The household gods, or *terafim* (the etymology of the term is still in doubt), are small figurines representing the
deities responsible for the well-being and prosperity of the household. The
often-cited parallel with the Roman *penates* seems quite pertinent. There is no
reason to assume that Rachel would have become a strict monotheist through
her marriage, and so it is perfectly understandable that she would want to take
with her in her emigration the icons of these tutelary spirits, or perhaps, sym-
bols of possession.

20. *Jacob deceived Laban.* Rachel makes off with, or steals, the household gods;
Jacob deceives—literally, "steals the heart of Laban" (the heart being the organ
of attentiveness or understanding). This verb, *ganav,* which suggests appropriating someone else's property by deception or stealth, will echo through the
denouement of the story. Jacob, in his response to Laban, will use a second
verb, *gazal,* which suggests taking property by force, "to rob." In heading for
Canaan with his wives, children, and flocks, Jacob is actually taking what is
rightly his (note the emphasis of legitimate possession in verse 18), but he has
good reason to fear that the grasping Laban will renege on their agreement,
and so he feels compelled to flee in stealth, making off not with Laban's property but with his "heart."

   Laban the Aramean. For the first time Laban is given this gentilic identification. The stage is being set for the representation of the encounter between
Jacob and Laban as a negotiation between national entities.

21. *the Euphrates.* The Hebrew says "the River," a term which refers specifically to the Euphrates.

22 toward the high country of Gilead. And it was told to Laban on the third
23 day that Jacob had fled. And he took his kinsmen with him and pursued
him a seven days' journey, and overtook him in the high country of
24 Gilead. And God came to Laban the Aramean in a night-dream and said
to him, "Watch yourself, lest you speak to Jacob either good or evil!"

25 And Laban caught up with Jacob, and Jacob had pitched his tent on the
height, and Laban had pitched with his kinsmen in the high country of
26 Gilead. And Laban said to Jacob, "What have you done, deceiving me,
27 and driving my daughters like captives of the sword? Why did you flee

---

the high country of Gilead. The region in question is east of the Jordan, a little south of Lake Tiberias, and was part of Israelite territory in the First Commonwealth period. It is thus quite plausible as the setting for a border
encounter between Laban the Aramean and Jacob the Hebrew.

23. *pursued him a seven days' journey.* Although it would have taken Jacob,
encumbered with his flocks and family, far longer to cross this distance of
nearly three hundred miles, it might have been feasible for a pursuit party traveling lightly, and so the formulaic seven days actually serves to convey the terrific speed of the chase. Jacob himself will allude to this speed when instead
of the more usual verb for pursuit, he refers to Laban's "racing" after him
(*dalaq,* a term that also means "to burn" and appears to derive from the rapid
movement of fire).

24. *either good or evil.* As in 24:50, the idiom means "lest you speak . . . anything at all."

26. *driving my daughters.* The common translation "carrying off" fudges the
brutality of Laban's language. The verb *nahag* is most often used for the driving of animals and is in fact the same term used in verse 18 to report Jacob's
driving his livestock.
like captives of the sword? The daughters had spoken of their father's treating them like chattel. Laban on his part chooses a simile with ominous military implications, suggesting that Jacob has behaved like a marauding army
that seizes the young women to serve as sexual and domestic slaves. It is surely
not lost on Jacob that Laban is leading a group of armed men ("My hand has
the might to do you harm").

in stealth and deceive me and not tell me? I would have sent you off
with festive songs, with timbrel and lyre. And you did not let me kiss   28
my sons and my daughters. O, you have played the fool! My hand has   29
the might to do you harm, but the god of your father said to me last
night, 'Watch yourself, lest you speak to Jacob either good or evil.' And   30
so, you had to go because you longed so much for your father's house,
but why did you steal my gods?" And Jacob answered and said to   31
Laban, "For I was afraid, for I thought, you would rob me of your
daughters. With whomever you find your gods, that person shall not   32
live. Before our kinsmen, make recognition of what is yours with me,
and take it." But Jacob did not know that Rachel had stolen them. And   33
Laban came into Jacob's tent, and into Leah's tent, and into the tent of

---

27. *deceive me*. At this point, Laban drops the object "heart" from the verb "to
steal" or "to make off with," and says instead "me," either because he is using
the idiom elliptically, or because he wants to say more boldly to Jacob, you
have not merely deceived me ("stolen my heart") but despoiled me ("stolen
me").

    with festive songs, with timbrel and lyre. The extravagance of this fantastic
scene conjured up by a past master of fleecing is self-evident. "Festive songs"
is a hendiadys: the Hebrew is literally "with festivity and with songs."

28. *my sons*. In this case, the reference would have to be to grandsons, despite
the fact that the term is bracketed with "my daughters," which would refer to
Rachel and Leah.

30. *but why did you steal my gods?* Laban once more invokes the crucial verb
ganav at the very end of his speech. Now the object is something that really
has been stolen, though Jacob has no idea this is so. Laban refers to the missing figurines not as *terafim*, a term that may conceivably have a pejorative connotation, but as *'elohai*, "my gods," real deities.

32. *that person shall not live*. Jacob does not imagine that anyone in his household could be guilty of the theft. If he is not unwittingly condemning Rachel
to death, his peremptory words at least foreshadow her premature death in
childbirth.

    make recognition. The thematically fraught verb *haker*, which previously fig-
ured in Jacob's deception of Isaac, will return to haunt Jacob, in precisely the
imperative form in which it occurs here.

the two slavegirls, and he found nothing. And he came out of Leah's
34 tent and went into Rachel's tent. And Rachel had taken the household
gods and put them in the camel cushion and sat on them. And Laban
35 rummaged through the whole tent and found nothing. And she said to
her father, "Let not my lord be incensed that I am unable to rise before
you, for the way of women is upon me." And he searched and he did
36 not find the household gods. And Jacob was incensed and voiced his
grievance to Laban, and Jacob spoke out and said to Laban:

> "What is my crime, what is my guilt,
>   that you should race after me?
37 Though you rummaged through all my things,
>   what have you found of all your household things?
> Set it here before my kin and yours
>   and they shall determine between us two.

---

34. *put them in the camel cushion and sat on them.* The camel cushion may be
a good hiding place, but Rachel's sitting on the *terafim* is also a kind of satiric
glance by the monotheistic writer on the cult of figurines, as necessity compels Rachel to assume this irreverent posture toward them.

35. *for the way of women is upon me.* The impotence of the irate father vis-à-
vis his biologically mature daughter is comically caught in the device she hits
upon, of pleading her period, in order to stay seated on the concealed figurines. Her invention involves an ironic double take because it invokes all
those years of uninterrupted menses before she was at last able to conceive
and bear her only son.

36. *voiced his grievance.* The verb here (there is no object noun in the Hebrew)
is cognate with *riv,* a grievance brought to a court of law. Jacob's speech is manifestly cast as a rhetorically devised plea of defense against a false accusation.
Although previous commentators have noted that his language is "elevated"
(Gerhard von Rad), it has not been observed that Jacob's plea is actually formulated as poetry, following the general conventions of parallelism of biblical
verse.
   What is my crime, what is my guilt . . . ? These cadenced parallel questions
signal the beginning of the formal plea of defense.

These twenty years I have been with you,   38
　　your ewes and your she-goats did not lose their young,
　　　the rams of your flock I have not eaten.
What was torn up by beasts I brought not to you,   39
　　I bore the loss, from my hand you could seek it—
　　　what was stolen by day and stolen by night.
Often—by day the parching heat ate me up   40
　　and frost in the night,
　　　and sleep was a stranger to my eyes.

These twenty years in your household I served you, fourteen years for 41
your two daughters and six years for your flocks, and you switched my

---

39. *What was torn up by beasts . . . I bore the loss.* After stating in the previous verse that he took exemplary care of the flocks, Jacob goes on to declare that he assumed a degree of responsibility above and beyond what the law requires of a shepherd. Both biblical and other ancient Near Eastern codes indicate that a shepherd was not obliged to make good losses caused by beasts of prey and thieves, where no negligence was involved.

　what was stolen by day and stolen by night. Again, the key verb *ganav* is invoked. The grammatical form of the construct state here—*genuvati*—uses an archaic suffix that is a linguistic marker of poetic diction.

40. *Often.* The Hebrew is literally "I was," but, as E. A. Speiser notes, this verb at the beginning of a clause can be used to impart an iterative sense to what follows.

　sleep was a stranger to my eyes. The Hebrew says literally, "sleep wandered from my eyes." It is a general idiom for insomnia.

41. *These twenty years in your household.* When Jacob begins to work out the calculation of how many years he has served Laban in return for what, he switches from verse to prose. This enables him to repeat verbatim the words he had used in his (prose) dialogue with his wives, when he said that Laban had "switched my wages ten times over." Understandably, what he deletes from that earlier speech is the blunt accusation that Laban "tricked me."

42 wages ten times over. Were it not that the God of my father, the God of Abraham and the Terror of Isaac, was with me, you would have sent me off empty-handed. My suffering and the toil of my hands God has

43 seen, and last night He determined in my favor." And Laban answered and said to Jacob, "The daughters are my daughters, and the sons are my sons, and the flocks are my flocks, and all that you see is mine. Yet for my daughters what can I do now, or for their sons whom they bore?

44 And so, come, let us make a pact, you and I, and let it be a witness

45 between you and me." And Jacob took a stone and set it up as a pillar.

46 And Jacob said to his kinsmen, "Gather stones." And they fetched

47 stones and made a mound and they ate there on the mound. And Laban

48 called it Yegar-Sahudutha but Jacob called it Gal-Ed. And Laban said, "This mound is witness between you and me this day." Therefore its

49 name was called Gal-Ed, and Mizpah, for he said, "May the LORD look

---

42. *He determined in my favor.* Jacob uses the same verb of legal vindication that he invoked in his poetic self-defense—"they shall determine between us two."

43. *The daughters are my daughters.* Laban begins his response by refusing to yield an inch in point of legal prerogative. But he concedes that there is nothing he can do about his daughters and all his grandsons—on the face of it, because of their evident attachment to Jacob, and, perhaps, because he fears to use the force he possesses against Jacob after the divine warning in the night-vision.

45. *Jacob took a stone.* Invited to make a pact, Jacob immediately resorts to the language of stones, as after the Bethel epiphany and in his first encounter with Rachel at the well. Thus, in sequence, the stones are associated with religious experience, personal experience, and now politics. Here, there is a doubling in the use of stones: a large stone as a commemorative pillar (and border marker) and a pile of smaller stones as a commemorative mound.

47. *Yegar-Sahadutha . . . Gal-Ed.* The international character of the transaction is nicely caught in Laban the Aramean's use of an Aramaic term while Jacob uses Hebrew. Both names mean "mound of witness."

49. *and Mizpah.* This is an alternate name for the height of Gilead. The meaning is "lookout point," as Laban's next words make etymologically clear.

out between you and me when we are out of each other's sight. Should 50
you abuse my daughters, and should you take wives besides my daughters though no one else is present, see, God is witness between you and
me." And Laban said to Jacob, "Look, this mound, and, look, the pillar 51
that I cast up between you and me, witness be the mound and witness 52
the pillar, that I will not cross over to you past this mound and you will
not cross over to me past this mound, and past this pillar, for harm.
May the god of Abraham and the god of Nahor"—the gods of their 53
fathers—"judge between us." And Jacob swore by the Terror of his
father Isaac. And Jacob offered sacrifice on the height and called to his 54
kinsmen to eat bread, and they ate bread and passed the night on the
height.

51–52. *Look, this mound, and, look, the pillar . . . witness be the mound and witness the pillar*. The studied repetitions and rhetorical flourishes that characterize Laban's speech throughout reflect its function as a performative
speech-act, stipulating the binding terms of the treaty.

I will not cross over to you . . . past this pillar. At this point, the story of bitter familial struggle is also made an etiology for political history. What Laban
is designating here is clearly an international border.

53. *the gods of their fathers*. These words, with the pronoun referent "they,"
could not be part of Laban's dialogue and so must be a gloss, perhaps occasioned by the discomfort of a scribe or editor with the exact grammatical equation between the god of Abraham and the god of Nahor in Laban's oath.

Jacob swore by the Terror of his father Isaac. This denomination of the deity,
which occurs only in this episode, is strange enough to have prompted some
biblical scholars to argue, unconvincingly, that the name has nothing to do with
terror or fear. What is noteworthy is that Jacob resists the universal Semitic
term for God, *'elohim*, and the equation between the gods of Nahor and Abraham. He himself does not presume to go back as far as Abraham, but in the
God of his father Isaac he senses something numinous, awesome, frightening.

54. *offered sacrifice . . . ate bread*. The treaty-vow is solemnly confirmed by a
sacred meal. The term *zevah* refers both to a ceremonial meal of meat and to
sacrifice. In effect, the two are combined: the fat of the animal is burned as an
offering, the meat is consumed by those who offer the sacrifice. As frequently
elsewhere in biblical usage, "bread" is a synecdoche for the whole meal.

CHAPTER 32

¹ And Laban rose early in the morning and kissed his sons and his daughters and blessed them, and Laban went off and returned to ² his place. And Jacob had gone on his way, and messengers of God ³ accosted him. And Jacob said when he saw them, "This is God's camp,"

---

1. The verse numbering reflects the conventional division used in Hebrew Bibles. The King James Version, followed by some modern English Bibles, places the first verse here as a fifty-fifth verse in chapter 31, and then has verses 1–32 corresponding to verses 2–33 in the present version.

2. *messengers of God accosted him*. There is a marked narrative symmetry between Jacob's departure from Canaan, when he had his dream of angels at Bethel, and his return, when again he encounters a company of angels. That symmetry will be unsettled when later in the chapter he finds himself in fateful conflict with a single divine being.

God's camp . . . Mahanaim. The Hebrew for "camp" is *maḥaneh*. Mahanaim is the same word with a dual suffix and thus means twin camps, a signification that will be played out in a second narrative etymology when Jacob divides his family and flocks into two camps. The entire episode is notable for its dense exploitation of what Martin Buber and Franz Rosenzweig called *Leitwortstil,* key-word style. J. P. Fokkelman (1975) has provided particularly helpful commentary on this aspect of our text. The crucial repeated terms are *maḥaneh,* "camp," which is played against *minḥah,* "tribute"; *panim,* "face," which recurs not only as a noun but also as a component of the reiterated preposition "before," a word that can be etymologically broken down in the Hebrew as "to the face of"; and *'avar,* "cross over" (in one instance here, the translation, yielding to the requirements of context, renders this as "pass").

and he called the name of that place Mahanaim. And Jacob sent mes- 4
sengers before him to Esau his brother in the land of Seir, the steppe
of Edom. And he charged them, saying, "Thus shall you say—'To my 5
lord Esau, thus says your servant Jacob: With Laban I have sojourned
and I tarried till now. And I have gotten oxen and donkeys and sheep 6
and male and female slaves, and I send ahead to tell my lord, to find
favor in your eyes.'" And the messengers returned to Jacob, saying, "We 7
came to your brother, to Esau, and he is actually coming to meet you,
and four hundred men are with him." And Jacob was greatly afraid, and 8
he was distressed, and he divided the people that were with him, and
the sheep and the cattle and the camels, into two camps. And he 9

---

4. *Jacob sent messengers before him.* These are of course human messengers,
but, in keeping with a common principle of composition in biblical narrative,
the repetition of the term effects a linkage with the immediately preceding
episode, in which the messengers, *mal'akhim,* are angels.

5. *Thus shall you say.* The syntactic division indicated by the cantillation markings in the Masoretic Text is: "Thus shall you say to my lord Esau." But E. A.
Speiser has convincingly demonstrated that "To my lord Esau, thus says your
servant Jacob," precisely follows the formula for the salutation or heading in
ancient Near Eastern letters and so must be part of the text of the message.
  my lord Esau . . . your servant Jacob. The narrator had referred to Esau as
Jacob's "brother," as will the messengers. An elaborate irony of terms underlies
the entire reunion of the twins: Jacob, destined by prenatal oracle and paternal blessing to be overlord to his brother, who is to be subject (*'eved*) to him,
repeatedly designates himself *'eved* and his brother, lord (*'adon*). The formulas
of deferential address of ancient Hebrew usage are thus made to serve a complex thematic end.

7. *he is actually coming . . . and four hundred men are with him.* There is no verbal response from Esau, who has by now established himself as a potentate in
the trans-Jordanian region of Edom, but the rapid approach with four hundred
men looks ominous, especially since that is a standard number for a regiment
or raiding party, as several military episodes in 1 and 2 Samuel indicate.

8. *two camps.* A law of binary division runs through the whole Jacob story: twin
brothers struggling over a blessing that cannot be halved, two sisters struggling
over a husband's love, flocks divided into unicolored and particolored animals,
Jacob's material blessing now divided into two camps.

thought, "Should Esau come to the one camp and strike it, the remain-
10 ing camp will escape." And Jacob said: "God of my father Abraham and
God of my father Isaac! Lord who has said to me, 'Return to your land
11 and your birthplace, and I will deal well with you.' I am unworthy of all
the kindness that you have steadfastly done for your servant. For with
my staff I crossed this Jordan, and now I have become two camps.
12 O save me from the hand of my brother, from the hand of Esau, for I
13 fear him, lest he come and strike me, mother with sons. And You Yourself said, 'I will surely deal well with you and I will set your seed like
14 the sand of the sea multitudinous beyond all count.'" And he passed
that same night there, and he took from what he had in hand a tribute
15 to Esau his brother: two hundred she-goats and twenty he-goats, two
16 hundred ewes and twenty rams; thirty milch camels with their young,
17 forty cows and ten bulls, twenty she-asses and ten he-asses. And he put
them in the hands of his servants, each herd by itself, and he said to
his servants, "Pass on before me, and put distance between one herd
18 and the next." And he charged the first one, saying, "When Esau my
brother meets you and asks you, saying, 'Whose man are you, and
19 where are you going, and whose are these herds before you?', you shall
say, 'They are your servant Jacob's, a tribute sent to my lord Esau, and,
20 look, he is actually behind us.'" And he charged the second one as
well, and also the third, indeed, all those who went after the herds,
saying, "In this fashion you shall speak to Esau when you find him.

---

10. *and I will deal well with you.* The first part of the sentence is in fact a direct
quotation of God's words to Jacob in 31:3 deleting only "of your fathers." But
for God's general reassurance, "I will be with you," Jacob, in keeping with his
stance as bargainer (who at Bethel stipulated that God must provide him food
and clothing) substitutes a verb that suggests material bounty.

14. *a tribute.* The Hebrew *minḥah* also means "gift" (and, in cultic contexts,
"sacrifice"), but it has the technical sense of a tribute paid by a subject people
to its overlord, and everything about the narrative circumstances of this "gift"
indicates it is conceived as the payment of a tribute. Note, for instance, the
constellation of political terms in verse 19: "They are *your servant* Jacob's, *a
tribute sent to my lord* Esau."

And you shall say, 'Look, your servant Jacob is actually behind us.'" For 21
he thought, "Let me placate him with the tribute that goes before me,
and after I shall look on his face, perhaps he will show me a kindly
face." And the tribute passed on before him, and he spent that night in 22
the camp.

And he rose on that night and took his two wives and his two slavegirls 23
and his eleven boys and he crossed over the Jabbok ford. And he took 24
them and brought them across the stream, and he brought across all
that he had. And Jacob was left alone, and a man wrestled with him 25
until the break of dawn. And he saw that he had not won out against 26
him and he touched his hip-socket and Jacob's hip-socket was

---

21. *Let me placate him with the tribute that goes before me, and after I shall look
on his face, perhaps he will show me a kindly face.* The Hebrew actually has
"face" four times in this brief speech. "Placate" is literally "cover over his face"
(presumably, angry face); and "before me" can be broken down as "to my face."
To "look on his face" is a locution generally used for entering the presence of
royalty; and "show me a kind face," an idiom that denotes forgiveness, is literally "lift up my face" (presumably, my "fallen" or dejected face).

23. *the Jabbok ford.* The word for "ford," *ma'avar,* is a noun derived from the
reiterated verb *'avar,* "to cross over." The Jabbok is a tributary of the Jordan
running from east to west. Jacob has been traveling south from the high country of Gilead, Esau is heading north from Edom to meet him.

25. *a man.* The initial identification of the anonymous adversary is from Jacob's
point of view, and so all he knows of him is what he sees, that he is a "man."
    wrestled with him. The image of wrestling has been implicit throughout the
Jacob story: in his grabbing Esau's heel as he emerges from the womb, in his
striving with Esau for birthright and blessing, in his rolling away the huge
stone from the mouth of the well, and in his multiple contendings with Laban.
Now, in this culminating moment of his life story, the characterizing image of
wrestling is made explicit and literal.

26. *he touched his hip-socket.* The inclination of modern translations to render
the verb here as "struck" is unwarranted, being influenced either by the context or by the cognate noun *nega',* which means "plague" or "affliction." But the
verb *naga'* in the *qal* conjugation always means "to touch," even "to barely

27   wrenched as he wrestled with him.And he said, "Let me go, for dawn
      is breaking." And he said, "I will not let you go unless you bless me."
28,29 And he said to him, "What is your name?" And he said, "Jacob." And he
      said, "Not Jacob shall your name hence be said, but Israel, for you have

---

touch," and only in the *pi'el* conjugation can it mean "to afflict." The adversary
maims Jacob with a magic touch, or, if one prefers, by skillful pressure on a
pressure point.

27. *Let me go, for dawn is breaking.* The folkloric character of this haunting
episode becomes especially clear at this point. The notion of a night spirit that
loses its power or is not permitted to go about in daylight is common to many
folk traditions, as is the troll or guardian figure who blocks access to a ford or
bridge. This temporal limitation of activity suggests that the "man" is certainly
not God Himself and probably not an angel in the ordinary sense. It has led
Claus Westermann to conclude that the nameless wrestler must be thought of
as some sort of demon. Nahum Sarna, following the Midrash, flatly identifies
the wrestler as the tutelary spirit (*sar*) of Esau. But the real point, as Jacob's
adversary himself suggests when he refuses to reveal his name, is that he
resists identification. Appearing to Jacob in the dark of the night, before the
morning when Esau will be reconciled with Jacob, he is the embodiment of
portentous antagonism in Jacob's dark night of the soul. He is obviously in
some sense a doubling of Esau as adversary, but he is also a doubling of all with
whom Jacob has had to contend, and he may equally well be an externalization of all that Jacob has to wrestle with within himself. A powerful physical
metaphor is intimated by the story of wrestling: Jacob, whose name can be
construed as "he who acts crookedly," is bent, permanently lamed, by his
nameless adversary in order to be made straight before his reunion with Esau.

28. *What is your name?* Whatever the realm from which he comes, the stranger
exercises no divine privilege of omniscience and must ask Jacob to tell him his
name.

29. *Not Jacob . . . but Israel.* Abraham's change of name was a mere rhetorical
flourish compared to this one, for of all the patriarchs Jacob is the one whose
life is entangled in moral ambiguities. Rashi beautifully catches the resonance
of the name change: "It will no longer be said that the blessings came to you
through deviousness [*'oqbah,* a word suggested by the radical of "crookedness"
in the name Jacob] but instead through lordliness [*serarah,* a root that can be

striven with God and men, and won out." And Jacob asked and said,   30
"Tell your name, pray." And he said, "Why should you ask my name?"
and there he blessed him. And Jacob called the name of the place   31
Peniel, meaning, "I have seen God face to face and I came out alive."

---

extracted from the name Israel] and openness." It is nevertheless noteworthy—and to my knowledge has not been noted—that the pronouncement
about the new name is not completely fulfilled. Whereas Abraham is invariably called "Abraham" once the name is changed from "Abram," the narrative
continues to refer to this patriarch in most instances as "Jacob." Thus, "Israel"
does not really replace his name but becomes a *synonym* for it—a practice
reflected in the parallelism of biblical poetry, where "Jacob" is always used in
the first half of the line and "Israel," the poetic variation, in the second half.

    striven with God. The Hebrew term *'elohim* is a high concentration point of
lexical ambiguity that serves the enigmatic character of the story very well. It
is *not* the term that means "divine messenger" but it can refer to divine beings,
whether or not it is prefixed by "sons of" (as in Genesis 6). It can also mean
simply "God," and in some contexts—could this be one?—it means "gods." In
a few cases, it also designates something like "princes" or "judges," but that is
precluded here by its being antithetically paired with "men." It is not clear
whether the anonymous adversary is referring to himself when he says *'elohim*
or to more-than-human agents encountered by Jacob throughout his career. In
any case, he etymologizes the name *Yisra'el,* Israel, as "he strives with God." In
fact, names with the *'el* ending generally make God the subject, not the object,
of the verb in the name. This particular verb, *sarah,* is a rare one, and there is
some question about its meaning, though an educated guess about the original sense of the name would be: "God will rule," or perhaps, "God will prevail."

    and won out. In almost all of his dealings, Jacob the bargainer, trader,
wrestler, and heel-grabber *has* managed to win out. His winning out against
the mysterious stranger consists in having fought to a kind of tie: the adversary
has been unable to best him, and though he has hurt Jacob, he cannot break
loose from Jacob's grip.

31. *Peniel.* The name builds on "face to face" (*panim 'el panim*), the "face" component being quite transparent in the Hebrew.

    God. Again the term is *'elohim,* and there is no way of knowing whether it
is singular or plural.

    I came out alive. The Hebrew says literally: "My life [or, life-breath] was
saved."

32 And the sun rose upon him as he passed Penuel and he was limping on
33 his hip. Therefore the children of Israel do not eat the sinew of the
thigh which is by the hip-socket to this day, for he had touched Jacob's
hip-socket at the sinew of the thigh.

---

32. *And the sun rose upon him.* There is another antithetical symmetry with the
early part of the Jacob story, which has been nicely observed by Nahum Sarna:
"Jacob's ignominious flight from home was appropriately marked by the setting
of the sun; fittingly, the radiance of the sun greets the patriarch as he crosses
back into his native land."

he was limping on his hip. The encounter with the unfathomable Other
leaves a lasting mark on Jacob. This physical note resonates with the larger
sense of a man's life powerfully recorded in his story: experience exacts many
prices, and he bears his inward scars as he lives onward—his memory of fleeing alone across the Jordan, his fear of the brother he has wronged, and, before
long, his grief for the beloved wife he loses, and then, for the beloved son he
thinks he has lost.

33. *Therefore the children of Israel do not eat the sinew.* This concluding etiological notice is more than a mechanical reflex. For the first time, after the
naming-story, the Hebrews are referred to as "the children of Israel," and this
dietary prohibition observed by the audience of the story "to this day" marks a
direct identification with, or reverence for, the eponymous ancestor who wrestled through the night with a man who was no man.

CHAPTER 33

And Jacob raised his eyes and saw and, look, Esau was coming, and   1
with him were four hundred men. And he divided the children
between Leah and Rachel, and between the two slavegirls. And he   2
placed the slavegirls and their children first, and Leah and her children
after them, and Rachel and Joseph last. And he passed before them   3
and bowed to the ground seven times until he drew near his brother.

---

1. *he divided the children between Leah and Rachel*. Again, the principle of
binary division running through the whole story comes into play. Here, there
is a binary split between the two wives on one side and the two concubines on
the other. The former of these categories is itself split between Rachel and
Leah. Although the division at this point, unlike the previous day's division
into two camps, appears to be for purposes of display, not defense, it looks as
though Jacob retains a residual fear of assault, and so he puts the concubines
and their children first, then Leah and her children, and Rachel and Joseph at
the very rear.

2. *Leah and her children after them*. The Masoretic Text reads "last" instead of
"after them" (in the Hebrew merely the difference of a suffix), but the context
requires "after them," a reading that is supported by at least one ancient
version.

3. *bowed to the ground seven times until he drew near*. This practice of bowing
seven times as one approaches a monarch from a distance was common court
ritual, as parallels in the Amarna letters and the Ugaritic documents (both
from the middle of the second millennium B.C.E.) indicate.

4 And Esau ran to meet him and embraced him and fell upon his neck
5 and kissed him, and they wept. And he raised his eyes and saw the
women and the children and he said, "Who are these with you?" And
6 he said, "The children with whom God has favored your servant." And
the slavegirls drew near, they and their children, and they bowed down.
7 And Leah, too, and her children drew near, and they bowed down, and
8 then Joseph and Rachel drew near and bowed down. And he said,
"What do you mean by all this camp I have met?" And he said, "To find
9 favor in the eyes of my lord." And Esau said, "I have much, my brother.
10 Keep what you have." And Jacob said, "O, no, pray, if I have found favor

---

4. *Esau ran to meet him and embraced him and fell upon his neck.* This is, of
course, the big surprise in the story of the twins: instead of lethal grappling,
Esau embraces Jacob in fraternal affection. The Masoretic Text has both
brothers weeping, the verb showing a plural inflection, but some scholars have
conjectured that the plural *waw* at the end of the verb is a scribal error, dupli-
cated from the first letter of the next word in the text, and that Esau alone
weeps, Jacob remaining impassive.

5. *The children.* Jacob's response makes no mention of the women. It would
have been self-evident that the women were the mothers of the children and
hence his wives, and one senses that he feels impelled to answer his brother
as tersely as possible, not spelling out what can be clearly inferred.

8. *What do you mean by all this camp.* The Hebrew is literally, "Who to you is
all this camp," but both "who to you" (*mi lekha*) and "what to you" (*mah lekha*)
have the idiomatic sense of, what do you mean, or want. "Camp" in this context means something like "retinue" or "procession of people," but the continuity with the twin camps of the preceding episode is obviously important for
the writer.

9. *I have much, my brother.* Esau in fact has become a kind of prince, despite
his loss of birthright and blessing, and he can speak to Jacob in princely generosity. It is striking that he addresses Jacob as "my brother"—the familial term
with the first-person possessive suffix is generally a form of *affectionate* address
in biblical Hebrew—while Jacob continues to call him "my lord," never swerv-
ing from the deferential terms of court etiquette.

in your eyes, take this tribute from my hand, for have I not seen your face as one might see God's face, and you received me in kindness? Pray, take my blessing that has been brought you, for God has favored 11 me and I have everything." And he pressed him, and he took it. And he 12 said, "Let us journey onward and go, and let me go alongside you." And 13 he said, "My lord knows that the children are tender, and the nursing sheep and cattle are my burden, and if they are whipped onward a single day, all the flocks will die. Pray, let my lord pass on before his ser- 14

---

10. *for have I not seen your face as one might see God's face, and you received me in kindness?* This most extravagant turn in the rhetoric of deferential address pointedly carries us back to Jacob's reflection on his nocturnal wrestling with the nameless stranger: "for I have seen God face to face and I came out alive." "And you received me in kindness" (just one word in the Hebrew) is significantly substituted for "I came out alive," the very thing Jacob feared he might not do when he met his brother.

11. *take my blessing.* The word for "blessing," *berakhah,* obviously has the meaning in context of "my gift," or, as Rashi interestingly proposes, invoking as an Old French equivalent, *mon salud,* my gift of greeting. But the term chosen brilliantly echoes a phrase Jacob could not have actually heard, which Esau pronounced to their father two decades earlier: "he's taken my blessing" (27:36). In offering the tribute, Jacob is making restitution for his primal theft, unwittingly using language that confirms the act of restitution.

I have everything. Jacob of course means "I have everything I need." But there is a nice discrepancy between his words and the parallel ones of his brother that is obscured by all English translators (with the exception of Everett Fox), who use some term like "enough" in both instances. Esau says he has plenty; Jacob says he has everything—on the surface, simply declaring that he doesn't need the flocks he is offering as a gift, but implicitly "outbidding" his brother, obliquely referring to the comprehensiveness of the blessing he received from their father.

13. *are my burden.* The Hebrew says literally, "are upon me."

vant, and I, let me drive along at my own easy pace, at the heels of the livestock before me and at the heels of the children, till I come to my
15 lord in Seir." And Esau said, "Pray, let me set aside for you some of the people who are with me." And he said, "Why should I find such favor
16 in the eyes of my lord?" And Esau returned that day on his way to Seir,
17 while Jacob journeyed on to Succoth. And he built himself a house, and for his cattle he made sheds—therefore is the name of the place called Succoth.

18 And Jacob came in peace to the town of Shechem, which is in the land of Canaan, when he came from Paddan-Aram, and he camped before

---

14. *at the heels*. Literally, "at the foot."

till I come to my lord in Seir. This is a "diplomatic" offer, for in fact Jacob will head back northward to Succoth, in the opposite direction from Seir.

15. *Why should I find such favor in the eyes of my lord?* In this protestation of unworthiness, Jacob preserves the perfect decorum of deferential address to the very end of his dialogue with his brother. Clearly, he is declining the offer of Esau's retainers because he still doesn't trust Esau and intends to put a large distance between himself and Esau or any of Esau's men. One should note that the very last word (one word in the Hebrew) spoken by Jacob to Esau that is reported in the story is "my lord."

16. *Succoth*. The Hebrew *sukkot* means "sheds."

18. *came in peace*. The adjective *shalem* elsewhere means "whole," and this has led many interpreters to understand it here as "safe and sound." A tradition going back to the Septuagint, and sustained by Claus Westermann among modern commentators, construes this word as the name of a town, Salem, understood to be a synonym for Shechem. (The claim has been made that a *tell* about two and a half miles from the site of Shechem is the biblical Salem.) But the Salem where Abraham meets Melchisedek is at an entirely different location, and if that were also a designation for Shechem, one would expect here at the very least the explanatory gloss, "Salem, that is, the town of Shechem" (*Shalem, hi' 'ir Shekhem*). Because these three verses are an introduction to the story of the rape of Dinah, where in fact Hamor and Shechem say of the sons of Jacob, "these men come in peace (*sheleimim*) to us," it is more likely that "came in peace" is the sense here. Abraham ibn Ezra argues for this meaning, similarly noting the link between the two passages.

the town. And he bought the parcel of land where he had pitched his 19
tent from the sons of Hamor, father of Shechem, for a hundred kesitahs. And he set up an altar there and called it El-Elohei-Israel.   20

---

when he came from Paddan-Aram. Now that Jacob has at last crossed the
Jordan (Succoth is in trans-Jordan) and has taken up residence outside a
Canaanite town, the long trajectory of his journey home is completed.

19. *a hundred kesitahs.* These are either measures of weight for gold and silver,
or units for the barter of livestock, or a term derived from the latter which has
been transferred to the former. The purchase of real estate, as with Abraham
at Hebron, signals making a claim to permanent residence.

20. *El-Elohei-Israel.* The name means "El/God, God of Israel." Claus Westermann makes the interesting argument that Jacob marks his taking up residence in Canaan by subsuming the Canaanite sky god in his monotheistic
cult: "El, the creator God, the supreme God in the Canaanite pantheon, now
becomes the God of the people of Israel."

CHAPTER 34

1 And Dinah, Leah's daughter, whom she had borne to Jacob, went
2 out to go seeing among the daughters of the land. And Shechem
the son of Hamor the Hivite, prince of the land, saw her and took

---

1. *to go seeing among the daughters of the land.* The infinitive in the Hebrew is
literally "to see," followed not by a direct object, as one might expect, but by a
partitive (the particle b^e), which suggests "among" or "some of." Although the
sense of the verb in context may be something like "to make the acquaintance
of" or "travel around among," the decision of several modern translations to
render it as "to visit" is misconceived. Not only does that term convey anachronistic notions of calling cards and tea, but it obliterates an important repetition of terms. This is one of those episodes in which the biblical practice of
using the same word over and over with different subjects and objects and a
high tension of semantic difference is especially crucial. Two such terms are
introduced in the first sentence of the story: "to see" and "daughter." Dinah,
Jacob's daughter, goes out among the daughters of the land, an identity of
terms that might suggest a symmetry of position, but the fact that she is an
immigrant's daughter, not a daughter of the land, makes her a ready target for
rape. (In the Hebrew, moreover, "sons" and "daughters," *banim* and *banot,* are
differently inflected versions of the same word, so Dinah's filial relation to
Jacob is immediately played against Shechem's filial relation to Hamor, and
that in turn will be pointedly juxtaposed with the relation between Jacob and
his sons.) Shechem's lustful "seeing" of Dinah is immediately superimposed on
her "seeing" the daughters of the land.

2. *saw . . . took . . . lay with . . . abused.* As elsewhere in Genesis, the chain of
uninterrupted verbs conveys the precipitousness of the action. "Took" will
become another thematically loaded reiterated term. "Lay with" is more brutal
in the Hebrew because instead of being followed by the preposition "with" (as,
for example, in Rachel's words to Leah in 30:15), it is followed by a direct

her and lay with her and abused her. And his very self clung to Dinah 3
daughter of Jacob, and he loved the young woman, and he spoke to the
young woman's heart. And Shechem said to Hamor his father, saying, 4
"Take me this girl as wife." And Jacob had heard that he had defiled 5
Dinah his daughter, and his sons were with his livestock in the field,
and Jacob held his peace till they came. And Hamor, Shechem's father, 6
came out to Jacob to speak with him. And Jacob's sons had come in 7
from the field when they heard, and the men were pained and they
were very incensed, for he had done a scurrilous thing in Israel by lying
with Jacob's daughter, such as ought not be done. And Hamor spoke 8

---

object—if the Masoretic vocalization is authentic—and in this form may
denote rape.

3. *his very self clung*. The Hebrew *nefesh* (life-breath) is used here as an intensifying synonym of the personal pronoun. ("His very self" in verse 8 represents
the same Hebrew usage.) The psychology of this rapist is precisely the opposite of Amnon's in 2 Samuel 13, who, after having consummated his lust for his
sister by raping her, despises her. Here, the fulfillment of the impulse of unre-
strained desire is followed by love, which complicates the moral balance of the
story.

4. *Take me this girl*. "Take," which indicated violent action in the narrator's
report of the rape, now recurs in a decorous social sense—the action initiated
by the father of the groom in arranging a proper marriage for his son. In verse
17, Jacob's sons will threaten to "take" Dinah away if the townsmen refuse to
be circumcised, and in the report of the massacre, they take first their swords
and then the booty. Shechem refers to Dinah as *yaldah*, "girl" or "child," a
term that equally suggests her vulnerability and the tenderness he now feels
for her.

7. *a scurrilous thing in Israel*. This use of this idiom here is a kind of pun. "A
scurrilous thing in Israel" (*nevalah beYisra'el*) is in later tribal history any
shocking act that the collective "Israel" deems reprehensible (most often a sexual act). But at this narrative juncture, "Israel" is only the other name of the
father of these twelve children, and so the phrase also means "a scurrilous
thing against Israel."
    *for he had done a scurrilous thing in Israel by lying with Jacob's daughter, such
as ought not be done.* This entire clause is a rare instance in biblical narrative

with them, saying, "Shechem my son, his very self longs for your daugh-
9 ter. Pray, give her to him as wife, and ally with us by marriage—your
daughters you will give to us and our daughters, take for yourselves,
10 and among us you will settle, and the land is before you: settle and go
11 about it and take holdings in it." And Shechem said to her father and
to her brothers, "Let me find favor in your eyes, and whatever you say
to me, I will give. Name me however much bride-price and clan-gift, I
12 will give what you say to me, and give me the young woman as wife."

---

of free indirect discourse, or narrated monologue. That is, the narrator conveys
the tenor of Jacob's sons' anger by reporting in the third person the kind of language they would have spoken silently, or to each other. It is a technical means
for strongly imprinting the rage of Jacob's sons in the presence of their father
who has kept silent and, even now, gives no voice to his feelings about the violation of his daughter.

10. *go about it*. The Hebrew verb *saḥar* has the basic meaning of "to go around
in a circle" and the extended meaning of "to trade." But at this early point of
tribal history, Jacob and his sons are seminomadic herdsmen, not at all merchants, so the commercial denotation of the term seems unlikely in context.

11. *And Shechem said . . . ". . . whatever you say to me, I will give."* The father
had begun the negotiations by asking for Dinah as wife for his son and then
immediately opened up the larger issue of general marriage-alliances with
Jacob's clan and the acquisition of settlement rights by the newcomers.
Shechem now enters the discussion to speak more personally of the marriage
and the bride-price. (According to biblical law, a man who raped an unbetrothed girl had to pay a high fine to her father and was obliged to marry her.)
After the two instances of "taking" earlier in the story, he insists here on "giving": he will give whatever the brothers stipulate in the expectation that they
will give him Dinah as wife.

12. *give me the young woman*. Addressing the brothers, Shechem does not refer
to Dinah now as *yaldah,* "girl," but as *na'arah,* the proper term for a nubile
young woman.

And the sons of Jacob answered Shechem and Hamor his father deceit- 13
fully, and they spoke as they did because he had defiled Dinah their sister, and they said to them, "We cannot do this thing, to give our sister 14
to a man who has a foreskin, as that is a disgrace for us. Only in this 15
way may we agree to you—if you will be like us, every male to be circumcised. Then we can give our daughters to you and your daughters 16
we can take for ourselves, and we can settle among you and become
one folk. But if you will not listen to us, to be circumcised, we will take 17
our daughter and go." And their words seemed good in the eyes of 18
Hamor and in the eyes of Shechem son of Hamor.

And the lad lost no time in doing the thing, for he wanted Jacob's 19
daughter, and he was most highly regarded of all his father's house. And 20
Hamor, with Shechem his son, came to the gate of their town, and they
spoke to their townsmen, saying, "These men come in peace to us. Let 21
them settle in the land and go about it, for the land, look, is ample
before them. Their daughters we shall take us as wives and our daughters we shall give to them. Only in this way will the men agree to us, to 22

---

13. *deceitfully*. This is the same term, *mirmah*, that was first attached to Jacob's
action in stealing the blessing, then used by Jacob to upbraid Laban after the
switching of the brides.

they spoke as they did because he had defiled Dinah their sister. "As they did
because" is merely a syntactically ambiguous "that" in the Hebrew—quite possibly a means for introducing another small piece of free indirect discourse.

14. *We cannot do this thing*. They begin as though their response were a flat
refusal. Then they ignore the offer of generous payment and instead stipulate
circumcision—to be sure, a physical sign of their collective identity, but also
the infliction of pain on what is in this case the offending organ.

16. *become one folk*. This ultimate horizon of ethnic unification was perhaps
implied but certainly not spelled out in Hamor's speech.

19. *the lad*. There was no previous indication of Shekhem's age. The term *na'ar*
is the masculine counterpart of the term he used for Dinah in verse 12 and
suggests that he, too, is probably an adolescent.

settle with us to be one folk, if every male of us be circumcised as they
23 are circumcised. Their possessions in livestock and all their cattle, will
they not be ours, if only we agree to them and they settle among us?"
24 And all who sallied forth from the gate of his town listened to Hamor,
and to Shechem his son, and every male was circumcised, all who sallied forth from the gate of his town.

25 And it happened on the third day, while they were hurting, that Jacob's
two sons, Simeon and Levi, Dinah's brothers, took each his sword, and
26 came upon the city unopposed, and they killed every male. And Hamor
and Shechem his son they killed by the edge of the sword, and they
27 took Dinah from the house of Shechem and went out. Jacob's sons

---

23. *Their possessions in livestock and all their cattle.* Although, in keeping with
the biblical convention of near verbatim repetition, Hamor's speech repeats
the language used by the sons of Jacob, there had been no mention before of
the Hivites becoming masters of the newcomers' livestock. This may reflect a
tactic of persuasion on the part of Hamor; it may equally reflect the Hivites'
cupidity.

24. *all who sallied forth.* In Abraham's negotiations with the Hittites in chapter
23, the town elders or members of the city council are referred to as "all the
assembled [or, those who come in] in the gate of [the] town." Here they are
designated as "all who go out from the gate." There are good grounds to suppose that the latter idiom has a *military* connotation: troops came out of the
gates of walled cities to attack besiegers or to set out on campaigns, and "to go
out and come in" is an idiom that means "to maneuver in battle." The reference to the Hivites as fighting men makes sense in context because they are
about to render themselves temporarily helpless against attack through the
mass circumcision.

26. *by the edge of the sword.* The Hebrew idiom is literally "the mouth of the
sword"—hence the sword is said to "consume" or "eat" in biblical language.
    and they took Dinah from the house of Shechem. Meir Sternberg (1985), who
provides illuminating commentary on the interplay of opposing moral claims
in this story, shrewdly notes that this is a shocking revelation just before the
end of the story: we might have imagined that Shechem was petitioning in
good faith for Dinah's hand; now it emerges that he has been holding her captive in his house after having raped her.

came upon the slain and looted the town, for they had defiled their sister. Their sheep and their cattle and their donkeys, what was in the 28
town and in the field, they took, and all their wealth, and all their young 29
ones and their wives they took captive, and they looted everything in
their houses. And Jacob said to Simeon and Levi, "You have stirred up 30
trouble for me, making me stink among the land's inhabitants, among
Canaanite and Perizzite, when I am a handful of men. If they gather
against me and strike me, I shall be destroyed, I and my household."
And they said, "Like a whore should our sister be treated?" 31

---

27. *for they had defiled their sister.* This angry phrase becomes a kind of refrain
in the story. Again, it sounds like the free indirect discourse of Simeon and
Levi, offered as a justification for the massacre they have perpetrated. Precisely in this regard, the element of exaggeration in these words should be
noted: only one man defiled Dinah, but here a plural is used, as though all the
males of the town could in fact be held accountable for the rape.

30. *stirred up trouble.* The root meaning of the verb is "to muddy."

31. *Like a whore should our sister be treated?* The very last words of the story are
still another expression—and the crudest one—of the brothers' anger and their
commitment to exact the most extravagant price in vindication of what they
consider the family's honor. (The Hebrew might also be rendered as "shall he
treat our sister," referring to Shechem, but the third-person singular does
sometimes function in place of a passive.) It is surely significant that Jacob,
who earlier "kept his peace" and was notable for his failure of response, has
nothing to say, or is reported saying nothing, to these last angry words of his
sons. (Only on his deathbed will he answer them.) This moment becomes the
turning point in the story of Jacob. In the next chapter, he will follow God's
injunction to return to Bethel and reconfirm the covenant, but henceforth he
will lose much of his paternal power and will be seen repeatedly at the mercy
of his sons, more the master of self-dramatizing sorrow than of his own family. This same pattern will be invoked in the David story: the father who fails
to take action after the rape of his daughter and then becomes victim of the
fratricidal and rebellious impulses of his sons.

CHAPTER 35

1   $\mathbf{A}$nd God said to Jacob, "Rise, go up to Bethel and dwell there and
make an altar there to the God Who appeared to you when you
2   fled from Esau your brother." And Jacob said to his household and
to all who were with him, "Put away the alien gods that are in your

---

AFTER Jacob's disastrous inaction in response to his daughter's rape in the face
of his vengeful sons, the narrative unit demarcated by this chapter is a collection of miscellaneous notices about Jacob and his household: the consecration
of the altar at Bethel; the death of Rebekah's nurse; a reiteration of Jacob's
name change coupled with a repetition of the covenantal promise delivered to
his father and grandfather; Rachel's death in childbirth; Reuben's cohabitation
with his father's concubine; the death of Isaac. This miscellaneous overview of
Jacob's later career—just before his sons entirely preempt the narrative foreground—bears the earmarks of a literary source different from that of the
immediately preceding material. Nevertheless, thematic reverberations from
the pivotal catastrophe at Shechem sound through it.

1. *Who appeared to you when you fled from Esau your brother*. This clause,
which takes us back to the dream-vision revelation and promise vouchsafed
the young Jacob in chapter 28, signals this injunction to build an altar as a ritual completion of that early promise. (See the comment on verse 3.)

2. *the alien gods*. Although many interpreters associate these icons or figurines
with the booty taken from Shechem, Rachel's attachment to her father's
household gods suggests that others in this large retinue of emigrating relatives
and slaves may have brought cultic figurines with them from Mesopotamia.

midst and cleanse yourselves and change your garments. And let us rise 3
and go up to Bethel, and I shall make an altar there to the God Who
answered me on the day of my distress and was with me on the way
that I went." And they gave Jacob all the alien gods that were in their 4
hands and the rings that were in their ears, and Jacob buried them
under the terebinth that is by Shechem. And they journeyed onward, 5
and the terror of God was upon the towns around them, and they did
not pursue the sons of Jacob. And Jacob came to Luz in the land of 6
Canaan, that is, Bethel, he and all the people who were with him. And 7
he built there an altar and he called the place El-Bethel, for there God
was revealed to him when he fled from his brother.

And Deborah, Rebekah's nurse, died, and she was buried below Bethel 8
under the oak, and its name was called Allon-Bacuth.

---

cleanse yourselves. Nahum Sarna aptly notes, "chapter 34 is dominated by
the theme of defilement; this chapter opens with the subject of purification."

3. *to the God Who answered me on the day of my distress and was with me.* When
Jacob approximately echoes God's words to him in verse 1, he replaces God's
revelation with God's answering him in his trouble and being with him, thus
confirming that God has fully responded to the terms he stipulated in 28:20,
"If the LORD God be with me and guard me on this way that I am going."

4. *the rings . . . in their ears.* As archeology has abundantly discovered, earrings
were often fashioned as figurines of gods and goddesses.
  buried. The verb *taman* is generally used for placing treasure in a hidden or
safe place, and is quite distinct from the term for burial that appears in verses
8, 19, and 29, which is a verb reserved for burying bodies.

5. *the terror of God.* Perhaps, in the view of this writer, which is more insistently theological than that of the immediately preceding narrative, the phrase
means literally that God casts fear on the Canaanites in order to protect Jacob
and his clan. But the phrase is deliberately ambiguous: it could also be construed as meaning "an awesome terror," with *'elohim* serving as an intensifier
rather than referring to divinity. In that case, the shambles to which Simeon
and Levi reduced Shechem might be sufficient reason for the terror.

8. *Allon-Bacuth.* The name means "oak of weeping." Beyond the narrative etiology of a place-name, there is not enough evidence to explain what this lonely
obituary notice is doing here.

9   And God appeared to Jacob again when he came from Paddan-Aram,
10 and He blessed him, and God said to him, "Your name Jacob—no
longer shall your name be called Jacob, but Israel shall be your name."
11 And He called his name Israel. And God said to him,

"I am El Shaddai.
Be fruitful and multiply.
A nation, an assembly of nations shall stem from you,
and kings shall come forth from your loins.

12 And the land that I gave to Abraham and to Isaac, to you I will give it,
13 and to your seed after you I will give the land." And God ascended from
14 him in the place where He had spoken with him. And Jacob set up a
pillar in the place where He had spoken with him, a pillar of stone, and

---

9. *And God appeared to Jacob again when he came from Paddan-Aram.* The
adverb "again," as Rashi notes, alludes to God's appearance to Jacob at this
same place, Bethel, when he fled to Paddan-Aram. This second version of the
conferring of the name of Israel on Jacob is thus set in the perspective of a
large overview of his career of flight and return, with both his eastward and
westward trajectory marked by divine revelation and promise at the same spot.
The first story of Jacob's name change is folkloric and mysterious, and the new
name is given him as a token of his past victories in his sundry struggles with
human and divine creatures. Here, the report of the name change is distinctly
theological, God's words invoking both the first creation ("be fruitful and multiply") and His promise to Abraham ("kings shall come forth from your loins").
In this instance, moreover, the new name is a sign of Jacob's glorious future
rather than of the triumphs he has already achieved, and the crucial element
of struggle is not intimated. As elsewhere in biblical narrative, the sequencing
of different versions of the same event proposes different, perhaps complementary views of the same elusive subject—here, the central and enigmatic
fact of the origins of the theophoric name of the Hebrew nation.

14. *And Jacob set up a pillar.* The cultic or commemorative pillar, *matsevah*, figures equally in the first episode at Bethel, in chapter 28. There, too, Jacob consecrates the pillar by pouring oil over it, but here, in keeping with the more
pervasively ritualistic character of the story, he also offers a libation, and he
builds an altar before setting up the pillar.

he offered libation upon it and poured oil on it. And Jacob called the 15
name of the place where God had spoken with him Bethel.

And they journeyed onward from Bethel, and when they were still some 16
distance from Ephrath, Rachel gave birth, and she labored hard in the
birth. And it happened, when she was laboring hardest in the birth, that 17
the midwife said to her, "Fear not, for this one, too, is a son for you."
And it happened, as her life ran out, for she was dying, that she called 18
his name Ben-Oni, but his father called him Benjamin. And Rachel 19

---

in the place where He had spoken with him. This phrase occurs three times
in close sequence. The underlining of "place" recalls the emphasis on that key
term in the earlier Bethel episode, where an anonymous "place" was transformed into a "house of God." In the present instance, "place" is strongly
linked through reiteration with the fact of God's having spoken to Jacob:
before the place is consecrated by human ritual acts, it is consecrated by
divine speech.

16. *some distance.* The Hebrew, *kivrat ha'arets,* occurs only three times in the
Bible, and there has been debate over what precisely it indicates. Abraham ibn
Ezra, with his extraordinary philological prescience, suggested that the initial
ki was the prefix of comparison (*kaf hadimyon*) and that the noun *barat* was
"the royal measure of distance." In fact, modern Semitic philologists have discovered an Akkadian cognate, *beru,* which is the ancient mile, the equivalent
of about four and a half English miles.

17. *for this one, too, is a son for you.* Rachel, in her naming-speech for Joseph,
had prayed for a second son, just as in her earlier imperious demand to her
husband, she had asked him to give her sons, not a son. The fulfillment of her
uncompromising wish entails her death.

18. *Ben-Oni.* The name can be construed to mean either "son of my vigor" or,
on somewhat more tenuous philological grounds, "son of my sorrow." Given
the freedom with which biblical characters play with names and their meanings, there is no reason to exclude the possibility that Rachel is punningly
invoking both meanings, though the former is more likely: in her death agony,
she envisages the continuation of "vigor" after her in the son she has born (the
tribe Benjamin will become famous for its martial prowess).
but his father called him Benjamin. In the reports given in biblical narrative,
it is more often the mother who does the naming. This is the sole instance of

died and she was buried on the road to Ephrath, that is, Bethlehem.
20 And Jacob set up a pillar on her grave, it is the pillar of Rachel's grave
to this day.

21 And Israel journeyed onward and pitched his tent on the far side of
22 Migdal-Eder. And it happened, when Israel was encamped in that land,
that Reuben went and lay with Bilhah, his father's concubine, and
Israel heard.

---

competing names assigned respectively by the mother and father. Jacob's
choice of *Bin-yamin* also presents a possibility of double meaning. The most
likely construal would be "son of the right hand," that is, favored son, the one
to whom is imparted special power or "dexterity." But the right hand also designates the south in biblical idiom, so the name could mean "dweller in the
south." Again, the *yamin* component might be, as some have proposed, not the
word for right hand but a plural of *yom,* day or time, yielding the sense "son of
old age."

22. *Reuben went and lay with Bilhah.* This enigmatic notice of Reuben's violation of his father's concubine is conveyed with gnomic conciseness. The Talmud saw in the story an intention on the part of Reuben to defile the slavegirl
of his mother's dead rival, Rachel, and so to make her sexually taboo to Jacob.
More recent commentators have observed with justice that in the biblical
world cohabitation with the consort of a ruler is a way of making claim to his
authority (as when the usurper Absalom cohabits with his father David's concubines), and so Reuben would be attempting to seize in his father's lifetime
his firstborn's right to be head of the clan.

    and Israel heard. The same verb is used when the report of the rape of
Dinah is brought to Jacob. In both instances, he remains silent. The fact that
he is referred to in this episode as Israel, not Jacob, may be dictated by the
context of sexual outrage, for which the idiom "a scurrilous thing in Israel,"
nevalah beYisra'el, is used, as in the story of Dinah.

And the sons of Jacob were twelve. The sons of Leah: Jacob's firstborn   23
Reuben and Simeon and Levi and Judah and Issachar and Zebulun.
The sons of Rachel: Joseph and Benjamin. And the sons of Bilhah,   24,25
Rachel's slavegirl: Dan and Naphtali. And the sons of Zilpah, Leah's   26
slavegirl: Gad and Asher. These are the sons of Jacob who were born to
him in Paddan-Aram. And Jacob came to Isaac his father in Mamre, at   27
Kiriath-Arba, that is, Hebron, where Abraham, and Isaac, had
sojourned. And Isaac's days were a hundred and eighty years. And Isaac   28,29
breathed his last, and died, and was gathered to his kin, old and sated
with years, and Esau and Jacob his sons buried him.

And the sons of Jacob were twelve. The genealogical list of the sons of Jacob,
followed by the list of the sons of Ishmael in the next chapter, marks a major
transition in the narrative. When the story picks up again at the beginning of
chapter 37, though old Jacob is very much alive and an important figure in the
background of the narrative, it will become the story of Joseph and his brothers—a tale that in all its psychological richness and moral complexity will take
up the rest of the Book of Genesis.

29. *And Isaac breathed his last.* The actual chronological place of this event is
obviously considerably earlier in the narrative. The biblical writers observe no
fixed commitment to linear chronology, a phenomenon recognized by the rabbis in the dictum, "there is neither early nor late in the Torah."

    Esau and Jacob his sons buried him. At this end point, they act in unison,
and despite the reversal of birthright and blessing, the firstborn is mentioned
first.

CHAPTER 36

1,2   **A**nd this is the lineage of Esau, that is, Edom. Esau took his wives
3   from the daughters of Canaan—Adah daughter of Elon the Hittite
     and Oholibamah daughter of Anah son of Zibeon the Hivite, and

---

CHAPTER 36 offers the last of the major genealogies in Genesis. These lists of generations (*toledot*) and of kings obviously exerted an intrinsic fascination for the ancient audience and served as a way of accounting for historical and political configurations, which were conceived through a metaphor of biological propagation. (In fact, virtually the only evidence we have about the Edomite settlement is the material in this chapter.) As a unit in the literary structure of Genesis, the genealogies here are the marker of the end of a long narrative unit. What follows is the story of Joseph, a continuous sequence that is the last large literary unit of Genesis. The role of Esau's genealogy is clearly analogous to that of Ishmael's genealogy in chapter 25: before the narrative goes on to pursue the national line of Israel, an account is rendered of the posterity of the patriarch's son who is not the bearer of the covenantal promise. But Isaac had given Esau, too, a blessing, however qualified, and these lists demonstrate the implementation of that blessing in Esau's posterity.

The chapter also serves to shore up the narrative geographically, to the east, before turning its attention to the south. Apart from the brief report in chapter 12 of Abraham's sojourn in Egypt, which is meant to foreshadow the end of Genesis and the beginning of Exodus, the significant movement beyond the borders of Canaan has all been eastward, across the Jordan to Mesopotamia and back again. Esau now makes his permanent move from Canaan to Edom—the mountainous region east of Canaan, south of the Dead Sea and stretching down toward the Gulf of Aqabah. Once this report is finished, our attention will be turned first to Canaan and then to Egypt.

1–8. This is the first of the six different lists—perhaps drawn from different archival sources by the editor—that make up the chapter. Though it does record Esau's sons, the stress is on his wives. There are both overlap and

Basemath daughter of Ishmael, sister of Nebaioth. And Adah bore to 4
Esau Eliphaz while Basemath bore Reuel, and Oholibamah bore Jeush 5
and Jalam and Korah. These are the sons of Esau who were borne to
him in the land of Canaan. And Esau took his wives and his sons and 6
his daughters and all the folk of his household and his livestock and all
his cattle and all the goods he had gotten in the land of Canaan and he
went to another land away from Jacob his brother. For their substance 7
was too great for dwelling together and the land of their sojournings
could not support them because of their livestock. And Esau settled in 8
the high country of Seir—Esau, that is, Edom.

And this is the lineage of Esau, father of Edom, in the high country of 9
Seir. These are the names of the sons of Esau: Eliphaz son of Adah, 10
Esau's wife, Reuel son of Basemath, Esau's wife. And the sons of Elip- 11
haz were Teman, Omar, Zepho, and Gatam and Kenaz. And Timna was 12

---

inconsistency among the different lists. These need not detain us here. The
best account of these sundry traditions, complete with charts, is the discussion of this chapter in the Hebrew *Encyclopedia ʿOlam haTanakh*, though
Nahum Sarna provides a briefer but helpful exposition of the lists in his
commentary.

2. *Anah son of Zibeon.* The Masoretic Text has "daughter of," but Anah is
clearly a man (cf. verse 24), and several ancient versions read "son."

6. *another land.* The translation follows the explanatory gloss of the ancient
Targums. The received text has only "a land."
   away from. Or, "because of."

7. *the land . . . could not support them.* The language of the entire passage is
reminiscent of the separation between Lot and Abraham in chapter 13. It is
noteworthy that Esau, in keeping with his loss of birthright and blessing, concedes Canaan to his brother and moves his people to the southeast.

9–14. The second unit is a genealogical list focusing on sons rather than wives.

12. *Timna . . . a concubine . . . bore . . . Amalek.* If Amalek is subtracted, we
have a list of twelve tribes, as with Israel and Ishmael. Perhaps the birth by a
concubine is meant to set Amalek apart, in a status of lesser legitimacy.

a concubine of Eliphaz son of Esau, and she bore to Eliphaz Amalek.
13 These are the sons of Adah, Esau's wife. And these are the sons of
Reuel: Nahath and Zerah, Shammah and Mizzah. These were the sons
14 of Basemath, Esau's wife. And these were the sons of Esau's wife
Oholibamah, daughter of Anah son of Zibeon—she bore to Esau Jeush
and Jalam and Korah.

15 These are the chieftains of the sons of Esau. The sons of Eliphaz, firstborn of Esau: the chieftain Teman, the chieftain Omar, the chieftain
16 Zepho, the chieftain Kenaz, the chieftain Korah, the chieftain Gatam,
the chieftain Amalek. These are the chieftains of Eliphaz in the land of
17 Edom, these are the sons of Adah. And these are the sons of Reuel son
of Esau: the chieftain Nahath, the chieftain Zerah, the chieftain
Shammah, the chieftain Mizzah. These are the chieftains of Reuel in
18 the land of Edom, these are the sons of Basemath, Esau's wife. And
these are the sons of Oholibamah, Esau's wife: the chieftain Jeush, the
chieftain Jalam, the chieftain Korah. These are the chieftains of
19 Oholibamah daughter of Anah, Esau's wife. These are the sons of Esau,
that is, Edom, and these their chieftains.

Amalek becomes the hereditary enemy of Israel, whereas the other Edomites
had normal dealings with their neighbors to the west.

15–19. The third unit is a list of chieftains descended from Esau.

15. *chieftains.* It has been proposed that the Hebrew *'aluf* means "clan," but
that seems questionable because most of the occurrences of the term elsewhere in the Bible clearly indicate a person, not a group. The difficulty is obvi-
ated if we assume that an *'aluf* is the head of an *'elef,* a clan. The one problem
with this construction, the fact that in verses 40 and 41 *'aluf* is joined with a
feminine proper noun, may be resolved by seeing a construct form there
("chieftain of Timna" instead of "chieftain Timna").

These are the sons of Seir the Horite who had settled in the land: Lotan 20
and Shobal and Zibeon and Anah, and Dishon and Ezer and Dishan. 21
These are the Horite chieftains, sons of Seir, in the land of Edom. And 22
the sons of Lotan were Hori and Hemam, and Lotan's sister was
Timna. And these are the sons of Shobal: Alvan and Manahoth and 23
Ebal, Shepho and Onam. And these are the sons of Zibeon: Aiah and 24
Anah, he is Anah who found the water in the wilderness when he took
the asses of his father Zibeon to graze. And these are the children of 25
Anah: Dishon and Oholibamah daughter of Anah. And these are the 26
sons of Dishon: Hemdan and Eshban and Ithran and Cheran. These 27
are the sons of Ezer: Bilhan and Zaavan and Akan. These are the sons 28
of Dishan: Uz and Aran. These are the Horite chieftains: the chieftain 29
Lotan, the chieftain Shobal, the chieftain Zibeon, the chieftain Anah,
the chieftain Dishon, the chieftain Ezer, the chieftain Dishan. These 30
are the Horite chieftains by their clans in the land of Seir.

20–30. *The fourth unit of the chapter is a list of Horite inhabitants of Edom.*
The Horites—evidently the term was used interchangeably with Hittite—
were most probably the Hurrians, a people who penetrated into this area from
Armenia sometime in the first half of the second millennium B.C.E. They seem
to have largely assimilated into the local population, a process reflected in the
fact that, like everyone else in these lists, they have West Semitic names.

20. *who had settled in the land.* "Settlers [or inhabitants] of the land" is closer
to the Hebrew. That is, the "Horites" were the indigenous population by the
time the Edomites invaded from the west, during the thirteenth century B.C.E.

24. *Aiah.* The Masoretic Text reads "and Aiah."
    who found the water in the wilderness. The object of the verb in the Hebrew,
yemim, is an anomalous term, and venerable traditions that render it as
"mules" or "hot springs" have no philological basis. This translation follows
E. A. Speiser's plausible suggestion that a simple transposition of the first and
second consonants of the word has occurred and that the original reading was
mayim, "water." Discovery of any water source in the wilderness would be
enough to make it noteworthy for posterity.

26. *Dishon.* The Masoretic Text reads "Dishan," who is his brother, and whose
offspring are recorded two verses later. There is support for "Dishon" in some
of the ancient versions.

31 These are the kings that reigned in the land of Edom before any king
32 reigned over the Israelites. And Bela son of Beor reigned in Edom and
33 the name of his city was Dinhabah. And Bela died and Jobab son of
34 Zerah from Bozrah, reigned in his stead. And Jobab died, and Husham
35 from the land of the Temanite reigned in his stead. And Husham died
and Hadad son of Bedad reigned in his stead, he who struck down Mid-
36 ian on the steppe of Moab, and the name of his city was Avith. And
37 Hadad died and Samlah of Masrekah reigned in his stead. And Samlah
died and Saul from Rehoboth-on-the-River reigned in his stead.
38 And Saul died and Baal-Hanan son of Achbor reigned in his stead.
39 And Baal-Hanan son of Achbor died and Hadad reigned in his stead,
and the name of his city was Pau and the name of his wife was
Mehetabel daughter of Matred daughter of Me-Zahab.

---

30. *by their clans.* The translation revocalizes the Masoretic *'alufeyhem* as *'alfey-hem* (the consonants remain identical) to yield "clans."

31–39. The fifth unit of the chapter is a list of the kings of Edom. They do not constitute a dynasty because none of the successors to the throne is a son of his predecessor.

31. *before any king reigned over the Israelites.* The phrase refers to the establishment of the monarchy beginning with Saul and not, as some have proposed, to the imposition of Israelite suzerainty over Edom by David, because of the particle *le* ("to," "for," "over"), rather than *mi* ("from") prefixed to the Hebrew for "Israelites." This is one of those brief moments when the later perspective in time of the writer pushes to the surface in the Patriarchal narrative.

37. *Rehoboth-on-the-River.* Rehoboth means "broad places": in urban contexts, in the singular, it designates the city square; here it might mean something like "meadows." Rehoboth-on-the-River is probably meant to distinguish this place from some other Rehoboth, differently situated.

39. *Hadad.* The Masoretic Text has "Hadar," but this is almost certainly a mistake for the well-attested name Hadad, as Chronicles, and some ancient versions and manuscripts, read. In Hebrew, there is only a small difference between the graphemes for *r* and for *d*.

And these are the names of the chieftains of Esau by their clans and 40
places name by name: the chieftain of Timna, the chieftain Alvah, the
chieftain Jetheth, the chieftain of Oholibamah, the chieftain Elah, the 41
chieftain Pinon, the chieftain Kenaz, the chieftain Teman, the chieftain 42
Mibzar, the chieftain Magdiel, the chieftain Iram. These are the chief- 43
tains of Edom by their settlements in the land of their holdings—that
is, Esau, father of Edom.

40–43. The sixth and concluding list of the collection is another record of the
chieftains descended from Esau. Most of the names are different, and the list
may reflect a collation of archival materials stemming from disparate sources.
This sort of stitching together of different testimonies would be in keeping
with ancient editorial practices.

CHAPTER 37

1   And Jacob dwelled in the land of his father's sojournings, in the
2   land of Canaan. This is the lineage of Jacob—Joseph, seventeen
years old, was tending the flock with his brothers, assisting the
sons of Bilhah and the sons of Zilpah, the wives of his father. And
3   Joseph brought ill report of them to their father. And Israel loved
Joseph more than all his sons, for he was the child of his old age, and

---

1–2. *And Jacob dwelled in the land of . . . Canaan. This is the lineage of Jacob.*
The aptness of these verses as a transition from the genealogy of Esau to the
story of Joseph is nicely observed by Abraham ibn Ezra: "The text reports that
the chieftains of Esau dwelled in the high country of Seir and Jacob dwelled
in the Chosen Land. And the meaning of 'This is the lineage of Jacob' is,
'These are the events that happened to him and the incidents that befell him.'"
Ibn Ezra's remark demonstrates that there is no need to attach these two
verses to the end of the preceding genealogy, as some modern scholars have
argued. The writer exploits the flexibility of the Hebrew *toledot,* a term that
can equally refer to genealogical list and to story, in order to line up the beginning of the Joseph story with the *toledot* passage that immediately precedes it.

2. *assisting.* The literal meaning of the Hebrew is "he was a lad with the sons
of Bilhah." But the Hebrew for "lad," *naʿar,* has a secondary meaning, clearly
salient here, of assistant or subaltern. The adolescent Joseph is working as a
kind of apprentice shepherd with his older brothers.
    brought ill report. The first revelation of Joseph's character suggests a
spoiled younger child who is a tattletale. The next revelation, in the dreams,
intimates adolescent narcissism, even if the grandiosity eventually is justified
by events.

3. *And Israel loved Joseph . . . for he was the child of his old age.* The explanation is a little odd, both because the fact that Joseph is the son of the beloved

he made him an ornamented tunic. And his brothers saw it was he their 4
father loved more than all his brothers, and they hated him and could
not speak a kind word to him. And Joseph dreamed a dream and told it 5
to his brothers and they hated him all the more. And he said to them, 6
"Listen, pray, to this dream that I dreamed. And, look, we were binding 7
sheaves in the field, and, look, my sheaf arose and actually stood up,

---

Rachel is unmentioned and because it is the last-born Benjamin who is the
real child of Jacob's old age. It is noteworthy that Jacob's favoritism toward
Joseph is mentioned immediately after the report of questionable behavior on
Joseph's part. One recalls that Jacob was the object of his mother's unex-
plained favoritism.

an ornamented tunic. The only clue about the nature of the garment is
offered by the one other mention of it in the Bible, in the story of the rape of
Tamar (2 Samuel 13), in which, incidentally, there is a whole network of
pointed allusions to the Joseph story. There we are told that the *ketonet pasim*
was worn by virgin princesses. It is thus a unisex garment and a product of
ancient *haute couture*. E. A. Speiser cites a cuneiform text with an apparently
cognate phrase that seems to indicate a tunic with appliqué ornamentation.
Other scholars have pointed to a fourteenth-century B.C.E. Egyptian fresco
showing captive Canaanite noblemen adorned with tunics made of longitudi-
nal panels sewn together.

5. *And Joseph dreamed.* As has often been noted, the dreams in the Joseph story
reflect its more secular orientation in comparison with the preceding narratives in Genesis. They are not direct messages from God, like His appearance
in the dream-visions to Abimelech and to Jacob: they may be literally portentous, but they require human interpretation (here the meaning is obvious
enough), and they may also express the hidden desires and self-perception of
the dreamer.

6. *Listen, pray, to this dream that I dreamed.* In keeping with the rule about the
revelatory force of a character's first words, this whole speech shows us a
young Joseph who is self-absorbed, blithely assuming everyone will be fascinated by the details of his dreams.

7. *And, look.* It is standard technique for the dreamer reporting his dream to
use the presentative *hineh*, "look," to introduce what he has "seen" in the
dream. But Joseph repeats the term three times in a single sentence, betraying his own wide-eyed amazement, and perhaps his naïveté. The same attitude
is reflected in his exclamatory "arose and actually stood up."

8 and, look, your sheaves drew round and bowed to my sheaf." And his
   brothers said to him, "Do you mean to reign over us, do you mean to
   rule us?" And they hated him all the more, for his dreams and for his
9 words. And he dreamed yet another dream and recounted it to his
   brothers, and he said, "Look, I dreamed a dream again, and, look, the
10 sun and the moon and eleven stars were bowing to me." And he
   recounted it to his father and to his brothers, and his father rebuked
   him and said to him, "What is this dream that you have dreamed? Shall
   we really come, I and your mother and your brothers, to bow before you

---

8. *for his dreams and for his words.* It is misguided to construe this as a hendiadys ("for speaking about his dreams") since the sharp point is that they hated
him both for having such dreams and for insisting on talking about them.

9. *And he dreamed yet another dream.* Later (41:32) we shall learn that the doubling of the dream is a sign that what it portends will really happen, but it
should also be observed that doublets are a recurrent principle of organization
in the Joseph story, just as binary divisions are an organizing principle in the
Jacob story. Joseph and Pharaoh have double dreams; the chief butler and the
chief baker dream their pair of seemingly parallel, actually antithetical dreams.
Joseph is first flung into a pit and later into the prison-house. The brothers
make two trips down to Egypt, with one of their number seemingly at risk on
each occasion. And their descent to Egypt with goods and silver mirrors the
descent of the merchant caravan, bearing the same items, that first brought
Joseph down to Egypt.

   the sun and the moon and eleven stars. Both Hermann Gunkel and Gerhard
von Rad have proposed that the eleven stars are actually the eleven constellations known in the ancient Near East, but these should then be twelve, not
eleven, and at least in the biblical record, knowledge of definite constellations
is reflected only in postexilic literature. The two parallel dreams operate on
different levels of intensity. The agricultural setting of the first one reflects the
actual setting—Freud's "day's residue"—in which Joseph does his dreaming,
and so is attached to the first part of the story, even if the brothers detect in it
aspirations to regal grandeur. The second dream shifts the setting upward to
the heavens and in this way is an apt adumbration of the brilliant sphere of the
Egyptian imperial court over which Joseph will one day preside. From a strict
monotheistic view, the second dream teeters on the brink of blasphemy.

10. *I and your mother.* This particular episode seems to assume, in flat contradiction of the preceding narrative, that Rachel is still alive, though Benjamin

to the ground?" And his brothers were jealous of him, while his father 11
kept the thing in mind.

And his brothers went to graze their father's flock at Shechem. And 12,13
Israel said to Joseph, "You know, your brothers are pasturing at
Shechem. Come, let me send you to them," and he said to him, "Here
I am." And he said to him, "Go, pray, to see how your brothers fare, and 14
how the flock fares, and bring me back word." And he sent him from
the valley of Hebron and he came to Shechem. And a man found him 15
and, look, he was wandering in the field, and the man asked him, saying, "What is it you seek?" And he said, "My brothers I seek. Tell me, 16
pray, where are they pasturing?" And the man said, "They have jour- 17
neyed on from here, for I heard them say, 'Let us go to Dothan.'" And
Joseph went after his brothers and found them at Dothan. And they 18
saw him from afar before he drew near them and they plotted against

---

has already been born (there are eleven brothers in the dream bowing to
Joseph). Attempts to rescue consistency on the ground that dreams may con-
tain incoherent elements are unconvincing, because it is a perfectly lucid
Jacob who assumes here that Rachel is still alive.

12. *Shechem.* As several medieval commentators note, Shechem has already
been linked with disaster in these stories.

14. *the valley of Hebron.* The validity of this designation can be defended only
through ingenious explanation because Hebron stands on a height.

15. *And a man found him.* The specificity of this exchange with an unnamed
stranger is enigmatic. Efforts to see the "man" as an angel or messenger of fate
have little textual warrant. What it is safe to say is that the question and
answer in a field outside Shechem reinforce the sense that Joseph is being
directed, unwitting, to a disastrous encounter.

17. *for I heard them.* The Masoretic Text has only "I heard," but several ancient
versions supply the *mem* suffix to the verb that would indicate "them" as its
object.

19 him to put him to death. And they said to each other, "Here comes that
20 dream-master! And so now, let us kill him and fling him into one of the
pits and we can say, a vicious beast has devoured him, and we shall see
21 what will come of his dreams." And Reuben heard and came to his res-
22 cue and said, "We must not take his life." And Reuben said to them,
"Shed no blood! Fling him into this pit in the wilderness and do not
raise a hand against him"—that he might rescue him from their hands
23 to bring him back to his father. And it happened when Joseph came to
his brothers that they stripped Joseph of his tunic, the ornamented

---

19. *that dream-master!* Although time-honored tradition renders this in English
simply as "dreamer," the Hebrew term *ba'al hahalomot* is stronger, and thus in
context more sarcastic. The *ba'al* component suggests someone who has a special proprietary relation to, or mastery of, the noun that follows it.

20. *let us kill him and fling him into one of the pits.* The flinging after the killing
underscores the naked brutality of the brothers' intentions. The denial of
proper burial was among the Hebrews as among the Greeks deeply felt as an
atrocity.

21–22. *We must not take his life. . . . Shed no blood!* Reuben eschews the two
verbs for killing used respectively by the narrator and the brothers and instead
invokes language echoing the primal taboo against taking—literally, "striking
down"—life and spilling human blood (compare the powerful prohibition in
9:6). In the event, the substitute blood of the slaughtered kid will figure prominently in the brothers' course of action.
    Fling him into this pit. At the same time, Reuben tries not to contradict the
violence of his brothers' feelings toward Joseph and uses the same phrase, to
fling him into a pit, with the crucial difference that in his proposal it is a live
Joseph who will be cast into the pit. This is precisely the verb used for Hagar
(21:15) when she flings Ishmael under a bush in the wilderness.

23. *his tunic, the ornamented tunic that he had on him.* Only now do we learn
that Joseph has the bad judgment to wear on his errand the garment that was
the extravagant token of his father's favoritism. Thus he provokes the brothers'
anger, and they strip him—not part of their original plan—and thus take hold
of what will be made into the false evidence of his death as their plan changes.

tunic that he had on him. And they took him and flung him into the pit, 24
and the pit was empty, there was no water in it. And they sat down to 25
eat bread, and they raised their eyes and saw and, look, a caravan of
Ishmaelites was coming from Gilead, their camels bearing gum and
balm and ladanum on their way to take down to Egypt. And Judah said 26
to his brothers, "What gain is there if we kill our brother and cover up
his blood? Come, let us sell him to the Ishmaelites and our hand will 27
not be against him, for he is our brother, our own flesh." And his broth-

---

24. *they . . . flung him into the pit.* Contrary to the original plan, they do not
kill him straight away. Perhaps they have decided instead to let him perish
trapped in the pit.

the pit was empty, there was no water in it. Deep cisterns of this sort—too
deep to climb out of—were commonly used for water storage.

25. *Ishmaelites.* This is a generic term for the seminomadic traders of Arab
stock whose homeland was east of the Jordan, but it is also an anachronism,
since at the time of the story, the eponymous Ishmael, the great-uncle of the
twelve brothers, was still alive (though he would be near the end of his 127-
year life span), and the only "Ishmaelites" would be their second cousins.

gum and balm and ladanum. The precise identity of these plant extracts
used for medicinal purposes and as perfume is in doubt, but it is clear that
they are costly export items.

26. *What gain is there if we kill our brother and cover up his blood?* Judah's argument for sparing Joseph's life—which most scholars regard as the manifestation of an originally different version of the story from the one in which the
firstborn Reuben tries to save Joseph—is based on the consideration of gain,
not on the horror of the taboo against shedding blood that Reuben invokes. To
cover up blood means to conceal bloodguilt.

27. *for he is our brother, our own flesh.* It is, of course, a dubious expression of
brotherhood to sell someone into the ignominy and perilously uncertain future
of slavery.

28 ers agreed. And Midianite merchantmen passed by and pulled Joseph
up out of the pit and sold Joseph to the Ishmaelites for twenty pieces
29 of silver, and they brought Joseph to Egypt. And Reuben came back to
the pit and, look, Joseph was not in the pit, and he rent his garments,
30 and he came back to his brothers, and he said, "The boy is gone, and I,
31 where can I turn?" And they took Joseph's tunic and slaughtered a kid
32 and dipped the tunic in the blood, and they sent the ornamented tunic
and had it brought to their father, and they said, "This we found. Rec-

---

28. *And Midianite merchantmen . . . pulled Joseph up out of the pit and sold Joseph to the Ishmaelites*. This is the one signal moment when the two literary strands out of which the story is woven seem awkwardly spliced. Up to this point, no Midianites have been mentioned. Elsewhere, Midianites and Ishmaelites appear to be terms from different periods designating the selfsame people (compare Judges 8:22 and 24), so the selling of Joseph to the Ishmaelites looks like a strained attempt to blend two versions that respectively used the two different terms. And the Midianite intervention contradicts the just stated intention of the brothers to pull Joseph out of the pit themselves and sell Joseph to the Ishmaelites for profit.

29. *And Reuben came back to the pit*. The contradiction between the two versions continues, since one is driven to assume that Reuben was not present at the fraternal meal during which the selling of Joseph was discussed, though there is no textual indication of his absence.

30. *The boy is gone*. The Hebrew says literally, "the boy is not." The phrase could be a euphemism for death or could merely indicate disappearance. It is a crucial ambiguity the brothers themselves will exploit much later in the story.

31. *slaughtered a kid and dipped the tunic in blood*. Jacob had used both a slaughtered kid and a garment in the deception he perpetrated on his own father.

32. *they sent . . . and had it brought*. The brothers operate indirectly, through the agency of a messenger, letting the doctored evidence of the blood-soaked tunic speak for itself.
  Recognize. When the disguised Jacob deceived his father, we were told, "he did not recognize him."

ognize, pray, is it your son's tunic or not?" And he recognized it, and he   33
said, "It is my son's tunic.

> A vicious beast has devoured him,
> Joseph is torn to shreds!"

And Jacob rent his clothes and put sackcloth round his waist and   34
mourned for his son many days. And all his sons and all his daughters   35
rose to console him and he refused to be consoled and he said, "Rather
I will go down to my son in Sheol mourning," and his father keened for
him.

But the Midianites had sold him into Egypt to Potiphar, Pharaoh's   36
courtier, the high chamberlain.

---

33. *And he recognized it, and he said . . . "A vicious beast has devoured him."*
Jacob's paternal anxiety turns him into the puppet of his sons' plotting. Not
only does he at once draw the intended false conclusion, but he uses the very
words of their original plan, "a vicious beast has devoured him." It is noteworthy that his cry of grief takes the form of a line of formal verse, a kind of compact elegy that jibes with the mourning rituals which follow it.

33–35. All this language of mourning and grieving suggests a certain extravagance, perhaps something histrionic. As the next verse tersely indicates, at the
very moment Jacob is bewailing his purportedly dead son, Joseph is sold into
the household of a high Egyptian official.

36. *Pharaoh's courtier, the high chamberlain.* The word for "courtier" in other
contexts can also mean "eunuch," but the evidence suggests that the original
use was as the title of a court official and that the sense of "eunuch" became
associated with the term secondarily because of an occasional Mesopotamian
practice of placing eunuchs in court positions. (The Hebrew *saris* is a loanword from the Akkadian *sa resi,* "royal official.") The second title attached to
Potiphar is associated with a root involving slaughter and in consequence
sometimes with cooking (hence the "chief steward" or, alternately, "chief exe-
cutioner" of various English versions). The actual responsibilities of this high
imperial post remain unclear.

CHAPTER 38

1   And it happened at this time that Judah went down from his broth-
2   ers and pitched his tent by an Adullamite named Hirah. And
Judah saw there the daughter of a Canaanite man named Shua,
3 and he took her and came to bed with her. And she conceived and bore
4 a son and called his name Er. And she conceived again and bore a
5 son and called his name Onan. And she bore still another son and
6 called his name Shelah, and he was at Chezib when she bore him. And
Judah took a wife for Er his firstborn, and her name was Tamar.

---

1. *And it happened at this time.* The formulaic indication of time is deliberately
vague. The entire story of Judah and the sons he begets spans more than
twenty years. It reads as though it began after the moment Joseph is sold down
to Egypt, but the larger chronology of the Joseph story and the descent into
Egypt suggests that the first phase of this story about Judah may considerably
antedate Joseph's enslavement. Many readers have sensed this tale of Judah
and Tamar as an "interruption" of the Joseph story, or, at best, as a means of
building suspense about Joseph's fate in Egypt. In fact, there is an intricate
network of connections with what precedes and what follows, as close attention to the details of the text will reveal.

    went down. The verb is justified by topography because Judah is coming
down from the hill country to the eastern edge of the coastal plain inhabited
by the Canaanites. But "going down" is also the verb used for travel to Egypt
(compare the end of verse 25 in the preceding chapter), and the next episode,
which returns to the Joseph story, will begin with the words, "And Joseph was
brought down to Egypt."

3. *she . . . called.* The Masoretic Text has "he called," but the more likely naming of the child by the mother, as in verse 4, is supported by several manuscript
traditions.

And Er, Judah's firstborn, was evil in the eyes of the LORD, and the 7
LORD put him to death. And Judah said to Onan, "Come to bed with 8
your brother's wife and do your duty as brother-in-law for her and raise
up seed for your brother." And Onan knew that the seed would not be 9
his and so when he would come to bed with his brother's wife, he
would waste his seed on the ground, so to give no seed to his brother.
And what he did was evil in the eyes of the LORD, and He put him 10
to death as well. And Judah said to Tamar his daughter-in-law, "Stay a 11
widow in your father's house until Shelah my son is grown up," for he

---

7. *And Er, Judah's firstborn, was evil in the eyes of the* LORD. The nature of his
moral failing remains unspecified, but given the insistent pattern of reversal of
primogeniture in all these stories, it seems almost sufficient merely to be firstborn in order to incur God's displeasure: though the firstborn is not necessarily evil, he usually turns out to be obtuse, rash, wild, or otherwise disqualified
from carrying on the heritage. It is noteworthy that Judah, who invented the
lie that triggered his own father's mourning for a dead son, is bereaved of two
sons in rapid sequence. In contrast to Jacob's extravagant grief, nothing is said
about Judah's emotional response to the losses.

8. *do your duty as brother-in-law*. In the Hebrew, this is a single verb, *yabem*,
referring to the so-called levirate marriage. The legal obligation of *yibum*,
which was a widespread practice in the ancient Near East, was incurred when
a man died leaving his wife childless. His closest brother in order of birth was
obliged to become his proxy, "raising up seed" for him by impregnating his
widow. The dead brother would thus be provided a kind of biological continuity, and the widow would be able to produce progeny, which was a woman's
chief avenue of fulfillment in this culture.

9. *the seed would not be his*. Evidently, Onan is troubled by the role of sexual
proxy, which creates a situation in which the child he begets will be legally
considered his dead brother's offspring.
    he would waste his seed on the ground. Despite the confusion engendered by
the English term "onanism" that derives from this text, the activity referred to
is almost certainly *coitus interruptus*—as Rashi vividly puts it, "threshing
within, winnowing without."

11. *Stay a widow in your father's house*. The childless Tamar is not only
neglected but must submit to a form of social disgrace in having to return to
her father's house after having been twice married. Since enough time elapses

thought, Lest he, too, die like his brothers. And Tamar went and stayed at her father's house.

12 And a long time passed and the daughter of Shua, Judah's wife, died, and after the mourning period Judah went up to his sheepshearers, he
13 with Hirah the Adullamite his friend, to Timnah. And Tamar was told, saying, "Look, your father-in-law is going up to Timnah to shear his
14 sheep." And she took off her widow's garb and covered herself with a veil and wrapped herself and sat by the entrance to Enaim, which is on the road to Timnah, for she saw that Shelah had grown up and she had

---

for Shelah to grow from prepuberty to at least late adolescence (see verse 14), this period of enforced return to the status of an unmarried daughter proves to be a very long one. Amos Funkenstein has observed to me that Tamar remains silent in the face of her father-in-law's condemnation, saying nothing of Onan's sexual aberration and leaving Judah to suppose that the death of both sons is somehow her fault. And though he banishes her to her father's house, she evidently remains under his legal jurisdiction, as his issuing of a death sentence against her (verse 24) indicates.

12. *after the mourning period.* The Hebrew says literally, "and Judah was consoled," a verb that may refer to actual feelings or to the simple end of the prescribed period of mourning. Either way, we pick up the antithetical echo of Jacob's refusal of consolation at the end of the previous chapter. The death of Judah's wife and the ensuing mourning set up the condition of sexual neediness that motivates his encounter with Tamar.

sheepshearers. As we know from elsewhere in the Bible, sheepshearing was the occasion for elaborate festivities, with abundant food and drink. In this way, Judah's going up to join his sheepshearers is itself an indication that he is done with the rites of mourning and is perhaps in a holiday mood. The verb twice used for this journey is to "go up," the complementary opposite of the going down with which the chapter begins.

14. *sat by the entrance to Enaim.* If, as is quite likely, this place-name means "Twin Wells," we probably have here a kind of wry allusion to the betrothal type-scene: the bridegroom encountering his future spouse by a well in a foreign land. One wonders whether the two wells might resonate with her two marriages, or with the twins she will bear. In any case, instead of a feast and the conclusion of a betrothal agreement, here we have a brusque goods-for-services business dialogue, followed by sex.

not been given to him as wife. And Judah saw her and he took her for   15
a whore, for she had covered her face. And he turned aside to her by   16
the road and said, "Here, pray, let me come to bed with you," for he
knew not that she was his daughter-in-law. And she said, "What will
you give me for coming to bed with me?" And he said, "I personally will   17
send a kid from the flock." And she said, "Only if you give a pledge till
you send it." And he said, "What pledge shall I give you?" And she said,   18
"Your seal-and-cord, and the staff in your hand." And he gave them to
her and he came to bed with her and she conceived by him. And she   19

---

16. *Here, pray, let me come to bed with you.* Despite the particle of entreaty *na'*, "pray," this is brutally direct: there is no preface of polite greeting to the woman, and the Hebrew idiom, repeatedly used in this story, says literally, "let me come into you." Judah's sexual importunacy becomes a background of contrast for Joseph's sexual restraint in the next chapter.

What will you give me for coming to bed with me? Tamar is careful to speak in character with her role as a roadside whore, but as the events unfold, it becomes clear that she also has an ulterior consideration in mind.

17. *a kid from the flock.* Though this is plausible enough payment coming from a prosperous pastoralist in a barter culture, it also picks up the motif of the slaughtered kid whose blood was used by Judah and his brothers to deceive Jacob (as Jacob before them used a kid to deceive his father). This connection was aptly perceived a millennium and a half ago in the Midrash Bereishit Rabba. The other material element in the brothers' deception of their father was a garment; Tamar uses a garment—the whore's dress and veil—to deceive her father-in-law.

Only if you give a pledge. Tamar is not only bold and enterprising in getting for herself the justice Judah has denied her but also very shrewd: she realizes it is crucial for her to retain evidence of the paternity of the child she may conceive.

18. *Your seal-and-cord, and the staff in your hand.* The seal was a cylinder seal attached to a cord and usually worn around the neck. Rolled over documents incised in clay, it would be the means of affixing a kind of self-notarized signature. It is less clear that the staff had a legal function, though of course in political contexts it is a symbol of authority. Tamar's stipulated pledge, then, is an extravagant one: taking the instruments of Judah's legal identity and social standing is something like taking a person's driver's license and credit cards in modern society.

he gave them to her and he came to bed with her and she conceived by him.

rose and went her way and took off the veil she was wearing and put on
20 her widow's garb. And Judah sent the kid by the hand of his friend the
Adullamite to take back the pledge from the woman's hand, and he did
21 not find her. And he asked the men of the place saying, "Where is the
cult-harlot, the one at Enaim by the road? "And they said, "There has
22 been no cult-harlot here." And he returned to Judah and said, "I could
not find her, and the men of the place said as well, "There has been no
23 cult-harlot here." And Judah said, "Let her take them, lest we be a
laughingstock. Look, I sent this kid and you could not find her."

24 And it happened about three months later that Judah was told, saying,
"Tamar your daughter-in-law has played the whore and what's more,
she's conceived by her whoring." And Judah said, "Take her out to be

---

The rapid chain of verbs suggests the pragmatically focused nature of the
transaction for both participants. The last of the three verbs reveals that Tamar
gets exactly what she has aimed for.

20. *by the hand . . . the woman's hand*. As elsewhere, the physical concreteness
of the terms of the narrative is salient: Hirah brings in his hand a kid in order
to take back the pledge from the hand of the roadside whore. Since she
remains anonymous for Judah, the narrator is careful to refer to her here as
"the woman" rather than by name.

21. *the place*. The Masoretic Text has "her place," but the more plausible "the
place," as in the next verse, is supported by several of the ancient versions.
   the cult-harlot. Hirah substitutes the more decorous term *qedeshah*, a
woman who practices ritual prostitution in a fertility cult, for the narrator's
frank *zonah*, "whore."

23. *Let her take them, lest we be a laughingstock*. Let her keep the pledge, and
we will keep our mouths shut, lest it become known that I have given such
valuable objects for a fleeting pleasure. Abraham ibn Ezra shrewdly observes:
"In his great lust, he gave three [precious] things for a trivial thing."

24. *played the whore . . . conceived by her whoring*. The very term that Hirah
fastidiously avoided is twice thrust into Judah's attention, *zantah* (played the
whore) and *zenunim* (whoring).
   And Judah said, "Take her out to be burned." The precipitous speed of

burned." Out she was taken, when she sent to her father-in-law, saying, 25
"By the man to whom these belong I have conceived," and she said,
"Recognize, pray, whose are this seal-and-cord and this staff?" And 26
Judah recognized them and he said, "She is more in the right than I, for
have I not failed to give her to Shelah, my son?" And he knew her again
no more.

And it happened at the time she gave birth that, look, there were twins 27
in her womb. And it happened as she gave birth that one put out his 28
hand and the midwife took it and bound a scarlet thread on his hand,

---

Judah's judgment, without the slightest reflection or call for evidence, is
breathtaking. The peremptory character of the death sentence—and burning
was reserved in biblical law only for the most atrocious crimes—is even more
evident in the Hebrew, where Judah's decree consists of only two words, a verb
in the imperative ("take-her-out") followed by "that-she-be-burned," *hotsi'uha
wetisaref.*

25. *Out she was taken.* There is no pause between the enunciation of the death
sentence and the beginning of its implementation. This speed is highlighted
grammatically in the Hebrew by the unusual use of a passive present participle
(cognate with "take her out")—*hi' muts'eit,* literally, "she is-being-taken-out."
    when she sent . . . "Recognize, pray." Like a trap suddenly springing closed,
the connection with the preceding story of the deception of Jacob is now fully
realized. In precise correspondence to Judah and his brothers, Tamar "sends"
evidence—in this case, true evidence—to argue her case. Like them, she confronts the father figure with the imperative, "Recognize, pray" (*haker-na'*)—this
echo, too, was picked up by the Midrash—and, like his father, Judah is compelled to acknowledge that he recognizes what has been brought to him.

26. *She is more in the right than I.* The verb used, *tsadaq,* is a legal term: it is
she who has presented the convincing evidence. But in the next clause Judah
also concedes that he has behaved unjustly toward Tamar, so that in a sense
her taking the law into her own hands, however unconventional the act, is vindicated by his words.

27–30. The twins of course recall Jacob and Esau and the whole chain of
paired brothers struggling over the right of the firstborn. Zerah, sticking his
hand out first, seems to be the firstborn, but he is overtaken by Perez, who

29 to say, this one came out first. And as he was drawing back his hand, look, out came his brother, and she said, "What a breach you have
30 made for yourself!" And she called his name Perez. And afterward out came his brother, on whose hand was the scarlet thread, and she called his name Zerah.

---

makes a "breach" or "bursts forth" (the meaning of the Hebrew *Perets*). Tamar seems to address the energetic newborn in a tone of wondering affection in the exclamation she pronounces as preface to naming him. Again, the Masoretic Text has "he called his name," but the reading of several of the ancient versions, "she called," makes much better sense. Perez will become the progenitor of the kings of Judea. The name Zerah means "shining," as in the dawning of the sun, and so is linked with the scarlet thread on his hand. The scarlet in turn associates Zerah with Esau-the-Red, another twin displaced from his initial position as firstborn.

CHAPTER 39

And Joseph was brought down to Egypt, and Potiphar, courtier of 1
Pharaoh, the high chamberlain, an Egyptian man, bought him
from the hands of the Ishmaelites who had brought him down
there. And the LORD was with Joseph and he was a successful man, and 2
he was in the house of his Egyptian master. And his master saw that the 3

THIS chapter is the most elegantly symmetrical episode in Genesis. It comprises an introductory narrative frame (verses 1–6), a closing frame (20–23) that elaborately echoes the introductory verses, and the central story of the failed seduction, which is intricately linked to the framing verses by a network of recurring thematic key words.

1. *an Egyptian man.* This slightly odd designation of the high chamberlain might perhaps be used here in order to be played off against the derogatory identification of Joseph as "a Hebrew man" in verse 14. The household staff are also referred to as "men" (see verse 11), though that plural form can include both sexes, which it probably does when the mistress calls in the "people of the house" in verse 14, as she will go on to stress their collective sexual vulnerability to the Hebrew intruder.

2–6. The thematic key words, emphatically repeated in phrase after phrase, are: all, hand, house, blessing, succeed—the last two terms being the manifestation of the reiterated "the LORD was with Joseph."

2. *master.* Only in the introductory verse is Potiphar referred to by name. Afterward he is designated consistently as Joseph's master. Although the source critics may be right in attributing this difference between verse 1 and the rest of the chapter to a difference in literary strands, the stylistic peculiarity of referring to Joseph's lord only by role serves the thematic purpose of constantly highlighting the master-slave relationship and the concomitant issue of trust and stewardship.

LORD was with him, and all that he did the LORD made succeed in his
4 hand, and Joseph found favor in his eyes and he ministered to him, and
he put him in charge of his house, and all that he had he placed in his
5 hands. And it happened from the time he put him in charge of his
house and of all he had, that the LORD had blessed the Egyptian's
house for Joseph's sake and the LORD's blessing was on all that he had
6 in house and field. And he left all that he had in Joseph's hands, and he
gave no thought to anything with him there save the bread he ate. And
Joseph was comely in features and comely to look at.

7 And it happened after these things that his master's wife raised her eyes
8 to Joseph and said, "Lie with me." And he refused. And he said to his
master's wife, "Look, my master has given no thought with me here to
what is in the house, and all that he has he has placed in my hands.
9 He is not greater in this house than I, and he has held back nothing
from me except you, as you are his wife, and how could I do this great

---

6. *And Joseph was comely in features and comely to look at.* These are exactly
the words used to describe Joseph's mother in 29:17. They signal an unsettling
of the perfect harmony of Joseph's divinely favored stewardship—that comprehensive management of "all" that is in the "house"—as they provide the
motivation for the sexual campaign of his mistress.

7. *Lie with me.* The extraordinary bluntness of this sexual imperative—two
words in the Hebrew—makes it one of the most striking instances of revelatory initial dialogue in the Bible. Against her two words, the scandalized (and
perhaps nervous) Joseph will issue a breathless response that runs to thirty-
five words in the Hebrew. It is a remarkable deployment of the technique of
contrastive dialogue repeatedly used by the biblical writers to define the differences between characters in verbal confrontation.

8. *in the house . . . all that he has . . . placed in my hands.* Joseph's protestation
invokes the key terms "house," "all," "hand" of the introductory frame, reminding us of the total trust given him as steward.

evil and give offense to God?" And so she spoke to Joseph day after day, 10
and he would not listen to her, to lie by her, to be with her. And it hap- 11
pened, on one such day, that he came into the house to perform his
task, and there was no man of the men of the house there in the house.
And she seized him by his garment, saying, "Lie with me." And he left 12
his garment in her hand and he fled and went out. And so, when she 13
saw that he had left his garment in her hand and fled outside, she 14
called out to the people of the house and said to them, saying, "See, he
has brought us a Hebrew man to play with us. He came into me to lie
with me and I called out in a loud voice, and so, when he heard me 15

10. *to lie by her*. The narrator, by altering the preposition, somewhat softens the bluntness of the mistress's sexual proposition. This led Abraham ibn Ezra to imagine that she adopted the stratagem of inviting Joseph merely to lie down in bed next to her.

12. *she seized him by his garment, saying, "Lie with me."* The two-word sexual command, which is all she is ever reported saying to Joseph, is now translated from words into aggressive action. "Garment" (*beged*) is a generic term. It is certainly not an outside garment or "coat," as E. A. Speiser has it, though the Revised English Bible's "loincloth" probably goes too far in the opposite direction. In any case, Joseph would be naked, or nearly naked, when he runs off leaving the garment behind in her grasping hand.

13. The narrator repeats the terms of the preceding sentence both in order to build up momentary suspense—what will she do now?—and in order to review the crucial evidence and sequence of events, which she is about to change.

14. *he has brought us a Hebrew man to play with us*. Rather contemptuously, she refers to her husband neither by name nor title. The designation "Hebrew" is common when the group is referred to in contradistinction to other peoples, but it may well have had pejorative associations for Egyptians. "Play" can mean sexual dalliance or mockery, and probably means both here. "Us" suggests they all could have been game for this lascivious—or, mocking—barbarian from the north and is an obvious attempt on her part to enlist their sense of Egyptian solidarity. She is probably suggesting that the very supremacy of this foreigner in the household is an insult to them all.

He came into me. She plays shrewdly on a double meaning. Though all she is saying is that he came into the house, or chamber, where she was alone, the idiom in other contexts can mean to consummate sexual relations. (It is the

raise my voice and call out, he left his garment by me and fled and went
16 out." And she laid out his garment by her until his master returned to
17 his house. And she spoke to him things of this sort, saying, "The
Hebrew slave came into me, whom you brought us, to play with me.
18 And so, when I raised my voice and called out, he left his garment by
19 me and fled outside." And it happened, when his master heard his

---

expression that in sexual contexts is rendered in this translation as "come to
bed with.")

15. *when he heard me raise my voice.* We, of course, have been twice informed
that the raising of the voice came after the flight, as a strategy for coping with
it, and not before the flight as its cause.

  he left his garment by me. She substitutes the innocent "by me" for the narrator's "in her hand." A verbal spotlight is focused on this central evidentiary
fact that she alters because of the earlier "left all that he had in Joseph's hands"
(the Hebrew actually uses the singular "hand"), and we are repeatedly
informed that trust was placed in his hand. Now we have a literal leaving of
something in *her* hand, which she changes to by her side.

16. *she laid out his garment by her.* She carefully sets out the evidence for the
frame-up. This is, of course, the second time that Joseph has been stripped of
his garment, and the second time the garment is used as evidence for a lie.

17. *The Hebrew slave came into me.* Talking to her husband, she refers to
Joseph as "slave," not "man," in order to stress the outrageous presumption of
the slave's alleged assault on his mistress. She avoided the term "slave" when
addressing the household staff because they, too, are slaves. Again, she uses
the ambiguous phrase that momentarily seems to say that Joseph consummated the sexual act.

  whom you brought us, to play with me. The accusation of her husband in her
words to the people of the house is modulated into a studied ambiguity. The
syntax—there is of course no punctuation in the Hebrew—could be construed
either with a clear pause after "brought us," or as a rebuke, "you brought us to
play with me."

wife's words which she spoke to him, saying, "Things of this sort your slave has done to me," he became incensed. And Joseph's master took 20 him and placed him in the prison-house, the place where the king's prisoners were held.

And he was there in the prison-house, and God was with Joseph and 21 extended kindness to him, and granted him favor in the eyes of the prison-house warden. And the prison-house warden placed in Joseph's 22 hands all the prisoners who were in the prison-house, and all that they were to do there, it was he who did it. The prison-house warden had to 23 see to nothing that was in his hands, as the LORD was with him, and whatever he did, the LORD made succeed.

---

19. *Things of this sort your slave has done to me.* Rashi is no doubt fanciful in imagining that the first words here are to be explained by the fact that she is talking to her husband in the midst of lovemaking, but the comment does get into the spirit of her wifely manipulativeness.

20. *the prison-house.* The reiterated Hebrew term for prison, *beyt sohar,* occurs only here. It should be noted that the term includes a "house" component which helps establish a link with the opening frame and the tale of attempted seduction. Joseph, though cast down once more, is again in a "house" where he will take charge.

And he was there in the prison-house. The division of the text follows the proposal of the nineteenth-century Italian Hebrew scholar S. D. Luzzatto in attaching these words to the concluding frame. In this way, the last part of verse 20 together with verse 21 becomes a perfect mirror image of verse 2.

21–23. The great rhythm of Joseph's destiny of successful stewardship now reasserts itself as the language of the introductory frame is echoed here at the end: "God was with Joseph," "granted him favor in the eyes of," "placed in Joseph's hands," "all," and, as the summarizing term at the very conclusion of the narrative unit, "succeed."

CHAPTER 40

1   And it happened after these things that the cupbearer of the king of
Egypt and his baker gave offense to their lord, the king of Egypt.
2   And Pharaoh was furious with his two courtiers, the chief cup-
3   bearer and the chief baker. And he put them under guard in the house
of the high chamberlain, the prison-house, the place where Joseph was
4   held. And the high chamberlain assigned Joseph to them and he ministered to them, and they stayed a good while under guard.

5   And the two of them dreamed a dream, each his own dream, on a single night, each a dream with its own solution—the cupbearer and the

---

4. *And the high chamberlain assigned Joseph to them and he ministered to them.*
The source critics take this as a flat contradiction of the end of chapter 39,
where Joseph is appointed as general supervisor of the prison, serving as a kind
of managing warden. But, in fact, Joseph's "ministering" to the two courtiers
need not imply a menial role. These two prisoners had occupied important
places in the court, and Pharaoh may yet pardon them, so it makes perfect
sense that they should be singled out for special treatment in prison, to be
attended personally by the warden's right-hand man. There is another seeming discrepancy with the preceding report of Joseph's incarceration: there, the
prison was run by a prison warden (*sar beyt hasohar*) whereas here it is gov-
erned by the high chamberlain (*sar hatabahim*), the title assigned to Potiphar
himself at the beginning of chapter 39. But it is easy enough to imagine the
high chamberlain as a kind of minister of justice, bureaucratically responsible
for the royal prisons, with the warden answering to him.

5. *solution.* Although a long tradition of translations opts for "interpretation"
here, the Hebrew verb *patar* and its cognate noun suggest decipherment (compare the related term *pesher* used in the Dead Sea Scrolls). There is one con-

baker to the king of Egypt who were held in the prison-house. And 6
Joseph came to them in the morning and saw them and, look, they were
frowning. And he asked Pharaoh's courtiers who were with him under 7
guard in his lord's house, saying, "Why are your faces downcast today?"
And they said to him, "We dreamed a dream and there is no one to 8
solve it." And Joseph said to them, "Are not solutions from God? Pray,
recount them to me." And the chief cupbearer recounted his dream to 9
Joseph and said to him, "In my dream—and look, a vine was before me.
And on the vine were three tendrils, and as it was budding, its blossom 10
shot up, its clusters ripened to grapes. And Pharaoh's cup was in my 11

---

clusive decoding for every dream, and a person who is granted insight can
break the code.

6. *they were frowning.* The Hebrew *zo'afim* can refer either to a grim mood or
to the grim facial expression that it produces. Because both the narrative
report in this verse and Joseph's words in the next verse make clear that he
sees something is wrong when he looks at their faces, this translation opts for
facial expression, against all the previous English versions.

8. *Are not solutions from God?* Joseph in Egyptian captivity remains a good
Hebrew monotheist. In Egypt, the interpretation of dreams was regarded as a
science, and formal instruction in techniques of dream interpretation was
given in schools called "houses of life." Joseph is saying, then, to these two
high-ranking Egyptians that no trained hermeneut of the oneiric—no professional *poter*—is required; since God possesses the meanings of dreams, if He
chooses, He will simply reveal the meanings to the properly attentive person.
But one should note that Joseph immediately proceeds to ask the cupbearer
to recount his dream, unhesitantly assuming that he, Joseph, is such a person
whom God will favor with insight into the meaning of the dream.

10. *and as it was budding, its blossom shot up, its clusters ripened to grapes.* Like
Joseph's pair of dreams, both these dreams are stylized, schematic, and nearly
transparent in regard to meaning. The only item requiring any effort of interpretation is the three tendrils representing three days. (Numbers stand out in
each of the three sets of dreams in the Joseph story—first twelve, here three,
and then seven.) The one manifestly dreamlike element in the cupbearer's
dream occurs at this point, when time is speeded up as he looks at the vine,
and in a rapid blur the vine moves from bud to blossom to ripened grapes to
wine.

hand. And I took the grapes and crushed them into Pharaoh's cup and
12 I placed the cup in Pharaoh's palm." And Joseph said, "This is its solu-
13 tion. The three tendrils are three days. Three days hence Pharaoh will
lift up your head and restore you to your place, and you will put
Pharaoh's cup in his hand, as you used to do when you were his cup-
14 bearer. But if you remember I was with you once it goes well for you,
do me the kindness, pray, to mention me to Pharaoh and bring me out
15 of this house. For indeed I was stolen from the land of the Hebrews,
and here, too, I have done nothing that I should have been put in the
16 pit." And the chief baker saw that he had solved well, and he said to
Joseph, "I, too, in my dream—and look, there were three openwork
17 baskets on my head, and in the topmost were all sorts of food for
Pharaoh, baker's ware, and birds were eating from the basket over my

---

13. *lift up your head.* As almost any reader of the Hebrew quickly sees, the biblical idiom, here rendered quite literally, is doubly punned on in the story. To
lift up someone's head, in administrative and royal contexts, means to single
out (as in a census), to invite, to grant favor or extend reconciliation (as when
a monarch lifts up with a gesture the downcast head of a contrite subject).
When Joseph addresses the baker in verse 19, he begins as though he were
using the idiom in the same positive sense as here, but by adding "from upon
you," he turns it into a reference to beheading, the first such reference in the
Bible. In verse 20, when both courtiers are the object of the idiom, it is used
in the neutral sense of "to single out."

15. *put in the pit.* In the previous verse, Joseph refers to the place of his incarceration as "this house" (invoking elliptically the "house" component of
"prison-house"). Now he calls it a pit, perhaps because it is a kind of underground dungeon, but also to make us see the link with the empty cistern into
which he was flung by his brothers—twice he has been put in a pit for what
he must feel is no good reason.

17. *in the topmost . . . all sorts of food for Pharaoh . . . and birds were eating.* The
cupbearer in his dream performs his normal court function, though at fast-
forward speed. The baker executes a kind of bizarre parody of his normal function, balancing three baskets of bread one on top of the other. This precarious
arrangement may imply, as Amos Funkenstein has proposed to me, a sense
that the baker has been negligent in his duties. The pecking of birds at this
tower of baked goods is of course an explicitly ominous element. The two

head." And Joseph answered and said, "This is its solution. The three ₁₈
baskets are three days. Three days hence Pharaoh will lift up your head ₁₉
from upon you and impale you on a pole and the birds will eat your
flesh from upon you."

And it happened on the third day, Pharaoh's birthday, that he made a ₂₀
feast for all his servants, and he lifted up the head of the chief cupbearer and the head of the chief baker in the midst of his servants. And ₂₁
he restored the chief cupbearer to his cupbearing, and he put the cup
in Pharaoh's hand; and the chief baker he impaled—just as Joseph had ₂₂
solved it for them. But the chief cupbearer did not remember Joseph, ₂₃
no, he forgot him.

---

dreams parallel Joseph's two dreams in that the first is anchored in an agricul
tural setting and involves harvesting while the second is oriented toward the
sky above. But instead of the glorious celestial bodies, here we have the
swooping down of ravenous birds from the sky.

19. *impale*. Despite the fact that the Hebrew verb generally means "to hang,"
hanging was not a common means of execution anywhere in the ancient Near
East, and there is evidence elsewhere that the same verb was used for impalement, which was frequently practiced. The baker's dire fate would seem to be
first decapitation and then exposure of the body on a high stake.

23. *did not remember Joseph, no, he forgot him.* The verb for remembering also
means "to mention," and Joseph employs both senses of the root in his words
to the cupbearer in verse 14. Now, with the emphasis of synonymity (did not
remember, forgot), attention is drawn to the cupbearer's failure to respond to
the plea of the man who helped him in prison. It will take another pair of
dreams—with which the next episode begins—to elicit that mention/remem-
bering. It should also be kept in mind that remembering is central to the larger
story of Joseph and his brothers. When he sees them again after more than
twenty years of separation, this same crucial verb of memory, *zakhar,* will be
invoked for him, and the complicated strategy he adopts for treating his brothers is a device for driving them into a painful process of moral memory.

CHAPTER 41

1   ![A]nd it happened at the end of two full years that Pharaoh dreamed,
2   and, look, he was standing by the Nile. And, look, out of the Nile
     came up seven cows, fair to look at and fat in flesh, and they
3 grazed in the rushes. And, look, another seven cows came up after them
out of the Nile, foul to look at and meager in flesh, and stood by the
4 cows on the bank of the Nile. And the foul-looking meager-fleshed
5 cows ate up the seven fair-looking fat cows, and Pharaoh awoke. And

---

1. *at the end of two full years*. The Hebrew says literally "two years of days." The expression might simply mean "two years' time," but it is equally plausible, as the King James Version surmised, that the addition of "days" emphasizes that a full period of two years has elapsed before the course of events compel the chief cupbearer to recall his neglected promise to Joseph.

    by the Nile. Given the Nile's importance as the source of Egypt's fertility, it is appropriate that this dream of plenty and famine should take place on its banks, a point made as long ago as the thirteenth century in Narbonne by the Hebrew exegete David Kimhi. As this story set in the pharaonic court unfolds, its Egyptian local color is brought out by a generous sprinkling of Egyptian loanwords in the Hebrew narrative: "Nile" (*ye'or*), "soothsayers" (*ḥartumim*), "rushes" (*'aḥu*), "ring" (*taba'at*), "fine linen" (*shesh*).

3. *and stood by the cows*. There is a small ominous note in the fact that the second set of seven cows do not graze in the rushes, as the first seven do, and as one would expect cows to do. In a moment, they will prove themselves carnivores.

4. *and Pharaoh awoke*. Although Pharaoh's dreams, like Joseph's, are quite stylized, the one element of psychological realism is his being shaken out of sleep by the nightmarish turn of the dream plot.

he slept and dreamed a second time, and, look, seven ears of grain came up on a single stalk, fat and goodly. And, look, seven meager ears, 6 blasted by the east wind, sprouted after them. And the meager ears 7 swallowed the seven fat and full ears, and Pharaoh awoke, and, look, it was a dream. And it happened in the morning that his heart pounded, 8 and he sent and called in all the soothsayers of Egypt and all its wise men, and Pharaoh recounted to them his dreams, but none could solve them for Pharaoh. And the chief cupbearer spoke to Pharaoh, saying, 9 "My offenses I recall today. Pharaoh had been furious with his servants 10 and he placed me under guard in the house of the high chamberlain— me and the chief baker. And we dreamed a dream on the same night, 11 he and I, each of us dreamed a dream with its own solution. And there 12 with us was a Hebrew lad, a slave of the high chamberlain, and we recounted to him and he solved our dreams, each of us according to his

---

6. *blasted by the east wind.* The desert lies to the east, and the wind that blows from there (the *hamsin*) is hot and parching.

7. *And the meager ears swallowed the seven fat and full ears.* The nightmare image of carnivorous cows is intensified in the second dream by this depiction of devouring stalks of grain. The imagery of Pharaoh's second dream corresponds to the grain imagery of Joseph's first dream, but an act of depredation is substituted for the ritual of obeisance.

8. *his heart pounded.* The literal meaning of the Hebrew is "his spirit pounded."
none could solve them for Pharaoh. Since it is implausible to imagine that the soothsayers had no interpretation at all to offer, one must assume that none could offer a convincing decipherment, as Rashi observes: "they interpreted [the dreams] and he was dissatisfied with their interpretation, for they would say: seven daughters you will beget, seven daughters you will bury."

9. *I recall.* The verb means both "to mention" and "to cause to remember" and so is linked with the theme of remembrance and forgetting that is central both to this episode and to the larger Joseph story.

12. *a slave.* Although the Hebrew *'eved* is the same term the chief cupbearer has just used in the sense of "servant" (and which is used in verses 37 and 38 to refer to Pharaoh's courtiers), it is likely that he invokes it here to highlight Joseph's status as slave.

13 dream he solved it. And it happened just as he had solved it for us, so it came about—me he restored to my post and him he impaled."

14 And Pharaoh sent and called for Joseph, and they hurried him from the pit, and he shaved and changed his garments and came before
15 Pharaoh. And Pharaoh said to Joseph, "I dreamed a dream and none can solve it, and I have heard about you that you can understand a
16 dream to solve it." And Joseph answered Pharaoh, saying, "Not I! God
17 will answer for Pharaoh's well-being." And Pharaoh spoke to Joseph:
18 "In my dream, here I was standing on the bank of the Nile, and, look, out of the Nile came up seven cows fat in flesh and fair in feature, and
19 they grazed in the rushes. And, look, another seven cows came up after them, gaunt and very foul-featured and meager in flesh, I had not seen
20 their like in all the land of Egypt for foulness. And the meager, foul

---

14. *and he shaved and changed his garments.* It is obvious that an imprisoned slave would have to make himself presentable before appearing in court, but, in keeping with the local color of the story, he does this in a distinctively Egyptian fashion. In the ancient Near East, only the Egyptians were clean-shaven, and the verb used here can equally refer to shaving the head, or close-cropping it, another distinctive Egyptian practice. The putting on of fresh garments is realistically motivated in the same way, but we are probably meant to recall that each of Joseph's descents into a pit was preceded by his being stripped of his garment. When Pharaoh elevates him to viceroy, he will undergo still another change of clothing, from merely presentable dress to aristocratic raiment.

15. *I have heard about you that you can understand a dream.* "Heard" and "understand" are the same verb (*shama'*), which has both these senses, precisely like the French *entendre.* Though the second clause has often been construed as a kind of hyperbole—you need only hear a dream to reveal its meaning—the straightforward notion of understanding dreams makes better sense.

19. *gaunt and very foul-featured and meager in flesh, I had not seen their like in all the land of Egypt.* In keeping with the biblical convention of near verbatim repetition, Pharaoh, in recounting his dreams to Joseph, uses virtually the same words that the narrator used in first reporting them. The piquant difference, as Meir Sternberg (1985) has noted, is that his language underlines his own sense of horror at what he has seen in his dream: "foul to look at and mea-

cows ate up the first seven fat cows, and they were taken into their bel- 21
lies and you could not tell that they had come into their bellies, for
their looks were as foul as before, and I woke. And I saw in my dream, 22
and, look, seven ears of grain came up on a single stalk, full and goodly.
And, look, seven shriveled, meager ears, blasted by the east wind, 23
sprouted after them. And the meager ears swallowed the seven goodly 24
ears, and I spoke to my soothsayers and none could tell me the meaning." And Joseph said to Pharaoh, "Pharaoh's dream is one. What God 25
is about to do He has told Pharaoh. The seven goodly cows are seven 26
years, and the seven ears of grain are seven years. The dream is one.
And the seven meager and foul cows who came up after them are seven 27
years, and the seven meager ears of grain, blasted by the east wind, will
be seven years of famine. It is just as I said to Pharaoh: what God is 28
about to do He has shown Pharaoh. Look, seven years are coming of 29

---

ger in flesh" is elaborated and intensified in Pharaoh's repetition, and he adds
the emphatic exclamation, "I had not seen their like. . . . " (The phrase "in all
the land of Egypt" will become a verbal motif to indicate the comprehensiveness of the plenty, of the famine, and of the measures that Joseph adopts.) The
comment in verse 21 about the unchanging lean look of the cows after swallowing their fat predecessors again reflects Pharaoh's horrified perspective.

    meager in flesh. Here, and again in verses 20 and 27, I read *daqot,* "meager,"
instead of the Masoretic *raqot* ("flat," or perhaps "hollow"). The Hebrew
graphemes for *d* and *r* are similar in form, and several of the ancient versions
reflect *daqot* in these verses.

24. *and none could tell me the meaning.* The Hebrew uses an ellipsis here, "and
none could tell me."

25. *Pharaoh's dream is one.* Joseph, it should be observed, doesn't miss a beat
here. The moment he has heard the dreams, he has everything in hand: the
meaning of all their details, and the explanation for the repetition.

28. *what God is about to do He has shown Pharaoh.* Although the framework of
the Joseph story is "secular" in comparison to the preceding narratives, and
though Joseph's exercise of *ḥokhmah* (wisdom) in dream interpretation and
economic planning has led scholars to detect a strong imprint of ancient Near
Eastern Wisdom literature, he himself is careful to attribute the determination
of events as well as his own "wisdom and discernment" to God (compare verse

30 great plenty through all the land of Egypt. And seven years of famine
will arise after them and all the plenty will be forgotten in the land of
31 Egypt, and the famine will ravage the land, and you will not be able to
tell there was plenty in the land because of that famine afterward, for
32 it will be very grave. And the repeating of the dream to Pharaoh two
times, this means that the thing has been fixed by God and God is has-
33 tening to do it. And so, let Pharaoh look out for a discerning, wise man
34 and set him over the land of Egypt. Let Pharaoh do this: appoint overseers for the land and muster the land of Egypt in the seven years of
35 plenty. And let them collect all the food of these good years that are
coming and let them pile up grain under Pharaoh's hand, food in the
36 cities, to keep under guard. And the food will be a reserve for the land
for the seven years of famine which will be in the land of Egypt, that

---

16). Whatever the considerations of source criticism, moreover, the name he
uses for the deity in speaking with Pharaoh is *'elohim,* the term that has general currency among polytheists and monotheists, and not the particularist
YHWH.

33. *And so, let Pharaoh look out for a discerning, wise man.* The advice after the
interpretation has not been requested. Joseph perhaps runs the risk of seeming presumptuous, but he must have a sense that he has captivated Pharaoh
by the persuasive force of his interpretation, and he sees that this is his own
great moment of opportunity. One wonders whether Pharaoh's two dreams
also make him remember his own two dreams of future grandeur.

34. *muster the land of Egypt.* The meaning of the verb *ḥimesh* is disputed. It
could be derived from *ḥamesh,* "five," and thus refer to a scheme of dividing
the land into fifths or perhaps taking a levy of 20 percent from the crops of the
good years. (In chapter 47, once the great famine is under way, Joseph insti-
tutes a 20 percent tax on the produce of the lands that have been made over
to Pharaoh.) But the same root is also used for the arming or deployment of
troops, and the idea here may be that Joseph is putting the whole country on
a quasimilitary footing in preparation for the extended famine.

35. *under Pharaoh's hand.* Joseph deferentially and diplomatically indicates
that everything will be under Pharaoh's jurisdiction, though it will really be the
"hand"—authority, power, trust—of the "discerning, wise man" that will run
the country.

the land may not perish in the famine." And the thing seemed good in 37
Pharaoh's eyes and in the eyes of his servants. And Pharaoh said to his 38
servants, "Could we find a man like him, in whom is the spirit of God?"
And Pharaoh said to Joseph, "After God has made known to you all 39
this, there is none as discerning and wise as you. You shall be over my 40
house, and by your lips all my folk shall be guided. By the throne alone
shall I be greater than you." And Pharaoh said to Joseph, "See, I have 41
set you over all the land of Egypt." And Pharaoh took off his ring from 42
his hand and put it on Joseph's hand and had him clothed in fine linen
clothes and placed the golden collar round his neck. And he had him 43

---

38. *Could we find a man like him, in whom is the spirit of God?* Pharaoh produces exactly the response Joseph would have hoped for. Again, the flexibility
of *'elohim* serves the dialogue well. The Egyptian monarch has not been
turned into a monotheist by Joseph, but he has gone along with Joseph's idea
that human wisdom is a gift of God, or the gods, and the expression he uses
could have the rather general force of "divine spirit."

40. *by your lips all my folk shall be guided.* The Hebrew says literally "by your
mouth." The clear meaning is "by your commands," "by the directives you
issue." There is some doubt about the verb *yishaq.* The usual sense of "will
kiss" is extremely unlikely here, unless this is a peculiar idiom for civil obedience not otherwise attested. It is best to associate it with the noun *mesheq*
(15:2), which appears to refer to economic administration.

41. *And Pharaoh said to Joseph, "See I have set you."* This is a nice deployment
of the convention of a second iteration of the formula for introducing direct
discourse without an intervening response from the interlocutor. Joseph for
the moment has remained silent, uncertain what to say to Pharaoh's astounding proposal, even if eliciting such a proposal may have been his express intention. So Pharaoh must repeat himself—this time in a performative speech-act
in which he officially confers the high office on Joseph and confirms the act
by adorning the Hebrew slave with regal insignia: the signet ring, the golden
collar, and the fine linen dress.

42. *the golden collar.* Although English translators have repeatedly rendered this
as "chain," Egyptian bas-reliefs show a more elaborate ceremonial ornament
made out of twisted gold wire that covered part of the shoulders and upper
chest as well as the neck. In fact, the Hebrew word is not the normal term for
"chain," and reflects a root that means "to plait," "to cushion," "to pad."

ride in the chariot of his viceroy, and they called out before him *Abrekh,*
44 setting him over all the land of Egypt. And Pharaoh said to Joseph, "I
am Pharaoh! Without you no man shall raise hand or foot in all the land
45 of Egypt." And Pharaoh called Joseph's name Zaphenath-Paneah, and
he gave him Asenath daughter of Potiphera, priest of On, as wife, and
Joseph went out over the land of Egypt.

46 And Joseph was thirty years old when he stood before Pharaoh king of
Egypt, and Joseph went out from Pharaoh's presence and passed

---

43. *Abrekh.* Despite the ingenuity of traditional commentators in construing
this as a Hebrew word, it is evidently Egyptian (in consonance with the loanwords in the surrounding narrative) and may mean something like "make way."
Gerhard von Rad calls attention to this meaning while canvassing other possibilities and sensibly concluding that the term is not entirely certain.

44. *I am Pharaoh!* Most commentators and translators have construed this as
an implied antithesis: though I am Pharaoh, without you no man shall raise
hand or foot. . . . But this is unnecessary because we know that royal decrees
in the ancient Near East regularly began with the formula: I am King X. The
sense here would thus be: By the authority invested in me as Pharaoh, I
declare that without you, etc.

45. *Zaphenath-Paneah.* The change to an Egyptian name is of a piece with the
assumption of Egyptian dress and the insignia of high office. The name may
mean "God speaks, he lives," as Moshe Weinfeld, following the lead of Egyp-
tologists, surmises.
   Potiphera. This is the full form of the same name born by Joseph's old master, Potiphar, but evidently refers to a different person, since Potiphar was
identified as courtier and high chamberlain, not as priest. *On* is not a deity but
the name of a city, later designated Heliopolis by the Greeks because of the
sun worship centered there.
   Joseph went out over the land. The wording is a little odd. It may be associated with the end of verse 46.

46. *when he stood before Pharaoh.* This could mean, idiomatically, when he
entered Pharaoh's service, though it is equally possible that the verb refers literally to the scene just reported, when he stood before Pharaoh and made his
way to greatness by interpreting the dreams.

through all the land of Egypt. And the land in the seven years of plenty 47
made gatherings. And he collected all the food of the seven years that 48
were in the land of Egypt and he placed food in the cities, the food
from the fields round each city he placed within it. And Joseph piled 49
up grain like the sand of the sea, very much, until he ceased counting,
for it was beyond count.

And to Joseph two sons were born before the coming of the year of 50
famine, whom Asenath daughter of Potiphera priest of On bore him.
And Joseph called the name of the firstborn Manasseh, meaning, God 51
has released me from all the debt of my hardship, and of all my father's

---

47. *made gatherings.* The Hebrew *qematsim* elsewhere means "handfuls," and
there is scant evidence that it means "abundance," as several modern versions
have it. But *qomets* is a "handful" because it is what the hand gathers in as it
closes, and it is phonetically and semantically cognate with *wayiqbots*, "he collected," the very next word in the Hebrew text. The likely reference here, then,
is not to small quantities (handfuls) but to the process of systematically gathering in the grain, as the next sentence spells out.

49. *like the sand of the sea, very much, until he ceased counting.* The language
here is strongly reminiscent of the covenantal language in the promise of progeny to Abraham and thus provides a kind of associative link with the notice of
Joseph's progeny in the next three verses. Upon the birth of Ephraim, Joseph
himself will invoke the verb for making fruitful that is featured in the repeated
promises of offspring to the patriarchs.

51. *Manasseh . . . released me from all the debt.* The naming pun is on the verbal stem *n-sh-h*. The virtually universal construal of this term here is "made me
forget," but it must be said that the root in that sense occurs only five times in
the biblical corpus, and at least two or three of those are doubtful. It is also
somewhat odd that Joseph should celebrate God for having made him forget
his father's house. But a very common usage of *n-sh-h* is "to hold in debt," and
a natural meaning of that stem in the *pi'el* conjugation, as here, would be "to
relieve from the condition of debt." Such an unambiguously positive verb is a
better parallel to "made me fruitful" in the next verse. I am grateful to Amos
Funkenstein for this original suggestion.

52 house. And the name of the second he called Ephraim, meaning, God has made me fruitful in the land of my affliction.

53 And the seven years of the plenty that had been in the land of Egypt
54 came to an end. And the seven years of famine began to come, as Joseph had said, and there was famine in all the lands, but in the land
55 of Egypt there was bread. And all the land of Egypt was hungry and the people cried out to Pharaoh for bread, and Pharaoh said to all of Egypt,
56 "Go to Joseph. What he says to you, you must do." And the famine was over all the land. And Joseph laid open whatever had grain within and sold provisions to Egypt. And the famine grew harsh in the land of
57 Egypt. And all the earth came to Egypt, to Joseph, to get provisions, for the famine had grown harsh in all the earth.

---

52. *Ephraim . . . made me fruitful.* The naming pun is on the verbal stem *p-r-h*.

55. *all the land of Egypt was hungry.* The contradiction between this report and the preceding statement that there was bread in Egypt is pointed. There is food in storage, not to be had from the wasted fields, but Joseph metes it out to the populace, and at a price.

56. *Joseph laid open whatever had grain within.* The Masoretic Text, which lacks "whatever had grain," is problematic at this point. The Aramaic Targums supply these missing words. Other ancient versions presume a phrase like "stores of grain."

CHAPTER 42

And Jacob saw that there were provisions in Egypt, and Jacob 1
said to his sons, "Why are you fearful?" And he said, "Look, 2
I have heard that there are provisions in Egypt. Go down
there, and get us provisions from there that we may live and not die."

---

1. *provisions*. Most of the biblical occurrences of this noun *shever*, as well as
the transitive verb *shavar* (verse 3, "to buy") and the causative verb *hishbir*
(verse 6) are in this story. The root means "to break," and the sense seems to
be: food provisions that serve to break an imposed fast, that is, a famine
(hence "provisions to stave off the famine," *shever ra'avon*, in verse 19). The
term "rations" adopted by at least three recent translations has a misleading
military connotation.

fearful. All English versions construe this as a reflexive of the verb for seeing (*r-'-h*) and render it along the lines of "staring at one another." But the four
other occurrences of this root in the reflexive in the Bible invariably link it with
panim ("face"), and staring as a gesture of inaction is not characteristically biblical. The Targum of Yonatan derived the verb from the root meaning "to fear"
(*y-r-'*), a construal feasible without emendation because the *yod* can be elided.
Fearing and the injunction to fear not are recurrent elements in the story of
the brothers' descent to Egypt.

2. *And he said*. The repetition of the formula introducing speech with no intervening response from the person or persons addressed accords with the general biblical convention we have observed elsewhere: such repetition is an
indication of a failure of response by the interlocutors. The brothers here do
not know how to respond to their father's challenge.

that we may live and not die. The almost excessive spelling out in Jacob's
words may reflect his impatience with his sons, who are acting as though they
did not grasp the urgency of the situation.

3,4 And the ten brothers of Joseph went down to buy grain from Egypt. But Benjamin, Joseph's brother, Jacob did not send with his brothers, for he thought, Lest harm befall him.

5 And the sons of Israel came to buy provisions among those who came,
6 for there was famine in the land of Canaan. As for Joseph, he was the regent of the land, he was the provider to all the people of the land. And Joseph's brothers came and bowed down to him, their faces to the
7 ground. And Joseph saw his brothers and recognized them, and he played the stranger to them and spoke harshly to them, and said to them, "Where have you come from?" And they said, "From the land of
8 Canaan, to buy food." And Joseph recognized his brothers but they did

---

3. *the ten brothers.* Biblical narrative is meticulous in its choice of familial epithets. When the ten go down to Egypt to encounter the man who will prove to be their supposedly dead brother, they are identified as Joseph's brothers, not Jacob's sons.

4. *Benjamin, Joseph's brother.* The identification of Benjamin as Joseph's brother is formally identical to the familial epithet in the previous verse, with the pointed difference that only Benjamin is Joseph's full brother.

5. *among those who came.* This economical phrase indicates a great crowd of people, from "all the earth," driven by the famine to Egypt, where there was food to be bought.

7. *and recognized them, and . . . played the stranger to them.* The verb for "recognize" and the verb for "play the stranger" are derived from the same root (the latter being a reflexive form of the root). Both uses pick up the thematically prominent repetition of the same root earlier in the story: Jacob was asked to "recognize" Joseph's blood-soaked tunic and Tamar invited Judah to "recognize" the tokens he had left with her as security for payment for sexual services.

8. *And Joseph recognized his brothers but they did not recognize him.* Given the importance of the recognition theme and the verb to which it is linked, it is fitting that the fact of Joseph's recognizing his brothers should be repeated, along with their failure to recognize him (in other words, the success of his playing the stranger).

not recognize him. And Joseph remembered the dreams he had 9
dreamed about them, and he said to them, "You are spies! To see the
land's nakedness you have come." And they said to him, "No, my lord, 10
for your servants have come to buy food. We are all the sons of one 11
man. We are honest. Your servants would never be spies." And he said 12
to them, "No! For the land's nakedness you have come to see." And they 13
said, "Twelve brothers your servants are, we are the sons of one man in
the land of Canaan, and, look, the youngest is now with our father, and

---

9. *And Joseph remembered the dreams.* This brief memory-flashback is a device
rarely used in biblical narrative. Its importance here is that the brothers, prostrated before Joseph, are, unbeknownst to them, literally fulfilling his two
prophetic dreams, the very dreams that enraged them and triggered the vio
lence they perpetrated against him. There is surely an element of sweet triumph for Joseph in seeing his grandiose dreams fulfilled so precisely, though
it would be darkened by his recollection of what the report of his dreams led
his brothers to do. The repetition of Joseph's angry accusation thus has psychological resonance: he remembers, and he remembers the reason for his
long-standing anger.

the land's nakedness. The idiom refers to that which should be hidden from
an outsider's eyes, as the pudenda are to be hidden from all but the legitimate
sexual partner. Joseph's language thus casts the alleged spies as *violators* of the
land.

11. *We are all the sons of one man. We are honest. Your servants would never be
spies.* This series of three brief sentences, without connecting "and's," is
uncharacteristic of biblical style, and may well be intended to reflect the
brothers' emphatic, anxious defensiveness in the face of Joseph's wholly unexpected accusation.

13. *Twelve brothers your servants are.* The Hebrew places the number twelve at
the very beginning of the brothers' speech. They use the euphemism "is no
more" (literally, "is not") to indicate that Joseph is dead, not imagining, in the
strong dramatic irony of the scene, that the brother who makes the full complement of twelve stands before them. It is thematically pointed that they
identify themselves as "twelve brothers," although only ten of them stand
before Joseph.

14 one is no more." And Joseph said to them, "That's just what I told you,
15 you are spies. In this shall you be tested—by Pharaoh! You shall not
16 leave this place unless your youngest brother comes here. Send one of
you to bring your brother, and as for the rest of you, you will be
detained, and your words will be tested as to whether the truth is with
17 you, and if not, by Pharaoh, you must be spies!" And he put them
18 under guard for three days. And Joseph said to them on the third day,
19 "Do this and live, for I fear God. If you are honest, let one of your
brothers be detained in this very guardhouse, and the rest of you go
forth and bring back provisions to stave off the famine in your homes.
20 And your youngest brother you shall bring to me, that your words may
21 be confirmed and you need not die." And so they did. And they said
each to his brother, "Alas, we are guilty for our brother, whose mortal
distress we saw when he pleaded with us and we did not listen. That is
22 why this distress has overtaken us." Then Reuben spoke out to them in
these words: "Didn't I say to you, 'Do not sin against the boy,' and you

---

15–16. Joseph's swearing by Pharaoh at first seems merely part of his playing
his role as Egyptian. Not until verse 23 do we learn that he is addressing them
through an interpreter, so the locution also probably reflects the fact that he is
speaking Egyptian.

20. *And your youngest brother you shall bring to me.* The "test" of bringing Benjamin to Egypt is actually a test of fraternal fidelity. Joseph may have some lingering suspicion as to whether the brothers have done away with Benjamin,
the other son of Rachel, as they imagine they have gotten rid of him.

21. *Alas, we are guilty.* The psychological success of Joseph's stratagem is confirmed by the fact that the accusation and the hostage taking immediately trigger feelings of guilt over their behavior toward Joseph. Notably, it is only now,
not in the original report (37:23–24), that we learn that Joseph pleaded with
them when they cast him into the pit, a remarkable instance of withheld narrative exposition. Reuben, who tried to save him, now becomes the chief
spokesman for their collective guilt.

would not listen? And now, look, his blood is requited." And they did   23
not know that Joseph understood, for there was an interpreter between
them. And he turned away from them and wept and returned to them   24
and spoke to them, and he took Simeon from them and placed him in
fetters before their eyes.

And Joseph gave orders to fill their baggage with grain and to put back   25
their silver into each one's pack and to give them supplies for the way,
and so he did for them. And they loaded their provisions on their don-   26
keys and they set out from there. Then one of them opened his pack to   27
give provender to his donkey at the encampment, and he saw his silver
and, look, it was in the mouth of his bag. And he said to his brothers,   28
"My silver has been put back and, look, it's actually in my bag." And
they were dumbfounded and trembled each before his brother, saying,
"What is this that God has done to us?" And they came to Jacob their   29

---

23. *And they did not know that Joseph understood.* The verb for understanding,
which also means "to hear" or "to listen," plays ironically against its use in the
immediately preceding verse, "and you would not *listen*."

24. *And he turned away from them and wept.* This is the first of three times, in
a clear crescendo pattern, that Joseph is moved to tears by his brothers.

25. *to put back their silver into each one's pack.* The return of the silver is also
associated with the brothers' guilt, for it repeats their receiving of silver from
the Ishmaelites for the sale of Joseph as a slave. If the story reflects the realia
of the Patriarchal period, the silver would be weights of silver, not coins, and
the weighing out of silver in Abraham's purchase of the burial site from the
Hittites suggests that is what is to be imagined here.

28. *My silver has been put back and, look, it's actually in my bag.* These words
of astonishment, with their virtual redundance and their locutions of emphasis—*wegam hineh be'amtaḥti*, "it's actually in my bag"—ironically correspond
to the language of amazement used by the young Joseph in reporting his dream
(compare 37:7).
    dumbfounded. The Hebrew says literally, "their heart went out."
    What is this that God has done to us? This is a kind of double dramatic irony.
It is of course Joseph who has done this to them, but we are also invited to
think of him as God's instrument—an idea he himself will emphasize after he

father, to the land of Canaan, and they told him all that had befallen
30 them, saying, "The man who is lord of the land spoke harshly to us and
31 made us out to be spies in the land. And we said to him, 'We are hon-
32 est. We would never be spies. Twelve brothers we are, the sons of our
father. One is no more and the youngest is now with our father in the
33 land of Canaan.' And the man who is lord of the land said to us, 'By this
shall I know if you are honest: one of your brothers leave with me and
34 provisions against the famine in your homes take, and go. And bring
your youngest brother to me that I may know you are not spies but are
honest. I shall give you back your brother and you can trade in the
35 land.'" And just as they were emptying their packs, look, each one's
bundle of silver was in his pack. And they saw their bundles, both they
and their father, and were afraid. And Jacob their father said to them,
36 "Me you have bereaved. Joseph is no more and Simeon is no more, and

---

reveals himself to his brothers. Thus a double system of causation, human and
divine, is brought to the fore.

31–34. The near verbatim repetition of reported speech, as we have seen elsewhere, is standard biblical practice, though more commonly there are subtly
significant variations in the repetition. Here, the one notable change is that in
addressing Jacob directly, they substitute "our father" for "one man."

33. *provisions against the famine.* The Hebrew here uses an ellipsis, simply,
"famine."

34. *trade.* The primary meaning of the verb is "to go around," and by extension,
"to engage in commerce." Given the situation of going back and forth to Egypt
to buy grain, the sense of trading seems more likely here.

35. *look, each one's bundle of silver was in his pack.* The second discovery of the
silver in the baggage of course contradicts the first discovery at the encampment and probably reflects the splicing together of two variant traditions—
unless one assumes that the brothers deliberately act out a discovery in the
presence of their father in order to impress upon him how they are all at the
mercy of a superior power.

36. *Me you have bereaved.* As earlier in the story, Jacob speaks as a prima donna
of paternal grief: hence the "me" at the beginning of his discourse (the Hebrew

Benjamin you would take! It is I who bear it all." And Reuben spoke to 37
his father, saying, "My two sons you may put to death if I do not bring
him back to you. Place him in my hands and I will return him to you."
And he said, "My son shall not go down with you, for his brother is 38
dead, and he alone remains, and should harm befall him on the way
you are going, you would bring down my gray head in sorrow to Sheol."

---

has an accusative pronoun before the verb instead of the normal accusative
suffix appended to the verb), and hence the emphatic rhythmic arrangement
of his speech in a formal symmetry that verges on poetry: "Joseph is no more
and Simeon is no more, and Benjamin you would take!" In a small envelope
structure, the "me" at the beginning is balanced by the "It is I" at the end (the
last sentence is literally: "Upon me they all were"). Jacob's equation of Joseph
and Simeon with the verb "is no more" teeters ambiguously between two possibilities: either he gloomily assumes that Simeon is already as good as dead,
or, despite his protestations of grief, he clings to the hope that Joseph, like
Simeon, is absent, not dead.

37. *My two sons you may put to death.* Reuben, as usual, means well but stum-
bles in the execution: to a father obsessed with the loss of sons, he offers the
prospect of killing two grandsons. David Kimhi catches this nicely: "[Jacob]
said: 'Stupid firstborn! Are they your sons and not my sons?'" This is not the
only moment in the story when we sense that Reuben's claim to preeminence
among the brothers as firstborn is dubious, and he will be displaced by Judah,
the fourth-born.

38. *My son shall not go down with you.* The extravagant insensitivity of Jacob's
paternal favoritism continues to be breathtaking. He speaks of Benjamin as
"my son" almost as though the ones he is addressing were not his sons. This
unconscious disavowal of the ten sons is sharpened when Jacob says, "he alone
remains," failing to add "from his mother." The histrionic refrain of descending in sorrow to Sheol, the underworld, is one Jacob first recited when he was
handed Joseph's blood-soaked tunic. "Should harm befall him" is a formula
first spoken by Jacob in an interior monologue (verse 4) and now repeated in
actual speech to the sons. Jacob is of course fearful of another dreadful accident like the one in which he believes Joseph was torn to pieces by a wild
beast. There is, then, an ironic disparity between Jacob's sense of a world of
unpredictable dangers threatening his beloved son and Joseph's providential
manipulation of events, unguessed by his father and his brothers.

CHAPTER 43

1,2   **A**nd the famine grew grave in the land. And it happened when they had eaten up the provisions they had brought from Egypt, that
3   their father said to them, "Go back, buy us some food." And Judah said to him, saying, "The man firmly warned us, saying, 'You shall not
4   see my face unless your brother is with you.' If you are going to send
5   our brother with us, we may go down and buy you food, but if you are not going to send him, we will not go down, for the man said to us, 'You
6   shall not see my face unless your brother is with you.'" And Israel said, "Why have you done me this harm to tell the man you had another
7   brother?" And they said, "The man firmly asked us about ourselves and

---

3. *The man firmly warned us.* "The man" refers elliptically to the phrase the brothers previously used in their report to their father, "the man who is lord of the land" (42:30). Their repeated use of this designation aptly dramatizes their ignorance of Joseph's identity. In the second half of this chapter, there is pointed interplay between the references to the brothers as "the men"—almost as though they were represented from an Egyptian point of view—and to Joseph's majordomo as "the man."

You shall not see my face. The Hebrew idiom has distinct regal overtones: you shall not come into my presence.

5. *You shall not see my face unless your brother is with you.* Judah reiterates this sentence word for word, at the end of his first speech to Jacob as at the beginning. The effect is to spell out the inexorable condition with heavy emphasis for the reluctant Jacob: it is only by bringing Benjamin along that we can return to Egypt.

6. *Why have you done me this harm.* Consistent with his character from chapter 37 onward, Jacob flaunts his sense of personal injury.

our kindred, saying, 'Is your father still living? Do you have a brother?' And we told him, in response to these words. Could we know he would say, 'Bring down your brother?'" And Judah said to Israel his father, 8 "Send the lad with me, and let us rise and go, that we may live and not die, neither we, nor you, nor our little ones. I will be his pledge, from 9 my hand you may seek him: if I do not bring him to you and set him before you, I will bear the blame to you for all time. For had we not 10 tarried, by now we could have come back twice." And Israel their 11 father said to them, "If it must be so, do this: take of the best yield of the land in your baggage and bring down to the man as tribute some balm and some honey, gum and ladanum, pistachio nuts and almonds.

---

8. *that we may live and not die, neither we, nor you, nor our little ones.* The phrase "live and not die" was used by Jacob to his sons before their first journey to Egypt (42:2), and Judah now throws it back in his face. By adding to it, "neither we, nor you, nor our little ones," Judah makes a vividly persuasive point: as Rashi sees, the implicit argument is that if we risk taking Benjamin, he may or may not be seized, but if we stay here, every one of us will perish from hunger.

9. *I will be his pledge, from my hand you may seek him.* The repetition through synonymity signals a performative speech-act, a legally binding vow. Judah, who conceived the scheme of selling Joseph into slavery, now takes personal responsibility for Benjamin's safety. But befitting the son who will displace Reuben as the progenitor of the kings of Israel, he asserts solemn responsibility without Reuben's rash offer to put two of his own sons to death if harm befalls Benjamin.

11. *the best yield of the land.* The Hebrew *zimrat ha'arets* occurs only here. The most plausible construal of the first term links it with a root that means "strength" or "power," though it could be related to *zemorah*, "branch" or "sprout."

   some balm and some honey, gum and ladanum. The tribute or gift (*minḥah*) to Joseph includes three of the same items as those in the briefer list of luxury export goods carried by the Ishmaelite traders (37:25) who bought Joseph from the brothers and sold him as a slave in Egypt. As with the silver sent back and forth, the brothers are thus drawn unwittingly into a process of repetition of and restitution for their fraternal crime.

12 And double the silver take in your hand, and the silver that was put
back in the mouths of your bags bring back in your hand. Perhaps it was
13 a mistake. And your brother take, and rise and go back to the man.
14 And may El Shaddai grant you mercy before the man, that he discharge
to you your other brother, and Benjamin. As for me, if I must be
bereaved, I will be bereaved."

15 And the men took this tribute and double the silver they took in their
hand, and Benjamin, and they rose and went down to Egypt and stood

---

12. *And double the silver take.* Now they are to go to Egypt with three times the
original amount of silver: the amount they intend to return to Joseph, and double that amount besides. Nahum Sarna construes the second clause, "and the
silver that was put back . . . ," as an explanation of the first, concluding that
only double the amount in sum was taken, but his reading dismisses the clear
additive sense of "and" in "and the silver." Rashi, with characteristic shrewd-
ness, suggests that extra silver was taken because the brothers were fearful
that the price of grain might have gone up steeply—a plausible possibility,
given Egypt's monopoly of food supplies and the persisting famine.

take in your hand. The addition of "in your hand," which is not strictly
required by Hebrew idiom, is repeated several times in the story. One suspects
it is linked with the theme of restitution: the very hands that were "raised
against" Joseph (37:22 and 27) now bear tribute to him.

13. *And your brother take.* Jacob holds back the detail that is most painful to
him, the sending down of Benjamin, until the very end of his instructions.
Pointedly, he does not refer to Benjamin by name but instead calls him "your
brother," stressing the fraternal responsibility his nine older sons have for their
half brother.

14. *he discharge to you your other brother, and Benjamin.* Jacob's fearful formulation virtually presupposes that Benjamin will be seized by the Egyptians, just
as Simeon was.

As for me, if I must be bereaved, I will be bereaved. Jacob is of course remembering his grief over the loss of Joseph and perhaps as well his concern over
Simeon's imprisonment. But he is also once more playing his role as histrion
of paternal sorrow, echoing his dirgelike words to his sons (42:36), "Me you
have bereaved," using the same verb that refers specifically in Hebrew to the
loss of children and again placing the first-person singular pronoun at the
beginning of his statement.

in Joseph's presence. And Joseph saw Benjamin with them and he said 16
to the one who was over his house, "Bring the men into the house, and
slaughter an animal and prepare it, for with me the men shall eat at
noon." And the man did as Joseph had said, and the man brought the 17
men to Joseph's house. And the men were afraid at being brought to 18
Joseph's house, and they said, "Because of the silver put back in our
bags the first time we've been brought, in order to fall upon us, to
attack us, and to take us as slaves, and our donkeys." And they 19
approached the man who was over Joseph's house, and they spoke to
him by the entrance of the house. And they said, "Please, my lord, we 20

---

16. *the one who was over his house.* Virtually all the English versions represent
this as "steward," but the Hebrew opts for this more circumlocutionary phrase
(which does occur, in a clear administrative sense, in notices about the later
Israelite royal bureaucracy) instead of one of the available biblical terms for
steward or majordomo. This roundabout designation reflects an Egyptian title
and may at the same time intimate the perspective of the Hebrew brothers
toward this Egyptian "man who was over the house" with whom they have to
deal. It also enables the writer to play "man" against "men" in his narrative
report.

17. *Joseph's house.* The phrase is repeated three times in rapid sequence, and
amplified by the secondary references to "the man who was over his house."
For the ten Hebrew men to go into Joseph's house is a momentous thing, politically and thematically. Since they are aware that it is not customary for foreigners who have come to buy grain to be introduced into the residence of the
viceroy, they are afraid it may be a trap (verse 18). Their last encounter with
Joseph in Canaan, more than two decades earlier, was in an open field, where
he was entirely in their power. Now, crossing the threshold of his house, they
will be entirely in his power—whether for evil or for good they cannot say.
Pointedly, their actual sitting down at Joseph's table is prefaced by a literally
liminal moment: they stand at the entrance, expressing their anxiety to
Joseph's steward.

18. *to fall upon us.* The Hebrew verb might well have the sense of "to find a
pretext against us," as many English versions render it, but it is at least as plausible to construe it as a verb of physical assault, in apposition to the term that
follows it.

    and our donkeys. This odd addendum at the very end of the sentence looks
suspiciously like a comic inadvertency.

21 indeed came down the first time to buy food, and it happened when we
came to the encampment that we opened our bags and, look, each
man's silver was in the mouth of his bag, our silver in full weight, and
22 we have brought it back in our hand, and we have brought down more
23 silver to buy food. We do not know who put our silver in our bags." And
he said, "All is well with you, do not fear. Your God and the God of your
father has placed treasure for you in your bags. Your silver has come to
24 me." And he brought Simeon out to them. And the man brought the
men into Joseph's house, and he gave them water and they bathed their
25 feet, and he gave provender to their donkeys. And they prepared the
tribute against Joseph's arrival at noon, for they had heard that there
26 they would eat bread. And Joseph came into the house, and they
brought him the tribute that was in their hand, into the house, and they
27 bowed down to him to the ground. And he asked how they were, and
he said, "Is all well with your aged father of whom you spoke? Is he still
28 alive?" And they said, "All is well with your servant, our father. He is
29 still alive." And they did obeisance and bowed down. And he raised his
eyes and saw Benjamin his brother, his mother's son, and he said, "Is
this your youngest brother of whom you spoke to me?" And he said,

---

23. *has placed treasure for you in your bags*. The majordomo dismisses their
fears by introducing a kind of fairy-tale explanation for the silver they found in
their bags.

Your silver has come to me. These words take the form of a legal declaration
meaning "I have duly received payment."

25. *they would eat bread*. "Bread," as in the English expression, "to eat the king's
bread," is obviously a synecdoche for food, but it diminishes the literary dignity of the narrative to render this, as many modern translations have done,
simply as "dine."

"God be gracious to you, my son." And Joseph hurried out, for his feel- 30
ings for his brother overwhelmed him and he wanted to weep, and he
went into the chamber and wept there. And he bathed his face and 31
came out and held himself in check and said, "Serve bread." And they 32
served him and them separately and the Egyptians that were eating
with him separately, for the Egyptians would not eat bread with the
Hebrews, as it was abhorrent to Egypt. And they were seated before 33
him, the firstborn according to his birthright, the youngest according to

---

29. *God be gracious to you, my son.* Benjamin, though considerably younger
than Joseph, would be at least in his late twenties at this point. In addressing
him as "my son," Joseph faithfully maintains his role as Egyptian viceroy,
though "my brother" is hiding in the word he uses. The great medieval Hebrew
poet Shmuel Hanagid (eleventh-century Granada) would brilliantly catch this
doubleness in a moving elegy to his brother by altering the end of the phrase:
"God be gracious to you, my brother."

30. *And Joseph hurried out . . . and he wanted to weep, and he went into the
chamber and wept there.* In the pattern of incremental repetition, this second
weeping of Joseph's is much more elaborately reported than the first (42:24),
including as it does the flight to a private chamber and (in the next verse), his
bathing his face to remove evidence of the tears and his effort of self-restraint
when he returns to the brothers.
   his feelings . . . overwhelmed him. The literal meaning of the Hebrew is "his
mercy [the same term used by Jacob in verse 14] burned hot."

32. *for the Egyptians would not eat bread with the Hebrews.* The dietary exclu-
sionism of the Egyptians is also attested by Herodotus. Both medieval and
modern commentators have linked this taboo with an Egyptian prohibition
against eating lamb, a staple of Hebrew diet.
   as it was abhorrent to Egypt. The consensus of English translations treats
this as "to the Egyptians," but the Masoretic vocalization of the final noun—
mitsrayim and not *mitsrim*—construes it as "to Egypt," which makes perfectly
good sense.

33. *And they were seated before him.* The seating in order of age of course has
been done at Joseph's direction: it constitutes a kind of dramatization of the
contrast between knowledge and ignorance—"and he recognized them but
they did not recognize him"—that has been paramount from the moment the
brothers first set foot in Egypt.

34 his youth, and the men marveled to each other. And he had portions
passed to them from before him, and Benjamin's portion was five times
more than the portion of all the rest, and they drank, and they got
drunk with him.

---

34. *they drank, and they got drunk with him.* In the Hebrew, these are two
entirely distinct verbs. The meeting between the eleven brothers and the man
who is lord of the land of Egypt appears to end on a note of conviviality, which
will quickly be reversed in the next scene of the drama Joseph has carefully
devised for his brothers. It should be noted that the drinking at the conclusion
of this scene anticipates the mechanism of what is to follow, for it is the
alleged theft of Joseph's silver goblet that will bring the brothers back to his
house under strict arrest.

CHAPTER 44

And he charged the one who was over his house, saying, "Fill the men's bags with as much food as they can carry, and put each man's silver in the mouth of his bag. And my goblet, the silver goblet, put in the mouth of the bag of the youngest, with the silver for his provisions." And he did as Joseph had spoken. The morning had just brightened when the men were sent off, they and their donkeys. They had come out of the city, they were not far off, when Joseph said to the

1. *put each man's silver in the mouth of his bag.* This detail is a small puzzle because nothing is made of the discovery of silver when the majordomo searches through the bags. This seeming indiscrepancy has led critics to write off the return of the silver as a later addition made to harmonize this episode with the one in chapter 42, but that is by no means a necessary conclusion. Joseph's scheme, after all, is to make the brothers feel they are trapped in a network of uncanny circumstances they can neither control nor explain. A repetition of the device of returning the silver would nicely serve this purpose. The majordomo, however, is exclusively focused on the retrieval of a particular silver object, the divining goblet, and so does not even deign to mention the weights of silver in the bags, as though their appearance there were a matter of course, whatever consternation it might cause the brothers. Meanwhile, as in dream logic—or perhaps one should say, guilt logic—the brothers, who once took silver when they sold Joseph down into Egypt, seem helpless to "return" the silver to Egypt, as much as they try. The returned silver, moreover, makes the purported stealing of the silver goblet look all the more heinous.

2. *And my goblet, the silver goblet.* The double formulation highlights both the fact that the goblet is Joseph's special possession and that it is made of silver.

3. *they and their donkeys.* Again the donkeys are tacked onto the end of the sentence, perhaps because the donkeys are carrying the packs, which will have to

one who was over his house, "Rise, pursue the men, and when you

5 overtake them, say to them, 'Why have you paid back evil for good? Is not this the one from which my lord drinks, and in which he always

6 divines? You have wrought evil in what you did.'" And he overtook them

7 and spoke to them these words. And they said to him, "Why should our lord speak words like these? Far be it from your servants to do such a

8 thing! Why, the silver we found in the mouth of our bags we brought back to you from the land of Canaan. How then could we steal from

9 your master's house silver or gold? He of your servants with whom it be found shall die, and, what's more, we shall become slaves to our lord."

10 And he said, "Even so, as by your words, let it be: he with whom it be

---

be set down on the ground and then reloaded (verses 11 and 12), in one of which the goblet has been secreted.

5. *Is not this the one from which my lord drinks, and in which he always divines?* The fact that the goblet is referred to only by a demonstrative pronoun ("the one from which") may reflect a flaunting of the assumption that, as all concerned should recognize, the only thing at issue here is the goblet. The brothers may well have seen Joseph drinking from the goblet at the dinner the day before, whereas its use for divination would have been news to them. The probable mechanism of divination in a goblet would be to interpret patterns on the surface of the liquid it contained or in drops running down its sides. Divination would have been a plausible activity on the part of a member of the high Egyptian bureaucracy, with its technology of soothsaying, but the emphasis it is given here is also linked with Joseph's demonstrated ability to predict the future and his superiority of knowledge in relation to his brothers.

9. *He of your servants with whom it be found shall die.* This pronouncement of a death sentence for stealing may be excessive in relation to the standards of ancient Near Eastern law, though Gerhard von Rad has proposed that stealing a sacred object would have been deemed a capital crime. The brothers' words are quite similar to those spoken by their father to Laban (31:32) before he rummaged through the belongings of Jacob's wives in search of his missing household gods. It is a teasing parallel with crucial differences: Laban does not find what he is looking for, but the death sentence pronounced on the actually guilty party—Benjamin's mother, Rachel—appears to be carried out later when she dies bearing him.

and . . . *we shall become slaves to our lord.* This gratuitous additional condition, a reflex of their perfect confidence in their innocence of the theft, car-

found shall become a slave to me, and you shall be clear." And they hur- 11
ried and each man set down his bag on the ground and each opened his
bag. And he searched, beginning with the oldest and ending with the 12
youngest, and he found the goblet in Benjamin's bag. And they rent 13
their garments, and each loaded his donkey and they returned to the
city.

And Judah with his brothers came into Joseph's house, for he was still 14
there, and they threw themselves before him to the ground. And 15
Joseph said to them, "What is this deed you have done? Did you not
know that a man like me would surely divine?" And Judah said, "What 16

---

ries forward the great theme of moral restitution: the brothers who sold Joseph
into slavery now offer themselves as slaves. The term 'eved means both servant
and slave, and the speeches in this episode pointedly play the two meanings
against each other. When the brothers refer to themselves as "your servants,"
they are clearly using courtly language of self-abasement; when they, or Judah,
offer to be slaves, they are proposing to surrender their freedom and enter into
a condition of actual servitude.

10. *Even so, as by your words, let it be.* These first words of response by the
majordomo may constitute a kind of bureaucratic, or legal, flourish. He begins
by seeming to concur in the stern sentence the brothers have pronounced on
themselves should the goblet be found among them; but, having accepted the
principle they enunciated that the guilty party should be punished and a dis
tinction made between him and his brothers, the majordomo modifies the sentence to make it more reasonable—the guilty brother will be made a slave and
the others allowed to go free.

14. *And Judah with his brothers came.* The Hebrew says, "Judah and his brothers" but uses a characteristic grammatical device, a verb conjugated in the singular instead of the plural, to indicate that the first-stated noun (Judah) is the
principal agent, the thematically focused subject of the verb. In a moment,
Judah will step forward and become the spokesman for all the brothers, the
ringing voice of their collective conscience.

15. *Did you not know that a man like me would surely divine?* Like much else
in this story, Joseph's words are contrived to yield a double meaning. He is saying they should have known that a person of his standing would practice divination and so the goblet they purloined was no mere silver cup but a

shall we say to my lord? What shall we speak and how shall we prove ourselves right? God has found out your servants' crime. Here we are, slaves to my lord, both we and the one in whose hand the goblet was
17 found." And he said, "Far be it from me to do this! The man in whose hand the goblet was found, he shall become my slave, and you, go up
18 in peace to your father." And Judah approached him and said, "Please, my lord, let your servant speak a word in my lord's hearing and let your
19 wrath not flare against your servant, for you are like Pharaoh. My lord

---

dedicated instrument of divination. But, in keeping with the sustained theme of his knowledge and his brothers' ignorance, he is also suggesting that a man of his powers would be able to divine such a theft, and its perpetrator.

16. *God has found out your servants' crime.* In this case, the double meaning expresses a buried psychological dimension in Judah's plea to Joseph. On the surface, he is simply conceding guilt as his only recourse because one of his brothers had been caught with the evidence and he has no counterarguments to offer. But he speaks out of the consciousness of a real guilt incurred by him and his brothers more than two decades earlier—compare their response at their first detention, 42:21—and thus expresses a real sense that God has at last exacted retribution for that act of fraternal betrayal. He of course cannot guess that the man whom he is addressing perfectly understands both references. One should note that guilt is assumed by Judah in the first-person plural and is not restricted to "the one in whose hand the goblet was found."

Here we are, slaves to my lord. Again, an unconscious principle of retribution asserts itself: the ten who condemned Joseph to slavery offer themselves as slaves to him, together with Benjamin.

in whose hand the goblet was found. In fact, it was found in the mouth of his bag. But the reiterated image of the hand holding the goblet links up with all the previous focusing on hands in the story and stresses the idea of agency and responsibility.

17. *he shall become my slave.* This is, of course, the last turn of the screw in Joseph's testing of his brothers: will they allow Rachel's other son to be enslaved, as they did with her elder son?

had asked his servants, saying, 'Do you have a father or brother?' And 20
we said to my lord, 'We have an aged father and a young child of his old
age, and his brother being dead, he alone is left of his mother, and his
father loves him.' And you said to your servants, 'Bring him down to me, 21
that I may set my eyes on him.' And we said to my lord, 'The lad can- 22
not leave his father. Should he leave his father, he would die.' And you 23
said to your servants, 'If your youngest brother does not come down
with you, you shall not see my face again.' And it happened when we 24
went up to your servant, my father, that we told him the words of my

---

20. *an aged father and a young child of his old age*. The phrase suggests the intimate connection between father and child ("aged," "old age") as well as Benjamin's vulnerability as youngest (the Hebrew for "young" also means "little").

his brother being dead, he alone is left of his mother, and his father loves him.
Either Judah assumes that after more than twenty years of slavery in a foreign
land Joseph is likely to be dead or he states Joseph's absence as death for the
sake of rhetorical simplicity, to make clear that the son is irrevocably lost to his
doting father. What is remarkable is that now Judah can bring himself, out of
concern for his old father, to accept the painful fact of paternal favoritism ("and
his father loves him") that was the root of the brothers' hostility to Joseph.

21. *that I may set my eyes on him*. This phrase, which in other contexts can
mean something like showing royal favor toward someone, and which for
Joseph has the personal meaning of wanting to behold his full brother,
momentarily seems to have been given a sinister twist by the course of events.

22. *The lad cannot leave his father*. Although Benjamin is considerably beyond
adolescence, "lad" (*na'ar*), as in a number of other notable occurrences, is a
designation that suggests tenderness, and perhaps the vulnerability of the person so designated, and Judah also uses it here because Benjamin is the
youngest. Joseph, it should be noted, had coldly referred to the purportedly
guilty Benjamin as "the man" (verse 17).

Should he leave his father, he would die. The translation reflects the ambiguity of the Hebrew, and one may be skeptical of the often-made claim that
the second "he" must refer to Jacob. It seems more likely that this is a studied
ambiguity on Judah's part: he leaves it to Joseph to decide whether the old man
would die if he were separated from Benjamin, or whether Benjamin could not
survive without his father, or whether both dire possibilities might be
probable.

25,26 lord. And our father said, 'Go back, buy us some food.' And we said, 'We cannot go down. If our youngest brother is with us, we shall go down. For we cannot see the face of the man if our youngest brother is not
27 with us.' And your servant, our father, said to us, 'You know that two did
28 my wife bear me. And one went out from me and I thought, O, he's
29 been torn to shreds, and I have not seen him since. And should you take this one, too, from my presence and harm befall him, you would
30 bring down my gray head in evil to Sheol.' And so, should I come to your servant, my father, and the lad be not with us, for his life is bound
31 to the lad's, when he saw the lad was not with us, he would die, and your servants would bring down the gray head of your servant, our
32 father, in sorrow to Sheol. For your servant became pledge for the lad to my father, saying, 'If I do not bring him to you, I will bear the blame

---

25. *Go back, buy us some food.* Judah quotes Jacob's words to his sons (43:2) verbatim. The report of their response in the next verse is a more approximate quotation.

27. *two did my wife bear me.* In Judah's report, Jacob speaks characteristically as though Rachel were his only wife. Judah appears now to accept this outrageous favoritism as part of what his father is, part of the father he must still love.

28. *he's been torn to shreds, and I have not seen him since.* In the first clause, Jacob is represented as quoting verbatim his actual response to Joseph's supposed death, yet the second clause has the look of clinging to the hope that Joseph has merely disappeared but has not been killed.

31. *when he saw the lad was not with us.* The Masoretic Text lacks "with us," though it is reflected in the Septuagint and in one version of the Samaritan Bible.

32. *For your servant became pledge.* Judah then proceeds to quote the actual formula of his pledge of surety to Jacob. As many commentators have noted, his invocation of his pledge is a way of explaining why he should have put himself forward as spokesman for the brothers.

to my father for all time.' And so, let your servant, pray, stay instead of 33
the lad as a slave to my lord, and let the lad go up with his brothers. For 34
how shall I go up to my father, if the lad be not with us? Let me see not
the evil that would find out my father!"

---

33. *let your servant, pray, stay instead of the lad as a slave.* Judah, who conceived
the plan of selling Joseph into slavery, now comes around 180 degrees by offering himself as a slave in place of Benjamin.

34. *Let me see not the evil that would find out my father!* This of course stands
in stark contrast to his willingness years before to watch his father writhe in
anguish over Joseph's supposed death. The entire speech, as these concluding
words suggest, is at once a moving piece of rhetoric and the expression of a
profound inner change. Joseph's "testing" of his brothers is thus also a process
that induces the recognition of guilt and leads to psychological transformation.

CHAPTER 45

1   And Joseph could no longer hold himself in check before all who
     stood attendance upon him, and he cried, "Clear out everyone
     around me!" And no man stood with him when Joseph made him-
2   self known to his brothers. And he wept aloud and the Egyptians heard
3   and the house of Pharaoh heard. And Joseph said to his brothers, "I am
     Joseph. Is my father still alive?" But his brothers could not answer him,
4   for they were dismayed before him. And Joseph said to his brothers,

---

2. *And he wept aloud*. The Hebrew says literally, "and he gave his voice in
weeping." This is the third, climactic weeping of Joseph: now he no longer
turns aside to weep in secret but sobs uncontrollably in the presence of his
brothers, so audibly that he is heard by the Egyptians outside and heard all the
way to the palace of Pharaoh. As in English, "house" may refer either to the
physical structure or to the people associated with it.

3. *I am Joseph. Is my father still alive?* His very first utterance, after his sobs
have subsided, is the essential revelation of identity, a two-word (in the
Hebrew) bombshell tossed at his brothers. He follows this by asking whether
his father is alive, as though he could not altogether trust the assurances they
had given him about this when he questioned them in his guise of Egyptian
viceroy. His repeated reference to "my father" serves double duty: the first-
person singular possessive expresses his sense of personal connection with old
Jacob (he is, after all, *my* father, he is saying to his brothers); but it is also
idiomatic usage for the familiar "Father" in biblical Hebrew (rather like *'abba*
in Aramaic and later Hebrew).

4. *And Joseph said to his brothers, "Come close to me, pray."* The purblindness to
which a mechanical focus on source criticism can lead is nowhere more vividly
illustrated than in the contention of some critics that this verse reflects a different source from the preceding verse because it is a "doublet" of it. What

"Come close to me, pray," and they came close, and he said, "I am
Joseph your brother whom you sold into Egypt. And now, do not be   5
pained and do not be incensed with yourselves that you sold me down
here, because for sustenance God has sent me before you. Two years   6
now there has been famine in the heart of the land, and there are yet
five years without plowing and harvest. And God has sent me before   7
you to make you a remnant on earth and to preserve life, for you to be
a great surviving group. And so, it is not you who sent me here but God, 8
and He has made me father to Pharaoh and lord to all his house and

---

should be obvious is that this repeated speech is a brilliant realization of the
dramatic moment. When Joseph first reveals himself to his brothers, they are,
quite understandably, "dismayed." And so he must speak again, first asking
them to draw close. (The proposal of the Midrash Bereishit Rabba that he
invites them to come close in order to show them that he is circumcised is of
course fanciful, but the closing of physical space does reflect his sense that he
must somehow bridge the enormous distance he has maintained between
himself and them in his Egyptian persona.)

   I am Joseph your brother whom you sold into Egypt. The qualifying clause
Joseph now adds to his initial "I am Joseph" is surely a heart-stopper for the
brothers, and could be construed as the last—inadvertent?—gesture of his test
of them. Their most dire imaginings of retribution could easily follow from
these words, but instead, Joseph immediately proceeds in the next sentence to
reassure them.

5. do not be incensed with yourselves. The literal Hebrew wording is "let it not
be incensed in your eyes."

   for sustenance God has sent me before you. Joseph's speech is a luminous
illustration of the Bible's double system of causation, human and divine. Commentators have tended to tilt the balance to one side, making Joseph a mouthpiece of piety here. His recognition of a providential plan may well be
admirable from the viewpoint of monotheistic faith, but there is no reason to
assume that Joseph has lost the sense of his own brilliant initiative in all that
he has accomplished, and so when he says "God" ('elohim, which could also
suggest something more general like "providence" or "fate"), he also means
Joseph. "Before you" is the first intimation that he intends the whole clan to
come down to Egypt after him.

8. father to Pharaoh. The obvious meaning of "father" is "authority," and there
are biblical parallels for this sense of the term. It is a matter of debate among

9 ruler over all the land of Egypt. Hurry and go up to my father and say
   to him, 'Thus says your son Joseph: God has made me lord to all Egypt.
10 Come down to me, do not delay. And you shall dwell in the land of
   Goshen and shall be close to me, you and your sons and the sons of
11 your sons and your flocks and your cattle and all that is yours. And I
   will sustain you there, for yet five years of famine remain—lest you lose
12 all, you and your household and all that is yours.' And, look, your own
   eyes can see, and the eyes of my brother Benjamin, that it is my very
13 mouth that speaks to you. And you must tell my father all my glory in
   Egypt and all that you have seen, and hurry and bring down my father

---

specialists whether the term also reflects an actual Egyptian administrative
title. Joseph's characterization of his political power moves outward through
concentric circles from Pharaoh to the court ("all his house") to the whole land
of Egypt.

9. *Thus says your son Joseph*. This is the so-called messenger formula that is
regularly used in biblical Hebrew as a kind of salutation to introduce letters or
orally conveyed messages.

10. *the land of Goshen*. "Land" here obviously means a region, not a country.
The area referred to is the rich pastureland of the Nile Delta, which would
also be close to the border of the Sinai. In historical fact, Semitic nomads from
the Sinai were granted permission by the Egyptian government to graze their
flocks in this region.

11. *lest you lose all*. The Hebrew verb here has often been confused with
another one, with which it shares two consonants, meaning "to become poor."
The literal meaning of the verb used by Joseph is "to be inherited," that is, to
lose all of one's possessions, either through bankruptcy or by being conquered
by an enemy.

12. *it is my very mouth that speaks to you*. As Abraham ibn Ezra nicely observed,
until the crucial moment when Joseph said, "Clear out everyone around me,"
all his communications with the brothers would have been through an interpreter, as we were reminded in 42:23. Now he has been speaking to them
directly in their native Hebrew, a fact they may have barely assimilated in their
dumbfounded condition, and of which he reminds them now at the end of his
speech as confirmation of his identity.

here." And he fell upon the neck of his brother Benjamin and he wept, 14
and Benjamin wept on his neck. And he kissed all his brothers and 15
wept over them. And after that, his brothers spoke with him.

And the news was heard in the house of Pharaoh, saying, "Joseph's 16
brothers have come." And it was good in Pharaoh's eyes and in his servants' eyes. And Pharaoh said to Joseph, "Say to your brothers: 'This 17
now do. Load up your beasts and go, return to the land of Canaan. And 18
take your father and your households and come back to me, that I may
give you the best of the land of Egypt, and you shall live off the fat of
the land.' And you, charge them: 'This now do. Take you from the land 19
of Egypt wagons for your little ones and for your wives, and convey your
father, and come. And regret not your belongings, for the best of all the 20
land of Egypt is yours.'"

---

14. *and he wept, and Benjamin wept.* After the three times Joseph wept apart
from his brothers, there is at last a mutual weeping in the reunion of the two
sons of Rachel.

15. *And after that, his brothers spoke with him.* The brothers' silence through
Joseph's long speech is an eloquent expression of how overwhelmed they are
by this amazing revelation. Only now, after he embraces them and weeps over
them, are they able to speak, but the writer preserves the dramatic asymmetry
between Joseph and his brothers by merely referring to their speaking without
assigning actual dialogue to them.

18. *the best of the land of Egypt.* The source critics have noted an apparent contradiction with Joseph's instructions, which are to settle specifically in the
region of Goshen—unless one construes "the best of the land" as a reference
to that fertile area, something supported by 47:11.
    live off the fat of the land. The Hebrew says literally, "eat the fat of the land."

19. *And you, charge them.* The Masoretic Text has "And you [singular] are
charged," which is a little incoherent in light of what follows. Both the Septuagint and the Vulgate read "charge them." Evidently, Joseph is enjoined by
Pharaoh to transmit this royal directive to his brothers conferring special status on their clan (Nahum Sarna).

20. *regret not your belongings.* The literal meaning of the Hebrew idiom used
is "let not your eye spare."

21 And so the sons of Israel did, and Joseph gave them wagons, as Pharaoh
22 had ordered, and he gave them supplies for the journey. To all of them,
each one, he gave changes of garments, and to Benjamin he gave three
23 hundred pieces of silver and five changes of garments. And to his father
he sent as follows: ten donkeys conveying from the best of Egypt, and
ten she-asses conveying grain and bread and food for his father for the
24 journey. And he sent off his brothers and they went, and he said to
them, "Do not be perturbed on the journey."

25 And they went up from Egypt and they came to the land of Canaan to
26 Jacob their father. And they told him, saying, "Joseph is still alive," and
that he was ruler in all the land of Egypt. And his heart stopped, for he

---

21. *as Pharaoh had ordered*. This reflects the Hebrew locution that means literally "according to Pharaoh's mouth."

22. *he gave changes of garments, and to Benjamin he gave three hundred pieces
of silver*. The bestowal of garments, as Nahum Sarna notes, is a kind of antithetical response to Joseph's having been stripped of his garment. The regal
amount of silver given to Benjamin is the final gesture of "restitution" for the
twenty pieces of silver the brothers took for the sale of Joseph.

23. *as follows*. Because a whole list of items is being introduced, the narrator
announces it with *kezo't*, a term prefaced to catalogues or inventories.

24. *Do not be perturbed on the journey*. There has been some dispute about the
meaning of the verb here. It is occasionally used in contexts that associate it
with anger, and so many interpreters have imagined that Joseph is warning his
brothers not to yield to mutual recrimination and perhaps fall to blows on the
way home. But the primary meaning of the verb is "to quake" or "to shake,"
either physically (as a mountain in an earthquake) or emotionally (as a person
trembling with fear), and it is the antonym of being tranquil or at peace. In all
likelihood, Joseph is reassuring his brothers that they need not fear any lurking residue of vengefulness on his part that would turn the journey homeward
into a trap.

26. *his heart stopped*. Translations like "his heart fainted" (King James Version),
"his heart was numb" (Speiser and New Jewish Publication Society), and "he
was stunned" (Revised English Bible) blunt the force of the original. The

did not believe them. And they spoke to him all the words of Joseph 27
that he had spoken to them, and he saw the wagons that Joseph had
sent to convey him, and the spirit of Jacob their father revived. And 28
Israel said, "Enough! Joseph my son is still alive. Let me go see him
before I die."

Hebrew verb plainly means to stop, or more precisely, to intermit. Judah had
warned that the loss of Benjamin would kill the old man. Now the tremendous
shock of this news about Joseph, which at first he cannot believe—does he
imagine his less-than-trustworthy sons are perpetrating a cruel hoax?—
induces a physical syncope.

27. *And they spoke to him all the words of Joseph . . . and he saw the wagons.*
Jacob's incredulity begins to yield to the circumstantial account of Joseph's
own story that his sons give him. Then he fully registers the presence of the
wagons, which would have been oxen-drawn vehicles of a distinctive Egyptian
design that would not normally be seen in Canaan and that mere foreign buy-
ers of grain would surely not be able to obtain. At this point his "spirit. . . .
revived," that is, came back to life: he emerges from the state of temporary
heart failure, or heart pause, triggered by the astounding report. One should
note that the only hint of direct discourse given to the brothers in this scene
is "Joseph is still alive" (just three words, four syllables, in the Hebrew). The
effect is to keep them in the background, even though they are actually speaking to Jacob. Joseph looms in the foreground in the first half of the chapter, as
does Jacob—the father from whom he has been so long separated—in the second half.

28. *Joseph my son is still alive. Let me go see him before I die.* The wonderful
poignancy of these words should not deflect us from noting that Jacob is again
invoking a kind of self-defining motif. Ever since Joseph's disappearance
twenty-two years earlier in narrated time, he has been talking about going
down to the grave. By now, he has in fact attained advanced old age (see 47:9),
and so the idea that he has little time left is quite reasonable. The brief seizure
he has just undergone is of course evidence of his physical frailty. Jacob's story,
like David's, is virtually unique in ancient literature in its searching representation of the radical transformations a person undergoes in the slow course of
time. The powerful young man who made his way across the Jordan to
Mesopotamia with only his walking staff, who wrestled with stones and men
and divine beings, is now an old man tottering on the brink of the grave, bearing the deep wounds of his long life.

CHAPTER 46

¹ And Israel journeyed onward, with all that was his, and he came to Beersheba, and he offered sacrifices to the God of his father ² Isaac. And God said to Israel through visions of the night, "Jacob, ³ Jacob," and he said, "Here I am." And He said, "I am the god, God of your father. Fear not to go down to Egypt, for a great nation I will make

---

1. *And Israel journeyed onward.* The choice of the verb is a little surprising, as one might have expected something like "he arose and set out" or "he went forth." It seems likely that this particular verb, with its etymological background of pulling up tent pegs and moving from one encampment to another, is intended to signal that the beginning of the sojourn in Egypt is to be construed as a resumption of the nomadic existence that characterized the lives of Abraham and Isaac. Thus the clan of Jacob does not head down to Egypt as a permanent place of emigration but as a way station in its continued wanderings.

2. *Jacob, Jacob . . . Here I am.* This is an exact verbal parallel, as Amos Funkenstein has observed to me, to the exchange between God and Abraham at the beginning of the story of the binding of Isaac. Perhaps there is a suggestion that the sojourn in Egypt is also an ordeal, with an ultimately happy ending.

3. *Fear not . . . for a great nation I will make you.* Both the language and the action of this whole scene are framed as an emphatic recapitulation of the earlier Patriarchal Tales now that they are coming to an end as the last of the patriarchs with his offspring leaves Canaan for the long stay in Egypt. Jacob, traveling south from Hebron, stops at Beersheba, where his father built an altar, and offers sacrifice just as both Isaac and Abraham did. God appears to him and speaks to him, as He did to Abraham and Isaac. The language of the dream-vision strongly echoes the language of the covenantal promises to Jacob's father and grandfather.

you there. I Myself will go down with you to Egypt and I Myself will   4
surely bring you back up as well, and Joseph shall lay his hand on your
eyes." And Jacob arose from Beersheba, and the sons of Israel conveyed   5
Jacob their father and their little ones and their wives in the wagons
Pharaoh had sent to convey him. And they took their cattle and their   6
substance that they had got in the land of Canaan and they came to
Egypt, Jacob and all his seed with him. His sons, and the sons of his   7
sons with him, his daughters and the daughters of his sons, and all his
seed, he brought with him to Egypt.

---

4. *I Myself will go down with you.* The first-person pronoun is emphatic
because God uses the pronoun *'anokhi,* which is not strictly necessary, followed as it is by the imperfect tense of the verb conjugated in the first-person
singular. The reassurance God offers—which is already the kernel of a theological concept that will play an important role in national consciousness both
in the Babylonian exile and after the defeat by the Romans in 70 C.E.—is necessary because in the polytheistic view the theater of activity of a deity was
typically imagined to be limited to the territorial borders of the deity's worshippers. By contrast, this God solemnly promises to go down with His people
to Egypt and to bring them back up.

   Joseph shall lay his hand on your eyes. The reference is to closing the eyes at
the moment of death.

5. *and the sons of Israel conveyed Jacob their father.* The repeated stress, in the
previous chapter and in this one, on "conveying" or carrying Jacob, together
with the women and children, reminds us that he is very old and infirm, no
longer an active participant in the journey.

7. *His sons, and the sons of his sons.* This last verse of the narrative report of the
departure for Egypt becomes an apt transition to the genealogy, purposefully
inserted at this point from what scholarly consensus deems a different literary
source.

8 And these are the names of the children of Israel who came to Egypt,
9 Jacob and his sons: Jacob's firstborn, Reuben, and the sons of Reuben,
10 Enoch and Pallu and Hezron and Carmi. And the sons of Simeon,
Jemuel and Jamin and Ohad and Jachin and Zohar and Saul the son of
11 the Canaanite woman. And the sons of Levi, Gershon, Kohath, and
12 Merari. And the sons of Judah, Er and Onan and Shelah and Perez and
Zerah—and Er and Onan died in the land of Canaan—and the sons of
13 Perez were Hezron and Hamul. And the sons of Issachar, Tola and
14 Puvah and Iob and Shimron. And the sons of Zebulun, Sered and Elon
15 and Jahleel. These are the sons of Leah whom she bore to Jacob in
Paddan-Aram, and also Dinah his daughter, every person of his sons
16 and daughters, thirty-three. And the sons of Gad, Ziphion and Haggi,
17 Shuni and Ezbon, Eri and Arodi and Areli. And the sons of Asher,
Imnah and Ishvah and Ishvi and Beriah and Serah their sister, and the
18 sons of Beriah, Heber and Malchiel. These are the sons of Zilpah
whom Laban gave to Leah his daughter, and she bore these to Jacob,
19 sixteen persons. The sons of Rachel, Jacob's wife, Joseph and Ben-
20 jamin. And to Joseph were born in the land of Egypt, whom Asenath
daughter of Potiphera priest of On bore to him, Manasseh and
21 Ephraim. And the sons of Benjamin, Bela and Becher and Ashbel,
Gera and Naaman, Ehi and Rosh, Muppim and Huppim and Ard.
22 These are the sons of Rachel who were born to Jacob, fourteen persons
23,24 in all. The sons of Dan, Hushim. And the sons of Naphtali, Jahzeel
25 and Guni and Jezer and Shillem. These are the sons of Bilhah whom
Laban gave to Rachel his daughter, and she bore these to Jacob, seven
26 persons in all. All the persons who came with Jacob to Egypt, issue of
his loins, aside from the wives of Jacob's sons, sixty-six persons in all.

8–27. Once again, the genealogical list is used to effect closure at the end of
a large narrative unit. The tales of the patriarchs in the land of Canaan are now
concluded, and as Jacob and his clan journey southward for the sojourn in
Egypt, we are given an inventory of his offspring, a large family already exhibiting in embryo the configuration of the future tribes of Israel.

23. *The sons of Dan, Hushim.* Only one son is mentioned, but this need not
reflect a contradiction in the text, as "the sons of" may be a fixed formula for
each new item in the list.

And the sons of Joseph who were born to him in Egypt, were two per- 27
sons. All the persons of the household of Jacob coming to Egypt were
seventy.

And Judah he had sent before him to show him the way to Goshen, 28
and they came to the land of Goshen. And Joseph harnessed his char- 29
iot and went up to meet Israel his father in Goshen, and appeared

---

27. *All the persons of the household of Jacob coming to Egypt were seventy.* The
traditional commentators resort to interpretive acrobatics in order to make the
list come out to exactly seventy—debating as to whether Jacob himself should
be included in the count, whether Joseph and his two sons are part of the sum,
and so forth. In fact, the insistence on seventy at the end of the list vividly
illustrates the biblical use of numbers as symbolic approximations rather than
as arithmetically precise measures. Seventy is a fullness, a large round number, ten times sacred seven, and its use here indicates that Jacob, once a solitary fugitive, has grown to a grand family, the nucleus of a nation.

28. *And Judah he had sent before him to show him the way.* Judah, who pledged
to guarantee Benjamin's safety (and from whose descendants the royal line will
spring) is now Jacob's choice as guide for the rest. The phrase "to show him
the way" is a little odd in the Hebrew (there are two variant readings reflected
in the ancient versions), and its meaning is not entirely certain.

29. *And Joseph harnessed his chariot.* The specification of the vehicle is another
strategic reminder of the Egyptian accoutrements Joseph employs as a matter
of course, even as he hurries to meet his father, who comes from a world
where there are neither chariots nor wagons. Realistically, "harnessed," as
Abraham ibn Ezra and many others have noted, would mean, "he gave orders
to harness." Nevertheless, there is thematic point in the sense of immediacy
conveyed by the transitive verb with Joseph as subject, and Rashi registers this
point, even if his reading is too literal, when he says: "He himself harnessed
the horses to the chariot in order to make haste in honor of his father."
    and appeared before him. This is a slightly odd phrase, since it is more typ-
ically used for the appearance of God before a human. Perhaps the sight of the
long-lost Joseph, in Egyptian royal raiment, riding in his chariot, is a kind of
epiphany for Jacob. In any case, "appearing before" accords with Jacob's own
emphasis on seeing Joseph's face.

before him and fell on his neck, and he wept on his neck a long while.
30 And Israel said to Joseph, "I may die now, after seeing your face, for you
31 are still alive." And Joseph said to his brothers and to his father's household, "Let me go up and tell Pharaoh and let me say to him, 'My brothers and my father's household that was in the land of Canaan have
32 come to me. And the men are shepherds, for they have always been
handlers of livestock, and their sheep and their cattle and all that is
33 theirs they have brought. And so, when Pharaoh calls for you and says,
34 'What is it you do?' you should say, 'Your servants have been handlers of
livestock from our youth until now, we and our fathers as well,' that you
may dwell in the land of Goshen. For every shepherd is abhorrent to
Egypt.

---

and fell on his neck, and he wept on his neck a long while. The absence of
reciprocal weeping on the part of Jacob can scarcely be attributed to ellipsis or
inadvertent narrative omission, for in the identically worded report of Joseph's
falling on Benjamin's neck and weeping, we are told, "and Benjamin wept on
his neck" (45:14). We are invited to imagine, then, a sobbing Joseph who
embraces his father while the old man stands dry-eyed, perhaps even rigid, too
overcome with feeling to know how to respond, or to be able to respond spon-
taneously, until finally he speaks, once more invoking his own death, but now
with a sense of contentment: "I may die now, after seeing your face, for you
are still alive."

32. *handlers of livestock.* The Hebrew phrase, *'anshei miqneh,* which occurs
only here and in verse 34, literally means "men of livestock." It is perhaps influenced by the designation of the brothers as "the men" at the beginning of this
verse.

34. *that you may dwell in the land of Goshen. For every shepherd is abhorrent to
Egypt.* This claim is puzzling because there is an indication in the next chapter that Pharaoh had his own flocks (see 47:6b), and there is no extrabiblical
evidence that shepherding was a taboo profession among the Egyptians, as the
categorical language of the last sentence here appears to suggest. The least
convoluted explanation is that the Egyptians, who were by and large sedentary
agriculturalists and who had large urban centers, considered the seminomadic
herdsmen from the north as inferiors (an attitude actually reflected in Egyptian sources) and so preferred to keep them segregated in the pasture region of
the Nile Delta not far from the Sinai border.

CHAPTER 47

And Joseph came and told Pharaoh and said, "My father and my   1
brothers and their flocks and their cattle and all that is theirs have
come from the land of Canaan and here they are in the land of
Goshen." And from the pick of his brothers he took five men and pre-   2
sented them to Pharaoh. And Pharaoh said to his brothers, "What is it   3

---

2. *And from the pick of his brothers.* The Hebrew prepositional phrase, *miqtseh*
'eḥaw, has elicited puzzlement, or evasion, from most translators. The common
meaning of *miqtseh* is "at the end of," but it is also occasionally used in the
sense of "from the best of" or "from the pick of," which would be appropriate
here, since Joseph wants to introduce the most presentable of his brothers to
Pharaoh. The use of *miqtseh* in Judges 18:2 in reference to elite soldiers nicely
illustrates the likely meaning in our own text: "and the Danites sent from their
clan five men of their pick [*miqtsotam,*] capable men . . . to spy out the land."
It might be noted that this term in Judges is associated with "capable men"
(*benei ḥayil*)—a phrase that in a military context might also be rendered
"valiant men"—just as an equivalent phrase, *'anshei ḥayil,* is associated with
Joseph's brothers at this point. There are, however, other occurrences of *miqt-*
seh or *miqtsot* that suggest it might also have the sense of "a representative
sample."

five men. The insistence of various modern commentators that "five" both
here and earlier in the story really means "several" is not especially convincing.
One should note that the whole Joseph story exhibits a fondness for playing
with recurrent numbers: the fraternal twelve, first signaled in Joseph's dreams,
then subtracted from by his disappearance, with the full sum made up at the
end; the triple pairs of dreams; the two pairs of seven. Five is one half the
number of the brothers who enslaved Joseph; Benjamin was given a fivefold
portion at Joseph's feast and five changes of garments; and the Egyptians are
obliged to pay a tax of one-fifth of their harvest.

4 you do?" And they said to Pharaoh, "Your servants are shepherds, we,
and our fathers as well." And they said to Pharaoh, "We have come to
sojourn in the land, for there is no pasture for your servants' flocks
because the famine is grave in the land of Canaan. And so, let your ser-

[5a–6b] vants, pray, dwell in the land of Goshen." *And Pharaoh said to Joseph,
saying,* "Let them dwell in the land of Goshen, and if you know there
are able men among them, make them masters of the livestock, over
what is mine." *And Jacob and his sons had come to Egypt, to Joseph, and*

5 *Pharaoh king of Egypt heard.* And Pharaoh said to Joseph, saying, "Your
[6a] father and your brothers have come to you. The land of Egypt is before
you. In the best of the land settle your father and your brothers. Let

7 them dwell in the land of Goshen." And Joseph brought Jacob his

8 father and stood him before Pharaoh, and Jacob blessed Pharaoh. And
Pharaoh said to Jacob, "How many are the days of the years of your

9 life?" And Jacob said to Pharaoh, "The days of the years of my sojourn-

---

4. *to sojourn in the land . . . dwell in the land.* First they use a verb of temporary residence, then one of fixed settlement.

[5a-6b.] The Masoretic Text is clearly problematic at this point because it has
Pharaoh speaking to Joseph, appearing to ignore the brothers who have just
addressed a petition to him, and also announcing, quite superfluously in light
of verse 1, "Your father and your brothers have come to you." Coherence in the
sequence of dialogues is improved by inserting the clauses italicized here,
which are reflected in the Septuagint and by changing the order of the verses.

7. *and Jacob blessed Pharaoh.* The Hebrew verb here also has the simple meaning of "to greet," but it seems likely that in this context it straddles both senses.
Jacob of course accords Pharaoh the deferential greeting owed to a monarch,
but it would be entirely in keeping with his own highly developed sense of his
patriarchal role that he—a mere Semitic herdsman chief addressing the head
of the mighty Egyptian empire—should pronounce a blessing on Pharaoh.

9. *The days of the years of my sojournings.* The last noun here probably has a
double connotation: Jacob's life has been a series of wanderings or "sojournings," not a sedentary existence in one place, and human existence is by nature
a sojourning, a temporary dwelling between non-being and extinction.

ings are a hundred and thirty years. Few and evil have been the days of
the years of my life, and they have not attained the days of the years of
my fathers in their days of sojourning." And Jacob blessed Pharaoh and   10
went out from Pharaoh's presence.

And Joseph settled his father and his brothers and gave them a holding   11
in the land of Egypt in the best of the land, in the land of Rameses, as
Pharaoh had commanded. And Joseph sustained his father and his   12

Few and evil have been the days of the years of my life. Jacob's somber summary of his own life echoes with a kind of complex solemnity against all that
we have seen him undergo. He has, after all, achieved everything he aspired
to achieve: the birthright, the blessing, marriage with his beloved Rachel, progeny, and wealth. But one measure of the profound moral realism of the story
is that although he gets everything he wanted, it is not in the way he would
have wanted, and the consequence is far more pain than contentment. From
his "clashing" (25:22) with his twin in the womb, everything has been a struggle. He displaces Esau, but only at the price of fear and lingering guilt and long
exile. He gets Rachel, but only by having Leah imposed on him, with all the
domestic strife that entails, and he loses Rachel early in childbirth. He is given
a new name by his divine adversary, but comes away with a permanent wound.
He gets the full solar year number of twelve sons, but there is enmity among
them (for which he bears some responsibility), and he spends twenty-two
years continually grieving over his favorite son, who he believes is dead. This
is, in sum, a story with a happy ending that withholds any simple feeling of
happiness at the end.

and they have not attained the days of the years of my fathers. In fact, Jacob,
long-lived as he is, will not attain the prodigious life spans of Abraham and
Isaac. At this point, however, he can scarcely know how much longer he has
to live (seventeen years, as it turns out), and so his words must reflect that
feeling of having one foot in the grave that he has repeatedly expressed before.
One should not exclude the possibility that Jacob is playing up the sense of
contradiction, making a calculated impression on Pharaoh, in dismissing his
own 130 years as "few." The ideal life span for the Egyptians was 110.

11. *the land of Rameses.* Medieval and modern commentators agree that this
designation is a synonym for Goshen. The term looks like an anachronism
because Rameses is the city later built with Israelite slave labor. Perhaps its
use here is intended to foreshadow the future oppression.

brothers and all his father's household with bread, down to the mouths
13 of the little ones. And there was no bread in all the earth, for the famine
was very grave, and the land of Egypt and the land of Canaan languished
14 because of the famine. And Joseph collected all the silver to be found in
the land of Egypt and in the land of Canaan in return for the provisions
they were buying, and Joseph brought the silver to the house of Pharaoh.
15 And the silver of the land of Egypt and of the land of Canaan ran out,
and all Egypt came to Joseph, saying, "Let us have bread, for why should
16 we die before your eyes? For the silver is gone." And Joseph said, "Let me
have your livestock, that I may give you in return for your livestock if the
17 silver is gone." And they brought their livestock to Joseph, and he gave
them bread in return for the horses and the stocks of sheep and the
stocks of cattle and the donkeys, and he carried them forward with
18 bread in return for all their livestock that year. And that year ran out and
they came to him the next year and said to him, "We shall not conceal
from my lord that the silver has run out and the animal stocks are my
lord's. Nothing is left for our lord but our carcasses and our farmland.

---

13. *And there was no bread in all the earth.* The tension with the preceding
verse, in which Joseph is reported sustaining his whole clan, down to the little ones, with bread, is of course pointed, and recalls a similar surface contradiction between verses 54 and 55 in chapter 41. The writer shuttles here
between the two common meanings of *'erets,* "earth" and "land," as in his previous accounts of the famine.

15. *why should we die before your eyes?* The last term in the Hebrew is literally
"opposite you." In the parallel speech in verse 19, the Egyptians actually say
"before your eyes."

17. *he carried them forward with bread.* The usual meaning of the verb is "to
lead"; the context here suggests it may also mean something like "to sustain."

18. *our carcasses and our farmland.* Previous translations have rendered the first
of these terms blandly as "our bodies" or "our persons." But the Hebrew
gewiyah refers specifically to a dead body and is often used in quite negative
contexts. The Egyptians here are speaking sardonically of their own miserable
condition: they have nothing left but their carcasses, they have been reduced
to walking corpses. The present translation uses "farmland" for the Hebrew
'adamah. That term usually means arable land—it is the reiterated "soil" of the

Why should we die before your eyes? Both we and our farmland— 19
take possession of us and our farmland in return for bread, and we
with our farmland will be slaves to Pharaoh, and give us seed, that we
may live and not die, and that the farmland not turn to desert."
And Joseph took possession of all the farmland of Egypt for Pharaoh, 20
for each Egyptian sold his field, as the famine was harsh upon them,
and the land became Pharaoh's. And the people he moved town by 21
town, from one end of the border of Egypt to the other. Only the 22
farmland of the priests he did not take in possession, for the priests
had a fixed allotment from Pharaoh and they ate from their allotment
that Pharaoh had given them. Therefore they did not sell their
farmland. And Joseph said to the people, "Look, I have taken posses- 23

Garden story—but "soil" would be a little off in these sentences. It cannot be
rendered throughout simply as "land" because that would create a confusion
with "land" (*'erets*), which is also used here several times to refer to Egypt as a
country. The fact that the farmland referred to by the Egyptians is not yielding
much produce suggests that in their eyes it is scarcely worth more than the
"carcasses" with which it is bracketed.

19. *slaves to Pharaoh.* The reduction of the entire population to a condition of
virtual serfdom to the crown in all likelihood was meant to be construed not
as an act of ruthlessness by Joseph but as an instance of his administrative
brilliance. The subordination of the Egyptian peasantry to the central government, with the 20 percent tax on agriculture, was a known fact, and our story
provides an explanation (however unhistorical) for its origins.

 that the farmland not turn to desert. As the famine continues, without seed-
grain to replant the soil, the land will turn to desert.

21. *And the people he moved town by town.* Despite many English versions, it
is problematic to construe the last term as "into the towns," for it would make
no sense to move all the farmers into the cities if there are to be crops in the
future, unless one imagines a temporary gathering of the rural population in
the towns for the distribution of food. But the Hebrew particle *le* in *le'arim* can
also have the sense of "according to"—that is, Joseph rounded up rural populations in groups according to their distribution around the principal towns
and resettled them elsewhere. The purpose would be to sever them from their
hereditary lands and locate them on other lands that they knew were theirs to
till only by the grace of Pharaoh, to whom the land now belonged.

sion of you this day, with your farmland, for Pharaoh. Here is seed
24 for you, and sow the land. And when the harvests come, you shall give
a fifth to Pharaoh and four parts shall be yours for seeding the field and
for your food, for those in your households and for your little ones to
25 eat." And they said, "You have kept us alive! May we find favor in the
26 eyes of our lord, in being Pharaoh's slaves." And Joseph made it a fixed
law, to this very day, over the farmland of Egypt, that Pharaoh should
have a fifth. Only the farmland of the priests, it alone did not become
Pharaoh's.

27 And Israel dwelled in the land of Egypt, in the land of Goshen, and
28 they took holdings in it, and were fruitful and multiplied greatly. And
Jacob lived in the land of Egypt seventeen years, and Jacob's days, the
29 years of his life, were one hundred and forty-seven years. And Israel's
time to die drew near, and he called for his son, for Joseph, and he said
to him, "If, pray, I have found favor in your eyes, put your hand, pray,
under my thigh and act toward me with steadfast kindness—pray, do
30 not bury me in Egypt. When I lie down with my fathers, carry me from
Egypt and bury me in their burial place." And he said, "I will do as you
31 have spoken." And he said, "Swear to me." And he swore to him. And
Israel bowed at the head of the bed.

---

25. *in being Pharaoh's slaves*. Most translations construe this as a future verb,
"we shall be." But the introductory clause of obeisance, "May we find favor . . . ,"
does not necessarily preface a declaration about a future action, and the Egyptians are already Pharaoh's slaves, both by their own declaration (verse 19) and
Joseph's (verse 23). In point of historical fact, Egypt's centralization of power, so
unlike tribal Israel and Canaan with its city-states, must have astounded and
perhaps also troubled the Hebrew writer.

28. *And Jacob lived in the land of Egypt seventeen years*. The symmetry with
Joseph's seventeen years until he was sold into Egypt was aptly observed in the
Middle Ages by David Kimhi: "Just as Joseph was in the lap of Jacob seventeen years, Jacob was in the lap of Joseph seventeen years."

CHAPTER 48

And it happened after these things that someone said to Joseph, 1 "Look, your father is ill." And he took his two sons with him, Manasseh and Ephraim. And someone told Jacob and said, "Look, your 2 son Joseph is coming to you." And Israel summoned his strength and sat up in bed. And Jacob said to Joseph, "El Shaddai appeared to me at 3 Luz in the land of Canaan and blessed me, and said to me, 'I am about 4 to make you fruitful and multiply you and make you an assembly of peoples, and I will give this land to your seed after you as an everlasting holding.' And so now, your two sons who were born to you in the 5 land of Egypt before I came to you in Egypt, shall be mine—Ephraim and Manasseh, like Reuben and Simeon, shall be mine. And those you 6

---

1. *And he took his two sons with him.* Joseph, even before he receives any word from his father in this regard, anticipates that Jacob will confer some sort of special eminence on his own two sons in a deathbed blessing, and so he brings them with him.

3. *Luz.* This is the older name for Beth-El, where Jacob was vouchsafed his dream-vision of divine messengers ascending and descending the ramp to heaven.

5. *your two sons . . . shall be mine—Ephraim and Manasseh, like Reuben and Simeon, shall be mine.* These words are equally fraught with thematic and legal implications. Jacob explicitly equates Joseph's two sons with his own firstborn and second-born, intimating that the former are to have as good an inheritance, or better, as the latter, and thus once more invokes the great Genesis theme of the reversal of primogeniture. (Note that he already places Ephraim, the younger, before Manasseh when he names Joseph's sons.) The fact that Reuben has violated Jacob's concubine and Simeon (with Levi) has initiated

begot after them shall be yours; by their brothers' names they shall be
7 called in their inheritance. As for me, when I was coming from Paddan,
Rachel died to my grief in the land of Canaan on the way, still some
distance from Ephrath, and I buried her there on the way." Ephrath

---

the massacre at Shechem may suggest that they are deemed unworthy to be
undisputed first and second in line among Jacob's inheritors. The language
Jacob uses, moreover, is a formula of legal adoption, just as the gesture of placing the boys on the old man's knees (see verse 12) is a ritual gesture of adoption. The adoption is dictated by the fact that Ephraim and Manasseh will
become tribes, just as if they were sons of Jacob.

6. *And those you begot after them.* It is difficult to square this phrase with the
narrative as we have it, which indicates that Joseph has only two sons. The
efforts of some commentators to make the verb a future is not at all warranted
by the Hebrew grammar, and, in any case, Joseph has been married more than
twenty-five years.

by their brothers' names they shall be called in their inheritance. Although the
idiom is familiar, the meaning is not entirely transparent. What Jacob probably is saying is that it is Ephraim and Manasseh who will have tribal status in
the future nation, and thus any other sons of Joseph would be "called by their
name," would have claim to land that was part of the tribal inheritance of
Ephraim and Manasseh and so designated.

7. *As for me, when I was coming from Paddan, Rachel died.* This verse is one of
several elements in this chapter that have been seized on by textual critics as
evidence of its highly composite nature and of what is claimed to be a concomitant incoherence in its articulations. But such conclusions seriously
underestimate the degree of integrative narrative logic that the writer—or perhaps one must say, the redactor—exhibits. At first glance, Jacob's comment
about the death of his beloved Rachel in the midst of blessing his grandsons
seems a non sequitur. It is, however, a loss to which he has never been reconciled (witness his extravagant favoritism toward Rachel's firstborn). His vivid
sense of anguish, after all these decades, is registered in the single word *'alai*
("to my grief," but literally, "on me," the same word he uses in 42:36, when he
says that all the burden of bereavement is on him), and this loss is surely
uppermost in his mind when he tells Pharaoh that his days have been few and
evil. On his deathbed, then, Jacob reverts obsessively to the loss of Rachel,
who perished in childbirth leaving behind only two sons, and his impulse to
adopt Rachel's two grandsons by her firstborn expresses a desire to compen-
sate, symbolically and legally, for the additional sons she did not live to bear.

is Bethlehem. And Israel saw Joseph's sons and he said, "Who are 8
these?" And Joseph said to his father, "They are my sons whom God 9
has given me here." And he said, "Fetch them, pray, to me, that I may
bless them." And Israel's eyes had grown heavy with age, he could not 10
see. And he brought them near him, and he kissed them and embraced
them. And Israel said to Joseph, "I had not thought to see your face, 11
and, look, God has also let me see your seed!" And Joseph drew them 12
out from his knees, and he bowed, his face to the ground. And Joseph 13
took the two of them, Ephraim with his right hand to Israel's left and
Manasseh with his left hand to Israel's right, and brought them near
him. And Israel stretched out his right hand and placed it on Ephraim's 14
head, yet he was the younger, and his left hand on Manasseh's head—
he crossed his hands—though Manasseh was the firstborn. And he 15
blessed them and said,

"The God in whose presence my fathers walked,
   Abraham and Isaac,
the God who has looked after me
   all my life till this day,

---

8. *Who are these?* Perhaps, as several commentators have proposed, he could
barely make out their features because he was virtually blind (see verse 10).
"And Israel saw," then, would mean something like "he dimly perceived," and
it need not be an out-and-out contradiction of the indication of blindness in
verse 10. But the question he asks might also be the opening formula in the
ceremony of adoption.

14. *he crossed his hands*. This image, extended in the exchange with Joseph in
which the old man says he knows what he is doing, is a kind of summarizing
thematic ideogram of the Book of Genesis: the right hand of the father conferring the blessing reaches across to embrace the head of the younger brother,
and the elder, his head covered by the old man's left hand, receives a lesser
blessing.

15. *he blessed them*. The Masoretic Text has, illogically, "he blessed Joseph," but
"them" as object of the verb is reflected in the Septuagint, the Syriac, and the
Vulgate.

16   the messenger rescuing me from all evil,
    may He bless the lads,
  let my name be called in them
    and the name of my fathers, Abraham and Isaac,
  let them teem multitudinous in the midst of the earth."

17 And Joseph saw that his father had placed his right hand on Ephraim's
head, and it was wrong in his eyes, and he took hold of his father's hand
18 to remove it from Ephraim's head to Manasseh's head. And Joseph said
to his father, "Not so, my father, for this one is the firstborn. Put your
19 right hand on his head." And his father refused and he said, "I know,
my son. I know. He, too, shall become a people, and he, too, shall be
great. But his younger brother shall be greater than he, and his seed
20 shall be a fullness of nations." And he blessed them that day, saying,

  "By you shall Israel bless, saying,
    'May God set you as Ephraim and Manasseh,'"

and he set Ephraim before Manasseh.

---

16. *the name of my fathers, Abraham and Isaac, / let them teem multitudinous.*
Jacob, after recapitulating the story of his personal providence in the first line
of the blessing-poem, invokes the benediction of the patriarchal line, and
then, going back still further in the biblical history, the promise, or injunction,
of fertility from the Creation story.

20. *And he blessed them that day.* The introduction of a second blessing is
hardly evidence of a glitch in textual transmission. After the exchange with
Joseph, which follows the full-scale blessing and also explains its implications,
Jacob reaffirms his giving precedence to Ephraim over Manasseh (a real
datum of later tribal history) by stating a kind of summary blessing in which
the name of the younger precedes the name of the elder. "By you shall Israel
bless" is meant quite literally: when the future people of Israel want to invoke
a blessing, they will do it by reciting the words, "May God set you as Ephraim
and Manasseh."

And Israel said to Joseph, "Look, I am about to die, but God shall be 21
with you and bring you back to the land of your fathers. As for me, I 22
have given you with single intent over your brothers what I took from
the hand of the Emorite with my sword and with my bow."

---

22. *I have given you with single intent over your brothers what I took from the hand of the Emorite.* The phrase represented here by "with single intent" is a notorious crux, but previous interpreters may have been misled by assuming it must be the object of the verb "have given." The Hebrew *shekhem 'aḥad* means literally "one shoulder." Many commentators and translators, with an eye to the immediate context of inheritance, have construed this as "one portion," but the evidence elsewhere in the Bible that *shekhem* means "portion" is weak. Others have proposed, without much more warrant than the shape of the shoulder, that the word here means "mountain slope." A substantial number of scholars, medieval and modern, read this as a proper noun, the city of Shechem, encouraged by the fact that the Joseph tribes settled in the vicinity of Shechem. That construction, however, entails two difficulties: if the city were referred to, a feminine form of the word for "one" (not *'aḥad* but *'aḥat*) would be required; and at least according to the preceding narrative, Jacob, far from having conquered Shechem with his own sword, was horrified by the massacre his sons perpetrated there. But the very phrase used here, *shekhem 'aḥad*, occurs at one other place in the Bible, Zephaniah 3:9, where it is used *adverbially* in an idiomatic sense made clear by the immediate context: "for all of them to invoke the name of the LORD, / to serve Him *shekhem 'eḥad* [King James Version, with one consent; Revised English Bible and New Jewish Publication Society Bible, with one accord]." This is, then, an expression that indicates concerted, unswerving intention and execution, and as such is perfectly appropriate to the legal pronouncement of legacy by Jacob in which it appears. Once the phrase is seen as adverbial, the relative clause, "what I took . . . ," falls into place with grammatical preciseness as the object of the verb "have given," and in this reading, no particular city or region need be specified.

CHAPTER 49

1 And Jacob called his sons and said, "Gather round, that I may tell you what shall befall you in the days to come.

As with the life-histories of Moses and David, the extended narrative of Jacob and his sons (with the entire Patriarchal Tale behind it) is given literary closure by the introduction of a long poem. Although the poem chiefly looks forward to the future tribal history of Jacob's twelve sons, it begins by harking back to incidents in the preceding narrative and so preserves some sense of the sons as individual characters, not merely eponymous founders of the tribes. There is debate among scholars as to whether the poem is a single composition or rather a kind of cento of poetic fragments about the fate of the various tribes that were in circulation in the early phase of Israelite history. It is generally agreed, however, that this is one of the oldest extended texts in the Bible. The representation of Levi as a tribe deprived of inheritance, with no hint of its sacerdotal function and the concomitant privileges, suggests a very early date—conceivably even before the completion of the conquest and settlement, as Nahum Sarna has proposed. The royal imagery, on the other hand, associated with Judah seems to reflect a moment after David's founding of his dynasty shortly before 1000 B.C.E. In any case, the antiquity of the poem, as well as the fact that it may be a collage of fragments, means that there are words, phrases, and occasionally whole clauses that are not very well understood. Sometimes this is because of the use of a rare, presumably archaic, term, though there are also at least a few points where the received text looks defective. Differences of interpretive opinion are such that in two instances there is no agreement about whether the language refers to animal, vegetable, or mineral! At such junctures, a translator can do no more than make an educated guess. In any event, the poetic beauty and power of Jacob's testament cannot be separated from its lofty antique style—its archaic grammatical forms and strange turns of syntax, its rare poetic terms, its animal and vegetal imagery, at some points recalling the old Ugaritic poems—and an English version should seek at least to intimate these qualities.

Assemble and hearken, O Jacob's sons,   2
    and hearken to Israel your father.
Reuben, my firstborn are you—   3
    my strength and first yield of my manhood,
        prevailing in rank and prevailing in might.
Unsteady as water, you'll no more prevail!   4
    for you mounted the place where your father lay,
        you profaned my couch, you mounted!
Simeon and Levi, the brothers—   5
    weapons of outrage their trade.

---

2. *Assemble and hearken . . . hearken.* It is a common convention of biblical poetry to begin with a formal exhortation for those addressed to listen closely. What is slightly odd about the opening line here is that "hearken" is repeated in the second half of the line instead of introducing a synonym like "give ear" (compare the beginning of Lamech's poem, Genesis 4:23).

3. *first yield of my manhood.* The word for "manhood," *'on,* means "vigor," but it is particularly associated with male potency. "First yield," *rei'shit,* is a word also used for crops. The biological image of Reuben as the product of Jacob's first inseminating seed sharpens the evocation in the next line of his violation of his father's concubine

4. *you'll no more prevail!* The verb here may rather mean "you'll not remain" (or pun on that meaning)—a reference to the early disappearance of the tribe of Reuben, perhaps before the period of the monarchy.
    the place where your father lay. The plural form used, *mishkevei 'avikha,* has an explicitly sexual connotation, whereas the singular *mishkav* can also mean simply a place where one sleeps.
    you profaned my couch, you mounted! The translation here emends *'alah* ("he mounted") to *'alita* ("you mounted"), though there is some possibility that the archaic poetic style permitted this sort of abrupt switch in pronominal reference.

5. *their trade.* The meaning of *mekheroteyhem* is highly uncertain. The translation here conjecturally links the term with the root *m-kh-r,* "to sell."

6   In their council let me never set foot,
            their assembly my presence shun.
        For in their fury they slaughtered men,
            at their pleasure they tore down ramparts.
7   Cursed be their fury so fierce,
            and their wrath so remorseless!
        I will divide them in Jacob,
            disperse them in Israel.
8   Judah, you, shall your brothers acclaim—
            your hand on your enemies' nape—
               your fathers' sons shall bow to you.

---

6. *let me never set foot.* Literally, "let my person not come."

their assembly my presence shun. The Hebrew says literally, "in their assembly let my presence not join," but this is clumsy as English, and in any case the point is that Jacob is ostracizing the two brothers.

they tore down ramparts. With many critics, the translation here reads *shur*, a poetic term for "wall," instead of *shor*, "ox," as the Masoretic Text has it. The verb, if it refers to oxen, would mean "to maim" or "to hamstring." It was sometimes the ancient practice to hamstring the captured warhorses of an enemy, but it would have been foolish to hamstring captured oxen, which could be put to peaceful use. Moreover, since Jacob is speaking of the massacre at Shechem, the narrative there explicitly noted that the cattle and other livestock were carried off, not maimed.

8. *Judah, you, shall your brothers acclaim.* This line in the Hebrew is a fanfare of sound-play, including a pun on Judah's name, *Yehudah, 'atah yodukha 'aḥekha.* Up to this point, Jacob's testament to his first three sons has actually been nothing but curses. Rashi neatly catches the transitional force of "Judah, you . . ." when he notes, "Inasmuch as he had heaped condemnations on the previous ones, Judah began to back away and his father called to him with words of encouragement, 'Judah, you are not like them.'" Judah now displaces the three brothers born before him, and his claim to preeminence ("your brothers acclaim") is founded on his military prowess ("your hand on your enemies' nape"). All this has a distinctly Davidic coloration. "Acclaim" is a more precise equivalent for the verb in context than the usual "praise" because what is involved is recognition of Judah's royal status.

A lion's whelp is Judah, 9
    from the prey, O my son, you mount.
He crouched, he lay down like a lion,
    like the king of beasts, and who dare arouse him?
The scepter shall not pass from Judah, 10
    nor the mace from between his legs,
that tribute to him may come
    and to him the submission of peoples.

---

9. *from the prey, O my son, you mount.* Amos Funkenstein has astutely suggested to me that there is an ingenious double meaning here. The Hebrew could also be construed as "from the prey of my son you mounted," introducing a shadow reference to Judah's leading part in the plan to pass off Joseph as dead. When the bloodied tunic was brought to Jacob, he cried out, "Joseph is torn to shreds" (*tarof toraf*), and the term for "prey" here is *teref*.

you mount. This is the same verb that is used above for Reuben's act of sexual violation, but here it refers to the lion springing up from the prey it has slain. The proposal that the verb means "to grow" is forced, with little warrant elsewhere in the Bible.

the king of beasts. This English kenning is necessary in the poetic parallelism because there are no English synonyms for "lion," whereas biblical Hebrew has four different terms for the same beast.

10. *mace.* The Hebrew *meḥoqeq* refers to a ruler's long staff, a clear parallel to "scepter." There is no reason to construe it, as some have done, as a euphemism for the phallus, though the image of the mace between the legs surely suggests virile power in political leadership.

that tribute to him may come. This is a notorious crux. The Masoretic Text seems to read "until he comes to Shiloh," a dark phrase that has inspired much messianic interpretation. The present translation follows an exegetical tradition that goes back to the Middle Ages, which breaks up the word "Shiloh" and vocalizes it differently as *shai lo*.

11   He binds to the vine his ass,
          to the grape-bough his ass's foal.
       He washes in wine his garment,
          in the blood of the grape his cloak.
12   O eyes that are darker than wine
          and teeth that are whiter than milk!
13   Zebulun near the shore of the sea shall dwell,
          and he by the haven of ships,
             his flank upon Sidon.
14   Issachar, a big-boned donkey,
          crouched amidst hearths.
15   He saw that the homestead was goodly,
          that the land was delightful,
       and he put his shoulder to the load,
          became a toiling serf.

---

11. *He binds to the vine his ass.* The hyperbole has been explained most plausibly by Abraham ibn Ezra, "The yield of his vineyards will be so abundant that his ass can turn aside to the vine and he won't care if it eats the grapes." This explanation jibes nicely with the next image of washing garments in wine—the wine will be so plentiful that it can be treated as water.

    the blood of the grape. This vivid poetic epithet for wine, with its intensifying effect, is reminiscent of the Ugaritic kenning for wine, "blood of the tree," and hence a token of the stylistic antiquity of the poem.

12. *O eyes that are darker than wine.* The Hebrew, like this English version, gives no pronoun references for these striking images, though they presumably refer to Judah, whose descendants will flourish in beauty in the midst of their viticultural abundance. The word for "darker," *ḥakhlili,* is still another rare poetic term, cognate with the Akkadian *elelu,* "to be dark."

14. *hearths.* The term occurs only here and in Judges 5:16. Because of the pastoral setting of the latter text, it is frequently construed as "sheepfolds," but the verbal stem from which it appears to derive means "to set a pot on the fire."

Dan, his folk will judge   16
    as one of Israel's tribes.
Let Dan be a snake on the road,   17
    an asp on the path,
that bites the horse's heels
    and its rider topples backward.
Your deliverance I await, O LORD!   18
Gad shall be goaded by raiders   19
    yet he shall goad their heel.
Asher's bread shall be rich   20
    and he shall bring forth kingly dishes.

---

16. *Dan, his folk will judge.* Dan has always been construed as the subject of the verb "judge" (or "govern"), not its object. But Hebrew grammar makes it equally possible to read "Dan" as object of the verb, and that would explain the otherwise obscure second clause: in historical fact, the tribe of Dan, far from assuming a role of leadership, was obliged to migrate from south to north. Despite its marginal existence, the Israelite people will judge or govern it as one of Israel's tribes.

17. *Let Dan be a snake on the road.* The sudden lethal attack from below on the roadside is an image of the tactic of ambush in guerilla warfare adopted against invaders by the Danite fighters. Again, the image suggests that this tribe, unlike the others, did not enjoy the security of fortified settlement.

19. *Gad shall be goaded by raiders.* The sound-play in the Hebrew is *gad gedud yegudenu.*

    yet he shall goad their heel. The phrase may be a reminiscence of "and you shall bite his heel," which is addressed to the serpent in the Garden. There would be a carryover, then, from the snake imagery of the preceding lines. The snake, one should keep in mind, is not "demonic" but an image of darting, agile, lethal assault.

20. *Asher's bread.* The Masoretic Text reads "from Asher, his bread," but several ancient versions, quite plausibly, attach the initial consonant *mem* ("from") to the end of the preceding word *'aqev* ("heel"), turning it into "their heel."

21　Naphtali, a hind let loose
　　who brings forth lovely fawns.
22　A fruitful son is Joseph,
　　　a fruitful son by a spring,
　　　　daughters strode by a rampart.

---

21. *lovely fawns*. The Hebrew *'imrei shafer* is in doubt. The translation follows one prevalent conjecture in deriving the first word from the Aramaic *'imeir,* which usually means "lamb."

22. *A fruitful son*. The morphology of the reiterated noun in this line is so peculiar that some scholars have imagined a reference to branches, others to a wild ass. There is little philological warrant for the former, and the connection between the term used here, *porat,* and *pere',* "wild ass," seems strained. (The main argument for the wild ass is that it preserves the animal imagery, but there are several other tribes in the poem that have no animal icons.) A link between *porat* and the root *p-r-h,* "to be fruitful," is less of a grammatical stretch, and is encouraged by Joseph's play on that same root in naming his son Ephraim. Joseph and Judah, as the dominant tribes of the north and the south respectively, get far more elaborate attention in the poem than do any of their brothers.

　　daughters strode. This is another crux because the verb "strode" appears to be in the feminine singular. But there are good grounds to assume that the verbal suffix *ah,* which in normative grammar signals third-person feminine singular perfect tense, was also an archaic third-person plural feminine form. There are a number of instances in which the consonantal text (*ketiv*) shows this form with a plural subject and the Masoretes correct it in the *qeri* (the indicated pronunciation) to normative grammar: e.g., Deuteronomy 21:7, "Our hands did not shed [*ketiv: shafkhah*] this blood." Without emendation, then, the text suggests that Joseph has the twin blessing of fruitfulness and military security. The young women of the tribe can walk in safety alongside the rampart because they will be protected by Joseph's valorous skill in battle (verses 23–24).

　　by a rampart. This is the same word as the one at the end of verse 6. There is scant warrant for extending it metonymically to "hillside," as some translators have done.

They savaged him, shot arrows   23
   and harassed him, the archers did.
But taut was his bow,   24
   his arms ever-moving,
through the hands of the Champion of Jacob,
   through the name of the Shepherd, and Israel's Rock.
From the God of your fathers, may He aid you,   25
   Shaddai, may He bless you—
blessings of the heavens above,
   blessings of the deep that lies below,
     blessings of breasts and womb.
Your father's blessings surpassed   26
   the blessings of timeless heights,
     the bounty of hills everlasting.
May they rest on the head of Joseph,
   on the brow of the one set apart from his brothers.

---

24. *taut was his bow, / his arms ever-moving*. There is some doubt about "taut," though the context makes this a reasonable educated guess. There is also some dispute over the verb represented here as "ever-moving," but its likely literal meaning is "to move about rapidly," "to be nimble."

   through the hands. This picks up the previous phrase, referring to Joseph, which is literally, "the arms of his hands" (unless "of his hands" is a scribal slip, a dittography of the next word in the text). In any case, the idea is that the hands of the human warrior are given strength by God's hands.

   through the name. Along with some of the ancient versions, the translation here reads *mishem* for the Masoretic *misham*, "from there," which is obscure.

25. *blessings of breasts and womb*. The fertility of the female body is aligned with the fertility of creation, the heavens above and the deep below—a correspondence not lost on the bawdy fourteenth-century Hebrew poet Emanuel of Rome, who exploited this verse in an erotic poem.

26. *the blessings of timeless heights, / the bounty of hills everlasting*. The Masoretic Text is not really intelligible at this point, and this English version follows the Septuagint for the first part of the verse, which has the double virtue of coherence and of resembling several similar parallel locutions elsewhere in biblical poetry. Instead of the Masoretic Text's *horai 'ad* ("my fore-

27   Benjamin, ravening wolf,
            in the morn he consumes the spoils,
            at evening shares out plunder."

28 These are the tribes of Israel, twelve in all, and this is what their father
    spoke to them, blessing them, each according to his blessing, he
29 blessed them. And he charged them and said to them, "I am about to
    be gathered to my kinfolk. Bury me with my fathers in the cave that is

---

bears" [?] "until" [?]), the Septuagint has the equivalent in Greek of the
idiomatic *harerei ʿad* ("timeless heights"). The noun *taʾawat* that immediately
follows may also reflect a defective text, but it could mean "that which is
desired," hence, "bounty" or "riches." The apparent sense of the whole line is:
the blessings granted Joseph and his fathers will be even greater than the
blessings manifested throughout time in the natural world, as seen in the ver-
dant, fruit-bearing hillsides.

    the brow. The Hebrew is actually a poetic synonym for "head" (something
like "pate"), but "brow" is used here for the sake of the English idiom of blessings, or honors, resting on that part of the anatomy.

27. *Benjamin, ravening wolf.* The last brief vignette of the poem, for the
youngest of the twelve sons, is one of its sharpest images of death-dealing animals, and later biblical accounts, especially in Judges, indicate that the tribe
of Benjamin was renowned for its martial prowess.

    the spoils. The rare noun *ʿad* has been variously construed as "prey"
(because of the wolf image) and "enemy," and the compactness of the line
even leaves doubt as to whether it is a noun and not an adverb (revocalizing
ʿad as *ʿod,* "still"). But both its sole other occurrence in the Bible (Isaiah 33:23)
and the poetic parallelism argue for the sense of spoils.

29. *in the cave that is in the field of Ephron the Hittite.* Jacob in his last words
to his sons exhibits an elaborate consciousness of the legal transaction
between his grandfather and Ephron the Hittite. Like the account of the purchase in chapter 25, he emphasizes the previous owner, the exact location of
the property, and the fact that it was acquired as a permanent holding. Thus,
at the end of Genesis, legal language is used to resume a great theme—that
Abraham's offspring are legitimately bound to the land God promised them,
and that the descent into Egypt is no more than a sojourn.

in the field of Ephron the Hittite, in the cave that is in the field of 30
Machpelah, which faces Mamre, in the land of Canaan, the field that
Abraham bought from Ephron the Hittite as a burial-holding. There 31
they buried Abraham and Sarah his wife, there they buried Isaac and
Rebekah his wife, and there I buried Leah—the field and the cave 32
within it, bought from the Hittites." And Jacob finished charging his 33
sons, and he gathered his feet up into the bed, and he breathed his last,
and was gathered to his kinfolk.

CHAPTER 50

1 And Joseph flung himself on his father's face and wept over him
2 and kissed him. And Joseph charged his servants the physicians to
3 embalm his father, and the physicians embalmed Israel. And forty
full days were taken for him, as such is the full time of embalming, and
4 the Egyptians keened for him seventy days. And the days for keening
him passed, and Joseph spoke to the household of Pharaoh, saying, "If,

---

1. *And Joseph flung himself on his father's face and wept over him and kissed him.*
These three gestures by now are strongly associated with Joseph's character. In
the great recognition scene in chapter 45, he flings himself on Benjamin's
neck, embraces and kisses him, and then does the same with his ten half
brothers, and before this he has wept three times over the encounter with his
brothers. Joseph is at once the intellectual, dispassionate interpreter of dreams
and central economic planner, and the man of powerful spontaneous feeling.
At his father's deathbed, he only weeps, he does not speak.

2. *his servants the physicians.* Although the Hebrew term means "healer," these
are obviously experts in the intricate process of mummification, and the wording indicates that Joseph had such specialists on his personal staff. Mummification would be dictated by Jacob's status as father of the viceroy of Egypt and
also by the practical necessity of carrying the body on the long trek to central
Canaan.

3. *forty full days.* A Hebrew formulaic number is used rather than the number
of days prescribed by Egyptian practice.
   seventy days. Evidently, the Egyptian period of mourning for a royal person-
age, seventy-two days, has been rounded off to the Hebrew formulaic seventy.

4. *Joseph spoke to the household of Pharaoh.* It is a little puzzling that Joseph,
as Pharaoh's right-hand man, is compelled to approach him through interme-

pray, I have found favor in your eyes, speak, pray, in Pharaoh's hearing,
as follows: 'My father made me swear, saying, Look, I am about to die. 5
In the grave I readied me in the land of Canaan, there you must bury
me.' And so, let me go up, pray, and bury my father and come back."
And Pharaoh said, "Go up and bury your father as he made you swear." 6
And Joseph went up to bury his father, and all Pharaoh's servants, the 7
elders of his household, and all the elders of the land of Egypt, went up
with him, and all the household of Joseph, and his brothers, and his 8
father's household. Only their little ones and their flocks and their cat-

---

diaries. Some commentators have explained this by invoking Joseph's condition as mourner, which, it is claimed, would prohibit him from coming directly
into Pharaoh's presence. A more reliable key to his recourse to go-betweens
may be provided by the language of imploring deference with which he introduces his message to Pharaoh—"If, pray, I have found favor in your eyes,
speak, pray. . . ." Joseph is aware that he is requesting something extraordinary
in asking permission to go up to Canaan with his entire clan, for Pharaoh
might be apprehensive that the real aim was repatriation, which would cost
him his indispensable viceroy and a whole guild of valued shepherds. Joseph
consequently decides to send his petition through the channel of Pharaoh's
trusted courtiers, to whom he turns in deferential court language.

5. *In the grave I readied me.* The usual meaning of the Hebrew verb *karah* is "to
dig," though it can also mean "to purchase." The latter sense is unlikely here
because it would be confusing to use *karah* for buying a grave, when it is so
naturally applied to digging the grave. But since the burial site in question is
actually a cave, one must assume an extrapolation from the primary meaning
of the verb to any preparation of a place for burial.
     and come back. This final verb is of course a crucial consideration for
Pharaoh.

7. *and all Pharaoh's servants, the elders of his household, and all the elders of the
land of Egypt, went up with him.* This vast entourage of Egyptian dignitaries
betokens Pharaoh's desire to accord royal honors to Jacob. The presence of
chariots and horsemen (verse 9) might also serve as protection against hostile
Canaanites, but the whole grand Egyptian procession is surely an effective
means for ensuring that Joseph and his father's clan will return to Egypt.

8. *Only their little ones.* The children and flocks are left behind as a guarantee
of the adults' return.

9 tle they left in the land of Goshen. And chariots and horsemen as well
went up with him, and the procession was very great. And they came
10 as far as Goren ha-Atad, which is across the Jordan, and there they
keened a great and heavy keening, and performed mourning rites for
11 his father seven days. And the Canaanite natives of the land saw the
mourning in Goren ha-Atad and they said, "This heavy mourning is
Egypt's." Therefore is its name called Abel-Mizraim, which is across the
12,13 Jordan. And his sons did for him just as he charged them. And his sons
conveyed him to the land of Canaan and buried him in the cave of the
Machpelah field, the field Abraham had bought as a burial holding
14 from Ephron the Hittite, facing Mamre. And Joseph went back to
Egypt, he and his brothers and all who had gone up with him to bury
his father, after he had buried his father.

15 And Joseph's brothers saw that their father was dead, and they said, "If
Joseph bears resentment against us, he will surely pay us back for all
16 the evil we caused him." And they charged Joseph, saying, "Your father

---

10. *Goren ha-Atad*. The place name means "threshing-floor of the bramble."

across the Jordan. The logical route from Egypt would be along the Mediterranean coast, which would necessitate construing this phrase from the perspective of someone standing to the east of the Jordan. That, however, is
implausible because "across the Jordan" in biblical usage generally means just
what we mean by trans-Jordan in modern usage—the territory east of the Jordan. Perhaps a circuitous route through the Sinai to the east and then back
across the Jordan is intended to prefigure the itinerary of the future exodus
and return to Canaan. Perhaps local traditions for the etiology of a place-name
Abel-Mizraim in trans-Jordan led to the intimation of this unlikely route.

11. *Abel-Mizraim*. This is construed in the folk etymology as "mourning of
Egypt," though *'abel* is actually a watercourse. *Mizraim* means "Egypt."

16. *And they charged Joseph*. The verb, which most commonly refers either to
giving instructions or delivering the terms of a last will and testament, is a little peculiar. If the received text is reliable here, the choice of verb would be
influenced by the fact that the brothers are conveying to Joseph the terms of
what they claim (perhaps dubiously) is their father's "charge" before his death.
In any case, they send this message through an intermediary, for only in verse

left a charge before his death, saying, 'Thus shall you say to Joseph, We   17
beseech you, forgive, pray, the crime and the offense of your brothers,
for evil they have caused you. And so now, forgive, pray, the crime of
the servants of your father's God.'" And Joseph wept when they spoke
to him. And his brothers then came and flung themselves before him   18
and said, "Here we are, your slaves." And Joseph said, "Fear not, for am   19
I instead of God? While you meant evil toward me, God meant it for   20
good, so as to bring about at this very time keeping many people alive.
And so fear not. I will sustain you and your little ones." And he com-   21
forted them and spoke to their hearts.

And Joseph dwelled in Egypt, he and his father's household, and   22
Joseph lived a hundred and ten years. And Joseph saw the third gener-   23
ation of sons from Ephraim, and the sons, as well, of Machir son of
Manasseh were born on Joseph's knees. And Joseph said to his broth-   24

---

18 are they represented as coming before Joseph—"And his brothers then
[*gam*] came"—so perhaps the odd use of the verb indicates indirection here.

17. *the servants of your father's God.* In the imploring language of their plea for
forgiveness, they conclude by calling themselves not his brothers but the faithful servants of the God of Jacob. Rashi nicely observes, "If your father is dead,
his God exists, and they are his servants."

20. *While you meant evil toward me, God meant it for good.* This whole final
scene between Joseph and his brothers is a recapitulation, after Jacob's death,
of the recognition scene in Egypt. Once more the brothers feel guilt and fear.
Once more Joseph weeps because of them. Once more they offer to become
his slaves. (The physical act of prostration, as the early-twentieth-century
German scholar Hermann Gunkel observes, carries us back full circle to
Joseph's two dreams at the beginning of the story.) And once more Joseph
assures them that it has been God's purpose all along to turn evil into good, for
the end of "keeping many people alive," with Joseph continuing in his role as
sustainer of the entire clan.

23. *were born on Joseph's knees.* This gesture serves either as a ritual of adoption or of legitimation.

ers, "I am about to die, and God will surely single you out and take you
25 up from this land to the land He promised to Isaac and to Jacob." And
Joseph made the sons of Israel swear, saying, "When God indeed sin-
26 gles you out, you shall take up my bones from this place." And Joseph
died, a hundred and ten years old, and they embalmed him and he was
put in a coffin in Egypt.

---

24. *God will surely single you out and take you up from this land.* The ground is
laid at the end of Genesis for the great movement out of Egypt in Exodus.

25. *take up my bones.* Although Joseph knows that Egyptian science will turn
his body into a mummy, he still thinks of his remains in Hebrew terms as he
invokes his eventual restoration to the land of the Hebrews.

26. *a hundred and ten years.* This is a last Egyptian touch, since this is the ideal
Egyptian life span, as against 120 in the Hebrew tradition.
    and he was put in a coffin in Egypt. The book that began with an image of
God's breath moving across the vast expanses of the primordial deep to bring
the world and all life into being ends with this image of a body in a box, a
mummy in a coffin. (The Hebrews in Canaan appear not to have used coffins,
and the term occurs only here.) Out of the contraction of this moment of mortuary enclosure, a new expansion, and new births, will follow. Exodus begins
with a proliferation of births, a pointed repetition of the primeval blessing to
be fruitful and multiply, and just as the survival of the Flood was represented
as a second creation, the leader who is to forge the creation of the nation will
be borne on the water in a little box—not the *'aron,* "the coffin," of the end of
Genesis but the *tevah,* "the ark," that keeps Noah and his seed alive.

EXODUS

INTRODUCTION

A s the long historical narrative of the Five Books of Moses moves from the patriarchs to the Hebrew nation in Egypt, it switches gears. The narrative conventions deployed, from type-scenes and thematic keywords to the treatment of dialogue, remain the same, but the angle from which events are seen and the handling of characters are notably different. Genesis ended with the death, and the distinctly Egyptian mummification, of Joseph. Exodus begins with a listing of the sons of Jacob who came down to Egypt, thus establishing a formal link with the concluding chapters of Genesis in which a more detailed list of the emigrants from Canaan (46:8–27) is provided. The rapid enumeration here of the sons of Jacob is concluded by a notation of the formulaic number of seventy said to constitute the Hebrew migration from Canaan to Egypt, and this is followed by a restatement of the death of Joseph—a device that biblical scholars call "resumptive repetition," whereby, after an interruption of narrative continuity, a phrase is repeated from the point at which the narrative broke off (the phrase here is "And Joseph died") in order to mark the resumption of the story. In this second report of Joseph's death, however, the focus is not on the mummy in the coffin but on the dying out of a whole generation, which thus propels us forward in historical time (four centuries, according to God's prophetic revelation to Abraham in Genesis 15) to a moment when *beney yisra'ael*, the sons of Israel (or Jacob), have swelled to a people, the Israelites, which is the meaning of that Hebrew phrase from now on in the narrative. Instead of the sharply etched individuals who constituted a family in all its explosive dynamics in Genesis, we now have teeming multitudes of Israelites whose spectacular prolificness introduces to the story the perspective of the whole wide world of creation announced at the beginning of Genesis: "And the sons of Israel were fruitful and swarmed and multiplied and grew very vast, and the land [the Hebrew word also means "earth," as in Genesis] was filled with them" (Exodus 1:7).

In keeping with this new wide-angle lens through which the characters and the events are seen, the narrative moves from the domestic, moral, and psychological realism of the Patriarchal Tales to a more stylized, sometimes deliberately schematic, mode of storytelling that in a number of respects, especially in the early chapters of the book, has the feel of a folktale. At the beginning of the story, Pharaoh is referred to several times as "the king of Egypt" rather than by his Egyptian title, which was used in Genesis and will become his set designation as the story goes on. This has the effect of casting him as the archetypal evil king (one who kills babies) in a folktale confrontation between the forces of good and of evil. Other folktale elements are evident: the many thousands of childbearing Hebrew women are attended to, in the charming schematic simplicity of a folktale, by just two virtuous midwives; in a folkloric motif that has been profusely documented in many traditions of the ancient Near East and elsewhere, the future hero is threatened with death by the evil king and is saved by being hidden and then rescued. The betrothal type-scene of the young woman encountered at the well in a foreign land, which in the instances of Rebekah and (the absent) Isaac and of Rachel and Jacob was pregnant with intimations of the character and the future relationship of the two people involved, here has undergone a certain stylization. Aspects of Moses's subsequent career as national leader are adumbrated, but there are no indications about his future relationship with Zipporah, and her character is not in the least at issue. Indeed, it is only here that the young woman at the well is multiplied into seven young women, Zipporah and her six sisters, a move that diminishes her individuality while recasting the encounter between the future spouses as a meeting between one man and seven maidens, according to the sanctified formulaic number.

The general rule in Exodus, and again in Numbers when the story continues, is that what is of interest about the character of Moses is what bears on his qualities as a leader—his impassioned sense of justice, his easily ignited temper, his selfless compassion, his feelings of personal inadequacy. Alone among biblical characters, he is assigned an oddly generic epithet, "the man Moses." There may be some theological motive for this designation, in order to remind us of his plainly human status, to ward off any inclination to deify the founding leader of the Israelite people, but it also suggests more concretely that Moses as forger of the nation and prince of prophets is, after all, not an absolutely unique figure but a man like other men, bringing to the soul-trying tasks of leadership both the moral and temperamental resources and the all-too-human weaknesses that many men may possess. In regard to our experience of the character and the story, all this means that "the man Moses" remains somewhat distanced from us, that we never get the sense of intimate acquaintance with his inner life and his distinctive traits of personality that we are so memorably afforded in the stories of Jacob and Joseph.

There is a certain correlation between the distancing of the central character and the distancing of the figure of God in Exodus (a procedure that, again, is continued into Numbers). God in Genesis, as one detects in a glimpse of Him in the Garden story and as one can see quite clearly in His encounter with Abraham in Genesis 18, walks about the earth looking very much like a man—indeed, being easily mistaken for a man until He chooses to reveal His identity—and at some points engaging a human being in what is clearly represented as face-to-face conversation. God in Exodus has become essentially unseeable, overpowering, and awesomely refulgent. Barriers to access accompany Him everywhere, just as they will be instituted architecturally in the tripartite structure of the sanctuary that He orders the Israelites to build. The first manifestation of God's presence to Moses is in the anomaly of the fire burning in a bush without consuming it, and then the divine voice enjoins Moses, "Come no closer here," and proceeds to speak to him without being in any way visible to him. Fire, which betokens potent energy and which is something one cannot touch without being hurt or destroyed, is the protective perimeter out of which God addresses Moses and the Israelites throughout the story: all of Mount Sinai will be smoking like a firebrand, with celestial fireworks of lightning and thunder crackling round its peak, when God reveals the Ten Commandments to Moses. Later, as we shall see, Deuteronomy, for its own theological reasons, will pick up and dramatically amplify this image of a barrier of fire around God at the defining moment of revelation. God in Exodus has become more of an ungraspable mystery than He seems in Genesis; and as He moves here from the sphere of the clan that is the context of the Patriarchal Tales to the arena of history, His sheer power as supreme deity and His implacability against those who would thwart His purposes emerge as the most salient aspects of the divine character.

Exodus, like Genesis, is made up of two large panels, though they are notably different in nature from the two panels that constitute Genesis. The first unit, running from chapter 1 through chapter 20, is a grand narrative sweep that culminates in what is, at least in national-historical and theological terms, the great climax and point of reference of all biblical literature—the revelation through Moses to Israel of the Ten Commandments on Mount Sinai. There are, one should note, legal passages along the way in chapters 12 and 13 regarding the spring rituals of the paschal offering and the Festival of Flatbread as well as the dedication of the firstborn, but these are to a large degree integrated into the general narrative, coming as they do when the first Passover rite is observed in Egypt and when the Israelite firstborn have been spared while Egypt's are stricken. This narrative is one of national triumph after the most painful abjection, though the triumph is complicated by the fact that it concludes with the imposition of a set of imperatives which for the Israelites will prove to be a great challenge to obey.

The narrative is organized around three thematically defined spaces: Egypt, the place of bondage; the wilderness, a liminal space where freedom will be realized and new obligations incurred, where a tense struggle between leader and people will play out as part of the initiatory experience of nationhood; and the promised destination of the Exodus from Egypt, the land that remains beyond the horizon of this book. Egypt is associated with water, almost everything there being linked with its central waterway, the Nile, where baby Moses is saved from drowning and where the Ten Plagues begin; and a barrier of water must be crossed to effect the escape of the Israelites, with that very water then drowning the pursuing Egyptian hosts as they had sought to drown the Israelite infant boys. The wilderness is, antithetically, a zone of parched dryness—arid sand and rugged rock formations, where the people more than once desperately thirst for water and are dependent on its miraculous discovery. The shepherd Moses first encounters God in the wilderness on a mountain later called Sinai (a name perhaps meant to recall *seneh*, the Hebrew word for "bush") but in this episode referred to as Horeb, which as the twelfth-century Hebrew exegete Abraham ibn Ezra shrewdly saw, means "dryness" or "parched place." God appears to Moses through a token of supernatural burning on the mountain of the parched place. He will then lead the Israelites through the wilderness with a pillar of fire by night that banks down to a pillar of cloud by day. The culmination of this narrative in the Sinai epiphany, as we have already noted, will make the mountain itself incandescent and rake the sky around its summit with divine fire. The climax of this whole story is a set of lapidary legal injunctions, but they are in no way anticlimactic for being that. Framed as a series of imperatives in the second-person singular and thus addressing every man and woman of the Israelite nation, they express the keenest sense of urgency, much like the urgency in dialogue between human characters that marks many of the dramatic high points of biblical narrative elsewhere. Later, in the episode of the Golden Calf, we learn that God has incised the ten imperative utterances on two tablets of stone (32:15–16), but here no mention is made of writing. The omission is dictated, I think, by a desire to convey the potent immediacy of God's speech to Israel through Moses: "And God spoke these words, saying" is the formula pointedly used to introduce the Decalogue.

Finally, beyond well-watered Egypt and the burning desert where uncanny fires flare, the new Israelite nation is repeatedly told of a third space, a land flowing not with water but, hyperbolically, with milk and honey. This utopian space will be beyond reach for forty years, and in a sense it can never be fully attained. When the twelve spies enter it on a reconnaissance mission in Numbers, they confirm its fabulous fecundity, but ten of the twelve also deem it unconquerable, calling it "a land that consumes its inhabitants." As the biblical story continues through Numbers and Deuteronomy and ultimately on to the history of the kingdoms of Judah and Israel, the land flowing with milk and honey will begin to seem something like the Land of Cockaigne of medieval European folklore, a dream of delighted, unimpeded fulfillment beyond the grating actualities of real historical time. Treated with poetic hyperbole by the Prophets, it will eventually generate eschatological visions not within the purview of these early books of the Bible.

It is the second large panel of Exodus that is likely to cause perplexity for a good many modern readers. After the riveting narrative of liberation and revelation, the second half of the book, with the exception of the Golden Calf story (chapters 32–34), is devoted to legal material—first a code of criminal and tort law, with some ritual injunctions at the end (chapters 21–23), which is often referred to by scholars as the Book of the Covenant, and then the elaborate instructions for the building of the Tabernacle (chapters 25–31), instructions that will be carried out, more or less word for word, just as one would expect, after the resolution of the confrontation over the Golden Calf (chapters 35–40). Readers attached to the notion of story are bound to find these seventeen chapters of laws and architectural instructions something of a letdown, but one must assume that the ancient writers and their audience had different ideas about literary unity and about how story related to law.

The Book of the Covenant could be understood as a detailed extension of the Decalogue, but the Tabernacle passages pose more of a problem. The easiest explanation for this lavishing of attention on the construction of the Tabernacle is that it reflects the professional interests of the Priestly writers who were responsible for the bulk of this material. That explanation seems plausible enough, but it is too simple a way of stating the case. An analogy between the two-panel structure of Exodus and the complementary interaction between the two versions of the Creation story in Genesis may be helpful. The Priestly editors of Genesis had inherited J's old story (beginning in chapter 2, the middle of the fourth verse) full of dynamism and danger, in which the acts of creation are represented in powerfully concrete anthropomorphic terms. This story, one may infer, represented a strong set of traditional truths for the editors, but truths that had to be complemented by a different perspective on the same events. And so, before the first human male shaped out of clay and Eve built from his rib and the seduction by the serpent, the Priestly writer placed his own magisterial version of creation, in which the world is called into being through a succession of divine speech-acts and in which everything proceeds in harmonious order, registered in the balanced cadences of the stately prose, from the first day to the seventh, coming to a formal conclusion in the primordial Sabbath. The first half of Exodus is a compelling story, punctuated, as some scholars have proposed, by certain epic gestures, that moves from enslavement to liberation to epiphany. It is also a story marked by danger, doubt, and what looks like a national destiny of endless trouble. Moses the future leader barely escapes being murdered as an infant; kills a man, an act that compels him to flee Egypt; harbors grave doubts about his capacity for the daunting mission God imposes on him; and on occasion is angry, impatient, almost despairing in his leadership. The Israelites on their part can scarcely bring themselves to trust Moses and Aaron when the two brothers come to lead them out of slavery, and once in the wilderness, the people will repeatedly prove to be recalcitrant in a long series of backslidings or "murmurings," both in Exodus and in Numbers. The crowning instance of these episodes of rebellion is the incident of the Golden Calf, carefully introduced between the instructions for the building of the Tabernacle and the carrying out of the instructions.

The Tabernacle, I would suggest, was imagined by these writers as a vision of perfectly orchestrated harmony, enacted through the meticulous crafts of architecture, weaving, dying, woodcarving, and metalwork—an implementation by human artisans, following divine directives, of the sort of comprehensive harmony figured in the Priestly account of creation. After the tense story of rupture and recrimination of national experience in history, the Priestly writers, themselves intimately associated with a realm of ordered ritual, provide an elaborately imagined representation of the beautiful ordering of sacred space, a zone of choreographed repetition set off against the unsettled peregrinations of the Wilderness generation. The satisfaction this material gives its audience is not story but pageantry: the splendor of the many-colored textiles displayed along the walls of the Tabernacle, the bronze loops on which they are hung, the wrought precious metals and inlaid gems of the various ritual implements. When at the end of all the building we are told, "And Moses completed the task" (40:33), we hear a significant echo of "And God completed on the seventh day the task He had done" (Genesis 2:2). Human labor, scrupulously following a divine plan, creates an ordered space that mirrors the harmony of God's creation. But the concluding image of the book is the pillar of cloud by day and fire by night that leads the Israelites on their march through the wilderness. On that long way, more trouble awaits them, as readers will discover when the narrative resumes in Numbers.

CHAPTER 1

And these are the names of the sons of Israel who came to Egypt ₁
with Jacob, each man with his household they came. Reuben, ₂
Simeon, Levi, and Judah. Issachar, Zebulun, and Benjamin. Dan ₃,₄
and Naphtali, Gad and Asher. And all these persons springing from the ₅
loins of Jacob were seventy persons, but Joseph was in Egypt. And ₆

---

1. *And these are the names.* The initial "and" (the particle *waw*) serves an important thematic end, as several of the medieval Hebrew commentators have noticed. It announces that the narrative that follows is a direct continuation of the Book of Genesis, which ended with Joseph's death. The list of Jacob's sons harks back to the longer list of sons and grandsons at the moment of the descent into Egypt in Genesis 46:8–27. It should be noted that the dominant Hebrew tradition assigns names to each of the Five Books of Moses based on the first significant word in the text, and so this book is called *Shemot*, "Names." The English tradition of titles follows the Greek practice, which is to use topical names, hence Exodus.

the sons of Israel. Although the masculine plural form of the Hebrew *ben* could also mean "children," it is clear here and in Genesis 46 that only the male offspring are used to make up the count of seventy, and only the names of sons are given.

2–4. *Reuben, Simeon . . . Asher.* In order to endow the list of eleven with formal symmetry, the writer arranges them in two groups of four with a group of three in the middle.

5. *the loins.* The Hebrew *yarekh* means "thigh" and is probably a euphemistic metonymy for testicles, as in Genesis 24:2.

seventy persons. Some ingenuity is required to come up with an exact total of seventy, but the Bible uses numbers as symbolic approximations: after seven and ten, one moves to forty (which is used for units of time rather than peo-

7 Joseph died, and all his brothers with him, and all that generation. And the sons of Israel were fruitful and swarmed and multiplied and grew very vast, and the land was filled with them.

8,9 And a new king arose over Egypt who knew not Joseph. And he said to his people, "Look, the people of the sons of Israel is more numerous

10 and vaster than we. Come, let us be shrewd with them lest they multiply and then, should war occur, they will actually join our enemies and

---

ple), then ten times seven, or seventy—here indicating a substantial clan, the nucleus of a people. (See the comment on Genesis 46:27.)

but Joseph was in Egypt. The particle *waw*, which usually means "and," either is the indication of a pluperfect or, as here, has an adversative sense when it is followed by the subject and then a perfective verb (instead of the normal imperfective verb in initial position and then the subject).

7. *the sons of Israel.* Though the phrase is identical with the one used at the beginning of verse 1, historical time has been telescoped and so the meaning of the phrase has shifted: now it signifies not the actual sons of Israel/Jacob but Israelites, the members of the nation to which the first Israel gave his name. In subsequent occurrences this translation will use "Israelites."

were fruitful and swarmed and multiplied. These terms are all of course pointed verbal allusions to the Creation story, as is the final clause of the verse since the Hebrew for "land," *'arets,* can also mean "earth." Despite exile and impending slavery, the dynamic of the first creation is resumed by the Israelites in Egypt. In fact, the thematic grounds of the Patriarchal Tales have notably shifted: instead of the constantly perilous struggle for procreation of the patriarchs, the Hebrews now exhibit the teeming fecundity of the natural world. It is for this reason that the verb "swarm" (*sharats*), which in the Creation story is attached to creeping things, is assigned to the Israelites. The verbal root for becoming vast (King James Version, "mighty") does not figure at the beginning of Genesis, but it is part of God's covenantal promise—"For Abraham will surely be a great and mighty nation" (Genesis 18:18).

9. *the people of the sons of Israel.* This oddly redundant phrase—it should be either "sons of Israel" or "people of Israel"—is explained by Pharaoh's alarmed recognition that the sons, the lineal descendants, of Israel have swelled to a people.

10. *be shrewd with them.* The Hebrew says "it," i.e., the people, but later switches to the plural.

fight against us and go up from the land." And they set over them 11
forced-labor foremen so as to abuse them with their burdens, and they
built store-cities for Pharaoh: Pithom and Ramases. And as they abused 12
them, so did they multiply and so did they spread, and they came to
loathe the Israelites. And the Egyptians put the Israelites to work at 13
crushing labor, and they made their lives bitter with hard work with 14
mortar and bricks and every work in the field—all their crushing work
that they performed. And the king of Egypt said to the Hebrew mid- 15
wives, one of whom was named Shiphrah and the other was named

---

they will actually join our enemies. The adverb *gam,* which generally means
"also," here has an emphatic sense. Compare Genesis 37:7.

go up from the land. The most plausible meaning, as the consensus of
medieval Hebrew commentators understood, is that after joining the enemy,
the Israelites would leave Egypt—probably to return to their country of origin
in the north, as the verb "go up" may suggest. The notion that the phrase could
mean "rise up from the ground" (New Jewish Publication Society) or "become
masters of the land" (Revised English Bible) seems far-fetched.

12. *as they abused them, so did they multiply.* Like a force of nature (compare
verse 7), the Israelites respond to oppression by redoubling their procreative
surge. Compare Rashi: "The Divine Spirit says, 'So—you say, "lest they multi
ply," and I say, "so did they multiply." ' "
    and they came to loathe the Israelites. William H. C. Propp has made the
ingenious suggestion that the loathing is a response to the reptilian "swarming"
of reproductive activity exhibited by the Israelites.

13. *at crushing labor.* The Hebrew is an adverbial form derived from a root that
means "to break into pieces," "to pulverize."

14. *work . . . work . . . work.* Following a prevalent stylistic practice of Hebrew
narrative, the writer underscores his main topic, the harshness of slavery, by
repeating a central thematic keyword. Indeed, the Hebrew literally says, "their
crushing work that they worked," but in English that cognate accusative form
sounds awkward except for a limited number of idioms (e.g., "sing a song").

15. *the Hebrew midwives.* "Hebrew" is regularly the designation of Israelites
from a foreign perspective.
    Shiphrah . . . Puah. The first name suggests "beauty," the second name, as
the Ugaritic texts indicate, might originally have meant "fragrant blossom" and

16 Puah. And he said, "When you deliver the Hebrew women and look on
the birth-stool, if it is a boy, you shall put him to death, and if it is a girl,
17 she may live." And the midwives feared God and did not do as the king
18 of Egypt had spoken to them, and they let the children live. And the
king of Egypt called the midwives and said to them, "Why did you do
19 this thing and let the children live?" And the midwives said to Pharaoh,
"For not like the Egyptian women are the Hebrew women, for they are
20 hardy. Before the midwife comes to them they give birth." And God

---

hence "girl." But since the root *pa'ah* can also mean "to murmur" or "to gur-
gle," Rashi inventively suggests it is the sound a nurturing woman makes to
soothe an infant. In any case, the introduction of just two heroic midwives
reflects the way this entire narrative, in contrast to Genesis, has been stylized
and simplified. Abraham ibn Ezra appears to grasp this principle of schematization when he proposes that Shiphrah and Puah in fact would have had to be
supervisors of whole battalions of midwives.

16. *birth-stool*. Literally, "double stones." Although there is some debate about
the meaning of the term, there are persuasive grounds to understand it as the
double stone or brick structure that the childbearing woman gripped as she
kneeled, the standard position to give birth. There is an Egyptian magical
papyrus that announces it is to be recited "over the two bricks of birthing."

19. *for they are hardy*. "Hardy," *ḥayot*, is derived from the verb "to live," which
has just been used twice in connection with the newborn. (Hence the King
James Version's "lively," though in modern English that unfortunately suggests
vivaciousness or bounciness.) The fact that *ḥayot* as a noun means "animals"
may reinforce the strong connection between the Israelites and the procreative
forces of the natural world: like animals, the Hebrew women need no midwife.

made it go well with the midwives, and the people multiplied and
became very vast. And inasmuch as the midwives feared God, He made   21
households for them. And Pharaoh charged his whole people, saying,   22
"Every boy that is born you shall fling into the Nile, and every girl you
shall let live."

---

21. *He made households for them.* Although some have seen Pharaoh as the
antecedent of "he," God seems considerably more likely. The sense would then
be that they were rewarded for their virtue with social standing, establishing
their own families, or something of the sort.

22. *Pharaoh charged his whole people.* Despairing of cooperation from the
Hebrew midwives in his genocidal project, Pharaoh now enlists the entire
Egyptian population in a search-and-destroy operation.
    Every boy . . . you shall fling into the Nile, and every girl you shall let live. The
schematic—as against historical or even historylike—character of the narrative is evident in this folktale antithetical symmetry. The idea is presumably
that the people would be eradicated by cutting off all male progeny while the
girls could be raised for the sexual exploitation and domestic service of the
Egyptians, by whom they would of course be rapidly assimilated. Pharaoh's
scheme will again be frustrated, as the future liberator of the Hebrews will be
placed (not flung) in the Nile and emerge eventually to cause grief to Egypt.
There is also an echo here of Abram's words to Sarai when they come down to
Egypt, adumbrating the destiny of their descendants, during a famine: "they
will kill me while you they will let live" (Genesis 12:12).

CHAPTER 2

1
2
3

And a man from the house of Levi went and took a Levite daughter, and the woman conceived and bore a son, and she saw that
he was goodly, and she hid him three months. And when she
could no longer hide him, she took a wicker ark for him and caulked
it with resin and pitch and placed the child in it and placed it in the
4 reeds by the banks of the Nile. And his sister stationed herself at a dis-

---

1. *took.* This verb is commonly used in biblical Hebrew for taking a wife, even
when "wife" is elided, as here. It is worth translating literally because the verb
is echoed in the woman's "taking" the wicker ark (verse 3) and in the Egyptian
slavegirl's "taking" the ark (verse 5).

3. *she took a wicker ark . . . and caulked it with resin and pitch.* The basket in
which the infant is placed is called a *tevah*, ark, the same word used for Noah's
ark. (It may be an Egyptian loanword. Such borrowed terms abound in the
story, giving it local color. The most prominent is the word for "Nile," *ye'or.*) As
numerous commentators have observed, the story of Moses begins with a
pointed allusion to the Flood story. In Genesis, a universal deluge nearly
destroys the whole human race. Here, Pharaoh's decree to drown every
Hebrew male infant threatens to destroy the people of Israel. As the ark in
Genesis bears on the water the saving remnant of humankind, the child borne
on the waters here will save his imperiled people. This narrative recapitulates
the Flood story, itself a quasi-epic narrative of global scope, in the transposed
key of a folktale: the story of a future ruler who is hidden in a basket floating
on a river has parallels in Hittite, Assyrian, and Egyptian literature, and
approximate analogues in many other cultures. Otto Rank sees the basket as a
womb image and the river water as an externalization of the amniotic fluid.
Psychoanalytic speculation apart, it is clear from the story that water plays a
decisive thematic role in Moses's career. He is borne safely on the water,
which Pharaoh had imagined would be the very means to destroy all the

tance to see what would be done to him. And Pharaoh's daughter came 5
down to bathe in the Nile, her maidens walking along the Nile. And
she saw the ark amidst the reeds and sent her slavegirl and took it.
And she opened it up and saw the child, and, look, it was a lad weep- 6
ing. And she pitied him and said, "This is one of the children of the
Hebrews." And his sister said to Pharaoh's daughter, "Shall I go and 7
summon a nursing woman from the Hebrews that she may suckle the
child for you?" And Pharaoh's daughter said to her, "Go." And the girl 8
went and summoned the child's mother. And Pharaoh's daughter said 9
to her, "Carry away this child and suckle him for me, and I myself will
pay your wages." And the woman took the child and suckled him.
And the child grew, and she brought him to Pharaoh's daughter and he 10
became a son to her, and she called his name Moses, "For from the
water I drew him out."

Hebrew male children. His floating among the reeds (*suf*) foreshadows the
miraculous triumph over the Egyptians that he will lead in the parting of the
Sea of Reeds (*yam suf*). His obtaining water for the thirsting people will figure
prominently in the Wilderness stories.

6. *and saw the child*. The Masoretic text has "she saw him, the child," but other
ancient versions show "saw" without the accusative masculine suffix.
    and, look, it was a lad weeping. "Lad," *na'ar*, is more typically used for an
older child or a young man, but it may be employed here to emphasize the discovery—"and look," *wehineh*—that this is a male child. (It might also be relevant that *na'ar* occurs elsewhere as a term of parental tenderness referring to
a vulnerable child.) The fact that this is a male child left hidden in a basket
would be the clue to the princess and her entourage that he belongs to the
Hebrews against whom the decree of infanticide has been issued. Nahum
Sarna notes that this is the sole instance in the Bible in which the verb "to
weep" is used for an infant, not an adult.

10. *And the child grew*. The verb clearly indicates his reaching the age of wean-
ing, which would have been around three. This might have been long enough
for the child to have acquired Hebrew as his first language. The same verb
"grew" in verse 11 refers to attaining adulthood.
    became a son to her. The phrase indicates adoption, not just an emotional
attachment.
    Moses. This is an authentic Egyptian name meaning "the one who is born,"

11   And it happened at that time that Moses grew and went out to his
brothers and saw their burdens. And he saw an Egyptian man striking
12   a Hebrew man of his brothers. And he turned this way and that and saw
that there was no man about, and he struck down the Egyptian and
13   buried him in the sand. And he went out the next day, and, look, two
Hebrew men were brawling, and he said to the one in the wrong, "Why
14   should you strike your fellow?" And he said, "Who set you as a man
prince and judge over us? Is it to kill me that you mean as you killed
the Egyptian?" And Moses was afraid and he thought, "Surely, the thing

and hence "son." The folk etymology relates it to the Hebrew verb *mashah*, "to
draw out from water." Perhaps the active form of the verb used for the name
mosheh, "he who draws out," is meant to align the naming with Moses's future
destiny of rescuing his people from the water of the Sea of Reeds.

12. *and saw there was no man about*. Although the obvious meaning is that he
wanted to be sure the violent intervention he intended would go unobserved,
some interpreters have proposed, a little apologetically, that he first looked
around to see if there was anyone else to step forward and help the beaten
Hebrew slave. "About" is merely implied in the Hebrew. In any case, there is
a pointed echoing of "man" (*'ish*)—an Egyptian man, a Hebrew man, and no
man—that invites one to ponder the role and obligations of a man as one man
victimizes another. When the fugitive Moses shows up in Midian, he will be
identified, presumably because of his attire and speech, as "an Egyptian man."

13. *Why should you strike your fellow?* The first dialogue assigned to a character in biblical narrative typically defines the character. Moses's first speech is
a reproof to a fellow Hebrew and an attempt to impose a standard of justice
(*rasha'*, "the one in the wrong," is a legal term).

14. *Who set you as a man prince and judge over us?* These words of the brawler
in the wrong not only preface the revelation that Moses's killing of the Egyptian is no secret but also adumbrate a long series of later incidents in which the
Israelites will express resentment or rebelliousness toward Moses. Again,
"man" is stressed. Later, "the man Moses" will become a kind of epithet for
Israel's first leader.
   thing. The Hebrew *davar* variously means "word," "thing," "matter," "affair,"
and much else.

has become known." And Pharaoh heard of this thing and he sought to   15
kill Moses, and Moses fled from Pharaoh's presence and dwelled in the
land of Midian, and he sat down by the well. And the priest of Midian   16
had seven daughters, and they came and drew water and filled the
troughs to water their father's flock. And the shepherds came and drove   17
them off, and Moses rose and saved them and watered their
flock. And they came to Reuel their father, and he said, "Why have you   18

---

15. *Midian.* The geographical location of this land in different biblical references does not seem entirely fixed, perhaps because the Midianites were
seminomads. Moses's country of refuge would appear to be a semidesert
region bordering Egypt on the east, to the west by northwest of present-day
Eilat.

    sat down by the well. The verb *yashav*, "sat down," is identical with the pre-
vious verb in this sentence, where it reflects its other meaning, "to dwell" or
"to settle." It makes sense for the wayfarer to pause to rest and refresh himself
at an oasis as Moses does here. "The well" has the idiomatic force of "a certain well."

16. *seven daughters . . . came and drew water.* By this point, the ancient audience would have sufficient signals to recognize the narrative convention of the
betrothal type-scene (compare Abraham's servant and Rebekah, Genesis 24,
and Jacob and Rachel, Genesis 29): the future bridegroom, or his surrogate,
encounters a nubile young woman, or women, at a well in a foreign land; water
is drawn; the woman hurries to bring home news of the stranger's arrival; he is
invited to a meal; the betrothal is agreed on. In keeping with the folktale stylization of the Moses story, the usual young woman is multiplied by the formulaic number seven.

17. *the shepherds came and drove them off.* Only in this version of the betrothal
scene is there an actual struggle between hostile sides at the well. Moses's
intervention to "save" (*hoshi'a*) the girls accords perfectly with his future role
as commander of the Israelite forces in the wilderness and the liberator,
moshi'a, of his people.

18. *Why have you hurried back today?* With great narrative economy, the
expected betrothal-scene verb, "to hurry," *miher*, occurs not in the narrator's
report but in Reuel's expression of surprise to his daughters.

19 hurried back today?" And they said, "An Egyptian man rescued us from
the hands of the shepherds, and, what's more, he even drew water for
20 us and watered the flock." And he said to his daughters, "And where is
21 he? Why did you leave the man? Call him that he may eat bread." And
Moses agreed to dwell with the man, and he gave Zipporah his daugh-
22 ter to Moses. And she bore a son, and he called his name Gershom, for
he said, "A sojourner have I been in a foreign land."

23 And it happened when a long time had passed that the king of Egypt
died, and the Israelites groaned from the bondage and cried out, and

---

19. *he even drew water for us and watered the flock.* Their report highlights the
act of drawing water, the Hebrew stressing the verb by stating it in the infinitive before the conjugated form—*daloh dalah* (in this translation, "even drew").
The verb is different from *mashah*, the term associated with Moses's name,
because it is the proper verb for drawing water, whereas *mashah* is used for
drawing something out of water. In any case, this version of the scene at the
well underscores the story of a hero whose infancy and future career are
intimately associated with water.

20. *Call him that he may eat bread.* "Call" here has its social sense of "invite,"
and "bread" is the common biblical synecdoche for "food." Reuel's eagerness
to show hospitality indicates that he is a civilized person, and in the logic of
the type-scene, the feast offered the stranger will lead to the betrothal.

21. *Zipporah.* The name means "bird."

22. *Gershom . . . A sojourner have I been.* In keeping with biblical practice, the
naming-speech reflects folk etymology, breaking the name into *ger,*
"sojourner," and *sham,* "there," though the verbal root of the name *g-r-sh* would
appear to refer to banishment.

23. *bondage.* The Hebrew *'avodah* is the same term rendered as "work" in
chapter 1.

their plea from the bondage went up to God. And God heard their 24
moaning, and God remembered His covenant with Abraham, with
Isaac, and with Jacob. And God saw the Israelites, and God knew.   25

---

24. *moaning*. The Hebrew *na'aqah* is a phonetic cousin (through metathesis)
to the word for groaning, *'anahiah*, reflected in the previous verse, an effect
this translation tries to simulate through rhyme.

24–25. Until this point, God has not been evident in the story. Now He is the
subject of a string of significant verbs—hear, remember (which in the Hebrew
has the strong force of "take to heart"), see, and know. The last of these terms
marks the end of the narrative segment with a certain mystifying note—sufficiently mystifying that the ancient Greek translators sought to "correct" it—
because it has no object. "God knew," but what did He know? Presumably, the
suffering of the Israelites, the cruel oppression of history in which they are
now implicated, the obligations of the covenant with the patriarchs, and the
plan He must undertake to liberate the enslaved people. And so the objectless
verb prepares us for the divine address from the burning bush and the beginning of Moses's mission.

CHAPTER 3

¹ And Moses was herding the flock of Jethro his father-in-law, priest of Midian, and he drove the flock into the wilderness and came to ² the mountain of God, to Horeb. And the LORD's messenger appeared to him in a flame of fire from the midst of the bush, and he saw, and look, the bush was burning with fire and the bush was not

---

1. *Jethro*. In the previous episode he was Reuel. Modern critics generally attribute the difference in names to different literary sources.

into the wilderness. The Hebrew preposition 'ahar is odd. Because it usually means "behind," the King James Version bizarrely translated this phrase as "the back side of the desert." The claim that here it means "to the west" is rather strained. Perhaps it may suggest something like "deep into."

Horeb. This appears to be a synonym for Sinai—it is the name used in the E document, whereas Sinai is J's term. The name is transparently derived from a root signifying dryness and so means something like "Parched Mountain." Abraham ibn Ezra acutely notes that this parched desert location is a full three days' journey (verse 18) from the Nile, the great source of water. That contrast points to a spatial-thematic antithesis: Moses, the man associated with water from infancy on, now encounters the God of all creation in the dry desert, and in flame.

2. *the LORD's messenger*. In what follows, it is God Himself reported as speaking to Moses from the burning bush. Either God first assigns a divine emissary to initiate the pyrotechnic display that will get Moses's attention, or the piety of early scribal tradition introduced an intermediary into the original text in order to avoid the uncomfortable image of the LORD's revealing Himself in a lowly bush.

the bush. The Hebrew *seneh*, a relatively rare word, intimates Horeb's other name, Sinai, by way of a pun. Some have conjectured that the name Sinai is actually derived from *Seneh*. In the ancient Near East, deities were often asso-

consumed. And Moses thought, "Let me, pray, turn aside that I may see ₃
this great sight, why the bush does not burn up." And the LORD saw ₄
that he had turned aside to see, and God called to him from the midst
of the bush and said, "Moses, Moses!" And he said, "Here I am." And ₅
He said, "Come no closer here. Take off your sandals from your feet,
for the place you are standing on is holy ground." And He said, "I am ₆
the God of your father, the God of Abraham, the God of Isaac, and the
God of Jacob." And Moses hid his face, for he was afraid to look upon
God. And the LORD said, "I indeed have seen the abuse of My people ₇
that is in Egypt, and its outcry because of its taskmasters. I have heard,

---

ciated with sacred trees, but not with bushes. Rashi construes this epiphany
in the humble bush as an expression of God's identification with the abasement of Israel enslaved.

and the bush was not consumed. The epiphanies to the patriarchs did not
involve supernatural events, but Moses is destined to lead Israel out of slavery
through great signs and wonders. If one recalls the later image in Jeremiah of
God's word as fire in the bones of the prophet (chapter 20), one might see in
the divine fire that does not consume the bush a reassuring portent for Moses
of the daunting prophetic role to which he is called, for the bush invested with
divinity is not destroyed. Rashi makes a similar inference here. In much of the
Exodus story, one senses strong symbolic implications in the concrete images,
but the symbolism is never explicit.

3. *Let me . . . turn aside that I may see.* Moses is initially drawn by curiosity
about the anomalous sight, scarcely imagining what he is getting into.

6. *Moses hid his face.* The gesture reflects the reiterated belief of biblical figures that man cannot look on God's face and live. What should be noted is
how God's manifestation has shifted from Genesis. God spoke to Abraham
face to face in implicitly human form. Here He speaks from fire, and even that
Moses is afraid to look on.

7. *I . . . have seen . . . I have heard, for I know its pain.* The three verbs in this
sequence pick up three of the four highlighted verbs used at the end of the
previous chapter. As Rashi notes, the objectless "knew" of 2:25 here is given its
object—pain.

8 for I know its pain. And I have come down to rescue it from the hand
   of Egypt and to bring it up from that land to a goodly and spacious land,
   to a land flowing with milk and honey, to the place of the Canaanite
   and the Hittite and the Amorite and the Perizzite and the Hivite and
9 the Jebusite. And now, look, the outcry of the Israelites has come to
   Me and I have also seen the oppression with which the Egyptians
10 oppress them. And now, go that I may send you to Pharaoh, and bring
11 My people the Israelites out of Egypt." And Moses said to God, "Who
   am I that I should go to Pharaoh and that I should bring out the
12 Israelites from Egypt?" And He said, "For I will be with you. And
   this is the sign for you that I Myself have sent you. When you bring
   the people out from Egypt, you shall worship God on this mountain."

---

8. *I have come down to rescue . . . to bring it up*. Ibn Ezra neatly observes that
the coming down is directly followed by the antithetical bringing up.

flowing with milk and honey. The honey in question is probably not bee's
honey, for apiculture was not practiced in this early period, but rather a sweet
syrup extracted from dates. The milk would most likely have been goat's milk
and not cow's milk. In any case, these two synecdoches for agriculture and animal husbandry respectively become a fixed epithet for the bounty of the
promised land.

the place of the Canaanite and the Hittite . . . and the Jebusite. This imposing and repeated list of the peoples of the land of Canaan serves as a notice
that this is far from an uninhabited country, that it contains resident peoples
who will need to be confronted militarily.

11. *Who am I*. Moses's profession of unworthiness is the first instance of a
recurring scene in which the future prophet responds to the divine call by an
initial unwillingness to undertake the mission (compare Isaiah 6 and Jeremiah
1). Moses has particular cause to feel unworthy. Having been reared as an
Egyptian prince, he has become an outlaw, an exile, and a simple shepherd.
His one intervention, moreover, with his Hebrew brothers elicited only a
resentful denunciation of him as a murderer.

12. *For I will be with you. And this is the sign*. Rashi proposes that God
"answered the first question first and the second question second." That is, to
the question "Who am I?", God responds that He will be with Moses, so
Moses will have divine authority invested in him. To the question about bringing out the Israelites from Egypt, God responds that the fire in the bush is the
concrete token of the miraculous power Moses will exert as God's agent in res-

And Moses said to God, "Look, when I come to the Israelites and say 13
to them, 'The God of your fathers has sent me to you,' and they say
to me, 'What is His name?', what shall I say to them?" And God said to 14
Moses, "*'Ehyeh-'Asher-'Ehyeh*, I-Will-Be-Who-I-Will-Be." And He said,
"Thus shall you say to the Israelites, '*Ehyeh* has sent me to you.'"

---

cuing his people. It should be observed, however, that the reference of "this is
the sign" is quite ambiguous, and perhaps was intended to be so. It could refer
simply to the previous clause: "I will be with you" and *that* will be the sign you
require. It could refer to the very burning bush out of which God speaks, as
Rashi infers. Or, it could refer to the following clause: the sign that it is God
Who has sent Moses will be realized when Moses succeeds in the extraordinary undertaking of bringing the Hebrews out of Egypt and leads them all the
way to the mountain on which he now stands.

13. *What is His name?* The name of course implies identity, distinctive essence,
and in the case of someone giving orders, official authorization (the emissary
can claim to be carrying out his mission in the name of So-and-so).

14. *'Ehyeh-'Asher-'Ehyeh*. God's response perhaps gives Moses more than he
bargained for—not just an identifying divine name (the implication of offering
one such name might be that there are other divinities) but an ontological
divine mystery of the most daunting character. Rivers of ink have since flowed
in theological reflection on and philological analysis of this name. The following brief remarks will be confined to the latter consideration, which in any
case must provide the grounding for the former. "I-Will-Be-Who-I-Will-Be" is
the most plausible construction of the Hebrew, though the middle word,
'asher, could easily mean "what" rather than "who," and the common rendering
of "I-Am-That-I-Am" cannot be excluded. ("Will" is used here rather than
"shall" because the Hebrew sounds like an affirmation with emphasis, not just
a declaration.) Since the tense system of biblical Hebrew by no means corresponds to that of modern English, it is also perfectly possible to construe this
as "I Am He Who Endures." The strong consensus of biblical scholarship is
that the original pronunciation of the name YHWH that God goes on to use
in verse 15 was "Yahweh." There are several good arguments for that conclusion. There is an independent name for the deity, Yah, which also appears as a
suffix to proper names, and that designation could very well be a shortened
form of this name. Greek transcriptions reflect a pronunciation close to "Yahweh." In that form, the name would be the causative or *hiph'il* form of the verb
"to be" and thus would have the theologically attractive sense of "He Who
Brings Things into Being." All this is plausible, but it is worth registering at

15 And God said further to Moses, "Thus shall you say to the Israelites:
'The Lord God of your fathers, the God of Abraham, the God of Isaac,
and the God of Jacob, sent me to you.

That is My name forever
and thus am I invoked in all ages.'

---

least a note of doubt about the form of the divine name. Here God instructs
Moses to tell Israel 'Ehyeh, "I-Will-Be," has sent him. The deity, if the
Masoretic vocalization is to be trusted, refers to Himself not with a causative
but with the qal ("simple") conjugation. This could conceivably imply that others refer to him in the qal third person as Yihyeh, "He-Will-Be." (The medial y
sound in this conjugated form would have had considerable phonetic interchange with the w consonant in YHWH.) This in turn would make the name
fit a common pattern for male names in the third-person masculine singular,
qal conjugation, imperfective form: Yitshaq (Isaac), "he will laugh"; Ya'aqov
(Jacob), "he will protect," or "he will grab the heel"; Yiftah (Jephthah), "he will
open"; and many others. If this were the case, then the name "Yah" could have
been assimilated to YHWH by folk etymology and then perhaps even affected
its pronunciation. Whether the pronunciaton of this name later in the Hellenistic period, by then restricted to the high priest on the Day of Atonement,
Yahweh, as indicated in Greek transcriptions, reflects its original sound is at
least open to question. The logic of Yihyeh as the essential divine name would
be that whereas particular actions may be attributed to humans through the
verbal names chosen for them, to God alone belongs unlimited, unconditional
being. This conjecture, inspired by the use here by God of the qal conjugation
rather than the causative conjugation in naming Himself, is far from certain,
but it might introduce at least some margin of doubt about the consensus
opinion regarding the divine name.

15. *and thus am I invoked.* The Hebrew of this brief poetic inset preserves strict
grammatical-syntactical parallelism with the preceding verset: "and that is my
appellation in all ages," but English synonyms for "name" (Hebrew *zekher*),
such as "appellation" and "designation," are too ponderously polysyllabic for
the little poem.

Go and gather the elders of Israel and say to them, 'The LORD God of   16
your fathers has appeared to me, the God of Abraham, Isaac, and
Jacob, saying, "I have surely marked what is done to you in Egypt, and   17
I have said, I will bring you up from the abuse of Egypt to the land of
the Canaanite and the Hittite and the Amorite and the Perizzite and
the Hivite and the Jebusite, to a land flowing with milk and honey."'
And they will heed your voice, and you shall come, you and the elders   18
of Israel, to the king of Egypt, and together you shall say to him: 'The
LORD, God of the Hebrews, happened upon us, and so, let us go, pray,
three days' journey into the wilderness, that we may sacrifice to the
LORD our God.' And I on My part know that the king of Egypt will not   19
let you go except through a strong hand. And I will send out My hand   20
and strike Egypt with all My wonders that I shall do in his midst, and
afterward will he send you out. And I will grant this people favor in   21
the eyes of Egypt, and so when you go, you will not go empty-handed.

---

18. *they will heed your voice*. God is responding to Moses's understandable concern that the Hebrews will simply dismiss him with his crazy-sounding claims.

and together you shall say. "Together" has been added to make clear what is
evident in the Hebrew through the plural form of "say," that the elders will be
speaking together with Moses to Pharaoh.

happened. They use a verb that elsewhere suggests chance encounter,
rather than the more definite "appeared." This might imply that they want to
intimate to Pharaoh that they did not seek this meeting with the divinity.

let us go . . . three days' journey. They do not say that they intend to return,
though these words bear the obvious implication that they are requesting only
a furlough (weeklong furloughs were actually sometimes extended to Egyptian
slaves). To ask for absolute manumission would have been outrageous.

20. *send out My hand*. A more idiomatic rendering would be "stretch out," but
it is important to preserve the symmetry of God's sending at the beginning of
the verse and Pharaoh's sending at the end.

22 But each woman will ask of her neighbor and of the sojourner in her house ornaments of silver and ornaments of gold and robes, and you shall put them on your sons and on your daughters and you shall despoil Egypt."

---

22. *each woman will ask of her neighbor and of the sojourner.* Both "neighbor" and "sojourner" are feminine nouns. The verse reflects a frequent social phenomenon—also registered in the rabbinic literature of Late Antiquity—in which women constitute the porous boundary between adjacent ethnic communities: borrowers of the proverbial cup of sugar, sharers of gossip and women's lore. It must be said that this situation, in which Egyptian women are lodgers in Israelite houses, does not jibe with the Plagues narrative, in which the Israelites live in a segregated region. Some readers have felt discomfort at the act of exploitation recorded here. The most common line of defense is that this is restitution for the unpaid labor exacted from the Hebrew slaves. In any case, it seems wise not to view the story in terms of intergroup ethics. From beginning to end, it is a tale of Israelite triumphalism. The denizens of the simple farms and the relatively crude towns of Judea would have known about imperial Egypt's fabulous luxuries, its exquisite jewelry, and the affluent among them would have enjoyed imported Egyptian linens and papyrus. It is easy to imagine how this tale of despoiling or stripping bare Egypt would have given pleasure to its early audiences. In each of the three sister-wife stories in Genesis that adumbrate the Exodus narrative, the patriarch and his wife depart loaded with gifts: the presence of that motif suggests that the despoiling of Egypt was an essential part of the story of liberation from bondage in the early national traditions.

CHAPTER 4

And Moses answered and said, "But, look, they will not believe me nor will they heed my voice, for they will say, 'The LORD did not appear to you.'" And the LORD said to him, "What is that in your hand?" And he said, "A staff." And He said, "Fling it to the ground." And he flung it to the ground and it became a snake and Moses fled

---

2. *What is that in your hand?* The shepherd's staff is his familiar possession and constant practical tool. Its sudden metamorphosis into a reptile is thus a dramatic demonstration to Moses of God's power to intervene in the order of nature that will be repeatedly manifested in the Plagues narrative. The staff itself will be wielded by Moses as a magician's wand, and Moses's mission to Egypt, an international capital of the technology of magic, will be implemented through the exercise of divinely enabled magic. In verse 20, the staff will be called "God's staff," not because it is a staff belonging to God that was given to Moses, as some scholars have contended, but because from this moment of the Horeb epiphany, the simple shepherd's staff has been transmuted into both the theater and the conduit of divine power.

3. *Fling it to the ground*. There is an odd semantic "rhyming" in the recycling for the staff of the violent verb that Pharaoh used for the Hebrew male infants (1:22).

   it became a snake and Moses fled. The trusty support turns into something dangerous and alien, triggering a primal fear in Moses—the very fear that is figured in the primordial reptile of the Garden story (Genesis 3:15). Although this particular transformation has the look of a conjuror's trick (and Pharaoh's soothsayers will replicate it), it is an intimation of the awesome power to unleash the zoological and meteorological realms that God will manifest in Egypt.

4 from it. And the LORD said to Moses, "Reach out your hand and grasp
   its tail." And he reached out his hand and held it and it became a staff
5 in his grip. "So that they will believe that the LORD God of their fathers,
   the God of Abraham, the God of Isaac, and the God of Jacob, has
6 appeared to you." And the LORD said further to him, "Bring, pray, your
   hand into your bosom." And he put his hand back into his bosom and
7 brought it out and, look, his hand was blanched like snow. And He said,
   "Put your hand back into your bosom." And he put his hand back into
   his bosom and brought it out and, look, it came back like his own flesh.
8 "And so, should they not believe you and should they not heed the
   voice of the first sign, they will believe the voice of the second sign.
9 And should it be that they do not believe even both these signs and do
   not heed your voice, you shall take of the water of the Nile and pour it
   on the dry land, and the water that you take from the Nile will become

---

4. *grasp its tail*. As has often been noted, this is the most dangerous place to
seize a venomous snake, and thus requires Moses to trust implicitly that God
will keep him from harm.

6. *his hand was blanched like snow*. The Hebrew *metsora'at*, here represented
as "blanched," is rendered as "leprous" in many older translations, but the
modern scholarly consensus is that what is involved is some disfiguring skin
disease other than leprosy. The comparison with snow would not refer to flak-
ing, as some have claimed, because "like snow" is a known biblical simile for
total whiteness—in the case of skin, loss of all pigmentation. A skin disease
will figure among the plagues with which God will strike the Egyptians, and
so is the second of the two metamorphic "signs" here. God appropriately is
both a sudden bringer of disease and a healer.

8. *heed the voice of the first sign*. Signs don't have voices, but the formulation
is determined by the momentum of the idiom "heed the voice." It is a case, as
Abraham ibn Ezra observes, when "Torah speaks like the language of
humankind."

9. *the water that you take from the Nile will become blood*. Thus, the enactment
of this third sign coincides with the implementation of the first plague. If the
metamorphoses of Moses's own staff and hand do not convince the Hebrews,
the spectacular transformation of the Nile—an Egyptian deity, as Rashi notes,
and the very source of life in Egypt—will eliminate any lingering skepticism.

blood on the dry land." And Moses said, "Please, my LORD, no man of   10
words am I, not at any time in the past nor now since You have spoken
to Your servant, for I am heavy-mouthed and heavy-tongued." And the   11
LORD said to him, "Who gave man a mouth, or who makes him mute
or deaf or sighted or blind? Is it not I, the LORD? And now, go, and I   12
Myself will be with your mouth and will instruct you what to say." And   13
he said, "Please, my LORD, send, pray, by the hand of him You would

---

The predominance of blood in this entire narrative should be observed. Moses
has already spilled Egyptian blood (the phrase is not used, but it is a fixed biblical idiom for both manslaughter and murder). The Ten Plagues will begin
with a plague of blood and end with one in which blood is heavily involved.
On the way to Egypt (verses 24–26), Moses's life will be saved by a rite carried
out through blood. The story of liberation from Egyptian bondage is consistently imagined as a process of violent oppression to be broken only by violent
counterstrokes. The portent here seems to be to turn the Nile water into blood
when it is scooped up and scattered on dry land. In the event, a more cataclysmic turning of the water of the river in its channel into blood will take
place. "Dry land" and "water" prefigure the Sea of Reeds miracle.

10. *heavy-mouthed and heavy-tongued.* It seems futile to speculate, as so many
commentators have, whether Moses suffered from an actual speech impedi-
ment or merely was unaccustomed to public speaking. The point is that he
invokes these Hebrew idioms for impeded speech—whether as hyperbole or
as physiological fact scarcely matters—to express his feeling of incapacity for
the mission, which is his new reason for refusal now that God has settled the
question of the skepticism of the Israelites. In the subsequent narrative,
Moses actually appears to be capable of considerable eloquence.

12. *I Myself will be with your mouth.* This rather unusual idiom is a way of
focusing in on God's initial promise that He will be with Moses. Since Moses
has now made an issue of his mouth and tongue, God assures him that the
promised divine sustaining aid will be specifically palpable in the organ of
speech.

13. *send, pray, by the hand of him You would send.* The implication, of course,
is: but not me. Moses resorts to this vague and slightly cryptic phrase because
he doesn't dare to say in so many words that he is still unwilling. But God
immediately recognizes this as a refusal—hence the flare-up of anger in His
immediate response.

14 send." And the wrath of the LORD flared up against Moses, and He
said, "Is there not Aaron the Levite, your brother? I know that he can
indeed speak, and, what's more, look, he is coming out to meet you, and
15 when he sees you, his heart will rejoice. And you shall speak to him and
put the words in his mouth, and I Myself will be with your mouth and
with his mouth and I will instruct you both what you should do,
16 and he will speak for you to the people, and so he, he will be a mouth
17 for you, and you, you will be for him like a god. And this staff you shall
take in your hand, with which you will do the signs."

---

14. *Is there not Aaron the Levite, your brother?* The innocent reader might be
impelled to ask, "Is there?", since no previous report of Aaron's existence had
been made. The account of Moses's conception and birth in 2:2 is elliptic
because it is made to sound as though they directly followed the marriage of
his parents, whereas Moses is actually the youngest of three siblings, Miriam
being the oldest.

his heart will rejoice. Are we to infer that the brothers had secret contact
and hence an established fraternal bond during the years that Moses was
growing up as the Egyptian princess's adopted son? The narrative data provided in chapter 2 at least allow the possibility that Moses's family could have
found ways to stay in touch with him, and this in turn would explain why he
felt a sense of identification with his Hebrew "brothers" when he witnessed
the beating of the Hebrew slave by the Egyptian taskmaster. In any case,
Aaron's joy at the brothers' reunion after Moses's years as a fugitive suggests
that the two will work together in fraternal unison.

16. *you will be for him like a god.* Moses will convey "oracular" messages to
Aaron who will transmit them as official spokesman to the people. This rather
audacious way of stating the communications relay is enabled by the fact that
'elohim, which has the primary meaning of "god," extends to merely angelic
divine beings and even to human eminences.

And Moses went and returned to Jether his father-in-law, and he said 18
to him, "Let me go, pray, and return to my brothers who are in Egypt
that I may see whether they still live." And Jethro said, "Go in peace."
And the LORD said to Moses in Midian, "Go, return to Egypt, for all the 19
men who sought your life are dead." And Moses took his wife and 20
his sons and mounted them on the donkey, and he returned to the land
of Egypt, and Moses took God's staff in his hand. And the LORD said to 21
Moses, "When you set out to return to Egypt, see all the portents that
I have put in your hand and do them before Pharaoh. But I on
my part shall toughen his heart and he will not send the people away.

---

18. *Jether*. This is a variant form of Jethro, which is more often used in the
narrative.

    return to my brothers who are in Egypt that I may see whether they still live.
Moses does not mention that he had fled Egypt for having committed a capital crime, and perhaps one may infer that he never divulged that part of his
Egyptian past to his father-in-law. In the very next verse, God will give Moses
assurance that he no longer is in danger of execution for the act of manslaughter. The last clause here is a pointed allusion to Joseph's anxious question to
his brothers (Genesis 45:3) about whether his father is still alive: the familial
bond that induced Joseph to bring his father and brothers down to Egypt will
now be manifested in Moses's actions as he sets out to reverse the process,
bringing his "brothers" up out of Egypt and back to Canaan. His wondering
whether his brothers still live is more than a way of saying that he wants to find
out how they are faring because he is aware that they have been the target of
a genocidal plan.

20. *his sons*. Only one son was previously mentioned, and only one son figures
in verses 24–26. Some textual critics, noting an ambiguity in early Hebrew
orthography, propose "his son" as the original reading.

21. *But I on My part shall toughen his heart*. This phrase, which with two synonymous variants punctuates the Plagues narrative, has been the source of
endless theological debate over whether Pharaoh is exercising free will or
whether God is playing him as a puppet and then punishing him for his puppet's performance. The latter alternative surely states matters too crudely. The
heart in biblical idiom is the seat of understanding, feeling, and intention. The
verb rendered here as "toughen" (King James Version, "harden") has the primary meaning of "strengthen," and the most frequent synonym of this idiom
as it occurs later in the story means literally "to make heavy." God needs

22 And you shall say to Pharaoh, 'Thus said the LORD: My son, my first-
23 born, is Israel. And I said to you, Send off my son that he may worship
Me, and you refused to send him off, and, look, I am about to kill your
son, your firstborn.'"

24 And it happened on the way at the night camp that the LORD encoun-
25 tered him and sought to put him to death. And Zipporah took a flint

---

Pharaoh's recalcitrance in order that He may deploy the plagues, one after
another, thus humiliating the great imperial power of Egypt—the burden of
the triumphalist narrative we have already noted—and demonstrating the
impotence of all the gods of Egypt. But Pharaoh is presumably manifesting his
own character: callousness, resistance to instruction, and arrogance would all
be implied by the toughening of the heart. God is not so much pulling a mar-
ionette's strings as allowing, or perhaps encouraging, the oppressor-king to persist in his habitual harsh willfulness and presumption.

22. *My son, my firstborn is Israel.* Framing the relationship in these terms lays
the ground in measure-for-measure justice for the lethal tenth plague predicted at the end of the next verse, since Pharaoh has sought to destroy Israel.

23. *to kill your son, your firstborn.* This dire threat, to be fulfilled in the tenth
plague, also inducts us to the narrative episode that follows in the next three
verses, in which the LORD seeks to kill Moses, and the blood of the firstborn
intercedes.

24. *on the way at the night camp that the LORD . . . sought to put him to death.*
This elliptic story is the most enigmatic episode in all of Exodus. It seems
unlikely that we will ever resolve the enigmas it poses, but it nevertheless plays
a pivotal role in the larger narrative, and it is worth pondering why such a
haunting and bewildering story should have been introduced at this juncture.
There is something starkly archaic about the whole episode. The LORD here is
not a voice from an incandescent bush announcing that this is holy ground but
an uncanny silent stranger who "encounters" Moses, like the mysterious
stranger who confronts Jacob at the Jabbok ford, in the dark of the night (the
Hebrew for "place of encampment" is phonetically linked to *laylah*, "night").
One may infer that both the deity here and the rite of circumcision carried out
by Zipporah belong to an archaic—perhaps even premonotheistic—stratum of
Hebrew culture, though both are brought into telling alignment with the story
that follows. The potently anthropomorphic and mythic character of the

episode generates a crabbed style, as though the writer were afraid to spell out its real content, and thus even the referents of pronominal forms are ambiguous. Traditional Jewish commentators seek to naturalize the story to a more normative monotheism by claiming that Moses has neglected the commandment to circumcise his son (sons?), and that is why the LORD threatens his life. What seems more plausible is that Zipporah's act reflects an older rationale for circumcision among the West Semitic peoples than the covenantal one enunciated in Genesis 17. Here circumcision serves as an apotropaic device, to ward off the hostility of a dangerous deity by offering him a bloody scrap of the son's flesh, a kind of symbolic synecdoche of human sacrifice. The circumciser, moreover, is the mother, and not the father, as enjoined in Genesis. The story is an archaic cousin of the repeated biblical stories of life-threatening trial in the wilderness, and, as modern critics have often noted, it corresponds to the folktale pattern of a perilous rite of passage that the hero must undergo before embarking on his mission proper. The more domesticated God of verse 19 has just assured Moses that he can return to Egypt "for all the men who sought your life are dead." The fierce uncanny YHWH of this episode promptly seeks to kill Moses (the same verb "seek"), just as in the previous verse He had promised to kill Pharaoh's firstborn. (Here, the more judicial verb, *himit*, "to put to death," is used instead of the blunt *harag*, "kill.") The ambiguity of reference has led some commentators to see the son as the object of this lethal intention, though that seems unlikely because the (unspecified) object of the first verb "encountered" is almost certainly Moses. Confusions then multiply in the nocturnal murk of the language. Whose feet are touched with the bloody foreskin? Perhaps Moses's, but it could be the boy's, or even the LORD's. The scholarly claim, moreover, that "feet" is a euphemism for the genitals cannot be dismissed. There are again three male candidates in the scene for the obscure epithet "bridegroom of blood," though Moses strikes me as the most probable. William H. C. Propp correctly recognizes that the plural form for blood used here, *damim*, generally means "bloodshed" or "violence" (though in the archaic language of this text it may merely reflect intensification or poetic heightening). He proposes that the deity assaults Moses because he still bears the bloodguilt for the act of involuntary manslaughter he has committed, and it is for this that the circumcision must serve as expiation. All this may leave us in a dark thicket of bewildering possibilities, yet the story is strikingly apt as a tonal and motivic introduction to the Exodus narrative. The deity that appears here on the threshold of the return to Egypt is dark and dangerous, a potential killer of father or son. Blood in the same double function it will serve in the Plagues narrative is set starkly in the foreground: the blood of violent death, and blood as the apotropaic stuff that wards off death—the bloody foreskin of the son will be matched in the tenth plague by the blood smeared on the lintel to ward off the

and cut off her son's foreskin and touched it to his feet, and she said,
26 "Yes, a bridegroom of blood you are to me." And He let him go. Then did she say, "A bridegroom of blood by the circumcising."

27 And the LORD said to Aaron, "Go to the wilderness to meet Moses." And he went and encountered him on the mountain of God and he
28 kissed him. And Moses told Aaron all the LORD's words with which He
29 sent him and all the signs with which He charged him. And Moses, and Aaron with him, went, and they gathered the elders of the Israelites.
30 And Aaron spoke all the words that the LORD had spoken to Moses, and
31 he did the signs before the people's eyes. And the people believed and heeded, that the LORD had singled out the Israelites and that He had seen their abuse. And they did obeisance and bowed down.

---

epidemic of death visiting the firstborn sons. With this troubling mythic encounter, we are ready for the descent into Egypt.

27. *And the* LORD *said to Aaron*. We return to the welcome sphere of a God Who speaks, and directs men to act through speech. After the reunion of the brothers, they will promptly implement God's instructions as Moses imparts the words to Aaron and Aaron then speaks the words to the people.

31. *And the people believed and heeded*. In the event, the two signs of the staff and the hand are sufficient to win their trust ("believe" does not have any doctrinal sense here), and the third sign, of water turned to blood, can be reserved for the first plague.

CHAPTER 5

And afterward Moses and Aaron came and said to Pharaoh, "Thus   1
said the LORD, God of Israel: 'Send off Israel My people that they
may celebrate to Me in the wilderness.'" And Pharaoh said, "Who   2
is the LORD, that I should heed His voice to send off Israel? I do not

---

1. *Thus said the* LORD. This is the so-called messenger formula, the conventional form for introducing the text, oral or written, of a message. The conveyor of the message may be divine, as here and repeatedly in the Prophets, or human, as in verse 10, where the message comes from Pharaoh. The phrase was regularly used at the beginning of letters.

Send off. The Hebrew verb *shileaḥ* has a range of meanings: "to let go or dismiss," "to divorce," "to send guests decorously on their way," "to grant manumission to a slave." There is probably some ironic tension in this narrative between the positive and the negative senses of the verb, and since it is repeatedly played off against God's "sending" out His hand or sending ministers of destruction, this translation represents the reiterated request to Pharaoh as "send off."

The abruptness of Moses and Aaron's address to the king of Egypt is noteworthy. They use none of the deferential forms of speech, none of the third-person bowing and scraping, which are conventional in biblical Hebrew for addressing a monarch. Instead, they immediately announce, "Thus said the LORD," and proceed to the text of the message, which begins with an imperative verb, without the polite particle of entreaty, *na'*. William H. C. Propp observes that in doing this, Moses is not following God's orders: he was to have spoken together with the elders, who appear to be absent; he was to have performed his two portents; he was to have threatened Pharaoh's firstborn in God's name. As to the absence of the elders, Rashi, following the Midrash, suggests that they slipped away in fear one by one as Moses and Aaron approached the palace.

2. *Who is the* LORD, *that I should heed His voice.* The very name, YHWH, of this Semitic deity may be news to Pharaoh, and even if he grants that there is

3 know the Lᴏʀᴅ, nor will I send off Israel." And they said, "The God of
the Hebrews happened upon us. Let us go, pray, a three days' journey
into the wilderness, that we may sacrifice to the Lᴏʀᴅ our God, lest
4 He hit us with pestilence or sword." And the king of Egypt said to
them, "Why, Moses and Aaron, do you disturb the people from its
5 tasks? Go to your burdens!" And Pharaoh said, "Look, the people of
the land are now many, and you would make them cease from their

---

such a god, there is no reason that he, as an Egyptian polytheist and as a figure thought to have divine status himself, should recognize the authority of
this Hebrew deity. ("I do not know the Lᴏʀᴅ" has the sense of "I refuse to recognize his divine authority.") Pharaoh speaks here in quasipoetic parallel
clauses, and D. N. Friedman has proposed that this may be coded as an aristocratic style of speech, a token of his regal stature.

3. *Let us go, pray, a three days' journey into the wilderness.* Speaking in God's
name, they had made the request unconditionally, without stipulation of time
limits. Now answering Pharaoh's indignation in their own voice, they use the
jussive verb form ("let us go") with the particle of entreaty ("pray") and mention the three days, which they presumably should have done at the outset.

lest He hit us with pestilence or sword. The proposal of some scholars that
"us" be emended to "you" (because of the impending plagues) should be
resisted. It was a perfectly understandable religious concept for peoples of the
ancient Near East that a national deity might need to be propitiated through
sacrifice. By couching their request for a furlough for the slaves in these terms,
Moses and Aaron are saying to Pharaoh that the cultic expedition into the
wilderness is no mere whim but a necessary means to avert the punishing
wrath of the god of the Hebrews. In this fashion, they are pitching their argument to Pharaoh's self-interest, for dead slaves would be of no use to him.

5. *the people of the land are now many.* This phrase remains a little obscure.
Because of the end of the sentence, it has to refer to the Hebrews. The most
likely sense is that the Hebrew workforce has become vast (compare all the
references to their proliferation in chapter 1), and so the Egyptian economy
has come to depend on this multitude of slave laborers and can scarcely afford
an interruption of their work.

burdens!" And Pharaoh on that day charged the people's taskmasters 6
and its overseers, saying, "You shall no longer give the people straw to 7
make the bricks as in time past. They themselves will go and scrabble
for straw. And the quota of bricks that they were making in the past you 8
shall impose upon them, you shall not deduct from it, for they are
idlers. Therefore do they cry out, saying, 'Let us go sacrifice to our god.'
Let the work be heavy on the men and let them do it and not look to 9
lying words!" And the people's taskmasters and its overseers went out 10
and said to the people, saying, "Thus said Pharaoh: 'I give you no straw.
As for you, fetch yourselves straw wherever you find it, because not a 11
thing is to be deducted from your work.'" And the people spread out 12
through all the land of Egypt to scrabble for stubble for straw. And the 13

---

6. *taskmasters . . . overseers.* As becomes clear in what follows (e.g., verse 14),
the taskmasters are Egyptian slave drivers, the overseers are Hebrew foremen.
The former term, *noges,* derives from a root that means "to oppress," the latter
term, *shoter,* is associated with a root meaning to "record in writing."

7. *as in time past.* The literal meaning of this common Hebrew idiom is "as yesterday [or] the day before." At the end of verse 14, these two components of
the idiom are broken out from the fixed formula, each being prefaced by the
emphatic *gam* ("even," "also").
  scrabble for straw. The verb *qosheshu* is linked with its usual cognate-
accusative object *qash,* "stubble" (see verse 12). "Straw" (*teven*) and "stubble"
(*qash*) appear to be the same substance, with the latter in the condition of not
having been picked from the ground. Crushed straw was used to give cohesiveness to the bricks before baking.

8. *for they are idlers.* The contemptuous term invoked here by Egypt's head
slave owner, *nirpim,* is derived from a verbal root that means "to relax," "to
loosen one's grip," "to let go." It is the very verb that is used in 4:26, when the
threatening deity of the Bridegroom of Blood episode "let him go."

12. *And the people spread out through all the land of Egypt to scrabble for stubble.* Even in this measure of aggravated oppression, the language of the story
picks up the initial imagery of animal-like proliferation, which in turn harks
back to the injunction in the Creation story to fill the land/earth.

taskmasters were urging them, saying, "Finish your tasks at the same
14 daily rate as when there was straw." And the overseers of the Israelites,
whom Pharaoh's taskmasters had set over them, were beaten, saying,
"Why have you not completed your tally for making bricks as in time
15 past, neither yesterday nor today?" And the Israelite overseers came
and cried out to Pharaoh, saying, "Why should you do this to your ser-
16 vants? Straw is not given to your servants, and bricks they tell us,
make, and, look, your servants are beaten and the fault is your peo-
17 ple's." And he said, "Idlers, you are idlers! Therefore you say, 'Let us go
18 sacrifice to the LORD.' And now, go work, and no straw will be given

---

14. *the overseers of the Israelites . . . were beaten.* The Egyptians have instituted
an effective chain of command for forced labor. It would not be feasible to
beat all the teeming thousands of Hebrew slaves, so when they fail to produce
their daily quota, the Israelite overseers are made personally responsible and
are beaten by the Egyptian slave drivers. The overseers then turn in protest to
Pharaoh, "crying out" (or "screaming"), which is the predictable reaction to a
beating.

16. *Straw is not given . . . bricks they tell us, make, and, look, your servants are
beaten.* There is a colloquial immediacy in the language with which the overseers express their outrage to Pharaoh, positioning "straw" and "bricks" at the
beginning of the first and second clauses.
    the fault is your people's. Presumably, the fault for the failure to fulfill the
quota of bricks is the Egyptians' because they are not providing the straw.

17. *Idlers, you are idlers! Therefore you say, "Let us go sacrifice to the LORD."* In
keeping with a common procedure of Hebrew narrative, phrases of previous
dialogue are pointedly recycled. Pharaoh sarcastically quotes the phrase from
Moses and Aaron's request about sacrificing to the LORD, and in a kind of
incremental repetition, he picks up his own term, "idlers," and expands it to
"Idlers, you are idlers!" These repetitions nicely convey a sense of inflexibly
opposed sides in the conflict.

18. *no straw will be given . . . but the quota of bricks you will give.* By this point,
"give" (*natan*) has emerged as a thematic keyword of the episode. Pharaoh had
announced in his message brought by the taskmasters, "I give you no straw."
The Hebrew overseers then complained, "Straw is not given," and Pharaoh,
picking up their very words, lashes back at them, "no straw will be given,"

to you, but the quota of bricks you will give." And the Israelite over- 19
seers saw themselves coming to harm, saying, "You shall not deduct
from your bricks, from the same daily rate." And they encountered 20
Moses and Aaron poised to meet them as they came out from Pharaoh.
And they said to them, "Let the LORD look upon you and judge, for you 21
have made us repugnant in the eyes of Pharaoh and in the eyes of his
servants, putting a sword in their hand to kill us." And Moses went 22
back to the LORD, and said, "My lord, why have you done harm to this
people, why have you sent me? Ever since I came to Pharaoh to speak 23

---

again stipulating that the slaves have the same obligation as before to "give"
their quota of bricks.

19. *saw themselves coming to harm.* This is the understanding of the somewhat
cryptic Hebrew *wayir'u . . . 'otam bera'* proposed by Abraham ibn Ezra and
many other commentators. Still smarting from their recent whipping, they are
acutely aware that they will be the first to suffer for the inability of the Hebrew
slaves to maintain their usual quota of bricks.

20. *And they encountered Moses and Aaron poised to meet them.* Moses and
Aaron, who previously had acted as bold spokesmen, now wait awkwardly, perhaps nervously, outside the palace while the delegation of overseers brings its
petition before Pharaoh. The verb for "encounter," *paga',* has both a neutral
and a violent meaning. It indicates the meeting of persons or substances—
including the "meeting" of forged iron with flesh, when it has the sense of
"stab" or "hit," as at the end of verse 3, above.

21. *made us repugnant.* The literal meaning of this common Hebrew idiom is
"made our odor stink," but the fact that the idiom is twice linked here with
"eyes" suggests that the writer is not much thinking of its olfactory force.
    putting a sword in their hand to kill us. Moses and Aaron, we should recall,
had expressed the fear to Pharaoh that, without due sacrifice, the LORD would
hit the people with pestilence or sword.

22. *why have you sent me?* Moses's initial hesitancy to accept the mission
imposed on him at Horeb seems to him perfectly confirmed now by the
events. God has only made things worse for the Hebrew slaves (Moses, as it
were, passes the buck he has received from the accusing overseers), and the
whole plan of liberation shows no sign of implementation.

in Your name, he has done harm to this people and You surely have not
6:1 rescued Your people." And the LORD said to Moses, "Now will you see
what I shall do to Pharaoh, for through a strong hand will he send them
off and through a strong hand will he drive them from his land."

6:1. *And the* LORD *said.* Although the conventional division puts this verse at
the beginning of a new chapter, it actually sums up the preceding speech,
whereas 6.2 marks the beginning of a new speech in which God offers a quasi-
historical summary of His relationship with Israel and His future intentions
toward Israel.

*through a strong hand will he send them off and through a strong hand will he
drive them from his land.* The "strong hand"—that is, violent force—becomes
a refrain in the story, here repeated in quasipoetic parallelism. The phrase
refers to the violent coercion that God will need to exert on Pharaoh. It is noteworthy that the semantically double-edged "send" (to send away ceremoni-
ously, to release, to banish) is here paired with the unambiguous "drive them
from his land." In the event, God's strong hand will compel Pharaoh to expel
the Hebrews precipitously, so that "let my people go" is reinterpreted as something like "banish my people." The Exodus, in other words, extorted from a
recalcitrant Egyptian monarch by an overpowering God, will prove to be a continuation of hostility, a fearful and angry expulsion of the slaves rather than a
conciliatory act of liberation.

CHAPTER 6

And God spoke to Moses and said to him, "I am the LORD. 2 And I appeared to Abraham, to Isaac, and to Jacob as El 3 Shaddai, but in My name the LORD I was not known to them.

2. *I am the LORD.* This formula "I am X"—has been found in a variety of ancient Near Eastern documents, both royal proclamations and pronouncements attributed to sundry deities. The force of the words is something like "By the authority invested in me as X, I make the following solemn declaration." The content of this particular declaration is a rehearsal of the binding covenant in which God entered with the patriarchs and an expression of His determination now to fulfill the covenantal promise by freeing the Israelites from slavery and bringing them up to the land of Canaan. In terms of the narrative rhythm of the Exodus story, this grand proclamation by the deity is inserted after the frustration of Moses and Aaron's initial effort, suspending the action while providing depth of historical background before the unleashing of the first of the plagues.

3. *as El Shaddai, but in My name the LORD I was not known to them.* The designation El Shaddai, which is in fact used a total of five times in the Patriarchal Tales, is an archaic, evidently Canaanite combination of divine names. El was the high god of the Canaanite pantheon, though the Hebrew term is also a common noun meaning "god." No satisfactory explanation for the meaning or origin of the name Shaddai has been made, but some scholars link it with a term for "mountain," and others associate it with fertility. The usage of "in My name" is a little odd because there is no equivalent here for "in" (b^e) in the Hebrew. Willam H. C. Propp has proposed that the ellipsis implies a distinction of meaning, but the grounds for such an inference seem rather tenuous. Were the patriarchs in fact ignorant of the name YHWH? It is true that Genesis has no special episode involving the revelation of the syllables and mystery of this divine name, as we have here in 3:13–16; but there is also no indication that the name was withheld from the patriarchs, and the Primeval

4 And I also established My covenant with them to give them the land of
5 Canaan, the land of their sojournings in which they sojourned. And
  also I Myself have heard the groaning of the Israelites whom the Egyp-
6 tians enslave, and I do remember My covenant. Therefore say to the
  Israelites: 'I am the LORD. I will take you out from under the burdens
  of Egypt and I will rescue you from their bondage and I will redeem you
7 with an outstretched arm and with great retributions. And I will take
  you to Me as a people and I will be your God, and you shall know that
  I am the LORD your God Who takes you out from under the burdens of

---

History reports that the invocation of this name goes back to the time of Enosh son of Seth (Genesis 4:26). Source critics see this passage as striking evidence for the original autonomy of the Priestly source, which does not share J's assumption that the name YHWH was known to the patriarchs. All the sources drawn together in the Exodus narrative assume that it was only on the threshold of God's intervention in history to liberate Israel that He revealed His unique name to the whole people.

4. *sojournings in which they sojourned*. God's language stresses the character of temporary residence of the nomadic forefathers in the land. Now temporary residence, *megurim*, will be transformed into fixed settlement, *yeshivah*.

6. *I am the LORD*. The repetition of this initiating formula is dictated by its marking the beginning of a declaration within a declaration—the divine proclamation that Moses is to carry to the people. In this instance, "I am the LORD" will be repeated at the end of the proclamation (verse 8) in an envelope structure.

7. *you shall know that I am the LORD your God Who takes you out from under the burdens of Egypt*. This idea is emphasized again and again, in the Torah as well as in later books of the Bible. It is the cornerstone of Israelite faith—that God has proven His divinity and His special attachment to Israel by the dramatic act of liberating the people from Egyptian slavery. Some modern scholars, arguing from the silence of Egyptian sources on any Hebrew slave population, not to speak of any mention of an exodus, have raised doubts about whether the Hebrews were ever in Egypt. The story is surely a schematization and simplification of complex historical processes. There is no intimation of the quite likely existence of a sizeable segment of the Hebrew people in the high country of eastern Canaan that never was in Egypt. Yet it is also hard to imagine that the nation would have invented a story of national

Egypt. And I will bring you to the land that I raised My hand in 8
pledge to give to Abraham, to Isaac, and to Jacob, and I will give it to
you as an inheritance. I am the LORD!'" And Moses spoke thus to the 9
Israelites, but they did not heed Moses out of shortness of breath and
hard bondage.

And the LORD spoke to Moses, saying, "Come, speak to Pharaoh 10,11
king of Egypt, that he send off the Israelites from his land." And Moses 12
spoke before the LORD, saying, "Look, the Israelites did not heed
me, and how will Pharaoh heed me, and I am uncircumcised of lips?"

---

origins involving the humiliation of slavery without some kernel of historical
memory. Virgil in the *Aeneid* may invent a tale of Rome rising from the ruins
of a defeated Troy, but the defenders of Troy are heroic warriors foiled by trick-
ery, which is scarcely the same as abject slavery.

8. *I raised My hand in pledge.* The Hebrew has only "raised My hand," which
by idiomatic usage implies a pledge or vow.

9. *out of shortness of breath.* The Hebrew *ruaḥ* can mean "breath," "wind," or
"spirit." This translation follows Rashi's understanding of the phrase, a construction that is attractive because of its concreteness: the slaves, groaning
under hard bondage—a condition made all the harder by Moses's bungled
intervention—can scarcely catch their breath and so are in no mood to listen
to Moses. Others render this term as "impatience" or "crushed spirit."

12. *And Moses spoke before the LORD.* The preposition "before," instead of "to,"
is sometimes used in addressing a superior (it can also mean "in the presence
of").
    I am uncircumcised of lips? The phrase is an approximate parallel (the doc-
umentary critics would say, in P's vocabulary as against J's) of the "heavy-
mouthed and heavy-tongued" we encountered in chapter 4. It is a mistake,
however, to represent this upward displacement of a genital image simply as
"impeded of speech" because the metaphor of lack of circumcision suggests
not merely incapacity of speech but a kind of ritual lack of fitness for the
sacred task (like Isaiah's "impure of lips" in his dedication scene, Isaiah 6). The
idiom is clearly intended to resonate with the Bridegroom of Blood story, in
which Moses is not permitted to launch on his mission until an act of circumcision is performed. Syntactically, this last clause of the verse dangles
ambiguously: Moses's thought was already complete in the *a fortiori* relation

13 And the L ORD spoke to Moses and to Aaron and He charged them regarding the Israelites and regarding Pharaoh king of Egypt to bring out the Israelites from the land of Egypt.

14 These are the heads of their fathers' houses: The sons of Reuben, Israel's firstborn—Enoch and Pallu, Hezron and Carmi, these are the
15 clans of Reuben. And the sons of Simeon—Jemuel and Jamin and Ohad and Jachin and Zohar and Saul, son of the Canaanite woman,

---

between the first and second clauses (if the Israelites wouldn't listen to me, how much more so Pharaoh . . .), and now Moses offers a kind of reinforcing afterthought—and anyway, I am uncircumcised of lips.

13. *and the L ORD spoke to Moses and to Aaron.* God offers no explicit response to Moses's reiteration of his sense of unfitness as spokesman, but, as Rashi notes, God's joint address at this point to Moses and Aaron may suggest Aaron's previously indicated role as mouthpiece for Moses.

14. *These are the heads of their fathers' houses.* Genealogical lists, as one can see repeatedly in Genesis, serve an important compositional role to mark the borders between different narrative segments. The story of Moses's early history and the prelude to the plagues is now completed, and before the unleashing of the first of the ten fearful divine blows against Egypt, the genealogical list constitutes a long narrative caesura. Although this list begins with the sons of Reuben and Simeon, because they are the two firstborn in the order of Jacob's sons, it is not a complete roll call of the tribes but is meant only to take us to the tribe of Levi, and then to culminate in the two sons of the tribe of Levi, Moses and Aaron, who are poised to carry out their fateful mission to Pharaoh. Other Levites appear to be singled out because they are to play roles in the subsequent narrative. "Father's house" (*beyt 'av*) in this list, as elsewhere in biblical Hebrew, refers to the social unit of the extended family presided over by the father.

these are the clans of Simeon. And these are the names of the sons of 16
Levi according to their lineage—Gershon and Kohath and Merari. And
the years of the life of Levi were a hundred and thirty-seven years. The 17
sons of Gershon—Libni and Shimei, according to their clans. And the 18
sons of Kohath—Amram and Izhar and Hebron and Uzziel. And the
years of the life of Kohath were one hundred and thirty-three years.
And the sons of Merari—Mahli and Mushi. These are the clans of the 19
Levite according to their lineage. And Amram took him as wife 20
Jochebed his aunt, and she bore him Aaron and Moses. And the years
of the life of Amram were a hundred and thirty-seven years. And the 21
sons of Izhar—Korah and Nepheg and Zichri. And the sons of Uzziel— 22
Mishael and Elzaphan and Sithri. And Aaron took him Elisheba daugh- 23
ter of Amminadab sister of Nahshon as wife, and she bore him Nadab
and Abihu, Eleazar and Ithamar. The sons of Korah—Assir and Elka- 24
nah and Abiasaph, these are the clans of the Korahite. And Eleazar son 25
of Aaron had taken him a wife from the daughters of Putiel, and she

---

16. *a hundred and thirty-seven years.* The life spans are schematized (either 133
or 137) and, as in Genesis, rather hyperbolic. Propp notes that the figures mentioned are approximately a third of the total period of four hundred years supposed to be the duration of the sojourn in Egypt.

20. *Amram took him as wife Jochebed his aunt.* Such a marriage was banned as
incestuous by the Priestly writers, to whom scholarship attributes this passage.
This is not the only instance in which a union prohibited by later legislation is
recorded without comment (compare Jacob's marrying two sisters), and might
well reflect an authentic memory of a period when the prohibition was not in
force. Only now is the anonymous "Levite daughter" of 2:1 given a name.

    she bore him Aaron and Moses. Her sons are listed by order of birth. Three
ancient versions add "Miriam their sister," but the list, like the one in chapter
1, is interested only in sons.

25. *Putiel . . . Phinehas.* These are the two names in the list of Egyptian origin
(though Putiel has the Semitic theophoric suffix -*el*). One might infer that taking a wife "from the daughters of Putiel" suggests that Eleazar's marriage is
exogamous—another indication that the Hebrews were not altogether segregated from the Egyptians—and thus the wife might understandably give an
Egyptian name to their son. Later, this possible product of intermarriage will
show himself to be a fierce zealot on behalf of Israelite purity.

bore him Phinehas. These are the heads of the fathers of the Levites
26 according to their clans. It was the very Aaron and Moses to whom the
LORD said, "Bring out the Israelites from the land of Egypt in their bat-
27 talions." It was they who were speaking to Pharaoh king of Egypt to
bring out the Israelites from Egypt, the very Moses and Aaron.

28 And it happened on the day the LORD spoke to Moses in the land of
29 Egypt, that the LORD spoke to Moses, saying, "I am the LORD, Speak to
30 Pharaoh king of Egypt all that I speak to you." And Moses said before
the LORD, "Look, I am uncircumcised of lips, and how will Pharaoh
heed me?"

26–27. *It was the very Aaron and Moses . . . It was they . . . the very Moses and Aaron.* As we move from the end of the list back to the narrative, the writer emphasizes the focus on Moses and Aaron with a triple structure of rhetorical highlighting, putting an indicative pronoun at the head of each clause: *hu' aharon umosheh, hem hamedabrim, hu' mosheh we'aharon.*

29. *I am the* LORD. See the comment on verse 2.

30. *Look, I am uncircumcised of lips, and how will Pharaoh heed me?* This sentence repeats verbatim Moses's demurral in verse 12, reversing the order of the two clauses and omitting the first clause about Israel's failure to heed Moses. The recurrent language is a clear-cut instance of a compositional technique that biblical scholars call "resumptive repetition": when a narrative is interrupted by a unit of disparate material—like the genealogical list here—the point at which the story resumes is marked by the repetition of phrases or clauses from the point where the story was interrupted. Moses's report of Israelite resistance to his message is not repeated because the focus now is on the impending confrontation between him and Pharaoh. For the same reason, "how will Pharaoh heed me?" is repositioned at the end of Moses's speech because it will be directly followed by God's enjoining Moses and Aaron to execute the first portent intended to compel Pharaoh's attention.

CHAPTER 7

And the Lord said to Moses, "See, I have set you as a god to 1
Pharaoh, and Aaron your brother will be your prophet. You it is 2
who will speak all that I charge you and Aaron your brother will
speak to Pharaoh, and he will send off the Israelites from his land. And 3
I on My part shall harden Pharaoh's heart, that I may multiply My signs

---

1. *I have set you as a god to Pharaoh.* The reiteration of this bold comparison
may have a polemic motivation: Pharaoh imagines himself a god, but I have
made you a god to Pharaoh.

3. *I . . . shall harden Pharaoh's heart, that I may multiply My signs and My portents.* Whatever the theological difficulties, the general aim of God's allowing,
or here causing, Pharaoh to persist in his harshness is made clear: without
Pharaoh's resistance, God would not have the opportunity to deploy His great
wonders and so demonstrate His insuperable power in history and the emptiness of the power attributed to the gods of Egypt. It should be noted that three
different verbs are used in the story for the action on or in Pharaoh's heart:
hiqshah, "to harden" (the verb here), *hizeq,* "to toughen," or in other contexts,
"to strengthen" (the verb used in earlier passages), and *kaved,* literally, "to be
heavy," which in English unfortunately suggests sorrow when linked with the
heart, and so has been rendered "harden" in this translation (as in verse 14).
The force of all three idioms is to be stubborn, unfeeling, arrogantly inflexible,
and there doesn't seem to be much differentiation of meaning among the
terms, though elsewhere *hizeq* linked with heart has a positive meaning—"to
show firm resolve."

4 and My portents in the land of Egypt. And Pharaoh will not heed you,
and I shall set My hand against Egypt and I shall bring out My battalions, My people the Israelites, from the land of Egypt with great retri-
5 butions, that the Egyptians may know that I am the LORD, when I
stretch out My hand over Egypt and bring out the Israelites from their
6 midst." And Moses, and Aaron with him, did as the LORD had charged,
7 thus did they do. And Moses was eighty years old and Aaron was eighty-
three years old when they spoke to Pharaoh.

8,9 And the LORD said to Moses and to Aaron, saying, "Should Pharaoh
speak to you, saying, 'Give you a portent,' you shall say to Aaron, 'Take
your staff and fling it down before Pharaoh, let it become a serpent.'"
10 And Moses, and Aaron with him, came to Pharaoh, and they did as
the LORD had charged, and Aaron flung down his staff before Pharaoh
11 and before his servants, and it became a serpent. And Pharaoh, too,
called for the sages and sorcerers and they, too, the soothsayers of
12 Egypt, did thus with their spells. And each flung down his staff and

---

4. *I shall bring out My battalions, My people the Israelites.* The opposition
expresses a wry and surprising identification. God bears the epithet "LORD of
Battalions" ("LORD of Hosts," "LORD of Armies," *YHWH tseva'ot*), but here the
"battalions" God calls His own turn out to be the people of Israel—in fact, a
mass of wretched slaves who will be fleeing from their taskmasters.

9. *let it become a serpent.* The noun used here, *tanin*, is not the ordinary
nahash, snake, of the Burning Bush story. (When God in verse 15 refers to the
staff that turned into a snake [*nahash*], He may be alluding to the Burning
Bush episode.) The *tanin* is usually a larger threatening reptile, as William
H. C. Propp correctly observes, and is sometimes used for the Egyptian croc-
odile, or for a mythological dragon. The Hebrew zoological reference is clearly
slippery, allowing a couple of commentators to see a Nilotic cobra in the transformed shepherd's staff.

11. *and they, too, the soothsayers of Egypt, did thus with their spells.* The Hebrew
word for "soothsayers," *hartumim*, is a direct borrowing from the Egyptian designation for priest-magicians. The term translated as "spells," *lehatim*, either is
related to the root *l-'-t* that means "to conceal" or, if one follows a proposal of
Abraham ibn Ezra, is derived from the root *l-h-t*, "to flame out," which he links
with the fire-and-flash technique of the illusionist. Ibn Ezra, a rationalist, thus

they became serpents, and Aaron's staff swallowed their staffs. And 13
Pharaoh's heart toughened, and he did not heed them, just as the LORD
had spoken.

And the LORD said to Moses, "Pharaoh's heart is hard. He refuses to 14
send off the people. Go to Pharaoh in the morning. Look, he will be 15
going out to the water, and you shall be poised to meet him on the bank
of the Nile, and the staff that turned into a snake you shall take in your
hand. And you shall say to him, 'The LORD god of the Hebrews sent 16
me to you, saying, Send off my people, that they may worship Me in
the wilderness, and look, you have not heeded us yet. Thus said the 17
LORD, By this shall you know that I am the LORD: Look, I am about to

---

implies that the soothsayers' success in transforming their staffs into serpents
was an act of legerdemain. The ancient writer, however, seems to have assumed
the efficacy of magic as a kind of technology: the point of the story is that the
capacity of this technology was limited, and hence the authentically miraculous
serpent into which Aaron's staff has turned swallows up the other serpents.

13. *Pharaoh's heart toughened*. In any case, Pharaoh is not impressed. Moses
and Aaron, after all, have done no more than trump his sorcerers at their own
game. What is called for in order to shake him is a series of truly cataclysmic
miraculous events.

15. *Look, he will be going out to the water*. This narrative presupposes, at least
on the information about Egypt available to the Hebrew writers, that Egyptian
royalty regularly went down to the Nile to bathe, unless the purpose was, as
ibn Ezra proposes, to check the level of the Nile. Pharaoh's encounter with
Moses by the riverside looks back to the discovery of Moses by Pharaoh's
daughter when she went down to the Nile.

16. *Send off my people, that they may worship Me . . . you have not heeded*. It
should be observed that this prose narrative, in a style not evident in most
other biblical stories, proceeds through the solemn, emphatic reiteration of
refrainlike phrases and entire clauses, both in the language of the narrator and
in the dialogue.

18 strike with the staff in my hand on the water that is in the Nile and it
will turn into blood. And the fish that are in the Nile will die and the
Nile will stink, and the Egyptians will not be able to drink water from
19 the Nile.'" And the LORD said to Moses, "Say to Aaron: 'Take your staff
and stretch out your hand over the waters of Egypt, over their rivers and
over their Nile channels and over their ponds and over all the gathering of their waters, that they become blood. And there shall be blood in
20 all the land of Egypt, and in the trees and in the stones.'" And Moses
and Aaron did thus as the LORD had charged. And he raised the staff
and struck the water that was in the Nile before the eyes of Pharaoh
and the eyes of his servants, and all the water that was in the Nile

---

17. *water . . . blood.* For Egypt as a nation dependent on irrigation, the Nile
with its fresh water is literally a lifeline. Blood in the Bible is imagined in radically ambiguous terms—the source and substance of life, an apotropaic and
redemptive agent, the token of violence and death. It is manifestly the third of
these meanings that is brought into play here, as the first plague symbolically
anticipates the last one and deprives Egypt of life-sustaining water.

19. *Nile channels.* The Hebrew here converts the Egyptian loanword, *ye'or*,
"Nile," into a plural. Elsewhere, in occasional poetic usage, this plural form is
simply an elegant synonym for "streams" or "rivers." In this Egyptian context,
it seems more likely that it designates both the Nile itself and the system of
irrigation canals built out from the Nile.

in the trees and the stones. Many construe this as a reference to wooden and
stone vessels or receptacles, but the plural form *'etsim* suggests trees rather
than wood. In any case, trees and stones as objects in nature accord better
with the catalogue of bodies of water that precedes than would household
utensils. It has also been noted that the Hebrew pairing here, *'etsim
wa'avanim,* is often used to refer to the material out of which idols are made.

20. *he raised the staff.* This would have to be Aaron.

before the eyes of Pharaoh and the eyes of his servants. The first spectacular
cataclysm is devised so that they will be eyewitnesses to the fearful event. In
most of these contexts, "servants" (it can also mean "slaves") refers to
Pharaoh's courtiers.

turned to blood. And the fish that were in the Nile died and the Nile 21
stunk, and the Egyptians could not drink water from the Nile, and the
blood was in all the land of Egypt. And the soothsayers of Egypt did 22
thus with their spells, and Pharaoh's heart toughened and he did not
heed them, just as the LORD had spoken. And Pharaoh turned and 23
came into his house, and this, too, he did not take to heart. And all of 24
Egypt dug round the Nile for water to drink, for they could not drink
the water of the Nile.

---

21. *and the Egyptians could not drink water from the Nile.* One of the most frequently employed conventions of biblical narrative is the verbatim repetition
of whole clauses, or even sequences of clauses, of narrative material—often,
as here, once in dialogue and once in the narrator's report. But the characteristic handling of this convention is to introduce small but quite revelatory
divergences from verbatim replication as the material is repeated (see the
comments on the elaborate near verbatim repetitions in Genesis 24 as a textbook illustration of this technique). Here, however, the point of the repetition
seems to be that every term of God's dire prediction (verse 18) is implemented
as an accomplished event (verse 21), only the temporal aspects of the verbs
shifting, with one minor substitution of a synonym—instead of "will not be
able" (*nil'u*), "could not" (*lo'-yakhlu*). The summary clause at the end of the
verse here, "and the blood was in all the land of Egypt," is not part of the prediction in verse 18 but appears to be a digest of the panorama of sites to be
struck in God's instructions for Aaron in verse 19.

22. *the soothsayers of Egypt did thus with their spells.* Ibn Ezra wonders where
they got water to turn into blood if Moses and Aaron had already done the trick
for the Nile and all the rivers and ponds. His answer is that they performed
their magic on water dug up from subterranean sources (verse 24), a conjuror's
act of transmutation that is not to be compared with the miraculous conversion of streams of flowing water into blood. Again, the reality of a technology
of magic is not called into question but it is noteworthy that the soothsayers
can do no more than effect a pale imitation of the destructive act of the God
of the Hebrews; what they are powerless to do is to reverse the process of
destruction.

25,26 And seven full days passed after the Lord struck the Nile. And the
Lord said to Moses, "Come to Pharaoh, and you shall say to him, 'Thus
27 said the Lord: Send off My people that they may worship Me. And if
you refuse to send them off, look I am about to scourge all your region
28 with frogs. And the Nile will swarm with frogs and they will come up
and come into your house and into your bedchamber and onto your
couch and into your servants' house and upon your people and into your

---

25. *And seven full days passed.* The literal sense of the Hebrew is "and seven
days were filled." Many commentators infer that during this period the waters
of the Nile returned to their original state; otherwise, the first plague alone
would have been sufficient to make things utterly intolerable for Pharaoh.

26. Although the King James Version begins chapter 8 at this point, the
Masoretic Text continues chapter 7 for four more verses, as here.

28. *the Nile will swarm with frogs.* The verb in the Hebrew is transitive ("will
swarm frogs"). Several commentators have noticed that this word choice
echoes the "swarming" of the proliferating Hebrews in chapter 1. There, the
orgy of propagation seems to have struck the Egyptians as repellently reptilian;
here, they are assaulted with a nauseating plague of amphibians. In this, as in
other details of the Plagues narrative, the allusions to the Creation story,
initially sounded in the first chapter of Exodus, turn into a network of reversals of the original creation. It would be excessive to insist that every detail of
the narrative, or even every plague, confirms this pattern. Nevertheless, the
allusions to early Genesis that are detectable trace a possibility that much
exercised the imaginations of the biblical writers: if creation emerged at a particular moment in a process with discriminated stages, one could imagine an
undoing of this event and this process, apocalypse being the other side of the
coin of creation. The benign swarming of life in Genesis turns into a threatening swarm of odious creatures, just as the penultimate plague of darkness,
prelude to mass death, is a reversal of the first "let there be light." Alexander
Pope, at the end of his great anticreation poem, *The Dunciad*, writes thoroughly in the spirit of these reversals when he announces of the new reign of
anarchy, "Light dies before thy uncreating word."
    into your house . . . your bedchamber . . . your couch . . . your servants' house.
The all-powerful Pharaoh should be invulnerable to such violation and should
be able to protect his people. Instead, what this fearful catalogue of penetra-
tions conveys is the absolute, helpless exposure of all Egypt, from king to slave,
from the intimate place of sleep and procreation to the places where food is
prepared, in the face of God's onslaught.

ovens and into your kneading pans. And upon you and upon your peo- 29
ple and upon all your slaves the frogs will come up.'"

---

29. *upon you.* The Hebrew preposition would normally mean "into you," which
led the Talmud (Sanhedrin 80) to amplify the idea of grotesque penetration by
saying that the frogs would croak from inside the guts of the Egyptians.

CHAPTER 8

1 And the Lᴏʀᴅ said to Moses, "Say to Aaron: Stretch out your hand with your staff over the rivers, over the Nile channels and over the 2 ponds, and bring up the frogs over the land of Egypt." And Aaron stretched out his hand over the waters of Egypt, and the frogs came up 3 and covered the land of Egypt. And the soothsayers did thus with their 4 spells and brought up frogs over the land of Egypt. And Pharaoh called to Moses and to Aaron and said, "Entreat the Lᴏʀᴅ that He take away

---

1. *Stretch out your hand with your staff over the rivers.* The explicit repetition of language and gestures from the first plague has the emphatic effect of a formal refrain, with an overlap between the first two plagues in the location of the Nile as source of the catastrophe. The report of the Ten Plagues—other biblical traditions appear to have known a smaller number—exhibits a high degree of literary shaping and symmetry. Umberto Cassuto offers a good early synthesis of the scholarly literature that has been devoted to following these formal patterns, and subsequent discussions by Moshe Greenberg and William H. C. Propp are also noteworthy. The plagues are organized in three triads, followed by the climactic and most devastating tenth plague. Only in the first triad is Aaron with his outstretched staff the executor of the plagues. In each triad, in the first plague of the series Moses encounters Pharaoh going out early in the morning; in the second plague of the series, Moses comes into Pharaoh's palace; and in the third plague of the series, the disaster is unleashed without warning. Cassuto also observes that the plagues are equally arranged in pairs: two involving the Nile, two plagues of insects, two epidemics affecting beasts and humans respectively, two plagues devastating the crops, and the final darkness paired with the death of the firstborn.

4. *take away the frogs from me.* Unlike the water turned to blood, the frogs actually invade the homes of Pharaoh and his subjects, thus impelling him to his first offer of terms to Moses.

the frogs from me and from my people, and I shall send off the people, that they may sacrifice to the LORD." And Moses said to Pharaoh, "You 5 may vaunt over me as for when I should entreat for you and for your servants and for your people to cut off the frogs from you and from your houses—only in the Nile will they remain." And he said, "For tomor- 6 row." And he said, "As you have spoken, so that you may know there is none like the LORD our God. And the frogs will turn away from you and 7 from your houses and from your servants and from your people—only in the Nile will they remain." And Moses, and Aaron with him, went 8 out from Pharaoh's presence, and Moses cried out to the LORD concerning the frogs that He had put upon Pharaoh. And the LORD did 9 according to Moses's word, and the frogs died, out of the houses and out of the courtyards and out of the fields, and they piled them up 10 heap upon heap, and the land stank. And Pharaoh saw that there was 11 relief and he hardened his heart and did not heed them, just as the LORD had spoken.

---

5. *You may vaunt over me as for when.* The Hebrew "vaunt over me" (*hitpa'er 'ulai*) is a little odd. The construction of the consensus of commentators, medieval and modern, which seems plausible, is that Moses is offering Pharaoh the limited "triumph" of choosing the moment when the plague will cease. This choice, of course, in fact demonstrates God's absolute power and Moses's perfect efficacy as intercessor. "When" refers not to the time of entreaty but to the time of cessation of the plague, a distinction indicated in the Hebrew, as Rashi nicely observes, by affixing the prefix *le* ("for") to *matay* ("when"). It is a bit surprising that Pharaoh does not choose to have the plague ended at once. Perhaps he is trying Moses's powers: can Moses really stipulate a given moment of cessation in the near future and make it come about?

   cut off the frogs. In Moses's proposal to Pharaoh, he uses a word that suggests abrupt extirpation of the frogs. In the prediction that he goes on to spell out (verse 7), he uses a less violent verb of evacuation or retreat ("turn away"). Finally, the narrator in his report of the event (verse 9) says, with plain descriptive accuracy, "die" because his account includes a discomfiting idea not mentioned by Moses to Pharaoh—the piles of dead frogs throughout the country.

9. *and the land stank.* The stench of the putrefying dead frogs provides another link with the preceding plague, in which the stench was produced by the dead fish from the Nile.

12 And the LORD said to Moses, "Say to Aaron: Stretch out your staff and strike the dust of the land and there will be lice in all the land of
13 Egypt." And thus they did, and Aaron stretched out his hand with his staff and struck the dust of the land, and there were lice in man and in
14 beast, all the dust of the land became lice in all the land of Egypt. And thus the soothsayers of Egypt did with their spells, to take out the lice,
15 but they were unable, and the lice were in man and in beast. And the soothsayers said to Pharaoh, "God's finger it is!" And Pharaoh's heart toughened, and he did not heed them, just as the LORD had spoken.

---

12. *lice.* At least in postbiblical Hebrew, the terms *kinam* (a collective noun) and *kinim* (a plural) mean "lice," though some have suggested that in this text they might mean "gnats" or "mosquitoes." The plagues began with a profoundly ominous, symbolically portentous, and life-threatening transformation of water into blood. The next three plagues are afflictions of maddening or disgusting discomfort rather than actual threats to survival. The tone of the Plagues narrative is that of harsh (indeed, gloating) monotheistic satire against the pagan imperial power, and so pains are taken to show the Egyptians squirming before they are exposed to destruction.

14. *And thus the soothsayers of Egypt did...to take out the lice.* The syntax directs us to a kind of comic discovery: at first we imagine that still again the soothsayers are engaged in their own pathetic imitation of Moses and Aaron's destructive act, bringing forth their own lice; then we realize that this time they are attempting to get rid of the plague, but to no avail.

15. *God's finger it is!* Now that they have tried futilely to get rid of a plague instead of replicating it, they have been forced to recognize that they are contending with a greater power. As Rashi neatly paraphrases their perception, "This plague is not through magic but from the Deity." It is noteworthy that the preceding narrative repeatedly spoke of God's hand or arm; the soothsayers appear to concede a lesser trace of divine action in mentioning God's finger.

And Pharaoh's heart toughened. The repeated formula for Pharaoh's obduracy takes on added meaning here because he willfully ignores the testimony of his soothsayers. The narrative provides no indication as to whether the plague of lice comes to an end, like the previous two, or whether the Egyptians simply continue to live with the infestation as God proceeds to launch the next blow.

And the LORD said to Moses, "Rise early in the morning and station 16
yourself before Pharaoh—look, he will be going out to the water—and
say to him, 'Thus said the LORD: send off My people, that they may
worship Me. For if you do not send off My people, I am about to send 17
against you and against you servants and against your people and
against your houses the horde, and the houses of Egypt will be filled
with the horde and the soil, too, on which they stand. But I shall set 18
apart on that day the land of Goshen upon which My people stands so
that no horde will be there, that you may know that I am the LORD in
the midst of the land. And I shall set a ransom between My people and 19

---

17. *if you do not send off . . . I am about to send*. Although the two verbs are in
different conjugations, the pun, with its measure-for-measure emphasis, is
quite explicit in the Hebrew.

the horde. The Hebrew term *'arov* occurs only here, and the only plausible
derivation is from the verbal root that means "to mix." Some medieval Hebrew
commentators imagined this as a mingling of sundry beasts of prey, but this
seems unlikely because, as verse 27 makes clear, the *'arov* has infested the
Egyptians rather than torn them limb from limb, and "not one remained" probably suggests minuscule constituents of the horde. A plague of maddeningly
noxious insects also makes a much better pair with the preceding plague. The
King James Version's "swarm of flies" is as good a guess as any, though it seems
wise to avoid "swarm" in order not to introduce a misleading echo of the verb
"swarm" in Exodus 1:7 and 7:28.

18. *But I shall set apart on that day the land of Goshen*. Goshen is the region of
northeastern Egypt that, according to the account in Genesis (46:34), was set
aside for Hebrew settlement. This is the first clear indication in Exodus that
the Hebrews lived in a segregated area in Egypt. That geographical segregation
will play a crucial role in the climactic ninth and tenth plagues.

19. *I shall set a ransom*. Most interpreters understand the Hebrew *pedut* to
mean something like "separation" or "distinction." Everywhere else, however,
this root means "to ransom," "to redeem," "to rescue from danger," including
the three other occurrences in the biblical corpus in this form of a verbal
noun. It seems wise to retain the semantic force of "ransom" and assign the
indication of separation to the preposition "between" that follows—that is,
God will grant ransom or rescue from the horde to the Israelites, and that
saving act will set them apart from the afflicted Egyptians.

20 your people. Tomorrow this sign will be.'" And thus the LORD did, and
a heavy horde came into the house of Pharaoh and the house of his servants, and in all the land of Egypt the land was ravaged in the face of
21 the horde. And Pharaoh called to Moses and to Aaron and said, "Go,
22 sacrifice to your god in the land." And Moses said, "It is not right to do
thus, for the abomination of Egypt we shall sacrifice to the LORD our
God. If we sacrifice the abomination of Egypt before their eyes, will
23 they not stone us? A three days' journey into the wilderness we shall go,
and we shall sacrifice to the LORD our God as He has said to us."
24 And Pharaoh said, "I myself will send you off, that you may sacrifice to
the LORD your god in the wilderness, only you must not go far away.
25 Entreat on my behalf." And Moses said, "Look, I am going out from
your presence and I shall entreat the LORD, that the horde may turn

---

20. *the land was ravaged*. This indication of general devastation suggests that
the second of the two plagues of insects is somehow more intense than the
first.

22. *for the abomination of Egypt we shall sacrifice*. The most likely meaning is
that the Hebrews will sacrifice cattle or other beasts considered taboo by the
Egyptians and so infuriate them. There is some evidence that Egypt in the late
Bronze Age was in fact quite tolerant about different kinds of sacrifice. The
Hebrew writer could well be reflecting the awareness of a later age, when
Egyptian attitudes may have shifted. By the time of Herodotus, the Egyptians
had developed a reputation for rigid sacrificial restrictions.

24. *I myself will send you off*. The desperate Pharaoh now uses a new turn of
urgent speech, prefacing the first-person imperfective verb with an emphatic
'anokhi, "I myself."
  only you must not go far away. Having yielded to Moses's argument on the
three days' journey, he still stipulates that the Hebrews should go no farther,
for he is unwilling to contemplate the permanent loss of this population of
slave workers.

25. *Look, I am going out from your presence*. There is temporal urgency in
Moses's response, as he uses a participial verbal form to indicate that he is
already on his way to entreat the LORD. The coy game of asking Pharaoh to
stipulate a time of deliverance that marked the previous plague is set aside as
Pharaoh's own sense of desperation grows.

away from Pharaoh and from his servants and from his people tomorrow. Only let not Pharaoh continue to mock by not sending the people
off to sacrifice to the LORD." And Moses went out from Pharaoh's pres- 26
ence and entreated the LORD. And the LORD did according to Moses's 27
word, and the horde turned away from Pharaoh and from his servants
and from his people, not one remained. And Pharaoh hardened his 28
heart this time, too, and he did not send off the people.

Only let not Pharaoh continue to mock. Moses's "only" clause is a clearly
marked formal rejoinder to Pharaoh's "only" clause in the previous verse. The
verb here, *hatel,* is rendered as "deal deceitfully" by the King James Version
and some modern versions, but elsewhere it means "to mock," "to toy with,"
and, from Moses's point of view, that would be a reasonable representation of
Pharaoh's repeated reflex of seeming to yield and then reasserting his
intransigence.

CHAPTER 9

1 And the LORD said to Moses, "Come into Pharaoh and you shall speak to him, 'Thus said the LORD, God of the Hebrews: Send off 2 My people, that they may worship Me. But if you refuse to send 3 them off and you still hold on to them, look, the hand of the LORD is about to be against your livestock which is in the field, against the horses, against the donkeys, against the camels, against the cattle, and

---

2. *and you still hold on to them.* As we move to the end of the first half of the Ten Plagues, a note of impatience is introduced into God's words through Moses to Pharaoh as this clause is added to the formulaically repeated language. Perhaps this new emphasis on Pharaoh's continuing torment of Israel is the reason that Rashi surprisingly glosses the transparent verb "hold on to," *maḥaziq,* by citing a bizarre parallel from Deuteronomy 25: "should she hold on to [or seize] his pudenda."

3. *the hand of the LORD is about to be against your livestock.* The Hebrew verb here has a spine-tingling effect for which there is no obvious English equivalent. The verb "to be" in Hebrew is not supposed to have a participial, or present, tense. At this ominous and supernatural juncture, however, that verbal stem *h-y-h* yields an anomalous *hoyah,* rendered in this translation as "about to be." This strange usage involves a kind of fearsome pun on the divine name YHWH that was mysteriously highlighted in the Burning Bush episode. God's intrinsic and unique capacity for being, we are made to see, is not just a matter of static condition but an awesome power of action—the hand that is "about to be" against all the livestock of Egypt.

camels. As in Genesis, the reference is anachronistic. Though camels were widely introduced to Mesopotamia and the land of Israel by early in the first millennium B.C.E., they were not used in Egypt until several centuries later; and in any case, the actual setting of the Exodus story would be some time in the thirteenth century B.C.E.

against the sheep—a very heavy pestilence. And the LORD will set apart 4
the livestock of Israel from the livestock of Egypt, and nothing of the
Israelites' will die.'" And the LORD set a fixed time, saying, "Tomorrow 5
the LORD will do this thing in the land." And the LORD did this thing 6
on the next day, and all the livestock of Egypt died, but of the livestock
of Israel not one died. And Pharaoh sent and, look, not a single one had 7
died of the livestock of Israel, and Pharaoh's heart hardened, and he did
not send off the people.

And the LORD said to Moses and to Aaron, "Take you handfuls of soot 8
from the kiln and let Moses throw it toward the heavens before
Pharaoh's eyes, and it shall become a fine dust over all the land of 9
Egypt and it shall become on man and on beast a burning rash erupting in boils in all the land of Egypt." And they took the soot from the 10
kiln and stood before Pharaoh, and Moses threw it toward the heavens

---

4. *the LORD will set apart.* The theme of the setting apart of the Hebrews from
the Egyptians, first introduced in the previous plague, is again stressed.

7. *Pharaoh's heart hardened.* This is one of many instances in which the literal
meaning of the verb is "became heavy." That usage in turn echoes ironically
against the qualifying adjective of "a very *heavy* pestilence" (verse 3).

8. *Take you handfuls of soot from the kiln and let Moses throw it toward the heavens.* The beginning of the second half of the Ten Plagues is marked by a switch
from the set formula for launching the plague with an outstretched staff. This
scooping up of soot and casting it skyward intensifies the ominousness of the
moment and has the look of an act of sympathetic magic. The black dust from
the kiln turns into broadcast contamination, a plague clearly paired with the
preceding plague of livestock pestilence but affecting man as well as beast.

9. *burning rash.* The Hebrew *shehin* obviously refers to a painful skin disease,
but no definitive identification of the malady has been made. The noun is
probably related to a root that means "to be hot"—Rashi cites the rabbinic
idiom *shanah shehunah*, "a torrid year"—and hence this translation represents
it as "burning rash." The fact that the plague is inaugurated with soot taken
from a kiln may reinforce an association between burning heat and the skin
disease in question.

and it became a burning rash with boils erupting on man and on beast.

11 And the soothsayers could not stand before Moses because of the burning rash, for the burning rash was on the soothsayers and in all of

12 Egypt. And the LORD toughened Pharaoh's heart, and he did not heed them, just as the LORD had spoken to Moses.

13 And the LORD said to Moses, "Rise early in the morning and station yourself before Pharaoh, and you shall say to him, 'Thus said the LORD, God of the Hebrews: Send off my people, that they may worship me.

14 For this time I am about to send all My scourges to your heart and against your servants and against your people, so that you may know

15 that there is none like Me in all the earth. For by now I could have sent forth My hand and I could have struck you and your people with pesti-

---

11. *the soothsayers could not stand before Moses because of the burning rash.* Their repeated gesture in the earlier plagues of a weak imitation of Moses vanishes. After "could not," on the basis of 8:14, we might have expected something like "cure the burning rash." In fact, the soothsayers, themselves painfully smitten by the maddening skin disease, are in no condition to make any effort of the sort but instead flee from Moses's presence. There is added irony in the idiom used, for "to stand before" elsewhere has the sense of "stand in attendance upon." In any case, what was noxious in the earlier plagues has now become physically unbearable.

12. *And the LORD toughened Pharaoh's heart.* For the first time, it is not Pharaoh, or his heart, that is the subject of the verb of obduracy but God. However, in the biblical perspective this may amount to the same thing because God is presumed to be the ultimate cause of human actions, and Pharaoh's stubborn arrogance can still be understood as the efficient cause. It is striking that Pharaoh persists in his resistance even as his afflicted soothsayers, the experts upon whom he has been depending, flee the scene.

14. *I am about to send.* The Hebrew writer cannot resist any opportunity to confront the two senses of "send"—the sending off or dismissal that Pharaoh is unwilling to implement and the dire sending by God of plague after plague.

lence, and you would have been wiped off the face of the earth. And 16
yet, for this I have let you stand—so as to show you My power, and so
that My name will be told through all the earth. You still block the way 17
to My people, not sending them off. Look, I am about to rain down very 18
heavy hail at this time tomorrow, the like of which there has not been
in Egypt from the day of its founding until now. And now, send, gather 19
in your livestock and everything you have in the field. Every man and
the beasts that will be in the field and that are not taken indoors,

---

16. *so as to show you My power, and so that My name will be told through all the earth.* Here we are given an emphatic summary of the theological rationale for the elaborate and excruciating sequence of plagues. The God of Israel is above all a God of history. His unrivaled supremacy as God is manifested for the Hebrew writers by His powerful acts in the arena of history. The Exodus story is conceived as an establishing of the credentials of the God of Israel for all humankind. Hence his awesome power has to be demonstrated in one plague after another, and Pharaoh's repeated resistance is a required condition of the demonstration. The scope of the demonstration is also noteworthy. The elastic Hebrew term *'erets*, which until this point in the Plagues narrative had meant "land" (as in "the land of Egypt"), clearly here means "earth": YHWH's mighty acts in Egypt are to confirm his reputation as omnipotent deity throughout the world.

17. *You still block the way to My people.* The meaning of the Hebrew verb here, *mistolel*, has long been in dispute. This translation presumes a connection with the military term *soleleh*, "siege-ramp," which might imply that Pharaoh is keeping the Hebrews penned in as a besieging army would do to the population trapped within a city.

18. *from the day of its founding until now.* As the plagues are intensified, rhetorical drumrolls such as this punctuate the report of the catastrophes. Compare verse 24, "the like of which there had not been in all the land of Egypt from the time it became a nation."

19. *Every man and the beasts.* The beasts are a little puzzling because verse 6 clearly reports a total destruction of Egyptian livestock. Perhaps all the reports of general destruction are meant to be taken as hyperboles; in any case, it seems unwise to look for absolute logical consistency in this narrative, which is chiefly focused on conveying a sense of grand cumulative catastrophe.
    indoors. The literal meaning of the Hebrew is "in the house." The

20 the hail shall come down on them and they shall die.'" Whoever feared
the LORD's word among Pharaoh's servants sheltered his slaves and his
21 livestock indoors. And whoever paid no mind to the LORD's word left
22 his slaves and his livestock in the field. And the LORD said to Moses,
"Stretch out your hand over the heavens, that there be hail in all the
land of Egypt, upon man and upon beast and upon all the grass of the
23 field in the land of Egypt." And Moses stretched out his staff over the
heavens, and the LORD let loose thunder and hail, and fire went along
24 earthward, and the LORD rained hail on the land of Egypt. And there
was very heavy hail, with fire flashing in the midst of the hail, the like
of which there had not been in all the land of Egypt from the time it
25 became a nation. And the hail struck through all the land of Egypt
whatever was in the field, from man to beast, and all the grass of the

---

house/field antonyms in biblical Hebrew (*bayit/sadeh*) also have the idiomatic
sense in some contexts of inside and outside.

20. *Whoever feared the LORD's word.* Elsewhere, this is an idiom that indicates
piety (as in "God-fearing"), but here the idiom has been stripped down to its
literal meaning: whoever was struck with terror by this grim threat of God's
took the necessary steps to protect his slaves and livestock. The existence of a
contingent of Egyptians now genuinely terrified by the dire predictions of the
Hebrews is an indication of developing cracks in the pharaonic front.

23. *the LORD let loose thunder and hail, and fire went along earthward.* The dramatic nature of this plague is another manifestation of the pattern of intensification. Instead of disaster welling up from the Nile or somehow coming
through the air, it appears here as a direct and violent assault from above
against the land of Egypt. In biblical poetry, as in its Canaanite antecedents,
thunder and lightning are the characteristic weapons of the sky god. The rain-
ing down of celestial fire also sets up an allusive correspondence with the story
of the destruction of Sodom.

    went along earthward. Instead of the standard form for the Hebrew verb "to
go" (*telekh*), the writer uses a dialectic variant form (*tihalakh*) rarely employed
in the Bible and perhaps felt to be archaic, as a kind of epic gesture. "Went
along earthward" seeks to produce an equivalent strangeness of effect while
replicating the rhythm of the Hebrew.

field did the hail strike, and every tree of the field did it smash. Only in 26
the land of Goshen, in which the Israelites were, was there no hail.

And Pharaoh sent and called to Moses and to Aaron and said to them, 27
"I have offended this time. The LORD is in the right and I and my
people are in the wrong. Entreat the LORD, and no more of God's thun- 28
der and hail! And let me send you off, and you shall not continue to
stay." And Moses said to him, "As I go out of the city, I shall spread out 29
my hands to the LORD. The thunder will stop, and the hail will be no
more, so that you may know that the earth is the LORD's. And as for you 30
and your servants, I know that you still do not fear the LORD God."

---

26. *Only in the land of Goshen . . . was there no hail.* The setting apart of
Israelite Goshen from the rest of Egypt is extended here into an implicit image
of a kind of protective canopy—we would say, umbrella—shielding the
Hebrews from the destructive wrath pouring down from the sky.

27. *I have offended this time.* The terrifying display of celestial violence for the
first time triggers a confession of wrongdoing from Pharaoh (and the terms "in
the right," *tsadiq*, and "in the wrong," *resha'im*, reflect legal usage). But "this
time" is restrictive, as though Pharaoh were suggesting: I did nothing to offend
before now, but I admit, in the face of the destruction hurled from the heavens, that this time I have done wrong.

28. *no more.* Literally, "enough" or "much."

29. *spread out my hands.* Spreading out the hands (literally, "palms") is a gesture of prayer or supplication.
    the earth is the LORD's. Again, the scope of the theological argument reaches
beyond the confines of the land of Egypt: the God Who has wreaked such
inconceivable destruction on the great empire of Egypt is surely the God of all
the earth.

30. *And as for you and your servants, I know that you still do not fear the LORD
God.* Moses appears to be shrewdly reading the grudging nature of Pharaoh's
admission, "I have offended this time." And Pharaoh's reversal of direction
after each of the previous plagues scarcely inspires confidence that he has now
undergone a change of heart. The phrase "you still do not fear the LORD God"
neatly straddles both senses of the idiom (see the comment on verse 20);
Pharaoh is far from fearing the LORD, as Moses recognizes, in the sense of

31 And the flax and the barley were struck, for the barley was in bud and
32 the flax was in ear. But the wheat and the emmer were unripened.
33 And Moses went out from Pharaoh's presence out of the city and
spread out his hands to the LORD, and the thunder stopped and the hail
34 and the rain were not sluiced earthward. And Pharaoh saw that the rain
and the hail and the thunder had stopped, and he continued to offend,
35 and he hardened his heart, both he and his servants. And Pharaoh's
heart toughened, and he did not send off the Israelites, just as the
LORD had spoken through Moses.

---

pious submission to divine authority. He does fear the LORD's destructive
power—that is why he is pleading with Moses—but probably not sufficiently
to prevent him from renewing his obduracy.

31. *flax and barley*. Umberto Cassuto reminds us that flax was used to make
linen, a principal Egyptian fabric for clothing (and also an important Egyptian
export item), and goes on to suggest that the barley would have been used for
cheap bread to feed slaves.

34. *and he continued to offend*. This phrase was not used in the earlier reports
of the hardening of Pharaoh's heart. It is directly motivated by the language of
his confession: after saying "I have offended this time" as the thunder and hail
rattle down, he finds himself once more under blue skies and directly proceeds to offend again by reneging on his promise to send off the Hebrews.

CHAPTER 10

And the LORD said to Moses, "Come into Pharaoh, for I Myself ₁
have hardened his heart and the heart of his servants, so that I
may set these signs of Mine in his midst, and so that you may tell ₂
in the hearing of your son and your son's son how I toyed with Egypt,
and My signs that I set upon them, and you shall know that I am the
LORD." And Moses, and Aaron with him, came into Pharaoh, and they ₃
said to him, "Thus said the LORD, God of the Hebrews: 'How long can

---

1. *for I Myself have hardened his heart and the heart of his servants*. This is the
first time that God informs Moses before his audience with Pharaoh that He
has hardened (once again, the literal sense is "made heavy") the heart of the
Egyptian monarch. This is a signal that the elaborate "toying" (verse 2) with
Egypt is approaching endgame: Pharaoh is showing himself ever more fiercely
recalcitrant, and the plagues are becoming more fearful as we draw near the
last plague that will break Pharaoh's will.

2. *so that you may tell in the hearing of your son and your son's son*. The rationale of establishing God's enduring fame shifts here from the global scope of
Exodus 9:16 ("that My name be told through all the earth") to a consideration
of educating the future nation. Confirming the LORD's supremacy throughout
the world might be viewed as a kind of monotheistic ideal, though not a very
realistic one. The particular importance of the Exodus story is that it served as
the foundational narrative for the nation.

3. *How long can you refuse to humble yourself before Me?* These words are a
translation into other terms of the just announced hardening of Pharaoh's
heart by God, and thus constitute a strong indication that events caused by
God and events flowing from human will, or willfulness, are merely different
biblical ways of accounting for the same phenomenon. It should be noted that
the language God directs to Pharaoh through Moses and Aaron has become

you refuse to humble yourself before Me? Send off My people, that
4 they may worship Me. For if you refuse to send off My people, look, I
5 am about to bring tomorrow locust in all your territory. And it will cover
the eye of the land, and one will not be able to see the land. And it will
consume the rest of the remnant left you from the hail, and it will con-
6 sume every tree you have growing in the field. And they will fill your
houses and the houses of all your servants and the houses of all of
Egypt, the like of which your fathers did not see nor your fathers'
fathers from the day they were on the soil until this day.'" And he

---

more confrontational: now Pharaoh is inveighed against not only for blocking
Israel from fulfilling its obligations to God but for failing to humble himself
before God—humble submission being the last thing the supreme monarch of
Egypt would imagine he would ever have to do.

4. *locust.* The Hebrew, like this translation, uses a collective noun. In verse 6,
when the narrator wants to emphasize the multiplicity of the locusts invading
every nook and cranny of Egypt, he switches to a plural verb.

5. *it will cover the eye of the land.* This striking Hebrew metaphor seems worth
preserving in English. The Hebrew 'ayin, which has the primary meaning of
"eye," obviously suggests something like "surface," "aspect," or "look" in this
context. It is a linguistic usage common to many languages in which the object
of the organ of perception shares a designation with the organ of perception.
The cloud of locusts is so thick ("very heavy," as in verse 14, still another
instance of heavy disaster answering the heaviness/hardness of Pharaoh's
heart) that it covers the whole surface, or eye, of the land, in effect, blinding
Egypt. This image, of course, makes the plague of locusts adumbrate the next
plague, darkness, a link that becomes explicit in verse 15, "and the land went
dark."

6. *the like of which your fathers did not see nor your fathers' fathers.* Several commentators have noticed that this is a neat antithesis to "your son and your son's
son" of verse 2. More important, however, is that this sentence, like the one in
verse 14, amplifies the grand drumroll of pronouncements begun in the previous chapter that declare that the catastrophe about to descend is unequaled
in all the long annals of Egyptian history.

turned and went out from Pharaoh's presence. And Pharaoh's servants   7
said to him, "How long will this fellow be a snare to us? Send off the
men, that they may worship the LORD their god. Do you not yet know
that Egypt is lost?" And Moses, and Aaron with him, were brought back   8
to Pharaoh, and he said to them, "Go, worship the LORD your god. Just
who is going?" And Moses said, "With our lads and with our old men   9
we will go. With our sons and with our daughters, with our sheep and

---

7. *How long will this fellow be a snare to us?* The impatient "how long" of
Pharaoh's courtiers, in the elegant symmetry of the narrative, echoes God's
words in verse 3, "How long can you refuse to humble yourself before Me?"
Pharaoh persists in his arrogance, but the Egyptian united front against Israel
is visibly coming apart at the seams as the courtiers, who have ample reason
to believe the direness of Moses's latest threat, try to tell their king that Egypt
is on the brink of total disaster. "This fellow" reflects the indicative pronoun
zeh, "this one," which is often used in biblical Hebrew to express contempt.

8. *And Moses, and Aaron with him, were brought back to Pharaoh.* Moses, after
concluding his annunciation of the impending plague of locusts, had turned
on his heels and left—the clear implication being that he was rebuffed by
Pharaoh, or did not for a moment expect a positive response from Pharaoh.
Now, after the courtiers conclude their rebuke to Pharaoh with "Do you not
yet know that Egypt is lost?", the Egyptian king appears to concede the justice
of their argument and has Moses and Aaron brought back into his presence. It
is noteworthy, however, that Pharaoh's agency, coerced and grudging, is left
rather vague by the passive construction ("were brought back")—presumably,
Pharaoh issued the order, but perhaps he merely acquiesced as his courtiers
sent after Moses and Aaron.
    Go, worship the LORD your god. His acceptance of their petition expresses
itself in an impatient imperative, quite in keeping with the "How long will this
fellow be a snare" of his courtiers.
    Just who is going? The literal meaning of the Hebrew is "Who and who are
going?" Pharaoh's agreement to Moses's request is immediately followed by this
question that clearly implies he is not prepared to have the entire people leave.

9. *With our lads and with our old men we will go . . .* Moses, at this point fully
confident that God has dealt him the stronger hand, responds to Pharaoh's
implied reservation uncompromisingly. In a reversal of their initial speech pos-
tures, it is now Pharaoh who speaks in brief, unadorned sentences, and it is
Moses who deploys quasipoetic parallelism—lads and old men, sons and

10   with our cattle we will go, for it is a festival of the LORD for us." And he
     said to them, "May the LORD be with you the way I would send you off
11   with your little ones! For evil is before your faces. Not so. Go, pray, the
     men, and worship the LORD, for that is what you seek." And he drove
     them out from Pharaoh's presence.

12   And the LORD said to Moses, "Stretch out your hand over the land of
     Egypt for the locust, that it may come up over the land of Egypt and
13   consume all the grass of the land that the hail left behind." And Moses
     stretched out his staff over the land of Egypt, and the LORD drove an
     east wind into the land all that day and all the night. When it was morn-

---

daughters, sheep and cattle—in a rhetorical flourish that makes it plain he will
yield in nothing.

10. *May the LORD be with you the way I would send you off with your little ones!*
The effect is sarcasm: that is, as much as I am prepared to send off your little
ones may the LORD be with you—which is not at all.
    For evil is before your faces. These words are ambiguous. The most likely
meaning is "You are headed for mischief," i.e., embarked on a scheme to escape
with all the Hebrew slaves, but it could also mean something like "Harm is
going to befall you." Some commentators have detected in the word for mis-
chief/harm/evil, *ra'ah*, a pun on the name of the Egyptian deity Re or Ra.

11. *the men.* The word used here, *gevarim*, is a different one from *'anashim*, the
one used by the courtiers in verse 7. It has a stronger connotation of maleness
(*'anashim* can also mean "people"), but "males" will not do as an English equivalent because the Hebrew term means adult males, definitely excluding the
"little ones."
    he drove them out from Pharaoh's presence. Some critics, in an effort to serve
logic, emend the Hebrew text to read "they were driven out." But it is not out
of keeping with biblical usage to have "Pharaoh's presence" spelled out as the
place from which they were driven even though Pharaoh is also the antecedent
of the "he" who does the driving. Moses and Aaron were brought back into the
court in a passive construction, but now Pharaoh actively and unambiguously
drives them out.

13. *an east wind.* The Hebrew idioms were coined in the geography of Canaan,
not of Egypt. In Canaan, locusts and parching winds come from the deserts to

ing, the east wind bore the locust. And the locust went up over all the   14
land of Egypt, and settled, very heavy, over all the territory of Egypt.
Before it there had never been locust like it and after it there never
would be. And it covered the eye of the land, and the land went dark.   15
And it consumed all the grass of the land and every fruit of the tree that
the hail had left, and nothing green in tree or in grass of the field was
left in all the land of Egypt. And Pharaoh hastened to call to Moses and   16
to Aaron, and he said, "I have offended before the LORD your god and
before you. And now, forgive, pray, my offense, just this time, and   17
entreat the LORD your god, that He but take away from me this death."
And he went out from Pharaoh's presence and entreated the LORD.   18
And the LORD turned round a very strong west wind, and it bore off the   19
locust and thrust it into the Sea of Reeds, not a locust remained in all
the territory of Egypt. And the LORD toughened Pharaoh's heart, and he   20
did not send the Israelites off.

---

the east. In Egypt, such winds and blights would typically come from the
Sudan, to the south.

15. *it consumed all the grass of the land and every fruit of the tree.* In this
instance, the account of total devastation would have sounded neither hyperbolic nor miraculous to the ancient audience, who would have had some
familiarity with the comprehensive destruction of all growing things that a vast
infestation of locusts could effect.

16–17. *I have offended . . . forgive, pray, my offense just this time . . . take away
from me this death.* The mastery of dialogue so often manifested in biblical narrative is striking here. Pharaoh's confident, imperious, aristocratic speech has
now broken down into contrite confession and short urgent pleas. The dense
layer of consuming locusts, blinding the eye of the land and penetrating every
crevice, is given no name by Pharaoh except its palpable meaning for him and
his people: "this death." That choice of name for it, of course, is an unwitting
anticipation of the last of the plagues, which will soon come.

19. *west wind.* The literal meaning is "sea wind," but because of the geographical situation of ancient Israel, "sea" (that is, the Mediterranean) is often used
to designate the west. Again, the wind reference reflects the geography of
Canaan.

21 And the LORD said to Moses, "Stretch out your hand over the heavens,
that there be darkness upon the land of Egypt, a darkness one can
22 feel." And Moses stretched out his hand over the heavens and there
23 was pitch dark in all the land of Egypt three days. No one saw his
fellow and no one rose from where he was three days, but all the
24 Israelites had light in their dwelling places. And Pharaoh called
to Moses and said, "Go, worship the LORD. Only your sheep and
your cattle will be set aside. Your little ones, too, may go with you."

---

21. *the LORD said to Moses.* As in each third plague in the three triads that make
up the sequence of nine, this plague is implemented without warning: the
ominousness of three days of total darkness, suddenly enveloping Egypt without advance notice, prepares the ground psychologically for the climactic
tenth plague.

a darkness one can feel. The force of the hyperbole, which beautifully conveys the claustrophobic palpability of absolute darkness, is diminished by
those who try to provide a naturalistic explanation for this plague (or indeed,
for any of the others)—i.e., a desert wind bearing particles of sand and dust
darkens the land and makes the darkness palpable. Nor would solar eclipse
work as an explanation, since the darkness persists for three days. Although
elements of nature are used in all of the plagues—except, perhaps, this one
and the next—they are all emphatically presented as extraordinary interventions by God in the order of nature, "signs and portents" that demonstrate His
power over the created world.

23. *No one saw . . . no one rose.* Abraham Ibn Ezra and Nahmanides both
shrewdly infer that this total incapacity through darkness would logically have
had to include the disabling of candlelight as well as sunlight—another manifestation of the miraculous character of the event.

but all the Israelites had light in their dwelling places. This previously reiterated opposition between the Israelites and the Egyptians is here made boldly
schematic, as the dramatic manifestation of God's miraculous intervention.
The contrast between light in Goshen and terrifying darkness in the rest of
Egypt then sets the stage for the distinction between life for the Israelites and
death for the Egyptians in the tenth plague.

24. *Only your sheep and your cattle will be set aside.* Pharaoh now concedes that
the children and, implicitly the womenfolk (which some claim are included in
the Hebrew term *taf*) may go, but he still wants to keep back the livestock as
a material guarantee for the return of the slaves.

And Moses said, "You yourself too shall provide us sacrifices and burnt   25
offerings, that we may do them to the LORD our God. And our livestock,   26
too, shall go with us, not a hoof shall remain. For from it we shall take
to worship the LORD our God, and we ourselves cannot know with what
we shall worship the LORD our God until we come there." And the   27
LORD toughened Pharaoh's heart and he did not want to send them
off. And Pharaoh said to him, "Go away from me. Watch yourself. Do   28
not again see my face, for on the day you see my face, you shall die."
And Moses said, "Rightly have you spoken—I will not see your face   29
again."

---

25. *You yourself . . . shall provide*. Moses is at least as uncompromising as in his previous encounter with Pharaoh. His immediate rejoinder to Pharaoh's stipulation about the livestock is that the Egyptian monarch himself will provide the sacrifices. This pugnacious response might nevertheless have allowed Pharaoh momentarily to infer that Moses was agreeing to the condition about leaving the livestock behind. But in his next sentence, Moses vigorously disabuses Pharaoh of this illusion ("not a hoof shall remain").

28–29. *Do not again see my face . . . I will not see your face again*. This is the final squaring-off between these adversaries. No further negotiations are possible, and the scene has now been set for the unleashing of the terrible last plague.

CHAPTER 11

1   A nd the LORD said to Moses, "Yet one more plague shall I bring upon Pharaoh and upon Egypt. Afterward he will send you off from here; when he sends you off altogether, he will surely drive 2 you out from here. Speak, pray, in the hearing of the people, that every man borrow from his fellow man and every woman from her fellow

---

1. *And the* LORD *said to Moses.* There is a problem about where to locate this speech temporally and spatially. In the immediately preceding verses, Pharaoh had warned Moses on pain of death never to see him again, and Moses had grimly concurred that he would never again see the Egyptian king. Verse 8, however, makes it clear that Moses is standing in Pharaoh's presence and announcing the tenth plague to Pharaoh. This speech to Pharaoh (verses 4–8), then, would have to be the continuation and conclusion of the angry confrontation reported at the end of the previous chapter. God's words to Moses (verses 1–3) do not seem smoothly integrated into the narrative progress, at any rate, not according to modern expectations of narrative continuity. Abraham ibn Ezra points out that most of this material is a restatement of God's predictions to Moses in the Burning Bush episode. The passage thus may be understood as a summarizing recapitulation—Umberto Cassuto sees it as a kind of flashback in Moses's mind—of God's initial promise to confound Egypt and to liberate Israel before the annunciation of the last plague.

send you off . . . drive you out. Again, the semantically multiple "send" ("to dismiss," "to free," "to divorce," "to take ceremonious leave of") is interpreted as brutal expulsion.

woman, ornaments of silver and ornaments of gold. And the LORD will 3
grant the people favor in the eyes of the Egyptians. The man Moses,
too, is very great in the land of Egypt in the eyes of Pharaoh's servants
and in the eyes of the people."

And Moses said, "Thus said the LORD: 'Around midnight I am going out 4
in the midst of Egypt. And every firstborn in the land of Egypt shall die, 5
from the firstborn of Pharaoh sitting on his throne to the firstborn of
the slavegirl who is behind the millstones, and every firstborn of the
beasts. And there shall be a great outcry in all the land of Egypt, the 6
like of which there has not been and the like of which there will not be
again. But against the Israelites no dog will snarl, from man to beast, so 7

---

3. *The man Moses, too, is very great.* This expression is a little odd because God
is, after all, addressing Moses. It is best construed as a kind of free indirect
discourse—the way the Egyptians, impressed as they are by Moses's stature,
might refer to him. The logical connection with the preceding sentence seems
to run along the following lines: just as the rank-and-file Israelites have made
the sort of appealing or superior impression on the Egyptians that encourages
the bestowal of gifts, the leader of the Hebrews exerts a powerful charisma
that confirms or enhances the standing of his followers in Egyptian eyes.

5. *from the firstborn of Pharaoh sitting on his throne to the firstborn of the slavegirl... behind the millstones.* Of all the catalogues to indicate the comprehensiveness of the plague about to be enacted, this is of course the scariest.
Cassuto locates the phrase "the slavegirl behind the millstones" in an Egyptian document and suggests it may have been proverbial in Egypt for the low-
est of the low; this would be another instance of an authentic touch of
Egyptian local color in this narrative.

6. *outcry.* The Hebrew *tse'aqah*, which has also been used for the cries of
anguish of the Israelites in their oppression, has a semantic range that goes
between "cry" and "scream."

7. *But against the Israelites no dog will snarl.* That is, not even a menacing gesture toward them will be made. The literal meaning of the idiom used here is
"no dog will sharpen its tongue." Dogs, which were not kept as pets in ancient
Israel, have a consistently negative valence in biblical literature as images of
malefic hostility or of abasement.

8 that you may know how the LORD sets apart Egypt and Israel. And all
these servants of yours shall come down to me and bow to me, saying,
Go out, you and all the people that is at your feet. And afterward I will
go out.'" And he went out from Pharaoh's presence in a flare of anger.

─────────────────────────────

8. *And all these servants of yours.* Since the beginning of Moses's speech, "And
Moses said," lacks the usual "to Pharaoh" (perhaps because this piece of dialogue is a direct continuation of their previous exchange), it is only now that
we can be certain that these words are addressed to Pharaoh, "your servants"
referring to Pharaoh's courtiers.

Go out . . . I will go out . . . And he went out. The Hebrew for the Exodus
from Egypt is *yetsi'at mitsrayim*, "the going-out from Egypt." Here that crucial
verbal stem becomes the thematic keyword of Moses's "last confrontation"
with Pharaoh before the actual exodus. The first two occurrences of the verb
in this verse refer to the Hebrews' leaving Egypt; the third occurrence indicates Moses's angry departure from the court, which through the very repetition of the verb also is made a kind of foreshadowing of the Israelite departure
from Egypt. All three of these uses of the verb play against God's "going out in
the midst of Egypt" (verse 4), where the same verb appears to have a military
sense—"to go out on a sortie," or, as elsewhere in this translation, "to sally
forth."

in a flare of anger. Both Rashi and ibn Ezra link this causally to Pharaoh's
"Do not again see my face." Since Pharaoh has offered no response to Moses's
terrifying announcement of the death of the firstborn, he clearly remains
implacable, and hence Moses's anger—the first explicit indication of such a
reaction by him in all his clashes with Pharaoh.

And the L<small>ORD</small> said to Moses, "Pharaoh will not heed you, so that 9
My portents may be multiplied in the land of Egypt." And Moses 10
and Aaron had done these portents before Pharaoh, and the L<small>ORD</small>
toughened Pharaoh's heart and he did not send off the Israelites from
his land.

9–10. *Pharaoh will not heed you . . . Moses and Aaron had done these portents
. . . the* L<small>ORD</small> *toughened Pharaoh's heart.* All this material in virtually the same
verbal formulation appears earlier in the narrative—indeed, as early as the initiating episode of the Burning Bush, like the material enunciated here in
verses 1–3. Its function at this point before the last night in Egypt is, as Cassuto suggests, a summarizing recapitulation. The first three verses of the chapter and these last two thus form a kind of recapitulative framework for Moses's
final confrontation with Pharaoh, reminding us that it is the prelude to the climactic fulfillment of the divine promise given to Moses at Horeb. The function of recapitulation is grammatically indicated by the use of a pluperfect
verb: "Moses and Aaron had done these portents." The portents, of course,
have proved unavailing, and so the stage is set for carrying out God's grim
pledge to Moses at Horeb to kill the firstborn of Egypt.

CHAPTER 12

1   **A**nd the Lord said to Moses and to Aaron in the land of Egypt, say-
2   ing, "This month is for you head of months, it is the first for you
3   of the months of the year. Speak to all the community of Israel,
saying: 'On the tenth of this month, let every man take a lamb for a

---

1. *in the land of Egypt.* This phrase is usually explained (by Nahmanides and others) as an indication of the unusual setting for the annunciation of this set of legal regulations in contradistinction to the body of Hebrew law that is given in the wilderness. But the phrase also serves to position this passage in the narrative sequence: as the Israelites are poised for the great escape, in the penultimate moment of their 430-year sojourn in Egypt (verse 40), God directs Moses and Aaron to deliver to them, while they are still on Egyptian soil, this law that will be binding on all their descendants.

2. *This month is for you head of months.* The reasonable inference of many scholars is that this calendric announcement reflects a moment in early Israelite history when there was at least one other competing system that designated a different month as the beginning of the year. (The Talmud later would speak of four different new years, and subsequent Jewish practice sets the beginning of the year in the early fall month of Tishrei, evidently making the calendar correspond to the agricultural cycle rather than to a historical event.) The point of beginning the annual sequence of months with the one in which the Exodus occurred is to coordinate the annual cycle with the event of liberation that is construed as the foundational act for the nation.

3. *a lamb.* Though the Hebrew *seh* can refer to both lamb and mature sheep, the indication that the animal should be in its first year—this is Rashi's plausible construction of the term *ben shanah*—makes "lamb" the appropriate translation. It is a slightly peculiar lamb, however, because in verse 5 we learn that it also includes "kid."

father's house, a lamb for a household. And should a household be too ₄
small to have a lamb, it must take together with its neighbor who is
close to its house, in proportion to the persons, each man according to
what he eats shall take his portion of the lamb. An unblemished lamb, ₅
a yearling male you shall have, from the sheep or from the goats you
may take it. And it shall be a thing to be kept by you until the four- ₆
teenth day of this month, and the whole congregation of the community of Israel shall slaughter it at twilight. And they shall take from the ₇
blood and put it on the two doorposts and on the lintel, on the houses
in which they will eat it. And they shall eat the meat on this night fire- ₈
roasted, with flatbread on bitter herbs shall they eat it. Do not eat from ₉
it raw, nor in any way cooked in water, but fire-roasted, its head with its

---

6. *a thing to be kept.* The Hebrew *mishmeret* is an abstract noun derived from
the verbal stem *sh-m-r*, which has meanings that range from "keep" to "watch"
to "observe" (in the ritual sense); all these meanings come into play as the root
is repeated through the passage.

8. *flatbread.* The etymology of the Hebrew *matsot* remains uncertain. The conventional translation of "unleavened bread" is less than felicitous not only
because of its excess of syllables but because it explicitly defines the bread by
negation, the lack of leavening, whereas the Hebrew is a positive term. In Genesis 19 Lot serves *matsot* to the two anonymous guests who were to his house
at nightfall, and the implication is that this is a kind of bread that can be baked
hastily, with no need to wait for the dough to rise before putting it in the oven.

9. *Do not eat from it raw, nor in any way cooked in water, but fire-roasted.* Eating raw meat, still suffused with blood, would in any case have been prohibited, but elsewhere there is no restriction on boiled meat (here that would be
lamb stew), whether for sacrificial or profane purposes. William H. C. Propp
offers what may be the best explanation for this insistence on fire-roasting by
observing that it is a more archaic method of cooking meat, without the use
of a pot, cooking utensils being the instruments of a more complex culinary
technology. In this fashion, he goes on to suggest, fire-roasting would be associated with a kind of purity in the preparation of the meal, just as flatbread
(probably baked over an open fire, nomad-style) without any admixture of
leaven, might be associated with purity. One could add that these archaically
prepared foods enhance the sense of ritual reenactment of what amounts to
an archaic moment of national history, when the nation itself was awaiting its

10 shanks and with its entrails. And you shall leave nothing from it by
11 morning, and what is left of it by morning in fire you shall burn. And
    thus shall you eat it: your loins girded, your sandals on your feet, your
    staff in your hand, and you shall eat it in haste. It is a passover offering
12 to the LORD. And I will cross through the land of Egypt on this night,
    and I will strike down every firstborn in the land of Egypt from man
    to beast, and from all the gods of Egypt I will exact retributions. I am
13 the LORD. And the blood will be a sign for you upon the houses in
    which you are, and I will see the blood and I will pass over you, and no
    scourge shall become a Destroyer amongst you when I strike in the

---

foundational liberation as a destroying angel stalked through the Egyptian
night and passed over the houses of the Israelites.

10. *in fire you shall burn*. This seemingly redundant idiom has the force of
"burn till utterly consumed" and so when applied to buildings means something like "burned to the ground."

12. *I will cross through the land*. The Hebrew verb 'avarti means to "pass" (over,
through, or by) or to "cross." The usual translation of "pass through" or "pass
over" has been avoided in order to obviate the misleading impression that it is
the same word as "Passover," which in the Hebrew reflects an entirely unrelated root, *p-s-ḥ*.
    from all the gods of Egypt I will exact retributions. The least strained con-
struction of this clause is that the absolute impotence of the supposed, or
perhaps merely petty, gods of Egypt to protect their adherents will expose
their nullity as gods. The idea of some commentators, that the Egyptian idols
were smashed in the course of this fateful night, seems fanciful: and the
exposure of the inefficacy of the Egyptian gods is in keeping with the preceding plagues.

13. *And the blood will be a sign*. Much anthropologically informed commentary
has been made on the smearing of blood at the entrance of the house to ward
off evil spirits, the "Destroyer" (*mashḥit*) of our narrative being a particularly
scary instance of such a spirit. It is equally important, however, to keep in
mind the deployment of blood as a recurrent motif in the literary structure of
the larger narrative. Moses is thrust from Egypt, and set on the road toward
his vocation as prophet, after he sheds the blood of the Egyptian taskmaster.
On the way back to Egypt, it is the blood of circumcision that saves his life—
a strong foreshadowing of the tenth plague that evidently interprets circumci-

land of Egypt. And this day shall be a remembrance for you, and you 14
shall celebrate it as a festival to the LORD through your generations, an
everlasting statute you shall celebrate it. Seven days shall you eat flat- 15
bread. The very first day you shall expunge leaven from your houses, for
whosoever eats leavened bread, that person shall be cut off from Israel,
from the first day to the seventh day. And on the first day a sacred con- 16
vocation and on the seventh day a sacred convocation you shall have,
no task shall be done on them, only what each person is to eat, that
alone will be prepared for you. And you shall observe the Flatbread, for 17
on this very day I brought out their battalions from the land of Egypt,
and you shall observe this day through your generations, an everlasting
statute. In the first month, on the fourteenth day of the month in 18
the evening you shall eat flatbread, until the twenty-first day in the

---

sion as a kind of substitute for the sacrifice of the firstborn. Then the plagues
begin with the turning of the water of the Nile into blood.

I will pass over you. The primary meaning of the Hebrew verb *pasaḥ* is to
"skip," "hop," "step over." (There is one occurrence in the biblical corpus
where it might mean "defend," which is scant basis for the claim of some
scholars that this is what it means here.) "Pass over" is used in this translation
to preserve the pun on the time-honored English name for the festival. It is
quite possible that the Hebrew *pesaḥ* was the independent name for this particular lamb sacrifice and for a spring festival, and that the narrative links that
name with the Exodus story through folk etymology.

15. *that person shall be cut off from Israel.* This punishment (the Hebrew term
is *karet*) will be invoked for a whole series of infractions as the Mosaic law is
promulgated. Perhaps the most likely reference is to some form of ostracism,
though both medieval and modern commentators have speculated about
whether premature death or childlessness might be suggested by the phrase.

17. *the Flatbread.* Here the term *matsot* is the name of the festival, which is
also called *pesaḥ*. Some have plausibly conjectured that these were originally
two different holidays—*matsot* agricultural and *pesaḥ* pastoral—that were
drawn together in the literary formulation of this text and hence in Israelite
practice.

19   evening. Seven days no leaven shall be found in your houses, for
     whosoever eats what is leavened, that person shall be cut off from the
20   community of Israel, sojourner and native of the land alike. Nothing
     that is leavened shall you eat, in all your dwelling places you shall eat
     flatbread.'"

21   And Moses called all the elders of Israel and said to them, "Draw out
     and take yourselves sheep according to your clans and slaughter the
22   Passover offering. And you shall take a bundle of hyssop and you shall
     dip it in the blood that is in the basin and you shall touch the blood that
     is in the basin to the lintel and to the two doorposts, and as for you,
     none of you shall go out from the entrance of his house till morning.
23   And the LORD shall cross through to scourge Egypt, and He shall see
     the blood on the lintel and on the two doorposts, and the LORD shall
     pass over the entrance, and He shall not allow the Destroyer to come
24   into your houses to scourge. And you shall keep this thing as a statute
25   for you and your sons, everlasting. And so when you come to the land
     that the LORD will give you as He has spoken, you shall keep this ser-

---

19. *sojourner*. As elsewhere, the Hebrew *ger* refers to a resident alien.

native of the land. The Hebrew reflected in "native," *'ezraḥ*, probably refers
to a plant (many think, a grapevine), and so would be a metaphor for the
autochthonous character of the native, springing from the soil in purity.

21. *Draw out and take*. The precise nuance of the first of these two verbs is elusive. It has been proposed that "draw" (*mashakh*) preceding another verb may
have the idiomatic force of "hasten," "perform urgently."

22. *touch the blood . . . to the lintel*. This is precisely the same verb that is used
in 4:25 for Zipporah's placing or smearing the blood of circumcision at someone's feet. The usage is unusual enough to suggest the possibility of an explicit
allusion here to the earlier episode.

25. *And so when you come to the land*. This is a pointed rupture of the time
frame of the story. In the midst of the breathless moment that is the last
evening of the Israelites in Egypt, as Moses enjoins them to smear their
entranceways with protective blood, the narrative briefly leaps forward to a
time when the Israelites, long ago liberated from Egyptian servitude, dwell in

vice. And so should your sons ask you, 'What is this service to you?', 26
you shall say, 'A Passover sacrifice to the LORD, who passed over the 27
houses of the Israelites in Egypt when he scourged Egypt and our
households He rescued.'" And the people bowed and did obeisance.
And the Israelites went and did as the LORD had charged Moses and 28
Aaron, thus did they do.

And it happened at midnight that the LORD struck down every firstborn 29
in the land of Egypt, from the firstborn of Pharaoh sitting on his throne
to the firstborn of the captive who was in the dungeon, and every firstborn of the beasts. And Pharaoh rose at night, he and all his servants 30
and all Egypt, and there was a great outcry in Egypt, for there was no
household in which there was no dead. And he called to Moses and to 31
Aaron at night and said, "Rise, go out from the midst of my people,
both you and the Israelites, and go worship the LORD as you have spoken. Both your sheep and your cattle take as you have spoken, and go, 32
and you shall bless me as well." And Egypt bore down on the people 33
to hurry to send them off from the land, for they said, "We are all

---

their land, and when a generation arises that scarcely knows the meaning of
the commemorative Passover ritual, so that telling has to supplement the ritualistic showing.

29. dungeon. The literal meaning of the Hebrew is "house of the pit."

32. and you shall bless me as well. As both Rashi and Abraham ibn Ezra note,
the desperate Pharaoh appears to feel in need of intercession: when you pro-
pitiate your god in the wilderness, he is saying, remember to put in a good
word for me.

33. Egypt bore down on the people. The literal meaning of the verb is "was
strong." This same verb, ḥazaq, was repeatedly used for the "toughening" of
Pharaoh's heart, and the redeployment here in a different context, with a different grammatical object, is a virtually ironic echo.
    We are all dead men. Coupled with the wrenching grief over the death of
the firstborn is a note of panic: "the disasters are becoming more and more
intolerable, and after the loss of our sons, the next thing that will happen is
that we shall all be killed."

34 dead men." And the people carried off their dough before it rose, their
35 kneading pans wrapped in their cloaks on their shoulders. And the
Israelites had done according to Moses's word, and they had asked of
the Egyptians ornaments of silver and ornaments of gold and cloaks.
36 And the Lord had granted the people favor in the eyes of the Egyp-
37 tians, who lent to them, and they despoiled Egypt. And the Israelites
journeyed from Rameses to Succoth, some six hundred thousand men
38 on foot, besides the little ones. And a motley throng also went up with
39 them, and sheep and cattle, very heavy livestock. And they baked the
dough that they had brought out of Egypt in rounds of flatbread, for it
had not leavened, since they had been driven out of Egypt and could
40 not tarry, and provisions, too, they could not make for themselves. And
the settlement of the Israelites which they had settled in Egypt was

---

35. *and cloaks.* The cloaks were not included in the preceding instructions
about this event. The mention here is evidently triggered by the report of the
cloaks in which the kneading pans were wrapped, as an explanation of where
the Hebrews got them. Perhaps it is assumed that as a matter of course abject
slaves would possess no more than simple work-tunics, and not the cloaks they
would need for a journey. (In Egyptian paintings slaves are often depicted
wearing only a short skirt and naked from the waist up.)

36. *six hundred thousand men on foot, besides the little ones.* "On foot" (*ragli*),
which functions adverbially here, is a military term with the usual meaning as
a noun of foot soldier and thus reinforces the idea that the fleeing Hebrews are
"the Lord's battalions." "The little ones" in this instance would logically have to
imply or include the women who nurtured them. The total figure of Israelites
thus would be considerably more than two million. This is scarcely credible as
a historical datum, but ancient literature (Greek as well as Hebrew) has little
notion of numerical accuracy in the way it conjures with numbers.

38. *motley throng.* Umberto Cassuto plausibly suggests that the Hebrew ʿerev
rav has no component that means "multitude" (King James Version, "mixed
multitude") but rather that the last syllable is not an independent word but a
duplication of the ultimate syllable of the main word—thus, ʿerevrav—which
is a Hebrew formation for pejoratives. (The English "riffraff" comes close.)
    very heavy livestock. "Heavy" is a word that shuttles back and forth through
the themes of the story, from Pharaoh's heavy/hard heart to the sundry heavy
plagues to the heaviness of the Israelite possessions.

four hundred and thirty years. And it happened at the end of four hun- 41
dred and thirty years and it happened on that very day, all the battalions
of the LORD went out from the land of Egypt. It is a night of watch for 42
the LORD, for His taking them out of the land of Egypt, this night is the
LORD's, a watch for all the Israelites through their generations.

And the LORD said to Moses and Aaron, "This is the statute of the 43
Passover offering: no foreigner shall eat of it. And every man's slave, 44
purchased with silver, you shall circumcise, then shall he eat of it.
A settler or hired worker shall not eat of it. In one house shall it be 45,46
eaten, you shall not take out any meat from the house, and no bone

---

42. *a night of watch.* The Hebrew *leyl shimurim* may suggest a vigil or simply a
night on which this complex of commemorative rituals is scrupulously kept or
observed. In any case, the last phrase of the verse, "through their generations"
(or "through their eras") serves as a transition from the preceding narration of
the event of Exodus to the passage of legislation that frames it (verses 43–51),
which will be followed by a second unit of legislative material (13:1–16).

43. *no foreigner shall eat of it.* The Exodus story defines the nation. The
Passover ritual, which commemorates that story, is the cultic enactment of
membership in the nation.

44. *purchased with silver.* Literally, the Hebrew is "purchase of silver."

45. *A settler.* The Hebrew *toshav* appears to mean the same thing as *ger*, that
is, "resident alien." The two words are often coupled in a hendiadys, *ger
wetoshav*, which plainly means resident alien.
    hired worker. The obvious implication is a non-Israelite hired worker.

46. *no bone shall you break in it.* This is often linked to the haste of the eating:
there is no time to break bones and suck out the marrow. It may be more likely,
however, that the prohibition is meant to preserve the idea of the wholeness
of the sacrificial meal. The lamb is fire-roasted whole, after which only the
meat that can be cut away is consumed.

47,48 shall you break in it. All the community of Israel thus shall do. And
should a sojouner sojourn with you and make the Passover offering to
the Lord, he must circumcise every male of his, then may he draw near
to do it and he shall be like a native of the land, but no uncircumcised
49 man shall eat of it. One law shall there be for the native and for the
50 sojourner who sojourns in your midst." And all the Israelites did as the
51 Lord had charged Moses and Aaron, thus did they do. And it happened
on that very day that the Lord brought the Israelites out of the land of
Egypt in their battalions.

---

48. *he must circumcise every male.* Circumcision is the mark of belonging to the
covenantal community, as God announced to Abraham when He enjoined the
practice (Genesis 17); and so circumcision is a prerequisite to participation in
the community-defining Passover ritual. But the mention of circumcision also
ties in this law with the Bridegroom of Blood episode that was the prelude to
Moses's mission in Egypt: there is a symbolic overlap between the apotropaic
blood of circumcision, the apotropaic blood of the lamb on the doorposts, and
God's saving Israel from the bloodbath of Egypt to make them His people.

    then may he draw near. In ritual contexts, this verb is often an ellipsis for
"draw near to the altar" (to offer sacrifice). The Hebrew for "sacrifice," *qorban*,
is cognate with the verb "draw near," *qarav*.

49. *One law.* The Hebrew term here is *torah*, which has the primary meaning
of "teaching" or "instruction."

CHAPTER 13

And the Lord spoke to Moses, saying, "Consecrate unto Me each 1,2
firstborn, breach of each womb among the Israelites in man and
in beast—it is Mine."

And Moses said to the people, "Remember this day on which you went 3
out of Egypt, from the house of slaves, for by strength of hand the Lord
brought you out from here, and unleavened stuff shall not be eaten.

---

2. *Consecrate unto me each firstborn.* As Nahum Sarna notes, there are indications elsewhere—e.g., Numbers 3:12—that the firstborn originally served as
priests, until they were replaced by the members of the tribe of Levi, and so
consecration here has a double meaning: the human firstborn are to be dedicated to God's cult and the animal firstborn are to be sacrificed to God. These
first two verses of the chapter appear to be a separate unit, editorially inserted
because of the connection with the instructions about the redemption of the
firstborn and the sacrifice of firstborn animals in the next unit (verses 12–13, 15).

breach of each womb. The Hebrew *peter* means "opening" and is related, by
metathesis, to *perets*, "bursting." It is a vivid idiom for the firstborn.

3. *Remember this day.* The Hebrew verb *zakhar* suggests both the cognitive act
of remembering and the ritual act of commemoration. This entire projection
into the future in the promised land of the Passover observance clearly duplicates some of the material in 12:14–28, though it stresses even more centrally
the function of memory/commemoration.

unleavened stuff. This rendering of *hamets* is preferable to "unleavened
bread" used by some translations because the term probably includes grain-
based foods other than bread, as later Jewish tradition would extravagantly
stipulate in its Passover regulations.

4,5 Today you are going out, in the month of the New Grain. And so when the LORD brings you to the land of the Canaanite and the Hittite and the Emorite and the Hivite and the Jebusite which He swore to your fathers to give to you, a land flowing with milk and honey, you shall per-
6 form this service in this month. Seven days shall you eat flatbread and
7 on the seventh day a festival to the LORD. Flatbread shall be eaten through the seven days and no leavened stuff of yours shall be seen and
8 no leavening of yours shall be seen in all your territory. And you shall tell your son on that day, saying, 'For the sake of what the LORD did for me
9 when I went out of Egypt.' And it shall be a sign for you on your hand and a remembrance between your eyes, so that the LORD's teaching will be in your mouth, for with a strong hand the LORD brought you out of

---

5. *this service.* The reference is to the Passover ritual. As has often been noted, the Hebrew *'avodah*, the term for service or worship, is also the word repeatedly used for the labor or slavery in Egypt; so the narrative traces a move from coerced manual service to service of the deity.

6. *on the seventh day a festival to the LORD.* Surprisingly, there is no indication here, as in the previous chapter, of a festival on the *first* day. Either this is an ellipsis, which would be untypical for legal injunctions, or it reflects a variant tradition.

9. *a sign for you on your hand and a remembrance between your eyes.* The concrete reference of these famous words remains in doubt. The original intention could conceivably be metaphorical: the story of the Exodus is to be forever present on the hand (or arm), the idiomatic agent of power and action, and between the eyes, the place of perception and observation. Here the keyword for our passage, "remembrance" (*zikaron*), is used for what should be between the eyes. In verse 16 the term used is *totafot*, "circlets" or "frontlets," a word of obscure origin and not entirely certain meaning: many imagine it as a headband, although a headband would be worn above, not between, the eyes, whereas there are Egyptian ornaments, as some scholars have noted, that were worn between the eyes. Subsequent Jewish tradition construed this phrase to enjoin the wearing of small leather boxes containing scriptural passages written on parchment (*tefillin*, conventionally translated as "phylacteries").

the LORD's teaching. Here *torah* has the clear meaning of "teaching" because it is said to be in the mouth (learning in the ancient world would have involved recitation out loud).

Egypt. And you shall keep this statute at its fixed time year after year. 10,11
And so when the LORD brings you to the land of the Canaanite as He
swore to you and to your fathers and gives it to you, you shall pass every 12
womb-breach to the LORD and every breach of spawn of beast that you
will have—the males to the LORD. And every donkey's breach you shall 13
redeem with a lamb, and should you not redeem it, you shall break its
neck, and every human firstborn of your sons you shall redeem. And so 14
should your son ask you tomorrow, saying, 'What is this?', you shall say
to him, 'By strength of hand the LORD brought us out of Egypt, from

---

12. *pass . . . to the LORD*. The verb, which is the causative form of the verb used
for God's crossing or passing through Egypt, means in this context "to transfer
possession."

13. *every donkey's breach*. Since the donkey was an impure animal for both
dietary and ritual purposes, it could not be sacrificed, and a lamb (or sheep)
had to be sacrificed in its stead. As William H. C. Propp observes, a donkey
was worth several times the value of a sheep, so the sheep substitution would
almost certainly be embraced rather than the alternative of destroying the donkey that is put forth in the next clause.

   you shall break its neck. The Hebrew verb 'araf clearly derives from 'oref, the
nape. It could conceivably refer to slaughter with a knife at the back of the
neck rather than at the front, as is ritually prescribed. In postbiblical Hebrew,
the verb means "to behead." In any case, the idea is that if a person should
refuse to perform the substitute sacrifice for the donkey, he should be
deprived of its use—which no sane owner of this ubiquitous and valuable
beast of burden and means of transportation would do.

14. *What is this?* Again and again, these texts emphasize the educational and
commemorative function of the Exodus story and of the Passover ritual
embedded in it. The story encodes the very matrix and rationale of Israelite
national existence, and it becomes a sustained exercise in collective remembering. The educational formulas here reiterate the verbal motif of "a strong
hand" or "strength of hand" that punctuates the Exodus narrative proper.

15 the house of slaves. And it happened, when Pharaoh was hard about
sending us off, that the LORD killed every firstborn in the land of Egypt
from the firstborn of man to the firstborn of beast. Therefore do I sacrifice to the LORD every womb-breach of the male and every firstborn
16 of my sons I must redeem. And it shall be a sign on your hand and circlets between your eyes, that through strength of hand the LORD
brought us out of Egypt.'"

17 And it happened when Pharaoh sent the people off that God did not
lead them by way of the land of the Philistines though it was close, for
God thought, "Lest the people regret when they see battle and go back
18 to Egypt." And God turned the people round by way of the wilderness
of the Sea of Reeds, and the Israelites went up armed from the land of

---

15. *every firstborn of my sons I must redeem.* The permanent "redemption" of
every firstborn son, in remembrance of all the firstborn Hebrew sons rescued
from death on that dire night in Egypt, is evidently a payment in silver or goods
to the priests. The notion that this is a substitute for human sacrifice of the
firstborn, as Sir James Frazer contended, is at best part of the shadowy archaic
antecedents of this practice, here firmly anchored in historical
commemoration.

17. *And it happened when Pharaoh sent the people off.* We now return to the
story, with an indication of the escape route that will be important as we
approach the dramatic event at the Sea of Reeds.
    by way of the land of the Philistines. This would have been the most direct
route to Canaan, along what amounted to a coastal highway up through the
area that is the present-day Gaza Strip. This route was in fact heavily fortified
by the Egyptians as the principal avenue for their varying imperial enterprises
to the north, and so would have immediately confronted the fleeing slaves with
the prospect of "battle." The Philistines in this period are an anachronistic reference, for they arrived from the Aegean region (and thus are known as the Sea
Peoples) in this coastal strip during the twelfth century B.C.E., perhaps as
much as a hundred years after the conjectured date of the Exodus in the later
thirteenth century.

18. *the Sea of Reeds.* This is not the Red Sea, as older translations have it, but
most likely a marshland in the northeastern part of Egypt. (Marshes might provide some realistic kernel for the tale of a waterway that is at one moment

Egypt. And Moses took the bones of Joseph with him, for he had 19
solemnly made the sons of Israel swear, saying, "God will surely single
you out, and you shall take up my bones with you from here." And they 20
journeyed from Succoth and encamped at Etham at the edge of the
wilderness. And the LORD was going before them by day in a pillar of 21
cloud to lead them on the way and by night in a pillar of fire, to give
them light to go by day and by night. The column of cloud would not 22
budge by day nor the pillar of fire by night from before the people.

---

passable and in the next flooded.) But it must be conceded that elsewhere *yam
suf* refers to the Red Sea, and some scholars have recently argued that the
story means to heighten the miraculous character of the event through the
parting of a real sea. Even if the setting is a marsh, the event is reported in
strongly supernatural terms.

19. *he had solemnly made the sons of Israel swear.* Here the reference of *beney
yisra'el* would have to be Joseph's brothers, the actual sons of Israel/Jacob. But
the double sense of the term works nicely by stressing the continuity of obligation between the original sons of Israel who swore to bring Joseph's bones
up out of Egypt and these "sons of Israel" who are the Israelites, the Hebrew
nation.

21. *And the LORD was going before them.* The participial form of the verb in the
Hebrew suggests constant action. This effect is complemented by the verb at
the very beginning of (in the Hebrew) the next verse, *lo' yamish*, which has an
iterative force, "would not budge." The twin images of a pillar of cloud and a
pillar of fire going before the people extend the representation of the Israelites
as "the LORD's battalions" because in biblical idiom the commander of an army
is said to "go out and come in" before it, that is, lead it in battle.
   a pillar of cloud . . . a pillar of fire. This spectacular panoramic picture of
the Israelite throngs following these miraculous guides through the wilderness
nicely counterpoints the plagues that preceded. Several of the plagues
involved destruction descending from the sky. Here a great mass of cloud
descends from the sky to lead Israel. The penultimate plague plunged Egypt
into terrifying darkness, and now a column of divine fire serves as a huge bea-
con to show Israel the way through the dark of the wilderness.

CHAPTER 14

1,2   nd the Lᴏʀᴅ spoke to Moses, saying, "Speak to the Israelites, that
         they turn back and encamp before Pi-Hahiroth between Migdol
         and the sea, before Baal-Zephon, opposite it you shall camp, by
3   the sea. And Pharaoh had said of the Israelites,

> 'They are confounded in the land,
> The wilderness has closed round them.'

---

2. *They are confounded in the land / The wilderness has closed round them.* Since
God has just given the most precise instructions as to where the Israelites
should establish their camp, this quotation of what Pharaoh says when he
hears of the Israelites' movements is a strong indication that God has set up
what amounts in military terms to an ambush. Pharaoh, seeing that the
Hebrews have not followed the short and obvious coastal route to get out of
Egypt northward, concludes that they have lost their way ("they are confounded in the land") and have inadvertently allowed themselves to be pinned
down on the shore of the Sea of Reeds ("The wilderness has closed round
them"), where the pursuing troops will easily surround them and recapture the
whole mass of runaway slaves. Note that Pharaoh, in his regal confidence,
speaks in verse—two semantically complementary clauses with three nicely
scanning beats in each, *nevukhím hém ba'árets / sagár 'aleihém hamidbár.* What
the Egyptian leader can scarcely foresee is that the Hebrews will be able to
flee into the sea, which then will turn into a death trap for the pursuing Egyptian troops. The place-names stipulated in God's instructions to Moses have
not been identified, though it might be noted that they are all Hebrew names,
with the exception of Pi-Hahiroth, which appears to have an Egyptian prefix.

And I shall toughen Pharaoh's heart, and he will pursue them, that I 4
may gain glory through Pharaoh and through all his force, and the
Egyptians will know that I am the LORD." And thus they did do.

And it was told to the king of Egypt that the people had fled, and 5
Pharaoh and his servants had a change of heart about the people, and
they said, "What is this we have done, that we sent off Israel from our
service?" And he harnessed his chariot, and his troops he took with 6
him. And he took six hundred picked chariots, and all the chariots of 7
Egypt, and captains over it all. And the LORD toughened the heart of 8
Pharaoh king of Egypt, and he pursued the Israelites, the Israelites
going out with a high hand. And the Egyptians pursued them and over- 9

---

4. *that I may gain glory.* The Hebrew verb *'ikavdah*, as anyone reading the story
in the original would notice, plays on the same word *kaved*, "heavy," that has
been repeatedly used for the severity of the plagues, the hardness of Pharaoh's
heart, and the density of the Israelites' livestock.

5. *about the people.* It is noteworthy that through this section the Israelites are
several times referred to simply as "the people," the perspective of the narrative, the audience, and of God having become thoroughly an Israelite national
perspective.
     from our service? Literally, "from serving us." The multivalent "send" is now
given its explicit legal sense of manumission.

6. *his troops.* The literal meaning of *'amo* is "his people," but *'am* in military
contexts regularly refers to troops, and Pharaoh clearly has not taken the entire
people with him, only his army.

7. *and all the chariots of Egypt.* That is, Pharaoh took not only the elite chari-
otry, but in fact the entire Egyptian chariot corps.
     captains. The Hebrew *shalishim* has never been definitively explained. It
appears to be derived from *sheloshah*, "three," and may refer to the division of
the army into command units of three and thirty (compare 2 Samuel 23:9–23).
Some have conjectured that the *shalish* would be the third man or commander
in a war chariot, but Egyptian chariots appear to have had crews of only two
men. A few scholars have suggested a Ugaritic cognate meaning "bronze," as in
bronze armor, the term by metonymy referring to a warrior or officer.

8. *with a high hand.* Nahum Sarna proposes that the idiom is drawn from
depictions of ancient Near Eastern gods brandishing a weapon in the upraised

took them encamped by the sea—all the horses of Pharaoh's chariots
10 and his riders and his force—at Pi-Hahiroth before Baal-Zephon. And
Pharaoh drew near, and the Israelites raised their eyes and, look, Egypt
was advancing toward them, and they were very afraid, and the Israelites
11 cried out to the LORD. And they said to Moses, "Was it for lack of graves
in Egypt that you took us to die in the wilderness? What is this you have
12 done to us to bring us out of Egypt? Isn't this the thing we spoke to you
in Egypt, saying, 'Leave us alone, that we may serve Egypt, for it is bet-
13 ter for us to serve Egypt than for us to die in the wilderness'?" And
Moses said to the people, "Do not be afraid. Take your station and see
the LORD's deliverance that He will do for you today, for as you see the

---

right hand. The English "high-handed" has some kinship with the notion of
defiance conveyed by the Hebrew expression. "Hand" has figured centrally in
the entire Exodus narrative both in God's powerful hand against Egypt and
Moses's outstretched hand (or arm, the Hebrew *yad* often covering both)
unleashing the plagues, as here it will split the sea.

11. *Was it for lack of graves in Egypt.* After the initial complaints of the Israelites
against Moses, we have been given no information about their collective mental state. Now we see them as fearful and as recalcitrant as they were at the
beginning. This moment becomes the first of a whole series of "murmurings"
that will punctuate the Wilderness narrative.

What is this you have done to us . . . ? These words are a pointed echo of the
words of Pharaoh's courtiers, "What is this we have done?" (verse 5).

12. *Isn't this the thing we spoke to you in Egypt.* These words amount to delayed
narrative exposition since, before this revelation in the people's dialogue, there
was no report of their having said they would perish in the wilderness and so
should stay in slavery. Alternately, they may be inventing words that they never
said, but now imagine what they may never actually have said.

13. *Do not be afraid.* Moses has already proven himself an irascible figure, and
he will be quick to anger in subsequent episodes. Here, however, he recognizes that the complaint of the newly freed slaves stems from fear, and so he
reassures them.

for as you see the Egyptians today you shall not see them again for all time. The
defeat will be so crushing that Egypt will never again attain this zenith of
imperial power. This ringing statement is not the least of the exercises in grat-
ifying historical fantasy in the story. Egypt in fact continued to be an intermittent military threat to Israel throughout the First Commonwealth period.

Egyptians today, you shall not see them again for all time. The LORD 14
shall do battle for you, and you, you shall keep still."

And the LORD said to Moses, "Why do you cry out to me? Speak to the 15
Israelites, that they journey onward. As for you, raise your staff and 16
stretch out your hand over the sea and split it apart, that the Israelites
may come into the midst of the sea on dry land. As for me, look, I am 17
about to toughen the heart of the Egyptians, that they come after them,
and I shall gain glory through Pharaoh and through all his force,
through his chariots and through his riders. And the Egyptians shall 18
know that I am the LORD when I gain glory through Pharaoh, through
his chariots and through his riders. And the messenger of God that was 19
going before the camp of Israel moved and went behind them, and the
pillar of cloud moved from before them and stood behind them. And it 20
came between the camp of Egypt and the camp of Israel, and there was
the cloud and the dark, and it lit up the night, and they did not draw

---

15. *Why do you cry out to me?* This is a little puzzling because there has been
no report of Moses's crying out to the LORD. The least strained solution is that
of Abraham ibn Ezra, who argues that since Moses is the spokesman of the
people, if the people cry out, God can readily attribute the crying out to
Moses.

19. *the messenger of God that was going before the camp.* In the initial report of
the pillars of cloud and of fire, God Himself was going before the Israelite
camp. The introduction of an agent of the deity here is either an explanation
in the original narrative of what God's presence before the people actually
meant or an interpolation of later tradition in order to mitigate the
anthropomorphism.

20. *and it lit up the night.* This clause is ambiguous, especially because the
antecedent would have to be the pillar of cloud, which does not give off light.
Perhaps one might view these words as a telescoping of a temporal shift: the
Egyptians approach the Israelites, who are clearly in full view, in daylight, perhaps, one may infer, in the late afternoon. The pillar of cloud swings around
from Israelite front to rear in order to form a barrier between the Hebrews and
the Egyptians. As night falls, the pillar of cloud ("and there was the cloud") in
response to the gathering darkness ("and the dark") turns into fire ("and it lit
up the night").

21 near each other all night. And Moses stretched out his hand over the
sea, and the LORD led the sea with a mighty east wind all night, and He
22 made the sea dry ground, and the waters were split apart. And the
Israelites came into the sea on dry land, the waters a wall to them on
23 their right and on their left. And the Egyptians pursued and came after
them, all Pharaoh's horses, his chariots, and his riders, into the sea.
24 And it happened in the morning watch that the LORD looked out over
the camp of Egypt in a pillar of fire and cloud and He panicked the

---

21. *wind . . . sea dry ground*. The key terms here hark back to the first creation
(God's breath-spirit-wind, *ruaḥ*; the dividing between sea and dry land). His
power over the physical elements of the world He created is again manifested,
this time in a defining event in the theater of history.

  split apart. Not merely "divided," for the Hebrew verb *baqaʿ* is a violent one,
the word that would be used for splitting wood with an axe.

22. *the waters a wall to them on their right and on their left*. Ilana Pardes persuasively identifies birth imagery in this whole story. The passage through
waters—led by a man who has been saved from water, after a genocidal decree
in which water was to be the means of killing the babies—is the beginning of
the birth of the nation, and Pardes aptly sees the large narrative from Exodus
to Numbers as the "biography of a nation."

24. *in the morning watch*. By Israelite reckoning, the last third of the night,
from 2:00 A.M. to 6:00 A.M. The Hebrews, then, would have marched through
the Sea of Reeds during the night, literally plunging into the dark, for the pillar of fire would have been behind them rather than leading them on their way.

  the LORD looked out. The Hebrew verb *hishqif* is generally reserved for looking down or out from a high vantage point.

  in a pillar of fire and cloud. The double identification is presumably because
of the moment of transition toward daybreak when the fire becomes cloud.
The narrative sequence at this point is not entirely clear, but it might be sorted
out as follows: during the night, the Israelites make their way across the sea,
with the protective pillar of fire following after them. The Egyptians, seeing
their movement, which would be joined with the receding pillar of fire, begin
pursuit. As day breaks, God looks down on them from the pillar of fire just as
it turns back into a pillar of cloud. As the water begins to seep back, the Egyptians turn round and flee.

camp of Egypt. And He took off the wheels of their chariots and drove 25
them heavily, and Egypt said, "Let me flee before Israel, for the LORD
does battle for them against Egypt." And the LORD said to Moses, 26
"Stretch out your hand over the sea, that the waters go back over the
Egyptians, over their chariots and over their riders." And Moses 27
stretched out his hand over the sea, and the sea went back toward
morning to its full flow, with the Egyptians fleeing toward it, and the
LORD shook out the Egyptians into the sea. And the waters came back 28

---

25. *He took off the wheels of their chariots.* There is some dispute about the
sense of the verb, which usually means to "take away," "take off," "remove."
The simplest explanation is that as the water begins to seep back and before
it becomes a flood that engulfs the Egyptians, it turns the dry ground into
muck. The chariot wheels rapidly become stuck in the mud ("He . . . drove
them heavily") and break off from the axles. In all this tale of the utter destruction of the Egyptian chariots, there is a kind of allaying of a recurrent Israelite
fear. From a number of references in the Book of Judges, we can infer that the
highland-based Hebrews were poorly equipped with chariots and vulnerable,
at least when they fought on level terrain, to the chariots of the Canaanites,
which would have been a rough ancient equivalent of armored corps in a modern army. The heavy chariots must have often appeared terrifying to the lightly
armed Israelites. In the story of the victory at the Sea of Reeds, the mighty
Egyptian chariot corps is rendered helpless, and this particular aspect of the
Egyptian defeat is made a focal point of the narrative.

27. *the Egyptians fleeing toward it.* The Hebrew preposition used here clearly
means "toward." What is suggested is the following sequence: the Egyptian
troops are struck with panic, perhaps at the sight of the pillar of cloud and fire,
surely by the fact that their chariots have lost traction on what had briefly been
dry land in the sea; they flee, presumably in the direction from which they had
come, but the flood of water comes down on them from that very direction.
The male warriors of the nation that had sought to drown every Hebrew male
child now meet a fate of death by drowning.

and covered the chariots and the riders of all Pharaoh's force who were

29 coming after them in the sea, not a single one of them remained. And the Israelites went on dry land in the midst of the sea, the waters a wall

30 to them on their right and on their left. And the LORD on that day delivered Israel from the hand of Egypt, and Israel saw Egypt dead on the

31 shore of the sea, and Israel saw the great hand that the LORD had performed against Egypt, and the people feared the LORD, and they trusted in the LORD and in Moses His servant.

---

29. *the waters a wall to them.* This key phrase serves as a formal refrain, and will be picked up in the Song of the Sea.

31. *the great hand.* "Hand" here obviously means something like "demonstration of power," but it picks up all the previous uses of "hand," both literal and figurative, in this story of liberation from bondage.

they trusted in the LORD and in Moses His servant. The whole story had begun with Moses's understandable doubt as to whether the people would trust, or believe, him. Now all doubt is banished (for the moment) in the great triumph at the Sea of Reeds.

CHAPTER 15

Then did Moses sing, and all the Israelites with him, this song to the 1
Lord, and they said, saying:

"Let me sing unto the Lord for He surged, O surged—
horse and its rider He hurled into the sea.

---

1. *Then did Moses sing.* The conclusion of many large narrative units in the Bible is marked with a relatively long poem (*shirah*). After the destruction of Pharaoh's army, the Egyptian phase of the Exodus story is completed, and the sequence of Wilderness tales (the very first is the Marah story, verses 22–26) that is the narrative skeleton of the rest of the Torah begins.

Let me sing unto the Lord. This poetic beginning reflects an ancient Near Eastern literary convention of announcing the topic and the act of song at the beginning of the poem, roughly parallel to the Greek and Latin convention for beginning an epic (as in Virgil's "Of arms and the man I sing").

for He surged, O surged. The poem begins with a vivid pun. The Hebrew verb *ga'ah* means something like "to triumph," "to be exalted," "to be proud," but it is also the verb used for the rising tide of the sea, a concrete image that is especially apt for representing God's overwhelming the Egyptians with the waters of the Sea of Reeds.

horse and its rider. Perhaps, as many scholars have argued, rider (*rokhev*) should be translated as "driver" because chariots are stressed, and the evidence appears to indicate that in the late second millennium B.C.E. the Egyptians did not make much use of cavalry. Nevertheless, the plain meaning of the Hebrew word is "rider," and only with some strain can it be made to mean "chariot driver." Anachronism about such details is familiar enough in the Bible—witness the ubiquity of camels in Genesis in a historical period before they were generally domesticated.

2   My strength and my power is Yah,
     and He became my deliverance.
   This is my God—I extol Him
     God of my fathers—I exalt Him.

3   The LORD is a man of war,
     the LORD is His name.

4   Pharaoh's chariots and his force
     He pitched into the sea
   and the pick of his captains
     were drowned in the Reed Sea.

5   The depths did cover them over,
     down they went in the deep like a stone.

6   Your right hand, O LORD, is mighty in power.
     Your right hand, O LORD, smashes the enemy.

---

2. *power*. Scholarly consensus is that this is the most likely sense here of the Hebrew *zimrah*, but it is probably a pun on the more common meaning of the word "song"—God, Who is the source of the speaker's power, is for that very reason the theme of his song.

3. *The LORD is a man of war*. The representation of God as a fierce warrior is recurrent in biblical poetry and draws on a literary background of Ugaritic/Canaanite mythological poetry.

4. *He pitched into the sea*. The vivid hyperbolic image of God's "pitching" or "hurling" the Egyptian troops into the sea provides a hint to the representation in the preceding prose narrative (which is later in composition) of God's "shaking out" the Egyptians into the sea.

5–6. *down they went in the deep like a stone. / Your right hand . . . mighty in power*. The Song of the Sea is a rare instance in the Bible of a poem that has clearly marked strophic divisions, as Umberto Cassuto and others have noted. Near the end of each strophe one encounters the simile "like a stone" or "like lead." The simile is followed by lines that celebrate the LORD's triumphal supremacy. The first strophe (verses 1–6) offers a kind of summary version of the victory at the sea. The second strophe (verses 7–11) goes over the event in more concrete terms, providing some dialogue for the pursuing Egyptians as well as a more particular account of how God's breath or wind (the same word in the Hebrew) first heaped up the waters in a mound or wall and then sent

In Your great surging You wreck those against You,   7
    You send forth Your wrath, it consumes them like straw.
And with the breath of your nostrils waters heaped up,   8
    streams stood up like a mound,
        the depths congealed in the heart of the sea.
The enemy said: 9
    'I'll pursue, overtake, divide up the loot,
        my gullet will fill with them, I'll bare my sword, my hand
          despoil them.'
You blew with Your breath—the sea covered them over.   10
    They sank like lead in the mighty waters:

---

them back to engulf the Egyptians. The right hand smashing the enemy derives from the martial imagery used for representing battling deities in ancient Near Eastern poetry, but it also resonates with all the references to God's powerful hand in the preceding narrative.

7. *In Your great surging.* Or, "in Your great triumph." The use of the noun derived from the verb *ga'ah* aligns the beginning of the second strophe with the beginning of the first.

    it consumes them like straw. The straw simile might appear to conflict with the stone simile, but it is generated, almost formulaically, by the language of "wrath" and, in the next line, "breath of Your nostrils," because in Hebrew poetic idiom, wrath is represented as a kind of fiery emanation from the nostrils. The Hebrew *'af* thus means both "nose" and, by metonymy, "flaring anger."

8. *waters . . . streams . . . depths.* The Hebrew word for water is always plural. The various synonyms used by the poet for the depths or the bottom of the sea are all in the plural as well—possibly a poetic plural of intensification but in any case a form that imparts a sense of grandeur or epic sublimity.

11   Who is like You among the gods, O Lᴏʀᴅ,
         who is like You, mighty in holiness?
            Awesome in praise, worker of wonders.
12   You stretched out Your hand—
         earth swallowed them up.
13   You led forth in Your kindness
         this people that You redeemed.
            You guided them in Your strength to Your holy abode.

---

11. *Who is like You among the gods*. This line has inspired a good deal of rather nervous commentary. The most unapologetic way of explaining it is that in the early part of the first millennium B.C.E., or possibly even earlier, to which the composition of this poem may plausibly be assigned, Hebrew writers had no difficulty in conceding the existence of other deities, though always stipulating, as here, their absolute inferiority to the God of Israel.

Awesome in praise. The Hebrew uses a plural, "praises." The word may refer in a kind of ellipsis to the tremendous acts performed by God that make Him the object of praise.

12. *You stretched out Your hand— / earth swallowed them up*. The hand that smashes the foe here works like Moses's hand, signaling to the sea to engulf the Egyptians. Since it is the sea, not the land, that does the swallowing, there is probably a play on the secondary meaning of the Hebrew *'arets*, "underworld." But in a doubling of the pun, *'arets*, which also means "land," points forward to the prospect of the promised land to which the people will be brought that is the topic of this third strophe.

13. *You led forth . . . You guided*. The Hebrew exhibits a sequence of three phonetically overlapping verbs—*natita*, "You stretched out," *naḥita*, "You led forth," *neihalta*, "You guided." This sound pattern helps to effect the temporal and spatial transition as the beginning of the third strophe moves from the Sea of Reeds to Canaan and, in the space of a single line, from this event in the thirteenth century B.C.E. to the establishment of God's temple on Mount Zion in the tenth century.

Peoples heard, they quaked,   14
   trembling seized Philistia's dwellers.
Then were the chieftains of Edom dismayed,   15
    the dukes of Moab, shuddering seized them,
     all the dwellers of Canaan quailed.
Terror and fear did fall upon them,   16
    as Your arm loomed big they were like a stone.
Till Your people crossed over, O LORD,
    till the people you made Yours crossed over.

---

14. *Peoples heard, they quaked, / trembling seized Philistia's dwellers.* The national triumphalism of the whole Exodus story comes to a climax here as the victory at the Sea of Reeds is imagined to reverberate throughout the region, panicking the peoples of Canaan who will face a Hebrew invasion led by the unconquerable LORD of Israel. (These lines will be echoed in the speech of Rahab, the harlot of Jericho, in Joshua 2 as a kind of on-the-ground "confirmation" of the terrific impact in Canaan of the event at the Sea of Reeds.) The reference to Philistia is an anachronism because the Philistines did not arrive on the coastal strip of Canaan from the Aegean until about a century after the Exodus.

15. *quailed.* The literal meaning of the Hebrew verb is "melted."

16. *they were like a stone.* It is also possible to construe the verb to yield "they were still as a stone." However, the image of the Canaanites petrified with fear seems stronger, and plays against the (literal) "melting" of the previous line.
   Till Your people crossed over . . . / till the people You made Yours crossed over. The use of this sort of incremental repetition is particularly characteristic of the older strata of biblical poetry. (The Song of Deborah, which is older still than this poem, abounds in such patterns.) The Hebrew for "You made Yours," *qanita*, means "to acquire," "to purchase," and occasionally "to create." The liberation from Egyptian slavery is taken as the great historical demonstration that God has adopted Israel as His special people.

17   You'll bring them, you'll plant them, on the mount of Your estate,
          a firm place for Your dwelling You wrought, O Lord,
             the sanctum, O Sovereign, Your hands firmly founded.

18   The Lord shall be king for all time!"

19   For Pharaoh had come with his chariots and his riders into the sea, and
      the Lord turned the waters of the sea back upon them, but the

20   Israelites went on dry land in the midst of the sea. And Miriam the
      prophetess, Aaron's sister, took the timbrel in her hand, and all the

21   women went out after her with timbrels and dances. And Miriam sung
      out to them:

---

17. *a firm place for Your dwelling . . . / . . . Your hands firmly founded.* The
Hebrew noun *makhon* and the related verb *konen* are regularly associated in
biblical idiom with the solid establishment of a throne or dynasty. Since a
mountain is also referred to here, and a sanctum, *miqdash*, is mentioned at the
end of the verse, it is highly likely that what the poet has in mind is the temple on Mount Zion, which is imagined as God's earthly throne or dwelling
place.

18. *The Lord shall be king for all time!* Although some construe this line as a
kind of epilogue to the poem (it lacks the parallelistic structure of a complete
line of poetry), its celebration of God's supremacy corresponds to the endings
of the two previous strophes (verses 6 and 11). God's regal dominion is confirmed both by the victory over the Egyptians and the establishing of a terrestrial throne in Jerusalem.

20. *And Miriam the prophetess, Aaron's sister, took the timbrel in her hand.* One
surmises that she is called "prophetess" (*nevi'ah*) because the singing and
dancing are an ecstatic activity, and one of the established meanings of the
Hebrew term for "prophet" is an ecstatic who typically employed dance and
musical instruments to induce the prophetic frenzy. Miriam is designated as
Aaron's sister in accordance with a practice of identifying a woman in relation
to her oldest brother. The custom of women's going out in song and dance to
celebrate a military victory was common in ancient Israel and the surrounding
peoples and figures significantly in the David story. The women here sing out
the opening lines of the song we have just heard as a kind of antiphonal
refrain. Everett Fox notes that Miriam is a witness by the water both at the
beginning of the Moses story and now.

"Sing to the LORD for He has surged, O surged,
Horse and its rider He hurled into the sea!"

And Moses made the Israelites journey onward from the Sea of Reeds,   22
and they went out to the Wilderness of Shur, and they went three days
in the wilderness and did not find water. And they came to Marah and   23
could not drink water from Marah, for it was bitter. Therefore is its
name called Marah. And the people murmured against Moses, saying,   24
"What shall we drink?" And he cried out to the LORD, and the LORD   25
showed him a tree, and he flung it into the water, and the water turned
sweet. There did He set him a statute and law, and there did He test

---

22. *the Wilderness of Shur.* The name means "wall" in Hebrew and evidently
refers to a fortified region on the northern border of Egypt. (The Egyptian
Hagar flees toward this region, Genesis 16:7.)

23. *Marah.* The name means "bitter," as the story goes on to explain.
    could not drink water from Marah. The desperate need for water in the
desert, which is a recurrent feature of the stories that follow, is of course a
realistic aspect of the Wilderness narrative. At the same time, it links the tribu-
lations of the Hebrews in the wilderness with the Plagues narrative. Here
there is an explicit echo of the first plague when the Egyptians "could not
drink water from the Nile." Moses, who as an infant was "drawn from the
water," and who has just led the people between walls of water, is now called
upon to provide them water to drink in the wilderness.

25. *There did He set him a statute and law, and there did He test him.* Nearly
everything about this gnomic sentence is uncertain. Since the only plausible
candidate for setting statutes and laws is God, He would logically be the subject of the verb in the parallel clause, though some have claimed it could be
Moses. "Him" might be Moses or a collective reference to Israel. The meaning of "statute and law" is obscure because, at least in this episode, no legislation is stipulated. The phrase might merely refer to the idea that it became a
set practice in the wilderness that, as in this incident, Israel's urgent needs
would be filled by God, if only Israel trusted in Him. The "testing," then,
would be the testing of Moses's, or Israel's, trust in God's power to provide for
the people's needs, though that is far from clear. In the famous parallel incident in Numbers 20, Moses will fail the test by angrily striking the rock in
order to bring forth water.

26   him. And He said, "If you really heed the voice of the LORD your God,
      and do what is right in His eyes, and hearken to His commands and
      keep all His statutes, all the sickness that I put upon Egypt I will not
      put upon you, for I am the LORD your healer."

27   And they came to Elim where there were twelve springs of water and
      seventy date palms, and they encamped there by the water.

---

26. *If you really heed . . . and do what is right in His eyes.* The language sounds
like Deuteronomy, but William H. C. Propp is prudent in calling this "quasi-
Deuteronomic diction," and associating it with the Wisdom overtones of the
episode. Wisdom literature, as he goes on to observe, is much concerned with
medicine. Here, God concludes by promising He will shield Israel from all the
sicknesses that visited the Egyptians. The allusion to the first plague at the
beginning of the episode associatively points to the others.

27. *twelve springs of water and seventy date palms.* After the scary incident at
Marah, in which it seemed there was only brackish water, the next stage of the
journey is more encouraging, for the Israelites arrive at a real oasis, with an
abundance of springs and fruit-bearing trees. Twelve and seventy are, of
course, formulaic numbers, perhaps here particularly echoing the twelve tribes
and the seventy elders of Israel.

CHAPTER 16

nd they journeyed onward from Elim, and all the community of   1
Israelites came to the Wilderness of Sin, which is between Elim
and Sinai, on the fifteenth day of the second month of their going
out from Egypt. And all the community of Israelites murmured against   2
Moses and against Aaron in the wilderness. And the Israelites said to   3
them, "Would that we had died by the LORD's hand in the land of Egypt
when we sat by the fleshpots, when we ate our fill of bread, for you
have brought us out to this wilderness to bring death by famine on all

---

2. *murmured*. The Hebrew verb *wayilonu* is distinctive of the Wilderness narrative. The various contexts in which it occurs suggest it means something like "complain" (its meaning in modern Hebrew) or "express resentment." Some modern translations opt for "grumble," which may be too low as diction, and there is no good reason to relinquish the time-honored "murmur."

3. *Would that we had died by the LORD's hand in . . . Egypt*. In the admirable efficiency of the dialogue, their formulation suggests that the LORD is about to kill them in the wilderness, so He might as well have done the job back in Egypt, where at least they would have died on a full stomach.

fleshpots. The Hebrew indicates something like a cauldron in which meat is cooked, but the King James Version's rendering of "fleshpots" ("flesh" of course meaning "meat" in seventeenth-century English) has become proverbial in the language and deserves to be retained.

when we ate our fill of bread. Bread and meat here are the two staples. God will provide both—quail in the evening and manna in the morning. By this point, in the second month of the departure from Egypt, the supply of unleavened bread that the Israelites brought with them in their precipitous flight might well have been exhausted. Commentators have puzzled over the nostalgia for meat because the Israelites have taken large flocks with them. Perhaps, as a people whose principal wealth is their flocks, they are loath to make heavy

4 this assembly." And the LORD said to Moses, "Look, I am about to rain down bread for you from the heavens, and the people shall go out and gather each day's share on that day, so that I may test them whether 5 they will go by My teaching or not. And it will happen, on the sixth day, that they will prepare what they bring in, and it will be double what 6 they gather each day." And Moses, and Aaron with him, said to the Israelites, "At evening, you shall know that it was the LORD Who 7 brought you out of the land of Egypt. And in the morning you shall see the LORD's glory as He hears your murmurings against the LORD, and

---

inroads into their livestock for the purpose of food on the journey. In any case, there seems to be a note of panic in the claim that they are on the point of death from starvation. That note would be plausible for a population of newly freed slaves who had been accustomed to having all meals provided by their masters and who now find themselves in the arid moonscape of the Sinai Desert.

4. *I am about to rain down*. This promise of divine benefaction may have a double edge because previous uses of this verb, *mamtir*, have been associated with God's showering destruction on humanity—in the Flood story, the Sodom story, and in the Plagues narrative.

    so that I may test them. The most plausible construction of this phrase is the one proposed by Rashi—that Israel will have to observe the restrictions regarding leaving over manna for the next day and not attempting to gather it on the Sabbath. The underlying conception of the deity in ancient Israel, beginning with the Garden story, is of a God who offers humankind a great abundance of gifts but always stipulates restrictions to be observed in their enjoyment.

6. *it was the LORD Who brought you out*. The people in their murmuring had directed their complaint against Moses and Aaron, saying it was the two brothers who brought them out from the land of Egypt (verse 2), while in the same breath accusing God of intending to kill them all. Now, the miraculous provision of meat at evening will make it clear to the people that all these events are directed by God.

7. *in the morning you shall see the LORD's glory*. There has been some puzzlement among interpreters about the evening and morning clauses and what actually is referred to in the latter. The evening-morning sequence may be a reminiscence of the first Creation story: in both, an omnipotent God providentially conducts the progress of events, though here, in contrast to the poised

as for us, what are we that you should murmur against us?" And Moses   8
said, "When the Lord gives you meat in the evening to eat and your fill
of bread in the morning, when the Lord hears your murmurings that
you murmur against him—and what are we?—not against us are your
murmurings but against the Lord." And Moses said to Aaron, "Say to   9
all the community of Israelites, 'Draw near before the Lord, for He has
heard your murmurings.'" And it happened as Aaron was speaking to all   10
the community of Israelites, that they turned toward the wilderness,
and, look, the Lord's glory appeared in the cloud. And the Lord said   11
to Moses, saying, "I have heard the murmurings of the Israelites. Speak   12
to them, saying 'At twilight you shall eat meat and in the morning you
shall have your fill of bread, and you shall know that I am the Lord
your God.'" And it happened in the evening that the quail came up and   13
covered the camp, and in the morning there was a layer of dew

---

harmony of the Creation story, there is palpable tension between the celestial
and the terrestrial realms. Seeing the Lord's glory may well be a threat as well
as a promise because the manifestation of God's numinous presence in the pillar of cloud (verse 10) might easily be rather terrifying to the people.

8. *and what are we?—not against us are your murmurings.* The Hebrew syntax,
which is reproduced in this translation, has a jagged and discontinuous look,
and may be intended, as Benno Jacob suggests, to mimic Moses's sense of per-
turbation in responding to the people's accusation directed at him and Aaron.

9. *Draw near before the Lord.* Since the preposition used here implies "presence," the location indicated is most probably the cloud that will be mentioned in verse 11 which is invested with God's glory.

12. *I have heard the murmurings of the Israelites.* This statement cuts two ways:
"to hear" in biblical idiom can mean "to heed" (i.e., "to obey"), but God may at
the same time be expressing annoyance with the people, for He has heard
their unreasonable complaint and their accusation that all along He meant to
destroy them.

13. *quail.* As with the plagues, generations of commentators have exerted considerable effort to explain all these events in naturalistic terms. Large flocks of
migratory quail, it is contended, are sometimes found in the Sinai, and the
manna is identified as a sugarlike secretion of desert aphids. One may concede

14 around the camp. And the layer of dew lifted, and, look, on the surface
15 of the wilderness—stuff fine, flaky, fine as frost on the ground. And the
Israelites saw, and they said to each other, *"Man hu,* What is it?" For
they did not know what it was. And Moses said to them, "It is the bread
16 that the LORD has given you as food. This is the thing that the LORD
charged: 'Gather from it each man according to what he must eat, an
omer to a head, the number of persons among you, each man for those
17 in his tent you shall take.'" And the Israelites did thus, and they gathered, some more and some less.

18 And they measured it by the *omer,* he who took more had no extra and
he who took less had no lack, each according to what he must eat did
19 they gather. And Moses said to them, "Let no man leave over from it
20 till morning." But they did not heed Moses, and some men left over
from it till morning, and it bred worms and stank, and Moses was furi-

---

that some kernels of actual memories of improvised sustenance during the
Wilderness wanderings might be preserved in these stories, but the point that
the narrative makes is to convert them into miraculous occurrences. No migration of quail, after all, would repeat itself every evening, and no edible gran-
ules secreted by aphids would mysteriously cease every seventh day.

14. *flaky.* The Hebrew *meḥuspas* is in dispute (in later Hebrew it means
"rough"). Umberto Cassuto links it to the root *ḥ-s-f* "to lay bare," and to a
Ugaritic cognate and proposes that it means "revealed."

15. Man hu, *What is it?* The scholarly consensus is that this is still another
instance of folk etymology. The general assumption is that there was a non-
Hebrew term, *man,* for this particular food-substance, perhaps related to an
Arabic root that means "to feed." *Man,* in this bit of dialogue, is an archaic
form of *mah,* the Hebrew for "what."

16. *omer.* This dry measure would have been a bit more than two quarts.

20. *some men left over from it till morning, and it bred worms and stank.* The
refractory nature of the people—or perhaps one should say their anxiety and
their greed—is manifested even in their response to this bounty from God that
has come to answer their complaints. In this case, it turns out that the prohi-

ous at them. And they gathered it morning after morning every man 21
according to what he must eat, and when the sun grew hot, it melted.
And it happened on the sixth day, that they gathered a double portion 22
of bread, two *omers* for each, and all the chiefs of the community came
and told Moses. And he said to them, "That is what the LORD has spo- 23
ken. A day of rest, a holy sabbath to the LORD is tomorrow. What you
bake, bake, and what you cook, cook, and whatever is left over leave for
yourselves to be kept until morning." And they left it until morning as 24
Moses had charged, and it did not stink, and there were no worms in
it. And Moses said, "Eat it today, for today is a sabbath to the LORD, 25
today you will not find it in the field. Six days you shall gather it, and 26
on the seventh day, the sabbath, there will be none then." And it hap- 27
pened on the seventh day that some of the people went out to gather
and they found nothing. And the LORD said to Moses, "How long do 28
you refuse to keep My commands and My teachings? See, for the LORD 29
has given you the sabbath. Therefore does He give you on the sixth
day bread for two days. Sit each of you where he is, let no one go out
from his place on the seventh day." And the people ceased from 30

---

bition announced by Moses is actuated by a perfectly practical consideration:
the manna will not keep overnight (except, miraculously, on the sabbath).

26. *Six days you shall gather it, and on the seventh day, the sabbath*. The sabbath
—the word means "cessation time"—has not yet been enjoined in the Ten
Commandments, but it is assumed by the story (with the Creation story
behind it) to be part of the very structure of nature. Thus the double portion
of manna gathered on the sixth day is preserved through the seventh, and no
manna is to be found on the seventh day.

there will be none then. The literal meaning of the Hebrew is: "there will be
none in it."

28. *How long do you refuse*. "You" in the Hebrew is plural, so although God is
addressing Moses, He is levying his accusation against the people for whom
Moses serves as spokesman.

29. *where he is*. Literally, "under him," that is, in his place.

31   work on the seventh day. And the house of Israel called its name
manna, and it was like coriander seed, white, and its taste was like a
32   wafer in honey. And Moses said, "This is the thing that the LORD commanded: a full *omer* of it to be kept for your generations, so that they
may see the bread with which I fed you in the wilderness when I
33   brought you out of the land of Egypt." And Moses said to Aaron, "Take
one jar and put in it a full *omer* of manna and set it before the LORD to
34   be kept for your generations." As the LORD had charged Moses, Aaron
35   set it before the Covenant to be kept. And the Israelites ate manna forty
years until they came to settled land, the manna did they eat until they
36   came to the edge of the land of Canaan. And the *omer* is one-tenth of
an *ephah*.

----

31. *the house of Israel*. This locution (instead of "the people of Israel" or "the
children of Israel [Israelites]") is unusual. Cassuto proposes that it is meant to
indicate that the Israelite posterity of the original desert-wanderers preserved
this name of manna for the wilderness food.

32. *for your generations*. Here the translation of *dorot* as "ages" in several modern versions is a little misleading because the point is that the ʿ*omer* of manna
is to be kept in order to be seen by posterity. The miraculous, and surely unhistorical, character of the memorial device is patent, for the evanescent manna
is the last thing one could imagine to survive through the centuries, however
tightly sealed.

34. *before the Covenant*. This phrase is clearly an ellipsis for "before the Ark of
the Covenant." The problem is that the Ark of the Covenant, in which the two
tables of the Law are kept, does not yet exist. The injunction here, then, must
be read as an anticipation of the time when the Ark will be an established fact
and a sacrosanct cultic focus.

CHAPTER 17

Ａnd all the community of Israelites journeyed onward from the 1
Wilderness of Sin on their journeyings by the LORD's direction,
and they encamped at Rephidim, and there was no water for the
people to drink. And the people disputed with Moses and they said, 2
"Give us water, that we may drink." And Moses said to them,

> "Why do you dispute with me
> and why do you test the LORD?"

---

1. *by the* LORD's *direction*. The literal sense of the Hebrew is "by the LORD's
mouth." God sets the itinerary, not Moses.

there was no water for the people to drink. In an alternating structure (A B
A), the sequence of three "murmuring" episodes exhibits respectively complaints about lack of water, lack of food, and again lack of water.

2. *disputed*. The Hebrew verb often appears in judicial contexts, where it
means to bring a legal complaint or disputation (the cognate noun *riv*). *Riv* is
the term used in verse 7 in the phrase translated as "the disputation of the
Israelites"; the name given the place there, Meribah, derives from the same
root and means something closer to "contention."

Give us water. The Masoretic Text shows a plural form of the verb, which
might suggest that Aaron is implicated with Moses in the complaint the people make. But several ancient manuscripts have a singular form for "give,"
which seems more plausible, since the people have "disputed" or quarreled
with Moses alone.

Why do you dispute with me / and why do you test the LORD? Moses gives
weight and solemnity to his words by casting his reply in a neatly scannable
line of parallelistic verse, as he does again in speaking to God a moment later.
As in the episode at Elim, he identifies the complaint against him (first verset)
as a complaint against God (second verset). Thus, the poetic parallelism

3 And the people thirsted for water there, and the people murmured against Moses and said, "Why is it you brought us up from Egypt to
4 bring death on me and my children and my livestock by thirst?" And Moses called out to the LORD, saying,

> "What shall I do with this people?
> Yet a little more and they will stone me."

5 And the LORD said to Moses, "Pass before the people and take with you some of Israel's elders, and the staff with which you struck the Nile take in your hand, and go.

---

becomes a vehicle for expressing the inseparability of Moses's leadership from God's.

3. *brought us up . . . to bring death on me and my children.* This sort of switch from first-person plural to first-person singular is good idiomatic usage in biblical Hebrew, especially in dialogue assigned to a collective entity. The switch allows the sharpness of the complaint to become more vivid as the prototypical individual speaker representing the people laments his own imminent death and that of his children.

4. *Yet a little more and they will stone me.* From the very beginning, at the burning bush, Moses had been doubtful that the people could trust him and accept his leadership. Now he feels something like desperate fear—that the people will actually kill him (an idea that Freud would understand as an accomplished fact).

5. *Pass before the people.* As both Rashi and Abraham ibn Ezra note, this might well be a direct response to Moses's expression of fear that the people will kill him: passing before the enraged people would be rather like running the gauntlet, and it is this that God compels him to do as the prelude to the demonstration of divine saving power.
    the staff with which you struck the Nile. This staff was recognized by the people as the instrument Moses used to unleash awesome destruction against Egypt. Now, as Rashi observes, they will see that it can also be an instrument of benefaction.

Look, I am about to stand before you there on the rock in Horeb, and   6
you shall strike the rock, and water will come out from it and the peo-
ple will drink." And thus did Moses do before the eyes of Israel's elders.
And he called the name of the place Massah and Meribah, Testing and   7
Dispute, for the disputation of the Israelites, and for their testing the
LORD, saying, "Is the LORD in our midst or not?"

And Amalek came and did battle with Israel at Rephidim. And Moses   8,9
said to Joshua, "Choose men for us and go out, battle against Amalek
tomorrow. I shall take my station on the hilltop, with the staff of God
in my hand." And Joshua did as Moses had said to him to battle against   10
Amalek, and Moses, Aaron and Hur had gone up to the hilltop. And so,   11
when Moses would raise his hand, Israel prevailed, and when he would

---

7. *Testing and Dispute . . . disputation . . . testing.* The arrangement of the terms
is neatly chiastic, just as the first pair of nouns here stand in a chiastic relation to the verbs "dispute" and "test" in verse 2. Ibn Ezra, who reads with the
eye of an accomplished poet as well as that of a philologist, firmly identifies
the pattern.

8. *And Amalek came and did battle with Israel.* Rashi comments astutely on the
sequence of episodes, the attack by a fierce enemy following upon the provision of water to the thirsty people: "You say, 'Is the LORD in our midst or not?'
By your life, the dog comes and bites you and you come and cry out to Me,
and you will know where I am."

9. *tomorrow.* The Masoretic cantillation marking places "tomorrow" at the
beginning of the next clause, which makes the adverb a modifier of when
Moses will take up his station, but it probably makes better sense as part of
the instruction to Joshua about when he will be fighting.

11. *when Moses would raise his hand.* This gesture neatly cuts two ways. It
could merely be the gesture of a general holding up a commander's baton or a
standard (compare the reference to a "banner" in verse 15) in order to encourage his troops to attack, or the hand holding the staff could be the conduit, as
in the earlier portents, for an influx of divine power. Throughout the passage,
the Hebrew noun *yad* characteristically slides between "hand" (verse 9) and
"arm" (probably here and surely in verse 12). It is worth retaining "hand" in all
instances to catch the sense of thematized repetition in the Hebrew: Umberto

12 put down his hand, Amalek prevailed. And Moses's hands grew heavy,
and they took a stone and put it beneath him and he sat upon it. And
Aaron and Hur supported his hands, one on each side, and it happened
13 that his hands were steady till the sun came down. And Joshua disabled
Amalek and its people by the edge of the sword.

14 And the Lord said to Moses, "Write this down as a remembrance in a
record, and put it in Joshua's hearing, that I will surely wipe out the

---

Cassuto, who has a certain fixation on the discovery of repeated terms exhibiting formulaic numbers, notes that *yad* recurs precisely seven times in this
episode.

12. *And Moses's hands grew heavy*. This could also be construed as "were heavy,"
i.e., they were heavy to begin with because Moses was an old man. The plural
suggests that he raised both hands simultaneously, the one with the staff and
the empty one, in a kind of spread-eagle gesture.

  his hands were steady. The Hebrew appears to use an abstract noun instead
of an adjective—conceivably, an emphatic form: "his hands were steadiness."

13. *disabled*. Several commentators have observed that the unusual verb here,
ḥalash (evidently derived from a root that means "weak") has a punning echo
in Deuteronomy 25:18, where the Israelite stragglers attacked by Amalek are
referred to as *neheshalim* (the same root with a reversal of the last two consonants). It should be noted that others, from Rashi to several twentieth-century
scholars, think that this odd verb means "to decapitate." In any case, this
image of a sword-wielding Hebrew commander cutting down the enemy is the
first representation of Israelites evincing martial prowess rather than watching
as God performs wonders and does battle for them.

14. *Write this down as a remembrance in a record*. In Genesis, with a certain
degree of historical verisimilitude, the patriarchs give no evidence of using
writing. Here it is assumed that writing is a primary mode of commemoration
in the culture. It must be said that literacy is an early phenomenon in ancient
Israel, though it is difficult to determine how far it might have extended, or
whether it extended, beyond a learned elite. (In Judges 8, Gideon appears to
assume that any lad he would encounter on the road would be capable of writing things down.) "Record" here reflects Hebrew *sefer*, which is used for anything cast in writing—a parchment or papyrus scroll that might contain
narrative, inventorial, or genealogical material; a letter; and also what we
would call a book.

name of Amalek from under the heavens." And Moses built an altar 15
and he called its name *YHWH Nissi,* the Lord is My Banner. And he 16
said, "For hand upon Yah's throne: War for the Lord against Amalek
from all time."

I will surely wipe out the name of Amalek. The noun *zekher,* though cognate
with "remembrance," *zikaron,* in the previous clause, here bears its usual
meaning of "name," as in 3:15. The written record will continue to memorial-
ize odious Amalek, but the nation will lose its "name," its posterity—an ultimate curse in the ancient Near East. In all this, as in the Plagues narrative,
history is transformed into symbolic typology. Ancient Israel was surrounded
by enemies—the Canaanite peoples with whom it fought for territory, mau-
rauders like the Midianites to the east and the Amalekites to the south, and
the great empires of Mesopotamia and Egypt. Historical survival required
nearly continual armed conflict. But distinctions are made among enemies,
and Amalek here becomes the very type of the ruthless foe that seeks to anni-
hilate Israel. (Hence much later, in the Book of Esther, Haman will be cast as
a descendant of the Amalekite king Agag.) This nation, then, becomes the
enemy of God Himself, Who pledges its utter destruction.

16. *For hand upon Yah's throne.* The hand is most likely an image of vow taking
in this obscure, and probably archaic, sentence. There has even been some
speculation that these words could be a quotation from the lost "Book of the
Battles of YHWH" mentioned elsewhere (see p. 790, as well as Numbers 21).
The meaning of *kes,* the word translated as "throne," has been widely disputed,
and the term has been sometimes emended. The interpretation that goes back
to Late Antiquity that it is a variant—archaic form?—of *kis'ei,* "throne," has
the attraction of not exhibiting excessive ingenuity, and the idea of God's taking a vow by placing His hand on the divine throne is plausible.

from all time. The Hebrew noticeably says "from," *mi,* and not *le,* "for." Perhaps the meaning is the same, though this formulation could suggest a kind of
mythic recess of ages, God warring against Amalek as far back as anyone can
conceive and until this foe is destroyed.

CHAPTER 18

1   And Jethro priest of Midian, Moses's father-in-law, heard all that
    God had done for Moses and for Israel His people, that the LORD
2   had brought Israel out of Egypt. And Jethro, Moses's father-in-
3   law, took Zipporah, Moses's wife, after her being sent away, and her two

---

1. *Jethro*. As Umberto Cassuto and others have noticed, this episode stands in
neat thematic antithesis to the preceding one. After a fierce armed struggle
with a hostile nation that Israel is enjoined to destroy, we have an encounter with
a representative of another people, Midian, that is marked by harmonious
understanding, mutual respect, and the giving of sage counsel. Cassuto points
out that this antithesis is underscored through thematic keywords: the
Amalek episode begins and ends with a repetition of "battle" (or "war"). The
Jethro episode begins with inquiries of "well-being" or "peace" (*shalom*) and
near the end, "this people will come to its place in peace." Moses "chooses"
men for war in the first episode and men for justice in the second. He sits on
a stone at the battle and then sits in judgment. His hands are "heavy" in the
battle scene and the judicial burden is "heavy" in the judgment scene. As for
Midian, the later biblical record shows them acting as marauders crossing the
Jordan to attack Israelite farms, but Jethro belongs to the Kenite clan of Midianites that had a particular relationship of loyal alliance with Israel.

2. *after her being sent away*. What this phrase refers to is uncertain. As we saw
repeatedly in the Exodus narrative, "send" (the verbal stem *sh-l-ḥ*) has multiple meanings. The verbal noun used here, *shiluḥim*, sometimes means
"divorce," but that is an unlikely scenario for Moses and Zipporah. The rare
use of the term as "marriage gift" makes even less sense in this context. The
most reasonable inference is that Moses, though he had started out for Egypt
with his wife and sons, at some point thought better of it and sent her and the
boys home to stay in safety with her father. *The Midrash HaGadol* (seventh
century) vividly dramatizes such a reading: When Aaron first comes out to the

sons, one of whom was named Gershom, for he said, "A sojourner I have been in a foreign land," and the other was named Eliezer, "For the ₄ God of my fathers was my aid and rescued me from Pharaoh's sword." And Jethro, Moses's father-in-law, and his sons and his wife with him, ₅ came to Moses, to the wilderness in which he was encamped, the mountain of God. And he said to Moses, "I, your father-in-law Jethro, ₆ am coming to you, and your wife and her two sons with her."

---

wilderness to meet Moses, he sees his brother's wife and sons and says: "'Where are you taking them?' He said to him, 'To Egypt.' He said to him, 'For the previous ones we are sorrow-stricken and now you are bringing us still others?' Immediately Moses said to her, 'Return to your father's house.'"

3. *Gershom.* In this poetic etymology, *ger*, "sojourner," is broken out from the rest of the name, which in fact appears to derive from the root *g-r-sh*, "to banish."

4. *was my aid and rescued me from Pharaoh's sword.* The name Eliezer means "my God is aid." The rescue from Pharaoh's sword probably refers, as Nahmanides proposes, to Moses's flight from Pharaoh's executioners after his killing of the Egyptian taskmaster. It could not refer to the victory at the Sea of Reeds because Eliezer had been born earlier, and it does not comfortably refer to the rescue of the infant Moses because swords were not involved in the decree of infanticide by drowning.

5. *the mountain of God.* There is a patent disruption of chronology here, as Abraham ibn Ezra and many others have noted, because in the immediately preceding episode the Israelites were at Rephidim, and it is only in the next chapter that they are reported to have arrived at Mount Sinai. This entire passage is thus a perfect illustration of the rabbinic dictum that "there is neither early nor late in the Torah," that is, that chronology may be violated in order to bring out certain thematic emphases (here, the antithesis between war/Amalek and peace/Jethro).

6. *And he said to Moses.* It is in the next verse that the two men meet, embrace, and inquire of each other's well-being. This has led Nahmanides and many others after him to infer that "said" here actually means something like "sent word."

7 And Moses went out to meet his father-in-law, and he bowed down and
    kissed him, and each of them asked of the other's well-being, and they
8 went into the tent. And Moses recounted to his father-in-law all that
    the LORD had done to Pharaoh and to Egypt for the sake of Israel, all
    the hardship that had come upon them on the way, and the LORD
9 had rescued them. And Jethro exulted over all the bounty that the LORD
    had done for Israel, that He had rescued them from the hand of Egypt.
10 And Jethro said, "Blessed is the LORD, Who has rescued you from the
    hand of Egypt and from the hand of Pharaoh, Who rescued the people
11 from under the hand of Egypt. Now I know that the LORD is greater
    than all the gods, for in this thing that they schemed against them—."
12 And Jethro, Moses's father-in-law, took a burnt offering and sacrifices
    for God, and Aaron came, and all the elders of Israel with him, to eat
    bread with Moses's father-in-law before God.

---

7. *and they went into the tent.* After Moses's respectful and affectionate public
greeting of his father-in-law, the two men withdraw to the privacy of Moses's
tent, where the leader of the Hebrews will give Jethro a full account of the
extraordinary events that occurred in Egypt and afterward.

11. *Now I know that the LORD is greater than all the gods.* Jethro's response to
Moses's narrative is a perfect confirmation of the reiterated theme in the Exodus story that the LORD's great acts against Egypt will demonstrate His
supremacy over all other imagined gods. Jethro, as a Midianite priest, appears
to speak here as a henotheist rather than a monotheist, conceding the reality
of other gods but affirming YHWH's unrivaled greatness.
    for in this thing that they schemed against them. These words are quite
obscure, and may well reflect a textual corruption. The chief problem is that
the syntax breaks off, and an expected clause to complete it appears to be
missing. The Targum Onkelos, in its explanatory Aramaic paraphrase, ingeniously proposes that "in this thing" refers to water—the Egyptians plotted to
destroy the Hebrews by drowning and they themselves were then drowned.

12. *to eat bread.* Here "bread" is clearly a synecdoche for food (as in the English expression, "to eat the king's bread"), since the ceremonial meal after a
sacrifice would have included meat saved from the *zevaḥim,* "sacrifices" (the
burnt offering, by contrast, would have been entirely consumed by fire on the
altar).

And it happened on the next day that Moses sat to judge the people, 13
and the people stood over Moses from the morning till the evening.
And Moses's father-in-law saw all that he was doing for the people, and 14
he said, "What is this thing that you are doing for the people? Why are
you sitting alone while all the people are poised over you from morning
till evening?" And Moses said to his father-in-law, "For the people come 15
to me to inquire of God. When they have some matter, it comes to me 16
and I judge between a man and his fellow and I make known God's
statutes and His teachings." And Moses's father-in-law said to him, 17
"The thing that you are doing is not good. You will surely wear yourself 18
out—both you and this people that is with you—for the thing is too
heavy for you, you will not be able to do it alone. Now, heed my voice— 19
I shall give you counsel, and may God be with you. Be you for the people over against God, and it shall be you who will bring the matters to
God. And you shall warn them concerning the statutes and the teach- 20
ings, and you shall make known to them the way in which they must
go and the deed which they must do. As for you, you shall search out 21
from all the people able, God-fearing men, truthful men, haters of

---

15. *to inquire of God*. Frequently, this is the phrase used for inquiry of an oracle, though here it obviously refers to obtaining a different sort of revelation of
recalcitrant truth—a judge's determination of what is right according to the
law.

18. *You will surely wear yourself out*. The literal meaning of the Hebrew verb is
"to wither"—an appropriate idiom in an agricultural society for exhaustion
from work as "burnout" is in a modern technological society.

19. *Be you for the people over against God, and it shall be you who will bring the
matters to God*. Jethro, a priest by profession, assumes that the ultimate source
of judicial insight for the chief justice is from God, and so Moses is to serve
as a kind of intercessor between the people and God.

21. *search out*. The Hebrew is literally "envision."
    able, God-fearing men, truthful men, haters of bribes. Quite similar language
for the recruitment of judges occurs in both Hittite and Egyptian documents
dating from the late second millennium B.C.E.

bribes, and you shall put over them chiefs of thousands, chiefs of hun-
22   dreds, chiefs of fifties, and chiefs of tens. And they shall judge the people at all times, and so, every great matter they shall bring to you, and
every small matter they themselves shall judge, and it will lighten from
23   upon you and they will bear it with you. If you will do this thing, God
will charge you and you will be able to stand, and also all this people
24   will come to its place in peace." And Moses heeded the voice of his
25   father-in-law, and did all that he had said. And Moses chose able men
from all Israel and he set them as heads over the people, chiefs of thou-
26   sands, chiefs of hundreds, chiefs of fifties, and chiefs of tens. And they
judged the people at all times. The hard matters they would bring to

---

put over them. That is, over the people as a whole.

chiefs of thousands. The Hebrew for "chief," *sar*, is usually a military term
("commander"), and this neat, numerically divided judicial organization has
the look of a military command structure. Scholars have noted that it is far better suited to the royal bureaucracy of the First Commonwealth period than to
the rough-and-ready conditions of nomadic life in the wilderness.

22. *every great matter*. Throughout, "matter" is the polyvalent Hebrew *davar*,
which means "word," "thing," "matter," "affair," "mission," and more. Cassuto
observes that *davar* in the singular occurs exactly ten times in this episode and
that it might be a kind of coded prelude to the immediately following episode
of the Ten Commandments, which in the Hebrew are called the Ten Words,
'*Aseret haDibrot*.

it will lighten . . . they will bear it. Both "it's" are supplied for purposes of
clarity in the translation. The language of course reflects the image of judicial
responsibility as a heavy burden.

23. *will come to its place in peace*. Evidently: will go home at the end of the day
in a state of well-being or mental contentment. But some have proposed that
the clause could refer to coming into the promised land.

26. *The hard matters*. The replacement of "great" by "hard" is a kind of explanatory gloss. Lest we think that "great" meant "important"—let us say, involving
large issues of wealth—this substitution informs us that it is the legal cases
that are difficult to resolve which would be given to Moses.

Moses, and every small matter they themselves would judge. And 27
Moses sent off his father-in-law, and he went away to his land.

---

27. *And Moses sent off his father-in-law.* The "sending off" is obviously a ceremonious and amicable leave-taking, though it is precisely the verb used
repeatedly in the Exodus narrative for what Pharaoh is implored to do for
Israel. The verb also neatly closes the episode in a ring structure, picking up
the "being sent away" of verse 2.

    he went away. The Hebrew uses an ethical dative, literally "he went him"
(as in "Go forth [go you] from your land," Genesis 12:1). Its effect seems to be
something like "away" or "on his way."

CHAPTER 19

O
n the third new moon of the Israelites' going out from Egypt, on
this day did they come to the Wilderness of Sinai. And they journeyed onward from Rephidim and they came to the Wilderness of
Sinai, and Israel camped there over against the mountain. And Moses
had gone up to God, and the LORD called out to him from the moun-

1. *On the third new moon . . . did they come.* Umberto Cassuto aptly observes
that instead of the usual "and it happened" (*wayehi*) that marks the beginning
of narrative units, this portentous moment—the pivotal one in the whole
Torah—begins abruptly (using the perfective instead of the expected imperfective verb form), "as though to notify us that here begins a theme that stands
alone, that is unique."

new moon. This is the common biblical meaning of *ḥodesh*, though it can
also mean "month," its usual meaning in later Hebrew. The fact that the
phrase in apposition, "on this day," refers to one particular day makes the sense
of "new moon" inevitable, and this is also the consensus of medieval Hebrew
commentators.

2. *And they journeyed onward from Rephidim.* After the stark statement of the
crucial narrative datum in the preceding verse that the Israelites had arrived
in the Wilderness of Sinai, we get a report that picks up the itinerary of wanderings, tracing the trajectory from the previous stage, Rephidim, to Sinai, and
now specifying that the place of encampment is not just the Wilderness of
Sinai but over against the mountain.

3. *And Moses had gone up to God.* The Hebrew, like this translation, has an
indication of pluperfect tense, suggesting that even as the people were pitching their tents opposite the mountain, Moses, who after his epiphany at the
burning bush knew this place as "the mountain of God," had made his way to
the heights to speak with God.

tain, saying, "Thus shall you say to the house of Jacob, and shall you tell
to the Israelites: 'You yourselves saw what I did to Egypt, and I bore you   4
on the wings of eagles and I brought you to Me. And now, if you will   5
truly heed My voice and keep My covenant, you will become for Me a
treasure among all the peoples, for Mine is all the earth. And as for you,   6
you will become for Me a kingdom of priests and a holy nation.' These
are the words that you shall speak to the Israelites."

Thus shall you say to the house of Jacob, and shall you tell to the Israelites. The
perfect poetic parallelism, both semantic and rhythmic, of this sentence signals the lofty, strongly cadenced language, akin to epic in its grandeur, of the
entire episode.

4. *I bore you on the wings of eagles.* Although no one has succeeded in squar-
ing this grand image with ornithological behavior, the soaring eagle's
supremacy among birds is meant to suggest the majestic divine power that
miraculously swept up the Hebrews and bore them off from the house of
bondage. The metaphorical implication is that the Hebrews themselves are
helpless fledglings, unable to fly on their own. (Compare Deuteronomy 32:11.)

5. *you will become for Me a treasure among all the peoples, for Mine is all the
earth.* "Treasure" (*segulah*), as Yitzhak Avishur has pointed out, is paired in a
Ugaritic document with "vassal" (Hebrew, *'eved*), and seems to be a term borrowed from the realm of precious objects for contexts of covenants: the faithful vassal becomes the cherished treasure of his sovereign. Because the LORD
is, as He declares here, sovereign of all the earth, it is His prerogative to privilege one people among the many as His special treasure.

6. *a kingdom of priests and a holy nation.* The implementation of the divine
promise that Israel will become God's treasure is conditional on Israel's
upholding the terms of the Covenant. In the covenantal passages in Genesis,
it was stipulated that Abraham's seed must do justice and righteousness. The
aspiration here is wound to a still higher pitch, envisaging an Israel that will
earn its special status before the deity by becoming a kingdom of priests and
a holy nation. Should this be construed as divine hyperbole? In any case, the
chasm between that ideal and the actual behavior of the people will continue
to preoccupy the biblical writers, through to the Prophets.

7 And Moses came and he called to the elders of the people, and he set
8 before them all these words that the LORD had charged him. And all the
people answered together and said, "Everything that the LORD has spoken we shall do." And Moses brought back the people's words to the
9 LORD. And the LORD said to Moses, "Look, I am about to come to you
in the utmost cloud, so that the people may hear as I speak to you, and
you as well they will trust for all time." And Moses told the people's
10 words to the LORD. And the LORD said to Moses, "Go to the people and
consecrate them today and tomorrow, and they shall wash their cloaks.
11 And they shall ready themselves for the third day, for on the third day
the LORD will come down before the eyes of all the people on Mount

---

7. *he set before them all these words.* Words (*devarim*) are imagined in biblical
Hebrew to be virtually palpable entities, which can be put before people,
which have powerful consequences from the moment they are spoken. It may
well be, as Cassuto proposes, that the highlighting of *devarim* in this episode
is a kind of prelude to the giving of the Ten Words that immediately follows.

8. *Moses brought back the people's words to the LORD.* Presumably, God would
have had no trouble hearing what the people said without Moses's help. This
formulation, however, stresses Moses's crucial role as intermediary in this
episode: God is up on the mountain, the people are down below, and Moses
shuttles up and down between the two. Herein lies a principal justification for
the recurrence of "go up" and "come down" as thematic keywords, a feature of
the chapter noted by Everett Fox.

9. *in the utmost cloud.* The Hebrew 'av he'anan brackets together two words
that mean the same thing and that elsewhere are paired in poetic parallelism.
The effect would seem to be a kind of epic intensification. (Compare 10:22,
"pitch dark," which similarly puts together two synonyms, *hoshekh 'afelah*.) It
should be noted that 'av means "cloud" and is not the same as 'aveh, "thick,"
as most translations have assumed.

10. *their cloaks.* The Hebrew *semalot* means "cloaks" or some sort of outer
wrap, and is not the general word for garments, *begadim*, though it may well
be a synecdoche for garments here. The choice of this term is probably dictated by the fact that it is *semalot* that the Hebrews borrow from their Egyptian neighbors as they flee. It thus makes particular sense that they are
enjoined now as part of the process of consecration to launder these cloaks
they took off the backs of Egyptian idolators.

Sinai. And you shall set bounds for the people all around, saying, 12
'Watch yourselves not to go up on the mountain or to touch its edge.
Whosoever touches the mountain is doomed to die. No hand shall 13
touch him, but He shall surely be stoned or be shot, whether beast or
man, he shall not live. When the ram's horn blasts long, they it is who
will go up the mountain.'" And Moses came down from the mountain 14
to the people, and he consecrated the people, and they washed their
cloaks. And he said to the people, "Ready yourselves for three days. Do 15
not go near a woman." And it happened on the third day as it turned 16
morning, that there was thunder and lightning and a heavy cloud on the
mountain and the sound of the ram's horn, very strong, and all the peo-

---

13. *No hand shall touch him.* Some construe the Hebrew masculine pronoun
bo as "it," referring to Mount Sinai, because the previous verse has pronounced a ban on touching even the edge of the mountain. The clear syntactical connection of this clause, however, as Abraham ibn Ezra sees, is with the
two clauses that follow: the transgressor is to be killed from a distance, by
stoning or arrows—perhaps because by violating this taboo he has set himself
irrevocably apart from the community.

they it is who will go up the mountain. The pronoun *hemah*, "they," is placed
in an emphatic position. The most plausible referent is Moses and Aaron, in
contradistinction to the rest of the people.

16. *there was thunder and lightning and a heavy cloud on the mountain and the
sound of the ram's horn.* It trivializes the grand solemnity and the epic sweep of
this narrative moment to "explain" it through the purported origins of YHWH
as a desert-storm god. In the Syro-Palestinian tradition of mythological poetry
upon which the Hebrew writer drew for his imagery, thunder and lightning
were the martial accoutrements of the sky god, as they are often in biblical
poetry. Literature being an essentially conservative and self-recapitulative
medium, a continuity of poetic tropes does not necessarily mean a continuity
of theology—the pagan epic apparatus of Milton's *Paradise Lost* is a central
case in point. The Sinai encounter is imagined as the decisive moment in
human history when the celestial and terrestrial realms are brought into
panoramic engagement, and as God comes down on the mountain, every sort
of natural fireworks is let loose, so that trembling seizes not only the people
but the mountain itself. The word for "lightning," *qolot*, is not the usual *ra'am*
but the word that generally means "voices" or "sounds," and so it is orchestrated with "the sound of the ram's horn" (*qol hashofar*) that reverberates so
strongly against the ground-base of the thunder. (The word for "ram's horn"

17 ple who were in the camp trembled. And Moses brought out the people toward God from the camp and they stationed themselves at the
18 bottom of the mountain. And Mount Sinai was all in smoke because
the Lord had come down on it in fire, and its smoke went up like the
19 smoke from a kiln, and the whole mountain trembled greatly. And the
sound of the ram's horn grew stronger and stronger. Moses would
20 speak, and God would answer him with voice. And the Lord came
down on Mount Sinai, to the mountaintop, and the Lord called Moses
21 to the mountaintop, and Moses went up. And the Lord said to Moses,
"Go down, warn the people, lest they break through to the Lord to see

---

here is different from *yovel*, the term used in verse 13, but there does not seem
to be any important difference in meaning.) It is something of a mystery as to
where this ram's horn comes from and who is blowing it. Since ram's horns
were used both in calls to arms and in coronation ceremonies, one may
assume this blast is of celestial origin, probably blown by a member of God's
angelic entourage, to announce the awe-inspiring descent of the King of all the
earth to deliver the Ten Words to His people.

19. *with voice.* The same multivalent Hebrew word *qol* has encouraged some
interpreters to render this as "in thunder." That translation may sound more
impressive, but it is unlikely for two reasons. *Qol* in the singular, as against
qolot in the plural, means "voice" or "sound," not "thunder." And the heart of
the whole story of the Sinai epiphany is that God addresses Moses with words
(*devarim*), not with *son et lumière*, which are merely the atmospheric prelude
to divine speech. The sense, then, of "Moses would speak, and God would
answer him with voice" is that Moses and God actually exchange speech on
the mountain, as a man would speak with his fellow man. This speech evidently is endowed with miraculous audibility, since it takes place against the
most intense background noise of thunder and the constantly mounting blast
of the ram's horn.

21. *Go down, warn the people, lest they break through.* God is repeating instructions that have already been carried out, a fact registered by Moses in his
response (verse 23: "You Yourself warned us . . ."). The point of the repetition
is to underscore the absolute inviolability of the boundary between the mountain where the deity is so awesomely manifested and the people, and to dramatize Moses's necessary role as intermediary going down to the people and
up to the mountaintop.

and many of them perish. And the priests, too, who come near to the 22
LORD, shall consecrate themselves, lest the LORD burst forth against
them." And Moses said to the LORD, "The people will not be able to 23
come up to Mount Sinai, for You Yourself warned us, saying, 'Set
bounds to the mountain and consecrate it.'" And the LORD said to him, 24
"Go down, and you shall come up, you and Aaron with you, and the
priests and the people shall not break through to go up to the LORD, lest
He burst forth against them." And Moses went down to the people and 25
said it to them.

---

perish. The literal sense of the Hebrew is "fall." The deity is imagined as setting up a sort of terrific force field that, when violated, "bursts forth"—the
same verb is used elsewhere as a response to violation of sancta—to destroy
the trespasser.

22. *And the priests.* This reference is a little puzzling because as yet there has
been no report of the establishment of a priestly caste. Perhaps the priesthood
was so fundamental to the constitution of the people for the later writer that
he assumed it must always have existed. Perhaps Moses already designated
priests from the tribe of Levi, for sacrifices were offered after the victory over
Amalek. Ibn Ezra solves the problem by identifying "priests" here with the
firstborn—a proposal that may have some historical merit, presupposing an
archaic period in which priestly functions were performed by the firstborn.
   who come near to the LORD. Even though their priestly role allows them to
approach the LORD by offering sacrifices to Him, in this overwhelming manifestation of God's presence, they are to consecrate themselves like the rest of
the people and remain within the boundary Moses has marked at the bottom
of the mountain.

25. *And Moses went down to the people and said it to them.* The object of "said"
("it") is supplied by the translation, which follows the decisive consensus of
traditional Hebrew commentators that assumes the content of the saying is
the warning about not crossing the boundary which God has just asked Moses
to convey to the people. Normally, the verb "to say" would be followed by
quoted speech, whereas the verb "to speak" (*diber*) does not typically require
quoted speech after it. Perhaps "to say" is used here for Moses in order to
avoid any overlap with God's speech-act in the very next verse: "And God
spoke (*wayedaber*) these words (*devarim*)." It should be kept in mind that the
chapter breaks are medieval, so the original text moved directly from Moses's
saying to God's speaking.

CHAPTER 20

[1,2] And God spoke all these words, saying: "I am the LORD your God Who brought you out of the land of Egypt, out of the house of [3,4] slaves. You shall have no other gods beside Me. You shall make you no carved likeness and no image of what is in the heavens above or what is on the earth below or what is in the waters beneath the earth.

---

1. *all these words*. The number ten is not stipulated, but the formulaic number ten, despite other ancient numerations of the commandments, exerted a powerful force. Jewish and Christian traditions have different ways of dividing the "words," here called *devarim* but in later Hebrew usage usually referred to as *dibrot* (singular, *diber*), which means something like "utterance" or perhaps even "inspired speech." The formulation of the ten injunctions is, in the most literal sense, lapidary—terse enough to be carved in stone. There is a good deal of plausibility, then, in the inference of some scholars that the wordier commandments here embody explanatory glosses on or elaborations of the original succinct formulations. Moshe Weinfeld proposes that the original version might have looked something like this:

1. I am the LORD your God; you shall have no other gods beside Me.
2. You shall make you no carved likeness.
3. You shall not take the name of the LORD your God in vain.
4. Remember the sabbath day to hallow it.
5. Honor your father and your mother.
6. You shall not murder.
7. You shall not commit adultery.
8. You shall not steal.
9. You shall not bear false witness against your fellow man.
10. You shall not covet.

The Hebrew, it should be said, is even more compact: commandments 6, 7, and 8, for example, are each only two words, three syllables. Other ancient

Near Eastern cultures customarily used tablets—as a rule, clay and not stone—for writing, whereas the Hebrews adopted the speedier and more efficient writing technology of ink on parchment or papyrus scrolls, which made detailed verbal elaboration easier. The Hebrews did, however, use stone tablets for monumental inscriptions, as a few recovered fragments indicate. The use of stone tablets (the medium will be mentioned later) is most probably dictated by the fact that these Ten Words amount to the text of a pact between God and Israel, and such covenantal texts were typically recorded on tablets of metal or stone.

But writing on stone is also an *archaic* medium of communication and as such lines up with the archaic cooking (fire-roasting) and the archaic baking (unleavened bread) earlier in the story.

2. *I am the* LORD. As we had occasion to note in earlier passages, this formal announcement of the identity of the sovereign whose authority underwrites what is to follow is a convention of ancient Near Eastern royal proclamations.

3. *You shall have no other gods.* Throughout the Ten Words the commands are cast in the second-person singular (elsewhere in Hebrew law, plurals or third-person singulars are often used): the commandments are addressed to each person in Israel.

beside Me. The literal meaning of the Hebrew is "upon my face." As Abraham ibn Ezra acutely observes, this same idiom, *'al peney*, is used in Genesis 11:28 in "Haran died in the lifetime of [*'al peney*] Terah his father." The sense here, then, may be something like this: I am eternally, and so you must have no other god alongside Me, instead of Me, infringing on My eternal presence that brooks no successors.

4. *the heavens above . . . the earth below . . . the waters beneath the earth.* These are the three realms of the biblical world-picture, each duly registered in the first Creation story. If the LORD in His initial proclamation announces himself as the God of history, "Who brought you out of the land of Egypt," here the language implies that He is equally the God of the cosmos, not limited to one of its realms (in contrast, for example, to Aton, elevated by Akhenaten over all other gods of Egypt but still a solar deity). In Canaanite mythology, as in the corresponding mythologies of other ancient peoples, different gods presided over the different realms of creation: Baal over the land, Yamm over the sea, Mot over the underworld. The invocation here of pagan pantheons argues strongly that the ban against fashioning images is a ban against cultic icons (verse 5, "You shall not bow to them . . .") and not, as some currents of later tradition concluded, a comprehensive prohibition of image-making.

5   You shall not bow to them and you shall not worship them, for I am the
    LORD your God, a jealous god, reckoning the crime of fathers with sons,
6   with the third generation and with the fourth, for My foes, and doing
    kindness to the thousandth generation for My friends and for those
7   who keep My commands. You shall not take the name of the LORD your
    God in vain, for the LORD will not acquit whosoever takes His name in

---

5. *a jealous god.* The Hebrew *qana'* can mean either "jealous" (including the
sexual sense) or "zealous," "ardent." The appearance of the term in connection
with God's banning all cultic rivals suggests that the leading edge of the word
here may in fact be jealousy. The revolutionary idea of a single God uniting all
the realms of creation may be a noble and philosophically bold idea, but it is
imagined in ancient Israel in powerfully anthropomorphic terms: God does not
tolerate rivals to the hearts of His people. The word "god" here is not capital-
ized because the Hebrew employs the generic term *'el*: this, the LORD is saying, is the kind of god I am, and you had better take that to heart.

   reckoning the crime of fathers with sons . . . for My foes. This troubling statement is explained by many Hebrew exegetes through reference to "my foes"
(or, "those who hate Me") at the end of the clause—it is often the way of the
world for sons to follow the path of their fathers, and as long as the offspring
of the original offenders qualify as God's foes, they will be subject to retribution. But the ancient view may well have been that God's mercy was manifest
in demanding retribution from only three or four generations while granting
kindness for a thousand generations. The word "foes" here is antithetically
paired with "for My friends," (or "those who love Me") in verse 6.

6. *doing kindness to.* This could also be rendered as "keeping faith with"—*ḥesed*
is an act of kindness and also the loyal performance of an obligation in an
alliance or treaty.

   the thousandth generation. The Hebrew *'alafim* would ordinarily mean
"thousands," but the parallel passage in Deuteronomy 7:9 plausibly glosses this
as a reference to generations, in parallel to the previous verse.

7. *take the name of the LORD your God in vain.* The Hebrew verb literally means
"bear" and indicates the taking of a vow or oath. The reference is to the use of
the potent divine name in adjuration and perhaps also in magical conjuration,
not to the mentioning of the name in casual speech. "In vain" has the sense of
"falsely."

vain. Remember the sabbath day to hallow it. Six days you shall work   8,9
and you shall do your tasks, but the seventh day is a sabbath to the   10
LORD your God. You shall do no task, you and your son and your daughter, your male slave and your slavegirl and your beast and your sojourner
who is within your gates. For six days did the LORD make the heavens   11
and the earth, the sea and all that is in it, and He rested on the seventh
day. Therefore did the LORD bless the sabbath day and hallow it.
Honor your father and your mother, so that your days may be long on   12
the soil that the LORD your God has given you. You shall not murder.   13

---

8. *Remember the sabbath day.* This sole ritual—or at least calendric—injunction among the Ten Commandments is a hinge that connects the two principal aspects of the deity already invoked: the God of creation and the God of
history. The observance of the sabbath is a commemoration or reenactment of
God's creation of the world, as verse 11 explains. At the same time, the liberation from labor, especially with the stipulation that one's male and female
slaves should equally be freed of labor on the seventh day, surely would have
brought to the mind of these newly freed slaves the blessings of freedom, of
cessation from labor. Jewish liturgy would pick up this clue by designating the
sabbath "a remembrance of the going out from Egypt."

9. *tasks.* In the Hebrew a collective noun in the singular.

12. *Honor your father and your mother.* This fifth commandment (according to
the numeration of Jewish tradition) effects a transition, as Nahmanides nicely
observes, from obligations vis-à-vis God to obligations vis-à-vis human beings,
beginning with the human pair through whom each of us comes into the
world. It is also the only commandment in which "no" or "not" (Hebrew *lo'*)
does not appear, though some have argued that prohibitions—e.g., not showing disrespect—are implicit. (In any event, the assumption of these Ten Words
is that the way to monotheistic loyalty and ethical behavior is paved with prohibitions, that human nature is fraught with impulses that must be resisted.)
It is hard to square the causal link between honoring parents and longevity
with empirical observation, and one probably has to regard this as part of the
traditional wisdom of the ancient Near East, the sort of hopeful moral calcu-
lus reflected in the Book of Proverbs.
    on the soil. The Hebrew *'adamah* could also mean "land" or "earth," but an
emphasis on soil (the same stuff of which the altar in verse 24 is fashioned)
sounds right for a people who will chiefly make their living from farming.

13. *You shall not murder.* Readers thoroughly conditioned by the King James

14,15,16   You shall not commit adultery. You shall not steal. You shall not bear false

17   witness against your fellow man. You shall not covet your fellow man's house. You shall not covet your fellow man's wife, or his male slave, or his slavegirl, or his ox, or his donkey, or anything that your fellow man has."

18   And all the people were seeing the thunder and the flashes and the sound of the ram's horn and the mountain in smoke, and the people

19   saw and they drew back and stood at a distance. And they said to Moses, "Speak you with us that we may hear, and let not God speak

20   with us lest we die." And Moses said to the people, "Do not fear, for in order to test you God has come and in order that His fear be upon you,

---

Version's "Thou shalt not kill" need to be reminded that the Hebrew verb *ratsah* clearly means "murder," not "kill," and so that ban is specifically on criminal acts of taking of life.

17. *You shall not covet.* The Hebrew verb *hamad* exhibits a range of meaning from "yearn for," "desire," even "lust after" (the usual sense in postbiblical Hebrew), to simply "want." But here, as in 34:24, it clearly suggests wanting to possess something that belongs to someone else, and so the King James Version rendering of "covet" still seems the best English equivalent. The attempted legislation of desire is problematic enough for Abraham ibn Ezra to devote what is almost a miniature essay to the subject in his commentary. His solution is along the following lines: Desire itself cannot be absolutely legislated but we all learn to condition ourselves as to what is realistic desire and what has to be confined to the realm of mere fantasy—for both moral and practical reasons. A peasant, ibn Ezra argues (perhaps a little too confidently), may be struck by the beauty of a princess, but knowing that she is inconceivably beyond his reach, " he will not covet her [or, lust after her] in his heart to go to bed with her."

18. *seeing the thunder and the flashes and the sound of the ram's horn.* Logically, of course, the objects of seeing would be only the lightning and the smoking mountain, but the writer presents the Sinai epiphany as one tremendous synesthetic experience that overwhelms the people while—the temporal force of the participial "seeing"—the Ten Words are enunciated. Just as *qolot*, "sounds" or "voices," is not the usual word for thunder, *lapidim*, " flashes," is not the usual designation for lightning but rather a term that generally means "torches," here conveying the visual immediacy of the lightning flashes.
   drew back. Literally "swayed," suggesting a motion of involuntary recoil.

so that you do not offend." And the people stood at a distance, and 21
Moses drew near the thick cloud where God was.

And the LORD said to Moses, "Thus shall you say to the Israelites: 'You 22
yourselves saw that from the heavens I spoke with you. You shall not 23
make with Me gods of silver and gods of gold, you shall not make them
for yourselves. An earthen altar shall you make for Me, and you shall 24
sacrifice upon it your burnt offerings and your communion sacrifices,
your sheep and your cattle. In every place that I make My name
invoked, I shall come to you and bless you. And should you make Me an 25
altar of stones, you shall not build them of hewn stones, for your sword

---

23. *with Me*. The preposition *'iti* appears to have approximately the same
meaning as *'al panai*, "beside Me," in the first commandment, and this prohibition of idol-making is a reiteration of the first of the Ten Words.
  make them. The accusative pronoun is merely implied in the Hebrew.

24. *An earthen altar*. These instructions have the effect of orienting the people
toward a temporal horizon when they will be planted on the soil (*'adamah*, the
material for building this altar). As Umberto Cassuto notes, this injunction
dissipates any sense the people might have that Sinai alone is God's dwelling
place and that the worship of the deity is a one-time event. The earthen material of the altar is also in stark antithesis to the silver and gold of the idols.
  In every place that I make My name invoked. As scholarship has abundantly
observed, the presumption here of a multiplicity of valid places for sacrifice
contrasts with the later insistence of Deuteronomy on a centralized cult "in
the place that I choose."

25. *your sword*. English translations from Tyndale in the early sixteenth century
to a spectrum of translations at the end of the twentieth century have rendered
this as "tool" because the context obviously requires an implement for hewing
stone. But the Hebrew *ḥerev* patently means "sword," here a kind of
metaphoric stand-in for "chisel," and pointedly used because of its association
with killing. Rashi succinctly catches the implication of the term: "The altar
was created to lengthen a man's days and iron was created to shorten a man's
days; it is not fit that the means of shortening should be brandished over the
means of lengthening."

26 you would brandish over it and profane it. And you shall not go up by steps upon My altar, that you may not expose your nakedness upon it.'"

---

26. *that you may not expose your nakedness.* The priests in fact wore linen breeches and so would not have had this problem, though this text probably antedates the introduction of trousers that the Priestly writers adopted. The prohibition, then, as Nahum Sarna notes, may envision a local altar where sacrifice is offered by laymen, who would have been wearing loose tunics without undergarments (like the dancing David in 2 Samuel 6). There is some evidence of ritual nudity in the ancient Near East, to which this injunction might be a response.

CHAPTER 21

And these are the laws that you shall set before them. Should you 1,2
buy a Hebrew slave, six years he shall serve and in the seventh he
shall go free, with no payment. If he came by himself, he shall go 3

---

1. *And these are the laws.* After the ten divine imperatives, couched in absolute terms and addressed to each Israelite in the second-person singular, we have a series of miscellaneous laws formulated casuistically (i.e., according to hypothetical case: "Should a man do X, . . ."). This collection of laws, which make up chapter 21 through chapter 23, is conventionally called the Book of the Covenant, in accordance with the phrase used in 24:7 ("And he [Moses] took the book of the covenant and read it in the hearing of the people"), though some scholars have questioned whether the text referred to that Moses reads to the people is really the same as this legal miscellany. It is probably one of the oldest collections of law in the Bible; it exhibits numerous parallels with (as well as divergences from) the Code of Hammurabi, with sundry other Sumerian and Akkadian codes, and with Hittite law, all of which have been abundantly studied in the scholarly literature.

you shall set before them. The "you" (singular) is Moses.

2. *Should you buy a Hebrew slave.* Pointedly, the first laws in the group deal with the regulation of slavery, addressed in the narrative situation to an audience of newly freed slaves. That situation may dictate the somewhat unexpected designation, "Hebrew slave" (rather than "a slave from your people" or "a slave from your brothers") because that was the identity of the Israelites in the eyes of their Egyptian masters, "Hebrew" generally being a foreigner's label for an Israelite.

and in the seventh he shall go free. What is clearly involved is not chattel slavery but what amounts to a kind of indentured servitude. The Bible does not question this institution but sets certain limits on it, and, as one can see in the subsequent laws, the slave retains basic human rights.

3. *by himself.* The unusual Hebrew term, *begapo*, might mean, according to Umberto Cassuto, "the corner, or wing [of a garment]." If this is the case, it

out by himself. If he was husband to a wife, his wife shall go out with

4 him. If his master should give him a wife and she bears him sons or
daughters, the wife and her children shall be her master's, and he shall

5 go out by himself. And if the slave should solemnly say, "I love my mas-

6 ter, my wife, and my children; I will not go free," his master shall make
him approach the gods and make him approach the door or the doorpost, and his master shall pierce his ear with an awl, and he shall serve

---

would have the idiomatic force of "with the shirt on his back" (and nothing
else).

4. *the wife and her children shall be her master's.* The evident implication is that
the master gave this slavegirl to the male slave for breeding purposes, not for
sentimental reasons. The next verse, however, reflects a recognition that even
in such brutally economic circumstances the man may develop an emotional
attachment to the woman and to their children.

5. *if the slave should solemnly say.* The emphatic force here of the infinitive followed by the conjugated verb *'amor yo'mar* is to indicate a performative
speech-act, a binding public declaration.

6. *make him approach the gods and make him approach the door or the doorpost.*
The word translated here as "gods" (*'elohim*) is a famous crux. Though plural in
form, when it is treated grammatically as a singular it usually means "God."
When it is treated as a plural it usually means "gods," though occasionally it
appears to designate some sort of celestial beings who are less than God. In this
sequence one cannot tell whether it is singular or plural. Rabbinic tradition
sought to avert any possible scandal in the verse by interpreting *'elohim* as
"judges," but the philological evidence for that understanding is slim. The most
plausible proposal that has been made is that the reference is to household
gods: there are several ancient Near Eastern documents indicating that these
were placed by the doorposts, and that certain legal declarations regarding a
person's relation to the household were made in their presence, at the doorway.
This premonotheistic detail may reflect the very old age of the law, and the
repetitive phrase "and make him approach the door or doorpost" may well be a
somewhat later gloss intended to explain what "made him approach the *'elohim*" meant. It certainly makes more sense that the door in question should be
the door of the household to which the slave is perpetually committing himself
and not, as others have claimed, the door of a sanctuary or of a judicial court.
    pierce his ear with an awl. There is no consensus on the symbolism, though

him perpetually. And should a man sell his daughter as a slavegirl, 7
she shall not go free as the male slaves go free. If she seem bad in the 8
eyes of her master, for whom she was intended, he shall let her be
redeemed; to an outsider he shall have no power to sell her since he
has broken faith with her. And if for his son he intended her, accord- 9
ing to the practice of daughters he shall do for her. If another woman 10
he should take for himself, he must not stint for this one her meals,
her wardrobe, and her conjugal rights. And if he does not do these 11
three for her, she shall go free without payment, with no money.

---

it is not implausible that the ear might be thought of as the organ of obedience. Perhaps no symbolism is intended, and piercing the ear is a way of permanently marking the perpetual slave without serious mutilation, or perhaps
the pierced ear might have been used to wear a ring bearing the master's mark
or initial.

7. *And should a man sell his daughter as a slavegirl.* From what follows, it is
clear that the impoverished father is selling her not to perform labor, as is the
case of the male slave, but as some sort of concubine. It is for this reason that
the conditions of her manumission differ from those of the male slave.

8. *If she seem bad in the eyes of her master.* That is, if he finds anything about
her that disinclines him to keep her as a sexual partner.
　an outsider. The Hebrew *'am nokhri* (elsewhere, it would mean "a foreign
people") is probably an archaic social term—another reflection of the ancient
character of the document—with *'am* meaning "kin."
　broken faith with her. Literally, "betrayed her." He has not honored his commitment to keep her as concubine.

10. *meals.* The Hebrew uses a relatively rare term for "meat," clearly a synecdoche for food.
　wardrobe. Literally, "covering."
　conjugal rights. Although this translation reflects the strong consensus of
Hebrew commentators, the term *'onah* is much in dispute. Since the master
has rejected the woman as a bedmate, it does seem odd to require him to make
conjugal visits. Some have interpreted the term as "housing" by relating it to
ma'on, "habitation." Others, noting a husband's threefold obligation in other
ancient Near Eastern documents to provide his wife food, clothing, and oil or
unguents, propose that *'onah* refers to such cosmetic necessities, though the
philological grounds for that claim are uncertain.

12,13 He who strikes a man and he dies is doomed to die. And he who did
not plot it but God made it befall him, I shall set apart for you a place
14 to which he may flee. And should a man scheme against his fellow man
15 to kill him by cunning, from My altar you shall take him to die. And he
16 who strikes his father or his mother is doomed to die. And he who kid-
naps a man and sells him or he is found in his hands, is doomed to die.
17,18 And he who vilifies his father or his mother is doomed to die. And
should men quarrel and a man strike his fellow man with stone or with
19 fist and he does not die but falls ill, if he gets up and goes about outside

---

12. *He who strikes a man.* Cassuto notes a general structural parallel to the
Decalogue. The list of laws begins with regulations about slavery, just as the
first commandment begins by mentioning the liberation from slavery. The next
group of laws begins with murder, just as the second half of the Decalogue
does.

13. *I shall set apart for you a place to which he may flee.* The presupposition of
this institution of places of sanctuary for people who have committed involuntary manslaughter is vendetta justice: the members of the family bent on
"redeeming the blood" (*ge'ulat hadam*) of their dead kinsman, even if the
killing was unintended, would not be permitted to penetrate these towns of
refuge. Eventually, the state took over all functions of executing justice and
these provisions became anachronistic.

14. *from My altar you shall take him.* As in other cultures, the altar was a place
of sanctuary, and someone accused of bloodguilt could flee to the altar and
cling to one of the carved horns at its corners in a plea to be held free of harm.
This is what Joab does in 1 Kings 2 in an effort to escape Solomon's henchmen.
Solomon orders him to be taken from the altar and executed—perhaps in
accordance with this law, for Joab has killed two commanders of Israel in cold
blood.

17. *vilifies.* The Hebrew *qilel* is the precise antithesis of "honor" (*kabed*) in
"honor your father and your mother," the word for "honor" being derived from
a root that means "heavy" or "important" and the word for "vilify" or "treat with
contempt" (King James Version, "curse") being derived from a root that means
"light" or "worthless."

18. *falls ill.* Literally, "falls to bed."

on his cane, the striker shall be clear, only he shall pay for his loss of
time, and he shall surely stand good for his cure. And should a man   20
strike his male slave or his slavegirl with a rod and they die under his
hand, they shall surely be avenged. But if a day or two they should sur-   21
vive, they are not to be avenged for they are his money. And should men   22
brawl and collide with a pregnant woman and her fetus come out but
there be no other mishap, he shall surely be punished according to what
the woman's husband imposes upon him, he shall pay by the reckoning.

---

19. *he shall surely stand good for his cure.* Literally, "he shall surely cure him."

20. *they die . . . they shall surely be avenged.* The Hebrew says "he" in each
instance because the masculine form has grammatical precedence, referring
to him or her. Since both the female and the male slave are mentioned as possible objects of the violence, the translation, in order to avoid the awkward "he
or she," switches to the plural. The same procedure is followed in several subsequent verses.

21. *But if a day or two they should survive.* The sad implication of this stipulation is that vigorous beating of slaves, male and female alike, was assumed to
be an acceptable practice. If the slave lasted a couple of days and then died,
the inference would be that the master had not intended the death but had
merely overdone the beating. If the slave died on the spot, this would be evidence that the master had meant to kill him, or at least was guilty of voluntary
manslaughter.
   for they are his money. That is, it would be counter to the master's own interest to take the life of a slave after having purchased him to perform service, so
the presumption is that unless the slave dies during the beating, there was no
clear intention on the part of the master to kill him.

22. *and her fetus come out.* The Masoretic Text reads *weyats'u yeladeha,* "and
her children came out," which amounts to the same thing but seems a little
odd, especially because of the plural "children." The Samaritan text and the
Septuagint both have *weyatsa' weladah,* "and her fetus came out."
   no other mishap. The reference would have to be to the death, or at least
grave impairment, of the pregnant woman. "Other" is supplied in the translation for the sake of clarity.
   by the reckoning. The meaning of the Hebrew *biflilim* is uncertain. Some
interpreters link the terms to judicial authority. The Code of Hammurabi is
equally concerned about liability for induced miscarriages but, unlike this law,
makes discriminations according to the social standing of the injured party.

23,24 And if there is a mishap, you shall pay a life for a life, an eye for
25 an eye, a tooth for a tooth, a hand for a hand, a foot for a foot, a burn
26 for a burn, a wound for a wound, a bruise for a bruise. And should a
man strike the eye of his male slave or the eye of his slavegirl and ruin
27 it, he shall send them off free for their eye. And if he should knock out
the tooth of his male slave or the tooth of his slavegirl, he shall send
28 them off free for the tooth. And should an ox gore a man or a woman
and they die, the ox shall surely be stoned and its flesh shall not be

---

23–25. *a life for a life, an eye for an eye . . . a bruise for a bruise.* The pitiless punishment by equivalent injury of this famous *lex talionis*—again, with a parallel
in the Code of Hammurabi—has created much discomfort and elicited tracts
of commentary. It should be observed that the connection with the pregnant
woman injured by brawlers is highly tenuous: burning, or even the loss of tooth
or eye, in that situation seems far-fetched; and in any case, someone who has
committed involuntary manslaughter would not be subject to the death
penalty. The notion, therefore, that this is a fragment of an archaic law code
stitched into this text seems plausible. The preponderant view of Jewish commentators in Late Antiquity and the Middle Ages is that in each of the cases
stipulated here, the intention is for the liable party to pay monetary compensation for the loss incurred. The possibility should not be excluded that this
was the original intention: monetary compensation for such losses was a widespread practice in ancient Near Eastern codes, and as some of the medieval
commentators point out, it would have been unfeasible to implement the *lex
talionis* literally with equity (e.g., how does one punish someone who has
caused a man a partial loss of eyesight in one eye?).

26. *should a man strike the eye of his male slave.* There is an obvious associative
link with the "eye for an eye" of the previous unit. Here it is perfectly clear that
the loss of a bodily faculty is assigned monetary value.

28. *an ox.* The ox is the exemplary instance of liability for one's animals in
ancient Near Eastern law (and afterward in the Talmud).
    the ox shall surely be stoned. This punishment in effect falls on the owner,
who loses the whole value of his animal. But there is also a sense that the ox
itself has been tainted by destroying a human life and so it is killed, not slaughtered, as a murderer would be killed, and it is unfit to be eaten.

eaten, and the ox's owner is clear. And if the ox is a gorer from time past 29
and was warned against to his owner, who did not keep it in, and it
caused the death of a man or a woman, the ox shall be stoned and its
owner, too, shall be put to death. If restitution be set for him, he shall 30
pay for the redemption of his life whatever will be set for him. Whether 31
a son it gore or a daughter it gore, according to this practice it shall be
done to him. If the ox should gore a male slave or a slavegirl, thirty 32
shekels of silver he shall give to their master and the ox shall be stoned.
And should a man open a pit or should a man dig a pit and not cover it 33
and an ox or donkey fall in, the owner of the pit shall pay silver, shall 34
make good to its owner, and the carcass shall be his. And should a man's 35
ox collide with his fellow man's ox and it die, they shall sell the live ox
and divide the money for it equally, and the carcass, too, they shall
divide equally. Or if it is known that the ox is a gorer from time past and 36
its owner did not keep it in, he shall surely pay an ox for the ox, and the
carcass shall be his. Should a man steal an ox or a sheep and slaughter 37
it or sell it, five cattle he shall pay for the ox and four sheep for the
sheep.'"

---

the ox's owner is clear. He has no further liability in the death because this
is a case in which there was no precedent for the ox's action and hence, given
the usually pacific nature of oxen, the owner could not be expected to anticipate the goring.

29. *a gorer from time past.* In the case of an ox known to be habitually violent,
the owner's failure to keep it safely penned in is an act of criminal negligence
resulting in death.

30. *If restitution be set for him.* There remains a loophole of monetary compensation for the negligent owner of the goring ox because even criminal negligence is not the same as malicious intention to kill.

37. *Should a man steal an ox or a sheep.* We now move on from torts to laws of
theft. The reason for a distinction in penalty between ox and sheep has been
debated, but the simplest explanation is that the ox, a draft animal as well as
an animal that can be slaughtered for its meat, is more valuable than the
sheep.

CHAPTER 22

1 "If while tunneling, a thief should be found and is struck down and
2 dies, there is no bloodguilt for him. If the sun rises upon him, there
is bloodguilt for him. He shall surely pay. If he has not the means,
3 he shall be sold for his theft. If what is stolen should indeed be found
alive in his hands, from ox to donkey to sheep, he shall pay double.

4 "'Should a man let his beast graze in a field or vineyard, and he send his
beast to graze in another's field, from the best of his field and the best

---

1. *If while tunneling.* This form of housebreaking by tunneling into the house
is clearly imagined as a nocturnal operation (the tunneler would surely risk
detection outside the house in daylight). If such a thief encountered a resident
of the house in the dark, there would be considerable danger that the thief
would try to kill him. Hence Rashi cites the rabbinic dictum "He who comes
to kill you, kill him first" to explain "there is no bloodguilt for him." But if this
encounter takes place in daylight, it would be much more likely that the
intruder would flee or surrender, depending on the balance of forces, and so
the householder cannot kill him with impunity.

2. *He shall surely pay.* Abraham ibn Ezra makes the plausible suggestion that
this and the following clauses refer not to the housebreaker but to the livestock thief of 21:37. If the stolen animal has already been sold, the thief must
pay fourfold or fivefold. If he still has the animal to restore to its owner, he is
nevertheless subject to a penalty of twofold payment for the theft. A thief
without the means to pay the penalty must be sold as a slave in order to make
good what he owes (in the Code of Hammurabi, a thief in such a case is to be
executed).

4. *Should a man let his beast graze.* The arrangement of laws in this more or
less miscellaneous list is largely determined either by thematic association or

of his vineyard he shall pay. Should a fire go forth and catch in thorns, 5
and stacked or standing grain or the field be consumed, he who set the
fire shall surely pay. Should a man give his fellow man money or goods 6
for safekeeping and they are stolen from the man's house, if the thief is
found, he shall pay double. If the thief is not found, the owner of the 7
house shall approach the gods to swear that he has not laid hands on

---

by recurring keywords. In the latter instance, one detects a convention that is
often used to link two adjacent units in biblical narrative: the same word is
used twice in succession in two different meanings. Thus the verb *hiv'ir*, "to
cause to graze," recurs in the next law in its other sense, "to set a fire." As to
thematic association, this law is connected, as Abraham ibn Ezra notes, with
the cluster of laws at the end of chapter 21 that also deal with damages caused
by one's beast.

    send his beast. The relatively rare Hebrew term for beast, *be'ir*, is a cognate
accusative of the verb for grazing. In the opening clause of this verse, the word
"beast" does not appear in the Hebrew but is implied by the verb *hiv'ir*.

5. *Should a fire go forth.* There is a thematic link (again noted by ibn Ezra) as
well as a verbal one with the preceding law because this is another instance in
which a person's negligence in supervising an activity in his own field—evidently, some sort of controlled burning—results in damage to someone else's
field.

    the field. Rashi plausibly suggests that this third category of damage is
scorching a plowed field, which would then have to be plowed out again.

7. *shall approach the gods.* Again, traditional commentators, and some modern
ones as well, interpret *'elohim* as a reference to judges, though if this is the case,
it would be a usage unique to the Book of the Covenant. This translation presumes that this is a vestige of premonotheistic verbal usage preserved in this
relatively archaic legal code. Here it would refer not to household gods, as in
21:6, but would seem to be a loose indication of deities at a local sanctuary. It
is noteworthy that when *'elohim* is the subject of a verb in the next verse, that
verb is conjugated in the plural. One should not make too much of this usage
theologically. Linguistic practice can often be more conservative than changing
perceptions of reality, and it is quite conceivable that an older stratum of biblical language should have preserved the polytheistic idiom for divine presence
at oracle or sanctuary without actually affirming a multiplicity of gods.

    to swear. The verb is not stated in the Hebrew but implied by the oath-
formula that follows.

8 his fellow man's effects. In every matter of breach of trust, for an ox, for
a donkey, for a sheep, for a cloak, for every loss about which one may
say, "This is it," the matter of both shall come before the gods. He
9 whom the gods find guilty shall pay double to his fellow man. Should a
man give to his fellow man a donkey or an ox or a sheep or any beast
for safekeeping and it die or be maimed or carried off, with no witness,
10 there shall be an oath by the LORD between the two of them, that he
has not laid hands on his fellow man's effects, and the owner shall
11 accept and he shall not pay. If it indeed be stolen from him, he shall
12 pay its owner. If it be torn up by beasts, he shall bring it in evidence,
13 he shall not pay for what was torn up by beasts. And should a man borrow it from his fellow man and it be hurt or die, its owner not being

---

effects. The Hebrew *mela'khah* (a collective noun) usually means "task" or
"labor," but in this legal context the clear meaning is the material possessions
that are the product of labor.

9, *maimed or carried off*. The word for "maimed," *nishbar*, usually means "broken" and hence is a little odd to apply to an animal. The choice of term is evidently dictated by the strong assonance with the next word, "carried off,"
nishbah.

10. *an oath by the LORD*. Literally, "an oath of the LORD"—not an oath taken in
the LORD's presence but rather an oath that invokes the LORD's name. At this
point, the legislator reverts to solid monotheistic language, and from his point
of view, there would have been no necessary contradiction with the preceding
use of *'elohim* in the plural.
    laid hands. The literal meaning is "sent out his hand."
    accept. Literally, "take."

12. *he shall bring it in evidence*. There are other indications in the Bible that
this was a common practice. A hired shepherd would bring some part of the
torn carcass of the beast to prove to the owner that he had not stolen and sold
the missing animal.

with it, he shall surely pay. If its owner is with it, he shall not pay. If he   14
is hired, he gets his hire. And should a man seduce a virgin who has not   15
been betrothed and lie with her, he shall surely pay a bride-price for her
as his wife. If her father utterly refuses to give her to him, he shall   16
weigh out silver according to the bride-price for virgins.

"'No witch shall you let live. Whosoever lies with a beast is doomed to   17,18
die. Whosoever sacrifices to a god, except to the LORD alone, shall be   19
put under the ban. You shall not cheat a sojourner and you shall not   20
oppress him, for you were sojourners in the land of Egypt. No widow   21

---

14. *if he is hired*. The term "hired" (*sakhir*) here has lent itself to different interpretations. The immediate context suggests that the most likely reference is to the person to whom the animal has been entrusted. If he has been hired to perform this task, and the loss of the beast occurs while its owner happens to be present to keep an eye on it, the person hired to do the safekeeping is still entitled to his fee.

15. *he shall surely pay a bride-price for her as his wife*. The seducer is obliged to make an honest woman of his victim, including the material benefit—the bride-price was a fund reserved for the use of the woman—accompanying marriage to a virgin. The penalty for raping rather than seducing an unbetrothed virgin is payment of a fine to the father and compulsory marriage without possibility of divorce (Deuteronomy 22:28–29).

17. *No witch shall you let live*. This verse marks the beginning of a second group of laws, no longer formulated casuistically but as absolute imperatives. The witch or sorceress is feminine because, as ibn Ezra and many others after him note, female practitioners predominated, though it may be inferred that male sorcerers are also implied. Ibn Ezra also proposes, somewhat fancifully, a thematic link with the previous law: a seducer might well resort to sorcery in order to have his way with a young woman. The practice of witchcraft had an understandable persistence in ancient Israel, as the tale of the necromancer of Endor (1 Samuel 28) illustrates. The monotheistic objection to the institution, whose efficacy was not necessarily denied, was to an occult technology that could manipulate the spirit realm which was reserved to God alone.

21. *No widow nor orphan*. Throughout biblical literature, and particularly in the Prophets, these are the paradigmatic cases of powerless members of society who are vulnerable to exploitation.

22 nor orphan shall you abuse. If you indeed abuse them, when they cry
23 out to Me, I will surely hear their outcry. And My wrath shall flare up
and I will kill you by the sword, and your wives shall be widows and
24 your children orphans. If you should lend money to My people, to the
pauper among you, you shall not be to him like a creditor, you shall not
25 impose interest on him. If you should indeed take in pledge your fellow
man's cloak, before the sun comes down you shall return it to him.
26 For it is his sole covering, it is his cloak for his skin—in what can he
lie? And so, when he cries out to Me, I will hear him, for I am com-
27 passionate. You shall not vilify God, nor shall you curse a chief among
28 your people. The first yield of your vats and the first yield of your grain
you shall not delay to give. The firstborn of your sons you shall give to

---

22. *abuse . . . cry out . . . hear their outcry.* The terms used here pointedly echo
the language used at the beginning of Exodus to describe the oppression of
Israel in Egypt and God's response to that suffering. This law, then, like the
previous one that explicitly invokes the Hebrews' condition of sojourners in
Egypt, touches on the experience of slavery as an enduring prod to social
conscience.

24. *you shall not impose interest.* The obvious presupposition of this law is an
agrarian economy with social groupings on the soil in extended families and
clans. Ancient Near Eastern societies with large urban populations in fact
have left records of sums regularly lent on interest at extortionate rates.

26. *For it is his sole covering, it is his cloak for his skin.* The anchorage of this
regulation in social reality is vividly illustrated in a fragmentary Hebrew
inscription from the seventh century B.C.E. uncovered at Yavneh-Yam. The person dictating the inscription, a formal complaint against his foreman, would
appear to be a corvée laborer doing agricultural work. Here are the most relevant lines (my translation): "And Hoshiahu son of Shobi came and took your
servant's garment when I had finished my harvesting. A full day he has taken
my garment, and all my brothers will answer for me, who harvest with me in
the heat [of the sun], my brothers will answer for me amen. I am guiltless. . . ."
One can make out in the highly fragmented two lines that follow a plea for the
garment to be returned.

28. *The first yield of your vats and the first yield of your grain.* The meaning of
the two Hebrew terms, *melei'ah* and *dema'*, is not entirely certain, though most

Me. Thus you shall do with your ox and your sheep: seven days it shall 29
be with its mother; on the eighth day you shall give it to Me. And con- 30
secrated men you shall be to Me: flesh in the field torn by beasts you
shall not eat; to the dog you shall fling it.'"

---

interpreters agree that they refer to two categories of agricultural produce from
which the farmer must offer the first yield as a sacrifice. (A word that would
make the idea of first yield explicit, such as *rei'shit* or *bikurey*, does not appear
in the text.) It has also been suggested that *melei'ah* and *dema'* are a single agricultural concept, a hendiadys.

to give. The verb is merely implied in the Hebrew.

The firstborn of your sons you shall give to Me. This could not be a command
to perform child sacrifice. In the archaic period of Hebrew culture, the firstborn officiated as priests. The standard practice then became to "redeem" the
firstborn by paying a fixed amount to the priests (compare Exodus 13:15).

30. *consecrated men.* Literally, "men of holiness" (*qodesh*). The root *q-d-sh* is the
same one used for the act of consecration just enjoined on the people before
the giving of the Law on Sinai. To eat carrion is seen as an act of self-
defilement.

flesh in the field torn by beasts. It is chiefly out in the field, as Rashi notes,
not in pen or barn, that a cow, sheep, or goat would be attacked by ravening
animals, though anthropologically inclined critics have also stressed the character of the field in the biblical imagination as a place beyond the pale of
human habitation, where wild beasts and impure spirits dwell.

to the dog you shall fling it. The biblical contempt for canines is again
detectable: the dog is an unseemly scavenger, an appropriately base receptacle
for carrion.

CHAPTER 23

"You shall not bear a false rumor. You shall not put your hand with the guilty to be a harmful witness. You shall not follow the many for evil, and you shall not bear witness in a dispute to go askew,

---

1. *You shall not bear a false rumor.* This injunction begins a group of laws intended to enforce the concept of equality before the law and equity in social behavior, regardless of social standing or condition of enmity or amity. The prohibition on bearing false rumor is reminiscent in formulation of the third of the Ten Commandments, but instead of pertaining to solemn oaths, it addresses the capacity of ordinary speech to do harm.

You shall not put your hand with the guilty. The Hebrew idiom, here literally translated, transparently means to be in league with someone. This injunction stands in a relation of intensifying parallelism (a typical pattern in biblical poetry) with the immediately preceding one. Distortion of the truth is involved in both, but there is an intensification from rumormongering to perjury.

2. *You shall not follow the many for evil.* The last word here could also be rendered "harm." The most straightforward way to construe this verse is as an injunction to cling to one's own sense of what is right despite the temptation to follow popular opinion, including when popular opinion is bent on the perversion of justice.

to go askew, to skew it in support of the many. The Hebrew, as the translation may suggest, seems a little awkward because "to go askew" (*lintot*) appears to be unnecessary and perhaps a little confusing when followed by the same verb in the causative form, *lehatot*, "to skew." It is conceivable that the repetition was introduced to underline formally the notion of skewing or tilting justice, which every person is enjoined to avoid.

4 8

to skew it in support of the many. Nor a poor man shall you favor in ₃ his dispute. Should you encounter your enemy's ox or his donkey stray- ₄ ing, you must surely return it to him. Should you see your adversary's ₅ donkey sprawling under its load and would hold back from assisting him, you shall surely assist him. You shall not skew the case of your ₆ indigent in his dispute. From a lying word stay far away, and ₇ the guiltless and innocent do not kill, for I will not acquit the guilty.

---

3. *Nor a poor person shall you favor in his dispute.* Throughout these laws, "dispute" (*riv*) refers to contention in a court of law. The principle of equality before the law requires the avoidance of any juridical "affirmative action"— one must give no preferential treatment in court either to the poor man because of his afflictions or to the rich man because of his power.

5. *your adversary's donkey sprawling under its load.* This is the first, but by no means the only, expression of humanitarian concern for animals in the Torah. The suffering of the beast must take precedence over a person's hostility toward the beast's owner.

   you shall surely assist him. The rare Hebrew verb '-z-b is the homonym of a common verb that means "to abandon." It occurs twice elsewhere in the Bible in the sense of "to perform," "to arrange," "to assist," and it has cognates with this meaning in both Ugaritic and Arabic. The object of the verb ("him") could be either the master or the donkey, but the former seems more likely: a heavily loaded donkey would not be wandering around by itself; the person would know to whom it belongs by seeing the owner; and the moral imperative would be all the more pressing because he is enjoined to give a hand to a man he hates.

6–9. Whereas verses 1–3 address the obligation of adherence to justice for all citizens, this related subgroup of injunctions is directed to judges.

6. *You shall not skew the case of your indigent in his dispute.* This formulation is the complement of verse 3. No one should grant preferential treatment to the poor man in justice, but here the judge is reminded that the poor should not be prejudicially mistreated in court. "Case," *mishpat*, can also mean "justice."

7. *I will not acquit the guilty.* The judge is implicitly thought of as a surrogate of God, obliged to enact only what is right, as God does.

8 No bribe shall you take, for a bribe blinds the sighted and perverts the
9 words of the innocent. No sojourner shall you oppress, for you know
the sojourner's heart, since you were sojourners in the land of Egypt.
10,11 And six years you shall sow your land and gather its produce. But in the
seventh you shall let it go and let it lie fallow, and your people's indigent may eat of it, and what is left, the beast of the field will eat. Thus
12 shall you do for your vineyard and your olive grove. Six days shall you
do your deeds and on the seventh day you shall cease, so that your ox
and your donkey may rest, and your bondman and the sojourner catch

---

8. *blinds . . . perverts.* The aphoristic parallelism sounds rather like the Book of
Proverbs.

    the sighted. The Hebrew adjective designates both those who have the fac-
ulty of sight and, by metaphorical extension, those who are keen-sighted. As a
kind of gloss on the term, a parallel law in Deuteronomy substitutes for
"sighted" the explicit "wise" (the sense of the term in modern Hebrew).

9. *the sojourner's heart.* The Hebrew is *nefesh,* "life," "inner nature," "essential
being," "breath."

11. *let it go.* The Hebrew verb *shamat* means "to release," "to allow to slip out
of one's grip." The noun derived from this verb, *shemitah,* is the general term
for sabbatical year.

    and your people's indigent may eat of it. The motive for the sabbatical year is
a partial redressing of social inequity, thus linking it with the immediately preceding laws. The ecological advantage of allowing fields to lie fallow is not
mentioned.

12. *so that your ox and your donkey may rest, and your bondman and the sojourner
catch their breath.* Unlike the Decalogue, but entirely in keeping with the context of the present code of laws, the rationale for the Sabbath offered here is
neither theological (God's resting after creation) nor historical (the liberation
from Egyptian slavery) but humanitarian. "Catch their breath" (*wayinafesh*) is
represented in most translations as "be refreshed." It is cognate with *nefesh,*
most probably in the sense of "breath," and is related to the verb *nashaf,* "to
breathe hard or pant." The idea of catching one's breath is consonant with the
representation in Job and elsewhere in the Bible of the laborer panting from
his work and longing to draw a long breath of relief after labor.

their breath. And in all that I have said to you, you shall watch your- 13
selves, and the name of other gods you shall not invoke nor shall it be
heard on your lips.

"Three times in the year shall you hold Me a festival. The Festival of 14,15
Flatbread you shall keep seven days; you shall eat flatbread as I have
charged you, at the fixed time of the month of the New Grain, for in it
you came out of Egypt, and they shall not appear in My presence
empty-handed. And the Festival of the Harvest, first fruits of your labor 16
that you sow in the field, and the Festival of Ingathering, as the year
goes out, when you gather in your labor from the field. Three times in 17
the year all your males shall appear in the presence of the Master, the
LORD. You shall not offer up the blood of My sacrifice with leavened 18
stuff, nor shall the fat of My festival offering be left till the morning.
The best of the first fruit of your soil you shall bring to the house of the 19
LORD your God. You shall not boil a kid in its mother's milk.

---

13. *And in all that I have said to you, you shall watch yourselves.* This summarizing command reintroduces, in the next clause, the obligation of loyalty to the single God and thus serves as a transition from the group of laws bearing on justice and social equity to the laws of the pilgrim festivals, which are national, seasonal expressions of fealty to God.

14. *Three times.* The word for "times" here, *regalim*, is different from *peʿamim*, the word used at the beginning of verse 17. Both terms mean "foot," the apparent connection with "time" being the counting of times with the tap of a foot.

15. *appear in My presence.* The original form of the Hebrew indicated "see My face [or presence]," but the Masoretes revocalized the verb as a passive, "to be seen" or "to appear," in order to avoid what looked like excessive anthropomorphism.

16. *Harvest . . . Ingathering.* The Festival of Flatbread ("Passover" is not used here) would be in April. The harvest (Shavuoth) of first fruits would occur in late May or early June, and Ingathering (Succoth) the harvest of most later crops, in late September or early October.

19. *You shall not boil a kid in its mother's milk.* This famous prohibition would become the basis in rabbinic dietary regulations for the absolute separation of

20 Look, I am about to send a messenger before you to guard you on the
21 way and to bring you to the place that I made ready. Watch yourself
     with him and heed his voice, do not defy him, for he will not pardon
22 your trespass, for My name is within him. But if you truly heed his
     voice and do all that I speak, I shall be an enemy to your enemies and
23 a foe to your foes. For My messenger will go before you and will bring

---

meat and dairy foods. Two different kinds of justification have been proposed
for the prohibition. Maimonides and many after him suggest that the law is a
response to a pagan cultic practice known to the ancients of eating a kid prepared in its mother's milk. There is no clear-cut archeological evidence of such
a practice—Maimonides merely inferred it interpretively. One fragmentary
mythological text in Ugaritic may in fact refer to this culinary item, though
that reconstruction of the text has been disputed. The other approach,
espoused by Abraham ibn Ezra (a little tentatively) and many others, is to
explain the prohibition on humanitarian grounds. The sensitivity toward animals previously evinced in this group of laws gives some plausibility to the
humanitarian possibility. Since no actual aggravation of the animals' suffering
is involved, the recoil from this commingling would be on the symbolic level:
the mixture of the mother animal's nurturing milk with the slaughtered flesh
of her offspring, a promiscuous joining of life and death.

20. *I am about to send a messenger before you.* Although modern rationalist commentators have sought to explain this as a metaphor for providential guidance,
the frankly mythological terms of the preceding narrative—the pillars of cloud
and fire, the Destroyer in Egypt—invite us to imagine the messenger as a fearsome agent of God, perhaps human in form like the divine messengers in Genesis, leading the people through the wilderness.

21. *he will not pardon your trespass, for My name is within him.* The messenger
is not only a guide for the Wilderness wanderings but an unblinking executor
of divine surveillance. The mention of the divine name is the earliest of a scattering of biblical references to a quasi-mythological notion of God's name as a
potent agency in its own right. This idea would be elaborately developed in
later Jewish mysticism.

22. *I shall be an enemy to your enemies and a foe to your foes.* The perfect parallelism of this statement recalls the symmetry of a line of biblical poetry, and
several verses in this concluding section of the Book of the Covenant approximate the formal balance and high solemnity of poetry.

you to the Amorite and the Hittite and the Perizzite and the Canaanite, the Hivite and the Jebusite, and I shall obliterate them. You shall 24
not bow to their gods and you shall not worship them, and you shall not
do as they do, but you shall utterly tear them down and you shall utterly
smash their pillars. And you shall worship the Lᴏʀᴅ your God, and He 25
will bless your bread and your water, and I shall take away sickness
from your midst. There shall be no woman miscarrying or barren in 26
your land. The count of your days I will fill. My terror I shall send 27
before you and I shall panic the whole people among whom you will
come, and I shall make all your enemies turn tail to you. And I shall 28
send the hornet before you and it will drive out the Hivite and the
Canaanite and the Hittite before you. I shall not drive them out before 29
you in one year, lest the land become desolate and the beasts of the

---

24. *tear them down*. The verb here, *haras*, indicates that the object is the idols,
not the idolators.

   pillars. The reference is to cultic pillars, or steles.

28. *I shall send the hornet before you*. There is some question about what is
sent: the noun *tsir'ah* appears in the Bible only three times, all in the context
of the conquest of Canaan. The strong consensus of later Hebrew tradition—
there is some dissent—is that it refers to a noxious stinging insect. In that
case, the word functions here as a collective noun (rather common biblical
usage for animals) and refers to dense swarms of hornets. An alternative I
would like to propose is that the root is related (with consonants reversed) to
the verb *ra'ats*, "to smash," and that this is a mythological rather than a zoological entity, the Smasher (or Smashing), which would be strictly parallel or
equivalent to "My terror" at the beginning of verse 27.

27. *turn tail*. The Hebrew refers to the nape of the neck, which the fleeing
enemy shows to his pursuer.

29. *lest the land become desolate*. The Hebrew writer, faced with the discomfiting report of the tradition available to him that the conquest of the land,
underwritten by solemn divine promise, took more than two centuries, is driven to find some explanation for the delay. (The Book of Judges will propose
three rather different explanations.) The prospect sketched here of a suddenly
depopulated land overrun by wild beasts and too big for the Hebrews seems
intrinsically implausible, and it is hard to square the notion of Israel awaiting

30 field multiply against you. Little by little shall I drive them out before
31 you until you are fruitful and inherit the land. And I shall fix its borders
from the Red Sea to the Sea of the Philistines, and from the wilderness
to the Euphrates, for I shall give into your hand the inhabitants of the
32 land and you will drive them out before you. You shall not make a pact
33 with them or with their gods. They shall not dwell in your land, lest
they cause you to offend Me, for should you worship their gods, it will
be a snare for you.'"

---

its own natural increase ("until you are fruitful") with the figure offered earlier
of 600,000 adult males, which implied a total population of well over two
million.

31. *I shall fix its borders.* These grandiose borders, which would make biblical
Israel seem a bit like Texas, do not correspond to any actual historical reality
but are rather a kind of imaginative nationalist fantasy of what a "spacious
land" (Exodus 3:8) might look like. Different, equally ideal borders are mentioned elsewhere.

   the Red Sea. In this context, this is the more plausible geographical reference of *yam suf*, rather than Sea of Reeds, which would probably be a marshland in northeastern Egypt.

32. *You shall not make a pact with them or with their gods.* Ibn Ezra, with his
keen eye for connections, relates the previous verse to this one: even though
God will give Israel this vast expanse of territory (presumably, filled with subject peoples), the temptation of embracing the gods of the native population
must be resisted.

CHAPTER 24

And to Moses He had said, "Go up to the Lord, you and Aaron, 1
Nadab and Abihu and seventy of the elders of Israel, and you shall
bow down from afar. And Moses alone shall come near to the 2
Lord but they shall not come near, and the people shall not go up with
him." And Moses came and recounted to the people all the Lord's 3
words and all the laws, and the people answered with a single voice and
said, "All the words that the Lord has spoken we will do." And Moses 4
wrote down all the Lord's words, and he rose early in the morning and
built an altar at the foot of the mountain with twelve pillars for the

---

1. *And to Moses He had said.* As is often the case in sequences of episodes in
the Bible, there is some ambiguity about the chronological location of this passage. The form of the verb (perfective instead of the usual imperfective prefixed by *waw*) may well indicate a pluperfect, and Rashi, no doubt noting that
what Moses does here is to go up the mountain and bring back God's words,
claims, "This passage was said before the Ten Commandments."

2. *Moses . . . shall come near . . . they shall not come near . . . the people shall
not go up.* There is evidently a tripartite deployment: Moses alone goes up to
the mountaintop; the seventy elders, Aaron, Nadab, and Abihu remain at a
stopping point partway up the mountain; and the people stay at the foot of the
mountain, as they were instructed to do in chapter 19.

3. *all the Lord's words and all the laws.* The two terms are strategically precise.
"Words" (*devarim*) refers to the Ten Words, or Commandments; "laws" (*mish-
patim*) is the term that announces (21:1) the catalogue of legal injunctions that
constitutes the Book of the Covenant.

4. *twelve pillars.* These pillars (*matsevot*) are not structural elements in the
altar but cultic pillars or steles, just like the ones that, when they are pagan,
the Israelites have been enjoined to smash (23:24).

5 twelve tribes of Israel. And he sent the lads of the Israelites and they
offered up burnt offerings and sacrificed sacrifices and communion
6 sacrifices, bulls to the LORD. And Moses took half the blood and put it
7 in basins, and half the blood he threw upon the altar. And he took the
book of the covenant and read it in the hearing of the people, and they
8 said, "All that the LORD has spoken we will do and we will heed." And
Moses took the blood and threw it upon the people, and he said, "Look,
the blood of the covenant that the LORD has sealed with you over all

5. *the lads.* This term, *ne'arim*, has a multiplicity of meanings, but a common
one, reflected here, is as a designation of anyone performing a subaltern or
assisting function—in the cult, an acolyte.

7. *the book of the covenant.* There are differing opinions as to whether this
phrase explicitly refers to the legal text of chapters 21–23, despite an established scholarly tradition for using it as a title for that literary unit. In any case,
this entire ritual, including the sacred feast and the epiphany that follow the
sacrifice, is a solemn confirmation of the covenant between God and Israel,
and it is conceivable that the "book of the covenant" is a spelling out of the
terms of that pact in language not necessarily incorporated in the preceding
narrative.

8. *And Moses took the blood and threw it upon the people.* Although splashing
blood on the altar is a standard sacrificial procedure, throwing blood on the
people is unique to this episode. Some squeamish modern commentators have
claimed that the blood is thrown on the pillars that represent the twelve tribes,
but such a notion surely undercuts the primal archaic power of the rite.
(Addressing the problem of how blood could be sprinkled over 600,000 adult
males, or more than two million people, Abraham ibn Ezra plausibly suggests
that the seventy elders served as ritual stand-ins for the whole people.) The
idea of two parties to a solemn, binding agreement confirming the mutual
obligation by dipping hands in the same blood, or exchanging blood smears, is
attested in many cultures. In this covenant of ontologically disparate partners,
the altar that is sprinkled with half the blood may serve as surrogate for the
deity to whose service the altar has been erected. The covenantal rite of casting blood on the people is a climax of the sundry occurrences of blood in this
narrative from the Bridegroom of Blood episode onward: the blood of circumcision (itself a covenantal act) that deflected the threat of death to Moses or
his child and the blood of the lamb that warded off the Destroyer in Egypt

these words." And Moses went up, and with him Aaron, Nadab and 9
Abihu and seventy of the elders of Israel. And they saw the God of 10
Israel, and beneath His feet was like a fashioning of sapphire pavement
and like the very heavens for pureness. But against the elect of the 11

---

reappear here as the blood of the sacrifice that confirms Israel's everlasting
bond with God.

9. *and with him Aaron, Nadab and Abihu, and seventy of the elders.* As often
elsewhere in this translation, "with him" is added to reflect the focusing function of the Hebrew verb: the verb is in the singular, indicating that the primary
or focused subject of the going up is Moses, and that the others join in, or are
subsidiary to, Moses's act of ascent. The indications of spatial deployment
here are minimal, but it appears that after the covenantal sacrifice, Moses led
his three followers and the elders to the mountaintop, or perhaps only near the
mountaintop, where they were vouchsafed their epiphany. Then they went
back down (verse 14), while Moses went back up the mountain, evidently
accompanied part of the way by Joshua (verse 13). In any event, it is Moses
alone who enters into the cloud at the mountaintop that conceals God's glory
or presence.

10. *And they saw the God of Israel.* The boldness with which this immediate
vision is stated is startling, especially against a biblical background in which
humans repeatedly fear that they cannot see God and live (compare the next
verse, "But against the elect of the Israelites He did not send forth His hand").
Such collective vision is reserved for this unique event. A symptom of how
shocking this frank anthropomorphism could be is Onkelos's evasive substitution in his Aramaic translation: "And they saw their sacrifices that had been
accepted favorably as though they had eaten and drunk." *Pace* Onkelos, the
eating and drinking after the beholding (verse 11 employs a verb of visionary
experience) are a communion feast enjoyed by the elders at God's feet.

and beneath His feet was like a fashioning of sapphire pavement. Mere flesh
and blood cannot long sustain the vision of God, and so the visual focus immediately slides down to the celestial brilliance beneath God's feet. Even for this
zone touched by the divine, direct linguistic reference is not possible, and so
the writer uses a doubled simile—"like a fashioning of . . . ," "like the very
heavens. . . ."

sapphire. Many scholars think that the Hebrew *sapir* refers to lapis lazuli. If
the Hebrew term is actually cognate with sapphire, the writer clearly has in
mind a blue sapphire.

Israelites He did not send forth His hand, and they beheld God and ate

12 and drank. And the LORD said to Moses, "Go up to me to the mountain and be there, that I may give you the stone tablets and the teaching and

13 the commandments that I have written to instruct them. And Moses arose, and Joshua his attendant with him, and Moses went up the

14 mountain of God. And to the elders he had said, "Sit here for us until we return to you, and, look, Aaron and Hur are with you. Whoever has

15 matters to air may approach them." And Moses went up, and the cloud

16 covered the mountain. And the LORD's glory abode on Mount Sinai, and the cloud covered it six days. And on the seventh day He called out to

17 Moses from the midst of the cloud. And the sight of the LORD's glory was like consuming fire at the mountaintop before the eyes of the

---

12. *the stone tablets and the teaching and the commandments that I have written.* Although the often repeated *devarim,* "words," implies speech (*dibur*), this central event of the giving of the Law places a strong stress on the act of writing as the vehicle for endowing words with permanence. Moses writes down the words and the laws, presumably with ink on parchment or papyrus. God now declares He will do His own inscription—presumably of the Ten Words— in the perdurable medium of stone.

14. *Whosoever has matters to air.* The Hebrew, *mi ba'al devarim,* literally means, "whosoever has/is possessor of words," but *devarim* here clearly means "legal matters," "cases to bring before the law," as the term is used in the Jethro episode (chapter 18). Since Moses seems to know he will be required to stay on the mountaintop a long time (the formulaic forty days), provision has to be made for the judicial needs of the people during his absence. The necessary implication is that the elders now have gone all the way down the mountain to where the people are waiting. Joshua will presumably stop somewhere short of the summit of the mountain.

17. *And the sight of the LORD's glory was like consuming fire . . . before the eyes of the Israelites.* After the direct epiphany to the elders, we get a long-distance view of God's presence from the perspective of the people at the foot of the mountain. There is more mystifying occlusion than revelation here: an enveloping cloud, flashes of fiery effulgence from within it. Even such distant glimpses of the deity must be qualified by simile—"like consuming fire."

Israelites. And Moses entered within the cloud and went up the moun- 18
tain, and Moses was on the mountain forty days and forty nights.

---

18. *and Moses entered within the cloud.* The terrifying gap between Moses and
the people is beautifully registered. They quail down below, seeing pulses of
consuming fire from within the cloud; on the mountaintop, Moses actually
enters into the cloud. His entering the cloud was already implied in verse 16
("He called out to Moses from the midst of the cloud"—perhaps what he
called out was the Ten Words), but now we get a kind of recapitulative summarizing report, strongly colored by the viewpoint of the assembled people at
the foot of the mountain who look up awestruck as Moses disappears into the
cloud for forty days and forty nights. That seemingly interminable absence of
the leader will in due course engender trouble down below.

CHAPTER 25

1,2   And the LORD spoke to Moses, saying: "Speak to the Israelites, that they take Me a donation from every man, as his heart may urge 3   him you shall take My donation. And this is the donation that you

---

2. *a donation*. The Hebrew *terumah* is a noun derived from a verb that means "to elevate," and, among several biblical terms for gift, it is the one that designates a donation for use in the cult or by the priests. This verse inaugurates an elaborate catalogue of instructions about the design of the Tabernacle and its furnishings that will take up the rest of the Book of Exodus, with the exception of the episode of the Golden Calf in chapters 32–34. Modern readers may well be perplexed as to why the compelling narrative of the liberation from Egypt and the revelation on Mount Sinai should be set aside for this lengthy account of cultic paraphernalia. The historical circumstances of the assembling of the Torah must surely be kept in mind. That editorial process in all likelihood took place in Priestly circles early in the period of the return from Babylonian exile (later sixth century B.C.E.). The strong scholarly consensus is that these chapters are the work of the Priestly writers (P), and the fascination with all the minute details of cultic paraphernalia seems a clear reflection of P's special interests. One may nevertheless ask why the editors, however sacerdotal their concerns, chose to introduce this large block of material at the very moment when Moses has disappeared into the cloud on the mountaintop to commune with God. That moment in the story is marked by the people's fearful distance from the fiery divine presence up above and the daring closeness of one man, Moses the intercessor, to the deity. Against this background, the architectural plan for the Tabernacle and its décor offers a reassuring antithesis. God will come down from above to dwell among His people within the securely designated sanctum of the Tabernacle, will sit enthroned on the cherubim carved above the Ark of the Covenant, from whence He will issue divine instruction (verse 22), and where He will be accessible through the cultic mediation of the priests. The divinely endorsed donations and cultic pro-

shall take from them: gold and silver and bronze, and indigo and pur- 4
ple and crimson, and linen and goat hair, and reddened ram skins and 5
ocher-dyed skins and acacia wood. Oil for the lamp, spices for the 6
anointing oil and for the aromatic incense. Carnelian stones and stones 7
for setting in the ephod and in the breastplate. And they shall make Me 8
a Tabernacle, that I may abide in their midst. As all that I show you, 9

---

cedures, moreover, set up a contrast with the transgressive donations that
enable the forbidden cult of the Golden Calf. For further comments on the
role of this long section, see the introduction to Exodus.

4. *indigo and purple and crimson.* These, at any rate, are the ends of the spectrum reflected by these color words, there being some margin of doubt about
the precise indication of chromatic terms and considerably more doubt about
the identification of precious stones in these lists. The first two colors indicate
dyes extracted from a species of murex, and of Phoenician manufacture; the
third is a dye derived from the eggs of scale insects found on oak trees. Both
processes of dye production were immensely laborious and costly, and hence
these colors were used especially for royal garments throughout the eastern
part of the Mediterranean (one may recall Agamemnon "treading on purple" in
the great welcome-carpet scene Clytemnestra stages for him near the beginning of the *Oresteia*). It is hard to imagine that these precious dyes would have
been accessible to the Hebrews in the wilderness—this is one of several indications that the picture of the Tabernacle is in many ways an ideal projection
rather than a strictly historical account.

5. *ocher-dyed skins.* Many translations interpret the Hebrew *tehashim* as "dol-
phins" or "dugongs," but a more plausible connection has been made with an
Akkadian term that indicates a yellow or orange dye. That would be in keeping with the focus on brilliantly dyed stuff in the previous verse.

8. *Tabernacle.* The Hebrew *mishkan* literally means "abode" ("that I shall abide
in their midst"). It is, of course, a portable sanctuary, to be carried from
encampment to encampment in the wilderness, and provisions are made for
carrying the Ark, beginning in verse 12. The *mishkan* looks like an amalgam of
recollections of an ancient portable sanctuary—Umberto Cassuto notes certain parallels in Ugaritic literature—and a retrojection to the Wilderness
period of the Jerusalem temple. More recent scholars detect a resemblance to
the bicameral design and proportions of Pharaoh Rameses II's tent used in
military campaigns.

the form of the Tabernacle and the form of all its furnishings, thus shall
10 you make it. And they shall make an ark of acacia wood, two and a half
cubits its length and a cubit and a half its width, and a cubit and a half
11 its height. And you shall overlay it with pure gold, inside and outside
you shall overlay it, and you shall make upon it a golden molding all
12 around. And you shall cast for it four golden rings and set them on its
four feet, and two rings on its one side and two rings on the other side.
13 And you shall make poles of acacia wood and overlay them with gold,
14 and you shall bring the poles through the rings on the side of the Ark
15 to carry the Ark with them. In the rings of the Ark the poles must be,
16 they shall not come out. And you shall set in the Ark the tablets of the
17 Covenant that I shall give you. And you shall make a cover of pure gold,
two and a half cubits its length, and a cubit and a half its width.
18 And you shall make two cherubim of gold, hammered work you shall
19 make them, at the two edges of the cover. And make one cherub at one
edge and one cherub at the other edge, from the cover you shall make
20 the cherubim at both its edges. And the cherubim shall spread wings
above, shielding the cover with their wings, and their faces toward each
21 other, toward the cover the faces of the cherubim shall be. And you
shall set the covering upon the Ark from above, and in the Ark you shall

---

12. *its four feet*. One may infer that there were actually small carved feet at the
four bottom corners so that the Ark would not rest directly on the ground.

16. *set in the Ark the tablets of the Covenant*. "Tablets" is merely implied by
ellipsis. The word for "covenant" here is *'edut*, a synonym for the more prevalent *berit*. The stone tablets of the Law are the document of the eternal contract between God and Israel, and their placement here reflects a common
ancient Near Eastern practice of placing documents of solemn contracts
within sacred precincts.

18. *cherubim*. The Hebrew *keruvim* is derived from a root that suggests hybrid
or composite and perhaps also "steed." These are fearsome winged beasts
(compare the Egyptian sphinx) that figure in poetry as God's celestial steeds
and that here serve as His terrestrial throne, "enthroned upon cherubim" being
an epithet for the deity. (See the comment on Genesis 3:24.)

set the tablets of the Covenant that I shall give you. And I shall meet 22
with you there and speak with you, from above the covering between
the two cherubim that are on top of the Ark of the Covenant, all that I
shall charge you regarding the Israelites. And you shall make a table of 23
acacia wood, two cubits its length and a cubit its width and a cubit and
a half its height. And you shall overlay it with pure gold, and make for 24
it a golden molding all around. And you shall make a frame for it, a 25
handsbreadth all around, and you shall make a golden molding for its
frame all around. And you shall make four gold rings for it and set the 26
rings at the four corners which are at its four legs. Facing the frame the 27
rings shall be, as housings for the poles to carry the table. And you shall 28
make the poles of acacia wood and overlay them with gold, and the
table shall be carried with them. And you shall make its bowls and its 29
shovels and its jars and its chalices, from which libation is done. Pure
gold you shall make them. And you shall set on the table the bread of 30
the Presence, before Me perpetually.

"And you shall make a lamp stand of pure gold, hammered work it shall 31
be made, its base and its shaft, its cups, its calyxes and its blossoms,
shall be from that work. And six shafts going out from its sides, three 32
shafts of the lamp stand from its one side and three shafts of the lamp
stand from its other side. Three cups shaped like almond blossoms in 33
the one shaft, calyx and blossom, and three cups shaped like almond
blossoms in the other shaft, calyx and blossom, thus for the six shafts

---

22. *And I shall meet with you there.* The "you" (singular) is Moses. The verb
translated as "meet" has the sense of appointing a fixed time and place.

29. *chalices.* Though the Hebrew *menaqiot* might seem to derive from the verb
that means "to clean" and so mean something like "scrapers," Cassuto argues
persuasively that these would have to be receptacles for pouring libations, and
he cites cognates in Akkadian and Ugaritic.

30. *the Presence.* Literally, "face," a word often used to designate "presence" for
royal, or divine figures.

31. *from that work.* Literally, "from it," the antecedent being "hammered work."

34 that go out from the lamp stand. And on the lamp stand four cups
35 shaped like almond blossoms, their calyxes and their blossoms. And a
calyx as part of it under every two shafts, a calyx as part of it under every
36 two shafts, for the six shafts coming out from the lamp stand. Their
calyxes and their shafts shall be part of it, all of it one hammered work,
37 pure gold. And you shall make its seven lamps, and its lamps shall be
38 mounted and give light in front of it, and its tongs and its fire-pans—
39 pure gold. With a talent of pure gold shall it be made together with all
40 these furnishings. And see, and make it by their pattern which you are
shown on the mountain."

---

40. *see, and make it by their pattern which you are shown on the mountain.* Rashi
comments here: "to tell us that Moses had difficulty with the fashioning of the
lamp stand, until the Holy One showed him a lamp stand of fire." It is in fact
no easy task to reconstruct the actual design of the lamp stand from these verbal instructions. The Priestly writer himself may have been aware of this difficulty and thus emphasizes that Moses was vouchsafed a vision ("you are
shown") of the precise pattern of the lamp stand. In any case, this reference
to Moses's being shown the pattern on the mountain reflects an effort to
anchor the instructions for the Tabernacle, which look like an independent literary unit, in the narrative context that in effect they disrupt.

CHAPTER 26

"And the Tabernacle you shall make with ten panels of twisted ₁
linen, and indigo and purple and crimson, with cherubim,
designer's work you shall make them. The length of the panel is ₂
twenty-eight cubits, and a width of four cubits to the one panel, a single measure for all the panels. Five of the panels shall be joined to each ₃
other and the other five joined to each other. And you shall make indigo ₄
loops along the edge of the outermost panel in the set, and thus shall
you do on the edge of the outermost panel in the other set. Fifty loops ₅
you shall make in the one panel and fifty loops you shall make in
the outermost panel which is in the other set, the loops opposite one
another. And you shall make fifty golden clasps, and you shall join ₆
the panels to one another with the clasps, that the Tabernacle be one

---

1. *panels of twisted linen*. The cloth panels, *yeri'ot*, invoke a term generally used
for tent coverings, and we are repeatedly reminded that this portable sanctuary, however splendid in gold and silver and bronze and acacia wood, is a tent,
'ohel. The twisting of linen evidently refers to a special technique in the weaving process devised to give the individual threads extra strength.

with cherubim, designer's work. These cherubim are woven as a tapestry
design into the cloth. The Hebrew for "designer," *ḥoshev*, indicates a person
with a special skill or someone who makes a purposeful plan (*maḥashavah*).

6. *that the Tabernacle be one whole*. More literally, "that the Tabernacle be
one." This phrase leads Abraham ibn Ezra to muse over how unity in the
greater world is constituted by an interlocking of constituent parts that
became a transcendent whole, as in the unity of microcosm and macrocosm.
One need not read this section homiletically, as he does, in order to see
the power of summation of this particular phrase. All the instructions for the
design of the Tabernacle—however much the learned interpreters have

7 whole. And you shall make goat-hair panels for a tent over the Taber-
8 nacle, eleven panels you shall make them. The length of the one panel,
thirty cubits, and a width of four cubits to the panel, a single measure
9 for the eleven panels. And you shall join five of the panels by themselves and six of the panels by themselves, and you shall double over
10 the sixth panel at the front of the tent. And you shall make fifty loops
along the edge of the outermost panel in the one set, and fifty loops
11 along the edge of the outermost panel in the other set. And you shall
make fifty bronze clasps and bring the clasps through the loops, and
12 you shall join the tent, that it become one whole. And the overhang left
over in the tent panels, half of the leftover panel you shall let hang over
13 the back of the Tabernacle. And the cubit on one side and the cubit on
the other in what is left over in the length of the tent panels shall hang
14 over both sides of the Tabernacle to cover it. And you shall make a covering for the tent of reddened ram skins and a covering of ocher-dyed
15 skins above. And you shall make boards for the Tabernacle of acacia
16 wood, upright. Ten cubits the length of the board, and a cubit and a

---

differed in explaining the concrete architectural details—point to a perfect
symmetry of nicely interlocking parts, posts fitting into sockets, clasps into
loops, with crossbars shooting from end to end on both sides of the structure,
and the dimensions of every component carefully measured.

7. *goat-hair panels*. Within the Tabernacle are splendid dyed hangings of
twisted linen. Covering the structure on the outside is a coarser cloth made of
woven goat hair, presumably black, a typical fabric for tents, with the capacity
to keep out bad weather.

10. *loops*. It is noteworthy that the Tabernacle passages abound in architectural
or structural terms such as this one (*lula'ot*) that do not appear elsewhere. The
plausible inference is that these passages reflect a specialized architectural (or
sacerdotal-architectural) literature.

half the width of the single board. Two tenons for the one board linked 17
to each other, thus you shall do for all the boards of the Tabernacle.
And you shall make the boards for the Tabernacle, twenty boards for 18
the southern end. And forty silver sockets you shall make beneath the 19
twenty boards, two sockets beneath the one board for its two tenons
and two sockets beneath the other board for its two tenons. And on the 20
other side of the Tabernacle at the northern end, twenty boards. And 21
their forty silver sockets, two sockets beneath the one board and two
sockets beneath the other board. And at the rear of the Tabernacle to 22
the west you shall make six boards. And two boards you shall make for 23
the corners of the Tabernacle at the rear. And they shall match below, 24
and together they shall end at the top inside the one ring, thus it shall
be for the two of them, at the two corners they shall be. And there shall 25
be eight boards with their silver sockets, sixteen sockets, two sockets
beneath the one board and two sockets beneath the next board. And 26
you shall make crossbars of acacia wood, five for the boards of the one
side of the Tabernacle. And five crossbars for the boards of the other 27
side of the Tabernacle, and five crossbars for the side of the Tabernacle at the rear to the west. And the central crossbar in the middle board 28
shall shoot through from end to end. And the boards you shall overlay 29
with gold, and their rings you shall make of gold, housings for the crossbars, and you shall overlay the crossbars with gold. And you shall set up 30
the Tabernacle according to the fashion of it that you were shown on
the mountain.

"And you shall make a curtain of indigo and purple and crimson and 31
twisted linen, designer's work it shall be made, with cherubim. And you 32
shall set it on the four acacia posts overlaid with gold, their hooks gold,

---

17. *tenons.* The Hebrew *yadot* (from *yad,* "hand") is another technical architectural term, indicating a projection at the end of the board made to fit into
another board in a kind of tongue-and-groove construction.

33 upon four silver sockets. And you shall set the curtain under the clasps
and you shall bring there, within the curtain, the Ark of the Covenant,
and the curtain shall divide for you between the Holy and the Holy of
34 Holies. And you shall set the cover over the Ark of the Covenant in the
35 Holy of Holies. And you shall put the table outside the curtain and the
lamp stand facing the table on the side of the Tabernacle to the south,
36 and the table you shall set on the northern side. And you shall make a
screen for the entrance of the tent, indigo and purple and crimson and
37 twisted linen, embroiderer's work. And you shall make for the screen
five acacia posts, and you shall overlay them with gold, their hooks
gold, and you shall cast for them five bronze sockets."

---

33. *the Ark of the Covenant . . . divide . . . between the Holy and the Holy of
Holies.* If the tent structure of the Tabernacle looks backward to an early
nomadic period, its dimensions—exactly half those of Solomon's temple—and
its divisions mirror the structure of the Jerusalem temple. Dividing—the same
word that is central to P's account of creation—between gradations of sanctity
is fundamental to the conception of sacred space put forth here. The 100-cubit
length (about 60 feet) of the Tabernacle is divided symmetrically between a
western half, or outer court, where there is an altar for burnt offerings, and an
eastern half, which constitutes the Holy Place (*maqom qadosh*), in which the
lamp stand, the table, and the altar of incense are located, and a small inner
zone, screened by a curtain, the Holy of Holies, in which the Ark of the
Covenant is kept. The verbal construct "X of X" has the idiomatic sense in biblical Hebrew of "the supreme X" (compare "the song of songs, which is
Solomon's").

CHAPTER 27

"And you shall make the altar of acacia wood, five cubits in length $_1$ and five cubits in width, the altar shall be square, and three cubits its height. And you shall make its horns on its four cor- $_2$ ners, from the same piece its horns shall be, and you shall overlay it with bronze. And you shall make its pails for its ashes and its shovels $_3$ and its basins and its flesh-hooks and its fire-pans, all its vessels you

---

2. *its horns.* The horn-shaped projections at the four corners of the altar were, as archeological investigation has established, a common feature of altars in the West Semitic world. One may surmise that the common Semitic association of horn (Hebrew *qeren,* the same word as Latin *cornu* and English "horn") with strength may have led to this particular practice of cultic ornamentation, the horns somehow confirming or focusing the strength flowing down from the deity to the cultic site. Blood from the sacrifices was sprinkled on the horns of the altar, and so perhaps the horns might have been regarded as the most sacred places on the altar. On that basis, some scholars have reasoned that this is why a person seeking sanctuary would cling to the horns of the altar, though a simpler explanation might be that the horns were the only places on the altar where there was something to hold on to.

3. *pails . . . shovels . . . basins . . . flesh-hooks . . . fire-pans.* Biblical narrative is notoriously stingy in providing details of the paraphernalia of everyday life, in marked contrast to Homer. Oddly and instructively, the one genre of biblical literature in which such details, with the particularizing lexicon needed to indicate them, are abundantly displayed is in cultic legislation. (Again, the Priestly writer remains true to his own professional interests.) Every one of the utensils required for the elaborate procedure of catching the blood of an animal, shoveling up the ashes and residual fat (*deshen*), turning over the meat as it burns, raking off the coals from the fire, is patiently catalogued in this nonnarrative material.

4 shall make of bronze. And you shall make for it a meshwork grating of
bronze, and you shall make on the mesh four bronze rings at its four
5 corners. And you shall set it beneath the ledge of the altar from below,
6 and the mesh shall come halfway up the altar. And you shall make poles
for the altar, poles of acacia wood and overlay them with bronze.
7 And its poles shall be brought through the rings, and the poles shall be
8 on the two sides of the altar when it is carried. Hollow boarded you
shall make it, as He showed you on the mountain, thus they shall do.

9 "And you shall make the Tabernacle court on the southern side. There
shall be hangings for the court of twisted linen, a hundred cubits in
10 length for one side. And its posts shall be twenty and their sockets
twenty, of bronze, the hooks for the posts and their bands shall be of
11 silver. And thus for the northern side, in length the hangings shall be a
hundred cubits, and its posts twenty and their sockets twenty, of
12 bronze, and the hooks for the posts, of silver. And the width of the court
on the western side, fifty cubits of hangings, their posts shall be ten and
13 their sockets ten. And the width of the court on the side to the very
14 east, fifty cubits. And fifteen cubits of hangings for the flank, their

---

8. *as He showed you on the mountain, thus they shall do*. This is a variation of
the formula at the very end of chapter 25: God is now the subject of a transitive verb "to show" instead of the passive form used for Moses in 25:40. Here,
moreover, there is a move from the singular "you" in the first clause to "they"
in the second, the Israelites. This switch may reflect an ambiguity about the
addressee of the laws of the Tabernacle. In narrative context, it would have to
be Moses on the mountain. In rhetorical formulation, the laws sound as
though they were addressed to an impersonal "you," the representative
Israelite who is obliged to perform all these instructions (and if this text was
originally an independent unit of Priestly legislation, it could well have been
directed to an impersonal Priestly "you"). This verse, then, appears to make an
effort to anchor the cultic laws in the narrative setting by reminding us that
everything is addressed to Moses, who will then pass on the orders to the
Israelite people for implementation.

14. *flank*. The Hebrew *katef* literally means "shoulder." Several of the recurring
architectural terms are transposed from anatomy to human constructions (e.g.,
tsela', one of two words translated here as "side," originally means "rib").

posts three and their sockets three. And for the other flank fifteen 15
cubits of hangings, their posts three and their sockets three. And for the 16
gate of the court a screen of twenty cubits, indigo and purple and crimson and twisted linen, embroiderer's work, their posts four and their
sockets four. All the posts around the court shall be banded in silver, 17
their hooks silver and their sockets bronze. The length of the court, a 18
hundred cubits, and the width fifty throughout, and the height five
cubits, twisted linen, and their sockets bronze. So for all the vessels of 19
the Tabernacle in all its service; and all its pegs and all the pegs of the
court, shall be bronze.

"As for you, you shall command the Israelites, that they take you 20
clear oil of beaten olives for the light, to kindle a lamp perpetually.

---

18. *fifty throughout.* The literal meaning is "fifty in [by?] fifty," evidently to
stress that the width shall measure fifty cubits throughout.

19. *So for all the vessels.* The "so" is probably implied by the initial *l*ᵉ, which
Umberto Cassuto, following Gesenius, characterizes as a *"lamed* of inclusion."

20. *clear oil of beaten olives.* Olive oil would have been the most expensive kind
of oil in the ancient Near East (sesame oil was cheaper and more common),
and in contrast to ordinary practice, in which cloudy oil would be used for
burning and clear oil for culinary purposes, only the best oil is to be burned in
the lamps. The olives are to be beaten (*katit*) with mortar and pestle rather
than crushed in a press, the latter being a less labor-intensive process. Egypt,
it should be noted, did not typically cultivate olive trees, and it imported olive
oil at a premium from Canaan and Phoenicia. It is thus extremely unlikely that
the fleeing slaves would have been able to bring with them supplies of fine
olive oil, or to obtain it in the wilderness, so this instruction is another clear
instance in which a detail of the later Jerusalem cult is retrojected onto the
Wilderness period.
    to kindle a lamp perpetually. The Hebrew *tamid* means "perpetually," or
"regularly repeated." Despite the attachment of later Jewish tradition to an
"eternal light" (the conventional English rendering of the two words here, *ner
tamid*), the clear indication of the next verse, confirmed by the sanctuary story
of young Samuel and Eli in 1 Samuel 2, is that the lamp burned from evening
until daybreak and was lit again each evening.

21   In the Tent of Meeting outside the curtain which is over the Ark of the
Covenant, Aaron with his sons shall lay it out, from evening to morning before the LORD, an everlasting statute for your generations incum-
bent on the Israelites."

---

21. *the Tent of Meeting.* This is a synonym for the Tabernacle, stressing the
notion that within this tent God "meets," or has fixed occasions of encounter
(*moʿed*) with the people through Moses and the high priest.

   the Ark of the Covenant. As before, "Ark" is merely implied in the Hebrew.

CHAPTER 28

"**A**nd you, bring you forward Aaron your brother and his sons with ₁
him from the midst of the Israelites to be priests to Me—Aaron,
Nadab, and Abihu, Eleazar and Ithamar, the sons of Aaron. And ₂
you shall make sacred garments for Aaron your brother for glory and for
splendor. And you, speak to every wise-hearted person whom I have ₃
filled with a spirit of wisdom, that they make Aaron's garments to consecrate him, to be priest to Me. And these are the garments that they ₄
shall make: breastplate and ephod and robe and checkwork tunic, turban and sash. And they shall make sacred garments for Aaron your
brother and for his sons to make him a priest to Me. And they, they ₅

---

1. *to be priests to Me*. Everywhere except perhaps in this chapter, the verb *kihen*
is intransitive and means "to perform the functions of a priest (*kohen*)." Here,
however, the infinitive has an accusative suffix and so might mean "to make
him a priest." In any case, the transformation of Moses's brother and nephews
into a distinctive sacerdotal caste is the burden of this passage, and it is the
brilliant priestly costume—note the refrain in verse 2 and verse 40, "for glory
and for splendor"—that most impressively effects this transformation.

3. *wise-hearted . . . wisdom*. The Hebrew for "wise/wisdom" suggests both a
craftsman's skill and insight or understanding.

4. *breastplate and ephod and robe and checkwork tunic*. The ancient audience
of this text had an immense advantage over modern readers because it would
have had some actual glimpses of all this splendid raiment and priestly ornamentation and thus would have had a concrete notion of what was being
referred to. There have been endless latter-day efforts to reconstruct the
wardrobe and to parse the technical sartorial terms that are used to represent
it, but these can be no more than amalgams of guesses and approximations.

shall take the gold and the indigo and the purple and the crimson and
6 the linen. And they shall make the ephod gold, indigo, and purple,
7 crimson and twisted linen, designer's work. Two joining shoulder-
8 pieces it shall have at its two edges, and attached. And the fastening
band that is on it shall be of the same fashioning, of one piece with it,
9 gold, indigo and purple and crimson and twisted linen. And you shall
take two carnelian stones and engrave on them the names of Israel's
10 sons. Six of their names on the one stone and the six remaining names
11 on the other stone in the order of their birth. Lapidary work, seal
engravings you shall engrave on the two stones the names of Israel's
12 sons, encased in filigree of gold you shall make them. And you shall set
the two stones on the shoulder-pieces of the ephod as remembrance
stones for Israel's sons, and Aaron shall carry their names before the
13 LORD on his two shoulders as a remembrance. And you shall make a fil-
14 igree of gold. And two chains of pure gold, intertwined you shall make
them in cordwork, and you shall set the corded chains on the filigree.
15 And you shall make a breastplate of judgment, designer's work, like the
work of the ephod you shall make it, gold, indigo and purple

Though the present translation assumes that "breastplate" is still plausible for
the Hebrew *hoshen* (etymology uncertain), others contend it is a smaller
"breastpiece" or even a "pouch." The ephod (the Hebrew root suggests "binding" or "wrapping around") evidently was a kind of apron, though opinions differ on this. It has a secondary meaning as an oracular device.

9. *the names of Israel's sons.* Here the recurrent ethnic designation *beney yisra'el*
clearly refers to the twelve sons of Jacob who are the eponymous founders of
the twelve tribes of Israel. This, too, reflects a momentous transformation,
enshrined in the magic of the cult: the twelve sons of Jacob have become a
consecrated people whose special status before the deity is evoked, "remembered," ritually enacted and confirmed in the engravings on the two precious
stones in the priest's shoulder-pieces that he carries before the LORD.

15. *a breastplate of judgment.* The judgment (*mishpat*) function of the breastplate is executed through the Urim and Thummim (verse 30) that are set in it.
Because the purpose of this device is oracular, some prefer to render *mishpat*
as "decision," though there is evidence elsewhere that the Urim and Thummim were often used to determine who was guilty of a particular trespass.

and crimson and twisted linen you shall make it. It shall be square 16
and doubled, a hand span its length and a hand span its width. And you 17
shall set in it a stone inset, four rows of stone, a row of ruby, topaz, and
malachite, the first row. And the second row, turquoise, sapphire, and 18
amethyst. And the third row jacinth, agate, and crystal. And the fourth 19,20
row, beryl and carnelian and jasper, framed in gold in their settings.
And the stones shall be according to the names of Israel's sons, twelve 21
according to their names, seal engravings, each with its name for the
twelve tribes. And you shall make on the breastplate intertwined cord- 22
work, chains of pure gold. And you shall make on the breastplate two 23
golden rings, and you shall set the two rings on the two edges of the
breastplate. And you shall set the two golden cords on the two rings at 24
the edges of the breastplate. And the two ends of the two cords you 25
shall set in the two frames and put them on the shoulder-pieces of the
ephod at the front. And you shall make two golden rings and put them 26
on the two edges of the breastplate, at its border which faces the ephod
on the inside. And you shall make two golden rings and set them on 27
the two shoulder-pieces of the ephod below in the front opposite its
seam above the band of the ephod. And they shall fasten the breast- 28
plate from its rings to the rings of the ephod with an indigo strand to
be upon the band of the ephod, that the breastplate not slip from the
ephod. And Aaron shall carry the names of Israel's sons in the breast- 29
plate of judgment over his heart when he comes into the sanctum as a

---

17–20. *ruby, topaz, and malachite . . . jasper.* For all the scholarly recourse to
conjectured etymologies and comparative philology, it is virtually impossible to
determine precisely what precious stones are referred to in this list of twelve
terms. We can do little more than revel in the gorgeousness of the words,
which is surely part of the intended response for the ancient audience.

21. *according to the names of Israel's sons.* The stones offer a reduplication—
reinforcing the ritual efficacy—of the device of incising the names of the
twelve tribes: in the first instance, six names were listed on each of two stones;
now every tribe has its own precious stone.

29. *over his heart.* "Heart" of course here means "chest," but the resonance of
the term as the organ of feeling and understanding should not be lost.

30 remembrance before the LORD perpetually. And you shall place in the
breastplate of judgment the Urim and the Thummim, that they be over
Aaron's heart when he comes before the LORD, and Aaron shall carry
the judgment for the Israelites over his heart before the LORD perpetu-
31,32 ally. And you shall make the robe for the ephod pure indigo. And the
opening for the head shall be in the middle of it, its opening shall have
a wovenwork border all around, like the opening of a coat of mail it
33 shall be, it must not tear. And you shall make on its hem pomegranates
of indigo and purple and crimson, on its hem all around, and golden
34 bells within them all around. A golden bell and a pomegranate, a golden
35 bell and a pomegranate, on the hem of the robe all around. And it shall
be upon Aaron when he serves, so that its sound be heard when he
comes into the sanctum before the LORD and when he goes out, that

---

30. *the Urim and the Thummim.* The precise character of this oracular device
has eluded identification. One common conjecture is that they were two
stones with different letters or words engraved on them, but unless someone
actually digs up a pair, there is no way of proving the conjecture. Traditional
interpretation associates the two words with roots that mean "light" and "perfection," but if they are opposites, they could be linked etymologically with
terms suggesting "curse" and "innocence." It is probably not coincidental that
these two words begin respectively with the first and the last letter of the
Hebrew alphabet. In any case, most of the references to the Urim and Thummim in narrative passages invite the inference that the device generated a
binary response to whatever question was posed: yes or no, guilty or innocent.

32. *like the opening of a coat of mail.* This is a prevalent traditional interpretation, but the crucial term in the phrase, *tahra*, does not appear elsewhere and
is of uncertain etymology and meaning.

33. *A golden bell and a pomegranate, a golden bell and a pomegranate.* The sheer
splendor of the ornamentation is evoked in poetic incantation through the repetition of the phrase. Judah Halevi, the great medieval Hebrew poet, echoes
these words in a delicate, richly sensual love poem, registering an imaginative
responsiveness to the sumptuous sensuality of the language here.

35. *so that its sound be heard . . . that he shall not die.* In the ancient Near East,
the inner sanctum was a dangerous place. Any misstep or involuntary trespass
of the sacred paraphernalia could bring death. (Compare verse 38: the device

he shall not die. And you shall make a diadem of pure gold and engrave 36
upon it with seal engravings: Holy to the LORD. And you shall put on it 37
an indigo strand, that it be on the turban, at the front of the turban it
shall be. And it shall be on Aaron's forehead, that Aaron may bear off 38
any guilt from the holy things that the Israelites consecrate, from all
their holy gifts, and it shall be on his forehead perpetually for their
acceptance before the LORD. And you shall weave the tunic checkwork 39
linen, and you shall make a linen turban, and a sash you shall make of
embroiderer's work. And for Aaron's sons you shall make tunics, and 40
you shall make sashes for them, and headgear you shall make them for
glory and for splendor. And you shall dress them, Aaron your brother 41
and his sons with him, and you shall anoint them, and you shall install
them and consecrate them, that they serve Me as priests. And make 42
them linen breeches to cover their naked flesh, from the hips to the

---

with the divine name on Aaron's golden diadem carries away any guilt that may
be incurred in violating "the holy things that the Israelites consecrate.") The
sound of the ringing golden bells on Aaron's hem goes before him as he enters
the sanctum, serving an apotropaic function to shield him from harm in this
zone of danger.

36. *diadem*. This is another term about which there is dispute. The primary
meaning of the Hebrew *tsits* is "blossom," and so this might be a blossom-
shaped gold ornament bound upon the forehead, of the sort the Egyptians
were known to use. In poetry, *tsits* appears in parallelism with *nezer*, "crown."

38. *any guilt*. If, for example, an Israelite consecrated to the cult an animal
marred by a blemish, "guilt" would be incurred.

41. *install them*. The literal meaning of the Hebrew is "fill their hands."

42. *linen breeches to cover their naked flesh*. Breeches were not worn except by
the priestly officials. The need to avoid exposing nakedness in the cult was
asserted earlier in 20:26. The Hebrew term here is literally "flesh of the nakedness," the word for nakedness, *'erwah*, referring specifically to the genitalia and
strongly associated with forbidden sexuality.

43 thighs they shall be. And they shall be upon Aaron and upon his sons
when they come into the Tent of Meeting or when they approach the
altar to serve in the sanctum, that they do not bear guilt and die—a perpetual statute for him and for his seed after him."

43. *that they do not bear guilt and die.* The phrase used pointedly puns on "bear
off . . . guilt" in verse 38. In the first instance, the idiom means to remove guilt.
Here, antithetically, it means to bear the onus of guilt. Even the golden diadem engraved with the divine name would not protect the priest from harm if
he were to violate the sanctity of the Tabernacle by exposing his sexual parts
as he performed his priestly functions.

CHAPTER 29

"And this is the thing you shall do for them to consecrate them to be priests to Me: take one bull of the herd and two unblemished rams, and flatbread and flatcakes mixed with oil and flatcake wafers brushed with oil, fine wheat flour you shall make them. And you shall place them in one basket and bring them forward in the basket, with the bull and with the two rams. And Aaron and his sons you shall bring forward at the entrance to the Tent of Meeting, and you shall bathe them in water. And you shall take the garments and dress Aaron in the tunic and the robe of the ephod and the ephod and the breast-plate, and you shall gird him with the band of the ephod. And you shall put the turban on his head and you shall set the holy diadem

---

1. *to consecrate them to be priests to Me.* This whole series of cultic regulations is arranged in concentric circles: first the donation of the sumptuous materials of the Tabernacle and the instructions for assembling the elaborate portable structure; then the directions for constructing the inner sanctum and the altar; then the vestments and sacred ornaments of the priests; now the priests themselves—their installation rite and the precise instructions for the animal sacrifices, the sundry meal offerings, and the libations. For the Priestly writer, the representation of Aaron and his sons actually performing the sacred service on the altar, installed in their sacerdotal function, butchering the animals and splashing gore on the altar and on themselves, would have surely been the climax of this entire sequence.

4. *you shall bring forward.* The Hebrew verb *hiqriv* generally means "to bring near" or "to cause to approach." Presumably what is implied is coming close to the sacred place of God's presence. It is also the common verb that means "to sacrifice."

7 on the turban. And you shall take the anointing oil and pour it over his
8 head and you shall anoint him. And his sons you shall bring forward
9 and dress them in tunics. And you shall belt them with sashes, Aaron
   and his sons, and set headgear on them, and the priesthood shall be for
10 them a perpetual statute, and you shall install Aaron and his sons. And
   you shall bring forward the bull before the Tent of Meeting, and Aaron,
11 and his sons, shall lay their hands on the bull's head. And you shall
   slaughter the bull before the LORD at the entrance to the Tent of Meet-
12 ing. And you shall take of the bull's blood and place it on the horns of
   the altar with your finger, and all the blood you shall spill upon the base
13 of the altar. And you shall take all the fats that cover the entrails and
   the lobe on the liver and the two kidneys and the fat that is on them

---

7. *anointing oil*. Oil poured over the head—presumably pure olive oil—was the
confirming act of consecration for both priests and kings. Hence in biblical
idiom the monarch is not the crowned king (though they did sometimes wear
crowns) but the anointed king (*mashiaḥ*).

9. *a perpetual statute*. The Hebrew *ḥoq*, which has the general meaning of
"statute," also sometimes suggests an allowance, a benefice that is regularly
paid to someone. Since the tribe of Levi from which the priests came would
have no lands, the priesthood was not only their spiritual inheritance but also
their allowance or dole.

10. *lay their hands on the bull's head*. The laying on of hands may simply have
betokened an affirmation of possession of the animal, though some commentators suggest a kind of magical transfusion of properties from the person
touching to the beast touched—perhaps, the sins for which the sacrificed animal is to atone.

12. *And you shall take of the bull's blood*. Blood, which has been so prominent
and so multivalent in the Exodus story, here serves a dedicatory and purgative
function, making the altar holy. Similarly, in verse 20 Aaron and his sons are
enjoined to daub the sacrificial blood symbolically on the organs of hearing
and holding and locomotion in order to dedicate themselves wholly to their
sacred task. (Presumably, the eye is omitted to avoid the danger of getting
blood in the eye, and the mouth is omitted because of the taboo against tasting blood.)
   all the blood. This obviously means all the rest of the blood.

and turn them to smoke on the altar. And the bull's flesh and its hide 14
and its dung you shall burn in fire outside the camp, it is an offense.
And the one ram you shall take, and Aaron and his sons shall lay their 15
hands on the ram's head. And you shall slaughter the ram and take its 16
blood and throw it upon the altar all around. And the ram you shall cut 17
up by its parts and wash its entrails and its limbs and put them on its
cut parts and its head. And you shall turn the ram to smoke on the 18
altar, it is a burnt offering to the LORD, a pleasing fragrance, a fire offering to the LORD. And you shall take the second ram, and Aaron, and his 19
sons, shall lay their hands on the ram's head. And you shall slaughter 20
the ram and take of its blood and put it on the right earlobe of Aaron
and on the right earlobe of his sons and on their right thumb and on
their right big toe, and you shall throw the blood on the altar all
around. And you shall take of the blood that is on the altar and of the 21
anointing oil and sprinkle them on Aaron and on his garments and on
his sons' garments and on his face together with them, and he shall be
consecrated, he and his garments and his sons and his sons' garments
together with him. And you shall take from the ram the fat, and the 22
broad tail and the fat that covers the entrails and the lobe on the liver
and the two kidneys and the fat that is on them, and the right thigh, for
it is the installation ram, and one loaf of bread and one cake of bread 23
made with oil and one wafer from the basket of flatbread that is before
the LORD. And you shall put it all on the palms of Aaron and on the 24

---

14. *burn in fire.* As elsewhere, this seeming redundance indicates total burning, burning to ashes.

18. *a pleasing fragrance.* This recurrent idiom clearly derives from pagan usage,
in which the fragrance of the sacrifices was imagined to ascend to the nostrils
of the deity and cause the deity bodily pleasure. What residue of the pagan
concreteness of the idiom may have been retained in its biblical usage is
impossible to know.

21. *blood . . . anointing oil.* The spectacle of the priests splattered all over with
blood and oil may be a repugnant one to the modern imagination, but for the
ancients both the clear olive oil and the sacrificial blood were thought of as
purifying agents.

palms of his sons and elevate it as an elevation offering before the
25 LORD. And you shall take them from their hands and turn them to
smoke on the altar, together with the burnt offering, as a pleasing fra-
26 grance before the LORD, it is a fire offering to the LORD. And you shall
take the breast from the installation ram which is Aaron's and elevate it
as an elevation offering before the LORD, and it shall be your portion.
27 And you shall consecrate the breast of the elevation offering and the
thigh of the donation, which were elevated and which were donated,
28 from the installation ram that is Aaron's and that is his sons'. And it
shall be a perpetual statute for Aaron and for his sons from the
Israelites, for it is a donation, and a donation shall it be from the
Israelites, from their communion sacrifices, their donation to the LORD.

29 "And the sacral garments that are Aaron's shall belong to his sons after
30 him, to be anointed in them and to be installed in them. Seven days the
priest in his stead among his sons shall wear them, who comes into the
31 Tent of Meeting to serve in the sanctum. And the installation ram you
32 shall take and you shall cook its flesh in a sacred place. And Aaron, and
his sons with him, shall eat the ram's flesh and the bread that is in the
33 basket at the entrance of the Tent of Meeting. And they for whom
atonement is made shall eat them, to install them, to consecrate them,
34 and no stranger shall eat them, for they are holy. And if something is
left over from the flesh of installation and from the bread until morning, you shall burn what is left in fire, it shall not be eaten, for it is holy.
35 And you shall do thus for Aaron and for his sons, as all that I have

---

29. *to his sons after him*. Here the priestly succession, from Aaron in the wilderness all the way to the Priestly writer in the sixth century, is envisaged. The
preposition "in his stead" (*taḥtaw*) in the next verse is another indication of a
chain of succession to the office of high priest.

33. *no stranger*. The reference here is clearly not to an ethnic alien but, as in
other ritual contexts, to anyone not belonging to the priestly caste and not consecrated to approach the sanctum.

charged you, seven days you shall install them. And an offense-offering   36
bull you shall prepare for each day, and you shall purge the altar as you
atone over it, and you shall anoint it to consecrate it. Seven days you   37
shall atone on the altar and consecrate it, and the altar shall be a holy
of holies, whoever touches it shall be consecrated. And this shall you   38
do on the altar: two yearling lambs each day, perpetually. The one lamb   39
you shall do in the morning and the other lamb you shall do at twilight.
And a tenth of a measure of fine flour mixed with a quarter-*hin* of   40
beaten oil, and a quarter-*hin* libation of wine for the one lamb. And the   41
other lamb you shall do at twilight, like the morning's grain offering and
its libation you shall do it, as a pleasing fragrance to the LORD, a per-   42
petual burnt offering for your generations at the entrance to the Tent of
Meeting before the LORD, where I shall meet with you there to speak
to you. And I shall meet there with the Israelites and it shall be conse-   43
crated through My glory. And I shall consecrate the Tent of Meeting   44

---

36. *purge.* The Hebrew verb is cognate with the noun for "offense" (*hata't*) and is used in the *pi'el* conjugation, which sometimes can mean to expunge or remove the substance or quality indicated by the verbal root.

37. *whoever touches it shall be consecrated.* This is commonly explained to mean that whoever touches the altar becomes consecrated, in a kind of contagion of holiness. It could equally mean, however, that whoever touches the altar must first be consecrated, the verb being construed as an imperative. Although contagious impurity is a common biblical idea, there is less basis for a notion of contagious sanctity.

42. *for your generations at the entrance to the Tent of Meeting.* The straddle of the Tabernacle laws between the Wilderness setting and the later cultic center in Jerusalem is especially evident here. The Tabernacle service, after all, was in effect just forty years, but the model it provides for the Temple service would be for the generations.

43. *it shall be consecrated through My glory.* One detects a certain tension between a conception of the sacred inherited from pagan cult and a new, monotheistic conception. According to the former, there exists an intricate technology of the sacred that confers holiness on a place and on the human officiants—the elaborate regimen of construction and dress and sacrifice and sprinkling with blood that has just been detailed. But now God reminds Israel

and the altar, and Aaron and his sons I shall consecrate to be priests to
45 Me. And I shall abide in the midst of the Israelites and I shall be God
46 to them. And they shall know that I am the LORD their God Who
brought them out from the land of Egypt for Me to abide in their midst.
I am the LORD their God."

---

that it is only through His glory, His free decision as deity to make His presence "abide"—a nomad's term of temporary residence—in this place, that the
altar becomes consecrated. Without this divine initiative, all the choreography
of the cult is unavailing. The manifestation of the "glory" of the deity has polytheistic antededents, though the strong emphasis on God's choice to abide in
the midst of Israel is new.

46. *I am the* LORD *their God.* Just as the royal proclamation of the Decalogue
began with this affirmation, the grand set of regulations for the creation of the
Tabernacle and the dedication of the priests concludes with the royal declaration of God's special relationship with Israel.

CHAPTER 30

"And you shall make an altar for burning incense, acacia wood you   1
shall make it. A cubit its length and a cubit its width, it shall be   2
square, and two cubits its height; from the same piece its horns.
And you shall overlay it with pure gold—its roof and its walls all around   3
and its horns, and you shall make for it a golden molding all around.
And two golden rings you shall make for it beneath its molding on its   4
two flanks, you shall make on its two opposite sides, and they shall be
housings for the poles with which to carry it. And you shall make the   5
poles of acacia wood and overlay them with gold. And you shall set it   6
before the curtain that is near the Ark of the Covenant in front of the
cover that is over the Ark of the Covenant where I shall meet you. And   7
Aaron shall burn upon it the aromatic incense morning after morning,
when he tends the lamps he shall burn it. And when Aaron lights the   8

---

1. *an altar for burning incense.* Like so many other features of the Tabernacle, small altars of this sort—two cubits square would be on the order of a foot and a half square—for the special purpose of burning incense were common in Canaanite sanctuaries, as archeological investigation has shown. Although the Hebrew word for "altar" is derived from the root that means "to slaughter" or "to sacrifice," its use here for a little golden square on which no sacrifices could be offered indicates that the term was applied to any raised platform dedicated to cultic purposes. The sacrificial altar was located in the outer court of the Tabernacle, the incense altar in the inner precinct directly in front of the Ark of the Covenant (verse 6). The placement of these regulations after the body of Tabernacle laws is commonly explained by the fact that they had nothing to do with the rites of installation. In any case, this chapter seems to be an appendix of miscellaneous items to the Tabernacle section: first instructions about the incense altar, then census regulations, then directions about the laver, and finally the recipe for the incense.

lamps at twilight he shall burn it, a perpetual incense before the LORD
9 for your generations. You shall not offer up on it unfit incense, nor
burnt offering nor grain offering, and no libation shall you pour upon it.
10 And Aaron shall atone on its horns once a year with the blood of the
offense offering of atonement, once a year he shall atone on it for your
generations. It is holy of holies to the LORD."

11,12 And the LORD spoke to Moses, saying, "When you count heads for the
Israelites according to their numbers, every man shall give ransom for
his life to the LORD when they are counted, that there be no scourge
13 among them when they are counted. This shall each who undergoes
the count give: half a shekel by the shekel of the sanctuary—twenty

---

9. *unfit incense*. Literally, "strange [*zarah*] incense." In the cultic passages, as
we have already seen, "strange" indicates not "alien" but either a person (layman) or, as here, a substance that is not proper for introduction into the
sanctum.

10. *once a year with the blood of the offense offering of atonement*. That one day
would be the Day of Atonement. Aaron would have to carry blood from the
outer court, where the animal sacrifice was offered, to conduct this ritual of
expiation or purgation in which the four horns of the incense altar were
daubed with blood.

12. *When you count heads*. The literal sense of the Hebrew is "lift up the head."
   every man shall give ransom for his life . . . when they are counted. It was a
belief common to Israel and to the Mesopotamian cultures that it was dangerous for humans to be counted. Perhaps it was felt that assigning individuals in a mass an exact number set them up as vulnerable targets for malefic
forces. The story of David's ill-fated census in 2 Samuel 24, which triggers a
plague, turns on this belief. The danger of destruction inherent in census taking could be averted by the payment of a "ransom" for each threatened life as
a donation to the sanctuary. The supposed danger of the census thus becomes
the rationale for the institution of a poll tax, which in turn will be an important source of revenue for the maintenance of the sanctuary and its officiants.

13. *half a shekel by the shekel of the sanctuary*. "Shekel" means "weight" in
Hebrew, and the stress on weights here is a clear indication that the reference
is to a fixed weight of silver rather than to a coin. (Coins came into use fairly
late in the biblical period.) It seems likely that the specified "shekel of the

gerahs to the shekel—half a shekel, a donation to the Lord. Whosoever 14
undergoes the count from twenty years old and up shall give the Lord's
donation. The rich man shall not give more and the poor man shall not 15
give less than half a shekel to atone for their lives. And you shall take 16
the atonement money from the Israelites and set it for the service of
the Tent of Meeting, and it shall be a remembrance for the Israelites
before the Lord to atone for their lives."

And the Lord spoke to Moses, saying, "And you shall make a laver of 17,18
bronze and a stand of bronze for washing and place it between the Tent
of Meeting and the altar, and place water there. And Aaron and his sons 19
shall wash their hands and their feet from it. When they come into the 20
Tent of Meeting, they shall wash with water, that they do not die, or
when they approach the altar to serve, to burn a fire offering to the
Lord. And they shall wash their hands and their feet, that they do not 21
die, and it shall be for them a perpetual statute, for him and for his
seed, for their generations."

And the Lord spoke to Moses, saying, "And you, take you choice 22,23
spices: five hundred weight wild myrrh, and aromatic cinnamon, half of
that, two hundred fifty weight, and aromatic cane, two hundred fifty
weight. And cassia, five hundred weight by the shekel of the sanctuary, 24

---

sanctuary" was a heavier weight than the "silver shekels at the merchants' tried
weight" (Genesis 23:16) that Abraham pays to Ephron the Hittite. The average
weight of actual shekels that have been unearthed is something over eleven
grams, which would make the *gerah*, its twentieth part, rather small change.

23–24. *myrrh . . . cinnamon . . . cassia.* As with the names for precious stones,
the exact identification of the sundry spices is uncertain (the items listed in
verse 34 are especially doubtful). The first two terms mentioned, however,
happily have cognates in other languages—*mor* and *qinamon*. The presence of
the latter term in biblical Hebrew demonstrates the vitality of ancient international trade: cinnamon was originally raised in Ceylon and elsewhere in
South Asia, and the word appears to have arrived in ancient Israel with the
luxury import from wherever the plant was grown.

25 and olive oil, a *hin*. And you shall make of it oil for sacred anointing, a
perfumer's compound, perfumer's work, sacred anointing oil it shall be.
26 And you shall anoint with it the Tent of Meeting and its furnishings and
27 the Ark of the Covenant, and the table and all its furnishings and the
28 lamp stand and its furnishings and the altar for incense, and the altar
for burnt offering and all its furnishings, and the laver and its stand.
29 And you shall consecrate them, and they shall be holy of holies, who-
30 ever touches them shall be consecrated. And Aaron and his sons you
31 shall anoint, and you shall consecrate them to be priests to Me. And to
the Israelites you shall speak, saying, 'Oil for sacred anointing this shall
32 be to Me for your generations. On a person's flesh it shall not be
poured, and in its proportions you shall make nothing like it. It is holy,
33 it shall be holy for you. The man who compounds its like and who puts
34 it on an unfit person shall be cut off from his people.'" And the LORD
said to Moses, "Take you the fragrances balsam and onycha and gal-
banum, fragrances, and clear frankincense, equal part for part it shall
35 be. And you shall make of it incense, a perfume compound, perfumer's
36 work, tinctured with salt, pure, sacred. And you shall pound it to fine
powder and place some of it before the Ark of the Covenant in the Tent
of Meeting where I shall meet you. Holy of holies it shall be to you.
37 And the incense that you will make, in its proportions you shall not
38 make for yourselves, holy it shall be for you to the LORD. The man who
makes its like to smell it shall be cut off from his people."

---

32. *On a person's flesh it shall not be poured*. The person (*'adam*) clearly means
a layperson, in contradistinction to a consecrated priest.

33. *unfit person*. Again, the term is *zar*, literally, "stranger," and serves as a definition of what is meant by "person" in the previous verse. There is a comple-
mentarity of notions of unfitness to the cult. An unfit person or substance may
not come or be brought before the altar. The sanctified compound of fragrances used for the incense to be burned on the altar may not be used outside the sanctuary for secular purposes, for the mere pleasure of enjoying the
aroma.

CHAPTER 31

And the LORD spoke to Moses, saying, "See, I have called by name [1,2] Bezalel son of Uri son of Hur, of the tribe of Judah. And I have [3] filled him with the spirit of God in wisdom and in understanding and in knowledge and in every task, to devise plans, to work in gold and [4] in silver and in bronze, and in stonecutting for settings and in wood [5]

---

1. *called by name.* The obvious sense of the idiom is to choose, to designate, or, as Rashi puts it, to summon "to perform a task." After the formal blueprints for the Tabernacle, God enlists the actual craftsmen who are to execute the plans.

3. *wisdom . . . understanding . . . knowledge.* As before, "wisdom" and its synonyms suggest both mastery of a craft and something like insight.

task. The two most common biblical terms for "work" are *mela'khah* (the word used here) and *'avodah* (the word used to designate the activity of the slaves in Egypt). *'Avodah* usually implies subservience—in political contexts, it means to be subject or vassal to a superior power, in cultic contexts, divine service—and it also often suggests strenuous physical labor (it is, for example, the verbal root used when Adam is cursed "to work the soil"). *Mela'khah* derives from the verbal root *l-'-k* found in Ugaritic but not used in the Bible as a verb, which means to carry out a designated task. Thus, a *mala'kh* is a messenger or agent (when his sender is God, an angel). In this immediate context, *mela'khah* has a clear connotation of craft, coupled with the requisite manual skill. The term, however, is meant to interact with its pointed recurrence in the immediately following passage about the sabbath, and so the present translation represents it by "task" in both cases.

6 carving, to do every task. And I, look, I have set by him Oholiab son of
Ahisamach, of the tribe of Dan, and in the heart of every wise-hearted
7 man I have set wisdom, that they make all that I have charged you: the
Tent of Meeting and the Ark of the Covenant and the covering that is
8 upon it and all the furnishings of the Tent, and the table and its furnishings and the pure lamp stand and all its furnishings and the
9 incense altar, and the burnt-offering altar and all its furnishings and the
10 laver and its stand, and the service garments and the sacred garments
11 for Aaron the priest and the garments of his sons to be priests, and the
anointing oil and the aromatic incense for the sanctum, as all that I
have charged you they shall do."

---

6. *in the heart of every wise-hearted man I have set wisdom.* The two master
craftsmen just mentioned by name would of course have needed large crews
of men with the requisite skills to work under them. Putting wisdom in the
hearts of wise-hearted men is a kind of positive counterpart to hardening the
heart of Pharaoh: the capacity for skillful artisanship is innate, one of the person's attributes, but God is the ultimate source of all such capacities and the
enabling force for their realization.

7–11. The list of everything that Bezalel and his workers are to execute follows
the instructions for the Tabernacle and the priests (chapters 25–30) in the
order they were given and thus serves as a recapitulative summary of the long
section that it now concludes.

10. *the service garments.* There is debate over the precise meaning of the
Hebrew *bigdey haserad.* Rashi—and many modern interpreters after him—
prefers to relate it to an Aramaic verb s-r-d, which means "to weave" or "to
braid." Others, beginning with the Aramaic Targums in Late Antiquity, connect it with the Hebrew root sh-r-t, "to serve." Because the term is bracketed
here with *bigdey qodesh,* "sacred garments," it is more likely that it indicates a
particular function rather than the weave or fabric of the clothing. It would
seem, then, that *bigdey haserad* are special garments worn while performing a
less sacrosanct service than that of the cult performed by the high priest.

And the LORD said to Moses, saying, "And you, speak to the Israelites,   12,13
saying, 'Yet My sabbaths you shall keep, for it is a sign between Me and
you for your generations to know that I am the LORD Who hallows you.
And you shall keep the sabbath, for it is holy to you. Those who pro-   14
fane it are doomed to die, for whosoever does a task on it, that person
shall be cut off from the midst of his people. Six days shall tasks be   15
done, and on the seventh day, an absolute sabbath, holy to the LORD.
Whosoever does a task on the sabbath day is doomed to die. And the   16

13–17. As is often the case in biblical passages of climactic thematic significance, the injunction about the sabbath is crafted with verbal symmetries that
are at once elegant and emphatic. The word *shabat* (in one instance, *shabaton*)
occurs precisely seven times and the verb "to keep" three times; and, as Yitzhak
Avishur has noted, the whole short section is chiastically structured—"for it is
a sign" (13) / "it is a sign for all time" (17); "between Me and you" (13) /
"Between Me and the Israelites" (17); "for your generations" (13) / "for their
generations" (16); etc.

13. *Yet My sabbaths you shall keep.* The force of the initial *'akh*, "yet" (or "only,"
"just") is to link this reiteration of the prohibition of work on the sabbath to the
preceding section on the construction of the Tabernacle. The Israelites have
been enjoined to undertake an elaborate set of labors in order to build God a
fit sanctuary. Nevertheless, this idea of a sanctuary, inherited from pagan
antecedents, for confirming the bond between man and God does not have
precedence over the original Israelite idea of the sabbath as the supreme confirmation of that bond, Israel's *imitatio dei*, "a sign between Me and you for
your generations."

14. *whosoever does a task on it.* All work, including even the "task" (*mela'khah*)
of the Tabernacle, must cease on the sabbath. The talmudic sages thus
showed themselves keen readers of these two adjacent passages in deriving the
thirty-nine primary categories of labor (*'avot mela'khah*) forbidden on the sabbath from the sundry activities necessary for the assemblage of the Tabernacle and its furnishings.
     doomed to die . . . cut off from the midst of his people. The vehemence of this
formulation is predicated on the notion that the sabbath is the ultimate sign
of the covenant between god and israel, so that one who violates the sabbath
violates the Covenant and renounces solidarity with the covenanted people.

15. *tasks.* The Hebrew uses a collective noun, singular in form.

Israelites shall keep the sabbath to do the sabbath for their generations,

17 a perpetual covenant. Between Me and the Israelites it is a sign for all time that six days did the LORD make heaven and earth and on the seventh day He ceased and caught His breath.'"

18 And He gave Moses when He had finished speaking with him on Mount Sinai the two tablets of the Covenant, tablets of stone written by the finger of God.

---

17. *caught His breath.* For a justification of this physical rendering of the verb, see the comment on Exodus 23:12. The flagrant anthropomorphism would not have been a problem for the ancient audience.

18. *when He had finished speaking.* The concise summary statement of this verse brings us back from the long catalogue of divine instructions—all that Moses was "shown on the mountain" during his forty days there—to the narrative situation that we left in chapter 20. Moses is now ready to come down to the foot of the mountain, where trouble is already brewing.

   written by the finger of God. The phrase "finger of God," previously used by Pharaoh's soothsayers, may suggest that God inscribed the stone tablets by tracing a finger over them, without chisel or stylus. Scholars have proposed that behind this image lie both mythological and political traditions of the ancient Near East: gods who inscribe human fate in stone and overlords who inscribe on tablets the conditions of vassalage for their vassals.

CHAPTER 32

nd the people saw that Moses lagged in coming down from the ¹ mountain, and the people assembled against Aaron and said to him, "Rise up, make us gods that will go before us, for this man Moses who brought us up from the land of Egypt, we do not know what

---

1. *And the people saw that Moses lagged in coming down from the mountain.* These words bring us back to the concrete narrative situation at the end of chapter 24, before the long interruption of cultic law: Moses had disappeared into the numinous cloud on the mountaintop; the people, awestruck, waited at the foot of the mountain, glimpsing the flashes of fire from the cloud above. It is understandable that after forty days they should wonder whether Moses would ever return, and that they should be terrified at the idea of being stranded in the wilderness without the leader on whom they had been entirely dependent.

make us gods that will go before us. Here, and repeatedly in the Golden Calf episode, *'elohim*, which regularly refers to God (in the singular) is used in the plural: despite all the spectacular demonstrations of the LORD's supreme power, the people have not liberated themselves from polytheistic notions. "Go before us" points to the urgently felt need for a guide through the wilderness, which should have been Moses or, more pointedly, the divine messenger God designated to lead Israel. The phrase is also a military idiom suggesting leadership in battle.

this man Moses. It is noteworthy that the most ordinary of terms, "man," becomes a kind of epithet for Moses, perhaps intimating the distance of puzzlement or wonder with which others regard him. Just before the tenth plague, we were told that "[t]he man Moses, too, is very great in the land of Egypt" (11:3). Now "this man Moses" is an object of exasperation and perplexity for the Israelites. The connection with the passage at the beginning of chapter 11 is reinforced by Aaron's request for the golden earrings, since the "borrowing" of gold and silver ornaments is mentioned in the same section of chapter 11.

2 has happened to him." And Aaron said to them, "Take off the golden
rings that are on the ears of your wives, your sons, and your daughters,
3 and bring them to me." And all the people took off the golden rings that
4 were on their ears and brought them to Aaron. And he took them from
their hand and he fashioned it in a mold and made it into a molten
calf. And they said, "These are your gods, O Israel, who brought you up
5 from the land of Egypt." And Aaron saw, and he built an altar before it,
and Aaron called out and said, "Tomorrow is a festival to the LORD."

---

4. *fashioned it in a mold.* The word represented as "mold," *ḥeret,* usually means
"stylus," but incising would not normally have been part of the process of making a molten image. Some scholars relate both the verb and the noun to
entirely different roots that yield the sense "wrapped it in a bag," but that reading is quite strained. Perhaps a term associated with a different image-making
process was then applied idiomatically to all kinds of metalwork image-
making. In any case, Aaron is pointedly represented as fashioning the image,
an idea that may have been reinforced by the use of the term *ḥeret,* in blatant
contradiction to the comically lame excuse he will make to Moses, "I flung it
into the fire, and out came this calf" (verse 24).

These are your gods, O Israel, who brought you up from the land of Egypt. This
is a provocative reversal of God's proclamation at the beginning of the Decalogue and elsewhere that He is the LORD Who brought the people out of
Egypt. The gods are plural while the calf is singular because ancient Near
Eastern people were polytheists, not fetishists: the golden icon was conceived
as the terrestrial throne or platform for the deity (singular or plural), having
precisely the same function as the cherubim over the Ark. The Golden Calf is
thus a kind of anti-Tabernacle or anti-Ark, meant for the same end of making
the divine dwell among the people but doing it in a prohibited fashion. It
should be noted that golden bulls or calves were often used as cultic seats for
deities in the ancient Near East. Scholarship has duly registered an implicit
polemic in this story against the northern kingdom of Israel, which set up
golden calves at its sanctuaries in Bethel and Dan—evidently, not at all as
images of pagan worship but as thrones for the God of Israel, in a competing
iconography to the one used in Jerusalem.

5. *a festival to the LORD.* Aaron tries both to placate the people and yet to preserve a sense of loyalty to the LORD, YHWH. They have already twice said that
they wanted him to make them "gods," but, rather desperately, he clings to the
notion that the Golden Calf should be seen as the LORD's throne and that this
celebration should be "a festival to the LORD."

And they rose early on the next day, and they offered up burnt offer- 6
ings and brought forward communion sacrifices, and the people came
back from eating and drinking and they rose up to play. And the LORD 7
said to Moses, "Quick, go down, for your people that I brought up from
Egypt has acted ruinously. They have swerved quickly from the way 8
that I charged them. They have made them a molten calf and bowed
down to it and sacrificed to it and said, 'These are your gods, O Israel,
who brought you up from the land of Egypt.'" And the LORD said to 9
Moses, "I see this people and, look, it is a stiff-necked people. And 10
now leave Me be, that My wrath may flare against them, and I will put
an end to them and I will make you a great nation." And Moses 11
implored the presence of the LORD his God and said, "Why, O LORD,
should your wrath flare against Your people that You brought out
from the land of Egypt with great power and with a strong hand?

---

6. *to play.* The Hebrew *letsaheq* suggests revelry and in some contexts sexual
play or license. The strong implication is a bacchanalian celebration (accompanied by food and drink) that involves shouting and song (verse 18) and dance
(verse 19) and probably orgiastic activity as well.

7. *your people that I brought up from Egypt.* Like a disgruntled parent disavow-
ing connection with a wayward child, God says to Moses that Israel is *your*
people.

9. *And the LORD said to Moses.* The formula for introducing quoted speech is
reiterated with no intervening response from Moses. According to this fixed
convention of biblical narrative, this repetition of the formula after the lack of
an answer points to Moses's incapacity to respond, dumbfounded as he is by
what God tells him.

10. *leave Me be . . . and I will put an end to them.* Either God, imagined in
frankly human terms, is so thoroughly fed up with the refractory people that
He really contemplates destroying them utterly and then starting from scratch
with Moses, or these words are a kind of test of Moses, who firmly declines to
be the progenitor of a new nation and shows himself a staunch advocate of
Israel.

12   Why should the Egyptians say, 'For evil He brought them out, to kill them in the mountains, to put an end to them on the face of the earth'? Turn back from Your flaring wrath and relent from the evil against 13   Your people. Remember Abraham, Isaac, and Israel Your servants, to whom You swore by Yourself and spoke to them, 'I will multiply your seed like the stars of the heavens, and all this land that I said, I will 14   give to your seed, and they will hold it in estate forever.'" And the LORD relented from the evil that He had spoken to do to His people. 15   And Moses turned and came down the mountain, with the two tablets of the Covenant in his hand written on both their sides, on the one 16   side and on the other they were written. And the tablets, God's doing they were, and the writing, God's writing it was, inscribed on the 17   tablets. And Joshua heard the sound of the people as it shouted, and he 18   said to Moses, "A sound of war in the camp!" And he said,

---

12. *Why should the Egyptians say.* Moses invokes what has been a leading motif of the Exodus story: God's liberation of Israel from slavery and His triumph over Egypt established His "glory," His unique status as supreme God of all the earth. To destroy Israel now would overturn all that has been achieved through the Exodus for God's standing in the eyes of humankind at large.

13. *Remember Abraham, Isaac, and Israel Your servants.* After the argument based on the preservation of God's reputation, Moses invokes a contractual obligation: God has promised to the patriarchs a grand future for their descendants in the terms of the Covenant, and He surely cannot revoke that promise.

15. *written on both their sides.* Despite Christian and Jewish iconography, the stone tablets, as archeology has discovered in remnants from the surrounding cultures, were thick enough to have inscriptions on both sides.

17. *And Joshua heard the sound of the people as it shouted.* Joshua, we should recall, was stationed partway up the mountain while Moses went on to the summit. Thus he hears the uproar of the Israelite revelry from a distance and is not close enough to see what is going on. Umberto Cassuto proposes that the single word for "as it shouted," *berei'oh,* is a pun on *bera'ah,* "for evil," which was used in verse 12.

   A sound of war in the camp! Joshua is a military man and so jumps to the conclusion that the uproar means battle.

> "Not the sound of crying out in triumph,
>   and not the sound of crying out in defeat.
>   A sound of crying out I hear."

And it happened when he drew near the camp that he saw the calf and   19
the dancing, and Moses's wrath flared, and he flung the tablets from
his hand and smashed them at the bottom of the mountain. And he   20
took the calf that they had made and burned it in fire and ground it fine
and scattered it over the water and made the Israelites drink it.
And Moses said to Aaron, "What did this people do to you that you   21
should have brought upon it great offense?" And Aaron said, "Let not   22
my lord's wrath flare. You yourself know that this people is in an evil

---

18. *triumph . . . defeat . . . crying out*. In the triadic line of poetry that Moses
uses to respond to Joshua, "triumph" (literally, "might") and "defeat" (literally,
"weakness") are antithetically bracketed, and then the third member of the
line, as often happens in poetic triads, introduces a new, unstable element.
The common claim that the Hebrew for "crying out," *'anot*, means "singing" is
dubious because the sound has just been described as shouting (though it
might include singing). The same term, *'anot*, occurs in 2 Samuel 22:36, where
it probably means "battle cry." Moses's response to Joshua, then, is that he
hears an indiscriminate uproar which has nothing to do with military matters.

19. *he saw the calf and the dancing . . . and he flung the tablets . . . and smashed
them*. Moses, of course, has already been informed about all this, but, as the
Hebrew proverb has it, "hearing is not the same as seeing." His wrath flares—
precisely what he implored God not to allow to occur with divine wrath—and
he responds in a paroxysm of anger, flinging and smashing. There is also a good
deal of evidence that in the ancient Near East smashing the tables on which
a binding agreement was written was a legal act of abrogating the agreement.

20. *scattered it over the water and made the Israelites drink it*. Numerous commentators have noted the (approximate) analogy to the ordeal by drinking to
which the woman suspected of adultery is submitted (Numbers 5:11–31).
Richard Elliott Friedman asks, what water?, and then interestingly proposes
that this would have to have been the water that Moses miraculously provided
for the people, which would be a compounding of irony.

23 way. And they said to me, 'Make us gods that will go before us, for this
man Moses who brought us up from the land of Egypt, we do not know
24 what has happened to him.' And I said to them, 'Whoever has gold, take
it off.' And they gave it to me, and I flung it into the fire, and out came
25 this calf." And Moses saw the people, that it was let loose, for Aaron
26 had let them loose as a shameful thing to their adversaries. And
Moses stood at the gate of the camp and said, "Whoever is for the
27 Lord, to me!" And the Levites gathered round him. And he said to
them, "Thus said the Lord God of Israel, 'Put every man his sword on
his thigh, and cross over and back from gate to gate in the camp, and
each man kill his brother and each man his fellow and each man his

---

24. *I flung it into the fire*. Aaron in his feeble attempt at an alibi uses the same
verb for violent or spasmodic throwing that was employed for Moses's casting
down the tablets.

25. *let loose, for Aaron had let them loose*. The basic meaning of the Hebrew
paru'a is "to unbind," as in the unbinding or letting loose of long hair. The
sense here is of a loosing of all inhibitions in orgiastic frenzy. Friedman sees in
"let them loose," *pera'oh,* a pun on "Pharaoh," while Cassuto detects in the
same word a pun on *bera'ah*, "in evil."
   as a shameful thing to their adversaries. The word translated as "shameful
thing," *shimtsah*, appears only here and so its meaning is uncertain, though it
seems to indicate something strongly negative. "To their adversaries" might
conceivably be a euphemism for "themselves," as the more common word for
enemies is sometimes used as a euphemistic substitution in curses.

27. *Put every man his sword on his thigh*. Typically, the short sword would have
been strapped in a scabbard to the left thigh for quick unsheathing by the right
hand. In rallying round him men of the tribe of Levi, his own tribe, Moses does
something analogous to what David will do in creating a power base within the
people through a kind of family militia recruited from his clan in Bethlehem.
We can no longer recover the historical roots of the biblical traditions about
Levi, later the sacerdotal tribe, as an implacably violent group. In the massacre
of the males of Shechem (Genesis 35), that violence was negative; here it is
represented in a positive light, supposedly exerting a necessary astringent
effect on the people that has been "let loose," that has surrendered to the
orgiastic release of a pagan cult.
   each man kill his brother . . . his fellow . . . his kin. This chilling command
enjoins the sword-wielding Levites to show no mercy to friend or kin, since the

kin.'" And the Levites did according to the word of Moses, and about 28
three thousand men of the people fell on that day. And Moses said, 29
"Dedicate yourselves today to the LORD, for each man is against his son
and against his brother, and so blessing may be given to you today."
And it happened on the next day that Moses said to the people, "You, 30
you have committed a great offense. And now I shall go up to the LORD.
Perhaps I may atone for your offense." And Moses went back to the 31
LORD and said, "I beg You! This people has committed a great offense,
they have made themselves gods of gold. And now, if You would bear 32
their offense . . . , and if not, wipe me out, pray, from Your book which

---

very nature of a pagan orgy engulfing the masses is that at least some of those
most deeply involved will be people close to the executors of retribution. The
figure of three thousand dead in the next verse indicates that this is not an
indiscriminate massacre but an assault on the ringleaders—or perhaps, those
guilty of the most egregious excesses—among the orgiasts.

29. *Dedicate yourselves.* This is the same idiom for priestly dedication, "fill your
hands," that in the context of the Tabernacle cult was rendered as "install."
    so blessing may be given to you. The Hebrew syntax is a little obscure, but
the evident sense is that the Levites, through their homicidal zealotry, confirm
their "dedication" as a priestly caste and thus as worthy recipients of God's
blessing.

31. *I beg You!* The Hebrew, a single word, is neither pronoun nor verb but is an
ejaculation, *'ana,* which is used to begin an entreaty. "Please" in English seems
matter-of-fact and merely polite, not sufficiently imploring.

32. *if You would bear their offense.* The thought stipulated after this conditional
clause is left incomplete, perhaps because Moses is uncertain what to say and
is in any case concentrating on the negative conditional clause: "if not, wipe
me out, pray, from Your book."
    Your book. Although most modern translators prefer to represent *sefer* as
"scroll" or "record," the word also sometimes means "book" in biblical Hebrew
(its regular sense in postbiblical Hebrew), and various ancient Near Eastern
peoples registered belief in a celestial book in which the fates of humankind
were inscribed. (The codex format of the book had not yet been invented, but
a text written on a scroll could nevertheless be conceptualized as a book.) This
entire exchange between Moses and God looks suspiciously like a duplication,
in part contradictory, of verses 9–13. There God offered to make Moses the

33 You have written." And the LORD said to Moses, "He who has offended
34 against Me, I shall wipe him out from My book. And now, lead this people to where I have spoken to you. Look, My messenger shall go before
you. And on the day I make a reckoning, I will make a reckoning with
35 them for their offense." And the LORD scourged the people for having
made the calf that Aaron made.

---

beginning of a new people after the destruction of all the Israelites. Here
Moses asks for death if God will not forgive Israel, and God replies that He
will exact retribution only from the offenders.

34. *My messenger shall go before you.* It is not the gods that the people wanted
Aaron to make for them that will go before them but, as stipulated earlier in
the story, God's messenger. That messenger, we should recall, is not only a
guide but also an inexorable and rather menacing monitor of the people's
behavior.

   on the day I make a reckoning. The exact reference is obscure. Three thousand of the offenders have already been killed by the Levites, and, momentarily, there will be a further "scourge" by God. For this archetypal sin of the
Golden Calf, a free-floating prospect of further retribution would seem to
hover over the people like a dark shadow.

35. *for having made the calf that Aaron made.* The repetition of the verb conveys the complicity of both the people and Aaron in the making of the calf.

CHAPTER 33

And the LORD said to Moses, "Go, head up from here, you and the 1 people that you brought up from the land of Egypt, to the land that I swore to Abraham, to Isaac, and to Jacob, saying, 'To your seed I will give it.' And I shall send a messenger before you and I 2 shall drive out the Canaanite, the Amorite, and the Hittite and the Perizzite, the Hivite and the Jebusite, to a land flowing with milk and 3 honey. But I shall not go up in your midst, for you are a stiff-necked people, lest I put an end to you on the way." And the people heard this 4 evil thing, and they mourned, and none of them put on their jewelry.

---

3. *But I shall not go up.* The initial Hebrew conjunction *ki* most often means "for" but also sometimes has an adversative sense, "though" or "but," which seems probable here: go up, and My messenger will go before you, but don't expect Me to go up with you.

lest I put an end to you on the way. These words seem to be dictated by a strongly anthropomorphic characterization of God: after the flaring of His anger over the Golden Calf, He prefers to keep a certain distance from this provoking people, whose behavior could easily push Him to destroy them entirely. Abraham ibn Ezra understands God's refusal to dwell in the midst of Israel as a cancellation of the construction project for the Tabernacle—a not unreasonable reading, because all along the Tabernacle was conceived as an institutionalized focus for God's presence in the midst of the people.

4. *none of them put on their jewelry.* Given the fact that they have just made a mass donation of gold earrings for the fashioning of the Golden Calf, one gets a sense that they have come out of Egypt bedecked with a rich abundance of precious ornaments.

5 And the LORD said to Moses, "Say to the Israelites, 'You are a stiff-
necked people. If but a single moment I were to go up in your midst, I
would put an end to you. And now, put down your jewelry from upon
6 you, and I shall know what I should do with you.'" And the Israelites
stripped themselves of their jewelry from Mount Horeb onward.

7 And Moses would take the Tent and pitch it for himself outside the
camp, far from the camp, and he called it the Tent of Meeting. And so,
whoever sought the LORD would go out to the Tent of Meeting which

---

5. *You are a stiff-necked people. If but a single moment I were to go up in your
midst.* This entire verse duplicates verse 3 and has the look of an uneven editorial splicing of sources. One difference, however, is that in the first instance
these words were addressed only to Moses, whereas now he is enjoined to
report them to the people, and with a certain note of intensification ("If but a
single moment . . ."). Another element of puzzling duplication is the injunction to remove the jewelry, an act that the Israelites have already executed.
Richard Elliott Friedman explains the contradiction by proposing that the verb
here, "put down from upon you," is meant to indicate not just a temporary
removal of the ornaments but a permanent renunciation of wearing them during the Wilderness period. This reading is supported by the odd prepositional
use in the next sentence of "stripped themselves of their jewelry from Mount
Horeb," where "from" probably has a temporal sense (which this translation
reflects by adding the adverb "onward").

7. *would take.* Biblical Hebrew has no specialized verbal form for the iterative
tense (that is, habitually repeated actions), but the use here of the imperfective followed by the perfective form and the contextual clues make it clear that
this whole passage is in the iterative.
　and he called it the Tent of Meeting. Elsewhere, this designation was synonymous with the Tabernacle, but here there is no question of erecting that
elaborate structure but rather of Moses's pitching his own tent outside the
camp and making it serve as a Tent of Meeting, a place where God meets or
encounters Moses as Israel's spokesman. Ibn Ezra proposes, with an eye to the
iterative character of the passage, that Moses has placed the second set of
tablets of the Law in this tent. The Tent itself is located outside the camp
because Israel, after the Golden Calf, is deemed unworthy to have God's
meeting place with them inside the camp.

was outside the camp. And so, when Moses would go out to the Tent, 8
all the people would rise and each man would station himself at the
entrance of his tent, and they would look after Moses until he came to
the Tent. And so, when Moses would come to the Tent, the pillar of 9
cloud would come down and stand at the entrance of the Tent and
speak with Moses. And all the people would see the pillar of cloud 10
standing at the entrance to the Tent, and all the people would rise and
bow down each man at the entrance of his tent. And the LORD would 11
speak to Moses face to face, as a man speaks to his fellow. And he
would return to the camp, and his attendant Joshua son of Nun, a lad,
would not budge from within the Tent.

---

8. *each man would station himself . . . they would look after Moses.* This setup
replicates horizontally the vertical setup in which Moses goes up on the mountain to encounter God and the people wait below, looking upward at the cloud
on the summit. The refractory people now appears to have resumed the stance
of obedient followers of Moses.

9. *the pillar of cloud would come down . . . and speak with Moses.* It is of course
God speaking from within the pillar of cloud. The oddness of the formulation
is dictated by the fact that it is a vividly faithful representation of the people's
visual perspective: as each man stands at the entrance of his tent looking after
Moses, and as he sees the pillar of cloud (verse 10), it seems to him as though
the pillar of cloud were speaking with Moses.

11. *And the LORD would speak to Moses face to face, as a man speaks to his fellow.* These two idioms for direct communication cannot be literally true
because the burden of what follows in this chapter is that no man, not even
Moses, can see God's face. The hyperbole is in all likelihood a continuation of
the visual perspective of the people so clearly marked in verses 8–10: as it
appears to the Israelites from their vantage point in front of their tents, Moses
conversing with the pillar of cloud is speaking to God as a man speaks to his
fellow.
   Joshua son of Nun, a lad. The preceding narrative conveys a strong impression that Joshua is a man of mature years. Ibn Ezra, who places him in his
fifties at this juncture, plausibly infers that the Hebrew *na'ar* here reflects its
not infrequent sense of someone in a subaltern position (it would thus be a
synonym for "attendant").

12 And Moses said to the Lord, "See, You say to me, 'Bring up this people,' yet You, You have not made known to me whom You will send with
me. And You, You have said, 'I know you by name, and you have also
13 found favor in My eyes.' And now, if, pray, I have found favor in Your
eyes, let me know, pray, Your ways, that I may know You, so that I may
14 find favor in Your eyes. And see, for this nation is Your people." And He
15 said, "My presence shall go, and I will grant you rest." And he said to
16 Him, "If Your presence does not go, do not take us up from here. And
how, then, will it be known that I have found favor in Your eyes, I and

---

12. *You have not made known to me whom You will send with me.* The verb "to
know," both in the *hiph'il* (causative) and *qal* (simple) conjugations, is the keyword of this section, which turns on Moses's urgent need to know both the
nature of the guidance God will provide Israel through the wilderness and
God's intrinsic nature. Moses appears to balk at God's previous declaration
that He will not go up in the midst of the people to the promised land but
instead will delegate a divine messenger for that task.

I know you by name. The Hebrew idiom suggests both special election and
intimate relationship.

13. *for this nation is Your people.* Moses seeks to remind God of His covenantal attachment to Israel, bearing in mind that in the flare-up of divine anger
when Israel made the Golden Calf, God had referred to the Israelites as "*your*
people."

14. *My presence shall go, and I will grant you rest.* The Hebrew is altogether
cryptic—and so compact that the whole sentence is only four words—and this
translation mirrors that cryptic effect. Presumably, what God is telling Moses
is that He will indeed go before the people through the wilderness, and thus
lighten Moses's burden, "grant you rest" (alternately, that verb could refer,
according to biblical idiom, to giving Moses, or the people, "rest" from their
enemies when they enter the land). But God, scarcely willing to concede that
He Himself will lead the people, words the response so laconically, suppressing the clarifying "before you" after "My presence shall go," that Moses is by
no means sure what God means, and so he goes on to say, "If Your presence
does not go, do not take us up from here." He then stipulates (verse 16) that it
is only through God's presence among the Israelites as they journey onward
that his own favored status before God can be confirmed, and the election of
Israel as well. In all this, it should be noted that "presence" and "face" are the
same Hebrew word, *panim.*

Your people? Will it not be by Your going with us, that I and Your people may be distinguished from every people that is on the face of the
earth?" And the LORD said to Moses, "This thing, too, which you have   17
spoken I will do, for you have found favor in My eyes and I have known
you by name." And he said, "Show me, pray, Your glory." And He said,   18,19
"I shall make all My goodness pass in front of you, and I shall invoke
the name of the LORD before you. And I shall grant grace to whom I
grant grace and have compassion for whom I have compassion." And   20
He said, "You shall not be able to see My face, for no human can see
Me and live." And the LORD said, "Look, there is a place with Me, and   21
you shall take your stance on the crag. And so, when My glory passes   22
over, I shall put you in the cleft of the crag and shield you with My

---

18. *Show me, pray, Your glory.* We are not likely to recover precisely what the key
term *kavod*—glory, honor, divine presence, and very literally, "weightiness"—
conveyed to the ancient Hebrew imagination. In any case, Moses, who first
fearfully encountered God in the fire in the bush, is now ready and eager to be
granted a full-scale epiphany, a frontal revelation of the look and character of
this divinity that has been speaking to him from within the pillar of cloud.

19. *I shall make all My goodness pass in front of you.* In response to the request
that God show Moses His glory, He offers instead to show him His "goodness"
(*tuv*), a manifestation of His moral attributes as divinity. But God's goodness
is not amenable to human prediction, calculation, or manipulation: it is God's
untrammeled choice to bestow grace and compassion on whom He sees fit, as
He has done with Moses.

21. *And the LORD said.* Extraordinarily, there are three consecutive iterations of
the formula for introducing speech (verses 19, 20, 21) with no response from
Moses. Moses, having asked to see God face to face, is in a daunting situation
where it is God Who will do all the talking and explain the limits of the revelation to be vouchsafed Moses.

22. *shield you with My palm.* The Hebrew *kaf* means the inside of the hand,
the part that holds objects, and is not the general word for hand (*yad*). The
conjunction of the verb "shield" (or "screen") with *kaf* is unusual, and perhaps
kaf is used here because it is the tender part of the hand. Another scholarly
proposal is that *kaf* in this instance is an assimilative spelling of *kanaf*, "wing"
(or "border," of a garment), a noun elsewhere idiomatically associated with
shielding or protection.

23 palm until I have passed over. And I shall take away My palm and you
will see My back, but My face will not be seen."

---

23. *you will see My back, but My face will not be seen.* Volumes of theology have
been spun out of these enigmatic words. Imagining the deity in frankly physical terms was entirely natural for the ancient monotheists: this God had, or at
least could assume, a concrete manifestation which had front and rear, face
and back, and that face man was forbidden to see. But such concreteness does
not imply conceptual naïveté. Through it the Hebrew writer suggests an idea
that makes good sense from later theological perspectives: that God's intrinsic
nature is inaccessible, and perhaps also intolerable, to the finite mind of man,
but that something of His attributes—His "goodness," the directional pitch of
His ethical intentions, the afterglow of the effulgence of His presence—can
be glimpsed by humankind.

CHAPTER 34

And the Lord said to Moses, "Carve you two stone tablets like the 1
first ones, and I shall write on the tablets the words which were
on the first tablets that you smashed. And be ready by morning, 2
and you shall go up in the morning to Mount Sinai and take your stance
for Me there on the mountaintop. And no man shall go up with you, 3
and also no man shall be seen in all the mountain. Neither shall the
sheep nor the cattle graze opposite that mountain." And he carved two 4
stone tablets like the first ones, and Moses rose early in the morning
and went up to Mount Sinai as the Lord had charged him, and he took

---

1. *Carve you two stone tablets.* The first set of tablets had been given by God to
Moses (31:18). Now, as Rashi aptly puts it, God says to Moses, "You smashed
the first ones, you, carve you others."

2. *take your stance.* The same verb, *nitsavta*, is used here as at the end of the
immediately preceding section (33:22); so it is reasonable to assume that the
revelation now on the mountaintop of God's moral attributes is precisely the just
promised revelation of God's "goodness" to Moses when he is to stand in the
cleft of the crag.

3. *no man shall be seen in all the mountain.* These instructions repeat the
injunction in chapter 19 to separate the people from Moses before God gives
the law to Moses on the summit of Sinai. Now, however, after the incident of
the Golden Calf, the separation is total—this time there are no attendants stationed partway up the mountain.

5 in his hand the two stone tablets. And the LORD came down in the
cloud and stationed Himself with him there, and He invoked the name
6 of the LORD. And the LORD passed before him and He called out: "The
LORD, the LORD! A compassionate and gracious God, slow to anger, and
7 abounding in kindness and good faith, keeping kindness for the thousandth generation, bearing crime, trespass, and offense, yet He does
not wholly acquit, reckoning the crime of fathers with sons and sons of
8 sons, to the third generation and the fourth." And Moses hastened and
9 prostrated himself on the ground and bowed down. And he said, "If,
pray, I have found favor in Your eyes, my Master, may my Master, pray,
go in our midst, for it is a stiff-necked people, and you shall forgive our

---

5. *stationed Himself with him there, and He invoked the name of the* LORD. Given
the propensity of biblical Hebrew to use verbs without making the grammatical subject explicit, either Moses or God could be doing the stationing and the
invoking. God makes better sense as the subject of "stationed" (the same verb
as the one used for Moses, "take your stance," but in the reflexive conjugation,
perhaps to distinguish God's action) because it immediately follows "came
down," of which God is the unambiguous subject. It might seem more plausible that Moses would be the one to invoke (*qara' b*e) God's name, but this is
precisely what God said He would do in the previous dialogue with Moses
(33:19). The exclamation "The LORD, the LORD!" would then be that invocation.

6. *The* LORD, *the* LORD! The translation follows the traditional understanding
of the two Hebrew words as an exclamatory repetition. It is also possible, as
Maimonides and others have noted, to read the sequence of words as follows:
"And the LORD called out, 'The LORD!'"

7. *keeping kindness for the thousandth generation . . . yet He does not wholly
acquit.* See the second comment on Exodus 20:5. "Wholly acquit" (which does
not appear in the version in the Decalogue) clearly implies that in cases where
the offenders persist in their offense they cannot expect to be acquitted, for
all of God's stated compassion.

9. *may my Master, pray, go in our midst.* Virtually every word Moses speaks here
harks back to his exchange with God after the fiasco of the Golden Calf. God
had said that He would not go in the midst of the people because it was stiff-
necked and that He would instead send a messenger; Moses invokes the same
attribute of being stiff-necked to argue that the people needs God's intimate
guiding presence. Moses had referred before to his finding favor in God's eyes;

crime and our offense, and claim us as Yours." And He said, "Look, I 10
am about to seal a covenant. Before all your people I will do wonders
that have not been created in all the earth and in all the nations, and
all the people in whose midst you are shall see the LORD's doing, for
fearsome is that which I do with you. Watch you that which I charge 11
you today. Look, I am about to drive out before you the Amorite and the
Canaanite and the Hittite and the Perizzite and the Hivite and the
Jebusite. Watch yourself, lest you seal a covenant with the inhabitant 12
of the land against which you come, lest he become a snare in your
midst. For their altars you shall shatter and their pillars you shall smash 13
and their cultic poles you shall cut down. For you shall not bow to 14
another god, for the LORD, His name is Jealous, a jealous God He is.

---

now he requests as confirmation of that favored status that God go in the
midst of the people.

10. *Look, I am about to seal a covenant.* Many scholars identify the verses that
follow, through to verse 28, as the Small Book of the Covenant. It manifestly
replicates material from the Book of the Covenant (chapters 21–23) as well as
from the Decalogue. It has also been proposed that these injunctions reflect a
variant set of Ten Commandments, but that interpretation seems strained
because some of the laws here—e.g., the redemption of firstborn animals and
the ban on the use of leavened stuff with sacrifices—are too secondary to be
part of a list of ten defining demands that God makes of Israel.

12. *lest you seal a covenant with the inhabitant of the land.* Such a covenant with
idolators would be a kind of anti-covenant to the one God is now making with
Israel. As many commentators have observed, in the aftermath of the Golden
Calf episode, this series of injunctions pointedly begins with a stern command
to keep a distance from the pagans and to destroy their cultic objects.

13. *pillars . . . cultic poles.* The pillars, *matsevot,* are sacred steles, probably made
of piled-up stones (hence the verb "smash"). The cultic poles, *'asherim,* were in
all likelihood initially associated with the worship of the fertility goddess
Asherah; their exact design and dimensions are not known, but it is clear that
they were made of wood (hence the verb "cut down," which also plays against
the verb in Hebrew for sealing a covenant, which is literally to "cut" a covenant).

14. *His name is Jealous.* See the first comment on Exodus 20:5. The fact that
the very next verses three times invoke the metaphor of whoring to represent

15 Lest you seal a covenant with the inhabitant of the land, and they
    whore after their gods and sacrifice to their gods, and he call you, and
16 you eat of his sacrifice, and you take from his daughters for your sons,
    and his daughters whore after their gods, and make your sons whore
17,18 after their gods. No molten gods shall you make for yourselves. The
    Festival of Flatbread you shall keep. Seven days you shall eat flatbread
    as I charged you, at the fixed time of the month of the New Grain, for
19 in the month of the New Grain you came out of Egypt. Every womb-
    breach is Mine, and all your livestock in which you have a male
20 womb-breach of ox or sheep. And a womb-breach of donkey you shall
    redeem with a sheep, and if you do not redeem it, you shall break its
    neck. Every firstborn of your sons you shall redeem, and they shall not
21 appear in My presence empty-handed. Six days you shall work and on
    the seventh day you shall cease. In plow time and in harvest you shall
22 cease. And a Festival of Weeks you shall make for yourself, first fruits
    of the harvest of wheat, and a Festival of Ingathering at the turn of the

---

idolatry strongly argues for a quasi-sexual sense of "jealous" (rather than
"impassioned"): the God Who has chosen Israel implicitly represents Himself
as Israel's husband and lover (a metaphor that both Hosea and Jeremiah will
make explicit), and when the Israelites betray Him by worshipping other gods,
they go "whoring," are unfaithful as an errant spouse is sexually unfaithful.

17. *No molten gods.* This reiterated prohibition has special resonance after
what has just happened with the Golden Calf.

20. *break its neck.* See the second comment on Exodus 13:13.

21. *In plow time and in harvest you shall cease.* This clause does not occur in
the earlier prohibitions of work on the seventh day. For the agriculturist, it is
a vivid way of stressing that the obligation of the sabbath day is binding
throughout the annual cycle, even when a farmer might feel the urgent temptation to go on with the plowing of his fields in the early spring or the harvesting of his crops in the fall.

year. Three times in the year all your males shall appear in the presence   23
of the Master, the LORD God of Israel. For I will dispossess nations   24
before you, and I will widen your territory and no man will covet your
land when you go up to appear in the presence of the LORD three times
in the year. You shall not slaughter with leavened stuff the blood of   25
My sacrifice, nor shall the sacrifice of the Festival of Passover be left
till the morning. The best of the first fruit of your soil you shall   26
bring to the house of the LORD your God. You shall not boil a kid in its
mother's milk."

And the LORD said to Moses, "Write you these words, for according to   27
these words I have sealed a covenant with you and with Israel." And he   28
was there with the LORD forty days and forty nights. Bread he did not
eat, nor water did he drink. And he wrote on the tablets the words of

---

23. *the Master*. The Hebrew *'adon* is an approximate synonym of *ba'al*, and
there may be a polemic point to the use of the term here in a legal document
that begins with a warning against the seductions of Canaanite cults: it is
before the Master, the *'adon*, the God of Israel, and not before any Baal that
Israel is to appear. For the double valence of "to appear in the presence of the
LORD," see the comment on 23:15.

24. *I will widen your territory and no man will covet your land*. As Abraham ibn
Ezra plausibly suggests, the fact that Israel will have ample, and secure, borders means that when people leave their holdings to go up to the sanctuary for
the pilgrim festivals, they will not have to fear incursions from marauders or
invaders.

26. *You shall not boil a kid in its mother's milk*. See the comment on Exodus
23:19.

28. *Bread he did not eat, nor water did he drink*. This parallelism is a kind of
epic flourish, stressing the superhuman heroism of "the man Moses" as he
undergoes his epiphany in a formulaic period of forty days.
   the words of the covenant, the Ten Words. This is the first time that what is
inscribed on the tablets is designated the Ten Words, or "Commandments."
(The Hebrew *devarim* means "words" or "things," and has several additional
senses.)

29 the covenant, the Ten Words. And it happened when Moses came
down from Mount Sinai, with the two tablets of the Covenant in
Moses's hand when he came down from the mountain, that Moses did
not know that the skin of his face had glowed when he spoke with Him.
30 And Aaron, and all the Israelites, saw Moses, and, look, the skin of
31 his face glowed, and they were afraid to come near him. And Moses
called to them, and Aaron and all the chiefs in the community came
32 back to him, and Moses spoke to them. And afterward all the Israelites

---

29. *Moses came down . . . Moses's hand . . . Moses did not know.* The triple repetition of the name is stylistically odd. It may serve here to throw a kind of
spotlight on Moses, who, after his forty days with God, is set off visibly from
the rest of humankind.

   the skin of his face had glowed. The sense of the verb would seem to be "had
begun to glow" since the condition continues. There is some question about
the precise meaning of the verb *qaran*, which occurs only here. The Greek
translation of Aquila and the Latin Vulgate famously understood it to mean
"sprouted horns" (from *qeren*, "horn"), a virtually impossible reading because
horns would grow from the head, not from "the skin of the face." Others have
imagined that the verb could indicate a hornlike toughness of the skin, a kind
of radiation burn after exposure to the divine effulgence. (Ibn Ezra indignantly
dismisses the rationalists who claim Moses's face had turned hornlike from the
forty days' fast.) It makes more sense to see something terrifyingly luminous—
a reflection of the divine fire glimpsed by the people from the foot of the
mountain—rather than a disfiguration in Moses's face. The notion of divine
radiance enveloping the head or face of a god, a king, or a priest appears in
numerous Mesopotamian texts, and so would probably have been a familiar
idea to the ancient Hebrew audience.

30. *and they were afraid to come near him.* If, as seems likely, Moses's face is
giving off some sort of supernatural radiance, the fear of drawing near him precisely parallels the people's fear of drawing near the fiery presence of God on
the mountaintop.

drew near and he charged them with what the LORD had spoken with
him on Mount Sinai. And Moses finished speaking with them, and he   33
put a veil on his face. And when Moses came before the LORD to speak   34
with Him, he would remove the veil until he came out, and he would
come out and speak to the Israelites that which he had been charged.
And the Israelites would see Moses's face, that the skin of Moses's face   35
glowed, and Moses would put the veil back on his face until he came
to speak with Him.

---

33. *a veil*. Richard Elliott Friedman interestingly connects this with the covering and curtain in the Tabernacle: the site of holiness, he proposes, has to be
partitioned off, enveloped in layers, and yet it remains accessible to the
people.

CHAPTER 35

¹ nd Moses assembled all the community of Israelites and said to ² them, "These are the things that the LORD has charged to do: Six days shall tasks be done and on the seventh day there shall be holiness for you, an absolute sabbath for the LORD. Whosoever does a ³ task on it shall be put to death. You shall not kindle a fire in all your dwelling places on the sabbath day."

---

1. *And Moses assembled all the community*. This initial clause, which brings us back to the interrupted instructions regarding the Tabernacle, beginning with the law of the sabbath that concluded those instructions (31:12–17), is a neat reversal of the inception of the Golden Calf episode: "the people assembled against Aaron" (32:1). Instead of a rebellious assembling of the people, their leader now assembles them in order to rehearse before them all that God has enjoined them.

2. *Six days*. This very brief version of the law of the sabbath is a kind of digest of the earlier iteration of the sabbath obligation. There is a good deal of summarizing repetition of earlier material in all that follows.

3. *You shall not kindle a fire*. This prohibition is a new specification. The lighting of fires might well be associated with the "tasks" involved in constructing the Tabernacle because fire would have been required for all the metalwork, and in one Ugaritic text, fire is burned six days in order to erect a sanctuary for Baal. But the kindling of fire—as against merely making use of fire that has been set accidentally—is clearly a primary labor of civilization, as the Prometheus myth suggests, a kind of inauguration of technology, and so it is understandable that a special prohibition of it on the sabbath should be spelled out.

And Moses said to all the community of Israelites, saying, "This is the 4
thing that the LORD has charged, saying, 'Take from what you have with 5
you a donation to the LORD. Whose heart urges him, let him bring it, a
donation of the LORD, gold and silver and bronze, and indigo and pur- 6
ple and crimson linen and goat hair, and reddened ram skins and ocher- 7
dyed skins and acacia wood, and oil for the lamp and spices for the 8
anointing oil and for the aromatic incense, and carnelian stones and 9
stones for setting in the ephod and in the breastplate. And every wise- 10
hearted man among you shall come and do all that the LORD has
charged: the tabernacle and its tent and its cover and its clasps and its 11
boards, its bolts, its posts, and its sockets; the Ark and its poles and all 12
its furnishings and the curtain for the screen; the table and its poles 13
and all its furnishings, and the bread of the Presence; and the lamp 14
stand for the light and its furnishings, and its lamps and the oil for the

---

5. *Take . . . a donation to the* LORD. *Whose heart urges him, let him bring it.* The
language here and in what follows takes us back to the beginning of the Tabernacle section, chapter 25, and then to passages from the subsequent chapters.
The structure of command and implementation in mirroring language is common to the Bible and other ancient Near Eastern literatures. The Priestly editor, now reverting to a Priestly text, seeks to make this a thematically
purposeful structure (though the return to cultic regulations is not likely to
please modern readers). That is, the design for a perfect earthly abode for God
in the midst of the Israelites has been traumatically disrupted by the story of
the Golden Calf and the shattering of the tablets of the Law. Now that divinely
mandated order has been restored with the making of the second set of
tablets, the text can return to the actual fashioning of the Tabernacle, once
again relishing every resplendent detail of indigo and crimson, gold and silver
and bronze.

    gold and silver and bronze. It is worth noting that though the Torah is a prod-
uct of the early Iron Age, the report of the metals used for the Tabernacle
remains faithful to the late Bronze Age setting of the Wilderness narrative.

10. *wise-hearted.* As before, the wisdom (*ḥokhmah*) in question slides from the
notion of insight or intelligence to skill in a craft—in part because intelligence
itself was thought of as a kind of teachable craft for those who had the capacity. The craft valence of the collocation used here is especially pronounced in
verse 25, which speaks of "every woman wise-hearted with her hands" in the
skill of spinning.

15 light; and the incense altar and its poles and the anointing oil and the
16 aromatic incense and the screen of the entrance to the Tabernacle; the
altar of burnt offering and the bronze grating that belongs to it, its poles
17 and all its vessels and the laver and its stand; the court hangings and its
18 poles and its sockets, and the screen of the court-gate; the pegs of the
19 Tabernacle and the pegs of the court and their cords; the service garments to serve in the sanctum, the sacred garments for Aaron the priest
and the garments of his sons to be priests."

20,21 And all the community of Israelites went out from before Moses. And
every man whose heart moved him and everyone whose spirit urged him
came, they brought a donation of the LORD for the task of the Tent of
22 Meeting and for all its work and for the sacred garments. And the men
came, besides the women, all whose heart urged them, they brought
brooches and earrings and rings and pendants, every ornament of gold,

---

19. *the service garments to serve in the sanctum.* In this instance, the writer puts
together *serad,* "service," and *sharet,* "to serve," either because he considered
them to reflect the same root or because he is punning on the phonetic
similarity.

21. *every man whose heart moved him and everyone whose spirit urged him.* The
impulse of generosity indicated in 25:2 is stated more emphatically here and in
the verses that follow. One may detect in this new emphasis a response to the
Golden Calf episode, in which the people were quick to offer their golden
rings for the fashioning of the molten image. Now they outdo themselves in
donations for the LORD's sanctuary.

22. *the men . . . besides the women.* The Hebrew construction, *ha'anashim 'al
hanashim,* is unusual. It would appear to suggest that the women queued up
first to offer their donations. Because of the gender-bound nature of impersonal constructions in Hebrew, all the preceding references to "everyone" were
masculine. Now we are alerted to the fact that women played an important
role in the outpouring of contributions for the Tabernacle—another way of
highlighting the comprehensiveness of the new impetus of generosity. The
women were also more likely to have possessed an abundance of ornaments
than the men.
  earrings. The item in question, *nezem,* was also worn on the nose.

and every man who raised an elevation offering of gold to the Lord. Every man with whom was found indigo and purple and crimson and 23 linen and goat hair and reddened ram skins and ocher-dyed skins brought it. Whoever donated a donation of silver and bronze brought a 24 donation of the Lord, and with whomever was found acacia wood for all the tasks of the work, they brought it. And every woman wise-hearted 25 with her hands spun and brought the threadwork of indigo and purple and crimson and linen. And all the women whose hearts moved them 26 with wisdom spun the goat hair. And the chieftains brought carnelian 27 stones and stones for setting in the ephod and in the breastplate, and the spice and the oil for the lamp and for the anointing oil and for 28 the aromatic incense. Every man and woman whose heart urged them 29 to bring for all the task that the Lord had charged to do by the hand of Moses, the Israelites brought a freewill gift to the Lord.

And Moses said to the Israelites, "See, the Lord has called by name 30 Bezalel son of Uri son of Hur from the tribe of Judah. And He has 31 filled him with a spirit of God in wisdom, in understanding, and in knowledge, and in every task, to devise plans, to work in gold and in sil- 32 ver and in bronze and in stonecutting for settings and in wood carv- 33 ing to do every task of devising, and He has given in his heart to 34 instruct—he and Oholiab son of Ahisamach from the tribe of Dan. He has filled them with heart's wisdom to do every task of carver and 35 designer and embroiderer in indigo and in purple and in crimson and in linen, and of weaver, doers of every task and devisers of plans.

---

25. *spun.* Spinning is of course the one craft particularly associated with women.

34. *to instruct.* God has endowed Bezalel, together with his chief assistant Oholiab, not only with the skill to execute all these sundry crafts but also with the capacity to instruct the crews of ordinary craftsmen how to carry out their work. Canaanite myth, like the Greek, had a craftsman god; here, instead, the Lord inspires a human being with the skill, or "wisdom," of the craft as well as with the ability to administer the project.

36:1 And Bezalel, and Oholiab and every wise-hearted man in whom the
Lord has given wisdom and understanding to know how to do the task
of the holy work, shall do all that the Lord has charged.

36:1. This verse is a summary of the nature of the workforce for constructing
the Tabernacle and therefore would seem to belong here rather than at the
beginning of the next chapter.

CHAPTER 36

And Moses called Bezalel and Oholiab and every wise-hearted man 2 in whose heart the LORD had given wisdom, everyone whose heart moved him, to approach the task to do it. And they took from 3 before Moses all the donation that the Israelites had brought for the task of the holy work to do it, and they on their part brought more freewill gifts morning after morning. And all the wise people who were 4 doing the holy task came, each man from his task that he was doing. And they said to Moses, saying, "The people are bringing too much for 5 the work of the task that the LORD charged to do." And Moses charged, 6 and they sent word through the camp, saying, "Let each man and woman do no further task for the holy donation," and the people were held back from bringing. And the task was enough to do all the task, 7 and more.

---

3. *freewill gifts.* The Hebrew *nedavah* (here a collective noun), which was mentioned in the previous chapter, 35:29, is derived from the same verb *nadav* that occurs repeatedly in the references to each man's heart "urging" him to offer a gift. In this passage, the theme of Israelite generosity for the construction of the Tabernacle as a resounding reversal of the ill-considered donations for the Golden Calf is given a climactic flourish: the donations go over the top (verse 5) and the people have to be "held back" (verse 6) from giving further.

6. *do no further task.* They are actually not "doing"—that is the responsibility of the craftsmen—but giving. "Task" (*mela'khah*) here is extended in meaning to refer to the materials necessary for the carrying out of the task that the people bring. That is clearly the meaning of the first occurrence of "task" in the next verse.

8 And every wise-hearted man among the doers of the task made the
Tabernacle—ten panels of twisted linen, and indigo and purple and
9 crimson, two cherubim, designer's work, they made them. The length
of the one panel twenty-eight cubits and a width four cubits to the
10 panel, a single measure for all the panels. And they joined the five pan-
11 els one to another, five panels they joined one to another. And they
made indigo loops along the edge of the outermost panel in the set, and
12 thus they did on the outermost panel in the other set. Fifty loops they
made in the one panel, and fifty loops they made in the outermost
13 panel which was in the other set, the loops opposite one another. And
they made fifty golden clasps and joined the panels to one another with
14 the clasps, and the Tabernacle became one whole. And they made goat-
hair panels for a tent over the Tabernacle, eleven panels they made
15 them. The length of the one panel, thirty cubits, and a width of four
16 cubits to the panel, a single measure for the eleven panels. And they
joined five of the panels by themselves and six of the panels by them-
17 selves. And they made fifty loops along the edge of the outermost panel
in the set, and fifty loops along the edge of the outermost panel in

8–38. The text now launches upon one of its most extravagant deployments of
verbatim repetition. This particular segment corresponds precisely to 26:1–32,
the only notable difference being that the imperative verbs of the instruction
passage are converted into past verbs for the implementation passage, with the
obvious implication that God's directions for the construction of the Tabernacle are now carried out with scrupulous fidelity to every single detail by Bezalel and his work crews. In biblical narrative—these lists scarcely qualify as
that—virtually every small swerve from verbatim repetition in repeated passages is a node of new meaning, but here the variance between the two versions is quite marginal and is by no means a vehicle of signification: what
really matters is the repetition itself, the fact that the Tabernacle is now faithfully assembled in all its prescribed splendid details. It should be noted that
all of the verbs for making in this passage, beginning with "they made them"
in verse 8, are in the singular in the Hebrew. The singular is presumably used
because the writer has in mind "every wise-hearted man" who is engaged in
the building. Hebrew usage slips back and forth easily from plural to singular
in such cases. The initial "made" in verse 8 is in the plural, but the end of the
verse uses a singular. English being more hidebound by logic, this translation
continues with the plural.

the other set. And they made fifty bronze clasps to join the tent to   18
become one whole. And they made a covering for the tent of reddened   19
ram skins and a covering of ocher-dyed skins above. And they made   20
boards for the Tabernacle of acacia wood, upright. Ten cubits the   21
length of the board, and a cubit and a half the width of the single board.
Two tenons for the one board linked to each other, thus they did for all   22
the boards of the Tabernacle. And they made the boards for the Taber-   23
nacle, twenty boards for the southern end. And forty silver sockets they   24
made beneath the twenty boards, two sockets beneath the one board
for its two tenons and two sockets beneath the one board for its
two tenons. And in the other side of the Tabernacle at the northern   25
end, twenty boards. And their forty silver sockets, two sockets beneath   26
the one board and two sockets beneath the one board. And at the rear   27
of the Tabernacle to the west they made six boards. And they made two   28
boards for the corners of the Tabernacle at the rear. And they matched   29
below, and together they ended at the top inside the one ring, thus they
did for the two of them, at the two corners. And there were eight   30
boards with their silver sockets, sixteen sockets, two sockets beneath
the one board. And they made five crossbars of acacia wood for the   31
boards of the one side of the Tabernacle. And five crossbars for the   32
boards of the other side of the Tabernacle, and five crossbars for the
boards of the Tabernacle at the rear to the west. And they made the   33
central crossbar to shoot through the boards from end to end. And the   34
boards they overlaid with gold, and their rings they made of gold, housings for the crossbars, and they overlaid the crossbars with gold. And   35
they made the curtain of indigo and purple and crimson and twisted
linen, designer's work they made it, with cherubim. And they made for   36
it four acacia posts and overlaid them with gold, their hooks gold, and
they cast for them four silver sockets. And they made a screen for the   37
entrance of the tent, indigo and purple and crimson and twisted linen,
embroiderer's work, and its five posts and its hooks, and they overlaid   38
their tops and their bands with gold, and their five sockets with bronze.

CHAPTER 37

₁ And Bezalel made the Ark of acacia wood, two and a half cubits its
length and a cubit and a half its width and a cubit and a half its
₂ height. And he overlaid it with pure gold, inside and outside, and
₃ he made for it a golden molding all around. And he cast for it four
golden rings on its four feet and two rings on its one side and two rings
₄ on its other side. And he made poles of acacia wood and overlaid them
₅ with gold. And he brought the poles through the rings on the side of the
₆ Ark to carry the Ark. And he made a cover of pure gold, two and a half
₇ cubits its length and a cubit and a half its width. And he made two
cherubim of gold, hammered work he made them, at the two edges of
₈ the cover. One cherub at one edge and one cherub at the other edge,
₉ from the cover he made the cherubim at both its edges. And the cherubim spread their wings above, shielding the cover with their wings, and
their faces toward each other, toward the cover their faces were.

1–28. As before, the implementation of the Tabernacle project mirrors verbatim
the instructions for the project, with only minuscule and insignificant variations
in formulation (e.g., "cast four golden rings" instead of the earlier "make four
golden rings"). The verses here correspond to 25:10–21, 25:23–40, and 30:1–10.

1. *And Bezalel made.* The instructions for the building were given in the
second-person singular to Moses or in the third-person plural for the
Israelites. Now Bezalel is represented executing all the details of design,
though it is to be understood that he would have been supervising crews of
craftsmen. Rashi explains the singling out of Bezalel by name by observing,
"Since he devoted himself to the task more than the other artisans, it was
linked with his name." Bezalel continues to figure in Hebrew tradition as the
archetypal dedicated artisan.

And he made the table of acacia wood, two cubits its length and a cubit   10
and a half its width and a cubit and a half its height. And he overlaid it   11
with pure gold and made for it a golden molding all around. And he   12
made a frame for it, a handsbreadth all around, and he made a golden
molding for its frame all around. And he cast for it four golden rings and   13
set the rings at the four corners which were at its four legs.
Facing the frame the rings were, as housings for the poles to carry the   14
table. And he made the poles of acacia wood and overlaid them with   15
gold, to carry the table. And he made the vessels that were on the table,   16
its bowls and its shovels and its chalices and its jars, from which libation is done, pure gold.

And he made the lamp stand of pure gold, hammered work he made   17
the lamp stand, its base and its shaft; its cups, its calyxes and its blossoms, were from that work. And six shafts going out from its sides,   18
three shafts of the lamp stand from its one side and three shafts of the
lamp stand from its other side. Three cups shaped like almond blos-   19
soms in the one shaft, calyx and blossom, and three cups shaped like
almond blossoms in the other shaft, and thus for the six shafts that go
out from the lamp stand. And on the lamp stand were four cups shaped   20
like almond blossoms, their calyxes and their blossoms. And a calyx   21
under every two shafts as part of it, and a calyx under every two shafts
as part of it, a calyx under every two shafts as part of it, for the six shafts
coming out of the lamp stand. Their calyxes and their shafts were part   22
of it, all of it one hammered work, pure gold. And he made its seven   23
lamps, and its tongs and its fire-pans—pure gold. With a talent of pure   24
gold he made it and all its furnishings.

And he made the altar for burning incense of acacia wood, a cubit its   25
length and a cubit its width, square, and two cubits its height; from the
same piece its horns. And he overlaid it with pure gold—its roof and its   26
walls all around and its horns, and he made for it a golden molding all
around. And two golden rings he made for it beneath its molding on its   27
two flanks, as housings for the poles with which to carry it. And he   28
made the poles of acacia wood and overlaid them with gold. And he   29
made the holy anointing oil and the pure aromatic incense, perfumer's
work.

CHAPTER 38

¹ And he made the burnt-offering altar of acacia wood, five cubits its length and five cubits its width, square, and three cubits its ² height. And he made its horns on its four corners, from the same ³ piece were its horns, and he overlaid it with bronze. And he made all the vessels of the altar, and the pails and the shovels and the basins and the flesh-hooks and the fire-pans, all its vessels he made of bronze. ⁴ And he made a meshwork bronze grating for the altar beneath its ledge ⁵ from below halfway up. And he cast four rings at the four corners of the ⁶ bronze grating as housings for the poles. And he made the poles of aca- ⁷ cia wood and overlaid them with bronze. And he brought the poles through the rings on the sides of the altar to carry it, hollow-boarded he made it.

⁸ And he made the laver of bronze and its stand of bronze from the mir- rors of the women who flocked to the entrance of the Tent of Meeting.

1–7. These verses correspond to Exodus 27:1–8 from the instruction passages.

8. *the mirrors of the women who flocked to the entrance.* The verb here, *tsav'u*, can mean either "to perform service," as in an army, *tsav'a*, or "to make up a multitude or crowd," as in the epithet for the stars, *tsev'a hashamayim*, the "host," or array, of the heavens. Although most modern interpreters opt for the sense of service, there are two difficulties with that construction. The cult was administered by males, and there is scant evidence of a quasi-sacerdotal func- tion performed outside the sanctuary by women. And if there really were such a group of women doing some sort of sacred service, their numbers would have had to be relatively limited, whereas the sanctuary required large quantities of bronze (see verse 28) donated by the masses. It thus seems more plausible to

And he made the court for the southern side, the hangings of the court 9
were twisted linen, a hundred cubits. Their posts twenty and their 10
sockets twenty, of bronze. The hooks of the posts and their bands were
silver. And for the northern side, a hundred cubits, their posts twenty 11
and their sockets twenty, of bronze. The hooks of the posts and their
bands were silver. And for the western side, hangings of fifty cubits. 12
Their posts ten and their sockets ten, the hooks of the posts and their
bands were silver. And to the very east, fifty cubits, hangings of fifteen 13,14
cubits to the flank, their posts three and their sockets three. And for the 15
other flank on each side of the gate of the court hangings of fifteen
cubits, their posts three and their sockets three. All the hangings of the 16
court all around were twisted linen. And the sockets for the posts were 17
bronze, the hooks of the posts and their bands silver and the overlay of
their tops silver, and they were banded with silver, all the posts of the
court. And the screen of the gate of the court was embroiderer's work, 18
indigo and purple and crimson and twisted linen. And it was twenty
cubits in length and a height in the width of five cubits over against the
hangings of the court. And their posts four and their sockets four, of 19
bronze. Their hooks were silver and the overlay of their tops and their
bands silver. And all the pegs for the Tabernacle and for the court all 20
around were bronze.

---

imagine crowds of devoted women flocking to the entrance of the Tent of
Meeting, where they would not have been permitted to go in. (Compare 1
Samuel 2:22, in which the same verb is used.) Mirrors in the ancient world
were made of polished bronze, not glass, and were an Egyptian luxury item.
Several medieval commentators note that the very objects used by the women
for the purposes of vanity, or in the cultivation of their sexual attractiveness,
are here dedicated to sacred ends. This verse complements the emphasis on
the prominent role of the women in the donations that was brought forth in
Exodus 35:22.

9–20. These verses correspond to 27:9–19 with some variation in the wording.

18. *and a height in the width of five cubits.* This is an odd way of describing the
height. One suspects that "in the width" (one word in the Hebrew) might be
a scribal error, though there are no ancient versions without it.

21 These are the reckonings of the Tabernacle, the Tabernacle of the
Covenant, that were reckoned by the word of Moses, the service of the
22 Levites in the hand of Ithamar son of Aaron the priest. And Bezalel son
of Uri son of Hur from the tribe of Judah made all that the Lord had
23 charged Moses. And with him was Oholiab son of Ahisamach from the
tribe of Dan, wood carver and designer and embroiderer in indigo and
24 in purple and in crimson and in linen. All the gold that was fashioned
for the task in every task of the sanctuary, the elevation-offering gold
was twenty-nine talents or seven hundred thirty shekels by the sanc-
25 turary shekel. And the silver reckoned from the community was a hundred talents or one thousand seven hundred seventy-five shekels by the

---

21. *These are the reckonings.* The term *pequdim*, immediately followed by the
cognate passive verb *puqad*, "reckoned," is difficult to translate because the
verbal stem *p-q-d* covers so many senses in biblical Hebrew. It means "to
count," "to inventory," "to take a census," "to single out," "to pay special attention," "to make a reckoning," and more. The most relevant sense in the present
context would be "inventory," but Hebrew idiom prefers to use general terms
for technical senses, and this translation honors that preference. When an
inventory is transferred from objects to people (verse 26), it becomes a census.
What is involved here are two categories of donation—freewill gifts and a poll
tax of a silver *beqa'* to the head. The poll tax serves simultaneously as a means
of extracting silver needed for the sanctuary and as an instrument for counting heads, or taking a census.

by the word of Moses. Literally, by the mouth.

24. *twenty-nine talents or seven hundred thirty shekels.* The conjunction *waw*
here and in what follows does not have its usual sense of "and" but rather
"or" since the weight in shekels is manifestly provided as an equivalent—
presumably, more familiar to the audience—of the weight in talents. As earlier, it is stipulated that this is the heavier sanctuary-weight shekel and not the
mercantile shekel.

sanctuary shekel. A *beqa* to the head, half a shekel by the sanctuary 26
shekel for each who underwent the reckoning from twenty years old
and above, for six hundred thousand and three thousand five hundred
and fifty. And the hundred talents of silver were for casting the sockets 27
of the sanctuary and the sockets of the curtain, a hundred sockets for
a hundred talents, a talent for a socket. And from the one thousand 28
seven hundred seventy-five shekels he made hooks for the posts and
overlaid their tops and banded them. And the elevation-offering bronze 29
was seventy talents or two thousand four hundred shekels. And he 30
made with it the sockets for the entrance of the Tent of Meeting and
the bronze altar and the bronze grating that belongs to it and all the furnishings of the altar, and the sockets of the court all around and the 31
sockets for the gate of the court, and all the pegs of the Tabernacle and
all the pegs of the court all around.

---

26. *for six hundred thousand and three thousand five hundred and fifty.* The previously given round number of 600,000 males is now made more precise in an
enhancement of the effect of exact census of the present context. The "for" (*l^e*)
that prefixes the number may be dictated by the beginning of the sentence: a
silver *beqa'* is paid for each head of the 603,550 males.

CHAPTER 39

1   And from the indigo and the purple and the crimson they made service garments to serve in the sanctuary, and they made the sacred
2 garments that were Aaron's as the LORD had charged Moses. And
he made the ephod of gold, indigo and purple and crimson and twisted
3 linen. And they pounded out the sheets of gold and cut strands to work
into the indigo and into the purple and into the crimson and into the
4 linen, designer's work. Joining shoulder-pieces they made for it, at its
5 two edges they were joined. And the ornamented band that was on it
was of a piece with it, fashioned like it, gold, indigo and purple and
6 crimson and twisted linen, as the LORD had charged Moses. And they
made the carnelian stones ringed with frames of gold, engraved with
7 seal engravings with the names of Israel's sons. And he set them on the
shoulder-pieces of the ephod, stones of remembrance for the sons of
8 Israel, as the LORD had charged Moses. And he made the breastplate,

---

1–31. These verses, which constitute the concluding section of the account of
implementing the building instructions, correspond to 28:5–42; again, the
material is repeated verbatim with only minor variations and, here, some limited abridgement.

1. *as the LORD had charged Moses.* This refrain, repeated, as Nahum Sarna
notes, seven times, is not part of the instruction passage in chapter 28.

3. *they pounded out the sheets of gold and cut strands.* This technical detail,
absent from chapter 28, is a faithful representation of how gold thread was
manufactured. The Egyptians were especially adept in this process, and the
word for "sheets," *paḥim*, which has a more common biblical homonym that
means "traps," may actually be an Egyptian loanword.

designer's work, like the work of the ephod, gold, indigo and purple and crimson and twisted linen. It was square, they made the breastplate 9 doubled, a span its length and a span its width, doubled. And they set 10 in it four rows of stones, a row of ruby, topaz, and malachite, the first row. And the second row, turquoise, sapphire, and amethyst. And the 11,12 third row, jacinth, agate, and crystal. And the fourth row, beryl, car- 13 nelian, and jasper, framed in gold in their settings. And the stones were 14 according to the names of Israel's sons, twelve according to their names, seal engravings, each with its name for the twelve tribes. And 15 they made on the breastplate intertwined cordwork, chains of pure gold. And they made two golden frames and two golden rings, and they 16 set the two rings on the two edges of the breastplate. And they set the 17 two golden cords on the two rings on the edges of the breastplate. And 18 the two ends of the two cords they set in the two frames, and they set them on the shoulder-pieces of the ephod at the front. And they made 19 two golden rings and set them on the two edges of the breastplate, at its border which faces the ephod on the inside. And they made two 20 golden rings and set them on the two shoulder-pieces of the ephod below in the front opposite its seam above the band of the ephod. And 21 they fastened the breastplate from its rings to the rings of the ephod with an indigo strand to be upon the band of the ephod, that the breast- plate not slip from the ephod, as the LORD had charged Moses. And he 22 made a robe for the ephod, weaver's work, through-and-through indigo. And the opening of the robe in the middle of it like the opening of a 23 coat of mail, a border for its opening all around, so it should not tear. And they made on the hem of the robe pomegranates of indigo and 24 purple and crimson, twisted linen. And they made bells of pure gold 25 and set the bells within the pomegranates on the hem of the robe all around, within the pomegranates. A bell and a pomegranate, a bell and 26 a pomegranate on the hem of the robe all around, to serve, as the LORD had charged Moses. And they made tunics of twisted linen, weaver's 27 work, for Aaron and for his sons, and the turban, linen, and the orna- 28 ments of the headgear, linen, and the breeches of linen, twisted linen,

---

21. The Samaritan version and an Exodus text found at Qumran insert here: "and they made the Urim and the Thummim as the LORD had charged Moses."

29 and the sash, twisted linen and indigo and purple and crimson, embroi-
30 derer's work, as the Lord had charged Moses. And they made a dia-
     dem, a sacred crown of pure gold, and wrote upon it in seal-engravings
31 inscription: "Holy to the Lord." And they put on it an
     indigo strand, to put on the turban above, as the Lord had charged
     Moses.

32 And all the work of the Tabernacle of the Tent of Meeting was com-
     pleted, and the Israelites did as all that the Lord had charged Moses,
33 thus they did. And they brought the Tabernacle to Moses, the Tent and
     all its furnishings, its clasps, its boards, its crossbars, and its posts and
34 its sockets, and the covering of reddened ram skins and the covering of
35 ocher-dyed skins and the curtain of the screen; the Ark of the Covenant
36 and its poles and the cover; the table and all its furnishings and the
37 bread of the Presence; the pure lamp stand, its lamps, lamps of the
38 array, and all its furnishings and oil for the light, and the golden altar
     and the anointing oil and the aromatic incense and the screen of the

---

32. *the work . . . was completed.* As Umberto Cassuto and others have noted, this passage that summarizes the completion of the Tabernacle echoes the report of God's completion of creation, Genesis 2:1–3, with completion of the work at the beginning and blessing at the end (verse 43). One should recall that the Hebrew for "Tabernacle," *mishkan*, means "dwelling"—God's dwelling place or abode in the midst of the people of Israel. Human effort, adhering to divine direction, emulates the Creator by applying human crafts to build God a harmonious, beautiful, and intricately constructed dwelling place on earth.

33–41. The report of the construction of the Tabernacle and the fashioning of all its furnishings as well as of the priestly garments now concludes, after all the abundance of architectural and sartorial detail, in a rapid catalogue that recapitulates in summary form the principal elements of the whole project. Throughout the Tabernacle passages, both in the directions and in the implementation, language has an incantatory or quasi-musical function in addition to the instructional aim, evoking in gorgeous syllables the sheer splendor and artisanal perfection of the sanctuary. This concluding catalogue is rather like the recapitulation of themes at the end of the last movement of a classical symphony, pulling all the previously stated elements together as the piece moves toward satisfying closure.

entrance of the tent; the bronze altar and the bronze grating that 39
belongs to it, its poles and all its furnishings, the laver and its stand; the
hangings of the court and its posts and its sockets and the screen for 40
the gate of the court and its pegs and all the furnishings of the service
of the Tabernacle for the Tent of Meeting; the service garments to serve 41
in the sanctuary and the sacred garments for Aaron the priest and the
garments of his sons to be priests. As all that the Lord had charged 42
Moses, thus the Israelites did all the work. And Moses saw all the 43
tasks, and, look, they had done it as the Lord had charged, thus they
had done it, and Moses blessed them.

CHAPTER 40

1,2 And the LORD spoke to Moses, saying, "On the day of the first
month, on the first of the month, you shall set up the Tabernacle
3   of the Tent of Meeting. And you shall put there the Ark of the
4   Covenant and screen the Ark with the curtain. And you shall bring the
table and lay out its array, and you shall bring the lamp stand and light
5   up its lamps. And you shall set the golden altar for the incense before
the Ark of the Covenant and you shall set up the screen for the

---

2. *the first month, on the first of the month.* Since the month of the New Grain
(Abib, or in later Hebrew usage, Nissan) has been fixed as the first month
(Exodus 12:2), one may infer that the Tabernacle was set up and consecrated
one year, less two weeks, after the departure from Egypt. Thus verse 17 refers
to "the first month in the second year," that is, the second year of the Exodus.

you shall set up the Tabernacle. After all the instructions concerning the
Tabernacle, followed, after the break of the Golden Calf episode, by the report
of the fashioning of all the components of the structure, according to the
divine instructions, God enjoins Moses to culminate all these labors by actually setting up the Tabernacle. These commands (verses 1–15) are followed by
the account of their implementation (verses 16–34), the latter repeatedly punctuated by the refrain "as the LORD had charged Moses." This perfect execution
of God's directions to make Him a dwelling place and a cultic center in the
midst of the Israelites would have been conceived, at least by the Priestly
writer, as a fitting conclusion to the Book of Exodus. The doubts as to whether
God would dwell among the people as it journeyed through the wilderness are
now settled, and that resolution is dramatically confirmed by the evocation of
the divine cloud and fire (verses 34–38) with which the book concludes.

4. *lay out its array.* The reference is to the twelve loaves of the bread of Presence, which were changed daily. See verse 23.

entrance of the Tabernacle. And you shall set the burnt-offering altar   6
before the entrance of the Tabernacle of the Tent of Meeting. And you   7
shall set the laver between the Tent of Meeting and the altar, and you
shall set water there. And you shall put up the court all around and set   8
up the screen of the court gate. And you shall take the anointing oil and   9
anoint the Tabernacle and all that is in it, and you shall consecrate it
and all its furnishings, that it be holy. And you shall anoint the burnt-   10
offering altar and all its furnishings, and you shall consecrate the altar,
that the altar be holy of holies. And you shall anoint the laver and its   11
stand and consecrate it. And you shall bring Aaron and his sons forward   12
to the entrance of the Tent of Meeting and wash them in water.
And you shall dress Aaron in the sacred garments and anoint him and   13
consecrate him, that he be a priest to Me. And his sons you shall bring   14
forward and dress them in tunics. And you shall anoint them as you   15
anointed their father, that they be priests to Me, and their anointing
shall become for them an everlasting priesthood for their generations."
And Moses did as all that the Lord had charged him, thus he did.   16

And it happened in the first month in the second year, on the first of   17
the month, that the Tabernacle was set up. And Moses set up the   18
Tabernacle and placed its sockets and put up its boards and fixed its
crossbars and set up its posts. And he spread the tent over the Taber-   19
nacle and put the covering of the tent over it from above, as the Lord
had charged Moses. And he took and set the Covenant in the Ark, and   20
he put the poles on the Ark, and he set the cover over the Ark from

----

15. *their anointing shall become for them an everlasting priesthood for their generations*. This rhetorical flourish makes clear that what the Priestly writer has
in view is not merely a report of the archaic era of origins in the Wilderness
wanderings but a model and permanent authorization of the privileged status
of the priestly caste for all time.

20. *set the Covenant in the Ark*. The Covenant, 'edut, is a synonym for *berit*, the
other common biblical term for pact, treaty, or covenant, and it clearly refers to
the two stone tablets on which the words of the Covenant were written by the
finger of God. The Tabernacle, then, has a double function: it is the place where
sacrifices are offered, as in all ancient Near Eastern cults, and it is the place

21 above. And he brought the Ark into the Tabernacle and placed the curtain of the screen and screened the Ark of the Covenant, as the LORD
22 had charged Moses. And he set the table in the Tent of Meeting on
23 the northern side of the Tabernacle outside the curtain. And he laid
out on it the array of bread before the LORD, as the LORD had charged
24 Moses. And he placed the lamp stand in the Tent of Meeting opposite
25 the table on the northern side of the Tabernacle. And he lit up the
26 lamps before the LORD, as the LORD had charged Moses. And he
placed the golden altar in the Tent of Meeting before the curtain.
27 And he burned on it aromatic incense, as the LORD had charged
28 Moses. And he put up the screen for the entrance of the Tabernacle.
29 And he put up the burnt-offering altar there at the entrance to the
Tabernacle of the Tent of Meeting, and offered up on it the burnt
30 offering and the grain offering, as the LORD had charged Moses. And
he placed the laver between the Tent of Meeting and the altar, and he
31 set water there for washing. And Moses and Aaron and his sons
32 washed their hands and their feet with it. When they came into the
Tent of Meeting and when they approached the altar, they would
33 wash, as the LORD had charged Moses. And he set up the court around
the Tabernacle and the altar, and he placed the screen of the court
gate. And Moses completed the task.

34 And the cloud covered the Tent of Meeting and the glory of the LORD
35 filled the Tabernacle. And Moses could not come into the Tent of
Meeting, for the cloud abode upon it and the glory of the LORD filled

---

where the material document of an eternal contract between God and Israel is
preserved. Though the burnt-offering altar is called "holy of holies" (verse 10),
the supreme locus of the sacrosanct, the concrete nexus between humanity and
the divine, is the Ark within which the tablets of the Covenant are kept.

33. *And Moses completed the task.* Once again, both the verb and the noun that
is its object hark back to the completion of creation in Genesis 2:1–3.

35. *the cloud abode . . . the glory of the LORD filled.* Throughout these four concluding verses, one hears the resonant cadences of a kind of epic narrative. As
is the rule in most literatures, when prose seeks grand effects, it tends to approx-

the Tabernacle. And when the cloud went up from over the Taberna- 36
cle, the Israelites would journey onward in all their journeyings. And if 37
the cloud did not go up, they would not journey onward until the day
it went up. For the LORD's cloud was over the Tabernacle by day, and 38
fire by night was in it, before the eyes of all the house of Israel in all
their journeyings.

---

imate the formal shape of poetry (compare Melville's repeated use of iambic
cadences, coupled with Shakespearian diction in *Moby-Dick*): these two clauses
almost scan (the Hebrew has a stress pattern of three beats in the first clause,
four in the second), and they exhibit the semantic parallelism that is one of the
most prominent features of biblical poetry. Analogous patterns are detectable in
the next three verses. The cloud and the glory appear to be virtual synonyms, or
at the very least, overlapping terms. The LORD's glory, *kavod*, is clearly a palpably concrete manifestation of the deity, for all the metaphysical attributes that
later theology would attach to it. It may have been imagined as a kind of mantle
of light enveloping God, with the cloud giving off a luminosity by day parallel to
the fire by night. (Thus the English word "glory," which suggests a nimbus or
halo, is an appropriate equivalent.) This cloudy effulgence is so daunting to
behold that even Moses does not dare enter the Tent until the cloud lifts.

38. *the LORD's cloud . . . by day, and fire by night was in it*. These words hark
back to the initial report of the pillar of cloud and fire (13:21–22) that marked
the very beginning of the Wilderness narrative, so this whole large segment of
text is cinched in an envelope structure. In chapter 13, the cloud and the fire
appear directly before the people to show them the way through the trackless
desert. Now, the cloud and the fire have been given a constructed, cultic focal
point—the Tabernacle that henceforth will be God's dwelling place in the
midst of the people.

in all their journeyings. Pointedly, "their journeyings," *mas'eyhem*, is the last
word of the Book of Exodus, just as this same verbal stem inaugurated the
Wilderness narrative in 13:20, "And they journeyed from Succoth." We have
been left with a sense of harmonious consummation in the completion of the
Tabernacle, likened by allusion to the completion of the tasks of creation; but
the condition in which the Israelites find themselves remains unstable, uncertain, a destiny of wandering through arduous wasteland toward a promised
land that is not yet visible on the horizon. The concluding words of Exodus
point forward not to the priestly regulations of the Book of Leviticus, which
immediately follows, but to the Book of Numbers, with its tales of Wilderness
wanderings, near catastrophic defections, and dangerous tensions between the
leader and the led.

LEVITICUS

INTRODUCTION

The book of Leviticus, the shortest of the five books that make up the Torah, sits squarely in the middle of the structure of the whole in a way that may be discomfiting to many modern readers. Poised between the completion of the Tabernacle after the Sinai epiphany in Exodus and the Wilderness wanderings in Numbers, it seems like a long moment of stasis dwelling chiefly on matters of ritual. After the brilliantly realized narrative impetus manifested throughout Genesis and, in a somewhat transformed manner, in the first half of Exodus, narrative is entirely set aside, apart from the monitory tales of the deaths of Nadab and Abihu in chapter 10 and of the brawling Egyptian husband who vilifies the divine name in chapter 24. Both those brief episodes, in any event, are introduced as exemplary precedent-setting illustrations of general principles of law, so they scarcely alter the general legal character of the book as a whole.

Most of the laws, moreover, are focused on topics that may seem less than urgent to audiences not part of the ancient world in which they were framed. There are, to be sure, interesting pieces of legislation here that regulate judicial probity, the administration of charity in an agricultural economy, sexual unions, and dietary practices, but the central concern of the book is the conduct of the cult, with elaborate stipulation of how the sacrificial animals are to be butchered, what parts of them are to be burned on the altar, how their blood is to be ritually sprinkled on the altar or in certain instances daubed on various extremities of the celebrant of the rite. Purification is a paramount consideration in all of this, and the legislation lays out elaborate procedures for cleansing both persons and substances of a rich variety of impurities. Stylistically, the authors of this text convey these laws with careful specification and dry precision, showing no hint of the Deuteronomic flair for rhetoric (apart from the admonitions of the penultimate chapter, which in fact are paralleled in more elaborate form in the concluding chapters of Deuteronomy), and having no recourse to the grand stately cadences that the Priestly writers elsewhere—in the first version of creation and in the story of the Deluge—impressively display.

If the Torah was assembled from its sundry literary sources by Priestly writers, as scholarly consensus holds, sometime during the sixth century B.C.E., in the decades following the fall of Judea in 586, it is understandable that these editors should want to make the concerns of their own sacerdotal guild the keystone of the literary structure they were establishing. The emphasis, moreover, on the regimen of sacrifices must have had a kind of historical poignancy and an ideological urgency for them: the Temple with all its splendid furnishings and accoutrements had been reduced to rubble by the Babylonian invaders, with much of the Judean population driven into exile, and these intricate legal instructions about ritual conduct within the sacred space of the Tabernacle were a means of reinstating the vanished Temple as a fact of the imagination and a blueprint for future restoration. Precisely this message was strongly carried forward into postbiblical Judaism. Two whole tractates of the Talmud, based on Leviticus, would be devoted to the laws of the cult and would remain the object of intensive study; and at least by the later Middle Ages, small Jewish boys were introduced to the Torah not through the great story of creation and the absorbing tales of the patriarchs in Genesis but through Leviticus—in Rashi's formulation of the pedagogic slogan, "Let the pure ones come and study laws of purity."

Does Leviticus, in all its legalism and all its focus on sacrificial and purgative procedures, have some sort of literary coherence? The liveliest attempt to define such a coherence is Mary Douglas's *Leviticus as Literature* (1999). As an anthropologist, she had long been fascinated by the system of laws in this book, addressing it in two long chapters of her celebrated book *Purity and Danger*. Eventually, she mastered an impressive body of the relevant biblical scholarship and even acquired some competence in biblical Hebrew in order to devote this full-length study to Leviticus. Her basic argument is that the book represents an extremely intricate and subtle deployment of a mode of thought that she calls "analogical," which, she contends, should not be deemed more primitive than the analytic thinking on which modern Western culture is largely based but rather seen as a different way of conceptually ordering the world, one that is exhibited in many cultures and to which we should not condescend. Reality is conceived as an elaborate system of correspondences—correspondences between Sinai and the cosmos, on the one hand, and the Tabernacle, on the other, and between all three of these and the body segments of the sacrificial animal. In the scheme of analogical thought that she proposes, no detail is adventitious or devoid of meaning, and so the most minute stipulations about the butchering of beasts and the regimen of ritual manifest an overarching symbolic system that differentiates the realms of the Creator, the human creature, and the priestly caste that serves as intermediary between the two. With this general scheme in constant view, Douglas claims that Leviticus as a book displays a consistently purposeful literary structure, one that follows the contours of this tripartite division of the cosmos.

One may grant the validity of the idea of analogical thought as a shaping force in the book and yet be skeptical about the presence of these proposed formal coherences, which in specific instances seem more the product of interpretive ingenuity than of persuasive reading. I would like to suggest, however, that Leviticus, even as a somewhat miscellaneous assemblage of cultic and other laws, and even as a joining of two distinct documents (the Priestly source and the Holiness Code, chapters 17–26), possesses a certain thematic, though not formal, unity.

There is a single verb that focuses the major themes of Leviticus— "divide" (Hebrew, *hivdil*). That verb, of course, stands at the beginning of the Priestly story of creation: "And God saw the light, that it was good, and God divided the light from the darkness. . . . And God made the vault and it divided the water beneath the vault from the water above the vault, and so it was." In this vision of cosmogony, the condition before the world was called into being was a chaotic interfusion of disparate elements, "welter and waste." What enables existence and provides a framework for the development of human nature, conceived in God's image, and of human civilization is a process of division and insulation—light from darkness, day from night, the upper waters from the lower waters, and dry land from the latter. That same process is repeatedly manifested in the ritual, sexual, and dietary laws of Leviticus. Thus, the summarizing statement at the end of the list of living creatures respectively permitted and prohibited for eating: "This is the teaching about beast and bird and every living creature that stirs in the water and every swarming thing that swarms on the earth [a whole string of phrases harking back to the Priestly story of Creation], to divide between the unclean and the clean and between the animal that is eaten and the animal that shall not be eaten" (11:46–47). Or again, right after the catalogue of forbidden sexual unions: "I am the LORD your God Who set you apart from all the peoples. And you shall set apart the clean from the unclean beast, and the unclean bird from the clean, and you shall not make yourselves despicable through beast and bird and all that crawls on the ground, which I set apart for you as unclean. And you shall be holy to Me, for I the LORD am holy" (20:24–26). (The same key Hebrew verb, *hivdil*, is used here, but because "divided you from all the peoples" sounds a little awkward, and might actually introduce an unintended idea of divisiveness, I have reluctantly abandoned consistency in this instance and represented it in English as "set apart.")

The verses just cited appear to straddle between the sexual prohibitions that precede them and the dietary prohibitions mentioned immediately afterward. Just as one has to set apart permissible sexual partners from forbidden ones—mothers, aunts, sisters, daughters, daughters-in-law, and every kind of animal—one must set apart what may be eaten in the great pullulation of living creatures from what may not be eaten—reptiles, amphibians, birds of prey, pigs, bats, rats. Israel, in its turn, by accepting these categorical divisions in the realm of appetite, sets itself apart from other peoples and becomes holy, like God. This last element of *imitatio dei* suggests that God's holiness, whatever else it may involve and however ultimately unfathomable the idea may be, implies an ontological division or chasm between the Creator and the created world, a concept that sets off biblical monotheism from the worldview of antecedent polytheisms, where at least the king could serve as mediator between human and divine.

Dividing, setting apart, the erection of barriers to access, are notions that suffuse all the regulations here about the Tabernacle (*mishkan*, more literally, God's terrestrial "dwelling place"). Again and again, we are reminded that ordinary Israelites are to keep their distance from the sacred space of the sanctuary, that no unauthorized person may "come forward" (Hebrew *qarav*, which in these contexts, as scholarship has noted, has much the sense of "encroach"). Even the priests must follow a careful regimen of dress and ablution and abstention from alcohol before entering the sanctuary, and the inner sanctum, conceived as the material point of linkage between God and the world, can be entered only by the high priest on the Day of Atonement after meticulous ritual preparation. What goes along with this rigorous setting apart of sacred space is an anxious concern about contamination from the sphere of the profane. Various body fluids; discharges and deformations of the skin and body caused by disease; mildew and other blights in fabrics, utensils, and buildings; violations of moral as well as ritual prohibitions—all these are lumped together in one large general category, according to the hierarchical division of the cosmos imagined here, of profane pollutants. These are thought of as an invisible cloud of contamination, or as some have proposed, a kind of miasma, that has the capacity to infiltrate into sacred space and compromise its holy character, which by definition involves a careful insulation from the realm of the profane.

The two brief narrative incidents incorporated in the book speak in different ways precisely to the fear of encroachment of the holy. Nadab and Abihu, Aaron's sons, bring forward "alien fire before the LORD, which He had not charged them" (10:1). Fire is a principal agency of the sacrificial cult, but even it may become a contaminant when it is unauthorized, when it is brought into the sacred zone from some secular source, and these two priests are punished for their invasive act by being consumed with an answering fire that comes out "from before the LORD." The case of the blaspheming Egyptian, who is also put to death (judicially, by stoning), involves a different sort of violation of the sacred. God has a dedicated, delimited space in the sanctuary, which must be guarded, but He also has a sacred name, which like other names, is understood to hold within it an adumbration or emanation of the distinctive essence of its bearer. The name, of course, cannot be sequestered within spatial barriers as the sanctuary is sequestered; it is always potentially available for circulation in linguistic usage. The Egyptian's vilification or profanation of the divine name is thus an act of encroachment, besmirching the holy with a vileness of the profane, and in the draconian terms of this division of realms, it is deemed a capital offense.

The chief instruments for protecting the separation of ontological spheres are fire, blood, oil, and water. These are all, of course, substances associated with the sacrificial cult that long antedate biblical monotheism, but one may follow Mary Douglas's general line of thought in viewing them as reflections of an implicit symbolic order. Fire, as we have seen abundantly in Exodus and will see even more emphatically in Deuteronomy, is associated with the deity: God reveals His commandments in an awesome pyrotechnic display, manifests His presence before the people in a pillar of fire by night and of cloud by day, and is appropriately worshipped through burnt offerings, entirely consumed by fire, and by other sacrifices that are "turned to smoke" (*hiqtir*) by the officiant. The heart of the sacred zone is a dangerous place from which divine fire may leap forth to protect the holy from contamination. Blood, as Leviticus emphatically reminds us, is the very life (*nefesh*) of the living animal. As such, it categorically must not be consumed as food, but in ritual procedure it has a purgative virtue and is to be sprinkled, cast, or smeared in designated ways during the sanctuary rite in order to effect purgation. Oil (it is specifically olive oil) has, by contrast, an association with the quotidian and with the social and political realms in ancient culture. A traveler, for example, after washing away the dust of the road, would rub himself with oil; and, of course, oil is the substance of dedication, poured on the head, for kings as well as for priests. It is chiefly the dedicatory function of oil that is carried over into its various stipulated uses here in the cult. Finally, the efficacy of water as a purifying agent is self-evident and universal. One should note that these four substances are drawn from four different realms of existence: fire is linked, as we have seen, with the divine; blood courses through the veins of living creatures, animal and human; olive oil is a product of agriculture, of the land, which sets it over against water, a manifestation of nature without human intervention (it is fresh running water that must be used for purification), recalling the primordial realm that must be set apart from dry land so that the world may come into existence.

None of this, I suspect, really mitigates the sense of strangeness that people of our own era are likely to feel in reading Leviticus. The preoccupation with dermatological conditions, genital discharges, mildew, the recipes for fritters and breads used in the cult, and the dissection of animals and the distinctions among their various inner organs does not correspond to modern assumptions about the content of great sacred literature. Nevertheless, all these regulations are reflections of a pervasive spiritual seriousness grounded in a comprehensive, coherent conception of reality. This ritual implementation of the monotheistic vision was a battle against the inchoate. Holiness could be achieved, and had to be protected, only by a constant confirmation of hierarchical distinction, by laying out reality in distinct realms and categories separated by barricades of prohibitions. Thus, Aaron and his surviving sons, immediately after the death of Nadab and Abihu, are warned never to come into the sanctuary when they have drunk "[w]ine and strong drink," for in the view of the Priestly writers, authorized ritual is in all respects the exact opposite of ecstatic orgy (another departure in principle from the pagan world as it was imagined by Israelite writers). This particular ban, like most of the injunctions of Leviticus, is framed to implement a general ideology of separation as "a perpetual statute for your generations, to divide between the holy and the profane, and between the unclean and the clean, and to teach the Israelites all the statutes that the LORD spoke by the hand of Moses" (10:9–11).

CHAPTER 1

Ａnd He called to Moses and the Lᴏʀᴅ spoke to him from the Tent   1
of Meeting, saying, "Speak to the Israelites and say to them,   2
'Should any person from you bring forward to the Lᴏʀᴅ an offering, of beasts from herd and from flock you shall bring forward your
offering. If his offering is a burnt offering, an unblemished male from   3

---

1. *And He called to Moses and the* Lᴏʀᴅ *spoke to him.* The translation reproduces the oddness of the Hebrew. According to normative usage, one would
have expected, "And the Lᴏʀᴅ called to Moses and He spoke to him." Is the
postponement of the subject a maneuver to isolate and emphasize the act of
calling? Several medieval commentators argue that the calling, or summoning,
is the necessary preceding stage before divine speech, and perhaps for that
reason it needs to be placed in the syntactic foreground. This verb, the first
word of the text (*wayiqra'*), is the prevalent Hebrew name for the book, though
another ancient designation, *torat kohanim*, "teaching of the priests," parallels
the Greek topical title "Leviticus." Rashbam, the twelfth-century French
Hebrew exegete, notes that Exodus ends by reporting Moses's being unable to
enter the Tent of Meeting because it was filled with the Lᴏʀᴅ's glory, and now
the Lᴏʀᴅ must address Moses from that very place in order to speak to him.

2. *any person.* The Hebrew *'adam* can refer to either sex. See the comment on
Genesis 1:27.
   bring forward. The verb *hiqriv* throughout this text has the technical sense
of "introduce," or "present," in the sacred space of the cult. The cognate noun,
qorban, "offering," is distinctive of Leviticus. Exodus concluded with a notice
of God's relationship with Israel in the wilderness, indicating how He led the
people on its peregrinations with the pillar of cloud by day and the pillar of fire
by night. Now, the Tabernacle having been completed (Exodus 35–37), attention is turned to how Israel on its part is to pursue its relationship with God
by offering sacrifices in the sanctuary that has been constructed.

the herd he shall bring it forward, at the entrance of the Tent of Meet-
4 ing, to be accepted for him before the LORD. And he shall lay his hand
on the head of the burnt offering, and it will be accepted for him to
5 atone for him. And he shall slaughter the male of the herd before the
LORD, and the sons of Aaron, the priests, shall bring forward the blood
and cast the blood round the altar which is at the entrance to the Tent
6 of Meeting. And he shall flay the burnt offering and cut it up into its
7 parts. And the sons of Aaron the priest shall place fire on the altar and
8 lay out the wood on the fire. And the sons of Aaron, the priests, shall
lay out the parts, the head and the fat, on the wood that is on the fire
9 which is on the altar. And its innards and its legs he shall wash in water,
and the priest shall turn it all to smoke on the altar, a fire offering, a fra-
10 grant odor to the LORD. And if his offering is from the flock,
from the sheep or from the goats, for a burnt offering, an unblemished
11 male he shall bring it forward. And he shall slaughter it on the north
side of the altar before the LORD, and the sons of Aaron, the priests,
12 shall cast its blood round the altar. And he shall cut it up into its parts,
its head and its fat, and the priest shall lay them out on the wood that
13 is on the fire which is on the altar. And the innards and the legs he shall
wash in water, and the priest shall bring it all forward and turn it to
smoke on the altar. It is a burnt offering, a fire offering, a fragrant odor
14 to the LORD. And if his burnt offering to the LORD is from the birds, he
shall bring forward his offering from the turtledoves or from the young
15 pigeons. And the priest shall bring it forward on the altar and
pinch off its head and turn it to smoke on the altar, and its blood shall

---

5. *he shall slaughter.* The person presenting the offering butchers the animal,
and then the priests take charge of laying out the parts on the altar and burning them.

7. *the sons of Aaron the priest.* Three ancient versions read here, "The sons of
Aaron, the priests," in the plural, "priests" modifying the sons and not Aaron,
as elsewhere in this chapter.

14. *from the birds.* The stipulation of this option appears to be, as several commentators have noted, an accommodation for the poor, who would have been
hard put to sacrifice something as valuable as a bull or a sheep.

be drained on the wall of the altar. And he shall remove its crop with 16
its feathers and fling it by the altar to the east, to the place of the ashes.
And he shall tear it open by its wings, he shall not divide them, and the 17
priest shall turn it to smoke on the altar, on the wood that is on the fire.
It is a burnt offering, a fire offering, a fragrant odor to the LORD.'"

---

16. *its crop with its feathers*. There is some question about the meaning of each
of these terms. Jacob Milgrom makes an elaborate argument that the first
term, *mur'ah*, means "crissum," i.e., the area around the cloacal opening
beneath the bird's tail. He is the author of a three-volume, 3000-page commentary on Leviticus that in its sheer comprehensiveness will remain a central reference for philological and historical issues involved in this book.
Consequently, his work will often be referred to here. He is an invaluable
guide but of course not infallible, and in the present instance there remains a
margin of conjecture in his identification of *mur'ah*, and since few readers will
understand what a crissum is without recourse to a dictionary, this translation
retains the more familiar "crop." The second term, *notsah*, has been linked
with the word for "excrement" by some medieval and modern commentators,
but it invariably means "feather" elsewhere in Hebrew usage. If the skin was
stripped from a large animal and not made part of the sacrifice, it is logical that
the feathers would be excluded in the sacrifice of a bird.

CHAPTER 2

¹ "Should a person bring forward a grain offering to the LORD, fine semolina his offering shall be, and he shall pour oil over it and ² place frankincense upon it. And he shall bring it to the sons of Aaron, the priests, and a handful from there shall be scooped up, from its fine semolina and from its oil, together with all its frankincense, and the priest shall turn its token portion to smoke on the altar, a fire offer- ³ ing, a fragrant odor to the LORD. And what is left of the grain offering is for Aaron and for his sons, holy of holies from the fire offerings of the

---

1. *Should a person bring forward a grain offering.* The early rabbis plausibly understood the grain offering as an accessible cultic vehicle for the common people, who might have been hard put to meet the expense of animal sacri- fice. The term for grain offering, *minḥah*, is borrowed from the political realm, where its primary meaning is "tributary payment," and thus it expresses Israel's relationship of vassal to God.

2. *a handful . . . shall be scooped.* The Hebrew says literally "he shall scoop," which could refer to a single priest. The third-person singular, however, with- out specified subject, is often used as an equivalent of the passive form of the verb.

its token portion. The general ancient Near Eastern practice, and perhaps the original Israelite one as well, was to burn the entire grain offering on the altar. Jacob Milgrom interestingly proposes that the limiting of the sacrificial fire to one small portion of the grain may have been a reaction to the wide- spread practice of burning cakes to Ishtar (denounced by Jeremiah [7:18]). The economic self-interest of the priests in preserving much of the offering for their own consumption may have also played a role in this prescription.

3. *holy of holies.* As elsewhere, this construction indicates a superlative: "most sacred." The meaning in this context is: strictly reserved for the priests.

LORD. And when you bring forward a grain offering, baked in an oven, 4
it is to be fine semolina, flatbread cakes mixed in oil or wafers of flatbread coated with oil. And if your offering is a grain offering on a grid- 5
dle, mixed in oil, flatbread it shall be. Break it into bits, and you shall 6
pour oil over it. It is a grain offering. And if your offering is a grain offer- 7
ing in a pan, with fine semolina in oil it shall be made. And you shall 8
bring the grain offering that will be made from these to the LORD, and
the priest shall bring it forward and put it out on the altar. And the 9
priest shall set aside from the grain offering its token portion and turn
it to smoke on the altar, a fire offering, a fragrant odor to the LORD. And 10
what is left of the grain offering is for Aaron and for his sons, holy of
holies from the fire offerings of the LORD. Any grain offering that you 11
bring forward to the LORD shall not be made leavened, for you shall not
turn to smoke any leaven nor any honey from it as a fire offering to the
LORD. You may bring them forward to the LORD as an offering of first 12
yield, but they shall not go up on the altar as a fragrant odor. And every 13
offering of your grain you shall season with salt. You shall not leave out
the salt of the covenant of your God from your grain offering. With
each of your offerings you shall offer salt. And if you bring forward an 14

---

11. *any leaven nor any honey.* No really convincing explanation for this prohibition has been offered. Though it might seem that there is some sort of connection between the ban on leaven in the sacrifice and the ban on leaven in
the Passover laws, honey—here, as elsewhere, the probable reference is to
date honey—does not appear to belong to the same category.

12. *but they shall not go up on the altar as a fragrant odor.* Leavened stuff and
honey are not intrinsically taboo substances, but they must be excluded from
the kind of offering that is burned on the altar.

13. *the salt of the covenant.* The indispensable presence of salt may ultimately
derive from the fact that the sacrifice was originally imagined as a divine meal,
and that seasoning with salt was felt to be necessary in order to make food
palatable (compare Job 6:6: "Can bland stuff be eaten without salt?"). But
throughout the Mediterranean, salt was associated with covenants, and the
phrase in Numbers 18:19, "a perpetual covenant of salt," suggests that the link
between salt and permanently binding covenants may have been reinforced by
salt's efficacy as a preservative.

offering of first fruits to the LORD, new ears of grain parched in fire, grits of fresh ears you shall bring forward the offering of your first fruits.

15   And you shall put oil upon it and you shall place frankincense on it. It
16   is a grain offering. And the priest shall turn its token portion to smoke, from its grits and from its oil together with all its frankincense, a fire offering to the LORD.'"

CHAPTER 3

"And if his offering is a communion sacrifice, if he brings it forward 1 from the herd, whether male or female, unblemished he shall bring it forward before the Lord. And he shall lay his hand on the 2 head of his offering and slaughter it at the entrance to the Tent of Meeting, and the sons of Aaron, the priests, shall cast the blood round the altar. And he shall bring forward from the communion sacrifice a 3 fire offering to the Lord, the fat covering the innards and all the fat that is on the innards, and the two kidneys and the fat that is on them, 4

---

1. *communion sacrifice*. There is some uncertainty as to precisely what category of sacrifice this is, especially since the second term of the Hebrew designa tion, *zevaḥ shelamim*, could be related to "whole," *shalem*, "repay," *shilem*, or "well-being," "greeting," or "peace," all meanings of *shalom*. Jacob Milgrom understands this as a "well-being sacrifice," but Baruch Levine argues plausibly, citing Ugaritic parallels, that it means "a sacred gift of greeting." The translation used here, "communion sacrifice," conveys that sense compactly and follows the rendering of the term in 1 Samuel by Kyle McCarter Jr.

3. *the fat covering the innards*. Modern readers may be perplexed as to why a sacred text should devote such attention to details of butchering and, in particular, why the suet covering the inner organs must be stripped from them (verse 4) and burned for the deity alone, taboo for human consumption (no suet pudding allowed in the Israelite diet). This is, of course, a Priestly text, and the officiants in the cult need to know precisely how to go about their business. But the anthropologist Mary Douglas proposes that all the details of sacrificial butchering are fraught with symbolic significance. For her, Leviticus is a prime instance of subtle and elaborate analogical thinking (in contradistinction to the analytic thinking with which we are more familiar). Thus, following Nahmanides, she sees a system of correspondences between the tripartite structure of the Tabernacle—Holy of Holies, sanctuary, and outer

which is on the sinews, and the lobe on the liver, together with the kid-
5 neys, he shall remove it. And the sons of Aaron shall turn it to smoke
on the altar together with the burnt offering that is on the wood which
6 is on the fire, a fire offering, a fragrant odor to the LORD. And if his
offering is from the flock as a communion sacrifice to the LORD, male
7 or female, unblemished he shall bring it forward. If a sheep he brings
8 forward as his offering, he shall bring it forward before the LORD. And
he shall lay his hand on the head of his offering and slaughter it before
the Tent of Meeting, and the sons of Aaron shall cast its blood round
9 the altar. And he shall bring forward from the communion sacrifice a
fire offering to the LORD, its fat, the entire broad tail opposite the back-
bone, he shall remove it, and the fat covering the innards and all the fat
10 that is on the innards. And the two kidneys and the fat that is on them,
which is on the sinews, and the lobe on the liver, together with the kid-
11 neys, he shall remove it. And the priest shall turn it to smoke on the
12 altar, fire-offering bread for the LORD. And if his offering is a goat, he
13 shall bring it forward before the LORD. And he shall lay his hand on its
head and slaughter it before the Tent of Meeting, and the sons of Aaron
14 shall fling its blood round the altar. And he shall bring forward his offer-

---

court—and Mount Sinai as it is represented in Exodus—the summit, where
only Moses may go, the perimeter of dense cloud, restricted to Aaron, his sons,
and the seventy elders, and the foot of the mountain, to which the people have
access. She goes on to propose that the animal sacrifice is correspondingly
divided in three—the entrails, intestines, and genitals at the summit of the
butchered pile, the midriff area with the covering of fat, to be burned on the
altar, and the head and meat sections, which may be consumed by the priests
and the people. "The suet," she contends, "that divides the body at the
diaphragm below the lower ribs is not just a covering. It corresponds in the
body to the boundary of a forbidden sacred space on the mountain."

11. *fire-offering bread*. The Hebrew *leḥem*, which has the primary meaning of
"bread," is often a synecdoche for food, as here, where the sacrifice is meat,
not cereal. In the pagan Near East, sacrifice was generally thought of as food
provided by man for the gods. It is not clear whether the religious elite of
monotheistic Israel preserved this belief—the idiom could be no more than a
linguistic fossil—though one may suspect some persistence of the idea in the
popular imagination.

ing from it, a fire offering to the LORD, the fat covering the innards and
the fat that is on the innards. And the two kidneys and the fat that is   15
on them, which is on the sinews, and the lobe on the liver, together
with the kidneys, he shall remove it. And the priest shall turn them to   16
smoke on the altar, fire-offering bread for the LORD, as a fragrant odor,
all the fat to the LORD. An everlasting statute for your generations in all   17
your dwelling places, no fat and no blood shall you eat.'"

---

17. *no fat and no blood shall you eat.* The prohibition on consuming blood is
grounded in the idea of the sacredness of life (see Genesis 9:4). The prohibition on eating fat seems strictly related to the fact that it is reserved for the
deity alone in the sacrificial rite—and, if one follows Douglas, because it
marks a barrier of exclusion in a system of analogies between body and sacred
cosmos. It is instructive that when the seventeenth-century antinomian messianic leader Sabbatai Zebi wanted to demonstrate to his followers that he was
empowered to abrogate the Torah, he chose to demonstrate this by the public
consumption of suet—the violation of a seemingly arbitrary prohibition, and a
violation that could scarcely have given him much pleasure.

CHAPTER 4

1,2   **A**nd the Lord spoke to Moses, saying, "Speak to the Israelites, saying, 'Should a person offend errantly in regard to any of the Lord's
3   commands that should not be done and he do one of these, if the
anointed priest should offend, incurring guilt for the people, he shall
bring forward for his offense that he has committed an unblemished
4   bull from the herd for the Lord as an offense offering. And he shall

---

1. *And the Lord spoke to Moses*. As Jacob Milgrom observes, this introductory
formula marks the beginning of a new category of offerings, those offered to
expunge the effects of an inadvertent offense.

2. *offend errantly*. The Hebrew adverb *bishegagah* has the sense of "unintentionally," "by mistake." The concern throughout this section is to preserve the
purity of the place of the cult. The inadvertent "offense" does not at all imply
an ethical transgression but rather the unwitting violation of a prohibition
("any of the Lord's commands that should not be done"), which, in ancient
Near Eastern terms, has the consequence of generating physical pollution that
must be cleansed. The rabbis aptly explained that the errancy could result
from either ignorance of the law or ignorance of the circumstances of the act
committed.

3. *the anointed priest*. This is an alternate designation for the high priest.
    as an offense offering. The traditional translation of this term is "sin offer-
ing." Milgrom argues in elaborate detail that this is a misrepresentation of the
Hebrew *ḥata't* and proposes "purification offering" as a precise English equivalent. The verb *ḥata'* in the *qal* conjugation, as in verse 2 here, means "to commit an offense," a term probably taken over from the political to the cultic
realm (as when a vassal people commits an offense against its overlords by
rebelling). The same root in the *pi'el* conjugation means to "remove" or "cancel" (one well-attested semantic function of this conjugation) the offense. The

bring the bull to the entrance of the Tent of Meeting before the LORD
and lay his hand on the head of the bull and slaughter the bull before
the LORD. And the anointed priest shall take from the blood of the bull   5
and bring it to the Tent of Meeting. And the priest shall dip his finger   6
in the blood and sprinkle from the blood seven times before the LORD
against the covering of the shrine. And the priest shall put some of the   7
blood on the horns of the altar of aromatic incense before the LORD,
which is in the Tent of Meeting, and all the blood of the bull he shall
pour out at the base of the burnt-offering altar which is at the entrance
to the Tent of Meeting. And all the fat of the bull of offense offering,   8
he shall set aside from it the fat covering the innards and all the fat that
is on the innards. The two kidneys and the fat that is on them, which   9
is on the sinews, and the lobe on the liver, together with the kidneys,
he shall take away, as it is set aside from the communion-sacrifice bull.   10
And the priest shall turn them to smoke on the burnt-offering altar,

---

noun *hata't* is derived from the *pi'el* conjugation and hence the canceling-out
effect ("purification") is in fact implied. But something is lost by using a designation for this offering that is not cognate with the verb "to offend," and the
context makes clear enough that an offense offering is a sacrifice that removes
the effects of the offense.

6. *dip his finger in the blood and sprinkle from the blood seven times before the*
LORD *against the covering of the shrine*. This sanguinary business may strike the
modern reader as an odd way to purify anything, but throughout the Bible
blood has powerfully antithetical valences, alternately identified as the stuff of
life and the manifestation of guilt. Perhaps because it was thought to be the
very bearer of the life force in animate creatures, it was understood to have
what Milgrom vividly calls a "detergent" effect. The sprinkling is of course performed seven times because of the sacredness of the number seven.

7. *the horns of the altar*. Ancient Near Eastern altars in fact have been uncovered that have stone horns carved at each of the four corners. Although no
definitive explanation of this general practice has been offered, since the animal's horn is a recurrent image in biblical poetry for power, the horned altar
may be a way of defining this space as a zone of power. Fugitives seeking asylum in the sanctuary would cling to one of the horns of the altar.
    all the blood. This phrase obviously means all of the remaining blood since
a small amount of the blood has been sprinkled on the altar.

11 and the hide of the bull together with its head and together with its
12 shanks and its innards and its dung. And he shall take the whole bull
out beyond the camp to a clean place, to the ash heap, and he shall
13 burn it on wood with fire, on the ash heap it shall be burned. And if all
the community of Israel should err, and the thing be hidden from the
eyes of the assembly, and they do one of all the LORD's commands that
14 should not be done, and they bear guilt, and the offense that they committed become known, the assembly shall bring forward a bull from the
herd as an offense offering, and they shall bring it before the Tent of
15 Meeting. And the elders of the community shall lay their hands on the
head of the bull before the LORD, and the bull shall be slaughtered
16 before the LORD. And the anointed priest shall bring from the blood of
17 the bull to the Tent of Meeting. And the priest shall dip his finger in
the blood and sprinkle from the blood seven times before the LORD
18 against the covering of the shrine. And some of the blood he shall put
on the horns of the altar that is before the LORD, which is in the Tent
of Meeting, and all the blood he shall pour out at the base of the burnt-
19 offering altar, which is at the entrance of the Tent of Meeting. And he
shall set aside all the fat from the bull and turn it to smoke on the altar.
20 And he shall do to the bull as he did to the offense-offering bull, so
shall it be done to it, and the priest shall atone for them and it shall be
21 forgiven them. And he shall take the bull out beyond the camp and
burn it as he burned the first bull. It is an offense offering of the assem-
22 bly. When a chieftain offends and does one of all the commands of the
LORD his God that should not be done, in errance, and he bears guilt,
23 or his offense that he committed is made known to him, he shall bring
24 his offering, an unblemished male goat. And he shall lay his hand on
the head of the goat and slaughter it in the place where the burnt offer-
25 ing is slaughtered before the LORD. It is an offense offering. And the
priest shall take from the blood of the offense offering on his finger and
place it on the horns of the burnt-offering altar, and he shall pour out
26 its blood at the base of the burnt-offering altar. And all its fat he shall

---

13. *if all the community of Israel should err.* As several commentators have
noted, this could occur if, for example, the high priest inadvertently misguided
them—say, about the day for observing a particular festival.

turn to smoke on the altar like the fat of the communion sacrifice, and
the priest shall atone for him for his offense, and it shall be forgiven
him. And if a single person from the common people should offend ²⁷
errantly in doing one of the LORD's commands that should not be done,
and bear guilt, or his offense that he committed is made known to him, ²⁸
he shall bring his offering, an unblemished female goat, for his offense
which he committed. And he shall lay his hand on the head of the ²⁹
offense offering and slaughter the offense offering in the place of the
burnt offering. And the priest shall take from its blood on his finger and ³⁰
place it on the horns of the burnt-offering altar, and he shall pour
out all its blood at the base of the altar. And all its fat he shall take away, ³¹
as the fat was taken away from the communion sacrifice, and the priest
shall turn it to smoke on the altar as a fragrant odor to the LORD, and
the priest shall atone for him and it shall be forgiven him. And if ³²
he brings a sheep as his offering for an offense, an unblemished female
he shall bring it. And he shall lay his hand on the head of the offense ³³
offering and slaughter it as an offense offering in the place where the
burnt offering is slaughtered. And the priest shall take from the blood ³⁴
of the offense offering on his finger and place it on the horns of the
altar, and all its blood he shall pour out at the base of the altar. And all ³⁵
its fat he shall take away as the fat of the sheep is taken away from the
communion sacrifice, and the priest shall turn it to smoke together
with the fire offerings of the LORD, and the priest shall atone for him,
for his offense that he committed, and it shall be forgiven him.'"

CHAPTER 5

1 "And should a person offend when he has heard a voice in adjuration, he being witness, or has seen or known, if he does not
2 tell, he shall bear his punishment. Or a person who touches any unclean thing, whether the carcass of an unclean beast or the carcass of an unclean domestic animal, or the carcass of an unclean crawling
3 thing, and it be hidden from him, and he is unclean and guilty, or should he touch human uncleanness, of any of the uncleannesses with which one may be defiled, and it be hidden from him, and he be guilty,
4 or should a person swear to utter with the lips, whether for evil or for good, of all that a human utters in a vow, and it be hidden from him,
5 and he know and be guilty of one of these, it shall be when he is guilty

---

2. *Or a person who touches.* The language of this entire chapter is characteristic of the uncompromising legal style of Leviticus, which makes no concession to rhetorical gesture (in contrast to Deuteronomy), lays out regulations with dry technical precision, and tries to cover a whole range of legal instances—in the present case, the incurring of unwitting guilt, whether through ritual impurity or in vow taking (the catalogue of possibilities, and then the cultic redress required, does not come to the end of a sentence until the conclusion of verse 5).

3. *any of the uncleannesses with which one may be defiled.* These would include contact with a corpse, with a menstruating woman, with a man who has just had a seminal emission.
   and he be guilty. The Hebrew *'ashem* (here, at the end of verse 2, and elsewhere in this chapter) primarily means to be in a state of guilt, to incur guilt. Because what is involved in these laws is unwitting infraction, many interpreters have understood the verb to indicate something like an acknowledgment of guilt, though it is not entirely clear that it bears that meaning.

of any of these, he shall confess that concerning which he has
offended. And he shall bring his guilt offering to the LORD for his 6
offense that he has committed, a female from the flock, a ewe or a she-
goat, as an offense offering, and the priest shall atone for him for his
offense. And if his hand cannot attain as much as a sheep, he shall 7
bring as his guilt offering for what he has committed two turtledoves or
two young pigeons to the LORD, one for an offense offering and one for
a burnt offering. And he shall bring them to the priest, who shall bring 8
forward first the one for the offense offering and pinch its head at its
nape but not sever it. And he shall sprinkle from the blood of the 9
offense offering against the wall of the altar, and what is left of the
blood shall be drained at the base of the altar. It is an offense offering.
And the second one he shall make a burnt offering according to regu- 10
lation, and the priest shall atone for him for his offense that he has
committed, and it shall be forgiven him. And if his hand cannot attain 11
two turtledoves or two young pigeons, he shall bring as his offering for
what he has committed a tenth of an ephah of fine semolina as offense
offering. He shall not put oil on it nor shall he place frankincense on it,
for it is an offense offering. And he shall bring it to the priest, and the 12
priest shall scoop up a fistful from it as its token and turn it to smoke
on the altar together with the fire offerings of the LORD. It is an offense
offering. And the priest shall atone for him for his offense that he has 13
committed of any of these, and it shall be forgiven him, and it shall be
for the priest like the grain offering.'"

And the LORD spoke to Moses, saying, "Should a person betray trust 14,15
and offend errantly in regard to any of the LORD's sancta, he shall bring

---

7. *if his hand cannot attain*. The primary sense of the verb is "reach." "Hand"
in biblical idiom is often used, as here, metonymically to indicate power or
capacity. The law that follows here is what the rabbis called "an ascending and
descending offering" (*qorban ʿoleh weyored*), that is, a sliding-scale offering
which is devised to accommodate people of limited means.

15. *betray trust*. The verb *maʿal* is used in Numbers 5 to indicate the betrayal of
marital trust in cases of infidelity. (In modern Hebrew, it has come to mean
embezzlement, reflecting a certain continuity with its ancient usage.) In this

his guilt offering to the LORD, an unblemished ram from the flock, or
its equivalent in silver shekels, according to the sanctuary shekel, as a
16 guilt offering. And that concerning which he has offended from the
sanctum he shall pay and a fifth part he shall add to it and give to the
priest, and the priest shall atone for him with the ram of the guilt offer-
17 ing, and it shall be forgiven him. And if a person offends and does any
one of all the commands of the LORD that should not be done and does
18 not know and is guilty, he shall bear his punishment. And he shall bring
an unblemished ram from the flock, or its equivalent, as a guilt offering, to the priest, and the priest shall atone for him for his errancy that
he has committed without knowing, and it shall be forgiven him.
19,20 It is a guilt offering. He has surely incurred guilt to the LORD." And the
21 LORD spoke to Moses, saying, "Should a person offend and betray the
LORD's trust and dissemble with his fellow about a deposit or pledge, or
22 by theft, or defraud his fellow, or should he find something lost and
dissemble about it and swear falsely about anything of what a person

---

verse, the sense is committing sacrilege, and the use of the verb may be dictated
by an assumption that preserving the sacred integrity of everything belonging to
the sanctuary is a special obligation with which all Israelites are entrusted. In
verse 21, betrayal of trust in its more obvious sense is at issue, although the
deception of one person by another is conceived as a betrayal of God's trust
because it is God who insists on a standard of honesty from humanity.

or its equivalent. The literal sense of the Hebrew is "in your estimation."
The possessive pronominal component of this expression ("your") reflects the
fact that it is, as Baruch Levine rightly observes, a bound expression, a colloquial "you" becoming fixed as a part of an idiom that means monetary
equivalences.

16. that concerning which he has offended from the sanctum he shall pay. A characteristic case that this law envisages is when someone eats food not realizing
it has been consecrated for cultic use. He would thus pay the monetary cost
of the food consumed plus a fine of 20 percent.

21. theft. Rabbinic interpretation distinguishes between gazel (the term used
here), "robbery" (taking another's property by main force), and geneivah, "theft"
(taking by stealth). However, the present context of fraud and dissembling
encourages the idea that theft is meant.

may do to offend, and it shall be, when he offends and is guilty, he shall 23
return the theft that he stole or the fraud that he committed or
the deposit that was placed with him or the lost thing that he found, or 24
anything that he swore about falsely, and he shall pay back the principal and add a fifth, to him to whom it belongs he shall give it, when his
guilt is confirmed. And his guilt offering he shall bring to the LORD, an 25
unblemished ram from the flock, or its equivalent, as a guilt offering,
to the priest. And the priest shall atone for him before the LORD, and it 26
shall be forgiven him for whatever he may have done to incur guilt
thereby."

---

23. *is guilty*. Again, many interpreters understand this to mean: acknowledges
his guilt. The sense could also be: he is found guilty, after which he acknowledges his guilt.

24. *when his guilt is confirmed*. The literal sense of the two Hebrew words
beyom 'ashmato is: the day of his guilt.

CHAPTER 6

1,2   **A**nd the Lord spoke to Moses, saying, "Charge Aaron and his sons, saying, 'This is the teaching of the burnt offering. It is the very burnt offering over its flame on the altar all night till morning, and 3   the fire of the altar shall keep burning on in it. And the priest shall wear

---

2. *This is the teaching*. Leviticus repeatedly introduces a particular set of regulations with the phrase "this is the teaching [*torah*]," this being the first occurrence. "Teaching" is, in fact, the primary meaning of *torah*, and this translation preserves that sense throughout, though in these contexts, "procedure," "ritual," "regulation," and similar terms used in sundry modern English versions are all justified. In any case, the reiteration of the term is a strong verbal symptom of how Leviticus differs formally from other biblical books. This is primarily a book of instructions, and one of its Hebrew names, *torah kohanim*, could aptly be translated as "Priestly Instructions."

It is the very burnt offering. The semantic force of the Hebrew phrase *hiʾ haʿolah* is to emphasize the noun (*ʿolah*) that follows the indicative pronoun (*hiʾ*).

flame. The literal sense is "place of burning" (though the translation "hearth" proposed by some modern scholars sounds altogether too domestic for a cultic setting). Stylistically, this entire passage about the burnt offering is dominated by terms related to burning, as if to focus the idea of a sacred fire that burns perpetually, coordinated with the sacrificial fire that entirely consumes the burnt offering. The word for burnt offering or holocaust, *ʿolah*, is not derived from a root that means "to burn" but rather from the verb "to go up," which, however, is metonymically linked to burning by suggesting the idea that the whole sacrifice "goes up" in smoke. Fire and blood are the two substances that are the key to the sacrificial rites, but the present passage gives preeminence to the nexus between cult and fire—the element associated with God's fiery epiphany at Sinai and with his first appearance to Moses in the burning bush. Hence an altar with a fire that "shall not go out."

his linen garb and linen breeches he shall wear on his body, and he
shall take away the ashes that the fire consumes from the burnt offering on the altar and put them beside the altar. And he shall take off his   4
clothes and wear other clothes and take out the ashes beyond the camp
to a clean place. And the fire on the altar shall keep burning on it, it   5
shall not go out, and the priest shall burn wood on it morning after
morning and lay out on it the burnt offering and turn the fat part of the
communion offerings to smoke. A perpetual fire shall keep burning on   6
the altar. It shall not go out.

" 'And this is the teaching of the grain offering. The sons of Aaron are to   7
bring it forward before the LORD in front of the altar. And a handful of   8
it shall be removed, from the semolina of the grain offering and from
its oil, with all the frankincense that is on the grain offering, and it shall
be turned to smoke on the altar, a fragrant odor, its token to the LORD.
And what is left of it Aaron and his sons shall eat, as flatcakes it shall   9
be eaten, in a holy place, in the court of the Tent of Meeting they shall
eat it. It shall not be baked leavened. As their share I have given it from   10
my fire offerings. It is holy of holies, like the offense offering and like
the guilt offering. Every male among the sons of Aaron shall eat it, a   11
perpetual portion for your generations from the fire offerings of the
LORD. Whatever touches them shall become holy.' "

---

9. *Aaron and his sons shall eat*. It must be kept in mind that in this agrarian
society, the landless members of the tribe of Levi needed the cult for the bread
and butter (or, more literally, the bread and meat) of their physical sustenance.
Throughout the sacrificial regulations, provisions are made for setting aside
portions to be consumed by the priests.

10. *It is holy of holies*. As elsewhere, this structure is a way of indicating a
superlative in biblical idiom, the sense being: supremely holy, sacrosanct.

11. *Whatever touches them shall become holy*. It is also possible to construe this
sentence, as Baruch Levine does, to mean: whoever touches them shall be
holy (i.e., no person is allowed to touch the flatcakes made from the grain
offerings who is not "holy," or a member of the priestly caste). Jacob Milgrom,
however, makes a persuasive case on philological and other grounds that the
reference is to objects rather than to persons. What is involved, then, is an

12,13 And the LORD spoke to Moses, saying, "This is the offering of Aaron
and his sons which they shall bring forward to the LORD on the day he
is anointed: a tenth of an ephah of semolina as a perpetual grain offer-
14 ing, half of it in the morning and half of it in the evening. On a griddle
in oil it shall be done, soaked through you shall bring it, as a grain offering of baked pieces you shall bring it forward, a fragrant odor to the
15 LORD. And the anointed priest, successor among his sons, shall do it,
a perpetual portion for the LORD, it shall be entirely turned to smoke.
16 And every priest's grain offering shall be entire, it shall not be eaten."

17,18 And the LORD spoke to Moses, saying, "Speak to Aaron and to his sons,
saying, 'This is the teaching of the offense offering. In the place
where the burnt offering is slaughtered, the offense offering shall be
19 slaughtered before the LORD. It is holy of holies. The priest performing
it as an offense offering shall eat it. In a holy place it shall be eaten,
20 in the court of the Tent of Meeting. Whatever touches its flesh shall
become holy, and when some of its blood is spattered on a garment,
21 that which has been spattered shall be laundered in a holy place. And

---

idea some scholars have described as a "contagion" of holiness symmetrical
with the more common idea of a contagion of impurity. Objects that come in
contact with consecrated substances such as the grain offering themselves
become consecrated and can no longer be used for profane purposes.

15. *successor among his sons.* The literal sense of the Hebrew is "in his stead
among his sons," but "in his stead" is regularly used in references to monarchy
to indicate the successor to the throne, and that must be the meaning here.

a perpetual portion for the LORD. Although the use of the noun ḥoq, "portion," may be a linguistic fossil harking back to a premonotheistic era when the
sacrifice was conceived as a way of offering food to the gods, its introduction
here is more probably dictated by the desire to use a complementary term: one
part of the grain offering was reserved for the priests to be eaten as their portion, and so the remaining part burned on the altar is described as "a perpetual portion for the LORD."

16. *every priest's grain offering shall be entire.* That is, when a priest presents a
grain offering on his own behalf rather than on behalf of a layperson, no part
is to be reserved for his consumption, all of it must be burned on the altar.

an earthen vessel in which it is boiled shall be broken, and if it was
boiled in a copper vessel, it shall be scoured and rinsed with water.
Every male among the priests shall eat it. It is holy of holies. And every   22,23
offense offering from which blood is brought into the Tent of Meeting
to atone in the sanctum shall not be eaten. In fire it shall be burned.'"

CHAPTER 7

_{1,2} And this is the teaching of the guilt offering. It is holy of holies. In
the place where they slaughter the burnt offering they shall
slaughter the guilt offering and its blood shall be cast on the altar
₃ all around. And all of its fat shall be brought forward, the broad tail and
₄ the fat covering the innards, and the two kidneys and the fat that is on
them which is over the loins and the lobe on the liver, together with the
₅ kidneys, it shall be removed. And the priest shall turn them to smoke
₆ on the altar, a fire offering to the LORD. It is a guilt offering. Any male
among the priests may eat it; in a holy place it shall be eaten. It is holy
₇ of holies. The offense offering like the sin offering, a single teaching do
₈ they have: the priest who atones through it, his shall it be. And the
priest bringing forward a man's burnt offering, the hide of the burnt
offering that the priest brought forward is the priest's, his it shall be.
₉ And every grain offering that is baked in an oven and everything made
in a pan and on a griddle is the priest's who brings it forward, his it shall
₁₀ be. And every grain offering, mixed with oil or dry, shall be for all the
sons of Aaron, each man of them alike.

₁₁ And this is the teaching of the communion sacrifice that is brought
₁₂ forward to the LORD. If in thanksgiving he brings it forward, he shall
bring forward with the thanksgiving sacrifice flatcakes mixed in oil and
flatcake wafers coated with oil and cakes of semolina soaked through,
₁₃ mixed in oil. With cakes of leavened bread he shall bring forward his
₁₄ offering with his thanksgiving communion sacrifice. And he shall bring
forward from it one kind of each offering, a levy to the LORD; for the
priest casting the blood of the communion sacrifice, his it shall be.
₁₅ And the flesh of his thanksgiving communion sacrifice shall be eaten
on the day of its offering; he shall not leave anything of it till the morn-

ing. And if his offering is a votive or a freewill offering, on the day he 16
brings forward his sacrifice it shall be eaten, and on the morrow what
is left of it may be eaten. And what is left of the flesh of the sacrifice 17
on the third day shall be burned in fire. And if some of the flesh of his 18
communion sacrifice should indeed be eaten on the third day, it will
not be acceptable, he who brings it forth, it will not be reckoned for
him, it is desecrated meat; and the person eating of it will bear his guilt.
And the flesh that touches anything unclean shall not be eaten, in fire 19
it shall be burned. And other flesh, whoever is clean may eat the
flesh. And the person who eats flesh from the communion sacrifice 20
which is the LORD's and his uncleanness is upon him, that person shall
be cut off from his kin. And should a person touch anything unclean 21
through human uncleanness or an unclean beast or any unclean abominable creature and eat of the flesh of the communion sacrifice which
is the LORD's, that person shall be cut off from his kin.

---

18. *desecrated meat*. The Hebrew *pigul* is a rare term of uncertain etymology
and without evident cognates in other Semitic languages. Most interpreters,
ancient and modern, assume it means something like "abomination" or "abhorrent thing," but Jacob Milgrom, carefully scrutinizing the other biblical occurrences with an eye to the present context, persuasively argues that the word
has the technical sense of "desecrated meat."

19. *And other flesh*. The Hebrew says, somewhat obscurely, only "the flesh."
The context compels one to infer that what is meant is the flesh of the communion sacrifice that has not been defiled by contact with something unclean.

21. *any unclean abominable creature*. The Hebrew noun is *sheqets*, which usually means "abomination." Some manuscript versions read *sherets*, "creeping
thing," which would be the more expected term here.

22,23 And the LORD spoke to Moses, saying, "Speak to the Israelites, saying,
24 'No fat of ox or sheep or goat shall you eat, and the fat of a beast
that has died and the fat of a beast torn by predators may be used for
25 any task but it shall by no means be eaten. For whoever eats fat from
the animal from which fire offering is brought forward to the LORD, the
26 person eating shall be cut off from his kin. And no blood shall you con-
27 sume in all your dwelling places, whether from fowl or beast. Any person who consumes any blood shall be cut off from his kin.'"

28,29 And the LORD spoke to Moses, saying, "Speak to the Israelites, saying,
'He who brings forward his communion sacrifice to the LORD shall
30 bring his offering to the LORD from his communion sacrifice. His own
hands shall bring the fire offerings of the LORD, the fat together with
the breast he shall bring it, the breast to elevate as an elevation offer-
31 ing before the LORD. And the priest shall turn the breast into smoke on
32 the altar, and the breast shall be Aaron's and his sons'. And the right
thigh you shall give as a levy to the priest from the communion sacri-
33 fices. He of the sons of Aaron who brings forward the blood of the
communion sacrifices and the fat, his shall be the right thigh as a

---

24. *a beast that has died*. This is a single word in the Hebrew, *neveilah*. The
basic meaning is "carcass," but with the necessary implication that the animal
has died from natural causes rather than violently.

   a beast torn by predators. Again, this is one word in the Hebrew, *tereifah*,
which means "something torn [by ravening beasts]." The taboo on eating torn
carcass was felt so strongly that, much later, in Yiddish usage, the word would
be adopted as the general term for forbidden foods.

26. *in all your dwelling places*. This introduction of this term is an indication
that the ban on ingesting blood is in no way restricted to animals or even categories of animals sacrificed in the cult but is comprehensively binding on the
Israelites wherever they dwell.

30. *to elevate*. This gesture was a public sign of conveying the part of the animal elevated to the LORD's jurisdiction or possession.

share. For the breast of the elevation offering and the thigh of the levy   34
I have taken from the Israelites, from their communion sacrifices, and
have given them to Aaron the priest and to his sons as a perpetual portion from the Israelites. This is the allotment of Aaron and the allot-   35
ment of his sons from the fire offerings of the LORD from the day they
were brought forward to be priests to the LORD, which the LORD   36
charged to give to them from the day they were anointed, from the
Israelites, a perpetual statute for their generations. This is the teaching   37
for the burnt offering, for the grain offering, and for the offense offering and for the guilt offering and for the installation offering and for the
communion sacrifice which the LORD charged Moses on Mount Sinai   38
on the day He charged the Israelites to bring forward their sacrifices to
the LORD in the Wilderness of Sinai.'"

---

34. *the breast . . . and the thigh.* The same two portions of the animal are
reserved for the Aaronides in the installation sacrifice about which instructions are given in Exodus 29:26–27. It is a token of how keenly the concrete
details of these seemingly dry cultic passages were reflected on by later generations that Moses ibn Ezra (c. 1055–c. 1135) should wittily invoke these body
parts in an erotic poem, transposing them from animal to woman, and proclaiming that he will take his due portion as did the priests of old. The ingenious allusion registers a sound exegetical understanding that the breast and
the thigh are the choice parts.

35. *from the day they were brought forward.* As elsewhere, the singular masculine verb (literally, "he brought them forward") is the equivalent of a passive
form. The verb *hiqriv,* "brought forward," is equally used for the sundry sacrifices and for the priests. In cultic contexts, it has the sense of presenting or
bringing forward into the sacred zone of the sanctuary, into the LORD's presence ("before the LORD"). Its cognate accusative is *qorban,* the general term
for "offering." Thus the priests are dedicated to God, brought forward into the
divine presence, just as the sacrifices are dedicated.

CHAPTER 8

1,2 **A**nd the Lᴏʀᴅ spoke to Moses, saying, "Take Aaron and his sons
      with him, and the garments and the anointing oil and the offense-
3   offering bull and the two rams and the basket of flatbread. And
assemble all the community at the entrance of the Tent of Meeting."
4 And Moses did as the Lᴏʀᴅ had charged him, and the community
5 assembled at the entrance of the Tent of Meeting. And Moses said
to the community, "This is the thing that the Lᴏʀᴅ charged to do."
6 And Moses brought forward Aaron and his sons and bathed them in
7 water. And he placed the tunics on them and girded them with the sash
and dressed them in the robe and put the ephod over it and girded
it with the ornamental band of the ephod, and tied it to him with it.

---

4. *And Moses did as the Lᴏʀᴅ had charged him.* A variant of this clause recurs
at the very end of the chapter, framing the whole in an envelope structure.
What is noteworthy is that in this chapter the Book of Leviticus for the first
time moves from lists of cultic regulations to narrative. It is, of course, a limited sort of narrative, strictly concentrating on the rite of consecration that
makes both the altar and Aaron and his sons fit for the cult of YHWH. The
details of this installation ceremony pick up Exodus 29.

7. *the tunics . . . the sash . . . the robe . . . the ephod.* The use of the definite
article before each of these items of attire is an indication that the item in
question has already been publicly stipulated (in Exodus) as part of the attire
the priests are to wear when officiating in the cult.
    to him. The Hebrew glides from the plural, used for all the sons of Aaron,
to the singular, Aaron the high priest, upon whom the focus will be in the next
verse.

And he put the breastplate on him and placed in the breastplate the 8
Urim and the Thummim. And he put the turban on his head, and he 9
put upon the turban at the front the golden diadem, the holy crown, as
the LORD had charged Moses. And Moses took the anointing oil and 10
anointed the Tabernacle and everything in it and consecrated them.
And he sprinkled from it on the altar seven times and anointed the altar 11
and all its implements and the laver and its stand to consecrate them.
And he poured from the anointing oil on Aaron's head and anointed 12
him to consecrate him. And Moses brought forward the sons of Aaron 13
and dressed them in tunics and girded them with sashes and bound
headdresses on them as the LORD had charged Moses. And he brought 14
close the offense-offering bull, and Aaron and his sons laid their hands
on the head of the offense-offering bull, and it was slaughtered. And 15
Moses took the blood and put it on the horns of the altar all around
with his finger and rid the altar of offense, and the blood he poured out
at the base of the altar and consecrated it to atone over it. And he took 16
all the fat that was on the innards and the lobe on the liver and the two

---

8. *the Urim and the Thummim.* See the comment on Exodus 28:30.

10. *Moses took the anointing oil and anointed the Tabernacle.* Some scholars
conjecture that anointment was the rite of consecration because, as some
ancient Near Eastern parallels suggest, coating with oil was thought to have a
prophylactic effect, warding off evil forces. There may, however, be a more
quotidian explanation. Rubbing the body with oil after bathing was a way of
both pleasuring the body and putting oneself in a festive state, as when David
renounces his ritual of mourning, bathes, rubs himself with oil, changes his
clothes, then comes to worship and finally to eat (2 Samuel 12:20). The same
procedure might have seemed appropriate to ready the altar and the officiants
for service. Anointing was also the ceremony for conferring kingship (rather
than crowning), perhaps as an extension of its cultic use. The anointing oil was
a special mix of olive oil and fragrant spices, with the latter predominating in
quantity.

15. *Moses took the blood and put it on the horns of the altar.* The two substances
upon which the dedication ritual turns are oil and blood. The function of the
former is, at least in the view of this commentary, purely consecrational,
whereas the blood is understood to have what Jacob Milgrom calls a "detergent" effect, ridding the altar of impurities.

kidneys and their fat, and Moses turned them to smoke on the altar.
17 And the bull and its hide and its flesh and its dung he burned in fire
18 outside the camp, as the LORD had charged Moses. And he brought forward the burnt-offering ram, and Aaron and his sons laid their hands
19 on the head of the ram. And it was slaughtered, and Moses cast the
20 blood on the altar all around. And the ram he cut up into its parts, and
21 Moses turned the head and the cut parts and the fat into smoke. And
the innards and the legs he washed in water. And Moses turned the
whole ram to smoke on the altar—a burnt offering it was—as a fragrant
odor to the LORD, a fire offering to the LORD it was, as the LORD had
22 charged Moses. And he brought forward the second ram, the installation ram, and Aaron and his sons laid their hands on the head of the
23 ram. And it was slaughtered, and Moses took from its blood and put it
on the right earlobe of Aaron and on the thumb of his right hand and
24 on the big toe of his right foot. And he brought forward the sons of
Aaron, and Moses put from the blood on their right earlobe and on the
thumb of their right hand and on the big toe of their right foot, and
25 Moses cast the blood on the altar all around. And he took the fat and
the broad tail and all the fat that is on the innards and the lobe on the
26 liver and the two kidneys and their fat and the right thigh. And from the
basket of flatbread that is before the LORD he took one loaf of flatbread
and one loaf of oil bread and one wafer and placed them on the fat and
27 on the right thigh. And he put everything on the palms of Aaron and on
the palms of his sons, and elevated them as an elevation offering before
28 the LORD. And Moses took them from their palms and turned them to
smoke on the altar together with the burnt offering—they were an

---

23. *Moses took from its blood and put it on the right earlobe of Aaron and on the thumb of his right hand and on the big toe of his right foot.* Both the altar and the priests are smeared with anointing oil and with blood. As Baruch Levine notes of the high priest, "In effect, he was the human counterpart of the altar." In fact, the ceremony as a whole is a strong instance of what Mary Douglas calls analogical thinking, in which sacerdotal body and altar are part of an intricate system of correspondences. The extremities daubed with blood correspond to the horns and the base of the altar on which blood is sprinkled. At the same time, the right hand and the right foot are the emblems of human agency as the right ear is the emblem of obedience or responsiveness.

installation offering for a fragrant odor, a fire offering they were to the LORD. And Moses took the breast and elevated it as an elevation offer- 29 ing before the LORD from the ram of installation. For Moses it was for a portion, as the LORD had charged Moses. And Moses took from the 30 anointing oil and from the blood that was on the altar and sprinkled it on Aaron, on his garments, and on his sons and on the garments of his sons, with him, and he consecrated Aaron with his garments and his sons and the garments of his sons, with him. And Moses said to Aaron 31 and to his sons, "Boil the flesh at the entrance to the Tent of Meeting, and there you shall eat it and the bread that is in the installation bas- ket, as I have charged, saying 'Aaron and his sons shall eat it.' And what 32 is left of the flesh and of the bread you shall burn in fire. And from the 33 entrance of the Tent of Meeting you shall not go out seven days, until the day of completion of the days of your installation, for seven days shall your installation be. As was done on this day, the LORD charged to 34 do to atone for you. And at the entrance of the Tent of Meeting you 35 shall sit day and night seven days, and you shall keep the LORD's watch and shall not die, for thus I have been charged." And Aaron, and his 36 sons with him, did all the things that the LORD had charged by the hand of Moses.

---

33. *until the day of completion of the days of your installation.* The Hebrew phrasing incorporates an untranslatable pun. The word for "installation," *milu'im,* literally means "fillings" and is linked to the idiom "fill the hands" (the phrase at the end of the verse, "shall your installation be" is literally "your hands will be filled," that is, you will be entrusted with the priestly functions, having been installed). "Completion" (*melo't*) is another form of this same ver- bal root, the idea being that a set period is completed when its days are filled out.

CHAPTER 9

And it happened, on the eighth day, that Moses called to Aaron and
to his sons and to the elders of Israel. And he said to Aaron, "Take
you a calf from the herd as an offense offering and a ram as a
burnt offering, both unblemished, and bring them forward before the
Lord. And to the Israelites you shall speak, saying, 'Take a he-goat as
an offense offering and a yearling unblemished calf and lamb as a burnt
offering, and a bull and a ram as communion offerings to sacrifice
before the Lord, and a grain offering mixed with oil, for today the Lord
will appear before you.'" And they took that which Moses had charged

---

1. *And it happened.* This formula (*wayehi*) is characteristically used to mark the
beginning of a unit of narrative. The present chapter completes the cultic narration inaugurated in chapter 7: after the rite of consecration of the altar and
of Aaron and his sons and the prescribed seven days of the installation period,
the priests are ritually fit to perform the sacrifices, which are reported here.

2. *both unblemished.* "Both" is added in the translation to indicate what is clear
in the Hebrew from the plural form of "unblemished," *temimim*, that the
adjective refers equally to the calf and the ram.

4. *for today the* Lord *will appear before you.* As Jacob Milgrom observes, the
revelation of God before all the people "renders the Tabernacle the equivalent
of Mount Sinai." Mary Douglas goes further, seeing a precise structural correspondence in the system of analogical thinking between Sinai and the Tabernacle: each is divided into three gradated zones of holiness—the Sinai
summit, where only Moses may ascend; partway up the mountain, where the
seventy elders come and are vouchsafed an epiphany; and the bottom of the
mountain where the people remain; corresponding to these vertically deployed
zones are the horizontal zones of the Tabernacle, from the Holy of Holies to
inner court to outer court. What is striking is that in Exodus God's manifesta-

in front of the Tent of Meeting, and all the community came forward
and stood before the LORD. And Moses said, "This is the thing that the 6
LORD charged, you shall do, that the glory of the LORD may appear to
you." And Moses said to Aaron, "Come forward to the altar and do your 7
offense offering and your burnt offering and atone for yourself and for
the people, and do the offering of the people and atone for them, as the
LORD has charged." And Aaron came forward to the altar and slaugh- 8
tered the offense-offering calf which was his. And the sons of Aaron 9
brought forward the blood to him, and he dipped his finger in the blood
and put it on the horns of the altar, and the blood he poured out at the
base of the altar. And the fat and the kidneys and the lobe from the liver 10
from the offense offering he turned to smoke on the altar as the LORD
had charged Moses. And the flesh and the hide he burned in fire 11
outside the camp. And he slaughtered the burnt offering, and the sons 12
of Aaron provided him with the blood, and he cast it on the altar all
around. And they provided him with the burnt offering in its cut pieces 13
and the head, and he turned it to smoke on the altar. And he washed 14
the innards and the legs and he turned them to smoke together with
the burnt offering on the altar. And he brought forward the offering of 15
the people and took the offense-offering he-goat which was the people's and slaughtered it and performed the offense offering with it as

---

tion of His fiery presence to the people comes from a divine initiative associated with the revelation of the Decalogue, whereas in this Priestly document
it is ritual—the scrupulous performance of the sacrifices by Aaron and his
sons—that brings about the grand epiphany.

6. *the LORD charged, you shall do*. Some commentators assume that *'asher,*
"that," between "charged" and "you shall do" has been inadvertently omitted.

9. *brought forward the blood to him*. This was obviously done by draining the
blood of the slaughtered animal into some sort of bowl.

12. *provided him*. The verb in the *hip'il* conjugation, *himtsi'*, is unique to this
chapter. The sense is: to make something available (literally, "to cause it to be
found").

16 with the previous one. And he brought forward the burnt offering and
17 did it according to the regulation. And he brought forward the grain
offering and filled his palm with it and turned it to smoke on the altar,
18 in addition to the morning's burnt offering. And he slaughtered the bull
and the ram of the communion sacrifice which was the people's, and
the sons of Aaron provided him with the blood, and he cast it on the
19 altar all around, and the fat from the bull and from the ram, the broad
20 tail and the covering fat and the kidneys and the lobe on the liver. And
they placed the fat on the breasts, and he turned the fat to smoke on
21 the altar. The breasts and the right thigh Aaron elevated in an elevation
22 offering before the LORD, as He had charged Moses. And Aaron raised
his hands toward the people and blessed them and came down from
having done the offense offering and the burnt offering and the com-
23 munion sacrifice. And Moses, and Aaron with him, came into the Tent
of Meeting, and they came out and blessed the people, and the glory of
24 the LORD appeared to all the people. And a fire came out from before
the LORD and consumed on the altar the burnt offering and the fat, and
all the people saw and shouted with joy and fell on their faces.

---

19. *the covering fat.* The received text has only the participle ("the covering").
This is probably a simple ellipsis, though the word for "fat" may have been
accidentally dropped in scribal transmission.

20. *the fat.* Here and at a couple of other points in the chapter, "the fat" is in
the plural (*haḥalavim*), indicating the fat stripped from the sundry inner
organs. Milgrom consequently represents this in English as "pieces of fat."

22. *Aaron raised his hands toward the people and blessed them.* A common view,
from Late Antiquity (*Sifra*) onward, is that he pronounces the tripartite priestly
blessing recorded in Numbers 6:24–26.

24. *a fire came out from before the LORD.* The cloud of the divine glory is lumi-
nescent, enveloping the fire into which it turns at night. Here, the emergence
of the fire is a dramatic sign of God's self-revelation and of divine favor in
accepting the sacrifice. In the next episode, when cultic procedure is violated,
this same fire from the LORD will be lethal.

CHAPTER 10

And the sons of Aaron, Nadab and Abihu, took each of them his 1
fire-pan and put fire in it and placed incense upon it and brought
forward alien fire before the Lord, which He had not charged
them. And fire came out from before the Lord and consumed them, 2

---

1. *And the sons of Aaron.* Now that the elaborate system of sacrificial regulations, capped by the rites of installation, is completed, we are reminded what
a dangerous business the cult is by the catastrophe that befalls the two sons
of Aaron when they violate cultic procedure. This is one of the two narrative
episodes in Leviticus.

put fire in it. Practically, as many modern commentators have observed, they
would have filled the fire-pans with glowing coals, not an actual fire. The literal
sense of "fire" (*'esh*) is worth preserving because it makes evident the measure-
for-measure enactment of divine justice: Nadab and Abihu introduce alien fire
to the sacred precinct, and a fire from the Lord comes out to destroy them.

incense upon it. The feminine form of "upon it" in the Hebrew tells us that
the incense is put on top of the coals since fire is feminine.

alien fire. The adjective *zarah*, "alien," "strange" (as in "stranger"), or "unfit,"
indicates in cultic contexts a substance or person not consecrated for entrance
or use in the sacred precinct (hence Jacob Milgrom's translation, "unauthorized"). The consensus of modern interpreters, with precedents in the classical Midrash, is that the fire is "alien" because it has been taken from a profane
source—e.g., coals taken from an ordinary oven. Incense has been put on top
of the coals, which leads Milgrom to conjecture that this story is a polemic
against a practice of burning incense to the astral deities (for which actually
there is scant archeological evidence) in the Assyrian period, probably through
Assyrian influence.

2. *And fire came out from before the Lord.* This is the same phrase used in 9:24
to report the act of divine acceptance by which a supernatural flame consumes

3 and they died before the LORD. And Moses said to Aaron, "This is just
what the LORD spoke, saying,

> 'Through those close to Me shall I be hallowed
>   and in all the people's presence shall I be honored.'"

4 And Aaron was silent. And Moses called to Mishael and to Elzaphan,
sons of Uzziel, Aaron's uncle, and he said to them, "Come forward.
Bear off your brothers from the front of the sacred precinct to outside
5 the camp." And they came forward and they bore them off in their
6 tunics outside the camp as Moses had spoken. And Moses said to
Aaron and to Eleazar and to Ithamar his sons, "Your heads you shall not
dishevel nor your garments rend, lest you die and the fury come upon

---

the offerings on the altar. The zone of the holy, where the divine presence
takes up its headquarters, is intrinsically dangerous and, from a certain point
of view, radically ambiguous. When proper procedures are followed—a virtual
obsession of these Priestly writers—miraculous signs of God's favor are manifested. When procedures are violated, God becomes a consuming fire.

3. *Through those close to Me.* The reference is to the cultic inner circle of the
designated priests, with an obvious pun on the verb from the same root
involved in *"brought forward* alien fire." The meaning of this cryptic one-line
poem is not entirely transparent, but the reference to being honored in all the
people's presence lends some support to the view of several medieval Hebrew
commentators that the spectacular punishment of Nadab and Abihu (who as
sons of Aaron would be "close to" God), evident to all the people, is what is
intended. God is "hallowed" by manifesting His power against transgressors.

4. *your brothers.* The term is used in its frequent extended sense of "kinsmen,"
since Mishael and Elzaphan are actually the cousins of Nadab and Abihu.

5. *in their tunics.* Rashi proposes that the divine fire miraculously killed Nadab
and Abihu without damaging their clothes. This interpretation may not be fanciful, for in an ordinary death by fire, the garments would surely have been
burned.

6. *Your heads you shall not dishevel nor your garments rend.* That is, you are not
to perform any of the conventional gestures of mourning, for your sons have

the whole community. And your brothers, the whole house of Israel, may keen for the burning that the LORD inflicted. And you shall not go 7 out from the entrance of the Tent of Meeting, lest you die, for the oil of the LORD's anointing is upon you." And they did according to the word of Moses. And the LORD spoke to Aaron, saying, "Wine and strong 8,9 drink you shall not drink, you and your sons with you, when you come into the Tent of Meeting, lest you die—a perpetual statute for your generations, to divide between the holy and the profane, and 10 between the unclean and the clean, and to teach the Israelites all the 11 statutes that the LORD spoke to them by the hand of Moses." And 12 Moses spoke to Aaron and to Eleazar and to Ithamar, his remaining sons, "Take the grain offering left from the fire offerings of the LORD and eat it as flatcakes by the altar, for it is holy of holies. And you shall 13 eat it in a holy place, for it is your portion and your sons' portion from the fire offerings of the LORD, for thus I have been charged. And the 14 breast of the elevation offering and the thigh of the levy you shall eat in a clean place, you and your sons and your daughters with you, for it has been given as your portion and your sons' portion from the communion sacrifices of the Israelites. The thigh of the levy and the breast of the 15 elevation offering together with the fire offerings of fat they shall bring to lift up as an elevation offering before the LORD. And it shall be for you and for your sons with you a perpetual portion, as the LORD has charged. And the offense-offering goat Moses had insistently sought 16 but, look, it had been burned, and he was furious with Eleazar and with

---

perished in violating the very trust of the sanctuary that has been given to you and your descendants. Instead, you may allow the people as a whole to take up the burden of mourning ("your brothers, the whole house of Israel, may keen").

the burning that the LORD inflicted. The Hebrew uses a cognate accusative: "the burning that the LORD has burned."

9. *strong drink.* It is not clear whether this term refers to a specific alcoholic beverage. It is transparently derived from the root *sh-k-r,* "to intoxicate."

17 Ithamar the remaining sons of Aaron, saying, "Why did you not eat the offense offering in a holy place? For it is holy of holies, and this did He give you to bear off the guilt of the community, to atone for them before
18 the LORD. Look, its blood was not brought within the sacred precinct.
19 You shall surely eat it in the sacred precinct as I have charged." And Aaron spoke to Moses, "Look, today they brought forward their offense offering and their burnt offering before the LORD, and things of this sort befell me. Had I eaten an offense offering today, would it have
20 seemed good in the eyes of the LORD?" And Moses heard, and it seemed good in his eyes.

---

17. *to bear off the guilt of the community.* The verb here plays against the "bearing off" of the bodies of Nadab and Abihu.

19. *and things of this sort befell me.* The obvious reference of this vague phrase is to the sudden deaths of Nadab and Abihu. Aaron cannot bring himself to report that painful event in explicit terms, and so he uses this circumlocution.

Had I eaten an offense offering today, would it have seemed good in the eyes of the LORD? One common understanding of these words is that he is, after all, mourning for his sons, so how could the LORD expect him to eat his fixed portion of the offering, or to eat at all (fasting being a practice of mourning)? Jacob Milgrom rejects this possibility because he notes that Aaron has been enjoined not to mourn. He proposes instead that the deaths of the two sons have contaminated the altar, transforming the offense offering into its archaic manifestation in which its "detergent" function was too potent to allow for human consumption. That explanation seems unduly complicated, and it is entirely possible that Aaron has been forbidden to engage in any public gesture of mourning (disheveling one's hair, tearing one's garments) but is still permitted this mourner's act of abstention. Such a reading makes the exchange here between Aaron and Moses more personally poignant: the grieving father asks his own brother whether God could really expect him to constrain himself to ingest meat in this moment of his grief, and Moses concedes that Aaron is right.

CHAPTER 11

And the Lord spoke to Moses and to Aaron, saying to them, "Speak 1,2
to the Israelites, saying, 'These are the beasts that you may eat of
all the animals that are on the land: Everything that has hooves 3
and that has split hooves, bringing up the cud, among beasts, this you
may eat. But this you shall not eat from those that bring up the cud or 4
have hooves, the camel for it brings up the cud but it has no hooves. It
is unclean for you. And the hare, for it brings up the cud but it has no 5
hooves. It is unclean for you. And the rock-badger, for it brings up the 6

---

2. *of all the animals that are on the land.* Though the last word in this chain,
'erets, often means "earth," the list that immediately follows makes clear that
the category in question is land animals.

3. *Everything that has hooves and that has split hooves.* The inventory of permitted and prohibited creatures and much of the language in which it is cast
are quite similar to what one finds in the dietary laws in Deuteronomy 14.
Jacob Milgrom makes a plausible argument that the author of the laws in
Deuteronomy was familiar with our text and offered what amounts to an
abridgement of it. Absent from the parallel passage in Deuteronomy is the
lengthy section here, beginning with verse 31, that is concerned not with
dietary taboos but with impurity ("uncleanness") imparted by contact with the
bodies of the forbidden animals. Purity and impurity, of course, are a preoccupation of the Priestly writers.

5–6. *the hare . . . the rock-badger.* Already at this point in the list, there is some
uncertainty about the identity of the animals named in the Hebrew, and this
uncertainty grows as the text moves on to birds, amphibians, reptiles, and
insects. See the comment on Deuteronomy 14:7. The use in translation of relatively rare zoological designations such as "gecko" and "skink" jibes with the
puzzlement that many of the Hebrew terms elicit.

7 cud but it has no hooves. It is unclean for you. And the pig, for it has
hooves and has split hooves, but it does not chew the cud. It is unclean
8 for you. Of their flesh you shall not eat and their carcass you shall not
9 touch. They are unclean for you. This you may eat of all that is in the
water: All that is in the water, in the seas and in the brooks that have
10 fins and scales, them you may eat. And all in the seas and in the brooks
that have no fins or scales, of all the swarming creatures of the water and
of all the living things that are in the water, they are an abomination for
11 you. And they shall be an abomination for you. Of their flesh you shall

---

7. *the pig.* It is only later, in the Hellenistic period, that the pig becomes the
prohibited animal par excellence, although the anonymous prophet of the
Babylonian exile whose words are recorded in Isaiah 66:17 brackets eaters of pig
and rat as participants in some unspeakable pagan rite. Pork was a common
food among the Philistines and was also sometimes eaten by Canaanites, as
archeological inspection of the bones of animals consumed has determined.
Interestingly, in the high country in the eastern part of Canaan, where Israelite
population was concentrated toward the end of the second millennium B.C.E.,
the percentage of pig bones discovered is only a fraction of what it is in the
Canaanite lowlands. This suggests that the taboo was already generally
embraced by the Israelites at an early period (well before the composition of
the Torah) and also that some Israelites chose to disregard it.

10. *that have no fins or scales, of all the swarming creatures of the water.* Mary
Douglas has proposed that what underlies the dietary prohibitions is a general
commitment of the Israelite mind-set to clear and distinct categories: forms of
animal life that appear to be ambiguous instances of their particular zoological class may not be eaten. That proposal seems a little strained for the land
animals because it is not self-evident that a nonruminant with hooves, such as
the pig, is somehow a violation of the category "land animal." Her argument is
more plausible for sea creatures, and, perhaps also, for amphibians and reptiles. Fish, possessing fins and scales, are the exemplary category instance of
denizens of the water. Yet the sea "swarms" or pullulates (Hebrew *shorets*) with
polymorphous creatures in shells and plasmic blobs and tentacles that seem
altogether unlike fish, and from this pullulation the Israelites are enjoined to
distance themselves. It is noteworthy that terms from the Creation story
abound here: "swarming creatures" (*sherets*), "according to its kind" (which is
to say, "of every kind"), "gathering of water," "stirs" (*romeset*, which in the different context of Genesis 1 was rendered as "crawling"). The dietary laws are
framed to make a statement about the Israelites' place in the created order of

not eat, and their carcass you shall abominate. Whatever in the water 12
has no fins and scales is an abomination for you. And these you shall 13
abominate of the birds, they shall not be eaten, they are an abomination: the eagle and the vulture and the black vulture, and the kite and 14
the buzzard according to its kind, and every raven according to its 15
kind, and the ostrich and the night hawk and the seagull and the hawk 16
according to its kind, and the horned owl and the cormorant and the 17
puff owl, and the hoot owl and the pelican and the fish hawk, and the 18,19
stork and the heron according to its kind and the hoopoe and the bat.
Every winged swarming thing that goes on all fours is an abomination 20
for you. But this you may eat of all winged swarming things that go on 21
all fours: that which has jointed legs above its feet on which to hop on
the ground. Of them, these you may eat: the locust according to its kind 22
and the bald locust according to its kind and the cricket according to
its kind and the grasshopper according to its kind. And every winged 23
swarming thing that has four feet is an abomination for you. And 24
through these you would become unclean. Whoever touches their car-

---

things that is a kind of qualifying addendum to the Priestly panorama of creation in Genesis 1. God's fecund world calls all sorts of living creatures into
existence, and man is one of these. But the Israelites are expected to set themselves apart from the natural world to which they belong just as they are
required to set themselves apart from the nations with which, of necessity, they
participate in political, economic, and cultural intercourse. Thus they are forbidden the flesh of whole classes of living creatures, especially when animal life
seems to manifest its most intense, category-dissolving pullulation. One may
wonder whether behind all this, at least for sea creatures, reptiles, insects, and
amphibians, there is some sort of horror of the inchoate, the seemingly form-
less, a horror akin to the revulsion in the face of the primordial serpent.

21. *that which has.* The Masoretic Text reads "that which does not have," *'asher
lo'*, almost certainly a scribal error for *'asher lo,* "that which has."

24. *Whoever touches their carcass shall be unclean.* It is the dead unclean animal that conveys this impurity by touch, not the living one. (Abraham ibn Ezra
expresses indignation against the Sadducees for imagining that living animals
are included.) Dead bodies of any sort impart ritual impurity, but in the present case, because a dead animal is potential food, the "uncleanness" inhering
in the prohibited creature assumes an especially dangerous potency. It is imag-

25   cass shall be unclean till evening. And whoever bears off anything from
26   their carcass shall wash his clothes and be unclean till evening. Of all
the beasts that have hooves but the hooves are not split and they do not
bring up the cud, they are unclean for you. Whoever touches them
27   becomes unclean. And whatever goes on its paws among all animals
that go on all four is unclean for you. Whoever touches their carcass
28   shall be unclean till evening. And he who bears off their carcass shall
launder his clothes and be unclean till evening. They are unclean for
29   you. This is unclean for you among the swarming creatures that swarm
on the ground: the mole and the rat and the great lizard according to its
30   kind, and the gecko and the spotted lizard and the lizard and the skink
31   and the chameleon. These are the unclean for you among all swarming
things. Whoever touches them when they are dead shall be unclean till
32   evening. And whatever upon which something from them falls
when they are dead shall be unclean. Of any vessel of wood or cloth or
skin or sackcloth, any vessel in which a task may be done, shall be

---

ined as a source of contamination transmitted by physical contiguity, rather
like a physical contagion.

25. *whoever bears off anything from their carcass.* As several medieval commentators note, the act of carrying off part of the carcass necessarily involves closer
and more sustained contact with the source of impurity and so it requires
laundering of the garments as well as bathing.

27. *whatever goes on its paws.* This category of prohibition is of course already
implied in the earlier stipulation regarding split hooves, but the Priestly writers seek to make the classes of proscribed animals as clear and explicit as
possible.

32. *whatever upon which something from them falls.* Here and in the subsequent verses the notion of contamination through contact is extended. Impurity is imparted not only to a person when he or she reaches out to touch or
pick up the carcass of a forbidden creature but also when any part of the carcass—say, a piece of decaying bird whose body is lodged in a tree—comes in
contact with any substance. Porous substances that can be suffused with
water in immersion—wood, cloth, skin, sackcloth—can be purified of the contamination through immersion. Earthen vessels, which are porous but cannot
be saturated, must be destroyed.

brought into water and be unclean till evening, and then be clean. And 33
any earthen vessel into which something from them falls, whatever is
in it shall be unclean, and you shall break it. Of any food that may be 34
eaten, when water comes on it, shall be unclean, and any liquid that
may be drunk in any vessel, shall be unclean. And whatever upon 35
which something from their carcass falls shall be unclean. Oven and
range shall be smashed. They are unclean, and they shall be unclean
for you. But a spring or a cistern, a gathering of water, shall be clean. 36
And he who touches their carcass shall be unclean. And should some- 37
thing from their carcass fall on any planted seed that may be planted,
it is clean. And should water be put on seed and something from their 38
carcass fall on it, it is unclean for you. And should one of the beasts die 39
which are your food, he who touches their carcass shall be unclean
till evening. And he who eats of its carcass shall launder his garments 40
and be unclean till evening. And he who bears off its carcass shall
launder his garments and be unclean till evening. And every swarming 41
thing that creeps on the earth is an abomination. It shall not be eaten.

---

36. *And he who touches their carcass shall be unclean.* This clause looks suspiciously out of place—perhaps an inadvertent scribal repetition from above.

38. *should water be put on seed.* This stipulation is an especially vivid illustration of how impurity is imagined as a contagion in quasimedical terms. Dry
planted seed in the ground is deemed part of the natural growing world and
resistant to contamination. Wet, softened seed becomes permeable to the contaminating substance.

39. *one of the beasts die which are your food.* Even the carcass of a permitted
animal (which has died rather than been deliberately slaughtered) conveys
impurity. Jacob Milgrom, noting the horror of the dead body and invoking the
ban on consuming blood and on eating a kid boiled in its mother's milk (neither of these mentioned here), argues that the dietary prohibitions are an affirmation of life over death. That claim seems apologetic, for it is not clear why,
say, the prohibition on eating nonruminants is an affirmation of life.

42 Whatever goes on its belly and whatever goes on all fours including the many-legged ones of all swarming things that swarm on the earth, you
43 shall not eat them, for they are an abomination. Do not make yourselves abominable through any swarming thing that swarms and do not
44 become unclean through them and be unclean. For I am the LORD your God, and you shall hallow yourselves and become holy, for I am holy. And you shall not make yourselves unclean through any swarming thing
45 that swarms on the earth. For I am the LORD Who has brought you up from the land of Egypt to be for you a God, and you shall be holy, for I
46 am holy. This is the teaching about beast and bird and every living creature that stirs in the water and every swarming thing that swarms on the
47 earth, to divide between the unclean and the clean and between the animal that is eaten and the animal that shall not be eaten.'"

---

42. *Whatever goes on its belly.* This phrase, of course, is another allusion to the Creation story, or rather, to the end of that story in the Garden of Eden, when an enmity between humankind and a representative of the animal kingdom (the serpent) is first introduced.

45. *you shall be holy, for I am holy.* This is a grand concluding generalization, but its precise application to the dietary prohibitions is not entirely clear. *Imitatio dei* is ringingly proclaimed. Perhaps because God is involved with creation yet loftily removed from it, Israelite man in his image in this cosmic hierarchy (compare Psalm 8) is enjoined to set himself at a certain distance from the natural world of which he is necessarily a part by restricting categories of animal food, by not ingesting all living creatures in the teeming polymorphous fullness of their pullulation. The reiterated verb "to divide" is a key to the Priestly account of creation in Genesis 1: the world comes into coherent being when God divides the chaotically interfused primal elements—light and darkness, the waters above and the waters below, the sea and dry land—from each other. Here the Israelites are commanded to emulate God by setting up a framework for daily life in which they are to "divide" (verse 47) between the unclean and the clean, between what is forbidden and permitted to be eaten.

CHAPTER 12

nd the LORD spoke to Moses, saying, "Speak to the Israelites, say- 1,2
ing, 'Should a woman quicken with seed and bear a male, she
shall be unclean seven days, as in the days of her menstrual
unwellness she shall be unclean. And on the eighth day the flesh of his 3
foreskin shall be circumcised. And thirty days and three she shall stay 4
in her blood purity. She shall touch no consecrated thing nor shall she
come into the sanctuary till the days of her purity are completed. And 5
if she bears a female, she shall be unclean two weeks, as in her menstruation, and sixty days and six she shall stay over her blood purity.

---

2. *she shall be unclean*. The notion that the blood of childbirth rendered the
parturient ritually impure was widespread in the ancient world, reflected in
texts by the Hittites to the north of Israel and by the Greeks to the west. Jacob
Milgrom notes that the ancients believed there was seed in the blood dis-
charged by the childbearing woman, and so he proposes that this loss of blood
was associated with death and hence conveyed impurity.

as in the days of her menstrual unwellness. The "in" is implied, for what is at
issue is not the number of days but the nature of the condition of impurity.

4. *thirty days and three she shall stay in her blood purity*. The Hebrew, empha-
sizing the counting, says literally "in thirty days and three days." When one
adds the initial seven days, the total period during which the woman is to avoid
contact with consecrated things (and also, evidently, refrain from marital relations) is the formulaic figure of forty days. The blood of the first seven days is
considered impure. Afterward, her blood is deemed pure ("her blood purity")
but she must remain in this state for thirty-three days before she is free of the
impurity contracted at childbirth.

5. *if she bears a female . . . sixty days and six she shall stay*. When one adds this
number to the initial fourteen days, the total period of sequestration comes to

6 And when the days of her purity are completed, whether for a son or for a daughter, she shall bring a yearling lamb for a burnt offering and a young pigeon or a turtledove for an offense offering to the entrance

7 of the Tent of Meeting, to the priest. And he shall bring it forward before the LORD and atone for her, and she shall be clean from the flow of her blood. This is the teaching about the childbearing woman,

8 whether of a male or of a female. And if her hand cannot manage enough for a sheep, she shall take two turtledoves or two young pigeons, one for a burnt offering and one for an offense offering, and the priest shall atone for her, and she shall be clean.'"

---

eighty, or twice forty. No entirely satisfactory explanation has been offered for why a female child requires twice the length of time for the mother to be free of impurity, though one suspects a general predisposition of the culture to see the female as a potential source of impurity. Seminal emission also imparts ritual impurity, but the period for ridding oneself of the impurity imparted by menstrual discharge is much longer.

6. *an offense offering*. The present case is a strategic instance of why it is misleading to render the Hebrew *hata't*, as almost all English versions do, as "sin offering." Surely the childbearing woman has done nothing that can be called a sin. The state of ritual impurity, however, imposed on her by biological circumstances makes her a potential source of violation of the sancta, which would be an offense to the cult and to its divine object, and so she is enjoined to present an offense offering that will mark the completion of her period of purification.

7. *the flow of her blood*. The literal sense of the Hebrew is "the source of her blood," the idiom exhibiting a common linguistic pattern in which there is an interchange between cause ("source") and effect ("flow").

8. *if her hand cannot manage*. More literally, "her hand cannot find" (elsewhere, "her hand cannot attain"), with "hand" having its frequent biblical sense of capacity or power.

CHAPTER 13

And the LORD spoke to Moses and to Aaron, saying, "Should a per-   1,2
son have on the skin of his body an inflammation or a rash or a
shiny spot and it become the affliction of skin blanch on the skin
of his body, he shall be brought to Aaron the priest or to one of his sons
the priests. And the priest shall see the affliction on the skin of the   3
body, and if the hair in the affliction has turned white and the affliction

---

2. *on the skin of his body.* The literal sense of the Hebrew is "on the skin of his
flesh." Though that sounds close to a redundancy in English, the point, as
Rashbam proposed, is probably to distinguish bare skin from the areas where
the skin is covered by hair.

   inflammation . . . rash . . . shiny spot. Throughout this long section on dermatological disorders, the precise identification of disease and even symptom
remains uncertain, and the approximations afforded by translation are chiefly
guided by etymology. ("Inflammation," for example, represents the Hebrew
se'et, which appears to exhibit the verbal root that means "to raise"; "shiny
spot" is proposed for *baharot* because the verbal stem on which that noun is
formed means "to shine" or "to be bright.") The fact of the matter is that the
ancients perceived and described diseases and their symptoms differently than
does modern Western medicine, and some conditions that they understood to
be a single malady may actually have been a variety of diseases, not all of them
intrinsically related. Scholarly attempts to equate the various conditions
reported here with specific dermatological disorders have had only limited
success. A certain lack of specificity in the translation of the quasi-medical
language of this section seems prudent and, indeed, appropriate.

3. *the priest shall see the affliction.* In most of its recurrences here, the verb
"see" has the obvious force of "examine," but this is still another instance in
which an ordinary all-purpose term is enlisted for a technical use—a stylistic
practice this translation emulates.

seems deeper than the skin of his body, it is skin blanch. When the
4 priest sees it, he shall declare him unclean. And if it is a white shiny
spot on the skin of his body and it does not seem deeper than the skin,
and its hair has not turned white, the priest shall confine the person
5 with the affliction seven days. And the priest shall see him on the seventh day, and, look, if the affliction has held its color, if the affliction
has not spread in the skin, the priest shall confine him another seven
6 days. And the priest shall see him again on the seventh day, and, look,
if the affliction has faded, if the affliction has not spread on the skin,
the priest shall declare him clean. It is a rash. And he shall launder his
7 clothes and be clean. But if the rash in fact has spread in the skin after
he has been seen by the priest and has been declared clean, he shall be
8 seen again by the priest. And if the priest sees and, look, the rash has
spread in the skin, the priest shall declare him unclean. It is skin
9 blanch. Should a person have the affliction of skin blanch, he shall be
10 brought to the priest. And if the priest sees, and, look, there is a white
inflammation in the skin in which the hair has turned white and there

---

skin blanch. Although older English translations represent the Hebrew
tsaraʿat (etymology uncertain) as "leprosy," modern scholars are virtually unanimous in rejecting this identification. The symptoms do not correspond, and
there is scant evidence that leprosy was present in the Near East before the
Hellenistic period. No positive identification with a disease known to modern
medicine has been made. In most biblical occurrences, tsaraʿat is associated
with a ghastly white loss of pigmentation, and hence this translation adopts
the coined term "skin blanch" (see the comment on Exodus 4:6). Loss of pigmentation in hair and skin is prominent here as a determining symptom.

When the priest sees it, he shall declare him unclean. The examining priest
determines the diagnosis, and perhaps one should think of him as performing
at least one function of a physician. But these regulations for skin conditions
reflect an ambiguous conception of disease that wavers between pathology
and ritual impurity (the general sense of tamʾe, "unclean"). Thus the quaranti-
ning of the afflicted person might involve a fear of contagion in the medical
sense or might be chiefly an avoidance of ritual contamination, and one suspects that the two were blurred in the Israelite imagination. Jacob Milgrom
proposes that the wasting of the flesh involved in tsaraʿat is associated with
death, and that these laws are an expression of the impulse in Leviticus to separate all deathlike phenomena from the living.

is exposed flesh in the inflammation, it is chronic skin blanch in the 11
skin of his body, and the priest shall declare him unclean. He shall not
confine him, for he is unclean. And if the skin blanch in fact erupts in 12
the skin, and the skin blanch covers all the skin of the person with the
affliction from head to toe, wherever the priest's eyes can see, the priest 13
shall see and, look, if the skin blanch has covered his whole body,
he shall declare the affliction clean. It has turned white; it is clean. On 14
the day exposed flesh is seen in it, he shall be unclean. When the 15
priest sees the exposed flesh, he shall declare him unclean. The
exposed flesh is unclean; it is skin blanch. Or, should the exposed flesh 16
recede and turn white, he shall come to the priest, and the priest shall 17
see him, and, look, if the affliction has turned white, the priest shall
declare the person with the affliction clean. He is clean. And a body in 18
which there be burning rash on the skin that is healed, and there be in 19
the place of the burning rash a white inflammation or a reddish white
shiny spot, and it be seen by the priest, and the priest see, and, look, 20

---

11. *chronic skin blanch.* The literal sense of the Hebrew is "old skin blanch,"
with the implication of its persistence—hence "chronic."

12. *the person with the affliction.* The Hebrew, as repeatedly elsewhere in this
passage, simply says "the affliction," but this is an obvious ellipsis or, as some
prefer to call it, a metonymy.
    from head to toe. The literal Hebrew idiom is "from his head to his feet."

13. *It has turned white; it is clean.* The referent of the second clause might be
either the affliction (*nega'*) or the person, in which case it should be translated
"he is clean." This criterion for being cured is a little confusing because white
has been associated with the disease—compare the preceding clause, "the
skin blanch has covered his whole body." Here, however, as Baruch Levine
explains, the whiteness is an indication of fresh skin that has grown instead of
"exposed flesh" (as in the next verse).

17. *the priest shall declare the person with the affliction clean. He is clean.* This
seeming redundancy probably reflects the attention to procedure of the law:
first we have the instructions about what the attending priest must do, then a
replication of the official, diagnostic declaration the priest is to make: "He is
clean."

if it appears lower than the skin and its hair has turned white, the priest
shall declare him unclean. It is the affliction of skin blanch. It has
21 erupted in the burning rash. And if the priest sees it and, look, there is
no white hair in it and it is not lower than the skin and it is faded, the
22 priest shall confine him seven days. And if in fact it has spread in the
23 skin, the priest shall confine him. It is an affliction. And if the shiny
spot remains in its place, does not spread, it is the scar of the burning
24 rash, and the priest shall declare him clean. Or, should there be a burn
from fire in the skin of a body, and the exposed flesh of the burn be a
25 reddish white or white shiny spot, the priest shall see it and, look, if
the hair has turned white in the shiny spot and seems deeper than the
skin, it is skin blanch, it has erupted in the burn, and the priest shall
26 declare him unclean. It is the affliction of skin blanch. And if the priest
sees him and, look, there is no white hair in the shiny spot and it is not
lower than the skin and it is faded, the priest shall confine him seven
27 days. And when the priest sees him on the seventh day, if in fact it has
spread in the skin, the priest shall declare him unclean. It is the afflic-
28 tion of skin blanch. And if the shiny spot remains in its place, does not
spread in the skin, and it is faded, it is the inflammation of the burn,
29 and the priest shall declare him clean, for it is the scar of the burn. And
30 should a man or a woman have an affliction in head or beard, and the
priest see the affliction and, look, it seems deeper than the skin and
there is thin yellow hair in it, the priest shall declare him unclean. It is

---

24. *burn from fire*. The introduction of actual burns here reflects how little
these regulations correspond to modern conceptions of disease. The previous
verse had dealt with "burning rash" (others: "boils"), *sheḥin*, a skin disease
which by etymology suggests heat or burning. This leads the Levitical legislator associatively to consider burns, which in his view have the potential to turn
into *tsaraʿat* (perhaps how he perceives an infected burn).

29. *a man or a woman . . . head or beard*. "Head" of course refers to either and
"beard" to the man alone.

30. *thin yellow hair*. This seems to indicate a loss of hair pigmentation that
gives the hair a flat discolored look without turning it altogether white. Black
hair was normative among ancient Israelites; Esau and David were said to have
red hair, but there is no indication of blonds in the population.

scurf. It is blanch disease of the head or of the beard. And should the 31
priest see the affliction and, look, it does not seem deeper than the skin
but it has no black hair, the priest shall confine the person with the
affliction of scurf another seven days. And the priest shall see the 32
affliction on the seventh day and, look, if the scurf has not spread and
there is no yellow hair in it and the scurf seems deeper than the skin,
the person with the scurf shall shave himself but the scurf he shall not 33
shave, and the priest shall confine the person with the scurf another
seven days. And the priest shall see the scurf on the seventh day and, 34
look, if the scurf has not spread in the skin and there is no yellow hair
in it and it does not seem deeper than the skin, the priest shall declare
him clean, and he shall launder his clothes and be clean. And if the 35
scurf has in fact spread in the skin after his being declared clean, and 36
the priest sees it and, look, the scurf has spread in the skin, the priest
shall not examine for the yellow hair—he is unclean. And if the scurf 37
has held its color and black hair has grown in it, the scurf is healed, he
is clean, and the priest shall declare him clean. And should a man or a 38
woman have on the skin of their body multiple white shiny spots, and 39
the priest sees and, look, on the skin of their body there are multiple
dull white spots, it is tetter. It has erupted in the skin. He is clean. And 40
should a man's hair fall out, he is bald on the pate. He is clean. And if 41
the front part of his hair falls out, he is bald on the forehead. He is
clean. And should there be on the bald pate or on the bald forehead a 42

---

33. *shave himself*. As Levine notes, the purpose of shaving all around the
affected area would be to allow the priest to examine it more readily.

39. *tetter*. This all-purpose term for skin diseases (herpes, impetigo, eczema),
adopted by many English translators, seems appropriate for the indeterminate
Hebrew *bohaq*, indicating a dermatological condition that for some reason was
not thought to impart uncleanness.

41. *he is bald*. As with the earlier association of burning rash and burns with
infectious diseases, the law here goes against the grain of modern understanding by placing a hereditary condition such as baldness in the category of
potentially contaminating skin diseases. Carefully taxonomic according to its
own lights, the law distinguishes between baldness fore and aft.

white affliction, it is erupting skin blanch on his bald pate or on his
43 bald forehead. And the priest shall see him and, look, the inflammation of the affliction is reddish white on his bald pate or on his bald
44 forehead, like skin blanch of the body in appearance, he is afflicted
with skin blanch. He is unclean. The priest shall surely declare him
45 unclean. His affliction is on his head. And the person afflicted with
skin blanch, in whom the affliction is, his clothes shall be torn and his
hair disheveled, and his moustache he shall cover, and he shall call out,
46 'Unclean! Unclean!' All the days that the affliction is on him he shall
remain unclean. He is unclean. He shall dwell apart. Outside the camp
shall his dwelling place be.

47 "And should a garment have in it a scaly affliction, whether in a wool
48 garment or a linen garment, whether in the warp or in the woof of the
49 linen or the wool, or in a skin or anything made of skin, and the afflic-

---

45. *his moustache he shall cover*. This rather odd expression seems to indicate
that the afflicted person is to pull some sort of scarf or head covering around
his mouth—according to Abraham ibn Ezra, so that he will bring no harm to
others from his contaminating breath. The law may stipulate moustache rather
than mouth to mark the line up to which the covering is to be pulled. The tearing of the garment and the disheveled hair are ordinarily signs of mourning,
but here their evident function is to set aside the afflicted person from the
healthy, like the bell that was rung by lepers in medieval times, and like the
cry of "Unclean! Unclean!" at the end of this verse.

46. *he shall remain unclean. He is unclean.* See the comment on verse 17.

47. *a scaly affliction*. The Hebrew is *nega' tsara'at*. Here the disparity between
ancient understanding and modern categories is most striking. This is the same
term for the condition that, when it appears on a human body, has been rendered here as "skin blanch." That translation obviously does not work for fabrics
and leather, and the law seems to have in mind some sort of mold or mildew,
which, however, is thought to exhibit the same pathology as the dermatological
condition, perhaps because of a sickly whiteness manifested in both.

48. *whether in the warp or in the woof*. Milgrom, who has actually consulted
weavers, notes that two kinds of threads of different textures and thicknesses
are often used, a fact that makes it possible for certain forms of decay to
spread through one set of threads and not the other.

tion be greenish or reddish in the garment or in the skin or in the warp
or in the woof or in any article of skin, it is the scaly affliction, and it
shall be shown to the priest. And the priest shall see the affliction and   50
sequester the article with the affliction seven days. And if he sees the   51
affliction on the seventh day, that the affliction has spread through the
garment or through the warp or through the woof or through the skin
for anything that the skin may serve for a task, the affliction is malignant scale disease. It is unclean. And the garment or the warp or the   52
woof in wool or in linen or in any article of skin in which the affliction
is shall be burned, for it is malignant scale disease. It shall be burned
in fire. And if the priest sees and, look, the affliction has not spread   53
through the garment or through the warp or through the woof or
through any article of skin, the priest shall charge, and they shall laun-   54
der that in which the affliction was and sequester it another seven days.
And the priest shall see after the article with the affliction has been   55
laundered, and, look, if the affliction has not changed color and
the affliction has not spread, it is unclean. In fire you shall burn it. It
is corrosion, whether on its inner side or its outer side. And if the priest   56
sees, and, look, the affliction has become faded after being laundered,
he shall tear it from the garment or from the skin or from the warp or
from the woof. And if it shall still appear in the garment or in the warp   57
or in the woof or in any article of skin, it is eruptive. In fire you shall
burn it—that in which the affliction is. And the garment or the warp   58
or the woof or any article of skin that you launder and from which the

---

50. *sequester.* The Hebrew verb is the same one used for "confining" an
afflicted person, but strict English usage does not permit "confining" objects.

55. *has not changed color and . . . has not spread.* The crucial criterion is the
color. Even if the blight has not spread, it is regarded as unclean because the
color has not changed.

 corrosion. The Hebrew *peḥetet* has not been identified but etymologically it
is associated with either a term that means "diminution" or one that means
"pit."

59 affliction disappears shall be laundered again and be clean. This is the teaching about the scaly affliction of a wool or linen garment or warp or woof or any article of skin, to declare it clean or unclean."

---

59. *This is the teaching about the scaly affliction of a wool or linen garment.* This verse formally marks the conclusion of the passage dealing with *tsara'at* in fabrics and leather. The chapter that follows will return to people afflicted with the disease.

CHAPTER 14

A nd the LORD spoke to Moses, saying, "This shall be the teaching 1,2 concerning the one struck with skin blanch on the day he becomes clean. He shall be brought to the priest, and the priest shall go out- 3 side the camp, and the priest shall see, and, look, if the affliction of skin blanch is healed in the afflicted one, the priest shall charge that 4 there be taken for him who is cleansing himself two live pure birds and cedar wood and crimson stuff and hyssop. And the priest shall charge 5 that one bird be slaughtered in an earthen vessel over fresh water.

---

2. *on the day*. This expression often has the sense of "when," and it occurs twice at the very end of the chapter, enclosing the entire unit in an envelope structure. The phrase might, however, specifically indicate the actual day of the purification rite, as some of the early rabbis contended. What follows is a set of procedures to be performed on that day.

3. *shall see*. As in the preceding chapter, the sense is "examine" or "inspect."

4. *that there be taken*. Here and repeatedly elsewhere in this chapter, the Hebrew third-person singular active verb without a specified subject is used as an equivalent of the passive.

   cedar wood and crimson stuff. Jacob Milgrom proposes that both are used in this rite of purification because of their red color, linked with blood, which also functions here as a purifying agent. Hyssop appears elsewhere in biblical literature as an instrument of purification, though it remains uncertain why it was thought to have that efficacy.

5. *fresh water*. The literal meaning of the Hebrew is "living water," which creates a link with the "live" bird. The sense of the idiom is flowing water, whether from a spring or a river. Since the entire ritual is designed to carry off the impurities from the place inhabited by the community, one may infer that the fresh water is to carry off the overflow of the blood.

6 The living bird—he shall take it, and the cedar wood and the crimson
stuff and the hyssop, and dip them and the living bird in the blood of
7 the slaughtered bird over fresh water. And he shall sprinkle upon him
who is cleansing himself of the skin blanch seven times, and cleanse
8 him, and he shall send out the living bird over the open field. And he
who is cleansing himself shall launder his garments and shave his hair
and wash in water and be clean. And afterward he shall come into the
9 camp and sit outside his tent seven days. And it shall be, on the seventh day, he shall shave all the hair of his head and his beard and his
eyebrows, and all his hair he shall shave, and he shall launder his gar-
10 ments and wash his flesh in water, and become clean. And on the
eighth day he shall take two unblemished sheep and one unblemished
yearling ewe and three-tenths of semolina flour, a grain offering mixed
11 with oil, and one *log* of oil. And the cleansing priest shall set the man
cleansing himself, together with them, before the LORD at the entrance

---

6. *The living bird—he shall take it.* The Hebrew syntax, reproduced in this
translation, is a little odd because the accusative "it" is redundant after "The
living bird" has already appeared as the object of the verb. The evident intention is to highlight the living bird in contrast to the slaughtered bird.

7. *he shall send out the living bird over the open field.* This rite of releasing the
bird in open country suggests an obvious analogy with the ritual of the scapegoat. The living bird, having been dipped in the blood of the slaughtered bird
that has also been sprinkled on the person to be cleansed, carries off any residual impurities to a place far from human habitation. There is something clearly
archaic about this entire ritual, and scholarship has detected antecedents in
Mesopotamian rites of magical purgation.

9. *he shall shave all the hair of his head and his beard and his eyebrows, and all
his hair.* The last seemingly redundant phrase probably indicates that he is to
shave all his body hair—the chest, the legs, and the pubic area. Such total
removal of hair was otherwise abhorrent in ancient Israel, but in this instance
it is enjoined as an expression of the encompassing thoroughness of the
cleansing process.

10. *three-tenths of semolina flour.* The ellipsis is for three-tenths of an *ephah*, a
dry measure roughly equivalent to 19 liters. A *log* is about $1\frac{1}{4}$ cups.

to the Tent of Meeting. And the priest shall take the one sheep and 12
bring it forward as a guilt offering, and the *log* of oil, and he shall elevate them as an elevation offering before the LORD. And he shall 13
slaughter the sheep in the place where the offense offering is slaughtered, and the burnt offering in the place of the sacred zone, for offense
offering and guilt offering alike are the priest's. It is holy of holies. And 14
the priest shall take from the blood of the guilt offering and the priest
shall put it on the right earlobe of him who is cleansing himself and on
the thumb of his right hand and on the big toe of his right foot. And the 15
priest shall take from the *log* of oil and pour it into the left palm of the
priest. And the priest shall dip his right finger into the oil that is in his 16
palm and sprinkle from the oil with his finger seven times before
the LORD. And from the rest of the oil that is in his palm the priest shall 17
put on the right earlobe of the one who is cleansing himself and
on the thumb of his right hand and on the big toe of his right foot,
together with the blood of the guilt offering. And what remains of the 18
oil that is in the palm of the priest he shall put on the head of the one
who is cleansing himself, and the priest shall atone for him before the

---

12. *guilt offering*. It may sound puzzling that a person who has suffered from a
skin disease is thought to have incurred guilt. It may be that the ancients imagined this particular disease as a punishment for some transgressive act, as
when Miriam is stricken with skin blanch for slandering her brother (Numbers
12:10–15).

14. *earlobe . . . thumb . . . big toe*. The ritual works by synecdoche: from the
protrusion of the head of the earlobe to the protrusions of hand and foot (all
on the "governing" right side), the person being cleansed is symbolically covered with the blood of the guilt offering from head to toe without actually
immersing in it.

17. *from the rest of the oil . . . the priest shall put on the right earlobe*. The two
purgative substances dominating the rite are blood and oil (to which one may
add the fresh water of the preceding ritual of the two birds). Blood belongs to
the animal kingdom, oil (olive oil) to the vegetable kingdom. Blood, as the life
substance, has purgative force; oil, elsewhere used for anointing the sacralia,
has both consecrating and purgative power. Here, both the blood and the oil
are part of the sacrifice.

19 LORD. And the priest shall do the offense offering and atone for the one cleansing himself from his uncleanness, and afterward he shall slaugh-
20 ter the burnt offering. And the priest shall offer up the burnt offering and the grain offering on the altar, and the priest shall atone
21 for him, and he shall be clean. And if he is poor and his hand cannot attain, he shall take one sheep as guilt offering for an elevation offering to atone for himself, and one-tenth of semolina flour mixed with oil as
22 a grain offering, and a *log* of oil, and two turtledoves or two young pigeons, as his hand may attain, and one shall be an offense offering
23 and one a burnt offering. And he shall bring them on the eighth day of his cleansing to the priest at the entrance of the Tent of Meeting before
24 the LORD. And the priest shall take the sheep of the guilt offering and the *log* of oil, and the priest shall elevate them as an elevation offering
25 before the LORD. And he shall slaughter the sheep of the guilt offering, and the priest shall take from the blood of the guilt offering and put it on the right earlobe of the one who is cleansing himself and on the
26 thumb of his right hand and on the big toe of his right foot. And from
27 the oil the priest shall pour into the left palm of the priest. And the priest shall sprinkle with his right finger from the oil that is in his left
28 palm seven times before the LORD. And the priest shall put from the oil that is in his palm on the right earlobe of the one who is cleansing himself and on the thumb of his right hand and on the big toe of his
29 right foot, on the place of the blood of the guilt offering. And what remains of the oil that is in the palm of the priest he shall put on the head of the one who is cleansing himself to atone for him before the
30 LORD. And he shall do one of the turtledoves or of the young pigeons,

---

21. *And if he is poor.* As with other kinds of sacrifice, special provision for a less costly offering is made for the person of limited means whose "hand cannot attain" (or "reach out," "manage") to bring the stipulated sacrifice.

26. *the priest shall pour into the left palm of the priest.* This odd wording led some traditional commentators to conclude that two priests are involved in the ritual, but perhaps the noun is repeated simply to make clear that the oil is not poured into the palm of the person cleansing himself.

27. *his right finger.* The rabbis plausibly inferred this was the index finger.

from which his hand attains, that which his hand attains, the one for 31
an offense offering and the other for a burnt offering, together with the
grain offering. And the priest shall atone for the one who is cleansing
himself before the LORD. This is the teaching concerning him in whom 32
there is an affliction of skin blanch whose hand cannot attain, when he
is being cleansed."

And the LORD spoke to Moses and to Aaron, saying, "When you come 33,34
into the land of Canaan which I am about to give you as a holding, and
I put the scaly affliction in the house of the land of your holding, he 35
whose house it is shall come and tell the priest, saying, 'Something like
an affliction has appeared to me in the house.' And the priest shall 36
charge that they clear the house so that nothing in the house is unclean
before the priest comes to see the affliction, and afterward the priest
shall come to see the house. And if he sees the affliction and, look, 37
the affliction is in the walls of the house, greenish or reddish hollows
that seem lower than the wall, the priest shall go out of the house to 38
the entrance of the house and sequester the house seven days. And the 39
priest shall come back on the seventh day and see and, look, if the

---

34. *I put the scaly affliction*. The Hebrew verb used here is identical with the
one just employed for God's "giving" the land. A theological notion is adumbrated in the pun: God bestows (verbal stem *n-t-n*) both great bounty and also
blight. The Midrash in Leviticus Rabba, seeking to rescue divine benevolence
for Israel, fancifully imagines that the Canaanites have hidden gold in the
walls of their houses which is discovered when the stones are pulled apart in
the ritual of purgation.

35. *Something like an affliction has appeared to me in the house*. The vagueness
of the phrasing reflects the uncertainty of the home owner's diagnosis. We
have already observed the peculiar extrapolation from scaly skin disease to
blight or mildew in fabrics. Now the owner of the house contemplates what is
evidently some sort of mold or mildew in the walls of his house and wonders
whether it exhibits a certain similarity—which the diagnosing priest could
establish as actually the very same pathology—to the skin disease called
tsara'at.

40 affliction has spread in the walls of the house, the priest shall charge
that they pull out the stones in which the affliction is and fling them
41 outside the town into an unclean place. And the house shall be scraped
from within all around, and they shall spill the earth that they
42 scraped off outside the town into an unclean place. And they shall take
different stones and bring them in place of the stones, and different
43 earth shall be taken and the house plastered. And if the affliction
comes back and erupts in the house after the pulling out of the stones
44 and after the scraping of the house and after the plastering, the priest
shall come and see and, look, if the affliction has spread, it is malignant
45 scale disease in the house. It is unclean. And he shall raze the house,
its stones, and its timbers and all the earth of the house, and he shall
46 have it taken out beyond the town to an unclean place. And whoever
comes into the house all the days it is sequestered shall be unclean
47 until evening. And whoever lies in the house shall launder his gar-
48 ments, and whoever eats in the house shall launder his garments. And
if the priest in fact comes and sees and, look, the affliction has not
spread in the house after the plastering of the house, the priest shall
49 declare the house clean, for the affliction has been healed. And he shall
take to purge the house two birds and cedar wood and scarlet stuff and
50 hyssop. And he shall slaughter the one bird into an earthen vessel
51 over fresh water. And he shall take the cedar wood and the hyssop and
the scarlet stuff and the living bird and dip them in the blood of the
slaughtered bird and in the fresh water and sprinkle on the house seven
52 times. And he shall purge the house with the blood of the bird and

---

40. *fling them outside the town into an unclean place.* As the emphatic language
suggests, what is involved is not a neutral act of removing contaminants but a
ridding the community of noxious impurities that are to be consigned, with
vehement energy, to a place of impurity outside the pale of the community.

51. *And he shall take . . . and dip them in the blood . . . and sprinkle on the house
seven times.* These linked rituals of purgation, from person to house, are motivated not medically but by a pervasive sense that the human community is
constantly threatened by forces of impurity which must be warded off or,
should they invade, which must be utterly purged through all the ritual gestures and detergent substances at the disposal of the priestly class. The shad-

with the fresh water and with the living bird and with the cedar wood
and with the hyssop and with the scarlet stuff. And he shall send out   53
the living bird beyond the town to the open field and atone for the
house, and it shall be clean. This is the teaching for every affliction of   54
skin blanch and for scurf, and for scale disease of garment and of   55
house, and for inflammation and for scab and for shiny spot, to teach   56,57
on the day of the unclean and on the day of the clean—this is the
teaching concerning scale disease."

---

owy antecedents of this vision of impurity lie in a pagan sense of a realm of
contamination dominated by demonic spirits. Although the ritual apparatus,
no doubt drawing on archaic precedents, remains in place, there is no indication here that impurity is associated with the demonic, though there appears
to be an association with decay, deformity, and death.

54. *This is the teaching for every affliction of skin blanch.* The little catalogue
that begins here and continues through the next two verses serves as a summary, enfolding the laws of this chapter with the preceding one (where scurf,
scale disease of garment, and inflammation, scab, and shiny spot are all mentioned).

57. *on the day of the unclean and on the day of the clean.* Less literally, and
adopting a minor shift in the vowel points proposed by Baruch Levine, this
could mean: when they are cleansed and when they are unclean.

CHAPTER 15

1,2   **A**nd the LORD spoke to Moses and to Aaron, saying, "Speak to the
Israelites, and you shall say to them, 'Should any man have a flux
3   from his member, he is unclean. And this shall be his uncleanness
in his flux: his member running with its flux or his member stopped up
4   with its flux—this is his uncleanness. Any bedding on which the man
with flux lies is unclean and any object on which he sits is unclean.

---

2. *from his member*. The primary meaning of the noun *basar* is "flesh." In the
preceding chapter, it was used as a synecdoche for "body." Here it is an obvious euphemism for the sexual organ.

3. *running with its flux or . . . stopped up with its flux*. Since the very term "flux"
(*zov*, the same root manifested in "a land *flowing with* milk and honey") suggests some sort of fluid discharge, there is a need to stipulate that this category of ailment also includes cases in which the discharge is scanty, slow, and
viscous ("stopped up").

4. *Any bedding*. As in the laws pertaining to skin disease and mildew, the concern is not a medical one of contagion but a ritual one of contamination
(*tum'ah*, "impurity" or "uncleanness"). The condition of ritual uncleanness
could be conveyed through secondary contact and, in some instances, even
tertiary contact. Here, a substance merely touched by the man with a genital
discharge does not contaminate, nor does he convey uncleanness if he touches
someone after rinsing his hands, but contact with a substance that has been
pressed against his genital area—bedding or a seat—does transmit the impurity. In all this, the overriding preoccupation of the Priestly writers is to protect the ritual purity of their special domain, the sanctuary, by instituting this
system of sequestering and ablution in order to prevent the spread of the contamination. In the pagan world, such contamination was imagined to be
imparted by demonic forces. Jacob Milgrom is certainly right in noting that the

And a man who touches his bedding shall launder his garments and 5
bathe in water and shall be unclean until evening. And he who sits on 6
an object that the man with flux has sat on shall launder his garments
and bathe in water and shall be unclean until evening. And he who 7
touches the body of the man with flux shall launder his garments and
bathe in water and shall be unclean until evening. And should a man 8
with flux spit upon a clean person, he shall launder his garments and
bathe in water and shall be unclean until evening. And any saddle upon 9
which the man with flux rides shall be unclean. And whoever touches 10
anything that has been under him shall be unclean until evening, and
he who carries these things shall launder his garments and bathe in
water and shall be unclean until evening. And anyone whom the man 11
with flux touches, not having rinsed his hands in water, shall launder
his garments and bathe in water and shall be unclean until evening.

---

monotheistic perspective of Leviticus precludes the notion of the demonic
from the conception of impurity. His contention, however, that the opposing
forces of life and death manifested in purity and impurity are the consequence
of man's moral actions is apologetic, for it is clear that certain pathological
conditions—not presented here as a punishment for sin—and even certain
normal physiological processes were thought to be intrinsic sources of
impurity.

5. *bathe*. The Hebrew verb *raḥats* can mean simply "to wash," but in these laws
it is evident that the whole body is to be immersed.

7. *he who touches the body*. Again, the noun used means "flesh," but the case
of touching the person's genitals is an unlikely one, so the term should be construed here as a synecdoche for body. Abraham ibn Ezra succinctly observes,
"Whatever member or limb it may be."

9. *saddle*. The Hebrew *merkav* refers to anything a person mounted on an animal would sit on, and so includes saddle cloths, pillows, and the like.

10. *these things*. The Hebrew says, rather tersely, "them," referring to anything
that would have been under the mounted person.

12 And an earthen vessel that the man with flux touches shall be broken,
13 and any wooden vessel shall be rinsed with water. And when the man
with flux becomes clean from his flux, he shall count him seven days
for his being clean and launder his garments and bathe his body in
14 fresh water, and he shall be clean. And on the eighth day he shall take
him two turtledoves or two young pigeons and come before the Lord
15 at the entrance to the Tent of Meeting and give them to the priest. And
the priest shall do them, one an offense offering and one a burnt offer-
16 ing, and the priest shall atone for him before the Lord for his flux. And
when a man has an emission of seed, he shall bathe his whole body in
17 water and be unclean until evening. And any fabric or any leather upon
which there has been an emission of seed shall be laundered in water
18 and be unclean until evening. And a woman whom a man has bedded
with emission of seed—they shall wash in water and be unclean until
19 evening. And a woman who has a flux of blood, her flux being from her
genitals, seven days she shall be in her menstruation, and whoever

---

12. *earthen . . . wooden vessel.* Milgrom suggests that the earthen vessel is to be
broken because such implements were cheap, whereas the more costly carved
wooden vessel was to be rescued for continued use through rinsing.

15. *offense offering.* As elsewhere, the context makes clear that the Hebrew ḥaṭ'at
does not mean "sin offering," for no sin has been committed. But being the
bearer of a source of contamination that could defile the sanctuary is at least a
potential offense, in a strictly mechanical sense, to the sacred zone of the deity.

16. *an emission of seed.* The Hebrew for "emission," *shikhvah,* is linked to the
verb for "lying down" *shakhav,* but may derive from what is "laid down" as the
result of a spurt or shower of anything liquid, as in the expression *shikhvat tal,*
"layer of dew" (Exodus 16:13).

18. *And a woman whom a man has bedded with emission of seed.* Sexual intercourse with ejaculation renders both parties temporarily impure in regard to
participation in the cult—a widespread idea in the ancient world. Hence the
Israelites are enjoined to refrain from sexual relations for three days before the
Sinai epiphany.

19. *her flux being from her genitals.* Again, the noun used is *basar.* The translation follows ibn Ezra in understanding this as a euphemism for the vagina and

touches her shall be unclean until evening. And whatever she lies upon 20
in her menstruation shall be unclean, and whatever she sits upon shall
be unclean. And whoever touches her bedding shall launder his gar- 21
ments and bathe in water and shall be unclean until evening. And 22
whoever touches any object upon which she has sat shall launder his
garments and bathe in water and shall be unclean until evening. And if 23
it is on the bedding or on the object that she is sitting on when he
touches it, he shall be unclean until evening. And if a man in fact beds 24
her, her menstruation shall be upon him, he shall be unclean seven
days, and any bedding upon which he lies shall be unclean. And should 25
a woman have a flux of blood many days, not in the time of her
menstruation, or should she have a flux in addition to her menstruation, all the days of the flux of her uncleanness she shall be as in the
days of her menstruation. She is unclean. Any bedding upon which she 26
lies all the days of her flux shall be like the bedding of her menstruation, and any object on which she sits shall be unclean like the
uncleanness of her menstruation. And whoever touches them shall be 27
unclean, and shall launder his garments and bathe in water and shall
be unclean until evening. And if she becomes clean from her flux, she 28
shall count her seven days and after shall be clean. And on the eighth 29
day she shall take her two turtledoves or two young pigeons and bring

---

uterus, which of course are the locus of the menstrual flow. The notion that
the menstruant is a source of contamination to be strenuously avoided is
shared by many ancient cultures. Even if the restrictions regarding menstruation are less extreme here than in some other cultures, the association of this
natural female function with uncleanness is one that has had problematic
social and perhaps psychological consequences continuing through postbiblical Judaism.

her menstruation. Though the noun nidah is conventionally derived from
the verbal stem n-d-h, which means "to banish," Levine proposes that it is cognate with n-z-h, "to sprinkle" or "to spatter," thus referring explicitly to the
menstrual flow.

24. her menstruation shall be upon him. Later, there will be a stipulation of
punishment for this act. Here, the man cohabiting with the menstruant
becomes a kind of male menstruant, conveying ritual impurity precisely as the
menstruating woman does and subject to the same process of purification.

30 them to the priest at the entrance to the Tent of Meeting. And the
priest shall do one an offense offering and one a burnt offering, and the
priest shall atone for her before the LORD for the flux of her unclean-
31 ness. And you shall set apart the Israelites from their uncleanness lest
they die through their uncleanness by making unclean My sanctuary
32 which is in their midst. This is the teaching about the man with flux
and about him who has an emission of seed by which he becomes
33 unclean, and about her who is unwell in her menstruation, and about
the person with flux, whether male or female, and about the man who
lies with an unclean woman.'"

CHAPTER 16

And the LORD spoke to Moses after the death of Aaron's two sons 1
when they came forward before the LORD and died. And the LORD 2
said to Moses, "Speak to Aaron your brother, that he not come at
all times into the sacred zone within the curtain in front of the cover
that is on the Ark, lest he die. For in the cloud I shall appear over the
cover. With this shall Aaron come into the sacred zone, with a bull from 3
the herd for an offense offering and a ram for a burnt offering. A sacral 4
linen tunic he shall wear and linen breeches shall be on his body and
with a linen sash he shall gird himself and a linen turban he shall don.
They are sacral garments. And he shall bathe his body in water and put

---

1. *after the death of Aaron's two sons.* As Rashi, Abraham ibn Ezra, and many
traditional and modern commentators variously observe, the death of Aaron's
sons when they presumptuously entered sacred space is mentioned to alert
Aaron to the mortal danger he and his successors run in entering the Holy of
Holies on the Day of Atonement.

when they came forward. This is the verb regularly used for coming before
the divine presence in the sanctuary. When the act is unauthorized, the implication of the verb is "to encroach."

2. *the sacred zone.* In the present context, the meaning of *haqodesh* ("the holy")
is clearly the Holy of Holies, where the Ark of the Covenant stands. Only on
this most sacred day of the calendar is the high priest granted access to this
dangerous space, and only when he follows a strict regimen of dress and
action.

the cover. The exact nature of this item is not entirely certain, though it
appears to have been some sort of carved lid to the Ark. Whatever the actual
etymology of the Hebrew term *kaporet*, this chapter surely exploits a punning
connection with *kipur*, "atonement" or "purgation."

5 them on. And from the community of Israelites he shall take two he-
6 goats for an offense offering and one ram for a burnt offering. And
   Aaron shall bring forward the offense-offering bull which is his and
7 atone for himself and for his household. And he shall take the two goats
   and set them before the LORD at the entrance to the Tent of
8 Meeting. And he shall put lots on the two goats, one for the LORD and
9 one for Azazel. And Aaron shall bring forward the goat for which the lot
10 for the LORD comes up, and he shall make it an offense offering. And
   the goat for which the lot for Azazel comes up shall be set live before
   the LORD to atone upon it, to send it off to Azazel in the wilderness.

---

6. *atone*. The verb *kiper*, as Jacob Milgrom explains, seems to derive from a
concrete notion of rubbing clean. In the cultic lexicon, it has the more
abstract—indeed, theological—sense of effecting atonement or expiation.
When it is applied to persons, it is followed either by the preposition *be'ad*
("for") or *'al* (literally "on," "over"). When it is applied to things (see verse 33),
it is followed by the noun as direct object, which has led some interpreters to
render it as "purge" in such cases.

8. *one for the* LORD *and one for Azazel*. As countless seals and other ancient
inscriptions unearthed by archeologists attest, the use of a proper name or
title, prefixed by the letter *lamed* ("for") as a *lamed* of possession, was a standard form for indicating that the object in question belonged to So-and-so (as
in *lamelekh*, "the king's"). These words, then (in the Hebrew, each is a single
word, *leYHWH* and *la'azaz'el*), are the actual texts written on the two lots.
Much ink since Late Antiquity has been spilled over the identity of Azazel,
but the most plausible understanding—it is a very old one—is that it is
the name of a goatish demon or deity associated with the remote wilderness.
The name appears to reflect *'ez*, goat.

9. *for which the lot for the* LORD *comes up*. This translation renders the Hebrew
verb literally. The use of that verb may be dictated by the fact that the lots
were in all likelihood pulled up out of a box or urn.

10. *to send it off to Azazel in the wilderness*. Approximate analogues to the so-
called scapegoat ritual, using different animals, appear in several different
Mesopotamian texts. The origins of the practice are surely in an archaic idea—
that the polluting substance generated by the transgressions of the people is
physically carried away by the goat. Azazel is not represented as a competing
deity (or demon) rivaling YHWH, but the ritual depends upon a polarity

And Aaron shall bring forward the offense-offering bull which is his, 11
and he shall atone for himself and for his household, and he shall
slaughter the offense-offering bull which is his. And he shall take a 12
panful of fiery coals from the altar, from before the LORD, and a double
handful of fine aromatic incense, and bring it within the curtain. And 13
he shall put the incense on the fire before the LORD, and the cloud of
incense shall envelope the covering that is over the Ark of the
Covenant, lest he die. And he shall take from the blood of the bull and 14
sprinkle with his finger over the surface of the cover on the east side,
and before the curtain he shall sprinkle seven times from the blood
with his finger. And he shall slaughter the offense-offering goat which 15
is the people's and bring its blood within the curtain, and do with its
blood as he did with the blood of the bull, and sprinkle it on the cover
and before the cover. And he shall atone over the sacred zone for the 16
uncleannesses of the Israelites and for their sins, according to all their
offenses, and thus he shall do for the Tent of Meeting that dwells with
them in the midst of their uncleannesses. And no person shall be in the 17

---

between YHWH/the pale of human civilization and Azazel/the remote wilderness, the realm of disorder and raw formlessness. An unapologetic reading
might make out the trace of a mythological plot, even if it is no more than ves-
tigial in this monotheistic context. It is as though the goat piled with impurities were being sent back to the primordial realm of "welter and waste" before
the delineated world came into being, but that realm here is given an animal-
or-demon tag. The early rabbis, extending the momentum of the ritual, imagined the goat as being pushed off a high cliff, but in our text it is merely sent
out, or set free, in the wild wilderness that is the realm of Azazel.

12. *double handful*. Since one hand holds the fire-pan, this is an indication of
dry measure rather than a direction that each of the priest's two hands should
be filled with incense.

16. *he shall atone over the sacred zone*. This clause is the conceptual heart of
the entire atonement ritual. During the year, the accumulated sins and transgressions and physical pathologies and inadvertencies of the Israelites have
built up a kind of smog of pollution that threatens the sanctity of the Tent of
Meeting and the Holy of Holies within it—by implication for later times, the
sanctity of the Temple. This elaborate rite of purgation scrubs everything clean
of impurity, making the sacred zone cultically viable for another year. Again,

Tent of Meeting when he comes into the sacred zone to atone until he goes out, and he shall atone for himself and for his household and

18 for the whole assembly of Israel. And he shall go out to the altar that is before the LORD and atone for it, and he shall take from the blood of the bull and from the blood of the goat and put it on the horns of the

19 altar all around. And he shall sprinkle over it from the blood with his finger seven times and cleanse it and consecrate it from the unclean-

20 nesses of the Israelites. And when he finishes atoning for the sacred zone and for the Tent of Meeting and for the altar, he shall bring for-

21 ward the live goat. And Aaron shall lay his two hands on the head of the live goat and confess over it all the transgressions of the Israelites and all their sins, according to all their offenses, and he shall put them on the head of the goat and send it off in the hand of a man for the hour

22 to the wilderness. And the goat shall bear upon it all their transgressions to a remote region, and he shall send off the goat to the wilder-

23 ness. And Aaron shall come into the Tent of Meeting and take off the linen garments that he wore when he came into the sacred zone and lay

24 them down there. And he shall bathe his body in water in a holy place and put on his garments and come out and do his burnt offering and the people's burnt offering, and he shall atone for himself and for the

25 people. And the fat of the offense offering he shall turn to smoke on

26 the altar. And he who sent off the goat to Azazel shall launder his garments and bathe his body in water, and after he may come into the

27 camp. And the offense-offering bull and the offense-offering goat whose blood has been brought to atone in the sacred zone shall be taken out beyond the camp, and they shall burn their hides in fire and

28 their flesh and their dung. And he who burns them shall launder his garments and bathe his body in water, and after he may come into the

---

evidence abounds of annual rites for cleansing the temple in Mesopotamian culture that may well have served as precedent for what we have here. Later Jewish tradition would transform this ritual for the purgation of a physical miasma of pollution into a process of spiritual repentance and atonement.

21. *a man for the hour*. The Hebrew *'ish 'iti* is a celebrated crux. The expression appears only here. The literal sense is "a timely man," and it probably indicates a man chosen to serve for this time and task.

camp. And it shall be a perpetual statute for you: in the seventh month 29
on the tenth of the month you shall afflict yourselves and no task shall
you do, the native and the sojourner who sojourns in your midst. For on 30
this day it will be atoned for you, to cleanse you of all your offenses,
before the LORD you shall be cleansed. It is a sabbath of sabbaths for 31
you, and you shall afflict yourselves, an everlasting statute. And the 32
priest shall atone, who will be anointed and who will be installed to
serve as priest in his father's stead, and he shall put on the linen garments, the sacral garments. And he shall atone for the holy sanctuary 33
and for the Tent of Meeting, and he shall atone for the altar, and for the
priests and for all the assembled people he shall atone. And this shall 34
be an everlasting statute for you to atone for the Israelites for all their
offenses once in the year." And he did as the LORD had charged Moses.

---

29. *afflict yourselves*. The evident meaning is fasting, though some have contended that the idiom is not restricted to fasting but could also represent other
forms of self-denial.

34. *And he did as the LORD had charged Moses*. The only logical antecedent for
"he" is Aaron, who as high priest is the person who has been enjoined to carry
out this ritual. It is unclear why the name is omitted. With it, the chapter
would be enclosed in a neatly chiastic envelope structure: "And the LORD said
to *Moses*, 'Speak to *Aaron*' . . . And *Aaron* did as the LORD had charged *Moses*."

CHAPTER 17

1,2   **A**nd the Lᴏʀᴅ spoke to Moses, saying, "Speak to Aaron and to his sons and to all the Israelites, and you shall say to them, 'This is 3   the thing that the Lᴏʀᴅ has charged, saying: Every man of the house of Israel who slaughters a bull or a sheep or a goat in the camp

---

2. *Speak to Aaron and to his sons and to all the Israelites.* In contrast to the preceding chapters, God here enjoins Moses to address not merely Aaron and the priestly caste but the whole Israelite people. This pitching of the divine message to the entire populace is one of many signals that have led scholars since the nineteenth century to conclude that chapters 17–26 constitute a distinctive unit—conventionally designated the Holiness Code because of its concern with the idea that the entire people shall make itself holy—possessing certain distinctive theological features and certain distinctive elements of vocabulary.

3. *Every man of the house of Israel.* This phrase, *'ish 'ish mibeyt yisra'el,* is reiterated in this chapter and does not appear at all in chapters 1–16. It is a stylistic device for insisting on the comprehensiveness of the obligation for all Israelites with which the Holiness Code is concerned.

    who slaughters. There has been debate since Late Antiquity about whether the verb refers to general slaughter for the purpose of eating or slaughter for the purpose of sacrifice. There are grounds to conclude that in the early biblical period there was no such thing as "secular" slaughter (*shehitat ḥulin*), for slaughter was regularly associated with offering some part of the animal as a sacrifice. That appears to be the assumption of this law. Slaughtering "outside the camp" entails the danger of sacrifice to the feral or vegetal deities of the open field, and so the animal must be brought to the sanctuary. This ban on secular slaughter, pointedly permitted by Deuteronomy, logically implies, as Jacob Milgrom argues at length, that local sanctuaries are envisaged by the law, where people living in the immediate region could bring the animals as offerings before consuming a large part of them.

616

or who slaughters outside the camp, and does not bring it to the ₄
entrance of the Tent of Meeting to bring it forward as an offering to the
LORD before the LORD's Tabernacle, it shall be counted as blood for
that man—he has spilled blood—and that man shall be cut off from
the midst of his people. So that the Israelites will bring their sacrifices ₅
which they sacrifice across the open field and bring them to the LORD,
to the entrance of the Tent of Meeting, to the priest, and they shall sacrifice them as communion sacrifices to the LORD. And the priest shall ₆
cast the blood on the LORD's altar at the entrance of the Tent of Meeting and turn the fat to smoke as a fragrant odor to the LORD. And they ₇
shall no longer sacrifice their sacrifices to the goat-demons after which
they go whoring. An everlasting statute shall this be for them for their
generations. And to them you shall say: every man of the house of Israel ₈
and of the sojourner who sojourns in their midst who offers up a burnt
offering or a sacrifice, and does not bring it to the entrance of the ₉
Tent of Meeting to do it for the LORD, that man shall be cut off from

---

4. *it shall be counted as blood . . . he has spilled blood.* The starkness of this formulation is quite startling, and very much in keeping with the emphasis
throughout the chapter on the sacrosanct character of blood as the principal
bearer and symbol of life. The person who slaughters an animal without having the priest cast some of its blood on the legitimate altar of YHWH is considered to have committed murder. The blood on the altar, then, offered up to
the deity together with the burnt suet, is an expiation for the blood of the animal spilled in the slaughtering process, a ritual recognition that the taking of
life, even for consumption as food, is a grave act that must be balanced by an
act of expiation.

7. *And they shall no longer sacrifice their sacrifices to the goat-demons.* This
clause provides persuasive evidence that the "slaughter" mentioned in verse 3
is not solely for eating but involves a cultic act. The "goat-demons" (*se'irim*) are
surely to be associated with Azazel in chapter 16. Though our knowledge of
their precise nature is limited, they are clearly archaic nature gods of the wild
realm "beyond the camp," outside the pale of monotheistic civilization that the
sundry Priestly writers are laboring to create. Monogamy, of course, is a reiterated biblical metaphor for monotheism, and so worship of the goat-demons
and other deities is an act of promiscuity, "whoring."

10 his kin. And every man of the house of Israel and of the sojourner who
    sojourns in their midst who consumes any blood, I shall set My face
    against the living person who consumes blood and cut him off from the
11 midst of his people. For the life of the flesh is in the blood. And as for
    Me, I have given it to you on the altar to ransom your lives, for it is the
12 blood that ransoms in exchange for life. Therefore have I said to the
    Israelites: no living person among you shall consume blood, nor shall
13 the sojourner who sojourns in your midst consume blood. And every
    man of the Israelites and of the sojourner who sojourns in their midst
    who hunts down prey, beast or fowl that may be eaten, he shall spill out
14 its blood and cover it with earth. For the life of all flesh, its blood is in
    its life, and I say to the Israelites: the blood of all flesh you shall not
    consume, for the life of all flesh is its blood, all who consume it shall

---

10. *the living person.* In similar contexts elsewhere, the polyvalent Hebrew
nefesh is rendered in this translation simply as "person," but here it is important to add the notion it implies of life because the use of the term puns on
nefesh in the sense of "life" as it appears in the next verse.

11. *I have given it to you on the altar to ransom your lives.* The conception of sacrifice as expiating substitution is made perfectly explicit here: the bloodshed,
equivalent to murder, involved in slaughtering the animal is "made good"
through divine provision by the sacrificial blood cast on the altar "to ransom
[or, atone for] your lives."

12. *no living person.* As in verse 10, the fraught term *nefesh* is pointedly used
rather than *'ish*, "man."

13. *he shall spill out its blood and cover it with earth.* In the case of game, perhaps typically downed with an arrow, the beast or bird is not fit to be brought
as an offering to the altar, so a different mechanism is employed to respect the
sacrosanct nature of the lifeblood—spilling it out on the ground and covering
it with earth.

14. *For the life of all flesh, its blood is in its life.* The syntax here, literally reproduced in the translation, is a little crabbed, leaving the relation of terms
slightly uncertain. One suspects that the writer was impelled by the desire to
insist repetitively on the equation of *dam*, "blood," and *nefesh*, "life."

be cut off. And any living person who eats an animal that has died or 15
been torn by predators, whether native or sojourner, shall launder his
garments and bathe in water and be unclean until evening, and then be
clean. And if he does not launder nor bathe his body, he shall bear his 16
punishment.'"

---

15. *any living person who eats . . . shall launder his garments and bathe.* The clear
implication of this verse, in contrast to other biblical legislation on this topic,
is that it is not forbidden to eat an animal that has died of natural causes or
has been killed by a beast of prey. The animal carcass does convey ritual impurity, so laundering of the garments and bathing are required of the person who
eats its flesh. The permissiveness concerning this category of meat may be
dictated by the consideration that an animal found dead would not be fit for
sacrifice and so, unlike animals slaughtered in open country, would not lead a
person into the danger of sacrificing to the feral deities.

CHAPTER 18

1,2   **A**nd the Lord spoke to Moses, saying, "Speak to the Israelites, and
3   you shall say to them: 'I am the Lord your God. Not like the
deeds of the land of Egypt in which you dwelt shall you do, and
not like the deeds of the land of Canaan into which I am about to
bring you shall you do, and according to their statutes you shall not

---

2. *I am the* Lord *your God*. As elsewhere in the Torah, this declaration at the
beginning, or the end, of a set of legal injunctions echoes the set form for royal
proclamations in the ancient Near East, and has the sense: "By the authority
invested in me as your sovereign I hereby enjoin you."

3. *the deeds of the land of Egypt . . . the deeds of the land of Canaan*. Were such
"deeds" (singular in the Hebrew) of incest and related forms of sexual license
endemic in Egypt and Canaan, and not prevalent in Mesopotamia and Phoenicia, which go unmentioned here? Despite the presence of sister-brother marriages in the Egyptian royal house, and perhaps even beyond it, the association
of both countries with unbridled sexuality surely cannot be grounded in historical observation. Egypt and Canaan are no doubt invoked because these are
the two pagan countries in which Israel has collectively resided. Otherwise,
the identification of both countries as theaters of sexual license may be attributed to a widespread reflex of projecting uncontrolled sexuality onto the cultural other (as Jews were sometimes thought of in Christian Europe, blacks in
America). This reflex would have been reinforced by the tendency to see the
polytheistic world as a realm lacking restraint, in contradistinction to the
Israelite conception of one God and one clearcut set of binding restrictions.
    their statutes. Ḥuqot, as elsewhere, is translated as "statutes," its etymologi-
cal primary sense ("things inscribed"), in order to maintain the counterpoint
with God's statutes in the next verse. The meaning in context, however, by a
kind of metonymic slide from law to action, is something like "habitual practice." When the same term occurs in the last verse of this chapter, the context
requires rendering it as "practices."

walk. My laws you shall do and My statutes you shall keep to walk by 4
them. I am the LORD your God. And you shall keep My statutes and 5
My laws which a person shall do and live through them. I am the LORD.
No man of you shall come near any of his own flesh to lay bare naked- 6
ness. I am the LORD. Your father's nakedness, which is your mother's 7
nakedness, you shall not lay bare. She is your mother; you shall not lay
bare her nakedness. The nakedness of your father's wife you shall not 8
lay bare. It is your father's nakedness. The nakedness of your sister, 9
your father's daughter or your mother's daughter, born in the household

---

6. *No man*. The male is singled out, one infers, because he is assumed to take
the initiative in sexual acts. An exception here (verse 23) is the woman engaging in bestiality.

his own flesh. This phrase follows an idiomatic pattern of placing two synonyms together in construct state—here, *she'er* and *basar*, both of which mean
"flesh"—in order to indicate emphasis or a superlative.

7. *nakedness*. The Hebrew noun *'erwah* transparently derives from a verbal root
that means "to be naked," but all its uses suggest either vulnerability (as in
Joseph's words to his brothers, "To see the land's nakedness you have come,"
Genesis 42:9) or shamefulness. Some characterize the term as a euphemism
for the genitalia, but if that is the case, it constitutes one of those instances in
which the euphemism itself becomes a potent and fraught term. When Saul
denounces Jonathan for disloyalty "to . . . the shame of your mother's nakedness" (1 Samuel 20:30) the term verges on an obscenity, as references to the
mother's pudenda are used in Arabic and other languages.

which is your mother's nakedness. Although the Hebrew uses *waw* here (usually, "and"), it is in this case the equivalent of an explanatory subordinate
clause, as the next sentence makes clear. A kind of contagion of nakedness is
envisaged. Because the mother's nakedness has been in contact with the
father's nakedness—and because in the patriarchal order her sexuality
"belongs" to him—she is taboo.

8. *your father's wife*. Especially given the circumstances of polygamy, one's
father's wife would not necessarily be one's mother.

10 or born outside—you shall not lay bare her nakedness. The nakedness
of your son's daughter or of your daughter's daughter—you shall not lay
11 bare her nakedness, for it is your nakedness. The nakedness of the
daughter of your father's wife, born in your father's household—she is
12 your sister; you shall not lay bare her nakedness. The nakedness of your
13 father's sister you shall not lay bare. It is your father's flesh. The nakedness of your mother's sister you shall not lay bare, for it is your mother's
14 flesh. The nakedness of your father's brother you shall not lay
15 bare, and you shall not come near his wife. She is your aunt. Your
daughter-in-law's nakedness you shall not lay bare. She is your son's
16 wife; you shall not lay bare her nakedness. The nakedness of your
17 brother's wife you shall not lay bare. It is your brother's nakedness. The
nakedness of a woman and her daughter you shall not lay bare. Her
son's daughter or her daughter's daughter you shall not take to lay bare
18 her nakedness. they are kin-flesh, it is depravity. And a woman with her
sister you shall not take to become rivals, to lay bare her nakedness
19 while her sister is still alive. And you shall not come near a woman in

---

10. *your son's daughter*. Presumably, a prohibition on intercourse with one's
own daughter is also assumed, but no satisfactory explanation has been offered
for why it is not explicitly stated.

18. *a woman with her sister*. As many interpreters have noted, this and several
other prohibitions in the list are explicitly violated by figures in the national
narrative of Israel: Jacob marries two sisters; Abraham claims that Sarah is his
half sister; David's daughter Tamar appears to think it possible that her father
can arrange a marriage between her and her half brother Amnon. Either these
laws represent a Priestly "reform" in sexual practice, as Jacob Milgrom proposes, or certain once acceptable sexual unions had come through evolving
social consensus to be regarded as taboo.

    to become rivals. This is the technical term, grounded in realism, for the
condition of co-wives in polygamy. In the clause "while her sister is still alive"
the words "her sister" are added for clarity.

her menstrual uncleanness to lay bare her nakedness. And you shall not   20
put your member into your fellow man's wife to spill seed, to be
defiled through her. And you shall not dedicate any of your seed to pass   21
over to Molech, and you shall not profane the name of your God. I am
the LORD. And with a male you shall not lie as one lies with a woman.   22

---

20. *to spill seed.* "Spill" is merely implied by the compact *lezara'*, "for seed." The
two defining elements for adultery, indicated here with legal precision, are
penetration and ejaculation. The potential consequence, of course, is that the
woman could produce a child of dubious paternity—a particularly problematic
condition in this patrilinear society.

21. *dedicate any of your seed to pass over to Molech.* Molech is a Canaanite deity
whose name suggests "king." The authentic form of the name may have been
Malik, revocalized by the Masoretes to make the word resemble *boshet*,
"shame." The most likely reference of the whole phrase is to child sacrifice,
which in fact was widely practiced in the Syro-Palestinian sphere, as vividly
attested by the vast number of children's graves uncovered at the site of
Carthage, the Phoenician colony in North Africa. The verb "pass over" would
then be an ellipsis for "pass over through fire," used in other texts for this
pagan practice. Some scholars, however, maintain that what was involved was
a dedication ceremony in which the child was passed over the fire but not
burned as a sacrifice. The metonymy "seed" for "child" links this law with the
preceding ones and those that follow in which seed in the sense of semen is
deposited in a forbidden place.

22. *with a male you shall not lie as one lies with a woman.* The explicitness of
this law—the Hebrew for "as one lies" is the plural construct noun *mishkevei*,
"bedding," used exclusively for sexual intercourse—suggests that it is a ban on
anal intercourse and intercrural intercourse (the latter often practiced by the
Greeks). Other forms of homosexual activity do not seem of urgent concern.
The evident rationale for the prohibition is the wasting of seed in what the law
appears to envisage as a kind of grotesque parody of heterosexual intercourse.
(Lesbianism, which surely must have been known in the ancient Near East, is
nowhere mentioned, perhaps because no wasting of seed is involved, though
the reason for the omission remains unclear.) There is scant textual evidence
to support the apologetic claim of some recent interpreters that the ban on
homosexual congress is limited to the preceding list of incestuous unions. One
may apply here the proposal of Mary Douglas that this is a culture that likes
to keep lines of categorical distinction clear: no human-beast couplings are

23 It is an abhorrence. And you shall not put your member into any beast
to be defiled through it. And a woman shall not present herself to a
24 beast to couple with it. It is a perversion. Do not be defiled through all
of these, for through all of these were the nations that I am about to
25 send away before you defiled. And the land was defiled, and I made a
reckoning with it for its iniquity, and the land spewed out its inhabi-
26 tants. And you on your part shall keep My statutes and My laws, and
you shall not do any of these abhorrences, neither the native nor the
27 sojourner who sojourns in your midst. For all these abhorrences did the
28 men of the land who were before you do, and the land was defiled. And
the land will not spew you out in your defiling it as it spewed out the
29 nation that was before you. For whosoever does any of these abhorrences, the person who does it shall be cut off from the midst of his
30 people. And you shall keep My watch not to do any of the abhorrent
practices that were done before you, and you shall not be defiled
through them. I am the LORD your God.'"

---

allowed (in contrast to the imaginative freedom on this topic of Greek myth),
and any simulation of procreative heterosexual intercourse by the insertion of
the male member in an orifice or fleshy crevice of another male is abhorrent.

23. *a woman shall not present herself to a beast.* The literal sense of the verb is
"stand before" (which in other contexts can mean "to perform service"), but in
fact she is crouching, with posterior toward the male beast, as the verb here
for coupling, *r-b-ʿ*, indicates, for it is cognate (possibly via the Aramaic) with
r-b-ts, the verb used for an animal's crouching. It is puzzling that no mention
is made in the present context of acts of bestiality by males, though in chapter 21 this is defined as a capital offense.

27. *the men of the land.* Perhaps the Hebrew *ʾanshey* also includes women, as
the taboo in verse 23 suggests, but it is surely meant to pick up the initial "No
man of you" in verse 6.

29. *the person who does it.* The Hebrew actually switches from the initial singular "whosoever does" to a plural "the persons who do it," but the singular is
used in the translation because of the requirement of consistency of English
usage.

CHAPTER 19

And the Lord spoke to Moses, saying, "Speak to all the community 1,2
of Israelites, and you shall say to them: 'You shall be holy, for I the
Lord your God am holy. Every man shall revere his mother and 3
his father, and My sabbaths you shall keep. I am the Lord your God.
Do not turn to the idols nor make molten gods for yourselves. I am the 4

---

2. *You shall be holy, for I . . . am holy.* Although the idea that the people of Israel
is to make itself holy by emulating God's intrinsic holiness is not unique to this
group of texts in Leviticus, its enunciation as the supreme rationale and didactic rallying point for God's commands is distinctive, and it is what has led
scholars to designate the textual unit from chapter 17 through chapter 26 as
the Holiness Code. When the sundry injunctions here conclude with the reiterated formula "I am the Lord," the implication is "I am the Lord your God
Who is holy."

3. *Every man shall revere his mother and his father, and My sabbaths you shall
keep.* It has been recognized since Late Antiquity that this section of laws,
beginning with this verse, constitutes a kind of paraphrase and elaboration of
the Ten Commandments, following a different order, using somewhat different turns of phrase, and introducing additional legal imperatives. Abraham ibn
Ezra, as usual with an eye to compositional links, notes that the previous section was focused on prohibited sexual relations that could lead to the expulsion of people from its land. The variegated laws of the present chapter, he
contends, came to remind Israel that there is a whole spectrum of commands
which must be observed if it is to remain rooted in its land.

4. *idols.* The Hebrew *'elilim* refers not to the carved likenesses of divinities but
to the nonentity of the pagan gods. Its most plausible derivation is from *'al*,
"not," and hence would suggest falsity or lack of being, but the term probably
also puns on *'el*, "god," using a diminutive and pejorative form that could mean
something like "godlet."

5 LORD your God. And when you sacrifice communion sacrifices to the
6 LORD, you should sacrifice it so that it will be acceptable for you. On
the day you sacrifice, it shall be eaten and on the morrow, and what is
7 left till the third day shall be burned in fire. And if in fact it is eaten on
8 the third day, it is desecrated meat, it shall not be acceptable. And he
who eats it shall bear his guilt, for he has profaned the LORD's holiness,
9 and that person shall be cut off from his kin. And when you reap your
land's harvest, you shall not finish off the edge of your field, nor pick
10 up the gleanings of your harvest. And your vineyard you shall not pluck
bare, nor pick up the fallen fruit of your vineyard. For the poor and for
11 the sojourner you shall leave them. I am the LORD your God. You shall
not steal. You shall not dissemble and you shall not lie, no man to his
12 fellow. You shall not swear falsely in My name, profaning the name of

---

5. *when you sacrifice.* It is characteristic of the sacerdotal milieu that produced
this paraphrase of the Decalogue that a sacrificial law is intertwined with the
fundamental moral and theological imperatives. The LORD's holiness is profaned no less by eating sacrificial meat on the third day than by dishonoring
one's parents or turning one's daughter into a whore.

   sacrifice it. The Hebrew thus switches to a distributive "it" after the plural
"sacrifices."

9. *you shall not finish off the edge of your field, nor pick up the gleanings of your
harvest.* In an agricultural economy without coined money (weights of silver
and gold could be used for exchange), the stipulation that an edge of the field
be left unharvested and that what was dropped by the reapers should not be
picked up amounted to a kind of poor tax. The indigent could follow the har-
vesters into the fields and pick up enough to sustain themselves, as we see dramatically in the Book of Ruth when the widowed Ruth, a newly arrived
resident alien, goes out into Boaz's fields.

10. *sojourner.* As elsewhere, the Hebrew term refers to a resident alien, who in
this tribal agrarian society would have been without real property.

12. *You shall not swear falsely in My name, profaning the name of your God.* The
main clause is a citation of the Decalogue. "Profaning the name of your God"
adds a Holiness Code rationale—to swear falsely is to compromise God's own
reputation of holiness through the malfeasance of the people purported to be
God's special treasure.

your God. I am the LORD. You shall not defraud your fellow man and 13 you shall not rob. You shall not keep the hired man's wages with you through the night till morning. You shall not vilify the deaf, and before 14 the blind you shall not put a stumbling block, and you shall fear your God. I am the LORD. You shall do no iniquity in justice. You shall not 15 favor the wretched and you shall not defer to the rich. In righteousness you shall judge your fellow. You shall not go about slandering your kin. 16 You shall not stand over the blood of your fellow man. I am the LORD.

---

13. *You shall not keep the hired man's wages with you through the night.* The presumption is that the hired man is without reserves. Holding back his wages not only subjects him to a night of anxiety as to whether he will be paid but could impose actual hardship, for he may need the wages for his evening meal.

14. *vilify the deaf, and before the blind . . . a stumbling block.* There is both a common denominator and a logical discrepancy (the rhetorical figure of zeugma) between these two prohibitions. In both instances, the sensory impairment of the victim prevents him from perceiving that someone is exploiting his weakness in a nasty way. But abusing or verbally insulting a deaf man gratuitously humiliates him in a fashion that he himself, unhearing, may never become aware of, whereas placing a stumbling block before a blind man causes him hurt of which he will immediately become aware. A long exegetical tradition sees both these cases as figurative instances of a more general category of moral turpitude: placing a bottle of whiskey, for example, in front of a recovering alcoholic would fall under the rubric of putting a stumbling block before the blind.

15. *You shall not favor the wretched and you shall not defer to the rich.* Both Hebrew verbs involve idioms that make "face" the object of the verb—literally "lift up the face," "glorify/honor the face." The term for "rich" more generally means "great," but in economic contexts (here as an antonym to "wretched" or "indigent") it regularly has the meaning of "wealthy."

16. *You shall not go about slandering . . . You shall not stand over the blood.* Jacob Milgrom neatly observes that the verbs are pointedly sequenced from going about to standing (and presumably doing nothing), both with the effect of complicity in doing harm. Though there is some dispute among interpreters about the meaning of "stand over the blood," there is a degree of consensus among traditional commentators, supported by the bracketing of the two sentences in this verse, that it means to stand by without intervening while your fellow man's blood—literally or figuratively—is spilled.

17 You shall not hate your brother in your heart. You shall surely reprove
18 your fellow and not bear guilt because of him. You shall not take
vengeance, and you shall not harbor a grudge against the members of
your people. And you shall love your fellow man as yourself. I am the
19 LORD. My statutes you shall keep. Your beasts you shall not mate with
a different kind. Your field you shall not sow with different kinds. And
a garment of different kinds of thread, *sha'atnez*, shall not be donned by
20 you. And should a man lie with a woman with emission of seed when
she is a slave previously assigned to a man but has not been ransomed
or given her freedom, there shall be an inquiry. They shall not be put to
21 death for she has not been freed. And he shall bring his guilt offering
22 to the entrance of the Tent of Meeting, a guilt-offering ram. And the
priest shall atone for him with the guilt-offering ram before the LORD
for his offense that he committed, and it will be forgiven him for his

---

17. *You shall surely reprove your fellow.* The obligation to reprove someone you
see engaged in a wrongful act may be linked psychologically with the immediately preceding injunction not to hate your brother in your heart: witnessing
immoral behavior without attempting to intervene, the observer may feel
resentment or contempt toward the perpetrator who in fact might conceivably
have been dissuaded from the act by reproof.

19. *sha'atnez.* This is evidently a loanword, and the etymology is uncertain. The
way it is used here suggests it might have required some explanation for ordinary Hebrew speakers of the time of writing, and in Deuteronomy 22:11 (its
only other biblical occurrence) it is explicitly glossed as a fabric made of interwoven threads of linen and wool (see the comment there). All the prohibitions
in this verse appear to reflect that general Israelite aversion to the mingling of
distinct categories on which Mary Douglas has written. It should be noted
that, as with some other prohibitions, what is forbidden for profane use is permitted for cultic use—the high priest's robe and the covering of the Ark were
linsey-woolsey.
      not be donned by you. The literal sense of the Hebrew is "not go up on you."

20. *put to death.* A betrothed woman having sex with another man would be
subject like her lover to capital punishment. A female slave, not being a free
agent, would not receive the death penalty, and evidently this crime, too, is
considered less grave. After an inquiry, a monetary penalty will be set to be
paid to the man who betrothed her.

offense that he committed. And when you come to the land and plant 23
any fruit-bearing tree, you shall leave its fruit uncircumcised. Three
years it shall be uncircumcised to you. It shall not be eaten. And in the 24
fourth year all its fruit shall be sacred, a jubilation before the LORD.
And in the fifth year you may eat its fruit, that its yield may be 25
increased for you. I am the LORD your God. You shall not eat over 26
the blood. You shall not divine nor interpret omens. You shall not round 27
off the edge-growth of your head nor ruin the edge of your beard.

---

23. *you shall leave its fruit uncircumcised.* This analogy of fruit to foreskin, a little startling to the modern ear, includes both the idea of leaving a natural
growth uncut and the notion, readily understandable in a society in which all
male infants were circumcised, of something prohibited. These three verses
reflect prudent arboricultural practice rather than any ethical imperative. Milgrom, who has consulted horticulturalists, reports that during the first three
years a tree is generally not thinned or pruned or harvested but that the closed
buds (from which the image of the foreskin would derive) are plucked before
fruit emerges.

24. *sacred, a jubilation before the LORD.* What is envisaged is a festival of first
fruit, to be offered in the sanctuary to God. Behind the term "jubilation," some
scholars have conjectured, may lie an old practice of festive celebrations at
harvesttime, perhaps involving matchmaking or even orgies, in the vineyards.

26. *You shall not eat over the blood.* The meaning of this sentence, represented
quite literally in this translation, has been disputed, but the most plausible
explanation is the one proposed by the medieval Hebrew exegete Nahmanides
and by Rashbam before him: what is involved is a pagan rite of divination—
this would be the link with the second half of the verse—in which a ritual
meal was consumed over a pit or large receptacle containing blood, perhaps
with the idea that spirits of the dead could be conjured up from the blood.

27. *round off the edge-growth of your head.* The word for "edge-growth," *pe'ah,*
is the same one used in verse 9 for the edge of the field, which is also not to
be cut. This is an instance of what Mary Douglas characterizes as analogical
thinking. This sort of bowl-shaped haircut does not appear to be the same
thing as shaving the head, but it should be noted that shaving the head, tearing or mutilating the beard, and gashing one's body are all pagan mourning
practices.

28 No gash for the dead shall you make in your flesh, and no tatoo shall
29 you make on yourselves. I am the LORD. Do not profane your daughter
to make a whore of her, lest the land play the whore and the land
30 be filled with depravity. My sabbath you shall keep and My sanctuary
31 you shall revere. I am the LORD. Do not turn to the ghosts, and of the
familiar spirits do not inquire to be defiled through them. I am the
32 LORD. Before a gray head you shall rise, and you shall defer to an elder
33 and fear your God. I am the LORD. And should a sojourner sojourn with
34 you, you shall not wrong him. Like the native among you shall be
the sojourner who sojourns with you, and you shall love him like yourself, for you were sojourners in the land of Egypt. I am the LORD your
35 God. You shall do no iniquity in justice—in measure, whether in weight
36 or liquid measure. Honest scales, honest weights, an honest
ephah and an honest *hin* you shall have. I am the LORD your God who
37 brought you out of the land of Egypt. And you shall keep all My statutes
and all My laws and do them. I am the LORD.'"

---

28. *for the dead*. The polyvalent Hebrew noun *nefesh* often means "person," but
in some contexts it refers to a dead person or corpse, and the implication of
mourning here points to that meaning.

32. *defer to an elder*. The idiom used is exactly the one that appears in verse 15
in the prohibition against deferring to the rich. Context is everything: in court
proceedings, no special consideration can be given to anyone, regardless of
status; in everyday interactions, an old person deserves deference. (Israeli
buses used to carry a sign with the words "Before a gray head you shall rise" as
a reminder that passengers should give up their seats to the elderly.)

35. *in measure, whether in weight or liquid measure*. The literal sequence of the
Hebrew is: "in measure, in weight, in liquid measure." Though some contend
that the first word, *midah*, refers to measures of length and breadth, it is a general term introducing the category of measurement, which is then followed by
different kinds of measure (hence "whether . . . or").

CHAPTER 20

And the LORD spoke to Moses, saying, "And to the Israelites you 1,2 shall say: 'Every man of the Israelites and of the sojourners who sojourn in Israel who gives of his seed to Molech is doomed to die. The people of the land shall stone him. And as for Me, I shall set My 3 face against that man and cut him off from the midst of his people, for he has given of his seed to Molech so as to defile My sanctuary and to profane My sacred name. And if the people of the land actually avert 4 their eyes from that man when he gives of his seed to Molech, not putting him to death, I Myself shall turn My face against that man and 5 his clan, and I shall cut him off and all who go whoring after him to whore after Molech, from the midst of their people. And the person 6 who turns to the ghosts and to the familiar spirits to go whoring after them, I shall set My face against that person and cut him off from the

---

2. *Every man of the Israelites . . . who gives of his seed to Molech*. The list of prohibited acts that begins here mirrors the one that takes up chapter 18. That chapter and the present one are two panels separated by the paraphrase of the Decalogue in chapter 19. What is couched in chapter 18 as a series of imperatives is recast here in the language of case law ("casuistically"), with the punishment for each offense now stipulated. That addition gives a focusing or quasi-narrative development to the relationship between the parallel lists of laws.

3. *I shall set My face*. The literal sense of the verb is "give," thus making it a measure-for-measure response to "gives of his seed to Molech."
so as to defile My sanctuary. Once more, we see the preoccupation of all the segments of Leviticus with preserving the sacred integrity of the sanctuary. A heinous act, such as child sacrifice, is not only intrinsically abhorrent, but also conveys pollution to the sanctuary of YHWH.

7 midst of his people. And you shall sanctify yourselves and become holy,
8 for I am the LORD your God. And you shall keep My statutes and do
9 them. I am the LORD Who makes you holy. For every man who vilifies
his father and his mother is doomed to die. He has vilified his father
10 and his mother—his bloodguilt is upon him. And a man who commits
adultery with a married woman, who commits adultery with his fellow
11 man's wife, the adulterer and the adulteress are doomed to die. And a
man who lies with his father's wife, his father's nakedness he has laid
bare. The two of them are doomed to die. Their bloodguilt is upon
12 them. And a man who lies with his daughter-in-law, the two of them
are doomed to die. They have done a perversion. Their bloodguilt is on
13 them. And a man who lies with a male as one lies with a woman, the
two of them have done an abhorrent thing. They are doomed to die.

---

8. *I am the* LORD *Who makes you holy.* This refrainlike line, which is the ultimate rationale for all the prohibited acts with their stipulated punishments, is
the thematic center of the chapter.

9. *who vilifies his father and his mother.* The verb *qalel*, "to treat with disrespect," "to vilify," or "to insult" (literally "to make light of") is the antonym of
"*honor* [literally, 'make heavy'] your father and your mother" in the Decalogue.

10. *a married woman.* The Hebrew says literally "a man's woman [or wife]."
   the adulteress. Abraham ibn Ezra shrewdly observes of the Hebrew term
hano'efet, which is an active verbal form, that had she been constrained by the
man to submit to the sexual act, she would not have been so designated.

11. *The two of them are doomed to die.* As with the preceding law, the assumption is that the woman is a willing participant.

13. *as one lies with a woman.* This locution, literally "the lying with a woman"
(as in 18:22, and see the comment there), plausibly leads the Talmud in Sanhedrin to characterize the act as "putting a brush into a tube"—that is, the particular homosexual act of anal penetration.

Their bloodguilt is upon them. And a man who takes a woman and her   14
mother, it is depravity. In fire shall he and they be burned, so that there
be no depravity in your midst. And a man who puts his member into a   15
beast is doomed to die, and the beast you shall kill. And a woman who   16
approaches any beast to couple with it, you shall kill the woman and
the beast. They are doomed to die. Their bloodguilt is on them. And a   17
man who takes his sister, his father's daughter or his mother's daughter,
and sees her nakedness and she sees his nakedness, it is vileness, and
they shall be cut off before the eyes of their kinfolk. His sister's nakedness he has laid bare. He shall bear his punishment. And a man who   18
lies with a woman while she is unwell and lays bare her nakedness, he
has exposed her flow and she has laid bare the flow of her blood, and
the two of them shall be cut off from the midst of their people. And   19
the nakedness of your mother's sister or your father's sister you shall not
lay bare, for his own flesh he has exposed. Their punishment they shall

---

14. *takes.* The use of this verb here and several times in subsequent verses is
an ellipsis for "takes as a wife," but its choice of the term may be dictated by
the way it stresses the male's taking the initiative.

15. *the beast you shall kill.* Commentators have wrestled with the reason for
executing the animal. As Rashi says, "If the person committed a wrong, what
wrong has the beast done?" The most plausible explanation is that the beast,
even without its volition, has been associated with a disgusting act and so must
be destroyed as a contaminated thing.

17. *and she sees his nakedness.* Ibn Ezra is surely right that this unusual addition is to emphasize her full complicity in the act of incest.

18. *he has exposed her flow.* The Hebrew noun *maqor* generally means "source,"
this being an instance of the common linguistic pattern in which there is an
exchange between cause (the source) and effect (the flow). It is reductive to
claim, as do Jacob Milgrom and others, that "source" is simply a euphemism
for the female genitalia. The point is that the menses are conceived not merely
as a contaminant but as some ultimate, intimate female mystery which the
woman has to keep secret—hence the condemnation, "for she has laid bare
her source/flow."

20 bear. And the man who lies with his aunt, his uncle's nakedness he has
21 laid bare. Their guilt they shall bear, barren they shall die. And the man
     who takes his brother's wife, it is a repulsive thing. His brother's naked-
22 ness he has laid bare. Barren they shall die. And you shall keep all My
     statutes and all My laws and do them, lest the land to which I bring you
23 to dwell there spew you out. And you shall not go by the statutes of the
     nation which I am about to send away before you, for all these things
24 they have done, and I loathed them. And I said to you, it is you who will
     take hold of their soil, and as for Me, I shall give it to you to take hold
     of it, a land flowing with milk and honey. I am the LORD your God
25 Who set you apart from all the peoples. And you shall set apart the
     clean from the unclean beast, and the unclean bird from the clean, and
     you shall not make yourselves despicable through beast and bird and all
26 that crawls on the ground, which I set apart for you as unclean. And
27 you shall be holy to Me, for I the LORD am holy. And any man or woman
     who has a ghost or a familiar spirit is doomed to die. They shall be
     stoned, their bloodguilt is upon them.'"

---

21. *a repulsive thing.* The Hebrew *nidah* is the term elsewhere used for menstruation. One infers that here it is intended metaphorically.

24. *it is you.* The use of the plural pronoun *'atem* before the conjugated verb
conveys this sense of emphasis.

24–25. *set you apart . . . you shall set apart.* There is a clear system of what one
might well describe as cosmic analogies functioning here. Holiness depends
upon distinction, upon being set apart and setting things apart. Israel has been
set apart by God to be holy, to be different from other nations. Israel in its turn
is enjoined to realize its distinctive character by relinquishing the indiscriminate
consumption of all living things and setting apart the unclean from the clean.

25. *you shall not make yourselves despicable.* Milgrom chooses to render this as
"you shall not defile your throats." This is a distinctly possible interpretation,
if not entirely compelling. The Hebrew *nefesh* means "life-breath," and then
synecdochically "person," but also metonymically "throat" (the passage
through which the breath is conducted). In the present context, however,
which stresses the imperative for Israel to preserve its holiness as a people set
apart, the defiling of the whole person rather than the throat seems more likely
as the intended meaning.

CHAPTER 21

And the LORD said to Moses, "Say to the priests, the sons of Aaron, 1 and say to them, 'For no dead person among his kin shall he be defiled, except for his own flesh that is close to him, for his mother and for his father and for his son and for his daughter and for 2 his brother, and for his virgin sister who is close to him, as she has not 3 become a man's, for her he may be defiled. He shall not be defiled 4 among his kin to profane himself. They shall not make a baldness on 5

---

1. *dead person*. The Hebrew *nefesh*, "person," is an abundantly attested ellipsis for *nefesh met*, "dead person," and the full phrase in fact is used in verse 11.

   defiled. It is possible, as many scholars have proposed, that the notion of corpses as a source of defilement is linked with a polemic against the cult of the dead evidently widespread in Canaan among both Canaanites and Israelites. But given the repeated affirmation through ritual in Leviticus of life against death, it is quite possible that dead bodies were thought of as intrinsically contaminating, even without reference to a cult of the dead.

3. *as she has not become a man's*. Once she is in the jurisdiction of her husband, it is his obligation in the case of her decease to see to her burial.

4. *He shall not be defiled among his kin*. The two Hebrew words *ba'al be'amaw* are a well-known crux. Literally, they mean "a master/husband among his kin." The various attempts to make this intelligible are strained, and it has been pointed out by several scholars that elsewhere *ba'al* is always used either as part of a collocation (Hebrew *smikhut*) or in a declined form. This translation adopts Meir Paran's plausible proposal that the received text reflects a dittography, the initial *beit* and *'ayin* of *be'amaw* inadvertently repeated by a scribe and then a *lamed* added in order to turn the two letters into a known word.

5. *baldness . . . the edge of their beard . . . shave . . . gash*. All these acts are pagan rites of mourning that must be avoided. There are other pagan gestures of

their head, and the edge of their beard they shall not shave, and in their
6 flesh they shall cut no gash. They shall be holy to their God, and they
shall not profane the name of their God, for the fire offerings of the
LORD, their God's bread, do they bring forward, and they shall be holy.
7 A woman degraded as a whore they shall not take as wife, and a woman
divorced from her husband they shall not take as wife, for he is holy to
8 his God, and you shall deem him holy, for he brings forward God's
bread. He shall be holy for you, for I the LORD Who hallows you am
9 holy. And should a priest's daughter degrade herself in whoring, she has
10 degraded her father, in fire she shall be burned. And the priest exalted
over his brothers, on whose head the anointing oil has been poured and
who has been installed to wear the garments, shall not dishevel his hair

---

mourning (as attested, for example, in Ugaritic texts) that are permitted to the
Israelites, such as putting ashes on the head and donning sackcloth. Presumably, the acts stipulated here are prohibited because they entail disfiguring some part of the body.

6. *God's bread*. As elsewhere, *leḥem* is a synecdoche for "food."

7. *A woman degraded as a whore*. This translation follows the proposal of many modern scholars that *zonah waḥalalah* (literally, "whore and degraded one") is a hendiadys used to convey the idea of the intrinsically degraded condition of the whore. Jacob Milgrom's proposal that *ḥalalah* means "raped woman" rests on rather flimsy philological evidence. Note that in verse 9 these same two roots are put together, this time as a verb and an infinitive, *taḥel liznot*, "degrade herself in whoring," strongly suggesting that they are a fixed collocation rather than designating two different possibilities.
    for he is holy. The Hebrew, like this translation, slips from the plural for all priests to the singular for the individual priest.

8. *holy . . . hallows . . . holy*. The verbal motif central to the Holiness Code is here redoubled as the text concentrates on the priests, the very heart of the holiness that is to extend to the entire people.

10. *exalted over his brothers*. More literally, "greater than his brothers."
    the garments. Though the Hebrew uses a general term for garments, the obvious reference is the priestly vestments worn in the cult.
    dishevel his hair nor rip his garments. Gestures of mourning permitted to

nor rip his garments. And near any dead person he shall not come in, 11
for his father or for his mother he shall not be defiled. And from the 12
sanctuary he shall not go out, and he shall not profane the sanctuary of
his God, for the mark of his God's anointing oil is upon him. I am the
LORD. And as for him, he must take as wife a woman in her virginity. 13
A widow or a divorced woman or a degraded whore, these he shall not 14
take as wife, but a virgin from his kin he shall take as wife. And he shall 15
not profane his seed among his kin, for I am the LORD Who hallows
him.'"

And the LORD spoke to Moses, saying, "Speak to Aaron, saying, 'No 16,17
man of your seed to their generations in whom there is a defect shall
come forward to offer his God's bread. For no man in whom there is a 18
defect shall come forward, no blind man nor lame nor disfigured nor

---

those who are not the high priest. The verb chosen for "rip," *param*, neatly allit-
erates with *para'*, "dishevel."

11. *he shall not come in*. The contamination of the corpse would be conveyed
to him if he were to enter any enclosed space in which the corpse was laid out.

for his father or for his mother he shall not be defiled. The syntactic positioning of the two nouns at the beginning of the clause suggests: not even for his
father or for his mother.

12. *mark*. The Hebrew *nezer* can also mean "diadem," but its etymology indicates "to be distinct, set apart," and the anointing oil is the priestly mark of
distinction.

14. *virgin*. On the basis of both the immediate context and usages elsewhere,
one must categorically reject Milgrom's claim that *betulah* simply means
"young woman" and does not imply virginity. The priest has to marry a virgin
to ensure the purity of the priestly line.

18. *no man in whom there is a defect*. The underlying notion, however objectionable to modern sensibilities, is one shared by many ancient religions: just
as the animal offered in sacrifice must be unblemished, the officiant offering
the sacrifice must be without physical blemish.

disfigured nor malformed. The two Hebrew terms, *harum* and *saru'a*, have
long been the objects of philological speculation. Their exact meaning remains
in doubt, though it is clear that they refer to some sort of physical deformity.

19,20 malformed, nor a man who has a broken leg or a broken arm, nor a
hunchback nor a midget nor one with a cataract in his eye nor scab nor
21 skin flake nor crushed testicle. No man from the seed of Aaron the
priest in whom there is a defect shall draw near to bring forward the
fire offerings of the LORD. There is a defect in him. He shall not draw
22 near to bring forward his God's bread. From the holy of holies and from
23 the holy, he may eat his God's bread. But he shall not come in by the
curtain nor shall he draw near to the altar, for there is a defect in him,
and he shall not profane My sanctuaries, for I am the LORD Who hal-
24 lows you.'" And Moses spoke to Aaron and to his sons and to all the
Israelites.

---

19. *a broken leg or a broken arm*. As Baruch Levine notes, given the limitations
of ancient medicine, broken bones would usually have resulted in a permanent
deformity.

22. *he may eat his God's bread*. The physical deformity does not disqualify the
man from his priestly perquisite of a share in the sacrifices. Otherwise, he
would have no source of sustenance. But he is not permitted (verse 23) to
approach the altar ("come in") to offer the sacrifice.

24. *And Moses spoke*. For editorial reasons that remain obscure to us, this chapter concludes atypically, with a report of Moses speaking that is not followed
by a speech and thus appears to refer retrospectively to the speech just
delivered.

CHAPTER 22

And the Lord spoke to Moses, saying, "Speak to Aaron and to his sons, that they keep apart from the sacred donations of the Israelites—lest they profane My holy name—which they consecrate to Me. I am the Lord. Say to them: 'To your generations, any man of all your seed who draws near the sacred donations that the Israelites consecrate to the Lord with his uncleanness upon him, that person shall be cut off from before Me. I am the Lord. Any man whosoever from the seed of Aaron when he is smitten with skin blanch or discharge from his member shall not eat of the sacred donations until he becomes clean, nor he who touches anything unclean through a dead

---

2. *that they keep apart.* The syntactical interpolation of the clause after this one makes the sentence slightly unclear, but the evident motive is to effect a strong thematic juxtaposition of the antonyms, *qodashim*, "sacred donations," and *yeḥalelu*, "profane," with the verb's direct object, *shem qodshi*, "My holy name," reinforcing the link between divine sacredness and the sacred donations. It may at first seem puzzling that the priests should be enjoined to keep apart from the sacred donations of sacrificial animals that were, after all, their sustenance, but the next verse makes clear that this warning to the priests obtains in cases when they are in a state of ritual impurity (and so Rashi observes).

3. *who draws near.* As Jacob Milgrom repeatedly notes, this all-purpose verb in contexts of ritual prohibition means "to encroach," though when the ritual act is permitted, it means, more neutrally, "to enter into the sacred zone."
    shall be cut off from before Me. The more common locution in Leviticus is "cut off from his kin." This variation may suggest divestment from priestly privileges, being cut off from the sacerdotal line.

5 person nor a man who has had an emission of seed, nor a man who has
touched any swarming thing by which one becomes unclean or a
6 human being by which one becomes unclean with any uncleanness. A
person who touches these shall be unclean till evening and shall not eat
7 of the sacred donations until he bathes his body in water, and the sun
sets and he becomes clean, and after he may eat of the sacred dona-
8 tions, for it is his bread. A beast that has died or one torn by predators
9 he shall not eat to be defiled by it. I am the LORD. And they shall keep
My watch and not bear offense for it and die through it when they pro-
10 fane it. I am the LORD Who hallows them. And no outsider shall eat a
sacred donation. A priest's resident hireling shall not eat the sacred
11 donation. And should a priest buy a person as the purchase of his silver, that person may eat of it, and he who is born in his household—
12 they may eat of his bread. And should a priest's daughter be married to
13 an outsider, she shall not eat of the levy of the sacred donations. And
should a priest's daughter become a widow or divorced, having no seed
and she come back to her father's house as in her youth, of her father's
14 bread she may eat, but no outsider shall eat of it. And should a man
eat the sacred donation in errance, he shall add a fifth of its value to it

---

5. *a human being*. This noun is the object of the double-duty verb "touched."

7. *for it is his bread*. As often elsewhere, "bread" is a synecdoche for "food." In
fact, the typical sacred donation would have been meat.

9. *bear offense for it and die through it*. Both of the pronouns here are masculine, though the only adjacent noun that might be a candidate for an
antecedent, "watch," is feminine. Various efforts to rescue grammatical consistency—e.g., that the antecedent is an elided *shem qodshi*, "My holy
name"—seem strained. It is more likely that the requirements of gender consistency of modern Western languages did not altogether obtain for biblical
grammar and that it seemed natural to use a masculine form for impersonal
constructions such as "bear offense for it" regardless of the antecedents.

10. *A priest's resident hireling*. Avraham Melamed, followed by Jacob Milgrom,
argues persuasively that the phrase *toshav kohen wesakhir*—literally, "priest's
resident and hireling"—is a hendiadys, like the use of *toshav* in other combi-
nations, and does not refer to two entities.

and give the sacred donation to the priest. And they shall not profane   15
the sacred donations of the Israelites that they set aside for the LORD,
causing them to bear the punishment of the guilt for having eaten of   16
their sacred donations, for I am the LORD Who hallows them.'"

And the LORD spoke to Moses, saying, "Speak to Aaron and to his sons   17,18
and to the Israelites, and you shall say to them: 'Every man of the house
of Israel and of the sojourner in Israel who brings forward his offering,
for any of their votive offerings or their freewill offerings that they bring
forward to the LORD as burnt offerings, to be acceptable for you, it shall   19
be an unblemished male from the cattle, the sheep, or the goats.
Whatever has a defect you shall not bring forward, for it will not be   20
acceptable for you. And should a man bring forward a communion sac-   21
rifice to the LORD to set aside as a votive offering or freewill offering
from the cattle or from the flock, it shall be unblemished to be acceptable, no defect shall there be in it. Anything blind or broken or lacer-   22
ated or with a wen or scab or skin-flake, these you shall not bring
forward to the LORD, and no fire offering from them shall you put on
the altar to the LORD. And a bull or sheep with a stretched or crimped   23

---

15. *And they shall not profane.* As the end of this sentence, in the next verse,
makes clear, "they" refers to the priests, who would profane the sacred donations by allowing unfit laypersons to incur guilt by eating them (thus Rashi).
This whole clause mirrors the language of the opening verse, thus forming an
envelope structure to bring this entire unit of the chapter to a close.

19. *to be acceptable for you.* Literally, "for your favor," i.e., for your finding favor,
being acceptable, in the eyes of God.

20. *Whatever has a defect you shall not bring forward.* As many commentators
have noted, the list of deformities for the animals unfit for the cult parallels
the list of deformities for priests unfit for the cult in the previous chapter. The
terms used, however, are different.

22. *Anything blind.* The Hebrew uses the term for the disease, "blindness," but
then switches to the male singular beast bearing the defect, "broken" (presumably, broken-limbed), and "lacerated," and then to symptoms of disease
("wen," "scab," "skin-flake"). Category consistency does not appear to have
been a requirement of ancient Hebrew idiomatic usage.

limb you may make a freewill offering but it shall not be acceptable as
24 a votive offering. And anything with crushed or smashed or torn-off or
cut-off testes you shall not bring forward to the LORD, and in your land
25 you shall not do it. And from the hand of a foreigner you shall not bring
forward your God's bread from any of these. Their deformity is in them,
a defect is in them. They shall not be acceptable for you.'"

26,27 And the LORD spoke to Moses, saying, "When a bull or a goat is born,
it shall be seven days under its mother, and from the eighth day onward
28 it is acceptable as a fire offering to the LORD. And a bull or sheep, you
29 shall not sacrifice it with its young on the same day. And when you sacrifice a thanksgiving sacrifice to the LORD, you shall sacrifice it so as to
30 be acceptable for you. On that day it shall be eaten, you shall leave
31 nothing of it till morning. I am the LORD. And you shall keep My com-
32 mands and do them. I am the LORD. And you shall not profane My holy
name, and I shall be hallowed in the midst of the Israelites. I am the
33 LORD Who hallows you, bringing you out of the land of Egypt to be God
for you. I am the LORD."

---

24. *crushed or smashed or torn-off or cut-off.* The list appears to be arranged in
ascending order of the severity of mutilation.

and in your land you shall not do it. This sounds like a general ban on geld-
ing, which, however, would have had a necessary role in animal husbandry.
One may tentatively adopt Milgrom's proposal that the reference is to regional
sanctuaries beyond the principal one, since Leviticus does not assume that
there is one exclusive sanctuary. "Do it," then, would mean perform the
sacrifice.

25. *from the hand of a foreigner you shall not bring forward . . . from any of these.*
This warning is intended to preclude the notion that a maimed animal is per-
mitted for sacrifice in cases where the maiming has not been done by an
Israelite but by a foreigner from whom the animal is purchased.

27. *it shall be seven days under its mother.* A humanitarian rationale for this law
is unconvincing because, after all, on the eighth day the suckling animal can
be slaughtered and offered up on the altar. It is more likely that the newborn
beast was not regarded as a viable living creature, and hence fit for sacrifice,
until it had attained its eighth day of life (the day designated for the circumcision of Israelite males). This correspondence of eight days between man and
beast may be another instance of analogical thinking.

CHAPTER 23

nd the LORD spoke to Moses, saying, "Speak to the Israelites, and 1,2 you shall say to them: 'These are the fixed times of the LORD which you shall call sacred convocations. These are My fixed times. Six days shall tasks be done, and on the seventh day, an absolute 3 sabbath, a sacred convocation. No task shall you do. It is a sabbath for the LORD in all your dwelling places. These are the fixed times of the 4 LORD, sacred convocations which you shall call in their fixed time.

---

3. *Six days shall tasks be done.* It is somewhat surprising, as commentaries from the Middle Ages onward have reflected, that after announcing a calendar of the sundry annual festivals (*mo'adim*, "fixed times"), the text proceeds to spell out the weekly obligation of the sabbath day. Rashi tries to reconcile the contradiction by proposing that the mention of the sabbath is to indicate that violation of the sabbath and violation of the festivals are equivalent in seriousness; but the consensus of modern scholarship is that these verses on the sabbath were added, perhaps out of later historical considerations, such as the impossibility of observing the pilgrim festivals in the Babylonian exile. This addition would have been facilitated by a certain ambiguity in the word *shabbat* (literally, "cessation"), which can apply, as it does elsewhere in this chapter, not only to the weekly day of rest but to a festival, when most everyday tasks are also prohibited.

an absolute sabbath. The Hebrew uses a doubled construct form that generally indicates a superlative, *shabbat shabbaton*.

4. *sacred convocations which you shall call.* In this recurring phrase, the verb, *tiqre'u*, and its object, *miqra'ey qodesh*, are cognates, something that the translation intimates at least etymologically because "convocation" is derived from a Latin term for calling. "Call" in this context obviously means to "proclaim," "convene," "invite."

5 In the first month on the fourteenth of the month at twilight a Passover
6 offering to the LORD. And on the fifteenth day of this month, a Festival
7 of Flatbread to the LORD. Seven days you shall eat flatbread. On
the first day a sacred convocation you shall have. No task of work shall
8 you do. And you shall bring forward a fire offering to the LORD seven
days. On the seventh day a sacred convocation, no task of work shall
you do.'"

9,10 And the LORD spoke to Moses, saying, "Speak to the Israelites, and you
shall say to them: 'When you come into the land that I am about to give
you and you reap its harvest, you shall bring a sheaf, first of your
11 harvest, to the priest. And he shall elevate the sheaf before the LORD to
be acceptable for you, from the morrow of the sabbath the priest
12 shall elevate it. And on the day you elevate the sheaf you shall do an

---

5. *the first month*. As elsewhere, the calendar begins with the spring month
that Exodus calls Abib and that will later be called Nisan. The present list does
not use names for the month, simply referring to them by ordinal numbers.

5–6. *Passover offering . . . a Festival of Flatbread*. The paschal offering (traditionally in English, "Passover offering") is stipulated for the first evening and
the flatbread for the seven days of the festival. On the historical relation
between the two aspects of observance, see the comment on Exodus 12:17.

6. *a Festival*. The Hebrew ḥag is a term reserved in biblical usage for pilgrim
festivals (evidently derived from a verb that means to "circle round" or "wend
one's way"), when the population of the countryside was enjoined to come to
the sanctuary.

10. *sheaf*. The early rabbis understood the term 'omer not as a reference to a
bundle of grain (in this case of a late spring harvest, probably barley) but as a
unit of dry measure.

11. *from the morrow of the sabbath*. This innocent-looking phrase is fraught with
ambiguity that generated historical schism. The early rabbis understood "sabbath" to refer to the first day of the Passover celebration (see the comment on
verse 3), and this has been the normative system in Judaism ever since for
counting forward to the Festival of Weeks, Shavuoth. The Karaites, among
others, understood *shabbat* here as a reference to the sabbath day, although the
question was raised whether this applied to the sabbath occurring in the week

unblemished yearling lamb as a burnt offering to the LORD, and its 13
grain offering, two-tenths of an *ephah* of semolina mixed with oil, a fire
offering to the LORD, a fragrant odor, and its wine libation, a quarter of
a *hin*. And bread and roast grain and fresh ears you shall not eat until 14
this very day, until you bring your God's offering, an everlasting statute
for your generations in all your dwelling places. And you shall count you 15
from the morrow of the sabbath, from the day you bring the elevation
sheaf, seven whole weeks shall they be. Until the morrow of the sev- 16
enth sabbath you shall count fifty days, and you shall bring forward
a new grain offering to the LORD. From your dwelling places you shall 17
bring two loaves of elevation bread, two-tenths of an *ephah* of semolina
they shall be, leavened they shall be baked, first fruits to the LORD. And 18
you shall bring forward with the bread seven unblemished yearling
lambs and one bull from the herd and two rams. They shall be a burnt
offering to the LORD and their grain offering and their libations, a fire
offering, a fragrant odor to the LORD. And you shall do one he-goat as 19
an offense offering and two yearling lambs as a communion sacrifice.
And the priest shall elevate them with the bread of first fruits as an ele- 20
vation before the LORD with the two lambs. They shall be holy for the
LORD, for the priest. And on this very day you shall call a sacred con- 21
vocation—it will be for you— no task of work shall you do, an everlast-

---

of the Passover festival or to the first sabbath after that week. (As a rule, issues
of calendar were often defining for schismatic divisions in Judaism.) Whatever
the reasons of the rabbis, their construction of *shabbat* as referring to "festival"
seems implausible. Baruch Levine and Jacob Milgrom have variously understood *shabbat* to mean "week" in the present context. In verse 16, the phrase
"seventh sabbath" in fact seems to mean "seventh week."

20. *They shall be holy for the LORD, for the priest.* The second phrase, which
syntactically is in apposition with the first, is a kind of gloss on it: in the case
of this offering of first fruits, the consecrated status of the foodstuffs ("holy for
the LORD") means not that they are to be consumed in fire on the altar but that
they are reserved exclusively for the use of the priests.

21. *a sacred convocation—it will be for you.* The oddness of the syntax might
conceivably reflect a scribal insertion here of a formula reiterated elsewhere. In
independent clauses, we find the complete syntactic unit, "A sacred convoca-

22 ing statute in all your dwelling places for your generations. And when you reap the harvest of your land, you shall not finish off the edge of your field in your reaping, nor gather the gleanings of your harvest. For the poor and for the sojourner you shall leave them. I am the LORD your God.'"

23,24 And the LORD spoke to Moses, saying, "Speak to the Israelites, saying: 'In the seventh month on the first of the month you shall have a
25 sabbath, a commemoration with horn blast, a sacred convocation. No task of work shall you do, and you shall bring forward a fire offering to
26,27 the LORD.'" And the LORD spoke to Moses, saying, "Yet on the tenth of this seventh month is the day of atonement, a sacred convocation it shall be for you, and you shall afflict yourselves and bring forward a fire
28 offering to the LORD. And no task shall you do on this very day, for it is
29 a day of atonement to atone for you before the LORD your God. For every person who is not afflicted on this very day shall be cut off from
30 his kin. And any person who does any task on this very day—I shall
31 make that person perish from the midst of his people. No task shall you do, an everlasting statute for your generations in all your dwelling
32 places. An absolute sabbath it is for you, and you shall afflict yourselves

---

tion it will be for you." Here, however, "a sacred convocation" is already the object of the verb "you will call," and so "it will be for you" seems not to belong.

24. *a commemoration with horn blast*. Although the instrument used is not specified here, the reasonable assumption is that it is the ram's horn, or *shofar*. The "commemoration" in question is the act of making God remember, or take note of, Israel through the ritual of horn blasts. Some biblical scholars have detected a hint of an annual ceremony for the coronation of God, but the historical evidence for that vivid conjecture is scant.

27. *Yet*. The Hebrew '*akh* ("yet," "however") expresses opposition but also a focusing emphasis ("only").
    you shall afflict yourselves. In legal-cultic contexts, this idiom refers primarily to fasting, a meaning perhaps reinforced by the fact that the noun in question, the ubiquitous *nefesh*, can also mean both "throat" and "appetite," though its most plausible sense in context is simply as an intensive form of the pronoun.

on the ninth of the month in the evening, from evening to evening you shall keep your sabbath.'"

And the Lord spoke to Moses, saying, "Speak to the Israelites saying: 'On the fifteenth day of this seventh month, a festival of huts, seven days, to the Lord. On the first day, a sacred convocation, no task of work shall you do. Seven days you shall bring forward a fire offering to the Lord. On the eighth day you shall have a sacred convocation and bring forward a fire offering to the Lord; it is a solemn gathering. No task of work shall you do. These are the fixed times of the Lord which you shall call sacred convocations to bring forward a fire offering to the Lord, burnt offering and grain offering, sacrifice and libation, each thing on its day, besides the Lord's sabbaths and besides your gifts and besides all your votive offerings and besides all your freewill offerings that you give to the Lord. Yet on the fifteenth day of the seventh month, when you gather in the yield of the land, you shall celebrate the Lord's festival seven days—on the first day a sabbath and on the eighth day a sabbath. And you shall take you on the first day the fruit of a stately tree, fronds of palm trees, and a branch of a leafy tree and wil-

33,34
35
36
37
38
39
40

---

32. *from evening to evening.* Only here is this phrase attached to the observance of a sacred day. Levine's reasonable inference is that the system of counting the day from sunset to sunset, standard in later Judaism, may not yet have been normative in the biblical period, and hence its binding application to the Day of Atonement had to be stipulated.

   you shall keep your sabbath. More literally, "you shall cease your cessation."

36. *solemn gathering.* This is a single word in the Hebrew, 'atseret, (elsewhere, also 'atsarah), which appears to refer specifically to the cultic assembly at the end of the festival, perhaps because the verb from which it derives means "to retain" or "to hold back."

40. *a stately tree.* In modern Hebrew, 'ets hadar has come to mean "citrus tree," but that is only because in the late Second Temple period this whole phrase was understood to refer to the citron, the somewhat larger and brighter-yellow cousin of the lemon. *Hadar,* however, is a general term referring to majesty, stateliness, or splendor, and it is probable that the original instruction was to take the fruit of any grand-looking tree, not necessarily the fruit of a specific genus of trees.

lows of the brook, and you shall rejoice before the LORD your God
41 seven days. And you shall celebrate it as a festival to the LORD seven
days in the year, an everlasting statute for your generations. In the sev-
42 enth month you shall celebrate it. In huts you shall dwell seven days.
43 All natives in Israel shall dwell in huts, so that your generations will
know that I made the Israelites dwell in huts when I brought them out
44 of the land of Egypt. I am the LORD your God.'" And Moses spoke the
fixed times of the LORD to the Israelites.

---

you shall rejoice before the LORD your God. The injunction to rejoice occurs
only in the case of Succoth, the fall Festival of Huts. One reason for this may
be that this was the final harvest festival of the agricultural cycle, and hence
the pilgrims, free from the need to hurry back to their farms to look after the
next crop, could spend the full week in celebration at the sanctuary where sacrifices were offered and attendant feasts enjoyed. In the climate of the Land
of Israel, this was the time (late September to early October) when the long
hot dry season came to an end and the welcome autumnal rains were imminent. In precisely this connection, we know from the Mishnah that the Succoth celebration in the Second Temple included an elaborate ritual for
invoking water for the land (*simḥat beyt hasho'evah*), a ritual explicitly represented as a peak of collective joy.

43. *I made the Israelites dwell in huts.* Huts were used for temporary shelter by
farmers watching over their crops about to be harvested and so may have been
associated with this festival of the fall harvest. Milgrom suggests that the flood
of pilgrims to the central sanctuary in this most popular of the pilgrim festivals
compelled many of them to spend the week in huts or other temporary shel-
ters because the town itself could not have possibly provided the bulk of them
with lodging. Whether the original explanation was in agricultural practice or
in the material necessities of pilgrimage, a historical-theological rationale is
now provided.

44. *Moses spoke the fixed times.* Here "spoke" has the obvious sense of
"enjoined," "proclaimed," "enunciated."

CHAPTER 24

A nd the Lord spoke to Moses, saying, "Charge the Israelites, that 1,2
they take clear beaten olive oil for the light to kindle a lamp perpetually. Outside the curtain of the Covenant in the Tent of Meet- 3
ing Aaron shall set it out from evening till morning before the Lord
perpetually, an everlasting statute for your generations. On the pure gold 4
lamp stand he shall set out the lamps, before the Lord perpetually.
And you shall take semolina flour and bake it into twelve loaves. Each 5
loaf shall be two-tenths of an *ephah*. And you shall place them in two 6

---

2. *beaten olive oil*. "Beaten" (*katit*), from a verb that means "to smash" or "to
pulverize," suggests that the olives are to be pounded with a pestle rather than
crushed in a press.

   perpetually. The Hebrew *tamid* implies that the light is to be constantly
renewed, not that it is to burn incessantly as an "eternal light."

3. *the curtain of the Covenant*. The last word here is a prevalent ellipsis for "Ark
of the Covenant."

4. *the pure gold lamp stand*. As both Rashi and Abraham ibn Ezra note, the
Hebrew phrase—literally, "the pure lamp stand"—is an ellipsis for "pure gold
lamp stand." The same is true of the phrase "pure [gold] table" in verse 6.

5. *twelve loaves*. This sanctified number of course reflects the number of the
tribes of Israel, as does the number of stones in the breastplate of the high
priest. The bread in question is the "bread of display" or "bread of the Presence" (King James Version, "shewbread"). Laying out bread on the altar daily,
or even several times a day, with the idea of symbolically feeding the deity, was
a widespread practice in ancient Near Eastern religions. Jacob Milgrom suggests that it was in order to distance this cherished cultic procedure from any
notion of providing sustenance to God that this version of the law stipulates

7 rows, six to a row, on the pure gold table before the LORD. And you shall
place clear frankincense together with the row and it shall become a
8 token offering for the bread, a fire offering to the LORD. Sabbath day
after sabbath day they shall be laid out before the LORD perpetually on
9 behalf of the Israelites, an everlasting covenant. And it shall be Aaron's
and his sons', and they shall eat it in a holy place, for it is holy of holies
for him from the LORD's fire offerings, an everlasting statute."

10 And the son of an Israelite woman, he being the son of an Egyptian
man, went out among the Israelites, and the son of the Israelite woman
11 and an Israelite man brawled in the camp. And the son of the Israelite
woman invoked the Name, vilifying it. And they brought him to Moses.

---

putting out fresh loaves only once a week. The inevitably stale bread could
then be consumed by the priests (perhaps one of the less attractive of their
sacerdotal perquisites).

7. *clear frankincense.* The adjective used, *zakh,* is the same one applied to olive
oil in verse 1, and translations that render it as "pure" run the risk of introducing a confusion with the pure (*tahor*) gold lamp stand and table. Since frankincense is a resin, this might be an indication that it should be translucent, a
visual attribute squarely within the semantic range of *zakh.*

  a token offering for the bread, a fire offering. Since the bread itself is not consumed on the altar but is left untouched until the following sabbath, when it
may be given to the priests, the frankincense, set alongside the bread, is
burned as a "token offering" in lieu of the bread.

8. *Sabbath day after sabbath day.* The literal contour of the Hebrew idiom is
"On the sabbath day, on the sabbath day."

10. *brawled.* This verb of violent altercation is the same one used for the two
Hebrew men whom the young Moses rebukes (Exodus 2:13). It is perhaps this
verbal trigger that led Rashi to claim, rather fancifully, that the blasphemer in
this episode was the son of the Egyptian taskmaster whom Moses killed on the
day before his encounter with the two brawling Israelites.

11. *invoked the Name, vilifying it.* "The Name," in an interesting biblical anticipation of later pious usage in Hebrew, is an ellipsis for "the Name of YHWH."
One suspects that the writer avoided using the complete phrase because the
idea of actually invoking and vilifying God's holy name was so abhorrent to

And his mother's name was Shelomith daughter of Dibri of the tribe of
Dan. And he left him under guard until it should be made clear to them   12
by the word of the LORD. And the LORD spoke to Moses, saying, "Take   13,14
out him who vilified beyond the camp, and all who heard shall lay their
hands on his head, and all the community shall stone him. And to the   15
Israelites you shall speak, saying, 'Should any man vilify his God, he
shall bear his offense. And he who invokes the LORD's name shall be   16
doomed to die; and the community shall surely stone him, sojourner
and native alike; for his invoking the Name he shall be put to death.

---

him. The object of "vilifying," it (the Name), is merely implied. Though it
might at first seem that the brawler is verbally abusing his adversary, super-
charging the abusive language by introducing God's sacrosanct name, verse 15
clearly makes "his God" the grammatical object of "vilify," and this direct verbal assault on the name YHWH is of course a graver transgression.

   Shelomith daughter of Dibri of the tribe of Dan. Mary Douglas ingeniously
detects in these names a kind of allegorical play: Compensation (or Retribution) daughter of Law-suit from the tribe of Judgment.

12. *until it should be made clear to them by the word of the LORD.* What is to be
made clear is what should be done with the malefactor. "By the word [literally,
by the mouth] of the LORD" in the present context obviously refers to an oracle,
and God's speech to Moses in the following verses is the message of the oracle.

14. *him who vilified.* God, too, suppresses the divine object of the verb of scurrilous speech.

   all who heard. That is, all who heard the blasphemous utterance.

   shall lay their hands on his head. In biblical idiom, bloodguilt rests "on the
head" of the perpetrator. The laying on of hands by the witnesses is the confirming of the guilt (and so Rashi observes).

16. *for his invoking the Name he shall be put to death.* The element of the idiom
that sticks in the craw of the pious writer, "and vilifying it," is merely implied.
This act of *lèse-majesté* aimed at God, Who is the very rationale for the existence of the community, is understood to be a threat to the community itself,
and so all are to be involved in the execution. In any case, this formulation,
which appears to hold the mere invoking of the Name as a sin, led later on to
a general ban against pronouncing the name YHWH except by the high priest
on the Day of Atonement in the Holy of Holies.

17 And should a man mortally strike down any human being, he is doomed
18 to die. And he who mortally strikes down a beast shall pay for it, life for
19 life. And should a man maim his fellow, as he has done so shall it be
20 done to him. A fracture for a fracture, an eye for an eye, a tooth for a
21 tooth—as he has maimed a human being, so shall he be maimed. And
he who strikes down a beast shall pay for it, but he who strikes down a
22 human being shall be put to death. One law shall there be for you, for
23 sojourner and native alike shall it be, for I am the LORD your God.'" And
Moses spoke to the Israelites, and they took out him who had vilified
beyond the camp and pelted him with stones. And the Israelites did as
all that the LORD had charged Moses.

---

17. *And should a man mortally strike down any human being.* The use of the
generic term *'adam*, "human being," sets up the contradistinction of killing a
domestic animal rather than a human being. But there may also be an implied
contrast with God in the preceding unit. God in principle cannot be hurt by
any human act, but His name, available for manipulation and debasement in
human linguistic practice, can suffer injury, and for this injury the death
penalty is exacted, as here in the case of murder.

18. *shall pay for it, life for life.* Since what is explicitly stated is providing restitution to the owner of the animal that has been killed, "life for life" here clearly
means the monetary value of the dead creature that will enable its owner to
acquire another one. Although the rabbis strenuously sought to extend this
notion of monetary compensation to all the cases of *lex talionis* that follow
here, the plain language of the text appears to call for an actual infliction of
injury for injury, as Milgrom plausibly concludes after an exhaustive survey of
the age-old interpretive debate. The formulation of the *lex talionis* in Exodus
21:23–25 may leave a bit more latitude for the possibility of monetary compensation because there is no verb for the act of maiming like what is used here,
"as he has maimed a human being so shall he be maimed." See the comment
on Exodus 21:23–25.

CHAPTER 25

And the Lord spoke to Moses on Mount Sinai, saying, "Speak to [1,2] the Israelites, and you shall say to them: 'When you come into the land that I am about to give you, the land shall keep a sabbath to the Lord. Six years you shall sow your fields and six years you shall [3] prune your vineyard and gather in its yield. And in the seventh year [4] there shall be an absolute sabbath for the land, a sabbath to the Lord. Your field you shall not sow and your vineyard you shall not prune. The [5] aftergrowth of your harvest you shall not reap and the grapes of your untrimmed vines you shall not pick. There shall be an absolute sabbath

---

1. *on Mount Sinai.* The mention here of Mount Sinai has become proverbial in Hebrew for a puzzling juxtaposition of two disparate terms—in Rashi's classic formulation: "What is the connection between Mount Sinai and the Year of Release?" The most plausible explanation, put forth by several recent scholars, is that there is an invocation of a Mesopotamian practice, in which a king assuming his throne would issue a general proclamation for the release of slaves. Thus God announcing His kingship at Sinai definitively releases the Israelites from the status of slaves to which they had been reduced in Egypt. They become instead God's slaves (a paradoxical definition of their new freedom), as the end of this chapter pointedly reminds us.

2. *the land shall keep a sabbath to the Lord.* More literally, "the land shall cease a cessation to the Lord."

4. *your vineyard you shall not prune.* The vines of course do not have to be planted annually like the grains, but without annual pruning, they will not yield an adequate crop of grapes.

5. *untrimmed vines.* A very literal representation of this phrase would be "nazirite vines." The Hebrew *nazir* reflects a root that means "to set apart," but

6 for the land. And the land's sabbath shall be food for you, for you and
   for your male slave and for your slavegirl and for your resident hirelings
7 who sojourn with you, and for your cattle and for the beasts that are in
8 your land, all its yield shall be for food. And you shall count you seven
   sabbaths of years, seven years seven times, and the days of the seven
9 sabbaths of years shall come to forty-nine years. And you shall send
   round a blasting ram's horn, in the seventh month on the tenth of the
   month, on the Day of Atonement, you shall send round a ram's horn
10 through all your land. And you shall hallow the fiftieth year and call a
   release in the land to all its inhabitants. A jubilee it shall be for you, and
   you shall go back each man to his holding and each man to his clan,

---

because the nazirite refrains among other things from cutting his hair, the
idiom here may be a simple analogical extension from uncut hair (because it
is forbidden) to untrimmed vines (because it is equally forbidden).

6. *the land's sabbath shall be food for you.* This phrasing is an obvious ellipsis
for "the land's sabbath yield shall be food for you."

   your resident hirelings. Throughout this section, the two nouns *sekhirkha
wetoshavkha*, connected by "and," should be understood not as separate items
("your hireling and your resident") but as a hendiadys, two terms indicating a
single concept.

7. *all its yield.* "Its" (feminine in the Hebrew) refers either to "land" or to "sabbath."

9. *send round.* This verb is chosen because what is suggested is that the ram's
horn is to be carried around the country from place to place by delegated her-
alds and to be appropriately sounded, so that everyone will know that the
jubilee year has arrived.

10. *call a release in the land to all its inhabitants.* One must regretfully forgo the
grandeur of the King James Version, inscribed on the Liberty Bell: "proclaim
liberty throughout *all* the land unto the inhabitants thereof." In fact, the passage is concerned with the legal arrangements regarding property in the jubilee
year, and modern scholarship has persuasively demonstrated that *deror* does
not mean "liberty" but is cognate with a technical Akkadian term, *anduraru*,
which means a release from, or moratorium on, debts and indenture.

   jubilee. Though scholarly debate persists about the etymology of this word
(which has entered English from the Hebrew), the noun *yovel* in Exodus 19:13

you shall go back. It is a jubilee, the fiftieth year it shall be for you. You 11
shall not sow and you shall not reap its aftergrowths and you shall not
pick its untrimmed vines. For it is a jubilee. It shall be holy for you. 12
From the field you may eat its yield. In this jubilee year you shall go 13
back, each man to his holding. And when you sell property to your fel- 14
low or buy from the hand of your fellow, you shall not defraud one
another. By the number of years after the jubilee you shall buy from 15
your fellow, and by the number of years of yield he shall sell to you. The 16
larger the number of years, the more you shall pay for its purchase and
the smaller the number of years the less you shall pay for its purchase,
since he is selling you the number of yields. And you shall not 17
defraud each other, and you shall fear your God, for I am the LORD your
God. And you shall do My statutes, and My laws you shall keep and do 18
them, and you shall dwell on the land securely. And the land will give 19
forth its fruits and you will eat to fullness, and you will dwell
securely on it. And should you say: What shall we eat in the seventh 20

---

clearly indicates a ram's horn (the alternate term is *shofar*), and thus it is plausible that the fiftieth year was called jubilee, *yovel*, because this was when loud
blasts of the ram's horn were sounded throughout the land.

12. *its yield*. The only proximate candidate for an antecedent of "its" (feminine)
is "jubilee year."

13. *you shall go back, each man to his holding*. Without the notion of inalienable property holdings, the whole system of permanent division of the land
according to tribes, and then clans, would have broken down. On the other
hand, the arrangements for the jubilee release entailed the most cumbersome
complications, as verses 16–17 concede, and once the tribal territories had disappeared as a historical fact in the Second Temple period, the rabbis devised
a legal mechanism that in effect abrogated the jubilee.

16. *since he is selling you the number of yields*. If, say, there remained only three
years till the jubilee, the buyer would enjoy only three harvests before the land
would revert to its original owner, and so the seller could demand only a limited purchase price (in all likelihood, $3/49$ of its intrinsic value).

19. *its fruit*. Here the term functions in its general sense of "produce."

21 year, if we do not sow and do not gather in our yield? I have charged
    My blessing for you in the sixth year, and it will produce yield for three
22 years. And you shall sow in the eighth year and eat of the old crop until
23 the ninth year, until its yield comes, you shall eat the old. And the land
    shall not be sold irreversibly, for Mine is the land, for you are sojourn-
24 ing settlers with Me. And in all the land of your holdings, you shall
25 allow a redemption for the land. Should your brother come to ruin and
    sell his holding, his redeemer who is related to him shall come and
26 redeem what his brother sold. And should a man have no redeemer and
27 his hand attain and find enough for its redemption, he shall reckon
    the years it was sold and give back the difference to the man to whom
28 he sold, and he shall go back to his holding. And if his hand cannot find
    enough to pay him back, what he sold shall be in the hands of the buyer
    till the jubilee year, and it shall be released in the jubilee, and he shall
29 come back to his holding. And should a man sell a dwelling house
    in a walled town, its redemption shall be till the end of the year of its

---

21. *I have charged My blessing for you in the sixth year, and it will produce yield for three years.* This miraculous intervention in order to generate a harvest in the sixth year sufficient for three years suggests that the legislation for the sabbatical year was in a way utopian, and could only have been observed imperfectly for compelling practical reasons.

23. *sojourning settlers.* As everywhere in biblical usage, the two Hebrew nouns (literally, "sojourner and settler") are a hendiadys with the modern legal sense of "resident alien."

24. *you shall allow a redemption for the land.* Land can be redeemed at any time either by its original owner or by a relative acting on behalf of the original owner, and the buyer is obliged to sell back the land, to "allow redemption." The jubilee, then, is a kind of backup system: if neither the original owner nor his kin can come up with the price of redemption, the land will in any case revert to its original owner in the jubilee.

28. *released.* The literal meaning of the verb *yatsaʾ* is "go out," but in contexts of property law it has this technical meaning, and the literal sense would not be intelligible in English.

sale. A year its redemption shall be. And if it is not redeemed by the 30
time a full year has elapsed for him, the house in the town that has a
wall shall pass over irreversibly to its buyer for his generations. It shall
not be released in the jubilee. And houses in the hamlets that have no 31
walls all around shall be reckoned as part of the land's open fields. They
shall have redemption and be released in the jubilee. And as to the 32
towns of the Levites, the houses of the towns of their holding, the
Levites shall have a redemption forever. And what is redeemed of the 33
Levites, the sale of house and the town of his holding, shall be released
in the jubilee, for the houses of the Levites' towns are their holding in
the midst of the Israelites. And the unenclosed fields of their towns 34
shall not be sold, for it is an everlasting holding for them.

"'And should your brother come to ruin and his hand buckle under you, 35
you shall hold him as sojourning settler, and he shall live under you. You 36
shall not take from him advance interest or accrued interest, and you
shall fear your God. You shall not give him your silver for advance 37
interest, and for accrued interest you shall not give him your food. I am 38

---

30. *the house in the town that has a wall shall pass over irreversibly to its buyer.*
In an agrarian economy, real property in open fields was a permanent and
indispensable source of livelihood, whereas urban real estate was primarily a
residence rather than a source of income. As a result, it was not regarded as
inalienable property and might be permanently relinquished if the seller could
not scrape together funds to buy it back within a year.

35. *his hand buckle under you.* The verb here is more typically associated with
the foot, where it has the sense of "stumble." Because "hand" is a metonym for
"power," the idea is that the person has suffered something we would call economic collapse.
    he shall live under you. That is, he shall live under your authority or power,
with the understanding that you shall take reasonable steps to allow him to
subsist.

36. *advance interest or accrued interest.* There is some uncertainty as to the precise differentiation between these two kinds of interest. The former term,
neshekh, etymologically means a "bite"; the latter, *marbit*, comes from the verb
that means "to multiply."

the Lord your God Who brought you out of the land of Egypt to give
39 you the land of Canaan to be God for you. And should your brother
come to ruin under you and be sold to you, you shall not work him the
40 work of a slave. Like a resident hireling he shall be under you, till the
41 jubilee year he shall work under you, and he shall be released from
you, he and his children with him, and go back to his clan, and to his
42 fathers' holdings he shall go back. For they are My slaves, whom I
brought out of the land of Egypt. They shall not be sold in a slave's sale.
43 You shall not hold crushing sway over him, and you shall fear your God.
44 And your male slave and your slavegirl whom you may have from the
nations that are around you—from them you may buy a male slave
45 or a slavegirl. And also from the children of the settlers sojourning
among them—from them and from their clan that is with them you
may buy whom they have begotten in your land, and they shall become
46 a holding for you. And you shall hold them in estate for your children
after you to inherit a holding forever. Them you may work, but your
brothers the Israelites—no man shall hold crushing sway over his
47 brother. And should the hand of a sojourning settler with you attain
means when your brother comes to ruin under you and is sold to a
sojourning settler under you, or to an offshoot of a sojourner's clan,

---

42. *For they are My slaves.* The parodoxical consequence of the fact that the
Israelites, as God's covenanted people, have assumed the condition of God's
slaves is that they are prohibited from treating each other as slaves. The status
outlined here, with mandatory release in the jubilee year, is a kind of indentured servitude. In contrast, however, to the sabbatical laws in Exodus and
Deuteronomy, manumission occurs only in the jubilee, so the maximum
period of servitude is forty-nine years, not six.

43. *You shall not hold crushing sway.* This idiom combines two locutions for
exercising absolute authority, the verb *radah* (see Genesis 1:26, with the second comment there) and the adverb *befarekh*, which is used for the harsh
enslavement of the Hebrews by the Egyptians (see the comment on Exodus
1:13).

47. *hand . . . attain means.* The object "means" has been added in the translation for the sake of intelligibility, the idea being that the resident alien has
amassed the wherewithal to purchase an impoverished Israelite.

after being sold, he shall have a redemption; one of his brothers may 48
redeem him. Or his uncle or his cousin may redeem him or any of his 49
own close kin from his clan may redeem him, or his hand may attain
the means and he shall be redeemed. And he shall reckon with his 50
buyer from the year of his sale to him till the jubilee year, and the silver of his sale shall be according to the number of the years, like the
time of a hireling he shall be under the other. If there are still many 51
years, according to them he shall pay back his redemption from the silver of his purchase. And if few years are left till the jubilee year, he shall 52
reckon for him, according to its years he shall pay back its redemption.
Like a hireling from year to year he shall be under you. No one shall 53
hold crushing sway over him before your eyes. And if he is not 54
redeemed through any of these ways, he shall be released in the jubilee
year, he and his children with him. For Mine are the Israelites as slaves, 55
they are My slaves whom I brought out of the land of Egypt. I am the
LORD your God.'"

---

48. *after being sold, he shall have a redemption.* This system, which envisages
Israelite domination of the land, is sharply asymmetrical. An Israelite sold into
slavery to an alien has the permanent right, without temporal restriction, to
have his freedom bought for him, whereas the alien sold to an Israelite may
become a permanent slave.

50. *reckon . . . from the year of his sale . . . till the jubilee year.* The procedure
is precisely parallel to that for the redemption of property. Since in the fiftieth
year the owner would in any event be obliged to release the Israelite slave, the
closer the time of buying back his freedom is to the jubilee, the less his mar-
ket value.

like the time of a hireling he shall be under the other. The value of the slave
shall be computed as though he were a hireling. If a hireling is paid x amount
of silver per year, and there are twelve years remaining until the jubilee, his
value is $12x$ of silver. In the translation, "the other" is added for clarification:
the Hebrew, a bit cryptically, simply says "under him."

CHAPTER 26

¹ "You shall make you no idols nor set up a sculpted image or a sacred pillar for yourselves, and you shall not put a figured stone ² in your land to bow over it, for I am the Lord your God. My sabbaths you shall keep, and My sanctuary you shall revere. I am the Lord. ^{3, 4} If you go by My statutes and keep My commands and do them, I shall give you rains in their season, and the land will give its yield and the tree of ⁵ the field will give its fruit. And your threshing will overtake the vintage, and the vintage will overtake the sowing, and you will eat your bread to

---

1. *You shall make you no idols.* These words signal a shift in the discourse to summarizing generalization, for the language of this verse and the next, as Jacob Milgrom observes, invokes three of the first five injunctions of the Decalogue, reverting, one may say, to first principles. These verses, then, may be construed as an overture to the grand epilogue to the laws of Leviticus that swings into full momentum with verse 3, the point at which Jewish tradition marks the beginning of the textual unit for communal reading. What follows is a rhetorically powerful evocation (the style switching from legalistic to rhetorical) of the blessings that will ensue if Israel keeps the covenant and the ghastly curses if it violates the covenant. Both in its placement in the book after the code of laws and in its own formal organization and language, the enire passage closely parallels Deuteronomy 28.

figured stone. The etymology of the word rendered as "figured," *maskit*, has long been debated, though it might derive from a verb that means "to look." Milgrom plausibly suggests that the stone in question is a paving stone (hence "bow *over it*"), perhaps with a mosaic design, set in the floor of a sanctuary.

5. *your threshing will overtake the vintage.* This image of a kind of fast-forward of the agricultural cycle as a hyperbolic representation of fertility is used in Amos 9:13.

your bread. Once again, this is a synecdoche for food in general.

the full, and you will dwell securely in your land. And I shall set peace 6
in the land, and you will lie down with none to cause terror, and I shall
make evil beasts cease from the land, and no sword will pass through
your land. And you will pursue your enemies and they will fall before 7
you by the sword. And five of you will pursue a hundred, and a hundred 8
of you will pursue ten thousand, and your enemies will fall before you
by the sword. And I shall turn toward you and make you fruitful 9
and multiply you and fulfill My covenant with you. And you will eat old 10
grain long stored, and you will clear out the old for the new. And I shall 11
place My tabernacle in your midst, and I shall not loathe you. And I 12

---

6. *I shall make evil beasts cease from the land.* As both biblical narrative and
poetry repeatedly attest, in the early period of Israelite settlement predatory
beasts—in particular, lions and bears—were a threat to the population (the
young David became a skilled fighter by learning how to contend with them).
In the hyperbolic language of the passage, predators, like invading enemies,
will entirely vanish. As in the Prophets, hyperbole points the way to later messianic constructions of an end-time in history.

9. *I shall turn toward you.* The rabbis supply "in favor," an idea clearly implied
by the idiom as it stands.
   make you fruitful and multiply you. The phrasing explicitly invokes God's
injunction to humankind in the Priestly version of the creation (Genesis 1:28).

10. *you will eat old grain long stored.* This appears to be an allusion to the preceding chapter (25:20–22) in which God promises to provide Israel sufficient
grain in the sixth year of the sabbatical cycle to tide people over the seventh
and eighth year until they can harvest new crops, planted in the eighth year,
during the ninth. This detail, perhaps oddly specific in context, is evidently put
forth as a particular instance of God's special providential care for Israel. The
punctilious observance of the sabbatical year, as the section of curses makes
clear, is a paramount concern of this writer.

11. *tabernacle.* Milgrom argues that *mishkan* (from the root *sh-k-n,* "to dwell")
means "presence" here, though elsewhere it is always a cultic structure, and
the fact that Israel in the wilderness already has a tabernacle by no means prevents God from promising that He will establish a sanctuary within the land
which the people is about to enter.
   loathe. The present translation concurs with Milgrom that the multivalent
nefesh here means "throat" and hence the phrase *lo tigʿal nafshi ʾetkhem* means

shall go about in your midst, and I shall be God to you, and as for you,
13 you will be My people. I am the LORD your God Who brought you out
of the land of Egypt, from your being slaves to them, and I broke the
bars of your yoke and made you walk upright.

14,15 "'But if you do not heed Me and do not do all these commands, and if
you reject My statutes and if you loathe My laws, not doing all My
16 commands, voiding My covenant, I on My part will do this to you: I will
direct panic against you, consumption and fever wasting the eyes and
making the throat ache, and you shall sow your seed in vain, and your
17 enemies shall eat it. And I will set My face against you and you shall be
routed before your enemies, and your foes shall hold sway over
18 you, and you shall flee with none pursuing you. And if even with these

---

literally "my throat will not expel you," i.e., I will not retch in disgust over you,
loathe you. Though it might at first seem surprising that so strongly negative a
locution would be used in a blessing, albeit prefaced by a "not," it is chosen in
order to stand in counterpoint to Israel's loathing God in verses 14 and 43 and
God's loathing Israel in return for its miscreance.

13. *I broke the bars of your yoke and made you walk upright.* In Hebrew, as in
other languages, "yoke" is a general symbol for subjugation (an English word
which itself means "being under the yoke"). But here the dead metaphor is
resuscitated: the two bars of the yoke connecting to the crosspiece are broken,
and enslaved Israel, forced to go about (in the metaphor) pulling heavy burdens on all four like a beast, can now stand up straight.

15. *voiding My covenant.* The antithesis to God's fulfilling the covenant (verse 9).

16. *making the throat ache.* Since a particular body part seems required to
match the wasted eyes, it is highly likely that the sense here of *nefesh* is once
again "throat."

17. *I will set My face against you.* This is the antithesis of "I shall turn toward
you" in verse 9. Throughout this section of curses, the translation uses "will"
in the first person and "shall" in the second because the modal force of the language seems more emphatic in the curses than in the blessings.

you do not heed Me, I will go on to chastise you sevenfold more for
your offenses. And I will break the pride of your strength and make your   19
heavens like iron and your earth like bronze. And your power shall be   20
spent in vain, and your land shall not give its yield, and the tree of
the land shall not give its fruit. And if you come in encounter against   21
Me and do not want to heed Me, I will go on with blows against you
sevenfold for your offenses. And I will unleash the beasts of the field   22
among you and they shall bereave you of your children and cut off
your cattle and diminish you, and your roads will be desolate. And if   23
through these you do not take chastisement by Me, and you come in
encounter against Me, I on My part will come in encounter against you   24
and I Myself will strike you sevenfold for your offenses. And I will bring   25
against you the avenging sword of the covenant's vengeance, and

---

19. *your heavens like iron and your earth like bronze.* This grim simile is a common feature in Assyrian treaty curses and is equally exploited in Deuteronomy
28:23.

21. *come in encounter against Me.* The exact origin of this phrase, unique to
this passage, *telkhu ʿimi beqeri,* is in dispute, though it obviously means something like "confront," "dispute," "rebel against." The most plausible etymology
of the noun *qeri* is from the verbal stem *q-r-h,* suggesting "encounter," "hap-
pening upon," or even "mishap," and so this translation uses the phrase "in
encounter" (which of course can also mean "duel"), preserving what may be a
slight idiomatic oddness in the Hebrew.

22. *your roads will be desolate.* If one pauses to reflect, this is a haunting image
(and one to which several of the Prophets revert): the once teeming highways
of the land will be bleak and empty after the devastation of the populace.

23. *And if through these you do not take chastisement.* The section of curses is
structured as a sequence of downward spiraling disasters. After each set of
punishing blows, God, as it were, pauses to see if Israel will correct its ways.
When this does not happen, He intensifies the catastrophes, which will culminate in exile.

25. *the avenging sword of the covenant's vengeance.* A covenant is both a promise
and a threat. From those who violate their covenantal obligations, vengeance
is exacted.

you shall gather into your towns, and I will send pestilence in your
26 midst, and you shall be given into an enemy's hands. When I break your
staff of bread, ten women shall bake your bread in one oven and dole
27 out your bread by weight, and you shall eat and not be sated. And if
despite this you do not heed Me and you come in encounter against
28 Me, I will come against you in wrathful encounter and I on My part
29 will chastise you sevenfold for your offenses. And you shall eat the flesh
30 of your sons, and the flesh of your daughters you shall eat. And I will
destroy your cult-places and cut off your incense stands, and I will put
your corpses on top of the corpses of your fetishes, and I will loathe
31 you. And I will turn your towns into ruins and lay waste your sanctuar-
32 ies, and I will not smell your fragrant odors. And I Myself will lay waste
to the land, and all your enemies who settle in it shall be appalled

---

28. *against you in wrathful encounter.* Ominously, God now adds the component of wrath, *ḥamah*, to the reiterated noun *qeri*, suggesting that divine hostility is now ready to trump Israelite hostility in a climactic set of disasters.

29. *you shall eat the flesh of your sons.* On this grisly detail, see the comment
on Deuteronomy 28:53. The verse is arranged as a neat chiasm—eat . . . flesh
of your sons . . . flesh of your daughters . . . eat—as a rhetorical means of
hammering home the horrific images.

30. *your corpses . . . the corpses of your fetishes.* Though logically fetishes cannot have corpses, not ever having been alive, the same word is pointedly
repeated, suggesting a bitter equation between the inert, heaped-up bodies of
the fetish worshippers and the inert, lifeless fetishes, which have been
"corpses" all along, and now deprived of worshippers, are all the more con-
spicuously sheer dead matter.

31. *sanctuaries.* The plural surely suggests that in this text a single central sanctuary is not presupposed.
    I will not smell your fragrant odors. The reference is to the fragrance of the
sacrifice burned on the altar and thought, at least in the pre-Israelite period,
to be a pleasing aroma in the nostrils of the gods. By the time of the writing of
this text, it may have become a dead metaphor simply meaning, I will not look
with favor on your sacrifices.

by it. And you I will scatter among the nations, and I will unsheath the 33
sword after you, and your land shall be a desolation, and your towns a
ruin. Then shall the land expiate its sabbath years all the days it is des- 34
olate while you are in the land of your enemies, then shall the land
keep a sabbath and expiate its sabbath years. All the days of the deso- 35
lation it shall keep a sabbath for not having kept your sabbath years
when you dwelled there. And those left among you, I will bring faint- 36
ness into their hearts in the lands of their enemies, and the sound of a
driven leaf shall pursue them, and they shall flee as in flight from the
sword and fall, with none pursuing. And each man shall stumble 37
against his brother as before the sword, with none pursuing, and there
shall be no standing up for you in the face of your enemies. And you 38
shall perish among the nations, and the land of your enemies shall consume you. And those left among you shall rot in their guilt in the lands 39
of your enemies, and also in the guilt of their fathers with them they
shall rot. And they shall confess their guilt and the guilt of their 40
fathers, in their betraying My trust, and also in their coming in

---

34. *Then shall the land expiate its sabbath years*. These words, and those of the
next two verses, reflect both a logic of restitution and mordant satiric irony.
The people has violated its obligation to keep the sabbatical year. Now, as the
depopulated land lies fallow year after year, all those violated sabbaths will be
made up for, numerically. But this is also a bitterly mocking image of the land,
violently divested of its Israelite inhabitants, compelled by grim history to keep
on its own a whole series of sabbatical years, in which nothing is sown or
reaped.

37. *there shall be no standing up for you in the face of your enemies*. This is a
vivid antithesis to "made you walk upright" in verse 13. The two Hebrew words
in question derive from the same root—"upright," *qomemiyut* and "standing
up," *tequmah*.

39. *guilt*. The Hebrew ʿ*awon* means "iniquity" (or "crime") and by causal extension, both "guilt" and "punishment."

41 encounter against Me. I on My part will come in encounter against
them and bring them into the land of their enemies, and then shall
their uncircumcised heart be humbled, and then shall they expiate
42 their guilt. And I will remember My covenant with Jacob and also My
covenant with Isaac and also My covenant with Abraham I will remem-
43 ber, and the land I will remember. And the land shall be forsaken of
them, and it shall expiate its sabbath years when it is desolate of them,
and they shall expiate their guilt, by very reason that they have rejected
44 My laws, and My statutes they have loathed. Yet even this, too—when
they are in the land of their enemies I will not reject them and I will
not loathe them to put an end to them, to void My covenant with them,
45 for I am the LORD their God. And I will remember for them the
covenant of the first ones whom I brought out from the land of Egypt
before the eyes of the nations to be God for them, I am the LORD.'"

46 These are the statutes and the laws and the teachings that the LORD set
out between Himself and the Israelites on Mount Sinai through the
hand of Moses.

---

41. *their uncircumcised heart*. This is a recurrent metaphor for obtuseness or
callousness. See the comment on Deuteronomy 10:16.

44. *My covenant*. The envelope structure formed by the reiteration of this key
term at the beginning and the end of the entire section is meant as a reassurance. God will respond in terrible wrath to Israel's dereliction, but the commitment to the covenant He expressed at the beginning will in the end lead
Him to rescue Israel from exile as He once rescued them from Egyptian slavery.

45. *the covenant of the first ones*. This somewhat opaque phrase refers to the
founding generation that stood at Sinai, but its very vagueness allows a certain
elision between these "first ones" and the patriarchs, with whom God initially
sealed the covenant that has just been mentioned.

46. *between Himself and the Israelites*. This locution of betweenness, in the
summation at the end of all the preceding laws and statutes, followed by this
chapter's catalogue of blessings and curses, is an indication of the two-sided
contractual nature of God's covenant with Israel that is repeatedly invoked in
the blessings and the curses.

CHAPTER 27

And the LORD spoke to Moses, saying, "Speak to the Israelites, and   1,2
you shall say to them, 'Should a man set aside a votive offering in
the value fixed for persons to the LORD, the value for the male   3

---

2. *Should a man set aside a votive offering.* This miscellany of laws seems, by
modern lights, an odd way to conclude a book. Interpretive attempts have
been made to rescue it as a thematically appropriate conclusion, but none is
altogether persuasive. This final chapter is best regarded as an appendix to
Leviticus focusing on a variety of laws pertaining to voluntary offerings and
taxed obligations to the sanctuary. Perhaps these monetary issues, necessary
for the maintenance of the sanctuary but not altogether agreeable for the audience of the book to contemplate, were deliberately tacked on at the very end

in the value fixed. The Hebrew term, at least as it has been vocalized by the
Masoretes, is *be'erkekha*, which means literally "in your value/valuation." It
seems likely (though there are other philological solutions) that this is a colloquial term—"as you would evaluate"—that became frozen and lexicalized as
an abstraction with the general sense of "assessed value." The verb used in
verse 8 and elsewhere for the priest's assessment of monetary value is cognate
with this noun and hence is translated here as "evaluate" in order to make that
connection clear.

the value fixed for. What follows is a table of fixed values in weights of silver (the meaning of "shekel"), the valuation being strictly according to age and
gender with no regard to the social or economic standing of the person. The
system of valuation, as Baruch Levine plausibly contends, reflects the potential economic productivity of a person of the stipulated age bracket and gender. A male has greater potential productivity than a female, a mature person
greater productivity than a child or than an aged person. The idea of setting
the amount of a votive offering of silver as the equivalent of the value of a person has symbolic and psychological force, for it expresses the idea that the
votary is offering to the sanctuary an equivalent of himself or herself.

from twenty years old up to sixty years old shall be fifty shekels by the

4 sanctuary shekel. And if it is for a female, the value shall be thirty

5 shekels. And if it is for someone from five years old up to twenty years old, the value shall be twenty shekels for the male and for the female

6 ten shekels. And if it is for someone from a month old up to a year, the value of the male shall be five silver shekels and for the female the

7 value three silver shekels. And if it is for someone from sixty years old and above, if a male, the value shall be fifteen shekels and for the

8 female ten shekels. And if one should become too impoverished to meet the value, he shall be set before the priest, and the priest shall evaluate him, according to what the hand of the votary can attain shall

9 the priest evaluate him. And if it is an animal that is brought forward as an offering to the Lord, any of which may be given to the Lord shall

10 be holy. He shall not exchange it and shall not replace it, whether good for bad or bad for good, and if in fact he replaces one animal for

11 another, both it and its replacement shall be holy. And if it is any unclean animal that is not to be brought forward as an offering to the

---

8. *if one should become too impoverished*. The verb, which in different contexts has been translated "fall to ruin," indicates a process of steep economic decline. What it logically means here is that the person in question made the vow to give the offering of his fixed value in silver but then fell on hard times, so that he now does not have the wherewithal to pay his pledge. The priest is therefore enjoined to assess the person's economic state and impose whatever limited amount it seems reasonable for him to pay.

9. *any of which may be given to the Lord*. That is, any of the specified kinds of animals acceptable as sacrifices. Such an animal, once pledged by the votary, becomes "holy," to be offered as a sacrifice with the greater part of its flesh reserved for the exclusive consumption of the priests.

10. *whether good for bad or bad for good*. The particular animal that the votary has pledged must be offered, and the substitution of, say a fatter animal for a scrawny one or the other way around, is not allowed.

11. *any unclean animal*. The animal in this case, which could not be used as a sacrifice, serves as a unit of value. Though Jacob Milgrom argues that unclean animals—for example, donkeys—could be used as beasts of burden in the

LORD, the animal shall be set before the priest. And the priest shall ₁₂
evaluate it, whether good or bad, according to the priest's valuation,
thus shall it be. And if he in fact redeems it, he shall add a fifth to its ₁₃
value. And should a man consecrate his house as holy to the LORD, the ₁₄
priest shall evaluate it, whether good or bad. As the priest evaluates it,
thus shall it stand. And if he who consecrates his house redeems it, he ₁₅
shall add a fifth to the silver of its value, and it shall be his. And if a ₁₆
man should consecrate anything from a field of his holding to the
LORD, its value shall be according to its seed—a *homer* of barley seed
at fifty silver shekels. If he consecrates his field from the jubilee year, ₁₇
it shall stand according to its value. And if he consecrates his field after ₁₈
the jubilee, the priest shall reckon the silver for him according to the
remaining years until the jubilee, and these shall be deducted from its
value. And if he who consecrates the field shall in fact redeem it, he ₁₉

---

sanctuary, the stipulation here of the priest's function as an assessor of value
suggests that what the law has in view is the equivalent in silver of the animal.

12. *whether good or bad.* This means, of course, whether high or low, but the
valuation itself is set according to the health, age, size, and so forth ("good or
bad") of the animal.

13. *if he in fact redeems it.* The votary may change his mind and decide he
wants to hang on to this particular animal. In that case, he is obliged to pay a
20 percent surcharge on top of its assessed value in silver.

16. *according to its seed.* That is, according to its capacity to be planted with a
particular quantity of seed.
      homer. The *homer*, derived from *hamor*, "donkey" (a load that a donkey can
carry), is a large unit of dry measure, well above a hundred liters.

17. *from the jubilee year, it shall stand according to its value.* This accords with
the preceding laws about the redemption of slaves and real property in relation
to the jubilee cycle. Consecration at the time of the jubilee would produce the
maximal value. Because the land is part of the person's ancestral, tribal holding, it must revert to him at the next jubilee.

20 shall add a fifth to its value, and it shall become his. And if he does not redeem the field and had sold the field to another man, it may no 21 longer be redeemed. And the field when it is released in the jubilee shall be holy to the LORD, as a proscribed field. His holding shall 22 become the priest's. And if he consecrates a field he has purchased, 23 which is not from the field of his holding, to the LORD, the priest shall reckon for him the amount of the value until the jubilee year, and he 24 shall give the value on that day, a sacred donation to the LORD. In the jubilee year the field shall revert to him from whom it was bought, to 25 him who has the holding of the land. And every valuation shall be by 26 the sanctuary shekel, twenty *gerahs* the shekel shall be. But the first-born of the animals, which is marked firstborn to the LORD, no man 27 shall consecrate. Whether ox or sheep, it is the LORD's. And if it is of an unclean animal, he shall ransom it by its value and add a fifth, and 28 if it is not redeemed, it shall be sold at its value. But anything pro-scribed, that a man may proscribe for the LORD, of anything he has, whether of humans or animals or of the field of his holding, shall not

---

20. *and had sold the field to another man*. The Hebrew is a little cryptic. Mil-grom, following Menahem Haran, plausibly argues that the person has first sold the field, which would ordinarily revert to him in the jubilee, and then consecrated it to the priests. The consecration following the sale (which was in effect no more than a lease) suggests that he is renouncing his right to have the property revert to him in the jubilee, as the next verse makes explicit.

22. *a field he has purchased*. This is a piece of property that is not part of his ancestral holding and hence need not revert to him in the jubilee.

25. *the sanctuary shekel*. As elsewhere, this phrase indicates a shekel that has a greater weight than the mercantile shekel.

26. *But the firstborn of the animals . . . no man shall consecrate*. Since the first-born in any case belongs to the deity, its owner is in no position to consecrate it as though it were his voluntary offering.

28. *anything proscribed*. The Hebrew term is *ḥerem*, which in martial contexts means the "ban" of total destruction to which a conquered population and its possessions are subjected. In the present context, a more pacific kind of *ḥerem* is intended: whatever a person irrevocably divests himself of and sets aside to

be sold and shall not be redeemed. Anything proscribed is holy of holies
to the Lord. No human who has been proscribed may be ransomed.   29
He is doomed to die. And all tithes of the land, of the seed of the land,   30
of the fruit of the land, are the Lord's, holy to the Lord. And if a man   31
in fact redeems something of his tithe, he shall add a fifth to it. And all   32
tithes of cattle and sheep, anything that passes under the staff, the
tenth shall be holy to the Lord. He shall not look out for good or bad,   33
and he shall not replace it. And if in fact he replaces it, it or its replacement shall be holy, it shall not be redeemed.'"

---

be dedicated to God. Thus "humans" (*'adam*) here must mean the one category of human beings that can become permanent property, non-Israelite
slaves, and their fate in this instance is not destruction but transfer to the
jurisdiction of the sanctuary. Thus three categories of property are listed:
slaves, livestock, and land.

29. *No human who has been proscribed*. In this case, the reference is by no
means limited to slaves, and the *ḥerem* referred to is the lethal kind. One clear-
cut example would be a prisoner taken from a conquered town that was to be
subjected to the ban of total destruction (like Agag the Amalekite king in 1
Samuel 15). The ban cannot be revoked, and hence the proscribed person is
"doomed to die." The appropriateness in this instance of the verb "ransomed,"
instead of the reiterated "redeemed" is clear.

32. *anything that passes under the staff*. The staff in question is obviously the
shepherd's staff, and the phrase as a whole, which appears with variations elsewhere in the Bible, is a kenning for herded animals. Both medieval and modern commentators, putting this phrase together with the next verse, have
understood the law to be that the shepherd actually counts the animals passing under his staff, marking every tenth one to be tithed to the sanctuary. As
the next verse makes clear, the tenth animal, whether it is robust or meager,
cannot be replaced by another creature, for better or for worse.

34 These are the commands that the LORD charged Moses for the Israelites on Mount Sinai.

---

34. *These are the commands that the LORD charged Moses.* Most commentators see this statement of closure as an explicit tie-in with the formal conclusion (21:46) of the previous textual unit, "These are the statutes and the laws and the teachings that the LORD set out between Himself and the Israelites on Mount Sinai through the hand of Moses." Since this chapter does not deal with covenantal material, the language of betweenness is omitted, and "commands" may have been introduced as a term that comprises the others. But as an editorial decision, this final verse equally points back to the whole Book of Leviticus and forward to the Book of Numbers. Leviticus begins not exactly on Mount Sinai but at the Tent of Meeting, after the Sinai epiphany and presumably still in spatial proximity to the mountain. The opening words of Numbers remind us of the link between God's revelation on Sinai and His further commands to Moses from the Tent of Meeting, locating God's speech to Moses "in the Wilderness of Sinai in the Tent of Meeting."

NUMBERS

INTRODUCTION

The Book of Numbers is in some respects the most miscellaneous of the five books of the Torah, but it also includes a series of uniquely fascinating episodes that exhibit distinctive literary features. The first ten chapters are, by scholarly consensus, the work of Priestly writers and in a certain sense constitute a continuation of Leviticus. The four initial chapters are taken up with a detailed tabulation of the census of the tribes conducted in the wilderness and are the warrant for the prevalent English title of the book, which goes back to the Vulgate and the Septuagint and is also reflected in a designation appearing in rabbinic sources, *homesh hapequdim*, "the Fifth [that is, one book of the Five] of Reckonings." (The generally used Hebrew title, *Bemidbar*, which is simply the first common noun in the text, means "in the wilderness.") The Priestly writers' enthusiasm for pageantry is manifested in this great initial roll call of the tribes, which is picked up in the review of the order of their march through the wilderness in chapter 10 and in the elaborately repetitive rehearsal of the gifts of the twelve chieftains in chapter 7. In between these, we are given laws intended to protect cultic purity in chapters 5 and 6, with considerable attention devoted to the trial by ordeal of the wife suspected of adultery and to the nazirite's vows of abstinence, and then the dedication of the Levites and the ritual of the Passover offering in chapters 8 and 9.

The book returns to the narrative impulse that marks the first half of Exodus—indeed, with certain pronounced parallels to episodes in Exodus—in chapter 11. Although some legal material, in large part concerned with the cult, will be introduced along the way, together with an additional chapter (26) devoted to census, narrative predominates to the end of the book. The Israelites, Sinai behind them, are on the

move, edging toward the prospect of the conquest of the land that is
first engaged here in the reconnaissance mission of the twelve spies
(chapters 13 and 14) and that will become imminent, forty years later
in narrated time, with actual combat against kingdoms to the east of
the Jordan, from chapter 21 onward. We are repeatedly reminded
of the passing of generations as the story carries us to the border of
the promised land. After the incident of the spies, the entire adult generation that came out of Egypt is fated to die before the promise of the
land can be realized. Moses, seconded by Aaron, fails the test of trust-
ing in God's provident intervention when he strikes the rock on his own
initiative in order to bring forth water (chapter 20), and as a result, he,
too, will not be privileged to enter the land. Miriam and Aaron die;
Moses's impending death on Mount Nebo is announced by God; and
Joshua is lined up to succeed him as leader (the logical narrative continuation of this book being the Book of Joshua).

But if Israel is on the move from chapter 11 to the end, it must be
said that this text associates movement with trouble. After the initial
choreographed procession of the teeming tribes, each arrayed in orderly
fashion around its own banner, we get repeated representations of a
motley crew of malcontents—the Hebrew pejorative *'asafsuf*, "riffraff"
(11:4), is aptly invoked to characterize them—a mob churning with
complaints and frustrated desires, restive under Moses's leadership, fed
up with the hardships of life in the wilderness, and nostalgic for the
material comforts of life in Egypt.

The incidents of Taberah (Conflagration) and Kibroth-Hattaavah
(the Graves of Desire) reported in chapter 11 establish a model for
much of what follows. The narrative motifs deployed, which first
appeared in Exodus and now recur in a whole series of episodes here
in Numbers, constitute such a fixed sequence that one is tempted to
say they qualify as a type-scene, like the type-scenes of betrothal and
annunciation in Genesis and Exodus. The one notable difference, however, from type-scene is that instead of the same scene, with significant
variations, featuring different characters, we have a repetition of
the same scene involving the same actors—Israel, Moses, and God—
manifesting a certain intensification more than significant variation
from one recurrence to the next. The scheme of the recurrent scene of
"murmuring" or complaint is as follows: the people bitterly protests its

misery in the wilderness or Moses's leadership or both; God's wrath
flares against the people, expressing itself in some sort of "scourge" that
decimates the Israelite ranks; Moses intercedes—in two instances,
after God actually threatens to wipe out the entire people and to begin
anew with Moses—and He relents. The two most salient episodes of
Israelite recalcitrance are the story of the spies, who report the fabulous bounty of the land but despair of conquering it, then seek to storm
it without divine authorization, and the story of the mutiny led by
Korah (respectively, chapters 13–14 and 16–17). Restiveness under
Moses's rule is so epidemic that even Miriam and Aaron are infected
by it, at one point resentfully rebelling against their brother (chapter
12). One suspects that all these repetitions of the scene of murmuring
are introduced because the writers conceived it as a paradigm for the
subsequent history of Israel: recurrent resentment of God's rule and
of the authority of His legitimate leaders, chronic attraction to objects
of base material desire, fearfulness, divisiveness, and the consequences
of national disaster brought about, in the view of the biblical writers, by
this whole pattern of constant backsliding.

For all the prominence of these scenes of rebellion, Numbers offers
a kind of dialectical counterimage to the representation of Israel as an
obstinate and refractory mob. This generation that cannot free itself
from the slave mentality it brought with it from Egypt also constitutes
the beginnings of a people meant to realize a grand historical destiny.
Imagery and acts of martial prowess, reinforced by sheer numbers that
daunt the other nations of the region, and more pacific images of well
watered vegetation luxuriantly burgeoning, are associated with the
assembled tribes of Israel. Many of these terms are introduced in
poetry, and it is the striking poetic insets in Numbers that account for
much of its distinctive quality among books of the Bible. The more typical convention of biblical literature is to insert a relatively long poem
at the end of a book, as happens with the Blessing of Jacob at the end
of Genesis and with the Song of Moses at the end of Deuteronomy, or
after a climactic narrative event, as in the instance of the Song of the
Sea in Exodus. Here, however, we are given snippets of what look like
very ancient Hebrew poems at unpredictable points in the narrative,
together with one relatively extended sequence of poems (it is not really
a single continuous poem), Balaam's oracles, a series of prophecies

about Israel's future that is pronounced, unlike any other biblical poetry, by a non-Israelite soothsayer.

It is worth reflecting on the ancient character of the poems and what role that plays in the narrative panorama of Numbers. The first of these (if one excepts God's oracular pronouncement in 12:6–8 to Miriam and Aaron on Moses's unique status as prophet) is a highly fragmentary quotation from a vanished work, the Book of the Battles of YHWH: "Against Waheb in a whirlwind and the wadis of Amon, /and the cascade of the wadis that turns down toward Ar's dwelling, / and clings to Moab's border" (21:14–15). These opaque lines are followed, two verses on, by the Song of the Well: "Rise up, O Well! / Sing out to it. / Well, that captains dug, / the people's nobles delved it, / with a scepter, with their walking stick." No one has offered a convincing explanation of what this is all about, and it is an interesting question why such scraps of old verse should have been incorporated in the Book of Numbers. The French literary critic Roland Barthes, in a much discussed essay, once provocatively claimed that many details of material reality in realist fiction are introduced not to signify anything or to serve any function of plot or theme but solely to invoke the category of the real, to produce a "reality effect." In a roughly analogous way, I would like to propose that these fragments of old poems are introduced into the narrative of Numbers at least in part in order to produce an "antiquity effect." There is no way of knowing whether Hebrew audiences in, say, the ninth century B.C.E. were still familiar with the Book of the Battles of YHWH, or whether it was already a lost work, surviving only in remembered fragments or perhaps tag-ends of manuscript. The point, in any case, of the fragmentary quotation, triggered in context by the geographical references, would have been to evoke a distant moment in early Israelite history, suffused with the aura of the historical era of the story's setting in the thirteenth century B.C.E. One may surmise that the Book of the Battles of YHWH was deemed too anthropomorphic or too mythological in character to be included in the canon that was evolving, perhaps (to judge by the title) featuring a warrior god wielding lightning as his weapon, as in some of the Psalms and in Ugaritic poetry, leading the assault against Israel's enemies. The enigmatic lines cited from this ancient text conjure up an era of fierce martial energies when Israel first established itself among the peoples of Canaan as a conquering nation. (The early-twentieth-century Hebrew poet Saul Tchernikhovsky would capture something of the spirit of this era by referring to the primordial deity of the Hebrews in a programmatically Nietzschean poem as "El, god of the conquerors of Canaan in a whirlwind.") The Song of the Well might possibly recall a particular incident of discovering water in the wilderness, but, more prominently, it evokes a whole nomadic way of life in the desert, and in its extreme brevity, it looks more like the refrain of an old song than the complete text.

Later in chapter 21 (verses 27–30), a third ancient poem is introduced, beginning with the words "Come to Heshbon, let it stand built, / may the city of Sihon be unshaken." What is striking about this particular text is that it is explicitly presented as coming from a non-Israelite source: it is said to be what the "rhapsodes" (*moshlim*) say; these would be West Semitic, possibly trans-Jordanian, bards of unspecified national identity, and the burden of their song is a celebration of the predominance of the Amorite city Heshbon over Moab that has no direct connection with Israelite history. These lines (which become somewhat obscure toward the end) are either a Hebrew translation of a foreign poem or a citation of a poem from a language so closely cognate with Hebrew that it required only minor adaptation. Given the foreign provenance of the poem, it is an especially striking instance of an antiquity effect, taking the story of the approach of the Israelite masses to the eastern border of Canaan back to a half-remembered time when many kingdoms rose and fell in this region.

The brilliant centerpiece among these citations of archaic poetry is the oracles of Balaam (chapters 23 and 24), which follow the story of Balaam and his she-ass, tracing a cunning network of analogies to it. That story has often been characterized as a folktale, and there are no other instances of talking animals in the historical narratives of the Bible (the only other candidate, the serpent in the Garden story, belongs to the primeval and hence more mythological phase of biblical literature). Especially because, according to prevalent preconceptions, there is no humor in the Bible, it should be noted that this story is quite funny. The humor serves the purposes of a monotheistic satire of pagan notions of the professional seer with independent powers to curse or bless: Balaam the celebrated visionary cannot see the sword-wielding divine messenger who is plainly visible to his ass, and he is reduced to spluttering frustration, finally engaging in an angry argument with his beast of burden. Balaam then plays the role of the ass whose eyes, and mouth, are opened by God vis-à-vis the thrice frustrated, and understandably fuming, Moabite king Balak, to whom Balaam's previous role as imperceptive satiric butt is assigned in this second story.

The very figure of Balaam is part of the antiquity effect cultivated in this narrative. This selfsame soothsayer is the principal character in an inscription discovered in Jordan in 1967, written in a language that is a close relative of Hebrew, with Aramaic elements, and dating from the eighth century B.C.E.; and so we may infer that he was known as a seer of fabled powers in the traditions of this region, perhaps going back to tales told centuries earlier. His appearance in Numbers, pronouncing blessings on Israel in lofty poetic language, sets this story of Israel on the threshold of its entrance into the land in the large context of the archaic traditions of the region. It is an Aramean prophet, summoned from "the eastern mountains," who beholds from a promontory the vast array of the tribes of Israel (a vivid narrative realization of the dry census figures at the beginning of the book) and projects spatial into temporal vision, prophesying the future greatness of Israel:

> [F]rom the top of the crags do I see them
>   and from the hills do I gaze on them.
> Look, a people that dwells apart,
>   amongst nations it is not reckoned.
> Who has numbered the dust of Jacob,
>   who counted the issue of Israel? (23:9–10)

The archaic coloration of Balaam's oracles is nicely conveyed through the names he uses for the deity. Balaam in the poems refers to God once, near the beginning of the first oracle, as YHWH, but then God is variously invoked as El, Shaddai, and Elyon, all names of deities from the Canaanite pantheon that have been, one might say, co-opted by the Hebrew monotheists. Balaam expresses his own identity as a seer schooled in the lore of West Semitic polytheists by using animal imagery for God (as the Psalms do), representing Him charging against Israel's enemies with "wild ox's antlers." And yet, this pagan prophet, both through the ingenious turns of the story and through the poetry that is put in his mouth, has been enlisted in the monotheistic cause. All prophetic utterance, all curses and blessings, come from YHWH alone: "What can I hex that El has not hexed, / and what can I doom that the LORD has not doomed?" (23:8). His prophecies about Israel move from sheer multitudinousness to martial fierceness—the people ravening like a lion, smashing the bones and crushing the loins of its foes—to a pacific vision of palm groves and gardens by a river followed by concluding reprise of martial imagery. Instructively, the sequence of oracles ends not with Israel but with a rapid panorama, couched in rather obscure vatic language, of sundry nations of the region plummeting to destruction. Once again, this chronicle of Israel poised for the conquest of the land God has promised it is set into an ancient world, whether remembered or reinvented through scraps of inherited literary tradition, where kingdoms rise and fall in the long reaches of history.

In the end, there are complementary parallels, counterpoints, and also strong tensions between the Priestly sections of the Book of Numbers and its narrative and poetic passages. The Priestly writers above all seek to establish a vision of order and stability—through the intricate system of laws regulating personal behavior and cultic practice, through the long lists of numbers and names, through the representation of the grand order of march of the tribes. They aspire to an ideal of Israel as a holy people, bound by Priestly ordinances, that is altogether unique among the nations of the earth. The poetry Balaam utters also registers the idea of "a people that dwells apart," yet his oracles, like the surrounding narrative, clearly see Israel as part of the unfolding history of the whole region. This is a theater in which great kingdoms have come and gone, long before the arrival of Israel: the biblical self-perception of the Israelite nation as a latecomer to the historical scene is palpably present here. Now, at this reported moment in the thirteenth century B.C.E., it is Israel's turn to establish itself through conquest. As the concluding chapters of Numbers take up issues of inheritance and the division of the land, and as the departure of Moses is announced, the narrative has prepared us for the defining moment of the crossing of the Jordan, with Joshua in command.

CHAPTER 1

   nd the Lord spoke to Moses in the Wilderness of Sinai in the   1
   Tent of Meeting on the first of the second month in the second
   year of their going out from Egypt, saying, "Count the heads of all   2
the community of the Israelites by their clans, by their fathers' houses,

---

1. *in the Wilderness*. The Hebrew word represented by these three English
words—*bemidbar*—is the prevalent Hebrew title for the book. Numbers, the
topical title, derives from the Greek rubric as well as a Hebrew equivalent that
appears in the Talmud. In this case, the convention of selecting the first significant word in the text as title fortuitously produces an apt characterization
of the book, which is all about Wilderness wanderings and trials and upheavals
in that liminal space for the nation in the making.

   on the first of the second month in the second year. The Tabernacle was completed one month earlier (Exodus 40:17). Now, after the Priestly legislation
that constitutes the Book of Leviticus, and which is not tied to a specific date,
the narrative turns its attention outward from the sanctuary to the people and
to the organization of a census.

2. *Count the heads*. Literally, "lift the heads." The word for "head" at the end
of this verse is not, as here, *ro'sh* but *gulgolet*, which means "poll" and also
"skull."

   their fathers' houses. The Hebrew *beyt 'av*, which some render as "patriarchal
house," designates a social unit considerably larger than a nuclear family. The
"clan" (*mishpaḥah*) would involve a large extended family, or several households of kinfolk. The most reasonable inference—there are differing opinions—is that the *beyt 'av* encompassed a number of clans, as verse 4 here may
suggest, since the head of a *beyt 'av* is chosen as representative of the whole
tribe.

3   according to the number of names, every male by their heads. From
     twenty years old and up, everyone who goes out in the army in Israel,
4   you shall reckon them by their battalions, you and Aaron. And with you
     let there be a man from each tribe, each man the head of his father's
5   house. And these are the names of the men who will stand with you:
6   for Reuben, Elizur son of Shedeur; for Simeon, Shelumiel son of Zur-
7,8 ishaddai; for Judah, Nahshon son of Amminadab; for Issachar,
9,10 Nethanel son of Zuar; for Zebulun, Eliab son of Helon; for the sons of
     Joseph—for Ephraim, Elishama son of Ammihud, for Manasseh,
11,12 Gamaliel son of Pedahzur; for Benjamim, Abidan son of Gideoni; for
13,14 Dan, Ahiezer son of Ammishaddai; for Asher, Pagiel son of Ochran; for

---

3. *everyone who goes out in the army.* That is, every male eligible for military
service. The purpose of the census here is to organize a general military conscription. The journeying from Sinai through the wilderness toward the
promised land, about to be initiated after the completion of the Tabernacle in
the second year of the Exodus, will necessarily be an extended military campaign. Thus, the Israelite males are to be counted "by their battalions."

you shall reckon them. The root *p-q-d*, which is used again and again in
connection with the census, is an all-purpose verb that variously means
"to muster," "to tally," "to single out," "to pay special attention to," "to requite,"
"to appoint," and more. The first two of these meanings are the ones strictly
relevant to our passage. This translation uses "reckon" precisely because it is
an English term not restricted to one semantic field and thus able to suggest
something of the overlapping senses of the Hebrew verb.

5. *And these are the names.* Jacob Milgrom notes that scarcely any of the names
of the tribal representatives appear elsewhere in biblical literature and that
none shows the theophoric suffix *yah.* He infers from this that the list reflects
an authentically ancient tradition.

10. *for the sons of Joseph.* In keeping with Jacob's deathbed promise to Joseph
that Joseph's two sons would be as his own sons, the descendants of the two
sons of Joseph are given tribal status (and are elsewhere designated as "half-
tribes"). Since the tribe of Levi will not be included in the census or the conscription, this device preserves the number of twelve for the tribes.

Gad, Eliasaph son of Deuel; for Naphtali, Ahira son of Enan. These 15,16
are the ones called from the community, chieftains of their fathers'
tribes, they are the heads of the kin-groups of Israel." And Moses, and 17
Aaron with him, took these men who had been marked out by name.
And all the community they assembled on the first of the second 18
month, and they were affiliated by their clans, by their fathers' houses
according to the number of names, from twenty years old and up, by
their heads, as the LORD had charged Moses, and he made a reckoning 19
of them in the Wilderness of Sinai.

And the sons of Reuben, Israel's firstborn, those born to them by their 20
clans, by their fathers' houses, according to the number of names, by
their heads, every male from twenty years old and up, everyone who
went out in the army, their reckoning for the tribe of Reuben, forty-six 21
thousand five hundred. For the sons of Simeon, those born to them by 22
their clans, by their fathers' houses according to the number of names,
by their heads, every male from twenty years old and up, everyone who
went out in the army, their reckoning for the tribe of Simeon, fifty-nine 23
thousand three hundred. For the sons of Gad, those born to them by 24
their clans, by their fathers' houses, according to the number of names,
from twenty years old and up, everyone who went out in the army, their 25
reckoning for the tribe of Gad, forty-five thousand six hundred and fifty.
For the sons of Judah, those born to them by their clans, by their 26
fathers' houses according to the number of names, from twenty years

---

16. *kin-groups*. Although there is scholarly consensus that the Hebrew term
'elef (in numerical contexts, "a thousand") indicates a group of kinfolk, the size
and configuration of the group and its relation to father's house and clan
remain uncertain.

18. *affiliated*. The unusual Hebrew verb, a reflexive form of the root that means
"to give birth," is interpreted by Rashi, and confirmed by modern scholarship,
to have the sense of sorting out birth lines or pedigrees.

21. *their reckoning*. Although the Hebrew *pequdim* may look like a past participle ("those reckoned"), this form is also used to express an abstraction.
Compare *zequnim*, "old age," from the root *z-q-n*, "to be old."

27 old and up, everyone who went out in the army, those reckoned for the
28 tribe of Judah, seventy-four thousand six hundred. For the sons of
Issachar, those born to them by their clans, by their fathers' houses,
according to the number of names, from twenty years and up, everyone
29 who went out in the army, their reckoning for the tribe of Issachar, fifty-
30 four thousand four hundred. For the sons of Zebulun those born to
them, by their clans, by their fathers' houses, according to the number
of names, from twenty years old and up, everyone who went out in the
31 army, their reckoning for the tribe of Zebulun, fifty-seven thousand
32 four hundred. For the sons of Joseph—for the sons of Ephraim, those
born to them by their clans, by their fathers' houses, according to the
number of names, from twenty years old and up, everyone who went
33 out in the army, their reckoning for the tribe of Ephraim, forty thou-
34 sand five hundred. For the sons of Manasseh, those born to them by
their clans, by their fathers' houses, according to the number of names,
35 from twenty years old and up, everyone who went out in the army, their
reckoning, for the tribe of Manasseh, thirty-two thousand two hun-
36 dred. For the sons of Benjamin, those born to them, by their clans, by
their fathers' houses, according to the number of names, from twenty
37 years old and up, everyone who went out in the army, their reckoning,
38 for the tribe of Benjamin thirty-five thousand four hundred. For the
sons of Dan, those born to them by their clans, by their fathers' houses,
according to the number of names, from twenty years old and up, every-
39 one who went out in the army, their reckoning for the tribe of Dan
40 sixty-two thousand seven hundred. For the sons of Asher, those born to
them, by their clans, by their fathers' houses, according to the number
of names, from twenty years old and up, everyone who went out in the
41 army, their reckoning for the tribe of Asher forty-one thousand five
42 hundred. The sons of Naphtali, those born to them by their clans, by
their fathers' houses, according to the number of names, from twenty
43 years old up, everyone who went out in the army, their reckoning for
44 the tribe of Naphtali, fifty-three thousand four hundred. These are the
reckonings that Moses, and Aaron and the chieftains of Israel, made,

---

44. *These are the reckonings*. The verb of which this noun is object ("made") is
a cognate to the accusative in the Hebrew, *paqad*, "reckoned."

twelve men, one man for each father's house they were. And all the 45
Israelites who were reckoned by their fathers' houses, from twenty years
old and up, everyone who went out in the army in Israel, all the reck- 46
onings came to six hundred three thousand five hundred and fifty. And 47
the Levites by the tribe of their fathers were not reckoned in their
midst. And the LORD spoke to Moses, saying, "But the tribe of Levi you 48,49
shall not reckon, and their heads you shall not count in the midst of the
Israelites. And you, make the Levites reckon with the Tabernacle of the 50
Covenant and with all its furnishings and with all that belongs to it.
They it is who shall bear the Tabernacle and all its furnishings, and they
shall serve it, and around the Tabernacle they shall camp. And when the 51
Tabernacle journeys onward, the Levites shall take it down, and when
the Tabernacle camps, the Levites shall set it up, and the stranger who
draws near shall be put to death. And the Israelites shall camp each 52
man with his camp and each man with his banner by their battalions.

---

49. *But.* The Hebrew *'akh* has a focusing and emphatic effect as well as an
adversative sense—"yet," "only."

50. *make the Levites reckon with the Tabernacle.* The obvious sense of the verb
is "to appoint" or "to install," but the Hebrew puns on the term *paqad* used for
the census, recasting it here in the *hiph'il* or causative conjugation: you are not
to reckon the Levites, but instead you must make them reckon with the Tabernacle, confer upon them the responsibility of its maintenance. The emphasis
on the central role of the Levites will continue through much of the Book of
Numbers.

51. *the stranger who draws near.* As is always the case in specifically cultic contexts, "stranger," *zar*, has the technical meaning of anyone unfit to enter the
sanctum, that is, a layman.

52. *banner.* This is the consensus of postbiblical Hebrew tradition for understanding the term *degel*. But Baruch Levine summons considerable comparative Semitic evidence, seconded by the Aramaic Targums, to argue that *degel*
actually designates a "sociomilitary unit" (perhaps something like "regiment"?).
It is also possible that a banner used to identify the military unit then became
interchangeable through metonymy with the unit—roughly, the way "regimen-
tals" in English came to be the term for the uniform of the regiment.

53 And the Levites shall camp around the Tabernacle of the Covenant,
that there be no fury against the community of Israelites, and the
54 Levites shall keep watch over the Tabernacle of the Covenant. And the
Israelites did as all that the LORD had charged Moses, thus did they do.

---

53. *that there be no fury.* The Hebrew term for "fury," *qetsef,* means, at least etymologically, "foam," as in a mouth foaming with rage. The fury in question is
God's punitive fury that would be triggered by any violation of the sacred space
of the sanctuary.

the Levites shall keep watch. The Hebrew again has a cognate accusative,
shamru mishmeret. Some understand the meaning to be that the Levites will
attend to all the necessary maintenance of the Tabernacle, and *mishmeret* does
sometimes have that meaning. But given the fact that the assignment of the
Levites to the Tabernacle is in lieu of military service, and given the just stated
need for them to ward off the unfit and thus prevent the unleashing of God's
fury, the sense of a military watch or vigil seems more likely: the Levites are
cast as a kind of elite corps guarding the sanctuary.

CHAPTER 2

And the LORD spoke to Moses and to Aaron, saying, "Every man by his banner with standards for his father's house, shall the Israelites camp opposite, round the Tent of Meeting they shall camp." And those that camp to the very east, the banner of the camp of Judah by its divisions, and the chieftain of the Judahites, Nahshon son of Amminadab. And his division and those reckoned with them,   1,2

3

4

---

2. *Every man by his banner with standards for his father's house*. After the preceding census lists, which provide the names of the tribal chieftains and then the head count of each of the tribes, with a stress on the census as a means of implementing military conscription, we are given a plan for the marching order of the Israelite forces, each tribe a military unit carrying its distinctive insignia.

round the Tent of Meeting they shall camp. The marching formation is a protective square, meant to ward off potential assaults from all directions, with the Tent of Meeting, the sacred locus of encounter between God and Moses and the site of the cult, inside the square.

3. *to the very east*. The Hebrew uses two successive synonyms for "east" (a procedure not followed for the other three directions), evidently with an effect of emphasis.

by its divisions. The Hebrew *tseva'ot* (singular *tsava'*) has elsewhere been rendered as "battalions" in order to convey the martial force of the term. In the present context, however, "battalion" would be too small a unit because the numbers involved run into tens of thousands, and hence "division" seems a better English approximation.

4. *those reckoned with them*. Although the language for each of the tribes is unvarying boilerplate, as befits a list of this sort, in some instances the text says "reckoned with them" and in some "reckoned with him." Abraham ibn Ezra rightly notes that there is no difference of meaning whatever—biblical

5 seventy-four thousand six hundred. And those camped by him, the
tribe of Issachar, and the chieftain of the Issacharites, Nethanel son of
6 Zuar. And his division and those reckoned with it, fifty-four thousand
7 four hundred. The tribe of Zebulun, and the chieftain of the Zebulu-
8 nites Eliab son of Helon. And his division and those reckoned with it,
9 seventy-five thousand four hundred. All the reckoning for the camp of
Judah one hundred eighty-six thousand four hundred by their divisions.
10 They shall journey first. The banner of the camp of Reuben to the
south by their divisions, and the chieftain of the Reubenites Elizur son
11 of Shedeur. And his division and those reckoned with it, forty-six
12 thousand five hundred. And those who camped by him, the tribe of
Simeon, and the chieftain of the Simeonites Shelumiel son of Zur-
13 ishaddai. And his division and their reckoning, fifty-nine thousand
14 three hundred. And the tribe of Gad, and the chieftain of the Gadites
15 Eliasaph son of Reuel. And his division and their reckoning with them,
16 forty-five thousand six hundred and fifty. All the reckoning for the
camp of Reuben, one hundred fifty thousand four hundred and fifty by

---

Hebrew indifferently construes collectives as singular or plural. Similarly, the
term rendered throughout in this passage as "fathers' houses" is literally
"fathers' house," though if linguistic usage followed logic, which it very often
does not, the phrase would be either "fathers' houses" or "father's house."

9. *They shall journey first.* Baruch Levine is surely right in arguing that here the
verb "journey" (*yisaʿu*) has the military sense of "march." But, by and large, biblical Hebrew adopts general terms for technical usages rather than coining
specialized technical terms—compare "reckoned" for "mustered"—and this
translation seeks to preserve that effect.

14. *Reuel.* In 1:13 this name appears as "Deuel." The letters indicating *d* and *r*
are similar in form and hence there are sometimes scribal errors in transcrib-
ing them. The more likely form is Reuel.

their divisions. And they shall journey second. And the Tent of Meet- 17
ing, the camp of the Levites, shall journey in the midst of the camps.
As they camp, so shall they journey, each in his own place, by their banners. The banner of the camp of Ephraim by their divisions to the 18
west, and the chieftain of the Ephraimites Elishama son of Ammihud.
And his division and their reckoning, forty thousand five hundred. And 19,20
by him the camp of Manasseh, and the chieftain of the Manassehites
Gamaliel son of Pedahzur. And his division and those reckoned with it 21
thirty-two thousand two hundred. And the tribe of Benjamin, and the 22
chieftain of the Benjaminites Abidan son of Gideoni. And his division 23
and their reckoning thirty-five thousand four hundred. And the reck- 24
oning for the camp of Ephraim one hundred eight thousand one hundred by their divisions. And they shall journey third. The banner of the 25
camp of Dan to the north by their divisions, and the chieftain of the
Danites Ahiezer son of Ammishaddai. And his division and their reck- 26
oning, sixty-two thousand seven hundred. And those who camped by 27
him, the tribe of Asher, and the chieftain of the Asherites Pagiel son of
Ochran. And his division and their reckoning forty-one thousand five 28
hundred. And the tribe of Naphtali, and the chieftain of the Naphtal- 29
ites Ahira son of Enan. And his division and their reckoning, fifty-three 30
thousand four hundred. All the reckoning for the camp of Dan one 31
hundred fifty-seven thousand six hundred. They shall journey last by
their banners. These are the reckonings of the Israelites by their 32
fathers' houses, all the reckonings of the camps by their divisions, six

---

17. *the Tent of Meeting, the camp of the Levites.* In the received Hebrew text,
these two phrases appear to be in apposition, yielding a rather curious characterization of the Tent of Meeting. The second phrase is best understood as
standing in a relation of metonymy to the first: the camp of the Levites sur-
rounds the Tent of Meeting, serving as a protective extension to it and thus
borrowing its name. This formulation sustains the notion put forth in 1:50–53
that the Levites fulfill a kind of military function in guarding the Tent of Meeting against all incursions. Thus in the marching plan for the army, the Levites
inside the square act as an elite corps or palace guard.

33 hundred three thousand five hundred and fifty. But the Levites were not reckoned in the midst of the Israelites, as the LORD had charged
34 Moses. And the Israelites did as all that the LORD had charged Moses, thus they camped by their banners and thus they journeyed, each man by his clans, together with his father's house.

---

33. *But the Levites were not reckoned in the midst of the Israelites.* This notation is in keeping with the differential instruction concerning the Levites in 1:49. The military role of the Levites is to serve as guards of the sanctuary, and as such they are not counted in the muster of the army that is assembled to confront external threats.

CHAPTER 3

And these are the generations of Aaron and Moses on the day the 1
LORD spoke with Moses on Mount Sinai. And these are the 2
names of the sons of Aaron: the firstborn Nadab, and Abihu,
Eleazar, and Ithamar. These are the names of the sons of Aaron, the 3
anointed priests whom he installed to serve as priests. And Nadab and 4
Abihu died before the LORD when they brought forward unfit fire
before the LORD in the Wilderness of Sinai, and sons they did not
have, and Eleazar and Ithamar served as priests in the lifetime of
Aaron their father.

And the LORD spoke to Moses, saying, "Bring forward the tribe of 5,6
Levi, and set them before Aaron the priest, that they may serve him.
And they shall keep his watch and the watch of all the community 7

---

1. *And these are the generations of Aaron and Moses.* Having completed the
marching formation of the eleven tribes, the writer now turns to the tribe of
Levi, listing its genealogy and its special duties. In keeping with his Priestly
perspective, considerably more space is devoted to the Levites than to any of
the other tribes.

4. *brought forward.* The Hebrew verb *hiqriv* has the overlapping meanings of
"bring forward," "bring near," "present," and "sacrifice." In cultic contexts it
suggests bringing before the divine presence or to the altar, and so it is appropriately followed here by "before the LORD." Compare verse 6, "bring forward
the tribe of Levi."
    unfit fire. Literally, "strange fire." In relation to the cult, "strange" means
"unconsecrated," "unfit." Compare "the stranger [the same word in the
Hebrew] who draws near" in verse 10.

8 before the Tent of Meeting to do the work of the Tabernacle. And they
shall keep watch over all the furnishings of the Tent of Meeting and the
9 watch of the Israelites to do the work of the Tabernacle. And you shall
give the Levites to Aaron and to his sons, wholly given shall they be from
10 the Israelites. And Aaron and his sons you shall single out, that they
keep their priesthood, and the stranger who draws near shall be put to
11,12 death." And the Lord spoke to Moses, saying, "And as for Me, look, I
have taken the Levites from the midst of the Israelites in place of every
13 firstborn womb-breach of the Israelites, that the Levites be Mine. For
Mine is every firstborn. On the day I struck down every firstborn in the
land of Egypt I consecrated to Me every firstborn in Israel from man to
beast—Mine they shall be. I am the Lord."

---

8. *keep . . . the watch of the Israelites.* The medieval commentators, like their
modern heirs, are divided on the interpretation of "keep watch" (*shamru mishmeret*) and how it relates to the Israelites. Rashi prefers the unmartial sense of
mishmeret as "maintenance" and explains that the sundry functions of the
Tabernacle were necessarily the actions of the Levites on behalf of the entire
community of Israelites. Abraham ibn Ezra, like the present translation,
prefers the military sense: "they will keep watch that no Israelite touch the
Tabernacle." The likelihood that the meaning here is "to guard against" is supported by the recurrence in the next verse of the formula, "the stranger who
draws near shall be put to death."

9. *wholly given shall they be.* The literal sense of the Hebrew is "given, given
shall they be." "Given" in this context obviously means "dedicated,"
"appointed," but again the translation seeks to reflect the stylistic tendency of
biblical Hebrew to use general terms for technical senses.

12. *that the Levites be Mine.* There may be an implicit etymological pun here.
"Levite" (*lewi*) is the name of Jacob's second son and hence of the tribe, but
the name could suggest the verbal stem *l-w-h*, "to accompany," "to attach to,"
which is the role of the Levites vis-à-vis the deity.

And the LORD spoke to Moses in the Wilderness of Sinai, saying, 14
"Reckon the Levites by their fathers' houses, by their clans, every male 15
from a month old and up you shall reckon them." And Moses reckoned 16
them according to the word of the LORD as he had been charged. And 17
these were the Levites by their names: Gershon and Kohath and Merari. And these are the names of the sons of Gershon by their clans: 18
Libni and Shimei. And the sons of Kohath by their clans: Amram and 19
Izhar, Hebron and Uzziel. And the sons of Merari by their clans: Mahli 20
and Mushi. These are the clans of Levi by their fathers' houses. To 21
Gershon, the Libnite clan and the Shimeite clan, these are the Gershonite clans. Their reckoning, in the number of every male from a 22
month old and up, their reckoning is seven thousand five hundred.
The Gershonite clans shall camp behind the Tabernacle to the west. 23
And the chieftain of the father's house for the Gershonite, Eliasaph son 24
of Lael. And the watch of the Gershonites in the Tent of Meeting, the 25
Tabernacle and the Tent, its cover and the screen of the entrance to the
Tent of Meeting, and the hangings of the court and the screen of the 26
entrance to the court which is around the Tabernacle and the altar and
its cords for all its service. And to Kohath, the Amramite clan and the 27
Izharite clan and the Hebronite clan and the Uzzielite clan, these are
the Kohathite clans. In the number of every male from one month old 28
and up, eight thousand six hundred, keepers of the watch of the sanctuary. The clans of the Kohathites shall camp on the side of the Taber- 29
nacle to the south. And the chieftain of the father's house for the clans 30
of the Kohathite, Elizaphan son of Uzziel. And their watch is the ark 31

---

15. *every male from a month old and up.* Unlike the other tribes, whose census
is the vehicle of an explicit military conscription and hence based on the age
of twenty and over, the Levites are dedicated to God for their whole lives. The
count begins not from birth but from one month because given the prevalence
of infant mortality, only after a month is the child regarded as a viable person
(an explanation duly noted by several of the medieval commentators).

16. *according to the word of the LORD.* The literal meaning of the Hebrew is "by
the mouth of the LORD." Jacob Milgrom's proposal that the phrase refers not
to divine command but to oracle has not found general acceptance. In verse
51, this phrase appears to be in apposition with "as the LORD had charged."

and the table and the lamp stand and the altars and the sacred vessels
32 with which they shall serve and the screen and all its work. And the
chieftain of the chieftains of the Levites is Eleazar son of Aaron the
33 priest, the charge of those who keep the watch of the sanctuary. To the
Merarite, the Mahlite clan and the Mushite clan, these are the Mer-
34 arite clans. And their reckoning, in the number of every male from one
35 month old and up, six thousand two hundred. And the chieftain of the
father's house for the clans of the Merarite, Zuriel son of Abihail. On
36 the side of the Tabernacle they shall camp to the north. And the charge
of the Merarites, the boards of the Tabernacle and its bars and its posts
37 and its sockets and all its furnishings and all its work, and the posts of
the court all around and their sockets and their pegs and their cords.
38 And those who camped before the Tabernacle to the east before
the Tent of Meeting to the east, Moses and Aaron and his sons, keeping the watch of the Tabernacle, for the watch of the Israelites, and the
39 stranger who draws near shall be put to death. All the reckonings of
the Levites that Moses and Aaron reckoned according to the word of
the LORD by their clans, every male from a month old and up—twenty-
two thousand.

40 And the LORD said to Moses, "Reckon every firstborn male of the
Israelites from a month old and up and count the number of their
41 names. And you shall take the Levites for Me—I am the LORD—instead
of every firstborn among the Israelites, and the cattle of the Levites
42 instead of every firstborn among the cattle of the Israelites." And Moses
reckoned as the LORD had charged him every firstborn among the
43 Israelites. And all the firstborn males in the number of names from a
month old and up in their reckoning came to twenty-two thousand two
44 hundred and seventy-three. And the LORD said to Moses, saying,

---

41. *instead of every firstborn among the Israelites.* This injunction picks up the idea
enunciated in Exodus 13 and elsewhere that, after the rescue of the Israelite
firstborn in Egypt, some form of "redemption" or substitution for the firstborn
was owed to God. Here the Levites, dedicated from infancy to the divine cult,
serve as substitutes. Behind this law stands an archaic background in which
cultic functions were performed by the firstborn instead of by a priestly caste.

"Take the Levites instead of every firstborn among the Israelites and 45
the cattle of the Levites instead of their cattle, and the Levites shall be
Mine. I am the Lord. And for the redemption of the two hundred 46
seventy-three of the firstborn of the Israelites who exceed the number
of the Levites, you shall take five shekels for each head, by the sanctu- 47
ary shekel, you shall take, twenty *gerahs* to the shekel, and you shall 48
give the silver to Aaron and his sons as redemption for those among
them who exceed the number." And Moses took the redemption silver 49
from those who exceeded the number of those redeemed by the
Levites. From the firstborn of the Israelites he took the silver, one thou- 50
sand three hundred and sixty-five shekels, by the sanctuary shekel.
And Moses gave the redemption silver to Aaron and to his sons accord- 51
ing to the word of the Lord, as the Lord had charged Moses.

---

46. *exceed the number*. The concept of "number" is in this context implied by
the Hebrew verb *'adaf*, which means to "go beyond the limit," "spill over the
edge," "exceed."

47. *you shall take five shekels for each head*. How would the Israelites know who
were the 273 who exceeded the number of the Levites and hence had to pay
this price of redemption? Several early rabbinic sources plausibly suggest that
a lottery was conducted to select the 273.
    by the sanctuary shekel. "Shekel" means "weight" and is not a coin, coinage
coming into Israelite life only in the late biblical period. The sanctuary shekel,
about 11.4 grams, was heavier than the commercial shekel.

48. *the silver*. Though this word has the approximate sense of "money" (the
meaning it frequently has in later Hebrew), what is given to Aaron and his sons
are weights of silver, so it is preferable to render the term as "silver."

CHAPTER 4

1,2 ＡA nd the LORD spoke to Moses and to Aaron, saying, "Count the
    heads of the Kohathites from the midst of the Levites by their
3   clans, by their fathers' houses. From thirty years old up till fifty
    years old, all who come to the army to do the task in the Tent of Meet-
4   ing. This is the work of the Kohathites in the Tent of Meeting, the holy
5   of holies. And Aaron shall come, and his sons, when the camp journeys
    onward, and take down the covering of the screen and cover with it the
6   Ark of the Covenant. And they shall place over it a cover of ocher-dyed

---

3. *From thirty years old up till fifty years old.* The Book of Numbers incorporates
three different traditions regarding the beginning age of levitical service. The
notion of the present unit that it begins at thirty seems to reflect a sense that,
in contradistinction to general military service, which begins at twenty, the
maintenance of the sanctuary as it is transported requires elaborate training or
perhaps something like spiritual maturity.

 all who come to the army. Throughout this chapter, the Hebrew word for
"army," *tzava'*, is a kind of pun. The term has a secondary meaning of "service,"
which is the primary sense in this context, but its repeated use reminds us that
the Levites' cultic service is an equivalent to fulfilling military obligations.

5. *take down the covering of the screen.* In both anthropological and literary
terms, the key to this entire passage is the idea of protective envelope, barrier,
covering. These terms are not only used repeatedly but a rich vocabulary of
synonyms is deployed: *mikhseh* and *kisui* (both meaning "covering"), *masakh*
("screen"), and, for the sheets of brilliant cloth used to wrap the sacred
objects, *beged*, "garment." This last term may reflect an anthropomorphizing
sense of solicitous concern for the sacralia, but, more pervasively, the extravagant emphasis on coverings (which may be more the literary articulation of a
theological idea than a record of the historical experience of early Israel) is
driven by a widespread ancient Near Eastern notion of the terrific danger of

skin and spread a garment of pure indigo above it and put in its poles. And on the table of the Presence they shall spread an indigo garment 7 and place on it the bowls and the ladles and the jars and the libation flasks, and the perpetual bread shall be upon it. And they shall spread 8 over them a crimson garment and cover it in a covering of ocher-dyed skin and put in its poles. And they shall take an indigo garment and 9 cover the lamp stand of the light and its lamps and its tongs and its fire-pans and all its oil vessels with which they serve. And they shall place 10 it and all its vessels in a covering of ocher-dyed skin and place it on a beam. And over the golden altar they shall spread an indigo garment 11 and cover it with a covering of ocher-dyed skin and put in its poles. And they shall take all the vessels of service with which they serve in 12 the sanctuary and place them in an indigo garment and cover them with a covering of ocher-dyed skin and place on a beam. And they shall 13 clear the ashes from the altar and spread over it a purple garment. And 14 they shall place on it all its vessels with which they serve upon it, the fire-pans and the flesh-hooks and the scrapers and the basins, all the vessels of the altar, and they shall spread over it a covering of ocher-dyed skin and put in its poles. And Aaron, and his sons, shall finish 15 covering the sanctuary and all the vessels of the sanctuary when the camp journeys onward, and afterward the Kohathites shall come to carry, so that they do not touch the holy and die. These make up the

---

the holy for all but the consecrated priests. Thus the transportation of the sanctuary from place to place, its disassembling and reassembling, was a moment of acute peril, for which our passage makes elaborate provision. Note how God exhorts Moses and Aaron (verse 18) to protect the Kohathites from being "cut off"—here, evidently, struck dead—by making sure not only that they avoid direct contact with the sacred objects but also that they not look at the sacred. This, too, is a taboo registered in other ancient Near Eastern texts. Only the consecrated Aaronite priests, not the Levites, may touch or behold the sacred objects.

7. *the table of the Presence.* This is a common ellipsis for the "table of the Bread of the Presence," that is the table on which the twelve loaves of "perpetual bread" (changed weekly by the officiants of the sanctuary) were placed.

16 carriage of the Kohathites in the Tent of Meeting. And what is appointed for Eleazar son of Aaron the priest—the oil for the lamp and the aromatic incense and the perpetual grain offering and the anointing oil, what is appointed for all the Tabernacle and all that is in it, in the sanctuary and in its vessels."

17,18 And the LORD spoke to Moses and to Aaron, saying, "Do not let the tribe of the clans of the Kohathites get cut off from the midst of the
19 Levites. And this shall you do for them, that they live and not die when they draw near the holy of holies: Aaron and his sons shall come and
20 set every man of them at his work and at his carriage. And they shall not come in to see the sanctuary for even a moment and die."

21,22 And the LORD spoke to Moses, saying, "Count the heads of the Ger-
23 shonites, too, by their fathers' houses, by their clans. From thirty years old up till fifty years old you shall reckon them, all who do army service
24 to do the work in the Tent of Meeting. This is the work of the Ger-
25 shonite clans, for work and for carriage: They shall carry the curtains of the Tabernacle and the Tent of Meeting, its covering and the cover-

---

19. *at his work and at his carriage.* These paired terms are repeated through the passage. Though some scholars have proposed that they are a hendiadys—two terms bound together to indicate one concept—it is more plausible to see them as the two complementary labors of the Levites: *'avodah,* "work," would be taking apart the sanctuary and perhaps also reassembling it; *masa',* "carriage," is the task of carrying it from place to place. It is misleading to render *'avodah* as "service" because hard physical labor is entailed, and only in later Hebrew does that noun come to mean the Temple service.

20. *even a moment.* The Hebrew *kevala'* (the verbal root means "to swallow" or "to destroy") is obscure. The translation follows a proposal of Baruch Levine, who compares the word with its occurrence in Job 7:19, but it should be said that in Job the verb, as an indication of a very brief moment, has a specific object: "You do not let go of me [even] to swallow my spittle." One would have to assume, then, that *kevala'* here is an ellipsis for an established idiom invoked more fully in Job, though there are scant grounds for confidence in that assumption. Others construe it as "dismantling," but that seems a long stretch from the basic meaning of "swallow" or "destroy."

ing of ocher-dyed skin that is over it above and the screen of the
entrance to the Tent of Meeting. And the panels of the court and the 26
screen for the entrance to the gate of the court which is all around the
Tabernacle and the altar, and their cords, and all the vessels for their
service and all that is done for them, and they shall do the work. By the 27
word of Aaron and his sons shall be all the work of the Gershonites, for
all their carriage and for all their work, and you shall oversee them
watchfully in all their carriage. This is the work of the Gershonite clans 28
in the Tent of Meeting, and their watch is in the hand of Ithamar son
of Aaron the priest. The Merarites by their clans, by their fathers' 29
houses, you shall reckon them. From thirty years old up till fifty years 30
old you shall reckon them, all who come to the army to do the work of
the Tent of Meeting. And this is the watch of their carriage for all their 31
work in the Tent of Meeting: the boards of the Tabernacle and its bars
and its posts and its sockets, and the posts of the court all around and 32
their sockets and their pegs and their cords, for all their vessels and for
all their work. And by name you shall reckon the vessels of their carriage watch. This is the work of the Merarites for all their work in the 33
Tent of Meeting, in the hand of Ithamar son of Aaron the priest."

And Moses, and Aaron and the chieftains of the community with him, 34
reckoned the Kohathites by their clans by their fathers' houses, from 35
thirty years old up till fifty years old, all who came to the army, to the
work in the Tent of Meeting. And their reckoning by their clans was 36
two thousand seven hundred and fifty. This is the reckoning of the 37
Kohathite clans, all who worked in the Tent of Meeting, which Moses,
and Aaron with him, reckoned, by the LORD's word, through the hand
of Moses. And the reckoning of the Gershonites by their clans and by 38
their fathers' houses, from thirty years old up till fifty years, all who 39
came to the army, to the work in the Tent of Meeting. And their reck- 40
oning by their clans, by their fathers' houses, came to two thousand six
hundred and thirty. This is the reckoning of the Gershonites, all who 41
worked in the Tent of Meeting, which Moses, and Aaron with him,
reckoned by the LORD's word. And the reckoning of the Merarite clans, 42
by their clans, by their fathers' houses, from thirty years old up till fifty 43
years old, all who came to the army, to the work in the Tent of Meeting. And their reckoning by their clans came to three thousand two 44

45 hundred. This is the reckoning of the Merarite clans that Moses, and Aaron with him, reckoned by the LORD's word, through the hand of
46 Moses. All the reckoning by which Moses, and Aaron and the chieftains of Israel with him, reckoned the Levites by their clans and by
47 their fathers' houses, from thirty years old up till fifty years old, all who came to do the work and the work of carriage in the Tent of Meeting.
48 And their reckoning came to eight thousand five hundred and eighty.
49 By the LORD's word did he reckon them through the hand of Moses, every man according to his work and according to his carriage, and his reckoning was as the LORD had charged Moses.

CHAPTER 5

A nd the Lord spoke to Moses, saying, "Charge the Israelites, that [1,2] they send out from the camp everyone infected with skin blanch and everyone suffering from genital flux and everyone defiled by a corpse. Whether male or female, you shall send them off, outside the [3] camp you shall send them, that they do not defile their camps in whose midst I abide." And thus did the Israelites do, and they sent them out- [4] side the camp. As the Lord had spoken to Moses, thus the Israelites did.

---

2. *skin blanch*. This English nonce term reflects the medical uncertainty of the Hebrew disease *tsara'at* (here in an adjectival form for the person suffering from it, *tsaru'a*). The symptoms listed in Leviticus 13–14 make it clear that it is not leprosy (Hansen's disease), as the older translations have it. Perhaps the term designated a group of diseases because the sundry skin lesions listed in Leviticus do not seem entirely compatible, with indications elsewhere (e.g., Exodus 4:6) that it involved a complete loss of pigmentation. In any case, the disease was regarded as contagious and, as other biblical texts record, required quarantine.

suffering from genital flux. This necessary clarification in translation does not do justice to the extraordinary compactness of the Hebrew, a single sylla-ble, *zav*, "flowing."

by a corpse. Literally, "for a [dead] person," *lanafesh*. All three of these cat-egories of impurity are clearly cultic, not moral. Pathology and death are viewed as contaminants, and the camp of Israel in the wilderness, in which God's presence dwells with a specific locus in the Tabernacle, must be kept free of them.

5,6 And the LORD spoke to Moses, saying, "Speak to the Israelites: Should man or woman commit any of the human offenses, to betray the trust

7 of the LORD, that person shall bear guilt. And they shall confess their offenses which they committed, and he shall render back for his guilt the sum of its principal, and a fifth part of it he shall add to it, and give

8 it to him whom he wronged. And if the man should have no redeemer to render back to him for his guilt, what is rendered back shall be the LORD's, the priest's, besides the ram of atonement with which he will

9 atone for himself. And every donation for all the sacred offerings of the

10 Israelites that they bring forward to the priest, his shall it be. And a man's sacred offerings shall be his. That which he gives to the priest shall be his."

---

6. *any of the human offenses, to betray the trust of the* LORD. The Hebrew *ḥato't ha'adam*, "human offenses," is unique to this text, and seems to indicate offenses of one person against another. The primary meaning of *lim'ol ma'al*, "to betray the trust," is to appropriate objects or goods that have been consecrated to the sanctuary. Here, the meaning has been extended to the illicit appropriation of another person's property, which is equally seen as betraying the LORD's trust.

7. *the sum of its principal.* "The sum of" represents the Hebrew particle *b*[e] ("with"), which here has the sense of a price or sum paid for something. "Principal" is the technical monetary sense of the Hebrew *ro'sh* (literally, "head"). The fact that the wrongdoer is to pay back the value of the appropriated goods plus a fine of 20 percent, rather than a fourfold or fivefold restitution, suggests that what may be involved is some sort of embezzlement rather than outright theft.

8. *if the man should have no redeemer.* The most plausible construction is that the man referred to is the wronged person, not the wrongdoer. "Redeemer" has the technical legal sense, as in the search for a redeemer for Naomi's deceased husband in Ruth 4, of a kinsman who can act as a surrogate for a deceased person. The case indicated, then, is one in which the wronged person is no longer alive to receive restitution and there is no relative who can be given the restitution in his stead. In such a case, the priest, God's agent, becomes the proxy to whom restitution is made.

And the LORD spoke to Moses, saying, "Speak to the Israelites and say   11,12
to them: 'Any man whose wife may stray and betray his trust, and a   13
man lie with her in seed-coupling and it be concealed from her husband's eyes and she hide and be defiled, with no witness against her,
and she herself be not apprehended—then a spirit of jealousy may   14
come over him and he will be jealous about his wife, with her being
defiled, or a spirit of jealousy may come over him and he will be jealous about his wife, she not being defiled. The man shall bring his wife   15
to the priest and bring her sacrifice for her, a tenth of an *ephah* of

---

12. *whose wife may stray and betray his trust*. The law of the wife suspected of
adultery is formally linked with the preceding section by the prominent use at
the beginning and then repeatedly of the idiom "to betray his trust." Similarly,
the repeated characterization of the unfaithful woman as "defiled" verbally
links this passage with the opening unit of this chapter concerning defilement
of the camp by contact with corpses or diseased persons.

13. *and a man lie with her in seed-coupling*. If the Masoretic vocalization of the
text can be trusted, the Hebrew makes "her" the direct object of "lie" ("lay her,"
"bed her"), a usage that may highlight the brutality of the act. "Seed-coupling,"
shikhvat-zera', is literally "seed-lying" or perhaps even "layer of seed." In any
case, the phrase clearly indicates vaginal penetration with emission of semen.
    concealed . . . hide . . . no witness . . . not apprehended. The deployment of
overlapping language stresses the clandestine nature of the act of adultery.
With no concrete evidence of the sexual betrayal, with no more than his suspicions to go on, the husband is overcome by a fit of jealousy (verse 14) and
has recourse to a trial by ordeal.

15. *The man shall bring his wife to the priest*. This troubling and also fascinating ritual is the only clear-cut instance of trial by ordeal in the Bible. It became
the basis for a whole tractate of the Talmud, Sotah ("the straying woman"), and
with the concern for the status of women in recent scholarship, it has been
the subject of voluminous discussion and debate. Apologetic approaches seem
questionable. The ritual reflects the strong asymmetry of sexual roles in the
biblical worldview: a woman must submit to this ordeal on the mere suspicion
of her husband, and the question of the man suspected of adultery is not even
raised in the legal system. The ordeal, moreover, is based on a kind of archaic
magic, however one seeks to square it with loftier versions of monotheism.
Parallels have been noted with the Code of Hammurabi, which provides for an
oath by the woman (compare verse 19 here) if her husband accuses her of

barley flour; he shall pour no oil over it nor put frankincense upon it, for it is a grain offering of jealousy, a grain offering of remembrance, a
16 remembering of guilt, and the priest shall bring her forward and stand
17 her before the LORD. And the priest shall take holy water in an earthen vessel, and from the earth that is on the floor of the sanctuary

---

unfaithfulness, and an ordeal of jumping into a river, sink or swim, if the accusation comes from someone else (compare the prominence of water here). Our passage powerfully records an ideology of marital relations, but in point of historical fact, there is no way of knowing to what extent it was actually practiced in ancient Israel. It is doubtful whether this was a living legal institution in the Second Temple period, and if the sanctuary setting of the ritual is the Tabernacle, it may even have not been observed in the First Temple period. In any case, it is a vivid male fantasy of testing and exposing sexual "defilement" in a woman.

her sacrifice . . . a tenth of an ephah of barley flour. A person seeking some sort of judicial or oracular determination from the sanctuary (understood to be from God through the priest) would have to come with an offering. But in consonance with the somber occasion for this visit to the sanctuary, this is a no-frills grain offering, not the usual semolina flour but barley, and devoid of oil and frankincense. As Rashi, citing Tractate Sotah, sharply puts it, "She did a beast's act, and her sacrifice is a beast's feed."

offering of remembrance, a remembering of guilt. The verbal stem z-k-r manifested in these paired nouns refers both to the cognitive act of remembering and to making a record or explicit indication of something. The word for "guilt," 'awon, which can also mean "crime" and even "punishment," is different from the term for "guilt," 'asham, used in verses 6–8.

17. holy water. This phrase does not occur elsewhere. It may plausibly be understood, as Abraham ibn Ezra and others have proposed, as a reference to the water in the basins of the sanctuary, set out for the use of the priests in ritual ablution. Two elements, then, of the sanctuary that are binary opposites are joined in the liquid vehicle of the trial by ordeal: water and earth. The latter, 'afar (also "dust" or "dirt") is not something one would ordinarily drink, and it is associated in biblical usage with mourning ('afar is placed on the head), and with death ("for dust you are / and to dust shall you return," Genesis 3:19).

the priest shall take and put into the water. And the priest shall stand   18
the woman before the LORD and undo her hair and place on her palms
the grain offering of remembrance, a grain offering of jealousy it is,
and in the hand of the priest shall be the bitter besetting water.
And the priest shall make her swear and shall say to the woman: If no   19
man has lain with you and if you have not strayed in defilement from
your husband, be cleared by this bitter besetting water. And you,   20
if you have strayed from your husband and if you have been defiled
and a man other than your husband has put his semen in you. . . .

18. *undo her hair*. The Hebrew says literally, "undo her head," a transparent
metonymy. The loosening of the hair is an act of public shaming, so the
woman in effect is exposed and vulnerable before she takes her oath and swallows the potion.

  the bitter besetting water. Punning sound-play is crucial in the Hebrew
phrase *mey hamarim hame'ararim*. The literal sense of the second of the two
Hebrew qualifiers of "water" is "cursing" or "curse-conveying." Verse 27 seems
to indicate that the water turns bitter only if the woman fails the trial by ordeal
("if she . . . betrayed her husband's trust, the besetting water will enter her as
bitter"). The ever-acute ibn Ezra proposes that "bitter" is used proleptically, in
analogy to "you stripped the garments of the naked" in Job 22:6. It should be
noted that in biblical idiom, bitter water is brackish or salt water that is unfit
for drinking.

19. *strayed . . . from your husband*. The Hebrew says literally "strayed under
your husband." Some have interpreted this as "under the authority of," a sense
of the preposition for which there is scant biblical evidence. One recent interpreter reads it as "in place of," one clear meaning of the Hebrew preposition,
but which strains the syntax here. One might infer a symbolic or even sexual
image of the husband on top, with the wife "straying" from under him.

20. *And you*. The woman is rhetorically buttonholed by this emphatic initial
"you" at the beginning of this statement of the negative alternative of the oath.

  put his semen in you. The term for "semen," *shekhovet*, is derived from the
verbal stem *sh-k-v*, "to lie," used at the beginning of the passage, and appears
to have this technical sexual sense. Its use, together with "seed-coupling"
above, may offer support to those commentators who propose that the suspected woman is actually pregnant. Either the husband thinks he has grounds
for suspicion that he is not the father (e.g., this wife has been frequently gone
from the house at odd hours), or, in a case where he has not been having sex

21 And the priest shall make the woman swear this oath of imprecation, and the priest shall say to the woman: May the LORD make you an imprecation and oath in the midst of your people through the LORD's

22 making your thigh sag and your belly swell. And this besetting water shall enter your innards to swell the belly and to sag the thigh. And the

23 woman shall say: Amen, amen. And the priest shall write these impre-

24 cations in a record and wipe them out in the bitter water. And he shall make the woman drink the bitter besetting water and the bitter beset-

25 ting water shall enter her. And the priest shall take from the woman's hand the grain offering of jealousy and elevate the grain offering before

26 the LORD and bring it forward to the altar. And the priest shall take a handful from the grain offering, its token, and turn it to smoke on the

---

with his wife (whether through mutual estrangement or because he has been away), he thinks he can be certain. Bathsheba and Uriah would be an instance of the second alternative.

21. *And the priest shall make the woman swear.* This clause interrupts the move from the conditional clause of the oath (verse 20) to the consequence clause ("May the LORD make you an imprecation . . .").

   your thigh sag and your belly swell. Much futile energy has been devoted to working out what sort of medical symptoms might be indicated. "Belly" is often womb in the Bible, and "thigh" might be a metonymic euphemism for vagina, but not necessarily. In any case, something physically dire immediately happens to the guilty woman after she swallows the potion, and it happens in or around the organs of generation. If in fact she is pregnant, that could be a miscarriage, the ordeal thus becoming an induced abortion, though this remains uncertain.

22. *this besetting water shall enter your innards.* The verb for entering or com- ing into is also a biblical idiom for consummated sexual intercourse, so the penetration of the ritual potion into the woman's innards answers to the act of which she has been accused.

23. *these imprecations.* Either the plural is a rhetorical intensification or it reflects the two symptoms, sagging thigh and swollen belly.

26. *its token.* Literally, "its remembrancing," *'azkaratah*.

altar and, after, shall make the woman drink the water. Once he has   27
made her drink the water, it shall come about that if she was defiled
and betrayed her husband's trust, the besetting water will enter her as
bitter and her belly will swell and her thigh sag, and the woman shall
become an imprecation in the midst of her people. And if the woman   28
has not been defiled and she is pure, she will be cleared and sown with
seed. This is the teaching of jealousy, should a woman stray from her   29
husband and be defiled. Or a man over whom a spirit of jealousy may   30
come and he be jealous about his wife. The priest shall stand her
before the LORD and do to her all this teaching, and the man shall be   31
clear of guilt, and that woman shall bear her guilt.'"

---

27. *the woman shall become an imprecation*. The ritual, for all its cruelty, does
not prescribe a death penalty for the adulterers. (In Genesis 38, Judah's judgment of Tamar presupposes the death penalty for such an act.) The punishment is public shaming and, one may infer, divorce without restitution of her
bride-price.

28. *sown with seed*. This is the literal meaning of the Hebrew. If one sustains
the assumption that the accused wife is pregnant, the phrase would mean that
she retains her pregnancy, now proven to be legitimate, and will be rewarded
with progeny. Otherwise, the phrase might suggest that her reward comes in
her conceiving afterward by her husband: in this reading, the trial by ordeal
would be a means of reconciliation between spouses separated by the husband's suspicion.

29. *This is the teaching*. Hebrew *torah* means "teaching," "regulation," "prescribed procedure."

31. *and the man shall be clear of guilt, and that woman shall bear her guilt*. The
asymmetry between the sexes is vividly summarized in this concluding verse.
If the woman should fail the trial by ordeal, she will of course bear her own
guilt, as the language of the oath that the priest has imposed on her makes
clear. But even if she is proven innocent, the husband incurs no guilt in subjecting her to the ordeal: if he thinks he has grounds for suspicion—indeed, if
he is simply caught up Othello-like in a "spirit of jealousy," a jealous passion—
it is his prerogative as husband to make her submit to the ordeal.

CHAPTER 6

1,2 Ａnd the Lᴏʀᴅ spoke to Moses, saying, "Speak to the Israelites and
say to them: 'Man or woman, should anyone act exceptionally to
3 make a nazirite vow to keep himself apart for the Lᴏʀᴅ, from both
wine and liquor he shall keep himself apart, neither wine vinegar nor
liquor vinegar shall he drink, no grape steepings shall he drink, and
4 grapes, whether wet or dry, he shall not eat. All the days of his naziritehood, of anything made from the grapevine, from seeds to skin, he shall

---

2. *should anyone act exceptionally*. Much of the biblical view of the institution
of the nazir depends on the interpretation of the verb *yafli* that is used here.
Some modern commentators make it relatively neutral by claiming that, in
conjunction with "vow," it merely means to state the vow expressly. The philological evidence, however, for this technical sense of the verb is slender, as
Baruch Levine argues. Some medieval commentators, whom Levine follows,
understand it as a synonymous reinforcer of the reiterated verb *hazir*, "to set
apart," assuming that the root *p-l-ʾ* is an orthographic variant of *p-l-h*, which
does mean "to set apart" or "to distinguish." But the common biblical use of
the verbal stem *p-l-ʾ* is in the sense of performing a wonder or acting in a way
that is profuse or extraordinary (thus Abraham ibn Ezra). If that is the most
likely meaning, then the biblical legislator sees the person who assumes these
obligations of self-restriction as doing something extraordinary. Whether this
extraordinary act is viewed with admiration or suspicion is not entirely clear.
   a nazirite vow. A nazir or nazirite is "someone set apart" (compare Joseph's
blessing, Genesis 49:26, "the one set apart from his brothers," *nezir ʾehaw*). The
word is a phonetic and etymological relative of the word that immediately
follows it, *neder*, "vow."

3. *from both wine and liquor*. The second of these two terms, *shekhar*, clearly
derives from the verb meaning "to intoxicate," but it is not clear what sort of
intoxicant it may have been. Some understand it as a form of ale, but Levine

not eat. All the days of his nazirite vow no razor shall pass over his head, 5
until the days come to term. That which he sets apart for the LORD shall
be holy, to grow loose the hair on his head. All the days of his setting 6
apart for the LORD, he shall not come to a dead person. For his father 7
and for his mother and for his brother and for his sister, he shall not be
defiled for them when they die, for the crown of his God is on his head.

---

rightly questions whether any kind of fermented grain would have been
allowed on the altar. The Targum of Onkelos renders *yayin weshekhar* as "new
wine and old wine," and since the restrictions on the nazirite are almost obsessively focused on anything connected with grapes, this understanding has a
certain plausibility.

5–6. *no razor shall pass over his head . . . he shall not come to a dead person.*
There are, then, three different restrictions involved in the vow of the nazirite:
abstention from all products of the grape, abstention from haircutting, and
avoidance of any sort of contact with a corpse. The last of these three restrictions reflects a general regulation regarding impurity, and is unambiguously
shared with the priesthood. The renunciation of wine is specific to the
nazirite: though the biblical writers variously register the dangers of drunken
excess, there is no general code of abstinence from drink, no biblical ethos of
asceticism. Allowing the hair to grow uncut has been the subject of much
anthropological speculation. The simplest inference is that it served as a very
visible outward sign of the nazirite's being "set apart," and that it then could
become a product of his body he could actually offer up—in flame—on the
altar. (There are no indications in these laws that the nazirite was to refrain
from sexual activity or joyous celebrations.) A late-ninth-century B.C.E.
Phoenician inscription seems to reflect an offering of hair to Astarte. One suspects that a practice roughly resembling that of the biblical nazirite, and
involving the renunciation of haircutting and then an offering of hair, was an
established devotional regimen among the West Semitic peoples. The Bible,
then, is by no means inventing or imposing this practice but recognizing it as
something that certain individuals, in emulation of established pagan tradition, might want to do. The aim of the legislation is to regulate the practice
and integrate it in the procedures of the official cult.

5. *the days come to term.* The literal sense of the Hebrew is "the days are filled."

7. *the crown of his God is on his head.* The Hebrew turns on a pun: *nezer* is a
common word for "crown," but in context it also means "naziritehood." The
abundance of uncut hair, crowning the head of the vow taker, is, as the visible

8,9 All the days of his naziritehood, he is holy to the LORD. And should a
dead person die near by him all of a sudden and he defile his nazirite
head, he shall shave his head on the day of his purification, on the sev-
10 enth day he shall shave it. And on the eighth day he shall bring two turtledoves or two pigeons to the priest at the entrance to the Tent of
11 Meeting. And the priest shall prepare one for an offense offering and
one for a burnt offering and shall atone for him, as he has offended
12 through the corpse, and he shall consecrate his head on that day. And
he shall keep apart for the LORD the days of his naziritehood, and he
shall bring a yearling lamb as a guilt offering, and the first days shall fall
13 away because he defiled his naziritehood. And this is the teaching for
the nazirite: When the days of his naziritehood come to term, he shall
14 be brought to the entrance of the Tent of Meeting, and he shall bring
forward his sacrifice to the LORD, one unblemished yearling lamb for a
burnt offering, and one unblemished yearling ewe as an offense offer-
15 ing, and one unblemished ram as a communion sacrifice, and a basket
of flatbread of fine flour, cakes mixed with oil, and flatbread wafers
16 coated with oil, and their grain offerings and their libations. And the
priest shall bring them forward before the LORD and do the offense
17 offering and its burnt offering. The ram he shall do as a communion

---

manifestation of his vow (*neder*), also a synecdoche for his naziritehood. Thus,
in verse 9, "his nazirite head" could also be rendered as "the crown of his
head."

12. *and the first days shall fall away*. That is, the days until the moment he
defiled himself by contact with the corpse are to be canceled, and he must
begin anew the count of days of the period he has vowed to be a nazirite.

14. *an offense offering*. What offense (*haṭaʾt*) has he committed? The consensus of medieval and modern commentators is that by now removing his person
from the realm of the consecrated to the ordinary realm of the profane, he is
taking something away from God and so must make an offense offering. An
antithetical construction is also possible: this "acting exceptionally" to set oneself apart for holiness, renouncing the pleasures of wine and letting one's hair
grow long, expresses a kind of presumption, an aspiration to spiritual superiority, and thus is an offense.

sacrifice to the LORD with the basket of flatbread, and the priest shall do his meal offering and his libation. And the nazirite shall shave his 18 nazirite head at the entrance of the Tent of Meeting, and he shall take the hair of his nazirite head and put it on the fire that is under the communion sacrifice. And the priest shall take the cooked shoulder from 19 the ram and one flatbread cake from the basket and one flatbread wafer and put them on the palms of the nazirite after he has shaved his crown. And the priest shall elevate them as an elevation offering before 20 the LORD. It is holy for the priest together with the breast of the elevation offering and the thigh of the donation. And afterward the nazirite shall drink wine. This is the teaching for the nazirite who vows his sac- 21 rifice to the LORD for his naziritehood besides what his hand may attain. According to his vow that he vows, so shall he do, together with the teaching for his naziritehood.'"

And the LORD spoke to Moses, saying, "Speak to Aaron and to his sons, 22,23 saying, 'Thus shall you bless the Israelites. Say to them:

---

20. *elevate them as an elevation offering*. This was a performative act of gesturing that formally conveyed what was elevated to God's jurisdiction. Practically, this meant that it was conveyed to God's agent, the priest.

21. *besides what his hand may attain*. The sacrifice just stipulated is the constitutive obligation of the nazirite vow. If the person who makes the vow has the means and desire to pledge more than this as an offering, he is free to do so.

23. *Thus shall you bless the Israelites*. This cadenced threefold blessing came to play a central liturgical role for both Jews and Christians, and probably began to serve that function even in the biblical period. Remarkable for its rhetorical stateliness and its emphatic use of repetition and overlapping terms, it is not, in strictly formal terms, a poem, but it does exhibit a remarkable degree of formal organization. Jacob Milgrom aptly characterizes its three clauses as embodying "a rising crescendo of 3, 5, and 7 words, respectively"; and this pattern, he goes on to observe, is coordinated with the number of stressed syllables (3, 5, and 7), and the total number of syllables (12, 14, and 16). A nearly identical version of this blessing was found on two silver filigree amulets in a burial cave at a site called Kateph Hinnom, in Jerusalem, in 1980. The amulets have been dated to the seventh century or early sixth century B.C.E. The version of the blessing on the amulets is somewhat abbreviated, which has led

24   May the L ord bless you and guard you.

25   May the L ord light up His face to you and grant grace to you;

26   May the L ord lift up His face to you and give you peace.'

27 And they shall set My name over the Israelites, and I Myself shall bless
     them."

---

some scholars to conclude that they register the "original" text. It seems more
plausible, however, that the text was abbreviated in order to fit it on the small
amulets: the shortened form does not preserve the just mentioned formal ele-
gance of the version in our text. Levine speculates that the prayer to be favored
and guarded by God may have been applied, given the fact that Kateph Hinnom was a burial place, to safeguarding in the underworld, though that is
hardly the original intention of the blessing.

25. *light up His face to you.* In biblical idiom, the shining of the face (or eyes)
toward someone is a showing of favor or affection. Lifting up the face has the
same meaning.

27. *and I Myself shall bless them.* The device of emphasis—the insertion of the
first-person pronoun *'ani* before the conjugated verb, which because of its conjugation would normally make the pronoun superfluous—is not reflected in
most translations. It is particularly important here because it underscores the
idea of God's special relationship with Israel: after the pronouncing of the
threefold blessing, God's name, a kind of divine proprietorship, will be set over
Israel, and God Himself will carry out the blessing.

CHAPTER 7

And it happened on the day Moses finished setting up the Taber- 1
nacle, that he anointed it and consecrated it and all its furnishings
and the altar and all its furnishings, and he anointed them and
consecrated them. And the chieftains of Israel—the heads of their 2
fathers' houses, they are the chieftains of the tribes, they are the ones
who stand over the reckoning—brought forward and set their offering 3
before the Lord: six covered wagons and twelve oxen, a wagon for every
two chieftains and an ox for each one, and they brought them before

---

1. *on the day Moses finished setting up the Tabernacle.* "On the day" (*beyom*) has
the semantic force of "when" but conveys a sense of epic solemnity lacking in
the more ordinary Hebrew term, *ka'asher*. (Compare Genesis 2:4, "On the day
the Lord God made earth and heavens.") The meaning here is obviously not
restricted to a single day because it will take the tribal chieftains twelve days
to present their offerings. Abraham ibn Ezra, characteristically looking for literary linkages, connects this entire passage with the immediately preceding
priestly blessing: once the threefold blessing was pronounced, the elaborate
proceedings of the dedication offerings could begin.

2. *stand over.* That is, supervise.

3. *six covered wagons.* The translation follows the Septuagint and the Aramaic
Targums in their understanding of *'eglot tsav*. They in turn seem to have based
their construction on the amphibian *tsav* in Leviticus 11:29, which many think
is a turtle. Some recent scholars instead connect *tsav* with a possible Akkadian
cognate that, like *'agalah*, means "wagon." It would then be an intensifier here.

4,5 the Tabernacle. And the LORD said to Moses, saying, "Take from them, and they shall be for doing the work of the Tent of Meeting, and you

6 shall give them to the Levites, each man according to his work." And

7 Moses took the wagons and the oxen and gave them to the Levites, the two wagons and the four oxen he gave to the Gershonites according to

8 their work. And the four wagons and the eight oxen he gave to the Merarites according to their work in the hand of Ithamar son of Aaron the

9 priest. And to the Kohathites he did not give, for the work of the sanc-

10 tuary was upon them, on the shoulder did they carry. And the chieftains brought forward the dedication offering of the altar on the day it was anointed, and the chieftains brought forward their offering for the ded-

11 ication of the altar. And the LORD said to Moses, "One chieftain each day, one chieftain each day, shall offer his offerings for the dedication of

12 the altar." And the one who brought forward his offering on the first day

13 was Nahshon son of Amminadab of the tribe of Judah. And his offering was one silver bowl, a hundred thirty shekels its weight, one silver basin, seventy shekels by the sanctuary shekel, both of them filled with fine

14 flour mixed with oil for a grain offering. One golden ladle of ten shekels

15 filled with incense. One bull from the herd, one ram, one yearling lamb

16,17 for the burnt offering. One goat for an offense offering. And for the communion sacrifice two oxen, five rams, five he-goats, five yearling

---

5. *each man according to his work.* As the subsequent verses show, the wagons are not distributed equally but according to the weight of the portage that the various levitical groups are to bear. The Kohathites, who carry the relatively light sanctuary furnishings on their shoulders, get no wagons.

12–88. This is the one signal instance in the entire Bible of extensive verbatim repetition without the slightest variation. (The single exception is that in verses 72 and 78, the word "day," *yom*, is—untranslatably—repeated after the formula "On the xth day," a usage perhaps dictated by the fact that the numeration has gone beyond ten to numbers that are compound in form in the Hebrew. The language in verse 12 reporting the first set of offerings also differs slightly from the formulas at the beginning of the subsequent eleven sets of offerings, but that is simply because it introduces the whole series.) Biblical narrative, as we have had many occasions to see, characteristically deploys significant swerves from verbatim repetition as it approximately repeats strings of phrases and whole clauses and sentences. This passage, however, is mani-

lambs. This is the offering of Nahshon son of Amminadab. On the 18
second day Nethanel son of Zuar, chieftain of Issachar, brought forward
his offering, and his offering was one silver bowl, a hundred thirty 19
shekels its weight, one silver basin, seventy shekels by the sanctuary
shekel, both of them filled with fine flour mixed with oil for a grain offering. One golden ladle of ten shekels filled with incense. One bull from 20,21
the herd, one ram, one yearling lamb for the burnt offering. One goat 22
for an offense offering. And for the communion sacrifice two oxen, five 23
rams, five he-goats, five yearling lambs. This is the offering of Nethanel
son of Zuar. On the third day, the chieftain of the Zebulunites, Eliab 24
son of Helon. His offering was one silver bowl, a hundred thirty shekels 25
its weight, one silver basin, seventy shekels by the sanctuary shekel,
both of them filled with fine flour mixed with oil for a grain offering.
One golden ladle of ten shekels filled with incense. One bull from the 26,27
herd, one ram, one yearling lamb for the burnt offering. One goat for an 28
offense offering. And for the communion sacrifice two oxen, five rams, 29
five he-goats, five yearling lambs. This is the offering of Eliab son of

---

festly not narrative but a kind of epic inventory. Each of the tribes, here
accorded absolutely equal status before the sanctuary without political hierarchy, brings exactly the same offering. One can readily imagine that the members of each tribe in the ancient audience of this text would be expected to
relish the sumptuousness of its own tribal offering exactly equal to all the others, as it hears the passage read. It is also well to remember that lists and the
repetitions they entail constitute an established literary form with its own aesthetic pleasures—as, for example, in the catalogue of the ships in the *Iliad* or
in the cumulative repetitive structures of songs like *Ḥad Gadya* ("An Only
Kid") and, more apposite to this catalogue of gifts, "On the Twelve Days of
Christmas." The offerings of the tribes encompass animal, vegetable, and mineral gifts (the sacrificial beasts, the grain offerings, the precious vessels) and
are punctuated by the solemn stipulation of weight and number. All this is
then totaled up in verses 84–88, after the twelve verbatim repetitions. Baruch
Levine notes, moreover, certain similarities in form with various West Semitic
temple inventories that have been uncovered by archeologists. (In the Hebrew,
for example, the ordinal numbers uncharacteristically follow the nouns rather
than precede them, evidently the set form for temple inventories.) This entire
passage, like almost all of the first ten chapters of Numbers, is the product of
Priestly writers, and it strongly reflects both their professional concerns and
the literary antecedents on which they drew.

30 Helon. On the fourth day, the chieftain of the Reubenites, Elizur son of
31 Shedeur. His offering was one silver bowl, a hundred thirty shekels its
weight, one silver basin, seventy shekels by the sanctuary shekel, both
32 of them filled with fine flour mixed with oil for a grain offering. One
33 golden ladle of ten shekels filled with incense. One bull from the herd,
34 one ram, one yearling sheep for the burnt offering. One goat for an
35 offense offering. And for the communion sacrifice two oxen, five rams,
five he-goats, five yearling lambs. This is the offering of Elizur son of
36 Shedeur. On the fifth day, the chieftain of the Simeonites, Shelumiel
37 son of Zurishaddai. His offering was one silver bowl, a hundred thirty
shekels its weight, one silver basin, seventy shekels by the sanctuary
shekel, both of them filled with fine flour mixed with oil for a grain offer-
38,39 ing. One golden ladle of ten shekels filled with incense. One bull from
40 the herd, one ram, one yearling lamb for the burnt offering. One goat
41 for an offense offering. And for the communion sacrifice two oxen, five
rams, five he-goats, five yearling lambs. This is the offering of Shelumiel
42 son of Zurishaddai. On the sixth day, the chieftain of the Gadites, Elias-
43 aph son of Deuel. His offering was one silver bowl, a hundred thirty
shekels its weight, one silver basin, seventy shekels by the sanctuary
shekel, both of them filled with fine flour mixed with oil for a grain offer-
44,45 ing. One golden ladle of ten shekels filled with incense. One bull from
46 the herd, one ram, one yearling lamb for the burnt offering. One goat
47 for an offense offering. And for the communion sacrifice two oxen, five
rams, five he-goats, five yearling lambs. This is the offering of Eliasaph
48 son of Deuel. On the seventh day, the chieftain of the Ephraimites,
49 Elishama son of Ammihud. His offering was one silver bowl, a hundred
thirty shekels its weight, one silver basin, seventy shekels by the sanctuary shekel, both of them filled with fine flour mixed with oil for a grain
50,51 offering. One golden ladle of ten shekels filled with incense. One bull
52 from the herd, one ram, one yearling lamb for the burnt offering. One
53 goat for an offense offering. And for the communion sacrifice two oxen,
five rams, five he-goats, five yearling lambs. This is the offering of
54 Elishama son of Ammihud. On the eighth day, the chieftain of the
55 Manassites, Gamaliel son of Pedahzur. His offering was one silver bowl,
a hundred thirty shekels its weight, one silver basin, seventy shekels by
the sanctuary shekel, both of them filled with fine flour mixed with oil
56 for a grain offering. One golden ladle of ten shekels filled with incense.

NUMBERS 7:57

One bull from the herd, one ram, one yearling lamb for the burnt offer- 57
ing. One goat for an offense offering. And for the communion sacrifice 58,59
two oxen, five rams, five he-goats, five yearling lambs. This is the offering of Gamaliel son of Pedahzur. On the ninth day, the chieftain of the 60
Benjaminites, Abidan son of Gideoni. His offering was one silver bowl, 61
a hundred thirty shekels its weight, one silver basin, seventy shekels by
the sanctuary shekel, both of them filled with fine flour mixed with oil
for a grain offering. One golden ladle of ten shekels filled with incense. 62
One bull from the herd, one ram, one yearling lamb for the burnt offer- 63
ing. One goat for an offense offering. And for the communion sacrifice 64,65
two oxen, five rams, five he-goats, five yearling lambs. This is the offering of Abidan son of Gideoni. On the tenth day, the chieftain of the 66
Danites, Ahiezer son of Ammishaddai. His offering was one silver bowl, 67
a hundred thirty shekels its weight, one silver basin, seventy shekels by
the sanctuary shckel, both of them filled with fine flour mixed with oil
for a grain offering. One golden ladle of ten shekels filled with incense. 68
One bull from the herd, one ram, one yearling lamb for the burnt offer- 69
ing. One goat for an offense offering. And for the communion sacrifice 70,71
two oxen, five rams, five he-goats, five ycarling lambs. This is the offering of Ahiezer son of Ammishaddai. On the eleventh day, the chieftain 72
of the Asherites, Pagiel son of Ochran. His offering was one silver bowl, 73
a hundred thirty shekels its weight, one silver basin, seventy shekels by
the sanctuary shekel, both of them filled with fine flour mixed with oil
for a grain offering. One golden ladle of ten shekels filled with incense. 74
One bull from thc herd, one ram, one yearling lamb for the burnt offer- 75
ing. One goat for an offense offering. And for the communion sacrifice 76,77
two oxen, five rams, five he-goats, five yearling lambs. This is the offering of Pagiel son of Ochran. On the twelfth day, the chieftain of the 78
Naphtalites, Ahira son of Enan. His offering was one silver bowl, a hun- 79
dred thirty shekels its weight, one silver basin, seventy shekels by the
sanctuary shekel, both of them filled with fine flour mixed with oil for a
grain offering. One golden ladle of ten shekels filled with incense. One 80,81
bull from the herd, one ram, one yearling lamb for the burnt offering.
One goat for an offense offering. And for the communion sacrifice two 82,83
oxen, five rams, five he-goats, five yearling lambs. This is the offering of
Ahira son of Enan. This is the dedication offering of the altar on the day 84
of its anointing from the chieftains of Israel: twelve silver bowls, twelve

85 silver basins, twelve golden ladles, one hundred thirty shekels each silver
bowl and seventy each basin; all the silver of the vessels, two thousand

86 four hundred by the sanctuary shekel. Twelve golden ladles filled with
incense, ten shekels the ladle by the sanctuary shekel; all the gold of the

87 ladles, one hundred twenty shekels. All the cattle for the burnt offering,
twelve bulls, twelve rams, twelve yearling lambs and their grain offering,

88 and twelve goats for an offense offering. And all the cattle for the communion sacrifice, twenty-four bulls, sixty rams, sixty he-goats, sixty yearling lambs. This is the dedication of the altar after it was anointed.

89 And when Moses came into the Tent of Meeting to speak with Him, he
would hear the voice being spoken to him from above the covering that
is over the Ark of the Covenant, from between the two cherubim, and
He would speak to him.

---

89. *And when Moses came into the Tent of Meeting to speak with Him.* This sentence about Moses's mode of communication with God in the Tent of Meeting
does not appear to be connected either with what precedes or what follows it.
The sentence also exhibits three rather puzzling turns of speech. The masculine pronoun that is the object of "to speak with" has to refer to God, but God
is not mentioned by name anywhere in this verse. One might have expected "to
speak with the LORD" in the initial clause of this little unit. Perhaps it is absent
because the unit has been excerpted from a larger literary document.

the voice being spoken. The second linguistic anomaly of this verse is the
use of the reflexive form of the verb, *midaber* (instead of the usual *medaber*,
"speaking"). Levine understands this form as an indication of "continually
speaking," though reflexive verbs in Hebrew are often used to indicate a passive sense. It is also possible that the meaning is genuinely reflexive: "the voice
speaking itself." There seems to be a theological impulse here to interpose
some kind of mediation between the divine source of the speech and the audi-
ble voice that is spoken to Moses.

and He would speak to him. The third linguistic knot in the strand of this
sentence is that the last two words, *wayedabar 'elaw*, a verb and a preposition
with no indication of proper nouns, could also be read the other way around:
"and he [Moses] would speak to Him." One wonders whether the cryptic style
of this verse might reflect a certain nervousness about the fraught topic of
direct communication between God and His prophet, as the highly cryptic
language of the Bridegroom of Blood fragment (Exodus 4:24–26) reflects a
nervousness about its potent mythic character.

CHAPTER 8

And the LORD spoke to Moses, saying, "Speak to Aaron and say to 1,2
him: 'When you light up the lamps, opposite the front of the lamp
stand shall the seven lamps give light.'" And thus Aaron did: oppo- 3
site the front of the lamp stand he lit up its lamps as the LORD had
charged Moses. And this is the fashioning of the lamp stand: ham- 4
mered work of gold, from its base to its petal it was hammered work,
according to the semblance that the LORD had shown Moses, thus did
he make the lamp stand.

---

2. *When you light up the lamps.* Rashi provides a vividly imaginative explanation for why this unit of four verses about the lamp stand should immediately
follow the dedicatory offering of the twelve tribes: "When Aaron saw the dedicatory offering of the chieftains, he was dismayed that he was not together
with them in the dedicatory offering, neither he nor his tribe. The Holy One
said to him, 'By your life, yours is greater than theirs, for you light and tend to
the lamps.'"

4. *petal.* This is a collective noun indicating the floral ornamentation of the
seven lamp holders.

5,6 And the LORD spoke to Moses, saying, "Take the Levites from the

7 midst of the Israelites and purify them. And thus you shall do to them
to purify them: sprinkle on them expiation water and pass a razor over

8 all their flesh and wash their clothes and be purified. And they shall
take a bull from the herd and its grain offering, fine flour mixed with
oil, and a second bull from the herd you shall take as an offense offer-

9 ing. And you shall bring the Levites forward before the Tent of Meet-

10 ing and you shall assemble all the community of Israelites. And you
shall bring the Levites forward before the LORD, and the Israelites shall

11 lay their hands on the Levites. And Aaron shall make of the Levites an
elevation offering before the LORD from the Israelites, and they shall

12 serve to do the work of the LORD. And the Levites, they shall lay their
hands on the head of the bulls and make the one an offense offering

13 and the one a burnt offering to the LORD to atone for the Levites. And
you shall stand the Levites before Aaron and before his sons and make

14 of them an elevation offering to the LORD. And you shall divide the

15 Levites from the Israelites and they shall be Levites to Me. And afterward the Levites shall come to work in the Tent of Meeting and you

---

6. *Take the Levites . . . and purify them.* If there is no biblical theology of original sin, there is, at least among the Priestly writers, a technology to deal with
original impurity. The dangerous inner zone of the sanctuary can be entered
only when a person has undergone an elaborate sequence of acts to rid himself of the impurity that is intrinsic to profane life: thus the Levites must be
sprinkled with expiation water, have their body hair shaven, their garments
washed, and a special sacrifice intended to remove even inadvertent offense
(ḥata't) offered up for them.

7. *expiation water.* Many medieval and modern interpreters understand this as
a reference to the water mingled with the ashes of the red heifer referred to in
Numbers 19:1–9, though Baruch Levine offers grounds for skepticism about
this identification. The term *ḥata't* means both offense (political, diplomatic,
social, moral, or cultic) and, especially in cultic contexts, any ritual means
employed to remove or cancel the effect of the offense committed.

10. *the Israelites shall lay their hands.* For practical reasons, as many commentators have noted, the laying on of hands would have to be performed by designated representatives of the people.

shall purify them and make of them an elevation offering. For wholly 16
given they are to Me from the midst of the Israelites instead of the
breach of every womb, firstborn of all of the Israelites, I have taken
them to Me. For Mine is every firstborn among the Israelites, in man 17
and in beast, on the day I struck down every firstborn in the land of
Egypt, I consecrated them to Me. And I took the Levites instead of 18
every firstborn among the Israelites. And I made the Levites wholly 19
given to Aaron and to his sons from the midst of the Israelites to do the
work of the Israelites in the Tent of Meeting, to atone for the Israelites,
that there be no scourge against the Israelites when the Israelites
approach the sanctuary." And Moses, and Aaron and all the commu- 20
nity of Israelites, did to the Levites as all that the LORD had charged
Moses concerning the Levites, thus did the Israelites do to them. And 21
the Levites did expiation and washed their clothes, and Aaron made of
them an elevation offering before the LORD, and Aaron atoned for them
to purify them. And afterward the Levites did come to do their work in 22
the Tent of Meeting before Aaron and before his sons; as the LORD had
charged Moses about the Levites, thus did they do to them.

---

19. *I made the Levites wholly given to Aaron and to his sons* Although "given"
(*netunim*) is not repeated (*netunim netunim*) as above, an analogous emphasis
is conveyed by the cognate verb (in the translation "made" but literally in the
Hebrew "gave"). This is the first clear indication of a hierarchical division of
cultic labor between the Aaronide priests (*kohanim*) and the Levites, who
serve them and do the heavy lifting in the sanctuary (the "work"), in contrast
to officiating in the ritual. Levine conjectures that historically this division
between Levites and priests began only at the time of Josiah's reforms around
621 B.C.E.

    that there be no scourge against the Israelites. This characteristically Priestly
notion is that profane persons, presuming to enter sacred space, would automatically trigger the devastating manifestation of divine fury (*qetsef*) in the
form of a scourge or epidemic. The presence of the Levites in the sanctuary is
thus properly represented as a "watch" or the equivalent of army service, for as
properly consecrated and purified cultic servitors, they act as a kind of protective phalanx that wards off danger from the Israelites who might otherwise
approach too close to the sacred zone.

23,24 And the LORD spoke to Moses, saying, "This is what regards the Levites: from twenty-five years old and up, each shall come to do army
25 service in the work of the Tent of Meeting. And from fifty years old he
26 shall come back from the army work and shall work no more. And he shall serve his brothers in the Tent of Meeting to keep watch, but work he shall not do. So shall you do to the Levites in their watch."

---

24. *from twenty-five years old and up.* Earlier, the beginning age for levitical service was stated as thirty. Various efforts have been made to harmonize the contradiction, but one suspects that the different passages reflect different traditions.

25. *he shall come back from the army work and shall work no more.* The provision made here is for a kind of phased retirement. The defining term of difference is "work." From the age of fifty, the Levite is relieved of heavy labor within the sanctuary, the responsibilities that were undertaken as a kind of equivalent for military service, but he continues to assist his brother Levites, evidently outside the sanctuary, in their guard duty.

CHAPTER 9

A nd the LORD spoke to Moses in the Wilderness of Sinai in the sec- 1
ond year of their going out from the land of Egypt in the first
month, saying, "Let the Israelites do the Passover offering at its 2
fixed time. On the fourteenth day in this month at twilight you shall do 3
it at its fixed time, according to all its statutes and according to all its
laws you shall do it." And Moses spoke to the Israelites to do the 4
Passover offering. And they did the Passover offering in the first month 5
on the fourteenth day of the month at twilight in the Wilderness of
Sinai, as all that the LORD had charged Moses, thus did the Israelites
do.

And it happened that there were men who were defiled by human 6
corpse and could not do the Passover offering on that day, and they

---

2. *Let the Israelites do the Passover offering.* The reiteration here of the instructions for the Passover offering picks up the first injunction about the Passover
offering on the eve of the departure from Egypt (Exodus 12:43–51). There is
narrative symmetry in the reiteration: the first Passover was celebrated just
before the Israelites set out on their journey from Egypt. Now they are about
to move onward from the Sinai encampment in their Wilderness itinerary—a
topic to which verses 15–23 alert us—and again the departure is marked by the
passover offering.

6. *And it happened that there were men who were defiled by human corpse.* The
injunction to offer the Passover sacrifice at its fixed time is followed by a piece
of case law. What is to be done for Israelites who find themselves in a state of
ritual impurity and hence excluded from the sacrificial ceremony?

7 drew near before Moses and before Aaron on that day. And these men
   said to him, "We are defiled by human corpse. Why should we be withheld from offering the LORD's sacrifice at its fixed time in the midst of
8 the Israelites?" And Moses said to them, "Stand by, that I may hear
9 what the LORD will charge you." And the LORD spoke to Moses, saying,
10 "Speak to the Israelites, saying, 'Any man who may be defiled by corpse
   or on a distant journey, of you or of your generations to come, and
11 would do the Passover offering to the LORD, in the second month on
   the fourteenth day at twilight they shall do it, with flatcakes and bitter
12 herbs they shall eat it. They shall leave nothing of it till morning, and
   no bone shall they break in it, according to all the statutes of the
13 Passover offering they shall do it. And the man who is pure and was not
   on a journey and fails to do the Passover offering, that person shall be
   cut off from his kin, for he did not offer the LORD's sacrifice at its fixed
14 time. That man will bear his punishment. And should a stranger
   sojourn with you and do the Passover offering to the LORD, according
   to the statute of the Passover offering and according to its law, thus
   shall he do. One statute shall you have, both for the stranger and for
   the native of the land.'"

---

7. *Why should we be withheld from offering the LORD's sacrifice at its fixed time in the midst of the Israelites?* The partaking in the Passover sacrifice is the primary act of affirming membership in the community of Israel, and so the people in question are distressed that a mere accident, contact with a corpse (or perhaps another source of ritual pollution), should exclude them from the community. Conversely, a person who deliberately neglects to perform the Passover offering is "cut off from his kin."

10. *or on a distant journey.* This is another circumstance, not that of the men who come to petition Moses, that would prevent someone from participating in the Passover offering. Baruch Levine plausibly infers that the stipulation of a distant journey presupposes the Deuteronomic requirement of a centralized cult. (The initial Passover sacrifice was performed in each household, and a person on a journey could presumably have participated with a household where he was a guest.)

14. *should a stranger sojourn with you.* This provision for the resident alien (*ger*) reflects a prevalent ancient Near Eastern practice of allowing such residents

And on the day the Tabernacle was set up, the cloud covered the 15
Tabernacle of the Tent of the Covenant, and in the evening it would be
over the Tabernacle like a semblance of fire until morning. Thus it 16
would be perpetually: the cloud would cover it, and a semblance of fire
at night. And as the cloud lifted from the tent, then the Israelites would 17
journey onward, and in the place where the cloud would abide, there
would the Israelites camp. By the LORD's word the Israelites would 18
journey onward and by the LORD's word they would camp, all the days
that the cloud would abide over the Tabernacle they would camp. And 19
when the cloud lingered over the Tabernacle many days, the Israelites
would keep the LORD's watch and would not journey onward. And 20
sometimes the cloud would be but a few days over the Tabernacle. By
the LORD's word they would camp and by the LORD's word they would
journey onward. And sometimes the cloud would be from evening till 21
morning and the cloud would lift in the morning and they would journey onward, or a day and a night and the cloud would lift and they
would journey onward. Or two days or a month or a year, when the 22
cloud lingered over the Tabernacle to abide over it, the Israelites would
camp and would not journey onward, and when it lifted, they would
journey onward. By the LORD's word they would camp and by the 23
LORD's word they would journey onward. The LORD's watch did they
keep by the LORD's word in the hand of Moses.

---

to adopt the local cult. No formal ceremony of "conversion," as in later times,
was required, though the law in Exodus stipulates that the stranger must be
circumcised before he can partake in the Passover offering. That requirement
is presumably implied here in "according to the statute of the Passover offering and according to its law" but it is not expressly stated.

15–23. This literary unit nicely sets the stage for the peregrinations and per-
turbations that will make up much of the Book of Numbers from chapter 10
onward. Until this point, the forward drive of narrative has been abandoned
for tabulation—census and military roster—and legislation in a long stasis in
the Wilderness of Sinai. Now the Israelites prepare to move on, and their
order of march, dictated by the descent upon the Tabernacle and the ascent
from the Tabernacle of the divine cloud, is reported in a series of verbs in the
iterative tense. The indication of the varying time periods during which the
cloud "abides" (or "tents," "dwells," a verb cognate with the noun *mishkan*,

"Tabernacle") over the Tabernacle may seem repetitious but in fact constitutes a grand rhetorical flourish: all of Israel's movements through the wilderness are prompted by the divine sign, with the duration of encampment varying from a night or two to a month to a year. Yitzhak Avishur neatly confirms the purposeful rhetorical organization of the passage by pointing to its studied use of numerically formulaic repetitions: the phrase "by the LORD's word" (literally, "by the LORD's mouth") occurs seven times—three times in conjunction with "they would journey onward," three times in conjunction with "they would camp," and at the very end of the passage, in conjunction with neither. "Tabernacle" occurs seven times; the root *sh-k-n* from which it derives, ten times; and, if one follows the Septuagint rather than the Masoretic Text, "cloud" also appears ten times. The carefully measured repetitions thus yield a tight thematic interweave of cloud, Tabernacle, camping, journeying, and God's word or direction.

CHAPTER 10

And the LORD spoke to Moses, saying, "Make you two silver trum- [1,2] pets, hammered work you shall make them, and they shall serve you for calling the community and for the journeying of the camps. And when they blow them, all the community shall meet with [3] you at the entrance of the Tent of Meeting. And if but one they blow, [4] the chieftains, the heads of Israel's thousands, shall meet with you. And if you blow a long blast, the camps that are encamped to the east [5] shall journey on. And if you blow a long blast a second time, the camps [6] that are encamped to the south shall journey on, a long blast they shall

---

2. *two silver trumpets*. After all the lists of the early chapters of Numbers, the visual pageantry of the Tabernacle furnishings, and the deployment of the tribal troops with their banners, sound enters the text—in essence, musical flourishes, a pageantry of sound. These particular sounds are in the first instance the signal for the forward movement of the camp, and so propel the whole story from the long stasis of the stay at Sinai into the narrative of wanderings that constitutes much of what follows. The hammered silver trumpets are more artfully wrought wind instruments than the *shofar*, the ram's horn, with which they share some functions. The *shofar* is used for the call to battle, and for coronations; these trumpets serve the distinctive purposes of signaling the march in the wilderness and accompanying cultic celebrations.

5. *a long blast*. There is no scholarly agreement as to whether the Hebrew *teru'ah* means "a long blast" and the other term, *teqi'ah*, "a short blast," or the other way around. The verb *taqa'* has the primary meaning of "stab," and by extension, a stabbing or penetration of breath through the aperture of a wind instrument. This sense might perhaps lend itself better to the idea of a short blast. *Teru'ah* also means "shout," without the aid of an instrument, and might be more prolonged.

7   blow for their journeyings. And when the assembly is gathered, you
8   shall blow but let out no long blast. And the sons of Aaron, the priests,
     shall blow the trumpets, and they shall become for you an everlasting
9   statute for your generations. And when you come in battle in your land
     against the foe who assails you, you shall let out a long blast with the
     trumpets and be remembered before the LORD your God and be res-
10 cued from your enemies. And on the day of your gladness and at your
     fixed seasons and on your new moons, you shall blow the trumpets over
     your burnt offerings and over your communion sacrifices, and they
     shall become for you a remembrance before your God. I am the LORD
     your God."

11 And it happened in the second year in the second month on the twen-
     tieth of the month that the cloud lifted from the Tabernacle of the
12 Covenant. And the Israelites began on their journeyings from the
     Wilderness of Sinai, and the cloud abided in the Wilderness of Paran.
13 And they journeyed on from the first by the word of the LORD through
14 the hand of Moses. And the banner of the camp of the Judahites jour-
     neyed first by their divisions, and over its division, Nahshon son of
15 Amminadab. And over the division of the tribe of Issacharites, Nethanel
16 son of Zuar. And over the division of the tribe of Zebulunites, Eliab son
17 of Helon. And the Tabernacle was taken down, and the Gershonites and
18 the Merarites, the bearers of the Tabernacle, journeyed on. And the
     banner of the camp of Reuben by their divisions journeyed on, and over
19 its division, Elizur son of Shedeur. And over the division of the tribe of
20 Simeonites, Shelumiel son of Zurishaddai. And over the division of the

---

9. *let out a long blast . . . and be remembered before the* LORD. Here the function of the trumpets is identical with that of the *shofar*. The trumpet blast ral-
lies the troops, perhaps frightens the enemy, and is imagined as a means for
alerting God's attention to Israel, calling them to mind, being a "remembrance"
before Him.

12. *And the Israelites began on their journeyings.* The marching order of the
tribes laid out in the next fifteen verses is a precise implementation of
the tribal deployment detailed in chapter 2.

tribe of Gadites, Eliasaph son of Deuel. And the Kohathites, the bear- 21
ers of the sanctuary, journeyed on, and they would set up the Tabernacle by the time they came. And the banner of the camp of the 22
Ephraimites by their divisions journeyed on, and over its division,
Elishama son of Ammihud. And over the division of the tribe of Man- 23
assehites, Gamaliel son of Pedahzur. And over the division of the tribe 24
of Benjaminites, Abidan son of Gideoni. And the banner of the tribe of 25
Danites journeyed on, the rear guard for all the camps by their divisions,
and over its division, Ahiezer son of Ammishaddai. And over the division 26
of the tribe of Asherites, Pagiel son of Ochran. And over the division of 27
the tribe of Naphtalites, Ahira son of Enan. These are the journeyings 28
of the Israelites by their divisions as they journeyed on.

And Moses said to Hobab son of Reuel the Midianite, Moses's father- 29
in-law, "We are journeying to the place of which the LORD said to us, 'It
will I give to you.' Come with us and we shall be good to you, for the

---

21. *bearers of the sanctuary.* In contradistinction to the Gershonites and the
Merarites, "bearers of the Tabernacle," the burden of the Kohathites is not the
structure itself but the cultic paraphernalia of the sanctuary.

and they would set up the Tabernacle by the time they came. As elsewhere,
biblical idiom is parsimonious in stipulating the antecedents of pronouns. The
first "they" would have to refer to the Gershonites and Merarites, who carry
the Tabernacle; the second "they" would be the Kohathites.

29. *And Moses said to Hobab son of Reuel the Midianite.* We now leave the
Priestly tabulations and pomp and ceremony and enter the first actual narrative episode of the Book of Numbers. The name of Moses's Midianite father-
in-law is a bafflement that has been resolved only by rather contorted
harmonizing explanations. In Exodus, he is called Jethro, who also seems to be
identical with Reuel, while here he is Hobab son of Reuel. It seems likely that
these narratives draw on authentic ancient traditions about an alliance and
kinship between Moses and the Kenite clan of the Midianites, and those traditions provided an etiological explanation for the peaceful cohabitation of the
Kenites with the Israelites (compare Judges 4:17–22). In the traditional variants of these stories about the Kenites, Moses's father-in-law may have been
assigned different names.

We are journeying to the place. No foreshadowing is allowed to intrude. At
this point, Moses, unwitting of the disasters that lie ahead, imagines that both

30 LORD has spoken a good thing for Israel." And he said to him, "I shall
31 not go, but to my land and to my birthplace I shall go." And he said to
   him, "Pray, do not leave us, for do you not know our encampment in the
32 wilderness? And you will serve us as eyes. And so, if you go with us, by
   that good which the LORD will do for us, we shall be good to you."

33 And they journeyed on from the mountain of the LORD a three days'
   march, with the Ark of the LORD's Covenant journeying before them a
34 three days' march to scout for a resting place for them. And the LORD's

---

he and the people he is leading are about to cross the wilderness and enter into
the promised land.

    the LORD *has spoken a good thing.* Literally, "spoken good," with the obvious
sense of "promised to confer all manner of good things." By repeating the root
in both verb and noun, Moses twice emphasizes (the second time in verse 32)
that he means to have Hobab share in the good that God has promised Israel.

30. *to my land and to my birthplace I shall go.* These words are probably an
explicit allusion to God's first command to Abraham, "Go forth from your land
and your birthplace" (Genesis 12:1). Hobab asserts the desire to reverse that
direction, to go back to his own homeland instead of forging on to the land
God has promised Israel.

31. *do you not know our encampment in the wilderness?* Previously in Numbers,
and before that in Exodus, there was a heavy stress on the idea that the cloud
over the Tabernacle would guide the people. Here, by contrast, human agency
is stressed: Hobab, himself indigenous to the great wilderness to the south of
Canaan, is to act as a native guide through this forbidding territory. It is conceivable that this story registers an actual historical memory of receiving help
of this sort from the Midianites. Hobab's response to Moses is not stated, but
the later presence of his descendants among the Israelites suggests that he
agreed to accompany them. Perhaps the end of this story was excised editorially in order not to diminish the idea conveyed in the next two verses that it was
the Ark with the accompanying cloud that led Israel through the wilderness.

33. *the Ark . . . journeying before them a three days' march.* Though the Ark was to
lead the way, this three days' distance is baffling, for in that case the Ark would
not have been visible to the people who were supposed to follow it. A common
scholarly solution to the problem is to see the second occurrence of "a three
days' march" as an inadvertent scribal repetition (dittography) of the first.

cloud was over them by day as they journeyed on from the camp. And 35
it happened, as the Ark journeyed on, that Moses would say,

> "Rise O Lord, and Your enemies scatter,
>   and Your foes flee before You!"

and when it came to rest, he would say, 36

> "Come back O Lord to Israel's teeming myriads."

---

35. *Rise O Lord.* These words attributed to Moses are often referred to as the Song of the Ark. Although one recent scholar, Richard Elliott Friedman, has expressed skepticism about whether this is actually a poem, there is sufficient evidence of poetic structure and diction even in the brief fragment. Rhythmically, these two versets contain, respectively, four and three stresses, a pattern sometimes found in lines of biblical poetry. The word pairings, enemies/foes, scatter/flee, are a hallmark of parallelistic poetry. The concluding line (verse 36) uses a bit of emphatic synonymity, "teeming myriads" (literally "myriads of thousands") that is marked as poetic diction and also appears, with the order of "myriads" and "thousands" reversed, in the poetic blessing for Rebekah, Genesis 24:60. "Rise," as several commentators have noted, also has a military sense of "attack," but the visual image of elevation is important—God, imagined as enthroned on the cherubim carved over the Ark, surges up like a warrior-king as the Ark is lifted to be carried forward. In the Hebrew text, the unit that verses 35–36 constitute is bracketed off from what precedes and follows by inverted letter *nuns.* This is a scribal device known from Late Antiquity for marking a piece of text that is out of place, or quoted from another source. Some have conjectured that the Song of the Ark is actually a quotation from the mysterious Book of the Battles of YHWH mentioned elsewhere. Whatever the source, the quotation may give only the opening lines of two poems rather than the integral text of the poems. In any case, this is the first of several fragments of archaic Hebrew poetry quoted in Numbers.

36. *Come back O Lord to Israel's teeming myriads.* There is no explicit "to" in the Hebrew connecting "come back" with Israel's myriads. The absence of the preposition has inspired a variety of ingenious interpretations, but one should keep in mind that biblical poetic diction—especially in the case of the more archaic layer of Hebrew poetry—exhibits a great deal of ellipsis, which is, after all, a means of eliminating extra syllables and heightening the compactness of the utterance. It thus seems reasonable to infer that "to" is implied here.

CHAPTER 11

And the people became complainers of evil in the ears of the
LORD, and the LORD heard and His wrath flared and the LORD's
fire burned against them and consumed along the edge of the
camp. And the people cried out to Moses, and Moses interceded with
the LORD, and the fire sunk down. And he called the name of that place
Taberah, for the LORD's fire had burned against them.

---

1. *And the people became complainers of evil.* The grammatical construction of
the Hebrew is unusual—literally, "And the people became [or were] as complainers of evil." Some understand this as an indication of persistence in the
activity of complaint, though it is at least as plausible to construe it as conveying the initiation of the activity. The likelihood of the latter construction is
reinforced by the fact that this episode is the first of the numerous episodes
of "murmuring" that punctuate Numbers. In this initial instance, no specific
content of the complaint is stipulated. This lack of specification may be
intended so that the episode can serve as a general paradigm for all the incidents that follow: unreasonable complaint triggering God's consuming wrath,
a plea for Moses's intercession, an end to the devastation.

3. *Taberah.* The place-name is derived from the verb *ba'ar*, "to burn," and so
means something like Conflagration.

And the riffraff that was in their midst felt a craving, and the Israelites, 4
too, again wept and said, "Who will feed us meat? We remember the 5
fish we used to eat in Egypt for free, the cucumbers and the melons and
the leeks and the onions and the garlic. And now our throats are dry. 6

---

4. *the riffraff.* The Hebrew *'asafsuf* is a noun in the reduplicative form (like the
English "riffraff") derived from the verb *'asaf*, "to gather." The reduplicative
form in Hebrew often has a pejorative sense: it is also used for the parallel
term in Exodus 12:38, *'erev rav* (perhaps originally *'ararav*, "motley throng.")
Richard Elliott Friedman has noted that the verb *'asaf* is especially prominent
in this chapter and the next. In the long second episode of the present chapter, Moses will strategically "gather" elders around him, and in an unusual
usage that appears to be dictated by the desire to repeat this verb, he does not
return to or enter the camp but is "gathered back into the camp" (verse 30).
The play between *'asafsuf* and *'asaf*, I would suggest, focuses the issues of leadership and national cohesiveness that are central both to this chapter and to
much of what follows in Numbers. There is a negative kind of "gathering" or
assembly, the ragtag collection of *'asafsuf* that congregates in order to voice
divisive gripes; and there is a positive gathering of leaders in which Moses del-
egates authority and imposes coherent governance on the people.

    and the Israelites, too. The subversive complaints of the riffraff, who are of
foreign origin, prove infectious and spread to the body of the Israelites proper.

    Who will feed us meat? This question may seem puzzling because the peo-
ple immediately go on to mention not meat but fish—a prominent source of
protein in the Egyptian diet—and its elaborate vegetable garnishings. In the
event, they get not fish, scarcely imaginable in this desert setting, but fowl.
Some interpreters contend, with a bit of a stretch, that "meat" means "fish." It
may make more sense to infer that the complainers, filled with craving or lust
(*ta'awah*) for the good old days of slavery, remember the sumptuous feasts of
Egypt and, in their appetitive recollection, are a little confused about the culinary terms: first they say "meat," the most substantial object of gluttonous
craving, but when they review the actual menu of their Egyptian meals, the
main course, plausibly enough along the banks of the Nile, turns out to be
fish.

5. *for free.* This term is a striking instance of selective memory. The slaves did
not have to pay for their food, which was provided by their owners, but of
course a brutally high price was exacted through the punishing labor imposed
upon them by their taskmasters.

7 There is nothing save the manna before our eyes." And the manna was
8 like coriander seed and its color like the color of bdellium. The people
would go about and gather it and grind it between millstones or pound
it in a pestle and cook it in a cauldron and make it into cakes. And its
9 taste was like the creaminess of oil. And when the dew would come
10 down on the camp at night, the manna would come down upon it. And
Moses heard the people weeping by its clans, every man at the entrance
of his tent, and the Lord's wrath flared fiercely, and in Moses's eyes it
11 was evil. And Moses said to the Lord, "Why have You done evil to Your
servant, and why have I not found favor in Your eyes, to put the burden

---

6. *before our eyes*. The Hebrew lacks "before" (a mere particle, *lᵉ*), whether
because this is an ellipsis or a scribal omission. In the Hebrew, there is an
anomalous "to" (*'el*) before "manna," and perhaps this preposition actually
belongs before "eyes."

7. *bdellium*. This English term may derive from the Hebrew *bedolaḥ* or its
Semitic cognates; it is a semitransparent yellowish gum. Later Hebrew, working from what is probably a misinterpretation of the biblical term, uses *bedolaḥ*
in the sense of "crystal."

8. *grind it . . . : pound it . . . cook it . . . make it into cakes*. This itemization of
processes of food preparation (the "it" is merely implied in the Hebrew) makes
one suspect that the reports of the manna reflect a real memory of some
improvised food in the Wilderness wanderings. A common conjecture is that
it might be the edible secretions of a particular insect found on trees in the
Sinai. However ingeniously processed, it would have offered poor competition
to the refinement and variety of Egyptian cuisine that riffraff and Israelites
alike recall.
   the creaminess of oil. In all likelihood, this refers to the thick upper layer of
the first press of olive oil.

10. *weeping by its clans*. Throughout this episode, "weep" has the obvious sense
of "complain," but it is used instead of several possible biblical alternatives
because it stresses the whining nature of the complaints.

11. *Why have You done evil to Your servant*. "Evil" here means "harm" but pointedly carries forward the perception by Moses in the previous verse that this
whole affair is evil, bad business.
   burden. The notion of the responsibility of leadership as a heavy load
repeats the emphasis of the parallel episode in Exodus 18.

of all this people upon me? Did I conceive all this people, did I give   12
birth to them, that You should say to me, 'Bear them in your lap, as the
guardian bears the infant,' to the land that You swore to their fathers?
From where shall I get meat to give to all this people when they weep   13
to me, saying, 'Give us meat that we may eat'? I alone cannot bear this   14
people, for they are too heavy for me. And if thus You would do with me,   15
kill me, pray, altogether, if I have found favor in Your eyes, and let me
not see my evil fate." And the LORD said to Moses, "Gather for Me   16
seventy men of the elders of Israel of whom you know that they are the
elders of the people and its overseers, and you shall take them to the
Tent of Meeting, and they shall station themselves there with you. And   17
I shall come down and speak with you there and I shall hold back some
of the spirit that is upon you and place it upon them, and they will bear
with you the burden of the people and you yourself will not bear it
alone. And to the people you shall say: 'Consecrate yourselves for the   18
morrow and you will eat meat, for you wept in the hearing of the LORD,

---

12. *Did I conceive all this people, did I give birth to them . . . ?* In an extravagant
metaphor that expresses Moses's sense of outrageous anomaly in the task he
is required to do, he asks whether he is the mother of all these teeming multitudes. He then goes on, in the words he attributes to God, to wonder
whether he is supposed to be an *'omen*, a guardian or private tutor of the sort
that wealthy families would hire to care for and instruct their children.

15. *kill me, pray, altogether, if I have found favor in Your eyes.* In Exodus 33, the
sign Moses sought that he had found favor in God's eyes was that God would
elect to go in the midst of the people and would show Moses something of the
divine nature. Now, Moses in his desperation imagines an end to his suffering
through death as the sign of God's favor.

17. *hold back some of the spirit.* The verb *'atsal*, which Esau uses when he asks
Isaac whether he has held in reserve some blessing for his real firstborn, suggests that a certain limited portion of the spirit vouchsafed Moses is taken
from him to be distributed among the elders. This is precisely what is involved
in the delegation of authority.

saying, Who will feed us meat? For it was good for us in Egypt. And the
19   LORD will give you meat and you will eat. Not one day will you eat and
not two days and not five days and not ten days and not twenty days,
20   but a full month of days, till it comes out of your noses and becomes a
loathsome thing to you, inasmuch as you have cast aside the LORD Who
is in your midst and you have wept before him, saying, "Why is it we
21   have come out of Egypt?" '" And Moses said, "Six hundred thousand
foot soldiers are the people in whose midst I am, and You, You said, 'I
22   shall give them meat and they will eat a month of days'? Will sheep and
cattle be slaughtered for them and provide for them? Will all the fish of
23   the sea be gathered for them and provide for them?" And the LORD said
to Moses, "Will the LORD's hand be too short? Now you will see whether
24   My word will come about or not." And Moses went out and spoke the
LORD's words to the people, and he gathered seventy men of the elders
25   of the people and stood them round about the Tent. And the LORD
came down in the cloud and spoke to him and held back some of the
spirit that was upon him and put it upon the seventy men of the elders,
and it happened, as the spirit rested upon them, that they prophesied,
26   but did it no more. And two men remained in the camp. The name of

---

21. *Six hundred thousand foot soldiers.* That is, 600,000 males the age of military conscription. This figure would then be multiplied through all the additional female and minor mouths to feed. The incredulity expressed in the
question indicates that even Moses cannot believe there is a way to provide
meat—both he and God take the people at their own initial word, forgetting
about the fish—for this vast populace.

22. *provide for them?* The Hebrew verb here usually means "find," but this
understanding of its meaning in context goes back to the Targum Onkelos and
is endorsed by most modern scholars.

23. *Will the LORD's hand be too short?* "Hand" here has the idiomatic sense of
"power" but also manifests a metaphorical image—the hand of God reaching
all the way to the sea to sweep up the quail and rain them down on the
Israelite camp.

25. *as the spirit rested upon them, that they prophesied.* To "prophesy" (*hitnabei'*)
is to exhibit ecstatic behavior—dancing, writhing, emitting vatic speech. In

the one was Eldad and the name of the other was Medad. And the spirit
rested upon them, and they were among those inscribed, but they did
not go out from the tent, and they prophesied in the camp. And the lad   27
ran to tell Moses and said, "Eldad and Medad are prophesying in the
camp." And Joshua son of Nun, attendant to Moses from his youth,   28
spoke out and said, "My lord Moses, restrain them!" And Moses said to   29
him, "Are you jealous on my part? Would that all the LORD's people were
prophets, that the LORD would place His spirit upon them." And Moses   30

---

this instance, the elders, who have been designated to share the burden of
leadership with Moses, don't do anything other than to make manifest through
prophesying, after they have gathered round Moses, that they, too, are invested
with the divine spirit and so share his responsibility. The end of the verse
makes clear that this is a one-time event: the elders demonstrate here that
they partake of the spirit, but they have no continuing role as prophets, in contrast to Moses.

26. *they were among those inscribed.* The most likely meaning is that they were
"inscribed" among the seventy elders but differed from them in not coming out
of the Tent. The particle *waw*, which usually means "and," can have an adversative sense, as it probably does here, when it prefixes a verb in the perfective
tense instead of the usual imperfective tense for historical narration (*welo'
yats'u*, "but they did not go out"). Abraham ibn Ezra helpfully glosses: "they did
not go out from the camp of Israel to the Tent of Meeting" (where the other
elders had gathered).

28. *from his youth.* The Hebrew *mibehuraw* could also mean "from his chosen
ones."

   My lord Moses, restrain them! The prophesying of the other sixty-eight elders
in the designated place of sanctity, before the Tent of Meeting, is one thing,
but the manifestation of prophecy in the midst of the Israelite camp is quite
another, for it could turn into a dangerously contagious threat to Moses's
leadership.

29. *Would that all the LORD's people were prophets.* Moses, just having surrendered a portion of the spirit invested in him to the seventy elders, now hyperbolically expresses the sense that holding on to a monopoly of power (equated
with access to the divine spirit) is not at all what impels him as leader.
Although he knows that there is scarcely any prospect that the entire people
will become prophets, he nevertheless points to an ideal of what we might call

31 was gathered back into the camp, he and the elders of Israel. And a wind moved onward from the LORD and swept up quail from the sea and left them over the camp, about a day's journey in every direction all round
32 the camp and about two cubits deep on the ground. And the people arose all that day and all that night and all the next day and gathered the quail. The most sparing gathered ten *homers*, and they laid them out for
33 themselves round about the camp. The meat was still between their teeth, it had not yet been chewed, when the LORD's wrath flared against the people, and the LORD struck a very great blow against the people.
34 And the name of the place was called Kibroth-Hattaavah, for there the
35 people buried the ones who had been craving. From Kibroth-Hattaavah the people journeyed on to Hazeroth, and they were in Hazeroth.

---

radical spiritual egalitarianism. Access to the realm of the spirit is granted by God, in principle to anyone God chooses. The "gathering" of the elders to share the spirit is the antithesis of the mob of riffraff that assembles to express in complaint the dictates of the belly, not the spirit.

31. *swept up quail from the sea.* There may be a realistic kernel to this miraculous event: flocks of migratory quail from the sea do cross over the Sinai, where, exhausted from their flight, they are easy to trap.

32. *ten* homers. This would be a huge amount, since the *homer* is ten *ephahs*, or more than five bushels.
    they laid them out. The evident purpose is to cure the meat in the hot desert sun. But two ancient versions read instead of *wayishtehu*, "and they laid out," *wayishhetu*, "and they slaughtered" (a reversal of the second and the third consonants of the verb).

33. *it had not yet been chewed.* The verb for "chew" or "consume," *yikaret*, is unusual, for its ordinary meaning is "to be cut off." It probably occurs here as an ominous bit of micro-foreshadowing, since the "blow" (or "plague") God strikes against the people will, in biblical idiom, cut off many of them.

34. *Kibroth-Hattaavah.* The Hebrew means Graves of Desire (or Lust). In both this episode and the preceding one of Taberah, as in many incidents to follow, the Israelites move across the trackless wastes of the Sinai peninsula ironically leaving a trail of new place-names that is the history of their own repeated derilections.

CHAPTER 12

Ａnd Miriam, and Aaron with her, spoke against Moses concerning 1
the Cushite wife he had taken, for he had taken a Cushite wife.
And they said, "Is it but through Moses alone that the LORD has 2
spoken? Has He not spoken through us as well?" And the LORD heard.

---

1. *And Miriam, and Aaron with her, spoke against Moses.* This is one of the most
striking instances of an expressive grammatical device in ancient Hebrew
prose: when there are two or more subjects of a verb but a singular verb is used
(here, feminine singular), there is a thematic focus on the first of the subjects
as the principal agent in the action stipulated through the verb. (This translation adds "with her" to suggest an equivalent effect.) Thus Abraham ibn Ezra:
"she spoke and Aaron assented or was silent, so he [too] was punished." It is
Miriam, of course, who will be stricken with the skin disease. The expression
diber be often means "to speak against," but in a punning usage, it can also
refer, as it does repeatedly in this episode beginning with Aaron's and Miriam's
dialogue in the next verse, to God's speaking *through* a prophet. Verse 8 here
also uses *diber be*, but because of the mouth to mouth idiom, in that one
instance it is translated as "speak with."

the Cushite wife. Is this Zipporah? Only if one locates Cush in Midian,
which some interpreters find grounds for doing. Otherwise, Cush might be a
designation for Nubia or Ethiopia, which would make this wife black. If she is
a second wife, the objection might be simply to the fact that Moses had com-
promised Zipporah's privileged status by this second marriage (Baruch Levine's
view), or it could reflect racial disapproval. If Miriam and Aaron are referring
to Zipporah, the objection would simply be to her coming from a different
ethnic-national group. In either case, they mean to suggest that Moses's marital behavior is unworthy of a prophetic leader and hence evidence that he
does not deserve to be the exclusive vessel of prophecy.

2. *Has He not spoken through us as well?* This familial "murmuring" should be
read against the background of the immediately preceding episode. There two
people, Eldad and Medad, were singled out as instruments of prophecy. Now

3   And the man Moses was very humble, more than any person on the
4   face of the earth. And the LORD said suddenly to Moses and to Aaron
     and to Miriam, "Go out, the three of you, to the Tent of Meeting." And
5   the three of them went out. And the LORD came down in the pillar of
     cloud and stood at the entrance of the tent and called, "Aaron and
6   Miriam!" And the two of them went out. And He said,

> "Listen, pray, to My words.
> If your prophet be the LORD's

---

these two siblings come forth to propose themselves as candidates for the
same role, though there is scant indication in the earlier narratives that God
has been speaking directly through them (despite Miriam's designation as
"prophetess" in Exodus 15:20). Moses responded to the prophesying of Eldad
and Medad by wishing that the whole people might be endowed with the spirit
of prophecy. In flagrant contrast, Miriam and Aaron pretend that their brother
has been treating prophecy as a private monopoly, and their view of the
prophetic spirit is of something one can seize as a means of privilege and
power. The great biblical theme of sibling rivalry, until now absent from the
story of Moses, Aaron, and Miriam, here makes an appearance.

3. *And the man Moses was very humble.* As we have noted before (see the comment on Exodus 32:1), "the man," quite exceptionally, is a kind of epithet for
Moses. His humble or unassuming character is reflected here in the fact that
he has not troubled to listen, or has paid no attention, to the malicious rumors
about him that Miriam and Aaron have initiated. God, however, has heard.

4. *the LORD said suddenly.* The use of "suddenly" to introduce divine speech is
quite unusual. Nahmanides proposes an interesting explanation: Miriam and
Aaron, having made their dubious declaration that through them, too, God
had spoken, "were not at the moment thinking of an expected prophecy, and
for Moses's sake it came upon them without invitation." Prophecy, that is,
proves to be an abrupt and frightening business, not the commodity of power
they had imagined. Thus, in the next verse, God, having called to all three siblings, singles out Miriam and Aaron in peremptory direct address.

6. *Listen, pray, to My words.* God's speech to Miriam and Aaron takes the exalted
form of poetry. One of the conventions for beginning a biblical poem is an exhortation for those addressed to hearken to the utterances of the poet. (Compare the
first of many instances, Genesis 4:23: "Adah and Zillah, O hearken my voice . . .")
     If your prophet be the LORD's. The Hebrew text is cryptic, perhaps through

in a vision to him would I be known,
  in a dream would I speak through him.
Not so My servant Moses,   7
  in all my house is he trusted.
Mouth to mouth do I speak with him,   8
  and vision, and not in riddles,
    and the likeness of the Lord he beholds.
And why did you not fear
  to speak against My servant Moses?"

And the Lord's wrath flared against them, and He went off. And the 9,10
cloud moved off from over the tent, and, look, Miriam was blanched as
snow, and Aaron turned to Miriam, and, look, she was struck with skin

---

scribal error, perhaps merely because of the compacted language of archaic
poetry. The literal Hebrew word sequence is: If-there-be your-prophet the-
Lord. The second and third of these word-units might be an ellipsis for
"prophet of the Lord," and both the Septuagint and the Vulgate show "of" or
"for" (the Hebrew particle l^e). A couple of other ancient versions also reflect a
reading of "a prophet among you." Various modern textual critics move "the
Lord" (YHWH) either back to the verb "said" at the beginning of the verse or
forward to the next clause, leaving "If there be a prophet [among you]."
  vision . . . dream. For an ordinary prophet, God reveals Himself through an
oblique imaging process, in vision or dream.

7. My servant Moses, / in all my house is he trusted. "Trusted," ne'eman, is an
expected qualifier for "servant," 'eved. Moses figures here as a kind of faithful
majordomo given the keys to God's household.
  and vision, and not in riddles. Although vision has been noted as one of the
two vehicles of communication with the ordinary prophet, in Moses's case it
is no enigmatic vision but a perfectly clear image, as he, and he alone, is privileged to look upon "the likeness of the Lord."

10. blanched as snow. If the Cushite woman is actually black, this sudden
draining of pigmentation, as Jacob Milgrom notes, would be mordant poetic
justice for Miriam's slander.

11 blanch. And Aaron said to Moses, "I beseech you, my lord, pray, do not
put upon us the offense which we did foolishly and by which we
12 offended. Let her not be, pray, like one dead who when he comes out
13 of his mother's womb, half his flesh is eaten away." And Moses cried
14 out to the LORD, saying, "God, pray, heal her, pray." And the LORD said
to Moses, "Had her father spat in her face, would she not be shamed
seven days, be shut up seven days outside the camp, and afterward she •
15 would be gathered back in?" And Miriam was shut up outside the camp
seven days, and the people did not journey onward until Miriam was
16 gathered back in. And afterward the people journeyed on from Hazeroth, and they camped in the Wilderness of Paran.

11–13. The rhetorical contrast between Aaron's petition to Moses and Moses's
petition to God is pointed. Aaron's speech is relatively lengthy and centers on
an elaborate, and horrifying, simile of stillbirth for Miriam's skin disease. (Perhaps that simile is dictated by Aaron's consciousness of the sibling bond
between Miriam and her two brothers, as though he were saying to Moses:
look, the three of us were born into life from the same womb, and now our sister is suffering a fate no better than that of a stillborn fetus.) Moses's prayer is
a mere five words and five syllables (both in the Hebrew and in this translation), devoid of any metaphorical elaboration or explanation of motive and circumstance, a kind of pure verbal distillate of imperatively urgent plea. The
starkness of the language makes it all the more affecting. Compare Rashi's
comment on the urgency of the language: "Why did not Moses pray at length?
So that the Israelites would not say, 'His sister is in distress and he is standing
and going on and on in prayer!'"

14. *shut up seven days outside the camp.* This does not appear to be the usual
medical quarantine for this disease, which would be fourteen days, but, to
judge by the immediate context, is rather a period of isolation until the public
shaming Miriam has undergone will no longer be fresh.

15. *gathered back in.* This is the same locution used for Moses's return to the
camp in Numbers 11:30. The repeated usage underscores a thematic antithesis: Moses was gathered back into the camp, from which he had gone out to
stand before the Tent of Meeting, after sharing his spirit of prophecy with the
seventy elders. Miriam is gathered back into the camp after having been
excluded from it in punishment because she had complained that Moses was
monopolizing the spirit that by right belonged equally to her and to Aaron. In
the first instance, we have a gesture of consolidating political unity; in the second instance, a divisive complaint.

CHAPTER 13

And the Lord spoke to Moses, saying, "Send you men, that they 1,2 scout the land of Canaan which I am about to give to the Israelites, one man each for his father's tribe, every one of them a chieftain." And Moses sent them from the Wilderness of Paran by the Lord's word, 3 all of them men, heads of the Israelites they were. And these are their 4 names: For the tribe of Reuben, Shammua the son of Zaccur. For the 5 tribe of Simeon, Shaphat the son of Hori. For the tribe of Judah, Caleb 6 son of Jephunneh. For the tribe of Issachar, Igal the son of Joseph. For 7,8 the tribe of Ephraim, Hosea son of Nun. For the tribe of Benjamin, Palti 9 son of Raphu. For the tribe of Zebulun, Gaddiel son of Sodi. For the 10,11 tribe of Joseph, the tribe of Manassah, Gaddi son of Susi. For the tribe 12 of Dan, Ammiel son of Gemalli. For the tribe of Asher, Sethur son of 13 Michael. For the tribe of Naphtali, Nahbi son of Vophsi. For the tribe 14,15 of Gad, Geuel son of Machi. These are the names of the men whom 16 Moses sent to scout the land. And Moses called Hosea the son of Nun

---

3. *all of them men*. Rashi, followed by several modern commentators, proposes that "men" has the connotation of men of stature. In the present context, that might mean military prowess—a trait that would make the fearful majority report of the scouts all the more shameful.

4. *And these are their names*. These names are entirely different from the names of the tribal chieftains previously reported. Most of the names, moreover, do not appear elsewhere in the Bible. This could be an authentic ancient list of tribal military leaders, distinct from the tribal political heads.

16. *And Moses called Hosea the son of Nun Joshua*. The names are phonetically closer in the Hebrew—*Hoshe'a* and *Yehoshu'a*. The latter is the variant of the former that bears the theophoric prefix, with the meaning "God-saves."

17 Joshua. And Moses sent them to scout the land of Canaan, and he said
to them, "Go up this way through the Negeb, and you shall go up into
18 the high country. And you shall see the land, what is it like, and the peo-
19 ple that dwells in it, are they strong or slack, are they few or many. And
what is the land in which they dwell, is it good or bad, and what are the
towns in which they dwell, are they in open settlements or in fortresses.
20 And what is the land, is it fat or lean, are there trees in it or not. And
you shall muster strength and take of the fruit of the land." And the season was the season of the first ripe grapes.

21 And they went up and scouted the land from the Wilderness of Zin to
22 Rehob at Lebo-Hamath. And they went up through the Negeb and
came to Hebron, and there were Ahiman, Sheshai, and Talmai, offspring of the giant. And Hebron had been built seven years before

---

17. *and you shall go up into the high country.* After crossing the Negeb desert,
the tribes would move into the mountainous region of Judea in eastern Canaan.

18. *are they strong or slack.* The formulation of the mission of the scouts in
terms of these binary opposites leads into the divided opinion of the report.
The majority of ten will focus on "strong" and "fortifications."

19. *in open settlements.* The Hebrew is literally "encampments." This nomad's
term was evidently extended to any settlement lacking fortified walls. Given
the fact that Canaan comprised a variety of city-states and regional mini-
kingdoms which were often in conflict with one another, the landscape
abounded in fortified cities.

20. *muster strength and take of the fruit of the land.* The notion that strength is
required to take a sample of the fruit of the land is the first hint that the fruit
is preternaturally heavy, just as the inhabitants are preternaturally large. The
hyperbolic—or legendary—indication in verse 23 is that a single cluster of
grapes is so heavy that it requires two men to carry it.

22. *offspring of the giant.* The second Hebrew term here, ʿ*anaq*, is understood
by some modern translators to be an ethnic designation ("Anakites"). The
words of the scouts, however, in verse 33, clearly place "offspring of the ʿ*anaq*"
in apposition with Nephilim, the legendary man-god hybrids mentioned in
Genesis 6:1–4, and there is no indication elsewhere of an ethnic group called
Anakites. (On the basis of this chapter, ʿ*anaq* in all subsequent strata of

Zoan in Egypt. And they came to Wadi Eshcol, and they cut off from 23
there a branch and one cluster of grapes—and bore it on a pole with
two men—and of the pomegranates and of the dates. That place was 24
called Wadi Eshcol because of the cluster that the Israelites cut off
there. And they came back from scouting the land at the end of forty 25
days. And they went and came to Moses and to Aaron and to all the 26
community of Israelites, at the Wilderness of Paran at Kadesh, and
they brought back word to them and to all the community, and showed
them the fruit of the land. And they recounted to him and said, "We 27
came into the land to which you sent us, and it's actually flowing with
milk and honey, and this is its fruit. But mighty is the people that 28
dwells in the land, and the towns are fortified and very big, and also
the offspring of the giant we saw there. Amalek dwells in the Negeb 29
land, and the Hittite and the Jebusite and the Amorite dwell in the
high country, and the Canaanite dwells by the sea and by the Jordan."

Hebrew is the standard term for "giant.") The legendary scale of the bounty of
the land, its "fatness," is matched by the legendary proportions of its inhabitants. It should be noted that this representation of Hebron inhabited by
giants swerves from the depiction of Hebron in Genesis 25, where the local
denizens are ordinary, and commercially shrewd, Hittites.

Zoan in Egypt. This city is usually identified as Tanis.

24. Wadi Eshcol. "Eshcol" is the Hebrew term for "grape cluster."

25. at the end of forty days. The number is of course formulaic, but it is also a
reasonably plausible time in which a contingent of men on foot might traverse
the Negeb, from its southernmost region (the Wilderness of Paran), make
their way to northern Canaan, and return.

27. they recounted to him. Although Aaron and the representatives of the community are present, and have been shown the spectacular samples of the fruit
of the land, it is to Moses as leader that they address the words of their report.

it's actually flowing with milk and honey. Moses, conveying the divine
promise, has repeatedly used this phrase for the fruitfulness of the land. Now
the eyewitnesses confirm that it is actually (gam) true.

29. the Canaanite dwells by the sea. This indication is historically accurate for
the thirteenth century B.C.E. because the Philistines, who would very soon
control most of the coastal area, had not yet arrived.

30 And Caleb silenced the people around Moses and said, "We will surely
31 go up and take hold of it, for we will surely prevail over it." But the men
who had gone up with him said, "We cannot go up against the people
32 for they are stronger than we." And they put forth an ill report to the
Israelites of the land that they had scouted, saying, "The land through
which we passed to scout is a land that consumes those who dwell in
33 it, and all the people whom we saw in it are men of huge measure. And
there did we see the Nephilim, sons of the giant from the Nephilim,
and we were in our own eyes like grasshoppers, and so we were in their
eyes."

---

30. *We will surely go up . . . we will surely prevail.* Caleb's vehement contradiction of the majority of the scouts does not deny the substance of their report but rather insists that even against such huge adversaries and such an array of fortified cities the Israelites will prevail. This martial resolution will be fulfilled in the biblical account a full generation later, under Joshua's leadership.

32. *a land that consumes those who dwell in it.* As several medieval commentators observe, the scouts now raise the ante in their negative report. At first, they duly noted the extravagant fruitfulness of the land together with the fearful aspect of its inhabitants. Now, in their rejoinder to Caleb, they put forth an ill report (*dibah*) of the land itself, saying that it consumes its inhabitants. Jacob Milgrom plausibly proposes that this phrase refers to a state of repeated war in which the inhabitants of this land find themselves, at the geographical crossroads between the Near Eastern empires to the south, to the east, and to the north. The multiple ethnic groups, moreover, of the land itself, indicated in the scouts' report, reflect armed conflict among the various natives. The land flowing with milk and honey, then, is seen in these words as a kind of death trap: even if the Israelites were to succeed in obtaining a foothold and themselves became dwellers of the land, it would "consume" them through internecine and international warfare.
    men of huge measure. "Huge" is merely implied in the Hebrew.

33. *and so we were in their eyes.* This judgment has to be sheer fearful projection, for they would scarcely have spoken with the Canaanites.

CHAPTER 14

And all the community lifted their voice and put it forth, and the ¹ people wept on that night. And all the Israelites complained ² against Moses and against Aaron, and all the community said to them, "Would that we had died in the land of Egypt, or in this wilderness would that we had died. And why is the LORD bringing us to this ³ land to fall by the sword? Our women and our little ones will become booty. Would it not be better for us to go back to Egypt?" And they ⁴ said one man to another, "Let us put up a head and return to Egypt."

---

1. *lifted their voice and put it forth*. The conjunction of these two verbs with "voice" as their grammatical object is unusual, though elsewhere one or the other commonly appears with that noun as object. The apparent aim of the synonymity is emphasis: thus the sense of the whole verse is something like "they wept loud and bitterly."

2. *Would that we had died*. The people's complaint is cast in quasi-poetic form, an indication of heightened, perhaps self-dramatizing, speech, in two semantically parallel clauses that are a neat chiasm: died—Egypt—wilderness—died.

3. *Our women and our little ones will become booty*. The complainers, in their terror of the imposing inhabitants of Canaan, neatly forget that in Egypt, where they long to return, a royal decree had been devised to destroy all their male children, leaving the girls and women to be exploited by their enslavers.

4. *Let us put up a head*. So Rashi, Targum Onkelos, and many other interpreters. The Hebrew *nitnah ro'sh* is a little cryptic. Others understand it as "let's pay attention" or even "let's set up a marching column." The New Jewish Publication Society, hanging on to the head in another sense, renders this as "let us head back." One should note that the same verb (*n-t-n*) used for "voice" in verse 1 recurs here with "head" for its object.

5 And Moses and Aaron fell on their faces before all the assembly of the
6 community of Israelites. And Joshua son of Nun and Caleb son of
Jephunneh from those who had scouted the land tore their garments.
7 And they said to all the community of Israelites, saying, "The land
8 through which we passed to scout, the land is very, very good. If the
LORD favors us, He will bring us to this land and give it to us, a land
9 that is flowing with milk and honey. Only do not rebel against the
LORD, and you, do not fear the people of the land, for they are our
bread, their shade has turned from them and the LORD is with us. Do
10 not fear them." And all the community meant to pelt them with stones,
but the glory of the LORD appeared in the Tent of Meeting to all the
11 Israelites. And the LORD said to Moses, "How long will this people
despise Me, and how long will they not trust Me, with all the signs that

---

5. *And Moses and Aaron fell on their faces before all the assembly.* For the most
part, this gesture is used to express submission to a greater power. Here evidently, as Nahmanides proposes, it is a desperate attempt by Moses and Aaron
to plead with the people not to undertake the disastrous course that they have
just threatened.

9. *for they are our bread, their shade has turned from them.* Caleb and Joshua's
words of exhortation conclude with what sounds like colloquial sting: as for
these supposedly fearsome Canaanites, we will just gobble them up, and they
are stripped of all protection, while the LORD is with us. "Shade," in the languages of this hot desert region, is a fixed metaphor for protection. Abraham
ibn Ezra, with an eye to the battlefield, suggests that the reference is to the
shadow of the warrior's shield.

10. *but the glory of the LORD appeared.* At the moment that Caleb and Joshua
are threatened with death by stoning, God interposes His earthly manifestation, the luminous cloud, and drives back the assailants, rather like the way
the two divine messengers to Sodom (Genesis 19) drive off the would-be
rapists by striking them with blinding light.

11. *How long will this people despise Me.* It is not clear whether these are the
words of an anthropomorphic God, sounding rather like an impatient parent,
a God now thoroughly fed up with the repeatedly rebellious Israelites, or
whether this divine proposal is intended as a test of Moses's selfless devotion
as leader. If the latter, he comes through with flying colors.

I have done in their midst? Let me strike them with the plague and dis- 12
possess them, and I shall make you a nation greater and mightier than
they." And Moses said to the Lord, "And the Egyptians will hear that 13
through Your power You brought up this people from their midst, and 14
will say to the inhabitants of this land, they have heard that You the
Lord are in the midst of this people, for eye to eye You are seen, Lord,
and Your cloud stands over them, and in a pillar of cloud You go before
them by day and in a pillar of fire by night. And you would put to death 15
this people as a single man? And the nations who have heard rumor of
You will say, saying, 'From the Lord's inability to bring this people to 16
the land that He swore to them, He slaughtered them in the wilderness.' And so, let the Lord's power, pray, be great, as you have spoken, 17
saying, "The Lord is slow to anger and abounding in kindness, bear- 18

---

13. *the Egyptians will hear.* Moses does not even bother to protest that he has
no ambitions to become the sole progenitor of a great people. Instead, he
immediately focuses on the issue of God's own global reputation. In the Exodus narrative, we were reminded again and again that the purpose of all the
prodigious signs and wonders that God worked against Egypt was to make His
uncontested supremacy known among all the nations. Were He now to destroy
the Israelites, the effect would be to unravel the great skein of the Exodus by
encouraging the nations to question whether the Lord has any real power.

16. *He slaughtered them.* Moses himself has just spoken of putting the people
to death, but he puts in the mouth of the contemptuous foreign nations a
stronger word, one usually reserved for the killing of animals.

17. *let the Lord's power, pray, be great.* Some interpreters, leaning on one marginal biblical parallel, claim that "power" here actually means "forbearance."
Rashi more plausibly glosses "power" as God's power to do what He has said.
That proposal makes particular sense in light of the jeering reference to God's
inability, or lack of power, in the words attributed to the surrounding nations.
That is, God, by standing by His word to Israel, will make the greatness of his
power manifest.

18. *The Lord is slow to anger.* Moses here recapitulates the declaration of
divine attributes made on Mount Sinai in Exodus 34:6–7, with some phrases
deleted (see the comments there). That declaration of attributes indicates that
God both exacts justice ("He does not wholly acquit") and is compassionate.
In the present urgent predicament, Moses cannot expect that God will simply

ing crime and trespass, yet He does not wholly acquit, reckoning the
crime of fathers with sons, with the third generation and the fourth.'
19 Forgive, pray, the crime of this people through Your great kindness
20 and as You have borne with this people from Egypt till now." And the
21 LORD said, "I have forgiven, according to your word. And yet, as I live,
22 let the LORD's glory fill all the earth. For all the men who have seen
My glory and My signs that I did in Egypt and in the wilderness yet
23 have tried Me ten times over and have not heeded My voice, they
shall never see the land that I swore to their fathers, and all who
24 despise Me shall not see it. But My servant Caleb, inasmuch as there
was another spirit with him, and he followed after Me, I shall bring
him to the land to which he comes and his seed will take hold of
25 it. And the Amalekite and the Canaanite dwell in the valley. Tomorrow turn and journey onward in the wilderness by the way of the Red

---

shrug off the people's rebelliousness, but the attributes, after all, begin with
"the LORD is slow to anger and abounding in kindness," an emphasis very
much to Moses's purpose as intercessor for a wayward Israel.

21. *as I live, let the* LORD's *glory fill all the earth.* Many interpreters, from Rashi
to the moderns, understood the second clause to mean "and as the LORD's
glory fills all the earth." The Hebrew, however, has no grammatical indication
of such an "as" structure, and there are no precedents for God's swearing not
merely by His life but by the fact that His glory fills all the earth. It is preferable to understand this clause as ibn Ezra does, to point forward in time to
God's unfolding historical plan: yes, the generation of adults in the wilderness
will perish there, but loyal Caleb, together with the next generation, will enter
the land, thus confirming God's glory, demonstrating that it was not out of
divine incapacity that the older Israelites failed to enter the land.

23. *they shall never see.* "Never" in the translation reflects the sense of solemn
emphasis conveyed by the negative oath form—prefixed by *'im*—that is used
in the Hebrew.

24. *followed after Me.* Literally "filled after"—an indication of absolute loyalty.

25. *by the way of the Red Sea.* In this case, the Israelites are directed toward
Eilat/Akaba. Unable to confront the Canaanite adversaries, they must make a
large sweep to the southeast and then ascend by stages through trans-Jordan,
from where they will eventually invade Canaan from the east. The "valley" in

Sea." And the LORD said to Moses and to Aaron, saying, "How long for 26,27
this evil community that raises against Me the complaints of the
Israelites? That which they complain against Me I have heard. Say to 28
them, 'As I live, the LORD declares, just as you have spoken in My hearing, so will I do to you. In this wilderness your corpses will fall and all 29
your reckoned ones from twenty years old and up, for you have complained against Me. You shall never come into the land about which I 30
lifted up My hand vowing to make you dwell within it, except for Caleb
son of Jephunneh and Joshua son of Nun. And your little ones, of 31
whom you said they would become booty, I shall bring them and they
will know the land that you cast aside. And your own corpses will fall 32
in this wilderness. And your sons will be herdsmen in the wilderness 33
forty years, and they will bear your whoring until your corpses come to

---

which the Amalekites and Canaanites dwell is a puzzle because the
Amalekites and the Canaanites at the end of this episode (verse 45) are said to
come from the high country.

26. *this evil community that raises against Me the complaints of the Israelites?*
Since a distinction is made between the "evil community" and the whole
Israelite people, the former phrase would have to refer to the spies, though it
is a little odd to call ten men a community *('edah)*.

29. *all your reckoned ones from twenty years old and up.* The laborious business
of the military census, laid out in such detail in the opening chapters of Numbers, is now to be undone by death.

30. *vowing.* This word does not appear in the Hebrew but is implied by the lifting of the hand.

32. *And your own corpses will fall in this wilderness.* It would have been sufficient, idiomatically and semantically, to say, 'And you will fall in this wilderness.' God's language, by making the corpses the grammatical subject, invites
the Wilderness generation to contemplate the concrete reality of their own
death, "you" turned into "corpses."

33. *they will bear your whoring.* Whoring is of course a standard biblical
metaphor for sinfulness—especially for betrayal (modeled on sexual betrayal).
Your offspring, then, will bear the consequences of your rebelliousness for
forty years until they are finally allowed to enter the land.

34 an end in the wilderness. By the number of days that you scouted the
land, forty days, a day for a year, a day for a year, you will bear your
35 crimes forty years, and you will know what it is to thwart Me. I the
LORD have spoken: will I not do this to all this evil community that
joins forces against Me? In this wilderness shall they come to an end,
36 and there shall they die." And the men whom Moses had sent to scout
the land, who came back and set all the community complaining
37 against him, putting forth an ill report about the land, the men who put
forth an ill and evil report of the land died in the scourge before the
38 LORD. And Joshua son of Nun and Caleb son of Jephunneh were left
39 alive from those men who had gone to scout the land. And Moses
spoke these words to all the Israelites, and the people mourned deeply.
40 And they rose early in the morning and went up to the mountaintop,
saying, "Here we are, and we shall go up to the place that the LORD
41 said, for we have offended." And Moses said, "Why is it you are over-

---

37. *the men*. This same word was emphasized at the beginning of the scouts'
expedition to express their standing as leaders and warriors. Now it is "the
men" who perish.

an ill and evil report. Previously, the noun *dibah*, which itself means "ill
report," had been used without an adjective. Here, for the sake of emphasis,
raʿah, "evil," is added to *dibah*.

40. *went up to the mountaintop*. The geographical indication here is rather
vague. There is a range of low mountains along the eastern axis of Canaan, but
the Israelites at this point are encamped to the south of Canaan. The unspecified mountain is probably intended to be doubly paradigmatic: an enemy
whose land is to be conquered would typically be situated in fortifications on
heights, and the unauthorized scramble up the mountainside toward the summit is an act of presumption, distantly related to the heaven-seeking Tower of
Babel.

we shall go up to the place that the LORD said, for we have offended. They recognize their own cowardice in having been persuaded by the scout's negative
report, but their resolution to storm the heights of Canaan is a misguided self-
correction, entirely ignoring God's declaration that none of this generation will
enter the land.

stepping the Lord's word, when it will not succeed? Do not go up, for   42
the Lord is not in your midst, lest you be routed before your enemies.
For the Amalekite and the Canaanite are there in front of you, and you   43
will fall by the sword, for have you not turned back from the Lord and
the Lord will not be with you?" And they strove to go up to the moun-   44
taintop, and the Ark of the Lord's Covenant and Moses did not budge
from the midst of the camp. And the Amalekite and the Canaanite,   45
who dwelled on that mountain, came down and struck them and shat-
tered them all the way to Hormah.

---

44. *strove*. The Hebrew verb *ya'pilu* is unique to this verse, and its meaning is
in dispute. One common etymology links it with *'ofel*, "height," assuming that
it means something like "strive upward."

    *the Ark of the Lord's Covenant and Moses did not budge from the midst of
the camp*. The would-be conquerors thus attack the heights without either
their leader or the object that is the token of God's potent presence in the
midst of the people. (Compare the Ark narrative in the early chapters of 1
Samuel, where the people believe they will be victorious if they carry the Ark
with them into battle.)

45. *all the way to Hormah*. Hormah may be a place-name, though its location
is unknown, or it could be a common noun, "destruction," in which case the
sense of the phrase would be "until they were utterly destroyed."

CHAPTER 15

1,2 Aᴺᴰ the Lᴏʀᴅ spoke to Moses, saying, "Speak to the Israelites, and you shall say to them: 'When you come to the land of your settle-
3 ment that I am about to give to you, you shall make a fire offering to the Lᴏʀᴅ, a burnt offering or a sacrifice to set aside a votive or a voluntary offering, or in your fixed seasons to make a fragrant odor to the
4 Lᴏʀᴅ from the cattle or from the flock. And he who brings forward his offering to the Lᴏʀᴅ shall bring forward a grain offering of fine
5 semolina, one-tenth measure mixed with one-fourth of a *hin* of oil. And wine for the libation, one-fourth of a *hin* you shall make with the burnt
6 offering or for the sacrifice for each sheep. Or for the ram you shall make a grain offering of fine semolina, two tenth measures mixed with

---

2. *When you come to the land.* After the incident of the spies, the narrative movement is broken off by the insertion of a miscellany of laws pertaining to the cult, the sabbath, and the mnemonic ritual fringes. The narrative of Wilderness rebellions will resume in the next chapter with the story of Korah's mutiny. It is not clear why the redactors deemed it appropriate to introduce this legal miscellany here, though the best effort of explanation has been made by Abraham ibn Ezra, with his characteristic alertness to possibilities of continuity in disjunct texts: "This section was juxtaposed to the previous because they [the ten scouts and their followers] had been cut down and people were mourning, to comfort the sons by letting them know that they would come to the land." Ibn Ezra goes on to say that the emphasis here on forgiveness (verse 25) is also a response to the sin of the ten scouts and their followers, and the reference to a "high hand" (verse 30) looks back to their arrogance in trying to storm the Canaanite heights without divine authorization.

4. *one-tenth measure.* This is evidently the dry measure *'ephah*, roughly a bushel.

a third of a *hin* of oil. And wine for the libation, a third of a *hin*, you 7
shall bring forward, a fragrant odor to the LORD. And should you make 8
a head of cattle as a burnt offering or a sacrifice to set aside a votive or
communion sacrifice to the LORD, the person shall bring forward with 9
the head of cattle a grain offering of fine semolina, three-tenths of a
measure mixed with half a *hin* of oil. And wine you shall bring forward 10
for the libation, half a *hin*, a fire offering, a fragrant odor to the LORD.
Thus shall be done for the one bull or the one ram or the lamb of the 11
sheep or the goats. For the number that you do, thus you shall do for 12
each one, according to their number. Every native shall do these thus, 13
to bring forward a fire offering, a fragrant odor to the LORD. And should 14
a sojourner reside with you, or anyone in your midst for your generations, he shall make a fire offering, a fragrant odor to the LORD, as you
do, so shall he do. The assembly—one statute for you and for the 15
sojourner who resides, a perpetual statute for your generations, you and
the sojourner alike, shall there be before the LORD. One teaching and 16
one practice shall there be for you and for the sojourner who resides
with you.'"

And the LORD spoke to Moses, saying, "Speak to the Israelites, and 17,18
you shall say to them: 'When you come to the land to which I am about
to bring you, when it happens that you eat of the bread of the land, you 19
shall present a donation to the LORD. The first yield of your kneading 20
troughs, a round loaf, you shall present in donation, like the donation
from the threshing floor, thus you shall present it. From the first yield 21
of your kneading troughs you shall give to the LORD, a donation for your

---

15. *one statute for you and for the sojourner.* Apologetic commentary has made
much of the egalitarianism of this reiterated formula. In fact, it was common
in the ancient Near East for resident aliens to participate in the cult of the
community in which they were, in effect, naturalized citizens. In this early
period, no special ceremony of conversion was involved, and as a matter of historical actuality, it is likely that the descendants of resident aliens in the course
of time would have become indistinguishable from native Israelites.

22 generations. And should you err and not do all these commandments
23 that the LORD spoke to Moses, all that the LORD has charged you by
the hand of Moses, from the day that the LORD charged and henceforth
24 for your generations, and should it happen that it was done as in
errancy away from the eyes of the community, the whole community
shall make one bull from the cattle as a burnt offering, a fragrant odor
to the LORD, and its grain offering and its libation according to fixed
25 practice, and one he-goat for an offense offering. And the priest shall
atone for all the community of the Israelites and it will be forgiven to
them, for it is an errancy, and they will have brought their offering, a
fire offering to the LORD, and their offense offering before the LORD,
26 for their errancy. And it will be forgiven to all the community of
Israelites and to the sojourner who resides in their midst, for the whole
27 people is errant. And if a single person errantly offends, he shall bring
28 forward a yearling she-goat as an offense offering. And the priest shall
atone for the person erring in his offense in errancy before the LORD,
29 to atone for him, and it will be forgiven him. And for the native among
the Israelites and for the sojourner who resides in their midst, one
30 teaching there shall be for them for him who does in errancy. And the
person who does it with a high hand, whether from the native or from
the sojourner—he reviles the LORD, and that person shall be cut off
31 from the midst of his people. For he has spurned the word of the LORD
and His commandment he has violated. That person shall surely be cut
off, his crime is upon him.'"

---

22. *And should you err.* The Hebrew root *sh-g-h* (here) or *sh-g-g* (in all the subsequent occurrences in this chapter) denotes an inadvertent offense, because
the person either is not aware of the law or is not cognizant of what he is doing.

24. *the whole community.* A prohibited act performed inadvertently by mem-
bers of the community incurs guilt on the whole group that must be expiated.
(Compare the plagues that descend on Thebes in *Oedipus the King* and
Antigone.)

30. *with a high hand.* This phrase, which suggests bold defiance, is the obvious legal antithesis to inadvertent transgressing, or erring.

And the Israelites were in the wilderness, and they found a man gath- 32
ering wood on the sabbath day. And those who found him gathering 33
wood brought him forward to Moses and to Aaron and to all the community. And they placed him under watch, for it had not been deter- 34
mined what should be done to him. And the LORD said to Moses, "The 35
man is doomed to die. Let all the community pelt him with stones outside the camp." And all the community took him outside the camp and 36
pelted him with stones and he died, as the LORD had charged Moses.

And the LORD said to Moses, saying, "Speak to the Israelites, and you 37,38
shall say to them that they should make them a fringe on the skirts of
their garments for their generations and place on the fringe of the skirt

---

32. *And the Israelites were in the wilderness*. This clause takes us back from the
listing of timeless laws to the narrative setting of the Wilderness tales. The
anecdote, however, proves to be a piece of case law indicating what is the sentence of a person willfully violating the sabbath.

35. *Let all the community pelt him with stones outside the camp*. The death sentence for violating the sabbath offers a grim prospect, which might well make
one think of the brutal enforcement of strict theological conformity in certain
modern theocracies. Ibn Ezra seeks to provide a palliative by linking this
episode with the "high hand" of the immediately preceding passage, suggesting that the wood gatherer had been duly warned but high-handedly went on
with his action. The larger narrative context comprises a series of acts of
mutiny, threatening both the authority of Moses and the cohesiveness of the
community, and this episode is conceived as a grave instance of such mutiny.
Israel as a community is in part defined by its adherence to the sabbath. In the
harsh reality of the Wilderness setting, he who has broken rank is taken outside the camp and executed by the whole community.

38. *make them a fringe on the skirts of their garments*. The "skirts" of the garment are literally "wings" (*kenafayim*). The garment would typically be a kind
of tunic (and so would not have "corners"), and the reference is thus to the
hem or bottom edge. The fringe—elsewhere the Hebrew *tsitsit* refers to a lock
of hair—is made up of uncut threads extending down from the hem.

39 an indigo twist. And it shall be a fringe for you, and you shall see it and
    be mindful of all the LORD's commandments and you shall do them.
    And you shall not stray after your heart and after your eyes, after which
40 you go whoring. So that you will be mindful and do My command-

---

an indigo twist. Though indigo may be a reasonable approximation of the
color in question, it should be noted that the dye is not derived from a plant,
as is indigo, but from a substance secreted by the murex, harvested off the
coast of Phoenicia (see the comment on Exodus 25:4). The extraction and
preparation of this dye were labor-intensive and thus made it quite costly. It
was used for royal garments in many places in the Mediterranean region, and
in Israel it was also used for priestly garments and for the cloth furnishings of
the Tabernacle. One may infer that the indigo twist was a token of the idea
that Israel should become a "kingdom of priests and a holy nation" and perhaps also that, as the covenanted people, metaphorically God's firstborn, the
nation as a whole had royal status. Remnants of clothing found in the caves
inhabited by Bar Kokhba's men demonstrate that such indigo twists were still
worn at the hems of ordinary outer garments in the second century C.E. Eventually, the indigo color was dropped as dye for the authentic hue became inaccessible. The fringes were transferred to the *talit* or prayer-shawl, though some
devout Orthodox men and boys still wear as an outer garment a sleeveless
piece of cloth with a large neckhole and fringes at its four corners.

39. *be mindful of all the LORD's commandments.* The key Hebrew verb *z-k-r*
means both "to remember" and "to be cognizant of." There is a continuing concern with mnemonic devices and stories in Numbers. This fringe with the
indigo twist is presumably meant to remind the Israelites of their obligation as
a holy people and of their quasi-royal status before God: when tempted to look
at the objects of desire, they are to look instead upon the mnemonic fringe.
    you shall not stray. The Hebrew verb here also has the more neutral mean-
ing of "to go about," "to explore," "to scout"; and, as many commentators have
noted, it is the very verb used for the expedition of the twelve spies. Perhaps
the "straying" is also intended, at least by the redactor, as a glance back at the
sabbath wood gatherer.

ments, and you shall be holy to your God. I am the LORD your God, 41
Who brought you out of the land of Egypt to become your God. I am
the LORD your God."

---

41. *I am the LORD your God, Who brought you out of the land of Egypt.* Throughout the Hebrew Bible, theology is an inseparable part of story. Israel's fealty to
God is not a consequence of abstract theological principle but of its experience of God's workings in history. The indigo twist—Rashi even seeks to link
it with the color of the sky on the night of the Exodus—is thus a reminder not
only of the commandments but of the liberation from slavery, prelude to the
Sinai epiphany through which Israel took on the obligation to become a kingdom of priests. The once enslaved people is henceforth to wear a constant
token of royalty and sanctity.

CHAPTER 16

¹ **A**nd Korah son of Izhar son of Kohath son of Levi, and Dathan and
Abiram sons of Eliab and On son of Peleth sons of Reuben, took
² up, and they rose before Moses, and two hundred fifty men of the

---

1. *And Korah . . . took up.* The verb (it is the first word here in the Hebrew text)
is in the singular, thus thematically focusing on the principal agent, Korah, who
becomes the archetype of the presumptuous rebel against just authority. The
function of the verb is nevertheless not entirely clear: the verb "to take" is transitive and should have a direct object but none appears in this sentence. Abraham ibn Ezra solves this difficulty by claiming that an elliptical object, "men,"
is implied. Others construe "take" to have the idiomatic sense of "take himself
aside" or "rebel." This translation replicates the ambiguity of the Hebrew.

Dathan and Abirman . . . sons of Reuben. The conjoining of Levites and
Reubenites is the first signal of an underlying problem in the entire episode,
abundantly registered by biblical scholars. This is a rare instance in which the
editorial orchestration of literary sources, instead of producing polyphonic complexity, generates repeated dissonance. Two rebellions have been combined, a
rebellion of Levites for priestly privilege and a rebellion of Reubenites for political power. It is fitting that the latter should come out of the tribe of Reuben,
for Reuben is the firstborn who has been passed over in the struggle for political preeminence. As the two stories twine around each other, it emerges that
there are two different places of confrontation—for Korah and his people, the
sanctuary ("before the LORD"), where the trial of the fire-pans occurs; and for
Dathan and Abiram and their followers, the entrance to their tents. And there
are also two different modes of destruction—a consuming fire engulfs the
Levites while the Reubenites are swallowed up by the earth. Perhaps this odd
weaving together of the two rebellions was intended to suggest that political
and sacerdotal power are inseparable (an idea that might have appealed to
Priestly editors), but from a modern perspective it makes peculiar reading.

Israelites, community chieftains, persons called up to meeting, men of renown. And they assembled against Moses and against Aaron and said 3 to them, "You have too much! For all the community, they are all holy, and in their midst is the LORD, and why should you raise yourselves up over the LORD's assembly?" And Moses heard and fell on his face. And 4,5 he spoke to Korah and to all his community, saying, "In the morning, the LORD will make known who is His, and him who is holy He will bring close to Him and him whom He chooses He will bring close to Him. Do this: take your fire-pans, Korah and all your community. And 6,7 place fire in them and put incense on them before the LORD tomorrow. And the man whom the LORD chooses, he is the holy one. You have too much, sons of Levi." And Moses said to Korah, "Listen, pray, sons of 8

---

3. *they are all holy.* Korah and his followers throw back in Moses's face the idea he has transmitted to them that all Israel should be "a kingdom of priests and a holy nation" (Exodus 19:6).

   raise yourselves up. The verb also could mean "play the chieftain."

4. *Moses heard and fell on his face.* This gesture of prostration ordinarily is an expression of reverence and self-abnegation, as indeed it is in verse 22; but here it would have to be a reflex of extreme dismay. Moses will promptly pick himself up and deliver an ominous prediction to the rebels.

5. *Korah and to all his community.* The Hebrew 'adato has often been rendered as his "band" or his "faction." But it is the term regularly used (as in "community chieftains" in verse 2) to indicate the legitimate organized collective of Israelites, and the point is that Korah has deflected a legitimate collectivity, the 'edah, into a mutinous break-off group, so the term needs to be preserved for both the legitimate organization and the rebellion.

   bring close. In ritual contexts, the verbal stem q-r-b almost always suggests the privilege of access to sanctified space and to the divine presence.

7. *You have too much, sons of Levi.* Moses is obviously flinging their own initial words of complaint against him (verse 3) back against them. This phrase will then be antithetically reversed at the very beginning of Moses's next speech (verse 8), "Is it too little . . . ?"

9 Levi. Is it too little for you that the God of Israel divided you from the community of Israel to bring you close to Him to do the work of the
10 LORD's Tabernacle, to stand before the community to serve them? And He brought you close, and all your brothers the sons of Levi with you.
11 And will you seek priesthood as well? Therefore you and all your community who band together against the LORD—and Aaron, what is he that you should murmur against him?"

12 And Moses sent to call to Dathan and Abiram, the sons of Eliab, and
13 they said, "We will not go up. Is it too little that you brought us up from a land flowing with milk and honey to put us to death in the wilderness,

---

9. *divided you . . . to bring you close . . . to do the work . . . to stand before the community to serve them?* The expansively synonymous character of Moses's language underscores the immense bounty that the Levites received in being charged with all the (nonpriestly) work of the Tabernacle. ("Stand before" has the idiomatic sense of "serve.")

11. *Therefore you and all your community . . . and Aaron, what is he.* The syntax here seems a bit disjunct, perhaps because the story of Korah is at this point interrupted by the story of Dathan and Abiram. Aaron is singled out here because from among the Levite clans it is upon Aaron and his sons that priesthood has been conferred.

12. *Moses sent to call.* The purpose of the summons is not stated, but it is clearly an expression of Moses's political authority over these Reubenites, which they categorically reject by declaring, "We will not go up." In this second story, where power rather than priestly privilege is at issue, the rebellion is directed against Moses, and Aaron now is not mentioned.

13. *Is it too little.* These words of course echo the phrase just used by Moses (verse 9) in addressing Korah and his followers and reflect an effort to pull the two strands together.
   from a land flowing with milk and honey. Previous recollections in the "murmurings" stories of the fleshpots of Egypt are now ratcheted up as the house of bondage is represented in the very terms of bounty that have been repeatedly used for the promised land. The claim that the wilderness is no more than a death trap for the liberated slaves has been made from the start.

that you should also actually lord it over us? What's more, to a land 14
flowing with milk and honey you have not brought us nor given us an
estate of fields and vineyards. Would you gouge out the eyes of these
men? We will not go up!" And Moses was very incensed and he said to 15
the LORD, "Do not turn to their offering. Not a donkey of theirs have I
carried off, and I have done no harm to any one of them."

And Moses said to Korah, "You and all your community, be before the 16
LORD, you and they and Aaron, tomorrow. And each man take his fire- 17
pan and you shall place on it incense and bring it forward before the
LORD, each man his fire-pan, two hundred fifty fire-pans, and you and
Aaron, each man his fire-pan." And each man took his fire-pan, and 18
they placed fire in them and put incense on them, and they stood at the
entrance of the Tent of Meeting, with Moses and Aaron. And Korah 19
assembled all the community by the entrance of the Tent of Meeting,
and the LORD's glory appeared to all the community. And the LORD 20
spoke to Moses and to Aaron, saying, "Divide yourselves from this 21
community, and I will put an end to them in an instant." And they fell 22

---

14. *to a land flowing with milk and honey you have not brought us.* This complaint is abundantly justified. They are still stuck in the pitiless rocky landscape of the Sinai Desert, and the effort of the ten scouts to lead an expedition
against the high country of Canaan has just been turned back in disastrous
defeat.

Would you gouge out the eyes of these men? "These men" is a euphemism for
"us," employed to avoid saying something dire about oneself. Gouging out the
eyes was sometimes a punishment of rebels in the ancient Near East, though
the Reubenites may simply be saying, as ibn Ezra proposes, that they are not
blind to Moses's outrageous behavior.

15. *Do not turn to their offering.* Dathan and Abiram have mentioned no offering, so this could be an attempt to harmonize this story with Korah's.

16. *And Moses said to Korah.* The narrative thread broken off at the end of verse
11 is now resumed.

21. *Divide yourselves from this community.* There is some ambiguity here about
the scope of the noun *'edah.* If it means Korah's faction, then in the next verse

on their faces and said, "El, God of the spirits for all flesh, should one
23 man offend and against all the community You rage?" And the LORD
24 spoke to Moses, saying, "Speak to the community, saying, 'Move up
25 from around the dwelling of Korah, Dathan, and Abiram.'" And Moses
arose and went to Dathan and Abiram, and the elders of Israel went
26 after him. And he spoke to the community, saying, "Turn away, pray,
from the tents of these evil men and touch nothing of theirs, lest you
27 be swept away in all their offense." And they moved up from the
dwelling of Korah, Dathan, and Abiram from all around, and Dathan
and Abiram went out, poised at the entrance of their tents, and their
28 wives and their sons and their little ones. And Moses said, "By this
shall you know that the LORD has sent me to do all these deeds, that it
29 was not from my own heart: If like the death of all human beings these
die, and if the fate of all human beings proves their fate, it is not the
30 LORD who has sent me. But if a new thing the LORD should create, and
the ground gapes open its mouth and swallows them and all of theirs
and they go down alive to Sheol, you will know that these men have
31 despised the LORD." And it happened, just as he finished speaking all

---

Moses and Aaron plead that only the ringleaders be punished, not all 250
rebels. But the subsequent occurrences of "community" in the story seem to
point to the whole Israelite people, so perhaps Moses and Aaron fear that God
is exhibiting another impulse to destroy the entire populace and to start again
with the two brothers.

24. *the dwelling.* The Hebrew *mishkan* is also the term for "Tabernacle." Its use
may be still another effort to tie the two stories together, as its application to
profane dwellings is generally in the plural (*mishkenot*).
    Korah, Dathan, and Abiram. The first of these names appears to be an inter-
polation, for Korah has been instructed to stand by the Tent of Meeting, not
in front of his own tent.

27. *they moved up.* This is the same verb as the rebels' "we will not *go up,*" used
here in a different conjugation to convey the sense of "removed themselves
from." It occurs equally in verse 24.
    Dathan and Abiram. Korah has now, properly, disappeared from the scene
in front of the tents.

these words, the ground that was under them split apart, and the earth 32
opened its mouth and swallowed them and their households and every
human being that was Korah's, and all the possessions. And they went 33
down, they and all that was theirs, alive to Sheol, and the earth covered
over them, and they perished from the midst of the assembly. And all 34
Israel that was round about them fled at the sound of them, for they
thought, "Lest the earth swallow us." And a fire had gone out from the 35
LORD, and consumed the two hundred fifty men bringing forward the
incense.

---

32. *the earth opened its mouth and swallowed them and their households.* This
justice by cataclysmic portent is pitiless, and scarcely accords with the discrimination of guilty agents elsewhere in the Mosaic Code—everyone associated with Dathan and Abiram is engulfed, down to the little children.

    and every human being that was Korah's. Once more the name is inserted in
order to try to splice the two strands, for one may infer that Korah should be
awaiting destruction by fire at the Tent of Meeting.

34. *And all Israel . . . fled at the sound of them.* The real thrust of the story is
not considered justice but monitory spectacle: terror surges through the whole
people as they witness the earth gaping, then closing (no mere earthquake!),
with the rebel Reubenites tumbling into the underworld.

35. *And a fire had gone out from the* LORD. Here we have the report of the
denouement of the trial of the fire-pans, suspended after verse 22. The use of
the pluperfect reflects an attempt to hold the two narrative lines together:
while Dathan, Abiram, and company were being swallowed by the earth, a
divine fire coming out from the sanctuary has consumed Korah and his people. But, pointedly, explicit reference to Korah is omitted from this verse
because verse 32 has just placed him alongside Dathan and Abiram. The consequent confusion is carried into postbiblical Hebrew tradition, where Korah
is sometimes represented as having been buried alive and sometimes as having been incinerated.

CHAPTER 17

1,2 And the LORD spoke to Moses, saying, "Say to Eleazar son of Aaron the priest that he should lift up the fire-pans from the midst of the burnt-out zone and scatter the fire abroad, for they have become
3 holy—the fire-pans of these offenders at the cost of their lives. And they shall make of them hammered sheets as plating for the altar, for they brought them forward before the LORD and they have become
4 holy, and they will become a sign for the Israelites." And Eleazar the priest took the bronze fire-pans that those burned to death had brought
5 forward, and they hammered them into a plating for the altar, a remembrance for the Israelites, so that no stranger, who was not of the seed

---

2. *lift up*. The idiomatic sense of this verb in context is "remove."

burnt-out zone. Literally, "the burning," but the fire of course has now died down.

scatter the fire. "Fire," *'esh*, sometimes can mean, as here, hot ashes.

3. *for they brought them forward before the Lord and they have become holy*. The first clause explains the second: the fire-pans, by virtue of having been carried into sacred space, even though by unauthorized persons who paid for the encroachment with their lives, have become holy.

they will become a sign for the Israelites. Again and again in the Book of Numbers, the narrative is concerned with collective mnemonic devices: ritual apparatus is meant to recall monitory events in the Wilderness wanderings— here, the bronze plating of the altar and, below, Aaron's staff, set before the altar in "safekeeping."

5. *stranger*. The general sense of *zar* is "alien" or "outsider." As always in ritual contexts, the term refers not to an ethnic foreigner but to anyone not a member of the consecrated priesthood.

of Aaron, should come forward to burn incense before the LORD, and
none should be like Korah and his community, as the LORD had spoken
to him in the hand of Moses.

And all the community of Israelites murmured on the next day against   6
Moses and against Aaron, saying, "You, you have put to death the
LORD's people." And it happened when the community assembled   7
against Moses and against Aaron, that they turned to the Tent of Meeting, and, look, the cloud had covered it and the LORD's glory appeared.
And Moses, and Aaron with him, came before the Tent of Meeting.   8
And the LORD spoke to Moses, saying, "Lift yourselves up from the   9,10
midst of this community and I will put an end to them in an instant."
And they fell on their faces. And Moses said to Aaron, "Take the fire-   11
pan and place fire upon it from the altar and put in incense and carry
it quickly to the community and atone for them, for the fury has gone

---

to him. The ambiguous antecedent is plausibly identified by Abraham ibn
Ezra as Aaron.

6. *all the community of Israelites*. Given the people's refractory nature, the violent suppression of a small band of rebels only triggers a general expression of
resentment against Moses's leadership. The repeated pattern of these stories
is a study in collective malcontent, in the psychology of resistance to authority.
    You, you have put to death the LORD's people. The insertion of the emphatic
second-person plural pronoun *'atem* vividly expresses the accusatory tone of
the Israelites' angry words to Moses and Aaron. As Richard Elliott Friedman
aptly notes, the accusation turns everything around in the story: the Israelites
are "the LORD's people" and Moses and Aaron are thus lined up against them
and God, saddled with the responsibility for the death of the rebels whom in
fact God killed.

10. *Lift yourselves up*. This idiom for "remove yourselves" pointedly picks up
the verb used for the removal of the fire-pans in verse 2. We have here a reiterated theme of the episodes of "murmuring": God's "fury"—literally, "foaming
wrath," *qetsef*—is on the point of consuming the whole rebellious people so
that He can start all over with Moses and Aaron, but they intercede on behalf
of the people.

12 out from before the LORD, the scourge has begun." And Aaron took as Moses had spoken, and he ran into the midst of the assembly, and, look, the scourge had begun against the people, and he put in incense
13 and atoned for the people. And he stood between the dead and the liv-
14 ing, and the scourge was held back. And those who died by the scourge came to fourteen thousand and seven hundred, besides those who died
15 because of Korah. And Aaron returned to Moses at the entrance of the Tent of Meeting, and the scourge was held back.

16,17 And the LORD spoke to Moses, saying, "Speak to the Israelites, and take from them a staff for every father's house from all their chieftains, according to their fathers' houses, twelve staffs—each man's name you
18 shall write on his staff. And Aaron's name you shall write on the staff of
19 Levi, for one staff there is for the head of their father's house. And you shall lay them down in the Tent of Meeting before the Ark of the
20 Covenant where I meet with you. And it will happen that the man whom I choose, his staff will flower. And I shall cause to subside from

---

12. *he put in incense and atoned for the people.* The burning of incense to drive off a plague should not be thought of as a sanitary technique. Since incense in ancient Near Eastern religions was imagined, like the burnt offerings it accompanied, as a fragrant odor in the nostrils of the gods, there would have been an expectation that the burning of incense had the power to assuage an angry deity. It is notable that this act of intervention to save the people is not dictated by God but is a device Moses on his own initiative orders Aaron to implement.

17. *a staff for every father's house.* The social unit "father's house" is used rather loosely here to designate "tribe," perhaps because the two Hebrew words for "tribe," *mateh* and *shevet*, both mean "staff," and hence the use of either in this context would have introduced confusion. In any case, we are made conscious that the staff, the tribal emblem, is a metonymy for tribe.

20. *I shall cause to subside from Me.* The unusual Hebrew verb (the same root is used for the receding waters of the Deluge) suggests that the murmurings of complaint are imagined as a kind of flood that rises up around the deity. In this sentence, God clearly aligns Himself with Moses and Aaron as object of the complaints—in precise antithesis to the people's attempt to put God on their side by identifying the two brothers as enemies of "the LORD's people."

Me the murmurings of the Israelites which they murmur against you."
And Moses spoke to the Israelites, and all their chieftains gave him a   21
staff for every single chieftain, according to their fathers' houses, twelve
staffs, and Aaron's staff was among their staffs. And Moses laid down   22
the staffs before the LORD in the Tent of the Covenant. And it hap-   23
pened on the next day that Moses came into the Tent of the Covenant,
and, look, Aaron's staff of the house of Levi had flowered, and it had
brought forth flower and had burgeoned in blossom and had borne
almonds. And Moses brought out all the staffs from before the LORD to   24
the Israelites, and they saw, and each man took his staff. And the LORD   25
said to Moses: "Bring back Aaron's staff before the Ark of the Covenant
as a safekeeping, as a sign for rebels, and let there be an end to their
murmurings against Me, and they shall not die." And Moses did as the   26

---

21. *Aaron's staff was among their staffs.* The tribe of Levi would not have been
reckoned among the twelve tribes. Thus, there are twelve staffs representing
the ten tribes and the two half-tribes of Ephraim and Manasseh, and Aaron's
staff is placed together with them in this trial.

23. *it had brought forth flower and had burgeoned in blossom and had borne
almonds.* The chronology of these stages of vegetal growth is a little obscure
because "flower," *perah,* and "blossom," *tsits,* are either synonyms, or *tsits* may
be an incipient *perah.* Perhaps the parallel clauses are encouraged by the practice of synonymity in poetry, where the more unusual term (here, *tsits*) is
always the second one. In any case, the bearing of fruit, the almonds, obviously follows in time the flowering, and this fast-forwarding of a slow process
of growth spectacularly confirms the miraculous character of the event. Flowering staffs also make an appearance in Herodotus. The divine favor accorded
the Levites is figured in this image of agricultural fertility linked with the tribe
whose sacerdotal duties in fact removed them from the soil.

27 Lᴏʀᴅ had charged him, thus did he do. And the Israelites said to
28 Moses, saying, "Look, we perish, we are lost, all of us are lost. Whoever
    so much as comes near the Lᴏʀᴅ's Tabernacle will die. Are we done
    with perishing?"

---

27. *Look, we perish, we are lost, all of us are lost.* Instead of embracing the monitory mnemonic of Aaron's staff that has just been offered them and accepting
God's assurance that if they renounce their murmurings, "they shall not die,"
the people conclude that they are about to be utterly destroyed. The panic
they feel is etched in the stark simplicity and the repetitions of their expression of fear: in these two concluding verses, they say "perish" twice, "lost"
twice, and (in the Hebrew) "approach" twice (*kol haqarev haqarev*). This whole
story, like so many others in Numbers, marks out a borderline between the
sacred and the profane, stressing that only the consecrated can cross into the
zone of the sacred. The people, however, who live alongside the sacred
precincts, are gripped with fear that at any time they might step over the line
and be struck down.

CHAPTER 18

nd the LORD said to Aaron, "You and your sons and your father's ₁
house with you, you shall bear the guilt of the sanctuary, and you
and your sons with you, you shall bear the guilt of your priesthood. And your brothers, too, the tribe of Levi, your father's tribe, bring ₂
forward with you, and they will be levied with you and serve you, and
you and your sons with you are to be before the Ark of the Covenant.
And they will keep your watch, the watch of all the Tent. Only they ₃
must not come near the sacred vessels and the altar, so that they do not

---

1. *And the* LORD *said to Aaron.* After the account of the rebellion against
Aaronite priestly privileges, concluding with the trial in which only Aaron's
staff blossoms, God directs this address not to Moses or to Moses and Aaron,
as is everywhere else the case, but to Aaron alone. The subject, appropriately,
is the grave responsibility of entering into the sanctuary and performing the
sacred work there.

bear the guilt of the sanctuary. This compressed Hebrew idiom refers to
bearing guilt, which is to say, the consequences of guilt, for any violation of the
sacred zone of the sanctuary. This whole series of instructions highlights the
intrinsic danger of the sacred zone, where any misstep can trigger divine "fury"
(verse 5), and hence the need to protect the sanctuary from the intrusion of
any unfit person (*zar*). The logic of placing these laws immediately after the
story of Korah's rebellion is manifest.

2. *the tribe of Levi, your father's tribe.* The Hebrew uses two synonyms for tribe,
first *mateh* (the characteristic Priestly term) and then *shevet*. Both words have
the primary meaning of "staff" and then become metonyms for tribe because
each tribe carries its distinctive staff.

3. *keep your watch.* As elsewhere, the Hebrew *mishmeret* has a military sense,
to keep watch or guard, but may also refer to something like "maintenance."

4   die, both they and you. And they will be levied with you and keep the
    watch of the Tent of Meeting for all the work of the Tent, and no
5   stranger shall come near them. And you shall keep the watch of the
    sacred zone and the watch of the altar, that there be no more fury
6   against the Israelites. And as for Me, look, I have taken your brothers
    the Levites from the midst of the Israelites, as a gift for you they are
7   given to the LORD, to do the work of the Tent of Meeting. And you and
    your sons with you, you shall keep your priesthood for every matter of
    the altar and for inside the curtain, and you shall do the work. As gift
    work I shall give your priesthood, and the stranger who comes near will
    be put to death."

8   And the LORD spoke to Aaron, "And as for Me, look, I have given you
    the watch of My donations for all the holy things of the Israelites, to
    you I have given them as a share and to your sons as a perpetual statute.
9   This will be yours from the most holy things from the fire, all their
    offerings, including all their grain offerings and all their offense offer-
    ings and all their guilt offerings that they give back to Me, most holy
10 things they are for you and for your sons. In the most holy precincts you
11 shall eat it, every male shall eat it. It will be holy for you. And this

---

4. *they will be levied with you.* The Hebrew verb *nilwu* means "to be joined" or
"associated," but it is an obvious pun on Levi (*lewi*), and "levied," in the sense
of "mustered," seems a close enough approximation that preserves the pun.

8. *as a share.* The Hebrew *lemoshḥah* is a homonym for a more common term
that has the sense of "for anointing." Baruch Levine has argued with especial
cogency that context requires the sense of "share" or "measure," which this
root has in several other Semitic languages.

is yours: their gift of donations including all the donation offerings of the Israelites, to you I have given them, and to your sons and to your daughters with you as a perpetual statute, every clean person in your household will eat it. All the richest of the oil and all the richest of the 12 wine and the grain, their prime yield that they give to the LORD, to you I have given them. The first fruits of all that is in their land, which they 13 bring to the LORD, for you it will be, every clean person in your household will eat it. Everything that has been proscribed in Israel, yours it 14 will be. Every womb-breach for all flesh that they offer to the LORD 15 whether human or beast, yours it will be. But you shall surely redeem every human firstborn, and the firstborn of unclean beasts you shall redeem. And its redemption price from a month old you shall redeem 16 at the value in silver of five shekels by the sanctuary shekel, which is twenty *gerahs*. But the firstborn of an ox or the firstborn of a sheep or 17 the firstborn of a goat you shall not redeem; they are holy. Their blood you shall throw upon the altar and their fat you shall turn to smoke, a fire offering with pleasing fragrance to the LORD. And their flesh will be 18 yours, like the best of the elevation offering and like the right thigh,

---

11. *perpetual statute.* The Hebrew noun *ḥoq* can mean either "statute" or "allotment," and it appears to straddle both meanings here. In verse 23, where no gifts to the priesthood are being doled out, the same phrase can mean only "perpetual statute."

every clean person. That is, everyone untainted by ritual impurity (such as having had contact with a corpse).

14. *Everything . . . proscribed.* Everything that has been declared *ḥerem*, "under ban," "set aside," and hence dedicated solely to the cult and not allowed for profane enjoyment.

15. *redeem every human firstborn, and the firstborn of unclean beasts.* Neither of these categories is acceptable for sacrifice, but for opposite reasons—human beings because their life is sacred, unclean beasts (pigs, scavengers) because it would be degrading to use them in the cult.

18. *their flesh will be yours.* For the landless Levites, the parts of the sacrificial animal not burned on the altar (only one class of sacrifices, the *'olah*, was wholly burned) become a special perquisite, and an important source of sustenance.

19 yours it will be. All the donations of the holy things that the Israelites donate to the LORD I have given to you and to your sons and to your daughters with you as a perpetual statute, a perpetual covenant of salt it is before the LORD, for you and for your seed with you."

20 And the LORD said to Aaron, "In their land you shall have no estate, and no portion shall you have in their midst. I am your estate and your por-
21 tion in the midst of the Israelites. And to the Levites, look, I have given every tithe in Israel as an estate in exchange for their work that they
22 perform, the work of the Tent of Meeting. And the Israelites will no
23 longer draw near to the Tent of Meeting to bear offense to die. And the Levite, he shall perform the work of the Tent of Meeting, and they will bear their guilt. It is a perpetual statute for your generations, and in the
24 midst of the Israelites they will have no estate. For the tithe of the Israelites which they donate to the LORD, I have given as a donation to the Levites for an estate. Therefore did I say to them, 'In the midst of the Israelites they will have no estate.'"

25,26 And the LORD spoke to Moses, saying, "And to the Levites you shall speak, and you shall say to them, 'When you take from the Israelites the tithe that I have given you from them as your estate, you shall donate
27 from it the LORD's donation, a tithe of the tithe. And it will be accounted for you as your donation, like the yield from the threshing

---

19. *a perpetual covenant of salt.* Although some commentators have argued for a reference to the actual consumption of salt as part of a covenantal feast, it is more likely that salt as a preservative is a figurative idiom that reinforces the idea of permanence equally invoked in "perpetual."

20. *no estate, and no portion.* The two Hebrew terms *naḥalah* and *ḥeleq* often occur (in reverse order) as a hendiadys meaning "permanent estate." Breaking out a hendiadys into two separate words for purposes of emphasis is a common stylistic maneuver both in Hebrew poetry and prose.

floor and like the matured wine from the vat. So shall you, too, donate 28
the LORD's donation from all your tithes that you take from the
Israelites, and you shall give from them the LORD's donation to Aaron
the priest. From all your gifts you shall donate the LORD's donation, 29
from all the richest of it, the consecrated part of it. And you shall say 30
to them, When you donate the richest of it, it will be accounted for the
Levites like the yield from the threshing floor and like the yield from
the vat. And you shall eat it in every place, you and your households, 31
for it is wages for you in exchange for your work in the Tent of Meeting. And you shall not bear offense for it when you donate the richest 32
of it, and you shall not profane the holy things of the Israelites and you
shall not die.'"

---

29. *from all the richest of it.* The literal meaning of the Hebrew is "from all the
fat of it," fat, *ḥelev*, being a common biblical idiom for the best part of anything
(as in "the fat of the land").

32. *you shall not bear offense for it . . . and you shall not profane the holy things
. . . and you shall not die.* This whole unit of instructions to the Aaronides
closes in an envelope structure: the danger of suffering the consequences of
violating the sanctuary, invoked at the beginning, recurs now on a note of reassurance: because these tithes of agricultural offerings are the priests' just
wages for their service in the cult, they run no risk of perishing for having
eaten consecrated foodstuffs.

CHAPTER 19

1,2   And the Lord spoke to Moses and to Aaron, saying, "This is the statute of the teaching that the Lord has charged, saying, 'Speak to the Israelites, that they take you a perfect red cow that has no 3 blemish and on which no yoke has been put. And you shall give her to Eleazar the priest, and he shall take her outside the camp and she shall 4 be slaughtered before him. And Eleazar the priest shall take of her blood with his finger and sprinkle toward the front of the Tent of Meet- 5 ing from her blood seven times. And the cow shall be burned in his

---

2. *a perfect red cow that has no blemish*. The traditional rendering of *parah* as "heifer" is not warranted by the Hebrew, which in no way suggests that the beast is not mature. The red color appears to be associated with the importance of blood in the purification ritual that follows, an association reinforced by the phonetic overlap in Hebrew between *dam*, "blood," and *'adom*, "red."

   on which no yoke has been put. The literal sense of the Hebrew is "on which no yoke has gone up." The manifest idea is that the cow should not have been used for profane purposes.

3. *she shall be slaughtered*. The Hebrew uses an impersonal third-person masculine verb, "one shall slaughter her," a fairly common equivalent of the passive. (The same form occurs at the beginning of verse 5). As verse 8 makes clear, some person other than Eleazar the priest does the burning: the priest himself is kept at a certain distance from this procedure, supervising it (the force of "before him" in this verse).

4. *her blood*. As elsewhere, blood has a purifying function, serving as what Jacob Milgrom calls a "spiritual detergent." The blood is sprinkled "toward" the Tent of Meeting because the whole ritual takes place at a considerable distance from it, outside the camp.

sight, her hide and her flesh and her blood together with her dung he
shall burn. And the priest shall take cedarwood and hyssop and crim- 6
son stuff and fling them into the burning of the cow. And the priest 7
shall wash his garments and bathe his flesh in water, and then he may
come into the camp, and the priest will be unclean till evening. And he 8
who burns her shall wash his garments in water and bathe his flesh in
water and will be unclean until evening. And a clean man shall gather 9
the cow's ashes and set them outside the camp in a clean place, and it
shall become for the community of Israelites a thing to be kept as riddance water; it is an offense offering. And he who gathers the cow's 10
ashes shall wash his garments and will be unclean until evening, and it
shall be for the Israelites and for the sojourner who dwells in their
midst a perpetual statute. He who touches a dead body of any human 11
person shall be unclean seven days. He shall cleanse himself with the 12
ashes on the third day and on the seventh day he will be clean, and if
he does not cleanse himself on the third day, on the seventh day he will
not be clean. Whosoever touches a dead body, a human being who has 13
died, and does not cleanse himself, he defiles the LORD's Tabernacle,

---

9. *it is an offense offering.* This comment is a kind of gloss. A normal offense
offering would be sacrificed on the altar to expiate an offense. These ashes
mixed with water serve a similar function of ridding the person of contamination. Both the corpse and the act of transgression are imagined as imparting a
polluting physical residue, a kind of miasma, that has to be cleansed.

11. *He who touches a dead body.* Baruch Levine has made a persuasive case that
the "hidden agenda" of this whole section is an attempt to discourage the cult
of the dead. Sundry Ugaritic and Mesopotamian documents suggest a widespread cult of the dead (especially, royal dead) in the ancient Near East, and
there are some hints of its presence in the Bible proper. These laws, then,
argue that the dead, far from being objects of worship and propitiation, are a
source of contamination, and that even accidental contact with corpse or grave
or bone requires a rite of purification. Without such purification, the defiled
person is proscribed from the community (verse 13).

12. *the ashes.* The Hebrew says only "it," but the antecedent of the pronoun has
been substituted for clarity in the translation. (The Hebrew for "ashes" is
singular.)

and that person shall be cut off from Israel, for riddance water was not thrown upon him. He is unclean; his uncleanness is still in him.

14 "'This is the teaching about a person who dies in a tent. Whosoever comes into the tent and all that is in the tent will be unclean seven
15 days. And every open vessel that has no tight lid on it will be unclean.
16 And whosoever in the open field touches a corpse slain by sword or a
17 dead body or a human bone or a grave will be unclean seven days. And they shall take for the unclean person from the dust of the burning of
18 the offense offering and fresh water shall be put into it in a vessel. And a clean person shall take a hyssop and dip it in water and sprinkle it on the tent and on all the vessels and on the people who were there and on him who touched the bone or the corpse or the dead person or the
19 grave. And the clean person shall sprinkle it over the unclean person on the third day and on the seventh day, and he shall cleanse him on the seventh day, and he shall wash his garments and bathe in water, and
20 he will be clean at evening. And a man who becomes unclean and does not cleanse himself, that person will be cut off from the midst of the assembly for he has defiled the LORD's sanctuary, riddance water has
21 not been thrown on him, he is unclean. And it shall become a perpet-

---

14. *all that is in the tent will be unclean*. The ritual impurity exuded by the corpse contaminates everything within the enclosed space of the tent, except for tightly sealed vessels. Although there is a similarity here to the modern understanding of the mechanism of contagion in highly communicable diseases, the similarity is a coincidence flowing from the ancient conception of impurity as a seeping miasma.

16. *a corpse slain by sword or a dead body or a human bone*. Any dead body, whether a victim of the sword or of natural causes, or any remnant of a dead body, is equally contaminant. The stress on "human," as some of the medieval commentators note, indicates that no distinction is intended between Israelite and non-Israelite corpses.

17. *the dust*. Dust and ashes, because they are a set collocation in biblical usage (see Genesis 18:27), exhibit a certain degree of interchangeability, though *'afar* does usually indicate dust of the earth and *'efer* the residue of burning.

ual statute for them, and he who sprinkles the riddance water shall wash his garments, and he who touches the riddance water will be unclean until evening. And whatever the unclean person touches will 22 be unclean, and the person who touches it will be unclean until evening.'"

CHAPTER 20

¹ And the Israelites, the whole community, came to the Wilderness of Zin, in the first month, and the people stayed in Kadesh. And Miriam died there and she was buried there.

² And the community had no water, and they assembled against Moses ³ and against Aaron. And the people disputed with Moses, and they said, saying, "Would that we had perished when our brothers perished before ⁴ the LORD. And why did you bring the LORD's assembly to this wilderness

---

1. *the whole community*. Both Rashi and Abraham ibn Ezra understand this phrase as intended to underline the fact that the Wilderness generation has died out and that a whole new community of Israelites is now poised to enter the land. The widely shared inference is that the story has now reached the fortieth year of Wilderness wanderings.

And Miriam died. This isolated obituary notice is inserted here to provide a symmetrical frame for the two stories of Moses's striking the rock and the rebuff of Israel by Edom. Miriam's death stands at the beginning and that of her brother Aaron at the end.

3. *And the people disputed with Moses*. This story is a close counterpart to the episode of complaint at the beginning of the Wilderness wanderings, Exodus 17:1–7. Even the place-names overlap: this place is called Meribah (Disputation); the site of the murmuring in Exodus is called Massah and Meribah (Testing and Dispute). In the present episode, the people provide a fuller description of the awfulness of the great desert (verse 5), and no mention is made here, as it is in Exodus 17, that Moses fears he will be stoned by the people, though perhaps fear is implied in the report that Moses and Aaron "came away from [*mipney*] the assembly into the Tent of Meeting," as into a place of refuge.

Would that we had perished when our brothers perished before the LORD. To mention the most recent episode, Dathan and Abiram and their followers were

to die here, we and our beasts? And why did you take us out of Egypt to 5
bring us to this evil place, not a place of seed or fig tree or vine or pomegranate, and no water to drink?" And Moses, and Aaron with him, came 6
away from the assembly to the entrance of the Tent of Meeting and fell
on their faces, and the LORD's glory appeared to them. And the LORD 7
spoke to Moses, saying, "Take the staff and assemble the community, 8
you and Aaron your brother, and you shall speak to the rock before their
eyes, and it will yield its water, and I shall bring forth water for them
from the rock and give drink to the community and to its beasts." And 9
Moses took the staff from before the LORD as He had charged. And 10
Moses and Aaron gathered the assembly in front of the rock, and he said
to them "Listen, pray, rebels! Shall we bring forth water for you from this
rock?" And Moses raised his hand and he struck the rock with his staff 11

---

swallowed up by the earth, Korah and his people incinerated—instantaneous
deaths that now seem preferable to slow death by thirst.

8. *Take the staff.* The fact that it is not referred to as "your staff" implies that
it is a staff—whether Moses's or Aaron's—that has been set aside for keeping
in the Tent of Meeting "before the LORD" (verse 9).

  assemble the community. The crucial verbal stem *q-h-l* has been used in a
negative sense: the mutinous assembling against Moses and Aaron. Now they
are enjoined to assemble the community to be united in witnessing God's
saving power.

10. *Shall we bring forth water for you from the rock?* The verb for taking out or
bringing out is the same one the people used (verse 5) to refer to their trajectory from Egypt into the wilderness. Both they and Moses attach the verb to
the wrong subject because in both cases it is God who does the bringing out,
not Moses and Aaron. Jacob Milgrom, building on an insight of the medieval
French Hebrew commentator Bekhor Hashor, persuasively argues that
Moses's sin, for which he is condemned to die outside the borders of the
promised land, is his presumptuous claim, at the very moment he is supposed
to "sanctify" God in the eyes of the people, that it is he and Aaron who will
bring forth the water from the rock. A venerable tradition sees Moses's sin in
his angry striking of the rock instead of speaking to it as he was instructed, but
in the twin episode in Exodus 17, he is actually told to strike the rock, and such
efficacious gestures with the staff have been an authorized part of Moses's role
as a worker of wonders from the beginning of his mission.

twice and abundant water came out, and the community, with its beasts,
12 drank. And the LORD said to Moses and to Aaron, "Inasmuch as you did
not trust Me to sanctify Me before the eyes of the Israelites, even so you
shall not bring this assembly to the land that I have given to them."
13 These are the waters of Meribah, where the Israelites disputed with the
LORD and He was sanctified through them.

14 And Moses sent messengers from Kadesh to the king of Edom: "Thus
said your brother Israel, 'You know all the hardship that has found us.
15 Our fathers went down to Egypt and we dwelled in Egypt many years
16 and the Egyptians did evil to us and to our fathers. And we cried out
to the LORD and He heard our voice and sent a messenger and brought

---

13. *and He was sanctified through them.* The antecedent of "them" is ambiguous, but the proximate noun that creates the fewest difficulties is "waters."
Moses and Aaron had the opportunity to proclaim God's power in bringing
forth the water from the rock. Though they failed in this, the gush of water
from the rock that revived the thirsting people nevertheless proved to be a confirmation of God's power, "sanctifying" Him, rather than being a demonstration of Moses's ability as an arch-magician.

14. *Thus said your brother Israel.* The first two words of this clause are the so-
called messenger formula that is conventionally used to introduce the text,
whether written or oral, of a message (roughly like the salutation in a modern
letter). Collective Israel identifies himself to Edom as "your brother" because
they are in fact ethnic kin; according to Genesis, the eponymous founders of
the two peoples, Jacob-Israel and Esau-Edom, were twins. The sending of
messengers to Edom, as many commentators have noted, recalls Jacob's sending messengers to his brother Esau after two decades of separation. This heir
of Esau, however, behaves quite differently from his ancestor, flatly rejecting
Israel's claim to brotherhood and its accompanying request of transit through
his territory.

15. *Our fathers went down to Egypt.* This recapitulation of history is in part
intended to enlist a sense of Semitic ethnic solidarity against the non-Semitic
Egyptian persecutors.

16. *sent a messenger.* In some of the varying accounts in Exodus, not God Himself but a divine messenger leads Israel out of slavery into the wilderness.

us out of Egypt. And look, we are in Kadesh, a town on the edge of your
territory. Let us, pray, pass through your land. We will not pass through 17
field or vineyard and we will not drink well water. On the king's road
we will go. We will not swerve to the right or the left until we pass
through your territory.'" And Edom said to him, "You shall not pass 18
through me, lest with the sword I come out to meet you." And the 19
Israelites said to him, "On the highway we will go up. And should we
drink your water, I and my livestock, I will pay its price. Only it is nothing. On foot let me pass through." And he said, "You shall not pass!" 20
And Edom came out to meet him with heavy troops and a strong hand.
And Edom refused to let Israel pass through his territory, and Israel 21
swung away from him.

---

territory. The Hebrew *gevul* means either "territory" or "border." In verse 23
the term obviously has the latter meaning.

17. *Let us, pray, pass through your land.* The Israelites are careful to use the
most polite and deferential forms in this diplomatic petition.
    the king's road. This is a major north-south route from Syria through trans-
Jordan to Egypt.

18. *And Edom said.* The obvious sense is "the king of Edom," just as "France"
in Shakespeare's plays can mean "the king of France."
    You shall not pass. Following the principle of contrastive dialogue often evi-
dent in biblical narrative, Edom's response, after Israel's elaborate petition, is
abrupt and blunt. His second response (verse 20) is even more abrupt, only
two words in the Hebrew, *lo' ta'avor,* "you shall not pass."

19. *highway.* The Hebrew *mesilah* is a beaten track, and appears to be a synonym for the king's road.
    I will pay its price. As Rashi suggests, Israel now proffers a possibility of eco-
nomic gain if Edom will grant transit rights.

21. *and Israel swung away from him.* In order to avoid a clash with the massed
Edomite forces, the Israelites, instead of proceeding north by northeast, swing
around (literally, "incline") to the east, coming to a place of encampment perhaps fifty miles eastward at Hor the mountain.

22 And they journeyed on from Kadesh, and the Israelites, all the com-
23 munity, came to Hor the mountain. And the LORD said to Moses and
to Aaron at Hor the mountain on the border of the land of Edom, say-
24 ing, "Let Aaron be gathered to his kin, for he shall not come into the
land that I have given to the Israelites because you both have rebelled
25 against My word at the Waters of Meribah. Take Aaron and Eleazar his
26 son and bring them up Hor the mountain. And strip Aaron of his garments and clothe with them Eleazar his son, and Aaron will be gath-
27 ered up and will die there." And Moses did as the LORD had charged,
and they went up Hor the mountain before the eyes of all the commu-
28 nity. And Moses stripped Aaron of his garments and clothed with them
Eleazar his son, and Aaron died there on the mountaintop, and Moses
29 came down, and Eleazar with him, from the mountain. And all the
community saw that Aaron had expired, and all the house of Israel
keened for Aaron thirty days.

---

22. *Hor the mountain*. This odd form reproduces the unusual word order of the
Hebrew, used only for this mountain.

24. *gathered to his kin*. This decorous euphemism is used instead of the plain
verb "die."

you both. "Both" is added in the translation to reflect the plural Hebrew
verb that addresses both brothers.

rebelled against My word. The Hebrew says literally "against My mouth."
God had said, "I shall bring forth water"; Moses on behalf of himself and
Aaron said, "Shall we bring forth water . . . ?"

26. *strip . . . clothe*. The divestiture of Aaron leaves him naked in his human
vulnerability, without accoutrement of office, before the universal fact of
death. But clothing his son in the priestly garb is also a concrete manifestation
of the continuity of his line and its sacerdotal authority. This is one reason that
traditional Hebrew commentaries see Aaron's demise as a blissful death.

die there. Only now is the blunt verb of death introduced, after Moses has
been twice prepared for the loss of his brother through the euphemism and
the instructions of divestiture.

29. *all the community saw . . . all the house of Israel keened*. The textual unit
that began with "all the community" arriving at Kadesh, where they disputed
with Moses and Aaron, ends with all the community joined in mourning for

Aaron. The biblical narrator's characteristic impassivity does not allow us to know confidently whether these thirty days of mourning are merely a formal ritual or an expression of real sorrow. Aaron was often enough a target of popular resentment, as in the very recent episode of the waters of Meribah. But he was also often a welcome intercessor for the people. Rashi neatly catches the second possibility, the people's reaction to the loss of a cherished leader: "When they saw Moses and Eleazar coming down and Aaron did not come down, they said, 'Where is Aaron?' He said to them, 'He's dead.' They said, 'Is it possible that the angel of death should conquer him who stood against the destroying angel and held back the scourge?'"

CHAPTER 21

1   **A**nd the Canaanite, king of Arad, the Negeb dweller, heard that
    Israel had come by way of Atharim, and he did battle with Israel
2   and took captives from him. And Israel made a vow to the Lord
and said, "If You indeed give this people in my hand, I will put its towns
3 under the ban." And the Lord hearkened to Israel's voice and He gave
the Canaanite in his hand, and he put them and their towns under the
ban, and called the name of the place Hormah.

---

1. *king of Arad*. Arad was a town in the central southern Negeb. Archeological
investigation raises doubts as to whether it existed in this early period. The
whole account here of battles and conquests around the southern and eastern
perimeters of Canaan appears to be a complicated interweaving of retrojec-
tions from a later period with fragmentary historical memories. The comments
here will concentrate on the literary articulation of the account without
attempting to sort out the layered phenomena of historical report.

he did battle with Israel. Although the way of Atharim has not been identified, the preceding narrative encourages the inference that the Israelites are
advancing eastward along the southern border of Canaan, avoiding any penetration into Canaan proper. The king of Arad, then, hearing of their movements, takes the initiative in leading an expeditionary force southward across
the border against them. This act of aggression, rewarded by the initial taking
of captives, is what prompts the Israelites to their vow of utter destruction.

2. *put its towns under the ban*. The Hebrew verb *heḥerim* (cognate noun,
ḥerem) means to devote to utter destruction, with any booty taken to be dedicated to the cult rather than retained for private enjoyment. The place-name
Hormah memorializes this grim practice.

3. *in his hand*. This clarifying phrase (a single Hebrew word) is lacking in the
Masoretic Text but is reflected in a couple of ancient versions.

And they journeyed on from Hor the mountain by way of the Red Sea   4
to skirt round the land of Edom, and the people grew impatient on the
way. And the people spoke against God and against Moses: "Why did   5
you bring us up from Egypt to die in the wilderness? For there is no
bread and there is no water, and we loathe the wretched bread." And   6
the LORD sent against the people the viper-serpents, and they bit the

---

4. *the Red Sea.* In the present context, *yam suf* could not refer to the Sea of
Reeds, the marshy lake region in northern Egypt, as it appears to do in Exodus, but would plausibly be the Red Sea, the body of water for which the term
is used in the Book of Kings.

5. *we loathe the wretched bread.* The probable literal sense of the Hebrew is
"our very self [*nafsheinu* as an intensive form of the first-person plural pro-
noun] loathes the wretched bread." The intensive sense is transferred in this
translation to the extremeness of the verb "loathe." But there are two more
physiological meanings of *nefesh* that are also possible here: "appetite" or "gul-
let." Perhaps the people are saying that they retch when they try to eat the
bread. The complaint here repeats the pattern of a whole series of murmuring
episodes that began in Exodus 17. The one notable difference in this instance
is that the people revile the very stuff that God has given them as a bounty to
sustain them in the wilderness—the manna. This denigration of a divine gift
may explain why, in contrast to the earlier episodes, God immediately
responds with lethal punishment.

6. *viper-serpents.* The Hebrew uses two words that, to judge by their bracketing elsewhere as parallel terms in poetry, are synonyms: *nehashim* and *serafim*.
The second word, transparently derived from the root that means "to burn," is
also used, in Isaiah 6, for "fiery angels" (from which the English "seraph" is
taken); that application of the term to snakes appears to come from the burning effect of the venom. Although it is unlikely that the *serafim* were fire-
breathing dragons, as some fanciful commentators have claimed, this is still
another instance in which kernels of historical recollection have been
expanded into myth. Israelites who wandered through the wilderness would
no doubt have been regularly exposed to the threat of venomous snakes native
to the desert. Here, however, the poisonous creatures are suddenly and miraculously dispatched by God against Israel as a relentless attacking force.

7 people, and many people of Israel died. And the people came to Moses and said, "We have offended, for we have spoken against the LORD and against you. Pray to the LORD that He take the serpents away from us."
8 And Moses interceded for the people. And the LORD said to Moses: "Make you a viper and put it on a standard, and so then, whoever is bit-
9 ten will see it and live." And Moses made a serpent of bronze and put it on a standard, and so then, if the serpent bit a man, he looked on the serpent of bronze and lived.

10,11 And the Israelites journeyed on and camped at Oboth. And they journeyed on from Oboth and camped at Iye-Abarim in the wilderness that
12 faced Moab, toward the rising sun. From there they journeyed onward
13 and camped at the wadi of Zered. From there they journeyed onward and camped across the Arnon, which is in the wilderness coming out from the territory of the Amorite, for the Arnon is the border of Moab
14 between Moab and the Amorite. Therefore is it said in the Book of the Battles of YHWH:

---

7. *the serpents.* The Hebrew employs a singular, collective noun, a common idiomatic pattern for animals in biblical usage.

9. *a serpent of bronze.* The Hebrew is *neḥash neḥoshet.* Rashi vividly catches the point of the wordplay: "It was not said to him 'of bronze,' but Moses said, 'The Holy One calls it *naḥash* and I'll make it out of *neḥoshet*'—a pun." The word magic of replicating serpent/*naḥash* in bronze/*neḥoshet* reinforces the device of sympathetic magic whereby the sight of the bronze image of the serpent becomes an antidote for the serpents' poisonous bite. Interestingly, a small bronze serpent, evidently used in the local cult, has been found at Timnah (where Solomon mined copper) near Eilat, the region in which this incident is reported to have taken place.

14. *the Book of the Battles of YHWH.* This is one of several lost books mentioned in the Bible. The tetragrammaton is represented in this instance as YHWH rather than as "the LORD" in order to intimate the archaic character of the book's title. One may conjecture that this ancient—probably poetic—book was not preserved for the canon because it was felt by later authorities to be too mythological in nature, representing YHWH as a warrior-god in direct combat with Israel's enemies—as He figures in the Song of the Sea—rather than working through the agency of Israel, as is the typical case in the Bible's historical narratives.

"Against Waheb in a whirlwind and the wadis of Arnon,
and the cascade of the wadis that turns down toward Ar's   15
    dwelling, and clings to Moab's border."

And from there to Be'er, which is the well of which the LORD said to   16
Moses, "Gather the people, that I may give them water." Then did   17
Israel sing this song:

"Rise up, O well!
    Sing out to it.
Well, that captains dug,   18
    the people's nobles delved it,
        with a scepter, with their walking stick."

Against Waheb in a whirlwind. The quotation from the Book of the Battles of YHWH is fragmentary, and it is not easy to determine what it might be about. The first two place-names are preceded by the accusative prefix *'et* but no verb is included in the quotation. It seems reasonable to infer that a verb of violent action, suggesting something like "to storm," with YHWH as subject, was present in the text immediately before the words actually quoted. In this translation, the implication of the accusative prefix is represented by "against." *Sufah,* the word for "whirlwind," is construed by many to be a place-name (otherwise unattested), but given the subject of divine battling, "whirlwind" makes better sense.

16. *Be'er, which is the well of which the LORD said.* Be'er means "well" in Hebrew. The narrative here invokes an apparently familiar episode of God's providing water in the desert but does not directly report it. Instead, we have the quotation of a second archaic poem that celebrates the discovery of the well. Such well-songs are actually current among later Bedouins: when life in the parched desert is so dependent on water, the discovery of an underground spring is an occasion for musical thanksgiving.

18. *Well, that captains dug, / the people's nobles delved it.* Although Abraham ibn Ezra wants to identify these leaders as Moses and Aaron, it is far more likely that this ancient bit of song registers a less historically anchored celebration by desert tribesmen and their chieftains, who, hyperbolically, are said to have dug into a water source using their staffs of authority as digging implements.

19 And from Midbar to Mattanah. And from Mattanah to Nahaliel, and
20 from Nahaliel to Bamoth. And from Bamoth to the valley that is in the
steppes of Moab, by the top of Pisgah looking out over the wasteland.

21,22 And Israel sent messengers to Sihon king of the Amorites, saying, "Let
me pass through your land. We will not turn off in field or vineyard. We
will not drink well water. On the king's road we will go until we pass
23 through your territory." And Sihon did not let Israel pass through his
territory, and Sihon gathered all his troops and went out to meet Israel
24 in the wilderness, and he came to Jahaz and did battle with Israel. And
Israel struck him down by the edge of the sword and seized his land
from the Arnon to the Jabbok to the Ammonites, for the border of the

---

20. *the steppes of Moab*. These notations of itinerary indicate that the Israelites
have at this point completed their march to the east and are poised for a northward drive. The Moabites and the Amorites inhabit the region that is part of
present-day Jordan; most of the towns mentioned are about a day's march to
the east of the Dead Sea. The northernmost area mentioned is Bashan, which
is above the Dead Sea.

22. *Let me pass through your land*. Although the language repeats the salient
elements of the diplomatic message to the king of Edom, there is no recapitulation of the enslavement in Egypt, perhaps because the Amorites are not a
"brother" people like the Edomites.

23. *Sihon did not let Israel pass through his territory*. His response is the same
as that of the king of Edom with one difference: he does not even honor the
Israelites' request for free passage with an answer but instead musters his
forces for an attack against them, like the king of Arad.

24. *the edge of the sword*. The literal sense of the Hebrew is "mouth of the
sword," an image correlated with the idiomatic usage in which the sword is
said to "consume."
    from the Arnon to the Jabbok. Both these rivers run north–south, the Jabbok
on the border of Canaan. The impregnable border of the Ammonites is to the
east.

Ammonites was strong. And Israel took all these cities and Israel set- 25
tled in all the cities of the Amorite, in Heshbon and in all its surrounding villages. For Heshbon is the city of Sihon king of the 26
Amorites, and he had done battle with the first king of Moab and he
took all his land from his hand as far as the Arnon. Therefore do the 27
rhapsodes say:

> "Come to Heshbon, let it stand built,
>   may the city of Sihon be unshaken.
> For fire has come out from Heshbon,   28
>   flame from the town of Sihon.
> It consumed Ar of Moab,
>   the notables of Arnon's high places.

---

25. *all its surrounding villages.* The literal meaning of the Hebrew is "all its
daughters." In biblical idiom, the city figures as a mother and the little settlements in its vicinity are daughters.

26. *the first king of Moab.* The expression could conceivably mean "the former
king of Moab," as Baruch Levine contends.

27. *Therefore do the rhapsodes say.* In the anthologizing spirit of this entire section, we are given still another quotation from an old poem, one that evidently
was a popular subject for recitation by the rhapsodes (*moshlim*) of this region.
The poem could not be Israelite in origin, for it celebrates the greatness of the
Amorite city Heshbon and its conquest of Moab. This text seems to be a
Hebrew translation or adaptation of Amorite epic material celebrating a military victory famous throughout the region.

28. *For fire has come out from Heshbon, / flame from the town of Sihon.* The
style of the poem is manifestly traditional, relying heavily on formulaic phrases
and formulaic word-pairings. This line, which has numerous analogues in the
poetry of the Prophets, is a textbook illustration of the formulaic construction
of a line of parallelistic verse: fire/flame; Heshbon/the town of Sihon, the verb
"come out" doing double duty for both versets, with the added element "town
of" (*qiryat*) providing an accented syllable that a second verb would yield and
thus preserving a three-beat rhythm in each verset.

29   Woe to you, Moab,
                    You are lost, O people of Chemosh.
                His sons he has turned into fugitives,
                    and his daughters to captive state
                        to the Amorite king Sihon.
30   And their mastery is lost,
                    from Heshbon to Dibon.
                We wrought havoc up to Nophah,
                    which is all the way to Medeba."

31,32 And Israel settled in the land of the Amorite. And Moses sent to spy out Jazer, and they captured its surrounding villages and dispossessed
33 the Amorite who was there. And they turned and went up on the road to Bashan, and Og king of Bashan came out to meet them in battle, he
34 and all his troops, at Edrei. And the Lord said to Moses, "Do not fear him, for in your hand I have given him and all his troops and his land, and you shall do to him as you did to Sihon king of the Amorites who
35 dwells in Heshbon." And they struck him down, and his sons and all his troops, till no remnant was left him, and they took hold of his land.

---

29. *You are lost.* The Hebrew verb means "to be lost," "to perish," "to vanish."
    Chemosh. He is the patron deity of Moab.
    His sons he has turned into fugitives. Although the verb could be a passive masquerading as a third-person singular transitive, it makes better poetic sense to construe Chemosh as the subject: the god of Moab has been compelled to make his own sons fugitives.

30. *And their mastery is lost.* The Hebrew *waniram* is obscure. The initial Masoretic vowel would make it a verb. This translation, following a construction endorsed by Rashi and many modern scholars, reads it as a noun, *weniram*. That noun, *nir*, has the primary meaning of "yoke," and then by metaphorical extension, "mastery" or "rule," and, alternately, by metonymic extension, "plowed field." An attractive alternative reading offered by the Septuagint is *weninam*, "and their descendants."

33. *Og king of Bashan.* According to the tradition registered in Deuteronomy 3:1–11, Og was a giant, but there is no indication of that in the present report.
    troops. The collective noun *'am* usually designates "troops" in any sort of military context, though the conjunction of *'am* with "land" in the next verse raises the possibility that it might reflect here its more general meaning of "people."

CHAPTER 22

And the Israelites journeyed onward, and they camped in the 1 steppes of Moab across the Jordan from Jericho. And Balak son of 2 Zippor saw all that Israel had done to the Amorite. And Moab was 3 very terrified of the people, for they were many, and Moab loathed the Israelites. And Moab said to the elders of Midian, "Now, this assembly 4 will nibble away everything around us as the ox nibbles the grass of the field." And Balak son of Zippor was king over Moab at that time. And he sent messengers to Balaam son of Beor at Pethor, which is on 5

---

2. *Balak . . . saw.* The thematic keyword of this entire episode is "to see," *ra'oh* (and in the poems that follow, its poetic synonym, "to gaze," *shur*). The Moabite king sees the vast expanse of the Israelite multitudes, which at the climax of the story Balaam, the hexer he has hired, will see as well; the ass sees the LORD's messenger in the road while her master, the professional seer, remains blind to the divine emissary until his eyes are "unveiled."

3. *Moab was very terrified of the people, for they were many, and Moab loathed the Israelites.* This report alludes pointedly to the response of the Egyptians to the Israelites in Exodus. There, too, the sheer magnitude of the Hebrews is stressed, with two terms, *rabim* and *'atsumim*, "many" and "mighty," that recur here, and the Egyptians, too, are said to "loathe" (verbal stem *quts*) the Israelites.

4. *nibble away everything.* The verb here for "chewing up" or "nibbling away" is generally reserved for animals, as the ox simile makes clear. The covering of the eye of the land in the next verse is an image borrowed from the plague of locusts in Exodus, which neatly catches the Moabites' fearful revulsion at the sight of the Hebrew multitudes. (In the Egyptian loathing in Exodus, the Hebrews are assimilated to the realm of crawling and creeping things by the verb "swarm.") In practical terms, though the Israelites have not actually

the Euphrates in his people's land, to call him, saying, "Look, a people
has come out of Egypt. Look, it has covered the eye of the land and it
6 is sitting over against me. And so, pray, go curse this people for me, for
it is mightier than I. Perhaps I shall be able to strike against it and drive
it out of the land. For I know that whom you bless is blessed and whom
7 you curse is cursed." And the elders of Moab and the elders of Midian
went, with spells in their hand, and they came to Balaam and spoke
8 Balak's words to him. And he said to them, "Lodge here tonight, and I
shall give you back an answer as the LORD will speak to me." And the

---

invaded Moab, Balak fears that this vast horde will eat up everything in sight
along the borders of his territory ("everything around us").

5. *the Euphrates*. The Hebrew says "the River," which usually is the designation for the Euphrates. In what follows, there is some ambiguity as to whether
Balaam's homeland is Aram in Mesopotamia or Ammon, to the southwest of
Aram, in trans-Jordan. In the latter case, "the River" might be the Jabbok. The
very next phrase here, "in his people's land" *'erets beney 'amo*, sounds a little
odd in Hebrew, and a reading reflected in the Vulgate and the Peshitta, *'erets
beney 'amon*, "land of the Ammonites," is a more idiomatic usage and would
place Balaam in trans-Jordan. That reading, however, may be merely an
ancient solution to the very textual difficulty delinated here.

6. *whom you bless is blessed and whom you curse is cursed*. Balak's concluding
words are the crux of this monotheistic fable. He assumes that he can employ
Balaam as a technician of the realm of spirits to put a hex on his enemies. The
emphatic point of the story is that God alone controls human destiny, and man
has no independent power to impose curses or blessings.

7. *the elders of Midian*. The addition of Midianites, not afterward mentioned,
to the delegation is perhaps puzzling. A couple of the medieval commentators
propose that the frightened king of Moab is rounding up allies from his
neighbors.

with spells in their hand. The meaning of this phrase has long been disputed.
Since the Middle Ages, many interpreters claim that this is an idiom that actually means "payment for spells to be cast," though one may wonder whether the
emissaries would really have brought Balaam his reward—to entice him?—
before he performed any service. The alternative view is that they brought along
spells to demonstrate their own expertise in magic as credentials for their
engaging him in informed fashion as a pastmaster of the craft.

chieftains of Moab stayed with Balaam. And God came to Balaam and 9
said, "Who are these men with you?" And Balaam said to God: "Balak 10
son of Zippor has sent to me: 'Look, the people that has come out of 11
Egypt has covered the eye of the land. So, go hex it for me. Perhaps I
shall be able to do battle against it and drive it out.'" And God said to 12

---

9. *And God came to Balaam.* This idiom, as Moshe Weinfeld notes, is reserved for God's appearance to non-Israelites. It is equally noteworthy that God typically comes to non-Israelites in night visions. (Compare the Gerarite king Abimelech in Genesis 20:3.) Otherwise, the entire story, with the fable of the talking ass that this commentary regards as integral to it, is altogether distinct from the surrounding narrative. Even the use of YHWH and *'elohim* as designations of the deity does not follow the pattern of discrete literary strands detectable elsewhere in the Torah. Baruch Levine conjectures that both story and poem are the special product of Israelite literary activity in Gilead, the central northern trans-Jordanian region. It is striking that an inscription on plaster, probably composed in the eighth century B.C.E., discovered in 1967 at Deir 'Alla, in this same region, about fifteen kilometers east of the Jordan River, speaks of a powerful soothsayer and seer named Balaam son of [the Aramaic *bar* is used rather than the Hebrew *ben*] Beor. The language of the inscription, which some scholars have called "Gileadite," is very close to Hebrew, perhaps merely a dialect of it with certain Aramaizing elements. Some terms in the inscription are quite similar to terms used in Balaam's poems in our text. The Deir 'Alla inscription, though fragmentary, clearly reflects a polytheistic outlook, which would by no means exclude an Israelite author. The well-known figure, then, of the pagan seer Balaam, whether legendary or historical, has been co-opted by the author of the Balaam story in Numbers to make a monotheistic point with considerable satirical brilliance. Balaam's first words reveal him as someone who assumes all answers and instructions come from "the LORD," YHWH (verse 8).

Who are these men with you? As elsewhere in dialogue between God and man (e.g., "Where is Abel your brother?"), God asks a question not in order to get information He needs but to elicit a response from his human interlocutor that will register some appropriate recognition of the situation at issue.

10. *has sent to me.* The verb here indicates: has sent me the following message. Balaam then goes on to quote the text of the message.

11. *Look, the people that has come out.* Although Balaam's report repeats Balak's words, he abbreviates the message, and, as Yitzhak Avishur neatly observes, he edits out elements that would unduly stress Balak's personal perspective.

Balaam, "You shall not go with them. You shall not curse the people, for

13 it is blessed." And Balaam rose in the morning and said to Balak's chieftains, "Go to your land, for the LORD has refused to let me go with

14 you." And the chieftains of Moab rose and came to Balak, and they

15 said, "Balaam refused to go with us." And Balak once more sent chief-

16 tains, more numerous and more honored than the others. And they came to Balaam and said to him, "Thus said Balak son of Zippor: 'Do

17 not, pray, hold back from going to me. For I will surely honor you greatly, and whatever you say to me, I will do. And, pray, go hex this

18 people for me.'" And Balaam answered and said to Balak's servants, "Should Balak give me his houseful of silver and gold, I could not cross the word of the LORD my God to do either a small thing or a great one.

19 And now, stay here, you, too, tonight, that I may know what the LORD

20 may speak further with me." And God came to Balaam in the night and said to him, "If these men have come to call you, rise, go with them.

21 But only the word that I speak to you shall you do." And Balaam rose in the morning and saddled his ass, and he went with the chieftains of

22 Moab. And God's wrath flared because he was going with them, and

---

Thus, "and it is sitting over against me" and "it is mightier than I" are both deleted.

17. *I will surely honor you.* "Honor" throughout suggests the generous bestowal of material rewards. The "more honored" emissaries of the second delegation may well be imagined as more splendid in raiment and personal ornament, explicitly chosen on these grounds in order to provide Balaam an intimation of the munificence from which he will benefit after rendering his services. One should note that Balak's second dispatch to Balaam is much briefer than the first, not repeating anything about the vastness of the Israelite hordes but instead stressing the promise of payment, not mentioned in the first dispatch.

20. *If these men have come to call you.* God of course realizes that the men have come to "call," or invite, Balaam. He has now determined to turn this invitation of a professional hexer into a trap to humiliate the polytheists, as the second sentence here ("But only the word that I speak . . .") makes clear.

22. *God's wrath flared because he was going with them.* This is a famous source of puzzlement because God has just told Balaam to go with them. Some bib-

the LORD's messenger stationed himself in the road as an adversary to him, and he was riding his ass, and his two lads were with him. And 23 the ass saw the LORD's messenger stationed in the road, his sword unsheathed in his hand, and the ass swerved from the road and went into the field, and Balaam struck the ass to steer her back to the road. And the LORD's messenger stood in the footpath through the vineyards, 24 a fence on one side and a fence on the other. And the ass saw the 25 LORD's messenger and was pressed against the wall and pressed Balaam's leg against the wall, and once more he struck her. And the 26

---

lical critics solve the problem by cutting the textual knot and assigning the tale of Balaam's ass that begins here to an entirely independent source. But could the God of this story be capable of capricious second thoughts? Or, to suggest more moral grounds for the seeming contradiction of God's act, when later He repeats what He had said in the night-vision, "Go with the men. But the word that I speak to you, it alone shall you do" (verse 35), the implication of the second sentence may be that Balaam was inwardly harboring other intentions. That is, he may have accepted the instructions of the dream-revelation in good faith, but now on the way to Moab, contemplating the profusion of wealth Balak has dangled before him, he could have begun to wonder whether he might not go ahead with a good professional execration. This shift of intention would then trigger God's wrath and the sword-wielding divine messenger.

24. *the footpath*. The Hebrew *mish'ol*, which occurs only here, is transparently derived from *sha'al*, "span," and so implies a narrow pedestrian way. The story assumes the folktale structure of a crescendo of three repetitions (like "Goldilocks and the Three Bears") with a climactic reversal or revelation in the third occurrence. What is noteworthy here is the progressive constriction: from road to footpath to a way so narrow that there is no room to move to either side. The spatial arrangement of the story becomes a dramatization of how man and beast are inexorably caught in God's design for them, from which there is no escape.

   a fence. The fences are, as one would expect in this region, low stone walls, and should not be imagined as picket fences or hedges. Their construction becomes clear in the next verse.

25. *and pressed Balaam's leg against the wall*. In the progression of three occurrences, first Balaam is caused to make an involuntary detour, now he is caused physical discomfort, and finally he will be totally stymied in his forward movement as the ass crouches down under him.

LORD's messenger crossed over and stood in a narrow place in which
27 there was no way to swerve right or left. And the ass saw the LORD's
messenger and crouched down under Balaam and Balaam's wrath
28 flared and he struck the ass with the stick. And the LORD opened the
ass's mouth, and she said to Balaam, "What have I done to you, that you
29 should have struck me these three times?" And Balaam said to the ass,
"Because you have toyed with me. Had I a sword in my hand, by now
30 I would have killed you." And the ass said to Balaam, "Am I not your ass
upon whom you have ridden your whole life till this day? Have I ever

---

27. *with the stick*. No stick was previously mentioned. Abraham ibn Ezra, ever
alert to minute textual details, infers that in the two previous instances Balaam struck the ass with a switch or branch and only now administers a more
serious beating with a stick.

28. *And the LORD opened the ass's mouth*. This is the only talking animal, if one
excludes the mythological serpent in the Garden story, in the entire Bible. The
early rabbis, sensitive to the anomaly, put the mouth of Balaam's ass on their
list of ten prodigies especially preordained from the time of creation. But the
talking ass is perfectly in accord with the theological assumptions of the story:
if God absolutely controls blessings and curses and vision, He can do the same
for speech. And the ensuing dialogue between master and ass opens up splendid comic possibilities.

29. *Because you have toyed with me*. The wonderful absurdity of this response
is that Balaam doesn't miss a beat. Confronted with the articulated speech of
his ass's eminently justified complaint, he answers irascibly as though he were
thoroughly accustomed to conducting debates with his beast.
Had I a sword in my hand. Even as he harangues his ass, Balaam remains
perfectly blind to something the ass has had no difficulty seeing all along: he
wishes he had a sword at the very moment the LORD's messenger stands in
front of him wielding an unsheathed sword.

30. *your whole life*. The Hebrew, a single word, means literally "as long as you
have been."
Have I ever been wont to do thus to you? The ass sounds altogether like an
aggrieved worker. Her service to her master has always been dependable, as
Balaam concedes in his one-word response, so these three deviations must
have special cause.

been wont to do thus to you?" And he said, "No." And the Lord unveiled ₃₁
Balaam's eyes, and he saw the Lord's messenger stationed in the road,
his sword unsheathed in his hand, and he prostrated himself and
bowed down on his face. And the Lord's messenger said to him, ₃₂
"For what did you strike your ass three times now? Look, I myself have
come out as adversary, for the road plunged before me. And the ass saw ₃₃
me and swerved away from me these three times. Had she not swerved
away from me, by now it is you I would have killed, while her I would
have let live." And Balaam said to the Lord's messenger, "I have ₃₄

---

31. *the Lord unveiled Balaam's eyes*. The unveiling or uncovering (verbal stem
g-l-h) of the eyes is of course crucial to the central theme of vision, and both
unveiling and eyes will recur in the prologue of Balaam's oracles.

he prostrated himself and bowed down on his face. This gesture of reverence
continues the comedy of man and beast, for Balaam unwittingly imitates what
his ass has already done in crouching down.

32. *the road plunged before me*. The reader should be warned that no one really
knows what this phrase means. The verb *yarat* occurs only one other time in
the Bible, in Job 16:11, and it is not even certain that the same root is manifested there. The context in Job suggests violent descent or some other catastrophic action. Many interpreters, medieval and modern, seek to smooth out
the meaning by understanding *derekh*, "road" or "way," as "mission" or "behavior," referring to Balaam. In that case, however, one would expect "your way"
instead of "the way." It seems best for the translation to reproduce the enigma
of the Hebrew.

33. *by now it is you I would have killed*. The divine messenger, sword in hand,
addressing the swordless Balaam, bounces back to him the very words he used
against the ass (verse 29).

while her I would have let live. The messenger's words are a virtual citation
of the words Abram says about himself and Sarai, "they will kill me while you
they will let live" (Genesis 12:12). This transposition of the predicament of
patriarch and matriarch to pagan prophet and his ass is still another bold gesture of comic incongruity in the shaping of the story.

offended, for I did not know that you were stationed to meet me in the

35 road. And now, if it is wrong in your eyes, let me turn back." And the LORD's messenger said to Balaam, "Go with the men. But the word that I speak to you, it alone shall you do." And Balaam went with Balak's

36 chieftains. And Balak heard that he had come, and he went out to meet him to the town of Moab, which is at the edge of the territory.

37 And Balak said to Balaam, "Did I not assuredly send to call you? Why

38 did you not go to me? Is it true that I cannot honor you?" And Balaam said to Balak, "Look, I have come to you now. Can I possibly speak anything? The word that God puts in my mouth, only that will I speak."

39,40 And Balaam went with Balak, and they came to Kiriath-Huzoth. And Balak slaughtered cattle and sheep and sent to Balaam and to the chief-

---

36. *And Balak heard that he had come.* Against the initial "seeing" (verse 2), he has now only this mediated report of Balaam's arrival at his border, and he has not the slightest idea of all that Balaam with his unveiled eyes has seen, so he blithely imagines that his design against Israel is moving forward.

37. *Why did you not go to me?* Although the ordinary logic of English usage would call for "come," this translation maintains "go" (verbal stem *h-l-k*) throughout because it is manifestly a thematic keyword in Balaam's story, the story of a man who goes on a questionable way.

38. *The word that God puts in my mouth.* Balaam, after his confrontation by the sword-wielding messenger of the LORD, is speaking in perfect good faith. Balak on his part no doubt assumes that this is the sort of pious twaddle that a top-notch execrator would invoke for the benefit of a client before proceeding to put a hex on someone.

40. *and sent to Balaam and to the chieftains who were with him.* Balak sends the dressed meat to Balaam and the chieftains as an act of hospitality and a prelude to the great ceremony of execration. It is unclear whether any of this slaughtering is sacrificial or whether it is purely a culinary measure, the same Hebrew verb serving both purposes.

tains who were with him. And it happened in the morning that Balak   41
took Balaam and brought him up to Bamoth-Baal, and he saw from
there the edge of the people.

---

41. *brought him up to Bamoth-Baal.* The place-name means "high places [that
is, sacrificial sites] of Baal," and so becomes the stage for the elaborate procedure of sacrifices that immediately follows. The bringing up is equally important because each of Balaam's oracles is delivered from a promontory where
he can look out over the multitudes of the Israelite camp.

and he saw from there the edge of the people. The narrative unit from the initial exposition of the story to the moment before the first oracle begins with
Balak's seeing Israel and concludes with Balaam's seeing Israel. But the professional visionary can see only the "edge" of the people, both because he is at
a considerable distance from them, on the heights, and because they constitute such a vast expanse that his eye can take in no more than the edge of their
encampment. The legendary notion that the total population of the Wilderness generation comes to well over two million is here both dramatized and
thematized.

CHAPTER 23

1 And Balaam said to Balak, "Build me here seven altars, and ready
2 me here seven bulls and seven rams." And Balak did as Balaam
had spoken, and Balak and Balaam offered up bull and ram on

---

1. *Build me here seven altars.* This elaborate cultic procedure turning on the
sacred number seven, and, as it emerges, repeated three times, may be Balaam's set professional regimen of preparation for delivering an efficacious
curse or blessing, but there is a suspicion that it could also be a delaying tactic through which he postpones the moment when the Lord, as he has good
reason to expect, will put a blessing and not a curse in his mouth. The number seven is also the number of times that Balaam's vatic utterances are formally introduced by "and he took up his theme and he said." The narrative also
establishes a satiric parallel between the three times that Balak and Balaam
set up altars and offer sacrifices and the three times that Balaam and his ass
are stymied by the Lord's messenger. Balak now plays the role of the thrice
frustrated Balaam in the preceding episode, and Balaam, whose eyes have
been "unveiled," plays the role of the ass. In each of the three instances, the
Lord "chances upon" or sets His spirit on Balaam, just as the Lord's messenger stationed himself before the ass. (The verb "to station oneself" is here
transferred to Balak, waiting by the sacrifice.) In the progression from instance
to instance, Balak's frustration mounts, just as Balaam's did with the ass, for
not only is the plan of execration repeatedly frustrated, but the blessings pronounced upon Israel become more extravagant from one oracle to the next.
The monotheist's satiric exposure of the polytheist's delusions could scarcely
be more brilliant.

each altar. And Balaam said to Balak, "Station yourself by your burnt ₃ offering, and let me go—perhaps the Lord will chance upon me and will show me something that I may tell you." And he went off in silence. And ₄ God met Balaam, and he said to Him, "The seven altars I have arrayed, and I have offered up bull and ram on each altar." And the Lord put a ₅ word in Balaam's mouth, and He said, "Go back to Balak and thus shall you speak." And he went back to him, and, look, he was stationed by his ₆ burnt offering, he and all the chieftains of Moab. And he took up his ₇ theme and he said:

> "From Aram did Balak lead me,
>   the king of Moab, from the eastern mountains:
> 'Go, curse me Jacob,
>   and go, doom Israel.'   ₈
> What can I hex that El has not hexed,
>   and what can I doom that the Lord has not doomed?

---

3. *in silence.* The Hebrew adverbial form *beshefi* occurs only here, and its meaning is not certain.

7. *he took up his theme.* The Hebrew term *mashal* represented by "theme" is variously used in the Bible for different kinds of poetic composition—aphoristic, proverbial, rhapsodic. (Thus the poets called *moshlim* in 21:27 are rendered as "rhapsodes.") Here the poetic utterance is oracular in nature. *Mashal* is not a term generally used for the pronouncements of the Hebrew prophets, and so it may have been deemed especially appropriate for this gentile seer.

8. *What can I hex that El has not hexed.* El, though it is also a Hebrew common noun that means "god," is the proper name of the head of the Canaanite pantheon. One may resist Baruch Levine's conclusion that the poem reflects a still polytheistic stage of thinking about gods in ancient Israel, but there is surely a certain teasing quality of hovering between two different theologies in the designations for God in the poem. A non-Israelite visionary such as Balaam might well speak of El in the old Canaanite sense, yet El appears to be a synonym, in the parallelism of the two versets of this line, with YHWH, the Lord, and in the second oracle (verse 22), El plays precisely the traditional role of YHWH in bringing Israel out of Egypt. This translation seeks to preserve the poem's gesture toward the archaic by using the proper noun El instead of "God."

9   For from the top of the crags do I see them
           and from the hills do I gaze on them.
       Look, a people that dwells apart,
           amongst nations it is not reckoned.
10   Who has numbered the dust of Jacob,
           who counted the issue of Israel?
       Let me but die the death of the upright,
           and may my aftertime be like his.”

11 And Balak said, “What have you done to me? I took you to curse
12 my enemies, and, look, you have done nothing but bless.” And he
   answered and said, “Why, that which the LORD puts in my mouth, only
13 that do I keep to speak.” And Balak said to him, “Go with me, pray, to
   another place, from which you will see him—only his edge will you see,
   but the whole of him you will not see, and hex him for me from there.”
14 And he took him to the Lookouts’ Field, on the top of Pisgah, and he

---

9. *see . . . gaze*. The synonymous language of the line highlights the theme of
seeing that was prominent in the tale of the ass.

   them. The Hebrew says “it/him,” the antecedent being the collective noun
“Israel.”

10. *who counted*. Reading, with the Septuagint *umi sapar* instead of the
Masoretic *umispar*, “and the number of.”

   the issue. The meaning of the unusual Hebrew term *rovaʿ* is in dispute. The
verbal stem *r-b-ʿ* (akin to *r-b-ts*) does sometimes apply to copulation and so,
perhaps, to the consequence of copulation. Others relate it to the number
four, *ʾarbaʿ* (thus Levine, “quarterland”); and still others, with an eye to a possible Akkadian cognate, understand it as another word for “dust,” or perhaps
“dust cloud.”

   the upright. An emendation of *yesharim* proposed by Levine produces *yeshurun*, “Jeshurun,” a synonym for Israel.

   my aftertime. The Hebrew *aharit* is an abstract noun derived from *ahar*,
“after.” It is misleading to translate it as “afterlife” because Israel in this period
had no real notion of an afterlife. What Balaam appears to be saying is that
when he dies (an eventuality mentioned in the first verset here), he would like
the name that lives after him to be as unassailable as that of the people of
Israel. This view of life and death is closer to Homer than to later Judaism or
Christianity.

built seven altars and he offered up bull and ram on each altar. And he 15
said to Balak, "Station yourself here by your burnt offering, and I myself
shall seek some chance. And the LORD chanced upon Balaam and put 16
a word in his mouth and said, "Go back to Balak, and thus shall you
speak." And he came back to him, and there he was stationed by his 17
burnt offering, and the chieftains of Moab with him. And Balak said to
him, "What has the LORD spoken?" And he took up his theme and he 18
said:

> "Rise, Balak, and listen,
>   give ear to me, O Zippor's son!
> El is no man who would fail, 19
>   no human who would show change of heart.
> Would he say and not perform
>   would he speak and not fulfill it?
> Look, to bless I was taken, 20
>   and He blessed, so I will not reverse it.
> He has beheld no harm in Jacob, 21
>   and has seen no trouble in Israel.
> The LORD his god is with him,
>   the king's trumpet blast in his midst,

---

18. *Zippor's son.* The poem uses an archaic-poetic construct form, *beno tsipor,*
instead of the usual *ben tsipor,* "son of Zippor."

19. *El is no man.* The monotheistic point briefly stated in the first oracle (verse
8) is here expanded to a full-fledged theological proposition on God's fixed
intentions that resist any human manipulation.

20. *I was taken.* Reading *luqaḥti* instead of the Masoretic *laqaḥti,* "I took."
    and He blessed. A change of one vowel in the consonantal text yields the
infinitive "bless," which might make a better syntactic parallelism with the
first verset.

22   El who brings them out from Egypt,
          like the wild ox's antlers for him.
23   For there is no divining in Jacob
          and no magic in Israel.
       Now be it said to Jacob
          and to Israel what El has wrought.
24   Look, a people like a lion arises,
          like the king of beasts, rears up.
       He will not lie down till he devours the prey,
          and blood of the slain he drinks."

---

22. *like the wild ox's antlers for him.* To'afot, the word translated as "antlers," usually means "mountain peaks" and perhaps is used metaphorically here for what juts out from the top of the wild ox's head. To whom does this simile refer? The more cautious reading is that it is a representation of the fiercely triumphant Israel, now a militant people after its liberation from Egyptian slavery. It may, however, be more in keeping with the archaic character of the poem to see the animal imagery as a representation, in accordance with the conventions of Canaanite epic, of the fierce God who has freed Israel from Egypt.

23. *Now be it said to Jacob . . . what El has wrought.* This line of verse follows directly from the assertion that there is no divining in Israel. Other nations may foolishly have recourse to soothsayers and word-magic professionals like Balaam, but Israel is immediately informed, whether through prophets or direct divine revelation, what God's designs are.

24. *like a lion arises.* This image of the rising, bloodthirsty lion is a stock metaphor for martial prowess in biblical and other ancient Near Eastern poetry. The kenning "king of beasts" in the second verset of this line reflects a single Hebrew word: biblical Hebrew has four synonyms for lion (whatever distinctions there may have been among them have been lost with the passage of time), whereas English, alas, has none.

blood of the slain he drinks. The language here is similar to the startling picture in Job 39:30 of the eagle's fledglings lapping up the blood of the slain. Altogether, Balaam's second oracle has raised the stakes of frustration for Balak. Israel is envisaged now not merely as vast but as a fiercely indomitable warrior people—Balak now has not just been led off the road into the field but feels his leg crushed against the wall.

And Balak said to Balaam, "Neither to curse shall you curse him nor 25
to bless shall you bless him." And Balaam answered and said to Balak, 26
"Did I not speak to you, saying, 'All that the LORD speaks, only that may
I do'?" And Balak said to Balaam, "Go, pray, let me take you to another 27
place. Perhaps it will be right in the eyes of the god and you will curse
him for me from there." And Balak took Balaam to the top of Peor, 28
which looks out over the wasteland. And Balaam said to Balak, "Build 29
me here seven altars and ready me here seven bulls and seven rams."
And Balak did as Balaam had said, and he offered up bull and ram on 30
each altar.

---

25. *Neither to curse.* Momentarily, Balak is so exasperated that he announces
that he is dispensing altogether with Balaam's professional services. But when
Balaam replies that he is, after all, bound to carry out whatever the LORD tells
him, Balak imagines that he may have better luck with this god on a third try.

27. *Perhaps it will be right in the eyes of the god.* Balak accepts the fact that Balaam's words are dependent on this particular deity, but he clings to the hope
that the deity at last will prove more favorably inclined to the plan of execration. The Hebrew *'elohim* could mean "God," but the fact that it is prefixed by
a definite article and that it is pronounced by a pagan makes the polytheistic
sense of the term more likely.

CHAPTER 24

¹ **A**nd Balaam saw that it was good in the eyes of the Lord to bless Israel, and he did not go as on the times before to encounter ² omens but turned his face to the wilderness. And Balaam raised his eyes and saw Israel dwelling by its tribes, and the spirit of God was ³ upon him. And he took up his theme and he said:

---

1. *he did not go as on the times before to encounter omens.* This constitutes new information about Balaam's two previous oracles. In each instance, as we now understand, he made his way along the promontory, in accordance with his usual professional procedures as seer and hexer or blesser, looking for signs (bird flight, cloud formations, or whatever) that would give him a clue about what to say. In each case, God intervened and "put a word in his mouth." Balaam's persistence in his seer's craft throws retrospective light on his intentions toward Israel during his journey from the east when he was stymied three times by his ass as she was confronted by the divine messenger. Now, in keeping with the folktale pattern of three repetitions with a climactic switch in the third occurrence, Balaam abandons his quest for omens, instead looking out straightaway to the wilderness where Israel is encamped.

2. *and the spirit of God was upon him.* In this altered third instance, God does not put a word in Balaam's mouth but sets His spirit upon him—the formula to designate inspiration used for the prophets (and the judges). With this spirit, he will now pronounce his most comprehensive blessing of Israel.

"Utterance of Balaam, Beor's son,
    utterance of the man open-eyed,
utterance of him who hears El's sayings,   4
    who the vision of Shaddai beholds,
        prostrate with eyes unveiled.
How goodly your tents, O Jacob,   5
    your dwellings, O Israel!
Like palm groves they stretch out,   6
    like gardens by a river,
Like aloes the Lord has planted,
    like cedars by the water.

---

3. *Utterance of Balaam.* Although this line and the next (verse 4) sound very much like the set self-introduction of a professional seer who feels he can lay claim to special visionary powers, there was no equivalent at the beginning of the previous oracles, and so the declaration may be motivated in narrative context by God's spirit having come upon Balaam.

4. *El's . . . Shaddai.* Elsewhere, El Shaddai is a compound name used for the God of Israel. As elsewhere in Balaam's oracles, these designations, as well as Elyon in verse 16, appear to be names once used for Canaanite deities (and hence neatly appropriate in the speech of this non-Israelite prophet) that have been co-opted for monotheistic usage.

prostrate with eyes unveiled. The unveiled eyes hark back to the unveiling of Balaam's eyes by the Lord's messenger. A certain irony is generated by the link between the two texts: Balaam's declaration here of his visionary power comes to remind us of his blindness when he was incapable of seeing what his ass plainly saw, until the Lord's messenger intervened. "Prostrate" (literally, "falling," *nofel*) most likely refers to the state of ecstasy in which the seer is flung to the ground. There are abundant indications elsewhere in the Bible that this sort of "falling" was expected as a consequence of the descent of the spirit on the seer or prophet.

6. *Like palm groves.* The Hebrew *nehalim,* most scholars agree, is a homonym for the much more common term that means "wadis" or "brooks." But the poet's decision to use this unusual word here, as the Israeli scholar Shlomo Morag has plausibly suggested, is motivated by a desire to reinforce through the pun on palm groves/brooks the imagery of abundant water in the next several versets. There is also a near pun in these lines between the verb *nitayu,* "stretch out," and *nata',* "planted."

7   Water drips from his branch,
            and his root in abundant waters.
      His king looms over Agag
            and his kingship is lifted high.
8   El who brings him out from Egypt,
            like the wild ox's antlers for him.
      He consumes nations, his foes,
            and their bones he does crush
            and smashes his loins.
9   He crouches, lies down like a lion,
            like the king of beasts, who can rouse him?
      Those who bless you are blessed,
            and your cursers are cursed."

10   And Balak's wrath flared against Balaam and he clapped his palms, and
      Balak said to Balaam, "To hex my enemies did I call you, and, look, you
11   have done nothing but bless now three times. And so, go flee to your
      place. I said I would surely honor you, and, look, the LORD has held you

---

7. *his root.* The noun *zera'*, which ordinarily means "seed," frequently designates "root" in poetry (repeatedly, in Job).
      Agag. King of Amalek at the time of Saul.

8. *their bones . . . his loins.* The switch from a plural to a singular object of the
verb is characteristic of the fluid Hebrew usage in this regard.
      and smashes his loins. The Masoretic Text reads "and smashes his arrows,"
weḥitsaw yimḥats. A compelling emendation adopted by many scholars cor-
rects this to *weḥalatsaw yimḥats* (the addition of a single consonant to the noun
in question). This not only yields a much more intelligible parallelism but also
reflects other lines of biblical poetry in which "loins," *ḥalatsayim*, is the direct
object of "smash," *maḥats*.

10. *clapped his palms.* In the biblical world, this is a conventional gesture of
despair.

11. *honor.* As before, "honor" refers to material reward. Balaam, having been
promised vast quantities of silver and gold, will now go home empty-handed.

back from honor." And Balaam said to Balak, "Did I not speak to your 12
messengers, too, whom you sent to me, saying, 'Should Balak give me 13
his houseful of silver and gold, I could not cross the word of the LORD
to do either a good thing or a bad one from my own heart. That which
the LORD speaks to me, it alone can I speak.' And so, I am about to go 14
to my people. Let me counsel you what this people will do to your people in days to come." And he took up his theme and he said, 15

> "Utterance of Balaam, Beor's son,
>   utterance of the man open-eyed.
> Utterance of him who hears El's sayings 16
>   and knows what Elyon knows.
> Shaddai's vision he beholds,
>   prostrate with eyes unveiled.

---

12. *Did I not speak to your messengers.* Following the established convention of
biblical narrative, Balaam does not simply summarize what he said to the messengers but actually quotes his earlier speech verbatim. The only substitution,
"a good thing or a bad one" instead of "a great thing or a small one," is merely
a synonymous variation, since both expressions have the sense of "anything at
all." This time, Balaam also adds "from my heart" by way of explanation.

13. *That which the* LORD *speaks to me, it alone can I speak.* This already
repeated sentence, recurring now just before Balaam pronounces his final oracles, has the force of a thematic refrain: the whole point of the story is that
there is no autonomous realm of word magic and vision that a technician of
the holy can manipulate; all blessings and curses are dictated by the LORD.

14. *people.* Balaam pointedly repeats this word three times, laying before Balak
a triangle of peoples: Moab, Israel, and his own people to the east, to whom
he will return once he has told Balak what Israel will do to Moab.

16. *and knows what Elyon knows.* The extravagance of this whole self-
advertisement, and especially of this clause, has a certain irony, given the previously unseeing Balaam's absolute dependence on God for everything he
manages to see and for everything he says.

17   I see him, but not yet now.
          I gaze on him, but not in time close.
          A star steps forth from Jacob,
              a meteor arises from Israel,
          and smashes the brow of Moab,
              and the pate of all the Sethites.
18   And Edom will be dispossessed,
              Seir dispossessed by its enemies.
          But Israel performs prowess,
19   and Jacob holds sway over them,
              and destroys the city's survivor."

---

17. *I see him . . . I gaze on him.* Once more, as Balaam launches on his final series of pronouncements, the thematic words of sight are highlighted.

A star steps forth. The meaning of this phrase has defied interpreters. The Septuagint's reading of *zarah,* "shines," instead of the Masoretic *darakh,* "steps forth" or "trods," is a transparent instance of evading a textual difficulty by substituting a simpler text. Some modern interpreters, arguing from a Semitic cognate, claim that *darakh* here means "rules," but that seems far-fetched because every other biblical instance has to do with treading or walking (or tightening a bow with pressure from a foot). It seems most sensible to imagine the star marching forth in military fashion or emerging from Jacob. The star is in all likelihood a metaphor for a king, something that Bar Kochba's followers assumed in using this verse as a rationale for his messianic name, which means "son of a star."

and the pate. The Masoretic Text here reads *weqarqar,* an infinitive form that might, only conjecturally, mean "and to raze." This translation embraces the widely accepted emendation of *weqodqod,* "and the pate," a neat parallel to "brow" and an apt object of the double-duty verb in the first verset, "smashes." (The ancient Hebrew graphemes for *d* and *r* are very similar.) The identity of the Sethites is uncertain and obscurities will grow as Balaam moves on to his oracles about the nations.

19. *and Jacob holds sway over them.* Instead of the Masoretic "and he holds sway from Jacob," *weyerd miya'aqov,* this translation reads *weyirdem ya'aqov,* moving the *mem* from the beginning of the noun to the end of the verb that precedes it.

And he saw Amalek, and he took up his theme and said,   20

    "First of nations was Amalek,
      and at his last unto destruction."

And he saw the Kenite, and he took up his theme and said,   21

    "Staunch is your settlement,
      and set in the rock your nest.
    But Cain will be for burning,   22
      how long will Asshur hold you captive?"

And he took up his theme and he said,   23

    "Woe, who can live more than El has set him,
      and ships from the hands of the Kittites,   24
    and they lay low Asshur and lay low Eber,
      and he, as well, unto destruction."

---

22. *Cain will be for burning, / how long will Asshur hold you captive?* The language of the second verset is especially crabbed and the meaning in doubt. There is also another way to construe the first verset. The verb *ba'er* can indicate either burning or grazing by cattle. Baruch Levine, adopting the second meaning, renders this as "Cain will be a trampled land."

23–24. *who can live more than El has set him, / and ships from the hands of the Kittites.* An honest translator must admit that the Hebrew text here is not intelligible, and that the nexus between the seemingly philosophical pronouncement of the first verset and the invocation of a Mediterranean fleet in the second verset is obscure. Some scholars have sought to recover the original meaning by performing radical surgery on the text.

24. *they lay low Asshur.* What one can glean from these last vatic words of Balaam is a vista of destruction in which once great kingdoms sink into oblivion while the people of Israel powerfully persists.

25 And Balaam rose and went and returned to his place, and Balak, too, went on his way.

---

25. *And Balaam rose and went and returned to his place.* This is a recurrent formula for marking the end of a narrative unit in the Bible. It should be noted that through much of the story, it was Balaam who was the subject of the verb "to go." Now he is seen, according to the set formula, returning to his place, resuming a condition of stasis outside the boundaries of what can be narrated, while Balak goes on his way, not toward any indicated destination or mission, as was the case with Balaam, but in the frustration of all his intentions.

CHAPTER 25

nd Israel stayed at Shittim, and the people began to go whoring   1
with the daughters of Moab. And they called the people to the   2
sacrifices of their gods, and the people ate and bowed down to
their gods. And Israel clung to Baal Peor, and the LORD's wrath flared   3

---

1. *Shittim.* The name means "acacias." The full place-name, given in 33:49, is
Abel-Shittim, which means "brook of the acacias."

began to go whoring with the daughters of Moab. The sexual metaphor of
"whoring" (verbal stem *z-n-h*) is regularly used in the Bible to represent Israel's
betrayal of cultic fidelity to its own God. This figurative usage leads Baruch
Levine to argue that no actual sexual activity is involved in the present
episode. That inference, however, is implausible because it offers no explanation of how or why it is the "daughters" (*banot*, "young women") of Moab who
lure the Israelite men to worship their god. Our story is rather an instance in
which the literal sense of the verb "to whore" leads to the figurative sense.
Rashi catches this double usage in the following vivid vignette: "When he was
seized by his sexual impulse and said, 'Submit to me,' she would pull out an
image of Peor from her lap and say to him, 'Bow down to this.'"

2. *they called.* The verb here has the technical sense of "invited."

3. *And Israel clung to Baal Peor.* There is no obvious link, beyond the trans-
Jordanian setting, between this episode of cultic infidelity and the preceding
tale of Balaam, and, indeed, the Baal Peor story seems clearly the product of
another hand, or in fact, of other hands. The editorial decision, however, to
insert this material here reflects the general predisposition of biblical literature
to represent Israel dialectically. If in Balaam's oracles Israel is a unique and
indomitable nation, here it is pathetically vulnerable to the seductions of the
surrounding pagan world. Perhaps most ironically apposite from Balaam's oracles is the grand declaration that Israel is "a people that dwells apart." Now,

4 against Israel. And the Lord said to Moses, "Take the chiefs of the people and impale them to the Lord before the sun, that the Lord's flar-
5 ing wrath turn away from Israel." And Moses said to the judges of
6 Israel, "Each of you kill his men who cling to Baal Peor." And look, a
man of the Israelites came and brought forth to his kinsmen the Midianite woman before the eyes of Moses and before the eyes of the whole
community of Israelites as they were weeping at the entrance to the
7 Tent of Meeting. And Phinehas son of Eleazar son of Aaron the priest
saw, and he rose from the midst of the community and took a spear in

---

immediately after that oracle, the Israelites show how intertwined they can be
with their pagan neighbors, both sexually and cultically. Baal is the Canaanite
god of the fields: Baal Peor means the Baal who is venerated at Peor. (One
wonders whether the story puns sexually on that place-name, which can be
related to the Hebrew verb that means "to gape open.") Jacob Milgrom notes
that this is the first mention in the Bible of Baal, a deity whose worship
became widespread only in the latter half of the second millennium B.C.E., and
he also observes that the story reflects the fact that Israel has now come to the
borders of Canaan, where it will be in contact with the Canaanite peoples.

4. *impale them to the Lord before the sun.* The clear implication of this grim
command is that the public impaling of the Israelite leaders is conceived in
quasi-ritual terms, "to the Lord," as a kind of expiatory sacrifice or execution.
In what follows, there is no report that this order of execution is carried out.

5. *the judges of Israel.* The Hebrew *shoftim* could mean "magistrates" or simply
"leaders," but in any case this has to be a group distinct from the "chiefs" (or
"heads," *ra'shim*) just mentioned.
   Each of you kill his men who cling to Baal Peor. Moses seems to alter God's
instructions that the chiefs of the people be killed. Milgrom sees this as
another instance of Moses's acting as intercessor, in this case making only the
malefactors the objects of the order of execution.

6. *the Midianite woman.* The story began with Moabite women, not Midianites, but this may reflect an assimilation of the two contiguous peoples rather
than a confusion. In the story of Balaam, the Moabite delegation that comes
to Balaam includes Midianite elders.

his hand. And he came after the man of Israel into the alcove and   8
stabbed the two of them, the man of Israel and the woman, in her
alcove, and the scourge was held back from the Israelites. And those   9
who died in the scourge came to twenty-four thousand. And the LORD   10
spoke to Moses, saying, "Phinehas son of Eleazar son of Aaron the   11
priest turned away My wrath from the Israelites when he zealously
acted for My zeal in their midst, and I did not put an end to the
Israelites through my zeal. Therefore say: 'I hereby grant him My   12
covenant of peace. And it shall be for him and for his seed after him a   13
covenant of perpetual priesthood in recompense for his acting zealously

---

8. *into the alcove . . . in her alcove.* The Hebrew *qubah* is unique to this text,
but it has been linked with the Arabic *qubbe*, which is a small tent of red
leather used for cultic purposes, or, alternately, for conjugal purposes. (The
English "alcove" actually derives from the Arabic *al-qubbe*.) The contention
that the term refers here to the Tabernacle, and hence that a violation of the
Israelite sanctum is at issue, is strained because the Tabernacle (*mishkan*) is
nowhere else referred to as *qubah*. The second occurrence of *qubah* in this
verse, if one follows the Masoretic vocalization, appears to be the same word,
though it obviously puns on *qebah*, "belly." One is warranted to understand the
second "alcove" as a rather transparent euphemisim for the woman's sexual
part: she is stabbed in her "alcove." Several of the medieval commentators follow this line of interpretation, invoking the principle of measure for measure.

 and the scourge was held back. There was no previous mention of a scourge,
and God's orders to kill the Israelite chiefs might seem to exclude the use of a
scourge as the agency of punishment. "The LORD's flaring wrath," (verse 4)
however, may imply scourge, as it does in the parallel episode of the Golden
Calf.

12. *I hereby grant him My covenant of peace.* Many understand the Hebrew *briti
shalom* as "My covenant of friendship" (or "of fellowship"). In any event, there
is some ironic dissonance between Phinehas's bloody act of retribution and
this covenant of *shalom* between his descendants and God. This is not the only
instance in which members of the priestly caste figure as militant—indeed,
military—champions of the LORD's exclusive cult. Such militancy scarcely
reflects the role of the priests in later Israelite history, though it may express
an image of their stern authority that they sought to impress on the people.

14 for his God and atoning for the Israelites.'" And the name of the man of Israel who was struck down, who was struck down with the Midianite woman, was Zimri son of Salu chieftain of the Simeonite father's

15 house. And the name of the Midianite woman who was struck down was Cozbi daughter of Zur, who was chieftain of the leagues of fathers'

16,17 houses in Midian. And the LORD spoke to Moses, saying, "Be foes to

18 the Midianites and strike them. For they have been foes to you through their wiles that they practiced upon you in the matter of Peor and in the matter of Cozbi daughter of the chieftain of Midian, their kinswoman, who was struck down on the day of the scourge over the matter of Peor."

14–15. *Zimri son of Salu chieftain of the Simeonite father's house . . . Cozbi daughter of Zur, who was chieftain of the leagues of fathers' houses in Midian.* The information about the name and lineage of the two culprits, given only at the end of the story, casts retrospective light on the implications of their act. This is not any "man of the Israelites," as we might have thought, but a Simeonite prince, cohabiting with a Midianite princess. The targeting of the Israelite chiefs for execution is perhaps to be understood in this connection: the sexual conjunction of an Israelite prince and a Midianite princess is not merely an encounter of desire between two individuals but a treacherous model for the populace on both sides, an emblem of the religious and sexual amalgamation of the two peoples. Her name, whatever actual Midianite provenance it might have, clearly points to the Hebrew root *k-z-b*, "to deceive" or "to lie." In all this, it is notable that Moses, who leaves the bloody work of execution to Phinehas, is himself married to the daughter of a Midianite priest, a figure who, far from promoting Baal, speaks of YHWH in virtually monotheistic terms. The Israelite attitude toward its neighbors appears to have oscillated over time and within different ideological groups, between xenophobia, a fear of being drawn off its own spiritual path by its neighbors, and an openness to alliance and interchange with the surrounding peoples.

CHAPTER 26

And it happened after the scourge that the Lord said to Moses and 25:18b;1
to Eleazar son of Aaron the priest, saying, "Count the heads of all 2
the community of Israelites from twenty years and up by their
fathers' houses, everyone who goes out in the army in Israel." And 3
Moses, and Eleazar the priest, spoke with them in the steppes of Moab
by the Jordan opposite Jericho, saying, "From twenty years and up, as 4
the Lord charged Moses and the Israelites who came out of the land
of Egypt. Reuben firstborn of Israel. The sons of Reuben: Enoch, clan 5

25.18b. *And it happened after the scourge.* Although these words occur at the end of chapter 25 in the conventional chapter break, they clearly belong here.

2. *Count the heads . . . from twenty years and up.* The principal narrative sequence of the Book of Numbers, consisting largely of a series of incidents of rebellion, is framed by a census at the beginning (chapter 1) and a census at the end. The aim of the first census was a military conscription for the march through the wilderness, and that function was reflected in the numbering of all males twenty years old and above. Here, on the other hand, the census is intended to lay the grounds for the division of the land as the Israelites encamp opposite Jericho, the first point of attack in the conquest; and the stipulation of males twenty years old is to indicate that the Wilderness generation fated not to enter the land has died out, with a new generation having grown up to take its place.

4. *as the Lord charged Moses and the Israelites who came out of the land of Egypt.* The most plausible construction of this clause is that the present census follows the pattern of the census that the Israelites were commanded to conduct at the beginning of the Wilderness wanderings for the generation that experienced the Exodus.

6 of the Enochite, for Pallu, clan of the Palluite. For Hezron, clan of the
7 Hezronite. For Carmi, clan of the Carmite. These are the clans of the
Reubenite, and their reckonings came to forty-three thousand seven
8,9 hundred and thirty. And the sons of Pallu, Eliab. And the sons of Eliab,
Nemuel and Dathan and Abiram, these are Dathan and Abiram, called
forth from the community, who incited against Moses and against
Aaron in the community of Korah, when they incited against the LORD.
10 And the earth opened its mouth and swallowed them and Korah when
the community died, when the fire consumed two hundred and fifty
11,12 men and they became a sign. But the sons of Korah did not die. The
sons of Simeon by their clans: For Nemuel, the clan of the Nemuelite.
For Jamin, the clan of the Jaminite. For Jachin, the clan of the Jachi-
13 nite. For Zerah, the clan of the Zerahite. For Saul, the clan of the
14 Saulite. These are the clans of the Simeonite, twenty-two thousand and
15 two hundred. The sons of Gad by their clans. For Zephon, the clan of
the Zephonite. For Haggi, the clan of the Haggite. For Shuni, the clan
16 of the Shunite. For Ozni, the clan of the Oznite. For Eri, the clan of the
17 Erite. For Arod, the clan of the Arodite. For Areli, the clan of the
18 Arelite. These are the clans of the sons of Gad by their reckonings,

---

9. *these are Dathan and Abiram*. Coming after a series of narrative incidents,
this census, unlike the earlier one, takes space for parenthetical glosses of figures in the lineage cut off by premature death.

10. *the earth opened its mouth . . . when the fire consumed*. The reference to the
two different agencies of destruction is a transparent effort to harmonize the
imperfectly blended accounts of the two different rebellions in chapter 16. In
fact, the Reubenites Dathan and Abiram and their followers were swallowed
up by the earth while the priestly rebels led by Korah were consumed by fire.
 a sign. The Hebrew *nes* generally means "banner" or "standard." Here the
sense is a sign of warning.

11. *But the sons of Korah did not die*. In fact, the Korahites ended up playing a
prominent role in the later temple cult.

forty thousand and five hundred. The sons of Judah, Er and Onan, and   19
Er and Onan died in the land of Canaan. And these are the sons of   20
Judah by their clans. For Shelah, the clan of the Shelanite. For Perez,
the clan of the Perezite. For Zerah, the clan of the Zerahite. And these   21
are the sons of Perez. For Hezron, the clan of the Hezronite. For
Hamul, the clan of the Hamulite. These are the clans of Judah by their   22
reckonings, seventy-six thousand and five hundred. The sons of   23
Issachar by their clans. Tola, the Tolaite clan. For Puvah, the clan of the
Punite. For Jashub, the clan of the Jashubite. For Shimron, the clan of   24
the Shimronite. These are the clans of Issachar by their reckonings,   25
sixty-four thousand and three hundred. The sons of Zebulun by their   26
clans. For Sered, the clan of the Seredite. For Elon, the clan of the
Elonite. For Jahleel, the clan of the Jahleelite. These are the clans of   27
the Zebulunite by their reckonings, sixty thousand and five hundred.
The sons of Joseph by their clans, Manasseh and Ephraim. The sons   28,29
of Manasseh. For Machir, the clan of the Machirite, and Machir begot
Gilead. For Gilead, the clan of the Gileadite. These are the sons of   30
Gilead: Iezer, clan of the Iezerite. For Helek, clan of the Helekite. And   31
Asriel, clan of the Asrielite. And Shechem, clan of the Shechemite.
And Shemida, clan of the Shemidaite. And Hepher, clan of the Hep-   32
herite. But Zelophehad son of Hepher had no sons but daughters, and   33
the names of the daughters of Zelophehad were Mahlah and Noa,
Hoglah, Milcah, and Tirzah. These are the clans of Manasseh by their   34

---

19. *Er and Onan died in the land of Canaan.* In this instance, the gloss on the
particular descendants of one of Jacob's sons who died without leaving offspring refers to an episode not in Numbers but in Genesis (chapter 38).

30. *Iezer.* This name is a contraction of Abiezer. In the parallel list in Joshua
17:2 the full form of the name is given.

33. *the names of the daughters of Zelophehad.* This exceptional stipulation of
daughters by name anticipates the issue of inheritance through daughters
raised in the next chapter with the case of Zelophehad's daughters as legal
precedent. Two of these names have been found on ostraca in Samaria dating
from around 800 B.C.E. and are the names of cities in the region. Other names
in this census list may also be place-names figuring as the designation of clans.

35 reckonings, fifty-two thousand and seven hundred. These are the sons
of Ephraim by their clans. For Shuthelah, the clan of the Shuthelahite.
For Becher, the clan of the Becherite. For Tahan, the clan of the Tahan-
36 ite. And these are the sons of Shuthelah. For Eran, the clan of the
37 Eranite. These are the clans of the sons of Ephraim by their reckonings, thirty-two thousand and five hundred. These are the sons of
38 Joseph by their clans. The sons of Benjamin by their clans. For Bela,
the clan of the Belaite. For Ashbel, the clan of the Ashbelite. For Ahi-
39 ram, the clan of the Ahiramite. For Shuphupham, the clan of the Shu-
40 phumamite. For Hupham, the clan of the Huphamite. And Bela's sons
were Ard and Naaman. The clan of the Ardite. For Naaman, the clan
41 of the Naamanite. These are the sons of Benjamin by their clans, and
42 their reckonings were forty-five thousand and six hundred. These are
the sons of Dan by their clans. For Shuham, the clan of the Shuhamite.
43 These are the clans of Dan by their clans. All the clans of the
Shuhamite by their reckonings, sixty-four thousand and four hundred.
44 The sons of Asher by their clans. For Imnah, the clan of the Imnite. For
45 Ishvi, the clan of the Ishvite. For Beriah, the clan of the Beriitite. For
the sons of Beriah. For Heber, the clan of the Heberite. For Malchiel,
46 the clan of the Malchielite. And the name of the daughter of Asher was
47 Serah. These are the clans of the sons of Asher by their reckonings,
48 fifty-three thousand and four hundred. The sons of Naphtali by their
clans. For Jahzeel, the clan of the Jahzeelite. For Guni, the clan of the
49 Gunite. For Jezer, the clan of the Jezerite. For Shillem, the clan of the
50 Shillemite. These are the clans of Naphtali by their clans, and their
51 reckonings were forty-five thousand and four hundred. These are the
reckonings of the Israelites: six hundred one thousand seven hundred
and thirty."

---

51. *six hundred one thousand seven hundred and thirty*. As in the earlier census,
the total number of adult males makes up a figure that is just a little over the
legendary and formulaic tally of 600,000.

And the LORD spoke to Moses, saying, "To these shall the land be 52,53
apportioned as an estate by the number of names. For the many you 54
shall make their estate large and for the few you shall make their estate
small, each according to his reckonings shall his estate be given. But by 55
lot shall the land be apportioned, by the names of their fathers' tribes
shall they inherit. According to lot shall their estate be apportioned, 56
whether many or few."

And these are the reckonings of the Levites by their clans. For Ger 57
shon, the clan of the Gershonite. For Kohath, the clan of the Kohathite.
For Merari, the clan of the Merarite. These are the clans of Levi. The 58
clan of the Libnite, the clan of the Hebronite, the clan of the Mahlite,
the clan of the Mushite, the clan of the Korahite. And Kohath begot
Amram. And the name of Amram's wife was Jochebed daughter of Levi 59
whom she bore to Levi in Egypt, and she bore to Amram Aaron and
Moses and Miriam their sister. And to Aaron were born Nadab and 60
Abihu, Eleazar and Ithamar. And Nadab and Abihu died when they 61
brought forward unfit fire before the LORD. And their reckonings were 62
twenty-three thousand, every male from a month old and up, for they
were not reckoned in the midst of the Israelites, for they were not given
an estate in the midst of the Israelites. These are the reckonings of 63
Moses and Eleazar the priest, who reckoned the Israelites in the
steppes of Moab by the Jordan opposite Jericho. And among these 64
there was not a man from the reckonings of Moses and Aaron the

---

53. *by the number of names.* That is, each clan here registered by name in the
census shall have territory inalienably assigned to it.

55. *But by lot shall the land be apportioned.* At first glance, this would seem to
contradict the condition just stated that the territory is to be divided according to the varying size of the clans and the tribes. The use of lots, however, is
in all likelihood restricted to the selection of particular regions and does not
apply to the size of the territories granted.

57. *the reckonings of the Levites.* As in the earlier census, the tally of the Levites
is given after the general census because the Levites had no land as estate
(and in the previous census, they were not subject to military conscription).

65   priest, who reckoned the Israelites in the Wilderness of Sinai. For the
LORD had said of them, "They are doomed to die in the wilderness."
And no man was left of them save Caleb son of Jephunneh and Joshua
son of Nun.

---

65. *save Caleb son of Jephunneh and Joshua son of Nun.* These two are, of
course, the sole exceptions to the death sentence on the adults of the Wilderness generation because they were the only scouts who brought back a positive report about the prospects for conquering the land. Mentioning them by
name here at the end of the census aligns this textual unit with the inception
of the conquest at the beginning of the Book of Joshua. Caleb will be the first
mentioned to take an inheritance in the land, and Joshua will lead the
conquest.

CHAPTER 27

A nd the daughters of Zelophehad son of Hepher, son of Gilead, son 1 of Machir, son of Manasseh of the clans of Manasseh, son of Joseph came forward, and these are the names of his daughters: Mahlah, Noa, and Hoglah and Milcah and Tirzah. And they stood 2 before Moses and before Eleazar the priest and before the chieftains and all the community at the entrance of the Tent of Meeting, saying, "Our father died in the wilderness, and he was not part of the commu- 3

---

1. *the daughters of Zelophehad*. Rashi, noting that this episode immediately follows a mention of the ten fearful spies, construes it as a special argument in behalf of the role of women as opposed to men in the Wilderness narrative: "The men say (Numbers 14), 'Let us make us put up a head and return to Egypt,' and the women say, 'Give us a holding.'"

3. *Our father died*. The choice of the favored instrument of biblical narrative—dialogue—for making this case has expressive consequences. The issue of daughters' inheritance in the absence of male offspring is not presented as an abstract legal precedent but as an impassioned plea for justice—"Why should our father's name be withdrawn . . . ? Give us a holding"—by these five young women who fear that the patriarchal system of inheritance will deprive them of their rights. Though the notion of daughters' inheriting was exceptional in the ancient Near East, this story is something other than a feminist argument. The chief concern is not to lose the inheritance pertaining to the clan, not to allow the "name" of the clan to disappear. But since the holdings of the clans were defined within tribal territories, the whole system would have been upset if the daughters were to marry outside the tribe. The follow-up to this episode in chapter 36 therefore stipulates that they are obliged to marry within the tribe.

nity that banded together against the LORD with the community of
4 Korah, for through his own offense he died, and he had no sons. Why
should our father's name be withdrawn from the midst of his clan
because he had no son? Give us a holding in the midst of our father's
5,6 brothers." And Moses brought forward their case before the LORD. And
7 the LORD said to Moses, saying, "Rightly do the daughters of Zelophehad speak. You shall surely give them a secure holding in the midst of
their father's brothers and you shall pass on their father's estate to
8 them. And to the Israelites you shall speak, saying, 'Should a man die
9 without having a son, you shall pass on his estate to his daughter. And
10 if he has no daughter, you shall give his estate to his brothers. And if
he has no brothers, you shall give his estate to his father's brothers.
11 And if his father has no brothers, you shall give his estate to his closest
kin from his clan and he shall take possession of it. And this shall be a
statute of law for the Israelites as the LORD has charged Moses.'"

---

for through his own offense he died. This would most plausibly be the
"offense" of all the adults of the Wilderness generation after the episode of the
spies. The daughters assume, as Abraham ibn Ezra notes, that the active con-
spirators against the LORD in the Korah rebellion are to be punished more
severely, by death and by denial of inheritance to their descendants.

5. *Moses brought forward their case before the LORD.* The idiom refers to inquiry
of an oracle, but, unlike the Urim and Thummin (evidently divinatory stones
or tokens) that Joshua is directed to employ at the end of this chapter, Moses
is represented as engaged in dialogue with God.

7. *a secure holding.* The Hebrew is literally "a holding of an estate." The two
terms, *'ahuzah* and *nahalah*, are virtual synonyms, and the use of two synonyms linked in the construct state often expresses an intensification of the
noun (compare *hoshekh 'afelah*, "pitch dark," in Exodus 10:22).

8. *Should a man die.* From the dramatized instance of the daughters of
Zelophehad, the divine response to Moses's inquiry now proceeds to a casuistically formulated law of inheritance that includes the contingency of a daughter as heir but also stipulates the lines of inheritance when the deceased has
neither sons nor daughters.

And the LORD said to Moses, "Go up to this Mount Abarim and see 12
the land that I have given to the Israelites. And you shall see it, and 13
you shall be gathered to your kin—you, too, as Aaron your brother was
gathered, since you rebelled against My word in the Wilderness of Zin 14
in the community's dispute, to sanctify Me through the water before
their eyes." These are the waters of Meribah at Kadesh in the Wilderness of Zin. And Moses said to the LORD, saying, "Let the LORD, God 15,16
of the spirits for all flesh, appoint a man over the community, who will 17
go out before them and come in before them and who will lead them
in and out on the march so that the LORD's community will not be like

---

14. *since you rebelled against My word . . . to sanctify Me through the water.* The
sense of the somewhat loose syntax of this sentence is: My instruction, against
which you rebelled, was to sanctify Me through the water (that is, by making
manifest that it was I bringing forth water from the rock rather than claiming
the deed for yourself and Aaron as you struck the rock).

16. *Let the LORD, God of the spirits for all flesh, appoint a man.* In this final dialogue between Moses and God, it is noteworthy that Moses, far from demur-
ring about the fate of imminent death that has just been pronounced upon
him, expresses his concern about the continuity of leadership and the future
of the people he has led. The relatively unusual epithet, "God of the spirits for
all flesh," points forward to the need for a man "who has spirit within him"
(either the "spirit of wisdom," *ruah hokhmah*, or the "spirit of God," *ruah 'elohim*). All living flesh has an animating spirit or life-breath in it, but only the
few are endowed with a spirit of understanding or visionary presence.

17. *go out before them and come in before them.* This idiom has the sense of "to
lead in battle," an appropriate role for Joshua, who will command the Israelite
forces in the conquest of the land. The same two verbs are used in the next
clause transitively, in the causative conjugation, and there the translation adds
"on the march" to underscore the military implication of the idiom.
   that the LORD's community will not be like a flock that has no shepherd.
Though the image of ruler as shepherd of the people is conventional in the
ancient Near East, it also harks back, as Richard Elliott Friedman aptly
observes, to Moses's own beginnings as a shepherd and his first dialogue with
God at the burning bush to which he had come while tending his sheep.

18 a flock that has no shepherd." And the LORD said to Moses, "Take you
   Joshua son of Nun, a man who has spirit within him, and lay your hand
19 upon him. And you shall stand him before Eleazar the priest and before
20 all the community, and you shall charge him before their eyes. And you
   shall set something of your grandeur upon him in order that all the
21 Israelite community will heed. And before Eleazar the priest he shall
   stand and inquire of him for the ruling of the Urim before the LORD.
   By it shall they go out and by it shall they come in—he and all the
22 Israelites with him and all the community." And Moses did as the LORD
   had charged him, and he took Joshua and stood him before Eleazar the
23 priest and before all the community. And he laid his hands upon him
   and charged him as the LORD had spoken through Moses.

---

18. *lay your hand upon him.* In the event, Moses will lay both hands on Joshua.
Jacob Milgrom, arguing that two hands were regularly used for the gesture of
passing on leadership, reads "hands" here, against the Masoretic text. Rashi
ingeniously makes an interpretive point out of the discrepancy between "hand"
and the plural "hands" in verse 23: "[Moses acted] more generously, more than
he had been commanded. For the Holy One said to him, 'and lay your hand'
but he did it with both his hands and turned [Joshua] into a chock-full vessel
and filled him with his wisdom generously."

20. *something of your grandeur.* The Hebrew *hod* ("grandeur," "majesty," "aura")
is typically associated with kings, or with God. The partitive *mem* that prefixes
the noun is a clear indication of the difference in stature between Moses and
Joshua—only a part of Moses's grandeur is to be conferred upon Joshua. In
any case, this notion of leadership presumes that the leader in his personal
presence must manifest some sort of charisma in order to enlist the loyalty of
those he would lead, "in order that the whole Israelite community will heed."

21. *inquire of him for the ruling of the Urim.* Joshua's lesser stature in comparison with Moses is reflected in the fact that he will be dependent upon an
institutionalized intermediary—the high priest manipulating the oracular
device of the Urim and Thummin—instead of speaking with God "as a man
speaks with his fellow man." The Urim and Thummin were evidently two
stones or dicelike carved objects that yielded yes-or-no responses to inquiries.
The two terms begin respectively with the first and last letters of the Hebrew
alphabet. More conjecturally, Urim might be related to the root '-*r-r*, "to curse,"
and Thummin to the root *t-m-m*, "innocent."

CHAPTER 28

Ａnd the Lᴏʀᴅ spoke to Moses, saying, "Charge the Israelites, and 1,2
you shall say to them, 'My offering, My bread, for My fire offerings,
My fragrant odor, you shall keep, to offer up to Me at its fixed time.'
And you shall say to them, 'This is the fire offering that you will offer to 3

---

2. *My offering, My bread*. Though Moses is to be the speaker, he is enjoined to
quote God's direct discourse to the Israelites.

My offering. The end of the previous chapter was clearly what should have
been the penultimate moment of the Moses story: Moses summoned to the
mountaintop where he will be gathered to his kin and where he is enjoined to
pass the leadership on to Joshua. Now, however, the Priestly redactors, pursuing their own professional concern with the cult, introduce a large block of
material stipulating regulations for sacrifices (chapters 28–29). This will be followed by a sequence of passages pertaining to the conquest and the division
of the land, but since in these sections Moses still holds the reins of leadership, they would have to be anterior to the end of chapter 27. One could
scarcely find a more emphatic illustration of the rabbinic principle that "there
is neither early nor late in the Torah," i.e., that the text of the Torah passed
down to us does not exhibit consistent chronological sequence.

My bread. As elsewhere, this is a synecdoche for food, since the burnt flesh
of animals as well as grain offerings is involved. The sacrificial laws reflect the
strongest nexus of biblical religion with antecedent paganism, and this link is
reflected in the archaic survivals of the language, in which the sacrifices are
represented as the food of the gods and the smoke from the altar as a "fragrant
odor" in the nostrils of the gods, predisposing them in favor of those who offer
the sacrifices. Although biblical monotheism by stages transcended this
mechanical conception of sacrifice, as polemic passages against it in the
Prophets demonstrate, one may assume that it had a powerful appeal, quite
literally understood, for many ordinary Israelite worshippers.

the LORD: two unblemished yearling lambs a day, a perpetual burnt
4 offering. One lamb you shall do in the morning and the second lamb
5 you shall do at twilight. And a tenth of an *ephah* of fine semolina flour
6 for the grain offering mixed with a fourth of a *hin* of beaten oil. A perpetual burnt offering like the one done on Mount Sinai as a fragrant
7 odor, a fire offering to the LORD. And its libation, a quarter of a *hin* for
each lamb in the sanctuary to pour out in libation of strong drink to the
8 LORD. And the second lamb you shall do at twilight like the grain offering of the morning and its libation, you shall do a fire offering, a fragrant
9 odor to the LORD. And on the sabbath day, two unblemished yearling
lambs and two-tenths of fine semolina flour, a grain offering mixed with
10 oil, and its libation. The burnt offering for one sabbath to the next,
11 besides the perpetual burnt offering and its libation. And on your new
moons you shall offer up a burnt offering to the LORD, two bulls from
12 the herd and one ram, seven unblemished yearling lambs. And three-
tenths of fine semolina flour, a grain offering mixed with oil for each
bull, and two-tenths of fine semolina flour, a grain offering mixed with
13 oil for each ram. And one-tenth of fine semolina flour, a grain offering
mixed with oil for every lamb, a burnt offering, a fragrant odor, a fire
14 offering to the LORD. And their libations, these will be half a *hin* for the
bull and a third of a *hin* for the ram and a quarter of a *hin* for the lamb—
wine. This is the burnt offering for the new moon on each new moon of
15 the year. And one goat as an offense offering to the LORD, besides the
perpetual burnt offering, will be done, and its libation.

---

3. *perpetual*. That is, a fixed and repeated requirement, performed daily.

5. *beaten oil*. The top-grade oil was produced with mortar and pestle rather
than extracted with a press.

6. *like the one done on Mount Sinai*. The literal sense of the somewhat enigmatic Hebrew is "that is done on Mount Sinai." Abraham ibn Ezra shrewdly
infers that the sacrifices, first established and performed at Sinai, were not
done during the forty years of wandering in the wilderness.

7. *strong drink*. The Hebrew *shekhar* is derived from the verbal root that means
"to intoxicate." Some think it means "beer" (widely used in the ancient Near
East), but since it is unlikely that beer, a fermented substance otherwise prohibited in the cult, was used for libations, it probably refers to some sort of
wine distinct from the ordinary kind.

"'And in the first month on the fourteenth day of this month, a Passover 16
offering to the LORD. And on the fifteenth day of this month, a festival, 17
seven days flatbread shall be eaten. On the first day a sacred assembly: 18
no task of work shall you do. And you shall offer up a fire offering, a 19
burnt offering to the LORD, two bulls from the herd and one ram and
seven yearling lambs, unblemished they shall be for you. And their 20
grain offering, fine semolina flour mixed with oil, three-tenths for the
bull and two-tenths for the lamb shall you do. One-tenth you shall do 21
for every lamb and two-tenths for the seven lambs you shall do. And 22
one offense-offering goat to atone for you. Besides the morning's burnt 23
offering which pertains to the perpetual burnt offering you shall do
these. Like these you shall do each day seven days, bread of the fire 24
offering, a fragrant odor to the LORD, besides the perpetual burnt offering shall it be done, and its libation. And on the seventh day a sacred 25
assembly shall you have, no task of work shall you do.

"'And on the day of First Fruits when you offer up an offering of new 26
grain to the LORD in your Festival of Weeks, a sacred assembly shall you
have, no task of work shall you do. And you shall offer up a burnt offer- 27
ing as a fragrant odor to the LORD, two bulls of the herd, one ram, seven
yearling lambs. And their grain offering mixed with oil, three-tenths for 28
the single bull, two-tenths for the single ram. A tenth for every single 29
lamb of the seven lambs. One goat to atone for you. Besides the per- 30,31
petual burnt offering and its grain offering you shall do. Unblemished
shall they be for you, and their libation.'"

---

17. *a festival*. The Hebrew *ḥag* implies a pilgrim festival. The noun derives from
the verb *ḥug*, "to move about in a circle," and in all likelihood refers to the trajectory of the pilgrim procession making its way to the sanctuary. As several
recent commentators have noted, *ḥag* is not mentioned in connection with the
feast of First Fruits, and this may not have been a pilgrim festival in the earlier biblical period.

26. *Festival of Weeks*. The Hebrew simply says "Weeks," *shavu'ot*. The name
refers to the seven weeks counted from the inception of Passover to this festival (hence the Christian Pentecost, festival of the fiftieth day, the day following seven weeks).

CHAPTER 29

1 "And in the seventh month on the first of the month you shall have a sacred assembly, no task of work shall you do. A day of trum-
2 peting it shall be for you. And you shall do a burnt offering, a fragrant odor to the LORD, one bull from the herd, one ram, seven
3 unblemished yearling lambs. And their grain offering mixed with oil,
4 three-tenths for the bull, two-tenths for the ram. And one-tenth for
5 each lamb of the seven lambs. And a goat for an offense offering to
6 atone for you. Besides the burnt offering of the new moon and its grain offering and the perpetual burnt offering and its grain offering and their libations according to their rule, as a fragrant odor, a fire offering to the

---

1. *in the seventh month on the first of the month.* In the postbiblical period, this sacred assembly would be designated Rosh Hashanah, New Year. The month in which it occurs, approximately equivalent to September, figures as the seventh month in biblical calculation because the agriculturally based calendar begins in the early spring.

A day of trumpeting. The Hebrew *teru'ah* in all likelihood refers to the sounding of the ram's horn, the *shofar*. Blasts on the ram's horn were used in coronation ceremonies, and as Moshe Weinfeld plausibly argues, this festival was probably linked with other ancient Near Eastern festivals that enacted an annual coronation of the principal deity. It is quite possible that as the biblical faith, evolving toward the form it took in rabbinic Judaism, became more monotheistically theological and less centered on agriculture, this theme of God's kingship led to the adoption of the first day of the seventh month as the beginning of the year—the time when God's majestic rule is ceremonially acknowledged and humanity vows fealty and submits itself (there are ancient Near Eastern precedents) to divine judgment.

LORD. And on the tenth of this seventh month you shall have a sacred   7
assembly, and you shall afflict yourselves, no task shall you do. And you   8
shall offer up a burnt offering to the LORD, a fragrant odor: one bull
from the herd, one ram, seven unblemished yearling lambs you shall
have. And their grain offering fine semolina flour mixed with oil, three-   9
tenths for the bull, two-tenths for the one ram. One-tenth for every   10
lamb of the seven lambs. One goat as an offense offering, besides the   11
offense offering of atonement and the perpetual burnt offering and its
grain offering and their libations.

"'And on the fifteenth day of the seventh month you shall have a sacred   12
assembly, no task of work shall you do, and you shall celebrate a festival to the LORD seven days. And you shall offer up a burnt offering, a   13
fire offering, a fragrant odor to the LORD, thirteen bulls from the herd,
two rams, fourteen yearling lambs, unblemished they shall be. And   14

---

7. *and on the tenth of this seventh month . . . you shall afflict yourselves*. The holiday referred to is the Day of Atonement, Yom Kippur, though that name is not
mentioned here. The idiom "you shall afflict yourselves," *we'initem 'et-
nafshoteikhem*, indicates fasting.

12. *on the fifteenth day of the seventh month*. The holiday in question is the
seven-day fall harvest festival of Succoth. Not only is that name not used here
but there is also no mention of the harvest aspect of the holiday in this Priestly
document, which focuses relentlessly on sacrificial procedures.

13. *And you shall offer up a burnt offering*. Throughout this cultic legislation,
the et cetera principle is strenuously avoided. Although all of the sacrifices,
except for the bulls, are identical on each day, for every day, as if to confirm
the high ceremonial scrupulousness of what is to be performed, each of the
items is restated verbatim. Only trivial variations in wording are allowed—
"and" sometimes appears and sometimes is deleted in the lists; the goat is
sometimes "one goat as an offense offering" (*se'ir 'izim 'ehad hata't*) and sometimes, more concisely, "one offense-offering goat" (*se'ir hata't 'ehad*). This is a
literature of meticulous protocol.
   thirteen bulls. The bulls, which decrease by one each day, begin with the
odd number thirteen in order that on the seventh day there will be a perfect
match of seven bulls for the seven days—a harmonious pairing of the sacred
number in the counting of the days and in the sacrificial animals.

their grain offering, fine semolina flour mixed with oil, three-tenths for each bull of the thirteen bulls, two-tenths for each ram of the two rams. And one-tenth for every lamb of the fourteen lambs. And one goat as an offense offering besides the perpetual burnt offering, its grain offering and its libation. And on the second day twelve bulls from the herd, two rams, fourteen unblemished yearling lambs. And their meal offering and their libations—for the bulls and for the rams and for the lambs by their number and according to their rule. And one goat as an offense offering besides the perpetual burnt offering and its grain offering and their libations. And on the third day eleven bulls, two rams, fourteen unblemished yearling lambs. And their grain offering and their libations—for the bulls and for the rams and for the lambs by their number according to their rule. And one offense-offering goat, besides the perpetual burnt offering and its grain offering and its libation. And on the fourth day ten bulls, two rams, fourteen unblemished yearling lambs. Their grain offering and their libations—for the bulls, for the rams, and for the lambs by their number according to their rule. And one goat as an offense offering, besides the perpetual burnt offering, its grain offering and its libation. And on the fifth day nine bulls, two rams, fourteen unblemished yearling lambs. And their grain offering and their libations—for the bulls, for the rams, and for the lambs by their number according to their rule. And one offense-offering goat, besides the perpetual burnt offering and its grain offering and its libation. And on the sixth day eight bulls, two rams, fourteen unblemished yearling lambs. And their grain offering and their libations—for the bulls, for the rams, and for the lambs by their number according to their rule. And one offense-offering goat, besides the perpetual burnt offering, its grain offering and its libations. And on the seventh day seven bulls, two rams, fourteen unblemished yearling lambs. And their grain offering and their libations—for the bulls, for the rams, and for the lambs, by their number according to their rule. And one offense-offering goat, besides the perpetual burnt offering, its grain offering and

its libation. On the eighth day you shall have a convocation, no task of 35
work shall you do. And you shall offer up a burnt offering, a fire offer- 36
ing, a fragrant odor to the Lord, one bull, one ram, seven unblemished
yearling lambs. Their grain offering and their libations—for the bull, for 37
the ram, and for the lambs, by their number according to their rule.
And one offense-offering goat, besides the perpetual burnt offering and 38
its grain offering and its libation. These shall you do for the Lord in 39
your fixed seasons, besides your votive offerings and your donations, as
your burnt offerings and your grain offerings and your libations and
your communion sacrifices.'" And Moses said to the Israelites as all 30:1
that the Lord had charged Moses.

---

35. *On the eighth day you shall have a convocation.* This eighth day's convocation, *'atseret,* is clearly marked in the cult as a separate holiday because it has
no part in the countdown of bulls, only one bull now being sacrificed. In postbiblical tradition, the holiday would come to be known as Shemini 'Atseret,
the Eighth-Day Convocation.

30:1. Hebrew Bibles set this as the beginning of chapter 30, but it is obviously
a conclusion of the present unit, summarizing what has preceded.

CHAPTER 30

² And Moses spoke to the heads of the tribes of the Israelites, say-
³ ing, "This is the thing that the LORD has charged: Should a man
take a vow or make an oath to the LORD, to take upon himself a
binding pledge, he shall not profane his word. According to all that
⁴ issues from his mouth he shall do. And should a woman take a vow to
the LORD and make a binding pledge in her father's house in her youth,
⁵ and her father hear her vow and her binding pledge that she took upon
herself, and her father remain silent to her, all her vows shall stand and

---

3. *Should a man take a vow.* Jacob Milgrom proposes that the editorial decision
to introduce this section on the laws of vows was dictated by the references to
vows or votive offerings (*nedarim*) at the end of the preceding section (29:39)
of laws about sacrifices.

vow . . . oath . . . binding pledge. The first term, *neder*, as Baruch Levine has
shown, refers to a conditional promise made to God: if God will do such-and-
such, the vow taker commits himself then to repay God by offering such-
and-such. (Jephthah's vow to sacrifice to God whoever or whatever comes out
of his house when he returns victorious from battle is a striking, if outrageous,
instance of a *neder*.) The second term, *shevu'ah*, is an oath binding from the
moment it is pronounced. The distinction between these two and the third
term, *'isar*, "binding pledge," is not entirely clear, though Levine suggests that
'isar is an oral pledge which is then set down in legally obligating written form.

4. *should a woman.* Though this section begins with a man who makes a vow
or pledge, its real subject is the woman who takes upon herself this sort of
obligation. The woman, clearly, has limited legal automony in this society.
Before marriage, her vows may be annulled by her father; after marriage, by
her husband.

in her youth. The abstract noun *ne'ureiha* refers to the period when she is a
na'arah, a nubile young woman, from puberty until marriage.

every binding pledge that she took upon herself shall stand. But should 6
her father restrain her when he hears all her vows and her binding
pledges that she took upon herself, it shall not stand, and the LORD will
forgive her, for her father restrained her. But should she indeed 7
become a man's with her vows upon her or her lips' utterance that she
made binding upon herself, and her husband hear of it at the time he 8
hears and remain silent to her, her vows shall stand, and her binding
pledges that she took upon herself shall stand. And if at the time her 9
husband hears, he restrains her and annuls her vow that is upon her
and her lips' utterance that she took upon herself as a binding pledge,
the LORD will forgive her. And the vow of a widow or a divorced 10
woman, all that she took upon herself as a binding pledge, shall stand.
And if she vowed in her husband's house or took upon herself a bind- 11
ing pledge by oath, and her husband heard and remained silent to her, 12
he did not restrain her, all her vows and every binding pledge that she
took upon herself shall stand. But if her husband indeed annulled them 13
at the time he heard, whatever issues from her lips in regard to her
vows and to her binding pledge shall not stand. Her husband has

---

6. *restrain.* That is, abrogate the vow she has made.

10. *the vow of a widow or a divorced woman.* This is the one category of woman
not subject to the authority of a man that biblical law imagines, since it does
not allow for the case of the spinster (presumably a great rarity in biblical society with its ubiquitous imperative to marry and procreate).

11. *And if she vowed in her husband's house.* The legal autonomy, however, of
the widow or the divorced woman is restricted to her present single state.
Commitments she made while married are still validated or voided by the say-
so of her deceased or former husband.

13. *whatever issues from her lips.* Throughout these laws, there is a sense that
the pronounced word, what comes out of the mouth, is a palpable entity with
legally binding force. Jephthah's daughter's words in Judges 11:36 perfectly
illustrate this notion.

14 annulled them and the LORD will forgive her. Every vow and every binding oath to afflict oneself, her husband shall let it stand and her hus-
15 band shall annul it. And if her husband indeed remains silent to her day
after day and lets all her vows stand or all her binding pledges that are
upon her, he has let them stand, for he remained silent to her when he
16 heard. But if he indeed annuls them after he has heard, he shall bear
17 her guilt." These are the statutes that the LORD charged Moses
between a man and his wife, between a father and his daughter in her
youth in her father's house.

---

14. *to afflict oneself.* As in 29:7, this idiom refers in the first instance to fasting.

16. *if he indeed annuls them after he has heard, he shall bear her guilt.* Though
the formulation is rather compressed, the clear sense is as follows: if the husband remains silent when he hears the woman's vows, and only afterward
annuls them, the vows are still binding, and should she now ignore the vow, it
is he who must bear the consequences of the violated commitment, having led
her to think that the vow was no longer binding.

CHAPTER 31

Ａnd the Lord spoke to Moses, saying, "Wreak the vengeance of the Israelites against the Midianites. Afterward you shall be gathered to your kin." And Moses spoke to the people, saying, "Send forth a vanguard of men from you for the army, for them to be against Midian to exact the Lord's vengeance from Midian. A thousand for every single tribe, for all the tribes of Israel you shall send to the army." And a thousand for the tribe, twelve thousand of the thousands of Israel, 1,2 3 4 5

---

1. *Afterward you shall be gathered to your kin.* In the rather intermittent narrative progress of the later chapters of Numbers, this military campaign against the Midianites, with the invocation of Moses's imminent death, should properly come after (or just before) God tells Moses of his impending demise in chapter 27 and after the Israelite involvement with the seductive Midianite women reported in chapter 25.

3. *Send forth a vanguard.* The verbal root *ḥ-l-ts* can mean either "to pull out" or "to gird." Either sense might lead to the specialized noun used in military contexts, *ḥaluts*, "vanguard." Here the root occurs strictly as a verb, but the likely meaning is that the men should constitute a vanguard.

to exact the Lord's vengeance from Midian. Rashi wonders why the Moabites, who after all were the ones who engaged Balaam to curse Israel, are not mentioned. His answer is that the Moabites acted out of fear of Israel, whereas the Midianites took up a quarrel that was not theirs. It may be more likely that the writer has in mind Midian's enticing the Israelites to join in pagan orgies in the Baal Peor incident, as Moses's angry words in verse 16 suggest.

4. *to the army.* Throughout this episode, this term could also be interpreted to mean "for military service."

6   were delivered as vanguards of the army. And Moses sent them out, a
    thousand for the tribe to the army—them and Phinehas son of Eleazar
    the priest, to the army, and the sacred vessels and the trumpets for
7   blasting were in his hand. And they arrayed against Midian, as the
8   LORD had charged Moses, and they killed every male. And they killed
    the kings of Midian, besides their slain men—Evi and Rekem and Tsur
    and Hur and Reba, the five kings of Midian, and Balaam son of Beor
9   they killed by the sword. And the Israelites took the Midianite women
    captive, and their little ones, and all their cattle and all their livestock
10 and all their wealth they plundered. And all their towns in their places
    of settlement and all their encampments they burned to the ground.
11 And they took all the booty and all the spoil both human and beast.
12 And they brought to Moses and to Eleazar the priest and to the com-
    munity of Israelites the captives and the spoil and the booty, to the
    camp in the steppes of Moab which are at the Jordan opposite Jericho.
13 And Moses and Eleazar the priest and all the chieftains of the com-
14 munity came out to meet them outside the camp. And Moses was furi-
    ous with the commanders of the force, the captains of the thousands
    and the captains of the hundreds who came from the battling army.
15,16 And Moses said to them, "You have let every female live! Look, these
    are the ones who led the Israelites by Balaam's word to betray the

---

6. *them and Phinehas son of Eleazar the priest.* One of several apparent dis-
crepancies between this story and the antecedent narrative is that a priest is
sent out as a frontline chaplain but there is no mention of a field commander,
and certainly not of Joshua.

the sacred vessels and the trumpets for blasting. It is not clear which sacred
vessels are to be brought, though it was common to bring instruments of divination, such as the Urim and Thummin, to the battlefield to guide tactical
decisions. Some medieval commentators, with the Ark narrative in 1 Samuel
in mind, propose that the Ark was taken on the campaign. The trumpets for
blasting would be used to muster the troops.

8. *besides their slain men.* The "slain" (*halalim*) is the term for those fallen in
battle. These kings were then killed after being taken captive.

Balaam son of Beor they killed. Here Balaam, in contrast to his performance
in the oracles narrative, appears as a negative figure, evidently assumed to
have instigated the actions of the Midianite women (verse 16).

LORD's trust in the affair of Peor, and there was a scourge against the
LORD's community. And now, kill every male among the little ones, and   17
every woman who has known a man in lying with a male, kill. And all   18
the little ones of the women who have not known lying with a male, let
live. And you, camp outside the camp seven days. Everyone who has   19
killed a person and everyone who has touched the slain, you shall
cleanse yourself on the third day and on the seventh day, you and your

---

17. *kill every male among the little ones, and every woman who has known a man.*
Moses's command—one should note that it is Moses's, not God's—to perpe-
trate this general massacre, excluding only virgin females, is bloodcurdling,
and the attempts of the interpreters, traditional and modern, to "explain" it
invariably lead to strained apologetics. The practice of massacring most or all
of a conquered population was widespread in the ancient Near East (the
Moabite Mesha stele records a similar "ban" or *herem* against a defeated
enemy, using certain Semitic terms cognate to ones that are employed here),
but that is not exactly a palliative. It is painfully evident that this is an instance
in which the biblical outlook sadly failed to transcend its historical contexts.
Many commentators have also puzzled over the fact that Moses, whose own
wife is Midianite, should now show such intransigence toward the Midianite
population. Either two conflicting traditions are present in these texts, or, if we
try to conceive this as a continuous story, Moses, after the Baal Peor episode,
reacts with particular fury against the Midianite women (not to speak of all the
males) because he himself is married to one of them and feels impelled to
demonstrate his unswerving dedication to protecting Israel from alien seduction. But it must be conceded that the earlier picture of the Midianite priest
Jethro, Moses's father-in-law, as a virtual monotheist and a benign councilor of
Israel does not accord with the image in these chapters of the Midianite
women enticing the Israelites to pagan excesses.

18. *all the little ones of the women.* This phrase is a literal representation of the
Hebrew, which sounds equally odd. The obvious sense is: all the young
females not yet nubile. This leads Rashi and others to infer that sexually
mature virgins were included in the massacre, though that inference seems to
be contradicted by the emphasis on "the women who have not known lying
with a male."

19. *you shall cleanse yourself.* The instructions here are in strict keeping with
the regulations in chapter 19 regarding purification from ritual contamination
imparted by contact with a corpse.

20 captives. And every garment and every article of leather and everything
21 made of goatskin and every wooden vessel you shall cleanse." And
Eleazar the priest said to the men of the army who came to the battle,
22 "This is the statute of teaching that the LORD charged Moses: Only the
gold and the silver and the bronze, the iron, the tin, and the lead,
23 everything that can come into fire you shall pass through fire and it will
be clean. Only in riddance water shall it be cleansed. And everything
24 that cannot come into fire you shall pass through water. And you shall
wash your garments on the seventh day and you shall be clean. After-
25 ward shall you come into the camp." And the LORD said to Moses, say-
26 ing, "Count the heads of the spoil of captives, both human and beast,
you and Eleazar the priest and the heads of the fathers of the commu-
27 nity. And you shall divide the spoil in half between those who bore
arms in battle, who went out to the army, and the whole community.
28 And you shall raise a levy for the LORD from the men of war who go out
to the army, one living creature out of five hundred from the humans
29 and from the cattle and from the donkeys and from the sheep. From
their half-share you shall take it and give to Eleazar the priest as the
30 LORD's donation. And from the half-share of the Israelites you shall take
one part of fifty from the humans, from the cattle, from the donkeys
and from the sheep, from all the beasts, and you shall give them to the

---

23. *everything that can come into fire.* That is, everything that can be passed
through fire without being destroyed. This seems to have been viewed as the
preferred process of purification.

Only in riddance water shall it be cleansed. The repetition of "only" (*'akh*)
from the previous sentence is a bit confusing. If the text is dependable, the
sense is that after having been passed through fire, the fireproof substances
are to be washed in the specially prepared "riddance water" (chapter 19) to
complete the process of purification. Other substances must simply be
cleansed with water.

28. *one living creature.* The Hebrew *'ehad nefesh* is peculiar on two counts: the
number precedes the noun instead of following it as it ordinarily does, and
the number is masculine whereas *nefesh* is feminine. There are, however,
instances in which numbers precede nouns, and the use of the masculine
number here may be influenced by the phrase for *"one part* of fifty" (verse 30),
which equally reverses the usual order of number and noun: *'ehad 'ahuz.*

Levites, keepers of the watch of the LORD's Tabernacle." And Moses, 31
and Eleazar the priest, did as all that the LORD had charged Moses. And
the spoil, over and above the plunder that the troops of the army had 32
plundered, came to six hundred seventy-five thousand sheep, and
seventy-two thousand head of cattle, and sixty-one thousand donkeys, 33,34
and human persons, of the women who had not known lying with a 35
male, all the persons came to thirty-two thousand. And the half, the 36
share of those who went out to the army, the number of sheep was
three hundred thirty-seven thousand and five hundred. And the levy for 37
the LORD from the sheep came to six hundred seventy-five. And the 38
cattle, thirty-six thousand head, and their levy to the LORD, seventy-
two. And donkeys, thirty thousand five hundred, and their levy to the 39
LORD, sixty-one. And human persons, sixteen thousand, and their levy 40
to the LORD, thirty-two persons. And Moses gave the levy of the LORD's 41
donation to Eleazar the priest as the LORD had charged Moses. And of 42
the half-share of the Israelites that Moses had split off from the men
serving in the army—the half-share of the community came to three 43
hundred thirty-seven thousand and five hundred sheep. And cattle, 44
thirty-six thousand head. And donkeys, thirty thousand five hundred. 45
And human persons, sixteen thousand. And Moses took from the half- 46,47
share of the Israelites one part of fifty from the humans and from the
beasts, and he gave them to the Levites, keepers of the watch of the
LORD's Tabernacle, as the LORD had charged Moses. And the com- 48
manders of the army's thousands, the captains of the thousands and the
captains of the hundreds, approached Moses. And they said to Moses, 49
"Your servants have counted the heads of the men of war who are in our

---

32. *six hundred seventy-five thousand.* The approximate correspondence to the
number of adult male Israelites in the wilderness is obvious. The numbers are
schematic and patently exaggerated, as are other details of the defeat of the
Midianites (most extravagantly, the report in verse 49 that the Israelites did not
suffer a single casualty).

50 hands, and not a man of them is missing. And we would offer up the Lord's offering, each man what he found of gold ornaments, armband and bracelet, ring, earring, and pendant, to atone for our lives before
51 the Lord." And Moses, and Eleazar the priest, took from them every
52 wrought ornament. And all the gold of the donation that they donated to the Lord came to sixteen thousand seven hundred and fifty shekels, from the captains of the thousands and from the captains of the hun-
53 dreds. But the men of the ranks had each of them taken booty for him-
54 self. And Moses, and Eleazar the priest, took the gold from the captains of the thousands and the hundreds, and they brought it to the Tent of Meeting as a remembrance for the Israelites before the Lord.

---

50. *armband and bracelet, ring, earring, and pendant.* Despoiling the defeated enemy of jewelry was a standard practice and is alluded to elsewhere as an expected procedure (compare David's elegy over Saul and Jonathan: "O daughters of Israel, weep over Saul, / who clothed you in scarlet and bangles, / who studded your garments with jewelry of gold." [2 Samuel: 1:24]). Of the items mentioned here, armbands and rings (that is, signet rings) could be worn by either sex, but the bracelets, earrings, and pendants are women's ornaments. The exact meaning of *kumaz*, the term translated as "pendant," is not entirely certain. Rashi imagines it is "an image of the vagina," which is perhaps fanciful but not completely off the mark, since ancient pendants have been found in this general region showing erotic female figures.

52. *all the gold of the donation.* As in the case of the Israelite donations for the making of the Tabernacle, the sundry gold ornaments are to be melted down and then refashioned as sacred vessels.

53. *But the men of the ranks.* More literally, "the men of the army." The form of the verb here clearly suggests contrast: the ordinary soldiers, in contrast to the officers, kept what they had taken as booty, the entire donation being made up by the officers.

CHAPTER 32

A nd the Reubenites and the Gadites had much livestock, very 1
numerous, and they saw the land of Jazer and the land of Gilead,
and, look, the place was a place for livestock. And the Gadites and 2
the Reubenites came to Moses and to Eleazar the priest and to the
chieftains of the community, saying, "Ataroth and Dibon and Jazer and 3
Nimrah and Heshbon and Elealeh and Sebam and Nebo and Beon, the 4
land that the LORD struck down before the community of Israel, is livestock land, and your servants have livestock." And they said, "If we have 5
found favor in your eyes, let this land be given to your servants as a hold-

---

1. *the land of Jazer and the land of Gilead.* The flexible Hebrew term *'erets,*
"land," often means "region," as it does here, rather than "country." The area of
settlement where these animal-breeding Israelites seek to stay is east of the
northern half of the Dead Sea and east of the Jordan River that flows down
into it, extending all the way up to the Sea of Galilee.

3. *Ataroth and Dibon and Jazer.* Perhaps out of a certain nervousness at presenting Moses with a request that might elicit his displeasure (this proves to
be the case), the Reubenites and Gadites begin their speech with a long catalogue of names of recently conquered places, not at first explaining what they
have on their mind.

5. *And they said.* As is generally the case, the repetition of the formula for introducing speech with no intervening response from the other party is an indication of temporary lack of response because of the nature of what has been
said. The Reubenites and Gadites present a catalogue of towns, then say that
this is good land for livestock and that they have livestock. This is a leading
statement, and Moses no doubt sees where their remarks are leading. He lis-
tens in stony silence: they hesitate, then resume their speech, now making the
explicit request to settle east of the Jordan.

6 ing. Do not make us cross the Jordan." And Moses said to the Gadites
and to the Reubenites, "Shall your brothers come to battle and you sit
7 here? And why would you hinder the heart of the Israelites from cross-
8 ing into the land that the LORD has given to them? Thus your fathers
9 did when I sent them from Kadesh-Barnea to see the land. And they
went up as far as Wadi Eshcol and saw the land, and they hindered the
heart of the Israelites from coming into the land that the LORD had given
10 them. And the LORD's wrath flared on that day and He swore, saying,
11 'These men who have come up from Egypt, from twenty years old and
up, shall not see the soil that I swore to Abraham, to Isaac, and to Jacob,
12 for they have not fulfilled My behest, save Caleb son of Jephunneh the
13 Kenizzite and Joshua son of Nun, for they fulfilled My behest.' And the
LORD's wrath flared against Israel, and He made them wander in the
wilderness forty years, until all the generation that had done evil in the
14 eyes of the LORD came to an end. And, look, you have arisen in your
fathers' stead, a breed of offending men, to add still more of the LORD's
15 flaring wrath against Israel. For you would turn back from Him, so that
He would continue to leave them in the wilderness, and you would
16 destroy all this people." And they approached him and said, "Sheep
enclosures we shall build here for our livestock, and towns for our little

---

6. *Shall your brothers come to battle and you sit here?* At least according to this
canonical account, the fighting in the region east of the Jordan (against the
Amorites, the Moabites, and the Midianites) has already been successfully
concluded, whereas the conquest of Canaan proper remains to be undertaken.

11. *the soil.* Here Moses chooses to have God say *'adamah*, which can mean
"land" or "country" but which has a strong connotation of "arable land" or
"soil," underlining the prospective fertility of the territory promised to Israel.
The more usual term in these texts of promise is *'erets*, "land."
    they have not fulfilled My behest. The literal meaning of this phrase is "they
have not filled after me," that is, implicitly followed Me.

15. *to leave them in the wilderness.* The Hebrew says, a little confusingly, "to
leave him," the evident antecedent being the collective noun "people."

ones. And as for us, we shall head out swiftly in the vanguard before the   17
Israelites until we bring them to their place, and our little ones will
dwell in the fortified towns because of the inhabitants of the land. We   18
will not return to our homes until the Israelites take possession every
man of his estate. For we will not take possession with them on the   19
other side of the Jordan and beyond, for our estate has come to us on
the side of the Jordan to the east." And Moses said to them, "If you will   20
do this thing, if you go out in the vanguard to battle before the LORD,
and every member of the vanguard among you crosses the Jordan before   21
the LORD until He dispossesses His enemies before Him, and the land   22
is conquered before the LORD, then you may return and you will be clear
of the LORD and of Israel, and this land will be a holding for you before
the LORD. And should you not do thus, look, you will have offended to   23
the LORD, and know your offense, which will find you. Build your towns   24
for your little ones and enclosures for your sheep, and the utterance of

---

17. *because of.* Or "in the face of," "against."

18. *We will not return to our homes until the Israelites take possession.* The existence of a substantial Israelite settlement east of the Jordan, whether one
attributes it to this early period or to later expansionist drives, clearly posed a
problem of national unity. The exemplary readiness of the Reubenites and
Gadites to head out in the vanguard to fight for their cis-Jordanian brothers is
intended as a rousing image of national solidarity.

19. *for our estate has come to us.* As Rashi notes, the idiom means "to come into
legal possession."

22. *you will be clear of the LORD and of Israel.* The idiom refers to being clear
of the obligations of a vow or pledge—in this case, because they will have been
fulfilled.

23. *know your offense, which will find you.* Although this agreement with the
trans-Jordanian tribes is strictly between them and Moses (in this case Moses
does not turn to God for guidance), the implicit guarantor of the pledge is
God. Violating the pledge would be an offense "to the LORD," and the consequences of the offense would be felt by the violators of the pledge.

24. *the utterance of your mouth.* More literally, "what goes out from your
mouth"—an idiom used for oaths, which cannot be retracted once they are
pronounced.

25 your mouth you shall do." And the Gadites and the Reubenites said to
26 Moses, saying, "Your servants will do as my lord charges. Our little ones,
our wives, our livestock, and all our beasts will be there in the towns of
27 Gilead. And your servants will cross over, all the vanguard of the army,
28 before the LORD to the battle, as my lord speaks." And Moses charged
them, with Eleazar the priest and Joshua son of Nun and the heads of
29 the fathers of the Israelite tribes. And Moses said to them, "If the
Gadites and the Reubenites cross the Jordan with you, all the vanguard
to the battle before the LORD, and the land is conquered before you, you
30 shall give them the land of Gilead as a holding. But if they do not cross
over with you as a vanguard, they shall find holdings in your midst in the
31 land of Canaan." And the Gadites and the Reubenites answered, saying,
"That which the LORD has spoken to your servants, so will we do.
32 We will cross over in the vanguard before the LORD to the land of
Canaan, while ours will be our secure holding on the other side of the
33 Jordan." And Moses gave to the Gadites and to the Reubenites and to
the half-tribe of Manasseh son of Joseph the kingdom of Sihon, king of
the Amorite, and the kingdom of Og, king of the Bashan, the land with
34 its towns within the borders of the towns of the land all around. And the
35 Gadites built Dibon and Ataroth and Aroer, and Atroth-Shophan and
36 Jazer and Jogbehah, and Beth-Nimrah and Beth-Haran—fortified towns
37 and sheep enclosures. And the Reubenites built Heshbon and Elealeh

---

28. *the heads of the fathers of the Israelite tribes.* "Fathers" apparently enters this string of phrases as a reference to the social-organizational unit, "father's house," or patriarchal house.

32. *our secure holding.* See the comment on 27:7 for an explanation of this phrase.

33. *the half-tribe of Manasseh.* Until this point, there was no mention of Manasseh as part of the trans-Jordanian group.

34. *built.* The implication is not that they built these towns from the ground up but that they rebuilt them after conquest and, one assumes, partial destruction. This is a common biblical use of this verb.

and Kiriathaim, and Nebo and Baal-Meon, changed in name, and 38
Sibmah. And they called by names, the names of the towns they had
built. And the sons of Machir son of Manasseh went to the Gilead and 39
captured it and dispossessed the Amorite who was in it. And Moses gave 40
the Gilead to Machir son of Manasseh, and he settled in it. And Jair son 41
of Manasseh went and captured their hamlets and called them Jair's
Hamlets. And Nobah went and captured Kenath and its surrounding vil- 42
lages and he called it Nobah, in his name.

---

38. *changed in name.* Some of these towns, as Rashi observed, bore names
associated with pagan gods (notably, the just mentioned Baal-Meon), so the
Israelites were impelled to rename them.

39. *the sons of Machir.* Although the obvious meaning is Machirites, in this
instance the translation literally reproduces the Hebrew "sons of" because of
the identification of Machir, twice, in what immediately follows as literally
"son of Manasseh."

CHAPTER 33

T1 hese are the journeyings of the Israelites who came out of the land
2 of Egypt by their battalions, in the hand of Moses and Aaron. And
Moses wrote down their departure points for their journeyings by
the word of the LORD, and these are their journeyings by their departure points.

3 And they journeyed from Rameses, in the first month on the fifteenth
day of the first month on the morrow of the Passover offering the
4 Israelites went out with a high hand before the eyes of all Egypt. And
the Egyptians were burying all the firstborn that the LORD had struck
down among them, and the LORD had dealt punishment to their gods.

---

1. *These are the journeyings.* Now at the end of the long chain of Wilderness
stories that began in Exodus, as the Israelites are poised to cross the Jordan
into the land of Canaan, we get a grand recapitulation of the whole narrative
in the form of an itinerary of all the way stations in the Wilderness march.
Such itineraries were a set literary form in the ancient Near East, with
Mesopotamian examples, akin in form to the document in this chapter, going
back to early in the second millennium B.C.E.

2. *Moses wrote down their departure points.* As elsewhere, the narrative reflects
a consciousness of the antiquity and primacy of writing in Hebrew culture.
   by the word. Literally, "by the mouth."

4. *the LORD had dealt punishment to their gods.* The conjecture of some scholars that this clause reflects a lost tradition in which the God of Israel battled
directly against the gods of Egypt seems unnecessary. From the story in Exodus, it is clear enough that the Ten Plagues and the freeing of the Hebrew
slaves are understood as a resounding demonstration of the impotence of the
gods of Egypt in the face of the all-powerful YHWH.

And the Israelites journeyed from Rameses and camped at Succoth. 5
And they journeyed from Succoth and camped at Etham, which is on 6
the edge of the wilderness. And they journeyed from Etham and went 7
back toward Pi-Hahiroth, which is opposite Baal-Zephon, and they
camped before Migdol. And they journeyed from Pi-Hahiroth and 8
crossed over through the sea to the wilderness, and they went three
days in the Wilderness of Etham and camped at Marah. And they jour- 9
neyed from Marah and came to Elim, and at Elim there were twelve
springs of water and seventy palm trees, and they camped there. And 10
they journeyed from Elim and camped by the Sea of Reeds. And they 11
journeyed from the Sea of Reeds and camped in the Wilderness of Sin.
And they journeyed from the Wilderness of Sin and camped at 12
Dophkah. And they journeyed from Dophkah and camped at Alush. 13
And they journeyed from Alush and camped at Rephidim, and there 14
was no water there to drink. And they journeyed from Rephidim and 15
camped in the Wilderness of Sinai. And they journeyed from the 16
Wilderness of Sinai and camped at Kibroth-Hattaavah. And they jour- 17
neyed from Kibroth-Hattaavah and camped at Hazeroth. And they jour- 18
neyed from Hazeroth and camped at Rithmah. And they journeyed 19
from Rithmah and camped at Rimmon-Perez. And they journeyed from 20
Rimmon-Perez and camped at Libnah. And they journeyed from Lib- 21

5–49. Most of the place-names occur in the narrative in Exodus and Numbers,
and the rehearsal of these names here constitutes a summary and recollection
of incidents that occurred at the sundry places. (Thus Kibroth-Hattaavah,
verse 16, which means Graves of Desire, hardly an ordinary place-name,
recalls the incident recorded in chapter 11.) But there are some important
episodes with their place-names that do not appear in this itinerary: even, surprisingly, the central stop at Mount Sinai is not actually mentioned, only a stay
in the Wilderness of Sinai. At the same time, a number of places are recorded
in the itinerary that do not appear in the preceding narrative. At least a few of
these are designations that don't sound like conventional place-names but
appear to refer to some event that occurred at the location in question (e.g.,
Haradah in verse 24 is the Hebrew word for "terror"). All this makes it likely
that, in keeping with a common compositional procedure of biblical literature,
an archival document has been spliced into the text, reflecting some traditions
about the Wilderness wanderings that were not incorporated in the canonical
narrative of Exodus and Numbers.

22 nah and camped at Rissah. And they journeyed from Rissah and
23 camped at Kehelath. And they journeyed from Kehelath and camped
24 at Mount Shepher. And they journeyed from Mount Shepher and
25 camped at Haradah. And they journeyed from Haradah and camped at
26 Makheloth. And they journeyed from Makheloth and camped at
27,28 Tahath. And they journeyed from Tahath and camped at Terah. And
29 they journeyed from Terah and camped at Mithkah. And they jour-
30 neyed from Mithkah and camped at Hashmonah. And they journeyed
31 from Hashmonah and camped at Moseroth. And they journeyed from
32 Moseroth and camped at Bene-Jaakan. And they journeyed from Bene-
33 Jaakan and camped at Hor-Haggidgad. And they journeyed from Hor-
34 Haggidgad and camped at Jothbathah. And they journeyed from Joth-
35 bathah and camped at Abronah. And they journeyed from Abronah and
36 camped at Ezion-Geber. And they journeyed from Ezion-Geber and
37 camped in the Wilderness of Zin, which is Kadesh. And they journeyed
from Kadesh and camped at Hor the Mountain at the edge of the land
38 of Edom. And Aaron the priest went up Hor the Mountain by the
LORD's word and died there in the fortieth year of the Israelites' going
39 out from Egypt, in the fifth month on the first of the month. And Aaron
was one hundred twenty-three years old when he died on Hor the
40 Mountain. And the Canaanite, the king of Arad, who dwelled in the
41 Negeb in the land of Canaan, heard when the Israelites came. And
42 they journeyed from Hor the Mountain and camped at Zalmonah. And
43 they journeyed from Zalmonah and camped at Punon. And they jour-
44 neyed from Punon and camped at Oboth. And they journeyed from
45 Oboth and camped at Iye-Abarim on the border of Moab. And they
46 journeyed from Iye-Abarim and camped at Dibon-Gad. And they jour-
47 neyed from Dibon-Gad and camped at Almon-Diblathaim. And they
journeyed from Almon-Diblathaim and camped in the high country of
48 Abarim, before Nebo. And they journeyed from the high country of
Abarim and camped in the steppes of Moab across the Jordan from
49 Jericho. And they camped by the Jordan from Beth-Jeshimoth to Abel-
Shittim, in the steppes of Moab.

50 And the LORD spoke to Moses in the steppes of Moab across the Jor-
51 dan from Jericho, saying, "Speak to the Israelites and you shall say to
them, 'You are about to cross the Jordan into the land of Canaan.

And you shall dispossess all the inhabitants of the land before you, and 52
you shall destroy all their carved figures and all their molten images you
shall destroy, and all their cult-places you shall demolish. And you shall 53
take possession of the land and dwell in it, for to you I have given the
land to take hold of it. And you shall settle the land by lot according to 54
your clans. For the many you shall make their estate large and for the
few you shall make their estate small. Wherever the lot falls, there it
will be his. By the tribes of your fathers you shall settle. And if you do 55
not dispossess the inhabitants of the land from before you, it will come
about that those of them you leave will become stings in your eyes and
thorns in your sides, and they will be foes to you on the land in which
you dwell. And it will come about that as I had thought to do to them, 56
I shall do to you.'"

---

52. *cult-places*. The *bamah* was an open-air altar on which sacrifices, to agricultural and other gods, were offered. Israelites in fact widely used *bamot* until
they were suppressed in the reforms of Josiah around 621 B.C.E.

55. *stings in your eyes and thorns in your sides*. Given the next clause, "they will
be foes to you on the land" (Onkelos interprets the verb here as "oppress"), the
reference of these metaphors appears to be strategic: unless you entirely
destroy or expel the Canaanites, they will continually attack you as you try to
dwell in the land. The parallels to this verse in Exodus 34:11–13, Deuteronomy
7:1, and Joshua 23:4–9 see the danger of the Canaanite presence as cultic
temptation rather than military harassment. In any case, the idea of wiping out
or totally banishing the Canaanites was never actually implemented, and it has
the look of a theological program retrojected onto a purportedly historical narrative as a desideratum presented by God to Israel.

CHAPTER 34

1,2 And the LORD spoke to Moses, saying, "Charge the Israelites, and
you shall say to them, 'When you come into the land of Canaan,
this is the land that will fall to you in estate, the land of Canaan
3 by its borders. And your southern limit shall be from the Wilderness of
Zin by Edom, and your southern border from the edge of the Dead Sea
4 to the east. And your border shall swing round south of the Ascent of
Akrabbim and pass through Zin, and its farthest reaches shall be south
of Kadesh-Barnea, and it shall extend out to Hazar-Addar and pass
5 through to Azmon. And the border shall swing round from Azmon

2. *fall to you*. As Rashi aptly notes, this verb is used because the apportionment of the land is to be carried out by lot.

3–12. As the Book of Numbers draws to a close, with the Israelites ready to begin the conquest of the land (a sequence of events that will not be reported until the Book of Joshua), the reality of the land in which Israel will dwell is concretized through this mapping out of its borders. Those borders are only partly consistent with the delineation of the borders in Joshua and Ezekiel, and it is questionable whether they completely correspond to any historical contours of Israelite dominion. The northern borders extend far into Syria, well north of Sidon. Though the Mediterranean as western border seems neat, it does not reflect the fact that for several centuries much of the coastal plain was Philistine territory. Some scholars have argued that these borders are substantially those of the Egyptian province of Canaan agreed on with the Hittites after the battle of Kedesh in 1270 B.C.E., but that proposal has not been universally accepted and it remains to be explained why a later writer would adopt those borders.

4. *the Ascent of Akrabbim*. The Hebrew means "Scorpion Ascent."

toward the Wadi of Egypt, and its farthest reaches to the Sea. And the 6
western border—the Great Sea shall be your border, this shall be your
western border. And this shall be your northern border, from the Great 7
Sea you shall trace a line to Hor the Mountain. From Hor the Moun- 8
tain you shall trace a line to Lebo-Hamath, and the farthest reaches of
the border to Zedad. And the border shall extend to Ziphron, and its far- 9
thest reaches, Hazar-Enan. This shall be your northern border. And you 10
shall trace for yourselves a line for the eastern border from Hazar-Enan
to Shepham. And the border shall go down from Shepham to the 11
Riblah, east of Ain, and the border shall go down and touch the slope
of Lake Chinnereth to the east. And the border shall go down to the 12
Jordan, and its farthest reaches at the Dead Sea. This shall be your land
by its borders all around.'"

And Moses charged the Israelites, saying, "This is the land of which 13
you will take possession by lot, as the LORD has charged to give to the
nine and a half tribes. For the tribe of the Reubenites by their fathers' 14
houses and the tribe of the Gadites by their fathers' houses and the
half-tribe of Manasseh have taken their estate. The two and a half 15
tribes have taken their estate beyond the Jordan across from Jericho to
the east." And the LORD spoke to Moses, saying, "These are the names 16,17
of the men who will share out estates of the land for you: Eleazar the
priest and Joshua son of Nun. And one chieftain, one chieftain from 18
each tribe you shall take to share out the estates of the land. And these 19
are the names of the men: For the tribe of Judah, Caleb son of Jephun-

---

6. *the western border*. The Hebrew term for "west," *yam*, actually means "sea."
That word, whether by itself or with the qualifier "great," always refers to the
Mediterranean, unless it is otherwise specified in the name (e.g., *yam suf*, Sea
of Reeds).

15. *have taken their estate beyond the Jordan*. The decision of the two and a half
tribes to settle east of the Jordan in the Gilead region was reported in detail in
chapter 32. Although this was a recognized area of Israelite settlement, there
is a sense here that it lies outside the land of Canaan proper, whose eastern
border is marked by Lake Kinneret (the Sea of Galilee) and the Jordan and the
Dead Sea below it.

20,21 neh. For the tribe of the Simeonites, Samuel son of Ammihud. For the
22 tribe of Benjamin, Elidad son of Chislon. And for the tribe of the Dan-
23 ites, chieftain Bukki, son of Jogli. For the Josephites of the tribe of the
24 Manassites, chieftain Hanniel son of Ephod. And for the tribe of the
25 Ephraimites, chieftain Kemuel son of Shiphtan. And for the tribe of the
26 Zebulunites, chieftain Elizaphan son of Parnach. And for the tribe of
27 the Issacharites, chieftain Paltiel son of Azzan. And for the tribe of the
28 Asherites, chieftain Ahihud son of Shelomi. And for the tribe of the
29 Naphtalites, chieftain Pedahel son of Ammihud. These are the ones
whom the Lord charged to share out estates to the Israelites in the
land of Canaan."

CHAPTER 35

nd the LORD spoke to Moses in the steppes of Moab by the Jor- 1
dan across from Jericho, saying, "Charge the Israelites, that they 2
give to the Levites from their secure holdings towns in which to
settle and pastureland for the towns around them you shall give to the
Levites. And the towns will be theirs to settle, and their pasturelands 3
will be for their cattle and for their goods and for all their beasts. And 4
the pasturelands of the towns that you give to the Levites are to be a
thousand cubits all around from the wall of the town. And you shall 5
measure outside the town the eastern limit two thousand in cubits and
the southern limit two thousand in cubits and the western limit two
thousand in cubits and the northern limit two thousand in cubits, with

---

2. *give to the Levites . . . towns in which to settle.* The Levites, it should be
recalled, had no tribal territory, and so the other tribes are enjoined to apportion towns for them.

5. *the eastern limit.* Both the invocation of the four points of the compass and
the use of the term "limit" (*pe'ah*) recall the apportionment of the land in the
preceding chapter. The juxtaposition—presumably, an editorial maneuver—is
significant. The division of the land into tribal territories and clan holdings
does not guarantee the creation of a stable, harmonious society. Provision
must be made, as it is in these regulations for towns of asylum, for acts of violence of Israelite against Israelite, with protection for the manslayer when the
act is not premeditated.
   two thousand in cubits. The seeming contradiction with the just stipulated
one thousand cubits is most simply resolved by assuming that the two thousand cubits are from perimeter to perimeter, with the breadth of the town
itself ("the town in the middle") excluded from the calculation. Rashi's solution is that in fact an area extending two thousand cubits beyond the town

6 the town in the middle. This will be their towns' pasturelands. And the
towns that you shall give to the Levites, the six towns of asylum you
shall give for a murderer to flee there, and in addition to them you shall
7 give forty-two towns. All the towns that you shall give to the Levites will
8 come to forty-eight towns, they and their pasturelands. And the towns
that you give from the holdings of the Israelites, from the many you
shall give much and from the few you shall give less, each according to
his estate of which he takes possession shall he give of his towns to the
9,10 Levites." And the LORD spoke to Moses, saying, "Speak to the
Israelites, and you shall say to them, 'When you cross over the Jordan
11 into the land of Canaan, you shall set out for yourselves towns, towns
of asylum you shall have, and a murderer may flee there, one who
12 strikes down a person in errance. And the towns will be an asylum for
you from the avenger, and the murderer will not die until he stands
13 before the community for judgment. And the towns that you give, six

---

walls is designated—an inner zone of one thousand cubits for pastureland and
an outer zone of another thousand cubits for planted fields and vineyards.

7. *forty-eight towns*. The total number amounts to four towns per tribe, though
the contribution of towns is to be implemented proportionately to the size of
the tribe (verse 8).

11. *set out*. The use of the verbal stem *q-r-h* here is a little unusual because it
generally indicates a chance event. Rashi proposes that the essential meaning
of the verb is "to determine," "to cause to happen" (*leshon hazmanah*).
    murderer. The Hebrew *rotseah* is used for both an intentional murderer and,
as here, for someone who has committed manslaughter.

12. *the avenger*. The term *go'el* is an abbreviated form of *go'el hadam*, "blood
avenger," used elsewhere in this chapter. Blood vengeance was a form of
vendetta justice executed by the family of the victim. The ritual motive beyond
the simple thirst for vengeance was an archaic sense that blood wrongfully
shed polluted the land, generated a kind of poisonous miasma, and had to be
"redeemed" by shedding the blood of the murderer. (Compare Genesis 9:6:
"He who sheds human blood / by humans his blood shall be shed.") The laws
here try to blend this older system of justice implemented by the family with
a system in which justice is administered by courts. Thus, the "community" is
given the responsibility for adjudicating between the accused person and the

towns of asylum you shall have. Three towns you shall give beyond the 14
Jordan and three towns in the land of Canaan, towns of asylum they
shall be. For the Israelites and for the sojourner and for the settler in 15
their midst these six towns shall be an asylum for everyone who strikes
down a person in errance, to flee there. But if he struck him with an 16
iron tool and he died, he is a murderer, the murderer is doomed to die.
And if he struck him with a hand stone by which one may die and he 17
died, he is a murderer, the murderer is doomed to die. Or with a 18
wooden hand tool by which one may die he struck him and he died, he

---

blood avenger by determining whether the accused has committed premeditated murder. If he has, capital punishment is then executed by the blood
avenger, not the community.

14. *Three towns . . . beyond the Jordan.* It is odd that the division should be
three on each side of the Jordan because nine and a half of the tribes reside
to the west of the Jordan. Rashi's suggestion that there was an unusually high
homicide rate among the trans-Jordanian Gileadites seems fanciful. Perhaps
three towns of asylum east of the Jordan made sense because this was the
region of Israelite settlement farthest removed from the main centers of
Israelite population, and thus a fugitive from vendetta justice was likely to feel
more safely distanced there from the reach of the avengers.

15. *for the sojourner and for the settler.* Although "for" is repeated before each
noun in the Hebrew, this is merely a variant form of the common hendiadys
ger wetoshav, which means "resident alien."

16. *with an iron tool.* As Jacob Milgrom reminds us, the historical setting for
these laws was the early Iron Age, when iron may have been chiefly used for
weapons. The prohibition in Exodus 20:25 against using iron tools in the construction of an altar reflects the same situation. If the fatal blow was delivered
with a lethal implement, the presumption is that the killing was intentional.

17. *a hand stone.* The translation literally reproduces the gnomic expression of
the Hebrew. The obvious meaning is a sizeable stone that can be grasped in
the hand and used as a weapon.

18. *Or with a wooden hand tool.* There appears to be a progressive extension of
the principle of lethal implement through these three instances. The iron tool
is designed as a weapon. The stone is an improvised weapon. The wooden

19 is a murderer, the murderer is doomed to die. The blood avenger shall
put the murderer to death, when he comes upon him he shall put him
20 to death. And if in hatred he should knock him down or fling some-
21 thing on him by design and he die, or in enmity he strike him with his
hand and he die, he who struck is doomed to die, he is a murderer. The
blood avenger shall put the murderer to death when he comes upon
22 him. But if on an impulse, without enmity, he knocked him down or
23 flung upon him any tool, without design, or with any stone by which
one may die, without seeing he dropped it on him and he died, he not
24 being his enemy nor seeking his harm, the community shall judge
between him who struck and the blood avenger on these matters of
25 judgment. And the community shall rescue the murderer from the
hands of the blood avenger and the community shall take him back to
the town of asylum where he fled, and he shall stay there until the
26 death of the high priest who was anointed with the holy oil. But if the
murderer should indeed go out beyond the border of his town of asy-
27 lum where he has fled, and the blood avenger finds him outside the

---

hand tool—say, a wooden mallet—is an implement meant for another purpose
that has been appropriated as a weapon.

19. *when he comes upon him.* The verb *p-g-ʿ* indicates an encounter between
two parties (or two material substances), but there may be a pun here because
the verb also means "to stab" (the sharp encounter of iron with flesh).

22. *But if on an impulse.* Or "suddenly," which is to say, the perpetrator of the
act himself did not foresee or plan it.

23. *with any stone by which one may die.* This stipulation recognizes that the
previously mentioned nature of the instrument of killing is not sufficient proof
of premeditation: a person could, for example, carelessly throw a "hand stone"
out a window, not realizing that someone was standing below.

26. *if the murderer should indeed go out beyond the border of his town of asylum.*
There is a link between the notion of levitical towns of asylum and the extension of protective sanctuary at the altar to manslayers and other accused crim-
inals. Baruch Levine suggests that once the cult was centralized in Jerusalem,
the levitical towns assumed the function of asylum previously associated with
local sanctuaries. In Mesopotamia there were analogous towns of asylum, and

border of his town of asylum and the blood avenger murders the murderer, he has no bloodguilt. But he shall stay in his town of asylum   28
until the death of the high priest, and after the death of the high priest
the murderer shall go back to the land of his holding. And these shall   29
be for you a statute of judgment for your generations in all your
dwelling places. Whoever strikes down a person, by witnesses shall the   30
murderer be murdered, and a single witness shall not testify against a
person to die. And you shall not take ransom for the life of a murderer   31
who is guilty to die, for he is doomed to die. And you shall not take ran-   32
som in lieu of flight to his town of asylum to let him go back to dwell
in the land, until the death of the high priest. And you shall not pollute   33
the land in which you are, for blood will pollute the land, and for the
land there will be no ransoming for the blood that has been shed in it
except through the blood of him who shed it. And you shall not defile   34
the land in which you dwell, in the midst of which I abide, for I am the
LORD, abiding in the midst of the Israelites.'"

Moshe Weinfeld notes that the Egyptians had zones of asylum, supervised by
priests, which may shed light on the linking of the duration of asylum here
with the life span of the high priest.

30. *by witnesses.* For capital crimes, at least two witnesses were necessary to
convict the accused.
   shall the murderer be murdered. The verb *ratsaḥ* reaches its longest semantic stretch here when it is used in the sense of "execute"—probably in order to
underline the notion of measure-for-measure justice. In verse 25 it is used to
designate an involuntary manslayer.

32. *ransom in lieu of flight.* The Hebrew says literally, "ransom to flee." Ransom
thus is equally prohibited as a substitute for the capital punishment of a murderer and as a substitute for a manslayer's settling in a town of asylum, which
would be a form of exile within the borders of the country (as in the sentence
of internal exile to a remote region in the Czarist system of justice).

CHAPTER 36

1 And the heads of the fathers' houses for the clan of the son of Gilead son of Machir son of Manasseh from the clans of the sons of Joseph came forward and spoke before Moses and before the chieftains,
2 heads of the fathers' houses of the Israelites. And they said, "The Lord charged my lord to give the land to the Israelites in estate by lot, and my lord was charged by the Lord to give the estate of our brother Zelophe-
3 had to his daughters. But should they become wives to any of the sons of the Israelite tribes, their estate would be withdrawn from our fathers' estate and added to the estate of the tribe to which they would belong,

---

1. *the heads of the fathers' houses*. In both occurrences of the phrase in this verse, the Hebrew uses an ellipsis, "heads of the fathers."

2. *the estate*. The issue of inheritance, so urgent in the later chapters of Numbers, is thematically focused in this concluding episode by the constant repetition of "estate," *naḥalah*. Yitzhak Avishur notes that the term recurs in two formulaic numbers—ten times in the dialogue of Zelophehad's kinsmen and seven times in Moses's response.

3. *any of the sons of the Israelite tribes*. The obvious reference is to husbands outside their own tribe and clan.

    their estate would be withdrawn . . . and added to the estate . . . from . . . our estate it would be withdrawn. The speech of the Gileadite leaders reflects an extraordinary degree of redundancy (and these recurring phrases are recycled still again in the next verse). Perhaps the repetition indicates nervousness on their part about the substance of their petition: they seem peculiarly anxious that some parcel of their tribal estate might slip away from them and be annexed by another tribe unless Moses takes immediate steps to rectify the situation. Moses's answer shows something of the same inclination to repeti-

and from the lot of our estate it would be withdrawn. And though the 4
jubilee comes for the Israelites, their estate would be added to the estate
of the tribe to which they would belong, and from the estate of our
fathers' tribe it would be withdrawn." And Moses charged the Israelites 5
by the word of the LORD, saying, "Rightly do the tribe of the sons of
Joseph speak. This is the thing that the LORD charged concerning the 6
daughters of Zelophehad, saying, 'To whomever is good in their eyes they
may become wives, only within the clan of their father's tribe must they
become wives. And an estate of the Israelites shall not turn round from 7
tribe to tribe, but the Israelites shall cling each man to the estate of the
tribe of his fathers. And every daughter inheriting an estate from the 8
tribes of the Israelites shall become wife to someone from the clan of her
father's tribe, so that the Israelites may inherit each man the estate of his

---

tion (compare verses 7 and 9), as though in response to their anxiety he wanted
to make absolutely clear what the governing principle must be.

the lot of our estate. The slightly odd collocation of these two nouns in the
construct state (*smikhut*) is dictated by the fact that the estate is divided by lot.

4. *though the jubilee comes for the Israelites.* In the jubilee year, the end of a forty-
nine year cycle, land that has been sold is supposed to revert to its original owners. This is not the case, however, for inherited land, and so the land inherited
by Zelophehad's daughters, were they to marry outside the tribe, would remain
attached to their husbands' tribes, even after the occurrence of the jubilee.

5. *by the word of the LORD.* Despite this phrase, there is no indication here that
Moses has consulted an oracle, which was the case in the initial legal issue of
the daughters of Zelophehad (chapter 27). Confronted with an unanticipated
consequence of the earlier ruling, a ruling said to be dictated by God, Moses
the judicial leader is compelled to engage in legal interpretation of how the ruling is to be applied. The act of interpretation itself is represented as a kind of
extension of the oracular revelation that was manifested in the earlier incident.
The phrase, "by the word [literally, mouth] of the LORD" here is a microcosmic
adumbration of the whole theology of legal interpretation that later will under-
gird the Talmud: every rabbinic ruling is *halakhah lemosheh misinai*, "a law
according to Moses from Sinai."

Rightly do the tribe of the sons of Joseph speak. As Richard Elliott Friedman
notes, these words are a pointed self-quotation by Moses of his response to the
petition of the young women in 27:7: "Rightly do the daughters of Zelophehad
speak."

9 fathers. And an estate shall not turn round from a tribe to another tribe,
10 but each man shall cling to his estate in the tribes of the Israelites.'" As
11 the LORD charged Moses, so did the daughters of Zelophehad do. And
    Mahlah, Tirzah, and Hoglah and Milcah and Noa the daughters of
12 Zelophehad became wives to their uncles' sons. Within the clans of the
    sons of Manasseh son of Joseph they became wives, and their estate was
    attached to the tribe of the clan of their father.

13 These are the commands and the regulations that the LORD charged
    the Israelites by the hand of Moses in the steppes of Moab by the Jor-
    dan across from Jericho.

---

12. *and their estate was attached to the tribe of the clan of their father.* Although
the legal anecdote of the marriage of Zelophehad's daughters is often characterized by scholars as an appendix to the Book of Numbers, it does serve as a
vivid focus for the prospect of inheriting the land that confronts the Israelites
as they await orders to begin their invasion. Not only does "estate" recur as a
keyword but also "clan," "tribe," and, it should be duly noted, "fathers" and
"sons." The case of inheriting daughters puts a certain strain on the patriarchal
system, but its patriarchal character remains firmly in place, as the reiteration
of "fathers" and "sons" makes clear, and thus a limitation on the choice of husband (to which noninheriting daughters would not be subject) is imposed on
these young women in order to preserve the integrity of the tribal configuration with its patriarchal definition. With the viability of the tribal division of
the land thus reaffirmed, the Israelites are prepared to begin the conquest.
First, however, in the redacted final form of the Five Books of Moses, they will
have to listen to Moses's long, recapitulative valedictory speech that makes up
the Book of Deuteronomy.

13. *These are the commands and the regulations.* This concluding summary is
more appropriate as a coda to the sections of law and cult procedure in the latter part of Numbers than to the book as a whole, with its many incidents of
rebellion and its account of military campaigns in the trans-Jordan region.
    in the steppes of Moab by the Jordan across from Jericho. This phrase of geo-
graphical location has been repeated several times, reminding us that the
Wilderness wanderings of the Israelites conclude with a long pause at this
final way station. It is fitting that "Jericho" should be the last word in the Book
of Numbers. Jericho will be the first military objective when the Israelites
cross the Jordan, and so the concluding word here points forward to the beginning of Joshua.

DEUTERONOMY

INTRODUCTION

The Book of Deuteronomy is the most sustained deployment of rhetoric in the Bible. It is presented, after all, as Moses's valedictory address, which he delivers across the Jordan from the promised land just before his death, as the people assembled before him are poised to cross the river into the land. It comprises a series of speeches, discourses, or, as some scholars actually call them, sermons. The two long poems that cap these speeches not only follow a biblical convention for concluding a book but are also a culmination of the rhetorical energies of this book, grandly echoing some of its major themes and even some of its recurring phrases. Only the code of laws in the middle of the book, from chapter 12 to chapter 26, does not participate in this manifestly rhetorical enterprise, though one function of the surrounding rhetoric is to underwrite the authority of the laws here promulgated, reminding the people again and again that their very lives and their collective survival on the land depend upon the punctilious observance of "this teaching" (*hatorah hazo't*).

If one tries to imagine, however, the actual audience for which Deuteronomy was first framed, it will begin to be evident that its impressive deployment of rhetoric serves another purpose. Rhetoric is an art of persuasion, and the rhetoric of Deuteronomy is meant to persuade audiences in the late First Commonwealth and exilic period of the palpable and authoritative reality of an event that never occurred, or at any rate surely did not occur as it is represented in this text—the national assembly in trans-Jordan that was a second covenant after the covenant at Sinai, in which Moses reviewed the whole code of law, rapidly rehearsed the story of the Wilderness wanderings, and exhorted the people to be loyal to God, with repeated predictions of the dire consequences if they should fail in their loyalty. There are, in fact, two equivalences that the language of Moses's address is devised to establish: an equivalence between this solemn convocation and the defining experience at Sinai, which is repeatedly referred to as *yom haqahal*, "the day of assembly," in order to line it up with this new assembly in the trans-Jordan; and an equivalence between the experience of this audience physically present to receive Moses's last words and that of the seventh-century B.C.E. audience and its prospective heirs listening to the Book of Deuteronomy and assenting to its authority. The resources of rhetoric are marshaled to create through a written text the memory of a foundational national event, so that the latter-day Israelites listening to "this book of teaching," *sefer hatorah hazeh*, will feel that they themselves are reenacting that event.

The role of stylistic indicators of temporal and spatial location and orientation—those "pointing words" that linguists refer to as *deictics*—is essential to the creation of this general effect. (Although critical scholarship views the opening section of the book through 4:44 as a somewhat later composition that was added as an introduction, there are significant stylistic continuities with the rest of the book, and it is those that will concern us here.) Moses's first discourse, beginning in chapter 1, is a rapid and highly selective recapitulation of elements of the Wilderness narrative reported in Exodus and in Numbers. The first discriminated episode in this recapitulation is the appointment of a judicial bureaucracy to help him carry the burden of administering justice to this multitudinous people. The prominent element of the parallel story in Exodus 18 pointedly omitted is the intervention of Moses's father-in-law Jethro as the person who proposes the delegation of judicial authority. Though a suspicious reader might wonder whether this change reflects an element of xenophobia in Deuteronomy (Jethro, of course, is a Midianite), the more urgent reason is that nothing must be allowed to diminish from the depiction here of Moses's strong leadership, grounded in his wisdom (a key value for Deuteronomy) and in his uniquely direct access to God. Moses concludes his account of creating this judicial system by declaring, "And I charged you at that time all the things that you must do" (1:18), right after having used the same phrase in relation to the magistrates, "And I charged your judges at that time saying, 'Hear between your brothers . . .'" (1:16). This seemingly minor deictic gesture, "at that time," *ba'et hahi'*, reflects an important, and recurring, rhetorical strategy in the book. There is no biblical text more generous than Deuteronomy in its use of demonstrative pronouns. "At that time" temporally positions both Moses and his audience in relation to the legal injunction he is delivering: you heard it then, the phrase tells us, or at any rate your parents, now died out, heard it, and its imperative force is exactly the same now as I repeat this injunction—and, again, it will be the same when these words of Moses are read out to their audience in the seventh century or later.

In the very next verse, 1:19, the deictic phrase functions in a more strictly narrative, rather than legal, context: "And we journeyed from Horeb and we went through all that great and fearful wilderness which you have seen, by way of the high country of the Amorite. . . ." Now, narrative report in the Bible is famously laconic, and one could plausibly argue that it would be more in keeping with characteristic biblical style for this verse to read, "And we journeyed from Horeb and we went through the wilderness, by way of the high country of the Amorite." What is the difference between this pared-down version and the one that is actually used in Deuteronomy? My more terse formulation follows a fairly typical biblical procedure of registering space traversed in a narrative report as essentially blank space: the idea is to get from point A to point B—say, to get Abraham and Isaac in a three days' journey from Hebron to Mount Moriah—without drawing attention to the spatial reality that lies in between because it is not deemed essential to the story. The Deuteronomic summary at this point of the Wilderness wanderings has a very different purpose. The demonstrative pronoun "that" which is attached to "wilderness" is both a temporal and an emotional deictic. Temporally, it points to something that has been undergone but that is now over and done with. The Israelites have completed their long and arduous trajectory through the wilderness and now stand before Moses in the Arabah, just east of the land of Canaan. Emotionally, the wilderness is a place to be remembered with fear and trembling, a place that tried the soul of the nation—"all that great and fearful wilderness," *kol-hamidbar hagadol wehanora' hahu'*, and the deictic "that" serves to keep it at arm's length as a haunting memory of a very palpable experience recently undergone. (The terror of the wilderness will be carried forward in Deuteronomy all the way to the Song of Moses, which speaks of "the wilderness land, . . . the waste of the howling desert [*tohu yeleil yeshimon*]" [32:10].) The little subordinate clause, again ostensibly gratuitous, that is added to the impressive phrase about the wilderness, is equally characteristic of the rhetorical strategy of national recollection in Deuteronomy. It is the wilderness, Moses says, '*asher re'item*, "which you have seen." Again and again, the audience of this national assembly is reminded that they have seen— or in a frequent variation, that their very eyes have seen, '*eyneikhem haro'ot*—the portentous events that Moses is rehearsing. At one remove, the members of the historical audience of the Book of Deuteronomy are implicitly invited to imagine what their forebears actually saw, to see it vicariously. The midrashic notion that all future generations of Israel were already present as witnesses at Sinai is adumbrated, perhaps actually generated, by this rhetorical strategy of the evocation of witnessing in Deuteronomy.

In precisely this connection, it should be noted that there is a purposeful ambiguity of reference in the use of the second person, whether plural as here, or singular as often elsewhere, in Moses's address. Since we are reminded of the episode of the spies early in the first discourse (1:22–45), with the consequent death sentence on the Wilderness generation, we know that all the people standing before Moses now would have been under the age of twenty, perhaps most of them, indeed, as yet unborn, at the time of the events recalled in his speech. Yet Moses repeatedly speaks as though they were all direct participants in or observers of the episodes he mentions. There is, I would say, a slide of identification between one generation and another. Most of those listening to Moses's words could not literally have seen the things of which he speaks, but the people is imagined as a continuous entity, bearing responsibility through historical time as a collective moral agent. It is this assumption that underwrites the hortatory flourish, repeated in several variations, "Not with our fathers did the Lord seal this covenant but with us—we that are here today, all of us alive" (5:3). Thus Moses can say of the witnessing, "you have seen" (my choice of a present perfect verb in the translation attempts to suggest the temporal doubleness of the seeing), and, in reporting actions, he can flatly state, referring to the route of Israel by the Amorites at Hormah, "you came back and wept before the Lord, and the Lord did not listen to your voice" (1:45), though it was the fathers, now deceased, not the living members of the audience, who did the weeping and were rebuffed by God. The implicit next link in this chain of identification is the generation in the twilight of the First Commonwealth, or perhaps immediately after it, which is invited to see itself experiencing what the Wilderness generations underwent, or at any rate, to see the experience of their forebears as a compelling model for its own historical predicament.

It is the unique event at Sinai that is the very matrix of collective memory in Deuteronomy. The Ten Words enunciated in Exodus are of course proclaimed again here, and though there are certain famous divergences in wording between the two texts, the restatement of these ten foundational imperatives reflects nothing of the strongly revisionary impulse that is so evident in the reformulation of antecedent laws elsewhere in the book. (One infers that the Decalogue was too fundamental to revise substantively.) Moses's valedictory transmission of God's commands to Israel is a second Sinai, and the written text that records his final discourses is in turn understood to be the permanent vehicle through which an approximation of the Sinai experience can be reenacted (thus laying the ground, one might observe, for the pervasive textualization of Jewish culture that would evolve in later centuries). As Israel's past is laid out in Moses's oratory, there is a sudden leap from summary to imaginative evocation when the story arrives at Sinai. The origins of the people in the Patriarchal period are almost entirely reduced to the reiterated reference to God's having sworn the land to "your fathers." The great signs and portents of the Exodus itself are mentioned in just those terms, but there are no vivid representations of the Ten Plagues or of the splitting of the Sea of Reeds. The Sinai epiphany, on the other hand, in all its terror and wonder, is a moment to which Moses's speech repeatedly reverts. Thus, the proclamation of the Decalogue in chapter 5 is prefaced by these words: "Face to face did the LORD speak with you on the mountain from the midst of the fire. I was standing between the LORD and you at that time to tell you the word of the LORD—for you were afraid in the face of the fire and did not go up the mountain" (5:4–5). Although the parallel account in Exodus has thunder and lightning and the whole mountain smoking, Deuteronomy chooses to emphasize the purer and even more unapproachable substance of divine fire from which God's words are emitted. Concomitantly, the issue of the separation of the people from the divine presence and the necessary role of Moses as mediator is reframed. In Exodus, God issues an explicit command before the epiphany that the people must keep their distance, that they are not so much as to touch the edge of the mountain. It is only after the tremendous fact of revelation that, awestruck, they implore Moses to act as their spokesman, thus confirming the rightness of the spatial restriction that God has already imposed on them. In Deuteronomy's version, there is no mention of a prior order from God that the people stay at a distance. On the contrary, their initial experience of the epiphany is almost too close for comfort: "Face to face did the LORD speak with you on the mountain from the midst of the fire." Moses here is obliged to interpose himself because the people are terrified by the fire and afraid to go up the mountain. The motive for keeping their distance is visceral response rather than divine taboo: their own eyes have seen, as future generations will be reminded, the full awesome force of God's descent upon the mountain, and this sight is too much to bear. Indeed, after the enunciation of the Decalogue, they are afraid to hear as well as to see: "And now, why should we die, for this great fire will consume us. If we hear again the voice of the LORD our God, we shall die" (5:22). In this fashion, the Deuteronomic story conveys both the indelible fact of witnessing and the indispensability of the lawgiver as mediator, including in that mediation "this book of teaching" that he will leave as legacy and implying the further need for authoritative mediation through those who will promulgate and expound the text he leaves.

The conjuring up of the Sinai experience through the powerful language of this oratory is brilliantly linked with the Deuteronomic polemic against the worship of images. Moses takes pains to remind his audience that the revelation they were vouchsafed was auditory, and in no way visual (another contrast to Exodus, where after the Decalogue is given, the elders of Israel come partway up the mountain and "beheld God" [Exodus 24:11]). This is how Moses here evokes the moment before the epiphany: "And you came forward and stood at the bottom of the mountain, and the mountain was burning with fire to the heart of the heavens—darkness, cloud, and dense fog. And the LORD spoke to you from the midst of the fire. The sound of words you did hear but no image did you see except the sound" (4:11–12). This is a moment of mystery, compounded of impenetrable obscurity—"darkness, cloud, and dense fog"—and blinding effulgence. The eye, which has seen so much from Egypt until this moment, can see nothing; the ear alone can receive the commanding divine words. The abiding residue of this voice is, as one might expect in Deuteronomy, a text:

> And He told you His covenant that He charged you to do, the Ten Words, and He wrote them on two tablets of stone. And me did the LORD charge at that time to teach you statutes and laws for you to do in the land into which you are crossing over to take hold of it. And you shall be very watchful of yourselves, for you saw no image on the day the LORD spoke to you from the midst of the fire, lest you act ruinously and make you a sculpted image of any likeness, the form of male or of female, the form of any beast that is on the earth, the form of any winged bird that flies in the heavens, the form of anything that crawls on the ground, the form of any fish that is in the waters under the earth, lest you raise your eyes to the heavens and see the sun and the moon and the stars, all the array of the heavens, and you be led astray and bow down to them and worship them, for the LORD your God allotted them to all the peoples under the heavens. But you did the LORD take and He brought you out from the iron's forge, from Egypt, to become for Him a people in estate as this day (4:13–20).

I have in this instance quoted at length because one needs the length in order to get a sense of Deuteronomy's sweeping oratorical power. Indeed, the heart of this passage is one grand sentence that rolls on, according to the conventional verse division, from the beginning of verse 15 to the end of verse 19. There are few biblical instances of this sort of sentence length outside of Deuteronomy, where the grand sentence is devised to catch up the listener in its sheer momentum of insistence. Let us try to follow the stages of the effort of persuasion inscribed in the language. God writes the text of the Ten Words in stone, then designates Moses, the continuing intermediary, as the leader and expounder of the laws—presumably, the reference is not to the Decalogue itself but to the code of laws, what in Exodus is the so-called Book of the Covenant, and to its counterpart in the code of laws in Deuteronomy. The narrative report of the Sinai experience in Exodus also emphasizes sound and speech, excluding any direct visual image of God, with the limited exception of the post-epiphanic vision on the mountain by the elders of Israel. Here, however, the imageless character of the revelation at Sinai is moved to the thematic center. The defining memory of the people of Israel is at once an overwhelming revelation of God and a memory of the absence of any image. That memory of an absence then becomes the warrant for an enduring imperative to avoid all worship of images, never to confuse the representation of any living thing in the created world with the exclusive divinity of the Creator. The language of the long central sentence here is profuse both in emphatic synonymity in regard to representations of deities—"a sculpted image of any likeness," *pesel temunat kol-samel*, and "form," *tavnit*—and in the hammering insistence of anaphora, *tavnit* standing at the head of five consecutive noun-phrases. The catalogue of images of things not to be worshipped also pointedly harks back to the Creation story, leading one to infer that the writer was familiar with the Priestly version of creation or some textual ancestor of it. Male and female, every beast that is on the earth, every winged bird that flies in the heavens, things crawling on the ground and fish in the waters under the earth are all part of the hierarchy of creation called into being by the Creator at the beginning of Genesis and not to be revered as though they had autonomous power as gods. The injunction not to raise one's eyes to the heavens and worship the celestial bodies probably had special urgency in the late First Commonwealth period when, particularly through Assyrian influence, the cult of astral deities had become widespread in the Israelite populace, at least according to one prevalent historical inference. Here, too, the language of the Priestly account of creation has special resonance: the eyes that have beheld God's portentous presence in history—but not His image— should avoid the temptation to see "the sun and the moon and the stars, all the array of the heavens . . . and bow down to them," for in the authoritative story all these celestial entities were ordained by God to exist in cosmic orderliness, with the process culminating when "the heavens and the earth were completed, and all their array" (Genesis 2:1). Israel, because of its unique historical experience from Egypt to Sinai, has been provided with an unprecedented vantage point to see that its imageless God is the God of all things. Fire plays a role both in

Egypt and at Sinai—in Egypt, figuratively, where the torment of slavery is represented as "the iron's forge," *kur habarzel,* and at Sinai, literally, where the mountain burns with fire to the heart of the heavens and God speaks from the midst of the fire. It is not the image of God but His incandescent presence that the people of Israel experience through their history, and the powerful rhetoric of the book is the means that evokes this presence.

CHAPTER 1

These are the words that Moses spoke to all the Israelites across the ₁
Jordan in the wilderness in the Arabah opposite Suph between
Paran and Tophel and Laban and Hazeroth and Di-Zahab, eleven ₂
days from Horeb by way of Mount Seir to Kadesh-Barnea. And it was ₃
in the fortieth year in the eleventh month on the first of the month that
Moses spoke to the Israelites according to all that the LORD had
charged him concerning them, after he had struck down Sihon king of ₄
the Amorite who dwelled in Heshbon and Og king of the Bashan who

---

1. *the words.* The prevalent Hebrew title for Deuteronomy, following the convention of using the first significant word in the text as title, is Devarim,
"Words." The title Deuteronomy, which is the Greek equivalent of an alternate
ancient Hebrew name for the book, means "second law" or "repetition of the
law" and is based on the Hebrew phrase in 17:18, *mishneh hatorah hazo't,* "a
copy [or repetition] of this teaching [or, law, *torah*]." Since Deuteronomy is in
fact a recapitulation of the law and narrative of the three preceding books (as
well as in certain important respects a revision of them), the Greek title is perfectly apt. But Devarim as a title has the advantage of highlighting the preeminently rhetorical character of this book, which is structured as a series of
long speeches delivered by Moses to Israel, and which also incorporates, as
the opening chapter illustrates, prominent elements of dialogue—words of
speech framed by words of oratory. More than any other biblical text, it is a
book of words, as the Hebrew title suggests.

2. *eleven days from Horeb.* Horeb is the alternate name for Sinai. These introductory verses of Deuteronomy swiftly situate Moses's discourse in time,
place, and sequence of events: at the end of the forty years' wandering, on the
east bank of the Jordan, where the Israelites were seen encamped at the conclusion of the Book of Numbers, and after the military victories over the trans-
Jordanian kings reported toward the end of Numbers.

5   dwelled in Ashtaroth in Edrei. Across the Jordan in the land of Moab
did Moses undertake to expound this teaching, saying:

6   "The LORD our God spoke to us in Horeb, saying, 'Long enough you
7   have stayed at this mountain. Turn and journey onward and come to
the high country of the Amorite and to all his neighbors in the Arabah,
in the high country, and in the lowland and in the Negeb and on the
shore of the sea, the land of the Canaanite, and the Lebanon, as far as
8   the Great River, the River Euphrates. See, I have given the land before
you. Come and take hold of the land that the LORD swore to your
fathers, to Abraham, to Isaac, and to Jacob, to give to them and to their

---

5. *to expound this teaching.* The verb *be'er,* "to expound" or "to explain," provides
a central rationale for the whole book. The teaching, *torah,* that has already
been enunciated is represented as requiring further exposition or explaining,
and hence the need for "the repetition of this teaching." *Torah* here is still a verbal noun that means "teaching," but the repeated stress of Deuteronomy on its
own textual character begins to push Torah in the direction of the meaning it
would subsequently have, the name not only of this book but of all the Five
Books of Moses. The act of expounding and explaining, moreover, announces
the intellectualist theme—in all likelihood, drawing on Hebrew Wisdom traditions—that sets off this book from the preceding four.

7. *the Amorite.* Deuteronomy uses this term to designate all the inhabitants of
Canaan, perhaps because the Amorites, on the eastern perimeter of the country, were the first people encountered by the invading Israelites.
    the Lebanon. This refers to the mountain range, not to a country.
    as far as the Great River, the River Euphrates. Needless to say, this grandiose
northeastern border does not correspond to the actual historical contours of
any Israelite state.

8. *See, I have given . . . you.* Significantly, the very first speech of God in
Moses's initial discourse is a ringing confirmation of the promise of the land
to the people. "I have given . . . you" has the legal force of a performative
speech-act, as if to say, By these words I hereby confer to you.

seed after them.' And I said to you at that time, saying, 'I cannot carry 9
you by myself. The LORD your God has multiplied you, and here you 10
are today like the stars of the heavens in multitude. May the LORD God 11
of your fathers add to you a thousand times more than you are and bless
you as He has spoken concerning you. O, how can I carry by myself 12
your trouble and your burden and your disputing? Get you wise and 13
understanding and knowing men according to your tribes, and I shall

---

9. *And I said to you at that time.* Though the adverbial phrase here does convey Moses's retrospective viewpoint, looking back to an event that occurred
four decades earlier, there is no connection, either narrative or thematic,
between the preceding unit concerning the promise of the land and the unit
now introduced, which reports the creation of a judiciary bureaucracy. It looks
as though "at that time" is a rhetorical ploy used to camouflage a lack of
transition.

10. *and here you are today like the stars of the heavens in multitude.* God's reiterated promise to Abraham to make his seed a multitudinous people is now
fully realized, and it confronts Moses with a grave practical problem of judicial oversight of these vast numbers.

11. *May the LORD . . . add to you a thousand times.* But Moses, not wanting to
construe the blessing of national fecundity negatively, hastens to wish for
Israel that it continue to proliferate in the spectacular fashion it already has
done.

12. *O, how can I carry.* The Hebrew does not use the ordinary form for "how,"
'eikh, but the elongated form *'eikhah,* which often marks the beginning of
laments. The translation seeks to suggest this effect of threnody by adding "O."

13. *Get you wise and understanding and knowing men.* This account of the
establishment of a judicial bureaucracy differs from the one in Exodus 18 in
several respects, all of which reflect the distinctive aims of Deuteronomy.
Jethro, Moses's father-in-law, who conceives the scheme in Exodus, is not
mentioned here. Instead, the plan is entirely Moses's idea, as this is the book
of Moses. Having hit on the idea, he entrusts the choice of magistrates to the
people, whereas in Exodus, he implements Jethro's directive by choosing the
judges himself. In Exodus the qualities to be sought in the judges are moral
probity and piety, whereas here intellectual discernment is stressed. "Knowing" in the Hebrew is a passive form ("known"), which led both Rashi and

14 set them at your head.' And you answered me and said, 'The thing that
15 you have spoken is good to do.' And I took the heads of your tribes,
wise and knowing men, and I made them heads over you, captains of
thousands and captains of hundreds and captains of fifties and captains
16 of tens and overseers for your tribes. And I charged your judges at that
time, saying, 'Hear between your brothers, and you shall judge rightly
17 between a man and his brother or his sojourner. You shall recognize no
face in judgment. You shall hear out the small person like the great one.
You shall have no terror of any man, for judgment is God's. And the
matter that will be too hard for you, you shall bring forward to me and
18 I shall hear it.' And I charged you at that time all the things that you
19 must do. And we journeyed from Horeb and we went through all that
great and fearful wilderness which you have seen, by way of the high
country of the Amorite, as the LORD our God had charged us, and we
20 came as far as Kadesh-Barnea. And I said to you, 'You have come to the
high country of the Amorite which the LORD our God is about to give
21 us. See, the LORD your God has given the land before you. Go up, take
hold, as the LORD God of your fathers has spoken to you. Be not afraid

---

Abraham ibn Ezra to understand the term as "well-known," but the word,
given the immediate context, could well have an active sense here (or could
be revocalized as an active verb), and it has been construed that way by many
interpreters, from the Aramaic Targums to contemporary scholars.

16. *Hear.* The Hebrew uses an infinitive form of the verb to serve as an imperative—a well-attested idiomatic option in biblical Hebrew but also a form that
nicely matches the impersonal rhetoric of authority in Deuteronomy, grammatically highlighting the action to be performed rather than those addressed.

17. *You shall recognize no face in judgment.* This vivid idiom, the meaning of
which is illustrated in the next sentence of this verse, has the obvious sense of
not showing partiality.

19. *all that great and fearful wilderness which you have seen.* This invocation of
the terrors of the great wilderness, experienced firsthand by the wandering
Israelites, emphatically recurs in Moses's speech as the people camp at the
edge of the wilderness at the end of the forty years looking into the land they
are about to enter.

nor be dismayed.' And you came forward to me, all of you, and you   22
said, 'Let us send men before us that they probe the land for us and
bring back word to us of the way on which we should go up and the
towns into which we should come.' And the thing was good in my   23
eyes, and I took from you twelve men, one man for each tribe. And they   24
turned and went up to the high country and came to Wadi Eshcol and
spied it out. And they took in their hand from the fruit of the land   25
and brought it down to us and brought back word to us, and they said,
'The land that the LORD our God is about to give us is good.' And you   26
did not want to go up and you rebelled against the word of the LORD
your God. And you grumbled in your tents and said, 'In the LORD's   27
hatred of us He took us out of the land of Egypt to give us into the hand
of the Amorite to destroy us. Where are we going up? Our brothers   28
have made our heart faint, saying, "A people greater and loftier than we,
towns great and fortified to the heavens; and also giants did we see
there."' And I said to you, 'You shall not dread and you shall not fear   29
them. The LORD your God Who goes before you, He it is Who will bat-   30
tle for you as all that He did with you in Egypt before your very eyes,

---

22. *Let us send men before us.* This version strikingly revises the story of the
twelve scouts reported in Numbers 13–14. There, the sending out of the scouts
was an order from God. Here, it is strictly the people's idea, their hesitant
response to Moses's flat imperative, "Go up, take hold."

   that they probe the land. More literally, "that they dig out the land." This verb,
which does not occur in Numbers 13–14, is in keeping with the strictly strategic purpose of the expedition here ("the way on which we should go up and the
towns into which we should come"). In Numbers, the scouts are especially
enjoined to ascertain the prosperity of the land and its natural resources. This
difference, however, is not strictly a "revision" on the part of Deuteronomy
because the present version is also a drastic *abridgement* of the story in Numbers, and it concentrates on what is deemed the essential matter of the episode.

27. *In the LORD's hatred of us.* The extreme vehemence of this phrase, which
does not appear in Numbers, again reflects the writer's tendency to incrimi-
nate the people in this book of admonishments that is Deuteronomy.

30. *The LORD your God Who goes before you, He it is Who will battle for you.* In
the version of the story in Numbers, it is Joshua and Caleb who defiantly
declare that they can successfully undertake an assault against the Canaan-

31 and in the wilderness that you have seen, where the LORD carried you as a man carries his son all the way that you went as far as this place.

32 And despite this thing you do not trust the LORD your God, Who goes

33 before you on the way to search out for you a place for you to camp in the fire by night to show you the way that you should go and in the

34 cloud by day.' And the LORD heard the sound of your words, and He

35 was furious and swore, saying, 'Not a man of these men, this evil gen-

36 eration, shall see the land that I swore to give to their fathers, save Caleb son of Jephunneh. He shall see it, and to him I will give the land on which he has trod, and to his sons, inasmuch as he fulfilled the

37 behest of the LORD.' Against me, too, the LORD was incensed because

38 of you, saying, 'You, too, shall not come there. Joshua son of Nun, who stands before you, he it is who will come there. Him you must

---

ites, "for they are our bread" (Numbers 14:9). In the more theologically pitched account here, the language of God's battling on behalf of Israel is borrowed from the victory at the Sea of Reeds (Exodus 14:14). This notion of God's overwhelming power is extended by Moses's reminder (verse 33) of the pillars of fire and cloud, an awesome phenomenon that in Numbers 14:14 is attributed to the rumor that has reached the fearful Canaanites.

36. *Caleb.* Curiously, for reasons that have been explained by many scholars as a drawing together of different sources, Joshua is not mentioned at all here but only in verse 38, in his function as Moses's personal attendant.

   the land on which he has trod. This phrase focuses the physical act of Caleb's walking through the land—evidently, only as far as Wadi Eshcol in the future tribal territory of Judah and not, as in Numbers, to the far north—on the espionage mission. Walking through territory was also an act of taking legal possession of it in a sale.

37. *Against me, too, the LORD was incensed because of you.* No mention is made here of the incident in which Moses struck the rock, and this appears to be an entirely new explanation of why Moses never entered the land. Once more, the change reflects the tendency of Deuteronomy to inculpate Israel. Moses is doomed to die east of the Jordan not because of his own unfortunate momentary impulse on which he acted but because he acceded to the people's plan to send out spies and was thus implicated in their subsequent guilt. Elsewhere in Deuteronomy, a different explanation will be offered for Moses's dying outside the land.

strengthen, for he will give it in estate to Israel. And your little ones of 39
whom you said they will become prey, and your sons who know not this
day good or evil, they it is who will come there, and to them I will give
it, and they will take hold of it. As for you, turn you and journey on to 40
the wilderness by way of the Red Sea.' And you answered and said to 41
me, 'We have offended the LORD. We ourselves will go up and do battle as all that the LORD our God has charged us.' And you girded, each
man, his weapons and you presumed to go up to the high country. And 42
the LORD said to me, 'Say to them: "You shall not go up and you shall
not do battle, for I am not in your midst, lest you be routed by your enemies."' And I spoke to you, and you did not heed, and you rebelled 43
against the LORD's word and you were defiant and went up to the high
country. And the Amorite who dwells in the high country came out to 44
meet you, and then pursued you as the bees do, and they pounded you
in Seir as far as Hormah. And you came back and wept before the 45
LORD, and the LORD did not listen to your voice and did not give ear to
you And you stayed in Kadesh many days, as the days that you stayed. 46
And we turned and journeyed on to the wilderness on the way to the 2:1
Red Sea, as the LORD had spoken to me, and we swung round the high
country of Seir many days."

---

43. *you were defiant and went up.* The choice of the verb here, *hazid,* "to be
defiant," "to act wickedly or maliciously," may reflect the fact that the present
text is a response to the one in Numbers. The previous verse is essentially a
quotation of Numbers 14:42. At this point in the version in Numbers (14:44),
an otherwise unattested verb, *ha'apil* ("to strive upward"?) is used, and this
writer appears to gloss that enigmatic term by substituting a more familiar
word.

46. *many days, as the days that you stayed.* The apparent sense of this Hebrew
idiom is: as many days as you ended up staying.

2:1. *the Red Sea.* The Hebrew *yam suf* in all likelihood refers to two different
bodies of water. In the Exodus story, it seems to be a lake or marshland in the
north of Egypt, the Sea of Reeds. Elsewhere, it does designate the Red Sea,
and here the Israelites are clearly being sent south toward Aqabah and the Red
Sea, not back to Egypt. This summarizing notation of the movements of the
Israelites makes it the conclusion of this whole literary unit, though the conventional chapter division sets it at the beginning of chapter 2.

CHAPTER 2

2,3
"And the Lord said to me, saying, 'Long enough you have swung round this high country. Turn you to the north. And charge the people, saying, "You are about to pass through the territory of your brothers the sons of Esau, who dwell in Seir. Though they fear you, you must take great care. Do not provoke them, for I will not give you of their land so much as a foot tread, for I have given the high country of Seir as an inheritance to Esau. Food you shall buy from them with silver, that you may eat, and water, too, you shall get from them with silver, that you may drink. For the Lord your God has blessed you in all the work of your hands. He has known your goings in this great wilderness these forty years. The Lord your God is with you. You have lacked

---

3. *Long enough.* This initial phrase pointedly echoes the one in 1:6, thus establishing a rhetorical link between God's command to Israel to move on from Sinai and His command thirty-eight years later for Israel to move on to the conquest after its peregrinations to the southeast of Canaan.

4. *Though they fear you.* Richard Elliott Friedman aptly notes that in Genesis 32, as Jacob/Israel drew near his brother after long years of separation, it was Israel who feared Esau and not the other way around.

7. *For the Lord your God has blessed you.* The initial "for" (*ki*) marks a clear logic of causation: because God has blessed all your enterprises, you have abundant wherewithal to pay for food and drink.

He has known. The Hebrew verb "to know" often suggests intimate knowledge—hence its use for sexual intercourse—and caring attention.

these forty years. Again and again in Moses's valedictory speech that constitutes this book, he invokes the palpable experience that the people has undergone in all its years of wandering "in this fearful wilderness."

nothing.'" And we passed onward away from our brothers the sons of 8
Esau, who dwell in Seir, from the way of the Arabah, from Eilath and
Ezion-Geber. And we turned and we passed through the Wilderness of
Moab. And the LORD said to me, 'Do not besiege Moab and do not 9
provoke them to battle, for I will not give you his land as an inheritance,
for to the sons of Lot I have given Ar as an inheritance. The Emim 10
used to dwell there, a great and multitudinous people, and lofty as
the giants. The Rephaim, they, too, are accounted as giants, and the 11
Moabites call them Emim. And in Seir the Horites used to dwell, and 12
the sons of Esau dispossessed them and destroyed them in their
onslaught and dwelled in their stead, as Israel did to the land of its

---

8. *Eilath and Ezion-Geber*. These are port cities at the northern end of the
Gulf of Aqabah.

10. *The Emim*. This designation, evidently of legendary creatures, is probably
related to the noun *'eymah*, "fear" or "terror." Rephaim in the next verse is a
well-attested Hebrew and Ugaritic term for ghosts or dwellers of the underworld. In verse 20, we are informed that the Ammonite name for these huge
creatures was Zamzummim. Jeffrey H. Tigay plausibly represents this as an
onomatopoeic term, "the Buzz-buzzers"—that is, people who speak an unintelligible, and perhaps frightening, language. This could also be, as Abraham
ibn Ezra proposes, the Hebraization of a foreign gentilic term. Moshe Weinfeld speculates that it was the presence of megaliths in the trans-Jordan region
that inspired these traditions of an aboriginal race of giants there.

12. *the sons of Esau dispossessed them . . . as Israel did to the land of its inheritance*. The writer confronts a theological problem posed by political history. All
around him, he sees a constant flux of warring peoples, one group laying waste
to another and seizing its territory. Upon this Hobbesian moral chaos of history, he strives to impose at least a degree of monotheistic order: it is God Who
determines the inheritance of peoples, not only in the case of Israel, which has
been promised it will succeed in overcoming the indigenous Canaanites and
possessing the land, but also in the case of the other peoples of the region. The
period of imperial incursions from the east from the late eighth century to the
late seventh century B.C.E. would have given special urgency to this effort to
account for the violent movements of history.
    in their onslaught. The literal sense of the Hebrew is "from before their
face," but the clear implication is fear, as from an attack, and this preposition
is often used after a verb such as "to banish."

13 inheritance which the LORD gave them. Now, rise up and cross over
14 the Wadi Zered.' And we crossed the Wadi Zered. And the time that
we went from Kadesh-Barnea until we crossed the Wadi Zered was
thirty-eight years until the whole generation, the men of war, came to
an end from the midst of the camp as the LORD had sworn concerning
15 them. And the hand of the LORD, too, was against them to panic them
16 from the midst of the camp until they came to an end. And it happened, when all the men of war had come to an end of dying from the
17,18 midst of the people, that the LORD spoke to me, saying, 'You are pass-
19 ing beyond the territory of Moab today, beyond Ar, and you will
approach opposite the Ammonites. You shall not besiege them and you
shall not provoke them, for I will not give you an inheritance of the land
of the Ammonites, for to the sons of Lot I have given it as an inheri-
20 tance. It is also accounted as the land of the Rephaim. The Rephaim
used to dwell there, and the Ammonites call them Zamzummim,
21 a great and multitudinous people, and lofty as the giants. And the LORD
destroyed them through the Ammonites' onslaught, and they dwelled in
22 their stead, as He did to the sons of Esau, who dwell in Seir, whom the
Horites destroyed in their onslaught and dispossessed them, and have

---

14. *came to an end.* The Hebrew verb *tum* means both "to come to an end," or
"to perish," and "to finish doing something." In verse 16 it is used in the latter
sense but coupled with "dying." The stylistic justification for the triple repetition is to convey emphatically the idea that this generation had absolutely and
entirely died out. This pattern of repetition is phonetically reinforced by the
word in verse 15 that means "to panic them," *lehumam*, which is a *rhyme riche*
with the last word of the verse, *tumam*, "they came to an end." Panicking is
what God regularly does to Israel's enemies in order to rout them in battle.
Thus, the Wilderness generation is not just left to die out but stricken with terror, impelling it to self-destruction.

18. *Ar.* If this is a precise site, it has not been located, but the context suggests
that it designates the whole region inhabited by the Moabites.

21. *through the Ammonites' onslaught.* The Hebrew says only "from before their
faces." As before, the element of fearfulness in that preposition is represented
by "onslaught," and "Ammonites' " is added to clarify an otherwise ambiguous
antecedent of the pronoun.

dwelled in their stead to this day—and the Avvim, who dwell in villages 23
as far as Gaza, the Caphtorim, who came out of Crete, destroyed them
and dwelled in their stead. Rise up, journey onward, and cross the 24
Wadi Arnon. See, I have given in your hand Sihon the Amorite king of
Heshbon, and begin, take hold of his land and provoke him to battle.
On this day will I begin to put the fear of you and the dread of you over 25
the peoples under all the heavens, so that when they hear rumor of you,
they will quake and shudder before you.'

"And I sent messengers from the Wilderness of Kedemoth to Sihon 26
king of Heshbon—words of peace, saying, 'Let me pass through your 27
land. On the road, on the road will I go. I will not swerve right or left.
Food for silver you shall sell me that I may eat, and water for silver you 28
shall give me, that I may drink. Only let me pass through on my own
feet, as the sons of Esau, who dwell in Seir, and the Moabites, who 29

---

23. *the Caphtorim, who came out of Crete.* Caphtor is the biblical name for
Crete. This notice is historically accurate. The coastal plain, including Gaza,
was invaded from the Mediterranean and successfully occupied by the
Philistines, one of the so-called Sea Peoples, in the later thirteenth century
and twelfth century B.C.E. They are first referred to explicitly in an Egyptian
inscription that has been dated to the 1180s or the 1170s. Although the Hebrew
writer does not directly ascribe this invasion of a Hellenic people to the LORD's
granting the territory to them as an inheritance, it does participate in the general pattern he is observing in which one well-established people is conquered
and displaced by another.

25. *the peoples under all the heavens.* The Septuagint opts for the more
expected idiom, "all the peoples under the heavens," and it is conceivable that
the Greek translators in fact had a Hebrew text before then which read that
way, but it is also quite possible that they decided to smooth out a little stylistic wrinkle actually chosen by the Deuteronomist, one that equally conveys
the sense of "everywhere on earth."

26. *words of peace.* The evident contradiction between this and verse 24, where
Israel is enjoined to provoke Sihon, has not been satisfactorily resolved.

27. *On the road, on the road.* The repetition clearly conveys the sense of
"strictly and exclusively."

dwell in Ar, did for me, until I cross the Jordan into the land that the
30 LORD our God is about to give us.' But Sihon king of Heshbon did not
want to let me pass through it, for the LORD your God hardened his
spirit and toughened his heart, in order to give him in your hand as on
31 this day. And the LORD said to me, 'See, I have begun to give Sihon
and his land before you. Begin—take hold—to take hold of his land.'
32 And Sihon sallied forth to meet us, he and all his troops, to battle at
33 Jahaz. And the LORD gave him before us, and we struck him down, and
34 his sons, and all his troops. And we captured all his towns at that time
and we put every town under the ban, menfolk and the women and the
35 little ones, we left no remnant. Only the beasts did we plunder, and
36 the booty of the towns that we captured. From Aroer which is on the
bank of the Wadi Arnon and the town in the wadi as far as the Gilead,

---

30. *hardened his spirit and toughened his heart.* The language is close enough
to the reiterated formula concerning Pharaoh in the Plagues narrative to suggest a typological connection between these two kings bent on Israel's destruction. Sihon's offensive against Israel, in the face of the Israelite proposal to
pass through his territory peacefully and pay for food and water, is taken as justification for the implementation of the brutal practice of the *herem* or "ban"
(verse 34)—the massacre of the entire population. The persistence of the
Amorites as a people suggests that this drastic report does not altogether
reflect historical reality. The supposed application of the *herem* to the Amorites may in fact have the function of defining political borders. The *herem* was
to be directed against the population of the promised land. In the parallel
account in Numbers, where the *herem* is not applied to Sihon's people, the
underlying assumption is that the promised land lies west of the Jordan, with
only a special concession made to two and a half tribes to settle in trans-
Jordan. As Moshe Weinfeld convincingly argues, the extension of Israelite
dominion east of the Jordan chiefly occurred during Davidic and Solomonic
times (tenth century B.C.E.), making it a long-established political reality by
the time our later writer framed his account, in which this region is included
in the promise of the land.

36. *the town in the wadi.* A wadi is a dry riverbed that fills with water during
the rainy season, but in this case, the reference seems to be to a riverbed, or
perhaps some small branch of it, that is no longer the site of seasonal
inundation.

there was no city that loomed too high for us, everything did the LORD our God give before us. Only the land of the Ammonites you did not approach, all along the Wadi Jabbok and the towns of the high country, as all that the LORD our God had charged." 37

---

there was no city that loomed too high for us. The looming high (a single verb in the Hebrew, *sagvah*) reflects the perspective of the besieging army looking up at the fortified city situated on a height. Looming high is also stressed as a response to the reiterated perception that the indigenous peoples are "lofty," a race of giants.

37. *Only the land of the Ammonites you did not approach.* This would be the hilly region farther to the east, whereas the Israelite advance is along the plain just east of the Jordan. Some recent scholars have accepted Jacob Milgrom's proposal that here the verb *q-r-b* ("approach") is used in a political extension of its cultic meaning, "to encroach upon," though there is no compelling necessity to see that sense of the word in this verse.

CHAPTER 3

1   "And we turned and we went up on the way to the Bashan, and Og
     king of Bashan sallied forth to meet us in battle, he and all his
2   troops, at Edrei. And the LORD said to me, 'Do not fear him, for
in your hand I have given him and all his troops and his land, and you
shall do to him as you did to Sihon the Amorite king who dwells in Hesh-
3   bon.' And the LORD our God gave in our hand Og king of the Bashan,
too, and all his troops, and we struck him down until no remnant was
4   left. And we captured all his towns at that time. There was not a city
that we did not take from them, sixty towns, all the district of Argob,
5   the kingdom of Og in the Bashan. All these were fortified towns with
high walls, double gates and bolt, besides the very many open towns.
6   And we put them under the ban as we had done to Sihon king of Heshbon, putting under the ban every town, menfolk, the women, and the

---

2. *Do not fear him, for . . . you shall do to him as you did to Sihon.* Although
Moses has already prevailed over Sihon, he has special reason to be afraid of
Og, for, as we learn in verse 11, Og, alone among these trans-Jordanian kings,
is a gigantic figure, the last scion of a legendary race.

5. *fortified towns with high walls, double gates and bolt.* The looming aspect of
the trans-Jordanian towns, which was stressed before, is here given architectural specification: despite the high walls and the firmly bolted gates, the
Israelites found ways to breach the defenses and capture every one of the enemies' towns. These passages might well be a wishful turning around of the
strategic telescope, for in the period in which they were composed—the last
century and a half of the First Commonwealth—it was the towns of Israel and
Judea that repeatedly faced assault and sometimes succumbed.
    open towns. That is, without walls or other fortifications.

little ones. But all the beasts and the booty of the towns we plundered 7
for ourselves. And we took the land at that time from the hand of the 8
two Amorite kings who were across the Jordan, from the Wadi Arnon as
far as Mount Hermon. The Sidonians call Hermon Sirion, and the 9
Amorites call it Senir. All the towns of the plateau and all the Gilead 10
and all the Bashan as far as Salcah and Edrei, the towns of the kingdom of Og in the Bashan. For only Og king of the Bashan remained 11
from the rest of the Rephaim. Look, his bedstead, an iron bedstead, is
it not in Rabbah of the Ammonites? Nine cubits its length and four
cubits its width by the cubit of a man. And this land we took hold of 12

---

8. *as far as Mount Hermon*. Repeatedly in these rehearsals of the Israelite conquest, the eye of the narrator—Moses—swings in a grand panorama from
trans-Jordan, where he and the people are standing and where the first victories took place, across the Jordan, and all the way to the fertile mountainous
region in the north of Canaan. The lushness of the Mount Hermon region is
attested by its invocation in erotic contexts in the Song of Songs.

11. *For only Og king of the Bashan remained from the rest of the Rephaim*. Since
the Rephaim, as we had occasion to note in 2:10–11, are a race of giants, and
also dwellers of the underworld, this makes Og virtually a mythological figure.
In a Phoenician mortuary inscription from the sixth or fifth century B.C.E.,
would-be violators of the tomb are warned that the great Og will exact retribution from them. He would appear to be some sort of fierce underworld god
or demon in the common lore of the region, and our text seeks to historicize
him while clinging to his legendary lineaments. Because of the link between
the Rephaim and the Nephilim of Genesis 6:4, several traditional commentators see Og as the last of the antediluvians.

his bedstead, an iron bedstead. The Hebrew noun 'eres is a poetic term for
bed, perhaps used here (instead of the more prosaic *mishkav* or *mitah*) to give
this declaration an epic flourish. Moshe Weinfeld proposes that it means
"bier," a secondary meaning that *mitah* has. Several scholars have noted that
late in the second millennium B.C.E., iron had been only recently introduced
and was still regarded as a rare metal. But the sheer hardness of the substance
might be meant to indicate the martial toughness of the gigantic king.

is it not in Rabbah of the Ammonites? The speaker points to this relic of the
gargantuan Og as concrete evidence of his actual existence, available for
inspection by the curious tourist.

by the cubit of a man. The disproportion between the giant and an ordinary
man is highlighted by giving the measurements of his bed according to "the

at that time. From Aroer which is on the Wadi Arnon and half the high
country of the Gilead and its towns, I gave to the Reubenite and to the
13 Gadite. And the rest of the Gilead and all of the Bashan, the kingdom
of Og, I gave to the half-tribe of Manasseh—all the district of Argob.
14 All of that Bashan is called Land of the Rephaim. Jair son of Manasseh
took all the district of Argob as far as the border of the Geshurite and
the Maacathites, and he called them—the Bashan—after his own
15 name, Jair's Hamlets, until this day. And to Machir I gave the Gilead.
16 And to the Reubenite and to the Gadite I gave from the Gilead as far
as Wadi Arnon, with the middle of the wadi the boundary, as far as
17 Wadi Jabbok, the boundary of the Ammorites, and the Arabah with the
Jordan the boundary, from Chinnereth as far as the Arabah Sea, the
18 Dead Sea, beneath the slopes of Pisgah to the east. And I charged you
at that time, saying, 'The LORD your God has given you this land to take
hold of it. As vanguard troops you shall cross over before your brothers

---

cubit of a man," that is, the length in an average man from the elbow to the
beginning of the knuckles. (The royal cubit was longer.) This would make the
bedstead around thirteen and a half feet long and approximately as wide as a
modern queen-size bed (in an era when all beds were single couches).

12. *And this land we took hold of at that time*. One of the earmarks of the
Deuteronomic style is the fondness it exhibits for demonstrative pronouns.
Moses, recapitulating the recent history of the Israelites for the benefit of the
people, likes to use what linguists call deictics—"pointing words"—to indicate
what is before their eyes, the familiar objects of their collective experience.

14. *until this day*. This little flourish is an inadvertent hint that for the moment
the writer is probably not thinking of Moses's time but of his own.

17. *the Arabah Sea, the Dead Sea*. The latter designation in the Hebrew is literally the Salt Sea.
  Pisgah. The other name for this mountain, from whose peak Moses will
look out on the promised land and then die, is Nebo.

the Israelites, all the warriors. Only your wives and your little ones and 19
your livestock—I know you have much livestock—shall stay in your
towns that I have given to you, until the LORD your God grants repose 20
to your brothers as to you, and they, too, take hold of the land that the
LORD your God is about to give to them across the Jordan. Then you
may go back, each man to his inheritance that I have given to you.' And 21
I charged Joshua at that time, saying, 'Your own eyes have seen all that
the LORD your God did to these two kings. So shall the LORD do to all
the kingdoms into which you are about to cross. You shall not fear 22
them, for it is the LORD your God Who does battle for you.'

"And I pleaded with the LORD at that time, saying, 'My Master, LORD, 23,24
You Yourself have begun to show Your servant Your greatness and Your

---

19. *Only your wives and your little ones and your livestock.* Most of the details
here of the military role assigned to the trans-Jordanian tribes correspond to
the account in Numbers 32, though this version is a good deal more succinct
and omits the indications of divine instruction in Numbers.

22. *it is the LORD your God Who does battle for you.* This clause, picked up from
Exodus 14:14, serves as a kind of refrain through this whole narrative of the
conquest.

23. *I pleaded.* Richard Elliott Friedman, noting the linkage between this verb
and "did not listen" in verse 26, interestingly detects an allusion to Genesis
42:21, where Joseph's brothers recall how he pleaded to them and they did not
listen when they sold him into slavery. Perhaps the point of the allusion is that
it recalls the moment when Joseph is violently thrust away from his homeland
of Canaan: Moses, who began where Joseph ended, in Egypt, will not be permitted to enter the homeland though, as we may recall, Joseph's bones will be
carried into the promised land to be buried there.

24. *My Master, LORD.* The Hebrew, as it is vocalized in the Masoretic Text,
reads *'adonai YHWH*, the first of these two words being another appellation of
God. This translation follows Weinfeld's persuasive suggestion that either the
original vocalization of the first word was *'adoni,* "my Master," a form of
address often used in supplications, or that the plural suffix *'adonai* is a plural
of majesty.

strong hand, for what god is there in the heavens and on the earth who
25   could do like Your deeds and like Your might? Let me, pray, cross over
that I may see the goodly land which is across the Jordan, this goodly
26   high country and the Lebanon.' And the LORD was cross with me
because of you, and He did not listen to me. And the LORD said to me,
27   'Enough for you! Do not speak more to Me of this matter. Go up to the
top of the Pisgah, and raise your eyes to the west and to the north and
to the south and to the east and see with your own eyes, for you shall
28   not cross this Jordan. And charge Joshua and strengthen him and bid
him take heart, for he shall cross over before this people and he shall
29   give them in estate the land that you will see.' And we stayed in the valley over against Beth Peor."

---

for what god is there in the heavens and on the earth. Given the Deuteronomist's rigorous monotheism, the plausible sense of these words is that the supposed gods of heaven and earth have no real substance and therefore no power
to perform any acts. Nevertheless, the formulation, perhaps as a kind of verbal fossil, carries a trace of the older view that there may be other gods, but
ones that are no match for YHWH.

25. *this goodly high country*. Still again one sees the Deuteronomist's fondness
for the demonstrative pronoun, here used with considerable poignancy as
Moses points verbally to the sweet land before him that he will not be allowed
to enter.

26. *and the LORD was cross*. Though the verb used in this translation—as by
Friedman—is a little too mild for the Hebrew *hit'aber*, which is closer to "was
angered," it has the virtue of preserving the pun, transparent in the Hebrew,
on the same verb ('-*b-r*) in the *qal* conjugation, "to cross" or "cross over," used
both for the advance of the Israelites (verse 21) and in Moses's plea to God
(verse 25). Such punning switches of meaning are a regular technique of biblical narrative employed to effect transitions and do not necessarily reflect thematic significance. (Compare, for example, Judges 3, in which Ehud first stabs
[*taqa'*] the Midianite king Eglon in the belly and then, having effected his
escape, blasts [*taqa'*] the ram's horn to muster the Israelites to rebellion.)
    Enough for you! This impatient phrase, *rav lekha*, pointedly echoes *rav
lakhem*, "Long enough you . . . ," addressed by God to the Israelites in 1:6 and
2:3.

CHAPTER 4

"And now, Israel, hear the statutes and the laws that I am about to ₁
teach you to do, so you may live, and you shall come and take hold
of the land that the LORD God of your fathers is about to give to
you. You shall not add to the word that I charge you and you shall not ₂
subtract from it, to keep the commands of the LORD your God which I

---

1. *And now, Israel, hear.* The first Hebrew word here, *we'atah*, "and now," is often
used in a logical rather than a temporal sense, to introduce a conclusion or mark
a transition in the stages of a discourse. At this point, it introduces the grand sermon that concludes this whole preamble to the main body of the Book of
Deuteronomy (chapters 5–31). The verb "to hear," often, as here, in the imperative (*shema'*), is one of the signature terms of Deuteronomy. The Hebrew verb
means "to hear," "to listen," "to heed," and "to understand," and quite frequently
all those meanings come into play. In this preeminently didactic book, the Israelites are repeatedly enjoined to devote careful attention to the exhortations and
the laws that Moses delivers to them—to listen, absorb, understand, and obey.

so you may live. This is another verbal refrain that punctuates the sermon.
For the Deuteronomist, with deportations and the destruction of nations
vividly on the political horizon, history has become a very dangerous realm,
and Moses repeatedly urges Israel to follow the only path that, according to
the Deuteronomic view, will avert impending disaster.

2. *You shall not add . . . you shall not subtract.* Jeffrey H. Tigay proposes that
this strict-constructionist view of the Mosaic teaching is intended to be limited to the injunction to worship a single God: one is not free to add other
objects of worship nor to remove YHWH as the object of worship. But such a
cultic sense of "subtract" is rather strained, and it is more likely that Moses
here is represented enjoining strict construction precisely in order to diminish
any impression (in fact, an abundantly warranted impression) that Deuteronomy is effecting a revision of a good many earlier laws and traditions.

3 charge you. Your own eyes have seen that which the LORD did at Baal Peor, for every man that went after Baal Peor did the LORD your God
4 destroy from your midst. But you, the ones clinging to the LORD your
5 God, are all of you alive today. See, I have taught you the statutes and the laws as the LORD my God has charged me, to do thus within the
6 land into which you are about to come to take hold of it. And you shall keep and do, for that is your wisdom and your understanding in the eyes of the peoples who will hear all these statutes and will say, 'Only
7 a wise and understanding people is this great nation.' For what great nation is there that has gods close to it like the LORD our God when-
8 ever we call to Him? And what great nation is there that has just statutes and laws like all this teaching that I am about to set before you
9 today? Only be you on the watch and watch yourself closely lest you forget the things that your own eyes have seen and lest they swerve from your heart—all the days of your life, and you shall make them
10 known to your sons and to your sons' sons: the day that you stood before the LORD your God at Horeb when the LORD said to me, 'Assemble the people to Me that I may have them hear My words, so that they learn to fear Me all the days that they live on the soil, and

---

4. *you, the ones clinging to the LORD your God, are all of you alive today.* The very physical existence of the audience for Moses's sermon is palpable proof of the principle he announced at the beginning of the sermon, "so you may live."

6. *Only a wise and understanding people is this great nation.* The primacy of wisdom in the worldview of Deuteronomy is sharply reflected here. Israel's greatness as the other nations come to recognize it is not in its fecundity and military might (as, for example, in Balaam's oracles in Numbers) but in its wisdom, demonstrated by its adherence to a set of just statutes and laws. The next lines (verses 7–8) are testimony to God's decision to be close to Israel through the statutes and teachings He reveals to them.

10. *the day that you stood before the LORD.* "The day" or "on the day" is an epic locution for "when." Having begun with a general exhortation to cling to God's laws, the sermon now focuses in on the defining moment four decades earlier when Israel stood at the foot of Mount Sinai and God revealed to them his law in thunder and lightning.

so that they teach their sons.' And you came forward and stood at the 11
bottom of the mountain, and the mountain was burning with fire to the
heart of the heavens—darkness, cloud, and dense fog. And the LORD 12
spoke to you from the midst of the fire. The sound of words you did
hear but no image did you see except the sound. And He told you His 13
covenant that He charged you to do, the Ten Words, and He wrote
them on two tablets of stone. And me did the LORD charge at that time 14
to teach you statutes and laws for you to do in the land into which you
are crossing over to take hold of it. And you shall be very watchful of 15
yourselves, for you saw no image on the day the LORD spoke to you
from the midst of the fire, lest you act ruinously and make you a 16
sculpted image of any likeness, the form of male or of female, the form 17

---

12. *The sound of words you did hear but no image did you see.* The account of
the Sinai epiphany in Exodus is less rigorous about excluding the aspect of
sight. The Israelites there are enjoined to keep their distance precisely in order
that they will see nothing, and then the seventy elders in the sacred feast on
the mountain are vouchsafed a vision of the effulgence surrounding God. The
Deuteronomist, by contrast, is sternly aniconic, in keeping with his steady
polemic against all cults of divine images; he is a writer who insists on hearing
the divine, and seeing only God's portentous acts in history.

except the sound. Abraham ibn Ezra ingeniously connects this slightly odd
turn of phrase with the synesthetic "and all the people saw the sounds [i.e.,
the thunder]" (Exodus 20:18).

15. *be very watchful of yourselves.* It should be noted that the Hebrew freely
swings between second-person plural and second-person singular, an oscillation perfectly idiomatic in biblical Hebrew and by no means to be attributed
to a collation of different sources. It may be that the speaker on occasion
switches to the singular form in order to emphasize the effect of imperative
address to each individual, but that is not certain.

16. *a sculpted image of any likeness, the form.* Philologists have sought to draw
technical differences among these terms, but the manifest point of their
deployment here is the stylistic force of their synonymity: any manner or shape
of image or icon will lead Israel on the path to ruin.

16–18. *the form of male or of female . . . of any beast . . . on the earth . . . of any
winged bird . . . in the heavens . . . of anything that crawls on the ground . . . of
any fish that is in the waters under the earth.* The ringing language of the ser-

of any beast that is on the earth, the form of any winged bird that flies
18 in the heavens, the form of anything that crawls on the ground, the
19 form of any fish that is in the waters under the earth, lest you raise
your eyes to the heavens and see the sun and the moon and the stars,
all the array of the heavens, and you be led astray and bow down to
them and worship them, for the LORD your God allotted them to all the

---

mon here is a grand evocation of the account of creation in Genesis 1, and the
precise recapitulation of phrases compels the conclusion that that account,
attributed to P, was familiar to the Deuteronomist in a textual form resembling
the one we know. The hierarchy of creation was ordained by God for human's
use and dominion, and man in turn was to recognize the single divine source
of all creation. The elevation of any component of the created world to an
object of worship is thus seen as a perversion of the whole plan of cosmogo-
nic harmony and hierarchy.

18. *the waters under the earth.* In keeping with the picture of the cosmos in
Genesis 1, water is imagined to be under the earth ("the great abyss"), beyond
the perimeters of the dry land (the sea), and erupting from within the dry land
itself in rivers and lakes.

19. *lest you raise your eyes to the heavens and see the sun and the moon and the
stars, all the array of the heavens.* Once again, the language harks back to the
first account of creation, which concludes with the completion of the earth
and the heavens "and all their array." In a historical period rife with religious
syncretism and cultural assimilation, the writer stresses the dangerous
enchantment of the beauty of the natural world, which could easily lead people to deify and worship the various manifestations of that beauty.

for the LORD your God allotted them to all the peoples under the heavens. This
notion, which will be picked up again in the Song of Moses (chapter 32), is a
curious one by the lights of later monotheism. To Israel the worship of the one
overmastering God was assigned, whereas the other nations were entrusted to
the supervision of lesser celestial beings, *beney ha'elohim* ("the sons of God")
and came to worship these intermediary beings as though they were
autonomous deities. Polytheism, in this view, is a reflection of the fact that the
sundry nations, unlike Israel, have not been chosen by the one God to serve
Him.

peoples under the heavens. But you did the LORD take and He brought 20
you out from the iron's forge, from Egypt, to become for Him a people
in estate as this day. And the LORD was incensed with me because of 21
your words and He swore not to let me cross the Jordan and not to let
me come into the goodly land that the LORD your God is about to give
you in estate. For I am about to die in this land, I am not to cross the 22
Jordan, but you are to cross over and you will take hold of this goodly
land. Be you on the watch, lest you forget the covenant of the LORD 23
your God which He has sealed with you, and you make for yourselves
a sculpted image of any sort, against which the LORD your God has
charged you. For the LORD your God is a consuming fire, a jealous god. 24
When you beget sons and sons of sons and are long in the land, and 25
you act ruinously and make a sculpted image of any sort and do evil
in the eyes of the LORD your God to anger Him, I have called to wit- 26
ness against you the heavens and the earth that you shall surely perish
quickly from upon the land into which you are about to cross the Jordan to take hold of it. You shall not long endure upon it, for you will

---

20. *But you did the LORD take and He brought you out from the iron's forge.* The
argument of the sermon now moves another step back in time, from Sinai to
the Exodus. The origins of Israel as a people subject to another people in
whose land it dwelled, rescued from the crucible of slavery by God, are
adduced as further evidence of God's unique election of Israel.

a people in estate. Literally, a people estate—God's special property.

21. *the LORD was incensed with me because of your words.* Again, the barring of
Moses from the promised land is attributed not to any act or gesture of his—
for here he is the impeccable leader, God's mouthpiece—but to the mistrust-
ful words of the Israelites in the incident of the spies.

26. *I have called to witness against you the heavens and the earth.* It was conventional in ancient Near Eastern treaties to invoke heaven and earth as witnesses, but the word pair here also nicely echoes the allusions to the Creation
story in previous verses. God's heaven and earth are everlasting, but Israel will
be all too ephemeral if it worships images of the natural world.

27   surely be destroyed. And the LORD will scatter you among the peoples
and you shall be left men few in number among the nations where the
28   LORD will drive you. And you shall worship there their gods that are
human handiwork, wood and stone, which neither see nor hear nor eat
29   nor smell. And you shall search for the LORD your God from there, and
you shall find him when you seek Him with all your heart and with all
30   your being. When you are in straits and all these things find you in
time to come, you shall turn back to the LORD your God and heed His
31   voice. For the LORD your God is a merciful god. He will not let you go
and will not destroy you and will not forget your fathers' covenant that

---

27. *And the* LORD *will scatter you among the peoples*. This dire prospect, which
is not within the purview of the Book of Exodus, haunts the Deuteronomist,
writing in a period after the neo-Assyrian empire had instituted a policy of
deporting substantial elements of subjugated populations in order to clear the
conquered territory for colonization. Indeed, some sections of the book,
including this one, may have been written in the Babylonian exile.

28. *And you shall worship there their gods that are human handiwork*. The ultimate catastrophe of exile is viewed as assimilation into the local pagan cults—
the fate, one may reasonably surmise, of most of those exiled from the ten
northern tribes after the neo-Assyrian conquest in 721 B.C.E. and some of those
exiled in 586 by the Babylonians.

    wood and stone, which neither see nor hear nor eat nor smell. In the earlier
books of the Torah, the gods worshipped by the other nations are imagined as
lesser entities, impotent in the face of YHWH's overwhelming superiority and
bound to be reduced to nullity in any competition with the God of Israel. In
the antipagan polemic of Deuteronomy, as in some of the contemporaneous
and slightly later Prophets, polytheism is jeeringly represented as imbecile
fetishism.

29. *with all your heart and with all your being*. This phrase, with its revivalist
fervor, is a recurrent one in the rhetoric of Deuteronomy.

30. *heed His voice*. The primary meaning of the verb, which has already
appeared several times in this sermon, is "hear," but the preposition b^e that follows it requires the specific sense of "heed."

He swore to them. For, pray, ask of the first days that were before you,   32
from the day God created a human on the earth and from one end of
the heavens to the other end of the heavens, has there been the like of
this great thing or has its like been heard? Has a people heard God's   33
voice speaking from the midst of the fire, as you yourself have heard,
and still lived? Or has God tried to come to take Him a nation from   34
within a nation in trials and signs and portents and in battle and with a
strong hand and an outstretched arm and with great terrors, like all that
the LORD your God did for you in Egypt before your eyes? You yourself   35
were shown to know that the LORD is God, there is none besides Him.
From the heavens He made you hear His voice to reprove you, and on   36
the earth He showed you His great fire, and His words you heard, from
the midst of the fire. And since He did love your fathers He chose their   37
seed after them and brought you out from Egypt through His presence
with His great power, to dispossess nations greater and mightier than   38
you from before you, to bring you to give to you their land in estate as

---

32–33. *from the day God created a human on the earth . . . Has a people heard God's voice speaking from the midst of the fire.* These sentences bind together in a summarizing flourish the topics of creation and the Sinai epiphany that were underscored earlier in this speech.

33. *still lived.* The "still" is added in the translation for clarity. The obvious sense of the verb is "survived" but the level of diction of that English term would betray the monosyllabic plainness of the Hebrew. "Still lived," it should be noted, takes us back to "so you may live" at the very beginning of the sermon.

34. *to take Him a nation from within a nation.* In the almost musical structure of this oratory, we now move back to the invocation of the Exodus as testimony in verse 20.

37. *their seed after them.* The Hebrew says literally "his seed after him," but there is no real confusion because the usage has simply moved to a grammatical singular for a collective entity.

39 on this day. And you shall know today and take to your heart that the
LORD, He is God in the heavens above and on the earth below, there is
40 none else. And you shall keep His statutes and His commands which I
am about to charge you today, that He do well with you and with your
sons after you and so that you long endure on the soil that the LORD
your God is about to give you for all time."

41 Then did Moses divide off three towns across the Jordan where the sun
42 rises for a murderer to flee there who murdered his fellow man without
knowing and he was not his enemy in time past, that he might flee to
43 one of those towns and live: Bezer in the wilderness in the land of the
plain for the Reubenite, and Ramoth in the Gilead for the Gadite, and
Golan in the Bashan for the Manassite.

44,45 And this is the teaching that Moses set before the Israelites. These are
the treaty terms and the statutes and the laws that Moses spoke to the
46 Israelites when they came out from Egypt, across the Jordan in the valley opposite Beth Peor in the land of Sihon king of the Amorite whom
Moses, and the Israelites, struck down when they came out from
47 Egypt. And they took hold of his land and the land of Og king of the
Bashan, the two kings of the Amorite who are across the Jordan where
48 the sun rises, from Aroer which is on the bank of the Wadi Arnon as far
49 as Sion, which is Hermon, and all the Arabah across the Jordan to the
east as far as the Arabah Sea, at the foot of the Pisgah slopes.

---

39. *take to your heart.* The literal sense of the verb before "heart" is "bring
back," aligning this usage with the references to turning back to God in exile.

41–43. This brief unit on the towns of asylum, repeating a regulation laid down
in greater detail in Numbers, appears to be out of place here and may have
originally belonged with the material on the apportioning of the land in chapter 3.

44. *And this is the teaching.* The preamble to Deuteronomy was completed at
verse 40. Verses 44–49 are a formal introduction to the long discourse that follows, which will begin with a reiteration of the Decalogue, to be followed by
exhortations to obey God's teaching and then by a series of specific laws.

CHAPTER 5

And Moses called to all Israel and said to them, "Hear, Israel, the 1 statutes and the laws that I am about to speak in your hearing today, and you shall learn them and watch to do them. The LORD 2 your God sealed a covenant with us at Horeb. Not with our fathers did 3 the LORD seal this covenant but with us—we who are here today, all of us alive. Face to face did the LORD speak with you on the mountain 4 from the midst of the fire. I was standing between the LORD and you at 5 that time to tell you the word of the LORD—for you were afraid in the face of the fire and did not go up the mountain,—saying,

---

2. *sealed a covenant.* As everywhere in biblical Hebrew, the literal sense of this idiom is "cut a covenant." The use of that verb may originate in the cutting of pieces of animals in the covenantal ritual, as in the solemn pact between Abraham and God in Genesis 15.

3. *with us—we who are here today, all of us alive.* The heavy emphasis of Moses's language, in which, exceptionally, "us" in the accusative is followed by "we" in the nominative and then the triple language of spatial and temporal presence, "here," "today," "alive," powerfully dramatizes the logic of reenactment at the heart of Deuteronomy. This book is framed as a renewal, through rehearsal, of the law. Its initial seventh-century B.C.E. audience is constantly invited to imagine itself in the shoes, or sandals, of the Israelites who stood before Moses just east of the Jordan as he repeated the law. Moses's rhetoric, in turn, repeatedly evokes the physical, witnessing presence of the audience he addresses as he reiterates the divine law revealed a generation earlier at Sinai.

5. *I was standing between the LORD and you . . . for you were afraid.* The seeming contradiction between this verse and the immediately preceding one ("Face to face did the LORD speak with you") has occasioned much exegetical ingenuity, but there is actually strong thematic and narrative logic in the move-

6 'I am the LORD your God Who brought you out of the land of Egypt,
7,8 out of the house of slaves. You shall have no other gods beside Me. You
shall make you no carved likeness, no image of what is in the heavens
above or what is on the earth below or what is in the waters beneath
9 the earth. You shall not bow to them and you shall not worship them,
for I am the LORD your God, a jealous god, reckoning the crime of
fathers with sons, and with the third generation and with the fourth, for

---

ment from verse 4 to verse 5. The parallel account in Exodus 19 places reiterated emphasis on the idea that the people must remain at a distance, not even
touching the base of the mountain, while Moses acts as their intermediary and
goes up to the heights to hear God's words. The Deuteronomist scarcely wants
to discard this notion of Moses's necessary mediation, but, with his own concern for dramatizing Israel as the living aural witnesses of the great epiphany,
he introduces two distinct, successive moments in the Sinai experience. God
actually addresses the people face to face, conveying to them from the midst
of the fire the words of revelation that they and their descendants are to
remember perpetually. The people, however, cannot tolerate the fearsome
directness of this divine address; they recoil from the ascent to the mountaintop and instead allow Moses to act as their intermediary.

in the face of. The verb "to fear" often is followed by a simple direct object.
The preposition *mipney*, "in the face of," pointedly glances back at "face to
face" and also amplifies the experience of fear because it suggests a frightened
drawing back from before, from the presence, from the face of, the feared
object.

6–18. This version of the Decalogue is in most respects textually identical with
the one that appears in Exodus 20:2–17. For elucidation of many of the significant details, see the commentary on those verses in Exodus. The comments
here will be limited to the points where the present version differs from the
one in Exodus.

8. *no carved likeness, no image*. The Hebrew syntax could also be construed as
a construct state—i.e., "no carved likeness of an image." The version in Exodus reads "no carved likeness and no image," which is probably a difference
without an important distinction.

9. *and with the third generation*. The initial "and" is an addition of our text. Its
absence in Exodus 20:5 produces a tighter rhythmic effect.

my foes, and doing kindness to the thousandth generation for My   10
friends and for those who keep My commands. You shall not take the   11
name of the LORD your God in vain, for the LORD will not acquit
whosoever takes His name in vain. Keep the sabbath day to hallow it   12
as the LORD your God has charged you. Six days you shall work and   13
you shall do your tasks, but the seventh day is a sabbath to the LORD   14
your God. You shall do no task, you and your son and your daughter and
your male slave and your slavegirl and your ox and your donkey and all
your beasts and your sojourner who is within your gates, so that your
male slave and your slavegirl may rest like you. And you shall remem-   15
ber that you were a slave in the land of Egypt, and the LORD brought

---

12. *Keep the sabbath day.* The Exodus version has "remember" (that is, be
mindful of) rather than "keep." The Midrash Mekhilta famously announced,
"'keep' and 'remember' in a singular utterance," and the two acts are, indeed,
joined in a tight nexus: because we remember or are mindful of something, we
keep it. But *shamor,* "keep," "observe," "watch," is a recurrent term in the
didactic rhetoric of Deuteronomy, and so it is hardly surprising that this verb
would be favored here.

as the LORD *your God has charged you.* This Deuteronomic clause of divine
injunction is absent in Exodus 20.

14. *and your male slave.* Again, the initial "and" is added in this version. Similarly, each of the last four commandments here (verses 17–18) is introduced by
an "and" lacking in the Exodus text. Though the difference is not major, the
lapidary abruptness of the version without the "and's" lends support to the
assumption that it is the primary text while the one here is a secondary elaboration, though one that in most respects hews very close to the original.

your ox and your donkey. Exodus has only "your beast." Ox and donkey are
a kind of synecdoche for all beasts of burden, and part of the legal vocabulary
of Deuteronomy.

so that your male slave and your slavegirl may rest like you. This entire clause
is absent in Exodus. It serves as a lead-in to the next verse, also lacking in Exodus, in which the liberation from Egypt and the memory of slavery are invoked
as the grounds for the sabbath. In Exodus, on the other hand, the sabbath is
explained as *imitatio dei*—just as God rested after the six days of creation,
Israel is enjoined to rest on the seventh day. The difference between these two
rationales is at least in part a difference in narrative location. The initial iteration of the Decalogue occurs in the direct narration of the awe-inspiring Sinai
epiphany, when God, descending from the heavens to make His words known

you out from there with a strong hand and an outstretched arm. There-
16 fore did the LORD charge you to make the sabbath day. Honor your
father and your mother, as the LORD your God charged you, so that your
days may be long and so that He may do well with you on the soil that
17 the LORD your God has given you. You shall not murder. And you shall
not commit adultery. And you shall not steal. And you shall not bear
18 vain witness against your fellow man. And you shall not covet your fellow man's wife, and you shall not desire your fellow man's house, his
field, or his male servant or his slavegirl, his ox or his donkey, or any-
19 thing that your fellow man has.' These words did the LORD speak to
your whole assembly at the mountain from the midst of the fire, the
cloud, and the dense fog, in a great voice, and nothing more. And He
20 wrote them on two tablets of stone and gave them to me. And it happened, when you heard the voice from the midst of the darkness, with

---

to Israel, powerfully manifests Himself as Creator of heaven and earth. The
present reiteration of the Decalogue takes place at the moment Israel is
poised to enter the promised land, establish a society, and exercise power over
others.

16. *as the* LORD *your God charged you.* Precisely as in verse 12, this clause is
added to the formulation of the corresponding commandment in Exodus.

and so that He may do well with you. This entire clause is absent in the Exodus version of this commandment, and, with its didactic emphasis of synonymity with the previous clause, is a strong indication that this formulation
of the Decalogue is a secondary elaboration.

17. *vain witness.* The Exodus version reads "false witness." The present formulation chooses a synonym for "false," "empty," "lying" that is the same word
used in "You shall not take [literally, bear] the name of the LORD your God in
vain." This translation preserves that repetition of terms.

18. *his field.* This specification is not part of the Exodus version.

his ox. This is one of only two points in this version of the Decalogue where
an initial w^e ("and" or "or") present in Exodus is deleted, rather than the other
way around.

19. *and nothing more.* The literal sense of the Hebrew is "and He did not add."

the mountain burning in fire, that you came forward to me, all the heads of your tribes and your elders. And you said, 'Look, the Lord our 21 God has shown us His glory and His greatness, and we have heard His voice from the midst of the fire. This day we have seen that the Lord can speak to man and he may live. And now, why should we die, for 22 this great fire will consume us. If we hear again the voice of the Lord our God, we shall die. For who is mortal flesh that has heard the voice 23 of the living God speaking from the midst of the fire as we did and has lived? You go near and hear all that the Lord our God says, and you it 24 is who will speak to us all that the Lord our God speaks to you, and we shall hear and do.' And the Lord heard the sound of your words when 25 you spoke to me, and the Lord said to me, 'I have heard the sound of the words of this people which they spoke to you. They have done well in all that they have spoken. Would that they had this heart of theirs to 26

---

21. *we have heard His voice from the midst of the fire*. This speech of the people is a detailed unpacking of what was indicated compactly, and proleptically, in verse 5. The people in this version of the story that stresses immediate witnessing have actually heard God's voice speaking the Ten Words from the summit of the mountain engulfed in fire. They draw back in terror—presumably, to the very bottom of the mountain or the approach to it—and make it clear, as they implore Moses to serve henceforth as their intermediary, that this is not an experience they would venture to undergo a second time. Thus the story succeeds in having it both ways—representing the people as having heard God's words with their own ears and firmly establishing Moses in his role as teacher and necessary intermediary between Israel and God.

23. *mortal flesh*. Literally, "all flesh."
    the living God . . . has lived? There is a striking play between God's overwhelmingly powerful, incandescent, eternal life and the fragile life of ephemeral man exposed to this terrific presence of the deity. Some scholars have also seen in the epitaph "living God" a counterpoint to the lifeless fetishes that the Deuteronomist often mocks.

25. *They have done well in all that they have spoken*. At the conclusion of the episode, God resoundingly confirms the rightness of the people's entreaty that Moses stand as go-between in all communications from the deity. One may detect in all this the interest of a royal scribal elite promoting itself as the necessary authoritative mediators of God's words for the people.

fear Me and to keep My commands for all time, so that it would go well
27 with them and with their sons forever. Go, say to them, Return you to
28 your tents. And you, stand here by Me and I shall speak to you all the
commands and the statutes and the laws that you will teach them, and
they will do them in the land that I am about to give them to take hold
29 of it. And you shall watch to do as the Lord your God has charged you.
30 You shall not swerve to the right or left. In all the way that the Lord
your God has charged you shall you go, so that you may live and it will
be well with you, and you will long endure on the land of which you
take hold.'"

---

30. *so that you may live and it will be well with you, and you will long endure on
the land*. This didactic flourish reflects an underlying view of history in
Deuteronomy. In this era of incursions by great empires, of deportations and
destruction of kingdoms, Israel's endurance on the land promised to it is constantly, dangerously, contingent on its faithfully hewing to all that God has
commanded.

CHAPTER 6

"And this is the command, the statutes and the laws that the Lord 1
your God has charged you to teach you to do in the land into
which you are about to cross to take hold of it. So that you will 2
fear the Lord your God to keep all His statutes and His commands
which I charge you—you and your son and your son's son, all the days
of your life; and so that your days will be long. And you shall hear, 3
Israel, and you shall keep to do, that it may go well with you, and that
you may greatly multiply, as the Lord God of your fathers has spoken
concerning you, a land flowing with milk and honey.

---

3. *that it may go well with you.* Again and again, the Deuteronomist stresses the
causal link between loyalty to God and prospering in the land. This notion is
variously adumbrated in earlier biblical texts but never given the central
emphasis it enjoys here as an overriding conception of history.

a land flowing with milk and honey. The syntactic connection of this phrase
with the whole clause is a little obscure, or at least elliptic. Some scholars supply "in" before "a land." The Septuagint and the Peshitta read, "to give you a
land."

4,5 Hear, Israel, the LORD our God, the LORD is one. And you shall love
the LORD your God with all your heart and with all your being and with
6 all your might. And these words that I charge you today shall be upon
7 your heart. And you shall rehearse them to your sons and speak of them

---

4. *Hear, Israel.* This entire passage, through to verse 9, has been aptly
described as a catechism, and it entirely fits its character as an exhortation to
hew to God's teachings that it later should have been incorporated in the daily
liturgy, recited twice each day in Jewish worship. Some translators render
'*eḥad*, "one," as "alone," but the evidence that this common Hebrew numeral
term ever meant that is questionable. The statement stands, then, as it has
been traditionally construed, as a ringing declaration of monotheism. Both
Rashi and Abraham ibn Ezra point to Zechariah 14:9 as an indication that in
days to come the LORD our God will be recognized as the one God by all.

5. *And you shall love the LORD your God.* It is a new emphasis of Deuteronomy
to add to the traditional fear of the LORD the emotion of love, perhaps in an
effort to deepen psychologically the conception of monotheism. Ibn Ezra links
this injunction with the immediately preceding declaration of God's oneness:
"Since we have no other god but only Him alone, you have to love Him, for we
have no other god." In this view, the lack of rivals obliges us to make this divine
suitor the object of our affection. But "love" also belongs to the ancient Near
Eastern language of international relations, appearing in treaties in which
fealty is sworn to a political overlord.
    with all your heart. The heart is the seat of understanding in biblical phys-
iology, but it is also associated with feelings.
    with all your being. The Hebrew *nefesh* means "life-breath" or "essential
self." The traditional translation of "soul," preserved in many recent versions,
is misleading because it suggests a body-soul split alien to biblical thinking.
    with all your might. The Hebrew *me'od* elsewhere is an adverb ("very"), not
a noun. It is not clear whether this distinctive Deuteronomic usage reflects
stylistic inventiveness in converting one part of speech to another or rather
records an idiomatic sense of the word that is simply not used elsewhere in the
biblical corpus.

7. *rehearse.* The Hebrew verb *shinen* is construed here, in accord with Jeffrey
H. Tigay, as a variant of *shanah*, "to repeat." Many commentators, medieval
and modern, insist on the fact that the root elsewhere means "sharp," and thus
that the meaning here would be "to teach incisively" or even "to incise upon."
It may well be that the writer is punning on the two phonetically related verbal roots in order to suggest something like "to rehearse with incisive effect."

when you sit in your house and when you go on the way and when you
lie down and when you rise. And you shall bind them as a sign on your 8
hand and they shall be as circlets between your eyes. And you shall 9
write them on the doorposts of your house and in your gates.

"And it shall come about when the LORD your God brings you to the 10
land that He swore to your fathers, to Abraham, to Isaac, and to Jacob,
to give to you—great and goodly towns that you did not build, and 11
houses filled with all good that you did not fill, and hewn cisterns that
you did not hew, vineyards and olive groves that you did not plant, you
will eat and be sated. Watch yourself, lest you forget the LORD Who 12
brought you out of the land of Egypt, from the house of slaves. The 13
LORD your God you shall fear, and Him shall you serve, and by His
name shall you swear. You shall not go after other gods, from the gods 14

---

house . . . way . . . lie down . . . rise. These two pairs of terms, each of which
is what is technically called a merism, two opposing terms that also imply
everything between them, obviously have the sense of wherever you are, whatever you do.

8. *a sign on your hand . . . circlets between your eyes.* Perhaps the original meaning is metaphorical, but inscribed amulets were in fact common in the ancient
Near East, and early rabbinic Judaism would interpret these words literally as
the injunction for wearing *tephillin,* small leather boxes on hand and forehead
containing this and other biblical passages written on parchment. The denotation and etymology of "circlet," *totafot,* are not entirely certain, though the
precedent of Egyptian ornaments worn on the forehead suggests itself. See
the comment on Exodus 13:9.

9. *in your gates.* These would be the gates of the city, since houses did not have
gates.

11. *you will eat and be sated.* The full belly is the enemy of faith in Deuteronomy. The comforts of prosperity are thought of as leading to complacency, or
perhaps even to cultic assimilationism—worshipping the gods of the previous
inhabitants who planted those groves and vineyards and hewed those cisterns.
Thus the history of Israel teeters on the edge of a precarious balance: if Israel
punctiliously adheres to the commands of its God, it will prosper; but when it
prospers, it runs the danger of falling away from its loyalty to God.

15 of the people who are all around you. For the LORD your God is a jealous god in your midst. Lest the wrath of the LORD your God flare
16 against you and He destroy you from the face of the earth. You shall not
17 try the LORD your God as you tried Him at Massah. You shall surely
keep the command of the LORD your God, and His treaty terms and
18 His statutes with which He charged you. And you shall do what is right
and good in the eyes of the LORD, so that it may go well with you, and
you shall come and take hold of the good land that the LORD swore to
19 your fathers to drive back all your enemies before you, as the LORD has
spoken.

20 "Should your son ask you tomorrow, saying, 'What are the treaty terms
and the statutes and the laws with which the LORD our God has
21 charged you?' You shall say to your son, 'Slaves were we to Pharaoh in

---

15. *For the LORD your God is a jealous God.* As in similar contexts elsewhere, it
is quite likely that the adjective *qanaʾ* refers to jealousy, even in the sexual
sense, rather than to "passion," as some have claimed, for what is at stake is
that the LORD will brook no rivals.

the face of the earth. The Hebrew *ʾadamah* could also mean "soil" or "land,"
referring to the tenure of this agricultural people in the land of Israel, but it
may be more plausible to see this verse as a threat of total destruction, thus
warranting the translation of *ʾadamah* as "earth."

16. *You shall not try the LORD your God.* For the incident at Massah (a name
that means "trial"), see Exodus 17:1–7. The trial in Exodus was the people's
lack of faith that God would provide for them in the wilderness. In this
prospective instance, all sorts of bounty would have already been provided to
them, and yet, with far less warrant than their ancestors, they would "try" or
provoke God by casting aside their obligations of loyalty to Him.

20. *Should your son ask you.* The didactic impulse of Deuteronomy is here
made perfectly explicit in the catechistic form of the entire passage. Appropriately, the passage was incorporated into the text of the Passover Haggadah
as part of the rationale for the ritual retelling of the Exodus story.

Egypt, and the LORD brought us out with a strong hand. And the LORD 22
wrought great and evil signs and portents against Egypt, against
Pharaoh and against all his house, before our eyes. But us did He take 23
out from there, so that He might bring us to give us the land that He
swore to our fathers. And the LORD charged us to do these statutes, to 24
fear the LORD our God for our own good always, to keep us in life as on
this day. And it will be a merit for us if we keep to do all this that is 25
commanded before the LORD our God as He has charged us.'"

---

22. *before our eyes.* The verse concluded by this phrase is a stringing together
of formulaic locutions repeatedly used in the Plagues narrative in Exodus.
What this final phrase adds is the reiterated emphasis in Deuteronomy on
Israel's having been ocular witness to God's saving power.

25. *a merit.* This is the most likely meaning here of the Hebrew *tsedaqah*,
which also means "righteousness" and "innocence." (For the sense of "merit,"
compare Genesis 15:6.) But it also occasionally means something like "boon"
(see Judges 5:11), and that sense could also work here.

CHAPTER 7

1 **"W**hen the Lord your God brings you to the land to which you are coming to take hold of it, He will cast off many nations from before you—the Hittite and the Girgashite and the Amorite and the Canaanite and the Perizzite and the Hivite and the Jebusite, seven 2 nations more numerous and mightier than you. And the Lord your God will give them before you and you shall strike them down. You shall surely put them under the ban. You shall not seal a covenant with 3 them and shall show them no mercy. You shall not intermarry with them. You shall not give your daughter to his son, nor shall you take his

---

1. *cast off.* The verbal root *n-sh-l* is elsewhere used for slipping off one's sandals or for an axe head slipping out of its haft.

nations more numerous and mightier than you. In earlier biblical accounts, the almost preternatural numerical growth of the Hebrew people is stressed. In the historical reality of the later seventh and sixth centuries B.C.E., a writer would have been keenly aware that Israel was a tiny nation surrounded by large and powerful peoples.

2. *You shall surely put them under the ban.* The verb *ḥaharim* implies both total destruction and a solemn vow to carry out that grim purpose without taking prisoners as slaves and with no secular exploitation of the booty. Moshe Weinfeld calls the emphasis on *ḥerem* (the ban) in Deuteronomy "utopian" and "wishful thinking." There is, thankfully, no archeological evidence that this program of annihilation was ever implemented, but the insistence on it here reflects an agenda of absolute separation of Israelite and Canaanite populations for the purpose of preserving cultic purity (compare verses 3–4).

3. *You shall not give your daughter to his son.* A moment before, the Canaanites were a plural, "them." But this characteristic easy switch from plural to singular is a way of focusing on the specific act of the individual Israelite about to

daughter for your son. For he will make your son swerve from follow- 4
ing Me, and they will worship other gods, and the LORD's wrath will
flare against you and He will swiftly destroy you. Rather, thus shall you 5
do to them: their altars you shall smash and their cultic pillars you shall
shatter and their sacred trees you shall chop down and their images you
shall burn in fire. For you are a holy people to the LORD your God. You 6
the LORD has chosen to become for Him a treasured people among all
the peoples that are on the face of the earth. Not because you are 7
more numerous than all the peoples did the LORD desire you and
choose you, for you are the fewest of all the peoples. But because of 8
the LORD's love for you and because of His keeping the vow that He
swore to your fathers He has brought you out with a strong hand and
ransomed you from the house of slaves, from the hand of Pharaoh, king

---

marry off his daughter to a Canaanite son. Marriages, of course, were arranged
by the families, not by the bride and groom.

4. *he will make your son swerve.* The antecedent is ambiguous: it could be the
just mentioned son who would marry your daughter, or it could be the singular, generic "Canaanite."
    from following Me. Literally, "from after me."

5. *their altars you shall smash.* This string of short clauses is a vivid instance of
the powerful rhetoric of iconoclastic theology that informs Deuteronomy. In
quasipoetic semantic parallelism, the statement moves from one verb of violent destruction to another, more intense one, ending with the utter consummation by fire of all pagan icons.

6. *a treasured people among all the peoples.* This is a variant formulation of the
phrase that appears in Exodus 19:5. The term for "treasure," *segulah,* is one
that is used in other ancient Semitic languages to designate a relationship of
privileged vassalage.

7. *Not because you are more numerous than all the peoples.* See the comment
on the related formulation in verse 1.

8. *ransomed.* This verb is chosen for the liberation from Egypt because it is
what one does to free a captive. In the event, God pays for the liberation not
with ransom money but with terrible acts of retribution.

9   of Egypt. And you shall know that the LORD your God, He is God, the
    steadfast god keeping the covenant and the faith for those who love
10 Him and keeping His commands to the thousandth generation, but He
    pays back those who hate Him to their face to make them perish. He
11 will not delay—him who hates Him to his face He will pay back. And
    you shall keep what is commanded and the statutes and the laws that
    I charge you today to do.

12 "And it shall come about in consequence of your heeding these laws
    when you keep and do them, that the LORD your God will keep the
13 covenant and the faith for you that he swore to your fathers. And He
    will love you and bless you and multiply you and bless the fruit of your
    womb and the fruit of your soil, your grain and your wine and your oil,
    the spawn of your herds and the calvings of your flock, upon the soil
14 that He swore to your fathers to give to you. Blessed shall you be more
    than all the peoples. There shall be no sterile male nor female among
15 you nor among your beasts. And the LORD shall turn away from you all
    illness, and all the evil ailments of Egypt which you knew He will not
16 put upon you but will set them on all who hate you. And you shall

---

9–10. These verses amount to a summarizing paraphrase of the revelation to
Moses of the divine attributes in Exodus 34 and in Numbers 14.

12. *in consequence of*. The relatively unusual Hebrew preposition ʿeqev literally
means "on the heel[s] of."

13. *multiply . . . bless the fruit*. These three terms hark back to the injunction
in Genesis, here reinterpreted as a blessing actively initiated by God, to be
fruitful and multiply.
     grain . . . wine . . . oil . . . spawn . . . calvings. Each of these five terms is not
the common one for the thing it designates. While redolent of the concrete
reality of agriculture and animal husbandry, each of these words is also the
name of a pagan deity associated with fertility. This usage is most evident in
the exceptional ʿashterot tsoʾnekha, "the calvings of your flock," for ʿashterot is
transparently the plural form of Ashtoreth, the Canaanite fertility goddess. In
the antipagan polemic impetus of the Deuteronomic oration, the God of Israel
supersedes all these agricultural deities as the source of fertility, reducing
them to mere common nouns.

devour all the peoples that the LORD your God is about to give to you. Your eye shall not pity them and you shall not worship their gods, for it is a snare to you. Should you say in your heart, 'These nations are more 17 numerous than I. How can I dispossess them?' You shall not fear 18 them. You shall surely remember what the LORD your God did to Pharaoh, and to all Egypt, the great trials that your own eyes saw, the 19 signs and the portents and the strong hand and the outstretched arm with which the LORD your God brought you out. So will the LORD your God do to all the peoples whom you fear. And the hornet, too, will the 20 LORD your God send against them, until those who remain and hide from you perish. You shall not be terrified by them, for the LORD your 21 God is in your midst, a great and fearsome god. And the LORD your God 22 will cast off these nations from before you little by little. You will not be able to put an end to them swiftly, lest the beasts of the field multi-

---

18. *You shall surely remember what the LORD your God did to Pharaoh.* Again and again in Deuteronomy, the Exodus story of the founding of the nation through liberation from slavery is invoked in order to exhort the people to confront their own frightening historical reality: threatened by overwhelmingly greater powers—most urgently, by the Assyrian and then the Babylonian empire—they are enjoined to recall the great narrative in which God's intervention enabled them to triumph over Egypt's imperial might. Hence the contemporary relevance of "these nations are more numerous than I," which surely goes beyond the immediate reference to the Canaanite peoples.

20. *the hornet.* The meaning of the Hebrew term *tsir'ah* is uncertain. See the philological comment on Exodus 23:28, where it is suggested that it might be a supernatural agency, the Smasher. Alternately, since the verb at the beginning of the next verse, "be terrified," reflects the same three consonants in reversed order ('-r-ts) and appears to play on the sound of *tsir'ah*, it might mean the Terror. Abraham ibn Ezra ingeniously identifies it as some kind of epidemic by relating it to *tsara'at* (which also has the root ts-r-'), a contagious skin disease.

22. *lest the beasts of the field multiply against you.* The biblical writers had to confront the repeated contradiction between the promise of a grand conquest of the Canaanite peoples and the historical fact that the conquest was only partial and gradual. Various explanations are offered in Exodus and in Judges, but this is one of the most strained.

23 ply against you. And the LORD your God will give them before you and
24 panic them with a great panic until they are destroyed. And He will give
their kings into your hand, and you shall make their name perish from
under the heavens. No man will stand up before you, until you destroy
25 them. The images of their gods you shall burn in fire. You shall not
covet the silver and gold upon them and take it for yourself, lest you be
26 snared by it, for it is an abhorrence to the LORD your God. And you
shall bring no abhorrent thing into your house or you will be under the
ban like it. You shall surely despise it and shall surely abhor it, for it is
under the ban."

---

26. *you shall bring no abhorrent thing into your house . . . for it is under the ban.*
Anything under the ban (*ḥerem*) is taboo and marked for utter destruction.
The antipagan polemic of Deuteronomy here extends to a fear that the material allure of the gold and silver images may lead Israelites to appropriate them,
an appropriation perhaps not initially intended for cultic purposes but that
could lead to the worship of the images.

CHAPTER 8

"All the commandment which I charge you today you shall keep to 1 do, in order that you may live and multiply and come and take hold of the land which the LORD has sworn to your fathers. And 2 you shall remember all the way on which the LORD your God led you these forty years in the wilderness, in order to afflict you, to test you, to know what was in your heart, whether you would keep His commands or not. And He afflicted you and made you hunger and fed you 3 the manna, which you did not know nor did your fathers know, in order to make you know that not on bread alone does the human live but on

---

2. *these forty years in the wilderness*. As in many previous passages, the deictic "these" (Hebrew *zeh*) positions Moses's audience as the group that has just undergone the long trial of wandering in the wilderness and has witnessed God's providential power. By implication, the writer's seventh-century B.C.E. audience is invited to imagine itself vicariously in the same position.

in order to afflict you, to test you. "To afflict" (*'inah*) is a verb that in other contexts means "to debase" or "to abuse." "To test" is precisely what the Israelites were warned not to do to God (6:16). It is also the verb used for what God does to Abraham in the story of the Binding of Isaac (Genesis 22:1). In both cases, either this is a God lacking the absolute foreknowledge ascribed to the deity by later theology, or the trial is essentially a means for man to show his mettle.

3. *the human*. The Hebrew *ha'adam* (literally, "the human") is grammatically masculine but refers to both sexes. (See the comment on Genesis 1:26.) "Man," *'ish*, in verse 5, is unambiguously masculine because in this society it is the father's role to discipline his son.

4 every utterance of the LORD's mouth does the human live. Your cloak
5 did not wear out upon you nor did your foot swell these forty years. And
   you knew in your heart that as a man chastises his son the LORD your
6 God chastises you. And you shall keep the commands of the LORD your
7 God, to walk in His ways and to fear Him. For the LORD your God is
   about to bring you to a goodly land, a land of brooks of water, springs
8 and deeps coming out in valley and in mountain, a land of wheat and
   barley and vines and figs and pomegranates, a land of oil olives and
9 honey, a land where not in penury will you eat bread, you will lack
   nothing in it, a land whose stones are iron and from whose mountains
10 you will hew copper. And you will eat and be sated and bless the LORD
11 your God on the goodly land that He has given you. Watch yourself,

---

4. *Your cloak.* The Hebrew *simlah* is not the general term for "garment," as
many English versions render it, but the very outer garment that the fleeing
Hebrews "borrowed" from their Egyptian neighbors and laundered before the
Sinai epiphany. Thus, the concreteness of the recollected experience of the
Exodus is sustained through the precise choice of terms.

7. *a goodly land, a land of brooks of water.* As a complement to the insistent
rhetoric of admonition in Deuteronomy ("watch yourself," "and you shall keep
the commands," etc.), one also finds a rhetoric of fulfillment, grandly evoking
the abundance of the rich land that God is giving to Israel. This long sentence,
which some scholars have characterized as "hymnic," rolls on resonantly all the
way to the end of verse 9, punctuating its catalogue of the bounty of Canaan
with an anaphoric reiteration of "land." The Israelites have been wandering
through a parched wilderness "where there is no water" (verse 15), so the catalogue strategically begins with "brooks of water, springs and deeps" before going
on to enumerate the agricultural produce and mineral resources of the land.

9. *not in penury.* The term *misken* ("poor man," here with the *ut* suffix of
abstraction) is an Akkadian loanword that is quite rare in the Bible, occurring
only here and in the late Ecclesiastes. Hence the choice in the translation of
a relatively uncommon word for poverty.

10. *And you will eat and be sated and bless the* LORD. This verse became the kernel for the grace after meals in later Jewish tradition, a practice, as the Qumran scrolls reveal, that goes back as far as the late Second Temple period. But
from the Deuteronomic viewpoint, the pleasure of eating one's fill carries with

lest you forget the LORD your God and not keep His commands and His laws and His statutes that I charge you today. Lest you eat and be sated 12 and build goodly houses and dwell in them. And your cattle and sheep 13 multiply, and silver and gold multiply for you, and all that you have multiply. And your heart become haughty and you forget the LORD your 14 God who brings you out of the land of Egypt from the house of slaves, Who leads you through the great and terrible wilderness—viper- 15 serpent and scorpions, and thirst, where there is no water—Who brings water out for you from flintstone. Who feeds you manna in the wilder- 16 ness, which your fathers did not know, in order to afflict you and in order to try you, to make it go well with you in your later time. And you 17 will say in your heart, 'My power and the might of my hand made me this wealth.' And you will remember the LORD your God, for He it is 18

---

it the danger of forgetting one's dependence on God—hence the quick transition to "watch yourself" at the beginning of the next verse.

12. *build goodly houses.* In the related passage in 6:10–14, the houses and all the other material benefits are the work of others, taken over by the Israelites. As Moshe Weinfeld notes, the emphasis in the earlier passage is on forgetting God through sheer effortless affluence, whereas here it is rather the Israelites' satisfaction in the abundance achieved through their own effort that leads them to imagine (verse 17), "My power and the might of my hand made me all this wealth."

15. *viper-serpent.* For a catastrophic episode involving these creatures, see Numbers 21:6–9, and note the comment on Numbers 21:6 for an explanation of this term.

16. *manna in the wilderness . . . in order to afflict you and in order to try you.* These phrases of course mirror verse 3. The rhetorical structure of this whole chapter, as several modern commentators have noted, is carefully contrived in a large chiasm: A: injunction to observe God's commands and live (verse 1); B: trial in the wilderness and the gift of manna (verses 2–5); A´: injunction to keep God's commands; C: prospering in the land and thanking God (verses 7–10); C´: danger of forgetting God through prosperity (verses 11–14); B´: gift of manna and trial in the wilderness (verses 15–16); A´´: danger of forgetting God's commands and perishing (verses 17–20).

Who gives you power to make wealth, in order to fulfill His covenant
19 that He swore to your fathers as on this day. And it will be, if you indeed
forget the LORD your God and go after other gods and worship them
and bow to them, I bear witness against you today that you shall surely
20 perish. Like the nations that the LORD causes to perish before you, so
shall you perish, inasmuch as you would not heed the voice of the LORD
your God."

CHAPTER 9

"Hear, Israel, you are about to cross the Jordan to dispossess nations 1
greater and mightier than you, great towns, and fortified to the
heavens, a great and lofty people, sons of giants, as you yourself 2
knew and you yourself heard: Who can stand up before the sons of
giants? And you shall know today that the LORD your God, He it is 3
crossing over before you, a consuming fire. He Himself will destroy
them and He will lay them low before you, and you will dispossess
them and make them perish swiftly as the LORD has spoken to you. Do 4
not say in your heart when the LORD your God drives them back before
you, saying, 'Through my merit did the LORD bring me to take hold of
this land and through the wickedness of these nations is the LORD dis-

---

1. *fortified to the heavens.* Literally, "in the heavens." The obvious force of this
recurring phrase is that to the Israelite invaders these lofty fortified cities loom
high as the sky.

3. *a consuming fire.* This epithet for God, which is coordinate with the
repeated emphasis on the notion that at Sinai God spoke from the midst of the
fire and that the mountain itself was continuously burning forty days and forty
nights (a detail not part of Exodus), reflects the fiercely militant monotheism
of Deuteronomy: the one God, Who is the God of Israel, will consume all
adversaries.

4. *before you.* Logically this should read "before me," and for that reason the
two words are placed here outside the quotation marks, as a reversion to
Moses's perspective. One proposed emendation changes *mipanekha*, "before
you" to *mipanai ki*, yielding "before me. For [not through your merit]."

5 possessing them' before you. Not through your merit nor through your heart's rightness do you come to take hold of their land but through the wickedness of these nations is the LORD your God dispossessing them before you and in order to fulfill the word that the LORD swore to your 6 fathers, to Abraham, to Isaac, and to Jacob. And you shall know that not through your merit is the LORD your God giving you this goodly land 7 to take hold of it, for you are a stiff-necked people. Remember, do not forget, that you infuriated the LORD your God in the wilderness from the very day you came out of the land of Egypt until you came to this 8 place, you have been rebellious against the LORD. And in Horeb you infuriated the LORD, and the LORD was incensed with you enough to 9 destroy you. When I went up the mountain to take the stone tablets, the tablets of the Covenant that the LORD sealed with you, and I stayed on the mountain forty days and forty nights, no bread did I eat nor

---

5. *merit . . . wickedness.* Perhaps these antonyms are meant to be understood in their judicial sense, referring to the respective attributes of the person in the right and the person in the wrong in a legal conflict.

6. *stiff-necked.* This idiom for stubbornness is characteristically associated with the episode of the Golden Calf, which will follow here. Various proposals have been made about the origins of the idiom, but the simplest explanation is in its suggestion of rigid pride: instead of bowing the head when submission is appropriate, the stiff-necked person remains presumptuously, defiantly, erect.

8. *enough to destroy you.* "Enough" is merely implied in the Hebrew, as it is again in the recurrence of this idiom in verses 19 and 20.

9. *the tablets of the Covenant.* Of the two equivalent Hebrew terms for "covenant," Exodus favors *'edut* and Deuteronomy *berit*. Perhaps the Deuteronomist prefers *berit* because it means only "covenant," whereas *'edut* has other meanings as well, and Deuteronomy presents itself in the most explicit terms as the great text of the renewal of Israel's Covenant with God.

water did I drink. And the LORD gave me the two stone tablets, writ- 10
ten with the finger of God, and on them all the words that the LORD
spoke with you from the midst of the fire on the day of the assembly.
And it happened at the end of forty days and forty nights, the LORD 11
gave me the two stone tablets, the tablets of the Covenant. And the 12
LORD said to me, 'Arise, go down quickly from here, for your people
that you brought out of Egypt has acted ruinously, they have quickly
swerved from the way that I charged them, they have made them a
molten image.' And the LORD said to me, saying, 'I have seen this peo- 13
ple and, look, it is a stiff-necked people. Leave me be, that I may 14
destroy them and wipe out their name from under the heavens and
make you into a greater and mightier nation than they.' And I turned 15
and came down from the mountain, the mountain burning in fire, and

---

10–21. This retelling of the story of the Golden Calf, as the Israeli Bible scholar
Moshe Tzippor has justly observed, presupposes the audience's familiarity
with the more elaborate account in Exodus 32–33. It is not a consecutive
report of the incident, and some significant details are elided. It is, moreover,
Moses's first-person account, reflecting what he is told by God on the mountain and then what he sees when he descends from the summit while not
directly conveying information that he learns only afterward.

10. *all the words.* The Masoretic Text reads "as all the words" but several
ancient versions lack the initial "as."

12. *for your people that you brought out of Egypt.* As Jeffrey H. Tigay and others
have noted, God here dissociates himself from Israel—indeed, attributes even
the liberation from Egypt to Moses rather than to Himself.

13. *And the LORD said to me.* According to the biblical convention, this reiteration of the formula for introducing speech, with no indication of an intervening response by the interlocutor, suggests that Moses is dumbfounded by
the devastating news God reports to him and doesn't know what to say. Now
God proceeds beyond announcing this one act of betrayal to a general condemnation of the character of Israel and to the proposal, as in Exodus, to anni-
hilate the people and to begin again with Moses. In this first-person version,
Moses does not immediately implore God to renounce the project of destruction as he does in Exodus. Instead, he must go down and see for himself; only
afterward will he turn back to God and intercede for Israel.

16 the two tablets of the Covenant in my two hands. And I saw and, look, you offended against the LORD your God, you made you a molten calf, 17 you swerved quickly from the way that the LORD charged you. And I seized the two tablets and flung them from my two hands and smashed 18 them before your eyes. And I threw myself before the LORD as at first, forty days and forty nights—no bread did I eat nor water did I drink— for all your offense which you committed, as you had offended, to do 19 what was evil in the eyes of the LORD, to anger Him. For I was terrified of the blazing wrath with which the LORD was furious enough with 20 you to destroy you, and the LORD listened to me that time as well. And the LORD was greatly enough incensed with Aaron to destroy him, and 21 I interceded in behalf of Aaron, too, at that time. And your offense that you made, the calf, I had taken and burned it in the fire and crushed it, grinding it well, till it was fine, into dust, and I had flung its dust into

---

16. *a molten calf.* God had given Moses the more general information that Israel had made a molten image, *masekhah*. Now, descending into the camp, Moses sees that it is the molten image of a calf, *'egel masekhah*, as the report continues to be faithful to his point of view.

18. *threw myself before the* LORD. This verb of prostration, *hitnapel*, is a technical term for supplication, both in biblical and rabbinic Hebrew.

19. *the blazing wrath.* This phrase reflects a hendiadys in the Hebrew, literally "the wrath and the hot-anger."

20. *incensed with Aaron to destroy him.* In this elliptical version of the Golden Calf episode, there is no direct report that it was Aaron who presided over the making of the icon, though that narrative datum is clearly implied by the divine wrath directed against Aaron which is mentioned here. In the parallel account in Exodus, we hear nothing of Aaron's being threatened with death for his complicity. It is likely that this detail is added here in keeping with the fervor of Deuteronomy's polemic against idol worship: any leader of Israel who fostered even a semblance of such cultic defection was worthy of a death sentence.

21. *your offense that you made, the calf.* It is characteristic of Deuteronomy's anti-iconic rhetoric to turn the negative terms "offense," "abhorrence," "abomination" into epithets for idols.
     crushed it, grinding it well, till it was fine, into dust. Although the language of the parallel account in Exodus 32:20 is approximately repeated, this version

the wadi that came down from the mountain. And at Taberah and at 22
Massah and at Kibroth-Hattaavah you infuriated the LORD. And when 23
the LORD sent you from Kadesh-Barnea, saying, 'Go up and take hold
of the land that I have given to you,' you rebelled against the word of
the LORD your God and you did not trust Him, and you did not heed
His voice. You have been rebellious against the LORD from the day I 24
knew you. And I threw myself before the LORD the forty days and the 25
forty nights that I threw myself, for the LORD had intended to destroy
you. And I interceded with the LORD and said, 'My master, LORD, do 26
not bring ruin on Your people and on Your estate that you ransomed
through Your greatness, that you brought out from Egypt with a strong
hand. Remember your servants, Abraham, Isaac, and Jacob. Turn not 27
to the stiffness of this people nor to its wickedness and its offense.

---

is more thoroughgoing in detailing the process of pulverization and utter
destruction—again, in accordance with the vehemence with which Deuteronomy in general conjures up the prospect of obliterating the paraphernalia of
pagan worship. Moshe Weinfeld notes linguistic similarities to a Ugaritic
account of the destruction of Mot, the god of death.

   I had flung its dust into the wadi that came down from the mountain. This
detail is a notable departure from the story in Exodus, which has the Israelites
forced to drink the water into which the ashes of the burnt idol have been cast.
Whatever the reason for that act—both medieval and modern commentators
have proposed a trial by ordeal—the very notion of imbibing the residue of an
object of wayward worship seems to be repugnant to the Deuteronomist, who
prefers to have the residue swept away by a mountain freshet.

24. *You have been rebellious.* The "rebellious" here and the "rebellious" in verse
7 are not mere repetitions but a formal frame (*inclusio*) that defines Israel's
behavior from the Exodus down to the episode of the spies.

27. *stiffness.* The Hebrew *qeshi* could also be rendered "hardness," but in all
likelihood it is an elliptical form of *qeshi 'oref*, the quality of being stiff-necked.

28 Lest the peoples of the land to which you brought us out from there
say, "From the LORD's inability to bring them into the land of which He
spoke to them or from His hatred of them He brought them out to put
29 them to death in the wilderness." And they are Your people and Your
estate that you brought out with Your great power and Your outstretched arm.'"

---

28. *the peoples of the land.* The Masoretic Text says only "the land," which
would normally require a singular feminine verb, whereas the verb "say" here
is conjugated as a masculine plural. The Samaritan Bible, the Septuagint, and
some other ancient versions have "the peoples of," *beney*, which seems
plausible.

From the LORD's *inability . . . or from His hatred of them.* This sentence is a
citation of the parallel story in Numbers 14:15–16, but no mention is made
there of hatred. Since the two alternatives are mutually contradictory, it is best
to construe the *waw* that introduces the second alternative not as "and" but as
"or."

29. *Your people and Your estate.* The conjunction of the two nouns, 'am and
naḥalah, which we have noted before in Deuteronomy, is probably a hendiadys, suggesting "Your very own people," "the people that is Your special acquisition."

CHAPTER 10

"At that time the LORD said to me, 'Carve you two stone tablets like the first ones and come up to Me on the mountain, and you shall make you a wooden ark, that I may write on the tablets the words that were on the first tablets which you smashed, and you shall place them in the Ark.' And I made an ark of acacia wood and I carved two stone tablets like the first ones, and I went up the mountain, the two tablets in my hand. And He wrote on the tablets, like the first writing, the Ten Words that the LORD had spoken to you on the mountain from the midst of the fire on the day of the assembly, and the LORD gave them to me. And I turned and came down from the mountain and I put the tablets in the Ark that I had made, and they were there as the LORD had charged me."

And the Israelites journeyed onward from Beeroth-Bene-Jaakan to Moserah. There Aaron died and he was buried there, and Eleazar his

---

3. *And I made an ark of acacia wood.* In the parallel account in Exodus, it is Bezalel, the master craftsman, who fashions the Ark. The version here may elide Bezalel simply to keep an uninterrupted focus on Moses, or, since this is, after all, Moses's first-person, abbreviated report of the earlier events, he may deem it unnecessary to mention the chief artisan who was, in effect, his agent in carrying out God's instructions for the making of the Ark.

6. *There Aaron died.* Abraham ibn Ezra notes a connection with the previous report of Moses's intercession on behalf of Aaron after the sin of the Golden Calf. He was not killed then, but after forty years he paid the price for his complicity when he died before the people crossed into the promised land.

7 son served as priest in his stead. From there they journeyed on to Gud-
8 god and from Gudgod to Jotbath, a land of brooks of water. At that time
the LORD divided off the tribe of Levi to bear the Ark of the LORD's
Covenant, to stand before the LORD, to minister unto Him and to bless
9 in His name, until this day. Therefore Levi has had no portion and
estate with his brothers, the LORD is his estate, as the LORD your God
10 had spoken to him. "As for me, I stood on the mountain as on the first
days forty days and forty nights, and the LORD heard me that time, too,
11 He did not want to bring ruin upon you. And the LORD said to me,
'Rise, go upon the journey before the people, that they may come and
take hold of the land that I swore to their fathers to give to them.'

12 "And now, Israel, what does the LORD your God ask of you but to fear
the LORD your God, to walk in all His ways, to love Him, and to wor-
13 ship the LORD your God with all your heart and with all your being, to
keep the LORD's commands and His statutes that I charge you today for

---

8. *to stand before the LORD, to minister unto Him*. The first of these two phrases
has the idiomatic sense of "stand in attendance," so the two phrases are virtual
synonyms, deployed to underscore the role of the Levites as authorized officiants in the LORD's cult.

10. *As for me*. The initial, emphatic first-person pronoun, *we'anokhi*, here
serves to mark a transition, taking us back to Moses's narration of his time on
the mountain before God after the interruption of the unit that begins with the
death of Aaron and ends with the designation of the Levites for cultic duties.
Perhaps a contrast may be suggested between the regularized ministrations of
the Levites "standing before the LORD" in the established cult and Moses's
lonely stand before God on the mountain, desperately pleading on behalf of
Israel.

12. *And now, Israel, what does the LORD your God ask of you*. These words signal
the beginning of a new unit: after Moses's narrative report of the events at
Sinai, we have an exhortation or sermon. Several commentators have noted the
similarity between these words and those of the prophet Micah: "He has told
you, man, what is good and what the LORD requires of you—only to do justice
and the love of kindness and walking humbly with your God" (Micah 6:8).

your own good? Look, the LORD your God's are the heavens and the 14
heavens beyond the heavens, the earth and all that is in it. Only your 15
fathers did the LORD desire to love them, and He chose their seed after
them, chose you from all the peoples as on this day. And you shall 16
circumcise the foreskin of your heart, nor shall you show a stiff neck
anymore. For the LORD your God, He is the God of gods and the 17
Master of masters, the great and mighty and fearsome God Who

---

14. *the heavens and the heavens beyond the heavens*. The literal sense of the
Hebrew is "the heavens of the heavens." This structure often indicates a
superlative (as in "the Song of Songs," which is to say, the finest of songs). The
basic meaning of the phrase, then, is something like "the utmost heavens," but
it is important to retain the repetition of "heavens" in order to suggest the powerful rhetorical flourish the Hebrew achieves through repetition.

15. *Only your fathers did the LORD desire*. Deuteronomy touches here on a
fraught theological paradox: its version of Creator and creation is resoundingly
monotheistic—YHWH is no local deity but the God of all the heavens and the
earth, and yet, unaccountably, He has decided to choose this one people and
show it special affection.
     chose you. This second "chose" is added in the translation in order to clar-
ify the syntax, which otherwise would be confusing in English.

16. *you shall circumcise the foreskin of your heart*. This bold metaphoric application of the idea of circumcision to the organ of understanding and feeling
amounts to a symbolic reinterpretation of the meaning of circumcision. Here
it is not merely the sign in the flesh of Abraham's covenant with God, as
enjoined in Genesis 17, but it also betokens the removal of an impeding mem-
brane, achieving a condition of responsive openness to God's word. Paul surely
had this verse in mind when he announced the replacement of the circumcision of the flesh by the circumcision of the heart in Romans.

17. *the God of gods and the Master of masters*. Although both these epithets in
all likelihood are linguistic fossils of an earlier view in which YHWH was conceived as the most powerful god, not the only one, the plausible sense here is
a superlative (as in "the heavens of the heavens"), i.e., "supreme God and
supreme Master."
     the great and mighty and fearsome God. The imperial monotheism of
Deuteronomy often is expressed in this sort of hymnic style, and it is scarcely
surprising that this book should have been mined by later Jewish liturgy (this

18 shows no favor and takes no bribe, doing justice for orphan and widow
19 and loving the sojourner to give him bread and cloak. And you shall love
20 the sojourner, for sojourners you were in the land of Egypt. The LORD
your God you shall fear, Him you shall worship, and to Him you shall
21 cleave, and in His name you shall swear. He is your praise and He is
your God Who did with you these great and fearsome things that your
22 eyes have seen. With seventy persons did your fathers go down to
Egypt, and now the LORD your God has set you like the stars of the
heavens for multitude."

---

string of divine epithets appears at the beginning of the Amidah prayer recited
three times daily).

shows no favor and takes no bribe. There may be a causal connection
between this affirmation about God and the previous one: because He is the
absolute master of all things, He is absolutely disinterested as judge of
humankind since He is beyond all dependence on human gifts and human
attempts to curry favor.

18. doing justice for orphan and widow and loving the sojourner. Divine disinterestedness is joined with divine compassion for those in the society who are
most vulnerable to exploitation—the widow and the orphan and the resident
alien. Israel is then exhorted (verse 19) to emulate this attribute of compassion
on the grounds of its own experience as an exploited alien people in Egypt.

21. He is your praise. Probably, this means that it is Israel's glory to worship the
one great God, though the phrase could also mean that the LORD is the object
of Israel's praise.

22. With seventy persons. This concluding sentence is an orchestrated invocation of three antecedent texts: the report of Jacob's descent into Egypt with
seventy persons in Genesis 46 and in Exodus 1 and the promise to Abraham
that his seed would be multitudinous as the stars in Genesis 15.

CHAPTER 11

"And you shall love the LORD your God and keep His watch and His ₁
statutes and His laws and His commands for all time. And you ₂
shall know today that it was not with your sons who did not know
and did not see the LORD your God's chastisement, His greatness, His
strong hand and His outstretched arm, and His signs and His deeds ₃
that He did in the midst of Egypt to Pharaoh king of Egypt and to all
his land, and that He did to Egypt's force, its horses and its chariots, ₄
when He made the waters of the Sea of Reeds flood over their faces as
they pursued after them, and the LORD made them perish to this day,
and that He did for you in the wilderness until you came to this place, ₅

---

2. *it was not with your sons*. The particle '*et* that prefixes *banim*, "sons," is either
a sign of the accusative or means "with." In either case, the verb that should
go along with '*et* is absent. Rashi plausibly infers an ellipsis, the implied phrase
being "I speak today." The omission of the verb may well be because the writer
has lost track of the verb as he is caught up in the grand sweep of this sentence, which is quite uncharacteristic of nonoratorical biblical prose and one
of the longest sentences in the biblical corpus: the long chain of clauses, gathering in a headlong rush the whole story of the Exodus and the forty years of
wandering, does not reach its period until the end of verse 7.

5. *and that He did for you*. The preposition *lakhem* could mean either "for you"
or "to you." Jeffrey H. Tigay argues for the latter alternative because the following clause mentions the rebels Dathan and Abiram (see Numbers 16) who
were the target of God's devastating punishment. But the phrase "until you
came to this place" is a strong indication that the preposition refers chiefly to
God's benevolent preservation of Israel through its adversities in the wilderness. Perhaps the writer may have also wanted to exploit the ambiguity of the
preposition, quickly indicating, in a manner quite in keeping with Deutero-

6 and that He did to Dathan and to Abiram, the sons of Eliab son of
Reuben, when the earth gaped open with its mouth and swallowed
them and their households and their tents and everything existing that

7 was at their feet, in the midst of all Israel, for your own eyes have seen

8 the LORD's great deed that He has done. And you shall keep all the
command which I charge you today, so that you may be strong and
come and take hold of the land into which you are about to cross to

9 take hold of it, and so that you may long endure on the soil that the
LORD your God swore to your fathers to give to them and to their seed,

10 a land flowing with milk and honey. For the land into which you are
coming to take hold of it is not like the land of Egypt from which you
went out, where you sow your seed and water it with your foot like a

11 garden of greens. But the land into which you are crossing to take hold
of it is a land of mountains and valleys. From the rain of the heavens

---

nomic theology, that the flip side of divine protection, if Israel rebels, is divine
retribution: what God does for Israel can easily turn into what God does to
Israel.

6. *to Dathan and to Abiram*. Korah is not mentioned, probably because the
Deuteronomist is interested in the popular tradition of a rebellion of Reuben-
ites for political power rather than in the priestly account of a rebellion of the
Korahite clan for sacerdotal privilege. In Numbers 16–17 the two rebellions are
intertwined. But the absence of Korah simply stems from the fact that the
Deuteronomist seems to have been familiar with J and E but not P.

10. *water it with your foot*. It is not entirely certain what this phrase means.
Some scholars have understood it as a reference to some sort of foot pedal
used in the Egyptian system of irrigation. Because "foot water" is a biblical
euphemism for urine, it has also been proposed that this might be a derisive
reference to irrigation with urine, though it is unclear that the Egyptians actually did this. In any case, the lush Nile Valley is elsewhere figured in the Bible
as a fertile garden. The fertility of the more rugged land of Israel is more
precarious.

11. *a land of mountains and valleys*. It is thus quite unlike the flat terrain of
Egypt, and not amenable to the sort of irrigation system used in Egypt.

you will drink water—a land that the LORD your God seeks out per- 12
petually, the eyes of the LORD your God are upon it from the year's
beginning to the year's end. And it shall be, if you indeed heed My 13
commands with which I charge you today to love the LORD your God
and to worship Him with all your heart and with all your being, I will 14
give the rain of your land in its season, early rains and late, and you
shall gather in your grain and your wine and your oil. And I will give 15
grass in your field to your beast, and you shall eat and be sated. Watch 16
yourselves, lest your heart be seduced and you swerve and worship
other gods and bow to them. And the LORD's wrath flare against you, 17
and He hold back the heavens and there be no rain and the soil give
not its yield and you perish swiftly from the goodly land that the LORD
is about to give to you. And you shall set these words on your heart and 18
in your very being and you shall bind them as a sign on your hand
and they shall become circlets between your eyes. And you shall teach 19
them to your sons, to speak of them, when you sit in your house and
when you walk on the way and when you lie down and when you arise.
And you shall write them on the doorposts of your house and in your 20
gates. So that your days may be many, and the days of your sons, on the 21
soil that the LORD swore to your fathers to give to them, as the days of
the heavens over the earth. For if you indeed keep all this command 22
which I charge you to do it, to love the LORD your God to walk in all
His ways and to cleave to Him, the LORD will dispossess all these 23
nations before you and you will dispossess nations greater and mightier

---

12. *the eyes of the* LORD *your God are upon it*. Against the reiterated assertion
that "your very eyes have seen" the LORD's great acts, the eyes of the LORD will
keep this land under constant watch. The phrase is double-edged: the LORD
attends to this land in order to bestow special bounty on it, causing the fruc-
tifying rains to fall (verse 14), and the LORD scrutinizes the land, withholding
the rains when the people is unfaithful (verse 17). The geographical fact, then,
that the land of Israel is dependent on rainfall rather than on irrigation from a
central river is both a blessing and a curse. Thus the reflections on divinely
guided meteorology set the stage for the binary opposition of the mountain of
the blessing and the mountain of the curse in verse 29.

24 than you. Every place where the sole of your foot treads, yours will be, from the wilderness and the Lebanon, from the River, the Euphrates
25 River, and as far as the Hinder Sea, this will be your territory. No man will stand up before you. Your fear and your dread the LORD your God will set over the face of the land in which you tread, as He has spoken to you.

26,27 "See, I set before you today blessing and curse: the blessing, when you heed the command of the LORD your God with which I charge you
28 today; the curse, if you heed not the command of the LORD your God and swerve from the way that I charge you today, to go after other gods
29 which you did not know. And it shall be, when the LORD your God brings you to the land into which you are coming to take hold of it, I shall set the blessing on Mount Gerizim and the curse on Mount Ebal.

---

24. *the Hinder Sea*. The reference is to the Mediterranean. The basic orientation—an English term which itself means facing the east—was toward the east, so one word for east was *qedem*, before, and a (relatively rare) term for west was *'aḥaron*, "hinder," what is behind.

29. *the blessing on Mount Gerizim and the curse on Mount Ebal*. Moshe Weinfeld, ever attentive to Mediterranean parallels, notes that the Greeks as well had foundation ceremonies when they entered into new territories. These ceremonies included inscribing divine instructions on steles, building commemorative stone pillars, and offering sacrifices. All of these elements appear in the ceremony involving the two mountains that is elaborated in chapter 27. The invocations of the mountains of the blessing and of the curse here and in chapter 27 frame the code of laws that constitutes the long central section of Deuteronomy. Weinfeld proposes two reasons for the association of these mountains respectively with the blessing and with the curse: in keeping with the orientation to the east, Gerizim is on the favored right hand and Ebal on the suspect left, and Gerizim is covered with vegetation whereas Ebal is desolate. The theology of Deuteronomy is beautifully concretized in the stark opposition of these two mountains, for the book repeatedly stresses the forking alternatives of prosperity and disaster, depending on Israel's faithfulness to God's laws.

Are they not across the Jordan beyond the sunset way in the land of the   30
Canaanite in the Arabah opposite the Gilgal beside the Terebinths of
Moreh? For you are about to cross the Jordan to come to take hold of   31
the land that the LORD your God is giving you, and you shall take hold
of it and dwell in it. And you shall keep to do all the statutes and the   32
laws that I set before you today."

----

30. *the sunset way.* That is, the westward way, a road leading from trans-Jordan
westward into Canaan.

CHAPTER 12

1 "These are the statutes and the laws that you shall keep to do in the land that the LORD, God of your fathers, has given you to take hold 2 of it all the days that you live on the soil. You shall utterly destroy all the places where the nations whom you are to dispossess worshipped their gods—on the high mountains and in the valleys and 3 under every lush tree. And you shall smash their altars and shatter their sacred pillars, and their cultic poles you shall burn in fire, and the images of their gods you shall chop down, and you shall destroy their

---

2. *You shall utterly destroy all the places*. The noun *maqom* is a general term for "place," both in biblical and postbiblical Hebrew, but it also has the more specialized sense in the ancient period of "cultic site," and that is its meaning throughout this passage. There have been exhortations earlier in Deuteronomy to eradicate all vestiges of the local pagan cults, but here that imperative of iconoclasm is coupled with a revolutionary insistence on the centralization of the Israelite cult (verse 5 and repeatedly thereafter). In point of historical fact, what the Israelite religion did was to take over places of Canaanite worship and adapt them for the worship of the God of Israel. (Abraham in Genesis similarly is reported to have built altars at a series of sites that were old Canaanite places of worship.) Later, as Christianity spread through Europe and then to the New World, it would follow the same practice. For the Deuteronomist, the very existence of such local places of worship carries with it the danger of syncretism—the mingling of pagan rituals and concepts with the worship of the one God, and, especially, a leakage of the adoration of natural deities ("on the high mountains and in the valleys and under every lush tree") into the cult of YHWH. Thus, the whole apparatus of the local cults must be utterly destroyed, and instead, one central, exclusive place is to be designated for the worship of Israel's God.

name from that place. You shall not do thus for the LORD your God. 4
But to the place that the LORD your God will choose of all your tribes 5
to set His name there, to make it dwell, you shall seek it and come
there. And you shall bring there your burnt offerings and your sacrifices 6
and your tithes and your hand's donation and your votive offerings and
your freewill gifts and the firstborn of your herd and your flock. And 7
you shall eat there before the LORD your God and you shall rejoice in
all that your hand reaches, you and your households, in which the
LORD your God has blessed you. You shall not do as all that we do here 8
today, each man what is right in his eyes. For you have not come as yet 9
to the abiding estate that the LORD your God is about to give to you.

---

4. *You shall not do thus for the LORD your God.* The preposition *le* can mean
either "for" or "to." If it had the latter meaning here, it would refer to smashing idols and cultic pillars and poles, but in any case one is not supposed to
use such appurtenances in the worship of YHWH. The reference, then, is to
the idea that the LORD is not to be worshipped in local sites (and in dangerously seductive natural settings), as the Canaanites worshipped their gods, but
rather in a single central sanctuary. Compare verse 31, where *le* can only mean
"for."

5. *to set His name there, to make it dwell.* It is characteristic of Deuteronomy's
scrupulous avoidance of pagan concretizations of the deity that God is not said
to dwell in the sanctuary He will choose, as He is represented repeatedly
doing in Exodus, but rather an intermediary agency, God's name, dwells there.
   you shall seek it. For clarity's sake, "it" is added.

7. *And you shall eat there before the LORD.* The burnt offerings were wholly consumed by fire on the altar, but in the case of other categories of sacrifice, only
some sections of the animal were burned and the rest were reserved for the
person bringing the sacrifice to be consumed in a sacred feast, after the sacrifice proper, "before the LORD."
   in all that your hand reaches. Still more literally, "all the reach of your hand."
The phrase *mishlah-yad* clearly refers to "undertakings," and to the material
yield of the undertaking. Appropriately, the phrase has come to mean "vocation" in modern Hebrew.

9. *the abiding estate.* The Hebrew is a hendiadys, *hamenuhah wehanahalah*, literally, "the haven [or the rest] and the estate," meaning secure, permanent
inheritance in the land.

10 And you shall cross the Jordan and dwell in the land that the LORD your
God is about to grant you in estate and He will give you abiding haven
11 from all your enemies around, and you shall dwell securely. And it will
be, the place that the LORD your God will choose in which to make His
name dwell, there you shall bring all that I charge you, your burnt offerings and your sacrifices, your tithes and your hand's donation and all
12 your choice votive offerings that you vow to the LORD. And you shall
rejoice before the LORD your God, you and your sons and your daughters and your male slaves and your slavegirls and the Levite who is
13 within your gates, for he has no portion or estate with you. Watch yourself, lest you offer up your burnt offerings in any place that you see.
14 Rather, in the place that the LORD will choose, in one of your tribes,
there you shall offer up your burnt offerings and there you shall do all
15 that I charge you. Only wherever your appetite's craving may be you
shall slaughter and eat meat, according to the blessing of the LORD your
God that He has given you within all your gates. The unclean and the

---

10. *grant you in estate . . . give you abiding haven*. The writer now plays with the
hendiadys introduced in the previous verse by breaking it apart and using each
of the roots as a verb instead of the two nouns. "Abiding" is added in the translation to "give haven" (*hiniaḥ*) in order to preserve this play on the previous
word pair.

12. *the Levite . . . for he has no portion or estate with you*. The Levites, as we are
repeatedly reminded, had no tribal territory. As long as the countryside was
dotted with local shrines, most Levites had a source of living close to hand,
officiating at the local cult and taking their share of the offerings brought by
the worshippers. One may infer that the centralization of the cult between the
late eighth century B.C.E. (Hezekiah's reform) and the late seventh century
(Josiah's reform) created a serious economic problem for Levites not employed
in the Jerusalem temple, and so they are included here in the category of vulnerable people who need to be the object of benefaction. The phrase "within
your gates" means "wherever you may live," and so refers to Levites outside of
Jerusalem.

15. *wherever your appetite's craving may be*. The versatile Hebrew *nefesh* ("life,"
"life-breath," "person," and also an intensive form of the personal pronoun) is
most plausibly construed here as "appetite," the sense it has in Psalms 107:9.
The other problem in understanding this phrase turns on the meaning of the

clean shall eat it, like the deer or like the gazelle. Only the blood you   16
shall not eat. On the earth you shall spill it like water. You shall not be   17
able to eat within your gates the tithe of your grain and of your wine
and of your oil and the firstborn of your herd and your flock and all your
votive offerings that you vow and your freewill gifts and your hand's
donation. But before the LORD your God you shall eat it in the place   18
that the LORD your God will choose, you and your son and your daughter and your male slave and your slavegirl and the Levite who is in
your gates, and you shall rejoice before the LORD your God in all that
your hand reaches. Watch yourself, lest you abandon the Levite all   19

---

initial particle *b^e*. Most translators understand it to refer to the degree of craving (Richard Elliott Friedman: "As much as your soul desires") or to the fre-
quency of the craving (New Jewish Publication Society: "whenever you
desire"). But *b^e* (primary meaning, "in") is more naturally a locative, and for an
indication of degree one would expect *k^e*, "as." The noun phrase itself, *'awat
nefesh*, suggests intense appetite, and the instructions that follow have to do
chiefly with place—that henceforth the Israelites will be allowed to slaughter
and eat meat wherever they happen to be, though sacrificial slaughter can take
place only on the central altar.

you shall slaughter and eat meat. The verbal root *z-b-ḥ* means both "to
slaughter" and "to sacrifice" because in ancient religion the two acts were
inseparable. But now that sacrifice at local shrines has been abolished, some
mechanism must be established to enable the Israelites to eat meat even when
they cannot come to the central place of worship. What follows are innovative
regulations for the practice that the rabbis called *sheḥitat hulin*, "secular
slaughter."

The unclean and the clean shall eat it. In the case of sacrificial meals, only
the ritually clean are allowed to partake. For secular meals the restriction does
not apply.

like the deer or like the gazelle. The one category of meat always permitted
outside the cult was game, neither deer nor gazelle being among the animals
specified for sacrificial use. Now, animals otherwise devoted to the cult
(sheep, bulls, goats, rams) may be eaten without sacrifice, just as game is
eaten.

16. *On the earth you shall spill it like water*. The draining of the blood on the
ground stands in contrast to sacrificial slaughter, in which the blood, as part of
the ritual, is splashed on the altar by the officiant. The reason for the draining
of the blood is spelled out in verse 23.

20 your days on your soil. When the LORD your God enlarges your territory as He has spoken to you, and you say, 'Let me eat meat,' when
your appetite craves eating meat, wherever your appetite's craving may
21 be, you shall eat meat. Should the place be far away from you that the
LORD your God will choose to set His name there, you shall slaughter
from your herd and from your flock that the LORD has given you as I
have charged and you shall eat within your gates wherever your
22 appetite's craving may be. Yet, as the deer or as the gazelle is eaten,
thus you shall eat it, the unclean and the clean together shall eat it.
23 Only be strong not to eat the blood, for the blood is the life and you
24 shall not eat the life with the meat. You shall not eat it. On the earth
25 you shall spill it like water. You shall not eat it, so that it will go well
with you and with your sons when you do what is right in the eyes of
26 the LORD. Only your holy things that you will have and your votive
offerings you shall bear and come to the place that the LORD will
27 choose. And you shall do your burnt offerings, the meat and the blood,
on the altar of the LORD your God, and the blood of your sacrifices shall
be spilled on the altar of the LORD your God, but the meat you may eat.
28 Watch and heed all these things that I charge you, so that it will go well
with you and with your sons after you for all time when you do what is
29 good and right in the eyes of the LORD your God. When the LORD your
God cuts off before you the nations which you are coming there to dis-

---

23. *Only be strong not to eat the blood.* The use of the verb "be strong" in conjunction with the prohibition against the consumption of blood is unusual,
something Rashi registers by offering two opposite interpretations (that it is
tempting to consume blood, that it is necessary to make a special effort even
for a prohibition of something altogether unappetizing). Given the repeated
emphasis on strong appetite, one may infer that the writer assumed that the
consumption of blood had some special attraction, either because of its appeal
to the palate (as, say, in blood sausages) or because, as the end of this verse
may suggest, there was a fetishistic belief that imbibing the blood meant
imbibing the life-force of the slaughtered beast.

possess, and you dispossess them and dwell in their land, watch your- 30
self, lest you be ensnared after them, after they are destroyed before
you, and lest you seek out their gods, saying, 'How do these nations
worship their gods? Let me, too, do thus.' You shall not do thus for the 31
LORD your God, for every abhorrence of the LORD that He hates they
have done for their gods. For even their sons and their daughters they
burn in fire to their gods.

"Everything which I charge you, that shall you keep to do. You shall not 13:1
add to it and you shall not subtract from it."

---

30. *lest you be ensnared after them.* The slightly odd preposition might simply
mean "by them," or it could suggest, as it sometimes does elsewhere, "following them," taking up their practices.

31. *You shall not do thus for the LORD your God.* This echo of verse 4 marks a
formal *inclusio* structure that frames this whole unit. It begins and now ends
with an injunction to avoid all contact with the practices of the local pagan
cults. To the paraphernalia of idol worship mentioned at the beginning the
writer here adds a moral abomination of pagan religion—child sacrifice. There
is at least some archeological evidence that child sacrifice was practiced
among the West Semites, and at the Phoenician colony of Carthage in North
Africa large numbers of urns have been unearthed containing the charred
bones of children.

13.1. This verse clearly belongs at the end of this unit as a concluding summary, a placement recognized in the New King James Version, which lists it as
verse 32 of chapter 12. Most Hebrew Bibles, however, set it as the first verse
of chapter 13.

CHAPTER 13

2 "Should there arise in your midst a prophet or a dreamer of dreams
3 and give you a sign or a portent, and the sign and the portent
which he speaks to you come about—saying, 'Let us go after
4 other gods that you do not know and worship them,' you shall not heed
the words of that prophet or of that dreamer of dreams, for the LORD

---

2. *a dreamer of dreams.* This would be a designation for a person who claims to have received a revelation from the deity through the medium of a dream. The Hebrew phrase *ḥolem ḥalom* does not mean a "diviner" or "interpreter of dreams," as some scholars have claimed. The term for someone with the special skill of deciphering the meaning of otherwise enigmatic dreams is *poter ḥalom*, as in the Joseph story.

3. *and the sign and the portent which he speaks to you come about.* This clause creates a certain theological problem because it suggests that the false prophet may have supernatural powers. Abraham ibn Ezra tries to solve the difficulty by proposing that the "sign" is merely a demonstrative gesture on the part of the prophet, as when Isaiah has his servants go naked and barefoot and gives his sons symbolic names. But the term "come about" argues for the fulfillment of some prediction. The idea stated in the next verse that God is "trying" Israel may intimate that He has allowed the fulfillment of the prediction as an element of the trial: even if the false prophet can show you a portent, the falsehood of his message should be evident in his urging you to worship other gods.
Let us go after other gods that you do not know. As Jeffrey H. Tigay aptly observes, this is "not a literal quotation of the prophet's proposal but Moses's pejorative paraphrase of it." To generalize the underlying stylistic principle, in Deuteronomy the boundaries between quoted speech and the framing speech of Moses are fluid (much more so than the boundaries between quoted speech and narrator's discourse elsewhere in the Bible) because everything here is thematically and structurally dominated by Moses's oratory: He quotes others

your God will be trying you to know whether you love the LORD your
God with all your heart and with all your being. After the LORD your   5
God shall you go and Him shall you fear and His commands shall you
keep and His voice shall you heed and Him shall you worship and to
Him shall you cleave. And that prophet or that dreamer of dreams shall   6
be put to death, for he has spoken falsehood against the LORD your God
Who brought you out of the land of Egypt and Who ransomed you from
the house of slaves, to thrust you from the way on which the LORD your
God charged you to go, and you shall root out the evil from your midst.
Should your brother, your mother's son, or your son or your daughter or 7
the wife of your bosom or your companion who is like your own self
incite you in secret, saying, 'Let us go and worship other gods' that you
did not know, neither you nor your fathers, from the gods of the peo-   8
ples that are all around them, the ones close to you or the ones far from
you from the end of the earth to the end of the earth, you shall not   9
assent to him and you shall not heed him and your eye shall not spare
him and you shall not pity and shall not shield him. But you shall   10
surely kill him. Your hand shall be against him first to put him to death

---

but readily bends the quotations to his own didactic purpose, quickly slipping
from the words of others to his own words. The example here of verses 7–8 is
even more extreme.

5. *After the* LORD *your God . . . Him shall you fear and His commands shall you
keep . . . Him shall you worship . . . to Him shall you cleave.* This sentence is a
vivid example of the vigorous hortatory style of Deuteronomy. God, or a personal pronoun standing in for God, is emphatically set at the head of each
brief clause, and the clauses themselves are a series of overlapping interlocked
imperatives.

6. *spoken falsehood.* This is the clear meaning of *diber sarah*, as parallel uses in
Jeremiah 28:16, 29:32, and in Isaiah 59:13 demonstrate, two of them coupling
the unusual *sarah* with the more common *sheqer*, "lie."

10. *But you shall surely kill him.* Your hand shall be against him first. The vehemence of this is startling, especially because the Hebrew does not use the
word for judicial execution, *hamit*, "put to death," but *harog*, "kill." No mention is made of a process of judicial review, as in the case of the town seduced

11 and the hand of all the people last. And you shall stone him and he
shall die, for he sought to thrust you away from the LORD your God who
12 brought you out of the land of Egypt, from the house of slaves. And all
Israel will hear and see, and they will not do this evil thing again in your
13 midst. Should you hear in one of your towns which the LORD your God
14 is about to give you to dwell there, saying, 'Worthless men have come
out from your midst and they have thrust away the inhabitants of their
town, saying, "Let us go and worship other gods" that you do not know.'
15 And you seek and inquire and ask well, and, look, the thing is true and
16 well-founded, this abhorrence has been done in your midst, you shall
surely strike down the inhabitants of that town by the edge of the
sword, putting it under the ban, it and everything in it, and its beasts,

---

into idolatry (verse 15). The impelling idea seems to be that in cases of incitement to idolatry, a person must overcome all natural feelings of compassion
(verse 8), even for his own offspring, for a best friend, for a brother (who came
out of the same womb), or for the woman who has shared his bed, and carry
out justice at once. In the three successive instances here of incitement to
idolatry, there is a progression in the enormity of the crime—from an individual who is a false prophet to the betrayal by close kin or beloved friend to the
seduction by a paganizing group of an entire community.

11. *And you shall stone him.* The verb by itself, *saqol*, means "to stone," but here
added to it is *ba'avanim*, "with stones," in a gesture of rhetorical emphasis.

16. *strike down the inhabitants of that town . . . putting it under the ban.* This
command of implacable, total destruction made the sages of the Talmud (Sanhedrin 10:4–5 and elsewhere) sufficiently uneasy that they proposed a whole
series of preconditions to the implementation of the injunction which rendered it nearly impossible to carry out. As in the case of the total destruction
of the Canaanite peoples, there is no evidence that the Israelites went about
wiping out their own cities when they discovered pagan practices, so this grim
law, too, must be understood as "utopian." It is, in other words, a legal expression of the unswerving antipagan polemic that animates Deuteronomy. The
eighteenth-century North African Hebrew commentator Or Hayim shows sensitivity to the darkest aspect of this law: its human executors, he observes, are
liable to become addicted to the frenzy of bloodthirstiness unleashed in the
massacre, captive to the "power of cruelty." (Or Hayim cites the murderous
Islamic sect of Assassins as an example.) He then imaginatively cites the

by the edge of the sword. And all its booty you shall collect in the 17
middle of its square and burn in fire—the town and all its booty—
altogether to the LORD your God, and it shall be an everlasting mound,
it shall never be rebuilt. And nothing shall cling to your hand from the 18
ban, so that the LORD may turn back from His blazing wrath and give
you compassion, and be compassionate to you and make you multiply
as He swore to your fathers, when you heed the voice of the LORD your 19
God to keep His commands with which I charge you today, to do what
is right in the eyes of the LORD your God."

---

phrase "give you compassion" in the verse 18 to argue that God's compassion
for Israel will be to save them, even in these terrible circumstances, from the
"power of cruelty" and to imbue them with compassion. This is scarcely a
likely historical scenario of mob psychology, but it is at least an exegetical
effort to conceive an ethos beyond bloodlust even in the midst of this theological militancy.

17. *an everlasting mound*. The Hebrew noun *tel* specifically designates the
mound of piled-up earth under which the remnants of a destroyed city are
buried. It has been appropriately adopted as a technical term by archeologists.

CHAPTER 14

"Y ou are children to the LORD your God. You shall not gash yourselves nor shall you make a bald place on the front of your head
for the dead. For you are a holy people to the LORD your God, and
you has the LORD chosen to be a treasured people to Him of all the
peoples that are on the face of the earth.

"You shall eat no abhorrent thing. These are the beasts that you may
eat: ox, lamb of sheep and lamb of goat, gazelle and deer and roebuck
and bison and antelope and mountain sheep, and every beast that has
hooves, that has hooves split in two, bringing up the cud; among beasts,

---

1. *You shall not gash yourselves nor shall you make a bald place on the front of
your head.* The consensus is that these were pagan rituals of mourning, specifically prohibited because they involved disfiguring the mourner's body, which
as the body of one of God's "children," should be guarded in its integrity. Ritual gashing is attested in the comportment of the Baal priests on Mount
Carmel in 1 Kings 18, though there the intention seems to be not mourning but
sympathetic magic (encouraging the descent of divine fire by spilling blood).
The Ugaritic texts do reflect gashing as a gesture of mourning. The bald place
"on the front of your head" (literally, "between your eyes") appears to be some
sort of tonsure, something that Abraham ibn Ezra, with an eye to his Christian neighbors, registers when he observes, "like the practice of the gentiles to
this day."

6. *hooves split in two, bringing up the cud.* Although the governing principles
that determine what creatures may not be eaten are not entirely consistent,
there appears to be a recoil from consuming land animals or birds that are
predators or scavengers. Thus, permissible animals must have genuine, split
hooves and nothing resembling claws, and they must be ruminants, as a kind
of guarantee that they are not carnivores. Some structuralist critics have pro-

it you may eat. But this you shall not eat from those that bring up the 7
cud or have a split hoof: the camel and the rock-badger and the hare,
for they bring up the cud but they have no hoof. They are unclean for
you. And the pig, for it has a hoof but no cud. It is unclean for you. Of 8
their flesh you shall not eat and their carcass you shall not touch. This 9
you may eat of all that is in the water: whatever has fins and scales you
may eat. And whatever has no fins and scales you shall not eat. It is 10
unclean for you. Every clean bird you may eat. And this you shall not 11,12
eat of them: the eagle and the vulture and the black vulture, and the 13
kite and the falcon and the buzzard according to its kind, and every 14
raven according to its kind, and the ostrich and the nighthawk and the 15
seagull and the hawk according to its kind, the horned owl and the puff 16
owl and the hoot owl, and the pelican and the fish hawk and the cor- 17
morant, and the stork and the heron according to its kind and the 18
hoopoe and the bat. And every swarming thing among winged creatures 19

---

posed that the Hebrews also had a strong predilection to keep things in neat
categories: a sea creature without fins or scales seemed to them, it is inferred,
a violation of appropriate categories and hence was forbidden. In any event, as
many commentators have noted, the dietary restrictions, coming as they do
after the prohibition of two prominent pagan mourning practices, are part of a
program for separating Israel from the surrounding peoples.

7–19. *the camel and the rock-badger and the hare.* In the long list that follows
of prohibited animals, once we get beyond the camel and the hare and the pig
(the rock-badger being a more questionable identification), it should be kept
in mind that most of the English equivalents are approximations or guesses
that reflect the tradition of translations more than ancient Hebrew zoology. In
verse 16, for example, the three birds mentioned, *kos, yanshuf,* and *tinshemet,*
may indeed be different kinds of owls (though even that is not entirely certain
for all three), but no one really knows precisely what they are. The present
translation improvises its own guesses, in the case of the second and third
terms guided by the suggestion of breathing, puffing, or emitting some sort of
respiratory sound in the Hebrew verbal roots of *yanshuf* and *tinshemet* (puff
owl and hoot owl). Other translations represent these as "the little owl, the
great owl, and the white owl," with scant evidence for the choices.

12. *And this you shall not eat.* The list comprises birds of prey and scavengers.

20 is unclean for you. They shall not be eaten. Every clean winged crea-
21 ture you may eat. You shall not eat any carcass. To the sojourner within
your gates you may give it and he may eat it, or sell it to a foreigner, for
you are a holy people to the LORD your God. You shall not boil a kid in
its mother's milk.

22 "You shall surely tithe all the yield of your seed that comes out in the
23 field year after year. And you shall eat before the LORD your God in the
place that He chooses to make His name dwell the tithe of your grain,
of your wine, and of your oil, and the firstborn of your cattle and your
sheep, so that you may learn to fear the LORD your God at all times.
24 And should the way be too much for you, for you cannot carry it, as the
place that the LORD your God chooses to make His name dwell there

---

21. *You shall not eat any carcass.* The Hebrew *nevelah* refers to the body of an
animal that has died of natural causes.

To the sojourner . . . you may give it. The resident alien, generally unable to
possess real property, is thought of here, as elsewhere in Deuteronomy, as economically disadvantaged and hence an appropriate object of charity. The foreigner, by contrast, is only a temporary resident or wayfarer and may bring with
him economic resources from elsewhere, so he is assumed to be in a position
to pay for the carcass.

You shall not boil a kid in its mother's milk. See the comment on the identical prohibition in Exodus 23:19.

22. *You shall surely tithe.* Ibn Ezra proposes a link with the preceding section
in regard to prohibited eating. The dietary restrictions forbid categories of animals, sea creatures, and birds; the Israelites are forbidden to eat the tithes
except "in the places that He chooses," that is, in the central temple.

23. *so that you may learn to fear the LORD your God.* This clause is most plausibly linked with the overriding principle of the centralization of the cult: the
pilgrim, by experiencing the cult at the central sanctuary and by contact with
the priestly caste there, will learn to fear the LORD.

24. *And should the way be too much for you.* The centralization of the cult
entailed a practical difficulty, which was the problem of carrying large quantities of agricultural produce over long distances to the central sanctuary. The
solution (verse 25) is to convert the tithed produce into easily portable silver,

will be too far for you, when the LORD blesses you, then you shall give 25
in silver, and you shall bundle the silver in your hand and you shall go
to the place that the LORD your God chooses. And you may give the sil- 26
ver for whatever your appetite craves—cattle and sheep and wine and
strong drink and whatever your appetite may prompt you to ask—and
you shall eat there before the LORD your God, and you shall rejoice, you
and your household. And the Levite who is within your gates, you shall 27
not abandon him, for he has no share and estate with you. At the end 28
of three years you shall take out all the tithe of your yield in that year
and set it down within your gates. And the Levite shall come, for he has 29
no share and estate with you, and the sojourner and the orphan and the
widow who are within your gates, and they shall eat and be sated, so
that the LORD your God may bless you in all the work of your hand that
you do."

---

which then could be reconverted at the sanctuary site into either comestible
animals or agricultural produce. (Hence the pragmatic need for money chang-
ers in the temple.)

the LORD *blesses you.* As very often, this phrase refers to material bounty, a
specific meaning that the context makes clear.

25. *bundle.* The weighted pieces of silver were carried in a leather bundle or
purse (*tsror*, the noun cognate with the verb used here). The husband of the
wayward wife in Proverbs 7 goes off on a long trip having taken "the bundle of
silver" (*tsror hakesef*) in his hand.

the silver. Coins did not come into use in ancient Israel until the Second
Temple period, so the reference is not to money but to readily exchangeable
weights of silver.

26. *may prompt you to ask.* More literally, "may ask you." In any case, the silver
equivalent of 10 percent of the annual agricultural yield would give the pilgrim
a great deal of money to spend in a few days, and thus enable him to purchase
abundantly whatever he craved.

CHAPTER 15

1,2 "At the end of seven years you shall make a remission. And this is the matter of the remission, the remitting by every loan holder, who holds a loan against his fellow man, he shall not dun his fellow man and brother, for a remission to the Lord has been proclaimed. 3 The foreigner you may dun, but that of yours which is with your brother

---

1. At *the end of seven years*. The Hebrew does not say "at the end of the seventh year" because the phrase, as Abraham ibn Ezra notes, is meant to indicate the beginning of the year that marks the end of the seven-year cycle.

a remission. The parallel passage in Exodus 23:10–11 has a verb with the root *sh-m-t* but not, as here, the noun *shemitah*. The basic meaning of the root is "to release," "to let slip out of one's hand." In the strictly agricultural context of Exodus 23, it was simply translated as "let it go," referring to the cultivated land. Deuteronomy's *shemitah* regulations, on the other hand, address a new urban and mercantile reality, and the focus of the law is consequently on debts rather than on allowing the land to lie fallow. For this business-oriented regulation, a more abstract English equivalent such as "remission" is required.

2. *dun*. The Hebrew verb is the same one reflected in the term for "taskmasters" in Exodus.

his fellow man and brother. These are equivalent terms here, and the one that will be favored through the rest of the passage is "brother." That word focuses the social ethic of Deuteronomy: whatever the social and economic differences, all Israelites should regard each other as brothers. The collocation "your brother the pauper" is especially telling in this regard—however wretched the pauper, he is still your brother.

your hand shall remit. Yet, there will be no pauper among you, for the 4
LORD will surely bless you in the land which the LORD your God is
about to give you in estate to take hold of it—only if you surely heed 5
the voice of the LORD your God to keep to do all this command that I
charge you today. For the LORD your God has blessed you as He spoke 6
to you, and you shall lend to many nations but you yourself shall not
borrow, and you shall dominate many nations, but you they shall not
dominate. Should there be a pauper among you, from one of your 7
brothers within one of your gates in your land that the LORD your God
is about to give you, you shall not harden your heart and clench your
hand against your brother the pauper. But you shall surely open your 8
hand to him and surely lend to him enough for his want that he has.

---

4. *there will be no pauper among you.* This extravagant statement, which may
have fueled the imaginations of some later social revolutionaries, seems flatly
contradicted, first, by "Should there be a pauper among you" (verse 7) and
then, more blatantly, by "For the pauper will not cease from the midst of the
land" (verse 11). Ibn Ezra neatly catches the utopian character of the pronouncement: "Know that I charged you not to dun your brother—there would
be no need for this if all Israel or most of them would heed God's voice, then
there would be no pauper among you who needs you to lend to him." As a realist, ibn Ezra registers the unlikelihood that a majority of the people will ever
actually heed God's words, hence "the pauper will not cease from the midst of
the land."

6. *you shall lend to many nations.* The Hebrew verb indicates a loan given
against security, with the pawned object of worth thus placing the borrower in
a palpable relationship of dependence to the lender.
   dominate. In the present context, the force of the verb *mashol* is obviously
economic rather than political domination.

7. *harden your heart.* The more literal sense is "strengthen your heart." Though
this is not one of the verbs used for Pharaoh's heart in the Exodus story, the
meaning is virtually the same.
   clench your hand. The language of this chapter focuses on the hand as the
synecdochic image of agency: debts are remitted when the hand releases or
lets them go (see verse 3); parsimony toward the indigent is figured as a
clenching tight of the hand, generosity as an opening of the hand.

9 Watch yourself, lest there be in your heart a base thing, saying, 'The seventh year, the year of remission is near,' and you look meanly at your brother the pauper and you do not give to him, and he call to the LORD

10 against you and it be an offense in you. You shall surely give to him, and your heart shall not be mean when you give to him, for by virtue of this thing the LORD your God will bless you in all your doings and in all

11 that your hand reaches. For the pauper will not cease from the midst of the land. Therefore I charge you, saying, 'You shall surely open your hand to your brother, to your poor, and to your pauper, in your land.'

12 Should your Hebrew brother or sister be sold to you, he shall serve you six years, and in the seventh year you shall send him out from you free.

13 And when you send him out from you, you shall not send him out

14 empty-handed. You shall surely provide him from your flock and from your threshing floor and from your winepress, as the LORD your God

15 has blessed you, you shall give to him. And you shall remember that you were a slave in Egypt and the LORD your God ransomed you.

16 Therefore I charge you with this thing today. And it shall be, should he

---

9. *a base thing.* Elsewhere, the Hebrew *bliya'al* is translated as "worthless," but the present context requires something like "base."

you look meanly. Literally, "your eye is evil."

10. *your heart shall not be mean.* Literally, "your heart shall not be evil."

12. *your Hebrew brother or sister.* Unlike the regulations concerning Hebrew slaves in Exodus 21, where distinctions are made between the sexes, evidently because the case in view is one in which the young woman has been sold into slavery with the intention of her becoming a concubine, here male and female slaves are regulated by an identical set of laws. Grammatically, masculine gender remains dominant, so even though both men and women have been mentioned, the text goes on to speak of "he" (as does this translation) representing both.

14. *You shall surely provide him.* The notion of what amounts to severance pay at the end of the period of indentured servitude is an innovation of Deuteronomy, again reflecting its humanitarian social ethos.

as the LORD your God has blessed you. That is, the bounty bestowed on the freed slave will be proportionate to the material "blessings" enjoyed by the slave owner.

say to you, 'I will not go out from you,' for he loves you and your household, as it is good for him with you, you shall take an awl and put it   17
through his ear and into the door, and he shall be your perpetual slave.
And to your slavegirl, too, thus you shall do. Let it not seem hard in   18
your eyes when you send him out from you free, for twice the value of
a hired man he served you six years, and the LORD your God will bless
you in all that you do. Every firstborn that is born in your herd or in   19
your flock, the male you shall consecrate to the LORD your God. You
shall not work the firstborn of your oxen nor shall you shear the firstborn of your flock. Before the LORD you shall eat it, year after year, in   20
the place that the LORD chooses, you and your household. And should   21
there be a defect in it, lameness or blindness or any bad defect, you
shall not sacrifice it to the LORD your God. Within your gates you may   22
eat it, the unclean and the clean together, like the gazelle and like the
deer. Only its blood you shall not eat. On the ground you shall spill it   23
like water."

---

17. *put it through his ear and into the door.* In Exodus 21:6, this ceremony is performed when the slave is made to "approach the gods" (or "God"), but the
frame of reference now is secular. If the phrase in Exodus refers to a local
sanctuary, the programmatic elimination of that institution in Deuteronomy
would necessitate the secularization of the ceremony as a practical matter. The
meaning, symbolic or otherwise, of the ceremony has been variously interpreted (see the first comment on Exodus 21:6).

    perpetual slave. At least according to rabbinic exegesis, even this condition
of servitude was abrogated in the jubilee year.

18. *twice the value of a hired man.* The word rendered as "value" usually means
"pay"—logically, what the employer would render to the hired man rather than
what he would extract from the laborer. But the most plausible sense is that a
paid worker over a period of six years would cost his employer twice what the
employer would have to lay out for the acquisition and upkeep of an indentured servant.

21. *lameness or blindness.* The Hebrew literally says "lame or blind." These
physical impairments render the animal unfit as an offering to God, but since
they do not necessarily involve any disease that might taint the flesh of the animals, the beasts are still fit for strictly secular consumption, "like the gazelle
and like the deer," which involves no restriction of ritual purity.

CHAPTER 16

¹ K eep the month of Abib, and you shall make a Passover to the Lᴏʀᴅ your God, for in the month of Abib the Lᴏʀᴅ your God brought ² you out of Egypt in the night. And you shall sacrifice a Passover offering to the Lᴏʀᴅ your God, sheep and cattle, in the place that the ³ Lᴏʀᴅ chooses to make His name dwell there. You shall not eat unleavened stuff with it. Seven days you shall eat with it flatcakes, poverty's bread, for in haste you did go out from the land of Egypt; so that you will remember the day of your going out from Egypt all the days of your ⁴ life. And no leavening will be seen with you in all your territory seven days, and nothing of the meat that you slaughter in the evening shall be

---

1. *Keep the month of Abib.* As noted in the commentary on Exodus, Abib, the month that corresponds to March–April, means "new grain" (in modern Hebrew, it comes to mean "spring"). The rabbis took the name as a warrant for introducing leap months in order to keep the lunar calendar in phase with the solar calendar. One could infer that some rudimentary mechanism of calendric correction was in place even in the early biblical period, or else the month of new grain would have fallen sometimes in midwinter, sometimes in late summer or fall. Unlike other biblical texts on the festivals, the law here does not specify which day in Abib marks the beginning of the festival—unless one interprets "month" as "new moon," a construction found among some ancient and modern commentators.

2. *sheep and cattle.* The option of cattle is new, perhaps reflecting a more sedentary form of animal husbandry than the earlier nomadic model.

3. *poverty's bread.* The noun *'oni* has the basic meaning of a lowly condition, and so it could equally refer to poverty, affliction, or debasement.

left overnight on the first day till the morning. You shall not be able to 5
sacrifice the Passover offering within one of your gates that the LORD
your God is about to give you. But to the place that the LORD your God 6
chooses to make His name dwell, there shall you sacrifice the Passover
offering in the evening, as the sun comes down, the hour of your coming out of Egypt. And you shall cook and eat in the place that the LORD 7
your God chooses, and you shall turn in the morning and go to your

---

5. *You shall not be able to sacrifice . . . within one of your gates.* This reiterated
emphasis in connection with Passover is understandable. Passover, unlike the
other festivals, was primarily a home ritual: each household sacrificed a
paschal lamb, and, at least in the earliest period, apotropaic blood was probably smeared on the lintel. Deuteronomy thus must take pains to relocate even
this domestic festival in the central sanctuary. The reiteration of the obligation
to go "to the place that the LORD chooses" contributes to the lengthiness of the
Passover section in comparison with the sections on the other two pilgrim festivals, though critical scholarship has also detected here a successive layering
into a single law of injunctions regarding a passover (*pesaḥ*) and injunctions
regarding a festival of flatbread (*matsot*), once separate observances.

6. *the hour of your coming out of Egypt.* Most traditional Hebrew commentators understand *moʿed* in its frequent sense of "fixed season," i.e., the date in
the month of Abib on which Israel left Egypt. The context, however, with the
stress on the time of sunset suggests that here the term means hour of the day.

7. *cook.* In other contexts, *bashel* means "boil," a mode of preparing the meat
prohibited by the Passover laws in Exodus, which insists that the meat be fire-
roasted. This may be another instance in which this legislation edges the
observance away from its archaic origins, not enjoining the preparation of the
meat in the old Bedouin fashion.

you shall turn in the morning and go to your tents. Although Deuteronomy
must insist on the pilgrim obligation to celebrate at the central sanctuary, it
also recognizes it could be a hardship for these agriculturalists to have to
remain at the temple site a whole week, so the pilgrims are permitted (in contrast to later laws about travel on the festivals) to return home the morning
after the sunset sacrifice. "Your tents" is a linguistic fossil; the actual fact of
fixed settlement is reflected in the more prevalent idiom, "within your gates."

8   tents. Six days you shall eat flatbread, and on the seventh day an assembly to the LORD your God. You shall do no task.

9   Seven weeks you shall count for yourself, from when the sickle begins
10   in the standing grain you shall begin to count seven weeks. And you
shall make a festival of weeks to the LORD your God, tribute of your
hand's freewill gift that you give as the LORD your God has blessed you.
11   And you shall rejoice before the LORD your God, you and your son and
your daughter and your male slave and your slavegirl and the Levite
who is within your gates and the sojourner and the orphan and the
widow who are in your midst in the place that the LORD your God
12   chooses to make His name dwell there. And you shall remember that
you were a slave in Egypt, and you shall keep and do these statutes.

13   A festival of huts you shall make for yourself seven days, when you
14   gather in from your threshing floor and from your winepress. And you
shall rejoice in your festival, you and your sons and your daughter and

---

8. *Six days you shall eat flatbread*. One would have expected "seven." Either it
is implied that the seventh day, the day of assembly, is included in the injunction, or the number six assumes a count that begins after the first day, on
which the Passover sacrifice is offered.

9. *from when the sickle begins in the standing grain*. Although Passover is not
mentioned, other biblical texts understand the counting to begin the day after
the first day of Passover (interpreted by some Jewish sectarians to mean the
first Sunday after the first day of Passover).

10. *your hand's freewill gift*. The repeated emphasis here, addressing a population of farmers and animal husbanders that is expected to enjoy a degree of
prosperity, is on voluntary gifts to the cult in proportion to the "blessing" that
the donor has enjoyed. The Priestly predilection for lists of stipulated sacrifices is entirely absent.

13. *A festival of huts*. The holiday is called Succoth, "huts" (others, "booths,"
"tabernacles") because as a harvest festival, there was evidently a celebration
at the site of huts in the field (feasting and perhaps in the earliest period some
sort of sacrifice). The Deuteronomist preserves the popular name (in Exodus
it is called the Festival of Ingathering) but makes no reference to any obser-

your male slave and your slavegirl and the Levite and the orphan and the widow who are within your gates. Seven days you shall celebrate to 15 the LORD your God in the place that the LORD chooses, for the LORD your God will bless you in all your yield and in all the work of your hands, and you shall be only joyful.

Three times in the year every one of your males shall appear in the 16 presence of the LORD your God in the place that He chooses: on the Festival of Flatbread and on the Festival of Weeks and on the Festival of Huts, and he shall not appear in the presence of the LORD empty-handed. Each man according to the gift of his hand, according to the 17 blessing of the LORD your God that He gives him.

Judges and overseers you shall set for yourself within all your gates that 18 the LORD your God is about to give to you according to your tribes, and

---

vance in huts, following his usual line on the obligation of pilgrimage to the central sanctuary, the sole legitimate place to celebrate the festival.

15. *Seven days you shall celebrate . . . in the place that the* LORD *chooses.* Unlike on Passover, the pilgrim is to remain at the temple site for the full seven days. Perhaps this is because after the completion of the autumn harvest, which this festival marks, the farmer has no urgent further work to do right away, as he would in the spring.

16. *Three times in the year every one of your males shall appear.* This and the next verse summarize the obligation of the three pilgrim festivals. As elsewhere, the phrase *yera'eh 'et pney-YHWH,* "will appear [or be seen] in the presence of the LORD," is a euphemistic revocalization of *yir'eh,* "will see," to avoid the anthropomorphism of the notion that the celebrant sees the presence, or face, of God. It should be noted that the pilgrim obligation, with the attendant hardships of travel, falls only on the male, but, in fact, the Israelite is encouraged to include his daughter and his slavegirl as well as male dependents (verses 11, 14) in the celebration.

18. *overseers.* The term *shotrim* is used in Exodus for the Hebrew overseers or foremen of the slave population. Since the word derives from a root meaning to "write down" or "record" (compare the Aramaic *shtar,* "document"), its meaning here might be an amanuensis, secretary, or administrator working alongside the judge.

19 they shall judge the people with just judgment. You shall not skew judgment. You shall recognize no face and no bribe shall you take, for a
bribe blinds the eyes of the wise and perverts the words of the inno-
20 cent. Justice, justice shall you pursue, so that you may live and take
21 hold of the land that the LORD your God is about to give you. You shall
plant you no cultic pole, no tree, by the altar of the LORD your God
22 which you will make you. And you shall set you up no pillar which the
LORD your God hates.

---

19. *You shall recognize no face.* As in Deuteronomy 1:17, not recognizing someone you know, or about whose guilt or innocence you might have some presumption, means showing no partiality.

for a bribe blinds the eyes of the wise and perverts the words of the innocent.
As Jeffrey H. Tigay justly observes, this declaration takes the form of a semantically balanced aphorism of the sort one finds in the Book of Proverbs. The
parallel verse in Exodus 23:8 has "sighted" instead of "wise." The change here
might be a kind of explanatory gloss on the original formulation because
"sighted" could refer merely to physical sight: Deuteronomy, with its intellectualist bent, wants to stress that even the wise lose the guidance of their wisdom if they succumb to bribery (whether *shohad* is construed as bribery proper
or as a fee paid a judge for his services).

20. *Justice, justice.* Though much ingenuity has been exercised by exegetes to
explain the repetition, its function as a verbal gesture of sheer emphasis is self-
evident: justice, and justice alone, shall you pursue.

21. *no cultic pole, no tree.* The *'asherah* may have been a carved pole. Either
"tree" could be in apposition to *'asherah*, an extended meaning of the word to
include artifacts made from trees, or it could refer to the sacred trees actually
planted at the sites of Canaanite worship and reflected in the Patriarchal stories in Genesis.

22. *you shall set you up no pillar.* The patriarchs and Moses did precisely that.
One way of resolving the contradiction (e.g., Abraham ibn Ezra) is to understand
"which the LORD your God hates" as a restrictive clause—it is specifically the
pillars (*matsevot*) associated with the pagan cult that are prohibited. But Rashi's
notion of a historical development seems more likely. "For it was a practice of
the Canaanites. And even though it was favored [by God] in the period of the
Patriarchs, now He hated it because these people made it a practice of idolatry."

CHAPTER 17

You shall not sacrifice to the LORD your God a bull or a sheep in   1
which there is a defect, anything wrong, for it is an abhorrence of
the LORD, your God. Should there be found in your midst, within   2
any of your gates that the LORD your God is about to give you, a man
or a woman who does evil in the eyes of the LORD your God to trans-
gress His covenant, and they go and worship other gods and bow to   3
them, to the sun or to the moon or to any of the array of the heavens
which I did not command, and it be told to you and you hear, and you   4
inquire well and, look, the thing is true, well-founded, this abhorrence
has been done in Israel, you shall take out that man or that woman who   5
has done this evil thing to your gates, the man or the woman, and you

---

2. *within any of your gates.* The recurrent phrase "within your gates" is the characteristic designation in Deuteronomy of the local town, wherever in the country it may be, in contradistinction to the place of the central sanctuary. Its use
in the present context after "in your midst" suggests a subversive source of
pagan contamination lurking somewhere within the closed walls of the
Israelite habitations. This would be in keeping with Abraham ibn Ezra's neat
observation that "After having mentioned the cultic pole by the altar, which is
public to all, he comes back to warn the *individual* about worship of abominations."

3. *to the sun or to the moon or to any of the array of the heavens.* There are some
indications, both biblical and extrabiblical, that worship of astral deities, a
practice probably influenced by the Assyrian cult, became especially widespread in Israel during the seventh century B.C.E.
    which I did not command. This clause may be a rebuke to a popular syn-
cretistic belief that YHWH enjoined the worship of astral deities alongside
worship of Him.

6 shall stone them to death. By the word of two witnesses or three witnesses shall the one who dies be put to death, he shall not be put to
7 death by the word of one witness. The hand of the witnesses shall be
against him first to put him to death and the hand of all the people
afterward and you shall root out the evil from your midst.

8 Should the matter be beyond you to judge, between blood and blood,
between case and case, and between injury and injury, affairs of grievances within your gates, you shall arise and go up to the place that the
9 LORD your God chooses, and you shall come to the levitical priests and
to the judge who will be in those days, and you shall inquire and they

---

6. *By the word*. The literal sense of the Hebrew is "by the mouth."

7. *The hand of the witnesses shall be against him first*. The frequently made
observation concerning this stipulation that it will compel the witnesses to be
very cautious about their testimony seems rather apologetic. Why, after all,
would this opportunity to be first among the executioners not encourage a
zealot or a person with a private grudge to offer hasty or even false testimony
against the accused idolater? The law in general reflects the antipagan animus
of Deuteronomy in an effort to forge a seamless anti-idolatrous Israelite front
in which a kind of "popular justice" is carried out by the whole community.

8. *between blood and blood, between case and case, and between injury and
injury*. These three phrases are meant to mark out the whole range of nonritual
law. "Between blood and blood" clearly indicates legal disputes or "grievances"
(*rivot*) involving accusations of capital crimes, and murder in particular. The
second category, "between case and case" (*beyn din ledin*), uses a general term
for a legal case, but sandwiched in between "blood" and "injury" (*negaʿ*), it
probably refers to torts involving property or money but not bodily injury.
  go up to the place that the LORD your God chooses. This set phrase, used
throughout the book to underscore the divine authorization of the centralized
cult, here serves to authorize a complementary notion—the centralization of
judicial power in a single court of appeals instituted at the site of the one chosen sanctuary.

9. *the levitical priests*. This somewhat odd designation—in the Hebrew it is, literally, "the priests, the Levites"—is distinctive of Deuteronomy. Scholarly consensus infers that in contradistinction to the three preceding books, which
variously envisage a priestly class from a particular Levite clan officiating in

will tell you the matter of the judgment. And you shall do according to 10
the thing that they tell you from that place which the LORD chooses,
and you shall keep to all that they instruct you. According to the teach- 11
ing that they instruct you and according to the judgment that they say
to you, you shall do, you shall not swerve from the word that they tell
you right or left. And the man who acts willfully not to heed the priest 12
standing to minister there to the LORD your God, or to the judge, that
man shall die, and you shall root out the evil from Israel. And all the 13
people shall listen and fear, and they shall no longer be willful.

When you come into the land that the LORD your God is about to give 14
you, and you take hold of it and dwell in it, and you say, "Let me put a
king over me like all the nations that are around me," you shall surely 15
put over you a king whom the LORD your God chooses, from the midst
of your brothers you shall put a king over you, you shall not be able to

---

the cult while the other Levites attend to maintenance chores in the sanctuary, Deuteronomy assumes that all Levites can potentially serve as priests.

    and to the judge. The simplest construction is that judicial authority was
shared by the priests and a layman jurist.

12. *the man who acts willfully.* Some interpreters take this as a reference to the
judge in the inferior court who refuses to recognize the authority of the central court. The repetition, however, of "willful" in the next verse in connection
with "all the people" suggests that it is rather an interested party in the case
appealed, who has come to hear the opinion of the supreme court and then,
when it proves unfavorable to him, has rejected it. Capital punishment in such
a case seems severe, at least by modern standards, but the Deuteronomist,
with his usual concern for the consolidation of power in one central place, is
fearful that flouting a decision of the supreme court will undermine the whole
system.

15. *a king whom the LORD your God chooses.* Thus, by using the same phrase
for both temple and king, the Deuteronomist effects an alignment between
the election of a central sanctuary and the election of the monarch. In keeping with the premise that all this is a Mosaic prediction, the fact that the king's
political capital and the sanctuary's location are one and the same place is not
spelled out, though the seventh-century B.C.E. audience would of course have
registered the connection.

16 set over you a foreign man who is not your brother. Only let him not
get himself many horses, that he not turn the people back to Egypt in
order to get many horses, when the LORD has said to you, "You shall not
17 turn back again on this way." And let him not get himself many wives,
that his heart not swerve, and let him not get himself too much silver
18 and gold. And it shall be, when he sits on his throne of kingship, that
he shall write for himself a copy of this teaching in a book before the

---

16. *let him not get himself many horses, that he not turn the people back to Egypt.*
The many horses, the many wives, the silver and gold, are all associated with
the extravagances of royal—indeed, imperial—pomp. Egypt is linked with
horses because of its celebrated chariot corps, prominent in the Exodus story,
and because it actually was an exporter of horses in the region. (In fact, the
Israelties were slow to adopt horses for travel and for warfare through much of
the First Temple period, preferring donkeys as mounts.) But turning the people back to Egypt may refer to a condition of virtual or actual slavery to which
a profligate monarch could reduce many of his overtaxed subjects through his
expenditures.

   You shall not turn back again on this way. No explicit statement to this effect
is recorded in the preceding books, though, as the Israeli Bible scholar David
Cohen-Zemach has proposed, there may be an approximation in Exodus 13:17:
"Lest the people regret when they see battle and they go back to Egypt."

17. *that his heart not swerve.* The precedent of Solomon suggests that a large
royal harem would involve a good many politically motivated marriages with
foreign princesses, and these could lead the king astray, as in the egregious
instance of Jezebel and Ahab.

18. *he shall write for himself a copy of this teaching.* The king is to be actively
engaged in personally producing a text of the teaching (translations that
embellish the simple verb "write" by representing it as "cause to be written"
miss the point). The location of religious authority in a text, a revolutionary
idea, is made dramatically clear. "A copy of this teaching," which might also be
construed as "a repetition of this teaching," is in Hebrew *mishneh hatorah
hazo't* and is the source of one of the Hebrew names as well as the Greek name
for Deuteronomy.

   in a book. The Hebrew *sefer* refers to anything written down, from letter to
record to what we would call a book. (The form in any case, would be a scroll.)
It may well designate here the whole book of Deuteronomy, the valedictory
rehearsal of the law delivered by Moses before his death. Some interpreters

levitical priests. And it shall be with him, and he shall read in it all the   19
days of his life, so that he may learn to fear the LORD his God, to keep
all the words of this teaching and these statutes, to do them, so that his   20
heart be not haughty over his brothers and so that he swerve not from
what is commanded right or left, in order that he may long endure in
his kingship, he and his sons, in the midst of Israel.

---

want to restrict "this teaching" to the just enunciated instructions to the king,
but that seems improbable, especially since the text goes on to say, "he shall
read *in it* all the days of his life," hardly something he would do with a few
lines about keeping tight reins on the royal budget.

19. *so that he may learn to fear the* LORD *his God.* Many commentators have
cited this whole section as a demonstration that the government of ancient
Israel was in essence a constitutional monarchy. Instructional texts for kings
had many precedents both in Mesopotamia and in Egypt, as Moshe Weinfeld
points out, so that element is scarcely an innovation. If the document that the
king is enjoined here to write and repeatedly read is the entire Book of
Deuteronomy, then he has not just a set of admonitions to a monarch but a
whole complex of laws and a covenantal vision of history that are binding on
him. This does make his regime a constitutional monarchy, but one founded
on theocratic authority, the Torah or constitution to be expounded by the
priests at the central sanctuary.

20. *so that his heart be not haughty over his brothers.* The language of brotherhood, earlier used to link affluent and indigent, here links monarch and subjects. Whatever power he exerts, he is not an absolute monarch, and he does
not differ in caste or in his relation to the divine from those over whom he
rules.

in order that he may long endure in his kingship. In the precarious historical
circumstances of the seventh century B.C.E., Deuteronomy makes the continuation of the monarchy conditional on the king's faithfulness to the words of
God's teaching, just as the people's continuation in the land promised them is
conditional on this fidelity to that same teaching.

CHAPTER 18

1 The levitical priests, all the tribe of Levi, shall have no share and estate with Israel. The fire offerings of the LORD and His estate 2 they shall eat. And he shall have no estate in the midst of his broth- 3 ers. The LORD is his estate, as He spoke to them. And this shall be the priests' due from the people, from the offerers of sacrifice, whether bull or sheep: to the priest shall be given the shoulder and the cheeks and 4 the stomach. The first of your grain, your wine, and your oil, and the 5 first shearing of your flock you shall give to him. For him did the LORD your God choose of all your tribes to minister in the name of the LORD, 6 him and his sons, always. And should the Levite come from one of your gates, from all of Israel, where he sojourns, he shall come as much as his appetite craves to the place that the LORD chooses, and shall min-

---

1. *The levitical priests*. Abraham ibn Ezra, with his penchant for identifying connections between consecutive passages (what we would call editorial principles), observes that this section on priests immediately follows the section on kings: the king, who acts as supreme judicial authority, is enjoined to make himself a copy of the teaching, or Torah, which the priests make available and which is their responsibility to expound.

His estate. The reference is not entirely clear, though Rashi plausibly proposes that the term indicates categories of sacrifice other than the fire offering.

6. *he shall come as much as his appetite craves to the place that the LORD chooses*. It is possible that the polyvalent *nefesh* ("appetite") here is simply an intensive substitute for the pronoun "he," though even in this case there may be a consideration of appetite because the central sanctuary is the place where all the choice cuts of meat are available for the Levites. There is to be no hindrance for any Levite who desires to come to the central place, even though presumably the cult could not have really offered positions as officiants to all of them.

ister in the name of the Lord his God like all his brothers, the Levites, ⁊ who stand there in attendance before the Lord. Share for share they shall eat, besides his sales from the patrimony. 8

When you come into the land that the Lord your God is about to give ⁹ you, you shall not learn to do like the abhorrent things of these nations. There shall not be found among you one who passes his son or his 10 daughter through fire, a speller of charms, a soothsayer, or a diviner or

---

7. *stand there in attendance.* "In attendance" is not explicitly stated in the Hebrew but is implied by the idiom "stand before."

8. *Share for share.* All the Levites at the sanctuary are to have an equal share of the animals, even those not directly employed in the cult.
    besides his sales from the patrimony. The Hebrew is obscure. This translation assumes the following general meaning: besides what the Levite may have realized by selling off property he has inherited from his fathers (the literal meaning of the word rendered as "patrimony"). Others revocalize *mimkaraw,* "his sales," as *mimakaraw,* "from his acquaintances"—i.e., funds or property the Levite has received from personal acquaintances, on top of whatever patrimony he has. That reading looks forced.

10. *who passes his son or his daughter through fire.* It is not certain whether this phrase refers to child sacrifice, elsewhere stringently forbidden, or to some pagan dedicatory rite in which the child was passed through or, more probably, over fire without harm.
    a speller of charms, a soothsayer. The precise demarcations among these terms are no longer known, though the last three in the series all clearly refer to necromancy. Stylistically, the series may function not as a legislative list of discriminated terms but as a grand drumroll of synonyms, conveying the idea that no shape or manner of divination will be tolerated. Making predictions based on a variety of techniques, from the inspection of the liver and the entrails of a slaughtered animal to tapping the supposed knowledge of departed spirits, was a major industry throughout the ancient Near East, as thousands of divinatory texts from Egypt to Mesopotamia attest. The biblical abhorrence of these practices stems not so much from a disbelief in their efficacy as from a sense that they violate God's prerogatives by establishing a technology of the realm of spirits, which is thus assumed to be wholly susceptible to human manipulation.

11 a sorcerer, or a chanter of incantations or an inquirer of ghost or famil-
12 iar spirit or one who seeks out the dead. For whosoever does these is
    the LORD's abhorrence, and because of these abhorrent things the
13 LORD your God is about to dispossess them before you. You shall be
14 wholehearted with the LORD your God. For these nations which you
    are about to dispossess heed soothsayers and spellers of charms, but
15 you, the LORD your God has not given such. A prophet like me from
    your midst, from your brothers, the LORD will raise up. Him shall you
16 heed. As all that you asked of the LORD your God at Horeb on the day
    of the assembly, saying, "Let me not hear again the voice of the LORD
    my God, and this great fire let me not see again, that I may not die."
17,18 And the Lord said to me, "Well have they spoken. A prophet I shall
    raise up for them from the midst of their brothers, like you, and I shall
    put My words in his mouth, and he shall speak to them all that I charge
19 him. And it shall be, the man who does not heed My words which he
20 will speak in My name, I Myself will requite it of him. But the prophet
    who willfully speaks a word in My name, which I have not charged him
    to speak, or who speaks in the name of other gods, that prophet shall

---

13. *wholehearted.* The word *tamim* means "whole," "without blemish" but the
root also appears in the collocation *tom levav,* "wholeness of heart." The idea
in context is that you cannot serve God and yet keep one foot in the pagan
realm by having recourse to necromancy and divination.

15. *A prophet like me.* The envisaged future prophet is not necessarily like
Moses in stature but in function—an intermediary between Israel and God
(verses 16–17) and someone who hears and then transmits God's words.

18. *I shall put My words in his mouth.* In contrast to the sundry techniques of
deciphering arcane patterns in entrails or smoke and pronouncing incantations, the idea of prophecy is based on articulated speech—from God to
prophet and from prophet to people—and hence the verb *daber,* "speak," and
the cognate noun *davar,* "word," are insisted on again and again here.

die. And should you say in your heart, 'How shall we know the word 21
that the Lord has not spoken?' That which the prophet speaks in the 22
name of the Lord and the thing does not happen and does not come
about, this is the word that the Lord did not speak. Willfully did the
prophet speak it: you shall have no dread of him."

---

22. *the thing does not happen and does not come about*. "Thing" here is also
"word," since *davar* refers both to speech and to the referent of speech, and in
vatic contexts also has the technical sense of "oracle." This criterion for detecting false prophecy presents notorious difficulties and seems to be put forth
here chiefly out of some general sense that a true prophet will speak the truth.
The literary prophets in the biblical canon are less in the business of prediction than of castigation. The predictions they make of national catastrophe are
almost always conditioned on Israel's failure to change its ways, and the predictions of glorious national restoration in the face of imminent disaster are
always projected beyond the immediate future. It is conceivable that this text
does not have in mind literary prophets but rather prophets who addressed
mundane issues of everyday life, making short-range predictions that might be
quickly verified or falsified by the events.

CHAPTER 19

1   When the Lᴏʀᴅ your God cuts off the nations whose land the Lᴏʀᴅ
your God is about to give you and you dispossess them and dwell
2   in their towns and in their houses, three towns you shall set aside
for yourself within your land that the Lᴏʀᴅ your God is about to give you
3   to take hold of it. You shall gauge for yourself the distance and divide in
three the territory of your land that the Lᴏʀᴅ your God will grant you in
4   estate, and it will be for every murderer to flee there. And this is the case

---

1. *the Lᴏʀᴅ your God . . . the Lᴏʀᴅ your God.* It is a stylistic peculiarity of
Deuteronomy that the Lᴏʀᴅ, YHWH, very rarely occurs without "your God,"
and even the substitution of a pronoun, as here, is generally avoided. This linguistic oddity reflects the didactic emphasis of the book, tirelessly reminding
Israel that YHWH is its God.

2. *three towns you shall set aside.* This provision of towns of asylum for involuntary manslayers parallels the law in Numbers 35. For a discussion of the
concept, its connections with vendetta justice, and its ancient Near Eastern
precedents, see the commentary on that chapter. As is often the case,
Deuteronomy shifts some of the grounds of the older law, and the comments
that follow will be limited to observing those changes as well as to elucidating
verbal formulations distinctive to this passage.

3. *You shall gauge for yourself the distance.* The verb *takhin*, which commonly
means "to make ready" and, in dynastic contexts, "to found firmly," also has the
occasional sense of "measure" or "gauge," clearly the relevant sense here. "Distance" is literally "way," an extended sense of that primary term current in
many languages. It is important to survey the land in order to space the three
towns equally from the centers of population. Too great a distance to the town
of asylum could prove fatal to the fugitive (see verse 6).

of the murderer who will flee there and live—he who strikes down his fellow man unwittingly and who was not a foe to him in time past, and 5 he who comes with his fellow man into the forest to hew wood and his hand slips on the axe cutting the wood and the iron springs from the wood and finds his fellow man and he dies, he shall flee to one of these towns and live. Lest the blood avenger pursue the murderer when his 6 heart is hot and overtake him should the way be long, and strike him down mortally, when he has no death sentence since he was not his foe in time past. Therefore do I charge you, saying: three towns you shall set 7 aside for yourself. And if the LORD your God enlarges your territory, 8 as He swore to your fathers, and gives you all the land that He spoke to give to your fathers, when you keep all this command which I charge you 9 today to do it, to love the LORD your God and to go in His ways for all time, you shall add for yourself another three towns to these three.

---

5. *and the iron springs from the wood.* As Rashi observes, it is ambiguous as to whether "the wood" refers to the tree being chopped down, from which the axe inadvertently, and lethally, rebounds, or to the haft of the axe, from which the axehead breaks loose. The former possibility seems a bit more likely because otherwise the writer would be using "the wood" in quick sequence in two different senses, and the slipping of the hand on the axe suggests that the person has lost his grip, not that the axe has come apart.

6. *Lest the blood avenger pursue the murderer . . . and strike him down mortally.* In Numbers 35, if the fugitive is careless enough to be caught in flight by the blood avenger, he is considered fair game. Here, the act of vengeance outside the asylum precincts seems to be viewed as a crime, and all possible steps should be taken to prevent it. One may surmise that the text in Numbers is a half-step closer to the archaic institution of vendetta justice and concedes it just a little more legitimacy. Here, as throughout the passage, the inadvertent killer is referred to as the *rotseah,* the murderer. There is no specialized biblical term for "manslayer," but the use here of *rotseah* may be meant to convey the gravity of having taken a human life, even unintentionally.

9. *to love the LORD your God and to go in His ways.* The constant reiteration of such formulaic phrases is still another manifestation of the didactic character of this book.
  you shall add for yourself another three towns to these three. In Numbers, it is stipulated from the outset that there are to be three towns of asylum in trans-Jordan and three west of the Jordan. Harmonistic interpreters infer that

10 And innocent blood will not be shed in the midst of your land that the
    LORD your God is about to give to you in estate, and there would be
11 bloodguilt upon you. And should a man be a foe to his fellow man and
    lie in wait for him and rise against him and strike him down mortally and
12 he die, and that man flee to one of these towns, the elders of his town
    shall send and they shall take him from there and give him into the hand
13 of the blood avenger, and he shall die. Your eye shall not spare him, and
    you shall root out innocent blood from Israel, and it will go well with you.

14 You shall not push back your fellow man's landmark that the first ones
    marked out on your estate that you will inherit in the land which the

---

the three trans-Jordanian sites are implied though not stated in verse 2, so that
now we come to a grand total of nine. It is more plausible to conclude that the
present law envisages only three towns of asylum, projecting the possibility of
an additional three to some fortunate future moment when the Israelite territory will be sufficiently expanded to justify another three.

10. *And innocent blood will not be shed in the midst of your land.* The innocent
blood would be the blood of the manslayer, who, because he has killed unintentionally, does not deserve to die. In the parallel law in Numbers, the stress
is on the idea that innocent blood shed pollutes the land, a sacral and archaic
idea. Here, by contrast, the emphasis is social; innocent blood is not to be shed
in "the midst of your land," evil must be expunged "from Israel" (verse 13).

11. *that man.* The Hebrew merely says "he," but English does not tolerate that
degree of ambiguity in pronominal reference.

12. *give him into the hand of the blood avenger.* The prerogative of vendetta justice is recognized insofar as the blood avenger is allowed to execute the death
sentence, but the implication is that the elders have first made a legal determination through a trial.

13. *root out innocent blood.* This is an ellipsis for rooting out the one who has
shed innocent blood.
    it will go well with you. This Deuteronomic pragmatic note is absent from
Numbers 35.

14. *landmark.* The Hebrew *gevul* means "border" and, by two different kinds of
metonymy, the territory marked out by the border and the stone pile that
marks the border.
    the first ones. The early generations that established the division of the land.

LORD your God is about to give you to take hold of it. A single witness 15
shall not rise up against a man for any crime and for any offense; in any
offense that he may commit, by the word of two witnesses or by the
word of three witnesses shall a case be established. Should a corrupt 16
witness rise up against a man, to testify against him falsely, the two men 17
who have a dispute shall stand before the LORD, before the priests and
judges who will be in those days, and the judges inquire well and, look, 18
the witness is a false witness, he has testified falsely against his brother,
you shall do to him as he plotted to do to his brother, and you shall root 19
out the evil from your midst. And those who remain will listen and be 20
afraid, and they will no longer do the like of this evil thing in your
midst. And your eye shall not spare—a life for a life, an eye for an eye, 21
a tooth for a tooth, a hand for a hand, a foot for a foot.

---

15. *by the word.* Literally, "by the mouth."

17. *before the LORD, before the priests and judges.* This apposition is not entirely
transparent. The normative sense of "before the LORD" in Deuteronomy is at
the central sanctuary, but it is doubtful that only a single court in the entire
country is envisaged. Rashi's proposal may capture the intended sense: "it
should seem to them as though they were standing before God" when the lit-
igants submit themselves to legal authority.

21. *a life for a life, an eye for an eye . . . a foot for a foot.* For a discussion of the
biblical *lex talionis*, see the comment on Exodus 21:23–25. There, however, the
reference is to someone who does bodily or mortal injury to another person.
Here, the reference is to the intention of doing grave injury by bearing false
witness. David Cohen-Zemach nicely observes that in our text first we have an
abstract juridical formulation ("You shall do to him as he plotted to do to his
brother.") and then a more popular, probably proverbial statement of the idea
("a life for a life," etc.). Exodus 21 uses a different preposition, *tahat* (literally,
"instead of"), whereas the present version employs *b^e*, which in all likelihood
expresses the function it sometimes has of "for the price of." The two formulations might be semantically identical, but it is also possible that the version
in Exodus assumes an archaic idea of a life taken or an injury inflicted literally
"replacing" or balancing out (*tahat*, instead) a life lost or an injury suffered,
whereas here the *talionis* may be viewed in quasi-monetary terms as payback.

CHAPTER 20

¹ **W**hen you go out to battle against your enemy and you see horse and chariot, troops more numerous than you, you shall not fear them, for the LORD your God is with you, Who has brought you ² up from the land of Egypt. And it shall be, when you approach the bat- ³ tle, that the priest shall come forward and speak to the troops and say to them, "Hear, Israel, you are approaching the battle today against your enemies. Let your heart be not faint. Do not fear and do not quake and ⁴ do not dread them. For the LORD your God goes before you to do bat-

---

1. *see horse and chariot*. As we are reminded elsewhere, especially in Exodus and Judges, chariots were the instruments of the great martial nations of the region, first the Egyptians and then the Canaanites, against whom the Israelites stood at a palpable disadvantage. In the early period of the conquest, the Israelites were mostly confined to the rocky high country of Canaan and often fought in what were essentially guerilla forces. This ancient equivalent of an armored corps could well have seemed terrifying to them. The allusion here to God's bringing Israel up out of Egypt, as Jeffrey H. Tigay notes, is probably meant to recall the great victory over Pharaoh's chariot corps at the Sea of Reeds.

troops. The collective noun *'am*, which has the more general meaning of "people," regularly designates "troops" in military contexts.

3. *Let your heart be not faint*. Rashi translates these exhortations into vividly concrete battlefield terms: "*Let your heart be not faint*—from the neighing of horses. *Do not fear*—from the clanging of shields. *And do not quake*—from the sound of the horns. *And do not dread*—the sound of the battle-cries." The "faint" heart is literally a "soft" heart in the Hebrew, but the obvious reference is to fear, not excessive compassion.

tle with your enemies to save you." And the overseers shall speak to the 5
troops, saying, "Whatever man has built a new house and not dedicated
it, let him go and return to his house, lest he die in the battle and
another man dedicate it. And whatever man has planted a vineyard and 6
not enjoyed it, let him go and return to his house, lest he die in the battle and another man enjoy it. And whatever man has betrothed a 7
woman and not wed her, let him go and return to his house, lest he die
in the battle and another man wed her." And the overseers shall speak 8
further to the troops and say, "Whatever man is afraid and faint of
heart, let him go and return to his house, that he not shake the heart
of his brothers like his own heart." And it shall be, when the overseers 9
finish speaking to the troops, they shall appoint the commanders of the

---

5. *the overseers*. These officials, *shotrim*, appear to be civilian authorities,
empowered both to allow exemptions from military service and to appoint
commanders (verse 9).

dedicated. The verb *hanakh* might refer to an actual ceremony of dedication, its fixed sense in later Hebrew usage, or might simply mean "to inaugurate," "to initiate use."

6. *enjoyed it*. The literal meaning of the Hebrew verb is "desacralize." The law
behind that linguistic usage is as follows: during the first three years after
planting a vineyard, its use was forbidden, presumably because the vines were
immature; in the fourth year, the product of the vineyard was considered "holy
to the Lord"; in the fifth year, its sacral status was voided and its fruits could
be enjoyed without hindrance.

7. *and another man wed her*. In all these identically couched statements, the
idea that someone else would enjoy what the man had anticipated enjoying
suggests that the rationale for all these military exemptions was humanitarian
consideration of the soldiers.

8. *and the overseers shall speak further*. This final exemption is set off from the
preceding three because the rationale is not humanitarian but pragmatic: the
presence of a coward in the ranks could undermine the morale of those around
him.

shake the heart. In keeping with the Hebrew idiom of a "soft" heart, the verb
here literally means "melt," but, again, the clear connotation is fear, not
compassion.

10   armies at the head of the troops. When you approach a town to do bat-
11   tle against it, you shall call to it for peace. And it shall be, if it answers
you in peace and opens up to you, all the people found within it shall
12   become forced labor for you and serve you. And if it does not make
13   peace with you, and does battle with you, you shall besiege it. And
when the LORD gives it into your hand, you shall strike down all its
14   males with the edge of the sword. Only the women and the little ones
and the cattle and everything that is in the town, all its booty you shall
plunder for yourself, and you shall consume the booty of your enemy
15   that the LORD your God gives to you. Thus shall you do to all the towns
16   far distant from you, which are not of the towns of these nations. Only,
of the towns of these people that the LORD your God is about to give
17   you in estate, you shall let no breathing creature live. But you shall
surely put them under the ban—the Hittite and the Amorite, the
Canaanite and the Perizzite, the Hivite and the Jebusite, as the LORD
18   your God has charged you. So that they will not teach you to do like
all the abhorrent things that they did for their gods, and you would
19   offend the LORD your God. Should you besiege a town many days to do
battle against it, you shall not destroy its trees to swing an axe against
them, for from them you shall eat, and you shall not cut them down.
For is the tree of the field a human, to come away from you in the

---

10. *peace*. As the next verse makes clear, "peace" (*shalom*) here amounts to
surrender.

13. *all its males*. As many commentators note, this would have to be adult
males, for we are told in the next verse that the little ones are to be spared
together with the women.

16. *you shall let no breathing creature live*. It is hard to find any mitigation for
the ferocity of this injunction to total destruction. The rabbis reinterpreted it,
seeking to show that it was almost never strictly applicable. Since the archeological evidence suggests that the "ban" was never actually implemented, it
seems to be the projection in legal imperative of a militant fantasy—but surely
a dangerous fantasy.

19. *its trees*. The Hebrew uses a collective noun, in the singular.

siege? Only a tree that you know is not a tree for eating, it you may   20
destroy and cut down and build a siege-work against the town that does
battle against you, until its fall.

---

20. *Only a tree that you know is not a tree for eating.* There may be an echo here
of "the tree was good for eating" (Genesis 3:6), evoking the Garden world in
which God provided all good things for human enjoyment, and prohibited the
fruit of two of the trees. Destroying fruit trees is a despoliation of God's natural gifts, and since the inhabitants of the besieged town would be economically dependent on the trees, it is a devastating blow against them for the
foreseeable future. In fact, it was quite common in the ancient world to cut
down the enemy's fruit trees, either for the practical purpose of erecting siege-
works or—as in some instances in which the Greeks destroyed olive groves—
out of sheer spite.

CHAPTER 21

¹ Should a slain person be found on the soil that the LORD your God is about to give you to take hold of it, lying in the field, it not being ² known who struck him down, your elders and your judges shall ³ go out and measure to the towns that are around the slain person. And it shall be, the town closest to the slain person, the elders of that town shall take a heifer of the herd that has not been worked, that has not ⁴ pulled in a yoke, and the elders of that town shall bring down the heifer to a swift-running wadi that is not worked and is not sown, ⁵ and there they shall break the neck of the heifer in the wadi. And the priests, sons of Levi, shall come forward, for them did the LORD

---

1. *on the soil.* Though *'adamah* has the extended meaning of "land" (and in some cases even "the earth"), its primary sense of "soil" is especially relevant to this and many passages in Deuteronomy. Violently shed blood soaks into the soil, pollutes it, cries out for justice (as in the murder of Abel), and when the murderer remains unknown, a special ritual is required to cleanse the polluted soil and atone for the blood shed. Abraham ibn Ezra notes that this law on bloodshed within the community of Israel immediately follows the laws pertaining to conduct in violent conflict with external enemies.

3. *the elders of that town.* The whole community is plagued with the miasma of bloodguilt—like Thebes at the beginning of *Oedipus the King*—and so must act as a community through its elders to purge the guilt.

4. *a swift-running wadi.* In all likelihood, this refers to a wadi that is filled with a powerful torrent during the rainy season and would not provide suitable terrain along its banks for cultivation. The wadi thus is a wilderness water-source, outside the pale of regular civilized undertakings, and therefore a suitable setting for this rite of expiation for an unsolved crime against humanity.

choose to minister to Him and to bless in the name of the LORD, and
by their word shall be every dispute and every injury. And all the elders   6
of that town, the ones close to the corpse, shall wash their hands over
the broken-necked heifer in the wadi. And they shall bear witness and   7
say, "Our hands did not shed this blood, and our eyes did not see.
Atone for Your people Israel whom You ransomed and do not put inno-   8
cent blood in the midst of Your people Israel, and let the blood be
atoned for them." As for you, you shall root out the innocent blood   9
from your midst, for you shall do what is right in the LORD's eyes.

Should you go out to battle against your enemies and the LORD   10
your God give him in your hand and you take captives from him,
and you see among the captives a woman of comely features and you   11
desire her and take her for yourself as wife, you shall bring her   12
into your house, and she shall shave her head and do her nails,

---

7. *Our hands . . . our eyes.* In this formula of exculpation, the elders declare
both that they—presumably this includes everyone in the community they
represent—have not committed the murder and that they have not witnessed
it, and so have no knowledge of the killer's identity.

11. *a woman of comely features.* The same epithet is attached to Joseph in Genesis 39 when the captive Hebrew becomes the object of his Egyptian mistress's
lustful gaze. Throughout the ancient Mediterranean world, captive women of
vanquished peoples were assumed to be the due sexual prerogative of the vic-
tors (compare Briseus at the beginning of the *Iliad*). This law exceptionally seeks
to provide for the human rights of the woman who falls into this predicament.

and take her for yourself as wife. This expression is proleptic: the victor,
desiring the woman, intends to make her his wife (or rather concubine), but
that intention, as the next two verses clearly indicate, cannot be realized until
the end of a thirty-day period after he returns home with her.

12. *she shall shave her head and do her nails.* Several of the medieval Hebrew
commentators construe this as intended to make her unattractive. That is, her
captor, having been smitten with desire when he first saw the beautiful
woman, may now have second thoughts about her desirability and change his
mind. But especially since trimming the nails would scarcely impair her attractiveness, it is more likely that this cutting of excrescences growing from the
body, together with the removal of the garment of captivity, is a rite of transi-

13 and she shall take off her captive's cloak and stay in your house and keen for her father and her mother a month of days. And afterward you shall come to bed with her, and you shall cohabit with her and she shall

14 become your wife. And it will be, if you like her not, you shall send her away on her own, but you shall certainly not sell her for silver, you shall not garner profit from her inasmuch as you have abused her.

15 Should a man have two wives, the one beloved and the other hated, and the beloved one and the hated one bear him sons, and the firstborn son

16 be the hated one's, it shall be, on the day he grants estate to his sons of

---

tion that marks the woman's transformation from the daughter of an alien people to a fit mate for an Israelite man. The period of thirty days—the set duration of all mourning—for her keening for the parents she has left behind is another indication that the law encodes a ritual of transition.

13. *come to bed with her.* Literally, "come into her." For the implication of this particular idiom for sexual intercourse, see the comment on Genesis 6:4.

cohabit with her. The verb *ba'al* means "to cohabit," "to master," "to exert the capacity of a husband."

14. *if you like her not.* The implication is that this disinclination toward the woman occurs at some point after she has become the man's sexual partner.

garner profit. The Hebrew verb *hit'amer* occurs only here and in 24:7 and its precise meaning is uncertain. Many understand it to mean "enslave" (Abraham ibn Ezra cites a supposed Persian cognate meaning "slavery"). This translation is based on the conjecture that the verb may be related to '*omer*, "sheaf of grain," and hence have something to do with extracting material benefit, as in a harvest.

abused her. The verb '*inah*, "abuse," "debase," "afflict," is also sometimes used for rape, and its employment here astringently suggests that the sexual exploitation of a captive woman, even in a legally sanctioned arrangement of concubinage, is equivalent to rape.

15. *beloved . . . hated.* There is some evidence that these ordinary Hebrew verbs, when applied to co-wives, have the technical sense of favored and unfavored wife. But it is worth preserving the literal meaning in translation because the language thus includes the possibility of an extreme case: even when you adore one wife and despise the other, you must grant the son of the woman you despise the rights of the firstborn if they are his due.

what he has, he shall not be able to make the beloved one's son the firstborn over the firstborn son of the hated one. For the firstborn, the 17 son of the hated one, he shall recognize to give him double of all that belongs to him, for he is his first yield of manhood, his is the birthright's due.

Should a man have a wayward and rebellious son, who does not heed 18 his father's voice and his mother's voice, and they punish him and he does not heed them, his father and his mother shall seize him and bring 19 him out to the elders of his town and to the gate of his place, and they 20 shall say to the elders of his town, "This son of ours is wayward and rebellious, he does not heed our voice, is a glutton and a drunk." All the 21 people of his town shall stone him to death, and you shall root out the evil from your midst, that all Israel may hear and be afraid.

---

17. *double*. Some interpreters argue that the Hebrew *pi shnayim* (literally, "the mouth of two") means two-thirds, as it does in Zechariah 13:8. The extant evidence is that there were varying proportional arrangements for favoring the firstborn in inheritance.

his first yield of manhood. This is the same phrase Jacob uses for his first-born Reuben in Genesis 49.3 (see the comment there on that phrase). The idiom may well have been proverbial, a kind of kenning for the firstborn, and it appears to reflect a belief that the first production of the virile vigor (Hebrew *'on*) of a man is endowed with special power.

20. *a glutton and a drunk* This designation is a clear indication that the carousing rebellious son is an adult.

21. *the people of his town shall stone him to death*. The sternness of this law surpasses that of ancient Near Eastern analogues, which variously punish the refractory son with public shaming, imprisonment, or disinheritance. The rabbis were sufficiently uncomfortable with this law to virtually disallow it. Thus the Babylonian Talmud: "The wayward and rebellious son never existed and never will exist. Then why is it written? To say, inquire and receive the reward [i.e., for strictly didactic purposes]" (*Sanhedrin* 71:A). It should be noted that the whole community (presumably after judicial proceedings) takes part in the execution, and in this instance the hand of the witnesses (the parents) is not first against the condemned, so justice is transferred from parental authority to the community.

22 And should there be against a man a death-sentence offense and he is
23 put to death, and you hang him on a tree, you shall not let his corpse
stay the night on the tree but you shall surely bury it on that day, for a
hanged man is God's curse, and you shall not pollute your soil that the
LORD your God is about to give you in estate.

---

22. *hang him on a tree*. One modern view, with an eye to Assyrian practice,
understands this as impalement on a pole or gibbet, though the Mishnah has
in view hanging the corpse to a kind of cross after the execution. "Tree," one
might recall, in older English usage, can refer to either a gallows or to the
cross.

23. *a hanged man is God's curse*. The meaning of these words is in dispute,
especially because of the polyvalence of *'elohim*—God, gods, divine beings,
spirits. Some modern commentators prefer the last of these alternatives, yielding the sense: a corpse left hanging is a curse or blight to the departed spirit
that once inhabited it. This suggestion, however, does not jibe well with "You
shall not pollute your soil," a clause suggesting that a corpse left unburied is a
violation of the sacredness of the human body, a violation that pollutes the
land. (In this connection, compare *Antigone*.) To leave a body hanging, then,
may simply be a disgrace or curse in the eyes of God. Alternately, *'elohim* might
even be simply a suffix of intensification: a hanged man is a supreme curse.

CHAPTER 22

You shall not see your brother's ox or his sheep slipping away and ₁ ignore them. You shall surely return them to your brother. And if ₂ your brother is not close to you and you do not know who he may be, you shall gather it into your house and it shall be with you until your brother inquires for it and you return it to him. And thus shall you do ₃ for his donkey and thus shall you do for his cloak and thus shall you do for any lost thing of your brother's that may be lost by him and that you find. You shall not be able to ignore it. You shall not see your ₄ brother's donkey or his ox falling on the way and ignore them. You shall surely raise them up with him.

---

1. *your brother's ox or his sheep*. This brief group of laws about the obligation to return lost property and help one's fellow man corresponds to Exodus 23:4–5 with an important terminological difference: Exodus posits the extreme case of finding the beast of your "enemy," whereas Deuteronomy, with its commitment to imagining a united community of the Israelite people, repeatedly uses the term "your brother."

ignore. The literal meaning is "hide yourself," i.e., pretend you don't see.

2. *gather it into your house*. Although this might simply mean "take into the jurisdiction of your household," in fact Canaanite domestic structures often had an enclosure used as a stable on the ground floor. The word thus emphasizes that the finder of the beast is to keep it safe and sheltered until the owner appears.

5 There shall not be a man's gear on a woman, and a man shall not wear
a woman's garment, for whoever does all these is an abhorrence of the
6 Lᴏʀᴅ your God. Should a bird's nest chance to be before you on the
way or in any tree or on the ground with fledglings or eggs and the
mother is crouched over the fledglings or over the eggs, you shall not
7 take the mother together with the children. You shall surely send off
the mother, and the children you may take for yourself, so that it may
8 go well with you and you will enjoy length of days. When you build a
new house, you shall make a parapet for your roof, that you not put

---

5. *There shall not be a man's gear on a woman, and a man shall not wear a
woman's garment.* The word *keli* ("gear") might mean clothing, as it does in rabbinic Hebrew, but it is an all-purpose term that could also refer to weapons,
as some scholars have contended. (The fact that a verb for wearing is not used
for the woman might lend support to this contention.) What is "abhorrent"
about the practice of cross-dressing could be an association with pagan orgiastic activities or even with pagan magic (a Hittite text prescribes cross-dressing
as the first stage in a ritual for curing impotence). In any case, the common
denominator shared by this law and those that follow is, as anthropological
critics have noted, a general recoil of ancient Hebrew culture from the commingling of distinct, often binary categories—male and female, nurture and
killing, seeds of different plants, wool (from animals) and linen (from plants),
conjugality and promiscuity.

6. *you shall not take the mother together with the children.* The often asserted
humanitarian motivation of this law is a little ambiguous because, after all, the
mother is separated from her fledglings or eggs, which are fated to end up on
someone's dinner table. This law has sometimes been compared with the prohibition against eating a kid boiled in its mother's milk: there appears to be a
sense that the order of nature is violated when the destruction of life includes
the biological producer and nurturer of life. Others have detected here a pragmatic, or ecological, consideration: if one makes a practice of killing both
fledglings and mother, the race of birds will not be able to reproduce itself.

8. *build a new house.* This particular law does not seem to be connected with
the surrounding laws that involve the separation of distinct categories. Perhaps
the editor linked it associatively with the discovery of the bird's nest because
of the idea of potential death on the heights.

bloodguilt in your house should someone fall from it. You shall not 9
plant your vineyard with mixed seeds, lest the ripe crop be proscribed—the seed that you plant and the yield of the vineyard. You 10
shall not plow with an ox and a donkey together. You shall not wear 11
sha'atnez, wool and linen together. You shall make yourself tassels on 12
the four corners of your garment with which you cover yourself.
Should a man take a woman, and come to bed with her and hate her, 13

---

should someone fall from it. The Hebrew literally says, "should he who falls
fall from it," the subject of the clause being, as Abraham ibn Ezra observes, a
proleptic usage.

9. lest the ripe crop be proscribed. This phrase, and any rationale for the law
other than the separation of distinct categories, are equally obscure. The
meaning of melei'ah, "ripe crop" (from the word that means "full") is in dispute. "Proscribed" is literally "sanctified," but to be sanctified, or set aside, can
also mean to be taboo, as Rashi notes, with several biblical instances. In any
case, no one has offered an entirely satisfactory explanation of why the crop of
mixed seeds should be sanctified or proscribed.

10. You shall not plow with an ox and a donkey together. In this case, the separation of the two kinds of beasts has a clear humanitarian motive, for the
smaller animal would suffer in this yoking.

11. sha'atnez. This term seems to be a foreign loanword, perhaps from the
Egyptian, and so, lest its sense be obscure, the rest of the verse is a gloss on
its meaning. Minglings of wool and linen were worn by the priests and used in
the sanctuary trappings, so the separation of categories here may be intended
to draw a line between the profane and the holy.

12. tassels. The Hebrew word gedilim differs from "fringe," tsitsit, used in Numbers 15:38–41, and here no mention is made that the tassel is a mnemonic
device for the believing Israelites. Fringes at the hems of garments were fairly
common in ancient Near Eastern apparel.

13. come to bed with her and hate her. The extreme concision of the sequence
of verbs in the Hebrew does not allow us to conclude whether the man was
immediately disaffected with the woman out of sexual dissatisfaction or
whether he simply came to be displeased with her with the passage of conjugal time.

14 and he impute to her misconduct and put out a bad name for her and
say, "This woman did I take and I came close to her and I found no
15 signs of virginity for her," the young woman's father and her mother
shall take and bring out to the elders of the town at the gate the signs
16 of the young woman's virginity. And the young woman's father shall say
to the elders, "My daughter I gave to this man as wife, and he hated
17 her. And look, he has imputed misconduct, saying, 'I found no signs of
virginity for your daughter,' but these are the signs of my daughter's virginity." And they shall spread out the garment before the elders of the
18 town. And the elders of that town shall take the man out and punish
19 him, and they shall fine him a hundred weights of silver and give it to
the young woman's father, for he put out a bad name for a virgin in

---

14. *I came close to her.* In his denunciation of the woman, the husband uses a
euphemism, an idiom not restricted to sex, instead of the narrator's plain
"came to bed with" (literally, "came into").

no signs of virginity. The Hebrew *betulim* means both the condition of virginity and the concrete evidence of virginity. In this case, the husband is
claiming that he found neither an intact hymen nor signs of blood after the
consummation of the act.

15. *bring out to the elders of the town at the gate the signs of . . . virginity.* One
infers that the bride would have entrusted to the safekeeping of her parents—
probably, her mother—as legal insurance the bloodied sheet or garment
(sleeping in one's garment being common in this culture) after the nuptial
night.

16. *and he hated her.* The parents of the bride, though recycling words already
used, understandably delete the verb for sexual intercourse.

18. *punish him.* The rabbinic understanding of this term, which is historically
plausible, is that it means public flogging.

19. *fine him.* A fine is appropriate because the man's calculation may have been
chiefly financial: he would have been able to divorce the woman without the
defamation but in that case would have been obliged to restore her dowry to
her, which served as a kind of divorce insurance for the wife.

give it to the young woman's father. One must keep in mind that in this society marriage was chiefly a transaction between the father of the bride and the

Israel. And she shall be his wife, he shall not be able to send her away
ever. But if this thing be true, no signs of virginity were found for the   20
young woman, they shall take the young woman out to the entrance of   21
her father's house and the men of her town shall stone her to death, for
she has done a scurrilous thing in Israel to play the whore in her own
father's house, and you shall root out the evil from your midst. Should   22
a man be found lying with a woman who has a husband, both of them
shall die, the man lying with the woman and the woman as well, and
you shall root out the evil from Israel. Should there be a virgin young   23
woman betrothed to a man, and a man find her in the town and lie with

---

groom (or the groom together with his father). The defamatory husband has
essentially suggested that the young woman's father passed off damaged goods
on him, and so now he owes the father an indemnity.

he shall not be able to send her away ever. "Send her away" here has the technical sense of "divorce." It might seem a dubious recompense for a woman to
continue as wife of a man who hates her and has tried to destroy her reputation. (Even more extremely, the unbetrothed victim of a rapist, verse 29, is to
become his wife, without possibility of divorce.) But in this society, the condition of a woman who is not a virgin and has no husband is quite desperate (witness Tamar's sense that her life is virtually ended after she has been raped,
2 Samuel 13). The law is no prescription for her happiness, but at least it
guarantees her social and economic security.

21. *stone her to death.* This is still another instance of a draconian law in
Deuteronomy—the capital punishment for premarital sex far exceeds even the
sternness of other ancient Near Eastern codes—which the rabbis sought to
mitigate through exegesis. Since death sentences are not supposed to be
issued without the firm testimony of at least two eyewitnesses, "if this thing
be true," the rabbis plausibly argued, means that the sentence could be pronounced only if two witnesses actually observed the illicit act of intercourse,
merely circumstantial evidence being excluded by principle. If that is the case,
implementation of the death sentence would have been extremely rare.

for she has done a scurrilous thing in Israel. This particular Hebrew phrase,
nevalah beyisra'el, is regularly used to indicate a shameful sexual act.

in her own father's house. The phrase might mean simply, while she was
under her father's jurisdiction, but the concreteness of the idiom leaves open
the more scandalous possibility that her assignations actually took place under
her father's roof.

24 her, you shall bring them both out to the gate of that town and stone
them to death—the young woman, for her not crying out in the town,
and the man, for his abusing his fellow man's wife, and you shall root
25 out the evil from your midst. But should the man find the betrothed
young woman in the field and the man seize her and lie with her, only
26 the man lying with her shall die. And to the young woman you shall do
nothing, the young woman bears no capital offense, for as a man rises
27 against his neighbor and murders him, so is this thing. For he found her
in the field: the young woman could have cried out and there would
28 have been none to save her. Should a man find a virgin young woman
who is not betrothed and take hold of her and lie with her, and they be
29 found, the man lying with her shall give to the young woman's father
fifty weights of silver, and she shall be his wife inasmuch as he abused
her. He shall not be able to send her away all his days.

---

24. *to the gate of that town.* Repeatedly, the gate is the place of public
judgment.

25. *in the field.* The obvious point is that out in the open, beyond the town,
there is no one else present to hear the woman's cry for help. But "the field,"
beyond the perimeters of safe communal existence, often figures in biblical
language as a dangerous zone where marauders, wild animals, even demons
prey on people.
    and the man seize her. This verb, indicating that the man is forcing himself
on her, is absent from the law about the woman in the town. There the presumption is that she is a willing partner since, had he forcibly "seized" her, she
would have called out for help and presumably gotten it. One should keep in
mind that Canaanite or Israelite towns were small and crowded, lacking the
desolate neighborhoods with empty streets one can find in a large modern city.
Precisely for that reason, this translation regularly renders the Hebrew term ʿir
as "town," not "city."

29. *the man . . . shall give to the young woman's father fifty weights of silver.*
Deflowering the unbetrothed young woman would make her unmarriageable
(see the comment on verse 19) and entail financial loss for her father, who would
be deprived of the bride-price. The double remedy of the law, however odd it
may seem to modern eyes in permanently binding the rape victim and the rapist,
is to decree that the man marry the woman without possibility of divorce, and
that he pay a bride-price to her father. It is not clear whether there was a standard bride-price in Israelite society, but fifty weights of silver sounds generous.

CHAPTER 23

man shall not wed his father's wife, and he shall not uncover his   1
father's skirt. No one with crushed testes or lopped member shall   2
come into the Lord's assembly. No misbegotten shall come into   3

---

1. *his father's wife.* Since the term "wed" could not be used for a man's mother or for a woman currently married to the man's father, the phrase would have to mean his father's widow (who might be fairly young, in light of the early age at which girls were married off) or a woman divorced from his father.

he shall not uncover his father's skirt. What is involved is taboo by metonymic contamination: a man should not come in contact with the female nakedness that was once in conjugal contact with his own father's nakedness. David Cohen-Zemach interestingly detects here an allusion to Ham's seeing his father Noah's nakedness (Genesis 9:22), Ham being the father of Canaan, the eponymous progenitor of the Canaanite peoples. What closely follows (verse 4) is a prohibition against ever accepting the Moabites and the Ammonites, two peoples purportedly engendered out of incestuous union with a father, into the Israelite community.

2. *crushed testes or lopped member.* This prohibition may simply express a vehement rejection of both forms of castration, in fact fairly commonly practiced in the ancient Near East. But the law as it is formulated also excludes from the assembly a man who is sexually mutilated through some accident. In this patriarchal culture, the integrity of the body is strongly connected with the integrity of the capacity for fatherhood. The prohibition, then, is thematically related to the immediately preceding prohibition against uncovering one's father's skirt, both expressing a horror of violation of the body of the father.

3. *misbegotten.* The Hebrew *mamzer* (etymology uncertain) later comes to mean "bastard," but the convincing consensus of both traditional and modern commentators is that it refers to the offspring of a taboo, or incestuous, union.

the Lord's assembly. Even his tenth generation shall not come into the
4 Lord's assembly. No Ammonite nor Moabite shall come into the
Lord's assembly. Even his tenth generation shall not come into the
5 Lord's assembly ever. Because they did not greet you with bread and
water on the way when you came out of Egypt, and for their hiring
6 against you Balaam son of Beor from Aram Naharaim to curse you. But
the Lord your God did not want to listen to Balaam, and the Lord your
God turned the curse into blessing for you, for the Lord your God loves
7 you. You shall not seek their well-being and their good all your days, for-
8 ever. You shall not abhor an Edomite, for he is your brother. You shall
9 not abhor an Egyptian, for you were a sojourner in his land. The sons
that are born to them, their third generation may come into the Lord's
assembly.

10 When you sally forth in a camp against your enemy, you shall keep
11 yourself from every evil thing. Should there be among you a man who
is not clean through nocturnal emission, he shall go outside the camp

---

4. *Ammonite nor Moabite.* It is not entirely clear why these two peoples should
be permanently excluded for their hostility toward the Israelites approaching
Canaan, whereas the Edomites, who were scarcely more friendly, and the
Egyptians, who wanted to murder the entire population of Hebrew male
infants, are to be accepted in the community. The issue is further complicated
by the fact that Boaz married a Moabite woman, Ruth, who then became progenitrix of David's royal line. (Abraham ibn Ezra's contention that the ban is
against Moabite men, not women, seems strained.) One must conclude that
as historical circumstances shifted, attitudes in ancient Israel toward the
sundry neighboring peoples also changed, and these changes are reflected in
the inconsistencies of the texts.

 shall not come into the Lord's assembly. Jeffrey H. Tigay argues persuasively
that the assembly is primarily a civic concept, roughly analogous to the *polis*
among the Greeks. To come into the assembly, then, means to become a naturalized citizen. That status, of course, would also have entailed worship of the
God of Israel.

11. *not clean through nocturnal emission.* This cluster of regulations about
remaining in a state of purity in the military camp is predicated on the notion
that "the Lord your God walks about in the midst of your camp" (verse 15),
acting as guarantor of victory. Soldiers on a campaign at least sometimes took

and not come into the camp. And it shall be, toward evening, he shall   12
bathe in water and as the sun sets he may come inside the camp. And   13
you shall have a marker outside the camp and shall go there outside.
And you shall have a spike together with your battle gear, and it shall   14
be, when you sit outside, you shall dig with it and go back and cover
your excrement. For the LORD your God walks about in the midst of   15
your camp to rescue you and to give your enemies before you, and your
camp shall be holy, that He should not see among you anything shamefully exposed and turn back from you.

You shall not hand over to his master a slave who escapes to you from   16
his master. With you he shall stay, in your midst, in the place that he   17
chooses within one of your gates wherever is good for him. You shall
not mistreat him. There shall be no cult-harlot from the daughters   18
of Israel, and there shall be no cult-catamite from the sons of Israel.

---

upon themselves a vow of sexual abstinence for the duration of the fighting, as
one sees in the David story (1 Samuel 21:5–6), and the ritual impurity imparted
by an involuntary emission of semen is related to that practice.

13. *a marker*. The Hebrew *yad* (primary meaning, "hand") also means "monument" or "marker." The common claim that here the sense is "place" stands on
scanty philological grounds.

14. *a spike*. The Hebrew *yated* usually means "tent peg."
    battle gear. The rare term *'azen* is probably an Aramaizing form of *zayin*,
"weapon."

15. *shamefully exposed*. The Hebrew is literally "nakedness of a thing," but the
word for "nakedness," *'erwah*, is specifically the term for prohibited sexual
nakedness, that which should never be exposed, and so carries a strong connotation of shame.

16. *You shall not hand over to his master a slave*. The scholarly consensus is that
this injunction to offer asylum to runaway slaves (an unusual law in the
ancient world) refers to foreign slaves. Israelite slaves, who were in essence
indentured servants, would have been freed after six years.

18. *cult-harlot . . . cult-catamite*. The precise meaning of these two terms,
qedeshah and *qadesh*, is disputed. There is no clear-cut evidence that ritual

19 You shall not bring a whore's pay nor a dog's price to the house of the
LORD your God for any votive offering, for both of them are the abhor-
20 rence of the LORD your God. You shall not exact interest from your
brother, interest of silver, interest of food, or interest of anything that
21 will bear interest. From the stranger you may exact interest but from
your brother you shall not exact interest, so that the LORD your God
may bless you in all that your hand reaches on the land to which you

---

prostitution was practiced in the ancient Near East, though it remains an
undeniable possibility. (Ritual prostitution was known in nearby Asia Minor,
the original homeland of the Hittites who often pass through the biblical
scene.) Exceptionally, the female *qedeshah* is presented here before the male
qadesh, suggesting she was the more familiar type. The story of Judah and
Tamar in Genesis 38 makes it clear that *qedeshah* was some sort of more
refined or dignified designation for a prostitute: Judah takes Tamar for a
"whore" (*zonah*); Hirah his emissary then refers to her more decorously as a
qedeshah. Since the root means "sacred," it is a reasonable inference that the
qedeshah was either a woman who prostituted herself as part of the cult (in
that case, a fertility cult) or a prostitute working near the site of a sanctuary
who devoted part of her professional income to the sanctuary. Since the pilgrim obligation to participate in the temple service was laid upon the males,
the *qadesh* would in all likelihood have been a homosexual prostitute, as the
translation "cult-catamite" is meant to indicate.

19. *a whore's pay nor a dog's price.* It is not clear whether the second of these
phrases refers literally to what is gained by selling or bartering a dog or whether
(perhaps more probably, because dogs had limited economic value in this society) "dog" is a contemptuous term for the *qadesh*. Dogs, we should recall, were
despised in ancient Hebrew culture, thought of chiefly as unpleasant scavengers. They were not kept as pets and may not have been used for hunting or
shepherding.

21. *From the stranger you may exact interest but from your brother you shall not
exact interest.* The prohibition against interest (the term, at least etymologically, means "bite") is predicated on an agrarian society of "brothers" in which
loans are extended as a form of temporary charity. The ban may not have
included properly mercantile loans, and it was not generally applied as
Israelite society became more fully urbanized. Foreigners can be required to
pay interest because the paradigmatic case would be foreign merchants traveling among the Israelites for business purposes.

are coming to take hold of it. Should you make a vow to the LORD your 22
God, you shall not delay fulfilling it, for the LORD your God will surely
require it of you and there would be an offense in you. And should you 23
refrain from making a vow, there will be no offense in you. The utter- 24
ance of your lips you shall keep, and you shall do as you have vowed to
the LORD your God, the freewill gift that you spoke with your mouth.
Should you come into your fellow man's vineyard, you may eat grapes 25
as much as you crave—to your fill—but you shall not put them in your
pouch. Should you come into your fellow man's standing grain, you may 26
pluck tender ears with your hand but you shall not wield a sickle on
your fellow man's standing grain.

---

23. *should you refrain from making a vow.* The vow is a "freewill gift," and no
one is under any obligation to make such a vow. But should a person in fact
undertake a vow, he is strictly responsible to fulfill it promptly.

25. *Should you come into your fellow man's vineyard.* This is by no means a
country crisscrossed with highways, and thus it would often have been necessary to pass through someone's vineyard or field on a narrow path in order to
reach one's destination.

26. *you may pluck tender ears.* The Hebrew *melilot* is derived from a verbal
stem that means to rub between the fingers and is distinct from *shibolim*,
"mature ears of grain." The *melilot* (like the grapes) are thus a kind of available
snack for the hungry pedestrian, but neither ears nor grapes are to be the
object of actual harvesting, by wielding a sickle or filling a pouch

CHAPTER 24

When a man takes a wife and cohabits with her, it shall be, if she
does not find favor in his eyes because he finds in her some
shamefully exposed thing, and he writes her a document of
divorce and puts it in her hand and sends her away from his house,
2 and she goes out from his house and goes and becomes another man's,
3 and the second man hates her and writes her a document of divorce
and puts it in her hand and sends her away from his house, or the sec-
4 ond man, who took her to him as wife, dies, her first husband, who sent
her away, shall not be able to come back and take her to be his wife
after she has been defiled, for it is an abhorrence before the LORD, and
you shall not lead the land to offend that the LORD your God is about

---

1–4. These verses are all one long run-on sentence, describing in quasinarra-
tive terms a special case of divorce, remarriage, and divorce rather than
addressing the general predicament of divorce.

1. *he finds in her some shamefully exposed thing.* This is the same idiom for
something disgraceful that appears in 23:15 (see the comment there). The
vagueness of the expression leaves open the possibility that the husband has
discovered something morally reprehensible in his wife or that what has
repelled him is a physical defect, perhaps something about her that displeases
him sexually.
   a document of divorce. The use of a written document for divorce (the actual
divorce procedure is not spelled out in biblical law) is registered only in
Deuteronomy and later texts. The reasonable inference is that in earlier periods divorce was effected by the act of banishing the woman from the house
and/or by an oral declaration on the part of the husband. The literal meaning
of the phrase used here, *sefer keritut*, is "document [or scroll] of cutting-off."
Since *keritut* is not one of the usual biblical terms for divorce, scholars have

to give you in estate. When a man takes a new wife, he shall not go out 5
in the army and shall not cross over on its account for any matter. He
shall be exempt in his house for a year and gladden his wife whom he
has taken. One may not take in pawn a hand mill or an upper millstone, 6
for one would be taking in pawn a life. Should a man be found stealing 7
a living person of his brothers, of the Israelites, and garner profit from
him and sell him, that thief shall die, and you shall root out the evil

---

conjectured that it refers to a ceremony in which the husband cut off a corner
of the wife's garment as a sign that he was severing relations with her. In 1
Samuel 15, when Saul inadvertently tears the hem of Samuel's garment, the
prophet immediately seizes on the act as a symbol that God is about to tear
away the kingship from Saul.

5. *When a man takes a new wife.* The thematic connection with the previous
law is the issue of sexual consummation in marriage.

shall not cross over on its account for any matter. The "it" may refer to the
army—i.e., the man shall stay put and not go off anywhere for military purposes—but the Hebrew is rather cryptic, as this literal translation indicates,
and no one has provided an entirely satisfactory interpretation.

gladden his wife. The verb here could refer specifically to giving her sexual
pleasure, though it does not exclude the more general pleasure of conjugal
sociability. This law differs from the parallel law of exemption from military
service for the newlywed in chapter 20 in introducing a humane concern for
the bride.

6. *a hand mill or an upper millstone.* Although the Hebrew *reihayim* is the general term for mill, the large agricultural mill, several feet in diameter, would be
too massive to move, so the reference must be to a hand mill. Even in that
case, the heavy netherstone (*shekhev*) would have been hard to carry off, but
it would have sufficed to seize the much lighter upper millstone (*rekhev*) in
order to disable the mill.

for one would be taking in pawn a life. A household typically ground its own
grain for bread, and hand mills were thus a necessary tool in even the poor
home, as the great number of them uncovered by archeologists confirms.

7. *a living person.* The term used here, *nefesh,* is the same one used for "life"
in the previous verse concerning the poor man and his hand mill and thus provides a link between the two laws. A human life is not to be disregarded for
the purpose of profit.

8   from your midst. Watch yourself in regard to the plague of skin blanch
to watch carefully and to do. According to all that the levitical priests
9   will teach you as I have charged them you shall watch to do. Remember what the LORD your God did to Miriam on the way when you came
10 out of Egypt. Should you make a loan of anything to your fellow man,
11 you shall not come into his house to take his pledge. You shall stand
outside, and the man to whom you have made the loan shall bring out
12 the pledge to you outside. And if he is a poor man, you shall not lie
13 down in his pledge. You shall surely give the pledge back to him as the
sun sets, that he may lie down in his cloak and bless you and it be a
14 merit for you before the LORD your God. You shall not oppress a poor
and needy hired worker from your brothers or from your sojourners who
15 are in your land within your gates. In his day you shall give his wages,
and the sun shall not set on him—for he is poor and his heart counts
on it—that he call not against you to the LORD and there be an offense

---

9. *Remember what the LORD your God did to Miriam.* The story in Numbers
12:10–15, in which Miriam is stricken with this disfiguring skin disease for
maligning Moses, is invoked because it provides an especially horrific representation of the disease, as Aaron's words to Moses make clear: "Let her not
be, pray, like one dead who when he comes out of his mother's womb, half his
flesh is eaten away."

11. *outside.* The seemingly redundant term of location at the very end of the
sentence—already clearly indicated in the verb "bring out"—serves to emphasize that the creditor must remain beyond the perimeters of the debtor's home
and not violate his private space.

12. *you shall not lie down in his pledge.* This is a kind of pun: you shall not go
to sleep, retaining his pledge, and you shall not sleep in it, as the poor man
himself would sleep in his cloak, his sole bedding.

14. *sojourners.* The Hebrew uses a singular form.

15. *his heart counts on it.* More literally: "his life [or his very self] lifts toward it."

in you. Fathers shall not be put to death over sons, and sons shall not be ₁₆ put to death over fathers. Each man shall be put to death for his own offense. You shall not skew the case of a sojourner or an orphan, and you ₁₇ shall not take as pawn a widow's garment. And you shall remember that ₁₈ you were a slave in Egypt, and the LORD your God ransomed you from there. Therefore do I charge you to do this thing. When you reap your ₁₉ harvest in your field and forget a sheaf in the field, you shall not go back to take it. For the sojourner and for the orphan and for the widow it shall be, so that the LORD your God may bless you in all the work of your hands. When you beat your olive trees, you shall not strip the branches ₂₀ of what is left behind you. For the sojourner, for the orphan, and for the widow it shall be. When you glean your vineyard, you shall not pluck the ₂₁ young grapes left behind you. For the sojourner, for the orphan, and for the widow it shall be. And you shall remember that you were a slave in ₂₂ Egypt. Therefore do I charge you to do this thing.

---

16. *Fathers . . . sons.* Collective punishment, or measure-for-measure punishment (you killed my son, your son shall be killed) was common in ancient Near Eastern legal codes, and this law is a protest against it.

17. *you shall not take as pawn a widow's garment.* This appears to be a greater restriction than the one for the poor man, in whose case the garment may be held by the creditor during the day but must be returned to the owner at sunset. Perhaps the law regarded it as a form of shameful exposure (*'erwat davar*) to deprive the widow of her (outer?) garment at any time, thus leaving her to go about insufficiently covered.

20. *beat your olive trees.* This was the general practice for harvesting ripe olives.
    you shall not strip the branches of what is left behind you. The relatively rare verb *pe'er* is derived from *po'rah*, "branch." It might have involved plucking the less ripe olives not shaken loose by beating. "What is left" is added in the translation to clarify the compact Hebrew.

21. *you shall not pluck the young grapes left behind you.* Another unusual verb, *'olel*, is derived from *'olelot*, "small grapes."

CHAPTER 25

W hen there is a dispute between men, they shall approach the
court of justice, and they shall judge them and find for the one
in the right and against the one in the wrong. And it shall be,
if the one in the wrong deserves blows, the judge shall make him lie
down and have him struck before him, according to his wrongdoing in
number. Forty blows he may strike him, he shall not go farther, lest he
go on to strike him beyond these a great many blows, and your brother
seem of no account in your eyes. You shall not muzzle an ox when it

---

1. *court of justice*. The single Hebrew word *mishpat* can mean "law," "judgment," "justice," "the institution or court of justice," besides several non-
judicial senses.

2. *deserves blows*. The corporal punishment would be either lashes or blows
delivered with a rod or cane. Biblical law is reticent about what infractions
merited this punishment, mentioning only the instance of a man who defames
his wife (22:18).

3. *Forty blows*. Rabbinic law stipulates thirty-nine lashes in order to avert the
possibility that the executor of the punishment might inadvertently exceed the
limit of forty. It also stipulates that if the guilty person is in any way infirm or
shows signs of losing physical control during the lashing, the number of blows
shall be reduced accordingly.
   a great many blows. Literally, "a multitudinous blow."

4. *You shall not muzzle an ox when it threshes*. The humanitarian motive of this
law is obvious. Threshing was done by oxen either with their hooves or pulling
a threshing sledge. In either case, the ox is not to be prevented from nibbling
during the work.

threshes. Should brothers dwell together and one of them die and 5
have no son, the wife of the dead man shall not become wife outside
to a stranger. Her brother-in-law shall come to bed with her and take
her to him as wife, and carry out a brother-in-law's duty toward her.
And it shall be, the firstborn whom she bears shall be established in 6
the name of his dead brother, that his name be not wiped out from
Israel. And if the man does not want to wed his sister-in-law, his sister- 7
in-law shall go up to the gate to the elders and say, "My brother-in-law
has refused to establish a name for his brother, a name in Israel. He
did not want to carry out a brother-in-law's duty toward me." And the 8
elders of his town shall call to him and speak to him, and if he stands
and says, "I do not want to wed her," his sister-in-law shall approach 9
him before the eyes of the elders and slip his sandal from his foot and

---

5. *Should brothers dwell together.* Though this might mean in the same
extended household, the probable reference is to contiguous properties or
properties in close proximity.

carry out a brother-in-law's duty toward her. This is a single verb in the
Hebrew *weyibmah,* derived from *yabum,* "brother-in-law." The institution
assumed here is the so-called levirate marriage (from the Latin *levir,* "brother-
in-law"). The continuity provided by male offspring in this patrilineal society
was the sole form of "immortality" a man could expect, which would also have
the economic ramification of bequeathing one's property to a son. A man who
dies without having begotten a son is thus cut off, his "name wiped out from
Israel." His brother serves as a kind of proxy for the dead man, and the son he
begets with the widow is to bear the name, that is, the patronymic, of the dead
brother. The practice of the levirate marriage seems to have shifted at different points in the biblical period. In the Book of Ruth, "brother" is clearly
extended to cover the nearest available kinsman, even a distant cousin.

6. *established.* The literal meaning of the verb is "to arise."

8. *if he stands.* Some interpreters understand this ordinary verb of physical
position to mean "persist" here.

9. *slip his sandal from his foot.* There are differing opinions about the symbolism of this gesture. Some understand it as a gesture of severance: as the widow
removes the sandal, she removes herself from obligatory connection with the
brother-in-law and is free to marry someone else. But calling his house the

spit in his face and speak out and say, "So shall be done to the man who
10 will not build his brother's house." And his name shall be called in
11 Israel: the House of the Slipped-off Sandal. Should men brawl
together, a man and his brother, and the wife of one of them come forward to rescue her man from the hand of the one striking him, and she
12 reach out her hand and seize his pudenda, you shall cut off her hand,
13 your eye shall not spare her. You shall not have in your pouch different
14 weight-stones, a big one and a small one. You shall not have in your
15 house different *ephah* measures, a big one and a small one. A whole

---

House of the Slipped-off Sandal clearly is a shaming act. Perhaps because only
the indigent would go about barefoot, slipping off the man's sandal in public
is a ritual of disgrace (especially since the law seems to assume that he and his
deceased brother are men who have property).

spit in his face. Abraham ibn Ezra, Rashi, and many modern commentators
interpret this as "before him," i.e., on the ground in front of him, which the
Hebrew preposition could definitely mean. But a more shocking gesture of
humiliation may be more in keeping with the harsh tenor of her declaration
"So shall be done to the man . . ."

11. *Should men brawl together.* Ibn Ezra shrewdly identifies this as an antithetical echo of "Should brothers dwell together (verse 5)."

pudenda. The Hebrew term *mevushim*, like the Latinate English term, is
derived from the root that means "shame."

12. *you shall cut off her hand.* Once again, the draconian severity of this law led
the rabbis to reinterpret it to mean monetary compensation. The law may register a vehement response to a breach of modesty on the part of the woman,
but a Middle Assyrian parallel suggests that the case in mind is one where the
woman inflicts serious injury on the man by seizing his testicles. If an impairment of reproductive function is involved, this would be grave, and would link
this law to the concern for the continuation of man's name in the levirate
marriage.

13. *weight-stones.* The Hebrew says simply "stones," but the meaning is unambiguous, and weight-stones were abundantly used for commercial transactions.

14. ephah *measures.* The Hebrew says simply "ephah," a unit of dry measure
equal to about 19 liters, though some think it might have been bigger.

and honest weight-stone you shall have; a whole and honest *ephah* measure you shall have, so that you may enjoy length of days on the soil that the LORD your God is about to give you. For the abhorrence of the 16 LORD your God is anyone who does all these things, who commits any fraud. Remember what Amalek did to you on the way when you came 17 out of Egypt, how he fell upon you on the way and cut down all the 18 stragglers, with you famished and exhausted, and he did not fear God. And it shall be, when the LORD your God grants you respite from all 19 your enemies around in the land that the LORD your God is about to give you in estate to take hold of it, you shall wipe out the remembrance of Amalek from under the heavens, you shall not forget.

---

17. *Remember what Amalek did to you.* It is not entirely clear why Amalek (compare Exodus 17:8–16) is singled out as the archenemy of Israel. In historical terms, the Amalekites, a seminomadic people of the Negeb and southern trans-Jordan region, carried out frequent and brutal marauding raids against Israelite settlements (see the story about the Amalekite raid against David's town of Ziklag in 1 Samuel 30). Deuteronomy here offers an explanation for the opprobrium of Amalek not mentioned in Exodus—that the Amalekites attacked the Israelite stragglers, who would have been the old, the infirm, and women and children, and slaughtered them.

18. *he fell upon you . . . and he did not fear God.* This language suggests an ambush of the stragglers. S. D. Luzatto, the nineteenth-century Italian Hebrew exegete, proposes that this injunction is connected to the previous one about false weights and measures through the idea of deception.

19. *when the LORD your God grants you respite from all your enemies.* Historically, a campaign to wipe out the Amalekites was undertaken in the time of Hezekiel, in the late eighth century B.C.E.

you shall wipe out the remembrance of Amalek. The noun *zekher*, which is also used in the parallel verse in Exodus 17:15, means "name" but derives from the root meaning "remembrance." Etymologically, a name is the remembrance a man leaves after him, and *zekher*, "remembrance," is strongly linked with *zakhar*, "male." (Compare the necessity of male offspring to prevent a name from being wiped out in the levirate marriage.) But it is important to retain the idea of remembering in translation because the writer is pointedly playing with "remembrance . . . do not forget."

CHAPTER 26

¹ A nd it shall be, when you come into the land that the Lord your God is about to give you in estate, and you take hold of it and ² dwell in it, you shall take from the first yield of all the fruit of the soil that you will bring from your land which the Lord your God is about to give you, and you shall put it in a basket and go to the place ³ that the Lord your God chooses to make His name dwell there. And you shall come to the priest who will be in those days, and you shall say to him, "I have told today to the Lord your God that I have come into ⁴ the land which the Lord swore to our fathers to give to us." And the priest shall take the basket from your hand and lay it down before the ⁵ altar of the Lord your God. And you shall speak out and say before the Lord your God: "My father was an Aramean about to perish, and

---

2. *from the first yield of all the fruit of the soil.* Neither the amount to be taken nor the kinds of produce are specified. The early rabbis understood this to refer to the seven kinds of agricultural produce (*shiv'at haminim*) for which the Land of Israel was famous.

3. *I have told today.* "Told" (*higid*) here has the obvious sense of making a formal declaration. In keeping with the textualization of biblical culture that is one of the central innovations of Deuteronomy, these verses and the next group of verses in this chapter offer an actual liturgy, the first full-fledged liturgy in the Torah, to be recited by each Israelite farmer.

5. *an Aramean about to perish.* The two most likely candidates for the Aramean are Abraham, who came from Mesopotamia, and Jacob, who spent twenty years there after fleeing from Esau. The surprising use of "Aramean" as an epithet for a patriarch may reflect the antiquity of this recited formula, since the Arameans later chiefly figured as enemies. The precise meaning of the verb *'oved* has long

he went down to Egypt, and he sojourned there with a few people, and
he became there a great and mighty and multitudinous nation. And the 6
Egyptians did evil to us and abused us and set upon us hard labor. And 7
we cried out to the Lᴏʀᴅ God of our fathers, and the Lᴏʀᴅ heard our
voice and saw our abuse and our trouble and our oppression. And the 8
Lᴏʀᴅ brought us out from Egypt with a strong hand and with an outstretched arm and with great terror and with signs and with portents.
And He brought us to this place and gave us this land, a land flowing 9
with milk and honey. And now, look, I have brought the first yield of the 10
fruit of the soil that You gave me, Lᴏʀᴅ." And you shall lay it down
before the Lᴏʀᴅ your God, and you shall bow before the Lᴏʀᴅ your

---

been in dispute. Some understand it to mean "wandering," though when it is
used elsewhere in that sense, the meaning appears to be closer to "lost," which
would not fit here. Because the end of the sentence registers going down into
Egypt, implicitly in a time of famine, which both Abraham and Jacob did, it is
likely that the intended reference is to the patriarch's being on the point of perishing. Thus the prosperous farmer, even as he brings to the sanctuary speci-
mens of the first yield of his crop, recalls how his forefathers were close to
dying from famine and were obliged to go down to Egypt, where in due course
they were enslaved. As Jeffrey H. Tigay notes, this liturgy shifts the grounds of
the ritual of first fruits from the agricultural cycle to a rehearsal of history. Some
scholars have gone a step farther in conjecturing that this emphasis on the God
of history in the presentation of the first fruits is an implied polemic against
pagan agricultural rites, in which the deities were invoked strictly in regard to
their function in guaranteeing the fertility of the crops.

10. *And you shall lay it down before the Lᴏʀᴅ your God.* This appears to contradict verse 4, in which, with the same verb used, the priest is the one who
lays down the basket. The explanation of the Mishnah, that both priest and
layman laid down the basket at different points in the ceremony, may well
reflect the actual biblical procedure: "With the basket still on his shoulder, he
recites from 'I have told today to the Lᴏʀᴅ your God' as far as 'My father was
an Aramean about to perish.' Then he puts down the basket from his shoulder
and grasps it by its edges, and the priest sets his hand beneath it and elevates
it, and then he recites from 'My father was an Aramean about to perish' until
he finishes the entire passage, and then lays it down alongside the altar and
bows and goes out" (Bikurim 3:6).

11 God. And you shall rejoice in all the bounty that the Lord your God
has given you and your household, you and the Levite and the sojourner
who is in your midst.

12 When you finish tithing all the tithe of your produce in the third year,
the year of tithing, you shall give it to the Levite, to the sojourner, to
the orphan, and to the widow, and they shall eat within your gates and
13 be sated. And you shall say before the Lord your God, "I have rooted
out what is to be sanctified from the house and, what's more, I have
given it to the Levite and to the sojourner, to the orphan, and to the
widow, according to all Your command that You charged me. I have not
14 transgressed Your command and I have not forgotten. I have not eaten
of it in mourning, and I have not rooted it out while unclean, and I have
not given of it for the dead. I have heeded the voice of the Lord my
15 God according to all that you charged me. Look down from Your holy
dwelling place, from the heavens, and bless your people Israel and the
soil that You have given us as You swore to our fathers, a land flowing
with milk and honey."

---

13. *I have rooted out what is to be sanctified.* The same verb, *biʿer*, that is repeatedly used for the uprooting of evil from the midst of Israel is employed here to
suggest how rigorous one must be in setting aside and not appropriating the
tithe dedicated to the poor ("what is to be sanctified").

14. *I have not eaten of it in mourning.* The mourner, having been in recent contact with the dead, might impart ritual impurity to the foodstuffs that must be
qodesh, "sanctified," for the consumption of the needy.
   I have not given of it for the dead. Food offerings intended to nourish the
spirits of the dead were a common practice in both Canaanite religion and
Israelite popular religion. It would be a violation of the tithe law to take any
part of what is supposed to be consecrated to the needy and use it for an offering to the dead. Such an offering would also be proscribed because the person
would become ritually impure ("unclean") by entering into a burial site.

15. *from Your holy dwelling place, from the heavens.* This identification of the
divine abode is important in the theology of Deuteronomy. The West Semitic
peoples often thought of the gods dwelling on a high mountain (like Olympus
among the Greeks). In Deuteronomy, God is to choose one place where He

This day the LORD your God charges you to do these statutes and these 16
laws, and you shall keep and do them with all your heart and with all
your being. The LORD you have proclaimed today to be your God, and 17
to go in His ways and to keep His statutes and His commands and His
laws and to heed His voice. And the LORD has proclaimed you today to 18
be to Him a treasured people, as He has spoken to you, and to keep all
His commands, and to set you high above all the nations that He made, 19
for praise and for reclaim and for glory, and for you to be a holy people
to the LORD your God, as He has spoken.

---

will make His name dwell (and the audience would have recognized that as a
mountaintop, Mount Zion), but that place is not to be thought of as God's
actual abode.

17. *you have proclaimed.* The verb *ha'amir* occurs only here. The most convincing construction of its meaning is to see it as a *hiph'il* form of *'amar*, "to
say." Since the *hiph'il* conjugation often has a causative sense, "cause to say"
would mean something like "to declare concerning," "to make a solemn proclamation about." The idea of solemn declarations on the part of both Israel and
God fits nicely with the move toward liturgical confessions of principle and
commitment that we encounter in this section of Deuteronomy.

CHAPTER 27

1 nd Moses, and the elders of Israel with him, charged the people,
2 saying, "Keep all the command that I charge you today. And it
shall be, on the day that you cross the Jordan into the land that
the LORD your God is about to give you, you shall set up for yourself
3 great stones and coat them with plaster. And you shall write on them
the words of this teaching when you cross over, so that you may come
into the land that the LORD your God is about to give you, a land flowing with milk and honey, as the LORD God of your fathers has spoken

---

2. *you shall set up for yourself great stones.* These would be steles, upright monumental stone slabs.

   coat them with plaster. Writing on plaster, in order to make the letters stand
out more distinctly (compare "very clearly" in verse 8), was a known procedure
in the ancient Near East. The Balaam inscription found at Deir 'Alla in Jordan
is written on plaster (see the comment on Numbers 22:9). Inscriptions on
plaster-coated steles of course would not have lasted too long under the
assault of the elements, but since the Deuteronomist presumably did not have
the actual inscriptions to display to his audience, that very fact of material
transience would have served his purpose, allowing him to evoke the idea of
monumental writing without the actual monuments.

3. *write on them the words of this teaching.* The most plausible reference of this
phrase is to the code of laws (chapters 12–26) that has just been enunciated,
though it could refer to the whole Book of Deuteronomy. Jeffrey H. Tigay
notes that two steles of the size on which the Code of Hammurabi are
inscribed could contain more than the entire text of Deuteronomy. In any
case, inscribing "the words of this teaching [*torah*]" on stone is a powerfully
concrete image of the idea of the text as the enduring source of authority,
which is a central ideological innovation of Deuteronomy.

to you. And it shall be when you cross the Jordan, you shall set up these 4
stones that I charge you today on Mount Ebal, and you shall coat them
with plaster. And you shall build there an altar to the LORD your God, 5
an altar of stones. You shall not wield iron over them. Whole stones you 6
shall build the altar of the LORD your God and offer up upon it burnt
offerings to the LORD your God. And you shall sacrifice communion 7
sacrifices, and you shall eat there and rejoice before the LORD your
God. And you shall write on the stones all the words of this teaching 8
very clearly." And Moses, and the levitical priests with him, spoke to all 9
Israel, saying, "Be still and listen, Israel. This day you have become a
people to the LORD your God. And you shall heed the voice of the 10
LORD your God and do His commands and His statutes which I charge
you today." And Moses charged the people on that day, saying, "These 11,12
shall stand to bless the people on Mount Gerizim as you cross the Jordan: Simeon and Levi and Judah and Issachar and Joseph and Ben-

---

5. *You shall not wield iron over them.* This injunction to make the altar of whole
stones is in keeping with Exodus 20:25. See the comment on that verse.

8. *very clearly.* The infinitive *ba'er* is the same verb used in Deuteronomy 1:5 in
the perfect tense, where it refers to clear expounding. Here the reference is
instead to clear writing.

9. *This day you have become a people to the LORD.* In Exodus, it is the Sinai
epiphany that transforms the Israelites into the people of the LORD. Deuteronomy must insist on "this day"—repeated several times in close sequence here
and frequently occurring elsewhere—as the transforming moment because it
is here, as the people stand ready to cross the Jordan, that Deuteronomy's
authoritative rehearsal/revision of the Law is given to them.

12. *These shall stand to bless.* In this solemn ceremony, the twelve tribes are
divided six and six on the two mountains, to pronounce respectively the blessing and the curse. Attempts to explain the division in terms of the genealogy
of the tribes or the moral behavior of their eponymous founders in Genesis
seem strained. Geography may be the best, if imperfect, explanation: all six
tribes stationed on the northern mountain, Ebal, had territories in the north or
east of the Jordan and became part of the northern kingdom of Israel; four of
the six tribes stationed on the southern mountain, Gerizim, ended up in territory south of the Jezreel Valley.

13 jamin. And these shall stand over the curse on Mount Ebal: Reuben,
14 Gad and Asher and Zebulun, Dan and Naphtali. And the Levites shall
15 call out and say to every man of Israel in a loud voice: 'Cursed be the
man who makes a statue or molten image, the LORD's abhorrence,
stonemason's handiwork, and sets it up in secret.' And all the people
16 shall call out and say, 'Amen.' 'Cursed be he who treats his father or
his mother with contempt.' And all the people shall say, 'Amen.'
17 'Cursed be he who moves his fellow man's landmark.' And all the peo-
18 ple shall say, 'Amen.' 'Cursed be he who leads a blind man astray on
19 the road.' And all the people shall say, 'Amen.' "Cursed be he who
skews the case of a sojourner, orphan, or widow.' And all the people
20 shall say, 'Amen.' 'Cursed be he who lies with his father's wife, for he
has uncovered his father's skirt.' And all the people shall say, 'Amen.'
21 'Cursed be he who lies with any beast.' And all the people shall say,
22 'Amen.' 'Cursed be he who lies with his sister, his father's daughter or
23 his mother's daughter.' And all the people shall say, 'Amen.' 'Cursed
be he who lies with his mother-in-law.' And all the people shall say,

---

13. *stand over the curse*. This phrase avoids the direct object (as in "to bless the
people"), introducing a slight obliquity into the dire act of cursing. Moshe
Weinfeld has shown that ceremonies of this sort, in which curses of just this
nature were invoked against those who strayed from the dictates of the gods,
were widely practiced by the Greeks when they established new colonies.

15. *and sets it up in secret*. Several commentators, medieval and modern, have
taken this indication of clandestine idolatry as a clue that all the transgressions
in this list that follows are acts performed in secret. (Compare the secret murderer in verse 24.) But one wonders whether secrecy is generally feasible in
denying legal justice to the helpless (verse 19).

20. *lies with his father's wife*. This would be either his father's ex-wife or widow
or, given the institution of polygamy, a wife of his father who was not the man's
mother.

22. *Cursed be he who lies with his sister*. The second half of the verse makes clear
that even a half sister is taboo. Tamar's attempt to ward off sexual assault from
her half brother Amnon (2 Samuel 13) by saying that perhaps their father David
might arrange a marriage between them is either an act of desperate stalling or
reflects an earlier moment in biblical law when such unions were acceptable.

'Amen.' 'Cursed be he who strikes down his fellow man in secret.' 24
And all the people shall say, 'Amen.' 'Cursed be he who takes payment 25
to strike down a life—innocent blood.' And all the people shall say,
'Amen.' 'Cursed be he who does not fulfill the words of this teaching to 26
do them.' And all the people shall say, 'Amen.' "

---

25. *who takes payment to strike down a life.* The word translated as "payment,"
shoḥad, usually means "bribe," and this has led most interpreters to under
stand this verse to refer to a judge's taking a bribe in a case involving capital
punishment. The problem with this view is that the idiom "strike down a
life"—i.e., mortally strike—means to kill, by a violent act, and only by questionable conjecture could it be extended to judicial murder. *Shoḥad*, however,
does not invariably mean "bribe." See, for example, 1 Kings 15:19, where Asa,
king of Judah, sends a message to the king of Aram, "I have sent you payment
[*shoḥad*] of silver and gold. Go, abrogate your treaty with Basha, king of Israel."
The most likely reference of our verse is to someone who takes payment in
order to carry out a murder (a "contract") on behalf of someone else. It may
well be that the phrase "innocent blood," which seems syntactically disjunct,
was added as a kind of gloss by an editor who understood *shoḥad* in its judicial
sense.

26. *Cursed be he who does not fulfill the words of this teaching.* The acts upon
which curses are pronounced come to twelve, one for each tribe. They encompass idolatry and moral and sexual turpitude. This twelfth curse is clearly a
summarizing one, which refers not to any specific transgression but to a general failure to uphold the words of the Law that Deuteronomy has conveyed.

CHAPTER 28

“And it shall be, if you truly heed the voice of the LORD your God to
keep to do all His commands that I charge you today, the LORD
your God will set you high above all the nations of the earth. And
all these blessings will come upon you and overtake you when you heed
the voice of the LORD your God. Blessed you will be in the town and
blessed you will be in the field. Blessed the fruit of your womb and the
fruit of your soil and the fruit of your beasts, the get of your herds and
the offspring of your flock. Blessed your basket and your kneading pan.
Blessed you will be when you come in and blessed you will be when you
go out. The LORD will render your enemies who rise against you routed
before you. On one way they will sally forth toward you and on seven

---

1. *set you high above all the nations of the earth*. The parallel statements of
divine favor to the Israelite people in Exodus stress the act of election itself
and the grant of the promised land but not this idea of supremacy—verses 7
and 12 make clear that this means military and economic supremacy—over all
other nations. The immediate political background for this conditional pronouncement is a period in which powerful nations to the east periodically
threatened Israel's national existence.

2. *overtake you*. The verb is a little surprising because it is the word used for
catching up with someone who is fleeing. The idea is that an unimaginable
profusion of bounties will come down on the Israelite in ways he could
scarcely expect, but the usage is also obviously dictated by the need to create
a precise verbal parallelism with verse 15, "all these curses will come upon you
and overtake you."

7. *On one way . . . on seven ways*. This formulaic numerical increase, sometimes found between the two versets in lines of poetry, offers, as Rashi notes,
a vivid image of the unity of the attack, the disarray of the retreat.

ways they will flee before you. The Lord will ordain the blessing with 8
you in your granaries and in all that your hand reaches, and He will bless
you in the land that the Lord your God is about to give you. The Lord 9
will set you up for Him as a holy people as He has sworn to you when
you keep the command of the Lord your God and walk in His ways.
And all the peoples of the earth will see that the name of the Lord is 10
called over you and they will fear you. And the Lord will give you an 11
extra measure for the good in the fruit of your womb and in the fruit of
your beasts and in the fruit of your soil on the soil that the Lord swore
to your fathers to give to you. The Lord will open for you His goodly 12
treasure, the heavens, to give your land's rain in its season and to bless
all your handiwork, and you will put many nations in your debt and you
will not be a debtor. And the Lord will set you as head and not as tail, 13
and you will be only above and you will not be below when you heed the
command of the Lord your God which I charge you today to keep and
to do. And you shall not swerve from all the words that I charge you 14
today to the right or to the left to go after other gods to worship them.

"And it shall be, if you do not heed the voice of the Lord your God to 15
keep to do all His commands and His statutes that I charge you today,
all these curses will come upon you and overtake you. Cursed you will 16

---

10. *the name of the Lord is called over you*. According to the biblical conception of naming, this means that the Lord has a special proprietary relationship
with the people, and will protect them.

12. *His goodly treasure, the heavens, to give your land's rain in its season*. Moses's
speech has already called attention to the strict dependence of agriculture in
the land of Israel upon rainfall (11:11).

15. *these curses*. Famously, four times more space is devoted to the curses than
to the blessings. Historically, the implementation of the curses seemed much
more imminent in the seventh century B.C.E. than the fulfillment of the blessings. In any case, the chief function of the entire verbal enactment of this stu-
pendous ceremony of blessings and curses is admonition, so it is not surprising
that a long catalogue of bloodcurdling catastrophes far outweighs the list of
happier events.

17 be in the town and cursed you will be in the field. Cursed your basket
18 and your kneading pan. Cursed the fruit of your womb and the fruit of
19 your soil, the get of your herds and the offspring of your flock. Cursed
       you will be when you come in and cursed you will be when you go out.
20 The LORD will send against you blight and panic and disaster in all that
       your hand reaches, that you do, until you are destroyed and until you
       perish swiftly because of the evil of your acts, as you will have forsaken
21 Me. The LORD will make the plague cling to you until He wipes you
       out from the face of the soil to which you are coming to take hold of it.
22 The LORD will strike you with consumption and with fever and with
       inflammation and with burning and with desiccation and with emacia-
23 tion and with jaundice, and they will pursue you till you perish. And
       your heavens that are over your head will be bronze and the earth that
24 is under you iron. The LORD will turn your land's rain into dust, and
       dirt from the heavens will come down upon you until you are

---

20. *The LORD will send against you blight*. After verses 15–19, which mirror verbatim the formulation of the blessings in verses 2–6, the pronouncement of
curses begins its own vivid elaborations of possibilities of disaster. The order
of the terms in verses 4–5 is reversed in verses 17–18, forming a kind of chiasm.
    until you perish. This phrase, or a close equivalent, becomes a kind of
refrain in the recitation of curses. The point is that not only will catastrophes
visit the people but that they will end by destroying its very national existence.

22. *desiccation*. Although the term *ḥerev* looks like the ordinary word for
"sword," a long tradition of interpreters, going back to Late Antiquity and the
Middle Ages, plausibly understands it in the present context of physical
pathologies as a variant of *ḥorev*, the condition of being parched.

23. *your heavens . . . bronze . . . the earth . . . iron*. This tremendous image of
devastating sterility is borrowed from the treaty of the Assyrian emperor
Assarhadon with his vassals (672 B.C.E.). Other phrases in the list of curses, as
Moshe Weinfeld has observed, also seem to have been inspired by the language
of that treaty, such as the acts of cannibalism against one's own near kin in time
of siege, the sightless stumbling, and the ravishing of the women by the enemy.

24. *turn your land's rain into dust*. Without rain, as Abraham ibn Ezra notes, the
winds would whip up vast clouds of dust that would cover the land. The similarity of this particular disaster with one of the Ten Plagues is pointed, and in
verse 27 "the burning rash of Egypt" will be explicitly mentioned.

destroyed. The LORD will render you routed before your enemies. On 25
one way you will sally forth toward him, and on seven ways you will flee
before him. And you will be a horror to all the kingdoms of the earth.
And your carcass will become food for the birds of the heavens and for 26
the beasts of the earth, with none to make them afraid. The LORD will 27
strike you with the burning rash of Egypt and with hemorrhoids and
with boils and with scabs from which you will not be able to be healed.
The LORD will strike you with madness and with blindness and with 28
confounding of the heart. And you will grope at noon as the blind man 29
gropes in darkness, and you will not make your ways prosper, and you
will be only exploited and robbed always with no rescuer. A woman you 30
will betroth and another man will bed her. A house you will build and
you will not dwell in it. A vineyard you will plant and you will not enjoy
its fruits. Your ox will be slaughtered before your eyes and you will not 31
eat of it. Your donkey will be robbed from you and will not come back
to you. Your sheep will be given to your enemies and you will have no
rescuer. Your sons and your daughters will be given to another people 32
with your own eyes seeing and wasting away for them all day long, and
your hand will be powerless. The fruit of your soil and all your enter- 33
prise a people that you knew not will eat up, and you will be only
exploited and crushed always. And you will be crazed by the sight of 34

---

26. *your carcass will become food for the birds.* To be denied burial and consumed as carrion is an ultimate curse throughout the Mediterranean, including Greece. Equivalents of this phrase abound in the Prophets.

 with none to make them afraid. That is, there will be no one to drive off the
vultures.

28. *madness . . . blindness . . . confounding of the heart.* All the physical afflictions are followed, causally, by the psychological devastation of the afflicted.

30. *A woman . . . A house . . . A vineyard.* As several commentators have noted,
this list of unfulfillments echoes the one in chapter 20 for which exemption
from military service is granted.

35 your eyes that you will see. The LORD will strike you with evil burning
rash on the knees and on the thighs, you will not be able to be cured,
36 from the sole of your foot to your pate. The LORD will lead you and
your king whom you set up over you to a nation that you knew not, neither you nor your fathers, and you will worship there other gods, wood
37 and stone. And you will become a derision, a byword, and an adage
38 among all the peoples where the LORD will drive you. Much seed the
field will bring forth and little will you gather, for the locust will con-
39 sume it. Vineyards you will plant and work, but wine you will not drink
40 and will not store up, for the worm will eat them. Olive trees you will
have throughout your territory but no oil will you rub on, for your olives
41 will drop away. Sons and daughters you will beget, but you will not
42 have them, for they will go off in captivity. All your trees and the fruit
43 of your soil the grasshopper will despoil. The sojourner who is in your
44 midst will rise up high above you and you will go down far below. He
will put you in debt and you will not put him in debt. He will become

---

35. *evil burning rash on the knees and on the thighs.* Before the culminating
political disaster of exile, and after a reiteration of the curse of madness, the
list reverts to an intolerable inflammation of the skin, here located on specific
parts of the body, as though the physical immediacy of the skin, as in the Job
story, were the best way to make suffering palpable.

36. *you will worship there other gods, wood and stone.* From the viewpoint of
Deuteronomy's militant monotheism, the ultimate curse is not exile itself but
being driven into a place where the exiles will be forced to turn into pagans or,
indeed, fetishists.

43. *The sojourner who is in your midst will rise up high.* At first blush, this may
seem odd because the sojourner has not elsewhere been regarded as a hostile
element in the population. The sojourner, however, is repeatedly mentioned as
legally and economically vulnerable, dependent on the benevolence of the
native Israelites. Now he will have the upper hand, and perhaps there is a hint
of the idea that an occupying force, having abrogated Israelite national sover-
eignty, will grant special privilege and power to the aliens residing in the land.

the head and you will become the tail. And all these curses will come 45
upon you and pursue you and overtake you until you are destroyed. For
you will not have heeded the voice of the LORD your God to keep His
commands and His statutes which He charged you. And they will be a 46
sign and a portent in you and in your seed for all time. Inasmuch as 47
you will not have served the LORD your God in joy and with a good
heart out of an abundance of all things, you will serve your enemies 48
whom the LORD will send against you in hunger and in thirst and in
nakedness and in the lack of all things, and he will put an iron yoke on
your neck until you are destroyed. The LORD will carry against you a 49
nation from afar, from the end of the earth, as the eagle swoops, a
nation whose tongue you will not understand, a fierce-faced nation 50
that will show no favorable face to an old man and will not pity a lad.
And he will eat the fruit of your beasts and the fruit of your soil until 51
you are destroyed, as he will not leave you grain, wine, and oil, the get
of your herds and the offspring of your flock, until he makes you perish. And he will besiege you in all your gates until your high and forti- 52
fied walls in which you trust come down throughout your land, and he
will besiege you in all your gates throughout your land which the LORD

---

45. *come upon you and pursue you and overtake you*. In a pattern of intensifying incremental repetition, "pursue" is now added to the previous iterations of
this formula.

48. *he will put an iron yoke on your neck*. In a characteristic move of biblical
Hebrew from plural to singular, "he" refers to "your enemy," which in the previous clause was a plural.

50. *a fierce-faced nation that will show no favorable face to an old man*. Showing no favorable face (literally, "lifting face"), i.e., showing no special consideration, is played off against the "fierce-faced" appearance of the invaders,
whose very language is unintelligible to their helpless victims.

52. *your high and fortified walls in which you trust*. The implication—standard
doctrine in the Bible—is that it is futile to trust in fortifications or weapons;
God alone can guarantee the nation's security.

53 your God gave you. And you will eat the fruit of your womb, the flesh
of your sons and your daughters whom the LORD your God gave you, in
54 the siege and in the straits in which your enemy will press you. The
tender and delicate man among you, his eye will be cast meanly on his
55 brother and on the wife of his bosom and on the remnant of his children that he will have left, not to give to a single one of them from his
children's flesh that he will eat because he will have nothing left in the
siege and in the straits in which your enemy will press you in your
56 gates. The tender and delicate woman among you, who has not ventured to set the sole of her foot on the ground from delicacy and from
tenderness, her eye will be cast meanly on the husband of her bosom
57 and on her son and on her daughter and on her afterbirth coming out
from between her legs and on her children whom she will bear, for she
will eat them in the lack of all things and in secret, in the siege and in
58 the straits in which your enemy will press you in your gates. If you do
not keep to do all the words of this teaching written in this book to fear
59 this solemn and fearsome name, the LORD your God, the LORD will
make your plagues and the plagues of your seed astounding, great and
60 relentless plagues, evil and relentless illnesses. And He will bring back
to you all the ailments of Egypt which you dreaded, and they will cling
61 to you. What's more, every illness and every plague that is not written

---

53. *the flesh of your sons and your daughters.* Such ghastly acts of cannibalism
did in fact occur in the desperation of starvation in time of siege, as they would
occur in other times and places (e.g., during the religious wars in France in the
sixteenth century).

55. *not to give to a single one of them.* The literal sense of the Hebrew is "from
giving to a single one of them."

56. *who has not ventured.* In the Hebrew, the subject of the verb is "sole of the
foot."

61. *What's more, every illness and every plague that is not written.* Lest the long
catalogue of terrifying plagues and disasters be incomplete, this clause is
added at the end to make it clear that all other conceivable plagues and disasters are included by implication.

in this book of teaching the Lord will bring down upon you until you
are destroyed. And you will remain a scant few instead of your being   62
like the stars of the heavens in multitude, for you will not have heeded
the voice of the Lord your God. And it shall be, as the Lord exulted   63
over you to do well with you and to multiply you, so will the Lord exult
over you to make you perish, to destroy you, and you will be torn from
the soil to which you are coming to take hold of it. And the Lord will   64
scatter you among all the peoples from one end of the earth to the
other, and you will worship there other gods that you did not know, neither you nor your fathers, wood and stone. And among those nations   65
you will have no quiet and the sole of your foot will have no resting
place, and the Lord will give you there a quaking heart and a wasting
away of the eyes and an anguished spirit. And your life will dangle   66
before you, and you will be afraid night and day and will have no faith
in your life. In the morning you will say, 'Would that it were evening,'   67
and in the evening you will say, 'Would that it were morning,' from your
heart's fright with which you will be afraid and from the sight of your
eyes that you will see. And the Lord will bring you back to Egypt in   68
ships, on the way that I said to you, 'You shall not see it again,' and you
will put yourselves up for sale there to your enemies as male slaves and
slavegirls, and there will be no buyer."

---

65. *a quaking heart and a wasting away of the eyes and an anguished spirit*. Physical suffering, bereavement, and finally exile are capped by the most unbearable inner torment. The closest analogue in the Bible to what is said here and
in the next two verses (especially, "In the morning you will say, 'Would that it
were evening' . . .") occurs in Job 7.

68. *bring you back to Egypt in ships*. The reference to ships is not entirely clear.
Perhaps, since all this constitutes a reversal of the narrative of national liberation in Exodus, the idea of an arduous trek on foot up out of Egypt is con-
trasted by the notion here of a rapid voyage by sea along the Mediterranean
coast back to Egypt.
     you will put yourselves up for sale there. This clause is obviously an ironic
recollection of Joseph, the first Hebrew to be sold down to Egypt as a slave,
and also invokes the enslavement of the whole people recounted at the beginning of Exodus. Jeffrey H. Tigay proposes as a rationale for the attempted sale

69 These are the words of the Covenant that the LORD charged Moses to seal with the Israelites in the land of Moab, besides the Covenant that He sealed with them at Horeb.

---

that the Israelites, presumably after having taken flight by sea to Egypt, will find themselves in a condition of such utter destitution that they will try to sell themselves as slaves. The sardonic conclusion of this curse is that no one will want to buy them—perhaps because they have become known throughout the earth as "a derision, a byword, and an adage," scarcely fit even for slavery.

CHAPTER 29

Annd Moses called to all Israel and said to them, "You have seen all 1
that the Lord did before your own eyes in the land of Egypt to
Pharaoh and to all his servants and to all his land, the great trials 2
that your own eyes have seen, those great signs and portents. But the 3
Lord has not given you a heart to know and eyes to see and ears to hear
until this day. And I led you forty years through the wilderness. Your 4
cloaks did not wear out upon you and your sandal did not wear out

---

1. *Moses called to all Israel*. As is often the case, this verb has the force of
"invoke" or "summon"—here, to a national assembly in which a solemn
covenant between God and Israel will be ratified—but its primary sense of
"calling out" is also important because, like the rest of Deuteronomy, this is
very much a piece of *oratory* delivered by Moses.

all that the Lord did. The rapid rehearsal here of the narrative of the
Wilderness experience corresponds to passages to the same effect in Moses's
discourse at the beginning of the book and is also similar to the mention of
royal triumphs in the Assyrian treaty texts with which this entire passage has
a generic kinship.

3. *But the Lord has not given you a heart to know*. This negative declaration is
hardly surprising. Abraham ibn Ezra succinctly explains, "Because they had
tried God ten times and never mentioned the signs they had seen." Moses
must balance the compelling importance of the idea that the Wilderness generation were eyewitnesses to God's great acts with their repeated recalcitrance
to follow God's ways. The underlying justification for this grand covenantal
ceremony, forty years after Sinai, is that now at last, on the verge of crossing
into the land, the people is granted the discernment to see God's real power.

4. *Your cloaks . . . your sandal*. This miraculous durability of clothing through
forty years of desert treks is a new detail.

5   upon your foot. Bread you did not eat, and wine and strong drink you
    did not drink, so that you might know that I am the LORD your God.
6   And you came to this place, and Sihon king of Heshbon and Og king
    of the Bashan sallied forth to meet us in battle, and we struck them
7   down. And we took their land, and we gave it in estate to the Reuben-
8   ite and to the Gadite and to the half-tribe of the Manassite. And you
    shall keep the words of this covenant and do them in order that you
9   may prosper in all that you do. You are stationed here today all of
    you before the LORD your God, your heads, your tribes, your elders,
10 and your overseers, every man of Israel. Your little ones, your wives,
    and your sojourner who is in the midst of your camps, from the hewer
11 of your wood to the drawer of your water, for you to pass into the
    Covenant of the LORD your God and into His oath that the LORD your
12 God is to seal with you today, in order to raise you up for Him today as
    a people, and He will be for you a God, as He spoke to you and as He
13 swore to your fathers, to Abraham, to Isaac, and to Jacob. And not
14 with you alone do I seal this covenant and this oath but with him who
    is here standing with us this day before the LORD our God and with him

---

5. *Bread you did not eat, and wine . . . you did not drink*. These words are
another reference to God's miraculous provision of the people's needs. They
did not eat bread but manna. They did not drink wine but water that God
brought forth from the rock. In the Song of Moses (chapter 32), this second
detail will be hyperbolically elevated to "He suckled them honey from the
rock / and oil from the flinty stone."

9. *your heads, your tribes*. Some ancient versions have a smoother phrasing,
"the heads of your tribes," and the Septuagint reads "your heads, your judges"
(a difference of one Hebrew consonant).

11. *for you to pass into the Covenant*. The relatively rare verb for concluding a
covenant is probably a linguistic fossil, reflecting an early practice in which a
covenant was sealed by cutting animals in two and, evidently, having the two
parties pass between the cut parts. (See Genesis 15 and the comments there.)
It is a reasonable guess that the old—perhaps archaic—idiom is used here to
underscore the binding solemnity of this covenant.

14. *but with him who is here standing with us this day . . . and with him who is
not here with us this day*. This idea is paramount for the whole theological-

who is not here with us this day. For you yourselves know how we 15
dwelled in the land of Egypt and how we passed through in the midst
of the nations through which you passed. And you saw their abomina- 16
tions and their foulnesses, wood and stone, silver and gold, that were
with them. Should there be among you a man or a woman or a clan or 17
a tribe whose heart turns away today from the LORD our God to go worship the gods of those nations, should there be among you a root bearing fruit of hemlock and wormwood, it shall be, when he hears the 18
words of this oath and deems himself blessed in his heart, saying, 'It
will be well with me, though I go in my heart's obduracy' in order to

---

historical project of the Book of Deuteronomy. The awesome covenant, evoked
through Moses's strong rhetoric, whereby Israel binds itself to God, is a timeless model, to be reenacted scrupulously by all future generations. The force
of the idea is nicely caught by the rabbinic notion that all unborn generations
were already standing here at Sinai.

15. *we passed . . . you passed*. The Hebrew exercises considerable freedom in
slipping from first person to second person, just as it does from Moses's discourse (the beginning of this entire speech) to God's discourse (e.g., verse 5,
"so that you might know that I am the LORD your God").

16. *their abominations and their foulnesses*. Deuteronomy, with its antipagan
polemic, is rich in terms of invective for idols. The second word here, *gilulim*,
may derive from a term that means "stele," but Rashi and others, with some
plausibility, link it to *gelalim*, "turds," and it is vocalized in the Masoretic text
to mirror the vowels of *shiqutsim*, "abominations."
    wood and stone, silver and gold. As elsewhere, the Deuteronomist reduces
the idols to their sheer materiality, turning them into fetishes.

17. *a root bearing fruit of hemlock and wormwood*. The image may correspond
to the idea in the next verse of an act of idolatry committed in the secrecy of
the heart: buried roots bear poisonous fruit; the secret idolator will end by having a pernicious effect on all around him. The metaphor of poison and wormwood will come back in the Song of Moses.

18. *It will be well with me*. Or: I shall have peace. That is, nothing will happen
to me, despite my betrayal of the cult of YHWH.
    in order to sweep away the moist with the parched. This sounds very much like
the citation of a proverbial saying, but lacking the original colloquial context,

19 sweep away the moist with the parched, the Lord shall not want to forgive him, for then shall the Lord's wrath and His jealousy smoulder against that man, and all the oath that is written in this book shall come down upon him, and the Lord shall wipe out his name from under the

20 heavens. And the Lord shall divide him off for evil from all the tribes of Israel according to all the oaths of the Covenant written in this book

21 of teaching. And a later generation will say—your children who will rise up after you and the stranger who will come from a distant land and will see the blows against this land and its ills with which the Lord

22 afflicts it, brimstone and salt, all the land a burning, it cannot be sown and it cannot flourish and no grass will grow in it, like the overturning of Sodom and Gomorrah, Admah and Zeboiim which the Lord over-

---

later readers have not been able to determine the precise reference. One often-repeated guess, citing the use of the same verb, "sweep away," in Abraham's bargaining with God over the survival of Sodom (Genesis 18), is that "the moist" are the innocent and "the parched" the wicked. The idea would then be that the behavior of the clandestine idolators will bring down destruction on others as well, good and bad alike. This interpretation, however, is by no means certain.

19. *oath*. The Hebrew term *'alah* can mean either "solemn oath" or "imprecation." In this case, the first sense leads to the second: if Israel takes upon itself this oath and then betrays the conditions to which it has committed itself, it will be the target of a terrible imprecation.

21. *And a later generation will say*. The sentence that begins with these words does not conclude until the end of verse 24, when the actual words of the later generation, together with the foreigners, are quoted. The fondness for long, breathless sentences, often employed to build up vehement rhetorical momentum, and with the syntactical ligaments somewhat slackened, is distinctive of the style of Deuteronomy.

    this land. Technically, the demonstrative pronoun used would mean "that land," but to translate it that way might give the impression that the reference is to the distant land from which the foreigners have come.

22. *brimstone and salt, all the land a burning, it cannot be sown and it cannot flourish*. This powerful image of the promised land turned into the Cities of the Plain, blasted and desiccated forever, is all the more shocking because this land is supposed to be the thematic and agricultural antithesis of Sodom and Gomorrah—a land flowing with milk and honey.

turned in His wrath and in His anger, all these nations will say, 'For 23
what has the LORD done this to this land? What is this great smouldering wrath?' And they will say, 'For their having abandoned the 24
Covenant of the LORD, God of their fathers, which He sealed with
them when He brought them out of the land of Egypt. And they went 25
and worshipped other gods and bowed to them, gods that they did not
know and that He did not apportion to them. And the LORD's wrath 26
flared against that land to bring upon it all the curse written in this
book. And the LORD tore them from upon their soil in wrath and in 27
anger and in great fury and flung them into another land as on this day.'

---

23. *smouldering wrath?* Though the link between wrath and burning or hot
breath is idiomatic, it is also vividly apt for the scorched Sodom-like landscape
that the speaker beholds.

25. *And they went and worshipped.* Repeatedly, the verb "to go" precedes the
indication of worshipping other gods. This usage is not just a stylistic tic but
serves to make a theological point: Israel, after having been made the object
of God's special favor and having been given God's law, must pick up its feet
and go off from the way upon which it has been set in order to serve alien gods.

and that He did not apportion to them. This is another recurring idea in
Deuteronomy—that God, having chosen Israel as His people, has also shared
out the worship of other gods to the sundry peoples all around. Why God
would want them to serve what the Deuteronomist must have regarded as
pseudo-gods is not entirely clear. Perhaps he is actually alluding here to a
notion that appears in the Song of Moses, a considerably older text, and one
that appears not to assume absolute monotheism.

27. *tore them . . . in great fury and flung them.* Onkelos represents the first of
these two verbs by the Aramaic term that means "to shake," "violently displace."
The uprooting of exile is clearly imagined as sudden, abrupt, and painful.

into another land as on this day. The temporal indicator here of course
reflects the perspective of those who behold the devastation of Israel, and it is
not strictly necessary to infer, as some critical scholars have done, that both
the phrase and the whole evocation of exile reflect the fact that this textual
unit was composed after 586 B.C.E. The entire Book of Deuteronomy was written in a period of ominous threats to national existence, after the destruction
of the Northern Kingdom of Israel in 722 B.C.E., and it took little effort of imagination to conjure up an imminent prospect of calamitous destruction and
exile, as is done at several points in the book.

28 Things hidden are for the LORD our God and things revealed for us and
for our children forever to do all the words of this teaching."

---

28. *Things hidden . . . things revealed.* This grim promise of future disasters if
Israel betrays the Covenant ends—if indeed this sentence is in its proper
place—with a gnomic declaration. What the declaration actually refers to is
disputed, but if the relevant context is the preceding passage on idolatry (and,
especially, its clandestine practice), then the consensus of the medieval
Hebrew commentators is plausible: acts of betrayal hidden from the eyes of
others will be visible to God, and He alone can exact retribution for them;
when such acts are committed publicly rather than in secret, it is the obligation of the community to take steps against the perpetrators. One must grant
that this construction of the verse is not assured, and the difficulty is compounded by the fact that the two Hebrew words which mean "for us and for
our children" have a row of dots above them in the Masoretic text, a device
often used by ancient scribes to indicate erasure.

CHAPTER 30

"And it shall be, when all these things come upon you, the blessing 1
and the curse that I have set before you, that your heart shall turn
back among all the nations to which the LORD your God will make
you to stray. And you shall turn back to the LORD your God and heed 2
His voice as all that I charge you today, you and your children, with all

---

1. *all these things come upon you, the blessing and the curse.* This opening clause
pointedly refers to the great catalogue of blessings and curses laid out in chapter 28. In fact, the immediate reference is to the curses because the end of the
verse assumes the condition of exile as an accomplished fact. The blessings
and the curses, presented in chapter 28 as alternatives between which Israel
is to choose by its future actions, here occur as a historical sequence: first the
curse of exile, then the blessing of restoration.

   that your heart shall turn back. Manifestly, the term "turn back" (*shuv*, reiterated in this chapter) is the thematic center of this passage, alternating
between Israel and God in dialectic interplay.

2. *And you shall turn back to the LORD your God and heed His voice as all that
I charge you today.* The grand exhortation of this whole speech, evoking the
prospect of Israel's return to God, exhorting Israel to choose life and good
rather than death and evil, and reminding Israel that the divine word is intimately accessible, makes it a fitting peroration to the series of speeches or sermons that constitute the bulk of the Book of Deuteronomy. Appropriately, the
closing of the frame here includes several verbal echoes of the frame at the
beginning, especially chapter 4. After this speech, the book moves on to matters pertaining to Moses's death and the transfer of authority and to the two
poems that mark the book's conclusion.

3 your heart and with all your being. And the LORD your God shall turn
   back your former state and have mercy upon you and He shall turn
   back and gather you in from all the peoples to which the LORD your
4 God has scattered you. Should your strayed one be at the edge of the
   heavens, from there shall the LORD your God gather you in and from
5 there shall He take you. And the LORD your God shall bring you to the
   land that your fathers took hold of, and you shall take hold of it, and
   He shall do well with you and make you more multitudinous than your
6 fathers. And the LORD your God shall circumcise your heart and the
   heart of your seed to love the LORD your God with all your heart and
7 with all your being for your life's sake. And the LORD your God shall set
   all these imprecations upon your enemies and your foes who pursued
8 you. And you, you shall turn back and heed the LORD's voice, and you
9 shall do all His commands which I charge you today. And the LORD
   your God shall give you an extra measure for the good in all your handiwork, in the fruit of your womb and in the fruit of your beasts and in
   the fruit of your soil, for the LORD shall turn back to exult over you for
10 good as He exulted over your fathers, when you heed the voice of the

---

3. *And the* LORD *your God shall turn back your former state*. The meaning of *she-vut*, here rendered as "former state," has long been disputed. Many inter-preters derive it from the root *sh-b-h* and hence understand it to mean "captivity." The use of the same verb (*shuv*) with this noun *shevut* in Jeremiah 48:47 immediately after the term *shivyah*, which unambiguously means "cap-tivity," would seem to lend support to this understanding. But precisely this idiom is employed for the restoration of the fortunes of Job (42:10), where there is no question of Job's having been in a prior state of captivity.

6. *And the* LORD *your God shall circumcise your heart*. A two-stage process is envisaged. First, the heart of Israel, in the depths of exile, will turn back to God. As a response to this spiritual renewal on the part of the people, God will restore them to their land and sensitize the heart that has already turned back to Him, endowing it with a heightened capacity to love Him and to cling to His teaching. This second stage seems to eliminate the prospect of another exile after the first.

7. *all these imprecations*. The noun invoked is *'alah*, the solemn oath men-tioned at the ceremony of the blessings and the curses, which when violated becomes dire imprecation.

LORD your God to keep His commands and His statutes written in this book of teaching, when you turn back to the LORD your God with all your heart and with all your being. For this command which I charge 11 you today is not too wondrous for you nor is it distant. It is not in the 12 heavens, to say, 'Who will go up for us to the heavens and take it for us and let us hear it, that we may do it?' And it is not beyond the sea, to 13 say, 'Who will cross over for us beyond the sea and take it for us and let us hear it, that we may do it?' But the word is very close to you, in your 14 mouth and in your heart, to do it. See, I have set before you today life 15 and good and death and evil, that I charge you today to love the LORD 16 your God, to go in His ways and to keep His commands and His statutes and His laws. And you shall live and multiply, and the LORD

---

11. *wondrous.* The force of the Hebrew root *p-l-'* is something hidden (as Abraham ibn Ezra says) or beyond human ken. The crucial theological point is that divine wisdom is in no way esoteric—it has been clearly set out in "this book of teaching" and is accessible to every man and woman in Israel.

12–13. *It is not in the heavens . . . it is not beyond the sea.* The Deuteronomist, having given God's teaching a local place and habitation in a text available to all, proceeds to reject the older mythological notion of the secrets or wisdom of the gods. It is the daring hero of the pagan epic who, unlike ordinary men, makes bold to climb the sky or cross the great sea to bring back the hidden treasures of the divine realm—as Gilgamesh crosses the sea in an effort to bring back the secret of immortality. This mythological and heroic era, the Deuteronomist now proclaims, is at an end, for God's word, inscribed in a book, has become the intimate property of every person.

15. *life and good and death and evil.* It is reductive to represent the primary terms "good" and "evil" as "prosperity" and "adversity" (New Jewish Publication Society). There is probably an echo here of "the tree of knowledge good and evil," and the point is that good, which may lead to prosperity, is associated with life just as evil, which may lead to adversity, is associated with death. The Deuteronomic assumptions about historical causation may seem problematic or, indeed, untenable, but this powerful notion of the urgency of moral choice continues to resonate.

your God shall bless you in the land into which you are coming to take
17 hold of it. And if your heart turns away and you do not listen, and you
18 go astray and bow to other gods and worship them, I tell you today that
you shall surely perish, you shall not long endure on the soil to which
19 you are about to cross the Jordan to come there to take hold of it. I call
to witness for you today the heavens and the earth. Life and death I set
before you, the blessing and the curse, and you shall choose life so that
20 you may live, you and your seed. To love the LORD your God, to heed
His voice, and to cling to Him, for He is your life and your length of
days to dwell on the soil which the LORD your God swore to your
fathers, to Abraham, to Isaac, and to Jacob, to give to them."

---

19. *I call to witness for you today the heavens and the earth.* These eternal witnesses will again be invoked at the beginning of the Song of Moses.

CHAPTER 31

A nd Moses finished speaking these words to all Israel. And he said 1,2
to them, "A hundred and twenty years old I am today. I can no
longer sally forth and come in, and the LORD has said to me, 'You
shall not cross this Jordan.' The LORD your God, He it is who crosses 3
over before you. He shall destroy these nations before you and you shall
dispossess them. Joshua, he it is who is to cross over before you as the
LORD has spoken. And the LORD will do to them as He did to Sihon 4
and to Og, the kings of the Amorite, and to their land, when He
destroyed them. And the LORD will give them before you, and you shall 5

---

1. *And Moses finished speaking.* The Masoretic text reads, "And Moses went
and spoke." This translation follows the Deuteronomy text found at Qumran,
which accords with the Septuagint. The third-person forms of the verb "went,"
wayelekh, and the verb "finished," *wayekhal,* have the same consonants, and
the order of the last two consonants could easily have been reversed in a
scribal transcription. The difference between the two versions is essential
because the Qumran version makes this a proper introduction to the entire
epilogue of Deuteronomy (chapters 31–34). Moses has *completed* his discourses—the monitory sermons, the Laws, the blessings and curses—and he
is not "going" anywhere to speak further words. Rather, the epilogue will now
concern itself with the following topics of closure: the transfer of authority to
Joshua, Moses's imminent death, the instructions for the public reading of
"this teaching" (the Book of Deuteronomy or at least substantial portions of it),
the recitation of the Song of Moses, which is to bear witness against Israel,
and the poem blessing the twelve tribes.

2. *I can no longer sally forth and come in.* The idiom "go out and come in" (elsewhere, "bring out and bring in") means to lead the forces in battle. It is an apt
phrase for Moses to use because Joshua, whom he is about to designate as his
successor, figures above all as the military commander of the conquest.

do to them according to all the command that I have charged you.
6 Be strong and courageous. Do not fear and do not dread them, for the
LORD your God, He it is Who goes with you. He will not let go of you
and He will not forsake you."

7 And Moses called to Joshua and said to him before the eyes of all
Israel, "Be strong and courageous, for you will come with this people
into the land which the LORD swore to their fathers to give to them, and
8 you will grant it to them in estate. And the LORD, He it is Who goes
before you. He will be with you and will not forsake you. You shall not
fear and you shall not be terrified."

9 And Moses wrote this teaching and gave it to the priests, the sons of
Levi, who bear the Ark of the LORD's Covenant, and to all the elders of

---

7. *Be strong and courageous.* These words of encouragement, used in verse 6 in
the plural for the Israelites, before the armed confrontation with the Canaanites are, as Abraham ibn Ezra properly notes, the same words Moses addresses
now to Joshua (verses 7 and 23).

    you will come with this people. Three ancient versions read here "you will
bring this people" (the same verb in a different conjugation), which matches
the use of the verb in verse 23.

8. *the LORD, He it is Who goes before you.* This is a recurring motif, picked up
from Exodus: God is imagined as a celestial warrior headed out in front of the
people against its enemies. The presence of that divine vanguard is the reassurance the people have when faced with adversaries superior in numbers.

9. *And Moses wrote this teaching.* As elsewhere in Deuteronomy, "this teaching,"
torah, refers to Deuteronomy itself. In verse 24, Moses is said to have written
"the words of this teaching in a book." That last noun, *sefer*, refers in biblical
Hebrew to anything recorded in writing, and it of course would not look physically like a book in our sense because the bound book or codex had not yet
been invented. But the scroll, or series of scrolls, on which the text of Moses's
valedictory discourses was set down clearly constitutes a book. Indeed, it may
well inaugurate the clear-cut concept of the book in ancient Israel.

Israel. And Moses charged them, saying, "At the end of seven years, in   10
the set season of the sabbatical year at the Festival of Huts, when all   11
Israel comes to appear before the presence of the LORD your God in the
place that He chooses, you shall read this teaching before all Israel, in
their hearing. Assemble the people, the men and the women and the   12
little ones and your sojourner who is within your gates, so that they may
hear and so that they may learn, and they will fear the LORD your God
and keep to do all the words of this teaching. And your children who   13
know not will hear and learn to fear the LORD your God all the days that
you live on the soil to which you are about to cross the Jordan to take
hold of it."

And the LORD said to Moses, "Look, your time to die has drawn near.   14
Call Joshua and station yourselves in the Tent of Meeting, that I may

---

10. *in the set season of the sabbatical year at the Festival of Huts.* In the sabbatical year the fields are allowed to lie fallow, and the Festival of Huts (Succoth),
the fall harvest festival, would conclude all harvesting from the previous year,
thus leaving the entire people, with its agriculturally based economy, free to
come to the central sanctuary and listen to the public reading of the book of
teaching. In later tradition, this reading of Deuteronomy once every seven years
would be replaced by the practice of reading all Five Books of Moses annually,
divided into weekly portions through the year. That practice has its roots in the
institution of the public reading of the Torah by Ezra in the fifth century B.C.E.

11. *in their hearing.* Literally, "in their ears."

12. *Assemble the people.* The assembly of the people to listen to the recitation
of the Mosaic teaching is, as David Cohen-Zenach aptly observes, a reenactment of the hearing of the Law at Sinai, an event that Deuteronomy calls "the
day of the assembly."

13. *your children who know not.* That is, your children who have not known,
have not witnessed, all these great signs and portents that you have seen with
your own eyes.

14. *Call Joshua . . . that I may charge him.* Critical scholarship has identified a
whole series of duplications, contradictions, interruptions, and shifts in terminology in this chapter and generally has attributed them to a collation of dif-

charge him." And Moses, and Joshua, went and stationed themselves
15 in the Tent of Meeting. And the LORD appeared in the Tent in a pillar
of cloud, and the pillar of cloud stayed over the entrance to the Tent.

16 And the LORD said to Moses, "Look, you are about to lie with your
fathers, and this people will rise and go whoring after the alien gods of
the land into the midst of which they are coming, and they will forsake
17 Me and break My covenant that I have sealed with them. And My
wrath will flare against them on that day, and I shall forsake them and
hide My face from them, and they will become fodder, and many evils
and troubles will find them, and they will say on that day, 'Is it not

---

ferent literary sources. The transfer of authority to Joshua is probably the most
salient of these contradictory repetitions. In verses 7–8, Moses confers authority on Joshua in a declaration made before the whole people and God plays no
direct role. Here it is God Who charges Joshua, and the investment of leadership is enacted away from the eyes of the people, in the sacrosanct space of
the Tent of Meeting. The intricacies of the interwoven sources in this chapter
need not detain us. Suffice it to say that there appear to be four layers: an old
source, well antedating the composition of Deuteronomy; a Deuteronomic
source; some work by the presumably exilic editor of Deuteronomy; and,
finally, the editorial intervention of the redactor of the Torah as a whole. An
orchestration of different strands may have been deemed necessary to provide
an adequate conclusion to the book. Modern readers must keep in mind that
the notion that most books were composite, heterogeneous in both authorship
and literary genre, the product of collage, was naturally assumed in ancient
Hebrew literature.

16. *and this people will rise and go whoring*. Abraham ibn Ezra emphatically
observes that "it could not possibly be connected with what precedes." We
might expect here a speech from God directed to Joshua, or to Joshua and
Moses, in the Tent of Meeting. Instead, we have a divine prediction of Israel's
future idolatry, leading to the withdrawal of the divine presence from Israel,
and cast in language reminiscent of the depiction of idolatry in Exodus and in
Numbers rather than in the distinctive style of Deuteronomy.

they are coming. Throughout this passage, "people" is singular, but the repetition of "it" would be awkward in English.

17. *they will become fodder*. Literally, "food," that is, easy prey for their enemies.

because our God is not in our midst that these evils have found us?'
And as for Me, I will surely hide My face on that day for all the evil that 18
they have done, for they turned to other gods. And now, write you this 19
song and teach it to the Israelites, put it in their mouths, so that this
song will be a witness against the Israelites. When I bring them to the 20
soil that I swore to their fathers, flowing with milk and honey, and they
eat and are sated and grow sleek and turn to other gods and worship
them and despise Me and break My covenant, it shall be, when many 21
evils and troubles find them, this song shall testify before them as witness, for it shall not be forgotten in the mouth of their seed, that I knew
their devisings that they do today before I brought them into the land

---

because our God is not in our midst. It is equally possible to understand this
as "because our gods are not in our midst." Jeffrey H. Tigay argues for this possibility, suggesting that the people persist in their idolatrous beliefs even after
disaster occurs. It may be more plausible, however, to coordinate the people's
sense of God's absence with His declaration that he will hide His face.

19. *this song will be a witness.* The sequence of verses from 18 to 22 are the first
preface to the Song of Moses (traditionally called in Hebrew Shirat Ha'azinu,
after the first word of the poem). But the text, instead of proceeding, as one
might have anticipated, to the lead-in line of verse 30 and then the Song
proper (chapter 32), will go on to two other topics first. Poetry is memorable
and formally articulated (in the Hebrew, through semantic and syntactic parallelism between halves of the poetic line) in ways that facilitate actual memorization. Thus, Moses is enjoined to "put it in their mouths," that is, to make
them learn it by heart. (A similar idiom for memorization is attested in other
ancient Semitic languages, and in postbiblical Hebrew, the idiom for "by
heart" is *be'al peh*, literally, "in/on the mouth.") But there is a fail-safe second
measure for permanence that Moses must take: he must not rely on memorization but must write the poem out, until the last word. The textual permanence of the poem thus makes it an eternal "witness" that will confront every
generation of the people of Israel.

20. *eat . . . grow sleek and turn to other gods . . . and despise Me.* The language
here abounds in terms that anticipate the actual language, not just the themes,
of the Song.

21. *I knew their devisings.* This relatively unusual word, *yetser*, is surely a
pointed allusion directing us to God's bleak words about human nature after

22 which I vowed." And Moses wrote down this song on that day and
23 taught it to the Israelites. And he charged Joshua son of Nun and said,
"Be strong and courageous, for you will bring the Israelites into the land
24 which He vowed to them, and I shall be with you." And it happened,
when Moses finished writing the words of this teaching in a book to
25 their very end, Moses charged the Levites, bearers of the Ark of the
26 LORD's Covenant, saying, "Take this book of teaching and place it
alongside the Ark of the Covenant of the LORD your God, and it shall
27 be there as witness against you. For I myself have known your rebelliousness and your stiff neck. Look, while I am still alive with you today
you have rebelled against the LORD, and how much more after my
28 death! Assemble to me all the elders of your tribes and your overseers,
and let me speak in your hearing these words, that I may call to witness

---

the Flood: "For the devisings of the human heart are evil from youth" (Genesis 8:21).

23. *And he charged Joshua*. This verse, which essentially repeats verse 8,
appears to interrupt the narrative continuity at this point.

26. *Take this book of teaching . . . and it shall be there as witness against you*.
First the Song is identified as witness; now it is the book of teaching, to be
placed alongside the Ark, which is to be the witness. At least from the viewpoint of the editor, the aim is to suggest an equivalence between these two
texts: the Song of Moses, culminating the Book of Deuteronomy, provides a
powerful focus in the concentrated form of poetry for the book's major themes,
and so both the larger text and the text within the text serve the same function.

27. *I myself have known your rebelliousness*. The emphatic *'anokhi*, "I myself"
before the conjugated verb has autobiographical resonance for the speaker
Moses, who through forty years has had to cope with the refractory nature of
the people and to be the repeated target of their resentment.

28. *that I may call to witness against you the heavens and the earth*. This clause
verbally anticipates the very beginning of the Song, "Give ear, O heavens, that
I may speak, / and let the earth hear my mouth's utterances." Thus Moses
segues from writing the book (verse 26) to declaiming the Song.

against you the heavens and the earth. For I know, after my death that 29
you will surely act ruinously and swerve from the way which I charged
you, and the evil will befall you in the latter days, for you will do evil in
the eyes of the Lord, to vex Him with your handiwork." And Moses 30
spoke in the hearing of all the assembly of Israel the words of this song
to their very end:

CHAPTER 32

ı   "**G**ive ear, O heavens, that I may speak,
          and let the earth hear my mouth's utterances.
2   Let my teaching drop like rain,
              my saying flow like dew,
          like showers on the green
              and like cloudbursts on the grass.

---

1. *Give ear, O heavens*. The high stylistic solemnity of the poem is signaled by
a formal beginning (verses 1–2) that calls attention to the poet's own act of
uttering sublime speech. This convention constitutes an approximate analogy
to the invocation of the muse and the proclamation of the subject of the poem
at the beginning of the Homeric epics. The address here to heaven and earth
as witnesses is replicated, as many commentators have noted, by the opening
lines of Isaiah 1. The Song of Moses (traditionally referred to in Hebrew, as we
have noted, as Shirat [the song of] Ha'azinu) is certainly older than the body
of Deuteronomy, though how much older is a matter of scholarly debate. Many
(though not all) of the grammatical and morphological features of the language
as well as certain aspects of the syntax are archaic, and numerous formulaic
word pairs in the parallel members of the lines are ones that also occur in the
prebiblical poetry of Ugarit. On stylistic grounds, then, the poem—or at least
much of it—could be as early as the period of the Judges, that is, the eleventh
century B.C.E. As with any archaic poem, one encounters rare terms of uncertain meaning and a number of points where the text appears to have been
scrambled in scribal transmission, whether out of sheer confusion or through
theological censorship of the ancient materials. The more salient instances of
these lexical and textual difficulties will be noted below.

2. *cloudbursts*. The only thing certain about the unique Hebrew noun *se'irim* is
that it has to be some form of precipitation. If it is cognate with *se'arah*,
"storm," then "cloudburst" would be a likely meaning.

For the name of the LORD do I call.   3
   Hail greatness for our God.
The Rock, His acts are perfect,   4
   for all His ways are justice.
A steadfast God without wrong,
   true and right is He.
Did He act ruinously? No, his sons' the fault—   5
   A perverse and twisted brood.
To the LORD will you requite thus,   6
   base and unwise people?
Is He not your father, your shaper,
   He made you and set you unshaken?
Remember the days of old,   7
   give thought to the years of times past.
Ask your father, that he may tell you,
   your elders, that they may say to you.
When Elyon gave estates to nations,   8
   when He split up the sons of man,
He set out the boundaries of peoples,
   by the number of the sundry gods.

---

4. *The Rock.* This epithet for God, with the obvious sense of bastion or strong-hold, is common in Psalms. It is used seven times in the poem, which exhibits a predilection for repeating key terms a formulaic number of times.

5. *Did He act ruinously? No, his sons' the fault.* The Hebrew syntax here is impacted and hence the meaning obscure. This translation—like all others, only a guess at the sense of the original—follows the sequence of Hebrew words fairly literally.

8. *When Elyon gave estates to nations.* Elyon (the High One) is the sky god of the Canaanite pantheon, who appears to have been assimilated into biblical monotheism as an epithet for the God of Israel (see the comment on Genesis 14:19–20). The use of this designation here probably reflects the antiquity of the poem.
   by the number of the sundry gods. The Masoretic Text here reads *lemispar beney yisra'el,* "by the number of the sons of Israel." It is hard to make much sense of that reading, though traditional exegetes try to do that by noting that

9   Yes, the Lord's portion is His people
                Jacob the parcel of His estate.

10   He found him in the wilderness land,
                in the waste of the howling desert.
          He encircled him, gave mind to him,
                watched him like the apple of His eye.

11   Like an eagle who rouses his nest,
                over his fledglings he hovers,
          He spread His wings, He took him,
                He bore him on His pinion.

12   The Lord alone did lead him,
                no alien God by His side.

Israel/Jacob had seventy male descendants when he went down to Egypt and that there are, at least proverbially, seventy nations. This translation adopts the reading of the text found at Qumran (which seems close to the Hebrew text used by the Septuagint translators): *lemispar beney 'elohim*. This phrase, which appears to reflect a very early stage in the evolution of biblical monotheism, caused later transmitters of the text theological discomfort and was probably deliberately changed in the interests of piety. In the older world-picture, registered in a variety of biblical texts, God is surrounded by a celestial entourage of divine beings or lesser deities, *beney 'elim* or *beney 'elohim*, who are nevertheless subordinate to the supreme God. The Song of Moses assumes that God, in allotting portions of the earth to the various peoples, also allowed each people its own lesser deity. Compare Moses's remark about the astral deities in Deuteronomy 4:19.

9. *Yes, the Lord's portion is His people*. This affirmation stands in contrast to the preceding statement that God has allotted different deities to the sundry peoples. The Lord has made Israel His special possession through His acts of historical providence toward them, and thus Israel must worship the Lord alone.

11. *who rouses his nest*. "Rouses" is the usual sense of this Hebrew verb. But some scholars have pointed to a possible Ugaritic cognate that would yield the sense "guard over."

He set him down on the heights of the land,   13
   and he ate the bounty of the field.
He suckled him honey from the crag
   and oil from the flinty stone,
Cattle's curd and milk of the flocks   14
   with the fat of lambs
and rams of Bashan and he-goats
   with the fat of kernels of wheat,
     and the blood of the grape you drank as mead.
And Jeshurun fattened and kicked—   15
   you fattened, you thickened, grew gross—
and abandoned the God who had made him
   and despised the Rock of his rescue.
He provoked Him with strangers,   16
   with abhorrences he did vex Him.

---

13. *He suckled him honey from the crag / and oil from the flinty stone.* This line is a lovely illustration of the dynamic of intensification that characterizes much of the semantic parallelism in biblical poetry. Because the verb "suckled" does double duty for both clauses, the poet has extra rhythmic room in the second verset—a unit of one word, one accented syllable—that he can exploit by elaborating or heightening the parallel object of the verb, moving from the general term "crag" to a particularly hard kind of rock, "the flinty stone." There is also a move from an image that can readily be understood in naturalistic terms, finding honeycombs in crevices, to one that seems more flatly miraculous, being suckled oil from flintstone. The effort of many commentators to "explain" the latter image as a reference to olive trees growing on crags may not be altogether beside the point, but diminishes the striking immediacy of the image.

14. *the fat of lambs . . . the fat of kernels of wheat.* In both cases, "fat" may mean what it says or may be idiomatic for "the best of" (as in "the fat of the land").

15. *Jeshurun.* An epithet for Israel. Since the etymology suggests "straight," its use here is ironic, as the poem pointedly associates crookedness with Israel.

17   They sacrificed to the demons, the ungods,
        gods they had not known,
    new ones just come lately,
        whom their fathers had not feared.
18   The Rock your bearer you neglected
        you forgot the God who gave you birth.
19   The Lord saw and He spurned,
        from the vexation of His sons and His daughters.
20   And He said, "Let Me hide My face from them,
        I shall see what their end will be.
    For a wayward brood are they,
        children with no trust in them.
21   They provoked Me with an ungod,
        they vexed Me with their empty things.
    And I, I will provoke them with an unpeople
        with a base nation I will vex them.
22   For fire has flared in My nostrils
        and blazed to Sheol down below,
    eaten up earth and its yield
        and kindled the mountains' foundations.

---

17. *the ungods.* The Hebrew is *lo' 'eloha.* One of the distinctive stylistic traits of this poem is the fondness it exhibits for such negative prefixes. Compare verse 21.

had not feared. The verb *se'arum* is unique to this text and its meaning is disputed. One interesting suggestion is that it plays on the noun *se'irim,* "demons" or perhaps "goat-gods," an approximate synonym for *shedim,* "demons," in this verse.

21. *their empty things.* Literally, "their mere vapors." The Hebrew *hevel* is the same word that will be repeatedly used in Ecclesiastes for "insubstantiality" ("vanity of vanities," King James Version), and here it glosses "ungod."

unpeople. The Hebrew is *lo'-'am.* Jeffrey H. Tigay thinks the reference may be to nomads, and hence would reflect the premonarchic period of nomadic mauraders, but the term might simply be a self-evident pejorative for an alien people.

I will sweep down evils upon them,   23
    my arrows, spending against them,
wasted with famine, withered by blight and bitter scourge,   24
    and the fang of beasts will I send against them,
      with the venom of creepers in the dust.
Outside will the sword bereave   25
    and within chambers—terror.
Both youth and virgin,
    suckling and gray-haired man.
I would have said, 'Let Me wipe them out,   26
    let Me make their name cease among men.'
Had I not feared the foe's provocation,   27
    lest their enemies dissemble,
      lest they say, 'Our hand was high,
        and not the LORD has wrought all this.'
For a nation lost in counsel are they,   28
    there is no understanding among them.

---

22. *For fire has flared in My nostrils.* This pyrotechnic representation of an angry warrior God, drawing on polytheistic antecedents, occurs frequently in biblical poetry (compare, for example, 2 Samuel 22:8–16). Thus, God's hiding His face from Israel (verse 20) is not merely a withdrawal of the divine presence but the opposite of showing favor (in biblical idiom, "lifting the face to")—a wrathful God actively assaults Israel. The weapons of the warrior deity are lightning (God's "arrows"), earthquake, a whole panoply of plagues and noxious beasts, and hostile nations.

26. *I would have said.* In this moment of fury, provoked by Israel's betrayal of its obligation of loyalty to YHWH, God expresses no compassion for His people; it is only concern for the divine reputation ("lest they say, 'Our hand was high, / and not the LORD has wrought all this'") that prevents Him from utterly destroying Israel.

28. *For a nation lost in counsel are they.* As the following lines make clear, the reference is not to Israel but to its triumphant enemy. Had they real understanding, they would realize that such a spectacular defeat as they inflicted on Israel could only have been God's doing.

29 Were they wise they would give mind to this,
  understand their latter days:
30 O how could one chase a thousand,
  or two put ten thousand to flight,
  had not their Rock handed them over,
  had the LORD not given them up?
31 For not like our Rock is their rock,
  our enemies' would-be gods.
32 Yes, Sodom's vine is their vine,
  from the vineyards of Gomorrah.
  Their grapes are grapes of poison,
  death-bitter clusters they have.
33 Venom of vipers their wine,
  and pitiless poison of asps.

---

30. *one chase a thousand, / or two put ten thousand to flight.* This paradigmatic line neatly illustrates the pattern of intensification that informs biblical poetic parallelism. Were the system based on actual synonymity, one would expect numerical equivalents in the two parallel versets, but the prevailing rule, precisely as with nonnumerical elements in poetic parallelism, is that something must be increased or heightened: from one to two, from a thousand to ten thousand.

31. *our enemies' would-be gods.* The second of the two Hebrew words here, *we'oyveinu pelilim*, is a notorious crux, evidently already a source of puzzlement to the ancient Greek translators. The ostensible verbal root of *pelilim* is related to the idea of judgment or assessment, but every attempt to construe the two words in light of that meaning seems strained. Tigay proposes an Akkadian cognate that means "leader" or "guardian" and serves as an epithet for deities. If one notes that *pelilim* rhymes richly with *'elilim*, "idols," and if one recalls this poet's verbal inventiveness in coining designations for the nonentity of the pagan gods, "would-be gods" is a distinct possibility.

32. *death-bitter.* The Hebrew *merorot* by itself suggests only bitterness, but in context the line is clearly referring to poison.

Look, it is concealed with Me,   34
   sealed up in My stores.
Mine is vengeance, requital,   35
   at the moment their foot will slip.
For their day of disaster is close,
   what is readied then swiftly comes.
Yes, the LORD champions His people,   36
   for His servants He shows change of heart
when He sees that power is gone,
   no ruler or helper remains.
He will say, 'Where are their gods,   37
   the rock in whom they sheltered,
who ate the fat of their offerings,   38
   drank their libation wine?
Let them arise and help you,
   be over you as a shield!'
See now that I, I am He,   39
   and no god is by My side.
I put to death and give life,
   I smash and I also heal
      and none rescues from My hand.
When I raise to the heavens My hand   40
   and say, 'As I live forever.'
When I hone the flash of My sword   41
   and My hand takes hold of justice,
I will bring back vengeance to My foes
   and My enemies I will requite.

---

34. *Look, it is concealed with Me, / sealed up in My stores.* The poet picks up an idea current in ancient Near Eastern mythology, also reflected in Job 38:22–23, that the deity stores up weapons in a cosmic armory or storehouse (Hebrew *'otsar*) for a day of apocalyptic battle.

36. *no ruler or helper.* The Hebrew phrase *'atsur we'azuv* has invited highly divergent interpretations, but its use elsewhere (compare 1 Kings 14:10 and 2 Kings 9:8) suggests a link with political leadership.

42   I will make My shafts drunk with blood,
      and My sword will eat up flesh,
    from the blood of the fallen and captive,
     from the flesh of the long-haired foe.

43   Nations, O gladden His people,
      for His servants' blood will He avenge,
    and vengeance turn back on His foes,
     and purge His soil, His people."

---

42. *I will make My shafts drunk with blood.* Now the warrior God turns His ferocity from Israel to its enemies. It is a commonplace of biblical figurative language that arrows drink blood, the sword consumes flesh.

from the flesh of the long-haired foe. The Masoretic Text says, very literally, "from the head of the long hair [or unbound hair] of the foe." This reading raises two problems: if the long hair is the object of the sword, not much blood would be involved; and "head" makes an odd parallel to "blood" in the preceding verset. This translation adopts a proposed emendation that simply reverses the order of consonants of "head," *ro'sh,* yielding *she'er,* "flesh."

43. *Nations, O gladden His people.* Though the formulation of the Hebrew is a little obscure, the sense seems to be something like "Nations, congratulate God's people as He exacts vengeance from their enemies and restores them to their place in their land." The Qumran text, again approximately confirming the Septuagint, has a partly divergent reading: "Gladden, O heavens, His people, / and let all divine beings bow before Him. // For His sons' blood He will avenge / and vengeance turn back on His foes. // And His enemies He will requite / and purge His people's soil." There are grounds for thinking this reading might be more authentic than the Masoretic Text. The invocation of the heavens at the end of the poem would correspond neatly to the apostrophe to the heavens at the beginning, whereas turning to the nations at the end is a little odd. As in the probable substitution of "sons of Israel" for "sundry gods" in verse 8, later editors for reasons of monotheistic rigor might have been impelled to delete the reference that follows to all divine beings (*kol 'elohim*) bowing before the triumphant LORD. Finally, "His people's soil" (*'admat 'amo,* in the construct state) makes better idiomatic sense than "His soil, His people" (*'admato 'amo* in seeming apposition).

And Moses came and spoke all the words of this song in the hearing of 44
the people—he and Hosea son of Nun. And Moses finished speaking 45
all these words to all Israel. And he said to them, "Set your hearts upon 46
all these words with which I bear witness against you today, that you
charge your sons with them to keep to do all the words of this teaching. For it is not an empty thing for you, but it is your life, and through 47
this thing you will long endure on the soil to which you are about to
cross the Jordan to take hold of it there."

And the LORD spoke to Moses on that very day, saying, "Go up to this 48,49
Mount Abarim, Mount Nebo, which is in the land of Moab by Jericho,
and see the land of Canaan that I am about to give to the Israelites as
a holding. And die on the mountain where you are going up and be 50
gathered to your kin, as Aaron your brother died in Hor the Mountain
and was gathered to his kin, because you two betrayed Me in the midst 51
of the Israelites through the waters of Meribath-Kadesh in the Wilderness of Zin, because you did not sanctify Me in the midst of the
Israelites. For from the far side you will see the land, but you will not 52
come there, to the land that I give to the Israelites."

---

44. *Hosea son of Nun.* Hosea is a variant form of Joshua.

46. *bear witness against you.* The poem, as chapter 31 makes clear, is the eternal witness. The phrase could also mean "warn you" or even "impose upon
you."

50. *And die on the mountain.* This a rare, and shocking, use of the verb "to die"
in the imperative.

51. *because you two betrayed Me.* The word "two" is added in the translation to
make clear in English what is transparent in the Hebrew through the plural
form of the verb—that both Moses and Aaron betrayed God at the waters of
Meribah and thus each was doomed to die on his own mountain.

CHAPTER 33

And this is the blessing that Moses the man of God, blessed the Israelites before his death. And he said:

1   2

---

1. *And this is the blessing that Moses . . . blessed the Israelites before his death.* This second, concluding poem is placed exactly in the same position, just before the end of the book, as Jacob's blessings before his death to the twelve future tribes. There are some precise echoes of Jacob's blessing here (compare verses 13, 15, and 16 with Genesis 49:25 and 26.) There are also some parallels to the Song of Deborah. These correspondences suggest that in the premonarchic period there may have been an oral reservoir of poetic sayings about the tribes from which poets could draw to celebrate them. The archaic nature of the language and the political situation envisaged by the poem argue for its origins in the era before the monarchy was established. Judah here (in contrast to Genesis 49) is not represented as the tribe of kings. The poem appears to assume some form of national federation of all twelve tribes. The centralization of the cult at a single national site, one of the great themes of Deuteronomy, is nowhere implied: on the contrary, Zebulun and Issachar are said to offer sacrifices in their tribal territory (verse 19). Finally, because of the antiquity of the poem, the text shows signs of having been mangled at several points—the most egregious of these will be noted below—and at these junctures all efforts to rescue intelligible meaning from the reading that has come down to us are liable to be unavailing.

"The LORD from Sinai came
　　and from Seir He dawned upon them,
He shone from Mount Paran
　　and appeared from Ribeboth-Kodesh,
　　　from His right hand, fire-bolts for them.
Yes, lover of peoples is He,　　　　　　　　　　　　　3
　　all His holy ones in your hand,
and they are flung down at Your feet,
　　he bears Your utterances.

---

2. *from Sinai.* This poem, like the Song of Deborah and a few Psalms, registers what looks like an early tribal memory that the grand inception of YHWH's relationship with Israel was to the south, in the Sinai peninsula and in a series of associated sites, though there are some indications in the poetic texts that Mount Sinai might have been placed in northern Arabia.

He shone. This choice of verb, like the preceding "dawned," reflects an early biblical poetic notion of the LORD's powerful appearance in awesome refulgence.

appeared from Ribeboth-Kodesh. It is safest to construe the last term here as an otherwise unattested place-name, though some scholars understand it as "the myriads of Kadesh" or "the myriads of holy ones." The verb for "appeared" (or "came") is the Hebrew cognate of the Aramaic *'atah,* which in early biblical Hebrew is restricted to poetic diction.

fire-bolts for them. The Hebrew *'eshdat,* anachronistically construed by later Hebrew exegetes to mean "fire of the law," is not intelligible. Since God in biblical poetry, following Canaanite conventions, is often represented coming down to earth hurling lightning bolts as His weapons, this translation embraces the proposal that the text originally read *'esh d[oleq]et* (burning, or racing, fire) or something similar.

3. *Yes, lover of peoples is He.* This entire verse is one of the most problematic in the poem. Its principal difficulties: the epithet "lover of peoples" for God is peculiar, and one is constrained by the nationalist character of the poem to understand "peoples" as "the tribes." The lines lurch from third-person to second-person references to God, leaving some doubt as to where the poet is talking about God and where about Israel. The verb rendered as "flung down" is uncertain of meaning. It is not entirely clear who the "holy ones" are and what is meant by "he bears Your utterances." The inevitable conclusion is that this verse suffered serious damage in transmission.

4 'A teaching did Moses charge us,
    a heritage for Jacob's assembly!'
5 And He became a king in Jeshurun
    when the chiefs of the people gathered,
      all together the tribes of Israel.
6 Let Reuben live and not die,
    though his menfolk be but few.
7 And this is for Judah, and he said:
    Hear, Lord, Judah's voice
      and to his people You shall bring him.
    With his hands he strives for himself—
      a help from his foes You shall be.

---

4. *A teaching.* Since Moses here is referred to in the third person, the simplest way to understand this without emending the line is as an exclamation of the people—hence the quotation marks in the translation.

5. *when the chiefs of the people gathered, / all together the tribes of Israel.* The poet clearly envisages a grand assembly of all the tribes—an obviously premonarchic event—to confirm God's kingship over Israel. (Jeshurun is of course an epithet for Israel.) This flourish concludes the introductory section of the poem and sets us up for the blessings of the tribes one by one.

6. *Let Reuben . . . not die, / though his menfolk be but few.* These urgent words, more prayer than blessing, obviously reflect a moment in early Israelite history when the tribe of Reuben, inhabiting territory east of the Jordan, habitually threatened by marauders, perhaps also in the process of being swallowed up by neighboring Gad, appeared to run the risk of extinction.

7. *to his people You shall bring him.* Jeffrey H. Tigay plausibly suggests that the reference is to bringing him back safe from battle. The next line in fact invokes combat.

And for Levi he said: 8
  Your Thummim and Your Urim
    for your devoted man,
  whom you tested at Massah,
    you disputed with him at the waters of Meribah,
  who says of his father and mother,   9
    I have not seen them,
  and his brothers he recognized not,
    and his sons he did not know.
  For they kept Your pronouncement
    and Your covenant they preserved.
  They shall teach Your laws to Jacob   10
    and Your teaching to Israel.
  They shall put incense in Your nostrils
    and whole offerings on Your altar.
  Bless, O Lord his abundance,   11
    and his handiwork look on with favor.
  Smash the loins of his foes,
    that his enemies rise no more.

---

8. *Your Thummim and Your Urim.* These oracular devices (see the comment on Exodus 28:30) appear in all other occurrences with Urim in first position. Perhaps the reversal was encouraged by the poetic form.

  whom You tested at Massah. The story of the waters of Massah and Meribah (Exodus 17:2–7) makes no mention of a crucial role for the Levites. One may infer that this early poem drew on a narrative tradition not reflected in the story told in the Torah.

9. *who says of his father and mother.* The reference is obscure, but this sounds rather like the Levites' ruthless denial of kinfolk in playing the role of the Lord's avengers in the episode of the Golden Calf (Exodus 32:26–29). Perhaps this same motif was attached to the Levites in an early story about Massah and Meribah that did not survive elsewhere.

11. *Smash the loins.* This violent image of martial triumph does not accord with the later sacerdotal role of the Levites, which exempted them from military duty. What it may pick up is the preceding allusion to the Levites as YHWH's special militia, wielding their swords against all who betrayed him, even against their own kin.

12   For Benjamin he said:
             The LORD's friend, may he dwell securely,
               He shelters him constantly,
                 and between His shoulders he dwells.
13   And for Joseph he said:
             Blessed of the LORD is his land,
               from the bounty of heavens, from dew,
                 and from the deep that couches below,
14   and from the bounty of yield of the sun
             and from the bounty of crop of the moon,
15   and from the top of the age-old mountains,
             from the bounty of hills everlasting,
16   and from the bounty of earth and its fullness
             and the favor of the bush-dwelling One.
             May these come on the head of Joseph,
               on the brow of him set apart from his brothers.

---

12. *between His shoulders he dwells.* This appears to be an image of Benjamin carried on God's shoulders. Rashi and others link the image with the proximity of Benjamin's tribal territory to the temple in Jerusalem, but that seems doubtful—especially because this poem does not envisage a central sanctuary.

13. *Blessed of the LORD is his land.* The tribal territory of Joseph was obviously proverbial for its fertility, and the language of the blessing to Joseph here strongly echoes the wording of Jacob's blessing for Joseph in Genesis 49, which similarly invokes the heavens above the watery deep (*tehom*) below, and the bounty of hills everlasting.
    from dew. Some manuscripts read *meʿal*, "above," instead of the Masoretic *mital*, "from dew." The attraction of that reading is that it makes a perfect parallelism with "below" at the end of the next verset.

16. *the bush-dwelling One.* This unique kenning for God is justified by the fact that it is Moses who is speaking. Moses first encountered God in the burning bush, and this poem begins by announcing that the LORD has come from Sinai—the mountain on which the bush (*seneh*) grew.

His firstborn bull is his glory,   17
   wild ox's antlers his horns.
With them he gores peoples,
   all together, the ends of the earth,
and they are the myriads of Ephraim
   and they are Manasseh's thousands.
And for Zebulun he said: 18
   Rejoice, Zebulun, when you go out
   and Issachar, in your tents.
Peoples they call to the mountain   19
   there they sacrifice offerings of triumph.
For the plenty of seas do they suckle
   and the hidden treasures of sand.

---

17. *His firstborn bull is his glory.* The idea of the firstborn bull as an embodiment of fierce power is clear enough, but the antecedent of "his" is ambiguous. Some attach it to Jacob, Joseph's father, but Joseph was not Jacob's firstborn, though he was Rachel's firstborn. The most likely candidate is Joseph himself, the image of the goring bull representing his son Ephraim, who displaces the firstborn (see Genesis 48) and thus has "myriads" while his brother Manasseh has only "thousands."

   the ends of the earth. There is an ellipsis here. The sense is: "he gores peoples, / all together [the inhabitants of] the ends of the earth."

   and they are. This explains the reference of the bull metaphor. The myriads and the thousands are of course the subject, not the object, of the goring.

18. *Rejoice, Zebulun, when you go out / and Issachar, in your tents.* The bracketing of these two tribes under one blessing, and in one poetic parallelism, is unique in this poem. It seems plausible that these two neighboring tribes, both offspring of Leah, were so intertwined at an early point in Israelite national history that it was deemed appropriate to join them in a single blessing.

19. *Peoples they call to the mountain.* Most commentators understand "peoples," *'amim*, as a poetic designation of the tribes, but one cannot exclude the possibility that Zebulun and Issachar actually invited (the sense of "call" here) neighboring peoples to participate in their sacrifices. It is unclear what mountain the poet has in mind, though it would have to be in the northern Galilee.

   the plenty of seas . . . the hidden treasures of sand. In light of what is known about the tribal territory of Zebulun and Issachar, the sea in question would

20   And for Gad he said:
      Blessed he who enlarges Gad.
        Like a lion he dwells
          and tears apart arm, even pate.
21   And he saw the prime for himself
        for there is the lot of the hidden chieftain.
      And the heads of the people came,
        he performed the Lord's benefaction,
          and His judgments for Israel.
22   And for Dan he said:
      Dan is a lion's whelp,
        he springs forth from the Bashan.
23   And for Naphtali he said:
      Naphtali is sated with favor
        and filled with the blessing of the Lord.
      To the west and the south his possession.

---

be the Sea of Galilee (Lake Kinneret). But "the hidden treasures of sand" must refer to the murex, from which the precious purple dye was extracted, and perhaps also to glass (Phoenicia was famous for both). These natural resources would bring us to the shore of the Mediterranean, not of Lake Kinneret. Some scholars have speculated that after Barak's victory over the Canaanites (Judges 4), these two tribes may have expanded westward to the seacoast.

21. *the prime*. The Hebrew *re'shit* usually means "beginning," but it also has the sense of the choice part or best, which the next verset seems to require.

for there is the lot of the hidden chieftain. This entire clause, and the rest of the verse as well, is one of the most obscure moments in the poem. Many traditional interpreters take this as a reference to the burial site of Moses, but difficulties abound: it is implausible that Moses would speak of his own future burial place; the term "chieftain," *meḥoqeq* (perhaps literally, "one who gives the statute"), is nowhere else linked with Moses, and some even think it actually refers here to a digging tool, as it appears to do in Numbers 21:18. These lines probably invoke a once well-known story, now irretrievably lost, about a hidden (or, in the term's rabbinic sense, important) leader, or even about some legendary spade, which explains the eminence of Gad. We remain equally in the dark about what event is alluded to when Gad is praised for performing "the Lord's benefaction, / and His judgments for Israel."

And for Asher he said: 24
   Blessed among sons is Asher,
     May he be favored of his brothers
     and bathe in oil his foot.
Iron and bronze your gate-bolts,   25
     and as your days be your might.
There is none like the God of Jeshurun   26
     riding through heavens as your help—
     and in His triumph through the skies.

---

24. *bathe in oil his foot*. Though this phrase might refer to an abundance of olive trees in Asher's territory, rubbing oneself with oil was a way of taking pleasurable care of the body, a kind of ancient Near Eastern antecedent to modern body lotions.

25. *Iron and bronze your gate-bolts*. The noun *min'alim* means "shoes" in rabbinic Hebrew. Rashi preserves this sense by understanding the whole clause metaphorically: your land is shod in iron and bronze by virtue of the mountains in it that yield those metals. It is more likely that the image is one of military security, and the verbal stem *n-'-l* does mean "to lock."

   your might. The Hebrew noun *dov'e* appears only here in the biblical corpus, and so one is compelled to infer its meaning from context. The inference of "might" is as old as Onkelos's Aramaic translation, which renders the word as *toqpakh*.

26. *There is none like the God of Jeshurun*. The Masoretic vocalization, *ka'el yeshurun* turns this into a vocative, "There's none like God, O Jeshurun." It seems more likely that this is an epithet for the God of Israel, *ke'el yeshurun*, the two nouns linked in the construct state. In any case, this clause signals the summarizing movement of the poem, the blessings of the individual tribes having been completed.

   riding through heavens. The image of God as a celestial warrior, riding a cherub through the skies, is drawn from Canaanite poetry and appears a number of times in Psalms and elsewhere. It is worth noting that the word for "help," *'ezer*, often has the sense of "rescue" from military threat.

27   A refuge, the God of old,
           from beneath, the arms everlasting.
       He drove from before you the enemy
           and He said, 'Destroy!'
28   And Israel dwelled securely,
           untroubled Jacob's abode,
       in a land of grain and wine,
           its heavens, too, drop dew.
29   Happy are you, Israel. Who is like you?
           A people delivered by the LORD,
       Your shield of help and the sword of your triumph.
           Your enemies cower before you
               and you on their backs will tread.' "

---

27. *from beneath, the arms everlasting*. That is, God embraces or physically supports Israel.

28. *untroubled Jacob's abode*. The normal meaning of *'eyn ya'qov* would be "Jacob's well," which makes little sense here. Most scholars construe the noun as a derivative of the root *'-w-n*, "to abide," which thus yields a neat parallelism with "Israel dwelled securely." This same root is reflected in *ma'on*, "refuge," at the beginning of verse 27.

29. *delivered*. This verb is frequently associated with military victory, and the rest of this verse emphatically confirms that sense. The poem concludes with a triumphalist flourish that is dictated by the geostrategic reality of the Land of Israel. The tribes may be blessed with an abundance of natural resources—grain and wine and oil and the treasures of the sea and its shore—but they are surrounded and interpenetrated by alien peoples with hostile intentions, so that in order to enjoy their land, they must above all be militarily powerful. This idea that the LORD is Israel's shield and sword betrays none of the concern expressed in the Song of Moses that Israel will swerve from God's covenant and be doomed to catastrophic defeat and exile as a punishment.

on their backs will tread. Although most biblical occurrences of the noun *bamot* use it in the sense of "high places," it appears that the topographical meaning of the term was an extension of its original anatomical sense (i.e., the "backs" of hills). Job 9:8 describes God "treading on the back of the sea," probably a reference to His triumph over the primordial sea-monster Yamm. The linking of exactly the same verb and noun here is a virtually iconographic representation of utterly subjugating a defeated enemy.

CHAPTER 34

And Moses went up from the steppes of Moab to Mount Nebo, to 1 the top of Pisgah, which faces Jericho. And the Lord let him see all the land, from the Gilead as far as Dan, and all Naphtali, and 2 the land of Ephraim and Manasseh, and all the land of Judah as far as the Hinder Sea, and the Negeb, and the plain of the Valley of Jericho, 3 town of the palm trees, as far as Zoar. And the Lord said to him, "This 4 is the land that I swore to Abraham, to Isaac, and to Jacob, saying, 'To

---

1. *And Moses went up.* He of course has to go up to reach the mountaintop from where he will see the grand panorama of the land which he will not enter. The action of ascent, however, also signals the trajectory of Moses's life: he is born in the Nile Valley, first encounters God in the burning bush on a mountain, returns from his mission in Egypt to that same mountain to receive the law there, and now dies on a mountaintop.

the Lord let him see. Elsewhere, this verb (the *hiph'il* or causative conjugation of the verb *r-'-h,* "to see") has been translated as "show," but here it is important to preserve the literal sense of allowing or causing to see because that is the pointed meaning of this verb when it occurs again in verse 4.

from the Gilead as far as Dan. Moses's gaze is directed first to the north, to the trans-Jordanian region of the Gilead, and then westward to the tribal territory of Dan in the northernmost part of the Land of Israel. Dan's original settlement was near the coastal plain in the south, and only later did the tribe migrate to the north; so the indication of tribal geography reflects the time of writing, not that of Moses.

2. *and all Naphtali.* The gaze now begins to sweep to the south, ending with the Negeb and the plain along the Dead Sea.

4. *the land that I swore to Abraham.* This final mention of the promise to the forefathers links the end of Deuteronomy with the beginning of the Patriarchal narrative in Genesis.

your seed I will give it.' I have let you see with your own eyes, but you
5 shall not cross over there." And Moses, the LORD's servant, died there
6 in the land of Moab by the word of the LORD. And he was buried in the
glen in the land of Moab opposite Beth-Peor, and no man has known
7 his burial place to this day. And Moses was one hundred and twenty
years old when he died. His eye had not grown bleary and his sap had

---

5. *by the word of the* LORD. The literal sense of this idiom, repeatedly used elsewhere in the Torah, is "by the mouth of the LORD," i.e., by divine decree. But
the use of "mouth" encouraged the Midrash to imagine here a "death by a kiss"
(*mitat neshiqah*), the ultimate favor granted to the righteous leader.

6. *And he was buried.* The Hebrew says literally, "and he buried him," but the
third-person singular verb without specified grammatical subject is not infre-
quently used in biblical Hebrew in place of a passive verb. Many interpreters
have understood this ostensibly active verb to mean that God buried Moses.
That possibility cannot be dismissed, but God's acting as a gravedigger for
Moses seems incongruous with the representation of the deity in these narratives, and thus construing the verb as a passive is more likely.

in the glen. This note of location is of a piece with the mystifying reticence
in the whole report of Moses's death. It is unclear how or by whom he was
brought down from the mountaintop to be buried in a glen, though the evident
purpose of this removal from the heights is to underline Moses's irreducible
humanity: we are not to imagine any act of "assumption" into the celestial
sphere; Moses is buried down below, like all his fellow men.

no man has known his burial place to this day. As many commentators have
observed, the occultation of the grave of Moses serves to prevent any possibility of a cult of Moses, with pilgrimages to his gravesite. The phrase "to this day"
is a giveaway of the temporal perspective from which this concluding chapter
of the Torah was written. Both the rabbis of the Talmud and the medieval
Hebrew commentators were perplexed about the authorship of the story of the
death of Moses. One opinion was that Joshua wrote this chapter; another, more
poignant one, was that God dictated it and Moses wrote it down, weeping
(Baba Batra 14:B). But the phrase "to this day" is regularly used in biblical narrative to signal a present moment shared by the writer and his audience that is
many generations removed from the time of the reported events.

7. *one hundred and twenty years old.* This is, of course, the typological number
for the extreme limit of a human life (see Genesis 6:3, which first sets this
limit), based on the Mesopotamian sexagesimal numerical system. Several

not fled. And the Israelites keened for Moses in the steppes of Moab 8
thirty days, and the days of keening in mourning for Moses came to an
end. And Joshua son of Nun was filled with a spirit of wisdom, for 9
Moses had laid his hands upon him, and the Israelites heeded him and
did as the LORD had charged Moses. But no prophet again arose in 10
Israel like Moses, whom the LORD knew face to face, with all the signs 11
and the portents which the LORD sent him to do in the land of Egypt
to Pharaoh and to all his servants and to all his land, and with all the 12
strong hand and with all the great fear that Moses did before the eyes
of all Israel.

---

eminent rabbinic sages are given biographies that divide their lives into three
large periods of forty (another formulaic number), and some commentators
have suggested that such a division may also be implied in the life of Moses:
forty years in Egypt, forty years in Midian until his return to Egypt, forty years
as leader of Israel in the wilderness.

10. *no prophet again arose in Israel like Moses*. This clause again reflects the
temporal distance of the writer from the event reported. There will be other
prophets in Israel, but none will enjoy the unique stature of Moses, whom
God knew (or embraced—the same verb that is used in different contexts for
sexual intimacy) face to face. Deuteronomy in this way concludes with an
implicit claim for its own irrevocable authority, for no subsequent revelation of
God's will to a prophet can equal the words conveyed to Israel by the one
prophet whom God knew face to face. Some interpreters detect here a clue to
the composition of this passage in the time of Ezra, when the period of
prophecy was deemed to have come to an end, but it is safer simply to infer
that the Book of Deuteronomy is confirming its own status, and that of the
entire Torah which it now concludes, as the product of an unparalleled
prophecy that suffers no amendment or replacement.

11–12. *with all the signs . . . to all his servants and to all his land, and with all the
strong hand . . . before the eyes of all Israel*. It is fitting that the Book of
Deuteronomy concludes with one last instance of the grand sweeping sentences that are characteristic of its style, here running from the beginning of
verse 10 to the end of verse 12. This final flourish flaunts the anaphora of "all"
to convey the comprehensiveness of Moses's epic undertaking: he executed all
the signs that God had directed him to do, made all their spectacular effects
manifest to all Pharaoh's servants in all the land of Egypt, before the eyes of

all Israel. It is beautifully apt that the last words of the book should be *le'eyney kol-yisra'el*, "before the eyes of all Israel," for these words pick up the strong rhetoric of witnessing that has informed the book. The claims of the book on the sense of history and the religious loyalty of its audience are founded on Israel's having witnessed God's great portents in the formative experience of national liberation. The envisaged result of that experience is a unified nation sharing the legacy of its supreme prophet—"all Israel," the concluding words of the book.

FOR FURTHER READING

Alter, Robert. *The Art of Biblical Narrative.* New York: Basic Books, 1981.
    An introduction to the major strategies and conventions of biblical narrative seen in literary terms.

————. *The Art of Biblical Poetry.* New York: Basic Books, 1985.
    An introduction to the organizing devices and the chief genres of biblical poetry seen in literary terms.

Alter, Robert, and Kermode, Frank. *The Literary Guide to the Bible.* Cambridge, Mass.: Harvard University Press, 1987.
    Includes essays on each of the Five Books of Moses, as well as on a variety of general topics relevant to a literary understanding of the Bible.

Auerbach, Erich. *Mimesis: The Representation of Reality in Western Literature.* Princeton: Princeton University Press, 1953.
    The first chapter, a seminal contrast between the modes of narration in the *Odyssey* and in Genesis, is a point of departure for the modern literary study of the Bible.

Barton, John. *Reading The Old Testament: Method in Biblical Study.* Philadelphia: Westminster, 1984
    A lucid critical survey of the various modern scholarly approaches to the Bible that sets them in a context of general intellectual history.

Damrosch, David. *The Narrative Covenant.* New York: Harper & Row, 1987.
    A lively study that, among other interests, seeks to fit Leviticus into the layered history of the Pentateuch and its literary structure.

Douglas, Mary. *In the Wilderness: The Doctrine of Defilement in the Book of Numbers.* Sheffield, UK: JSOT Press, 1993.
    An anthropological account of the concepts of purity and impurity.

————. *Leviticus as Literature.* Oxford: Oxford University Press, 1999.
    An anthropological reading of the priestly laws as a complex system of "analogical thinking."

Fishbane, Michael. *Biblical Interpretation in Ancient Israel.* Oxford: Clarendon Press, 1985.
    An important study of how biblical literature evolved in part through a process of interpreting its own earlier stages.

Friedman, Richard Elliot. *Who Wrote the Bible?* Englewood Cliffs, N.J.: Prentice Hall, 1987.
   A lucid account of the Documentary Hypothesis, which explains how the Pentateuch was woven together from four distinct literary strands.

Greenberg, Moshe. *Understanding Exodus.* New York: Behrman House, 1969.
   An alert, close reading of the first thirteen chapters of Exodus.

Hendel, Ronald. *Remembering Abraham: Culture, History, and Memory in Ancient Israel.* New York: Oxford University Press, 2004.
   A series of astute essays on the relation of the biblical texts to ideas of history and the discernible historical record.

Josipovici, Gabriel. *The Book of God.* New Haven: Yale University Press, 1988.
   An imaginative comprehensive approach to the Bible as a set of literary texts that makes unique claims on the life of the reader.

Levine, Baruch. *Numbers: The Anchor Bible.* 2 vols. New York: Doubleday, 1993–2000.
   A recent scholarly translation with elaborate notes and commentary on philological, historical, theological, and other issues. Particularly strong in its philological discriminations.

———. *Leviticus: The JPS Torah Commentary.* Philadelphia: Jewish Publication Society, 1989.
   A scholarly commentary directed to a popular audience, with helpful appended short essays on pertinent topics. Includes the Hebrew text and the New Jewish Publication Society translation.

Levinson, Bernard. *Deuteronomy and the Hermeneutics of Legal Innovation.* New York: Oxford University Press, 1997.
   An incisive account of how Deuteronomy effected a revolution in biblical law while seeming to follow its predecessors.

Milgrom, Jacob. *Leviticus: The Anchor Bible.* 3 vols. New York: Doubleday, 1991–2001.
   A recent scholarly translation with extremely elaborate notes and commentary on philological, historical, theological, and other issues. These three thousand pages strive for an exhaustive account of all topics relevant to the ancient Israelite cult.

———. *Numbers: The JPS Torah Commentary.* Philadelphia: Jewish Publication Society, 1989.
   A scholarly commentary directed to a popular audience, with helpful appended shorts essays on pertinent topics. Includes the Hebrew text and the New Jewish Publication Society translation.

Pardes, Ilana. *The Biography of Ancient Israel.* Berkeley: University of California Press, 2000.
   A perceptive reading of key episodes in Exodus, Numbers, and Deuteronomy as a narrative of the formation of the Israelite nation seen as analogous to the narration of an individual life.

Polzin, Robert. *Moses and the Deuteronomist.* New York: Seabury Press, 1980.

An application of the theory of language developed by M. M. Bakhtin to the deployment of rhetoric and strategies of address in Deuteronomy (and in Joshua as well).

Propp, William. *Exodus: 1–18*. New York: Doubleday, 1999.
A recent scholarly translation, at some points extravagantly literal, with elaborate notes and commentary on philological, historical, theological, and other issues.

Sarna, Nahum. *Exodus: The New JPS Commentary*. Philadelphia: Jewish Publication Society, 1991.
A scholarly commentary directed to a popular audience, with helpful appended short essays on pertinent topics. The approach is eclectic, including a literary perspective. Issues of the composite nature of the text are not addressed. Includes the Hebrew text and the New Jewish Publication Society translation.

———. *Genesis: The New JPS Commentary*. Philadelphia: Jewish Publication Society, 1989.
A scholarly commentary directed to a popular audience, with helpful appended short essays on pertinent topics. The approach is eclectic, including a literary perspective. Issues of the composite nature of the text are not addressed. Includes the Hebrew text and the New Jewish Publication Society translation.

Shanks, Hershel, ed. *Ancient Israel: A Short History from Abraham to the Roman Destruction of the Temple*. Washington, D.C.: Biblical Archaeology Society, 1988.
Chapters by eight leading scholars offer a concise historical account of the major phases of biblical history. The text is complemented by abundant illustrations and maps.

Sonnet, Jean-Pierre. *The Book Within the Book: Writing in Deuteronomy*. Leiden, Holland: Brill, 1997.
An analysis of the attention drawn to the act of writing and to the status of the book as book in Deuteronomy.

Speiser, E. A. *Genesis: The Anchor Bible*. New York: Doubleday, 1964.
A scholarly translation with notes and commentary on philological, historical, and other issues. Although some of the scholarship is now out of date, the notes and commentary include keen philological analysis. Considerable space is devoted to a presentation of sources according to the Documentary Hypothesis.

Sternberg, Meir. *The Poetics of Biblical Narrative*. Bloomington: Indiana University Press, 1985.
An elaborate, pioneering account of how biblical narrative constructs meanings, with lengthy analysis of examples.

Tigay, Jeffrey H. *Deuteronomy: The New JPS Commentary*. Philadelphia: Jewish Publication Society, 1996.
A scholarly commentary directed to a popular audience, with helpful appended short essays on pertinent topics. The commentary deals with the composite nature of the text and is particularly helpful on links with other ancient Near Eastern literatures. Includes the Hebrew text and the New Jewish Publication Society translation.

Weinfeld, Moshe. *Deuteronomy I–XI: The Anchor Bible*. New York: Doubleday, 1991.

A scholarly translation with notes on philological, historical, and other issues by one of the leading authorities on Deuteronomy.

Weitzman, Steven. *Song and Story in Biblical Narrative.* Bloomington: Indiana University Press, 1997.
A study of the biblical literary conventions that govern the introduction of relatively long poems into the narratives.